CurrentLaw

STATUTES

1994

VOLUME FOUR

AUSTRALIA
The Law Book Company
Brisbane : Sydney : Melbourne : Perth

CANADA
Carswell
Ottawa : Toronto : Calgary : Montreal : Vancouver

Agents:
Steimatzky's Agency Ltd., Tel Aviv;
N. M. Tripathi (Private) Ltd., Bombay;
Eastern Law House (Private) Ltd., Calcutta;
M.P.P. House, Bangalore;
Universal Book Traders, Delhi;
Aditya Books, Delhi;
MacMillan Shuppan KK, Tokyo;
Pakistan Law House, Karachi

Current Law

STATUTES

1994

VOLUME FOUR

SWEET & MAXWELL EDITORIAL TEAM
SARAH ANDREWS
MELANIE BHAGAT
ALASTAIR BRUNKER
CAROLINE EADIE
PHILIPPA JOHNSON
SOPHIE LOWE
CERI PICKERING
ALICE WILEY

W. GREEN EDITORIAL TEAM
ELANOR BOWER
CHARLOTTE HALL
PETER NICHOLSON

LONDON
SWEET & MAXWELL

EDINBURGH
W. GREEN

1995

Published by
SWEET & MAXWELL LIMITED
of South Quay Plaza, 183 Marsh Wall, London,
and W. GREEN LIMITED
of Alva Street, Edinburgh,
Typeset by MFK Typesetting Ltd., Hitchin, Herts.
and printed in Great Britain
by The Bath Press,
Bath, Avon.

ISBN This Volume only : 0 421 51940 1
As a set : 0 421 51900 2

All rights reserved.
U.K. statutory material in this publication is acknowledged as Crown copyright.
No part of this publication may be reproduced or transmitted in any form or by any means, or stored in any retrieval system of any nature, without prior written permission, except for permitted fair dealing under the Copyright, Designs and Patents Act 1988, or in accordance with the terms of a licence issued by the Copyright Licensing Agency in respect of photocopying and/or reprographic reproduction. Application for permission for other use of copyright material including permission to reproduce extracts in other published works shall be made to the publishers. Full acknowledgment of author, publisher and source must be given.

©
Sweet & Maxwell Ltd.
1995

CONTENTS

CHRONOLOGICAL TABLE

VOLUME FOUR

Private Acts

*c.*i. British Railways Order Confirmation Act 1994
ii. British Railways (No. 2) Order Confirmation Act 1994
iii. British Railways (No. 3) Order Confirmation Act 1994
iv. British Railways Act 1994
v. Church of Scotland (Properties and Investments) Order Confirmation Act 1994
vi. Greater Manchester (Light Rapid Transit System) Act 1994
vii. Commons Registration (East Sussex) Act 1994
viii. Dunham Bridge (Amendment) Act 1994
ix. London Underground (Green Park) Act 1994
x. Lerwick Harbour Order Confirmation Act 1994
xi. Croydon Tramlink Act 1994
xii. London Local Authorities Act 1994
xiii. London Docklands Development Corporation Act 1994
xiv. Hill Samuel Bank and United Dominions Trust Act 1994
xv. Greater Nottingham Light Rapid Transit Act 1994
xvi. University of London Act 1994

Church Measures

1. Pastoral (Amendment) Measure 1994
2. Care of Cathedrals (Supplementary Provisions) Measure 1994
3. Church of England (Legal Aid) Measure 1994

Commencement Orders

1. Commencement Diary 1994
2. Commencement Orders 1994 C.1–84

Numerical Table of Statutory Instruments

Listing of all Instruments released for 1994

Alphabetical Table of Statutes

Listing of all Public Acts passed, 1700–1994

Legislation Citator 1994

Statutory Instrument Citator 1994

Index 1994

CHRONOLOGICAL TABLE

VOLUMES 1–4

ALPHABETICAL INDEX OF SHORT TITLES

PUBLIC GENERAL ACTS 1994

(References are to chapter numbers of 1994)

ALPHABETICAL INDEX OF SHORT TITLES

PRIVATE ACTS 1994

(References are to chapter numbers of 1994)

BRITISH RAILWAYS ORDER CONFIRMATION ACT 1994

(1994 c. i)

An Act to confirm a Provisional Order under the Private Legislation Procedure (Scotland) Act 1936, relating to British Railways.

[24th March 1994]

PARLIAMENTARY PROGRESS
    The Bill's progress through Parliament was as follows:
    House of Commons: First Reading, March 8, 1994; Second Reading, March 16, 1994; Considered by Commons, March 17, 1994; Third Reading, March 21, 1994.
    House of Lords: First Reading, March 21, 1994; Considered by Lords, March 22, 1994; Third Reading, March 24, 1994.

INTRODUCTION
    The British Railways Board is required to provide railway services and other connected services in Great Britain. In accordance with this remit the Board wishes to undertake certain construction works in the Strathclyde region. In order to execute their functions properly it is necessary for the works and any connected interference with land to be sanctioned by Order of Parliament. This Act gives the Board the necessary permission to undertake the works specified in this Act and to purchase or use the lands specified herein.
    Part I contains preliminary measures. Part II details the works proposed and indicates the likely interference with existing amenities. Part III details the land likely to be affected by the Act. Part IV sets out protective provisions *vis-à-vis* amenities and Crown rights.

WHEREAS the Provisional Order set forth in the Schedule hereunto annexed has been made by the Secretary of State under the provisions of the Private Legislation Procedure (Scotland) Act 1936, and it is requisite that the said Order should be confirmed by Parliament:

    Be it therefore enacted by the Queen's most Excellent Majesty, by and with the advice and consent of the Lords Spiritual and Temporal, and Commons, in this present Parliament assembled, and by the authority of the same, as follows:—

Confirmation of Order in Schedule

1. The Provisional Order contained in the Schedule hereunto annexed is hereby confirmed.

Short title

2. This Act may be cited as the British Railways Order Confirmation Act 1994.

SCHEDULE

BRITISH RAILWAYS

Provisional Order to empower the British Railways Board to construct works and to purchase or use land; to confer further powers on the Board; and for other purposes.

WHEREAS—

(1) By the Transport Act 1962 the British Railways Board (hereinafter referred to as "the Board") were established:

(2) It is the duty of the Board under the said Act of 1962 (inter alia) to provide railway services in Great Britain and, in connection with the provision of railway services, to provide such other services and facilities as appear to the Board to be expedient, and to have due regard, as respects all those railway and other services and facilities, to efficiency, economy and safety of operation:

(3) It is expedient that the Board should be empowered to construct in the Strathclyde Region the works authorised by this Order and to purchase or use the land referred to in this Order and that the other provisions in this Order contained should be enacted:

(4) Plans and sections showing the lines or situations and levels of the works to be constructed under this Order, and plans of the lands authorised to be purchased or used by this Order, and a book of reference to those plans containing the names of the owners and lessees, or reputed owners and lessees, and of the occupiers of the said lands were duly deposited in the office of the Clerk of the Parliaments and in the Private Bill Office of the House of Commons and with the sheriff clerks of the sheriff court districts of Ayr and of Glasgow and Strathkelvin, which plans, sections and book of reference are respectively referred to in this Order as the deposited plans, the deposited sections and the deposited book of reference:

(5) The purposes of this Order cannot be effected without an Order confirmed by Parliament under the provisions of the Private Legislation Procedure (Scotland) Act 1936:

Now therefore, in pursuance of the powers contained in the last-mentioned Act, the Secretary of State orders as follows:—

PART I

PRELIMINARY

Short title

1. This Order may be cited as the British Railways Order 1994.

Interpretation

2.—(1) In this Order, unless the context otherwise requires, words and expressions to which meanings are assigned by the enactments incorporated herewith have the same respective meanings; and—

"the Act of 1845" means the Railways Clauses Consolidation (Scotland) Act 1845;

"the Act of 1991" means the New Roads and Street Works Act 1991;

"the Board" means the British Railways Board;

"enactment" includes any order, byelaw, rule, regulation, scheme or other instrument having effect by virtue of an enactment;

"the limits of deviation" means the limits of deviation shown on the deposited plans;

"the regional council" means the Strathclyde Regional Council;

"road" has the meaning assigned to it by section 107 of the Act of 1991;

"road works authority" has the meaning assigned to it by section 108 of the Act of 1991;

"the sheriff" means the sheriff principal of, or any sheriff appointed for, the Sheriffdom of South Strathclyde, Dumfries and Galloway or the Sheriffdom of Glasgow and Strathkelvin, as the case may be;

"the tribunal" means the Lands Tribunal for Scotland; and

"the works" means the works authorised by Part II (Works, etc.) of this Order.

(2) Except in relation to section 5 (Power to deviate) of this Order, all directions, distances and lengths stated in any description of works, powers or lands in this Order shall be construed as if the words "or thereby" were inserted after each such direction, distance and length and distances between points on a railway shall be taken to be measured along the railway.

(3) Any reference in this Order to a work identified by the number of that work shall be construed as a reference to the work of that number authorised by this Order.

(4) References in this Order to points identified by letters shall be construed as references to the points so lettered on the deposited plans.

(5) References in this Order to access to any place shall include reference to egress from that place.

Incorporation of enactments

3.—(1) The following enactments, so far as the same are applicable for the purposes of and are not inconsistent with, or varied by, the provisions of this Order, are incorporated with this Order, and this Order shall be deemed to be the special Act for the purposes of the said incorporated enactments:—

(a) the Lands Clauses Acts, except sections 120 to 124 and section 127 of the Lands Clauses Consolidation (Scotland) Act 1845;

(b) the Act of 1845, except sections 1, 7, 8, 9, 17, 19, 20, 22 and 23 thereof; and

(c) in the Railways Clauses Act 1863, Part I (relating to construction of a railway) except sections 13, 14, 18 and 19 thereof.

(2)(a) In the application of the enactments incorporated by subsection 1(b) and (c) above the expression "the company" means the Board.

(b) Sections 18 and 21 of the Act of 1845 shall not extend to regulate the relations between the Board and any other person in respect of any matter or thing concerning which those relations are regulated in any respect by the provisions of Part IV of the Act of 1991 or by section 30 (For protection of electricity, gas and water undertakers) of this Order.

PART II

WORKS, ETC.

Works

Power to make works

4. Subject to the provisions of this Order, the Board may, in the lines or situations and within the limits of deviation shown on the deposited plans and according to the levels shown on the deposited sections, make and maintain the following works in the Strathclyde Region, with all necessary works and conveniences connected therewith:—

In the Cumnock and Doon Valley District—

Work No. 1—A railway (10,922 metres in length), being a reinstatement of part of the railway between Auchinleck and Muirkirk, commencing at Auchinleck by a junction with the Kilmarnock and Dumfries Railway at a point 21 metres east of the bridge carrying that railway over Main Street and terminating at Powharnal at a point 52 metres south-west of the A.70 Road (Ordnance Survey National Grid reference point NG 6471:2553).

In the City of Glasgow District—

Work No. 2—A railway (1,570 metres in length), being in part a reinstatement of part of the railway between Maryhill Park and Knightswood South Junctions, commencing at Anniesland station at a point 91 metres north-east of the bridge carrying the Drumgelloch and Helensburgh Railway over Great Western Road and terminating at Maryhill by a junction with the railway between Cowlairs West and Knightswood North Junctions at a point 168 metres south-west of the bridge carrying Maryhill Road over the last-mentioned railway.

Work No. 3—A railway (82 metres in length) at Anniesland, commencing by a junction with the Drumgelloch and Helensburgh Railway at a point 264 metres north-east of the bridge carrying that railway over Great Western Road and terminating by a junction with Work No. 2 at a point 257 metres north-east of its commencement.

Power to deviate

5.—(1) In the construction of the works the Board may—
(a) deviate from the lines or situations thereof shown on the deposited plans to the extent of the limits of deviation; and
(b) subject to subsection (2) below, deviate vertically from the levels shown on the deposited sections to any extent not exceeding 3 metres upwards or downwards or to such further extent as may be approved by the Secretary of State.

(2) Subsection (1)(b) above shall not apply to the construction of Work No. 2 beneath the aqueduct included in the land numbered in the deposited plans 10 in the City of Glasgow District where the Board may deviate downwards only and then only to an extent not exceeding 0·5 of a metre.

Relief of certain obligations in respect of Work No. 1

6.—(1) In this section—
"the bridges" means the two bridges in the Cumnock and Doon Valley District, one of which carries the road from Auchinleck to Lugar over the former railway at Commondyke and the other of which carried the former railway over the road from Auchinleck to the A.70 road at Cronberry;
"the former railway" means the discontinued portion of the former railway between Auchinleck and Muirkirk on the course of, and coterminous with, Work No. 1 which was authorised and constructed under the original Act; and
"the original Act" means the Glasgow, Paisley, Kilmarnock, and Ayr Railway and Glasgow and Belfast Union Railway Amendment and Branches Act No. 1 1847.

(2) In the construction of Work No. 1 the Board shall be relieved of the obligations of sections 39 and 60 of the Act of 1845, as incorporated with the original Act, including any contractual obligations arising under the said section 60, in respect of the bridges and any other works on, or relating to, the former railway.

(3)(a) Notwithstanding anything in the original Act or in the Act of 1845, as incorporated with this Order, the Board may, in relation to the roads which cross or are crossed by the bridges and are mentioned in paragraph (b) below, retain the bridges with the dimensions therein specified.

(b) The roads and dimensions referred to in paragraph (*a*) above are—
- (i) the road at Commondyke, with a clear space between parapets of 4.62 metres; and
- (ii) the road at Cronberry, with a clear height above the surface of the road of 4.08 metres for a space of 3.05 metres.

Station works between Anniesland and Maryhill, Glasgow

7. In the construction of Work No. 2 and for the purpose of serving that work, the Board may, on any part of the land in the City of Glasgow District described in column (1) of Schedule 1 to this Order which lies within the lines marked "Limit of station works" on the deposited plans, make, maintain and operate the station works described in column (2) of that Schedule with all necessary works and conveniences connected therewith.

Power to open surface of Coal Road, Auchinleck

8. Subject to the provisions of this Order, the Board may, for the purpose of constructing Work No. 1, enter upon, open, break up and interfere with so much of the surface of Coal Road, Auchinleck, as is within the limits of deviation of that work.

Access to Work No. 1

9. The Board may, in relation to Work No. 1, or to all or any of the lands within the limits of deviation of that work, form and lay out means of access at the points specified in column (1) of Schedule 2 to this Order for the purposes mentioned in column (2) of that Schedule.

General works provisions

Temporary stoppage of roads

10.—(1) The Board, during and for the purpose of the execution of the works, may temporarily stop up and divert and interfere with any road and may for any reasonable time divert the traffic therefrom and prevent all persons other than those bona fide going to or from any land, house or building abutting on the road from passing along and using the same.

(2) The Board shall provide reasonable access for persons on foot bona fide going to or from any such land, house or building.

(3)(a) The Board shall not exercise the powers of this section without the consent of the road works authority.

(b)Any such consent may be given subject to such reasonable conditions as the road works authority may require but shall not be unreasonably withheld and any question whether such consent has been unreasonably withheld or whether any such condition is reasonable shall be determined by arbitration.

Underpinning of buildings near works

11. The Board at their own expense may, subject as hereinafter provided, underpin or otherwise strengthen any building within 30 metres of any part of the works and the following provisions shall have effect:—

(1) At least 14 days' notice shall (except in case of emergency) be given to the owner, lessee and occupier of the building intended to be so underpinned or otherwise strengthened:

(2) If any owner, lessee or occupier of any such building, within 10 days after the giving of such notice, gives a counter-notice in writing that he disputes the necessity of such underpinning or strengthening, the question of the necessity shall be determined by arbitration; and, if the arbiter decides that such underpinning or strengthening is not necessary, the Board shall not proceed therewith:

(3) In any case in which any building shall have been underpinned or strengthened under the powers of this section the Board may, from time to time after the completion of such underpinning or strengthening, and during the execution of the work in connection with which such underpinning or strengthening was done, or within five years after the opening for traffic of that work, after giving reasonable notice to the occupier enter upon and survey such building and, after complying with the foregoing provisions of this section, do such further underpinning or strengthening as they may deem necessary or expedient:

(4) The Board shall be liable to compensate the owner, lessee and occupier of every such building for any loss or damage which may result to them by reason of the exercise of the powers of this section:

(5) Nothing in this section shall affect liability to compensate under any enactment in respect of loss or damage arising from the execution of any works, except so far as compensation is payable under paragraph (4) above:

(6) Every case of compensation to be ascertained under this section shall be ascertained according to the provisions of the Land Compensation (Scotland) Act 1963.

Use of sewers, etc., for removing water

12.—(1) The Board may use for the discharge of any water pumped or found by them during the construction of the works any available stream or watercourse, or any sewer or drain vested in, or under the control of, the regional council, and for that purpose may lay down, take up and alter conduits, pipes and other works and may make any convenient connections with any such stream, watercourse, sewer or drain within the limits of deviation.

(2) The Board shall not—

(a) discharge any water into any such sewer or drain except with the consent of the regional council, whose consent shall not be unreasonably withheld, and subject to such terms and conditions (including the taking of steps to remove as far as may be reasonably practicable from water so discharged any gravel, soil or other solid substance or matter in suspension) as the regional council may reasonably impose; or

(b) make any opening into any such sewer or drain except in accordance with plans approved by, and under the superintendence (if given) of, the regional council but approval of those plans by the regional council shall not be unreasonably withheld.

(3) Any difference arising between the Board and the regional council under this section shall be determined by arbitration.

(4) Section 31 of the Control of Pollution Act 1974 shall apply to, or to the consequence of, a discharge under the powers of this section into any controlled waters within the meaning assigned to that expression by section 30A (1) of that Act as if this section were not a provision of a local Act or a statutory order for the purposes of section 31(2)(b)(ii) of that Act.

(5) Nothing in this section shall affect the operation of Part IV of the Act of 1991.

(6) Nothing in this section shall authorise the Board to discharge any water directly or indirectly into the Forth and Clyde Canal of the British Waterways Board.

PART III

LAND

Meaning of new rights

13. In this Part references to the purchase by the Board of new rights are references to the purchase of rights (whether heritable or moveable) to be created in favour of the Board.

Purchase of land

14.—(1) The Board may purchase compulsorily and use such of the land within the limits of deviation and described in the deposited book of reference as they require for the purposes of the works or their undertaking.

(2) The Board may enter upon, use and appropriate so much of the subsoil and undersurface of, or airspace over, any public road or place within the limits of deviation and described in the deposited book of reference as shall be necessary for the purposes of subsection (1) above without being required to purchase the same or any servitude or other right therein or thereunder or to make any payment therefor.

(3) For the purpose of section 28 of the Land Registration (Scotland) Act 1979 subsection (2) above shall be taken to create a real right over such land as is referred to in that subsection without any necessity to record a deed in the Register of Sasines or to register the right.

(4) The Board shall not exercise the powers of this section or sections 15 (Purchase of new rights over land) and 16 (Purchase of specific new rights over land) of this Order in relation to any land to which section 17 (Temporary use of land) of this Order applies.

Purchase of new rights over land

15.—(1) Subject to the provisions of this Order, the Board may for the purpose of constructing, maintaining, protecting, altering, renewing and using the works, or for the purpose of obtaining access to the works or for the purpose of doing any other thing necessary in connection with the works, purchase compulsorily and use so much of the subsoil and undersurface of, or may purchase compulsorily such new rights as they require in, under or over any of the land within the limits of deviation and described in the deposited book of reference instead of purchasing that land under section 14 (Purchase of land) of this Order.

(2) The Lands Clauses Acts, as applied by this Order, shall have effect with the modifications necessary to make them apply to the compulsory purchase of new rights under subsection (1) above and under section 16 (Purchase of specific new rights over land) of this Order as they apply to the compulsory purchase of land so that, in appropriate contexts, references in the Lands Clauses Acts to land are read as referring, or as including references, to the new rights or to land over which the new rights are, or are to be, exercisable, according to the requirements of the particular context.

Purchase of specific new rights over land

16.—(1) The Board may, in addition to such new rights as they may purchase under section 15 (Purchase of new rights over land) of this Order, purchase compulsorily such new rights as they require in or over any of the lands shown on the deposited plans within the lines marked "Limit of land to be used" and specified in Part I of Schedule 3 to this Order for the provision of means of access to the roads there mentioned.

(2) Where in column (3) of the said Part I reference is made to a lettered point, the Board may form and lay out means of access at that point to the road there named.

Temporary use of land

17. The provisions set out in Part II of Schedule 3 to this Order shall have effect with respect to the temporary use of land by the Board for working sites and related movement of equipment, materials and plant.

Time for compulsory purchase of land or rights over land

18. Except as may be provided under section 19 (Extension of time) of this Order, the powers of the Board of compulsory purchase of land and new rights in, under or over land under this Order shall cease on 31st December 1997.

Extension of time

19.—(1) In this section "lessee" means a lessee under a lease having a period of not less than 21 years to run at the date of his notice under subsection (3) below; and any reference to the purchase of an interest in land includes reference to the purchase of a new right in, under or over that land.

(2)(a) Subject to the provisions of this section, the Secretary of State may, by order under this subsection, extend the period for the exercise of powers of compulsory purchase of land and new rights in, under or over land under this Order.

(b) An order under this subsection shall be subject to special parliamentary procedure.

(3) If any owner or lessee of any land subject to an order under subsection (2) above shall give notice in writing to the Board of his desire for the purchase as soon as may be by the Board of his interest in any part of the land specified in the notice, the Board shall within a period of three months after the receipt of such notice—

(a) enter into a contract with him for the purchase of his interest in the land or such part thereof as may be specified in the contract; or

(b) serve on him a notice to treat for the compulsory purchase of his interest in the land specified in his notice, or in such part thereof as may be required by the Board; or

(c) serve on him notice in writing of the Board's intention not to proceed with the purchase of his interest in the land specified in his notice.

(4) Where notice is given under subsection (3) above by any owner or lessee, then—

(a) if the Board—

    (i) fail to comply with that subsection; or

    (ii) withdraw in pursuance of any statutory provision a notice to treat served on him in compliance with subsection (3)(b) above; or

    (iii) serve notice on him in compliance with subsection (3)(c) above;

the powers conferred by this Order for the compulsory purchase of his interest in the land so specified shall cease;

(b) if his interest in part only of the land so specified is purchased in pursuance of such a notice to treat, the powers conferred by this Order for the compulsory purchase of his interest in the remainder of the land so specified shall cease.

Correction of errors in deposited plans and book of reference

20.—(1) If the deposited plans or the deposited book of reference are inaccurate in their description of any land or in their statement or description of the ownership or occupation of any land, the Board, after giving not less than 10 days' notice to the owner, lessee and occupier of the land in question, may apply by summary application to the sheriff having jurisdiction in the place where the land is situated for the correction thereof.

(2) If on any such application it appears to the sheriff that the misstatement or wrong description arose from mistake, he shall certify accordingly and shall in his certificate state in what respect any matter is misstated or wrongly described.

(3) The certificate shall be deposited in the office of the Clerk of the Parliaments and a copy thereof in the Private Bill Office, House of Commons, the Scottish Office, London, the office of the Secretary of State for Scotland, Edinburgh, the office of the Health and Safety Executive, Edinburgh, and with the sheriff clerk of the sheriff court district of Ayr or of Glasgow and Strathkelvin, according to the place where the land is situated, and thereupon the deposited plans and the deposited book of reference shall be deemed to be corrected according to the certificate.

(4) Any certificate or copy deposited under this section with any person shall be kept by him with the other documents to which it relates.

Grant of servitudes by persons under disability

21.—(1) Any person empowered by the Lands Clauses Acts to sell and convey or discharge land may if he thinks fit, subject to the provisions of those Acts, grant to the Board any servitude, right or privilege required for the purposes of this Order in, under, over or affecting the land (not being a servitude, right or privilege of water in which some person other than the grantor has an interest).

(2) The provisions of the said Acts with respect to land and feu duties or ground annuals so far as they are applicable shall extend and apply to any such grant and to any such servitude, right or privilege as aforesaid.

Purchase of part of certain properties

22.—(1) Where a copy of this section is endorsed on, or annexed to, a notice to treat served under the Lands Clauses Acts, as incorporated with this Order, the following provisions of this section shall apply to the land subject to the notice instead of section 90 of the Lands Clauses Consolidation (Scotland) Act 1845.

(2) Where the land subject to the notice is part only of a house, building or factory, or part only of land consisting of a house together with any park or garden belonging thereto, then, if the person on whom the notice is served, within 21 days after the day on which the notice is served on him, serves on the Board a counter-notice objecting to the sale of the part and stating that he is willing and able to sell the whole (in this section referred to as "the land subject to the counter-notice"), the question whether he shall be required to sell the part shall, unless the Board agree to take the land subject to the counter-notice, be referred to the tribunal.

(3) If the said person does not serve such a counter-notice as aforesaid within 21 days after the day on which the notice to treat is served on him, or if on such a reference to the tribunal the tribunal determines that the part subject to the notice to treat can be taken without material detriment to the remainder of the land subject to the counter-notice or, in the case of part of land consisting of a house together with a park or garden belonging thereto, without such detriment and without seriously affecting the amenity and convenience of the house, the said person shall be required to sell the part.

(4) If, on such a reference to the tribunal, the tribunal determines that part only of the land subject to the notice to treat can be taken without material detriment to the remainder of the land subject to the counter-notice or, as the case may be, without such detriment and without seriously affecting the

amenity and convenience of the house, the notice to treat shall be deemed to be a notice to treat for that part.

(5) If, on such a reference to the tribunal, the tribunal determines that the land subject to the notice to treat cannot be taken without material detriment to the remainder of the land subject to the counter-notice but that the material detriment is confined to a part of the land subject to the counter-notice, the notice to treat shall be deemed to be a notice to treat for the land to which the material detriment is confined in addition to the land already subject to the notice, whether or not the additional land is land which the Board are authorised to purchase compulsorily under this Order.

(6) If the Board agree to take the land subject to the counter-notice, or if the tribunal determines that—

(a) none of the land subject to the notice to treat can be taken without material detriment to the remainder of the land subject to the counter-notice or, as the case may be, without such detriment and without seriously affecting the amenity and convenience of the house; and

(b) the material detriment is not confined to a part of the land subject to the counter-notice;

the notice to treat shall be deemed to be a notice to treat for the land subject to the counter-notice whether or not the whole of that land is land which the Board are authorised to purchase under this Order.

(7) In any case where, by virtue of a determination by the tribunal under subsection (4), (5) or (6) above, a notice to treat is deemed to be a notice to treat for part of the land specified in the notice or for more land than is specified in the notice, the Board may, within six weeks after the tribunal makes its determination, withdraw the notice to treat and, if they do so, shall pay to the said person compensation for any loss or expense occasioned to him by the giving and withdrawal of the notice to be determined, in default of agreement, by the tribunal:

Provided that the determination of the tribunal shall not be deemed to be made so long as—

(a) the time for requiring the tribunal to state a case with respect thereto has not expired and any proceedings on the points raised by a case so stated have not been concluded; or

(b) any proceedings on appeal from any decision on the points raised by a case so stated have not been concluded.

(8)(a) Where a person is under this section required to sell part only of a house, building or factory, or of land consisting of a house, together with any park or garden belonging thereto, the Board shall pay to him compensation for any loss sustained by him due to the severance of that part in addition to the value of his interest therein.

(b) Any dispute as to a person's entitlement to compensation under this section or as to the amount of the compensation shall be determined by the tribunal.

Disregard of recent improvements and interests

23. In determining a question with respect to compensation claimed in consequence of the compulsory purchase of land under this Order, the tribunal shall not take into account—

(a) any interest in land, or

(b) any enhancement of the value of any interest in land, by reason of any building erected, works executed or improvement or alteration made (whether on the land purchased or on any other land with which the claimant is, or was at the time of the erection, executing or making of the building, works, improvement or alteration, directly or indirectly concerned), if the tribunal is satisfied that the creation of the interest, the erection of the building, the execution of the works, or the making of the improvement or alteration, as the case may be, was not reasonably necessary and was undertaken with a view to obtaining compensation or increased compensation.

Set-off for enhancement in value of retained land

24.—(1) In this section "relevant land" means any land purchased, or any land in or over which any new rights are purchased, by the Board for the purposes of the works.

(2) In assessing the compensation payable to any person on the purchase by the Board from him of any relevant land, or any rights therein, the tribunal shall—
  (a) have regard to the extent to which the land or the remaining contiguous lands belonging to the same person may be benefited by the works; and
  (b) set off against the value of the relevant land any increase in value of the remaining contiguous lands belonging to the same person which will accrue to him by reason of the construction of any of the works.

(3) The Land Compensation (Scotland) Act 1963 shall have effect subject to the provisions of this section.

Power to enter, survey, etc., land

25.—(1) The Board and their surveyors and officers may at all reasonable times in the day, upon giving on the first occasion not less than 7 days', and on subsequent occasions not less than 3 days', previous notice in writing to the occupier and to the owner if he is not the occupier, enter upon, examine and lay open any land which may be purchased compulsorily under this Order for the purpose of surveying, measuring, taking levels, examining works and valuing that land or for any other purpose ancillary to the powers conferred by this Order.

(2) Any person entering land under subsection (1) above on behalf of the Board shall, if so required, produce written evidence of his identity and of his authority to do so.

(3) In the exercise of the powers of subsection (1) above the Board and their surveyors and officers shall cause as little detriment or inconvenience to any person as circumstances allow, and the Board shall, subject to the provisions of this Order, make compensation to the owners and occupiers of any land injuriously affected by the exercise of those powers, to be determined in case of dispute by the tribunal.

Further powers of entry

26. At any time after notice to treat has been served for any land which may be purchased compulsorily under this Order the Board may, after giving to the owner and occupier of the land not less than three months' notice, enter on and take possession of the land or such part thereof as is specified in the notice without previous consent or compliance with sections 83 to 89 of the Lands Clauses Consolidation (Scotland) Act 1845, but subject to the payment of the like compensation for the land of which possession is taken, and interest on the compensation awarded, as would have been payable if those sections had been complied with.

Extinction or suspension of private rights of way

27.—(1) All private rights of way over any land which may be purchased compulsorily under this Order shall be extinguished on the purchase of the land whether compulsorily or by agreement, or on the entry on the land under section 26 (Further powers of entry) of this Order.

(2) All private rights of way over any land of which the Board may take temporary possession under this Order shall be suspended and unenforceable against the Board for so long as the Board shall remain in lawful possession thereof.

(3) Any person who suffers loss by the extinction or suspension of any right under this section shall be entitled to be paid by the Board compensation, to be determined in case of dispute by the tribunal.

Service of notices, etc.

28. Paragraph 19 of Schedule 1 to the Acquisition of Land (Authorisation Procedure) (Scotland) Act 1947 shall apply and have effect with respect to any notice or other document required or authorised to be served under or by virtue of this Order as if such notice or other document were required or authorised to be served under that Schedule.

PART IV

PROTECTIVE PROVISIONS

Crown rights

29. Nothing in this Order affects prejudicially any estate, right, power, privilege or exemption of the Crown and, without prejudice to the generality of the foregoing, nothing in this Order authorises the Board to take, use, or interfere with, any land or rights—
    (a) belonging to Her Majesty in right of the Crown and under the management of the Crown Estate Commissioners; or
    (b) belonging to a government department, or held in trust for Her Majesty for the purposes of a government department;
without the consent in writing of those commissioners on behalf of Her Majesty or, as the case may be, that government department.

For protection of electricity, gas and water undertakers

30. For the protection of the several undertakers referred to in this section, the following provisions shall, unless otherwise agreed in writing between the Board and the undertakers concerned, have effect:—
    (1) In this section—
        "adequate alternative apparatus" means alternative apparatus adequate to enable the undertakers to fulfil their statutory functions in a manner not less efficient than previously;
        "apparatus" means—
            (a) in the case of electricity undertakers, electric lines or electrical plant (as defined in the Electricity Act 1989) belonging to or maintained by such undertakers; or
            (b) in the case of gas or water undertakers, any mains, pipes or other apparatus belonging to or maintained by such undertakers;
        (not being, except in paragraph (2) below, apparatus in respect of which the relations between the Board and the undertakers are regulated by the provisions of Part IV of the Act of 1991) and includes any structure for the lodging therein of apparatus or for giving access to apparatus;
        "functions" includes powers and duties;
        "in" in a context referring to apparatus or alternative apparatus in land includes a reference to apparatus or alternative apparatus under, over or upon land; and
        "undertakers" means any person authorised to carry on, in any area within which the Board are by this Order authorised to purchase land or execute works, an undertaking for the supply of gas or

water or for the generation, transmission or supply of electricity; and, in relation to any apparatus, means the undertakers to whom it belongs or by whom it is maintained:

(2) Notwithstanding the temporary stopping up or diversion of any road under the powers of section 10 (Temporary stoppage of roads) of this Order, the undertakers shall be at liberty at all times to execute and do all such works and things in, upon or under any such road as may be reasonably necessary or desirable to enable them to inspect, repair, maintain, renew, remove or use any apparatus which at the time of the stopping up or diversion was in that road:

(3) The Board, in the case of the powers conferred by section 11 (Underpinning of buildings near works) of this Order, shall, so far as is reasonably practicable, so exercise those powers as not to obstruct or render less convenient the access to any apparatus and, if by reason of the exercise of those powers any damage to any apparatus (other than apparatus the repair of which is not reasonably necessary in view of its intended removal or abandonment) or property of the undertakers or any interruption in the supply of electricity, gas or water, as the case may be, by the undertakers is caused, the Board shall bear and pay the cost reasonably incurred by the undertakers in making good that damage or restoring the supply; and shall—

   (a) make reasonable compensation to the undertakers for any loss sustained by them; and

   (b) indemnify the undertakers against all claims, demands, proceedings, costs, damages and expenses which may be made or taken against or recovered from or incurred by the undertakers;

by reason of any such damage or interruption:

Provided that—

   (i) nothing in this paragraph shall impose any liability on the Board with respect to any damage or interruption to the extent that the damage or interruption may be attributable to the act, neglect or default of the undertakers or their contractors or workmen;

   (ii) the undertakers shall give to the Board reasonable notice of any claim or demand as aforesaid and no settlement or compromise thereof shall be made without the prior consent of the Board:

(4) Notwithstanding anything in section 12 (Use of sewers, etc., for removing water) of this Order, no use shall be made by the Board in the construction of the works of pumping or other like modes of removing water except where reasonably necessary or in case of emergency or unforeseen accident or for the purpose of removing rainwater or other small amounts of water:

(5) Notwithstanding anything in this Order or shown on the deposited plans, the Board shall not acquire any apparatus under the powers of this Order otherwise than by agreement:

(6) If the Board, in the exercise of the powers of this Order, acquire any interest in any land in which any apparatus is placed, that apparatus shall not be removed under this section and any right of the undertakers to maintain, repair, renew or inspect that apparatus in that land shall not be extinguished until adequate alternative apparatus has been constructed and is in operation to the reasonable satisfaction of the undertakers:

(7) If the Board, for the purpose of executing any works in, on or under any land purchased, held, appropriated or used under this Order, require the removal of any apparatus placed in that land, they shall give to the undertakers written notice of that requirement, together with a plan and section of the work proposed, and of the proposed position of the alternative apparatus to be provided or constructed so as to provide adequate alternative apparatus in lieu of the apparatus to be removed, and in that case (or if in consequence of the exercise of

any of the powers of this Order, the undertakers reasonably require to remove any apparatus) the Board shall afford to the undertakers the necessary facilities and rights for the construction of the alternative apparatus in other land of the Board and thereafter for the maintenance, repair, renewal and inspection of that apparatus:

Provided that, if the alternative apparatus or any part thereof is to be constructed elsewhere than in other land of the Board, or the Board are unable to afford such facilities and rights as aforesaid in the land in which the alternative apparatus or part thereof is to be constructed, the undertakers shall, on receipt of a written notice to that effect from the Board, forthwith use their best endeavours to obtain the necessary facilities and rights in that last-mentioned land:

(8) (a) Any alternative apparatus to be constructed in land of the Board under this section shall be constructed in such manner and in such line or situation as may be agreed between the undertakers and the Board or in default of agreement determined by arbitration;

(b) The undertakers shall, after the alternative apparatus to be provided or constructed has been agreed or determined by arbitration as aforesaid and after the grant to the undertakers of any such facilities and rights as are referred to in paragraph (7) above, proceed with all reasonable dispatch to construct and bring into operation the alternative apparatus and thereafter to remove any apparatus required by the Board to be removed under the provisions of this section:

(9) Notwithstanding anything in paragraph (8) above, if the Board give notice in writing to the undertakers that they desire themselves to execute any part of so much of the work necessary in connection with the construction of the alternative apparatus, or the removal of the apparatus required to be removed, as will take place in any land of the Board, that work, in lieu of being executed by the undertakers, shall be executed by the Board with all reasonable dispatch under the superintendence, if given, and to the reasonable satisfaction of the undertakers:

Provided that nothing in this paragraph shall authorise the Board to execute the actual placing, installation, bedding, packing, removal, connection or disconnection of any apparatus, or execute any filling around the apparatus (where the apparatus is laid in a trench) within 300 millimetres of the apparatus:

(10) Where, in accordance with the provisions of this section, the Board afford to the undertakers facilities and rights for the construction, maintenance, repair, renewal and inspection in land of the Board of alternative apparatus in substitution for apparatus to be removed as aforesaid, those facilities and rights shall be granted upon such terms and conditions as may be agreed between the Board and the undertakers or in default of agreement determined by arbitration:

Provided that—

(a) in determining those terms and conditions in respect of alternative apparatus to be constructed in or along any railway of the Board, the arbiter shall—

(i) give effect to all reasonable requirements of the Board for ensuring the safety and efficient operation of the railway and for securing any subsequent alterations or adaptations of the alternative apparatus which may be required to prevent interference with any proposed works of the Board or the traffic on the railway; and

(ii) so far as it may be reasonable and practicable to do so in the circumstances of the particular case, give effect to the terms and conditions applicable to the apparatus, if any, constructed in or along the railway for which the alternative apparatus is to be substituted;

(b) if the facilities and rights to be afforded by the Board in respect of any alternative apparatus and the terms and conditions subject to which the same are to be granted are in the opinion of the arbiter less favourable on the whole to the undertakers than the facilities and rights enjoyed by them in respect of the apparatus to be removed and the terms and conditions to which those facilities and rights are subject, the arbiter shall make such provision for the payment of compensation by the Board to the undertakers in respect thereof as appears to him to be reasonable having regard to all the circumstances of the particular case:

(11) (a) Not less than 28 days before commencing to execute any works which are referred to in paragraph (7) above and are near to or will or may affect any apparatus the removal of which has not been required by the Board under the said paragraph (7), the Board shall submit to the undertakers a plan, section and description of the works to be executed;

(b) Those works shall be executed only in accordance with the plan, section and description submitted as aforesaid and in accordance with such reasonable requirements as may be made by the undertakers for the alteration or otherwise for the protection of the apparatus or for securing access thereto and the undertakers shall be entitled by their officer to watch and inspect the execution of those works:

Provided that—

(i) if the undertakers within 14 days after the submission to them of a plan, section and description shall, in consequence of the works proposed by the Board, reasonably require the removal of any apparatus and give written notice to the Board of that requirement, the foregoing provisions of this section shall apply as if the removal of the apparatus had been required by the Board under paragraph (7) above;

(ii) nothing in this sub-paragraph shall preclude the Board from submitting at any time or from time to time, but in no case less than 28 days before commencing the execution of any works, a new plan, section and description thereof in lieu of the plan, section and description previously submitted, and thereupon the provisions of this paragraph shall apply to and in respect of the new plan, section and description;

(c) The Board shall not be required to comply with sub-paragraph (a) above in a case of emergency but in that case they shall give to the undertakers notice as soon as reasonably practicable and a plan, section and description of those works as soon as reasonably practicable thereafter and shall comply with sub-paragraph (b) above so far as reasonably practicable in the circumstances:

(12) Where, by reason of this Order, any part of any road in which any apparatus is situate ceases to be part of a road, the undertakers may exercise the same rights of access to that apparatus as they enjoyed immediately before the passing of the Act confirming this Order, but nothing in this paragraph shall affect any right of the Board or of the undertakers to require removal of the apparatus under this section or the power of the Board to execute works in accordance with paragraph (11) above:

(13) Subject to paragraph (14) below, the Board shall pay to the undertakers the costs, charges and expenses reasonably incurred by the undertakers in or in connection with the inspection, removal, alteration or protection of any apparatus or the construction of any new apparatus which may be required in consequence of the execution of any such works as are referred to in paragraph (7) above, less the value of any apparatus removed under the provisions of this section (that

value being calculated after removal) and shall also make compensation to the undertakers—
  (a) for any damage caused to any apparatus (other than apparatus the repair of which is not reasonably necessary in view of its intended removal in accordance with the provisions of this section); and
  (b) for any other expenses, loss, damages, penalty or costs incurred by the undertakers;
by reason of the execution, maintenance, user or failure of those works or otherwise by reason of the exercise by the Board of the powers of this Order:

(14) If the cost of maintaining, using, repairing or renewing any apparatus is reduced by reason of any of the works, including the provision of alternative apparatus under this section, a capitalised sum representing that saving shall be paid by the relevant undertakers to the Board or set off against any sums payable by the Board to the relevant undertakers under this section:

(15) Where, by reason of the stopping up of any road under the powers of this Order, any apparatus belonging to the undertakers and laid or placed in the road or elsewhere is rendered derelict or unnecessary, the Board shall pay to the undertakers the then value of that apparatus (which shall thereupon become the property of the Board) and the reasonable cost of and incidental to the cutting off of that apparatus from any other apparatus and of and incidental to the execution or doing of any works or things rendered necessary or expedient by reason of that apparatus being so rendered derelict or unnecessary:

  Provided that the Board shall not under the provisions of this paragraph be required to pay to the undertakers the value of any apparatus rendered derelict or unnecessary, if, to the reasonable satisfaction of the undertakers, other apparatus has at the expense of the Board been provided and laid and made ready for use in substitution for the apparatus so rendered derelict or unnecessary:

(16) Any difference arising between the Board and the undertakers under this section (other than a difference as to the meaning or construction of this section) shall be determined by arbitration:

(17) Nothing in this section shall affect the provisions of any enactment or agreement regulating the relations between the Board and the undertakers in respect of any apparatus laid or erected in land belonging to the Board at the date of the passing of the Act confirming this Order.

For protection of roads and road traffic, etc.

31. The following provisions shall, unless otherwise agreed in writing between the Board and the road works authority or Cumnock and Doon Valley District Council or City of Glasgow District Council, as the case may be, have effect:—

(1) In this section—
  "the appropriate council" means the road works authority or the district council, as the case may be;
  "the district council" means the Cumnock and Doon Valley District Council and the City of Glasgow District Council, or either of them as the case may be;
  "road" has the same meaning as in the Roads (Scotland) Act 1984; and
  "road equipment" means any works or apparatus on or under any road comprising any refuge, lamp column, traffic sign, bollard, bin for refuse or road materials, surface water drain, gully or sewer for conducting road drainage or apparatus respectively connected therewith:

(2) Wherever in this section provision is made with respect to the approval or consent of the appropriate council, that approval or consent shall be in writing and shall not be unreasonably withheld:

(3) The Board shall not, without the consent of the road works authority, construct any part of the works which will involve interference with any road, except in accordance with plans and sections submitted to, and approved by, the road works authority:

Provided that, if within 56 days after those plans and sections have been submitted the road works authority have not approved or disapproved them, they shall be deemed to have approved the plans and sections as submitted:

(4) Before commencing to construct any part of the works, or any works or conveniences connected therewith, which will involve interference with a road, or the traffic in any road, the Board shall consult the road works authority as to the time when that part shall be commenced, and as to the extent of the surface of the road which it may be reasonably necessary for the Board to occupy or the nature of the interference which may be caused to the said traffic in the construction of that part, and as to the time during which, and the extent to which, the road shall be interfered with, and as to the conditions under which that part shall be constructed, so as to reduce so far as possible inconvenience to the public and to ensure the safety of the public, and that part shall not be constructed, and the surface of the road shall not be occupied by the Board, and the said interference with traffic shall not be caused, except at such time, to such extent, and in accordance with such conditions as may be agreed between the Board and the road works authority or determined by arbitration:

(5) At least 56 days before commencing to make any hole from the surface of any part of any road the Board shall serve notice in writing on the road works authority of their intention to commence the same, and that notice shall describe the place at which any hole is intended to be made, and the steps, if any, to be taken by the Board to safeguard pedestrians using any footway, footpath or other way in which the hole is intended to be made, and, if within 21 days after the receipt of the notice any objection is made by the road works authority, the matter shall (unless otherwise agreed) be determined by arbitration before the making of the hole is commenced, but if no objection is made the Board may proceed with the making of the hole:

(6) The Board shall secure that so much of the works as is constructed under, or so as to affect, any road is so designed, constructed and maintained as to carry the appropriate loading for that road recommended at the time of construction of those works by the Secretary of State, and the Board shall indemnify the road works authority against, and make good to the road works authority, all expenses which they may reasonably incur or be put to in the maintenance or repair of any road, or any tunnels, sewers, drains or apparatus therein, by reason of any non-compliance by the Board with the provisions of this paragraph:

(7) It shall be lawful for an authorised officer of the appropriate council at all reasonable times to enter upon and inspect any part of the works which is in or under any road or which may affect any road or any property or work of the appropriate council, during the execution thereof, and the Board shall give to that officer all reasonable facilities for such inspection and, if he is of the opinion that the construction of that part of the works is attended with danger to any road or to any road equipment or any other property or work belonging to, or under the jurisdiction or control of, the appropriate council on or under any road, the Board shall adopt such measures and precautions as may be reasonably necessary for the purpose of preventing any damage or injury thereto:

(8) The Board shall not alter, disturb or in any way interfere with any road equipment or any other property or work belonging to, or under the jurisdiction or control of, the appropriate council on or under any road, or the access thereto, without the consent of the appropriate council, and any alteration, adaptation, diversion, replacement or reconstruction of any road equipment or any other property or work as aforesaid which may be necessary shall be made by the appropriate council or the Board as the appropriate council think fit and any costs, charges and expenses reasonably incurred by the appropriate council in so doing shall be repaid to the appropriate council by the Board:

(9) The Board shall not remove any soil or material from any road except such as must be excavated in the execution of the works:

(10) (a) The Board shall not, except with the consent of the road works authority, deposit any soil, subsoil or materials, or stand any vehicle or plant, on any road so as to obstruct the use of such road by any person or, except with the like consent, deposit any soil, subsoil or materials on any road except within a hoarding;

(b) All costs, charges and expenses reasonably incurred by the road works authority in removing any soil, subsoil or materials deposited on any road in contravention of this paragraph shall be repaid to the road works authority by the Board:

(11) Where any part of any road has been temporarily broken up or disturbed by the Board, the Board shall make good the subsoil, foundations and surface of such part of the road to the reasonable satisfaction of the road works authority and maintain the same to the reasonable satisfaction of the road works authority for such time as may be reasonably required for the permanent reinstatement of the road:

Provided that the reinstatement of such part of the road shall in the first instance be of a temporary nature only and the permanent reinstatement thereof shall be carried out by the road works authority as soon as reasonably practicable after the completion of the temporary reinstatement, and the costs, charges and expenses reasonably incurred by the road works authority in so doing shall be repaid to the road works authority by the Board:

(12) The Board shall compensate the appropriate council for any subsidence of, or damage to, any road or any road equipment or any other property or work belonging to, or under the jurisdiction or control of, the appropriate council on or under any road which may be caused by, or in consequence of, any act or default of the Board, their contractors, servants or agents and whether such damage or subsidence happens during the construction of the works or at any time thereafter:

(13) Any difference arising between the Board and the appropriate council under this section (other than a difference as to the meaning or construction of this section) shall be determined by arbitration.

For protection of sewers of Strathclyde Regional Council

32. For the protection of the sewers of the regional council the following provisions shall, unless otherwise agreed in writing between the Board and the regional council, have effect:

(1) In this section—

"sewer" includes any manholes, ventilating shafts, pumps or other accessories of a sewer; and

"specified work" means any part of the works which will or may be situated within 15 metres measured in any direction of any sewer of the regional council:

(2) Wherever in this section provision is made with respect to the approval or consent of the regional council, that approval or consent shall be in writing and shall not be unreasonably withheld:

(3) The Board shall not commence the execution of any specified work until they have given to the regional council not less than 56 days' notice in writing of their intention to commence the same, together with plans as described in paragraph (8) below (in this section referred to as "the said plans"), for their approval and until the regional council have signified their approval of those plans:

Provided that, if within 56 days after the submission of the said plans the regional council have not approved or disapproved them, they shall be deemed to have approved the said plans as submitted:

(4) The Board shall comply with, and conform to, all reasonable orders, directions and regulations of the regional council in the execution of any specified work and shall provide new, altered or substituted works in such manner as the regional council reasonably require for the protection of, and for preventing injury or impediment to, any existing sewer of the regional council by reason of the specified work and shall indemnify the regional council against all expenses occasioned thereby:

(5) All new, altered or substituted works shall, where so required by the regional council, be done by or under the direction, superintendence and control of an officer of the regional council duly appointed for the purpose at the cost of the Board, and all costs, charges and expenses reasonably incurred by the regional council by reason of those works, whether in the execution thereof, or in the preparation or examination of plans or designs, or in such direction, superintendence or control as aforesaid, or otherwise, shall be paid to the regional council by the Board:

(6) When any new, altered or substituted works or any work of defence connected therewith are completed by or at the cost of the Board under the provisions of this section, they shall thereafter be as fully and completely under the direction, jurisdiction and control of the regional council as any sewers or works now or hereafter may be:

(7) The regional council may require the Board in constructing any specified work to make any reasonable deviation within the limits of deviation from the lines or levels shown upon the said plans for the purpose of avoiding injury, or risk of injury, to any sewer of the regional council, and the Board shall in constructing those works deviate accordingly:

(8) The plans to be submitted to the regional council for the purposes of this section shall be detailed plans, drawings, sections and specifications which shall describe the exact position and manner in which, and the level at which, any specified work is proposed to be constructed and shall accurately describe the position of all sewers of the regional council within the limits of deviation (for which purpose the regional council shall allow the Board access to plans in their possession and to any of their sewers in order to enable the Board to obtain reliable information) and shall comprise detailed drawings of every alteration which the Board may propose to make in any sewer:

(9) The regional council may require such modifications to be made in the said plans as may be reasonably necessary to secure the main drainage system of the district in which any specified work is situated against interference or risk of damage and to provide and secure proper and convenient means of access to any sewer:

(10) The Board shall be liable to make good, or, if the regional council so decide, to bear any expense reasonably incurred by the regional council in making good, all injury or damage caused by, or resulting from,

the construction of any specified work to any sewer, drain or work vested in the regional council:

(11) If the Board in the construction of any specified work or any new, altered or substituted work or any work of defence connected therewith provided in accordance with this section, damage or, without the consent of the regional council, alter or in any way interfere with any existing sewer of the regional council, the Board shall—

    (a) pay to the regional council any additional expense which may be reasonably incurred by the regional council in the maintenance, management or renewal of any new, altered or substituted sewer which may be necessary by reason of the said construction; and

    (b) give to the regional council full, free and uninterrupted access at all times to any such new, altered or substituted sewer and every reasonable facility for the inspecting, maintenance, alteration and repair thereof:

(12) It shall be lawful for an officer of the regional council duly appointed for the purpose at any reasonable time, on giving to the Board such notice as may in the circumstances be reasonable, to enter upon and inspect any specified work or any other work constructed under the powers of this section:

(13) The approval by the regional council of any plans, or the superintendence by them of any work, under the provisions of this section, shall not exonerate the Board from any liability or affect any claim for damages under this section or otherwise:

(14) Any difference arising between the Board and the regional council under this section (other than a difference as to the meaning or construction of this section) shall be determined by arbitration.

For protection of telecommunications operators

33. For the protection of telecommunications operators the following provisions shall, unless otherwise agreed in writing between the Board and the telecommunications operators concerned, have effect:—

(1) In this section expressions defined in the Telecommunications Act 1984 have the same meanings as in that Act:

(2) The temporary stopping up or diversion of any road under section 10 (Temporary stoppage of roads) of this Order shall not affect any right of a telecommunications operator under paragraph 9 of the telecommunications code to inspect, maintain, adjust, repair or alter any apparatus which, at the time of the stopping up or diversion, is in that road.

For protection of British Waterways Board

34. For the protection of the British Waterways Board (in this section referred to as "the waterways board") the following provisions shall, unless otherwise agreed in writing between the Board and the waterways board, have effect:—

(1) In this section—

    "the aqueduct" means the aqueduct conveying the canal over the former railway of the Board between Maryhill Park and Knightswood South Junctions;

    "the canal" means the Forth and Clyde Canal of the waterways board and any works connected therewith for the maintenance of which the waterways board are responsible and includes—

        (a) any lands held or used by the waterways board for the purposes of the canal; and

(b) the aqueduct (for the maintenance of which the Board are responsible);

"construction" includes execution, placing and altering and the maintenance and repair of the specified works and "construct" shall be construed accordingly;

"the designated land" means the land numbered on the deposited plans 14 in the City of Glasgow District;

"the engineer" means an engineer to be appointed by the waterways board;

"plans" includes sections, drawings and particulars (including descriptions of methods of construction); and

"the specified works" means so much of Work No. 2 and any works and conveniences connected therewith as may be situated upon, across or under, or may in any way affect, the canal:

(2) Notwithstanding anything in this Order or shown on the deposited plans, the Board shall not purchase compulsorily or use any land or other property of the waterways board or any new rights therein:

(3) The Board shall not use any land or property of the waterways board for the passage of vehicles, plant or machinery employed in the construction of the specified works except—

(a) with the consent in writing of the engineer, whose consent shall not be unreasonably withheld;

(b) subject to compliance with such reasonable requirements as the engineer may from time to time specify—

(i) for the prevention of damage to such land and property and of danger to persons thereon; and

(ii) in order to avoid or reduce any inconvenience to the waterways board, their officers and agents and all other persons lawfully on such land or property:

(4) The Board shall, before commencing the construction of the specified works, including temporary works, furnish to the waterways board proper and sufficient plans thereof for the reasonable approval of the engineer, and shall not commence the construction of the specified works until plans thereof have been approved in writing by the engineer or determined by arbitration:

Provided that, if within 56 days after such plans have been furnished to the waterways board the engineer shall not have notified his disapproval thereof and the grounds of his disapproval, he shall be deemed to have approved the plans as submitted:

(5) Upon signifying his approval or disapproval of the plans the engineer may specify any protective works, whether temporary or permanent, which in his opinion should be carried out before the commencement of the construction of the specified works to ensure the safety or stability of the canal and such protective works as may be reasonably necessary for those purposes shall be constructed by the Board with all reasonable dispatch:

(6) The Board shall pay to the waterways board a capitalised sum representing the increased or additional cost of maintaining and, when necessary, renewing any permanent protective works provided under paragraph (5) above, but, if the cost of maintaining, or of works of renewal on, the canal is reduced in consequence of any such protective works, a capitalised sum representing such saving shall be set off against any sum payable by the Board to the waterways board under this section:

(7) The Board shall give to the engineer not less than 28 days' notice of their intention to commence the construction of the specified works or any protective works, except in emergency (when they shall give such notice as may be reasonably practicable), of their intention to carry

out any works for the repair or maintenance of the specified works in so far as such works of repair or maintenance affect or interfere with the canal so that, in particular, the waterways board may where appropriate arrange for the publication of notices bringing those works to the attention of users of their inland waterways:

(8) The Board shall provide and maintain at their expense such temporary lighting of the canal and signal lights in the vicinity of the specified works as the engineer may reasonably require during the construction or failure of the specified works:

(9) The construction of the specified works shall, when commenced, be carried out with all reasonable dispatch in accordance with the approved plans and under the supervision (if given), and to the reasonable satisfaction, of the engineer, and in such manner as to cause as little damage as may be to the canal and as little interference as may be with the passage of vessels using the canal and, if any damage to the canal or any stoppage thereof or any interference with the passage of vessels using the canal shall be caused by the construction of the specified works, or by the passage of vehicles, plant and machinery used in connection therewith, the Board shall, notwithstanding any such approval as aforesaid, make good such damage and on demand pay to the waterways board all reasonable expenses to which they may be put and compensation for any loss which they may sustain by reason of any such damage, stoppage or interference:

(10) Without prejudice to paragraph (9) above the Board, following the completion of the initial construction of the specified works, shall restore the canal to a condition no less satisfactory than its condition immediately prior to the commencement of those works:

(11) The Board shall at all times afford reasonable facilities to the engineer for access to the specified works during their construction and shall supply him with all such information as he may reasonably require with regard to the specified works or the method of construction thereof:

(12) The Board shall not in the course of constructing the specified works or otherwise in connection therewith pollute or deposit any materials in the canal or do or permit anything which may result in such pollution and shall take such steps as the engineer may reasonably require to avoid or make good any breach of their obligations under this paragraph:

(13) The Board shall repay to the waterways board all costs, charges and expenses reasonably incurred by the waterways board—

(a) in respect of the employment of any inspectors, watchmen and other persons whom it shall be reasonably necessary to appoint for inspecting, watching and lighting the canal and for preventing, so far as may be reasonably practicable, interference, obstruction, danger or accident arising from the construction or failure of the specified works;

(b) in respect of the approval by the engineer of plans supplied by the Board under paragraph (4) above and the supervision by him of the construction of the specified works;

(c) in bringing the specified works to the notice of users of the canal:

(14) The Board shall be responsible for and make good to the waterways board all costs, charges, damages and expenses not otherwise provided for in this section which may be occasioned to, or reasonably incurred by, the waterways board—

(a) by reason of the construction of the specified works or the failure thereof; or

(b) by reason of any act or omission of the Board or of any persons in their employ, or of their contractors or others whilst engaged upon the construction of the specified works;

and the Board shall effectively indemnify and hold harmless the waterways board from and against all claims and demands arising out of, or in connection with, the construction of the specified works or any such failure, act or omission as aforesaid and the fact that any act or thing may have been done in accordance with plans approved by the engineer, or in accordance with any requirement of the engineer or under his supervision, shall not (if it was done without negligence on the part of the waterways board or of any person in their employ, or of their contractors or agents) excuse the Board from any liability under the provisions of this paragraph:

Provided that the waterways board shall give to the Board reasonable notice of any claim or demand as aforesaid and no settlement or compromise thereof shall be made without the prior consent of the Board:

(15) Nothing in this section shall extend to regulate—

(a) the alteration, maintenance and repair by the Board of the aqueduct; or

(b) the alteration, maintenance and repair by the Board of the specified works after completion of their initial construction in relation to the aqueduct;

and in these respects the rights and obligations as between the Board and the waterways board created by Schedule No. 1 to the Minute of Agreement between those Boards dated 10th April and 26th June and registered in the Books of the Lords of Council and Session for preservation on 9th July, all being months in the year 1964, shall be exercisable and observed between those Boards notwithstanding anything to the contrary in subclause (Two) (b) of clause X of that Agreement:

(16) Any difference arising between the Board and the waterways board under this section (other than a difference as to the meaning or construction of this section) shall be determined by arbitration.

PART V

GENERAL

Saving for town and country planning

35.—(1) The Town and Country Planning (Scotland) Act 1972, and any orders, regulations, rules, schemes and directions made or given thereunder and any restrictions or powers thereby imposed or conferred in relation to land shall apply and may be exercised in relation to any land notwithstanding that the development thereof is or may be authorised by this Order.

(2) Subject to subsection (3) below, in their application to development authorised by this Order, article 3 of, and Class 29 in Part 11 of Schedule 1 to, the Town and Country Planning (General Permitted Development) (Scotland) Order 1992 (which permit development authorised by any local or private Act or by any order approved by both Houses of Parliament, being an Act or order designating specifically both the nature of the development thereby authorised and the land on which it may be carried out) shall have effect as if the authority to develop given by this Order were limited to development begun within 10 years after the passing of the Act confirming this Order.

(3) Subsection (2) above shall not apply to the carrying out of any development consisting of the alteration, maintenance or repair of works or the substitution of new works therefor.

Arbitration

36. Where under any provision of this Order any difference (other than a difference to which the provisions of the Lands Clauses Acts apply) is to be determined by arbitration, then, unless otherwise provided, the difference shall be referred to, and settled by, a single arbiter to be agreed between the parties or, in default of agreement, to be appointed on the summary application of any party (after notice in writing to the other) by the sheriff.

Repeal and disapplication of enactments

37.—(1) The enactments specified in columns (1) and (2) of Part I of Schedule 4 to this Order are hereby repealed to the extent specified in column (3) of that Part.

(2) The enactments specified in Part II of the said Schedule 4 shall cease to have effect in their application to Work No. 2.

SCHEDULES

Section 7   SCHEDULE 1

STATION WORKS REFERRED TO IN SECTION 7 OF THIS ORDER

Land numbered on deposited plans (1)	Description of station works (2)
In the City of Glasgow District	
4	Bay platform at Anniesland station.
11 to 15, 17, 18	Station at Dalsholm Road.
21 to 25	Station at Maryhill.

Section 9   SCHEDULE 2

MEANS OF ACCESS REFERRED TO IN SECTION 9 OF THIS ORDER

Description of access (1)	Purpose for which access required (2)
In the district of Cumnock and Doon Valley	
Point A from Quarry Knowe, Auchinleck.	To construct Work No. 1 and thereafter for the general purposes of the Board.
Point B from the Auchinleck to Lugar road, Cronberry.	To construct Work No. 1 and thereafter for the general purposes of the Board.

Section 16   SCHEDULE 3

PART I

MEANS OF ACCESS REFERRED TO IN SECTION 16 OF THIS ORDER

Area (1)	Land numbered on deposited plans (2)	Road to which access to be provided (3)	Purpose for which access required (4)
In the Strathclyde Region			
District of Cumnock and Doon Valley.	10	Auchinleck to Lugar road.	To construct Work No. 1.
	11a	Auchinleck to Lugar road.	To construct Work No. 1.
	18	Rigg Road, Lugar.	To construct Work No. 1 and thereafter for the general purposes of the Board.
	23	Auchinleck to A.70 road, Cronberry, at point C.	To construct Work No. 1 and thereafter for the general purposes of the Board.
	28	A.70 road, Cronberry.	To construct Work No. 1 and thereafter for the general purposes of the Board.
	39	A.70 road, Cronberry.	To construct Work No. 1 and thereafter for the general purposes of the Board.
	41, 43	A.70 road, Powharnal.	To construct Work No. 1 and thereafter for the general purposes of the Board.
City of Glasgow District	1 to 3	Great Western Road, Anniesland.	To construct Works Nos. 2 and 3 and the bay platform at Anniesland station and the station at Dalsholm Road referred to in section 7 of, and Schedule 1 to, this Order, or any of them, and thereafter for the general purposes of the Board.
	24 to 26	Maryhill Road, Maryhill.	To construct Work No. 2 and the station at Dalsholm Road referred to in section 7 of, and Schedule 1 to, this Order, or either of them, and thereafter for the general purposes of the Board.

Section 17   PART II

TEMPORARY WORKING SITES

1. In this Part of this Schedule "the designated lands" means any of the lands shown on the deposited plans within a line marked "Limit of land to be used" and numbered on those plans 6, 8, 11, 19, 25a and 40 in the district of Cumnock and Doon Valley.

2. The Board, in connection with the construction of Work No. 1 and after giving to the owners and occupiers of the designated lands not less than 28 days' notice in writing of intended entry, may—

  (a) enter upon and take possession temporarily of the designated lands;
  (b) remove any structures and vegetation on the designated lands; and
  (c) construct on the designated lands such temporary works or structures as may be required by them.

3. The Board shall not, by reason of the exercise of the powers of paragraph 2 above, be required to purchase any part of the designated lands.

4. On the exercise of the powers conferred by paragraph 2 above, the following provisions shall have effect:—

  (1) The Board shall not, without the agreement of the owners and occupiers of the designated lands, remain in possession of any part thereof after a period of one year from the completion of the works for which such possession has been taken:
  (2) Before giving up possession of the designated lands, the Board shall remove all temporary works or structures and restore the designated lands to the reasonable satisfaction of the owners and occupiers thereof:
  (3) The Board shall compensate the owners and occupiers of the designated lands for any loss or damage which may result to them by reason of the exercise of the powers of this Part:
  (4) Nothing in this Part shall relieve the Board from liability to compensate under section 6 or 43 of the Act of 1845 or under any other enactment, in respect of loss or damage arising from the execution of any works, other than loss or damage for which compensation is payable under sub-paragraph (3) above:
  (5) Any dispute as to a person's entitlement to compensation under sub-paragraph (3) above or as to the amount thereof shall be determined by the tribunal.

Section 37   SCHEDULE 4

PART I

REPEALS

Chapter (1)	Short title (2)	Extent of repeal (3)
34 & 35 Vict. c.cvi.	North British Railway Act 1871.	Sections 27 to 36.

PART II

ENACTMENTS DISAPPLIED IN RESPECT OF WORK NO. 2

Chapter (1)	Short title (2)	Extent of disapplication (3)
34 & 35 Vict. c.cvi.	North British Railway Act 1871.	Sections 18 to 23.

INDEX

References are to section number of the Order

BRITISH RAILWAYS (NO. 2) ORDER CONFIRMATION ACT 1994

(1994 c. ii)

An Act to confirm a Provisional Order under the Private Legislation Procedure (Scotland) Act 1936, relating to British Railways (No. 2).

[24th March 1994]

PARLIAMENTARY PROGRESS
    The Bill's progress through Parliament was as follows:
    House of Commons: First Reading, March 9, 1994; Considered by Commons, March 15, 1994; Third Reading, March 16, 1994.
    House of Lords: First Reading, March 16, 1994; Considered by Lords, March 22, 1994; Third Reading, March 24, 1994.

INTRODUCTION
    This Act provides for the reinstatement of the railway between Cambus and Alloa in the Clackmannan District in order to allow the reopening of a passenger service line between Stirling and Alloa. This Act empowers the British Railways Board to undertake the works necessary to complete this development. Part I contains preliminary provisions. Part II details the works proposed and indicates the likely interference with existing amenities. Part III details the land likely to be affected by the Act. Part IV sets out protective provisions *vis-à-vis* amenities and Crown rights.

WHEREAS the Provisional Order set forth in the Schedule hereunto annexed has been made by the Secretary of State under the provisions of the Private Legislation Procedure (Scotland) Act 1936, and it is requisite that the said Order should be confirmed by Parliament:

Be it therefore enacted by the Queen's most Excellent Majesty, by and with the advice and consent of the Lords Spiritual and Temporal, and Commons, in this present Parliament assembled, and by the authority of the same, as follows:—

Confirmation of Order in Schedule

1. The Provisional Order contained in the Schedule hereunto annexed is hereby confirmed.

Short title

2. This Act may be cited as the British Railways (No. 2) Order Confirmation Act 1994.

SCHEDULE

BRITISH RAILWAYS (No. 2)

Provisional Order to empower the British Railways Board to construct works and to purchase or use land; to confer further powers on the Board; and for connected purposes.

WHEREAS—

    (1) It is the duty of the British Railways Board (hereinafter referred to as "the Board") under the Transport Act 1962 (inter alia) to provide railway services in Great Britain and, in connection with the provision of railway services, to provide such other services and facilities as appear to the Board to be expedient, and to have due regard, as respects all those railway and other services and facilities, to efficiency, economy and safety of operation:

    (2) It is expedient that the Board should be empowered to construct in the Central Region the works authorised by this Order and to purchase or use the land referred to in this Order and that the other provisions in this Order contained should be enacted:

    (3) A plan and section showing the line or situation and levels of the work to be constructed under this Order, and a plan of the lands authorised to be

purchased or used by this Order, and a book of reference to that plan containing the names of the owners and lessees, or reputed owners and lessees, and of the occupiers of the said lands were duly deposited in the office of the Clerk of the Parliaments and in the Private Bill Office of the House of Commons and with the sheriff clerk of the sheriff court district of Alloa, which plan, section and book of reference are respectively referred to in this Order as the deposited plan, the deposited section and the deposited book of reference:

(4) The purposes of this Order cannot be effected without an Order confirmed by Parliament under the provisions of the Private Legislation Procedure (Scotland) Act 1936:

Now therefore, in pursuance of the powers contained in the last-mentioned Act, the Secretary of State orders as follows:—

PART I

PRELIMINARY

Short title

1. This Order may be cited as the British Railways (No. 2) Order 1994.

Interpretation

2.—(1) In this Order, unless the context otherwise requires, words and expressions to which meanings are assigned by the enactments incorporated herewith have the same respective meanings; and—

>"the Act of 1845" means the Railways Clauses Consolidation (Scotland) Act 1845;
>
>"the Act of 1991" means the New Roads and Street Works Act 1991;
>
>"the Board" means the British Railways Board;
>
>"enactment" includes any order, byelaw, rule, regulation, scheme or other instrument having effect by virtue of an enactment;
>
>"the limit of deviation" means the limit of deviation shown on the deposited plan;
>
>"road" has the meaning assigned to it by section 107 of the Act of 1991;
>
>"the sheriff" means the sheriff principal of, or any sheriff appointed for, the Sheriffdom of Tayside, Central and Fife;
>
>"the tribunal" means the Lands Tribunal for Scotland;
>
>"the works" means the works authorised by Part II (Works, etc.) of this Order; and
>
>"Work No. 1" means the work of that number authorised by section 4 (Power to make railway) of this Order.

(2) Except in relation to section 6 (Power to deviate) of this Order, all directions, distances and lengths stated in any description of works, powers or lands in this Order shall be construed as if the words "or thereby" were inserted after each such direction, distance and length.

Incorporation of enactments

3.—(1) The following enactments, so far as the same are applicable for the purposes of and are not inconsistent with, or varied by, the provisions of this Order, are incorporated with this Order, and this Order shall be deemed to be the special Act for the purposes of the said incorporated enactments:—

>(a) the Lands Clauses Acts, except sections 120 to 124 and section 127 of the Lands Clauses Consolidation (Scotland) Act 1845;
>
>(b) the Act of 1845, except sections 1, 7, 8, 9, 17, 19, 20, 22 and 23 thereof; and
>
>(c) in the Railways Clauses Act 1863, Part I (relating to construction of a railway) except sections 13, 14, 18 and 19 thereof.

(2)(a) In the application of the enactments incorporated by subsection (1) (b) and (c) above the expression "the company" means the Board.

(b) Sections 18 and 21 of the Act of 1845 shall not extend to regulate the relations between the Board and any other person in respect of any matter or thing concerning which those relations are regulated in any respect by the provisions of Part IV of the Act of 1991 or by section 27 (For protection of electricity, gas, water and sewerage undertakers) of this Order.

PART II

WORKS, ETC.

Works

Power to make railway

4. Subject to the provisions of this Order, the Board may, in the line or situation and within the limit of deviation shown on the deposited plan and according to the levels shown on the deposited section, make and maintain the following work in the Clackmannan District, Central Region, with all necessary works and conveniences connected therewith:—

> Work No. 1—A railway (3,530 metres in length), being a reinstatement of part of the former Stirling to Dunfermline Railway, commencing at Cambus by a junction with the Stirling to Menstrie Railway at a point 14 metres north-west of Station Road and terminating at Alloa at a point on the former Stirling to Dunfermline Railway 142 metres east of the bridge carrying the footpath known as Station Bridge over the site of the last-mentioned railway.

Level crossings of Station Road, Cambus, and Grange Road, Alloa

5.—(1) In this section—

> "the level crossings" means the level crossings provided under subsection (2) below, or either of them; and

> "traffic sign" has the same meaning as in the Road Traffic Regulation Act 1984.

(2) The Board may in the construction of Work No. 1 provide level crossings comprising a single line of railway across and on the level of—

(a) Station Road, Cambus; and

(b) Grange Road, Alloa;

(which roads are respectively numbered on the deposited plan 3 and 5 in the Clackmannan District), but shall not be required to erect or maintain a station or lodge thereat.

(3)(a) The Board may, with the consent in writing of the Secretary of State and subject to such requirements as he may from time to time lay down, provide, maintain and operate at or near the level crossings such barriers, lights, traffic signs, and automatic or other devices and appliances as may be approved by the Secretary of State.

(b) So long as the consent referred to in paragraph (a) above continues in force, the provisions (in so far as they are inconsistent with any such consent) of the Highway (Railway Crossings) Act 1839, section 9 of the Railway Regulation Act 1842, section 40 of the Act of 1845 and section 6 of the Railways Clauses Act 1863 shall not apply to the level crossings.

(c) Section 65(1) of the Road Traffic Regulation Act 1984 (placing of traffic signs by highway authorities) shall have effect with respect to the erection and display of a traffic sign by the Board as if it were a traffic sign erected and displayed by a traffic authority within the meaning of that Act.

Power to deviate

6.—(1) In the construction of Work No. 1, the Board may—

(a) deviate from the line or situation thereof shown on the deposited plan to the extent of the limit of deviation; and

(b) subject to subsection (2) below, deviate vertically from the levels shown on the deposited section to any extent not exceeding 1 metre upwards or downwards.

(2) Subsection (1)(b) above shall not apply to the construction of Work No. 1 across and on the level of Station Road, Cambus, and Grange Road, Alloa.

Station works at Alloa

7. In the construction of Work No. 1, the Board may—

(a) on any part of the land numbered on the deposited plan 16, 17, 20 and 21 in the Clackmannan District which lies within the line marked "Limit of station works" on the deposited plan make, maintain and operate a station at Alloa for the purposes of serving that work, with all necessary works and conveniences connected therewith; and

(b) form and lay out means of pedestrian access at the point marked "A" on the deposited plan from and to Station Bridge to and from that station.

General works provisions

Temporary stoppage of roads

8.—(1) The Board, during and for the purpose of the execution of Work No. 1, may temporarily stop up and divert and interfere with the specified roads, or either of them, and may for any reasonable time divert the traffic therefrom and prevent all persons other than those bona fide going to or from any land, house or building abutting on the specified roads, or either of them, from passing along and using the same.

(2) The Board shall provide reasonable access for persons on foot bona fide going to or from any such land, house or building.

(3) (a) The Board shall not exercise the powers of this section without the consent of the road works authority.

(b) Any such consent may be given subject to such reasonable conditions as the road works authority may require but shall not be unreasonably withheld and any question whether such consent has been unreasonably withheld or whether any such condition is reasonable shall be determined by arbitration.

(4) In this section—

"the specified roads" means so much of Station Road, Cambus, and Grange Road, Alloa, as is numbered on the deposited plans 3 and 5, respectively, in the Clackmannan District; and

"road works authority" has the meaning assigned to it by section 108 of the Act of 1991.

Underpinning of buildings near works

9. The Board at their own expense may, subject as hereinafter provided, underpin or otherwise strengthen any building within 30 metres of any part of the works and the following provisions shall have effect:—

(1) At least 14 days' notice shall (except in case of emergency) be given to the owner, lessee and occupier of the building intended to be so underpinned or otherwise strengthened:

(2) If any owner, lessee or occupier of any such building, within 10 days after the giving of such notice, gives a counter-notice in writing that he disputes the necessity of such underpinning or strengthening, the question of the necessity shall be determined by arbitration; and, if the arbiter decides that such underpinning or strengthening is not necessary, the Board shall not proceed therewith:

(3) In any case in which any building shall have been underpinned or strengthened under the powers of this section the Board may, from time to time after the completion of such underpinning or strengthening, and during the execution of the work in connection with which such underpinning or strengthening was done, or within 5 years after the opening for traffic of that work, after giving reasonable notice to the occupier, enter upon and survey such building and, after complying with the foregoing provisions of this section, do such further underpinning or strengthening as they may deem necessary or expedient:

(4) The Board shall be liable to compensate the owner, lessee and occupier of every such building for any loss or damage which may result to them by reason of the exercise of the powers of this section:

(5) Nothing in this section shall affect liability to compensate under any enactment in respect of loss or damage arising from the execution of any works, except so far as compensation is payable under paragraph (4) above:

(6) Every case of compensation to be ascertained under this section shall be ascertained according to the provisions of the Land Compensation (Scotland) Act 1963.

Use of sewers, etc., for removing water

10.—(1) The Board may use for the discharge of any water pumped or found by them during the construction of the works any available stream or watercourse, or any sewer or drain vested in, or under the control of, the regional council, and for that purpose may lay down, take up and alter conduits, pipes and other works and may make any convenient connections with any such stream, watercourse, sewer or drain within the limit of deviation.

(2) The Board shall not—

(a) discharge any water into any such sewer or drain except with the consent of the regional council, whose consent shall not be unreasonably withheld, and subject to such terms and conditions (including the taking of steps to remove as far as may be reasonably practicable from water so discharged any gravel, soil or other solid substance or matter in suspension) as the regional council may reasonably impose; or

(b) make any opening into any such sewer or drain except in accordance with plans approved by, and under the superintendence (if given) of, the regional council but approval of those plans by the regional council shall not be unreasonably withheld.

(3) Any difference arising between the Board and the regional council under this section shall be determined by arbitration.

(4) Section 31 of the Control of Pollution Act 1974 shall apply to, or to the consequence of, a discharge under the powers of this section into any controlled waters within the meaning assigned to that expression by section 30A(1) of that Act as if this section were not a provision of a local Act or a statutory order for the purposes of section 31(2)(b)(ii) of that Act.

(5) Nothing in this section shall affect the operation of Part IV of the Act of 1991.

(6) In this section "the regional council" means the Central Regional Council.

PART III

LAND

Meaning of new rights

11. In this Part references to the purchase by the Board of new rights are references to the purchase of rights (whether heritable or moveable) to be created in favour of the Board.

Purchase of land

12.—(1) The Board may purchase compulsorily and use such of the land within the limit of deviation and described in the deposited book of reference as they require for the purposes of the works or their undertaking.

(2) The Board may enter upon, use and appropriate so much of the subsoil and undersurface of, or airspace over, any public road or place within the limit of deviation and described in the deposited book of reference as shall be necessary for the purposes of subsection (1) above without being required to purchase the same or any servitude or other right therein or thereunder or to make any payment therefor.

(3) For the purpose of section 28 of the Land Registration (Scotland) Act 1979 subsection (2) above shall be taken to create a real right over such land as is referred to in that subsection without any necessity to record a deed in the Register of Sasines or to register the right.

Purchase of new rights over land

13.—(1) Subject to the provisions of this Order, the Board may for the purpose of constructing, maintaining, protecting, altering, renewing and using the works, or for the purpose of obtaining access to the works or for the purpose of doing any other thing necessary in connection with the works, purchase compulsorily and use so much of the subsoil and undersurface of, or may purchase compulsorily such new rights as they require in, under or over any of the land within the limit of deviation and described in the deposited book of reference instead of purchasing that land under section 12 (Purchase of land) of this Order.

(2) Subject to subsection (3) below, the Lands Clauses Acts, as applied by this Order, shall have effect with the modifications necessary to make them apply to the compulsory purchase of new rights under subsection (1) above and under section 14 (Purchase of specific new rights over land) of this Order as they apply to the compulsory purchase of land so that, in appropriate contexts, references in the Lands Clauses Acts to land are read as referring, or as including references, to the new rights or to land over which the new rights are, or are to be, exercisable, according to the requirements of the particular context.

(3) Notwithstanding anything in subsection (2) above, section 90 of the Lands Clauses Consolidation (Scotland) Act 1845 shall not apply to any compulsory purchase by the Board under this section or section 14 (Purchase of specific new rights over land) of this Order.

Purchase of specific new rights over land

14.—(1) The Board may, in addition to such new rights as they may purchase under section 13 (Purchase of new rights over land) of this Order, purchase compulsorily such new rights as they require in or over the land numbered on the deposited plan 19 in the Clackmannan District within the line marked "Limit of land to be used" for the purpose of providing means of access—

    (a) in connection with the construction and maintenance of the works; and

(b) following completion of the works, for pedestrians proceeding to and from the station authorised by section 7 (Station works at Alloa) of this Order.

(2) For the avoidance of doubt, nothing in this section shall be taken as conferring a power to carry out works.

Time for compulsory purchase of land or rights over land

15. Except as may be provided under section 16 (Extension of time) of this Order, the powers of the Board of compulsory purchase of land and new rights in, under or over land under this Order shall cease on 31st December 1998.

Extension of time

16.—(1) In this section "lessee" means a lessee under a lease having a period of not less than 21 years to run at the date of his notice under subsection (3) below; and any reference to the purchase of an interest in land includes reference to the purchase of a new right in, under or over that land.

(2) (a) Subject to the provisions of this section, the Secretary of State may, by order under this subsection, extend the period for the exercise of powers of compulsory purchase of land and new rights in, under or over land under this Order.

(b) An order under this subsection shall be subject to special parliamentary procedure.

(3) If any owner or lessee of any land subject to an order under subsection (2) above shall give notice in writing to the Board of his desire for the purchase as soon as may be by the Board of his interest in any part of the land specified in the notice, the Board shall within a period of three months after the receipt of such notice—

(a) enter into a contract with him for the purchase of his interest in the land or such part thereof as may be specified in the contract; or

(b) serve on him a notice to treat for the compulsory purchase of his interest in the land specified in his notice, or in such part thereof as may be required by the Board; or

(c) serve on him notice in writing of the Board's intention not to proceed with the purchase of his interest in the land specified in his notice.

(4) Where notice is given under subsection (3) above by any owner or lessee, then—

(a) if the Board—

(i) fail to comply with that subsection; or

(ii) withdraw in pursuance of any statutory provision a notice to treat served on him in compliance with subsection (3)(b) above; or

(iii) serve notice on him in compliance with subsection (3)(c) above;

the powers conferred by this Order for the compulsory purchase of his interest in the land so specified shall cease;

(b) if his interest in part only of the land so specified is purchased in pursuance of such a notice to treat, the powers conferred by this Order for the compulsory purchase of his interest in the remainder of the land so specified shall cease.

Correction of errors in deposited plan and book of reference

17.—(1) If the deposited plan or the deposited book of reference are inaccurate in their description of any land or in their statement or description of the ownership or occupation of any land, the Board may apply by summary application to the sheriff for the correction thereof.

(2) If on any such application it appears to the sheriff that the misstatement or wrong description arose from mistake, he shall certify accordingly and shall in his certificate state in what respect any matter is misstated or wrongly described.

(3) The certificate shall be deposited in the office of the Clerk of the Parliaments and a copy thereof in the Private Bill Office, House of Commons, the Scottish Office, London, the office of the Secretary of State for Scotland, Edinburgh, the office of the Health and Safety Executive, Edinburgh, and with the sheriff clerk of the sheriff court district of Alloa and thereupon the deposited plan and the deposited book of reference shall be deemed to be corrected according to the certificate.

(4) Any certificate or copy deposited under this section with any person shall be kept by him with the other documents to which it relates.

Purchase of part of certain properties

18.—(1) Where a copy of this section is endorsed on, or annexed to, a notice to treat served under the Lands Clauses Acts, as incorporated with this Order, the following provisions of this section shall apply to the land subject to the notice instead of section 90 of the Lands Clauses Consolidation (Scotland) Act 1845.

(2) Where the land subject to the notice is part only of a house, building or factory, or part only of land consisting of a house together with any park or garden belonging thereto, then, if the person on whom the notice is served, within 21 days after the day on which the notice is served on him, serves on the Board a counter-notice objecting to the sale of the part and stating that he is willing and able to sell the whole (in this section referred to as "the land subject to the counter-notice"), the question whether he shall be required to sell the part shall, unless the Board agree to take the land subject to the counter-notice, be referred to the tribunal.

(3) If the said person does not serve such a counter-notice as aforesaid within 21 days after the day on which the notice to treat is served on him, or if on such a reference to the tribunal the tribunal determines that the part subject to the notice to treat can be taken without material detriment to the remainder of the land subject to the counter-notice or, in the case of part of land consisting of a house together with a park or garden belonging thereto, without such detriment and without seriously affecting the amenity and convenience of the house, the said person shall be required to sell the part.

(4) If, on such a reference to the tribunal, the tribunal determines that part only of the land subject to the notice to treat can be taken without material detriment to the remainder of the land subject to the counter-notice or, as the case may be, without such detriment and without seriously affecting the amenity and convenience of the house, the notice to treat shall be deemed to be a notice to treat for that part.

(5) If, on such a reference to the tribunal, the tribunal determines that the land subject to the notice to treat cannot be taken without material detriment to the remainder of the land subject to the counter-notice but that the material detriment is confined to a part of the land subject to the counter-notice, the notice to treat shall be deemed to be a notice to treat for the land to which the material detriment is confined in addition to the land already subject to the notice, whether or not the additional land is land which the Board are authorised to purchase compulsorily under this Order.

(6) If the Board agree to take the land subject to the counter-notice, or if the tribunal determines that—

(a) none of the land subject to the notice to treat can be taken without material detriment to the remainder of the land subject to the counter-notice or, as the case may be, without such detriment and without seriously affecting the amenity and convenience of the house; and

(b) the material detriment is not confined to a part of the land subject to the counter-notice;

the notice to treat shall be deemed to be a notice to treat for the land subject to the counter-notice whether or not the whole of that land is land which the Board are authorised to purchase under this Order.

(7) In any case where, by virtue of a determination by the tribunal under subsection (4), (5) or (6) above, a notice to treat is deemed to be a notice to treat for part of the land specified in the notice or for more land than is specified in the notice, the Board may, within 6 weeks after the tribunal makes its determination, withdraw the notice to treat and, if they do so, shall pay to the said person compensation for any loss or expense occasioned to him by the giving and withdrawal of the notice to be determined, in default of agreement, by the tribunal:

Provided that the determination of the tribunal shall not be deemed to be made so long as—

(a) the time for requiring the tribunal to state a case with respect thereto has not expired and any proceedings on the points raised by a case so stated have not been concluded; or

(b) any proceedings on appeal from any decision on the points raised by a case so stated have not been concluded.

(8)(a) Where a person is under this section required to sell part only of a house, building or factory, or of land consisting of a house, together with any park or garden belonging thereto, the Board shall pay to him compensation for any loss sustained by him due to the severance of that part in addition to the value of his interest therein.

(b) Any dispute as to a person's entitlement to compensation under this section or as to the amount of the compensation shall be determined by the tribunal.

Disregard of recent improvements and interests

19. In determining a question with respect to compensation claimed in consequence of the compulsory purchase of land under this Order, the tribunal shall not take into account—

(a) any interest in land, or

(b) any enhancement of the value of any interest in land, by reason of any building erected, works executed or improvement or alteration made (whether on the land purchased or on any other land with which the claimant is, or was at the time of the erection, executing or making of the building, works, improvement or alteration, directly or indirectly concerned),

if the tribunal is satisfied that the creation of the interest, the erection of the building, the execution of the works, or the making of the improvement or alteration, as the case may be, was not reasonably necessary and was undertaken with a view to obtaining compensation or increased compensation.

Set-off for enhancement in value of retained land

20.—(1) In this section "relevant land" means any land or new rights over land required by the Board for the purposes of, or in connection with, the works.

(2) In assessing the compensation payable to any person on the purchase by the Board from him of any relevant land, the tribunal shall set off against the value of the relevant land any increase in value of any contiguous or adjacent lands belonging to the same person in the same capacity, or of the land over which new rights are acquired, which will accrue to him by reason of the construction of any of the works.

(3) The Land Compensation (Scotland) Act 1963 shall have effect subject to the provisions of this section.

Power to enter, survey, etc., land

21.—(1) The Board and their surveyors and officers may at all reasonable times in the day, upon giving on the first occasion not less than 7 days', and on subsequent occasions not less than 3 days', previous notice in writing to the occupier and to the owner if he is not the occupier, enter upon, examine and lay open any land which may be purchased compulsorily under this Order for the purpose of surveying, measuring, taking levels, examining works and valuing that land or for any other purpose ancillary to the powers conferred by this Order.

(2) Any person entering land under subsection (1) above on behalf of the Board shall, if so required, produce written evidence of his identity and of his authority to do so.

(3) In the exercise of the powers of subsection (1) above the Board and their surveyors and officers shall cause as little detriment or inconvenience to any person as circumstances allow, and the Board shall, subject to the provisions of this Order, make compensation to the owners and occupiers of any land injuriously affected by the exercise of those powers, to be determined in case of dispute by the tribunal.

Further powers of entry

22. At any time after notice to treat has been served for any land which may be purchased compulsorily under this Order the Board may, after giving to the owner and occupier of the land not less than 3 months' notice, enter on and take possession of the land or such part thereof as is specified in the notice without previous consent or compliance with sections 83 to 89 of the Lands Clauses Consolidation (Scotland) Act 1845, but subject to the payment of the like compensation for the land of which possession is taken, and interest on the compensation awarded, as would have been payable if those sections had been complied with.

Extinction or suspension of private rights of way

23.—(1) All private rights of way over any land which may be purchased compulsorily under this Order shall be extinguished on the purchase of the land whether compulsorily or by agreement, or on the entry on the land under section 22 (Further powers of entry) of this Order.

(2) All private rights of way over any land of which the Board may take temporary possession under this Order shall be suspended and unenforceable against the Board for so long as the Board shall remain in lawful possession thereof.

(3) Any person who suffers loss by the extinction or suspension of any right under this section shall be entitled to be paid by the Board compensation, to be determined in case of dispute by the tribunal.

Service of notices, etc.

24. Paragraph 19 of Schedule 1 to the Acquisition of Land (Authorisation Procedure) (Scotland) Act 1947 shall apply and have effect with respect to any notice or other document required or authorised to be served under or by virtue of this Order as if such notice or other document were required or authorised to be served under that Schedule.

PART IV

PROTECTIVE PROVISIONS

Crown rights

25. Nothing in this Order affects prejudicially any estate, right, power, privilege or exemption of the Crown and, without prejudice to the generality

of the foregoing, nothing in this Order authorises the Board to take, use, or interfere with, any land or rights—
  (a) belonging to Her Majesty in right of the Crown and under the management of the Crown Estate Commissioners; or
  (b) belonging to a government department, or held in trust for Her Majesty for the purposes of a government department;
without the consent in writing of those commissioners on behalf of Her Majesty or, as the case may be, that government department.

For protection of telecommunications operators

26. For the protection of telecommunications operators the following provisions shall, unless otherwise agreed in writing between the Board and the telecommunications operators concerned, have effect:—
  (1) In this section expressions defined in the Telecommunications Act 1984 have the same meanings as in that Act:
  (2) The temporary stopping up or diversion of any part of Station Road, Cambus, or Grange Road, Alloa, under section 8 (Temporary stoppage of roads) of this Order shall not affect any right of a telecommunications operator under paragraph 9 of the telecommunications code to inspect, maintain, adjust, repair or alter any apparatus which, at the time of the stopping up or diversion, is in that part of the road.

For protection of electricity, gas, water and sewerage undertakers

27. For the protection of the several undertakers referred to in this section, the following provisions shall, unless otherwise agreed in writing between the Board and the undertakers concerned, have effect:—
  (1) In this section—
      "adequate alternative apparatus" means alternative apparatus adequate to enable the undertakers to fulfil their statutory functions in a manner not less efficient than previously;
      "apparatus" means—
        (a) in the case of electricity undertakers, electric lines or electrical plant (as defined in the Electricity Act 1989) belonging to or maintained by such undertakers; or
        (b) in the case of gas, water or sewerage undertakers any mains, pipes, sewers or other apparatus belonging to or maintained by such undertakers;
      (not being, except in paragraph (2) below, apparatus in respect of which the relations between the Board and the undertakers are regulated by the provisions of Part IV of the Act of 1991) and includes any structure for the lodging therein of apparatus or for giving access to apparatus;
      "functions" includes powers and duties;
      "in" in a context referring to apparatus or alternative apparatus in land includes a reference to apparatus or alternative apparatus under, over or upon land; and
      "undertakers" means any person authorised to carry on, in any area within which the Board are by this Order authorised to purchase land or execute works, an undertaking for the supply of gas or water, for the generation, transmission or supply of electricity or for the provision of sewerage services; and, in relation to any apparatus, means the undertakers to whom it belongs or by whom it is maintained:
  (2) The temporary or permanent stopping up or diversion of a road under the powers of this Order shall not affect any right of undertakers to inspect, maintain, renew, remove or use any apparatus which at the time of the stopping up or diversion was in that road:

(3) The Board, in the case of the powers conferred by section 9 (Underpinning of buildings near works) of this Order, shall, so far as is reasonably practicable, so exercise those powers as not to obstruct or render less convenient the access to any apparatus:

(4) Notwithstanding anything in section 10 (Use of sewers, etc., for removing water) of this Order, no use shall be made by the Board in the construction of the works of pumping or other like modes of removing water except where reasonably necessary or in case of emergency or unforeseen accident or for the purpose of removing rainwater or other small amounts of water:

(5) Notwithstanding anything in this Order or shown on the deposited plan, the Board shall not acquire any apparatus under the powers of this Order otherwise than by agreement:

(6) If the Board, in the exercise of the powers of this Order, acquire any interest in any land in which any apparatus is placed, that apparatus shall not be removed under this section and any right of the undertakers to maintain, repair, renew or inspect that apparatus in that land shall not be extinguished until adequate alternative apparatus has been constructed and is in operation to the reasonable satisfaction of the undertakers:

(7) If the Board, for the purpose of executing any works in, on or under any land purchased, held, appropriated or used under this Order, require the removal of any apparatus placed in that land, they shall give to the undertakers written notice of that requirement, together with a plan and section of the work proposed, and of the proposed position of the alternative apparatus to be provided or constructed so as to provide adequate alternative apparatus in lieu of the apparatus to be removed, and in that case (or if in consequence of the exercise of any of the powers of this Order the undertakers reasonably require to remove any apparatus) the Board shall, if it is reasonably practicable to do so, afford to the undertakers the necessary facilities and rights for the construction of the alternative apparatus in other land of the Board and thereafter for the maintenance, repair, renewal and inspection of that apparatus:

Provided that, if the alternative apparatus or any part thereof is to be constructed elsewhere than in other land of the Board, or the Board are unable to afford such facilities and rights as aforesaid in the land in which the alternative apparatus or that part thereof is to be constructed, the undertakers shall, on receipt of a written notice to that effect from the Board, forthwith use their best endeavours to obtain the necessary facilities and rights in that last-mentioned land:

(8) (a) Any alternative apparatus to be constructed in land of the Board under this section shall be constructed in such manner and in such line or situation as may be agreed between the undertakers and the Board or in default of agreement determined by arbitration;

(b) The undertakers shall, after the alternative apparatus to be provided or constructed has been agreed or determined by arbitration as aforesaid and after the grant to the undertakers of any such facilities and rights as are referred to in paragraph (7) above, proceed with all reasonable dispatch to construct and bring into operation the alternative apparatus and thereafter to remove any apparatus required by the Board to be removed under the provisions of this section:

(9) Notwithstanding anything in paragraph (8) above, if the Board give notice in writing to the undertakers that they desire themselves to execute any part of so much of the work necessary in connection with the construction of the alternative apparatus, or the removal of the apparatus required to be removed, as will take place in any land of the Board, that work, in lieu of being executed by the undertakers, shall

be executed by the Board with all reasonable dispatch under the superintendence, if given, and to the reasonable satisfaction of the undertakers;

Provided that nothing in this paragraph shall authorise the Board to execute the actual placing, installation, bedding, packing, removal, connection or disconnection of any apparatus, or execute any filling around the apparatus (where the apparatus is laid in a trench) within 300 millimetres of the apparatus:

(10) Where, in accordance with the provisions of this section, the Board afford to the undertakers facilities and rights for the construction, maintenance, repair, renewal and inspection in land of the Board of alternative apparatus in substitution for apparatus to be removed as aforesaid, those facilities and rights shall be granted upon such terms and conditions as may be agreed between the Board and the undertakers or in default of agreement determined by arbitration:

Provided that—

(a) in determining those terms and conditions in respect of alternative apparatus to be constructed in or along any railway of the Board, the arbiter shall—

(i) give effect to all reasonable requirements of the Board for ensuring the safety and efficient operation of the railway and for securing any subsequent alterations or adaptations of the alternative apparatus which may be required to prevent interference with any proposed works of the Board or the traffic on the railway; and

(ii) so far as it may be reasonable and practicable to do so in the circumstances of the particular case, give effect to the terms and conditions applicable to the apparatus, if any, constructed in or along the railway for which the alternative apparatus is to be substituted and to any other reasonable operational requirements of the undertakers;

(b) if the facilities and rights to be afforded by the Board in respect of any alternative apparatus and the terms and conditions subject to which the same are to be granted are in the opinion of the arbiter less favourable on the whole to the undertakers than the facilities and rights enjoyed by them in respect of the apparatus to be removed and the terms and conditions to which those facilities and rights are subject, the arbiter shall make such provision for the payment of compensation by the Board to the undertakers in respect thereof as appears to him to be reasonable having regard to all the circumstances of the particular case:

(11) (a) Not less than 28 days before commencing to execute any part of the works which will or may be within 15 metres of, or may otherwise affect, any apparatus the removal of which has not been required by the Board, the Board shall submit to the undertakers a plan, section and description of the works to be executed;

(b) Those works shall be executed only in accordance with the plan, section and description submitted as aforesaid and in accordance with such reasonable requirements as may be made by the undertakers for the alteration or otherwise for the protection of the apparatus or for securing access thereto and the undertakers shall be entitled by their officer to watch and inspect the execution of those works:

Provided that—

(i) if the undertakers within 14 days after the submission to them of a plan, section and description shall, in consequence of the works proposed by the Board, reasonably require the removal of any apparatus and give written notice to the Board of that requirement, the foregoing provisions of this section shall apply as if the removal of the apparatus had been required by the Board;

     (ii) nothing in this sub-paragraph shall preclude the Board from submitting at any time or from time to time, but in no case less than 28 days before commencing the execution of any works, a new plan, section and description thereof in lieu of the plan, section and description previously submitted, and thereupon the provisions of this paragraph shall apply to and in respect of the new plan, section and description;

   (c) The Board shall not be required to comply with sub-paragraph (a) above in a case of emergency but in that case they shall give to the undertakers notice as soon as reasonably practicable and a plan, section and description of those works as soon as reasonably practicable thereafter and shall comply with sub-paragraph (b) above so far as reasonably practicable in the circumstances:

(12) Subject to paragraph (13) below, the Board shall pay to the undertakers the costs, charges and expenses reasonably incurred by the undertakers in or in connection with the inspection, removal, alteration or protection of any apparatus or the construction of any new apparatus which may be required in consequence of the execution of any such works as are referred to in paragraph (7) above, less the value of any apparatus removed under the provisions of this section (that value being calculated after removal) and shall also make compensation to the undertakers—

     (a) for any damage caused to any apparatus (other than apparatus the repair of which is not reasonably necessary in view of its intended removal in accordance with the provisions of this section); and

     (b) for any other expenses, loss, damages, penalty or costs incurred by the undertakers;

by reason of the execution, maintenance, user or failure of those works or otherwise by reason of the exercise by the Board of the powers of this Order:

(13) If the cost of maintaining, using, repairing or renewing any apparatus is reduced by reason of any of the works, including the provision of alternative apparatus under this section, a capitalised sum representing that saving shall be paid by the relevant undertakers to the Board or set off against any sums payable by the Board to the relevant undertakers under this section:

(14) Any difference arising between the Board and the undertakers under this section shall be determined by arbitration:

(15) Nothing in this section shall affect the provisions of any enactment or agreement regulating the relations between the Board and the undertakers in respect of any apparatus laid or erected in land belonging to the Board at the date of the passing of the Act confirming this Order.

PART V

GENERAL

Saving for town and country planning

28.—(1) The Town and Country Planning (Scotland) Act 1972, and any orders, regulations, rules, schemes and directions made or given thereunder and any restrictions or powers thereby imposed or conferred in relation to land shall apply and may be exercised in relation to any land notwithstanding that the development thereof is or may be authorised by this Order.

(2) Subject to subsection (3) below, in their application to development authorised by this Order, article 3 of, and Class 29 in Part 11 of Schedule 1 to, the Town and Country Planning (General Permitted Development) (Scot-

land) Order 1992 (which permit development authorised by any local or private Act or by any order approved by both Houses of Parliament, being an Act or order designating specifically both the nature of the development thereby authorised and the land on which it may be carried out) shall have effect as if the authority to develop given by this Order were limited to development begun within 10 years after the passing of the Act confirming this Order.

(3) Subsection (2) above shall not apply to the carrying out of any development consisting of the alteration, maintenance or repair of works or the substitution of new works therefor.

Arbitration

29. Where under any provision of this Order any difference (other than a difference to which the provisions of the Lands Clauses Acts apply) is to be determined by arbitration, then, unless otherwise provided, the difference shall be referred to, and settled by, a single arbiter to be agreed between the parties or, in default of agreement, to be appointed on the summary application of any party (after notice in writing to the other) by the sheriff.

INDEX

References are to sections in the Order

BRITISH RAILWAYS (NO. 3) ORDER CONFIRMATION ACT 1994

(1994 c. iii)

PART IV

PROTECTIVE PROVISIONS

PART V

GENERAL

An Act to confirm a Provisional Order under the Private Legislation Procedure (Scotland) Act 1936, relating to British Railways (No. 3).

[24th March 1994]

PARLIAMENTARY PROGRESS
    The Bill's progress through Parliament was as follows:
    House of Commons: First Reading, March 9, 1994; Considered by Commons, March 15, 1994; Third Reading, March 16, 1994.
    House of Lords: First Reading, March 16, 1994; Considered by Lords, March 22, 1994; Third Reading, March 24, 1994.

INTRODUCTION
    This Act makes provision for the reinstatement of the railway between Hamilton and Larkhall in the Hamilton District to enable the reopening of a passenger service between Hamilton and Larkhall. A new station will be provided at Larkhall. Part I contains preliminary provisions. Part II details the works proposed and indicates the likely interference with existing amenities. Part III details the land likely to be affected by the Act. Part IV sets out protective provisions *vis-à-vis* amenities and Crown rights.

Whereas the Provisional Order set forth in the Schedule hereunto annexed has been made by the Secretary of State under the provisions of the Private Legislation Procedure (Scotland) Act 1936, and it is requisite that the said Order should be confirmed by Parliament:

    Be it therefore enacted by the Queen's most Excellent Majesty, by and with the advice and consent of the Lords Spiritual and Temporal, and Commons, in this present Parliament assembled, and by the authority of the same, as follows:—

Confirmation of Order in Schedule

1. The Provisional Order contained in the Schedule hereunto annexed is hereby confirmed.

Short title

2. This Act may be cited as the British Railways (No. 3) Order Confirmation Act 1994.

SCHEDULE

BRITISH RAILWAYS (NO. 3)

Provisional Order to empower the British Railways Board to construct works and to purchase or use land; to confer further powers on the Board; and for connected purposes.

WHEREAS—

(1) It is the duty of the British Railways Board (hereinafter referred to as "the Board") under the Transport Act 1962 (inter alia) to provide railway services in Great Britain and, in connection with the provision of railway services, to provide such other services and facilities as appear to the Board to be expedient, and to have due regard, as respects all those railway and other services and facilities, to efficiency, economy and safety of operation:

(2) It is expedient that the Board should be empowered to construct in the Strathclyde Region the works authorised by this Order and to purchase or use the land referred to in this Order and that the other provisions in this Order contained should be enacted:

(3) Plans and sections showing the lines or situations and levels of the works to be constructed under this Order, and a plans of the lands authorised to be purchased or used by this Order, and a book of reference to those plans containing the names of the owners and lessees, or reputed owners and lessees, and of the occupiers of the said lands were duly deposited in the office of the Clerk of the Parliaments and in the Private Bill Office of the House of Commons and with the sheriff clerk of the sheriff court district of Hamilton, which plans, sections and book of reference are respectively referred to in this Order as the deposited plans, the deposited sections and the deposited book of reference:

(4) The purposes of this Order cannot be effected without an Order confirmed by Parliament under the provisions of the Private Legislation Procedure (Scotland) Act 1936:

Now therefore, in pursuance of the powers contained in the last-mentioned Act, the Secretary of State orders as follows:—

PART I

PRELIMINARY

Short title

1. This Order may be cited as the British Railways (No. 3) Order 1994.

Interpretation

2.—(1) In this Order, unless the context otherwise requires, words and expressions to which meanings are assigned by the enactments incorporated herewith have the same respective meanings; and—

"the Act of 1845" means the Railways Clauses Consolidation (Scotland) Act 1845;

"the Act of 1991" means the New Roads and Street Works Act 1991;

"the Board" means the British Railways Board;

"enactment" includes any order, byelaw, rule, regulation, scheme or other instrument having effect by virtue of an enactment;

"the limits of deviation" means the limits of deviation shown on the deposited plans;

"the regional council" means the Strathclyde Regional Council;

"road" has, except in section 31 (For protection of roads and road traffic, etc.) of this Order, the meaning assigned to it by section 107 of the Act of 1991;

"road works authority" has the meaning assigned to it by section 108 of the Act of 1991;

"the sheriff" means the sheriff principal of, or any sheriff appointed for, the Sheriffdom of South Strathclyde, Dumfries and Galloway;

"the tribunal" means the Lands Tribunal for Scotland; and

"the works" means the works authorised by Part II (Works, etc.) of this Order.

(2) Except in relation to section 8 (Power to deviate) of this Order, all directions, distances and lengths stated in any description of works, powers or lands in this Order shall be construed as if the words "or thereby" were inserted after each such direction, distance and length.

(3) Any reference in this Order to a work identified by the number of that work shall be construed as a reference to the work of that number authorised by this Order.

(4) References in this Order to points identified by letters shall be construed as references to the points so lettered on the deposited plans.

(5) References in this Order to access to any place shall include reference to egress from that place.

Incorporation of enactments

3.—(1) The following enactments, so far as the same are applicable for the purposes of and are not inconsistent with, or varied by, the provisions of this Order, are incorporated with this Order, and this Order shall be deemed to be the special Act for the purposes of the said incorporated enactments:—

(a) the Lands Clauses Acts, except sections 120 to 124 and section 127 of the Lands Clauses Consolidation (Scotland) Act 1845;

(b) the Act of 1845, except sections 1, 7, 8, 9, 17, 19, 20, 22 and 23 thereof; and

(c) in the Railways Clauses Act 1863, Part I (relating to construction of a railway) except sections 13, 14, 18 and 19 thereof.

(2)(a) In the application of the enactments incorporated by subsection (1) (b) and (c) above the expression "the company" means the Board.

(b) Sections 18 and 21 of the Act of 1845 shall not extend to regulate the relations between the Board and any other person in respect of any matter or thing concerning which those relations are regulated in any respect by the provisions of Part IV of the Act of 1991 or by section 29 (For protection of electricity, gas and water undertakers) of this Order.

PART II

WORKS, ETC.

Works

Power to make railway

4. Subject to the provisions of this Order, the Board may, in the lines or situations and within the limits of deviation shown on the deposited plans

and according to the levels shown on the deposited sections, make and maintain the following works in the Hamilton District, Strathclyde Region, with all necessary works and conveniences connected therewith:—

> A reinstatement of part of the former railway between Hamilton and Stonehouse comprising—
>> Work No. 1   A railway (2,325 metres in length) commencing at Ferniegair by a junction with the Hamilton to Motherwell Railway at a point 160 metres north-east of the bridge carrying Carlisle Road (A74) over that railway and terminating at a point on the said former railway 130 metres west of the bridge carrying Lanark Road (A72) over that former railway; and
>> Work No. 2   A railway (2,328 metres in length) commencing by a junction with the termination of Work No. 1 and terminating at Larkhall at a point on the said former railway 68 metres north-west of the junction of Caledonian Road with Macneil Street.

Application of Act of 1845 to certain existing bridges

5.—(1) In this section "the existing bridges" means the bridges in Hamilton District carrying Clyde Avenue and Hamilton Road over the route of the former railway between Hamilton and Stonehouse.

(2) Nothing in the Act of 1845, as incorporated with this Order, shall be taken to—

  (a) require the Board in constructing Works Nos. 1 and 2 beneath the existing bridges to alter or reconstruct those bridges, or

  (b) impose any responsibility on the Board for the repair and maintenance of those bridges.

Station works at Larkhall

6. In the construction of Works Nos. 1 and 2, the Board may—

  (a) on any part of the land numbered 34 in the Hamilton District which lies within the line marked "Limit of station works" on the deposited plans make, maintain and operate at Larkhall a railway station for the purpose of serving those works, with all necessary works and conveniences connected therewith; and

  (b) form and lay out means of pedestrian access at points C, D and E from Caledonian Road to that station.

Stopping up of paths

7.—(1) Subject to the provisions of this Order, the Board may in connection with the construction of Works Nos. 1 and 2 stop up and discontinue—

  (a) so much of the path between Fairholm Street and High Avon Street, Larkhall, as lies between points X, Y and Z; and

  (b) so much of any other path as lies within the limits of deviation other than the path between Fairholm Street and Glen View Park, Larkhall.

(2) After any stopping up under subsection (1) above all rights of way over or along the path or portion thereof authorised to be stopped up shall be extinguished and the Board may, subject to the provisions of the Act of 1845 with respect to mines lying under or near the railway, appropriate without making any payment therefor and use for the purposes of their undertaking the site thereof.

(3) The Board shall, at least seven days before exercising the powers of subsection (1) above, post notices at each end of every defined path or portion thereof which they intend to stop up stating that they intend to stop it up and setting out the effect of subsection (4) below.

(4) Any person who suffers loss by the extinguishment of any private right under this section shall be entitled to be paid by the Board compensation to be determined in case of dispute by the tribunal.

Power to deviate

8. In the construction of the works the Board may—
(a) deviate from the lines or situations thereof shown on the deposited plans to the extent of the limits of deviation; and
(b) deviate vertically from the levels shown on the deposited sections to any extent not exceeding 3 metres upwards or downwards.

General works provisions

Temporary stoppage of roads

9.—(1) The Board, during and for the purpose of the execution of the works may temporarily stop up and divert and interfere with any road and may for any reasonable time divert the traffic therefrom and prevent all persons other than those bona fide going to or from any land, house or building abutting on the road from passing along and using the same.

(2) The Board shall provide reasonable access for persons on foot bona fide going to or from any such land, house or building.

(3)(a) The Board shall not exercise the powers of this section without the consent of the road works authority.

(b) Any such consent may be given subject to such reasonable conditions as the road works authority may require but shall not be unreasonably withheld and any question whether such consent has been unreasonably withheld or whether any such condition is reasonable shall be determined by arbitration.

(4) The provisions of this section shall not apply to any road of which temporary possession is taken under section 16 (Temporary use of land) of this Order.

Underpinning of buildings near works

10. The Board at their own expense may, subject as hereinafter provided, underpin or otherwise strengthen any building within 30 metres of any part of the works and the following provisions shall have effect:—
(1) At least 14 days' notice shall (except in case of emergency) be given to the owner, lessee and occupier of the building intended to be so underpinned or otherwise strengthened:
(2) If any owner, lessee or occupier of any such building, within 10 days after the giving of such notice, gives a counter-notice in writing that he disputes the necessity of such underpinning or strengthening, the question of the necessity shall be determined by arbitration; and, if the arbiter decides that such underpinning or strengthening is not necessary, the Board shall not proceed therewith:
(3) In any case in which any building shall have been underpinned or strengthened under the powers of this section the Board may, from time to time after the completion of such underpinning or strengthening, and during the execution of the work in connection with which such underpinning or strengthening was done, or within 5 years after the opening for traffic of that work, after giving reasonable notice to the occupier, enter upon and survey such building and, after complying with the foregoing provisions of this section, do such further underpinning or strengthening as they may deem necessary or expedient:
(4) The Board shall be liable to compensate the owner, lessee and occupier of every such building for any loss or damage which may result to them by reason of the exercise of the powers of this section:

(5) Nothing in this section shall affect liability to compensate under any enactment in respect of loss or damage arising from the execution of any works, except so far as compensation is payable under paragraph (4) above:

(6) Every case of compensation to be ascertained under this section shall be ascertained according to the provisions of the Land Compensation (Scotland) Act 1963.

Use of sewers, etc., for removing water

11.—(1) The Board may use for the discharge of any water pumped or found by them during the construction of the works any available stream or watercourse, or any sewer or drain vested in, or under the control of, the regional council, and for that purpose may lay down, take up and alter conduits, pipes and other works and may make any convenient connections with any such stream, watercourse, sewer or drain within the limits of deviation.

(2) The Board shall not—

(a) discharge any water into any such sewer or drain except with the consent of the regional council, whose consent shall not be unreasonably withheld, and subject to such terms and conditions (including the taking of steps to remove as far as may be reasonably practicable from water so discharged any gravel, soil or other solid substance or matter in suspension) as the regional council may reasonably impose; or

(b) make any opening into any such sewer or drain except in accordance with plans approved by, and under the superintendence (if given) of, the regional council but approval of those plans by the regional council shall not be unreasonably withheld.

(3) Any difference arising between the Board and the regional council under this section shall be determined by arbitration.

(4) Section 31 of the Control of Pollution Act 1974 shall apply to, or to the consequence of, a discharge under the powers of this section into any controlled waters within the meaning assigned to that expression by section 30A(1) of that Act as if this section were not a provision of a local Act or a statutory order for the purposes of section 31(2)(b)(ii) of that Act.

(5) Nothing in this section shall affect the operation of Part IV of the Act of 1991.

PART III

LAND

Meaning of new rights

12. In this Part references to the purchase by the Board of new rights are references to the purchase of rights (whether heritable or moveable) to be created in favour of the Board.

Purchase of land

13.—(1) The Board may purchase compulsorily and use such of the land within the limits of deviation and described in the deposited book of reference as they require for the purposes of the works or their undertaking.

(2) The Board may enter upon, use and appropriate so much of the subsoil and undersurface of, or airspace over, any public road or place within the limits of deviation and described in the deposited book of reference as shall be necessary for the purposes of subsection (1) above without being required to purchase the same or any servitude or other right therein or thereunder or to make any payment therefor.

(3) For the purpose of section 28 of the Land Registration (Scotland) Act 1979 subsection (2) above shall be taken to create a real right over such land

as is referred to in that subsection without any necessity to record a deed in the Register of Sasines or to register the right.

Purchase of new rights over land

14.—(1) Subject to the provisions of this Order, the Board may for the purpose of constructing, maintaining, protecting, altering, renewing and using the works, or for the purpose of obtaining access to the works or for the purpose of doing any other thing necessary in connection with the works, purchase compulsorily and use so much of the subsoil and undersurface of, or may purchase compulsorily such new rights as they require in, under or over, any of the land within the limits of deviation and described in the deposited book of reference instead of purchasing that land under section 13 (Purchase of land) of this Order.

(2) Subject to subsection (3) below, the Lands Clauses Act, as applied by this Order, shall have effect with the modifications necessary to make them apply to the compulsory purchase of new rights under subsection (1) above and under section 15 (Purchase of specific new rights over land) of this Order as they apply to the compulsory purchase of land so that, in appropriate contexts, references in the Lands Clauses Acts to land are read as referring, or as including references, to the new rights or to land over which the new rights are, or are to be, exercisable, according to the requirements of the particular context.

(3) Notwithstanding anything in subsection (2) above, section 90 of the Lands Clauses Consolidation (Scotland) Act 1845 shall not apply to any compulsory purchase by the Board under this section or section 15 (Purchase of specific new rights over land) of this Order.

Purchase of specific new rights over land

15. The Board may, in addition to such new rights as they may purchase under section 14 (Purchase of new rights over land) of this Order, purchase compulsorily such new rights as they require in or over the lands numbered on the deposited plans 5 to 7, 14, 15 and 17 in the Hamilton District within the lines marked "Limit of land to be used" for the purpose of providing means of access in connection with the construction and maintenance of the works.

Temporary use of land

16. The provisions set out in the Schedule to this Order shall have effect with respect to the temporary use of land by the Board for working sites and related movement of equipment, materials and plant.

Time for compulsory purchase of land or rights over land

17. Except as may be provided under section 18 (Extension of time) of this Order, the powers of the Board of compulsory purchase of land and new rights in, under or over land under this Order shall cease on 31st December 1999.

Extension of time

18.—(1) In this section "lessee" means a lessee under a lease having a period of not less than 21 years to run at the date of his notice under subsection (3) below; and any reference to the purchase of an interest in land includes reference to the purchase of a new right in, under or over that land.

(2) (a) Subject to the provisions of this section, the Secretary of State may, by order under this subsection, extend the period for the exercise of powers of compulsory purchase of land and new rights in, under or over land under this Order.

(b) An order under this subsection shall be subject to special parliamentary procedure.

(3) If any owner or lessee of any land subject to an order under subsection (2) above shall give notice in writing to the Board of his desire for the purchase as soon as may be by the Board of his interest in any part of the land specified in the notice, the Board shall within a period of three months after the receipt of such notice—

  (a) enter into a contract with him for the purchase of his interest in the land or such part thereof as may be specified in the contract; or

  (b) serve on him a notice to treat for the compulsory purchase of his interest in the land specified in his notice, or in such part thereof as may be required by the Board: or

  (c) serve on him notice in writing of the Board's intention not to proceed with the purchase of his interest in the land specified in his notice.

(4) Where notice is given under subsection (3) above by any owner or lessee, then—

  (a) if the Board—

      (i) fail to comply with that subsection; or

      (ii) withdraw in pursuance of any statutory provision a notice to treat served on him in compliance with subsection (3)(b) above; or

      (iii) serve notice on him in compliance with subsection (3)(c) above;

  the powers conferred by this Order for the compulsory purchase of his interest in the land so specified shall cease;

  (b) if his interest in part only of the land so specified is purchased in pursuance of such a notice to treat, the powers conferred by this Order for the compulsory purchase of his interest in the remainder of the land so specified shall cease.

Correction of errors in deposited plans and book of reference

19.—(1) If the deposited plans or the deposited book of reference are inaccurate in their description of any land or in their statement or description of the ownership or occupation of any land, the Board may apply by summary application to the sheriff for the correction thereof.

(2) If on any such application it appears to the sheriff that the misstatement or wrong description arose from mistake, he shall certify accordingly and shall in his certificate state in what respect any matter is misstated or wrongly described.

(3) The certificate shall be deposited in the office of the clerk of the Parliaments and a copy thereof in the Private Bill Office, House of Commons, the Scottish Office, London, the office of the Secretary of State for Scotland, Edinburgh, the office of the Health and Safety Executive, Edinburgh, and with the sheriff clerk of the sheriff court district of Hamilton and thereupon the deposited plans and the deposited book of reference shall be deemed to be corrected according to the certificate.

(4) Any certificate or copy deposited under this section with any person shall be kept by him with the other documents to which it relates.

Purchase of part of certain properties

20.—(1) Where a copy of this section is endorsed on, or annexed to, a notice to treat served under the Lands Clauses Acts, as incorporated with this Order, the following provisions of this section shall apply to the land subject to the notice instead of section 90 of the Lands Clauses Consolidation (Scotland) Act 1845.

(2) Where the land subject to the notice is part only of a house, building or factory, or part only of land consisting of a house together with any park or garden belonging thereto, then, if the person on whom the notice is served, within 21 days after the day on which the notice is served on him, serves on the Board a counter-notice objecting to the sale of the part and stating that he is willing and able to sell the whole (in this section referred to as "the land

subject to the counter-notice"), the question whether he shall be required to sell the part shall, unless the Board agree to take the land subject to the counter-notice, be referred to the tribunal.

(3) If the said person does not serve such a counter-notice as aforesaid within 21 days after the day on which the notice is served on him, or if on such a reference to the tribunal the tribunal determines that the part subject to the notice to treat can be taken without material detriment to the remainder of the land subject to the counter-notice or, in the case of part of land consisting of a house together with a park or garden belonging thereto, without such detriment and without seriously affecting the amenity and convenience of the house, the said person shall be required to sell the part.

(4) If, on such a reference to the tribunal, the tribunal determines that part only of the land subject to the notice to treat can be taken without material detriment to the remainder of the land subject to the counter-notice or, as the case may be, without such detriment and without seriously affecting the amenity and convenience of the house, the notice to treat shall be deemed to be a notice to treat for that part.

(5) If, on such a reference to the tribunal, the tribunal determines that the land subject to the notice to treat cannot be taken without material detriment to the remainder of the land subject to the counter-notice but that the material detriment is confined to a part of the land subject to the counter-notice, the notice to treat shall be deemed to be a notice to treat for the land to which the material detriment is confined in addition to the land already subject to the notice, whether or not the additional land is land which the Board are authorised to purchase compulsorily under this Order.

(6) If the Board agree to take the land subject to the counter-notice, or if the tribunal determines that—

(a) none of the land subject to the notice to treat can be taken without material detriment to the remainder of the land subject to the counter-notice or, as the case may be, without such detriment and without seriously affecting the amenity and convenience of the house; and

(b) the material detriment is not confined to a part of the land subject to the counter-notice;

the notice to treat shall be deemed to be a notice to treat for the land subject to the counter-notice whether or not the whole of that land is land which the Board are authorised to purchase under this Order.

(7) In any case where, by virtue of a determination by the tribunal under subsection (4), (5) or (6) above, a notice to treat is deemed to be a notice to treat for part of the land specified in the notice or for more land than is specified in the notice, the Board may, within 6 weeks after the tribunal makes its determination, withdraw the notice to treat and, if they do so, shall pay to the said person compensation for any loss or expense occasioned to him by the giving and withdrawal of the notice to be determined, in default of agreement, by the tribunal:

Provided that the determination of the tribunal shall not be deemed to be made so long as—

(a) the time for requiring the tribunal to state a case with respect thereto has not expired and any proceedings on the points raised by a case so stated have not been concluded; or

(b) any proceedings on appeal from any decision on the points raised by a case so stated have not been concluded.

(8)(a) Where a person is under this section required to sell part only of a house, building or factory, or of land consisting of a house, together with any park or garden belonging thereto, the Board shall pay to him compensation for any loss sustained by him due to the severance of that part in addition to the value of his interest therein.

(b) Any dispute as to a person's entitlement to compensation under this section or as to the amount of the compensation shall be determined by the tribunal.

Disregard of recent improvements and interests

21. In determining a question with respect to compensation claimed in consequence of the compulsory purchase of land under this Order, the tribunal shall not take into account—

(a) any interest in land, or

(b) any enhancement of the value of any interest in land, by reason of any building erected, works executed or improvement or alteration made (whether on the land purchased or on any other land with which the claimant is, or was at the time of the erection, executing or making of the building, works, improvement or alteration, directly or indirectly concerned),

if the tribunal is satisfied that the creation of the interest, the erection of the building, the execution of the works, or the making of the improvement or alteration, as the case may be, was not reasonably necessary and was undertaken with a view to obtaining compensation or increased compensation.

Set-off for enhancement in value of retained land

22.—(1) In this section "relevant land" means any land or new rights over land required by the Board for the purposes of, or in connection with, the works.

(2) In assessing the compensation payable to any person on the purchase by the Board from him of any relevant land, the tribunal shall set off against the value of the relevant land any increase in value of any contiguous or adjacent lands belonging to the same person in the same capacity, or of the land over which new rights are acquired, which will accrue to him by reason of the construction of any of the works.

(3) The Land Compensation (Scotland) Act 1963 shall have effect subject to the provisions of this section.

Power to enter, survey, etc., land

23.—(1) The Board and their surveyors and officers may at all reasonable times in the day, upon giving on the first occasion not less than 7 days', and on subsequent occasions not less than 3 days', previous notice in writing to the occupier and to the owner if he is not the occupier, enter upon, examine and lay open any land which may be purchased compulsorily under this Order for the purpose of surveying, measuring, taking levels, examining works and valuing that land or for any other purpose ancillary to the powers conferred by this Order.

(2) Any person entering land under subsection (1) above on behalf of the Board shall, if so required, produce written evidence of his identity and of his authority to do so.

(3) In the exercise of the powers of subsection (1) above the Board and their surveyors and officers shall cause as little detriment or inconvenience to any person as circumstances allow, and the Board shall, subject to the provisions of this Order, make compensation to the owners and occupiers of any land injuriously affected by the exercise of those powers, to be determined in case of dispute by the tribunal.

Further powers of entry

24. At any time after notice to treat has been served for any land which may be purchased compulsorily under this Order the Board may, after giving to the owner and occupier of the land not less than 3 months' notice, enter on and take possession of the land or such part thereof as is specified in the notice without previous consent or compliance with sections 83 to 89 of the Lands Clauses Consolidation (Scotland) Act 1845, but subject to the

payment of the like compensation for the land of which possession is taken, and interest on the compensation awarded, as would have been payable if those sections had been complied with.

Extinction or suspension of rights of way

25.—(1) All private rights of way over any land which may be purchased compulsorily under this Order shall be extinguished on the purchase of the land whether compulsorily or by agreement, or on the entry on the land under section 24 (Further powers of entry) of this Order.

(2) All public or private rights of way over any land of which the Board may take temporary possession under section 16 (Temporary use of land) of this Order shall be suspended and unenforceable against the Board for so long as the Board shall remain in lawful possession thereof:

Provided that the Board shall provide reasonable access for persons on foot bona fide exercising such rights to go to or from any land, house or building abutting on any such land.

(3) Any person who suffers loss by the extinction or suspension of any private right under this section shall be entitled to be paid by the Board compensation, to be determined in case of dispute by the tribunal.

Service of notices, etc.

26. Paragraph 19 of Schedule 1 to the Acquisition of Land (Authorisation Procedure) (Scotland) Act 1947 shall apply and have effect with respect to any notice or other document required or authorised to be served under or by virtue of this Order as if such notice or other document were required or authorised to be served under that Schedule.

PART IV

PROTECTIVE PROVISIONS

Crown rights

27. Nothing in this Order affects prejudicially any estate, right, power, privilege or exemption of the Crown and, without prejudice to the generality of the foregoing, nothing in this Order authorises the Board to take, use, or interfere with, any land or rights—

(a) belonging to Her Majesty in right of the Crown and under the management of the Crown Estate Commissioners; or

(b) belonging to a government department, or held in trust for Her Majesty for the purposes of a government department;

without the consent in writing of those commissioners on behalf of Her Majesty or, as the case may be, that government department.

For protection of telecommunications operators

28. For the protection of telecommunications operators the following provisions shall, unless otherwise agreed in writing between the Board and the telecommunications operators concerned, have effect:—

(1) In this section expressions defined in the Telecommunications Act 1984 have the same meanings as in that Act:

(2) The temporary stopping up or diversion of any road under section 9 (Temporary stoppage of roads) of this Order shall not affect any right of a telecommunications operator under paragraph 9 of the telecommunications code to inspect, maintain, adjust, repair or alter any apparatus which, at the time of the stopping up or diversion, is in that part of the road.

For protection of electricity, gas and water undertakers

29. For the protection of the several undertakers referred to in this section, the following provisions shall, unless otherwise agreed in writing between the Board and the undertakers concerned, have effect:—

(1) In this section—

"adequate alternative apparatus" means alternative apparatus adequate to enable the undertakers to fulfil their statutory functions in a manner not less efficient than previously;

"apparatus" means—

(a) in the case of electricity undertakers, electric lines or electrical plant (as defined in the Electricity Act 1989) belonging to or maintained by such undertakers; or

(b) in the case of gas or water undertakers any mains, pipes or other apparatus belonging to or maintained by such undertakers;

(not being, except in paragraph (2) below, apparatus in respect of which the relations between the Board and the undertakers are regulated by the provisions of Part IV of the Act of 1991) and includes any structure for the lodging therein of apparatus or for giving access to apparatus;

"functions" includes powers and duties;

"in" in a context referring to apparatus or alternative apparatus in land includes a reference to apparatus or alternative apparatus under, over or upon land; and

"undertakers" means any person authorised to carry on, in any area within which the Board are by this Order authorised to purchase land or execute works, an undertaking for the supply of gas or water or for the generation, transmission or supply of electricity; and, in relation to any apparatus, means the undertakers to whom it belongs or by whom it is maintained:

(2) The temporary or permanent stopping up or diversion of a road under the powers of this Order shall not affect any right of undertakers to inspect, maintain, renew, remove or use any apparatus which at the time of the stopping up or diversion was in that road:

(3) The Board, in the case of the powers conferred by section 10 (Underpinning of buildings near works) of this Order, shall, so far as is reasonably practicable, so exercise those powers as not to obstruct or render less convenient the access to any apparatus:

(4) Notwithstanding anything in this Order or shown on the deposited plans the Board shall not acquire any apparatus under the powers of this Order otherwise than by agreement:

(5) If the Board, in the exercise of the powers of this Order, acquire any interest in any land in which any apparatus is placed, that apparatus shall not be removed under this section and any right of the undertakers to maintain, repair, renew or inspect that apparatus in that land shall not be extinguished until adequate alternative apparatus has been constructed and is in operation to the reasonable satisfaction of the undertakers:

(6) If the Board, for the purpose of executing any works in, on or under any land purchased, held, appropriated or used under this Order, require the removal of any apparatus placed in that land, they shall give to the undertakers written notice of that requirement, together with a plan and section of the work proposed, and of the proposed position of the alternative apparatus to be provided or constructed so as to provide adequate alternative apparatus in lieu of the apparatus to be removed, and in that case (or if in consequence of the exercise of any of the powers of this Order the undertakers reasonably require to

remove any apparatus) the Board shall, if it is reasonably practicable to do so, afford to the undertakers the necessary facilities and rights for the construction of the alternative apparatus in other land of the Board and thereafter for the maintenance, repair, renewal and inspection of that apparatus:

Provided that, if the alternative apparatus or any part thereof is to be constructed elsewhere than in other land of the Board, or the Board are unable to afford such facilities and rights as aforesaid in the land in which the alternative apparatus or that part thereof is to be constructed, the undertakers shall, on receipt of a written notice to that effect from the Board, forthwith use their best endeavours to obtain the necessary facilities and rights in that last-mentioned land:

(7) (a) Any alternative apparatus to be constructed in land of the Board under this section shall be constructed in such manner and in such line or situation as may be agreed between the undertakers and the Board or in default of agreement determined by arbitration;

(b) The undertakers shall, after the alternative apparatus to be provided or constructed has been agreed or determined by arbitration as aforesaid and after the grant to the undertakers of any such facilities and rights as are referred to in paragraph (6) above, proceed with all reasonable dispatch to construct and bring into operation the alternative apparatus and thereafter to remove any apparatus required by the Board to be removed under the provisions of this section:

(8) Notwithstanding anything in paragraph (7) above, if the Board give notice in writing to the undertakers that they desire themselves to execute any part of so much of the work necessary in connection with the construction of the alternative apparatus, or the removal of the apparatus required to be removed, as will take place in any land of the Board, that work, in lieu of being executed by the undertakers, shall be executed by the Board with all reasonable dispatch under the superintendence, if given, and to the reasonable satisfaction of the undertakers;

Provided that nothing in this paragraph shall authorise the Board to execute the actual placing, installation, bedding, packing, removal, connection or disconnection of any apparatus, or execute any filling around the apparatus (where the apparatus is laid in a trench) within 300 millimetres of the apparatus:

(9) Where, in accordance with the provisions of this section, the Board afford to the undertakers facilities and rights for the construction, maintenance, repair, renewal and inspection in land of the Board of alternative apparatus in substitution for apparatus to be removed as aforesaid, those facilities and rights shall be granted upon such terms and conditions as may be agreed between the Board and the undertakers or in default of agreement determined by arbitration:

Provided that—

(a) in determining those terms and conditions in respect of alternative apparatus to be constructed in or along any railway of the Board, the arbiter shall—

(i) give effect to all reasonable requirements of the Board for ensuring the safety and efficient operation of the railway and for securing any subsequent alterations or adaptations of the alternative apparatus which may be required to prevent interference with any proposed works of the Board or the traffic on the railway; and

(ii) so far as it may be reasonable and practicable to do so in the circumstances of the particular case, give effect to the terms and conditions applicable to the apparatus, if any, constructed in or along the railway for which the alternative apparatus is to be substituted;

(b) if the facilities and rights to be afforded by the Board in respect of any alternative apparatus and the terms and conditions subject to which the same are to be granted are in the opinion of the arbiter less favourable on the whole to the undertakers than the facilities and rights enjoyed by them in respect of the apparatus to be removed and the terms and conditions to which those facilities and rights are subject, the arbiter shall make such provision for the payment of compensation by the Board to the undertakers in respect thereof as appears to him to be reasonable having regard to all the circumstances of the particular case:

(10) (a) Not less than 28 days before commencing to execute any part of the works which will or may be within 15 metres of, or may otherwise affect, any apparatus the removal of which has not been required by the Board, the Board shall submit to the undertakers a plan, section and description of the works to be executed;

(b) Those works shall be executed only in accordance with the plan, section and description submitted as aforesaid and in accordance with such reasonable requirements as may be made by the undertakers for the alteration or otherwise for the protection of the apparatus or for securing access thereto and the undertakers shall be entitled by their officer to watch and inspect the execution of those works:

Provided that—

(i) if the undertakers within 14 days after the submission to them of a plan, section and description shall, in consequence of the works proposed by the Board, reasonably require the removal of any apparatus and give written notice to the Board of that requirement, the foregoing provisions of this section shall apply as if the removal of the apparatus had been required by the Board;

(ii) nothing in this sub-paragraph shall preclude the Board from submitting at any time or from time to time, but in no case less than 28 days before commencing the execution of any works, a new plan, section and description thereof in lieu of the plan, section and description previously submitted, and thereupon the provisions of this paragraph shall apply to and in respect of the new plan, section and description;

(c) The Board shall not be required to comply with sub-paragraph (a) above in a case of emergency but in that case they shall give to the undertakers notice as soon as reasonably practicable and a plan, section and description of those works as soon as reasonably practicable thereafter and shall comply with sub-paragraph (b) above so far as reasonably practicable in the circumstances:

(11) Subject to paragraph (12) below, the Board shall pay to the undertakers the costs, charges and expenses reasonably incurred by the undertakers in or in connection with the inspection, removal, alteration or protection of any apparatus or the construction of any new apparatus which may be required in consequence of the execution of any such works as are referred to in paragraph (6) above, less the value of any apparatus removed under the provisions of this section (that value being calculated after removal) and shall also make compensation to the undertakers—

(a) for any damage caused to any apparatus (other than apparatus the repair of which is not reasonably necessary in view of its intended removal in accordance with the provisions of this section); and

(b) for any other expenses, loss, damages, penalty or costs
incurred by the undertakers;
by reason of the execution, maintenance, user or failure of those works
or otherwise by reason of the exercise by the Board of the powers of
this Order:

(12) If the cost of maintaining, using, repairing or renewing any apparatus
is reduced by reason of any of the works, including the provision of
alternative apparatus under this section, a capitalised sum representing that saving shall be paid by the relevant undertakers to the Board
or set off against any sums payable by the Board to the relevant undertakers under this section:

(13) Any difference arising between the Board and the undertakers under
this section shall be determined by arbitration:

(14) Nothing in this section shall affect the provisions of any enactment or
agreement regulating the relations between the Board and the undertakers in respect of any apparatus laid or erected in land belonging to
the Board at the date of the passing of the Act confirming this Order.

For protection of sewers of Strathclyde Regional Council

30. For the protection of the sewers of the regional council the following
provisions shall, unless otherwise agreed in writing between the Board and
the regional council, have effect:—

(1) In this section—
"sewer" means, subject to paragraph (2) below, any sewer of the
regional council and includes any manholes, ventilating shafts,
pumps or other accessories of a sewer; and
"specified work" means any part of the works which will or may
be situated within 15 metres measured in any direction of a sewer:

(2) Nothing in this section shall apply to apparatus of the regional council
in respect of which the relations between the Board and the regional
council are regulated by the provisions of Part IV of the Act of 1991:

(3) Wherever in this section provision is made with respect to the
approval or consent of the regional council, that approval or consent
shall be in writing and shall not be unreasonably withheld:

(4) The Board shall not commence the execution of any specified work
until they have given to the regional council not less than 56 days'
notice in writing of their intention to commence the same, together
with plans as described in paragraph (9) below (in this section referred
to as "the said plans"), for their approval and until the regional council
have signified their approval of those plans:
Provided that, if within 56 days after the submission of the said plans
the regional council have not approved or disapproved them, they
shall be deemed to have approved the said plans as submitted:

(5) The Board shall comply with, and conform to, all reasonable orders,
directions and regulations of the regional council in the execution of
any specified work and shall provide new, altered or substituted works
in such manner as the regional council reasonably require for the protection of, and for preventing injury or impediment to, any existing
sewer by reason of the specified work and shall indemnify the regional
council against all expenses occasioned thereby:

(6) All new, altered or substituted works shall, where so required by the
regional council, be done by or under the direction, superintendence
and control of an officer of the regional council duly appointed for the
purpose at the cost of the Board, and all costs, charges and expenses
reasonably incurred by the regional council by reason of those works,
whether in the execution thereof, or in the preparation or examination

of plans or designs, or in such direction, superintendence or control as aforesaid, or otherwise, shall be paid to the regional council by the Board:

(7) When any new, altered or substituted works or any work of defence connected therewith are completed by or at the cost of the Board under the provisions of this section, they shall thereafter be as fully and completely under the direction, jurisdiction and control of the regional council as any sewers or works now or hereafter may be:

(8) The regional council may require the Board in constructing any specified work to make any reasonable deviation within the limits of deviation from the lines or levels shown upon the said plans for the purpose of avoiding injury, or risk of injury, to any sewer and the Board shall in constructing those works deviate accordingly:

(9) The plans to be submitted to the regional council for the purposes of this section shall be detailed plans, drawings, sections and specifications which shall describe the exact position and manner in which, and the level at which, any specified work is proposed to be constructed and shall accurately describe the position of all sewers of the regional council within the limits of deviation (for which purpose the regional council shall allow the Board access to plans in their possession and to any of their sewers in order to enable the Board to obtain reliable information) and shall comprise detailed drawings of every alteration which the Board may propose to make in any sewer:

(10) The regional council may require such modifications to be made in the said plans as may be reasonably necessary to secure the main drainage system of the district in which any specified work is situated against interference or risk of damage and to provide and secure proper and convenient means of access to any sewer:

(11) The Board shall be liable to make good, or, if the regional council so decide, to bear any expense reasonably incurred by the regional council in making good, all injury or damage caused by, or resulting from, the construction of any specified work to any sewer, drain or work vested in the regional council:

(12) If the Board in the construction of any specified work or any new, altered or substituted work or any work of defence connected therewith provided in accordance with this section, damage or, without the consent of the regional council, alter or in any way interfere with any existing sewer, the Board shall—

    (a) pay to the regional council any additional expense which may be reasonably incurred by the regional council in the maintenance, management or renewal of any new, altered or substituted sewer which may be necessary by reason of the said construction; and

    (b) give to the regional council full, free and uninterrupted access at all times to any such new, altered or substituted sewer and every reasonable facility for the inspecting, maintenance, alteration and repair thereof:

(13) It shall be lawful for an officer of the regional council duly appointed for the purpose at any reasonable time, on giving to the Board such notice as may in the circumstances be reasonable, to enter upon and inspect any specified work or any other work constructed under the powers of this section:

(14) The approval by the regional council of any plans, or the superintendence by them of any work, under the provisions of this section, shall not exonerate the Board from any liability or affect any claim for damages under this section or otherwise:

(15) Any difference arising between the Board and the regional council under this section (other than a difference as to the meaning or construction of this section) shall be determined by arbitration.

For protection of roads and road traffic, etc.

31. The following provisions shall, unless otherwise agreed in writing between the Board and the road works authority or Hamilton District Council, as the case may be, have effect:—

(1) In this section—

"the appropriate council" means the road works authority or the district council, as the case may be;

"the district council" means the Hamilton District Council;

"road" has the same meaning as in the Roads (Scotland) Act 1984; and

"road equipment" means any works or apparatus on or under any road comprising any refuge, lamp column, traffic sign, bollard, bin for refuse or road materials, surface water drain, gully or sewer for conducting road drainage or apparatus respectively connected therewith:

(2) Wherever in this section provision is made with respect to the approval or consent of the appropriate council, that approval or consent shall be in writing and shall not be unreasonably withheld:

(3) The Board shall not, without the consent of the road works authority, construct any part of the works which will involve interference with any road, except in accordance with plans and sections submitted to, and approved by, the road works authority:

Provided that, if within 56 days after those plans and sections have been submitted the road works authority have not approved or disapproved them, they shall be deemed to have approved the plans and sections as submitted:

(4) Before commencing to construct any part of the works, or any works or conveniences connected therewith, which will involve interference with a road, or the traffic in any road, the Board shall consult the road works authority as to the time when that part shall be commenced, and as to the extent of the surface of the road which it may be reasonably necessary for the Board to occupy or the nature of the interference which may be caused to the said traffic in the construction of that part, and as to the time during which, and the extent to which, the road shall be interfered with, and as to the conditions under which that part shall be constructed, so as to reduce so far as possible inconvenience to the public and to ensure the safety of the public, and that part shall not be constructed, and the surface of the road shall not be occupied by the Board, and the said interference with traffic shall not be caused, except at such time, to such extent, and in accordance with such conditions as may be agreed between the Board and the road works authority or determined by arbitration:

(5) At least 56 days before commencing to make any hole from the surface of any part of any road the Board shall serve notice in writing on the road works authority of their intention to commence the same and that notice shall describe the place at which any hole is intended to be made, and the steps, if any, to be taken by the Board to safeguard pedestrians using any footway, footpath or other way in which the hole is intended to be made, and, if within 21 days after the receipt of the notice any objection is made by the road works authority, the matter shall (unless otherwise agreed) be determined by arbitration before the making of the hole is commenced, but if no objection is made the Board may proceed with the making of the hole:

(6) The Board shall secure that so much of the works as is constructed under, or so as to affect, any road is so designed, constructed and maintained as to carry the appropriate loading for that road recommended

at the time of construction of those works by the Secretary of State, and the Board shall indemnify the road works authority against, and make good to the road works authority, all expenses which they may reasonably incur or be put to in the maintenance or repair of any road, or any tunnels, sewers, drains or apparatus therein, by reason of any non-compliance by the Board with the provisions of this paragraph:

(7) It shall be lawful for an authorised officer of the appropriate council at all reasonable times to enter upon and inspect any part of the works which is in or under any road or which may affect any road or any property or work of the appropriate council, during the execution thereof, and the Board shall give to that officer all reasonable facilities for such inspection and, if he is of the opinion that the construction of that part of the works is attended with danger to any road or to any road equipment or any other property or work belonging to, or under the jurisdiction or control of, the appropriate council on or under any road, the Board shall adopt such measures and precautions as may be reasonably necessary for the purpose of preventing any damage or injury thereto:

(8) The Board shall not alter, disturb or in any way interfere with any road equipment or any other property or work belonging to, or under the jurisdiction or control of, the appropriate council on or under any road, or the access thereto, without the consent of the appropriate council, and any alteration, adaptation, diversion, replacement or reconstruction of any road equipment or any other property or work as aforesaid which may be necessary shall be made by the appropriate council or the Board as the appropriate council think fit and any costs, charges and expenses reasonably incurred by the appropriate council in so doing shall be repaid to the appropriate council by the Board:

(9) The Board shall not remove any soil or material from any road except such as must be excavated in the execution of the works:

(10) (a) The Board shall not, except with the consent of the road works authority, deposit any soil, subsoil or materials, or stand any vehicle or plant, on any road so as to obstruct the use of such road by any person or, except with the like consent, deposit any soil, subsoil or materials on any road except within a hoarding;

(b) All costs, charges and expenses reasonably incurred by the road works authority in removing any soil, subsoil or materials deposited on any road in contravention of this paragraph shall be repaid to the road works authority by the Board:

(11) Where any part of any road has been temporarily broken up or disturbed by the Board, the Board shall make good the subsoil, foundations and surface of such part of the road to the reasonable satisfaction of the road works authority and maintain the same to the reasonable satisfaction of the road works authority for such time as may be reasonably required for the permanent reinstatement of the road:

Provided that the reinstatement of such part of the road shall in the first instance be of a temporary nature only and the permanent reinstatement thereof shall be carried out by the road works authority as soon as reasonably practicable after the completion of the temporary reinstatement, and the costs, charges and expenses reasonably incurred by the road works authority in so doing shall be repaid to the road works authority by the Board:

(12) The Board shall compensate the appropriate council for any subsidence of, or damage to, any road or any road equipment or any other property or work belonging to, or under the jurisdiction or control of, the appropriate council on or under any road which may be caused by, or in consequence of, any act or default of the Board, their contractors,

servants or agents and whether such damage or subsidence happens during the construction of the works or at any time thereafter:

(13) Any difference arising between the Board and the appropriate council under this section (other than a difference as to the meaning or construction of this section) shall be determined by arbitration.

PART V

GENERAL

Saving for town and country planning

32.—(1) The Town and Country Planning (Scotland) Act 1972, and any orders, regulations, rules, schemes and directions made or given thereunder and any restrictions or powers thereby imposed or conferred in relation to land shall apply and may be exercised in relation to any land notwithstanding that the development thereof is or may be authorised by this Order.

(2) Subject to subsection (3) below, in their application to development authorised by this Order, article 3 of, and Class 29 in Part 11 of Schedule 1 to, the Town and Country Planning (General Permitted Development) (Scotland) Order 1992 (which permit development authorised by any local or private Act or by any order approved by both Houses of Parliament, being an Act or order designating specifically both the nature of the development thereby authorised and the land on which it may be carried out) shall have effect as if the authority to develop given by this Order were limited to development begun within 10 years after the passing of the Act confirming this Order.

(3) Subsection (2) above shall not apply to the carrying out of any development consisting of the alteration, maintenance or repair of works or the substitution of new works therefor.

Arbitration

33. Where under any provision of this Order any difference (other than a difference to which the provisions of the Lands Clauses Acts apply) is to be determined by arbitration, then, unless otherwise provided, the difference shall be referred to, and settled by, a single arbiter to be agreed between the parties or, in default of agreement, to be appointed on the summary application of any party (after notice in writing to the other) by the sheriff.

Section 16   SCHEDULE

TEMPORARY WORKING SITES

1. In this Schedule "the designated lands" means any of the lands shown on the deposited plans within a line marked "Limit of land to be used" and numbered on those plans 5 to 11, 22 and 23 in the Hamilton District.

2. The Board, in connection with the construction of Works Nos. 1 and 2 and after giving to the owners and occupiers of the designated lands not less than 28 days' notice in writing of intended entry, may—

(a) enter upon and take possession temporarily of the designated lands;
(b) remove any structures and vegetation on the designated lands; and
(c) construct on the designated lands such temporary works or structures as may be required by them.

3. The Board may form and lay out temporary means of access to the lands numbered 8 and 22 in the Hamilton District from—

(a) Carlisle Road, Ferniegair, at point A; and
(b) Merryton Road, Merryton, at point B.

4. The Board shall not, by reason of the exercise of the powers of paragraph 2 or 3 above, be required to purchase any part of the designated lands.

5. On the exercise of the powers conferred by paragraph 2 or 3 above, the following provisions shall have effect:—

(1) The Board shall not, without the agreement of the owners and occupiers of the designated lands, remain in possession of any part thereof after a period of one year from the completion of the works for which such possession has been taken:

(2) Before giving up possession of the designated lands, the Board shall remove all temporary works or structures and restore the designated lands to the reasonable satisfaction of the owners and occupiers thereof:

(3) The Board shall compensate the owners and occupiers of the designated lands for any loss or damage which may result to them by reason of the exercise of the powers of this Schedule:

(4) Nothing is this Schedule shall relieve the Board from liability to compensate under section 6 or 43 of the Act of 1845 or under any other enactment, in respect of loss or damage arising from the execution of any works, other than loss or damage for which compensation is payable under sub-paragraph (3) above:

(5) Any dispute as to a person's entitlement to compensation under sub-paragraph (3) above or as to the amount thereof shall be determined by the tribunal.

6. The provisions of paragraph 5 above are without prejudice to the powers conferred by section 15 (Purchase of specific new rights over land) of this Order in respect of the land numbered on the deposited plans 5 to 7 in the Hamilton District.

INDEX

References are to section numbers of the Order

BRITISH RAILWAYS ACT 1994

(1994 c. iv)

ARRANGEMENT OF SECTIONS

PART I

PRELIMINARY

PART II

WORKS, ETC.

Works

General works provisions

Miscellaneous

PART III

LAND

Purchase of land, etc.

General lands provisions

PART IV

PROTECTIVE PROVISIONS

PART V

GENERAL

An Act to empower the British Railways Board to construct works and to acquire land; to confer further powers on the Board; and for connected purposes.   [31st March 1994]

PARLIAMENTARY PROGRESS
   The Bill's progress through Parliament was as follows:
   House of Commons: First Reading, January 22, 1992; Suspended, March 12, 1992; Second Reading, February 8, 1993 and July 8, 1993; Bill Committed, July 8, 1993; Suspended, October 28, 1993; Unopposed Bill Committee, February 9, 1994; Bill as amended Considered, February 23, 1994; Third Reading, March 2, 1994.
   House of Lords: First Reading, March 2, 1994; Second Reading, March 17, 1994; Bill Committed, March 17, 1994; Unopposed Bill Committee, March 22, 1994; Third Reading, March 30, 1994.

INTRODUCTION
   This Act empowers the British Railways Board to undertake certain works in accordance with its duties as laid down in the Transport Act 1962. Part I contains preliminary provisions. Part II details the works proposed and indicates the likely interference with existing amenities. Part III details the land likely to be affected by the Act. Part IV sets out protective provisions *vis-à-vis* amenities and Crown rights.

WHEREAS—

   (1) It is the duty of the British Railways Board (hereinafter referred to as "the Board") under the Transport Act 1962 (inter alia) to provide railway services in Great Britain and, in connection with the provision of railway services, to provide such other services and facilities as appear to the Board to be expedient, and to have due regard, as respects all those railway and other services and facilities, to efficiency, economy and safety of operation:
   (2) It is expedient that the Board should be empowered to construct the works authorised by this Act and to acquire or use the land referred to in this Act:
   (3) It is expedient that the other powers in this Act contained should be conferred on the Board, and that the other provisions in this Act contained should be enacted:
   (4) Plans and sections showing the lines or situations and levels of the works to be constructed under this Act, and plans of the land authorised to be acquired or used by this Act, and a book of reference to such plans containing the names of the owners and lessees, or reputed owners and lessees, and of the occupiers of the said land were duly deposited in the office of the Clerk of the Parliaments and in the Private Bill Office of the House of Commons and with the proper officers of the councils of the counties within which the said works may be constructed or the said land is situated, which plans, sections and book of reference are respectively referred to in this Act as the deposited plans, the deposited sections and the deposited book of reference:
   (5) The purposes of this Act could not have been effected without the authority of Parliament when the Bill for this Act was deposited:
   May it therefore please Your Majesty that it may be enacted, and be it enacted, by the Queen's most Excellent Majesty, by and with the advice and consent of the Lords Spiritual and Temporal, and Commons, in this present Parliament assembled, and by the authority of the same, as follows:—

PART I

PRELIMINARY

Short title

1. This Act may be cited as the British Railways Act 1994.

Interpretation

2.—(1) In this Act, unless the context otherwise requires, words and expressions to which meanings are assigned by the enactments incorporated herewith have in relation to the related subject-matter the same respective meanings; and—

"the Act of 1845" means the Railways Clauses Consolidation Act 1845;

"the Act of 1965" means the Compulsory Purchase Act 1965;

"the Board" means the British Railways Board;

"enactment" includes any order, byelaw, rule, regulation, scheme or other instrument having effect by virtue of an enactment;

"the limits of deviation" means the limits of deviation shown on the deposited plans;

"reference point" means Ordnance Survey National Grid reference point;

"the tribunal" means the Lands Tribunal; and

"the works" means the works authorised by this Act.

(2) All directions, distances and lengths stated in any description of works, powers or lands shall be construed as if the words "or thereabouts" were inserted after each such direction, distance and length.

(3) Any reference in this Act to Work No. 2 shall be construed as a reference to the work of that number authorised by this Act.

(4) References in this Act to access to any place shall include reference to egress from that place.

(5) References in this Act to the purchase by the Board of new rights are references to the purchase of rights to be created in favour of the Board.

Incorporation of general enactments

3.—(1) The following enactments, so far as the same are applicable for the purposes of and are not inconsistent with this Act, are incorporated with this Act, and this Act shall be the special Act for the purposes of the said incorporated enactments:—

(a) the Act of 1845, except sections 1, 7, 8, 9, 11, 12, 15, 17, 19, 20, 22 and 23 thereof; and

(b) in the Railways Clauses Act 1863, Part I (relating to the construction of a railway), except sections 13 to 19 thereof.

(2)(a) For the purposes of the enactments incorporated by subsection (1) above the expression "the company" where used in those enactments means the Board.

(b) Sections 18 and 21 of the Act of 1845, as incorporated by subsection (1) above, shall not extend to regulate the relations between the Board and any other person in respect of any matter or thing concerning which those relations are regulated in any respect by the provisions of Part III of the New Roads and Street Works Act 1991 or by section 26 (For protection of electricity, gas and water undertakers) of this Act.

Application of Part I of Compulsory Purchase Act 1965

4.—(1) Part I of the Act of 1965 (except section 4 thereof and paragraph 3(3) of Schedule 3 thereto), so far as it is applicable for the purposes of and is not inconsistent with this Act, shall apply to the compulsory purchase of land under this Act as it applies to a compulsory purchase to which the Acquisition of Land Act 1981 applies and as if this Act were a compulsory purchase order under the said Act of 1981.

(2) In section 11(1) of the Act of 1965 (which empowers the acquiring authority to enter on and take possession of land the subject of a notice to treat after giving not less than 14 days' notice), as so applied, for the words "fourteen days" there shall be substituted "three months".

(3) The Lands Clauses Consolidation Act 1845 shall not apply to the purchase of land under this Act.

PART II

WORKS, ETC.

Works

Power to make works

5. The Board may, on lands in their ownership, or to be made available to them, and in the line or situation and within the limits of deviation shown on the deposited plans and according to the levels shown on the deposited sections, make and maintain the following work in Mid Glamorgan with all necessary works and conveniences connected therewith:—

In the borough of Cynon Valley—

Work No. 2   A railway (704 metres in length), being a deviation of the Cardiff to Aberdare Railway on the eastern side of that railway, commencing by a junction with that railway at a point 58 metres south of Town Bridge over that railway and terminating by a junction with that railway at a point 78 metres south of the junction of Bailey Street with Miskin Road including a crossing on the level of the footpath (PF 22) leading from Miskin Road (B4275) to Cardiff Road (A4059).

General works provisions

Power to deviate

6. In the execution of Work No. 2 the Board may deviate from the lines or situations thereof shown on the deposited plans to the extent of the limits of deviation and may deviate vertically from the levels shown on the deposited sections to any extent not exceeding 3 metres upwards or downwards or to such further extent as may be approved by the Secretary of State.

Stopping up highways

7.—(1) On the stopping up of any highway or part thereof under any provision of this Act, other than section 11 (Temporary stoppage of highways), all rights of way over or along the highway or part so stopped up shall be extinguished.

(2) Any person who suffers loss by reason of the extinguishment under this section of any private right shall be entitled to be paid by the Board compensation, to be determined in case of dispute by the tribunal.

Appropriating sites of highways

8. After a highway or part thereof is permanently stopped up under this Act, the Board may, subject to the provisions of the Act of 1845 with respect to mines lying under or near the railway, so far as the said highway or part thereof is bounded on both sides by lands of the Board, appropriate the site thereof without making any payment therefor and use it for the purposes of their undertaking.

Repair of highways

9. Any highway or part thereof made, diverted or altered under this Act (except the structure carrying any such highway over any railway of the Board) shall when completed, unless otherwise agreed, be maintained by and at the expense of the highway authority.

Agreements with highway authorities

10.—(1) Where a highway or part thereof is altered or stopped up or interfered with under this Act, the Board may enter into and carry into effect agreements with the highway authority with respect to such alteration, stopping up or interference, or the construction of any new highway to be made under this Act, contributions to the costs thereof or any other matters relating thereto.

(2) The Board may by agreement delegate to the highway authority the power of constructing and maintaining any such alterations or new highway, including the structure of any bridge over or under any railway.

(3) The purposes of this section shall be deemed to be purposes for which a highway authority may incur expenditure and borrow money.

Temporary stoppage of highways

11.—(1) The Board, during and for the purpose of the execution of the works, may temporarily stop up and divert and interfere with any highway and may for any reasonable time divert the traffic therefrom and prevent all persons other than those going bona fide to any land, house or building abutting on the highway from passing along and using the same.

(2) The Board shall provide reasonable access for persons on foot going bona fide to any such land, house or building.

(3)(a) The Board shall not exercise the powers of this section without the consent of the highway authority.

(b) Any such consent may be given subject to such reasonable conditions as the highway authority may require but shall not be unreasonably withheld and any question whether such consent has been unreasonably witheld, or whether any such condition is reasonable, shall be referred to and settled by arbitration.

Underpinning of buildings near works

12. The Board may at their own expense, subject as hereinafter provided, underpin or otherwise strengthen any house or building within 35 metres of Work No. 2 and the following provisions shall have effect:—

(1) At least 14 days' notice shall (except in case of emergency) be given to the owner, lessee and occupier of the house or building intended to be so underpinned or otherwise strengthened:

(2) Each such notice shall be served in a manner prescribed by section 6 of the Acquisition of Land Act 1981 as if required to be served under that Act:

(3) If any owner, lessee or occupier of any such house or building, within 10 days after the giving of such notice, gives a counter-notice in writing that he disputes the necessity of such underpinning or strengthening, the question of the necessity shall be settled by arbitration and, if the arbitrator decides that such underpinning or strengthening is not necessary, the Board shall not proceed therewith:

(4) In any case in which any house or building has been underpinned or strengthened under the powers of this section the Board may, from time to time after the completion of such underpinning or strengthening, and during the execution of the work in connection with which

such underpinning or strengthening was done, or within five years after the opening for traffic of that work, enter upon and survey such house or building and, after complying with the foregoing provisions of this section, do such further underpinning or strengthening as they may deem necessary or expedient:

(5) The Board shall be liable to compensate the owner, lessee and occupier of every such house or building for any loss or damage which may result to them by reason of the exercise of the powers of this section:

(6) Nothing in this section shall affect liability to compensate under section 6 of the Act of 1845, as incorporated with this Act, or section 10(2) of the Act of 1965, as applied by this Act, or under any other enactment in respect of loss or damage arising from the execution of any works, except so far as compensation is payable under paragraph (5) above:

(7) Every case of compensation to be ascertained under this section shall be ascertained according to the provisions of the Land Compensation Act 1961.

Use of sewers, etc., for removing water

13.—(1) In this section "relevant authority" means a sewerage undertaker, the National Rivers Authority, an internal drainage board of a local authority.

(2) The Board may use for the discharge of any water pumped or found by them during the construction of the works any available stream or watercourse, or any sewer or drain of a relevant authority, and for that purpose may lay down, take up and alter conduits, pipes and other works and may make any convenient connections with any such stream, watercourse, sewer or drain within the limits of deviation.

(3) The Board shall not—

(a) discharge any water into any sewer or drain vested in or under the control of a relevant authority except with the consent of that authority, which consent shall not be unreasonably withheld, and subject to such terms and conditions as that authority may reasonably impose; or

(b) make any opening into any such sewer or drain save in accordance with plans approved by, and under the superintendence (if given) of, the relevant authority in whom the sewer or drain is vested, but approval of those plans by that authority shall not be unreasonably withheld.

(4)(a) Section 85 of the Water Resources Act 1991 shall apply to, or to the consequence of, a discharge under the powers of this section into any controlled waters within the meaning given by section 104 of that Act as if this section were not a local statutory provision for the purposes of section 88(1)(f) of that Act.

(b) In the exercise of their powers under this section the Board shall not damage or interfere with the bed of any watercourse forming part of a main river or the banks thereof, within the meaning of section 113 of the Water Resources Act 1991.

(5) The Board shall take all such steps as may reasonably be required to secure that any water discharged by them under this section is as free as may be reasonably practicable from any gravel, soil or other solid substance or matter in suspension.

(6) Any difference arising between the Board and a relevant authority under this section shall be referred to and settled by arbitration.

Miscellaneous

Bridge at Hunslet East, Leeds

14.—(1) in this section—

"the existing bridge" means the bridge of the Board (numbered 4) carrying Fewston Avenue in the city of Leeds across the railway between Osmondthorpe and Stourton;

"the footway" means the western footway of Fewston Avenue; and

"the relevant enactments" means section 9 of the North Eastern Railway Act 1893, section 12 of the North Eastern Railway Act 1894, sections 46 and 50 of the Act of 1845 as incorporated with those Acts and any other enactment relating to the existing bridge.

(2) The Board may bar public access to any part of the existing bridge other than access for persons on foot using the footway.

(3) The relevant enactments shall cease to have effect in so far as they impose any obligation on the Board to provide a bridge on the site of the existing bridge of a width greater than that required for the accommodation of the footway or to allow public access to any part of the existing bridge other than the footway.

Wheal Bois level crossing, Redruth, Cornwall

15.—(1) In this section—

"the specified enactments" means the Highway (Railway Crossings) Act 1839, section 9 of the Railway Regulation Act 1842, section 47 of the Act of 1845, sections 5, 6 and 7 of the Railways Clauses Act 1863 and any other provision to the same or similar effect incorporated with, or contained in, any enactment; and

"Wheal Bois crossing" means the level crossing in the community of Redruth in the district of Kerrier, county of Cornwall, known as Wheal Bois level crossing (reference point SW 7117:4378) whereby the road leading from the A3047 to Radnor Road is crossed by the railway between Redruth and Truro stations.

(2) Subject to the provisions of this Act, the Board may stop up and discontinue so much of the road at Wheal Bois crossing as lies within the boundaries of their property.

(3) Upon the stopping up of Wheal Bois crossing the specified enactments shall cease to apply to that crossing.

(4) The stopping up under this section of Wheal Bois crossing shall not affect the right of persons to use that crossing on foot and the Board shall provide and maintain wicket gates or stiles on both sides of the railway at that crossing.

(5) Section 28 of the Great Western Railway (General Powers) Act 1909 is hereby repealed so far as it relates to Wheal Bois crossing.

PART III

LAND

Purchase of land, etc.

Purchase of land

16.—(1) The Board may purchase compulsorily and use for the purposes specified in column (3) of Part I of Schedule 1 to this Act, or for any purpose connected with or ancillary to their undertaking, all or any of the land specified in columns (1) and (2) of that Part.

(2) For the avoidance of doubt, nothing in this section or section 17 (Purchase of rights over land) of this Act shall be taken as conferring a power to carry out works.

Purchase of rights over land

17.—(1) The Board may purchase such new rights as they require in or over any of the lands shown on the deposited plans within the lines marked "Limit of land to be used" and specified in columns (1) and (2) of Part II of Schedule 1 to this Act for the provision of means of access to the highways mentioned in column (3) of that Part, for the purposes specified in column (4) thereof.

(2) The Act of 1965, as applied by this Act, shall have effect with the modifications necessary to make it apply to the compulsory purchase of new rights under subsection (1) above as it applies to the compulsory purchase of land so that, in appropriate contexts, references in the Act of 1965 to land are read as referring, or as including references, to the new rights or to land over which the new rights are, or are to be, exercisable, according to the requirements of the particular context.

(3) Without prejudice to the generality of subsection (2) above, in relation to the purchase of new rights under subsection (1) above—

(a) Part I of the Act of 1965 shall have effect with the modifications specified in Schedule 2 to this Act; and

(b) the enactments relating to compensation for the compulsory purchase of land shall apply with the necessary modifications as they apply to such compensation.

Temporary use of land

18. The provisions set out in Part III of Schedule 1 to this Act shall have effect with respect to the temporary use of land by the Board for working sites.

General lands provisions

Purchase of part of certain properties

19.—(1) Where a copy of this section is endorsed on, or annexed to, a notice to treat served under the Act of 1965, as applied by this Act, the following provisions of this section shall apply to the land subject to the notice instead of section 8(1) of that Act.

(2) Where the land subject to the notice is part only of a house, building or factory, or part only of land consisting of a house, together with any park or garden belonging thereto, if the person on whom the notice is served, within 21 days after the day on which the notice is served on him, serves on the Board a counter-notice objecting to the sale of the part and stating that he is willing and able to sell the whole (in this section referred to as "the land subject to the counter-notice"), the question whether he shall be required to sell the part shall, unless the Board agree to take the land subject to the counter-notice, be referred to the tribunal.

(3) If the said person does not serve such a counter-notice as aforesaid within 21 days after the day on which the notice to treat is served on him, or if, on such a reference to the tribunal, the tribunal determine that the part subject to the notice to treat can be taken without material detriment to the remainder of the land subject to the counter-notice or, in the case of part of land consisting of a house, together with a park or garden belonging thereto, without such detriment and without seriously affecting the amenity and convenience of the house, the said person shall be required to sell the part.

(4) If, on such a reference to the tribunal, the tribunal determine that part only of the land subject to the notice to treat can be taken without material

detriment to the remainder of the land subject to the counter-notice or, as the case may be, without such detriment and without seriously affecting the amenity and convenience of the house, the notice to treat shall be deemed to be a notice to treat for that part.

(5) If, on such a reference to the tribunal, the tribunal determine that the land subject to the notice to treat cannot be taken without material detriment to the remainder of the land subject to the counter-notice but that the material detriment is confined to a part of the land subject to the counter-notice, the notice to treat shall be deemed to be a notice to treat for the land to which the material detriment is confined in addition to the land already subject to the notice, whether or not the additional land is land which the Board are authorised to purchase compulsorily under this Act.

(6) If the Board agree to take the land subject to the counter-notice, or if the tribunal determine that—

(a) none of the land subject to the notice to treat can be taken without material detriment to the remainder of the land subject to the counter-notice or, as the case may be, without such detriment and without seriously affecting the amenity and convenience of the house; and

(b) the material detriment is not confined to a part of the land subject to the counter-notice;

the notice to treat shall be deemed to be a notice to treat for the land subject to the counter-notice whether or not the whole of the land is land which the Board are authorised to purchase compulsorily under this Act.

(7) In any case where, by virtue of a determination by the tribunal under subsection (4), (5) or (6) above, a notice to treat is deemed to be a notice to treat for part of the land specified in the notice or for more land than is specified in the notice, the Board may, within six weeks after the tribunal make their determination, withdraw the notice to treat and, if they do so, shall pay to the said person compensation for any loss or expense occasioned to him by the giving and withdrawal of the notice, to be determined in case of dispute by the tribunal:

Provided that the determination of the tribunal shall not be deemed to be made so long as—

(a) the time for requiring the tribunal to state a case with respect thereto has not expired or any proceedings on the points raised by a case so stated have not been concluded; or

(b) any proceedings on appeal from any decision on the points raised by a case so stated have not been concluded.

(8) (a) Where a person is required under this section to sell part only of a house, building or factory, or land consisting of a house, together with any park or garden belonging thereto, the Board shall pay him compensation for any loss sustained by him due to the severance of that part in addition to the value of his interest therein.

(b) Any dispute as to a person's entitlement to compensation under this section or as to the amount of compensation shall be determined by the tribunal.

Disregard of recent improvements and interests

20. In determining a question with respect to compensation claimed in consequence of the compulsory purchase of land under this Act, the tribunal shall not take into account—

(a) any interest in land; or

(b) any enhancement of the value of any interest in land by reason of any building erected, works executed or improvement or alteration made (whether on the land purchased or on any other land with which the claimant is, or was at the time of the erection, executing or making of the building, works, improvement or alteration, directly or indirectly concerned);

if the tribunal are satisfied that the creation of the interest, the erection of the building, the execution of the works or the making of the improvement or alteration, as the case may be, was not reasonably necessary and was undertaken with a view to obtaining compensation or increased compensation.

Extinction or suspension of private rights of way

21.—(1) All private rights of way over any land which may be purchased compulsorily under this Act shall be extinguished on the purchase of the land, whether compulsorily or by agreement, or on the entry on the land under section 11(1) of the Act of 1965 as applied by this Act, whichever is sooner.

(2) All private rights of way over any land of which the Board may take temporary possession under this Act shall be suspended and unenforceable against the Board for so long as the Board shall remain in lawful possession thereof.

(3) Any person who suffers loss by reason of the extinguishment or suspension under this section of any right shall be entitled to be paid by the Board compensation, to be determined in case of dispute by the tribunal.

Correction of errors in deposited plans and book of reference

22.—(1) If the deposited plans or the deposited book of reference are inaccurate in their description of any land, or in their statement or description of the ownership or occupation of any land, the Board after giving not less than 10 days' notice to the owner, lessee and occupier of the land in question may apply to two justices having jurisdiction in the place where the land is situated for the correction thereof.

(2) If on any such application it appears to the justices that the misstatement or wrong description arose from mistake, the justices shall certify the fact accordingly and shall in their certificate state in what respect any matter is misstated or wrongly described.

(3) The certificate shall be deposited in the office of the Clerk of the Parliaments, and a copy thereof in the Private Bill Office of the House of Commons, and with the proper officer or chairman of a local authority with whom a copy of the deposited plans has been deposited in accordance with the Standing Orders of the Houses of Parliament, or who has the custody of any such copy so deposited; and thereupon the deposited plans and the deposited book of reference shall be deemed to be corrected according to the certificate, and it shall be lawful for the Board to take the land and execute the works in accordance with the certificate.

(4) A person with whom a copy of the certificate is deposited under this section shall keep it with the other documents to which it relates.

Set-off for enhancement in value of retained land

23.—(1) In this section "relevant land" means any land or new rights over land acquired by the Board for the purposes of the works.

(2) In assessing the compensation payable to any person on the acquisition by the Board from him of any relevant land, the tribunal shall set off against the value of the relevant land any increase in value of any contiguous or adjacent lands belonging to the same person in the same capacity, or of the land over which new rights are acquired, which will accrue to him by reason of the construction of any of the works.

(3) The Land Compensation Act 1961 shall have effect subject to the provisions of this section.

Time for purchase of land and rights over land

24. The powers of the Board for the compulsory purchase of land and rights in or over land under this Act shall cease on 31st December 1997.

PART IV

PROTECTIVE PROVISIONS

Notice of interference with roads

25. Before breaking up or otherwise interfering with any road to which the public has access in connection with the construction of Work No. 2, the Board shall (except in case of emergency) give not less than 14 days' notice in writing to the chief officer of police.

For protection of electricity, gas and water undertakers

26. For the protection of the several undertakers referred to in this section, the following provisions shall, unless otherwise agreed in writing between the Board and the undertakers concerned, have effect:—

(1) In this section—
"adequate alternative apparatus" means alternative apparatus adequate to enable the undertakers to fulfil their statutory functions in a manner not less efficient than previously;
"apparatus" means—
  (a) in the case of electricity undertakers, electric lines or electrical plant (as defined in the Electricity Act 1989) belonging to or maintained by such undertakers; or
  (b) in the case of gas or water undertakers, any mains, pipes or other apparatus belonging to or maintained by such undertakers;
(not being, except in paragraph (2) below, apparatus in respect of which the relations between the Board and the undertakers are regulated by the provisions of Part III of the New Roads and Street Works Act 1991) and includes any structure for the lodging therein of apparatus or for giving access to apparatus;
"functions" includes powers and duties;
"in" in a context referring to apparatus or alternative apparatus in land includes a reference to apparatus or alternative apparatus under, over or upon land; and
"undertakers" means any person authorised to carry on, in any area within which the Board are by this Act authorised to purchase land or execute works, an undertaking for the supply of gas or water or for the generation, transmission or supply of electricity; and, in relation to any apparatus, means the undertakers to whom it belongs or by whom it is maintained:

(2) Notwithstanding the temporary stopping up or diversion of any highway under the powers of section 11 (Temporary stoppage of highways) of this Act, the undertakers shall be at liberty at all times to execute and do all such works and things in, upon or under any such highway as may be reasonably necessary or desirable to enable them to inspect, repair, maintain, renew, remove or use any apparatus which at the time of the stopping up or diversion was in that highway:

(3) The Board, in the case of the powers conferred by section 12 (Underpinning of buildings near works) of this Act, shall, so far as is reasonably practicable, so exercise those powers as not to obstruct or render

less convenient the access to any apparatus and, if by reason of the exercise of those powers any damage to any apparatus (other than apparatus the repair of which is not reasonably necessary in view of its intended removal or abandonment) or property of the undertakers or any interruption in the supply of electricity, gas or water, as the case may be, by the undertakers is caused, the Board shall bear and pay the cost reasonably incurred by the undertakers in making good such damage or restoring the supply; and shall—

(a) make reasonable compensation to the undertakers for any loss sustained by them; and

(b) indemnify the undertakers against all claims, demands, proceedings, costs, damages and expenses which may be made or taken against or recovered from or incurred by the undertakers;

by reason of any such damage or interruption:

Provided that—

(i) nothing in this paragraph shall impose any liability on the Board with respect to any damage or interruption to the extent that such damage or interruption may be attributable to the act, neglect or default of the undertakers or their contractors or workmen;

(ii) the undertakers shall give to the Board reasonable notice of any claim or demand as aforesaid and no settlement or compromise thereof shall be made without the prior consent of the Board:

(4) Notwithstanding anything in section 13 (Use of sewers, etc., for removing water) of this Act, no use shall be made by the Board in the construction of the works of pumping or other like modes of removing water except where reasonably necessary or in case of emergency or unforeseen accident or for the purpose of removing rainwater or other small amounts of water:

(5) Notwithstanding anything in this Act or shown on the deposited plans the Board shall not acquire any apparatus under the powers of this Act otherwise than by agreement:

(6) If the Board, in the exercise of the powers of this Act, acquire any interest in any land in which any apparatus is placed, that apparatus shall not be removed under this section and any right of the undertakers to maintain, repair, renew or inspect that apparatus in that land shall not be extinguished until adequate alternative apparatus has been constructed and is in operation to the reasonable satisfaction of the undertakers:

(7) If the Board, for the purpose of executing any works in, on or under any land purchased, held, appropriated or used under this Act, require the removal of any apparatus placed in that land, they shall give to the undertakers written notice of that requirement, together with a plan and section of the work proposed, and of the proposed position of the alternative apparatus to be provided or constructed so as to provide adequate alternative apparatus in lieu of the apparatus to be removed, and in that case (or if in consequence of the exercise of any of the powers of this Act the undertakers reasonably require to remove any apparatus) the Board shall afford to the undertakers the necessary facilities and rights for the construction of the alternative apparatus in other land of the Board and thereafter for the maintenance, repair, renewal and inspection of that apparatus:

Provided that, if the alternative apparatus or any part thereof is to be constructed elsewhere than in other land of the Board, or the Board are unable to afford such facilities and rights as aforesaid in the land in which the alternative apparatus or part thereof is to be constructed, the undertakers shall, on receipt of a written notice to that effect from the Board, forthwith use their best endeavours to obtain the necessary facilities and rights in that last-mentioned land:

(8) (a) Any alternative apparatus to be constructed in land of the Board under this section shall be constructed in such manner and in such line or situation as may be agreed between the undertakers and the Board or in default of agreement settled by arbitration;

(b) The undertakers shall, after the alternative apparatus to be provided or constructed has been agreed or settled by arbitration as aforesaid and after the grant to the undertakers of any such facilities and rights as are referred to in paragraph (7) above, proceed with all reasonable dispatch to construct and bring into operation the alternative apparatus and thereafter to remove any apparatus required by the Board to be removed under the provisions of this section:

(9) Notwithstanding anything in paragraph (8) above, if the Board give notice in writing to the undertakers that they desire themselves to execute any part of so much of the work necessary in connection with the construction of the alternative apparatus, or the removal of the apparatus required to be removed, as will take place in any land of the Board, that work, in lieu of being executed by the undertakers, shall be executed by the Board with all reasonable dispatch under the superintendence, if given, and to the reasonable satisfaction of the undertakers:

Provided that nothing in this paragraph shall authorise the Board to execute the actual placing, installation, bedding, packing, removal, connection or disconnection of any apparatus, or execute any filling around the apparatus (where the apparatus is laid in a trench) within 300 millimetres of the apparatus:

(10) Where, in accordance with the provisions of this section, the Board afford to the undertakers facilities and rights for the construction, maintenance, repair, renewal and inspection in land of the Board of alternative apparatus in substitution for apparatus to be removed as aforesaid, those facilities and rights shall be granted upon such terms and conditions as may be agreed between the Board and the undertakers or in default of agreement settled by arbitration:

Provided that—

(a) in settling those terms and conditions in respect of alternative apparatus to be constructed in or along any railway of the Board, the arbitrator shall—

(i) give effect to all reasonable requirements of the Board for ensuring the safety and efficient operation of the railway and for securing any subsequent alterations or adaptations of the alternative apparatus which may be required to prevent interference with any proposed works of the Board or the traffic on the railway; and

(ii) so far as it may be reasonable and practicable to do so in the circumstances of the particular case, give effect to the terms and conditions applicable to the apparatus, if any, constructed in or along the railway for which the alternative apparatus is to be substituted;

(b) if the facilities and rights to be afforded by the Board in respect of any alternative apparatus and the terms and conditions subject to which the same are to be granted are in the opinion of the arbitrator less favourable on the whole to the undertakers than the facilities and rights enjoyed by them in respect of the apparatus to be removed and the terms and conditions to which those facilities and rights are subject, the arbitrator shall make such provision for the payment of compensation by the Board to the undertakers in respect thereof as appears to him to be reasonable having regard to all the circumstances of the particular case:

(11) (a) Not less than 28 days before commencing to execute any works that are referred to in paragraph (7) above and are near to or will or may affect any apparatus the removal of which has not been required by the Board under the said paragraph (7), the Board shall submit to the undertakers a plan, section and description of the works to be executed;

(b) Those works shall be executed only in accordance with the plan, section and description submitted as aforesaid and in accordance with such reasonable requirements as may be made by the undertakers for the alteration or otherwise for the protection of the apparatus or for securing access thereto and the undertakers shall be entitled by their officer to watch and inspect the execution of those works:

Provided that—

(i) if the undertakers within 14 days after the submission to them of a plan, section and description shall, in consequence of the works proposed by the Board, reasonably require the removal of any apparatus and give written notice to the Board of that requirement, the foregoing provisions of this section shall apply as if the removal of the apparatus had been required by the Board under paragraph (7) above;

(ii) nothing in this sub-paragraph shall preclude the Board from submitting at any time or from time to time, but in no case less than 28 days before commencing the execution of any works, a new plan, section and description thereof in lieu of the plan, section and description previously submitted, and thereupon the provisions of this paragraph shall apply to and in respect of the new plan, section and description;

(c) The Board shall not be required to comply with sub-paragraph (a) above in a case of emergency but in that case they shall give to the undertakers notice as soon as reasonably practicable and a plan, section and description of those works as soon as reasonably practicable thereafter and shall comply with sub-paragraph (b) above so far as reasonably practicable in the circumstances:

(12) Where, by reason of this Act, any part of any highway in which any apparatus is situated ceases to be part of a highway the undertakers may exercise the same rights of access to such apparatus as they enjoyed immediately before the passing of this Act, but nothing in this paragraph shall affect any right of the Board or of the undertakers to require removal of such apparatus under this section or the power of the Board to execute works in accordance with paragraph (11) above:

(13) Subject to paragraph (14) below, the Board shall pay to the undertakers the costs, charges and expenses reasonably incurred by the undertakers in or in connection with the inspection, removal, alteration or protection of any apparatus or the construction of any new apparatus which may be required in consequence of the execution of any such works as are referred to in paragraph (7) above, less the value of any apparatus removed under the provisions of this section (that value being calculated after removal) and shall also make compensation to the undertakers—

(a) for any damage caused to any apparatus (other than apparatus the repair of which is not reasonably necessary in view of its intended removal in accordance with the provisions of this section); and

(b) for any other expenses, loss, damages, penalty or costs incurred by the undertakers;

by reason of the execution, maintenance, user or failure of those works or otherwise by reason of the exercise by the Board of the powers of this Act:

(14) If the cost of maintaining, using, repairing or renewing any apparatus is reduced by reason of any of the works, including the provision of alternative apparatus under this section, a capitalised sum representing that saving shall be paid by the relevant undertakers to the Board or set off against any sums payable by the Board to the relevant undertakers under this section:

(15) Where, by reason of the stopping up of any highway under the powers of this Act, any apparatus belonging to the undertakers and laid or placed in such highway or elsewhere is rendered derelict or unnecessary, the Board shall pay to the undertakers the then value of such apparatus (which shall thereupon become the property of the Board) and the reasonable cost of and incidental to the cutting off of such apparatus from any other apparatus, and of and incidental to the execution or doing of any works or things rendered necessary or expedient by reason of such apparatus being so rendered derelict or unnecessary:

Provided that the Board shall not under the provisions of this paragraph be required to pay to the undertakers the value of any apparatus rendered derelict or unnecessary if, to the reasonable satisfaction of the undertakers, other apparatus has at the expense of the Board been provided and laid and made ready for use in substitution for the apparatus so rendered derelict or unnecessary:

(16) Any difference arising between the Board and the undertakers under this section shall be referred to and settled by arbitration:

(17) Nothing in this section shall affect the provisions of any enactment or agreement regulating the relations between the Board and the undertakers in respect of any apparatus laid or erected in land belonging to the Board at the date of the passing of this Act.

For protection of telecommunications operators

27. For the protection of telecommunications operators the following provisions shall, unless otherwise agreed in writing between the Board and the telecommunications operators concerned, have effect:—

(1) In this section expressions defined in the Telecommunications Act 1984 have the same meanings as in that Act:

(2) The temporary stopping up or diversion of any highway under section 11 (Temporary stoppage of highways) of this Act shall not affect any right of a telecommunications operator under paragraph 9 of the telecommunications code to inspect, maintain, adjust, repair or alter any apparatus which, at the time of the stopping up or diversion, is in that highway.

Crown rights

28.—(1) Nothing in this Act affects prejudicially any estate, right, power, privilege, authority or exemption of the Crown and, in particular and without prejudice to the generality of the foregoing, nothing in this Act authorises the Board to take, use, enter upon or in any manner interfere with, any land or hereditaments or any rights of whatsoever description (including any river)—

(a) belonging to Her Majesty in right of Her Crown and under the management of the Crown Estate Commissioners, without the consent in writing of those commissioners; or

(b) belonging to a government department, or held in trust for Her Majesty for the purposes of a government department, without the consent in writing of that government department.

(2) A consent under subsection (1) above may be given unconditionally or subject to such conditions and upon such terms as shall be considered necessary or appropriate.

PART V

GENERAL

Planning permission

29.—(1) Subject to subsection (2) below, in their application to development authorised by this Act, article 3 of, and Class A in Part 11 of Schedule 2 to, the Town and Country Planning General Development Order 1988 (which permit development authorised by private Act designating specifically both the nature of the development thereby authorised and land on which it may be carried out) shall have effect as if the authority to develop given by this Act were limited to such development begun within 10 years after the passing of this Act.

(2) Subsection (1) above shall not apply to the carrying out of any development consisting of the alteration, maintenance or repair of works or the substitution of new works therefor.

Arbitration

30. Where under any provision of this Act any difference (other than a difference which falls to be determined by the tribunal) is to be referred to or settled by arbitration, then such difference shall be referred to and settled by a single arbitrator to be agreed between the parties or, failing agreement, to be appointed on the application of either party (after notice in writing to the other) by the President of the Institution of Civil Engineers.

SCHEDULES

Section 16

SCHEDULE 1

LANDS

PART I

LAND REFERRED TO IN SECTION 16 OF THIS ACT

Area (1)	Number on deposited plans (2)	Purpose for which land may be used (3)

In the county of Nottinghamshire—
  District of Bassetlaw,
    parish of Ranskill
	3	Provision of loop extension on railway between Doncaster and Retford.

In the county of Humberside—
  Borough of Glanford—
    Parish of Brigg
	3, 6, 8, 10, 12	Strengthening embankment of railway between Gainsborough and Grimsby.

Parish of Scawby	2, 4, 6, 9, 11 to 13	

Section 17

PART II

MEANS OF ACCESS REFERRED TO IN SECTION 17 (PURCHASE OF RIGHTS OVER LAND) OF THIS ACT

Area (1)	Land numbered on deposited plans (2)	Highway to which access to be provided (3)	Purpose for which access required (4)
In the county of Nottinghamshire— District of Bassetlaw, parish of Ranskill	1 and 2	Station Road	For loop extension on railway between Doncaster and Retford.
In the county of Cambridgeshire— District of East Cambridgeshire, parish of Ely	1, 2 5	Queen Adelaide Way Station Road	To reconstruct bridge no. 1569, the more south-westerly of the two bridges carrying the railway between Cambridge and Ely over the river Great Ouse.
In the county of Humberside— Borough of Glanford— Parish of Brigg Parish of Scawby	4 8	Mill Lane	To strengthen embankment of railway between Gainsborough and Grimsby.

Section 18

PART III

TEMPORARY WORKING SITES

1.—In this Part of this Schedule—
"the designated lands" means any of the lands shown on the deposited plans within the lines marked "Limit of land to be used" and numbered on those plans—
    2a, 3, 4 and 5a in the district of East Cambridgeshire, parish of Ely;
    1, 2, 5, 7, 9, 11, 13 and 14 in the borough of Glanford, parish of Brigg;
    1, 3, 5, 7, 10 and 14 in the borough of Glanford, parish of Scawby; and
    2a in the district of Bassetlaw, parish of Ranskill; and
"the relevant works" means—
    (a) the reconstruction of bridge number 1569, the more south-westerly of the two bridges carrying the railway between Cambridge and Ely over the river Great Ouse;
    (b) the strengthening of the embankment of the railway between Gainsborough and Grimsby; and
    (c) the provision of a loop extension on the railway between Doncaster and Retford.
2. The Board, in connection with the construction of the relevant works and after giving to the owners and occupiers of the designated lands not less than 28 days' notice in writing of intended entry, may—
    (a) enter upon and take possession temporarily of the designated lands;

(b) remove any structures and vegetation on the designated lands; and

(c) construct on the designated lands such temporary works or structures as may be required by them.

3. The Board shall not, by reason of the exercise of the powers conferred by paragraph 2 above, be required to purchase any part of the designated lands.

4. On the exercise of the powers conferred by paragraph 2 above, the following provisions shall have effect:—

(1) The Board shall not, without the agreement of the owners and occupiers of any part of the designated lands, remain in possession thereof after a period of one year from the completion of the works for which such possession has been taken:

(2) Before giving up possession of the designated lands, the Board shall remove all temporary works or structures and restore the designated lands to the reasonable satisfaction of the owners and occupiers thereof:

(3) The Board shall compensate the owners and occupiers of the designated lands for any loss or damage which may result to them by reason of the exercise of the powers of this Part:

(4) Nothing in this Part shall relieve the Board from liability to compensate under section 6 or 43 of the Act of 1845 or section 10(2) of the Act of 1965, as incorporated with or applied by this Act, or under any other enactment, in respect of loss or damage arising from the execution of any works, other than loss or damage for which compensation is payable under sub-paragraph (3) above:

(5) Any dispute as to a person's entitlement to compensation under sub-paragraph (3) above or as to the amount thereof shall be determined by the tribunal.

Section 17   SCHEDULE 2

MODIFICATION OF PART I OF COMPULSORY PURCHASE ACT 1965
FOR PURCHASE OF NEW RIGHTS

1. In the Compulsory Purchase Act 1965 (hereinafter in this Schedule referred to as "the Act") for section 7 (which relates to compensation) there shall be substituted the following:—

"7.—(1) In assessing the compensation to be paid by the acquiring authority under this Act regard shall be had not only to the extent (if any) to which the value of the land in or over which the right is purchased is depreciated by the purchase but also the damage, if any, to be sustained by the owner of the land by reason of injurious affection of other land of the owner by the exercise of the right.

(2) The modifications subject to which subsection (1) of section 44 of the Land Compensation Act 1973 is to have effect, as applied by subsection (2) of that section to compensation for injurious affection under this section, are that for the words 'land is acquired or taken' there shall be substituted 'a right in or over land is purchased' and for the words 'acquired or taken from him' there shall be substituted 'in or over which the right is exercisable'."

2. For section 8 of the Act (which relates to cases in which a vendor cannot be required to sell part only of a building or garden) there shall be substituted the following:—

"8.—(1) Where in consequence of the service on a person under section 5 of this Act of a notice to treat in respect of a right in or over land consisting of a house, building or manufactory or of a park or garden belonging to a house (hereafter in this subsection referred to as "the relevant land")—

(a) a question of disputed compensation in respect of the purchase of the right would apart from this section fall to be determined by the Lands Tribunal (hereafter in this section referred to as "the Tribunal"); and

(b) before the Tribunal has determined that question the person satisfies the Tribunal that he has an interest which he is able and willing to sell in the whole of the relevant land and—

(i) where that land consists of a house, building or manufactory, that the right cannot be purchased without material detriment to that land; or

(ii) where that land consists of such a park or garden, that the right cannot be purchased without seriously affecting the amenity or convenience of the house to which that land belongs;

the British Railways Act 1994 shall, in relation to that person, cease to authorise the purchase of the right and be deemed to authorise the purchase of that person's interest in the whole of the relevant land including, where the land consists of such a park or garden, the house to which it belongs, and the notice shall be deemed to have been served in respect of that interest on such date as the Tribunal directs.

(2) Any question as to the extent of the land in which the British Railways Act 1994 is deemed to authorise the purchase of an interest by virtue of subsection (1) above shall be determined by the Tribunal.

(3) Where, in consequence of a determination of the Tribunal that it is satisfied as mentioned in subsection (1) above, the British Railways Act 1994 is deemed by virtue of that subsection to authorise the purchase of an interest in land, the acquiring authority may, at any time within the period of six weeks beginning with the date of the determination, withdraw the notice to treat in consequence of which the determination was made; but nothing in this subsection prejudices any other power of the acquiring authority to withdraw the notice.

(4) The modifications subject to which subsection (1) of section 58 of the Land Compensation Act 1973 is to have effect, as applied by subsection (2) of that section to the duty of the Tribunal in determining whether it is satisfied as mentioned in subsection (1) above, are that at the beginning of paragraphs (a) and (b) there shall be inserted the words 'a right over', for the word 'severance' there shall be substituted 'right in or over the whole of the house, building or manufactory or of the house and the park or garden' and for the words 'part proposed' and 'part is' there shall be substituted respectively 'right proposed' and 'right is'."

3. The following provisions of the Act (which state the effect of a deed poll executed in various circumstances where there is no conveyance by persons with interest in the land), namely:—

section 9(4) (failure of owners to convey);

paragraph 10(3) of Schedule 1 (owners under incapacity);

paragraph 2(3) of Schedule 2 (absent and untraced owners); and

paragraphs 2(3) and 7(2) of Schedule 4 (common land);

shall be so modified as to secure that, as against persons with interests in the land which are expressed to be overridden by the deed, the right which is to be purchased compulsorily is vested absolutely in the acquiring authority.

4. Section 11 of the Act (powers of entry) shall be so modified as to secure that, as from the date on which the acquiring authority have served notice to treat in respect of any right, they have power, exercisable in the like circumstances and subject to the like conditions, to enter for the purpose of exercising that right (which shall be deemed for this purpose to have been created on the date of service of the notice); and sections 12 (penalty for unauthorised entry) and 13 (entry on sheriff's warrant in the event of obstruction) of the Act shall be modified correspondingly.

5. Section 20 of the Act (compensation for short term tenants) shall apply with the modifications necessary to secure that persons with such interests as are mentioned in that section are compensated in a manner corresponding to that in which they would be compensated on a compulsory acquisition of the interests but taking into account only the extent (if any) of such interference with such interests as is actually caused, or likely to be caused, by the exercise of the right in question.

6. Section 22 of the Act (protection of acquiring authority's possession of land where by inadvertence an interest in the land has not been purchased) shall be so modified as to enable that acquiring authority, in circumstances corresponding to those referred to in that section, to continue to be entitled to exercise the right in question, subject to compliance with that section as respects compensation.

INDEX

References are to section number

CHURCH OF SCOTLAND (PROPERTIES AND INVESTMENTS) ORDER CONFIRMATION ACT 1994

(1994 c. v)

ARRANGEMENT OF SECTIONS

An Act to confirm a Provisional Order under the Private Legislation Procedure (Scotland) Act 1936, relating to Church of Scotland (Properties and Investments).   [26th May 1994]

PARLIAMENTARY DEBATES
   The Bill's progress through Parliament was as follows:
   House of Commons: First Reading, May 4, 1994; Second Reading, May 10, 1994; Third Reading, May 11, 1994.
   House of Lords: First Reading, May 11, 1994; Considered by Lords, May 17, 1994; Third Reading, May 24, 1994.

INTRODUCTION
   This Act provides for the alteration of the constitution of the Church of Scotland Trust, conferring further powers on that body (Pt. II). The Act also incorporates the Church of Scotland Investors Trust and authorises the transfer of certain properties to the trust (Pts. III and IV). Part V provides for various powers of investment in relation to the Investors Trust and General Trustees, including the power to appoint managers and the power to categorise and appropriate property.

WHEREAS the Provisional Order set forth in the Schedule hereunto annexed has been made by the Secretary of State under the provisions of the Private Legislation Procedure (Scotland) Act 1936, and it is requisite that the said Order should be confirmed by Parliament:
   Be it therefore enacted by the Queen's most Excellent Majesty, by and with the advice and consent of the Lords Spiritual and Temporal, and Commons, in this present Parliament assembled, and by the authority of the same, as follows:—

Confirmation of Order in Schedule

1. The Provisional Order contained in the Schedule hereunto annexed is hereby confirmed.

Short title

2. This Act may be cited as the Church of Scotland (Properties and Investments) Order Confirmation Act 1994.

SCHEDULE

CHURCH OF SCOTLAND (PROPERTIES AND INVESTMENTS)

Provisional Order to alter the constitution of and to confer further powers on the Church of Scotland Trust; to incorporate the Church of Scotland Inves-

tors Trust and to transfer certain moveable property and to authorise the
transfer of toher property to such trust; to transfer certain heritable property
and to authorise the transfer of other property to the Church of Scotland
General Trustees; to confer further powers on the Church of Scotland General Trustees; and for other purposes.

Whereas the general work of the Church of Scotland (hereinafter referred to as "the Church") beyond the local spheres of kirk sessions and presbyteries is directed and controlled by the General Assembly of the Church:

And whereas The Church of Scotland General Trustees (hereinafter referred to as "the General Trustees") were incorporated by the Church of Scotland (General Trustees) Order 1921 to hold the properties belonging to the Church and described in the Schedule thereto for the same ends, uses and purposes as those for which they were held by the several trustees or persons by whom they were held previously:

And whereas The Church of Scotland Trust (hereinafter referred to as "the Trust") was incorporated by the Church of Scotland Trust Order 1932 (hereinafter referred to as "the Order of 1932") to hold the properties belonging to the Church and described in the Schedule thereto for the same ends, uses and purposes as those for which they were held by the several trustees or persons by whom they were held previously:

And whereas by the Order of 1932 the Trust was also authorised to accept and hold such other properties as any organisation or minister of any congregation of the Church might desire to transfer to the Trust:

And whereas the Trust holds assets which fall broadly into three categories, that is to say:—

(1) moveable property which largely comprises the assets of funds known as the general investment fund, the income fund, the deposit fund, the main pension fund, the contributors' pension fund and the special investment account of the Church;

(2) heritable or real property in the United Kingdom being mainly the functional properties and superiorities of the boards and committees of the General Assembly of the Church; and

(3) heritable or real property outside the United Kingdom being mainly churches in Europe and in the Americas and foreign mission properties in Asia, Africa and elsewhere:

And whereas the arrangements whereby some assets of the Church are held by the General Trustees and other assets are held by the Trust have become anomalous and inconvenient for the good management and efficient administration of the heritable property and moveable property belonging to the Church:

And whereas it is expedient to alter the constitution of and to confer further powers on the Trust:

And whereas it is expedient to establish a new statutory body with modern and appropriate powers of management and administration to hold all the moveable property (as in this Order defined) now held by the Trust and any other property which it is authorised by this Order to hold:

And whereas it is expedient to transfer to the General Trustees the heritable properties in Scotland now vested in the Trust and to authorise other property to be transferred to the General Trustees:

And whereas it is expedient for the new body to provide investment services to the Church and to bodies within or connected with the Church:

And whereas it is expedient that the new body should be able to act as trustee of certain church property and that other trustees should be authorised to transfer their trusteeships to the new body:

And whereas it is expedient to confer further powers on the General Trustees:

And whereas for the benefit of the Church and with the support and approval of the General Assembly of the Church, the Trust has resolved to promote legislation to give effect to the proposed changes aforesaid:

And whereas the purposes aforesaid cannot be effected without an Order confirmed by Parliament under the provisions of the Private Legislation Procedure (Scotland) Act 1936:

Now, therefore, in pursuance of the powers contained in the said Act, the Secretary of State hereby orders as follows:—

PART I

PRELIMINARY

Short title

1. This Order may be cited as the Church of Scotland (Properties and Investments) Order 1994.

Interpretation

2. In this Order, unless the context otherwise requires—
   "the appointed day" means such day as may, under section 3 (Appointed day) of this Order, be appointed for the purposes of this Order;
   "the Church" means the Church of Scotland as constituted by the union of the Church of Scotland and the United Free Church of Scotland on 2nd October 1929;
   "the General Assembly" means the General Assembly of the Church;
   "the General Trustees" means The Church of Scotland General Trustees incorporated by the Church of Scotland (General Trustees) Order 1921;
   "heritable property" means an interest in land which conforms to the definition of an interest in land in section 28 of the Land Registration (Scotland) Act 1979 and wheresoever situated;
   "the Investors Trust" means the body incorporated by section 13 (Incorporation) of this Order;
   "moveable property" means personal property, investments, rights and interests of any nature whatever and wheresoever situated not included in the term "heritable property" and not a right or interest of any nature in corporeal moveable property, or in heritable property, in Asia or Africa vested in the Trust on the appointed day;
   "the Order of 1932" means the Church of Scotland Trust Order 1932; and
   "the Trust" means The Church of Scotland Trust incorporated by the Order of 1932.

Appointed day

3.—(1) The Trust may appoint a day to be the appointed day for the purposes of this Order.

(2) Before the day so appointed the Trust shall publish in the Edinburgh Gazette notice of the day appointed, stating that it is the appointed day for the purposes of this Order.

PART II

CHURCH OF SCOTLAND TRUST

Constitution

4. On the appointed day the members of the Trust other than those named

below shall go out of office and subject to the provisions of this Order the following 10 members of the Church shall be members of the Trust, viz:

Ronald Stanton Blakey M.A., B.D., M.Th.
Robert Bow M.A., LL.B.
William Donald Bruce Cameron C.A.
William Steven Carswell M.A., LL.B.
George Fraser Davidson C.A.
David Douglas McKinnon B.Sc., F.F.A., F.I.M.A.
David Mackay Nicolson C.A.
James Alan Walker Somerville W.S.
James Leslie Weatherhead M.A., LL.B., D.D.
John Christopher Wigglesworth M.B.E., B.Sc., Ph.D., B.D.

and they and the survivors of them and their successors in office and any additional members to be appointed as hereinafter provided (all hereinafter referred to as "members of the Trust") shall continue to be a body corporate by the name of "The Church of Scotland Trust".

Qualification of members

5. From the appointed day only a member of the Church shall be eligible to be a member of the Trust and if a person who is a member of the Trust ceases to be a member of the Church he shall thereupon cease to be a member of the Trust.

Roll of members

6.—(1) The secretary and clerk of the Trust shall keep a roll of the members of the Trust and shall enter in it the names of the members of the Trust stated in section 4 (Constitution) of this Order in the same order as they appear in that section and the names of all persons who are appointed or co-opted as members of the Trust in terms of this Order in the order in which they are appointed or co-opted.

(2) When a person ceases to be a member of the Trust the secretary and clerk of the Trust shall amend the roll accordingly and when a person is re-appointed as a member of the Trust the secretary and clerk shall re-enter his name in the roll after the names of the other members of the Trust.

Retirement of members

7.—(1) After the appointed day two members of the Trust other than the chairman and vice-chairman shall retire annually on 31st May each year but shall be eligible for re-appointment by the General Assembly as hereinafter provided.

(2) The order in which the members of the Trust shall retire shall be the order in which their names appear in the roll of members of the Trust.

Appointment and removal of members

8.—(1) The Trust shall report to the General Assembly all vacancies in the membership of the Trust and may nominate persons for appointment by the General Assembly to fill any vacancies.

(2) The General Assembly shall appoint or re-appoint two persons to be members of the Trust in place of the two members of the Trust retiring in terms of this Order.

(3) If a member of the Trust dies, resigns or becomes disqualified or is removed from office, the General Assembly shall have power to appoint another member of the Trust.

(4) Subject to the provisions of subsection (6) of this section the General Assembly shall have power to appoint persons to be additional members of the Trust beyond the number specified in section 4 (Constitution) of this Order.

(5) Subject to the provisions of subsection (6) of this section the Trust may at any time co-opt persons to be additional members of the Trust provided that any person so co-opted shall not remain a member of the Trust after the next meeting of the General Assembly unless his co-option is then ratified by the General Assembly.

(6) The number of members of the Trust shall not exceed 20.

(7) The General Assembly shall have power to remove any member of the Trust from office.

Appointment of chairman and vice-chairman

9.—(1) The Trust shall whenever necessary appoint from among the members of the Trust a chairman and vice-chairman who shall hold office for a period of four years from the date of such appointment subject to such conditions as the General Assembly may from time to time determine and provided that the chairman and vice-chairman shall not remain chairman and vice-chairman respectively after the meeting of the General Assembly next following their appointment unless their appointment is then ratified by the General Assembly.

(2) The General Assembly shall have power to renew or extend such appointments or either of them for a period not exceeding four years.

Quorum

10. In subsection (3) of section 14 (Meetings of Trust) of the Order of 1932, the word "three" shall be substituted for the word "five".

Powers in relation to certain trusteeships

11.—(1) In this and the next section, "trust" means any trust of any kind whether public or private, inter vivos, contractual or mortis causa, including, without prejudice to the foregoing generality, executorship, administration, agency, factorship, curatory, receivership, guardianship, management and membership of a committee; and "trustee" and "co-trustee" shall be construed accordingly.

(2) The Trust may act, decline to act or resign from acting as trustee of any trust.

(3) In addition and without prejudice to such other powers and privileges as it may enjoy the Trust may, in, for and during the performance of any trusteeship accepted by it—

(a) charge the trust for acting as trustee;

(b) retain any share of brokerage or commission paid to it;

(c) retain remuneration paid in respect of its officers appointed as directors of a company whose shares or debentures are held in the trust;

(d) vest any assets of the trust in any person or corporate body as its nominee;

(e) insure the assets of the trust for such value and against such risks as it shall at its absolute discretion decide and charge the premiums against the capital or the income of the trust;

(f) carry on for such period as it thinks fit, or wind up when it thinks fit, any business held in the trust;

(g) refrain from intervention in the management or conduct of the business of any company in which it has an interest, whether or not representing or conferring exclusive or majority control, provided that it has no reason to believe that such management and conduct by the directors is not in accordance with their fiduciary obligations, and in particular refrain from exercising any powers to require the payment of dividends or other distributions to the members of the company;

(h) acquire, deal with and turn to account life or other policies of insurance or similar assets and reversionary or deferred property or rights of any description, whether by way of investment or otherwise;

(i) make loans from the trust to any beneficiary without requiring security and grant securities or guarantees on behalf of any beneficiary;

(j) allocate or set apart funds in which a beneficiary may have a particular interest;

(k) pay and satisfy in whole or in part any legacy or share of the trust by transferring or setting apart any investments or other assets at such values as it may decide;

(l) pay and make over in whole or in part any funds or other assets due or advanced to or on account of any beneficiary under legal disability or incapacity by reason of nonage to his or her legal guardian or to any person or persons de facto acting or willing to act as such, whether legally holding or entitled to that office or not, the acknowledgment of the recipient being a sufficient discharge;

(m) accept the receipt of a responsible official of any body (incorporated or unincorporated) which is a beneficiary of the trust;

(n) decide in all cases the apportionment of receipts, allowances, payments and charges as between one beneficiary and another;

(o) employ or appoint to any office in connection with the trust any person or otherwise transact in any manner and free of any restriction with any co-trustee and allow any person so employed or appointed reasonable remuneration for services other than as a trustee;

(p) act on the opinion or advice of or information obtained from a duly qualified professional person without liability; and

(q) delegate any decision relating to investment of any funds of the trust to any other person, firm, corporation or other body.

(4) In addition and without prejudice to such other privileges and immunities as it may enjoy the Trust shall not be liable for the acts or omissions of any co-trustee.

Scottish trusts

12. In the case of a trust of which the Trust is a trustee and which is governed by the laws of Scotland—

(1) notwithstanding its receipt of remuneration, the Trust shall have all the powers of a trustee, gratuitous or otherwise, including the power to resign office; and

(2) where the Trust is not the sole trustee, a quorum shall be—

    (a) one trustee, if there are two trustees; and

    (b) a majority of the trustees resident in Great Britain if there are more than two trustees:

Provided that in all cases such quorum shall include the Trust.

PART III

CHURCH OF SCOTLAND INVESTORS TRUST

Incorporation

13. Subject to the provisions of this Order the following 14 members of the Church viz:

Alan Archibald Aitchison

Charles Morrison Burnet

Rupert Gavin Burnett B.Com., C.A., F.C.M.A.
William Donald Bruce Cameron C.A.
Thomas Young Darling M.A., F.I.C.E., A.C.I.I.
John Brian Michael Dick A.C.I.B.
Donald Mackenzie Fortune C.A.
David Jeffrey Kirkpatrick F.F.A.
Thomas Macgill
David Douglas McKinnon B.Sc., F.F.A., F.I.M.A.
Andrew David Monteath O.B.E., T.D., C.A.
Robert Weir Spittal F.F.A., A.I.A.
Cecil Henry Stout O.B.E., Ph.D., B.Com., I.P.F.A.
Gerrard Webster Tait

and the survivors of them and their succcessors in office and any additional members to be nominated and appointed as hereinafter provided (all hereinafter referred to as "members of the Investors Trust") shall be and are hereby incorporated by the name of "The Church of Scotland Investors Trust" and by that name shall be a body corporate.

Qualification of members

14. Only a member of the Church shall be eligible to be a member of the Investors Trust and if a person who is a member of the Investors Trust ceases to be a member of the Church he shall thereupon cease to be a member of the Investors Trust.

Roll of members

15.—(1) The secretary of the Investors Trust shall keep a roll of the members of the Investors Trust and shall enter in it the names of the members of the Investors Trust stated in section 13 (Incorporation) of this Order in the same order as they appear in that section and the names of all persons who are appointed or co-opted as members of the Investors Trust in terms of this Order in the order in which they are appointed or co-opted.

(2) When a person ceases to be a member of the Investors Trust the secretary of the Investors Trust shall amend the roll accordingly and when a person is re-appointed as a member of the Investors Trust the secretary shall re-enter his name in the roll after the names of the other members of the Investors Trust.

Retirement of members

16.—(1) Three members of the Investors Trust other than the chairman and vice-chairman shall retire annually on 31st May each year but shall be eligible for reappointment by the General Assembly as hereinafter provided.

(2) The order in which the members of the Investors Trust named in section 13 (Incorporation) of this Order shall retire shall be the order in which their names appear in that section and the order in which any other members of the Investors Trust to be appointed hereafter shall retire shall be the order in which they are entered as a member of the Investors Trust on the roll of members of the Investors Trust after the date of their appointment.

Appointment and removal of members

17.—(1) The Investors Trust shall report to the General Assembly all vacancies in its membership and may nominate persons for appointment by the General Assembly to fill any vacancies.

(2) The General Assembly shall appoint or reappoint three persons to be members of the Investors Trust in place of the three members of the Investors Trust retiring in terms of this Order.

(3) If a member of the Investors Trust dies, resigns or becomes disqualified or is removed from office, the General Assembly shall have power to appoint another member of the Investors Trust.

(4) Subject to the provisions of subsection (6) of this section, the General Assembly shall have power to appoint persons to be additional members of the Investors Trust beyond the number specified in section 13 (Incorporation) of this Order.

(5) Subject to the provisions of subsection (6) of this section, the Investors Trust may at any time co-opt persons to be additional members of the Investors Trust provided that any person so co-opted shall not remain a member of the Investors Trust after the next meeting of the General Assembly unless his co-option is then ratified by the General Assembly.

(6) The number of members of the Investors Trust shall not exceed 20.

(7) The General Assembly shall have power to remove any member of the Investors Trust from office.

Appointment of chairman and vice-chairman

18.—(1) The Investors Trust shall whenever necessary appoint from among the members of the Investors Trust a chairman and vice-chairman who shall hold office for a period of four years from the date of such appointment subject to such conditions as the General Assembly may from time to time determine and provided that the chairman and vice-chairman shall not remain chairman and vice-chairman respectively after the meeting of the General Assembly next following their appointment unless their appointment is then ratified by the General Assembly.

(2) The General Assembly shall have power to renew or extend such appointments or either of them for a period not exceeding four years.

Treasurer

19.—(1) The general treasurer of the Church shall ex officio be the treasurer of the Investors Trust.

(2) In the event of a vacancy in the office of general treasurer of the Church, the Investors Trust shall appoint for its own purposes an interim treasurer to fill the vacancy who shall vacate office immediately upon a general treasurer of the Church being appointed.

Secretary

20. The Investors Trust shall appoint a secretary who shall keep minutes of all meetings of the Investors Trust and also a record of all deeds and documents to which the seal of the Investors Trust has been affixed.

Meetings of Investors Trust

21.—(1) The secretary of the Investors Trust, whom failing the treasurer, shall call all meetings of the Investors Trust and shall also call a meeting of the Investors Trust upon being requested in writing to do so by no fewer than five members of the Investors Trust.

(2) Not less than five days' notice shall be given for a meeting of the Investors Trust.

(3) At all meetings of the Investors Trust three shall be a quorum and any meeting at which a quorum is present shall be competent to exercise all or any of the authorities, powers and discretions exercisable by the Investors Trust.

(4) In the absence of the chairman and vice-chairman from any meeting of the Investors Trust those members of the Investors Trust who are present shall appoint a chairman for the meeting.

(5) The chairman presiding at any meeting of the Investors Trust shall in the event of an equality of votes have a casting vote in addition to his deliberative vote.

PART IV

TRANSFERS TO INVESTORS TRUST AND TO GENERAL TRUSTEES, ETC.

Transfers to Investors Trust

22.—(1) Subject to the provisions of this Order, all moveable property vested in and held by the Trust immediately before the appointed day shall, by virtue of this Order and without the necessity of any other instrument of transfer, on that day be transferred to and vest in the Investors Trust.

(2) The production of a copy of the Act confirming this Order shall be sufficient warrant to the registrar, directors or other officials of any corporation, firm, company, authority or concern as well out of Scotland as in Scotland to enter the Investors Trust upon the register thereof as proprietor or holder of the moveable property transferred to and vested in the Investors Trust by subsection (1) of this section without the production of any particular assignation, conveyance or transfer thereof and to grant and issue to the Investors Trust a certificate or other writing as evidence of the title of the Investors Trust to such moveable property:

Provided that in the case of any moveable property which is only transferable in a particular manner prescribed by or under an Act of Parliament or by or under the constitution or rules of any particular corporation, firm, company or concern such moveable property shall be transferred to and vested in the Investors Trust in the prescribed manner.

(3) In addition to the moveable property transferred to and vested in the Investors Trust by virtue of subsection (1) of this section, the Investors Trust may hold any heritable property or moveable property held at the commencement of this Order or subsequently acquired—

(a) by or on behalf of the Church, or any court of the Church or board or committee of the General Assembly or any association, fund or scheme of the Church or by or on behalf of any congregation, financial board of a congregation or other ecclesiastical body or organisation of the Church; or

(b) by any trustee or body of trustees for behoof of or in connection with the Church or any court of the Church, board or committee of the General Assembly, association, fund or scheme of the Church or any congregation, financial board of a congregation, ecclesiastical body or organisation of the Church under any settlement or deed of trust, gift or appointment whether granted inter vivos or mortis causa.

(4) The moveable property transferred to and vested in the Investors Trust by virtue of subsection (1) of this section and any property held by it by virtue of subsection (3) of this section shall be held by the Investors Trust for the same ends, uses and purposes as those for which they were held by the Trust or for which they are or may hereafter be held or acquired by or on behalf of the Church or any court of the Church, board or committee of the General Assembly, association, fund or scheme of the Church or by any congregation, financial board of a congregation or other ecclesiastical body or organisation of the Church or by a trustee or body of trustees as aforesaid prior to their being so transferred to the Investors Trust, where such ends, uses and purposes are expressed or defined and, failing such expression or definition, subject to the directions of the court of the Church, board or committee of the General Assembly, association, fund or scheme of the Church or the congregation, financial board of a congregation or other ecclesiastical body or organisation of the Church or trustee or body of trustees as aforesaid on whose behalf they were held or, failing such directions, then, with the

exception of any property held by them by virtue of subsection (3)(b) of this section, subject to the directions of the General Assembly.

Transfers to General Trustees

23.—(1) In this section "title sheet" means a title sheet of an interest in land under section 6 of the Land Registration (Scotland) Act 1979.

(2) Subject to the provisions of this Order all heritable property in Scotland vested in and held by the Trust immediately before the appointed day shall, by virtue of this Order, on that day be transferred to and vest in the General Trustees and all rights, obligations, claims and demands relative to the said heritable property including all accrued rents, income or interest and all arrears of rents, income or interest shall by virtue of this Order be deemed and taken to be validly transferred to and vested in the General Trustees.

(3) For the purpose of enabling the General Trustees if thought fit to complete a title to any heritable property in Scotland or to any part thereof by—

(a) expeding a notarial instrument or notice of title and recording the same in the appropriate division of the General Register of Sasines or by obtaining or granting a conveyance, assignation or transfer of such property and recording the same in like manner; or

(b) registering an interest in land in the Land Register of Scotland; or

(c) registering such amendment as is necessary to the title sheet of an interest in land registered in the Land Register of Scotland,

this Order shall be deemed to be and may be used as a general disposition or assignation as the case may be of such heritable property in favour of the General Trustees.

(4) In addition to the property transferred to the General Trustees by virtue of subsection (2) of this section, the General Trustees may hold any heritable property or moveable property held at the commencement of this Order or subsequently acquired—

(a) by or on behalf of the Church or any presbytery of the Church, or any board or committee of the General Assembly or any association, fund or scheme of the Church; or

(b) by any trustee or body of trustees for behoof of or in connection with the Church or any court of the Church, board or committee of the General Assembly, association, fund or scheme of the Church or any congregation, financial board of a congregation, ecclesiastical body or organisation of the Church under any settlement or deed of trust, gift or appointment, whether granted inter vivos or mortis causa.

(5) The property transferred to and vested in the General Trustees by virtue of subsection (2) of this section and any property held by them by virtue of subsection (4) of this section shall be held by the General Trustees for the same ends, uses and purposes as those for which they were held by the Trust or for which they are or may hereafter be held or acquired by the Church or any presbytery of the Church, or any board or committee of the General Assembly or any association, fund or scheme of the Church, or by a trustee or body of trustees as aforesaid, prior to their being so transferred to the General Trustees where such ends, uses and purposes are expressed or defined and, failing such expression or definition, subject to the directions of the presbytery, board or committee, association, fund or scheme of the Church, or trustee or body of trustees as aforesaid, on whose behalf they were held or, failing such directions, then, with the exception of any property held by them by virtue of subsection (4)(b) of this section, subject to the directions of the General Assembly.

Transfer of interests in heritable and other property

24.—(1) For the avoidance of doubt it is hereby declared that the transfer and vesting of any property to and in the Investors Trust or the General Trustees by virtue of this Order shall not—

(a) in relation to property in England and Wales constitute a purchase or creation of an interest in land for the purposes of section 30(2) of the Landlord and Tenant Act 1954; or

(b) constitute an assignation, assignment, transfer, devolution, parting with possession or other disposition of property or of an interest in property for the purposes of any provision relating to assignation, assignment, transfer, devolution, parting with possession or other disposition contained in any deed or other instrument or document concerning that property or that interest; or

(c) operate as a breach of covenant or condition against alienation; or

(d) give rise to any forfeiture or irritancy; or

(e) invalidate or discharge any contract or security; or

(f) operate so as to merge any leasehold interest (being the interest of the lessee of land under a lease or the interest of the sublessee of land under a sublease) in the interest of the immediate landlord under the lease or sublease.

Certain trusteeships not to pass with trust property

25. The powers, responsibilities and duties of any trustee or body of trustees (including where acting in that capacity the Trust) in relation to property held for behoof of or in connection with the Church or any court of the Church, board or committee of the General Assembly, association, fund or scheme of the Church or any congregation, financial board of a congregation, ecclesiastical body or organisation of the Church under any settlement or deed of trust, gift or appointment, whether granted inter vivos or mortis causa, shall continue to be exercisable and performed by the trustee or body of trustees for the time being of that settlement or deed of trust, gift or appointment notwithstanding any transfer to and vesting of such property in the Investors Trust or the General Trustees by virtue of section 22 or 23 of this Order.

Continuation of byelaws and regulations

26. On and after the appointed day all byelaws and regulations made by the General Assembly in respect of any heritable property and moveable property held by the Trust shall, until altered or revoked, continue to apply and have effect with respect to that property to the same extent and effect as if this Order had not been passed and shall be operated in relation to that property by the Investors Trust or the General Trustees as the case may be as if any references to the Trust in such byelaws and regulations were references to the Investors Trust or to the General Trustees.

Investors Trust and General Trustees may receive gifts, bequests, etc., on behalf of the Church

27. In the event of the Church, or any court of the Church or any board or committee of the General Assembly or any association, fund or scheme of the Church or any congregation, financial board of a congregation or other ecclesiastical body or organisation of the Church being or becoming entitled to any gift, legacy or bequest or to payment of any capital sum, or to payment of the income of any capital sum, or any annuity or annual payment it shall be competent for the Investors Trust or the General Trustees to receive such gift, legacy or bequest or such capital sum or such income, annuity or annual payment on behalf of the Church or such court, board, committee, association, fund or scheme, or such congregation, financial board of a congregation or such other ecclesiastical body or organisation of the Church as the case may be and by the hand of the treasurer or the secretary of the Investors Trust or the treasurer or the clerk of the General Trustees to grant a receipt, discharge or other writing therefor and a receipt, discharge or other writing

so granted in favour of any person or persons paying or transferring to the Investors Trust or the General Trustees any such gift, legacy or bequest or making payment of such capital sum or of such income, annuity or annual payment shall be a full and complete discharge to such person or persons who shall have no concern with the application of such gift, legacy or bequest or capital sum or of such income, annuity or annual payment.

Trustees to be entitled to transfer to Investors Trust property or funds held for behoof of Church, etc.

28.—(1) This section applies where a trustee or body of trustees shall hold any property or funds for behoof of or in connection with the Church or any court of the Church of any board or committee of the General Assembly or any association, fund or scheme of the Church or any congregation, financial board of a congregation, ecclesiastical body or organisation of the Church under any settlement or deed of trust, gift or appointment, whether granted inter vivos or mortis causa.

(2) Where a trustee or body of trustees acting for the time being under such a settlement or deed of trust, gift or appointment shall desire to be relieved of the trust thereby constituted or created or of the whole or a part of the property or funds of such trust it shall be competent for such trustee or body of trustees, unless expressly prohibited by the terms of such settlement or deed of trust, gift or appointment, to denude himself or themselves of such trust, property or funds and to pay or transfer and convey the whole property or funds held thereunder or comprising such part to and in favour of the Investors Trust to be held by the Investors Trust for the same ends, uses and purposes as such property or funds was or were held prior to the date of such payment or transfer and conveyance.

(3) Upon payment or transfer and conveyance under subsection (2) of this section being completed, the trustee or body of trustees making the same shall be fully exonerated, released and discharged of the trust constituted or created by such settlement or deed of trust, gift or appointment as aforesaid by any receipt, discharge, release or other writing to be granted by the Investors Trust under their hand and seal to and in favour of such trustee or trustees in respect of any property or funds paid, transferred or conveyed by him or them as aforesaid.

(4) Notwithstanding anything contained in any such settlement or deed of trust, gift or appointment, whether granted inter vivos or mortis causa, any such trustee or body of trustees (including the Investors Trust consequent upon its assumption of trusteeship of any trust in terms of subsection (2) of this section) may from time to time contribute the whole or any part of the property or funds held as aforesaid to any fund for the time being held or maintained by the Investors Trust under the provisions of section 32 (Power to categorise, etc., and appropriate, etc., property) of this Order.

(5) In the administration of any trust, the whole or any part of the property or funds of which has been contributed to any fund of the Investors Trust, all sums distributed from that fund as income shall be treated as income of the trust, and all sums distributed on withdrawal from or on the winding up of that fund shall, unless specifically designated by the General Assembly as income, be treated as capital of the trust.

(6) The contribution to or deposit in a fund of the Investors Trust of the whole or any part of any property or funds to which this section is applicable shall for all purposes be an authorised investment of such assets.

Power to transfer property from one body to another

29. The General Trustees, the Trust and the Investors Trust shall have power to transfer heritable property and moveable property to each other provided that any property so transferred shall, after any such transfer, be

held for the same ends, uses and purposes as those for which they had been held prior to such transfer.

PART V

POWERS OF INVESTMENT, ETC.

Powers of investment

30.—(1) The Investors Trust and the General Trustees may invest the whole or any part of the funds belonging to or held by them from time to time (including, in the case of the Investors Trust, the whole or any part of the property and funds held by it in terms of subsection (2) of section 28 of this Order)—

(a) in the purchase, or upon the security, of any heritable property or moveable property and whether involving liability or not (but not involving unlimited liability) and whether producing income or not as the Investors Trust or the General Trustees shall in their discretion think fit; or

(b) in depositing the whole or any part of the said funds with any bank, company, building society, authority or institution of any kind in any part of the world either at interest or otherwise and for such time and upon such terms in all respects as the Investors Trust or the General Trustees shall in their discretion think fit.

(2) In addition to investing in moveable property as aforesaid, the Investors Trust and the General Trustees may for fees, commission or other consideration underwrite or sub-underwrite the issue or disposal of any securities in which they may invest.

Power to appoint managers

31. The Investors Trust and the General Trustees may, upon such terms and conditions as they think fit, appoint investment or other managers (either from among their own number or otherwise) to manage any heritable property or moveable property held by them or held on their behalf.

Power to categorise, etc., and appropriate, etc., property

32. Subject to the provisions of this Order and of any byelaws and regulations governing the same made by the General Assembly, the Investors Trust may—

(1) categorise, classify, place in different funds, divide, consolidate or place in a common fund or pool any property held by them or held on their behalf by reference to its type, its origin, its amount, the purposes for which or the trusts upon which it is held, the duration for which it is expected to be held, the investment objectives relative thereto or to such other criteria and for such purposes and subject to such conditions as they think fit; and

(2) appropriate, allocate or attribute, either actually or notionally, and in whole or in part, any property held by them or held on their behalf, or any share or interest in such property, to any trustee or body of trustees or to any trust fund or to any court, board, committee, association, fund or scheme of the Church or to any congregation, financial board of a congregation or other ecclesiastical body or organisation of the Church for which or for whom they hold property in such manner and subject to such conditions as they think fit.

Additional powers as to heritable property

33.—(1) In this section "development" includes the carrying out of building, engineering, mining or other operations in, on, over or under heritable property or the making of any change in the use of any such property.

(2) In relation to heritable property, the Investors Trust and the General Trustees may exercise all the powers of development, improvement and management which could be exercised by an absolute owner holding the property beneficially.

PART VI

MISCELLANEOUS

Investors Trust and General Trustees entitled to sue for and recover property or funds, etc.

34. The Investors Trust and the General Trustees shall, without prejudice to any antecedent or existing right and title of the General Trustees or of the Trust or of the Investors Trust as regards any property or funds now or hereby vested or hereafter becoming vested in them, be entitled on behalf of the Church or of any court of the Church or any board or committee of the General Assembly or of any association, fund or scheme of the Church or of any congregation, financial board of a congregation or other ecclesiastical body or organisation of the Church to sue for and recover all property or funds to which the Church or such court, board or committee, association, fund, scheme of the Church, congregation, financial board of a congregation or other ecclesiastical body or organisation of the Church as the case may be may be entitled and also to enforce, compromise, settle or refer to arbitration all or any claims relating to such property or funds at the instance of or against the Church or such court, board or committee, association, fund, scheme of the Church or congregation, financial board of a congregation or other ecclesiastical body or organisation of the Church.

Execution of deeds

35.—(1) For any purpose other than those mentioned in subsection (2) below a document is validly executed by the Investors Trust if it is signed on its behalf by a member of the Investors Trust or its treasurer or secretary or by a person authorised to sign the document on its behalf.

(2) For the purposes of any enactment or rule of law relating to the authentication of documents under the law of Scotland, a document is validly executed by the Investors Trust if it is sealed with the seal of the Investors Trust and subscribed on its behalf by—

(a) two of the members of the Investors Trust; or

(b) a member and either the treasurer or the secretary of the Investors Trust,

and such execution shall be equally binding and effectual whether attested by witnesses or not.

(3) A document which bears to be executed by the Investors Trust in accordance with subsection (2) above is, in relation to such execution, a probative document.

Power to appoint nominees

36. The Investors Trust and the General Trustees may authorise that any property belonging to or held by them be held in the name or names of any other person or persons as nominees for them.

Power to delegate collection and distribution of income

37. The Investors Trust may grant all powers of attorney, mandates or other authorities necessary for the collection and distribution of income from the heritable property and moveable property for the time being held by it.

Costs of management and administration

38. All costs, charges and expenses incurred by the Investors Trust in managing and administering its affairs shall form a first charge upon the income of the trust funds and estate held and administered under or by virtue of the provisions of this Order except in so far as the same may in the discretion of the Investors Trust form a proper charge against any special or separate fund, property or estate forming part of such trust funds and estate or in so far as such costs, charges and expenses shall be provided by the General Assembly.

Questions or disputes referred to board of practice and procedure

39. In the event of any question or dispute arising—
(1) between the Investors Trust and any court of the Church (other than the General Assembly), any board or committee of the General Assembly, association, fund or scheme of the Church or any congregation, financial board of a congregation or other ecclesiastical body or organisation of the Church, or
(2) between the General Trustees and any presbytery of the Church, board or committee of the General Assembly, association, fund or scheme of the Church,
on whose behalf heritable property or moveable property is held by the Investors Trust or by the General Trustees respectively, the same shall be referred to the board of practice and procedure of the General Assembly or to any special committee who may be appointed by the said board of practice and procedure or by the General Assembly for the purpose and the decision of the board of practice and procedure or of such special committee, if and when so appointed, shall be final and binding on all parties unless an appeal against such decision shall, within 21 days from the date of such decision, be taken or intimated by any party or parties concerned to the General Assembly.

Investors Trust to be immune from liability

40. The Investors Trust shall not be liable for the acts, receipts, neglects, defaults or frauds of any member of the Investors Trust or of any treasurer, secretary, clerk, law agent or other agent, officer or servant of the Investors Trust or for any loss or expense resulting through any depreciation or loss arising upon any heritable property or moveable property taken or held by the Investors Trust or through the insufficiency or deficiency of title of or to any heritable property or moveable property.

Byelaws and regulations

41. It shall be lawful for the General Assembly from time to time to make byelaws and regulations to be observed by the Investors Trust in the discharge of its duties and functions under this Order.

Amendment of Companies Act 1985

42.—(1) Section 209 (interests to be disregarded) of the Companies Act 1985 shall be read and have effect as if, in subsection (10), for paragraph (b) there were substituted the following paragraph:
"(b) an interest of the Church of Scotland General Trustees, the Church of Scotland Trust or the Church of Scotland Investors Trust in shares held by them or of any other person in shares held by those Trustees or Trusts otherwise than as simple trustees;".
(2) Paragraph 12 of Schedule 13 to the Companies Act 1985 shall be read and have effect as if for paragraph (a) there were substituted the following paragraph:

"(a) of the Church of Scotland General Trustees, the Church of Scotland Trust or the Church of Scotland Investors Trust in shares or debentures held by them;",

and as if in paragraph (b) for the words "that Trust" there were substituted the words "those Trusts". Accordingly there shall be added at the end of the note to that paragraph—

'and "the Church of Scotland Investors Trust" is the body incorporated by Part III of the Order confirmed by the Church of Scotland (Properties and Investments) Order Confirmation Act 1994'.

Repeals

43. The enactments referred to in the first and second columns of the Schedule to this Order are hereby repealed to the extent specified in the third column of that Schedule.

Costs of Order

44. The costs, charges and expenses of and in connection with the preparation, obtaining and confirming of this Order shall be paid out of the funds of the Church.

Section 43 SCHEDULE

REPEALS

Chapter (1)	Short title (2)	Extent of repeal (3)
11 & 12 Geo. 5 c. cxxv.	Church of Scotland (General Trustees) Order Confirmation Act 1921.	Sections 17, 18 and 20 of the Order scheduled thereto.
22 & 23 Geo. 5 c. xxi.	Church of Scotland Trust Order Confirmation Act 1932.	Sections 4, 5, 6, 7 and 8 of the Order scheduled thereto.

INDEX

References are to paragraphs of the Schedule

GREATER MANCHESTER (LIGHT RAPID TRANSIT SYSTEM) ACT 1994

(1994 c. vi)

ARRANGEMENT OF SECTIONS

PART I

PRELIMINARY

PART II

FURTHER EXTENSION OF LIGHT RAPID TRANSIT SYSTEM

PART III

LANDS

PART IV

PROTECTIVE PROVISIONS

PART V

MISCELLANEOUS

An Act to empower the Greater Manchester Passenger Transport Executive to construct works and to acquire lands; to confer further powers on the Executive; and for other purposes.   [26th May 1994]

PARLIAMENTARY DEBATES
   The Bill's progress through Parliament was as follows:
   House of Lords: First Reading, January 15, 1991; Second Reading, February 26, 1991; Suspended, July 18, 1991; Unopposed Bill Committee, July 24, 1991; Suspended, March 12, 1992; Third Reading, June 3, 1992.

House of Commons: First Reading, June 3, 1992; Second Reading, May 13, 1993; Bill Committed, May 13, 1993; Unopposed Bill Committee, October 28, 1993; Suspended, November 2, 1993; Bill as Amended by Committee Considered, May 11, 1994; Third Reading, May 17, 1994.

INTRODUCTION

The Greater Manchester Passenger Transport Executive is charged with providing public passenger transport services for the metropolitan county of Greater Manchester. In order to fulfil its duties as set out under the Transport Act 1968 it is proposed that the light rapid transport system is further extended. This Act provides the authorisation for the relevant works to be undertaken and for land and rights over land to be acquired in order for those works to proceed.

WHEREAS the area of the Greater Manchester Passenger Transport Executive (hereinafter referred to as "the Executive") is the metropolitan county of Greater Manchester:

And whereas it is the duty of the Executive under the Transport Act 1968 to secure the provision of such public passenger transport services as they consider it appropriate to secure for meeting any public transport requirements within their area in accordance with policies formulated by the passenger transport authority for their area:

And whereas the further extension of the light rapid transit system which the Executive are authorised to provide would be of great public advantage:

And whereas it is expedient that the Executive should be empowered to construct the works authorised by this Act and to acquire or use the lands referred to in this Act:

And whereas it is expedient that the other powers in this Act contained should be conferred upon the Executive and that the other provisions in this Act should be enacted:

And whereas plans and sections showing the lines or situation and levels of the works authorised by this Act (other than the substituted portion of the tramroad (Work No. 5) as defined in this Act and hereinafter referred to as "the substituted portion of Work No. 5"), and a book of reference to such plans containing the names of the owners and lessees, or reputed owners and lessees, and of the occupiers of the lands which may be acquired or used compulsorily under the powers of this Act (other than the lands required for the purposes of the substituted portion of Work No. 5), were in the month of November 1990 deposited in the office of the Clerk of the Parliaments and in the Private Bill Office, House of Commons, and with the proper officer of the Oldham Borough Council and such plans, sections and book of reference are in this Act respectively referred to as the deposited plans, the deposited sections and the deposited book of reference:

And whereas a plan and section showing the line or situation and level of the substituted portion of Work No. 5 and also a book of reference to such plan containing the names of the owners and lessees, or reputed owners and lessees, and of the occupiers of the lands which may be acquired or used for the purposes of the substituted portion of Work No. 5 were deposited in the month of July 1991 in the office of the Clerk of the Parliaments and in the Private Bill Office, House of Commons, and with the proper officer of the Oldham Borough Council and such plan, section and book of reference are respectively referred to in this Act as the substituted plan, the substituted section and the substituted book of reference:

And whereas the purposes of this Act could not be effected without the authority of Parliament when the Bill for this Act was deposited:

And whereas the Greater Manchester Passenger Transport Authority have approved the promotion of the Bill for this Act pursuant to section 10(1)(xxix) of the Transport Act 1968:

May it therefore please your Majesty that it may be enacted, and be it enacted, by the Queen's most Excellent Majesty, by and with the advice and consent of the Lords Spiritual and Temporal, and Commons, in this present Parliament assembled, and by the authority of the same, as follows:—

Part I

Preliminary

Citation

1. This Act may be cited as the Greater Manchester (Light Rapid Transit System) Act 1994.

Interpretation

2.—(1) In this Act, unless the context otherwise requires—
"the authorised works" means the works authorised by this Act;
"the borough" means the borough of Oldham;
"the Executive" means the Greater Manchester Passenger Transport Executive;
"the railways board" means the British Railways Board or, as the case may require, any person who pursuant to the Railways Act 1993 succeeds (whether before or after the date of this Act) to any functions of the British Railways Board, or any other person who derives title to any property from the British Railways Board or such successor and holds that property for railway purposes;
"the substituted portion of Work No. 5" means the portion of the tramroad (Work No. 5) which is shown on the substituted plan and section commencing at reference point SD93194 05067 and terminating at reference point SD93329 05150;
"the tramroads" means Works Nos. 1, 2, 3 and 5, including the substituted portion of Work No. 5 but excluding the portion of that work for which that substituted portion is substituted;
"the tramway" means Work No. 4;
"the tribunal" means the Lands Tribunal.
(2) Where in this Act any distance or length is stated, or any reference point is referred to, in any description of works or functions, the reference to that distance, length or reference point shall be construed as if the words "or thereabouts" were inserted after such distance, length or reference point (as the case may be).
(3) Unless the context otherwise requires, any reference in this Act to a work identified by the number of the work shall be construed as a reference to the work of that number authorised by this Act.
(4) References in this Act to reference points shall be construed as references to National Grid reference points.

Application of Part I of Compulsory Purchase Act 1965

3.—(1) Part I of the Compulsory Purchase Act 1965 (except section 4 thereof and paragraph 3(3) of Schedule 3 thereto), in so far as it is applicable for the purposes of this Act and is not inconsistent with the provisions thereof, shall apply to the compulsory acquisition of land under this Act as it applies to a compulsory purchase to which Part II of the Acquisition of Land Act 1981 applies and as if this Act were a compulsory purchase order under the said Act of 1981.
(2) In subsection (1) of section 11 of the said Act of 1965, as so applied, for the words "fourteen days" there shall be substituted the words "three months".

(3) The Lands Clauses Consolidation Act 1845 shall not apply to the acquisition of land under this Act.

PART II

FURTHER EXTENSION OF LIGHT RAPID TRANSIT SYSTEM

Power to make works

4.—(1) Subject to the provisions of this Act, the Executive may make and maintain the works in the borough referred to in this section (together with all necessary works and conveniences connected therewith) in the lines or situations and according to the levels following (that is to say):—

(a) as regards the substituted portion of Work No. 5, the line or situation delineated on the substituted plan and the level shown on the substituted section; and

(b) as regards the remainder of the works hereafter in this section described (except the portion of Work No. 5 for which the substituted portion of that work is substituted), the lines or situations delineated on the deposited plans and the levels shown on the deposited sections.

(2) The works referred to in subsection (1) above are as follows:—

Work No. 1   A tramroad 1,307 yards (1,196 metres) in length (double line) commencing by a junction with the Hollinwood Branch Railway of the railways board at reference point SD91300 04762 and terminating at reference point SD92047 04796;

Work No. 2   A tramroad 272 yards (249 metres) in length (double line), partly in tunnel, commencing at the termination of Work No. 1 and terminating at reference point SD92274 04774;

Work No. 3   A tramroad 95 yards (87 metres) in length (double line) commencing at the termination of Work No. 2 and terminating at reference point SD92363 04771;

Work No. 4   A tramway 951 yards (870 metres) in length (double line) commencing at the termination of Work No. 3 and terminating at reference point SD93181 05059;

Work No. 5   A tramroad 291 yards (266 metres) in length (double line) commencing at the termination of Work No. 4 and terminating by a junction with the Middleton Junction to Rochdale Railway of the railways board at reference point SD93395 05178;

The substituted portion of Work No. 5;

Work No. 6   A pedestrian footpath and subway 55 yards (50 metres) in length commencing at reference point SD91955 04798 and terminating at reference point SD92004 04788;

Work No. 7   A pedestrian footpath and subway 33 yards (30 metres) in length commencing at reference point SD93323 05116 and terminating at reference point SD93346 05136;

Work No. 8   A widening of Cromwell Street 117 yards (107 metres) in length commencing at reference point SD92615 04733 and terminating at reference point SD92720 04764;

Work No. 9   A widening of Clegg Street 11 yards (10 metres) in length commencing at reference point SD92741 04863 and terminating at reference point SD92746 04871.

Further works and powers

5.—(1) Subject to the provisions of this Act, the Executive may make and maintain the further works in the borough described in this section, with all necessary works and conveniences connected therewith, and may exercise the powers hereinafter mentioned:—

(a) they may re-arrange the whole or any part of the footpath which lies between the points marked "J" and "K" on the deposited plans;

(b) they may stop up and discontinue the whole or any part of the footpath and subway which lie between the points marked "L" and "M" on the deposited plans;

(c) they may re-arrange the whole or any part of the junction of the streets known as Union Street West and King Street between the points marked "N" and "S" on the deposited plans;

(d) they may set back or re-arrange the whole or any part of the footway and kerblines at the junction of the streets known as King Street and George Street between the points marked "P" and "Q" on the deposited plans;

(e) they may set back or re-arrange the whole or any part of the footways and kerblines of the street known as Union Street which lie between the points marked "R" and "S", "S" and "T", "T" and "U", "V" and "W", "W" and "X", "X" and "Y", "AB" and "AC" and "Z" and "AA" respectively on the deposited plans;

(f) they may re-arrange the whole or any part of the footpaths which lie between the points marked "AH" and "AJ" on the deposited plans;

(g) they may set back or re-arrange the whole or any part of the kerblines of the street known as Oldham Way which lie between the points marked "AD" and "AE" and "AF" and "AG" respectively on the deposited plans.

(2) After the stopping up of any part of a footpath or street under subsection (1) above, all rights of way over or along the part of the footpath or street so stopped up shall be extinguished.

(3) In the exercise of the powers of subsection (1) above, the Executive may place such bollards or other obstructions for preventing the passage of vehicles as they consider appropriate and as may be agreed by the highway authority.

Gauge of tramroads and tramway

6. The tramroads and the tramway shall be constructed on a gauge of 4 feet 8½ inches (1·435 metres).

Power to deviate

7. Subject to the provisions of this Act, the Executive in constructing the authorised works may deviate from the lines thereof shown on the deposited plans or, as the case may be, the substituted plan to any extent within the limits of deviation shown on those plans and may deviate vertically from the levels shown on the deposited sections or, as the case may be, the substituted section to any extent not exceeding 3 metres upwards and to such extent downwards as may be found necessary or convenient and in constructing the tramroads and the tramway they may alter the radius of any curve described on the deposited plans and increase or diminish any inclination or gradient shown thereon.

Plans to be approved by Secretary of State before works commenced

8.—(1) Before constructing any of the tramroads or the tramway the Executive shall submit to the Secretary of State for his approval plans, sections and particulars of their proposals in respect of that work concerning—

(a) permanent way or track and stations;

(b) tunnels, lifts, escalators and stairways;

(c) signalling;

(d) lighting; and

(e) ventilation.

(2) Any such work shall be constructed and maintained in accordance with plans, sections and particulars approved by the Secretary of State.

Approval of Secretary of State

9. The tramroads and the tramway shall not be opened for public traffic until they have been inspected and certified to be fit for such traffic by the Secretary of State.

Certain works to be deemed tramways, etc.

10. For the purposes of the Regulation of Railways Act 1871 and Schedule 2 to the Telecommunications Act 1984 the tramroads shall be deemed to be tramways.

Extension of powers, etc.

11.—(1) The provisions of Part II of the Greater Manchester (Light Rapid Transit System) Act 1988 (except section 5(1) and (2) and sections 6, 7, 8, 11, 13, 21 and 22) and of section 43 (For protection of electricity, gas and water undertakers), section 44 (For protection of North West Water Authority) and section 46 (Carriages deemed to be public service vehicles) of that Act shall apply for the purposes of this Act.

(2) The provisions of the said Act of 1988 so applied shall have effect as if—

(a) any reference to the light rapid transit system included a reference to the authorised works;

(b) any reference to the tramroads or the tramways included a reference to the tramroads or, as the case may be, the tramway within the meaning of this Act;

(c) any reference to the said Act of 1988 (except a reference to a particular section of that Act) included a reference to this Act;

(d) section 10 (Power to cross streets on the level) included a reference to West Street and Winterbottom Street in the borough;

(e) for the purposes of section 14 (Application of Tramways Act 1870), the tramroads authorised by this Act were tramways;

(f) the references to section 23 of the said Act of 1988 in paragraph (2) of the said section 43 and to sections 15, 16 and 44 of the said Act of 1988 in paragraph (5) of the said section 43 included references to those sections as applied by this Act;

(g) in paragraph (1) of the said section 43, the words "(not being apparatus in respect of which the relations between the Executive and the undertakers are regulated by the provisions of Part II of the Public Utilities Street Works Act 1950)," were omitted;

(h) the reference to the deposited plans in paragraph (3) of the said section 43 included a reference to the plans deposited in connection with the Bill for this Act;

(i) in paragraph (12) of the said section 43, the words "in any street or controlled land within the meaning of the Public Utilities Street Works Act 1950" were omitted;

(j) in paragraph (13) of the said section 43, for the proviso there were substituted the following:—

"Provided that if in the course of the works of the undertakers hereinbefore in this paragraph mentioned apparatus of a better type, of greater dimensions or of greater capacity is placed in substitution for existing apparatus of a worse type, of smaller dimensions or of smaller capacity, or apparatus (whether existing apparatus or apparatus substituted for existing apparatus) is placed at a depth greater than the depth at which the existing apparatus was, and the placing of apparatus of that type, dimensions or capacity, or the placing of apparatus at that depth, as the case may be, had not been agreed or settled by arbitration under this section, then—

    (a) if it involves cost in the execution of works of the undertakers exceeding that which would have been involved if the apparatus placed had been of the existing type, dimensions or capacity, or at the existing depth, as the case may be, the amount which apart from this paragraph would be payable to the undertakers in respect of their works shall be reduced by the amount of that excess; and

    (b) if it involves cost in the execution of the works authorised by this Act exceeding the amount which would have been involved in that case, the undertakers shall pay to the Executive an amount equal to that excess.

For the purposes of this proviso—

    (i) an extension of apparatus to a length greater than the length of existing apparatus shall not be treated as a placing of apparatus of greater dimensions than those of the existing apparatus;

    (ii) where the provision of a joint in a cable is specified or agreed as necessary, the consequential provision of a jointing chamber or of a manhole shall be treated as if it also had been so specified or agreed; and

an amount which apart from this proviso would be payable to the undertakers in respect of their works shall, if the works include the placing of apparatus by way of renewal of apparatus placed more than seven-and-a-half years earlier so as to confer on the undertakers any financial benefit by deferment of the time for renewal of the apparatus in the ordinary course, be reduced by the amount which represents that benefit.".

(3) Section 9 (Agreements with railways board, etc.) of the Greater Manchester (Light Rapid Transit System) (No. 2) Act 1988 shall have effect as if the reference therein to the authorised works included a reference to the works authorised by this Act, the references therein to the light rapid transit system included references to those works and the references therein to the existing railways included a reference to so much of the Manchester South District Railway of the railways board as lies between the termination of Work No. 10B authorised by the Greater Manchester (Light Rapid Transit System) (No. 2) Act 1990 and the commencement of Work No. 11 authorised by that Act and all works and conveniences provided in connection with the said railway, as existing, altered or constructed (as the case may be) from time to time.

PART III

LANDS

Power to acquire lands

12. Subject to the provisions of this Act, the Executive may enter upon, take and use such of the lands respectively delineated on the deposited plans and the substituted plan and described respectively in the deposited book of reference and the substituted book of reference as they may require for the purposes of the authorised works or for any purpose connected with, or ancillary to, their undertaking.

Power to acquire new rights

13.—(1) In this section references to the purchase by the Executive of new rights are references to the purchase of rights to be created in favour of the Executive.

(2) The Executive may, for the purposes of constructing, maintaining, protecting, renewing and using any of the authorised works, purchase compulsorily such new rights as they may require over any of the lands that may be acquired compulsorily under this Act instead of acquiring those lands.

(3) The Compulsory Purchase Act 1965 as applied by this Act shall have effect with the modifications necessary to make it apply to the compulsory purchase of rights under subsection (2) above as it applies to the compulsory purchase of land so that, in appropriate contexts, references in that Act to land are read as referring, or as including references, to the rights or to land over which the rights are or are to be exercisable according to the requirements of the context.

(4) Without prejudice to the generality of subsection (3) above, in relation to the purchase of rights under subsection (2) above—

  (a) Part I of the said Act of 1965 shall have effect with the modifications specified in the Schedule to this Act; and

  (b) the enactments relating to compensation for the compulsory purchase of land shall apply with the necessary modifications as they apply to such compensation.

Correction of errors in deposited plans and book of reference

14.—(1) If the deposited plans or the deposited book of reference or the substituted plan or the substituted book of reference are inaccurate in their description of any land, or in their statement or description of the ownership or occupation of any land, the Executive after giving not less than 10 days' notice to the owner, lessee and occupier of the land in question may apply to two justices having jurisdiction in the place where the land is situated for the correction thereof.

(2) If on any such application it appears to the justices that the misstatement or wrong description arose from mistake, the justices shall certify the fact accordingly, and shall in their certificate state in what respect any matter is misstated or wrongly described.

(3) The certificate shall be deposited in the office of the Clerk of the Parliaments, and a copy thereof in the Private Bill Office, House of Commons, and with the proper officer of the Oldham Borough Council and thereupon the deposited plans and the deposited book of reference or, as the case may be, the substituted plan and the substituted book of reference shall be deemed to be corrected according to the certificate, and it shall be lawful for the Executive to take the land and execute the works in accordance with the certificate.

(4) A person with whom a copy of the certificate is deposited under this section shall keep it with the other documents to which it relates.

Disregard of recent improvements and interests

15. In determining a question with respect to compensation claimed in consequence of the compulsory acquisition of land under this Act, the tribunal shall not take into account any interest in land, or any enhancement of the value of any interest in land, by reason of any building erected, works executed or improvement or alteration made, whether on the land acquired or on any other land with which the claimant is, or was at the time of erection, executing or making of the building, works, improvement or alteration, directly or indirectly concerned, if the tribunal are satisfied that the creation of the interest, the erection of the building, the execution of the works or the making of the improvement or alteration, as the case may be, was not reasonably necessary and was undertaken with a view to obtaining compensation or increased compensation.

Extinction of private rights of way

16.—(1) All private rights of way over any land that may be acquired compulsorily under this Act shall be extinguished on the acquisition of the land, whether compulsorily or by agreement, or on the entry on the land in pursuance of section 11(1) of the Compulsory Purchase Act 1965, as applied by this Act, whichever is the sooner.

(2) Any person who suffers loss by the extinguishment of any right under this section shall be entitled to be paid by the Executive compensation to be determined in case of dispute by the tribunal.

Period for compulsory purchase of lands

17.—(1) The powers of the Executive for the compulsory acquisition of the lands which they are authorised to acquire by this Part of this Act shall not be exercised after the end of the period of 5 years commencing on the date of the passing of this Act.

(2) The powers of the Executive for the compulsory acquisition of the said lands shall for the purposes of this section be deemed to have been exercised when notice to treat has been served in respect of those lands.

PART IV

PROTECTIVE PROVISIONS

For protection of British Railways Board

18. For the protection of the railways board the following provisions shall, unless otherwise agreed in writing between the Executive and the railways board, have effect:—

(1) In this section—

"construction" includes execution, placing, alteration and reconstruction and "construct" and "constructed" have corresponding meanings;

"the engineer" means an engineer to be appointed by the railways board;

"plans" includes sections, drawings, specifications, soil reports, calculations and descriptions (including descriptions of methods of construction);

"railway property" means any railway of the railways board and any works connected therewith for the maintenance or operation of which the railways board are responsible and includes any land held or used by the railways board for the purposes of such railway or works;

"specified works" means so much of the authorised works as may be situated upon, across, under or over or within 15 metres of, or may in any way affect, railway property and includes the construction, maintenance, alteration and renewal of the specified works:

(2)(a) The Executive shall not under the powers of this Act acquire compulsorily any railway property or any other land of the railways board but they may, with the consent of the railways board, which consent shall not be unreasonably withheld, acquire such easements or other rights in any railway property or any other land of the railways board delineated on the deposited plans or, as the case may be, the substituted plan as they may reasonably require for the purposes of the specified works;

(b) The Executive shall fence off the specified works from railway property or any other land of the railways board to the reasonable satisfaction of the engineer where so required by him:

(3) During the construction of the specified works the Executive shall at all times ensure reasonable access to, and egress from—

    (a) any station, depot or other operational premises of the railways board for vehicles and pedestrians;

    (b) any other railway property for the railways board and their agents, contractors and employees (with or without vehicles, plant, machinery and materials):

(4) The Executive shall before commencing the specified works (other than works of maintenance or repair) furnish to the railways board proper and sufficient plans thereof for the reasonable approval of the engineer and shall not commence the specified works until plans thereof have been approved in writing by the engineer or settled by arbitration:

    Provided that if within 56 days after such plans have been furnished to the railways board the engineer has not intimated his disapproval thereof and the grounds of his disapproval he shall be deemed to have approved the same:

(5) If within 56 days after such plans have been furnished to the railways board, the railways board give notice to the Executive that the railways board desire themselves to construct any part of the specified works which in the opinion of the engineer will or may affect the stability of railway property or the safe operation of traffic on the railways of the railways board then, if the Executive desire such part of the specified works to be constructed, the railways board shall construct the same with all reasonable dispatch on behalf of and to the reasonable satisfaction of the Executive in accordance with the plans approved or deemed to be approved or settled as aforesaid:

(6) Upon signifying his approval or disapproval of the plans the engineer may specify any protective works (whether temporary or permanent) which in his opinion should be carried out before the commencement of the specified works to ensure the safety or stability of railway property and such protective works as may be reasonably necessary for those purposes shall be constructed by the railways board or by the Executive, if the railways board so desire, with all reasonable dispatch and the Executive shall not commence the construction of the specified works until the engineer has notified the Executive that the protective works have been completed to his reasonable satisfaction:

(7)(a) The Executive shall give to the railways board notice in writing of their intention to commence the construction of any of the specified works in accordance with sub-paragraph (b) below and, except in emergency (when they shall give such notice as may be reasonably practicable), also of their intention to carry out any works for the maintenance or renewal of the specified works;

(b) The period of notice required to be given by the Executive to the railways board by virtue of sub-paragraph (a) above shall be—

    (i) 6 months in any case where the engineer, upon signifying his approval or disapproval of plans furnished to the railways board under paragraph (4) above, has reasonably given it as his opinion that the construction, maintenance or renewal of the specified works will require the Executive to have temporary occupation of the permanent way of the railway (including land lying within a distance of 2 metres from any outer rail of the railway) or will necessitate the imposition of speed restrictions, or the substitution, diversion or suspension of train services; and

    (ii) 28 days in all other cases:

(8) The specified works shall, when commenced, be carried out—
    (a) with all reasonable dispatch in accordance with the plans approved or deemed to have been approved or settled as aforesaid;
    (b) under the supervision (if given) and to the reasonable satisfaction of the engineer;
    (c) in such manner as to cause as little damage to railway property as may be; and
    (d) so far as is reasonably practicable, so as not to interfere with or obstruct the free, uninterrupted and safe user of any railway of the railways board or the traffic thereon and the use by passengers of railway property;
and, if any damage to railway property or any such interference or obstruction is caused or takes place, the Executive shall, notwithstanding any such approval as aforesaid, make good such damage and shall on demand pay to the railways board all reasonable expenses to which they may be put and compensation for any loss which they may sustain by reason of any such damage, interference or obstruction:

(9) The Executive shall—
    (a) at all times afford reasonable facilities to the engineer for access to the specified works during their construction;
    (b) ensure access for the engineer at all reasonable times to all working sites, depots and premises at which materials to be employed in the construction of the specified works are being made, constructed or assembled;
    (c) supply the engineer with all such information as he may reasonably require with regard to the specified works or the method of construction thereof:

(10) The railways board shall at all times afford reasonable facilities to the Executive and their agents for access to any works carried out by the railways board under this section during their construction and shall supply the Executive with such information as they may reasonably require with regard to such works or the method of construction thereof:

(11) If any alterations or additions, either permanent or temporary to railway property are reasonably necessary in consequence of the construction of the specified works, such alterations and additions may be effected by the railways board after not less than 28 days' notice has been given to the Executive and the Executive shall pay to the railways board on demand the cost thereof as certified by the engineer including, in respect of permanent alterations and additions, a capitalised sum representing the increased or additional cost of maintaining, working and, when necessary, renewing any such alterations or additions:

(12) The Executive shall repay to the railways board all costs, charges and expenses reasonably incurred by the railways board—
    (a) in constructing any part of the specified works on behalf of the Executive as provided by paragraph (5) above or in constructing any protective works under the provisions of paragraph (6) above including, in respect of any permanent protective works, a capitalised sum representing the cost of maintaining and renewing those works;
    (b) in respect of the employment of any inspectors, signalmen, watchmen and other persons whom it is reasonably necessary to appoint for inspecting, watching, lighting and signalling railway property and for preventing as far as may be all interference, obstruction, danger or accident arising from the construction, maintenance, renewal, repair or failure of the specified works;

(c) in respect of any special traffic working resulting from any speed restrictions which are necessary as a result of the construction, maintenance, renewal, repair or failure of the specified works and which may in the opinion of the engineer be required to be imposed or from the substitution, suspension or diversion of services which may be necessary for the same reason;

(d) in respect of any additional temporary lighting of railway property in the vicinity of the specified works being lighting made reasonably necessary as a result of the specified works or the failure thereof;

(e) in respect of the approval by the engineer of plans submitted by the Executive and the supervision by him of the specified works:

(13) If at any time after the completion of the specified works, not being works vested in the railways board, the railways board give notice to the Executive informing them that the state of repair of the specified works appears to be such as prejudicially to affect railway property, the Executive shall, on receipt of such notice, take such steps as may be reasonably necessary to put the specified works in such state of repair as not prejudicially to affect railway property and, if and whenever the Executive fail to do so, the railways board may make and do in and upon the land of the railways board or of the Executive all such works and things as are requisite to put the specified works in such state of repair as aforesaid and the cost and expenses reasonably incurred by the railways board in so doing shall be repaid to them by the Executive:

(14) All temporary structures, erections, works, apparatus and appliances erected or placed by the Executive under the powers of this Act upon, over or under any railway of the railways board shall, as soon as reasonably practicable, be removed by the Executive at times to be agreed with, and to the reasonable satisfaction of, the engineer and in such a way as to cause as little damage to railway property and as little interference with, or delay or interruption to, the traffic on the railways of the railways board as may be; and if any damage to railway property or such interference, delay or interruption is caused by any such failure to remove any such temporary structures, erections, works, apparatus or appliances, the Executive shall forthwith make good such damage and pay to the railways board the reasonable costs and expenses to which they may be put and reasonable compensation for any loss which they may sustain by reason of such damage, interference, delay or interruption:

(15) If it is necessary for the protection and safety of railway property for the railways board to purchase any minerals for the support of such property or to pay compensation for any minerals to be left unworked for the support thereof and the specified works also derive support from such minerals, the Executive shall repay to the railways board a reasonable proportion of the amount paid by the railways board for or in respect of such minerals and the costs and expenses incurred by the railways board in relation to any such purchase or payment of compensation:

(16) Before providing any illumination or illuminated traffic sign on or in connection with the specified works or in the vicinity of any railway of the railways board, the Executive shall consult with the railways board and comply with their reasonable requirements in regard thereto with a view to ensuring that such illumination or illuminated sign could not be confused with any railway signal or other light used for controlling, directing or securing the safety of traffic on the railway:

(17) Any additional expense which the railways board may reasonably incur after giving 56 days' notice to the Executive in widening, altering, reconstructing or maintaining railway property under any powers existing at the passing of this Act by reason of the existence of the specified works shall be repaid by the Executive to the railways board:

(18) The Executive shall be responsible for and make good to the railways board all costs, charges, damages and expenses not otherwise provided for in this section which may be occasioned to or reasonably incurred by the railways board—

> (a) by reason of the specified works or the failure thereof; or
>
> (b) by reason of any act or omission of the Executive or of any persons in their employ or of their contractors or others whilst engaged upon the specified works;

and the Executive shall effectively indemnify and hold harmless the railways board from and against all claims and demands arising out of or in connection with the specified works or any such failure, act or omission as aforesaid and the fact that any act or thing may have been done by the railways board on behalf of the Executive or in accordance with plans approved by the engineer or in accordance with any requirement of the engineer or under his supervision shall not (if it was done without negligence on the part of the railways board or of any person in their employ or of their contractors or agents) excuse the Executive from any liability under the provisions of this section:

Provided that the railways board shall give to the Executive reasonable notice of any claim or demand as aforesaid and no settlement or compromise thereof shall be made without the prior consent of the Executive:

(19) Section 42 (For further protection of British Railways Board) of the Greater Manchester (Light Rapid Transit System) Act 1988 shall have effect as if the references therein to the light rapid transit system included references to Works Nos. 1 and 5 and to any parts of the railways of the railways board transferred to, and vested in, the Executive by agreement with the railways board under this Act:

(20) Any difference arising between the Executive and the railways board under this section (other than a difference as to the meaning or construction of this section) shall be referred to and settled by arbitration in the manner provided by section 47 of the Greater Manchester (Light Rapid Transit System) Act 1988.

For protection of telecommunications operators

19. For the protection of telecommunications operators the following provisions shall, unless otherwise agreed in writing between the Executive and the telecommunications operators concerned, have effect:—

(1) In this section expressions defined in the Telecommunications Act 1984 have the same meanings as in that Act:

(2) The temporary stopping up or diversion of any street or footpath under section 23 (Temporary stoppage of streets and footpaths) of the Greater Manchester (Light Rapid Transit System) Act 1988 as applied for the purposes of this Act shall not affect the right of a telecommunications operator under paragraph 9 of the telecommunications code to inspect, maintain, adjust, repair or alter any apparatus which, at the time of the stopping up or diversion, is in that street or footpath.

For protection of Trustees of King Street Baptist Church, Oldham

20. For the protection of the Trustees the following provisions shall, unless otherwise agreed in writing between the Executive and the Trustees, have effect:—

(1) In this section—
"the Act of 1951" means the Baptist and Congregational Trusts Act 1951;

"the Association" means the Lancashire and Cheshire Association of Baptist Churches (Incorporated), whose registered office is at Latchford Baptist Church, Loushers Lane, Warrington WA4 2RP;

"the present lands" means the land delineated and numbered 23 in the borough on the deposited plans and described in the deposited book of reference as the King Street Baptist Church, Oldham;

"the prior works" means the construction to the reasonable satisfaction of the Trustees' architects of buildings and facilities ready for use and occupation comparable and reasonably equivalent to those erected on the present lands including, for the avoidance of doubt, comparable ground level accommodation and the capability of extending the accommodation by 66 per cent. of the total accommodation;

"the replacement lands" means lands in a location which is reasonably equivalent to the location of the present lands having regard to their amenity, their proximity to the central area of the borough and their suitability for the purposes hereinafter specified and of a size capable of providing the buildings and facilities to be constructed thereon with public highway, vehicular and pedestrian access and other rights and appurtenances similar to those now enjoyed by the present lands for an estate in fee simple or for the term of years now held subject only to the ground rents now prevailing;

"the Trustees" means the Association and such individuals as are for the time being trustees of the King Street Baptist Church, Oldham:

(2) Whereas the Trustees hold the present lands by virtue of a Memorandum of Choice and Appointment dated 19th September 1984 for the residue of two long leasehold estates existing until or beyond 15th October 2859 subject to ground rents aggregating £48.95 upon trust subject to the provisions of section 6 of the Act of 1951 for occupation, use or enjoyment for all or any of the following purposes namely:—

(a) the public worship of God according to the principles and usages for the time being of Protestant Dissenters of the Baptist denomination;

(b) the instruction of children or adults or the promotion of other religious or charitable purposes in accordance with the principles and usages aforesaid:

Now it is hereby provided that until at the cost and expense of the Executive—

(i) the prior works have been completed and are ready for use and occupation on the replacement lands;

(ii) the Trustees' architects have certified that they have approved the design and specification of the prior works and the contract for and the construction of the prior works and are satisfied that the payments due under the said contract have been made or secured and the warranties in the contract enure for the benefit of the Trustees; and

(iii) the prior works and the replacement lands have for the estate aforesaid been vested in the Trustees by way of Deed of Exchange of the present lands;

the Executive shall not exercise in respect of the present lands the powers of this Act:

Provided that the issue of a certificate by the Trustees' architects shall not be unreasonably withheld and the completion of the said Deed of Exchange and the payment of the Trustees' architects' and legal fees shall be taken to satisfy the obligation of the Executive to pay compensation:

(3) Until the provisions of sub-paragraphs (i), (ii) and (iii) above have been complied with—

    (a) none of the authorised works shall be constructed within 15 metres of the present lands;

    (b) during the construction of any of the authorised works more than 15 metres from the present lands the Executive shall at all times—

        (i) ensure reasonable access to and egress from the present lands for vehicles and pedestrians;

        (ii) prevent the construction of the authorised works from interfering with acts of worship by noise and (so far as is reasonably practicable) by dust or other nuisance; and

        (iii) use their best endeavours to avoid disturbing or interfering with use being made of the present lands:

(4) Any difference arising between the Executive and the Trustees under this section (other than a difference as to the meaning or construction of this section) shall be referred to and settled by a single arbitrator to be agreed between the parties, or, failing agreement, to be appointed on the application of either party (after notice in writing to the other) by the President of the Royal Institution of Chartered Surveyors.

PART V

MISCELLANEOUS

Power to contract for police services

21.—(1) Agreements may be made—

(a) between the Executive and the chief officer of police of any police force and the police authority; or

(b) between the Executive and the railways board,

for making available to the Executive for the purposes of the operation of the light rapid transit system the services of members of the police force or, as the case may be, members of the British Transport Police Force on such terms as to payment or otherwise, and subject to such conditions, as the parties to them think fit.

(2) Where such an agreement has been made between the Executive and the railways board, members of the British Transport Police Force may act, in accordance with the terms of the agreement, as constables in, on or in the vicinity of any premises forming part of the light rapid transit system or other facilities used in connection with the light rapid transit system notwithstanding the provisions of section 53(1) of the British Transport Commission Act 1949 (which restricts them to acting in, on or in the vicinity of premises belonging to or leased to or worked by the railways board, etc.).

(3) In this section—

(a) "chief officer of police", "police authority" and "police force" have the same meaning as in the Police Act 1964;

(b) the British Transport Police Force means the force organised under the scheme set out in the Schedule to the British Transport Police Scheme 1963 (Approval) Order 1964 made under section 69 of the Transport Act 1962; and

(c) the reference to "premises forming part of the light rapid transit system" is a reference to premises of the Executive used for or in connection with the operation of the light rapid transit system and includes a reference to rolling stock and other vehicles used on that system.

Saving for town and country planning

22. In their application to development authorised by Part II (Further extension of light rapid transit system) of this Act, Article 3 of, and Class A in Part 11 of Schedule 2 to, the Town and Country Planning General Development Order 1988 shall have effect as if the authority to develop given by this Act in respect of the authorised works were limited to such development begun within 10 years after the passing of this Act.

SCHEDULE

ADAPTATION OF PART I OF THE COMPULSORY PURCHASE ACT 1965

1. In the Compulsory Purchase Act 1965 (hereafter in this Schedule referred to as "the Act") for section 7 (measure of compensation) there shall be substituted the following:—
    "7. In assessing the compensation to be paid by the acquiring authority under this Act regard shall be had not only to the extent (if any) to which the value of the land over which the right is to be acquired is depreciated by the acquisition of the right but also to the damage (if any) to be sustained by the owners of the land by reason of its severance from other land of his, or injuriously affecting that other land by the exercise of the powers conferred by this or the special Act.".
2. For section 8(1) of the Act (protection for vendor against severance of house, garden, etc.) there shall be substituted the following:—
    "(1) No person shall be required to grant any right over part only—
    (a) of any house, building or factory; or
    (b) of a park or garden belonging to a house;
    if he is willing to sell the whole of the house, building, factory, park or garden, unless the Lands Tribunal determines that—
      (i) in the case of a house, building or factory, the part over which the right is proposed to be acquired can be made subject to that right without material detriment to the house, building or factory; or
      (ii) in the case of a park or garden, the part over which the right is proposed to be acquired can be made subject to that right without seriously affecting the amenity or convenience of the house;
    and, if the Lands Tribunal so determine, the tribunal shall award compensation in respect of any loss due to the acquisition of the right, in addition to its value; and thereupon the party interested shall be required to grant to the acquiring authority that right over that part of the house, building, factory, park or garden.
    (1A) In considering the extent of any detriment to a house, building or factory, or any extent to which the amenity or convenience of a house is affected, the Lands Tribunal shall have regard not only to the right which is to be acquired over the land, but also to any adjoining or adjacent land belonging to the same owner and subject to compulsory purchase.".
3. The following provisions of the Act (being provisions stating the effect of a deed poll executed in various circumstances where there is no conveyance by persons with interests in the land)—
    section 9(4) (refusal by owners to convey);
    Schedule 1, paragraph 10(3) (owners under incapacity);
    Schedule 2, paragraph 2(3) (absent and untraced owners); and
    Schedule 4, paragraphs 2(3) and 7(2) (common land);
shall be so modified as to secure that, as against persons with interests in the land which are expressed to be overridden by the deed, the right which is to be compulsorily acquired is vested absolutely in the acquiring authority.

4. Section 11 of the Act (powers of entry) shall be so modified as to secure that, as from the date on which the acquiring authority have served notice to treat in respect of any right, they have power, exercisable in the like circumstances and subject to the like conditions, to enter for the purpose of exercising that right (which shall be deemed for this purpose to have been created on the date of service of the notice); and sections 12 (penalty for unauthorised entry) and 13 (entry on sheriff's warrant in the event of obstruction) of the Act shall be modified correspondingly.

INDEX

References are to sections

COMMONS REGISTRATION (EAST SUSSEX) ACT 1994

(1994 c. vii)

ARRANGEMENT OF SECTIONS

An Act to make provision for the reconstitution and validation of the registers of common land and of town or village greens maintained under the Commons Registration Act 1965 for the County of East Sussex; and for connected purposes.   [5th July 1994)

PARLIAMENTARY DEBATES

The Bill's progress through Parliament was as follows:

House of Lords: First Reading, January 12, 1994; Second Reading, February 16, 1994; Unopposed Bill Committee, April 13, 1994; Third Reading, April 26, 1994; Commons' Amendments, June 23, 1994.

House of Commons: First Reading, April 26, 1994; Second Reading, May 11, 1994; Bill Committed, May 11, 1994; Unopposed Bill Committee, May 25, 1994; Bill Amended by Committee, June 16, 1994; Third Reading, June 23, 1994.

INTRODUCTION

The East Sussex County Council is classed as the registration authority for the area affected by this Act under the provisions of the Commons Registration Act 1965(c. 64). Under that Act the county council is required to maintain registers of common land and of town or village greens. As a result of a fire in January 1993 these records were completely destroyed and it is now the responsibility of the county council to reconstitute the East Sussex register. Given the difficulties which will be encountered in reconstituting accurately the complete register, this Act provides for the necessary validation of the register as reconstituted, to avoid challenges to the authority of the new register.

WHEREAS—

(1) Under the Commons Registration Act 1965 (in this Act referred to as "the Act of 1965") the East Sussex County Council (in this Act referred to as "the county council") is the registration authority for its area, subject as mentioned in section 2(2) of that Act:

(2) In January 1993 the registers of common land and of town or village greens which the county council is required to maintain under the Act of 1965 (in this Act referred to as "the East Sussex registers") were completely destroyed by fire:

(3) The county council has begun to reconstitute the East Sussex registers by collecting evidence from various sources as to the contents of the East Sussex registers:

(4) The county council apprehends that although it will be possible accurately to reconstitute the major part of the East Sussex registers it will not be possible to effect a reconstitution of the East Sussex registers which can be proved to be complete and accurate in every detail:

(5) To avoid uncertainty as to the status of the matters recorded in the East Sussex registers as reconstituted and to enable the county council to comply with its duties under the Act of 1965 it is expedient to make provision with respect to the reconstitution, and for the validation, of the East Sussex registers and to make such other provision for these purposes as are contained in this Act:

(6) The purposes of this Act cannot be achieved without the authority of Parliament:

(7) On the promotion of the Bill for this Act the county council has observed the requirements of section 239 of the Local Government Act 1972:

May it therefore please Your Majesty that it may be enacted, and be it enacted, by the Queen's most Excellent Majesty, by and with the advice and consent of the Lords Spiritual and Temporal, and Commons, in this present Parliament assembled, and by the authority of the same, as follows:—

Citation and commencement

1. This Act may be cited as the Commons Registration (East Sussex) Act 1994.

Interpretation and general

2.—(1) In this Act, unless the context otherwise requires—

"the Act of 1965" means the Commons Registration Act 1965;

"concerned authority" in relation to a registration means a local authority (other than the registration authority) in whose area any part of the land affected by the registration lies;

"the county council" means the East Sussex County Council;

"the destroyed registers" means the East Sussex registers as destroyed by fire in January 1993;

"the East Sussex registers" means the registers of common land and of town or village greens which the county council is required to maintain under the Act of 1965;

"registration" means registration under section 4 of the Act of 1965 and an entry in the register made in pursuance of section 13 of the Act of 1965.

(2) A reference in any provision of this Act to the proper officer is a reference to the officer appointed by the county council for purposes which include the purpose of that provision.

(3) Except as otherwise provided in this Act, expressions used in this Act and in the Act of 1965, or the regulations made under that Act have the same meaning as in that Act and those regulations.

(4) Notice is duly given by or to the county council to or by any person under this Act if given in accordance with section 231 or, as the case may be, 233 of the Local Government Act 1972.

Reconstitution of East Sussex registers

3.—(1) As soon as may be after the commencement of this Act the county council shall reconstitute the East Sussex registers by drawing new registers in accordance with subsection (2) below.

(2) The new registers shall be drawn in such manner as to replicate as far as reasonably practicable the contents of the destroyed registers and to incorporate all such amendments, corrections or alterations as shall have been required by or under the Act of 1965 or the Common Land (Rectification of Registers) Act 1989 to be entered into the East Sussex registers since the destruction of the destroyed registers.

(3) Nothing in this Act shall prejudice the power of the county council to note in the new registers any matter authorised to be noted by or under the Act of 1965.

Invitation of requests for notification of new registration

4.—(1) Not later than one month from the commencement of this Act the county council shall publish, at least once in each of two successive weeks in one or more newspapers circulating in the county of East Sussex an advertisement stating—

(a) the general effect of this Act; and

(b) that any person who is or may be concerned by any registration in the East Sussex registers may request the county council to give him notice when the new registers have been drawn and to supply him with a copy of them so far as they relate to specified land, stating in his request—

    (i) his name and address;

    (ii) the land in relation to which he requests notice; and

    (iii) if he so desires, the name and address of any other person to whom such notice should be given on his behalf.

(2) The advertisement published under subsection (1) above shall also state the latest date, not less than six months from the commencement of this Act, for the making of a request to the county council as provided by subsection (1)(b) above.

(3) Not later than one month from the commencement of this Act the county council shall publish in the London Gazette notice of the commencement of this Act specifying a local newspaper in which the advertisement required by subsection (1) above will be found.

Notification of new registration

5.—(1) When the new registers have been drawn the county council shall give notice thereof—

(a) specifying at least one place in the county of East Sussex where copies of the new registers may be inspected by any person free of charge at all reasonable times during the period of six months from the date of the first publication of the notice; and

(b) stating the effect of section 6 (Determination of new registers) of this Act and the latest date for the submission of representations to the county council for the purposes of that section.

(2) Notice under subsection (1) above shall be given—

(a) by publishing the notice in a newspaper circulating in the county of East Sussex and, as soon as possible thereafter, in the London Gazette;

(b) by sending, not later than the date on which the notice is first published, a copy of the notice to each of the following:—

    (i) any concerned authority; and

    (ii) any person who has requested notice in accordance with section 4 (Invitation of requests for notification of new registration) of this Act, or any person nominated by such a person pursuant to section 4(1)(b)(iii), at the address for notification stated in the request.

(3) There shall be sent together with any copy of a notice sent pursuant to subsection (2)(b) above—

(a) in the case of a copy sent to a concerned authority pursuant to sub-paragraph (i), copies of the new registers in so far as they relate to land lying within the area of that authority; and

(b) in the case of a copy sent to any person pursuant to sub-paragraph (ii), copies of the new registers in so far as they relate to land specified in the request.

Determination of new registers

6.—(1) If, within the period of six months from the date of the first publication under section 5 (Notification of registration) of this Act of notice that the new registers have been drawn, representations are made to the county council that in respect of any matter the new registers do not comply with section 3 (Reconstitution of East Sussex registers) of this Act, the county council shall consider the representations and give to each authority or person by whom any such representations have been made, and to any other person who the county council has reason to believe (whether from information supplied by him or otherwise) has an interest in the matter, an opportunity of being heard by a person appointed by the county council for the purpose, at a time and place notified to them.

(2) The county council shall, after considering any such representations and, if a person is appointed to hear representations, the report of that person, determine whether or not to modify the new registers to take into account those representations.

(3) Upon the determination of any such matter under subsection (2) above the county council shall send to each authority and person concerned (including any relevant concerned authority) notice of its determination and, where it has determined to modify the new registers, a copy of the relevant portions of the new registers as modified.

(4) If required by any person, within seven days of the receipt by him of notice under subsection (3) above of any determination of the county council, the county council shall give to him a statement of the grounds upon which that determination is based.

Validity of new registers

7.—(1)(a) Upon the determination by the county council of all matters affecting the new registers under section 6 (Determination of new registers) of this Act, the new registers shall be certified by the proper officer.

(b) If, within the period of six months from the date of the first publication under section 5 (Notification of new registration) of this Act of notice of the drawing of the new registers, no such representations as are referred to in subsection (1) of the said section 6 are made to the county council in respect of any matter affecting the new registers, the new registers shall be certified by the proper officer at the expiration of that period.

(c) The certification of the new registers under this subsection shall be made by a note in the general parts of the new registers signed by the proper officer.

(2) On the certification by the proper officer of the new registers under subsection (1) above, then—

(a) the new registers shall become and be the registers of common land and of town or village greens for the registration area of the county council; and

(b) the destroyed registers shall cease to have effect.

(3) Nothing in this Act shall give a registration or other entry in the new registers any greater validity than it would have had if—

(a) it had appeared in substantially the same form in the destroyed registers; and

(b) the destroyed registers had been drawn in accordance with the statutory requirements made by or under the Act of 1965; and

(c) this Act had not passed.

Official searches before certification

8. Until certification by the proper officer of the new registers under section 7 (Validity of new registers) of this Act each certificate setting forth the results of a search in the East Sussex registers shall be indorsed with words substantially to the following effect:—

"The East Sussex registers have been destroyed by fire. This certificate is based on reconstituted registers not yet validated under the Commons Registration (East Sussex) Act 1994.".

INDEX

References are to sections and schedule

DUNHAM BRIDGE (AMENDMENT) ACT 1994

(1994 c. viii)

ARRANGEMENT OF SECTIONS

PART I

PRELIMINARY

PART II

CONSTITUTION OF COMPANY

PART III

LANDS

PART IV

TOLLS, ETC.

An Act to provide for the amendment of the existing constitution of the Dunham Bridge Company; to authorise the eventual dissolution of the Company and the vesting of its undertaking in a company registered under the Companies Act 1985; to provide for the vesting of further land in the Company and for the vesting of exchange land; to provide for new works constructed on the land so vested in the Company and on other land acquired by them to form part of the undertaking; to prescribe the level of tolls recoverable from users of Dunham Bridge and to modify the Transport Charges &c. (Miscellaneous Provisions) Act 1954 in its application to the undertaking; to amend or repeal certain of the local statutory provisions applicable to the undertaking and for related purposes.   [5th July 1994]

PARLIAMENTARY DEBATES
   The Bill's progress through Parliament was as follows:
   House of Commons: First Reading, January 22, 1993; Second Reading, January 28, 1993; Bill Committed, March 4, 1993; Unopposed Bill Committee, March 24, 1993; Bill Amended by Committee, May 5, 1994; Third Reading, May 11, 1994; Lords' Amendments, June 26, 1994.
   House of Lords: First Reading, May 11, 1994; Second Reading, June 7, 1993; Bill Committed, June 7, 1993; Suspended, October 28, 1993; Unopposed Bill Committee, June 9, 1994; Third Reading, June 21, 1994.

INTRODUCTION
   The Dunham Bridge Company have been charged with the levying of tolls for passage over the Dunham Bridge since the incorporation of the company in 1830. As a result of an increase in traffic over the bridge the current constitution of that company does not allow for the efficient management of the undertaking. This Act makes provision for the amendment of the constitution of the company, to incorporate various clauses of the Companies Clauses Consolidation Act 1845 (c. 16) and the Companies Clauses Act 1863 (c. 118) and to allow for the dissolution of the company if so resolved. Further provisions are made to effect the improvement of the bridge facilities, namely the improvement of toll collection facilities and the Act ensures that land necessary for that development is vested in the company free from existing rights.

WHEREAS—

(1) By an Act passed in the eleventh year of the reign of His late Majesty King George IV intituled "An Act for building a Bridge over the River Trent, from Dunham, in the County of Nottingham, to the opposite Shore, in the County of Lincoln" (hereinafter called "the Act of 1830") the Dunham Bridge Company (hereinafter called "the Company") were incorporated and authorised to construct the said bridge (hereinafter called "Dunham Bridge") and to levy tolls for passage thereover:

(2) The share capital of the Company is now £14,250:

(3) Dunham Bridge continues to serve the needs of an increasing volume of traffic and since the constitution of the Company as embodied in the Act of 1830 hinders the effective management of the undertaking it is expedient that the existing constitution of the Company be amended by the incorporation of provisions of the Companies Clauses Consolidation Act 1845 and the Companies Clauses Act 1863 and other provisions, that provision be made, if the Company should so resolve, for the Company to be dissolved and their undertaking transferred to a company registered under the Companies Act 1985 and that provisions in the Act of 1830 should be repealed:

(4) For the convenience of traffic using Dunham Bridge it is expedient that the Company should provide on the east side of the bridge a site for improved toll collection facilities and that these facilities when constructed should form part of the undertaking:

(5) Part of the land so required is in unknown ownership and registered as common under the Commons Registration Act 1965 and it is expedient to provide for the vesting of that land free from existing rights and for the provision of exchange land:

(6) The cost of maintaining and eventually replacing Dunham Bridge continues to increase and it is therefore expedient that, notwithstanding the provisions of the Locomotive Act 1861 (which have the effect of imposing inappropriate limits on the levels of toll which can be imposed at Dunham Bridge), the tolls recoverable in respect of traffic using Dunham Bridge may be up to the amounts allowed by the Act of 1830;

(7) It is expedient that the other provisions of this Act be enacted:

(8) The objects of this Act cannot be attained without the authority of Parliament:

(9) A plan showing the lands which are to be vested under the authority of this Act and the exchange land, and a book of reference to that plan containing the names of the occupiers and (so far as ascertainable) the owers of those lands, has been deposited in the office of the Clerk of the Parliaments and in the Private Bill Office of the House of Commons and with the Chief Executive of Lincolnshire County Council, which plan is in this Act referred to as "the deposited plan":

May it therefore please Your Majesty that it may be enacted, and be it enacted, by the Queen's most Excellent Majesty, by and with the advice and consent of the Lords Spiritual and Temporal, and Commons, in this present Parliament assembled, and by the authority of the same, as follows:—

PART I

PRELIMINARY

Short title

1. This Act may be cited as the Dunham Bridge (Amendment) Act 1994.

Interpretation

2.—(1) In this Act, unless otherwise expressly provided or the context otherwise requires—

"the Act of 1830" means the Act 11 Geo. 4 c. lxvi;
"the Act of 1845" means the Companies Clauses Consolidation Act 1845;
"the Act of 1863" means the Companies Clauses Act 1863;
"the appointed day" means such day as the Company may appoint for the purposes of section 51 of this Act;
"the Company" means the Dunham Bridge Company;
"Dunham Bridge" means the bridge of the Company authorised by the Act of 1830 together with the approaches thereto extending on either side of the river Trent for a distance of 180 yards from the centre of the river and all toll booths or other toll collection facilities constructed on the said bridge or approaches;
"the registered company" means such company, registered under the Companies Act 1985, as may be formed by the Company under section 50 (Formation of registered company) of this Act.
"share" means share in the capital of the Company and includes stock except where a distinction between stock and shares is expressed or implied; and "share capital" shall be construed accordingly;
"the undertaking" means the undertaking of the Company, or so much of the undertaking of any successor as comprises Dunham Bridge and any alteration or renewal thereof, and includes all the lands, easements, rights, signals, offices and other assets of whatever description for the time being held or used by the Company, or such successor, in connection with Dunham Bridge.

(2) For the purposes of this Act a special resolution of the Company means a resolution passed by a majority of not less than three quarters of such of the members of the Company as (being entitled to do so) vote (whether in person or by proxy) at a meeting of the Company of which not less than 21 days' notice, specifying the intention to propose the resolution, has been given.

PART II

CONSTITUTION OF COMPANY

Company to continue

3. Notwithstanding the repeals effected by section 61 (Repeals and consequential amendments) of this Act the Company shall remain incorporated with the same name and, subject to section 21 (Missing shareholders) of this Act, the same share capital as immediately before the coming into force of this Act, but the affairs of the Company shall henceforth be managed in accordance with the provisions of this Act and accordingly—

(a) the existing shares of the Company shall, subject to the said section 21, remain vested in the same persons as they were immediately before the coming into force of this Act but shall be deemed to have been issued under the provisions of this Act and any rights and liabilities previously attaching to those shares shall, so far as they are inconsistent with the provisions of this Act, cease to have effect;

(b) those persons who comprised the Committee of Management of the Company immediately before the coming into force of this Act are hereby appointed the directors of the Company for the purposes of this Act;

(c) all other officers of the Company shall continue in office as if they had been appointed by the directors of the Company under this Act until they are removed therefrom in accordance with the provisions of this Act;

(d) things done by the Company under the Act of 1830 shall be deemed to have been done under the equivalent provision of this Act:

Provided that, subject to paragraphs (b) and (c) above, nothing in this Part shall affect the rights and liabilities of the Company in relation to any person who is not a member of the Company in respect of anything done before the coming into force of this Act.

Incorporation of enactments

4.—(1) Subject to the provisions of this Part the following enactments are incorporated with this Act:—

(a) the Act of 1845, except sections 56 to 60 (which related to the conversion of borrowed money into capital), section 80 (which relates to the manner of ascertaining a majority of votes), sections 85 and 86 (which relate to the qualifications and interests of directors), sections 101 to 119 (which relate to auditors and accounts), sections 124 to 127 (which relate to byelaws) and sections 142 to 156 (which relate to recovery of damages and penalties);

(b) Part I (relating to cancellation and surrender of shares), Part II (relating to additional capital), except the provisions thereof which limit the rate of dividend or interest on preference capital, and Part III (relating to debenture stock) of the Act of 1863 except section 34 thereof:

Provided that—

(i) section 90 of the Act of 1845 (which relates to the powers of the directors), as so incorporated, shall have effect as if at the end thereof there were added the following sentence: "A resolution passed at any such general meeting shall require a majority of not less than three quarters of such of the members of the Company as (being entitled to do so) vote (whether in person or by proxy) at the meeting";

(ii) section 98 of the Act of 1845 (which requires proceedings to be entered in books), as so incorporated, shall have effect as if after the words "shall be signed by the chairman of such meeting" there were inserted the words "or of the next succeeding meeting";

(iii) section 14 of the Act of 1863 (which relates to dividends on preference capital), as so incorporated, shall have effect as if—

(A) after the words "each year" there were inserted the words "or out of the unappropriated profits from previous years or partly out of the one and partly out of the other"; and

(B) before the words "profits available" there were inserted the word "such";

(iv) section 122 of the Act of 1845 (which authorises the creation of a contingency fund), as so incorporated, shall have effect as if for the words from "as they" to the end of the section there were substituted the words "by way of reserve as they may think proper, and may divide the balance only among the shareholders";

(v) section 22 of the Act of 1863 (which contains regulations as to the creation and issue of debenture stock), as so incorporated, shall have effect as if the words "and to the same amount as" were omitted.

(2) In the construction of the enactments so incorporated with this Act the expression "the company" shall mean the Company.

(3) Nothing in this section affects the operation of section 718 of the Companies Act 1985 (which applies certain provisions of that Act to unregistered companies).

Share capital

5.—(1) The Company may from time to time by ordinary resolution authorise any of the alterations in the share capital of the Company mentioned in subsection (2) below.

(2) The alterations referred to in subsection (1) above are—

(a) any increase in the share capital of the Company by such sum to be divided into shares of such amount as the resolution prescribes;

(b) any consolidation and division of the share capital into shares of a greater nominal value;

(c) any sub-division of the share capital into shares of a smaller nominal value; and

(d) any cancellation of shares (being shares which, at the date of the passing of the resolution, have not been taken up or agreed to be taken up) together with the diminution of the share capital by the amount of the shares so cancelled.

(3) Any resolution under subsection (1) above shall include provision as to the incidents attaching to the shares to which it relates and in particular shall, whenever appropriate, make provision as to the relative rights attaching on the one hand to those shares and on the other to the remaining shares in the Company.

(4) If on an alteration of the sort mentioned in subsection (2)(b) or (c) above any fractions arise, they shall be dealt with in such way as the directors may determine including by way of sale of shares representing those fractions, the proceeds of such sale being distributed pro rata among those members of the Company who would otherwise have been entitled to the fractions.

Loan capital and borrowing powers

6. Subject to and in accordance with the provisions of this Act, the Company may from time to time raise by the creation and issue of loan capital or by borrowing, whether secured or unsecured, such sums as they may require for the purposes of the undertaking.

Purchase of own shares

7.—(1) The Company may, in accordance with the provisions of this section, purchase its own shares of any class (including any redeemable shares) at any price (whether at par or above or below par) and so that any shares to be so purchased may be selected in any manner whatsoever.

(2) The powers of this section—

(a) are subject to any relevant special rights attached to any class of shares; and

(b) shall be exercised in accordance with the provisions of Chapter VII of Part V of the Companies Act 1985 (which relate to the purchase of its own shares by a company registered under that Act).

(3) In its application to the Company the said Chapter VII shall have effect as if—

(a) reference to any account or reserve maintained by the Company included any equivalent account or reserve maintained by the Company pursuant to this Act;

(b) reference to any special resolution were to a special resolution of the Company as defined in section 2 (2) of this Act; and

(c) the Company were a private company limited by shares and registered under the said Act of 1985.

Power to reduce capital

8.—(1) The Company may, in accordance with the provisions of this section, by special resolution reduce its share capital, any capital redemption reserve and any share premium account in any way.

(2) The powers of this section shall be exercised in accordance with the provisions of Chapter IV of Part V of the Companies Act 1985 (which relate to the reduction of the share capital of companies registered under that Act).

Investment powers

9. The Company may (whether in the name of the Company or of any nominee for the Company) invest and deal with the monies of the Company not immediately required for the purposes of the undertaking in such manner as may from time to time be determined and may (whether in the name of the Company or of such nominee) hold or otherwise deal with any investments so made.

General powers of Company

10. In addition to powers conferred on the Company by any enactment (including this Act), the Company may do all such things as in the opinion of the directors are incidental to, or conducive to the attainment of, the profitable operation of the undertaking.

Debenture stock

11. Notwithstanding anything contained in the provisions of Part III of the Act of 1863, the interest on all debenture stock and on all mortgages at any time after the passing of this Act created and issued or granted by the Company under this or any subsequent Act shall, subject to the provisions of any subsequent Act, rank pari passu (without respect to the dates of the securities or of the Acts of Parliament or resolutions by which the stock and mortgages were authorised) and shall have priority over all principal monies secured by such mortgages. Notice of the effect of this enactment shall be endorsed on all mortgages and certificates of debenture stock issued after the passing of this Act.

Redeemable stock

12.—(1) The directors may from time to time by virtue of this Act and without further or other sanction or authority issue, so as to be redeemable at such times and in such manner and on and subject to such terms and conditions and to bear dividends or interest at such rate or rates as the directors at the time of the issue thereof determine, any preference shares or debenture stock (all of which are in this section referred to as and included in the expression "stock") created by the Company under the powers conferred by this Act.

(2) There shall be stated on each certificate of any such stock the time or times at which and the manner in which and the terms and conditions on and subject to which such stock is to be redeemed.

(3) If it is so provided in the said terms and conditions the Company may—

(a) call in and pay off the stock or any part thereof at any time before the date fixed for redemption; and

(b) redeem the stock or any part thereof either by paying off the stock or by issuing to the holder of any stock (subject to his consent) other stock in substitution therefor.

(4) For the purpose of providing money for paying off the stock or for the purpose of providing substituted stock, the Company may create and the directors may issue other stock (either redeemable or irredeemable) or the directors may re-issue any stock originally created and issued as aforesaid.

(5) The Company shall not redeem out of revenue any stock created and issued as aforesaid.

Interim dividends

13. The directors may in any year without calling a meeting of the Company for the purpose declare and pay an interim half-yearly dividend.

Incidents of new capital

14. Any additional capital raised under the powers of this Act and the shares therein and the holders thereof respectively shall (except as may be otherwise expressly provided by the resolution creating the same) be subject and entitled to the same powers, provisions, liabilities, rights, privileges and incidents whatsoever in all respects as if that capital were part of the capital of the Company as existing immediately before the creation of the additional capital, of the same class or description and as if the new shares were shares in that previously existing capital. The additional capital shall form part of the capital of the Company.

Application of premiums

15. Any sum of money which may arise from the issue of any shares under the provisions of this Act by way of premium after deducting therefrom the expenses of and incident to such issue shall not be considered as profits of the Company but shall be expended only on purposes to which capital is properly applicable or in paying off money borrowed or owing on mortgage or redeemable debenture stock by the Company and shall not be considered as part of the capital of the Company entitled to dividend.

Priority of mortgages and debenture stock

16. All monies raised or to be raised by the Company on mortgage or by debenture stock under the Act of 1830 or this Act shall have priority against the Company and the property from time to time of the Company over all other claims on account of any debts incurred or engagements entered into by them after the passing of this Act.

Appointment of receiver

17. The mortgagees of the Company may enforce payment of arrears of interest or principal, or principal and interest, due on their mortgages by the appointment of a receiver:

Provided that in order to authorise the appointment of a receiver in respect of arrears of principal the amount owing to the mortgagees by whom the application for a receiver is made shall not be less than ten thousand pounds.

Receipt in case of persons not sui juris

18. If any money is payable to a shareholder, debenture stockholder or mortgagee, being a minor or a person of unsound mind, the receipt of his guardian, receiver or duly appointed attorney or of the Court of Protection (as the case may be) shall be a sufficient discharge to the Company.

Company not bound to regard trusts

19. The Company shall not be bound to see to the execution of any trust, whether express, implied or constructive, to which any shares, debenture stock or mortgage may be subject and the provisions of section 20 of the Act of 1845 (which provides that the Company shall not be bound to regard trusts), shall extend and apply to any stock, debenture stock or mortgage of the Company as if the same were shares in the capital of the Company.

Joint holders

20.—(1) Notwithstanding anything in the Act of 1845, where several persons are jointly entitled to and registered as holders of any shares, any one of those persons may vote at any meeting at which holders of shares of the same class are entitled to vote either personally or by proxy in respect of the shares as if he were solely entitled thereto; but if more than one of the joint holders be present at any meeting personally or by proxy that one of the said persons so present whose name stands first on the register in respect of the shares shall alone be entitled to vote in respect thereof.

(2) For the purposes of this section, executors or administrators of a deceased member in whose name any share in the capital of the Company stands shall be deemed joint holders thereof.

Missing shareholders

21.—(1) In this section "the missing shareholders" means the shareholders of the Company named in column (1) of Schedule 1 to this Act and registered as shareholders of the Company on the dates specified in column (2) of that Schedule and "the notification period" means the period commencing on the passing of this Act and terminating on a date 56 days after the first publication of the newspaper notice referred to in subsection (2) below.

(2) As soon as reasonably practicable following the passing of this Act the Company shall publish in each of two successive weeks in a local newspaper circulating in the county of Nottinghamshire and a local newspaper circulating in the county of Lincolnshire a notice containing the names and addresses of the missing shareholders and an explanation of the effect of this section.

(3) Any person may at any time before the expiry of the notification period serve written notice on the Company claiming that he is entitled to the interest of one or more of the missing shareholders in any shares and any such notice shall be accompanied by a £50 deposit payable to the Company which shall be returned to the claimant in the event that he succeeds in establishing his claim.

(4) If any person, having duly served notice on the Company and paid a deposit in accordance with subsection (3) above within the notification period, establishes, within a further period of 56 days commencing on the expiry of the notification period, to the satisfaction of the Company in accordance with the provisions of the Act of 1845 that the interest of one or more of the missing shareholders in any shares has been transmitted to him the Company shall, subject to subsection (5) below, enter the name of such person in the register of shareholders and pay him so much of the arrears of dividend for the immediately preceding six years (which shall bear no interest) as are owing to him in respect of the shares to which he is entitled:

Provided that if it is necessary for a claimant to make any application for the purpose of establishing his claim to any shares the period for establishment of his claim shall be extended until the expiry of 30 days after proceedings on that application (including any proceedings on or in consequence of an appeal) have been determined and any time for appealing or further appealing has expired, or, as the case may be, until that application is abandoned or withdrawn.

(5) Before entering any claimant in the register of shareholders or paying him any arrears of dividends the Company may require him to provide an indemnity in respect of any subsequent claims made against the Company in respect of that registration or that payment.

(6) Any shares of the missing shareholders in respect of which notice and a deposit is not received in accordance with subsection (3) above before the expiry of the notification period, or in respect of which a claim is not established to the satisfaction of the company in accordance with subsection (4) above before the expiry of the further period referred to in that subsection, or in respect of which the claimant refuses to provide an indemnity in accordance with subsection (5) above, shall be cancelled and all rights and liabilities in, or arising from any entitlement to, those shares shall be extinguished.

(7) A sum equivalent to the nominal value of such shares as are cancelled under subsection (6) above shall be held by the Company and applied only

for the purposes for which premiums may be applied under section 15 (Application of premiums) of this Act.

Indemnity before issue of substituted certificates, etc

22. Notwithstanding anything in section 13 of the Act of 1845, the Company shall not be under any obligation to issue a new debenture or mortgage bond or a new certificate of any shares or debenture stock or a new warrant in respect of interest or dividend in lieu of any debenture, bond, certificate or warrant lost or destroyed, or alleged to be lost or destroyed, until they have received from the person to whom such new debenture, bond, certificate or warrant is to be issued such indemnity as the directors may require against any and every claim or expense which may be made against the Company or which the Company may incur in respect of such lost or destroyed debenture, bond, certificate or warrant or the debenture, mortgage, shares, debenture stock, dividend or interest represented thereby.

Register of transfers

23. Notwithstanding anything in sections 15 and 47 of the Act of 1845 and section 28 of the Act of 1863, the Company shall not be under any obligation to keep registers of transfers of ordinary shares, preference shares, debenture stock and mortgages respectively so long as the Company in lieu of those registers shall keep a file of all transfers and evidences of transmission of any ordinary shares, preference shares, debenture stock or mortgages of the Company which are sent to them for registration in accordance with the provisions of those Acts.

Closing of transfer books

24.—(1) The directors may close the register of transfers of ordinary shares and preference shares of any class and the register of transfers of debenture stock or mortgages for any time or times not exceeding in the case of each such register thirty days in each year and the directors may in any such case fix a day for the closing of any register which they are authorised to close under the provisions of this section.

(2) Any transfer of any ordinary shares, preference shares or debenture stock or mortgages lodged for registration with the Company after the register of transfers relating to shares, debenture stock or mortgages of the same class has been so closed and before the next date of payment of any dividend, interim dividend or interest, as the case may be, thereon shall as between the Company and the persons claiming under the transfer (but not otherwise) be considered as made subsequently to the payment of such dividend, interim dividend or interest.

(3) In this section the expression "register of transfers" includes any file of transfers kept by the Company in lieu of any such register.

Register of shareholders and shareholders' address book

25.—(1) Notwithstanding anything in sections 9, 10 and 63 of the Act of 1845, the Company shall not be under any obligation—
- (a) to keep separately a register of shareholders and a shareholders' address book; or
- (b) to authenticate by the affixing of their common seal or otherwise the register of shareholders or any register which the Company may keep in lieu thereof under the powers of this section.

(2) If the Company do not keep separately a register of shareholders and a shareholder's address book they shall in lieu thereof keep one register only containing such particulars as are required by the said Act to be entered in the register of shareholders and the shareholders' address book respectively.

Substitution of card index for shareholders' address book

26. Notwithstanding anything in section 10 of the Act of 1845, the Company may substitute for the shareholdes' address book provided under that section, or for the portion of any register which the Company may keep under section 25 (Register of shareholders and shareholders' address book) of this Act, containing such particulars as are required by the said Act of 1845 to be entered in the shareholders' address book, a card or other index (of a type to be approved by the auditors of the Company) containing the names and addresses of the several shareholders of the undertakers.

Ordinary meetings

27. Notwithstanding anything in section 66 of the Act of 1845, the ordinary general meeting of the Company shall be held in each year in the month of September or at such other time as the directors may appoint.

Quorum for general meetings

28. The quorum of every general meeting of the Company, whether ordinary or extraordinary, shall be at least six shareholders present in person or by proxy holding in the aggregate not less than twenty-five per cent. of the capital of the Company.

Extraordinary meetings

29. The number of shareholders on whose requisition an extraordinary meeting of the Company may be required to be convened shall be not less than fifteen holding in the aggregate not less than one hundred shares of £50 each.

Notice of meetings

30. Notwithstanding anything in section 71 of the Act of 1845, notice of all meetings of the Company (whether ordinary or extraordinary) may (if the directors so determine) be given by letter sent by ordinary post to each shareholder instead of by public advertisement:

Provided that the letters giving the notice shall be directed to the registered address or other known address of each shareholder and posted not later than seven clear days before the date of the meeting. In proving that any such notice has been given it shall be sufficient to prove that the letter containing the notice was properly addressed and posted by ordinary first class post as a prepaid letter not later than the time hereby prescribed.

Notices, etc., to shareholders abroad

31. Members of the Company who have no registered address within the United Kingdom shall not be entitled to receive notices of meetings and accounts unless they shall have supplied to the Company an address within the United Kingdom for the giving of notices to them.

Voting rights

32. At all meetings of the Company every holder of ordinary shares shall be entitled to one vote for each share held by him.

Proof of majority of votes only required when poll demanded

33. At any meeting of the Company a majority of votes shall only be required to be proved if a poll be demanded at the meeting, and if a poll be not demanded at the meeting then a declaration by the chairman that the resolution has been carried and an entry to that effect in the book of proceedings of the Company shall be sufficient and conclusive evidence of the fact without proof of the number or proportion of votes recorded in favour of or against the resolution.

Voting at general meetings

34. Where a body corporate, being a holder of ordinary or preference capital to which voting rights are attached, is present at a meeting of the Company by a proxy who is not a holder of capital of the Company, such proxy shall be entitled to vote for such body on a show of hands.

Appointment of proxies

35. Notwithstanding anything in section 76 of the Act of 1845, the attorney of any member duly authorised in writing or, in case of a corporation, an officer or attorney so authorised may appoint a proxy to vote for and on behalf of the member and for that purpose may execute on behalf of the member the necessary form of proxy.

Number of directors

36. The number of directors shall be eight but the Company may at any time and from time to time vary the number provided that the number be not at any time more than sixteen nor less than four.

Powers of directors

37.—(1) In addition to the powers of the directors under section 95 of the Act of 1845 (which authorises the appointment of committees exercising powers of the directors) the directors may delegate any of their powers to any director holding executive office, including any managing director appointed pursuant to section 39 (Appointment of managing director) of this Act.

(2) Any delegation under subsection (1) above may be made subject to such conditions as the directors may think fit and may from time to time be revoked, withdrawn, altered or varied.

(3) The directors may co-opt on to any committee appointed under the said section 95 persons other than directors (not exceeding half the total membership of the committee) who may enjoy voting rights in the committee:

Provided that a resolution of any such committee shall not be effective unless a majority of thosse present at the meeting of the committee at which the resolution is passed are directors.

(4) Subject to such conditions as may be imposed under subsection (2) above any recipient of delegated powers under the said section 95 or subsection (1) above may sub-delegate any of those powers to one or more directors (whether or not acting as a committee) or to any employee or agent of the Company.

Quorum of meeting of directors

38. A quorum of a meeting of directors shall be four.

Appointment of managing director

39.—(1) The directors may appoint one or more of their body to be managing director or managing directors of the Company either for a fixed term or without any limitation as to time and may remove or dismiss him or them from office and appoint another or others in his or their place or places.

(2) A managing director shall not while holding that office be subject to retirement by rotation and shall not be taken into account in determining the rotation of retirement of directors but if he ceases to hold the office of direc-

tor from any other cause he shall ipso facto immediately cease to be a managing director.

(3) The remuneration of a manging director shall from time to time be fixed by the directors and may be by way of salary or commission or participation in profits or by any or all of those modes.

Power of directors to determine remuneration of secretary

40. In addition to the powers which the directors may exercise under the Act of 1845, the Act of 1863 or otherwise, they may from time to time determine the remuneration of the secretary of the Company.

Vacation of office of director

41. If any director shall be made bankrupt or shall become of unsound mind the office of such director shall become vacant and thenceforth he shall cease from voting or acting as a director.

Directors holding office under or contracting with Company

42.—(1)(a) In the case of a director being or becoming interested in any contract with the Company, whether such interest arises before or after his appointment as a director, the nature of his interest in the contract shall be disclosed by him at the meeting of the directors at which the contract is decided upon if his interest then exists or in any other case at the first meeting of the directors after the acquisition of his interest or after his appointment.

(b) No director shall as a director vote in respect of any such contract and if he does so vote his vote shall not be counted, but this prohibition shall not apply to any contract by or on behalf of the Company to give to the directors or any of them any security by way of indemnity.

(2) For the purposes of subsection (1)(a) above, a general notice given to the directors by one of them to the effect that he is a member of a specified company or firm and is to be regarded as interested in any contract which may after the date of the notice be made with that company or firm shall be deemed to be a sufficient declaration of interest in relation to any contract so made.

Alteration of constitution of Company

43.—(1) The Secretary of State may on the application of the Company by order authorise the alteration of the constitution of the Company and any such order may for that purpose add to, amend, repeal or replace any provision—

(a) incorporated by subsection (1) of section 4 (Incorporation of enactments) of this Act; or

(b) of this Part; or

(c) of the Act of 1830.

(2) Application for an order under this section shall be authorised by a special resolution of the Company and shall be accompanied by a draft of the order which the Company desire the Secretary of State to make.

(3) The Secretary of State may make an order in the terms of the draft submitted to him or in those terms as modified in such manner as he thinks fit.

(4) The power to make orders under this section shall be exercisable by statutory instrument.

PART III

LANDS

Vesting of parish land and exchange land

44.—(1) In this section—

"the Council" means the Newton-on-Trent parish council;

"the exchange land" means plot number 2 on the deposited plan;
"the highway land" means plot number 3 on the deposited plan;
"the parish land" means plot number 1 on the deposited plan;
"the vesting day" means such day as the Company, or after the appointed day the registered company, may, after either has acquired an unencumbered freehold interest in the exchange land, appoint for the purposes of subsection (2) of this section.

(2) On the vesting day—

(a) the highway land and the parish land shall vest in the Company (or, if the vesting day is not earlier than the appointed day, the registered company) and all such land shall thereupon be discharged from all rights, interests, restrictions, trusts and incidents to which it was previously subject; and

(b) the exchange land shall vest in the Council and shall be held by them subject to such public or customary rights as attached to the parish land immediately before the vesting day.

(3) Any person who suffers loss by reason of the extinguishment under this section of any private right or interest other than a customary right shall be entitled to be paid compensation by the Company, or in the event of the dissolution of the Company in accordance with section 53 (Dissolution of Company) of this Act the registered company, the amount of such compensation to be determined in case of dispute by the Lands Tribunal.

Extended toll plaza to form part of Dunham Bridge

45.—(1) In this section "the extended toll plaza" means such structures, roads and other works as are constructed on the land marked "Site of extended toll plaza" on the deposited plan, for the purposes specified in subsection (2) below, in accordance with any planning consent from time to time in force in relation to that land.

(2) The purposes referred to in subsection (1) above are the purposes of and in connection with the collection of tolls under the Act of 1830 and this Act.

(3) Following completion of any part of the extended toll plaza that part shall, for so long as it is required for the purposes specified in subsection (2) above, be deemed to form part of Dunham Bridge and the Act of 1830 and this Act and all other enactments relating to Dunham Bridge shall apply to that part accordingly.

PART IV

TOLLS, ETC.

Tolls

46.—(1) Subject to section 6 of the Transport Charges &c. (Miscellaneous Provisions) Act 1954 (revision of charges), but notwithstanding anything in section 1 of the Locomotive Act 1861 the tolls recoverable from users of Dunham Bridge under the Act of 1830 shall be those specified in Schedule 2 to this Act.

(2) In section 69 (Tolls to be taken) of the Act of 1830—

(a) for the words "Horses, Beasts, Cattle, Carriages, or Foot Passengers" there shall be substituted the word "vehicle"; and

(b) after the words "not exceeding the" there shall be inserted the words "tolls recoverable in accordance with section 46 (Tolls) of the Dunham Bridge (Amendment) Act 1994".

Modification of Transport Charges &c. (Miscellaneous Provisions) Act 1954

47. In its application to the undertaking section 6(3) of the Transport Charges &c. (Miscellaneous Provisions) Act 1954 (revision of charges) shall have effect as if for the reference to the paid up share capital of the undertaking there were substituted a reference to any amounts invested in the undertaking by the Dunham Bridge Company and any successor company.

Toll booths

48.—(1) For the avoidance of doubt, in relation to any existing toll booth section 68 (Power to erect Toll Gates, &c.) of the Act of 1830 has effect as if the reference therein to the bridge were a reference to Dunham Bridge as defined in this Act.

(2) There shall no longer be a requirement to affix a table of tolls to each toll house or toll gate or to issue tickets to persons paying tolls and sections 75, 76 and 78 of the Act of 1830 shall accordingly cease to have effect.

Toll collectors

49. In the proviso (Penalty on obstructing Collectors) to section 90 (For preventing Toll Collectors from misbehaving) of the Act of 1830, for the words "assault, obstruct, hinder or molest" there shall be substituted the words "intentionally obstruct or hinder".

PART V

TRANSFER OF UNDERTAKING, ETC.

Formation of registered company

50.—(1) The Company may form an incorporated company with limited liability under the Companies Act 1985 for the purpose of effecting the transfer authorised by section 51 (Transfer of undertaking) of this Act.

(2) All costs, charges and expenses of and incidental to the formation of the registered company shall be paid by the Company and (with the exception of the cost of the subscription shares, which shall be paid out of capital) may in whole or in part be defrayed out of revenue.

Transfer of undertaking

51.—(1) The Company may by special resolution appoint a day on which the undertaking is transferred to the registered company and there shall thereupon vest in the registered company—

    (a) all that property vested in the Company which immediately before the appointed day was held by them;

    (b) subject to section 58 (Repeals for the purpose of Part V) of this Act, all rights, liabilities and obligations of the Company subsisting immediately before the appointed day.

(2) Not less than 28 days before the appointed day the Company shall publish in the London Gazette and in a local newspaper circulating in the district of Bassetlaw and a local newspaper circulating in the district of West Lindsey a notice containing a copy of the special resolution and explaining its effect.

Receipt of shares in Company

52. On or as soon as practicable after the appointed day each person registered immediately before the appointed day as a holder of shares in the Company shall receive in substitution therefor shares in the registered company, equal in amount to, and, so far as is applicable, having the same rights, privileges, liabilities and incidents as, his shares in the Company.

Dissolution of Company

53. On the appointed day the Company shall be dissolved.

Final accounts of Company

54.—(1) The accounts of the Company shall be made up to the appointed day and shall be audited by an auditor appointed by the Company, being a person eligible for appointment as a company auditor by virtue of section 25 of the Companies Act 1989.

(2) The auditor's fee shall be payable by the registered company.

(3) Any sum due from any person to the Company and certified by the auditor to be so due shall be paid to the registered company.

Books, etc., to remain evidence

55. All books and documents which, if this Act had not been passed, would have been evidence in respect of any matter for or against the Company shall be admissible in respect of that matter for or against the registered company.

Saving of agreements, etc.

56. All sales, conveyances, leases, grants, assurances, deeds, contracts, bonds, agreements, notices and demands affecting the undertaking and in force immediately before the appointed day shall on and from that day be as binding and of as full force and effect in every respect and may be enforced as fully and effectively against or in favour of the registered company as if the registered company were a party thereto or bound thereby or entitled to the benefit thereof.

Pending actions not to abate

57. Any action, arbitration or proceeding and any cause of action, arbitration or proceeding pending or existing immediately before the appointed day by or against or in favour of the Company in relation to the undertaking shall not abate or be discontinued or be in anywise prejudicially affected by the transfer to the registered company of the undertaking or by anything in this Act, but it may be continued, prosecuted and enforced by, against or in favour of the registered company as and when it might have been continued, prosecuted and enforced by, against or in favour of the Company if this Act had not been passed, but not further or otherwise.

Repeals for the purpose of Part V

58. On the appointed day sections 1 and 32 of the Act of 1830 and Part II of this Act shall be repealed and the remaining provisions of the Act of 1830 shall have effect as if for references to the Company there were substituted references to the registered company.

PART VI

MISCELLANEOUS AND GENERAL

Stopping up, etc., of Dunham Bridge: discontinuance of undertaking

59.—(1) If any order is made under any enactment for the stopping up of the highway over Dunham Bridge the Secretary of State may on the application of the Company, or in the event of the dissolution of the Company in accordance with section 53 (Dissolution of Company) of this Act the registered company, by order provide for the discontinuance of the undertaking, including provision for the repeal or amendment of the Act of 1830 or this Act (if the order is made on the application of the Company) for the dissolution of the Company.

(2) Application for an order under this section shall be authorised by a special resolution of the Company, or as the case may be the registered company, and shall be accompanied by a draft of the order which it is desired that the Secretary of State should make.

(3) The Secretary of State may make an order in the terms of the draft submitted to him or in those terms as modified in such manner as he thinks fit.

(4) The power to make orders under this section shall be exercisable by statutory instrument.

Amendment of section 2 of Act of 1830

60. In section 2 (Power to build the Bridge, &c.) of the Act of 1830 after the word "Bridge" in the last place where it appears there shall be inserted the words "works and approaches".

Repeals and consequential amendments

61.—(1) Subject to the provisions of section 3 (Company to continue) of this Act, so much of the Act of 1830 as is specified in column (3) of Part I of Schedule 3 to this Act (which includes provisions which are spent, obsolete or unnecessary) is hereby repealed.

(2) The consequential amendments of the Act of 1830 specified in Part II of Schedule 3 to this Act shall have effect.

Costs of Act

62. The costs, charges and expenses preliminary to, and of and incidental to, the preparing and passing of this Act shall be paid by the Company and may in whole or in part be defrayed out of revenue.

SCHEDULES

Section 21   SCHEDULE 1

MISSING SHAREHOLDERS

Name of shareholder	Date registered as shareholder
J. T. W. Bartholomew	29.5.1830
Edwd. Baxter	29.5.1830
St Jn. Cartwright	29.5.1830
Jas. Chambers	29.5.1830
John Clarke	29.5.1830
John Clater	29.5.1830
Benjn. Eddison Senior	29.5.1830
Jn. Fardell	29.5.1830
Thomas Fisher	29.5.1830
Saml. Fras. Flower	29.5.1830
Thomas Fox	29.5.1830
Executors of Jep^h. Greesham	29.5.1830
Wm. Quible Hall	29.5.1830
Executors of the Rev. Wm. Hett	21.11.1833
John Holmes	29.5.1830
Jn. Lesiter	29.5.1830

Name of shareholder	Date registered as shareholder
Fras. Marriott	29.5.1830
Sarah Ann Nelson	18.9.1834
Executors of John Nelson	18.9.1834
Thos. Nettleship	29.5.1830
Thomas Newton	29.5.1830
Jn. Parkinson	29.5.1830
William Scorah	29.5.1830
James Scott	29.5.1830
Robt. Sharpe	29.5.1830
Step^n. Camm. Short	29.5.1830
Francis Sissons	29.5.1830
William Smith	16.4.1831
Jno. Smith (Worksop)	29.5.1830
William Spencer	29.5.1830
Miss Sophia Swan	29.5.1830
Mrs Swan	29.5.1830
Richard Turner	29.5.1830
Jno. Smith (Retford)	29.5.1830

Section 46   SCHEDULE 2

LEVEL OF TOLLS

Car, or van under 10 cwt		20p
Car and 2-wheel trailer		30p
Tri-car		15p
Motorcycle		10p
Lorry	4 wheels	20p
Vans over 10 cwt	6 wheels	30p
or Coach	8 wheels	40p
Every extra pair of wheels (any vehicle)		10p

Section 61(1)   SCHEDULE 3

PART I

REPEALS

Chapter (1)	Title (2)	Extent of repeal (3)
11 Geo. 4 & 1 Will. 4 c. lxvi (1830)	An Act for building a Bridge over the River Trent, from Dunham in the County of Nottingham, to the opposite Shore, in the County of Lincoln.	In Section 1, the words "in manner by this Act directed" in both places where they appear and the words "without incurring any of the Penalties or Forfeitures of the Statutes of Mortmain". Section 5. In section 7, the words "or to provide a proper and convenient Ferry and Boats and Barges" and the words "or Ferry". Sections 9 to 31. In section 32 the words "or joint stock" in both places where they appear and the words from "; and every Body Politic," to the end of the section.

Chapter (1)	Title (2)	Extent of repeal (3)
		Sections 33 to 67. In section 69, the words "as soon as the said Bridge shall be made fit for the Passage of Carriages, Horses, Cattle, and Passengers," the words "respective sums following; (that is to say,)" and the list of tolls. Sections 70 to 76. In section 77 the words "in pursuance of this Act". Section 78. Section 80. In section 81 the words from "or for any Horse, Beast, Cattle, or Carriage travelling with Vagrants" to "any legal Warrant" and the words from "or for any Coach," to "or be concluded;". Section 90, except the proviso. Section 91. In section 92 the words from "shall wilfully or maliciously damage" to "may be injured, or" and the words from "and shall also pay and defray" to the end of the section. Sections 93 to 107.

Section 61(2)   Part II

CONSEQUENTIAL AMENDMENTS

1. In section 32 (The Money to be divided into Shares), for the words "said Capital" there shall be substituted the words "Capital of the said Company".

2. In section 92 (For preventing wilful Damage to the Bridge, &c.) for the words "the same" there shall be substituted the words "the Bridge".

INDEX

LONDON UNDERGROUND (GREEN PARK) ACT 1994

(1994 c. ix)

ARRANGEMENT OF SECTIONS

PART I

PRELIMINARY

An Act to empower London Underground Limited, for safety purposes and the relief of passenger congestion, to construct works to improve the underground station at Green Park and to acquire lands; and for connected purposes. [5th July 1994]

PARLIAMENTARY DEBATES
   The Bill's progress through Parliament was as follows:
   House of Commons: First Reading, January 22, 1992; Suspended, March 12, 1992; Second Reading, November 5, 1992; Bill Committed, November 12, 1992; Suspended, October 28, 1993; Opposed Bill Committee, March 2 to December 7, 1993; Bill Amended by Committee, December 15, 1994; Third Reading, January 12, 1994; Lord's Amendments, July 5, 1994.

House of Lords: First Reading, January 12, 1994; Second Reading, February 7, 1994; Bill Committed, February 7, 1994; Opposed Bill Committee, May 16, 1994; Unopposed Committee, June 9, 1994; Third Reading, June 27, 1994.

INTRODUCTION

London Regional Transport ("the Corporation") are charged with providing or securing the provision of public passenger transport services for Greater London. In doing so they must give due consideration to the transport needs of the area and efficiency, economy and safety. London Underground, which is a wholly owned subsidiary of the Corporation is responsible for operating that part of the system. Various works at Green Park station have been identified as necessary to improve safety and relieve passenger congestion. This Act makes provision to ensure that the necessary acquisition of and access to lands can be effected in order to carry out the necessary works, and that said works can be undertaken.

WHEREAS—

(1) By the London Regional Transport Act 1984 the London Transport Executive which were established by the Transport (London) Act 1969 were reconstituted on 29th June 1984 under the name of London Regional Transport (in this Act referred to as "the Corporation"):

(2) It is the general duty of the Corporation under the said Act of 1984, in accordance with principles from time to time approved by the Secretary of State and in conjunction with the British Railways Board, to provide or secure the provision of public passenger transport services for Greater London, and in carrying out that duty the Corporation is to have due regard to (a) the transport needs for the time being of Greater London and (b) efficiency, economy and safety of operation:

(3) London Underground Limited (in this Act referred to as "the Company") were incorporated as a wholly-owned subsidiary of the Corporation by virtue of the said Act of 1984 and the Companies Acts 1948 to 1981 (inter alia) to acquire and take over, as a going concern, that part of the undertaking of the Corporation responsible for operating the railway system of the Corporation (other than the Docklands Railway) and for the maintenance of such railway system and to carry on, develop and turn to account that part of that undertaking and all property and assets acquired from the Corporation in connection therewith:

(4) By the London Regional Transport Underground Railway Asset Transfer Scheme 1985 made under the provisions of section 4 (7) of the said Act of 1984 there were transferred from the Corporation to the Company all the property, rights and liabilities comprised in those parts of the Corporation's underground railway services (except as provided in the said Scheme) together with any functions under any statutory provision relating to the Corporation's underground railway:

(5) In order to improve safety and to relieve passenger congestion at the Company's Green Park station it is expedient that the Company should be empowered to construct in the city of Westminster the works authorised by this Act and to purchase or use the land in that city referred to in this Act:

(6) It is expedient that the other powers in this Act contained should be conferred on the Company as therein provided, and that the other provisions in this Act contained should be enacted:

(7) A substituted plan and substituted sections showing the lines or situations and levels of the works to be constructed under this Act, and a substituted plan of the land authorised to be purchased or used by this Act, and a substituted book of reference to such substituted plan containing the names of the owners and lessees or reputed owners and lessees and of the occupiers of the said land were duly deposited in the office of the Clerk of the Parliaments and in the Private Bill Office of the House of Commons and with the proper officer of the Westminster City Council which plan, sections and book of reference are respectively referred to in this Act as the substituted plan, the substituted sections and the substituted book of reference:

(8) The purposes of this Act could not have been effected without the authority of Parliament when the Bill for this Act was deposited:

May it therefore please Your Majesty that it may be enacted, and be it enacted, by the Queen's most Excellent Majesty, by and with the advice and consent of the Lords Spiritual and Temporal, and Commons, in this present Parliament assembled, and by the authority of the same, as follows:—

PART I

PRELIMINARY

Short title

1. This Act may be cited as the London Underground (Green Park) Act 1994.

Interpretation

2.—(1) In this Act, unless the context otherwise requires, the several words and expressions to which meanings are assigned by the enactments incorporated herewith have, in relation to the related subject-matter, the same respective meanings; and—

"the Act of 1845" means the Railways Clauses Consolidation Act 1845;
"the Act of 1963" means the London Transport Act 1963;
"the Act of 1964" means the London Transport Act 1964;
"the Act of 1965" means the London Transport Act 1965;
"the Act of 1966" means the London Transport Act 1966;
"the Act of 1969" means the London Transport Act 1969;
"the Act of 1976" means the London Transport Act 1976;
"the Act of 1981" means the London Transport Act 1981;
"the Company" means London Underground Limited;
"the limits of deviation" means the limits of deviation shown on the substituted plan; and
"the works" means the works authorised by Part II (Works, etc.) of this Act.

(2) Any reference to the London Transport Board or to the London Transport Executive in any of the provisions incorporated with this Act shall be construed as a reference to the Company.

(3) All distances, lengths and directions stated in any description of works, powers or lands, shall be construed as if the words "or thereabouts" were inserted after each such distance, length and direction.

(4) Unless the context otherwise requires, any reference in this Act to a work identified by the number of such work shall be construed as a reference to the work of that number authorised by this Act.

Incorporation of general enactments

3.—(1) The following enactments, so far as the same are applicable for the purposes and are not inconsistent with or varied by the provisions of this Act, are incorporated with and form part of this Act, and this Act shall be deemed to be the special Act for the purposes of the said incorporated enactments:—

(a) the Lands Clauses Acts, except sections 127 to 132 of the Lands Clauses Consolidation Act 1845; and
(b) the Act of 1845, except sections 7 to 9, 11 to 15, 17, 19, 20, 22, 23, 94 and 95 thereof;

(2) For the purposes of the provisions of the Act of 1845, as incorporated with this Act—

(a) the expression "the company" where used in the said incorporated provisions means the Company; and
(b) Works Nos. 4, 4A, 4B, 4C, 5 and 5A shall be deemed to be railways authorised by the special Act.

(3) Sections 18 and 21 of the Act of 1845, as incorporated with this Act, shall not extend to regulate the relations between the Company and any other person in respect of any matter or thing concerned which those relations are regulated in any respect by the provisions of—
(a) Part III of the New Roads and Street Works Act 1991; or
(b) section 42 (For protection of gas, water and electricity undertakers) of the Act of 1963, as incorporated with this Act.

PART II

WORKS, ETC.

Power to make works

4. The Company may, in the lines or situations shown on the substituted plan and according to the levels shown on the substituted sections, make and maintain in Greater London the works described in the Schedule to this Act, with all necessary works and conveniences connected therewith.

Access from Arlington Street

5. The Company may in the city of Westminster form and lay out means of access from Arlington Street at point A on the substituted plan for the purpose of constructing the works.

Power to open surface of and temporarily stop up streets

6.—(1) The Company may for the purpose of constructing the works—
(a) enter upon, open, break up and interfere with; and
(b) temporarily stop up and divert;
so much of the streets specified in subsection (3) below as is within the limits of deviation and may for any reasonable time divert the traffic therefrom and prevent all persons, other than those bona fide going to or from any land or building abutting on the street, from passing along and using the same.
(2) The Company shall provide reasonable access for persons on foot going bona fide to or from any such land or building.
(3) The streets referred to in subsection (1) above are—
In the city of Westminster—
Arlington Street;
Bennett Street;
Park Place; and
Piccadilly.

Notice of interference with streets

7. Before breaking up or otherwise interfering with any street to which the public has access in connection with the construction of any of the works, the Company shall (except in case of emergency) give not less than 14 days' notice in writing to—
(a) the London Fire and Civil Defence Authority; and
(b) the chief officer of police;
and make such arrangements with the chief officer of police as may be reasonably necessary so as to cause as little interference with the traffic in such street during the construction of such works as may be reasonably practicable.

Use of sewers, etc., for removing water

8.—(1) The Company may use for the discharge of any water pumped or found by them during the construction of the works any available stream or watercourse, or any sewer or drain of a relevant authority in or through whose area the works may be constructed or pass, and for that purpose may lay down, take up and alter conduits, pipes and other works and make any convenient connections with any such stream, watercourse, sewer or drain within the limits of deviation but—

(a) the Company shall not discharge any water into any sewer or drain vested in or under the control of a relevant authority except with the consent of the relevant authority and subject to such terms and conditions as the relevant authority may reasonably impose; and

(b) the Company shall not make any opening into any such sewer or drain save in accordance with plans approved by, and under the superintendence (if given) of, the relevant authority in whom the sewer or drain is vested and approval of those plans by the relevant authority shall not be unreasonably withheld.

(2) (a) Section 85 of the Water Resources Act 1991 shall apply to, or to the consequence of, a discharge under the powers of this section into any controlled waters within the meaning given by section 104 of that Act as if this section were not a local statutory provision for the purposes of section 88(1)(f) of that Act.

(b) In the exercise of their powers under this section the Company shall not damage or interfere with the bed of any watercourse forming part of a main river or the banks thereof within the meaning of section 113 of the Water Resources Act 1991.

(3) The Company shall take all steps reasonably required to secure that any water discharged by them under the powers of this section shall be as free as may be reasonably practicable from any gravel, soil or other solid substance or oil or matter in suspension.

(4) Any difference arising between the company and a relevant authority under this section shall be settled by arbitration.

(5) In this section "relevant authority" means Thames Water Utilities Limited, the National Rivers Authority or the Westminster City Council.

Power to deviate

9. In the execution of any of the works, the Company may deviate from the lines or situations thereof shown on the substituted plan to the extent of the limits of deviation and may deviate vertically from the levels shown on the substituted sections—

(a) to such extent downwards as may be found necessary or convenient; and

(b) to any extent upwards not exceeding 3 metres in the case of Works Nos. 4, 4A, 4B, 5 and 5A and to such extent upwards in the case of Work No. 4C as may be found necessary or convenient.

Safeguarding works to buildings

10.—(1) In connection with the works, the Company at their own cost may, subject as hereinafter provided, carry out safeguarding works to any building situated within 35 metres of the works and for that purpose may enter any such building or any land belonging thereto.

(2) In connection with the safeguarding works authorised by subsection (1) above, the following provisions shall have effect:—

(a) before exercising the powers of subsection (1) above at least 14 days' notice shall, except in cases of emergency, be given to the owners, lessees and occupiers of the building in respect of which safeguarding works are proposed;

(b) a notice shall be served in the manner prescribed by section 19 of the Lands Clauses Consolidation Act 1845;

(c) if any owner, lessee or occupier of any such building, within 10 days after the giving of such notice, gives a counter-notice in writing that

he disputes the necessity of such safeguarding works, the question
of necessity shall be referred to and settled by arbitration;

(d) the Company shall compensate the owners, lessees and occupiers of
every such building for any loss or damage which may result to them
by reason of the exercise by the Company of the powers of this section;

(e) in any case where safeguarding works have been carried out to any
building under the powers of this section, the Company may, from
time to time after the completion of such safeguarding works, and during the execution of the works in connection with which such safeguarding works were done, or before the expiry of five years after the
opening for public use of the works, enter upon and survey such building and do such further safeguarding works as they may deem necessary or expedient or, in case of dispute between the Company and the
owner, lessee or occupier of the building, as may be determined by
arbitration;

(f) if the safeguarding works carried out by the Company to any building
under the powers of this section prove at any time before the expiry of
five years from the opening for public use of the works in connection
with which such safeguarding works were carried out to be inadequate
for the support or protection of the building against further damage
arising from the execution of the works, the Company shall compensate the owner, lessee and occupier of the building for such damage;

(g) nothing in this section or in any dealing with any property in pursuance
of this section shall relieve the Company from liability to compensate
under section 68 of the Lands Clauses Consolidation Act 1845;

(h) every case of compensation to be ascertained under this section shall
be determined in accordance with Part I of the Land Compensation
Act 1961.

(3) For the purpose of determining whether and, if so, how to exercise their
powers and how to discharge their duties under this section, the Company
may at any reasonable time enter and survey any building to which subsection (1) above applies.

(4) To enable them to carry out the safeguarding works authorised by subsection (1) above, the Company may stop up, divert, break open and interfere with any street or footpath, whether public or private, or any other open
space which is adjacent to any building to which safeguarding works are to be
carried out.

(5) In this section—

(a) "building" includes any structure or any part of a building or structure
and, in the case of so much of the works as are constructed below the
surface of the ground, reference to any building within 35 metres of
those works includes reference to any building within 35 metres of the
point on the surface below which those works are situated;

(b) "safeguarding works" includes underpinning, strengthening and any
other works which in the reasonable opinion of the Company might
prevent damage to any building which may arise as a result of the construction of the works; and

(c) "the works" does not include safeguarding works.

Incorporation of works provisions

11. Section 15 (Power to make trial holes) of the Act of 1963 is, with necessary modifications, incorporated with this Act.

PART III

LANDS

Power to acquire lands

12.—(1) The Company may enter upon, take and use such of the lands delineated on the substituted plan and described in the substituted book of reference as they may require for the purposes of the works or for any purpose connected with or ancillary to their undertaking.

(2) The Company may enter upon, use and appropriate so much of the subsoil and under-surface of any public street, road, footway or place delineated on the substituted plan and described in the substituted book of reference as may be necessary for the purposes mentioned in subsection (1) above without being required to purchase the same or any easement therein or thereunder or to make any payment therefor.

Power to acquire subsoil or new rights only in certain cases

13.—(1) In this Part of this Act "new rights" in relation to any land means easements or other rights in, under or over such land, which are to be created in favour of the Company.

(2) Notwithstanding anything in this Act, the Company may, for the purposes of constructing, maintaining, protecting, renewing and using the works, enter upon, take and use so much of the subsoil and under-surface of or may acquire such new rights as they may require in, under or over any of the lands delineated on the substituted plan and described in the substituted book of reference without being obliged or compellable to acquire any greater interest in, under or over the same respectively and may give notice to treat in respect of such entry, taking and using.

(3) (a) If, in any case where the Company enter upon, take and use the subsoil and under-surface of, or acquire a new right in or under, any of the lands referred to in subsection (2) above they also require to take, use and pull down or open any cellar, vault, arch or other construction forming part of any such lands they may enter upon, take and use such cellar, vault, arch or other construction for the purposes of the works and (subject to the provisions of this Act) the provisions of the Lands Clauses Acts shall apply in relation to the purchase thereof as if such cellar, vault, arch or other construction were lands within the meaning of those Acts.

(b) Section 12 (Acquisition of part only of certain properties) of the Act of 1964, as incorporated with this Act, shall apply in respect of the acquisition by the Company under this subsection of any cellar, vault, arch or other construction as if the same were a part of land to which that section applies.

Subsoil or new rights only to be acquired under certain lands

14.—(1) In this section—
  "the specified lands" means the lands numbered on the substituted plan 2, 4, 5, 9, 10, 12, 13 and 15 to 18 in the city of Westminster; and
  "the level of the surface of the specified lands" means ground surface level or, in the case of a building on the specified lands, means the level of the surface of the ground adjoining the building.

(2) (a) Notwithstanding the provisions of subsection (1) of section 12 (Power to acquire lands) of this Act, the Company shall not acquire compulsorily under the powers of this Act any part of the specified lands, except as provided in paragraph (b) below.

(b) The Company may, within the limits of lateral deviation prescribed by this Act in respect of the works, enter upon, take and use so much of the subsoil and under-surface of the specified lands as they may require for the purposes of constructing, maintaining, protecting, renewing and using the works and any necessary works and conveniences connected therewith, or compulsorily purchase such new rights in the subsoil and under-surface of the specified lands as they may require for the said purposes without in either case being obliged or compellable to acquire any greater interest in, under or over the specified lands and may give notice to treat in respect of such entry, taking and using.

(c) For the purposes of this section the subsoil and under-surface of the specified lands shall be deemed not to include any such subsoil or under-surface which is within 9 metres of the level of the surface of the specified lands.

Application of Lands Clauses Acts to compulsory purchase of new rights

15.—(1) The Lands Clauses Acts, as incorporated with this Act, shall have effect with the modifications necessary to make them apply to the compulsory purchase of rights under sections 13 (Power to acquire subsoil or new rights only in certain cases) and 14 (Subsoil or new rights only to be acquired under certain lands) of this Act as they apply to the compulsory purchase of land so that, in appropriate contexts, references in those Acts to land are read as referring, or as including references, to the rights or to land in, under or over which the rights are or are to be exercisable, according to the requirements of the particular context.

(2) Without prejudice to the generality of subsection (1) above in relation to the purchase of new rights in pursuance of sections 13 (Power to acquire subsoil or new rights only in certain cases) and 14 (Subsoil or new rights only to be acquired under certain lands) of this Act—

(a) the Lands Clauses Consolidation Act 1845 shall, subject to the provisions of subsection (3) below, have effect with the modifications specified in Schedule 1 (except paragraph 4) to the Act of 1976 and as if for the word "over", wherever it occurs in paragraph 1 of that Schedule, there were substituted the words "in, under or over";

(b) the enactments relating to compensation for the compulsory purchase of land shall apply with the necessary modifications as they apply to such compensation.

(3) Notwithstanding anything in this section, section 92 of the Lands Clauses Consolidation Act 1845 shall not apply to any compulsory acquisition or purchase by the Company under sections 13 (Power to acquire subsoil or new rights only in certain cases) or 14 (Subsoil or new rights only to be acquired under certain lands) of this Act.

Set-off for enhancement in value of retained land

16.—(1) In this section "relevant land" means any land or any subsoil or under-surface of or new rights in, or over any land acquired by the Company for the purposes of the works.

(2) In assessing the compensation payable to any person on the acquisition by the Company from him of any relevant land, the Lands Tribunal shall—

(a) have regard to the extent to which the lands or the remaining contiguous lands belonging to the same person may be benefited by the works; and

(b) set off against the value of the relevant land any increase in the value of the remaining contiguous lands belonging to the same person which will accrue to him by reason of the construction of the works.

(3) The Land Compensation Act 1961 shall have effect subject to the provisions of this section.

Period for compulsory purchase of lands and new rights

17. The powers of the Company for the compulsory purchase of lands and new rights under this Act shall cease at the end of the period of six years commencing on the date of the passing of this Act.

Incorporation of lands provisions

18.—(1) The following of the undermentioned Acts are, with necessary modifications, incorporated with this Act:—

the Act of 1963—
    section 21 (Power to enter for survey or valuation; and
    section 28 (As to cellars under streets not referenced):

the Act of 1964—
    section 12 (Acquisition of part only of certain properties); and
    section 14 (Extinction of private rights of way):

the Act of 1965—
    section 13 (Correction of errors in deposited plans and book of
        reference):

the Act of 1966—
    section 14 (Power to expedite entry):

the Act of 1969—
    section 14 (Disregard of recent improvements and interests).

(2) The provisions of the said section 21 of the Act of 1963, as so incorporated, shall have effect as if after the word "acquire" there were inserted the words "or use".

PART IV

PROTECTIVE PROVISIONS

Incorporation of protective provisions

19.—(1) The following provisions of the undermentioned Acts, are, with necessary modifications, incorporated with this Act:—

the Act of 1963—
    section 42 (For protection of gas, water and electricity
        undertakers):

the Act of 1976—
    section 13 (For protection of sewers of Thames Water Authority):

the Act of 1981—
    section 17 (For protection of British Telecommunications).

(2) The provisions of paragraph (1) of the said section 42 of the Act of 1963, as so incorporated, shall have effect as if—

(a) for the definition of "the undertakers" there were substituted the following:—

" 'the undertakers' means any person authorised to carry on, in the area within which the Company are by this Act authorised to purchase land or execute works, an undertaking for the supply of gas or water or for the generation, transmission or supply of electricity;"; and

(b) in the definition of "apparatus"—

(i) in sub-paragraph (a) thereof for the words "electric lines or works" there were substituted "electric lines or electrical plant" and for the reference to the Electricity (Supply) Acts 1882 to 1936 there were substituted a reference to Part I of the Electricity Act 1989; and

(ii) in the words in parenthesis for the reference to the Public Utilities Street Works Act 1950 there were substituted a reference to Part III of the New Roads and Street Works Act 1991.

(3) The provisions of the said section 13 of the Act of 1976, as so incorporated, shall have effect as if—

(a) for references to Thames Water Authority there were substituted references to Thames Water Utilities Limited;

(b) for the reference in paragraph (8) thereof to section 7 (Incorporation of provisions of Acts of 1963, 1965, 1969 and 1974 relating to works) of the Act of 1976 there were substituted a reference to section 11 (Incorporation of works provisions) of this Act; and

(c) in the definition of "the specified works" in paragraph (1), for the reference to the works authorised by the Act of 1976 there were substituted a reference to the works.

(4) The provisions of the said section 17 of the Act of 1981, as so incorporated, shall have effect as if—

(a) paragraph (2) of that section were omitted;

(b) for references to Work No. 2 of the Act of 1981 there were substituted references to the works; and

(c) for the reference to British Telecommunications there were substituted a reference to any public telecommunications operator as defined in section 9(3) of the Telecommunications Act 1984.

Crown rights

20.—(1) Nothing in this Act affects prejudicially any estate, right, power, privilege or exemption of the Crown and in particular and without prejudice to the generality of the foregoing nothing in this Act authorised the Company to take, use or in any manner interfere with any land or hereditaments or any rights of whatsoever description—

(a) belonging to Her Majesty in right of Her Crown and under the management of the Crown Estate Commissioners without the consent in writing of those commissioners; or

(b) belonging to Her Majesty in right of Her Crown and under the management (pursuant to any statute or otherwise) of the Secretary of State without his consent in writing; or

(c) belonging to a government department or held in trust for Her Majesty for the purposes of a government department without the consent in writing of that government department.

(2) A consent under subsection (1) above may be given unconditionally or subject to such conditions and upon such terms as may be considered necessary or appropriate.

PART V

MISCELLANEOUS

Planning permission

21.—(1) In this section "Part 11 development" means development permitted by article 3 of, and Class A in Part 11 of Schedule 2 to, the Town and Country Planning General Development Order 1988 (which permits development authorised by private Act designating specifically both the nature of the development thereby authorised and the land on which it may be carried out).

(2) Subject to the provisions of subsection (3) below, in its application to development authorised by this Act, the planning permission granted for Part 11 development shall have effect as if the authority to develop given by this Act were limited to development begun within 10 years after the passing of this Act.

(3) Subsection (2) above shall not apply to the carrying out of any development consisting of the alteration, maintenance or repair of works authorised by this Act or the substitution of new works therefor.

Arbitration

22. Where under this Act any difference (other than a difference to which the provisions of the Lands Clauses Acts, as applied by this Act, apply) is to be referred to or settled by arbitration, then, unless otherwise provided, such difference shall be referred to and settled by a single arbitrator to be agreed between the parties or, failing agreement, to be appointed, on the application of either party (after notice in writing to the other), by the President of the Institution of Civil Engineers.

Costs of Act

23. All costs, charges and expenses of and incidental to the preparing for, obtaining and passing of this Act, or otherwise in relation thereto, shall be paid by the Company and may in whole or in part be defrayed out of revenue.

Section 4. SCHEDULE

DESCRIPTION OF WORKS REFERRED TO IN SECTION 4 OF THIS ACT

In the city of Westminster

Work No. 4   A passenger subway commencing by a junction with an existing subway serving the Piccadilly Line station/platform concourse beneath a point 27 metres south-east of the junction of Dover Street with Piccadilly and terminating by a junction with a cross-passage serving the Jubilee Line platform concourse beneath a point 37 metres south-east of the south-eastern end of Arlington Street.

Work No. 4A   A passenger subway commencing by a junction with a cross-passage serving the Jubilee Line station platform concourse beneath a point 36 metres south of the south-eastern end of Arlington Street and terminating by a junction with Work No. 4 beneath a point 34 metres south of that end of Arlington Street.

Work No. 4B   A shaft, incorporating a lift, with connecting subways commencing by a junction with a cross-passage serving the Jubilee Line station/platform concourse beneath a point 28 metres south of the south-eastern end of Arlington Street and terminating by a junction with Work No. 4 beneath a point 25 metres south of that end of Arlington Street.

Work No. 4C   A subway including an emergency escape shaft commencing by a junction with Work No. 4 beneath a point 48 metres south-east of the junction of Bennett Street with Arlington Street and terminating by a junction with Work No. 4 beneath a point 65 metres south-east of that road junction.

Work No. 5   A passenger subway commencing by a junction with a cross-passage serving the Piccadilly line station concourse beneath a point 31 metres south-west of the junction of Dover Street with Piccadilly and terminating by a junction with an existing subway serving the Piccadilly Line station/platform concourse beneath a point 32 metres south of that road junction.

work No. 5A   A shaft, incorporating a lift, with connecting subways commencing by a junction with a cross-passage serving the Piccadilly Line station concourse commencing beneath a point 19 metres south-west of the junction of Dover Street with Piccadilly and terminating by a junction with Work No. 5 beneath a point 25 metres south-west of that road junction.

INDEX

References are to sections and schedule

LERWICK HARBOUR ORDER CONFIRMATION ACT 1994

(1994 c. x)

ARRANGEMENT OF SECTIONS

SCHEDULE

LERWICK HARBOUR

An Act to confirm a Provisional Order under the Private Legislation Procedure (Scotland) Act 1936, relating to Lerwick Harbour. [21st July 1994]

PARLIAMENTARY PROGRESS
    The Bill's progress through Parliament was as follows:
    House of Commons: First Reading, July 7, 1994; Bill considered by Commons, July 13, 1994; Third Reading, July 14, 1994.
    House of Lords: First Reading, July 14, 1994; Bill considered by Lords, July 18, 1994; Third Reading, July 20, 1994.

INTRODUCTION
    The Trustees of the port and harbour of Lerwick were constituted to manage, maintain and regulate the port and harbour. It is expedient that the limits of the harbour and port are extended—the suggested extension is set out in s.3 and Pt. I of the Order. This Act gives the necessary confirmation to the Order to enable the developments set out to go ahead.

WHEREAS the Provisional Order set forth in the Schedule hereunto annexed has been made by the Secretary of State under the provisions of the Private Legislation Procedure (Scotland) Act 1936, and it is requisite that the said Order should be confirmed by Parliament:
    Be it therefore enacted by the Queen's most Excellent Majesty, by and with the advice and consent of the Lords Spiritual and Temporal, and Commons, in this present Parliament assembled, and by the authority of the same, as follows:—

Confirmation of Order in Schedule

1. The Provisional Order contained in the Schedule hereunto annexed is hereby confirmed.

Short title

2. This Act may be cited as the Lerwick Harbour Order Confirmation Act 1994.

SCHEDULE

LERWICK HARBOUR

Provisional Order to extend the limits of the port and harbour of Lerwick, and for connected purposes.

    Whereas by the Lerwick Harbour Improvements Act 1877 the Trustees of the port and harbour of Lerwick (hereinafter referred to as "the Trustees") were constituted for the purposes of the management, maintenance and regulation of the port and harbour of Lerwick:

And whereas it is expedient that the limits of the port and harbour of Lerwick should be extended as provided in this Order:

And whereas it is expedient that the Trustees should have powers with respect to the management, regulation and control of development within the harbour limits as extended by this Order:

And whereas it is expedient that the further provisions contained in this Order should be enacted:

And whereas the purposes aforesaid cannot be effected without an Order confirmed by Parliament under the provisions of the Private Legislation Procedure (Scotland) Act 1936:

Now therefore in pursuance of the powers contained in the last-mentioned Act the Secretary of State orders as follows:—

Short title and citation

1.—(1) This Order may be cited as the Lerwick Harbour Order 1994.

(2) This Order and the Lerwick Harbour Acts and Orders 1877 to 1993 may be cited together as the Lerwick Harbour Acts and Orders 1877 to 1994.

Interpretation

2. In this Order, unless the context otherwise requires, the following expressions have the meanings hereby assigned to them respectively:—

"added areas" means the areas by this Order added to the existing area and described in Part I of the Schedule to this Order;

"commencement of this Order" means the date of the passing of the Act confirming this Order;

"existing area" means the area of the limits of the harbour as described in Part II of the Schedule to the Order of 1975 as extended by the Lerwick Harbour Revision Order 1989;

"harbour" means the port and harbour of Lerwick as defined by the Harbour Acts;

"Harbour Acts" means the Lerwick Harbour Acts and Orders 1877 to 1994;

"level of high water" means the level of mean high-water springs;

"level of low water" means the level of mean low-water springs;

"Order of 1975" means the Lerwick Harbour (Miscellaneous Provisions) Order 1975;

"Trustees" means the Trustees of the harbour for the time being acting under the Harbour Acts.

Alteration of limits of harbour of Lerwick

3.—(1) As from the commencement of this Order the limits of the harbour and of the area within which the Trustees have authority to exercise powers by virtue of any jurisdiction or function conferred or imposed on or transferred to them by the Lerwick Harbour Acts and Orders 1877 to 1993 or by any other enactment shall be extended to include the added areas and thereafter the harbour shall comprise the area described in Part II of the said Schedule in lieu of the existing area.

(2) Subject as hereinafter provided, all enactments conferring rights, powers, privileges and immunities or imposing duties, obligations and liabilities upon the Trustees including provisions for the protection of any person and all byelaws and regulations made by the Trustees which relate to or are in

force in the existing area shall relate to and have effect in the harbour and in all lands and heritable properties from time to time in the ownership or occupation of the Trustees.

(3) Without prejudice to the generality of subsections (1) and (2) above, nothing in this Order shall affect the operation within the existing area of such of the provisions of the Harbours, Docks, and Piers Clauses Act 1847 as immediately before the coming into operation of this Order were operative within that area and the said provisions shall extend and apply to the added areas.

(4) A map showing the limits of the harbour as described in Part II of the Schedule to this Order of which four copies have been signed by Gavin Douglas, Q.C., Senior Counsel to the Secretary of State under the Private Legislation Procedure (Scotland) Act 1936, shall within one month after the commencement of this Order be deposited as follows, that is to say, one copy at the offices of the Secretary of State in Edinburgh, one copy at the office of the Chief Executive of the Shetland Islands Council, one copy with the Department of Transport and one copy with the Sheriff Clerk of the Sheriff Court District of Lerwick.

(5) In the event of any discrepancy between the description in words of the limits of the harbour as described in Part II of the Schedule to this Order and the limits delineated on the map referred to in subsection (4) above, the description in words shall prevail.

(6) Section 6 of and the Schedule to the Order of 1975 and the Lerwick Harbour Revision Order 1989 are hereby repealed.

Crown rights

4.—(1) Nothing in this Order shall affect prejudicially any estate, right, power, privilege, authority or exemption of the Crown and in particular and without prejudice to the generality of the foregoing nothing herein contained shall authorise the Trustees or any licensee of the Trustees to take, use, enter upon or in any manner interfere with any land or interest in land, or any rights of whatsoever description (including any portion of the shore or bed of the sea or of any river, channel, creek, bay or estuary)—

  (a) belonging to Her Majesty in right of her Crown and under the management of the Crown Estate Commissioners without the consent in writing of those Commissioners; or

  (b) belonging to a government department or held in trust for Her Majesty for the purposes of a government department without the consent in writing of that government department.

(2) A consent under subsection (1) above may be given unconditionally or subject to terms and conditions.

Section 3   SCHEDULE

PART I

ADDED AREA (NORTH)

An area of sea lying to the north-east of the existing area and bounded by an imaginary line commencing at the north-eastern extremity of the level of high water at Hawks Ness in the mainland of Shetland (latitude 60° 13.43′ north, longitude 01° 09.95′ west); thence due east (090° true) across the sea and foreshore to the position latitude 60° 13.43′ north, longitude 01° 03.98′ west; thence due south (180° true) across the sea and foreshore to the north-eastern extremity of the level of high water of the Island of Outer Score (latitude 60° 11.63′ north, longitude 01° 03.98′

west); thence north-westward (306° true) across the sea and foreshore to the northern extremity of the level of high water of the Island of Green Holm; thence west-north-westward (297° true) across the sea and foreshore to the point of commencement.

ADDED AREA (SOUTH)

An area of sea including all creeks, inlets and voes lying to the south of the existing area and bounded by an imaginary line commencing at the southern extremity of the level of high water of Kirkabister Ness in the Island of Bressay (latitude 60° 07.19′ north, longitude 01° 07.15′ west); thence due south (180° true) across the foreshore to the point of the level of low water at Kirkabister Ness; thence south-eastward along the line of low water mark passing the Ord and Maatruf to the southern extremity of the level of low water mark at Bard Head (latitude 60° 06.19′ north, longitude 01° 04.24′ west); thence west-south-westward (259° true) across Bressay Sound to a point at the eastern extremity of the level of low water of The Skeo on the mainland of Shetland (latitude 60° 05.42′ north, longitude 01° 12.30′ west); thence north-westward then north-eastward along the line of low water of Pund Geo, East Voe of Quarff, Wick of Burland, Burland to Ness of Setter; thence north-westward, northward and south-eastward along the line of low water of Gulber Wick and crossing the foreshore to the southern extremity of the level of high water at Ness of Trebister (latitude 60° 07.18′ north, longitude 01° 10.39′ west); thence due east (89° true) across Bressay Sound to the point of commencement at Kirkabister Ness.

PART II

LIMITS OF HARBOUR OF LERWICK

An area bounded by an imaginary line commencing at the level of high water on the south-east corner of The Breakwater, 15.24 metres or thereby east of the south-east corner of the Old Tolbooth; thence northward passing along the building line on the west side of South Esplanade and the west side of the Harbour Trust Offices and continuing northward following the building line on the west side of North Esplanade to the north-east extremity of the property formerly belonging to Messrs. J. & J. Tod Limited; thence westward along the northern boundary of the said property to the wall on the east side of Commercial Road opposite Fort Charlotte; thence northward along the said building line and the wall on the east side of the road leading to Northness to the south-western extremity of the property belonging to Malakoff Limited; thence eastward along the southern boundary of the said property to the level of high water of Lerwick harbour; thence northward along the level of high water passing Northness, the docks and pier belonging to Hay & Co. (Lerwick) Limited and the piers and docks at Garthspool, taking in the piers and jetties constructed after the date of the passing of the Lerwick Harbour Improvements Act 1877; thence northward along the level of high water on the east side of the mainland of Shetland passing Holmgarth and Gremista to the eastern extremity of the level of high water at Green Head (now incorporated and forming part of a new quay); thence westward, then northward along the line of high water to a point at the western extremity of the central line of the foreshore between the mainland of Shetland and the tidal islet of Easter Rova Head; thence eastward along the said centre line of foreshore to a point where it joins with the islet of Easter Rova Head; thence along the line of high water around the said islet in an anti-clockwise direction returning to the point of junction with the said centre line of foreshore; thence westward retracing the said centre line of foreshore to its point of departure from the mainland of Shetland; thence westward, then southward, then northward, along the line of high water of Bight of Vatsland to the northern extremity of the level of high water of Kebister Ness; thence south-westward, then north-eastward along the line of high water of Dales Voe passing Doos Cove, Kebister, Muckle Ayre, Dale Burn, South Califf, North Califf and Breiwick to the northern extremity of the level of high water of Fora Ness; thence westward, then northward along the line of high water of Foraness Voe, Brim Ness, Bight of Brimness to the north-eastern extremity of the level of high water of Hawks Ness (latitude 60° 13.43′ north, longitude 01° 09.95′ west); thence due east (090° true) across the sea and foreshore to the position latitude 60° 13.43′ north, longitude 01° 03.98′ west; thence due south (180° true) across the sea and foreshore to the northern extremity of the level of high water of the Island of Outer Score (latitude 60° 11.63′ north, longitude 01° 03.98′ west); thence south-westward along the line of high water to the south-western extremity of the level of high water of the Island of Outer Score; thence in a straight line south-westward across the sea and foreshores to the north-eastern extremity of the level of high water of the Island of Inner Score; thence south-westward, then southward along the line of high water to the southern extremity of the level of high water of the Island of Inner Score; thence westward ln a straight line across the sea and foreshores to the northern extremity of the level of high water of Aith Ness in the Island of Bressay; thence south-westward and southward, then generally westward along the line of high water of the north coast of the Island of Bressay passing Aith Voe, Sweyn Ness, Ness of Beosetter, Baa Berg, White Ayre, Scarfi Taing to the north-west extremity of the line of high water of Turra Taing; thence southward along the line of high water on the west coast of the Island of Bressay to the south-western extremity of the level of high water of the Point of Hogan (or Heogan); thence following the line of high water southward passing Cruster and Gardie to the southern extremity of the level of high water of Leira Ness taking in the piers and jetties constructed after the passing of the Lerwick Harbour Improvements Act 1877; thence in a straight line in a south-easterly direction across the sea and foreshores to the south extremity of the level of high water of Holm of Mel; thence in a straight line in a south-easterly direction across the sea and foreshores to the north-eastern extremity of Mel Pier; thence southward along the line of high water on the west coast of the Island of Bressay to the north-western extremity of the level of high water of the Head or Taing of Ham; thence southward along the line of high water to the southern extremity of the level of high water of Kirkabister Ness; thence continuing southward to the level of low water of Kirkabister Ness; thence south-eastward along the level of low water on the south-east coast of the Island of Bressay passing The Ord and Maatruf to the southern extremity of the level of low water of Bard Head (latitude 60° 06.19′ north, longitude 01° 12.24′ west); thence westward (259° true) across the sea to the eastern extremity of the level of low water of The Skeo on the mainland of Shetland (latitude 60° 05.42′ north, longitude 01° 12.30′ west); thence north-westward then north-eastward along the line of low water of Pund Geo, East Voe of Quarff, Wick of Burland, Burland to Ness of Setter; thence north-westward, northward and south-eastward along the line of low water of Gulber Wick and crossing the foreshore to the southern extremity of the level of high water of Ness of Trebister; thence northward, eastward and southward to the southern extremity of the level of high water of Ness of Sound; thence northward along the level of high water of Ness of Sound to the Bight of Clickimin; thence eastward and south-eastward along the level of high water at Bight of Clickimin and Breiwick to the southern extremity of the level of high water of the Horse of the Knab; thence northward, north-eastward and north-westward along the line of high water of the Knab, South Ness, Twageos to the point of commencement at the south-east corner of The Breakwater.

INDEX

References in roman type are to sections of this Act; those in italic are to sections of the Order

CROYDON TRAMLINK ACT 1994

(1994 c. xi)

ARRANGEMENT OF SECTIONS

An Act to empower London Regional Transport and Croydon London Borough Council to provide for the development and operation of a system of light rail transit in the London boroughs of Merton, Sutton, Croydon and Bromley; to authorise the construction of works and the acquisition of lands for that purpose; to confer further powers upon London Regional Transport and Croydon London Borough Council; and for other purposes.   [21st July 1994]

PARLIAMENTARY DEBATES
The Bill's progress through Parliament was as follows:

House of Lords: First Reading, January 13, 1992; Suspended, March 12, 1992; Second Reading, October 27, 1992; Bill Committed, October 27, 1992; Opposed Bill Committee, November 10, 1992–February 9, 1993; Unopposed Bill Committee, March 17, 1993; Third Reading, March 31, 1993; Commons' Amendments, July 12, 1994.

House of Commons: First Reading, March 31, 1993; Second Reading, July 21, 1993; Bill Committed, July 21, 1993; Suspended, November 2, 1993; Opposed Bill Committee, January 26–June 30, 1994; Bill as amended Considered, July 6, 1994; Third Reading, July 12, 1994.

INTRODUCTION
London Regional Transport ("the Corporation") was established under the London Regional Transport Act 1984. The duties of the Corporation are set out within that Act and include the provision or securing of public passenger transport for Greater London, having due regard for the transport needs of that area and the efficiency, economy and safety of operation. The Corporation, in consultation with Croydon borough council, have identified that public passenger needs can be best met by the construction of a light rail system linking the London boroughs of Merton, Sutton, Croydon and Bromley.

In order to undertake the necessary works to develop the light rail system it is expedient that certain works be undertaken and the acquisition or use of certain lands be facilitated. This Act gives the necessary authorisation for such works to be undertaken.

WHEREAS—
(1) By the London Regional Transport Act 1984 the London Transport Executive which were established by the Transport (London) Act 1969 were reconstituted on 29th June 1984 under the name of London Regional Transport (in this Act referred to as "the Corporation"):

(2) It is the general duty of the Corporation under the said Act of 1984, in accordance with principles from time to time approved by the Secretary of State and in conjunction with the British Railways Board, to provide or secure the provision of public passenger transport services for Greater Lon-

don, and in carrying out that duty the Corporation shall have due regard to (a) the transport needs for the time being of Greater London and (b) efficiency, economy and safety of operation:

(3) The London borough of Croydon (in this Act referred to as "the Council") is a London borough established by the London Government Act 1963 under the management and local government of the mayor and citizens of the borough and numerous statutory powers and duties have been conferred and imposed on the Council, including the functions of a local planning authority and a highway and traffic authority for the borough:

(4) Studies carried out jointly by the Corporation and the Council have established the feasibility of meeting public passenger transport requirements in the Croydon area by the provision of a system of light rail transit based on a route from Wimbledon through central Croydon to Elmers End, Beckenham and New Addington and constructed in the London boroughs of Merton, Sutton, Croydon and Bromley:

(5) It is accordingly expedient that the Corporation should be empowered to construct the works authorised by this Act, and to acquire or use lands referred to in this Act, for the development and operation of the system of light rail transit in the London boroughs of Merton, Sutton, Croydon and Bromley and that the other powers in this Act should be conferred upon the Corporation for the operation and development of the system:

(6) It is expedient that the other powers of this Act should be conferred upon the Corporation and that the other provisions of this Act should be enacted:

(7) The purposes of this Act could not have been effected without the authority of Parliament when the Bill for this Act was deposited:

(8) In relation to the promotion of the Bill for this Act by the Council the requirements of section 239 of the Local Government Act 1972 have been observed:

(9) Plans and sections showing the lines or situations and levels of the works to be constructed under the powers of this Act and plans of the lands authorised to be acquired or used by this Act, and a book of reference to such plans containing the names of the owners and lessees or reputed owners or lessees and of the occupiers of the said lands, were duly deposited in the office of the Clerk of the Parliaments and in the Private Bill Office of the House of Commons and with the proper officers of the London borough councils affected by the works, which plans, sections and book of reference are respectively referred to in this Act as "the deposited plans", "the deposited sections" and "the deposited book of reference":

May it therefore please Your Majesty that it may be enacted, and be it enacted, by the Queen's most Excellent Majesty, by and with the advice and consent of the Lords Spiritual and Temporal, and Commons, in this present Parliament assembled, and by the authority of the same, as follows:—

PART I

PRELIMINARY

Short title

1. This Act may be cited as the Croydon Tramlink Act 1994.

Interpretation

2.—(1) In this Act, unless the context otherwise requires, the several words and expressions to which meanings are assigned by the Acts wholly or partly incorporated herewith have the same respective meanings, and—

"the Act of 1845" means the Railways Clauses Consolidation Act 1845;
"the Act of 1870" means the Tramways Act 1870;

"the Act of 1965" means the Compulsory Purchase Act 1965;

"the Act of 1991" means the New Roads and Street Works Act 1991;

"the authorised railways" means the railways authorised by this Act, including, where the context so admits, any railway adapted for use, and worked as part of Tramlink under section 16 (Agreements with British Railways Board) of this Act;

"the authorised works" means the works authorised by this Act;

"carriageway" has the same meaning as in the Highways Act 1980;

"the Corporation" means London Regional Transport;

"the Council" means the Council of the London borough of Croydon;

"enactment" means any enactment, whether public general or local, and includes any order, byelaw, rule, regulation, scheme or other instrument having effect by virtue of an enactment;

"existing" means existing at the passing of this Act;

"highway authority" has the same meaning as in the Highways Act 1980;

"the limits of deviation" mean the limits so shown on the deposited plans and, where, in the case of a work in any street, no such limits are shown for that work, the boundaries of the street (including any verge or roadside waste adjoining it);

"the limits of land to be acquired or used" means the limits marked "Limit of land to be acquired or used" on the deposited plans;

"the railways board" means the British Railways Board, and, in relation to any land or other property, includes any person who holds or uses that property for railway purposes and who derives title to that property from or under the British Railways Board or under any person deriving title from the British Railways Board;

"sewerage undertaker" has the same meaning as in the Water Industry Act 1991;

"statutory undertaker" means a licence holder under Part I of the Electricity Act 1989, a public gas supplier within the meaning of Part I of the Gas Act 1986, the National Rivers Authority and a water undertaker within the meaning of the Water Industry Act 1991 or any of such bodies;

"street" has the meaning given by section 329 of the Highways Act 1980 and includes a bridleway, cycle track or footpath as defined in the said section 329 and any way laid out or used as a cycleway;

"traffic sign" has the meaning given by section 64 of the Road Traffic Regulation Act 1984;

"Tramlink" means the light rail transit system comprising the authorised railways including such railways designated as tramways, and all works and conveniences provided in connection with any of those railways, as that system is constructed, extended or altered from time to time;

"tramway" means any railway, or any part of a railway, authorised by this Act and thereby designated as a tramway;

"the tribunal" means the Lands Tribunal.

(2) Unless the context otherwise requires, any reference in this Act to a work identified by the number of the work shall be construed as a reference to the work of that number authorised by this Act.

(3)(a) Except as mentioned in paragraph (b) below, all distances and lengths stated in any description of works, powers or lands shall be construed as if the words "or thereabouts" were inserted after each such distance and length, and distances between points on a railway shall be taken to be measured along the railway.

(b) This subsection does not apply to distances or lengths stated in the following provisions of this Act:—

section 13 (Power to deviate);

section 15 (Gauge of railways and restrictions on working).

(4) Any reference in this Act to rights over land includes reference to the right to do, or to place and maintain, anything in, on or under the land, or in the air space above its surface.

(5) Any reference in this Act to access to any place includes egress from that place.

Incorporation and application of enactments relating to railways

3.—(1) The following enactments, so far as they are applicable for the purposes and are not inconsistent with or varied by the provisions of this Act, are incorporated with and form part of this Act, and this Act shall be deemed to be the special Act for the purposes of those enactments:—

> the Act of 1845 (except sections 7 to 9, 11 to 15, 17, 19, 20, 22, 23, 46 to 62, 94, 95, 112 to 124 and 138); and
>
> section 4 of the Railways Clauses Act 1863.

(2) In the enactments incorporated by subsection (1) above—

(a) the expression "the company" means the Corporation; and

(b) sections 18 and 21 of the Act of 1845 shall not extend to regulate the relations between the Corporation and any other person in respect of any matter or thing concerning which those relations are regulated in any respect by Part III of the Act of 1991; and

(c) in section 4 of the said Act of 1863, the words "and subject to the limitations contained in sections eleven, twelve and fifteen of those Acts respectively," and the proviso shall be omitted.

(3) The following enactments shall not apply to Tramlink:—

> the Highway (Railway Crossings) Act 1839;
>
> in the Railway Regulation Act 1842, sections 9 and 10;
>
> in the Regulation of Railways Act 1868, section 22;
>
> in the Regulation of Railways Act 1889, sections 1, 3, 4 and 6;
>
> in the Road and Rail Traffic Act 1933, sections 41 and 42.

Application of Tramways Act 1870

4.—(1) Subject as provided in subsection (2) below, the following provisions of Parts II and III of the Act of 1870, so far as they are applicable for the purposes and are not inconsistent with or varied by the provisions of this Act, apply to any tramway, and for that purpose are incorporated with and form part of this Act:—

> sections 25, 26, 29 and 30, 34, 41, 49, 50, 53, 54 and 57.

(2)(a) In the provisions of the Act of 1870 applied by subsection (1) above, the expression "the special Act" means this Act and "the promoters" means the Corporation.

(b) The provisions of the Act of 1870 applied by subsection (1) above shall have effect subject to the following modifications:—

(i) in section 25, for the words "the road", there shall be substituted the words "the part of the road in which it is laid" and the words from "and shall not be opened" to the end of that section shall be omitted;

(ii) in section 26, for the words from "the following regulations" to the end of the section, there shall be substituted the words "the provisions of the special Act";

(iii) in section 30, for the words from "also subject to" to the end of the section, there shall be substituted the words "the special Act";

(iv) in section 34, the words from "No carriage used" to the end of the section shall be omitted;

(v) in sections 49, 50, 53 and 54, for the penalty specified in each of those sections, there shall be substituted a fine not exceeding level 3 on the standard scale and in the said section 54 the words from "or under licence" to "by this Act provided" shall be omitted.

(3) This section shall have effect notwithstanding the repeal by the Transport and Works Act 1992 of the provisions of the Act of 1870 referred to in subsection (1) above.

Application of Part I of Compulsory Purchase Act 1965

5.—(1) Part I of the Act of 1965 (except section 4 and paragraph 3(3) of Schedule 3), in so far as it is applicable for the purposes and is not inconsistent with the provisions of this Act, shall apply to the compulsory acquisition of land under this Act as it applies to a compulsory purchase to which the Acquisition of Land Act 1981 applies and as if this Act were a compulsory purchase order under the said Act of 1981.

(2) Section 11(1) of the Act of 1965 (which empowers the acquiring authority to enter upon and take possession of land the subject of a notice to treat after giving not less than 14 days' notice) as so applied shall have effect as if for the word "fourteen" there were substituted, in respect of the lands over which rights only are required, the word "twenty-eight" and, in the case of any other lands, the word "ninety-one".

(3) The Lands Clauses Consolidation Act 1845 shall not apply to the acquisition of land under this Act.

PART II

WORKS

Power to make works

6.—(1) Subject to the provisions of this Act, the Corporation may, in the lines or situations shown on the deposited plans and according to the levels shown on the deposited sections, make and maintain the works in the London boroughs of Merton, Sutton, Croydon and Bromley specified in Part I of Schedule 1 to this Act, with all necessary works and conveniences connected therewith.

(2) Notwithstanding anything in this Act or shown on the deposited plans or the deposited sections but without prejudice to the provisions of section 13 (Power to deviate) of this Act, the Corporation may, with the consent of the owners, lessees and occupiers of the lands affected, construct the whole or part of Works Nos. 10 and 11 and so much of Work No. 7 as lies within the London borough of Bromley in lines or situations and in accordance with levels, dimensions and descriptions other than the lines or situations, levels, dimensions and descriptions shown on the deposited plans and the deposited sections or specified in Part I of Schedule 1 to this Act.

Further works and powers

7.—(1) Subject to the provisions of this Act (and, in so far as the same are shown on the deposited plans and the deposited sections, in the lines or situations and according to the levels so shown), the Corporation may exercise the powers and make and maintain the further works, described in Part II of Schedule 1 to this Act, in the London boroughs of Merton, Sutton, Croydon and Bromley with all necessary works and conveniences connected therewith.

(2) Without prejudice to the specific powers conferred by subsection (1) above, for the purposes of constructing or maintaining the authorised railways in or adjoining any street, the Corporation may, with the consent of the highway authority—

(a) increase the width of the carriageway of the street by reducing the width of any footway, cycle track or verge or other land within the boundary of the street;

(b) alter or interfere with the level of any kerb, footway, cycle track, verge or other land within the boundary of the street; or

(c) at any stopping place on a tramway reduce the width of the carriageway of the street by forming a reserved area in the street or by setting forward the kerbline of the street and providing access for vehicles to adjoining premises and a footway on the side of that kerbline nearest to those premises.

(3) No footway shall, under subsection (2) above, be reduced to a less width than 1·80 metres (5 feet 11 inches).

(4) Where the carriageway, or part of the carriageway, of any street in which a tramway is laid is of sufficient width to provide not less than 3 metres of width for vehicular traffic in each permitted direction clear of the tramway path (as determined in accordance with the clearance required by the Secretary of State), the Corporation may, with the consent of the highway authority, carry out such works as may be required to deter, but not prevent, the passage of vehicular traffic along the tramway, by raising the level of the part of the carriageway occupied by the tramway path above the level of the adjoining carriageway or by placing a kerb or other obstruction along the edge of that adjoining carriageway.

(5) Notwithstanding section 25 of the Act of 1870 as applied by this Act, in the case of any part of the length of a tramway which is situated clear of the carriageway or footway of any street, the Corporation may, with the consent of the highway authority, lay and maintain the tramway in such manner that the uppermost surface of the rails is not on a level with the surface of the ground in which it is laid.

(6) Subject to the provisions of this Act, the Corporation may—

(a) in relation to Work No. 3, lay down single, double or interlacing lines in lieu of triple lines, either when constructing that work or at any time thereafter;

(b) lay down double lines in lieu of single lines or single lines in lieu of double lines or interlacing lines in lieu of double or single lines on any of the tramways, either when constructing them or at any time thereafter, and construct or take up and reconstruct any such tramway or associated work in such position in the street or land in which it is authorised to be constructed as they think fit; and

(c) make, maintain, alter and remove such crossings, passing places, sidings, junctions and other works, in addition to those specified in and authorised by this Act, as they find necessary or convenient for the efficient working of Tramlink, for the purposes of the control of traffic or for providing access to any premises.

(7) The powers of subsection (6) above shall not be exercised in any street which is a highway without the consent of the highway authority.

Works in street

8.—(1) Subject to the provisions of this Act, the Corporation may, for the purposes of Work No. 4C, make and maintain permanent openings in so much of any street as is within the limits of deviation for that work.

(2) The Corporation shall not be required to purchase any part of the surface of, or any easement in, any street in which they are authorised by this section to make and maintain any permanent opening, or to make any payment in respect of any such permanent opening, or for breaking up or interfering with the surface of any such street.

Requirements applicable to tramways

9.—(1) The tramways shall be so laid and maintained that the distance between the sides of the widest carriages to be used on the tramways when passing one another thereon shall not be less than 380 millimetres (15 inches).

(2)(a) On completion of any tramway the Corporation shall provide traffic signs to give warning to other traffic of the presence of the tramway.

(b) Subject to any directions and any other requirements given or imposed by the Secretary of State with respect to such a traffic sign, the places at which the traffic signs are displayed shall be such as may be approved by the highway authority.

(3)(a) Where a tramway has been constructed in a street in such manner that—

    (i) the uppermost surface of the rails is level with the surface of the street; or

    (ii) the level of the width of the carriageway occupied by the tramway path is altered as provided in section 7(4) (Further works and powers) of this Act;

works for the purpose, or having the effect, of altering the level of the part of the street in which the tramway is situated shall not be carried out without the consent of the Corporation.

(b) Consent under paragraph (a) above may be given subject to such reasonable terms and conditions as the Corporation may require, but shall not be unreasonably withheld, and any difference arising under this paragraph shall be determined by the Secretary of State.

Level crossings

10.—(1) The Corporation may, in the construction of the authorised railways, carry the same with a single or double line across and on the level of the streets specified in Schedule 2 to this Act.

(2) The Corporation may, subject to such requirements as the Secretary of State may from time to time lay down, provide, maintain and operate at or near any such level crossing such barriers, lights, traffic signs and automatic or other devices and appliances as may be approved by the Secretary of State.

(3) In the exercise of the powers of this section, the Corporation may alter or interfere with the level of any street upon which any railway or associated work is to be laid.

Subsidiary works

11.—(1) Subject to the provisions of this Act the Corporation may, for the purposes of Tramlink and associated traffic control—

    (a) within the limits of deviation make, lay down, place, erect, repair, alter, renew, maintain, operate and use rails, rail fixings, plates, sleepers, channels, conduits, tubes, stations, platforms, islands, gates, junctions, points, turntables, turnouts, crossings, temporary or permanent cross-overs, passing places, pillars, posts, poles, brackets, wires, subways, manholes, shafts, engines, dynamos, substations, transformers, switchgear, cabling, signalling, monitoring and communications equipment, together with subsidiary and incidental machinery, apparatus, works and appliances; and

    (b) in, or under any street in which it may be necessary or convenient, or in other land over which the Corporation have or obtain sufficient rights, lay, place, form, erect, maintain, renew and repair drains, ditches and culverts, electric wires, conductors, cables, brackets, posts, tubes, substations, boxes and other electrical apparatus for connecting the authorised railways and associated works with any electricity generating station or substations or for the purposes of signalling, monitoring and communication in connection with Tramlink.

(2) The provisions of sections 158 and 159 of, and paragraph 3 of Schedule 13 to, the Water Industry Act 1991 (street works) shall apply to apparatus and works referred to in subsection (1) above as they apply to relevant pipes and service pipes but as if—

(a) for any reference to a water undertaker there were substituted a reference to the Corporation; and

(b) paragraph 3(6) of Schedule 13 were omitted.

(3) The Corporation may, for the purposes of Tramlink, alter, renew and maintain the parapet of any bridge under which the authorised railways are to be situated, or construct any other works for the safety of persons passing over any such bridge.

(4) In constructing stations and stopping places for the purposes of Tramlink the Corporation shall make provision, in so far as it is in the circumstances both practicable and reasonable and without prejudice to any requirement having effect under or by virtue of the Chronically Sick and Disabled Persons Act 1970, for the needs of members of the public using Tramlink who are disabled or elderly.

(5) Nothing in this section shall prejudice the generality of sections 6 (Power to make works) and 7 (Further works and powers) of this Act.

Provision of accommodation for apparatus

12. Where the Corporation lay down conduits for the accommodation of cables or other apparatus for the purposes of Tramlink or associated traffic control under section 11 (Subsidiary works) of this Act, they may, in pursuance of those powers, provide in, or in connection with, such conduits accommodation for the apparatus of any other person, and manholes and other facilities for access to such accommodation, and may permit the use of such conduits on such terms and conditions as may be agreed between the Corporation and such other person.

Power to deviate

13. In the execution of the authorised works the Corporation may, except as may be otherwise provided by this Act, deviate from the lines or situations thereof shown on the deposited plans to the extent of the limits of deviation and deviate vertically from the levels shown on the deposited sections to any extent not exceeding 3 metres upwards and to such extent downwards as may be found necessary or convenient.

Plans to be approved by Secretary of State before works commenced

14.—(1) Before constructing any of the authorised railways the Corporation shall submit to the Secretary of State for his approval plans, sections and particulars of their proposals concerning—

(a) permanent way or track;

(b) signalling; and

(c) lighting.

(2) Any such works shall be constructed and maintained in accordance with such plans, sections and particulars approved by the Secretary of State.

(3) The Corporation shall submit for the approval of the Secretary of State details of their proposals for the rolling stock to be used on Tramlink and any rolling stock so used shall be constructed and maintained in accordance with particulars approved by the Secretary of State.

Gauge of railways and restrictions on working

15.—(1) The authorised railways to be constructed shall be constructed on a gauge of 1,435 millimetres (4 feet 8½ inches) and the motive power to be used shall be electrical energy or such other motive power as the Secretary of State may approve.

(2) No part of Tramlink shall be used for, or in connection with, the conveyance of passengers without the written permission of the Secretary of State and the Corporation shall comply with the conditions (if any) which the

Secretary of State may from time to time prescribe for the safety of persons using Tramlink.

(3) If, without reasonable excuse, the Corporation contravene the provisions of subsection (2) above they shall for each offence be liable on summary conviction to a fine not exceeding level 2 on the standard scale.

(4) Without prejudice to the generality of subsection (2) above, traction cables of the overhead line equipment of any tramway, and of so much of any authorised railway as is comprised in any level crossing, shall be erected at a height agreed by the Secretary of State and, if at any place a height of less than 5·63 metres (18 feet 6 inches) above the surface of the ground is so agreed for a cable, the Corporation shall, in accordance with section 9(2) (Requirements applicable to tramways) of this Act, erect such traffic signs as may be directed by the Secretary of State to give warning of the cable.

Agreements with British Railways Board

16.—(1) In this section—

"the affected properties" means any land described in the deposited book of reference which is owned by the railways board or in which the railways board have an interest; and

"the specified works" means so much of Works Nos. 1, 1A, 1B, 1C, 1D, 2, 2A, 3, 3A, 7, 8 and 9 as will be constructed under, on or over any of the affected properties.

(2) Any work of alteration or adaptation of property of the railways board which may be necessary in order to construct the specified works and thereafter, the use, maintenance, repair and renewal of such property and of the specified works shall be carried out and regulated by the Corporation or the railways board, or by the Corporation and the railways board jointly, in accordance with such terms and conditions as may be agreed in writing between the Corporation and the railways board.

(3)(a) Any agreement made under this section may relate to the whole or part of the affected properties and may contain such incidental, consequential or supplementary provisions as may be so agreed, including (but without prejudice to the generality of the foregoing) provisions—

(i) with respect to the defraying of, or the making of contributions towards, the cost of such works of alteration or adaptation or the costs of such maintenance, repair and renewal as are referred to in subsection (2) above by the Corporation or by the railways board or by the Corporation and railways board jointly; and

(ii) for the exercise by the railways board, or by the Corporation, or by the railways board and the Corporation jointly, of all or any of the powers and rights of the railways board and the Corporation (as the case may be) in respect of any part of the specified works under any enactment or contract.

(b) The exercise by the Corporation or the railways board or by the Corporation and the railways board jointly, of any powers and rights under any enactment or contract pursuant to any such agreement as is authorised by paragraph (a) above shall be subject to all statutory and contractual provisions relating thereto as would apply if such powers and rights were exercised by the Corporation or the railways board (as the case may be) alone, and accordingly such provisions shall with any necessary modifications, apply to the exercise of such powers and rights by the Corporation or the railways board, or by the Corporation and the railways board jointly, as the case may be.

(4) In constructing the specified works the Corporation may, on such terms as shall be agreed with the railways board, re-align so much of the railways board's railway as lies within the limits of deviation of those works in such

position and on such terms as shall be agreed between the Corporation and the railways board.

(5) The Corporation and the railways board may enter into, and carry into effect, agreements for the transfer to the Corporation of—

(a) any part of the affected properties,

(b) any lands, works or other property held in connection with any part of the affected properties, and

(c) any rights and obligations (whether or not statutory) of the railways board relating to any part of the affected properties.

(6) Where agreement is made for the transfer to the Corporation of any railway or former railway comprised within the affected properties under subsection (5) above, the Corporation may adapt for use, maintain, use and work that railway as part of Tramlink in accordance with the provisions of the Act of 1845 and the Railways Clauses Act 1863 incorporated with this Act and the provisions of the Railway Regulation Acts 1840 to 1889 applicable to Tramlink.

Discontinuance of existing railway services

17. The provisions of section 54 of the Transport Act 1962 and section 37 of, and Schedule 5 to, the Railways Act 1993 (proposals to discontinue railway passenger services) shall not apply in respect of the discontinuance of any existing railway passenger services from any station or on any line or, as the case may be, the discontinuance of any railway passenger or goods services provided by the railways board, where such discontinuance is for the purposes of, or in connection with, the construction of the authorised works or the transfer of any parts of any existing railway to form part of Tramlink.

Temporary stoppage of streets

18.—(1) During and for the purpose of the execution of the authorised works, the Corporation may temporarily stop up and interfere with the whole or any part of any street to the extent of the limits of deviation, or the limits of land to be acquired or used, and may for any reasonable time divert the traffic therefrom and prevent all persons, other than those bona fide going to or from any land, house or building abutting on the said part of the street, from passing along and using the same.

(2) The Corporation shall provide reasonable access for foot passengers bona fide going to or from any such land, house or building.

Stopping up streets without providing substitute

19.—(1) This section applies in the case of any stopping up of a street or portion thereof authorised by the Act without the provision of a substitute.

(2) After any stopping up to which this section applies, all rights of way over or along the street, or portion thereof, authorised to be stopped up shall be extinguished and the Corporation may, without making any payment therefor, but subject to the provisions of the Act of 1845 incorporated with this Act with respect to mines lying under or near the railways, appropriate and use for the purposes of their undertaking the site of the street, or portion thereof, so stopped up.

(3) Any person who suffers loss by the extinguishment of any private right under this section shall be entitled to be paid by the Corporation compensation to be determined in case of dispute in accordance with Part I of the Land Compensation Act 1961.

(4) Without prejudice to the generality of subsection (1) above, this section applies, in particular, to the stopping up of a street or portion thereof mentioned in paragraphs (viii), (ix), (xi), (xii), (xiv), (xvi), (xx), (xxii) and (xxix) of Part II of Schedule 1 to this Act.

Stopping up streets in case of diversion or substitution

20.—(1) Except as provided in section 18 (Temporary stoppage of streets) of this Act, where this Act authorises the making of a new street, either by way of diversion of, or in substitution for, an existing street and the stopping up of the existing street or portion thereof, the stopping up shall not, in either case, take place until the highway authority are satisfied that the new street has been completed in accordance with their reasonable requirements and is open for public use or, in the case of any difference between the Corporation and the highway authority as to whether the said requirements have been complied with or as to their reasonableness, until the matter in dispute has been determined by arbitration and the new street has been completed accordingly.

(2) Before referring the matter to arbitration under this section the Corporation shall give to the highway authority 7 days' notice in writing of their intention to do so.

(3) As from the completion of the new street to the satisfaction of the highway authority or, in the case of dispute, according to the decision of the arbitrator, all rights of way over or along the existing street, or portion thereof, authorised to be diverted or stopped up shall be extinguished, and the Corporation may, without making any payment therefor, but subject to the provisions of the Act of 1845 incorporated with this Act with respect to mines lying under or near the railways, appropriate and use for the purposes of their undertaking the site of the street, or portion thereof, diverted or stopped up so far as the same is bounded on both sides by lands in the possession of the Corporation.

(4) Any person who suffers loss by the extinguishment of any private right under this section shall be entitled to be paid by the Corporation compensation to be determined in case of dispute in accordance with Part I of the Land Compensation Act 1961.

Notice of interference with streets

21. Before breaking up or interfering with any street to which the public has access in connection with the construction of any of the authorised works the Corporation shall (except in case of emergency) give 14 days' notice in writing to the chief officer of the fire and police authorities for the area in which such street is situated and make such arrangements with the chief officer of police as may be reasonably necessary so as to cause as little interference with the traffic in such street during the construction of such works as may be reasonably practicable.

Provisions as to repair of streets, etc.

22.—(1) Subject to subsections (2) and (3) below, any street, or portion thereof, made, diverted or altered under this Act shall, when completed, unless otherwise agreed, be maintained by and at the expense of the Corporation for a period of 12 months from its completion and at the expiration of that period shall be maintained by and at the expense of the highway authority.

(2) Subsection (3) below applies where the Corporation has under section 7(4) (Further works and powers) of this Act raised the level of part of the carriageway of a street in which a tramway is laid; and in that subsection, so much of the carriageway whose level has been so raised is referred to as "the raised tramway path".

(3) Unless otherwise agreed with the highway authority, the raised tramway path shall be maintained by and at the expense of the Corporation for as long as the raised tramway path is required to be used primarily for the purposes of Tramlink.

Underpinning of houses near works

23. The Corporation may, at their own expense, subject as hereinafter provided, underpin or otherwise strengthen any house or building within 30 metres of any of the authorised works, and for this purpose the following provisions shall have effect:—

(1) At least 14 days' notice shall (except in the case of emergency) be given to the owner, lessee and occupier of the house or building intended to be so underpinned or otherwise strengthened.

(2) Each such notice shall be served in manner prescribed by section 6 of the Acquisition of Land Act 1981 as if required to be served under that Act.

(3) If any owner, lessee or occupier of any such house or building, within 10 days after the giving of such notice, gives a counter-notice in writing that he disputes the necessity of such underpinning or strengthening, the question of the necessity shall be settled by arbitration.

(4) In any case in which any house or building has been underpinned or strengthened under the powers of this section the Corporation may, from time to time after the completion of such underpinning or strengthening, and during the execution of the authorised work in connection with which such underpinning or strengthening was done, or within five years after the opening for traffic of the authorised works, enter upon and survey such house or building and, after complying with the foregoing provisions of this section, do such further underpinning or strengthening as they may deem necessary or expedient.

(5) The Corporation shall be liable to compensate the owner, lessee and occupier of every such house or building for any loss or damage which may result to them by reason of the exercise of the powers of this section.

(6) Nothing in this section nor any dealing with any property in pursuance of this section shall relieve the Corporation from the liability to compensate under section 10(2) of the Act of 1965 as applied by this Act, or under any other enactment, in respect of loss or damage arising from the execution of any works, other than works of underpinning or strengthening authorised by this section.

(7) Every case of compensation under this section shall be determined in case of dispute in accordance with Part I of the Land Compensation Act 1961.

Use of sewers, etc., for removing water

24.—(1) The Corporation may use for the discharge of any water pumped or found during the construction of the authorised works any available stream or watercourse, or any sewer or drain of any sewerage undertaker or London borough council in or through whose area or district the works may be constructed or pass, and for that purpose may lay down, take up and alter conduits, pipes and other works and may make any convenient connections with any such stream, watercourse, sewer or drain within the limits of deviation.

(2)(a) The Corporation shall not—

(i) discharge any water into any sewer or drain vested in or under the control of a sewerage undertaker or London borough council except with the consent of that body and subject to such terms and conditions as that body may reasonably impose; or

(ii) make any opening into any such sewer or drain except in accordance with plans approved by, and under the superintendence (if given), of the sewerage undertaker or London borough council in which the sewer or drain is then vested.

(b) Consent to a discharge, or approval of plans submitted, under this subsection shall not be unreasonably withheld.

(3)(a) Section 85 of the Water Resources Act 1991 shall apply to, or to the consequence of, a discharge under this section into any controlled waters within the meaning given by section 104(1) of that Act as if this section were excluded from the reference to any local statutory provision in section 88(1)(f) of that Act.

(b) In the exercise of their powers under this section the Corporation shall not damage or interfere with the bed of any watercourse forming part of a main river of the National Rivers Authority or the banks thereof within the meaning of section 72 of the Land Drainage Act 1991 or forming part of a metropolitan watercourse within the meaning assigned to that expression by paragraph 1 of Schedule 5 to the Land Drainage Act 1976.

(4) The Corporation shall take all such steps as may be reasonably required to secure that any water discharged under this section shall be as free as may be reasonably practicable from any gravel, soil or other solid substance or matter in suspension.

(5) Any difference arising between the Corporation, National Rivers Authority, sewerage undertaker or London borough council, as the case may be, under this section shall be determined by arbitration.

Attachment of brackets, etc., to buildings for purposes of works

25. The Corporation may affix brackets, cables, wires and other apparatus required in connection with Tramlink to any building or structure; and for that purpose the provisions of subsections (2), (4) to (6), (8) and (9) of section 45 of the Public Health Act 1961 (affixing apparatus to buildings for street lighting) shall apply as if—
  (a) the attachments therein mentioned included any such apparatus;
  (b) for any reference to the street lighting authority there were substituted a reference to the Corporation; and
  (c) in the proviso to subsection (2), after the words "unreasonably withheld" there were inserted the words "or is not granted within a reasonable time".

Attachment of equipment to tramway buildings and structures

26.—(1) Subject to subsection (2) below, the Council may, with the consent of the Corporation, affix to any building or structure ancillary to any tramway comprised in Tramlink—
  (a) street lighting equipment;
  (b) decorative lighting equipment;
  (c) traffic signs within the meaning of section 64 of the Road Traffic Regulation Act 1984;
  (d) traffic guidance control equipment;
  (e) traffic monitoring equipment; or
  (f) any other apparatus or equipment of a like nature.

(2) The power in subsection (1) above shall not be exercised in such a way as to impair the safe and efficient operation of Tramlink.

(3) The consent of the Corporation under this section may only be withheld if the Corporation consider that the proposed exercise of the power would impair the safe and efficient operation of Tramlink.

Provisions as to use of electrical energy

27. The following provisions shall apply to the use of electrical energy for the purposes of Tramlink:—

(1) The Corporation shall employ either insulated returns or uninsulated metallic returns of low resistance.

(2) The Corporation shall take all reasonable precautions in designing, constructing, placing and maintaining their electric lines and circuits and other works of all descriptions and also in working Tramlink so as to minimise the discharge of electrical currents into the ground and not—

(a) injuriously to affect by fusion or electrolytic action any electric lines or any gas or water pipes, or other metallic pipes, structures or substances; or

(b) injuriously to interfere with, or with the working of—

(i) any wire, line or apparatus from time to time used for the purpose of transmitting electrical energy or of any telecommunication system; or

(ii) the currents in any such wire, line or apparatus.

(3) (a) The Secretary of State may make regulations under this section for regulating the use of electrical energy for the operation of Tramlink, and the design, voltage, testing and working of the overhead equipment and return circuits of the Tramlink system, including regulations—

(i) for preventing injurious affection (by the discharge of electrical currents into the ground, fusion or electrolytic action) of electric lines or gas or water pipes or other metallic pipes, structures or substances; and

(ii) for minimising, so far as is reasonably practicable, interference with, and with the working of, electric wires, lines and apparatus, whether such apparatus does or does not use the earth as a return.

(b) Before making regulations under this section the Secretary of State shall consult the Corporation and the statutory undertakers.

(4) The Corporation shall be deemed to take all reasonable and proper precautions against interference with, or with the working of, any wire, line or apparatus if and so long as they use, at the option of the Corporation, either such insulated returns, or such uninsulated metallic returns of low resistance and such other means of preventing injurious interference with, and with the working of, the electric wires, lines and apparatus, as may be prescribed by the regulations; and in prescribing such means the Secretary of State shall have regard to the expense involved in relation to the protection afforded.

(5) The provisions of this section shall not give any right of action in respect of injurious interference with, or with the working of, any electric wire, line or apparatus, or the currents therein, unless, in the construction, erection, maintaining and working of such wire, line and apparatus, all reasonable and proper precautions, including the use of an insulated return, have been taken to minimise injurious interference therewith, and with the currents therein, by or from other electric currents.

(6) If any difference arises between the Corporation and any other person with respect to anything in the foregoing provisions of this section, the difference shall, unless the parties otherwise agree, be determined by the Secretary of State, or, at his option, by an arbitrator to be appointed by him, and the costs of such determination shall be in the discretion of the Secretary of State or the arbitrator as the case may be.

(7) The power to make regulations conferred on the Secretary of State by this section shall be exercisable by statutory instrument.

(8) In this section—

    (a) reference to an insulated return includes reference to a return by means of a combined neutral and earth cable which is covered by an insulated sheath suitable for protection against corrosion and is approved for use below ground by the Secretary of State for the purpose of any regulations relating to the supply of electricity; and

    (b) telecommunication system has the same meaning as in the Telecommunications Act 1984.

PART III

ACQUISITION OF LAND

Power to acquire lands

28.—(1) Subject to the provisions of this Act, the Corporation may enter upon, take and use—

    (a) so much of the land shown on the deposited plans within the limits of deviation for the authorised works as they may require for the purposes of the authorised works or for any purpose connected with, or ancillary to, their undertaking; and

    (b) so much of any land specified in columns (1) and (2) of Part I of Schedule 3 to this Act shown on the deposited plans within the limits of land to be acquired or used as they may require for the purpose specified in relation to that land in column (3) of that Part of that Schedule.

(2) Without prejudice to section 51 (As to land of Council) of this Act, the Corporation shall not under the powers of this Act without the consent of the Council acquire compulsorily any interest of the Council in the lands in the London borough of Croydon referred to in the book of reference.

(3) The Corporation shall not under the powers of this Act without the consent of the railways board acquire or enter upon, take or use whether temporarily or permanently, or acquire any new rights or subsoil of—

    (i) the lands of the railways board delineated on the deposited plans and therein numbered 1, 2, 3, 4, 5, 6, 8, 10, 11, 55, 57 and 60 in the London borough of Merton;

    (ii) the lands of the railways board delineated on the deposited plans and therein numbered 6, 9, 10, 10A, 25 and 30 in the London borough of Croydon; or

    (iii) the lands of the railways board delineated on the deposited plans and therein numbered 6, 7, 8, 10, 11, 12, 14, 15, 16, 17, 18 and 21 in the London borough of Bromley.

(4) Without prejudice to subsection (3) above the Corporation may acquire the interest of any person other than the railways board in any of the lands specified in subsection (3) above for the purposes of the authorised works.

Extinction of private rights of way

29.—(1) All private rights of way over any land that may be acquired compulsorily under this Act shall be extinguished on the acquisition of the land, whether compulsorily or by agreement, or on entry on the land in pursuance of section 11(1) of the Act of 1965 as applied by this Act, whichever is the sooner.

(2) All private rights of way over any land of which the Corporation may take temporary possession under this Act shall be suspended and unenforceable against the Corporation for so long as the Corporation shall remain in lawful possession thereof.

(3) Any person who suffers loss by the extinguishment or suspension of any right under this section shall be entitled to compensation to be determined in case of dispute in accordance with Part I of the Land Compensation Act 1961.

Power to acquire new rights

30.—(1) In this section references to the purchase by the Corporation of new rights are references to the purchase of rights to be created in favour of the Corporation.

(2) The Corporation may, for the purposes of constructing, maintaining, protecting, renewing and using any of the authorised works, purchase compulsorily such new rights as they may require over any of the lands that may be acquired compulsorily under this Act instead of acquiring those lands.

(3) The Act of 1965 as applied by this Act shall have effect with the modifications necessary to make it apply to the compulsory purchase of rights under subsection (2) above as it applies to the compulsory purchase of land so that, in appropriate contexts, references in that Act to land are read as referring, or as including references, to the rights or to land over which the rights are or are to be exercisable, according to the requirements of the context.

(4) Without prejudice to the generality of subsection (3) above, in relation to the purchase of rights under subsection (2) above—

(a) Part I of the Act of 1965 shall have effect with the modifications specified in Schedule 4 to this Act; and

(b) the enactments relating to compensation for the compulsory purchase of land shall apply with the necessary modifications as they apply to such compensation.

Acquisition of part only of certain properties

31.—(1) Where a copy of this section is endorsed on, or annexed to, a notice to treat served under the Act of 1965 as applied by this Act, the following provisions of this section shall apply to the land subject to the notice instead of section 8(1) of that Act.

(2) Where the land subject to the notice is part only of a house, building or factory, or part only of land consisting of a house together with any park or garden belonging thereto, then, if the person on whom the notice is served, within 21 days after the day on which the notice is served on him, serves on the Corporation a counter-notice objecting to the sale of the part and stating that he is willing and able to sell the whole (hereafter in this section referred to as "the land subject to the counter-notice"), the question whether he shall be required to sell the part shall, unless the Corporation agree to take the land subject to the counter-notice, be referred to the tribunal.

(3) If the said person does not serve such a counter-notice as aforesaid within 21 days after the day on which the notice to treat is served on him, or if on such a reference to the tribunal the tribunal determine that the part subject to the notice to treat can be taken without material detriment to the remainder of the land subject to the counter-notice or, in the case of part of land consisting of a house together with a park or garden belonging thereto, without material detriment to the remainder of the land subject to the counter-notice and without seriously affecting the amenity and convenience of the house, the said person shall be required to sell the part.

(4) If, on such a reference to the tribunal, the tribunal determine that part only of the land subject to the notice to treat can be taken without material detriment to the remainder of the land subject to the counter-notice or, as the case may be, without material detriment to the remainder of the land subject to the counter-notice and without seriously affecting the amenity and convenience of the house, the notice to treat shall be deemed to be a notice to treat for that part.

(5) If, on such a reference to the tribunal, the tribunal determine that the land subject to the notice to treat cannot be taken without material detriment to the remainder of the land subject to the counter-notice but that the material detriment is confined to a part of the land subject to the counter-notice, the notice to treat shall be deemed to be a notice to treat for the land to which the material detriment is confined in addition to the land already subject to the notice, whether or not the additional land is land which the Corporation are authorised to acquire compulsorily under this Act.

(6) If the Corporation agree to take the land subject to the counter-notice, or if the tribunal determine that—

(a) none of the land subject to the notice to treat can be taken without material detriment to the remainder of the land subject to the counter-notice or, as the case may be, without material detriment to the remainder of the land subject to the counter-notice and without seriously affecting the amenity and convenience of the house; and

(b) the material detriment is not confined to a part of the land subject to the counter-notice;

the notice to treat shall be deemed to be a notice to treat for the land subject to the counter-notice, whether or not the whole of that land is land which the Corporation are authorised to acquire compulsorily under this Act.

(7) In any case where, by virtue of a determination by the tribunal under subsection (4), (5) or (6) above, a notice to treat is deemed to be a notice to treat for part of the land specified in the notice or for more land than is specified in the notice, the Corporation may, within six weeks after the tribunal make their determination, withdraw the notice to treat, and if they do so shall pay to the person on whom the notice was served compensation for any loss or expense occasioned to him by the giving and withdrawal of the notice, to be determined in default of agreement by the tribunal.

(8) For the purposes of subsection (7) above, the determination shall not be taken to have been made so long as—

(a) the time for requiring the tribunal to state a case with respect to the determination has not expired;

(b) any proceedings on points raised by a case stated have not been concluded; or

(c) any proceedings on appeal from any decision on points raised by a case stated have not been concluded.

(9) Where a person is required under this section to sell part only of a house, building or factory, or of land consisting of a house together with any park or garden belonging thereto, the Corporation shall pay him compensation for any loss sustained by him due to the severance of that part in addition to the value of his interest therein.

Disregard of recent improvements and interests

32. In determining a question with respect to compensation claimed in consequence of the compulsory acquisition of land (including rights) under this Act, the tribunal shall not take into account—

(a) any interest in land; or

(b) any enhancement of the value of any interest in land, by reason of any building erected, works executed or improvement or alteration made, whether on the land acquired, or, as the case may be, on the land over which rights are acquired, or on any other land with which the claimant is, or was, at the time of erection, executing or making of the building, works, improvement or alteration, directly or indirectly concerned;

if the tribunal are satisfied that the creation of the interest, the erection of the building, the execution of the works or the making of the improvement or alteration, as the case may be, was not reasonably necessary and was undertaken with a view to obtaining compensation or increased compensation.

Set-off for enhancement in value of retained land

33.—(1) In this section "relevant land" means any land or any new rights over any land purchased by the Corporation for the purposes of the authorised works.

(2) In assessing the compensation payable to any person on the purchase by the Corporation from him of any relevant land, the tribunal shall—

    (a) have regard to the extent to which the land or the remaining contiguous lands belonging to the same person may be benefited by any of the authorised works; and

    (b) set off against the value of the relevant land any increase in value of the remaining contiguous lands belonging to the same person which will accrue to him by reason of the construction of any of the authorised works.

(3) The Land Compensation Act 1961 shall have effect subject to the provisions of this section.

Temporary possession of land

34.—(1) In this section "the relevant land" means so much of any of the lands specified in Part II of Schedule 3 to this Act as is not within the limits of deviation for any of the authorised works.

(2) Subject to the provisions of this section, the Corporation may take temporary possession of and use the relevant land for the provision of working sites and access for construction purposes.

(3) Not less than 28 days before entering upon and taking temporary possession of the relevant land the Corporation shall give notice to the owners and occupiers of the land.

(4)(a) The Corporation shall not, without the agreement of the owners and occupiers, remain in possession of any part of the relevant land under the powers of this section after a period of 18 months from the completion of the authorised works.

(b) Before giving up possession of the relevant land, the Corporation shall remove all temporary works and restore the relevant land to the reasonable satisfaction of the owners and occupiers thereof; but the Corporation shall not be required to replace a building removed by them under this section.

(5)(a) The Corporation shall not be empowered to purchase compulsorily, or be required to purchase, any part of the relevant land.

(b) The Corporation shall compensate the owners and occupiers of the relevant land for any loss or damage which may result to them by reason of the exercise of the powers of this section in relation to the relevant land.

(c) Nothing in this section shall relieve the Corporation from liability to compensate under section 6 or 43 of the Act of 1845 or section 10(2) of the Act of 1965 as incorporated or applied by this Act, or under any other enactment, in respect of loss or damage arising from the execution of any works, other than loss or damage for which compensation is payable under paragraph (b) above.

(6) Every case of compensation under this section shall be determined in case of dispute in accordance with Part I of the Land Compensation Act 1961.

Provision for mortgagors in certain cases

35.—(1) This section applies where—

    (a) the whole or part of the interest of a resident owner occupier ("the relevant owner") in land is acquired in consequence of the construction of Tramlink;

(b) at the date of the passing of this Act the interest is subject to one or more mortgages;

(c) at the valuation date, the principal, interest and costs secured on the land by that mortgage or those mortgages ("the mortgage debt") exceeds 90 per cent. of the open market value of the whole of the relevant owner's interest in the land; and

(d) the whole of the mortgage debt is required by the mortgagee or mortgagees to be repaid on the disposal by the relevant owner of the interest in the land to be acquired as mentioned in paragraph (a) above.

(2) Where this section applies the acquiring authority may, if so required by the relevant owner, either—

(a) lend to him on the terms mentioned in subsection (3) below a sum equal to the amount by which the mortgage debt exceeds 90 per cent. of the open market value of the whole of his interest in the land at the valuation date; or

(b) if another person lends that sum to the relevant owner on the terms mentioned in subsection (3) or on other terms acceptable to the relevant owner, guarantee any default on the part of the relevant owner in the payment of that loan and of all interest payable under it.

(3) Any loan made under subsection (2)(a) above shall, unless otherwise agreed between the parties, be made on the same terms (except as to security) as those on which the mortgage (or, if there was more than one, the last mortgage) referred to in subsection (1)(b) above was made.

(4) Any loan made under subsection (2)(a) above shall, if the acquiring authority so require, be secured—

(a) by way of a second mortgage, on any land purchased by the relevant owner within two years from the valuation date; and

(b) where only part of the relevant owner's interest in the land has been acquired, by way of a first mortgage on the land retained by the relevant owner (in addition to the mortgage referred to in paragraph (a) above).

(5) Where the acquiring authority enter into a guarantee under subsection (2)(b) above, the relevant owner and his personal representatives shall indemnify the acquiring authority against all actions, proceedings, liability, claims, damages, costs and expenses in relation to or arising out of the guarantee.

(6) For the purposes of this section an interest in land shall be taken to be acquired in consequence of the construction of Tramlink if—

(a) it is acquired by the Corporation for the purposes of the Act; or

(b) it is acquired by the Corporation or the Council in pursuance of any undertaking given to a Parliamentary Committee during the passage through Parliament of the Bill for this Act or any undertaking or agreement given to a person in consideration of his refraining from opposition to that Bill.

(7) In this section—

"acquiring authority" means the Corporation or, as the case may be, the Council;

"the mortgage debt" means the principal, interest and costs referred to in subsection (1)(c) above;

"the relevant owner" means the owner occupier referred to in subsection (1) above;

"resident owner occupier" has the same meaning as in Chapter II of Part VI of the Town and Country Planning Act 1990; and

"valuation date" means the date on which the relevant owner's interest falls to be valued for the purposes of the acquisition (whether under the enactments relating to compulsory purchase or under the agreement or undertaking concerned).

Correction of errors in deposited plans and book of reference

36.—(1) If the deposited plans or the deposited book of reference are inaccurate in their description of any land, or in their statement or description of the ownership or occupation of any land, the Corporation, after giving not less than 10 days' notice to the owner, lessee and occupier of the land in question, may apply to two justices having jurisdiction in the place where the land is situated for the correction thereof.

(2) If on any such application it appears to the justices that the misstatement or wrong description arose from mistake or inadvertence, the justices shall certify the fact accordingly and shall in their certificate state in what respect any matter is misstated or wrongly described.

(3) The certificate shall be deposited in the office of the Clerk of the Parliaments, and a copy thereof in the Private Bill Office, House of Commons, and with the proper officer of the London borough council for the area in which the land is situated and thereupon the deposited plans and the deposited book of reference shall be deemed to be corrected according to the certificate, and it shall be lawful for the Corporation to take the land or, as the case may be, a right over the land and execute the works in accordance with the certificate.

(4) A person with whom a copy of the certificate is deposited under this section shall keep it with the other documents to which it relates.

Period of compulsory purchase of lands or rights

37.—(1) The powers of the Corporation for the compulsory acquisition of the lands and rights which they are authorised to acquire by this Part of this Act shall not be exercised after the expiration of five years from the passing of this Act.

(2) The powers of the Corporation for the compulsory acquisition of the said lands and rights shall, for the purposes of this section, be deemed to have been exercised if notice to treat has been served in respect of those lands and rights.

Extinguishment of powers of compulsory purchase of lands or rights

38.—(1) The compulsory purchase powers shall cease to have effect if—
  (a) a period of not less than 3 years beginning with the day on which this Act is passed has expired;
  (b) none of those powers has been exercised; and
  (c) after the expiry of the said period of 3 years, a resolution in pursuance of this section is passed by each of the following:—
      (i) the Council;
      (ii) the Council of the London borough of Merton; and
      (iii) the Council of the London borough of Bromley.
(2) For the purposes of this section—
  (a) "compulsory purchase powers" means the powers of the Corporation for the compulsory acquisition of lands or rights under this Part of this Act; and
  (b) the compulsory purchase powers shall be deemed to have been exercised if notice to treat has been served under those powers in respect of any land or rights.

PART IV

MISCELLANEOUS AND GENERAL

Crown rights

39.—(1) Nothing in this Act affects prejudicially any estate, right, power, privilege or exemption of the Crown and, without prejudice to the generality of the foregoing, nothing in this Act authorises the Corporation to take, use or in any manner interfere with any land or hereditaments or any rights of whatsoever description—

(a) belonging to Her Majesty in right of Her Crown and under the management of the Crown Estate Commissioners, without the consent in writing of those commissioners; or

(b) belonging to Her Majesty in right of Her Crown and under the management (pursuant to any statute or otherwise) of the Secretary of State, without his consent in writing; or

(c) belonging to a government department or held in trust for Her Majesty for the purposes of a government department, without the consent in writing of that government department.

(2) A consent under subsection (1) above may be given unconditionally or subject to such conditions and upon such terms as may be considered necessary or appropriate.

(3) Nothing in this section shall prejudice or affect the exercise of statutory powers to carry out works in or affecting any highway vested in or maintained by the Secretary of State.

Environmental protection

40. The following provisions shall, unless otherwise agreed in writing between the Corporation and the Council, have effect:—

(1) In this section—

"construction" includes placing, alteration and renewal;

"plans" includes sections, drawings, specifications, particulars and descriptions (including descriptions of methods of construction);

"the specified works" means so much of Works Nos. 3, 3A, 3B, 4, 5 and 6 as may be constructed in the London borough of Croydon.

(2) The Corporation shall, before commencing the construction of the specified works, supply to the Council proper and sufficient plans thereof for their approval and shall not commence the specified works until plans thereof have been approved in writing by the Council, or settled by arbitration in accordance with subsection (5) below:

Provided that if within 56 days after such plans have been supplied to the Council they shall not have notified their disapproval thereof and the grounds of their disapproval, they shall be deemed to have approved the plans as supplied:

(3) The construction of the specified works shall, when commenced, be carried out in accordance with the plans as approved by the Council or deemed to have been so approved or settled by arbitration in accordance with subsection (5) below.

(4) The Council may not withhold their approval under this section except in respect of any detail of the plans which—

(a) in their reasonable opinion will cause unacceptable detriment to the environment or to the amenity of the borough; and

(b) is susceptible of a reasonable alternative which will not in their reasonable opinion cause such detriment.

(5) Any difference arising between the Corporation and the Council under this section shall be referred to and settled by arbitration but the Corporation and the Council shall use their best endeavours to ensure that proceedings before an arbitrator commence in every case within 7 days of the Corporation or the Council registering such a difference.

Power to lop trees overhanging railway

41.—(1) The Corporation may cut and lop any trees in or near any railway forming part of Tramlink which may in any way interfere with the construction or working of the railway or cables, wires or other apparatus, or with the clear and safe passage of carriages and their passengers.

(2) In exercising the powers of this section the Corporation shall do no unnecessary damage to trees and shall pay compensation to any person who may sustain damage by reason of the exercise of the powers.

(3) Every case of compensation under subsection (2) above shall be determined in case of dispute in accordance with Part I of the Land Compensation Act 1961.

Traffic control

42.—(1) The Corporation shall not exercise the powers conferred by section 11 (Subsidiary works) of this Act in relation to any signalling, monitoring or communication equipment the purpose of which is to control traffic on any tramway comprised in Tramlink except with the consent of the Secretary of State.

(2) Subject to any general or specific directions given by the Secretary of State, the Corporation shall not exercise the powers conferred by that section in relation to any signalling, monitoring or communication equipment the purpose of which is to control general traffic on the street in which the tramway is laid as well as traffic on the tramway itself except with the consent of the highway authority.

(3) Subject to any general or specific directions given by the Secretary of State, the highway authority shall, unless otherwise agreed with the Corporation, operate any such signalling, monitoring or communications equipment as is referred to in subsection (1) above if the purpose of operating that equipment is to control general traffic on the street in which the tramway is laid as well as traffic on the tramway itself.

Removal of obstructions

43.—(1) If any obstruction to traffic on Tramlink is caused by—

(a) a vehicle on any tramway or at any level crossing waiting, loading, unloading or breaking down; or

(b) a load falling on any tramway or at any level crossing from a vehicle;

the person in charge of the vehicle shall forthwith remove the vehicle or the load so as to prevent the continuance of the obstruction and, if he fails to do so, the Corporation may remove the vehicle or load, taking all necessary steps for that purpose, and may recover from any person responsible the expenses reasonably incurred in doing so.

(2) In subsection (1) above "person responsible" means—

(a) in the case of a vehicle waiting, loading, unloading or breaking down—

(i) the owner of the vehicle at the time at which it became an obstruction to traffic on Tramlink unless he shows that he was not concerned in, or aware of, the vehicle being put or left in that place at that time; and

(ii) the person by whom the vehicle was put or left in the place in which it became an obstruction to traffic on Tramlink; and

(b) in the case of a load falling from a vehicle—

(i) the owner of the vehicle at the time of that event unless he shows that he was not concerned in, or aware of, the vehicle being put or left, or as the case may be, being in the place at which the load fell from it; and

(ii) the person in charge of the vehicle at the time when the load fell from it.

(3) For the purposes of this section the owner of a vehicle shall be taken to be the person by whom the vehicle is kept; and in determining, for those

purposes who was the owner of a vehicle at any time, it shall be presumed (unless the contrary appears) that the owner was the person in whose name the vehicle was at that time registered under the Vehicles (Excise) Act 1971.

For better prevention of trespass on railways

44.—(1) Any person who trespasses upon any railway lines or sidings or in any tunnel or upon any embankment, cutting or similar work forming part of any railway comprised in Tramlink which is not designated as a tramway, or upon any other lands of the Corporation to which the public are not admitted in dangerous proximity to any such lines or other works or to any electrical apparatus used for or in connection with the working of any such railway, shall be guilty of an offence and liable on summary conviction to a fine not exceeding level 3 on the standard scale.

(2) No person shall be convicted of an offence under this section unless it is proved to the satisfaction of the court before which complaint is laid that public warning has been given to persons not to trespass upon the railways comprised in Tramlink by notice clearly exhibited and maintained at the station on Tramlink nearest to the place where the offence is alleged to have been committed.

Penalty fares

45.—(1) The Secretary of State may, at the request of the Corporation, by order provide that any enactment (whether passed before or after this Act) relating to the imposition by the Corporation of penalty fares on passengers travelling on a bus service or a train service shall have effect, as from such date as may be specified in the order, with respect to passengers travelling on Tramlink with such modifications as may be specified in the order.

(2) Any order under subsection (1) above, and any order revoking such an order, may contain such supplementary, incidental and consequential provisions (including transitional provisions) as may appear to the Secretary of State to be necessary or expedient.

(3) The power to make an order conferred on the Secretary of State by subsection (1) above shall be exercisable by statutory instrument subject to annulment in pursuance of a resolution of either House of Parliament.

(4) The Secretary of State may recover from the Corporation payment of administrative costs reasonably incurred by him in connection with an application for an order under subsection (1) above and, where the order is made, in connection with the making of the order subject to a maximum payment of £5,000 in respect of the application for and making of any such order.

Byelaws relating to Tramlink

46.—(1) The Corporation may make byelaws regulating the use of and working of, and travel on, Tramlink, the maintenance of order on Tramlink and on the Corporation's premises or other facilities provided in connection with Tramlink and the conduct of all persons including officers and servants of the Corporation while on those premises.

(2) Without prejudice to the generality of subsection (1) above, byelaws under this section may contain provisions—
- (a) with respect to tickets issued for travel on Tramlink, the payment of fares and charges and the evasion of payment of fares and charges;
- (b) with respect to interference with, or obstruction of, the working of Tramlink or other facilities provided in connection with Tramlink;

(c) with respect to the use of tobacco or other substances and the prevention of nuisances;

(d) for regulating the passage of bicycles and other vehicles on ways and other places intended for the use of persons on foot within railway premises of the Corporation, not being premises within the boundary of any street;

(e) for the safe custody and delivery or disposal of property found in premises of the Corporation forming part of, or provided in connection with, Tramlink, or elsewhere on Tramlink and for fixing the charges which may be made in respect thereof; and

(f) for prohibiting or restricting the placing or leaving of any vehicle without its driver on any authorised railway, or in premises of the Corporation forming part of Tramlink.

(3) Byelaws made under this section may provide that any person contravening them shall be liable on summary conviction to a fine not exceeding for each offence level 3 on the standard scale.

(4) Without prejudice to the taking of proceedings under subsection (3) above, if the contravention of any byelaw having effect under this section is attended with danger or annoyance to the public, or hindrance to the Corporation in the conduct of Tramlink, it shall be lawful for the Corporation summarily to take action to obviate or remove the danger, annoyance or hindrance.

(5) The power of making byelaws under this section shall include power to vary or repeal any byelaw previously made under this section.

(6) Subsections (5) to (11) of section 67 of the Transport Act 1962 (confirmation of byelaws) shall apply to any byelaws made by the Corporation under this section as they apply to any byelaws made under that section.

Carriages on Tramlink deemed public service vehicles

47.—(1) On such day as may be appointed under subsection (2) below, regulations made, or having effect as if made, under section 25 or 60(1)(k) of the Public Passenger Vehicles Act 1981 (regulation of conduct of passengers and lost property) shall have effect as if the carriages used on Tramlink were public service vehicles used in the provision of a local service within the meaning of the Transport Act 1985.

(2)(a) The Corporation may by resolution appoint a day for the purpose of any regulation mentioned in subsection (1) above, the day so appointed being fixed in accordance with paragraph (b) below.

(b) The Corporation shall publish in a newspaper circulating in the area in which Tramlink is situated, notice—

(i) of the passing of any such resolution and of the day fixed thereby; and

(ii) of the general effect of the enactments for the purposes of which the day has been fixed;

and the day so fixed shall not be earlier than the expiration of 28 days from the date of the publication of the notice.

(c) A photostatic or other reproduction certified by the secretary of the Corporation to be a true reproduction of a page, or part of a page, of any newspaper bearing the date of its publication and containing the notice mentioned in paragraph (b) above shall be evidence of the publication of the notice and of the date of publication.

Proposed discontinuance of services on Tramlink

48. The provisions of Schedule 5 to the Railways Act 1993 (procedure for closure of certain railway passenger services) shall apply in relation to any passenger services operating on Tramlink as if those services were for the time being designated in an order under section 49(3) of that Act as railway passenger services in relation to which that Schedule is to have effect.

Application of Railways Act 1993

49. For the avoidance of doubt it is hereby declared that Tramlink shall be deemed to be a tramway for the purposes of Part I of the Railways Act 1993.

Transfer of functions

50.—(1) The Secretary of State may by order provide that all or any of the functions of the Corporation arising under this Act shall be transferred to and vested in any other person.

(2) A transfer order may be made so as to transfer and vest such functions in a person for such period as may be specified in that order or for so long as the order remains in force.

(3) Without prejudice to the power of the Secretary of State to revoke or amend a transfer order, a transfer order may specify circumstances in which that order shall cease to have effect before the expiry of any period specified in any such order.

(4) A transfer order may include such supplementary, incidental, transitional and consequential provisions as the Secretary of State may consider to be necessary or expedient.

(5) Upon expiry of any period specified in a transfer order in accordance with subsection (2) above or upon a transfer order being revoked or otherwise ceasing to have effect, the functions of the Corporation which were transferred by that order shall, by virtue of this subsection but subject to the effect of any further transfer order, be transferred to and vested in the Corporation but such vesting in the Corporation shall not make the Corporation subject to any of the liabilities of the person in whom those functions had previously been vested (other than liabilities which arise pursuant to any undertaking given to a Parliamentary Committee during the passage through Parliament of the Bill for this Act or any undertaking or agreement given to a person in consideration of his refraining from opposition to that Bill).

(6) Notwithstanding the provisions of section 50(2) of the Fair Trading Act 1973 the Director General of Fair Trading may make a monopoly reference, within the meaning of that Act, in respect of services consisting of the carriage of passengers or goods by rail on the authorised railways at any time during which the functions of the Corporation under this Act in respect of the provision of any of those services have been transferred to and are vested in any other person by virtue of a transfer order.

(7) Subject to subsection (8) below, while the functions of the Corporation under this Act in respect of the provision of passenger services are vested in a transferee by virtue of a transfer order, it shall be the duty of the Committee to consider and, where it appears to them to be desirable, make recommendations with respect to any matter affecting such services which is—

    (a) the subject of representations (other than representations appearing to the Committee to be frivolous) made to the Committee by or on behalf of users of those services; or

    (b) referred to the Committee by the Secretary of State or by the transferee; or

    (c) in the opinion of the Committee a matter to which consideration ought to be given;

and copies of the minutes, conclusions and recommendations of the Committee shall be sent to the Secretary of State, the transferee and to such person as may be directed by the Secretary of State.

(8)(a) Subsection (7) above shall apply only after the opening for passenger services of the railway comprised within the authorised works and nothing in that subsection shall entitle the Committee to consider the charges made for any services, or to consider any question relating to the discontinuance or reduction of railway services or, subject to paragraph (b) below, any matter which is the subject of a monopoly reference by the Director General of Fair Trading pursuant to subsection (6) above.

(b) Nothing in subsection (8)(a) above shall affect consideration under section 81 of the Fair Trading Act 1973 of any representations made by the Committee pursuant to that section or preclude the Committee from being heard orally under that section.

(9) The power to make a transfer order shall be exercisable by statutory instrument.

(10) The Secretary of State may recover from the Corporation payment of administrative costs reasonably incurred by him in connection with an application for an order under this section and, where the order is made, in connection with the making of the order subject to a maximum payment of £5,000 in respect of the application for and making of any such order.

(11) In this section—

"the Committee" means the London Regional Passengers' Committee;

"functions" includes powers, duties and obligations;

"transferee" means the person to whom the functions of the Corporation under this Act in respect of the provision of passenger services have been transferred by virtue of a transfer order; and

"transfer order" means an order made under this section.

As to land of Council

51.—(1) Notwithstanding the provisions of section 123(2) of the Local Government Act 1972, where land held by the Council is shown on the deposited plans within the limits of deviation for the authorised works or within the limits of land to be acquired or used, the Council may dispose of that land to the Corporation for a consideration less than the best that can reasonably be obtained.

(2) Where by virtue of subsection (1) above the Council dispose of land which is held—

(a) for the purposes of section 164 of the Public Health Act 1875 (pleasure grounds); or

(b) in accordance with section 10 of the Open Spaces Act 1906 (duty of local authority to maintain open spaces and burial grounds),

the land shall by virtue of the disposal be freed from any trust arising solely by virtue of its being land held in trust for enjoyment by the public in accordance with the said section 164 or, as the case may be, the said section 10.

(3) Subsection (4) below shall apply if—

(a) the construction of the authorised works shall not have begun within the period specified in section 55(2) (Planning permission) of this Act, or

(b) the provisions of this Act which confer power to construct, maintain and operate so much of Tramlink as is situated, or is to be situated, on the designated land are repealed, and

at the end of that period or (as the case may be) on the day on which the provisions are repealed any land which adjoins the designated land is held by the Council or any other person on terms (however expressed and whether imposed by or under statute or any other instrument) requiring the land to be preserved or regulated as a park, recreation ground or public open space for the enjoyment of the public.

(4) Where this subsection applies, the Secretary of State may, on an application made in accordance with subsection (5) below by any interested person, make an order vesting the designated land or any part of that land in such person as he may determine on the same terms as the adjoining land is held or on such other terms as he shall consider appropriate, being terms which secure that the designated land (or that part of it) is preserved or regulated as

a park, recreational ground or public open space for the enjoyment of the public.

(5) An application under subsection (4) above shall be made in writing and—

(a) in a case falling within paragraph (a) of subsection (3) above, within 12 months of the end of the period referred to in that paragraph, or

(b) in a case falling within paragraph (b) of that subsection, within 12 months of the repeal of the provisions referred to in that paragraph.

(6) The Secretary of State shall not make an order under subsection (4) above in relation to any land unless he is satisfied that the land is no longer required for the purposes of Tramlink; and before making such an order he shall give to the owner, lessee or occupier of the land the opportunity of making representations.

(7) In this section—

"the designated land" means so much of the land in the London borough of Croydon shown numbered 5A, 76, 78, 79, 81, 98, 99, 102, 104, 106, 108, 112, 118 and 126 on the deposited plans, and so much of the land in the London borough of Bromley shown numbered 1 on those plans, as may be acquired for the purposes of Tramlink pursuant to the powers conferred by this Act; and

"the adjoining land" means the land adjoining the designated land and referred to in subsection (3) above.

Power of Council to make agreements

52. The Council may enter into and carry into effect agreements with respect to the construction, maintenance, use and operation of Tramlink or any part or parts thereof and as to any other matters incidental or subsidiary thereto or consequential thereon.

As to application of certain railway enactments

53.—(1) Any enactment by which any railway or former railway of the railways board comprised within the affected properties was authorised shall have effect subject to the provisions of this Act.

(2) Nothing in subsection (1) above shall prejudice any express statutory provision for—

(a) the protection of the owner, lessee or occupier of any specifically designated property; or

(b) the protection or benefit of any public trustees or commissioners, corporation or other person, specifically named in such provision.

(3) In this section "affected properties" has the same meaning as in section 16 (Agreements with British Railways Board) of this Act.

Saving for Reservoirs Act 1975

54. Nothing in this Act shall affect the application of the Reservoirs Act 1975.

Planning permission

55.—(1) In this section "Part 11 development" means development permitted by article 3 of, and Part 11 of Schedule 2 to, the Town and Country

Planning General Development Order 1988 (which permits development
authorised by private Act designating specifically both the nature of the
development thereby authorised and the land on which it may be carried
out).

(2) Subject to the provisions of subsection (3) below, in its application to
development authorised by this Act, the planning permission granted for
Part 11 development shall have effect as if the authority to develop given by
this Act were limited to development begun within 10 years of the passing of
this Act.

(3) Subsection (2) above shall not apply to the carrying out of any development consisting of the alteration, maintenance or repair of works authorised
by this Act or the substitution of new works therefor.

(4) Without prejudice to the planning permission granted for Part 11
development, it is hereby declared for the avoidance of doubt that, for the
purposes of Part 17 of Schedule 2 to the said Order of 1988 (which permits
certain development by statutory undertakers)—

  (a) the tramways comprised in Tramlink and the works and conveniences
      connected with those tramways shall be taken to be a tramway under-
      taking within Class H of that Part of that Schedule; and

  (b) the authorised railways other than tramways comprised in Tramlink
      and the works and conveniences connected with those railways shall
      be taken to be a light railway undertaking within Class A of that Part
      of that Schedule.

For protection of British Railways Board

56. For the protection of the railways board the following provisions shall,
unless otherwise agreed in writing between the Corporation and the railways
board for the purposes of this section, have effect:—

  (1) In this section—
      "construction" includes reconstruction and, where the context so
      admits, includes maintenance and repair of the specified works;
      "the engineer" means an engineer to be appointed by the rail-
      ways board;
      "plans" includes sections, drawings, particulars and schedules of
      construction;
      "railway property" means any railway of the railways board, and
      any works, apparatus and equipment of the railways board connec-
      ted therewith and includes any land held or used by the railways
      board for the purposes of such railway or works; and
      "the specified works" means so much of the authorised works as
      may be situated upon, across, under, over or within 15 metres of
      railway property or may in any way affect railway property.

  (2) The exercise by the Corporation against the railways board of the
      powers of section 11(3) of the Act of 1965 shall be confined to lands
      which the Corporation are empowered to acquire compulsorily under
      section 28 (Power to acquire lands) of this Act.

  (3) In its application to the service on the railways board of notice of entry
      in respect of the following lands:—
      the lands of the railways board delineated on the deposited plans
      and therein numbered 56, 57, 58, 60, 62, 66, 84, 85, 86, 87, 88, 89, 90
      and 91 in the London borough of Croydon,
      section 11(1) of the Act of 1965 (as incorporated by section 5(1)
      (Application of Part I of Compulsory Purchase Act 1965) of this Act)
      shall have effect as if for the word "fourteen" there were substituted
      the words "one hundred and eighty".

(4) No part of the track formation of the authorised railways shall be constructed so as to pass beneath the track formation of any operational railway of the railways board:

Provided that this subsection shall not preclude the construction of track formation beneath a bridge carrying an operational railway of the railways board.

(5) Except with the consent of the railways board—

　　(a) the Corporation shall not in the exercise of the powers of this Act interrupt or prejudicially affect pedestrian or vehicular access to any operational station of the railways board or any other railway property; and

　　(b) the provisions of section 29 (Extinction of private rights of way) of this Act shall not apply to any right of access of the railways board to any railway property:

Provided that such consent shall not be unreasonably withheld but may be given subject to reasonable conditions.

(6) The Corporation shall not under the powers of this Act enter upon any railway property for the purpose of exercising its powers under section 41 (Power to lop trees overhanging railway) of this Act without the consent of the railways board which shall not be unreasonably withheld but which may be given subject to reasonable conditions.

(7) (a) The Corporation shall, before commencing the construction of the specified works, furnish to the railways board such proper and sufficient plans thereof (including, in the case of the works described in paragraphs (xiii), (xiv), (xx) and (xxi) of Part II of Schedule 1 to this Act, particulars as to the working methods and the regulation of traffic in the vicinity of the works) as may reasonably be required by the engineer and shall not commence the specified works until plans thereof have been approved in writing by the engineer or settled by arbitration as provided in paragraph (b) below;

(b) The engineer's approval under paragraph (a) above shall not be unreasonably withheld and any question of whether it has been unreasonably withheld shall be settled by arbitration, and in any event if within 56 days after such plans have been furnished to the railways board the engineer has not notified his disapproval thereof and the grounds of his disapproval, he shall be deemed to have approved the plans as submitted.

(8) If within 56 days after such plans have been furnished to the railways board, the railways board give notice to the Corporation that the railways board themselves desire to construct any part of the specified works, which in the opinion of the engineer will or may affect the stability of railway property and the safe operation of the railways of the railways board, then, if the Corporation desire such part of the specified works to be constructed, the railways board shall construct it with all reasonable dispatch on behalf of, and to the reasonable satisfaction of, the Corporation in accordance with the plans approved or deemed to be approved or settled as aforesaid.

(9) Upon signifying his approval or disapproval of the plans the engineer may specify any protective works, whether temporary or permanent, which in his opinion should be carried out before the commencement of the construction of the specified works to ensure the stability of railway property, the continuation of safe and effective operation of the railways of the railways board (including any relocation of works, apparatus and equipment necessitated by the specified works) and the comfort and safety of their passengers who may be affected by the specified works, and such protective works as may be reasonably necessary for those purposes shall be constructed by the railways board with all reasonable dispatch or, if the railways board so desire,

such protective works shall be carried out by the Corporation at their own expense, and the Corporation shall not commence the construction of the specified works until the engineer has notified the Corporation that the protective works have been satisfactorily completed.

(10) The Corporation shall give to the engineer not less than 56 days' notice of their intention to commence the construction of any of the specified works and also, except in emergency (when they shall give such notice as may be reasonably practicable), of their intention to carry out any works for the repair or maintenance of the specified works insofar as such works of repair or maintenance affect or interfere with railway property.

(11) The construction of the specified works and of any protective works carried out by the Corporation by virtue of the provisions of subsection (9) above shall, when commenced, be carried out with all reasonable dispatch in accordance with the plans approved or deemed to be approved or settled as aforesaid and under the supervision (if given), and to the reasonable satisfaction, of the engineer, and in such manner as to cause as little damage as may be to railway property and as little interference as may be with the conduct of traffic on the railways of the railways board and the use by passengers of railway property and, if any damage to railway property or any such interference is caused by the carrying out of the specified works, the Corporation shall, notwithstanding any such approval as aforesaid, make good such damage and shall pay to the railways board all reasonable expenses which the railways board may reasonably incur and compensation for any loss which they may sustain by reason of any such damage or interference:

Provided that nothing in this subsection shall impose any liability on the Corporation with respect to any damage, cost, expense or loss which is attributable to the act, neglect or default of the railways board or their servants or agents.

(12) Without prejudice to the generality of subsections (9) and (11) above, the railways board may, in approving the plans of or in supervising the carrying out of the specified works or of any protective works carried out by the Corporation by virtue of the provisions of subsection (9) above, impose reasonable conditions with a view to ensuring that—

(a) nothing shall be done by or on behalf of the Corporation which impedes the free, uninterrupted and safe flow of passengers to and from the Wimbledon, Mitcham Junction, West Croydon, East Croydon, Elmers End, Birkbeck and Beckenham Junction stations of the railways board;

(b) dust sheets and other works and working methods are used so as to prevent, so far as practicable, any dust or dirt from the relevant works affecting such passengers; and

(c) adequate signing of all alterations of routes for passengers and of any hazards or obstructions to the free movement of passengers is provided.

(13) The Corporation shall at all times afford reasonable facilities to the engineer for access to the specified works during their construction and shall supply him with all such information as he may reasonably require with regard to the specified works or the method of construction thereof.

(14) During the construction of any works by the railways board under this section the railways board shall at all times afford reasonable facilities to the Corporation and their agents for access to those works, and shall supply the Corporation with such information as they may reasonably require with regard to such works or the method of construction thereof.

(15) If any alterations or additions, either permanent or temporary, to railway property are reasonably necessary during the construction of the specified works, or during a period of 12 months after the completion thereof, by reason of the construction of the specified works, such alterations and additions may be carried out by the railways board and, if the railways board give to the Corporation reasonable notice of their intention to carry out such alterations or additions, the Corporation shall pay to the railways board the reasonable cost thereof including, in respect of permanent alterations and additions, a capitalised sum representing any increase in the costs which may be expected to be reasonably incurred by the railways board in maintaining, working and, when necessary, renewing any such alterations or additions:

Provided that, if the cost of maintaining, working or renewing railway property is reduced in consequence of any such alterations or additions, a capitalised sum representing such saving shall be set off against any sum payable by the Corporation to the railways board under this section.

(16) The Corporation shall repay to the railways board all reasonable costs, charges and expenses reasonably incurred by the railways board—

(a) in constructing any part of the specified works on behalf of the Corporation as provided by subsection (8) above or in constructing any protective works under the provisions of subsection (9) above, including, in respect of any permanent protective works, a capitalised sum representing the costs which may be expected to be reasonably incurred by the railways board in maintaining and renewing such works;

(b) in respect of the employment of any inspectors, signalmen, watchmen and other persons whom it is reasonably necessary to appoint for inspecting, signalling, watching and lighting railway property and for preventing, so far as may be reasonably practicable, interference, obstruction, danger or accident arising from the construction or failure of the specified works;

(c) in respect of any special traffic working resulting from any speed restrictions which may, in the opinion of the engineer, require to be imposed by reason of the construction or failure of the specified works, or from the substitution or diversion of services which may be reasonably necessary for the same reason;

(d) in respect of any additional temporary lighting of railway property in the vicinity of the specified works, being lighting made reasonably necessary by reason of the construction or failure of the specified works;

(e) in respect of the supervision by the engineer of the construction of the specified works.

(17) The Corporation shall be responsible for, and make good to the railways board, all reasonable costs, charges, damages and expenses not otherwise provided for in this section which may be occasioned to, or reasonably incurred by, the railways board—

(a) by reason of the construction of the specified works (as opposed to their existence) or the failure thereof; or

(b) by reason of any act or omission of the Corporation or of any person in their employ, or of their contractors or others whilst engaged upon the construction of the specified works;

and the Corporation shall indemnify the railways board from and against all claims and demands arising out of or in connection with the construction of the specified works or any such failure, act or omission as aforesaid, and the fact that any act or thing may have been done in accordance with any requirement of the engineer or under his supervision, shall not (if it was not attributable to the act, neglect or default of the railways board, or of any person in their employ, or of their

contractors or agents) excuse the Corporation from any liability under the provisions of this section:
    Provided that the railways board shall give to the Corporation reasonable notice of any claim or demand as aforesaid and no settlement or compromise thereof shall be made without the prior consent of the Corporation.
(18) Any difference arising between the Corporation and the railways board under this section (other than a difference as to the meaning or construction of this section) shall be referred to and settled by arbitration.

Protection of certain bodies and persons

57. Schedule 5 to this Act shall have effect for protecting the interests of the bodies and persons specified in that Schedule.

Arbitration

58. Where under this Act any difference (other than a difference to which the provisions of the Act of 1965 as applied by this Act apply) is to be determined by arbitration, then, unless otherwise provided, the difference shall be referred to and settled by a single arbitrator to be agreed between the parties or, failing agreement, to be appointed, on the application of either party (after notice in writing to the other), by the President of the Institution of Civil Engineers.

SCHEDULES

Section 6   SCHEDULE 1

THE AUTHORISED WORKS

Note: In the following descriptions:—
    "the South Western Railway" means the former London and South Western Railway (London to Southampton);
    "the Wimbledon Railway" means the Wimbledon to West Croydon Railway;
    "the Sutton Railway" means the Streatham Junction to Sutton Railway;
    "the West Croydon Railway" means the West Croydon to Epsom Railway;
    "the Brighton Railway" means the former London Brighton and South Coast Railway (London to Brighton);
    "the former Selsdon Railway" means that part of the former Woodside and South Croydon Railway between Woodside Junction and Selsdon;
    "the Mid Kent Railway" means that part of the former South Eastern Railway (Mid Kent Line) between Lewisham and Hayes;
    "the Addiscombe Railway" means that part of the former South Eastern Railway (Mid Kent Line) between Elmers End and Addiscombe;
    "the Norwood Spur" means the Victoria to Beckenham Junction (via Crystal Palace) Railway.

PART I

DESCRIPTION OF WORKS SPECIFICALLY AUTHORISED

In the London boroughs of Merton, Sutton and Croydon—
    Work No. 1   A railway (9,307 metres in length) commencing at a point 100 metres west of the junction of Hartfield Crescent with Hartfield Road, passing south-eastwards along

the course of the Wimbledon Railway, passing over the River Wandle by means of the existing bridges, passing beneath the existing bridge carrying Carshalton Road over the Sutton and Wimbledon Railways, then passing to the south of Mitcham Junction Station, passing over the Sutton Railway including a new bridge over that railway, then rejoining the course of the Wimbledon Railway, passing over the West Croydon Railway including a bridge over that railway, passing north-eastwards along the north-western side of Waddon New Road, then along that road from a point 30 metres north-east of the junction of that road with Lower Church Street to the junction of Waddon New Road and Cairo New Road, then passing south-eastwards along the course of that road and terminating at a point 115 metres north-west of the junction of that road with Reeves Corner.

In the London borough of Merton—

Work No. 1A   A footbridge (63 metres in length) commencing at a point 125 metres south of the junction of Wimbledon Bridge with St George's Road, passing south-eastwards and southwards over the South Western Railway, and terminating at a point 95 metres west of the junction of Hartfield Crescent with Hartfield Road;

Work No. 1B   A footpath (82 metres in length) commencing at a point 360 metres east of the bridge carrying Carshalton Road over the Sutton and Wimbledon Railways, passing south-westwards, then southwards by means of a subway beneath Work No. 1, then eastwards, and terminating at a point 46 metres south of its commencement.

In the London borough of Croydon—

Work No. 1C   A footbridge (63 metres in length) commencing at a point 50 metres north-west of the junction of Ridge's Yard with Waddon New Road passing south-eastwards beneath the bridge carrying Work No. 1, then southwards, then eastwards over the West Croydon Railway, then northwards and terminating at a point 20 metres north of that junction;

Work No. 1D   A new street (89 metres in length) forming a diversion of part of the carriageway of Waddon New Road and Cairo New Road, commencing at a point 30 metres north-east of the junction of Waddon New Road with Lower Church Street, passing eastwards beneath the existing bridge carrying Roman Way then southwards and terminating at a point 110 metres north-west of the junction of Cairo New Road with Reeves Corner.

In the London borough of Sutton—

Work No. 2   A railway (545 metres in length) commencing by a junction with Work No. 1 at a point 535 metres north-west of the footbridge carrying Therapia Lane over the Wimbledon Railway, passing eastwards and south-eastwards and terminating by a junction with Work No. 1 at a point 2 metres east of that footbridge forming, with sidings, a depot for Tramlink;

Work No. 2A   A railway (497 metres in length) commencing by a junction with Work No. 1 at a point 535 metres north-west of the footbridge carrying Therapia Lane over the Wimbledon Railway, passing south-eastwards and terminating by a junction with Work No. 1 at a point 40 metres west of that footbridge forming, with sidings, a depot for Tramlink with access provided by means of a new service road from Endeavour Way.

In the London borough of Croydon—

Work No. 3   A railway (1,941 metres in length) commencing by a junction with Work No. 1 at its termination, forming double lines of tramway (92 metres in length) passing southwards along Cairo New Road, a single line of tramway (720 metres in length) passing south-eastwards along that road, south-eastwards along Reeves Corner, south-eastwards and eastwards along Church Street, eastwards along Crown Hill, and eastwards along George Street and passing over the Croydon Underpass by means of the existing bridge, double lines of tramway (188 metres in length) passing eastwards along George Street, triple lines of tramway (92 metres in length) passing eastwards along that street and passing over the Brighton Railway by means of the existing bridge, a single line of tramway (165 metres in length) passing eastwards along Addiscombe Road, double lines of tramway (684 metres in length) passing eastwards along that road and terminating at a point 60 metres east of the junction of that road with Chepstow Road;

Work No. 3A   A railway (216 metres in length) commencing by a junction with Work No. 3 at the junction of George Street with Addiscombe Road, forming a single line of tramway, passing south-eastwards, eastwards, northwards and eastwards along Addiscombe Road and terminating by a junction with Work No. 3 at the junction of that road with Colson Road;

Work No. 3B   A railway (39 metres in length) commencing by a junction with Work No. 3 at a point 15 metres east of the junction of Cherry Orchard Road with Addiscombe Road, forming a single line of tramway, passing south-eastwards and southwards along that road and terminating by a junction with Work No. 3A at a point 40 metres south-west of the junction of that road with Colson Road;

Work No. 3C   A widening of Addiscombe Road on its southern side between its junction with Leyburn Gardens and a point 75 metres east of that junction;

Work No. 4   A railway (1,465 metres in length) commencing by a junction with Work No. 3 at a point 35 metres west of the junction of Tamworth Road with Reeves Corner, forming a single line of tramway, passing eastwards along Cairo New Road, north-eastwards along Tamworth Road and Station Road, southwards along Wellesley Road and eastwards along George Street and terminating by a junction with Work No. 3 at a point 45 metres east of the junction of Wellesley Road with George Street;

Work No. 4A   A widening of Tamworth Road on its north-western side between a point 85 metres south of its junction with Drayton Road and that junction;

Work No. 4B   A widening of Station Road on its north-western side between a point 90 metres south-west of its junction with Wellesley Road and that junction;

Work No. 4C   A subway (23 metres in length) commencing at a point 5 metres north of the junction of Lansdowne Road with Wellesley Road and passing north-east and north-west and terminating at a point 25 metres north of that junction;

Work No. 5   A railway (47 metres in length) commencing by a junction with Work No. 3 at a point 20 metres south-east of the junction of Tamworth Road with Reeves Corner, forming a single line of tramway, passing northwards along Reeves Corner and Tamworth Road and terminating by a junction with Work No. 4 at a point 30 metres north-east of the junction of Tamworth Road with Reeves Corner;

Work No. 6   A railway (46 metres in length) commencing by a junction with Work No. 3 at a point 15 metres west of the junction of Wellesley Road with George Street, forming a single line of tramway, passing eastwards along George Street and passing over the Croydon Underpass by means of the existing bridge, passing northwards along Wellesley Road and terminating by a junction with Work No. 3 at a point 30 metres north of the junction of Wellesley Road with George Street.

In the London boroughs of Croydon and Bromley—

Work No. 7   A railway (6,970 metres in length) commencing by a junction with Work No. 3 at its termination, passing eastwards on the southern side of Addiscombe Road, northwards along the course of the former Selsdon Railway, north-eastwards along the course of the Addiscombe Railway, north-westwards and north-eastwards through South Norwood Country Park, north-westwards on the south-western side of Beckenham Crematorium, north-eastwards and eastwards along the course of the Norwood Spur passing over the Mid Kent Railway by means of the existing bridge and terminating at a point 90 metres north-west of the junction of Southend Road with Rectory Road.

In the London borough of Croydon—

Work No. 7A   A new street (62 metres in length) forming a diversion of part of the carriageway of Woodbury Close, crossing Work No. 7 on the level, commencing at a point 10 metres west of the junction of Woodbury Close with Addiscombe Road, passing southwards on the western side of Woodbury Close and terminating at a point 65 metres south of that junction.

In the London boroughs of Croydon and Bromley—

Work No. 8   A railway (896 metres in length) commencing by a junction with Work No. 7 at a point 260 metres north-east of the junction of Albert Road with Estcourt Road, passing north-eastwards along the course of the Addiscombe Railway, and terminating at a point 110 metres west of the junction of Station Estate with Elmers End Road.

In the London borough of Croydon—

Work No. 9   A railway (2,300 metres in length) commencing by a junction with Work No. 7 at a point 85 metres south-west of the junction of Sandilands with Addiscombe Road passing southwards along the course of the former Selsdon Railway, partly in existing tunnels (Radcliffe Tunnel, Park Hill Tunnel and Coombe Road Tunnel) and passing over the Fairfield Path (FP 595) including a new bridge over that footpath then eastwards along the north side of Coombe Road and terminating at a point 35 metres north-east of the junction of Oaks Road with Coombe Road;

Work No. 10   A railway (1,552 metres in length) commencing by a junction with Work No. 9 at its termination, passing eastwards, south-eastwards and eastwards on the northern side of Coombe Lane and Sunken Road, then south-eastwards, partly in tunnel, passing beneath the junction of Coombe Lane with Gravel Hill and Shirley Hills Road, south-eastwards on the southern side of Gravel Hill and terminating at a point 120 metres west of the junction of Abbots Green with Gravel Hill;

Work No. 11   A railway (2,100 metres in length) commencing by a junction with Work No. 10 at its termination, passing eastwards on the southern side then the northern side of Gravel Hill, north-eastwards on the western side then the central reserve of Kent Gate Way, south-eastwards on the south-western side of Lodge Lane and terminating at a point 20 metres west of the junction of Field Way with Lodge Lane including the provision of a bus interchange;

Work No. 12   A railway (1,553 metres in length) commencing by a junction with Work No. 11 at its termination, passing south-eastwards on the south-western side of Lodge Lane, along the central reserve of Parkway and on the south-western side of Central Parade and terminating at a point 240 metres south-east of the junction of Parkway with Central Parade.

PART II

Section 7   DESCRIPTION OF FURTHER WORKS AND POWERS

In the London borough of Merton—

(i) Stop up and discontinue so much of the footpath at Mitcham Golf Course as lies between the points marked A, B, C and D on the deposited plans.

In the London borough of Croydon—

(ii) Stop up and discontinue the footbridge adjoining Vicarage Road between the points marked A, B, C and D on the deposited plans, substituting therefor a new level crossing between the points so marked A and E;

(iii) Stop up and discontinue the footbridge adjoining Waddon New Road between the points marked F, G and H, and G and J on the deposited plans;

(iv) Stop up and discontinue so much of Waddon New Road and Cairo New Road as lies within the limits of deviation of Work No. 1D;

(v) Set back so much of the kerb line on the south-western side of Cairo New Road as lies between the points marked A1 and A2 on the deposited plans;

(vi) Set back so much of the kerb line on the northern side of Church Street as lies—

     (a) between the points marked H1 and H2 on the deposited plans;

     (b) between the points so marked J1 and J2;

(vii) Set back so much of the kerb line on the northern side of Crown Hill as lies between the points marked K1 and K2 on the deposited plans;

(viii) Stop up and discontinue Surrey Street at the point marked K on the deposited plans;

(ix) Stop up and discontinue so much of Crown Hill as lies between the points marked L and M on the deposited plans;

(x) Set back so much of the kerb line on the northern side of George Street as lies between the points marked M1 and M2 on the deposited plans;

(xi) Narrow and stop up—

     (a) so much of the northern side of George Street as lies between the points marked N1 and N2 on the deposited plans;

     (b) so much of the southern side of George Street as lies between the points marked P1 and P2 on the deposited plans;

(xii) Stop up and discontinue so much of College Road as lies between the points marked N and P on the deposited plans;

(xiii) Set back so much of the kerb line—

     (a) on the southern side of George Street as lies between the points marked Q1 and Q2 on the deposited plans;

     (b) on the northern side of George Street as lies between the points marked S1 and S2 on the deposited plans;

(xiv) Narrow and stop up so much of George Street as lies between the points marked R1, R2, R3, R4, R5 and R6 on the deposited plans;

(xv) Set back so much of the footway and kerb line on the southern side of Addiscombe Road as lies between the points marked U1 and U2 on the deposited plans;

(xvi) Stop up and discontinue so much of Lebanon Road as lies between the points marked Q and R on the deposited plans;

(xvii) Set back so much of the kerb line on the southern side of Addiscombe Road as lies between the points marked T1 and T2 on the deposited plans;

(xviii) Set back so much of the footway and kerb line on the western side of Tamworth Road as lies between the points marked B1 and B2 on the deposited plans;

(xix) Set back so much of the kerb line on the western side of Tamworth Road as lies between the points marked C1 and C2 on the deposited plans;

(xx) Narrow and stop up so much of the western side of Station Road as lies between the points marked D1 and D2 on the deposited plans;

(xxi) Set back so much of the footway and kerb line on the north-western side of Station Road as lies between the points marked E1 and E2 on the deposited plans;

(xxii) Narrow and stop up—

(a) so much of the western side of the southbound carriageway of Wellesley Road as lies between the points marked F1, F2 and F3 on the deposited plans;

(b) so much of the eastern side of the northbound carriageway of Wellesley Road as lies between the points marked F4 and F5 on the deposited plans;

(xxiii) Stop up and discontinue so much of the pedestrian subway beneath Wellesley Road as lies within the limits of deviation of Work No. 4C;

(xxiv) Set back so much of the kerb line on the eastern side of Wellesley Road as lies between the points marked G1 and G2 on the deposited plans;

(xxv) Set back so much of the kerb line on the eastern side of Wellesley Road and the northern side of George Street as lies between the points marked L1 and L2 on the deposited plans;

(xxvi) Stop up and discontinue so much of Woodbury Close as lies within the limits of deviation of Work No. 7A;

(xxvii) Stop up and discontinue the footpath (No. PRW71) between the points marked S and V on the deposited plans, substituting therefor a new footpath between the points so marked S, T, U and V.

In the London borough of Bromley—

(xxviii) Stop up and discontinue the footpath (No. PRW71) between the points marked A and B on the deposited plans, substituting therefor a new footpath between the points so marked A, C and D;

(xxix) Narrow and stop up so much of the northern side of Rectory Road as lies between the points marked E, F, G and H on the deposited plans.

In the London borough of Croydon—

(xxx) Stop up and discontinue the footpath between the points marked W and X on the deposited plans, substituting therefor a new footpath between the points so marked W and Y;

(xxxi) Stop up and discontinue the cycle way between the points marked Y1 and Y2 on the deposited plans, substituting therefor a new cycle way between the points so marked Z1 and Z2.

Section 10   SCHEDULE 2

RAILWAY CROSSINGS IN STREETS

In the London borough of Merton—
Dundonald Road/Hartfield Crescent
Kingston Road
In the London boroughs of Merton and Sutton—
Beddington Lane
In the London borough of Croydon—
Substituted footpath between Vicarage Road and Wandle Park
Woodbury Close
Bingham Road
Lower Addiscombe Road
Substituted part of footpath between the rear of Macclesfield Road and Elmers End Station
Larcombe Close
Lloyd Park Avenue
Oaks Road
Sunken Road
Gravel Hill
Kent Gate Way
Roundabout (King Henry's Drive)
Parkway (Link Road No. 1)
Parkway (Link Road No. 2)
Parkway (Link Road No. 3)
Parkway
In the London borough of Bromley—
Footpath between Elmers End Station and Harrington Road

       SCHEDULE 3

LANDS TO BE ACQUIRED OR USED

PART I

LANDS OUTSIDE LIMITS OF DEVIATION WHICH MAY BE ACQUIRED OR USED

Location	Lands numbered on the deposited plans	Purpose
(1)	(2)	(3)
In the London borough of Merton		
Land at Wimbledon railway station.	1, 2, 3, 4, 5, 6 and 8	For the provision of station access.
Wimbledon Bridge and adjoining land.	7 and 9	For the provision of station access and access for construction purposes.
Hartfield Crescent and adjoining land, Wimbledon.	12, 13 and 18	For the provision of a working site and access for construction purposes and station access.
Land at the rear of Saxonbury Close.	41	For the provision of station access and access for construction purposes.
Willow Lane and adjoining land.	54 and 56	For the provision of a working site for construction purposes.
Carshalton Road and adjoining land.	58 and 59	For the provision of access for construction purposes.
In the London borough of Sutton		
Endeavour Way and adjoining land.	9 and 10	For the provision of access for construction purposes and for access to intended depot.
In the London Borough of Croydon		
Land at Wandle Park.	7A	For the provision of a working site for construction purposes.
Cuthbert Road and adjoining land.	10A and 11	For the provision of access for construction purposes.
Land adjoining Drummond Road.	19	For the provision of a working site for construction purposes.
London Road and adjoining land.	23 and 24	For the provision of a working site for construction purposes.
Land adjoining Station Road.	25	For the provision of a working site for construction purposes, station access and landscaping.
Lansdowne Road and Dingwall Road and adjoining land.	31 and 32	For the provision of a working site for construction purposes.
Land adjoining Addiscombe Road, Lebanon Road.	33A, 33D and 33E	For the provision of remedial works.
Lebanon Road and adjoining land.	33B and 33C	For the provision of station access, turning area and landscaping.
Land adjoining Addiscombe Road.	34	For the provision of a working site for construction purposes.
Blackhorse Lane and adjoining land.	65A and 66	For the provision of station access and access for construction purposes.
Land adjoining Macclesfield Road.	74	For the provision of station access.
Albert Road and adjoining land.	76A and 77	For the provision of a working site for construction purposes.
Harrington Road and adjoining land.	79A and 80	For the provision of access for construction purposes.
Gravel Hill and adjoining land.	117A	For the provision of station access and access for construction purposes.

Section 34   Part II

LANDS OF WHICH TEMPORARY POSSESSION ONLY MAY BE TAKEN

Area (1)	Lands numbered on the deposited plans (2)
In the London borough of Merton	54, 56, 58 and 59
In the London borough of Croydon	7A, 10A, 11, 19, 23, 24, 31, 32, 34, 76A, 77, 79A and 80

Section 30   SCHEDULE 4

ADAPTATION OF PART I OF THE COMPULSORY PURCHASE ACT 1965

1. For section 7 of the Act of 1965 (measure of compensation) there shall be substituted the following:—

"7. In assessing the compensation to be paid by the acquiring authority under this Act regard shall be had, not only to the extent (if any) to which the value of the land over which the right is to be acquired is depreciated by the acquisition of the right, but also to the damage (if any) to be sustained by the owner of the land by reason of its severance from other land of his, or injuriously affecting that other land by the exercise of the powers conferred by this or the special Act.".

2. For section 8(1) of the Act of 1965 (protection for vendor against severance of house, garden, etc.) there shall be substituted the following:—

"(1) No person shall be required to grant any right over part only—

(a) of any house, building or factory; or

(b) of a park or garden belonging to a house;

if he is willing to sell the whole of the house, building, factory, park or garden, unless the Lands Tribunal determine that—

(i) in the case of a house, building or factory, the part over which the right is proposed to be acquired can be made subject to that right without material detriment to the house, building or factory; or

(ii) in the case of a park or garden, the part over which the right is proposed to be acquired can be made subject to that right without seriously affecting the amenity or convenience of the house;

and, if the Lands Tribunal so determine, the tribunal shall award compensation in respect of any loss due to the acquisition of the right, in addition to its value; and thereupon the party interested shall be required to grant to the acquiring authority that right over that part of the house, building, factory, park or garden.

(1A) In considering the extent of any material detriment to a house, building or factory, or any extent to which the amenity or convenience of a house is affected, the Lands Tribunal shall have regard not only to the right which is to be acquired over the land, but also to any adjoining or adjacent land belonging to the same owner and subject to compulsory purchase.".

3. The following provisions of the Act of 1965 (being provisions stating the effect of a deed poll executed in various circumstances where there is no conveyance by persons with interests in the land):—

section 9(4) (refusal by owners to convey);

paragraph 10(3) of Schedule 1 (owners under incapacity);

paragraph 2(3) of Schedule 2 (absent and untraced owners); and

paragraphs 2(3) and 7(2) of Schedule 4 (common land);

shall be so modified as to secure that, as against persons with interests in the land which are expressed to be overridden by the deed, the right which is to be compulsorily acquired is vested absolutely in the acquiring authority.

4. Section 11 of the Act of 1965 (powers of entry) shall be so modified as to secure that, as from the date on which the acquiring authority have served notice to treat in respect of any right, they have power, exercisable in the like circumstances and subject to the like conditions, to enter for the purpose of exercising that right (which shall be deemed for this purpose to have been created on the date of service of the notice); and sections 12 (penalty for unauthorised entry) and 13 (entry on sheriff's warrant in the event of obstruction) shall be modified correspondingly.

5. Section 20 of the Act of 1965 (protection for interests of tenants at will etc.) shall apply with the modifications necessary to secure that persons with such interests as are mentioned in that

section are compensated in a manner corresponding to that in which they would be compensated on a compulsory acquisition under this Act of the interests, but taking into account only the extent (if any) of such interference with such an interest as is actually caused, or likely to be caused, by the exercise of the right in question.

6. Section 22 of the Act of 1965 (protection of acquiring authority's possession of land where by inadvertence an interest in the land has not been purchased) shall be so modified as to enable the Corporation, in circumstances corresponding to those referred to in that section, to continue to be entitled to exercise the right in question, subject to compliance with that section as respects compensation.

Section 57   SCHEDULE 5

PROTECTIVE PROVISIONS

FOR PROTECTION OF HIGHWAY AUTHORITIES

1. For the protection of highway authorities the following provisions shall, unless otherwise agreed in writing between the Corporation and the relevant highway authority, have effect:—
   (1) In this paragraph—
      "highway" means any highway vested in or repairable or maintainable by a highway authority;
      "specified works" means so much of the authorised works as may in any way affect any highway:
   (2) Notwithstanding anything in this Act or shown on the deposited plans, the Corporation shall not purchase compulsorily any estate or interest in land vested in a highway authority for highway purposes but they may purchase such easements or other rights in land of a highway authority in accordance with the provisions of section 30 (Power to acquire new rights) of this Act as they may reasonably require for the purposes of the specified works:
   (3) The Corporation shall give to the highway authority not less than 28 days' notice in writing of their intention permanently to stop up and discontinue any highway under the powers of this Act:
   (4) The Corporation shall not exercise the powers of section 23 (Underpinning of houses near works) of this Act, so as to interfere with any highway except with the consent of the highway authority, which consent shall not be unreasonably withheld or delayed:
   (5) Before commencing the construction of any of the specified works, the Corporation shall submit plans, sections and particulars relating thereto to the relevant highway authority for their approval, which shall not be unreasonably withheld, and, notwithstanding anything shown on the deposited plans and the deposited sections, the work to which those plans, sections and particulars relate shall not be constructed otherwise than in accordance with such plans, sections and particulars as may be approved by the highway authority, or, if such approval be refused, as may be settled by arbitration:
      Provided that, if within 56 days after the submission to them of plans, sections and particulars in accordance with the provisions of this sub-paragraph the highway authority do not signify their approval or disapproval thereof and the grounds for such disapproval, they shall be deemed to have approved thereof:
   (6) (a) Before commencing to construct any part of the specified works which will involve interference with a highway the Corporation shall consult the highway authority as to—
         (i) when that part shall be commenced;
         (ii) the extent of the surface of the highway which it may be reasonably necessary for the Corporation to occupy in the construction of that part; and
         (iii) the conditions under which that part shall be constructed so as to reduce so far as possible inconvenience to the public and to ensure the safety of the public;
      and such part shall not be constructed and the surface of the highway shall not be occupied by the Corporation except at the time, to the extent and in accordance with such reasonable conditions as may be agreed between the Corporation and the highway authority or, in default of agreement, as may be settled by arbitration;
   (b) Any such highway shall be reinstated by the Corporation in a manner approved by the highway authority, which approval shall not be unreasonably withheld, and to their reasonable satisfaction:
   (7) Any part of the construction of the specified works which may involve interference with a highway shall be carried out under the supervision (if given) and to the reasonable satisfaction of the highway authority:
   (8) The Corporation shall, at all reasonable times during the construction of any part of the specified works, afford to the engineer of the relevant highway authority or his duly auth-

orised representatives access to that part of the specified works for the purposes of inspection:

(9) The Corporation shall keep highway authorities indemnified against all actions, costs, claims and demands whatsoever brought or made against them by any person in respect of loss or damage caused by, or in consequence of the construction of any of the specified works and the fact that any act or thing may have been done in accordance with plans, sections and particulars approved by a highway authority or in accordance with any requirement of a highway authority or under their supervision shall not (if it was done without negligence on the part of the highway authority) excuse the Corporation from liability under the provisions of this paragraph:

   Provided that a highway authority shall give to the Corporation reasonable notice of any claim or demand as aforesaid and no settlement or compromise thereof shall be made without the prior consent of the Corporation:

(10) The Corporation shall repay to a highway authority all costs, charges and expenses reasonably incurred by the highway authority for the examination of the plans, sections and particulars submitted to the highway authority under this paragraph in relation to any of the specified works:

(11) Any differences arising between the Corporation and a highway authority under this paragraph shall be referred to and settled by arbitration.

FOR PROTECTION OF ELECTRICITY, GAS AND WATER UNDERTAKERS

2. For the protection of the several undertakers referred to in this paragraph, the following provisions shall, unless otherwise agreed in writing between the Corporation and the undertakers concerned, have effect:—

(1) In this paragraph—

   "adequate alternative apparatus" means alternative apparatus adequate to enable the undertakers to fulfil their statutory functions in a manner not less efficient than previously;

   "apparatus" means—

      (a) in the case of electricity undertakers, electric lines or electrical plant (as defined in the Electricity Act 1989) belonging to or maintained by such undertakers; or

      (b) in the case of gas or water undertakers, any mains, pipes or other apparatus belonging to or maintained by such undertakers; and includes any building, structure or works for the lodging therein of apparatus;

   "functions" includes powers and duties;

   "in" in a context referring to apparatus or alternative apparatus in land includes a reference to apparatus or alternative apparatus under, over or upon land;

   "the undertakers" means a licence holder under Part I of the Electricity Act 1989, a public gas supplier within the meaning of Part I of the Gas Act 1986 or a water undertaker within the meaning of the Water Industry Act 1991 or any of such bodies; and, in relation to any apparatus, means the undertakers to whom it belongs or by whom it is maintained:

(2) Notwithstanding the temporary stopping up or diversion of any street under section 18 (Temporary stoppage of streets) of this Act, the undertakers shall be at liberty at all times to execute and do all such works and things in, upon or under any such street as may be reasonably necessary or desirable to enable them to inspect, repair, maintain, renew, remove or use any apparatus which at the time of the stopping up or diversion was in that street:

(3) The Corporation, in the case of the powers conferred by section 23 (Underpinning of houses near works) of this Act, shall, so far as is reasonably practicable, so exercise those powers as not to obstruct or render less convenient the access to any apparatus and, if by reason of the exercise of those powers any damage to any apparatus (other than apparatus the repair of which is not reasonably necessary in view of its intended removal or abandonment) or property of the undertakers or any interruption in the supply of electricity, gas or water, as the case may be, by the undertakers shall be caused, the Corporation shall bear and pay the cost reasonably incurred by the undertakers in making good such damage or restoring the supply; and shall—

   (a) make reasonable compensation to the undertakers for any loss sustained by them; and

   (b) indemnify the undertakers against all claims, demands, proceedings, costs, damages and expenses which may be made or taken against or recovered from or incurred by the undertakers;

by reason or in consequence of any such damage or interruption:

Provided that—
    (i) nothing in this sub-paragraph shall impose any liability on the Corporation with respect to any damage or interruption to the extent that such damage or interruption may be attributable to the act, neglect or default of the undertakers or their contractors or workmen;
    (ii) the undertakers shall give to the Corporation reasonable notice of any claim or demand as aforesaid and no settlement or compromise thereof shall be made without the prior consent of the Corporation:

(4) Notwithstanding anything in section 24 (Use of sewers, etc., for removing water) of this Act, no use shall be made by the Corporation in the construction of the works of pumping or other like modes of removing water except where reasonably necessary or in case of emergency or unforeseen accident or for the purpose of removing rainwater or other small amounts of water:

(5) Notwithstanding anything in this Act or shown on the deposited plans the Corporation shall not acquire any apparatus under the powers of this Act otherwise than by agreement:

(6) If the Corporation, in the exercise of the powers of this Act, acquire any interest in any land in which any apparatus is placed, that apparatus shall not be removed under this paragraph and any right of the undertakers to maintain, repair, renew or inspect that apparatus in that land shall not be extinguished until adequate alternative apparatus shall have been constructed and be in operation to the reasonable satisfaction of the undertakers:

(7) If the Corporation, for the purpose of executing any works in, on or under any land purchased, held, appropriated or used under this Act, require the removal of any apparatus placed in that land, and shall give to the undertakers written notice of such requirement, together with a plan and section of the work proposed, and of the proposed position of the alternative apparatus to be provided or constructed so as to provide adequate alternative apparatus in lieu of the apparatus to be removed, or, if in consequence of the exercise of any of the powers of this Act the undertakers shall reasonably require to remove any apparatus, the Corporation shall afford to the undertakers the necessary facilities and rights for the construction of such alternative apparatus in other land of the Corporation and thereafter for the maintenance, repair, renewal and inspection of such apparatus:

Provided that, if the alternative apparatus or any part thereof is to be constructed elsewhere than in other land of the Corporation, or the Corporation are unable to afford such facilities and rights as aforesaid in the land in which the alternative apparatus or such part thereof is to be constructed, the undertakers shall, on receipt of a written notice to that effect from the Corporation, forthwith use their best endeavours to obtain the necessary facilities and rights in such last-mentioned land:

(8) (a) Any alternative apparatus to be constructed in land of the Corporation under this paragraph shall be constructed in such manner and in such line or situation as may be agreed between the undertakers and the Corporation or in default of agreement determined by arbitration;

(b) The undertakers shall, after the alternative apparatus to be provided or constructed shall have been agreed or determined by arbitration as aforesaid and after the grant to the undertakers of any such facilities and rights as are referred to in sub-paragraph (7) above, proceed with all reasonable dispatch to construct and bring into operation the alternative apparatus and thereafter to remove any apparatus required by the Corporation to be removed under the provisions of this paragraph:

(9) Notwithstanding anything in sub-paragraph (8) above, if the Corporation give notice in writing to the undertakers that they desire themselves to execute any part of so much of the work necessary in connection with the construction of the alternative apparatus, or the removal of the apparatus required to be removed, as will be situate in any land of the Corporation, such work, in lieu of being executed by the undertakers, shall be executed by the Corporation with all reasonable dispatch under the superintendence, if given, and to the reasonable satisfaction of the undertakers:

Provided that nothing in this sub-paragraph shall authorise the Corporation to execute the actual placing, installation, bedding, packing, removal, connection or disconnection of any apparatus, or execute any filling around the apparatus (where the apparatus is laid in a trench) within 300 millimetres of the apparatus:

(10) Where, in accordance with the provisions of this paragraph, the Corporation afford to the undertakers facilities and rights for the construction, maintenance, repair, renewal and inspection in land of the Corporation of alternative apparatus in substitution for apparatus to be removed as aforesaid, those facilities and rights shall be granted upon such terms and conditions as may be agreed between the Corporation and the undertakers or in default of agreement determined by arbitration:

Provided that—

(a) in determining such terms and conditions as aforesaid in respect of alternative apparatus to be constructed in or along any railways of the Corporation, the arbitrator shall—

(i) give effect to all reasonable requirements of the Corporation for ensuring the safety and efficient operation of the railway and for securing any subsequent alterations or adaptations of the alternative apparatus which may be required to prevent interference with any proposed works of the Corporation or the traffic on the railway; and

(ii) so far as it may be reasonable and practicable to do so in the circumstances of the particular case, give effect to the terms and conditions applicable to the apparatus, if any, constructed in or along the railway for which the alternative apparatus is to be substituted;

(b) if the facilities and rights to be afforded by the Corporation in respect of any alternative apparatus and the terms and conditions subject to which the same are to be granted are in the opinion of the arbitrator less favourable on the whole to the undertakers than the facilities and rights enjoyed by them in respect of the apparatus to be removed and the terms and conditions to which those facilities and rights are subject, the arbitrator shall make such provision for the payment of compensation by the Corporation to the undertakers in respect thereof as appear to him to be reasonable having regard to all the circumstances of the particular case:

(11) (a) Not less than 28 days before commencing to execute any such works as are referred to in sub-paragraph (7) above and are near to or will or may affect any apparatus the removal of which has not been required by the Corporation under the said sub-paragraph (7), the Corporation shall submit to the undertakers a plan, section and description of the works to be executed;

(b) Such works shall be executed only in accordance with the plan, section and description submitted as aforesaid and in accordance with such reasonable requirements as may be made by the undertakers for the alteration or otherwise for the protection of the apparatus or for securing access thereto and the undertakers shall be entitled by their officer to watch and inspect the execution of such works:

Provided that—

(i) if the undertakers within 14 days after the submission to them of any such plan, section and description, in consequence of the works proposed by the Corporation, reasonably require the removal of any apparatus and give written notice to the Corporation of such requirement, the foregoing provisions of this paragraph shall have effect as if the removal of such apparatus had been required by the Corporation under the said sub-paragraph (7);

(ii) nothing in sub-paragraph (11)(b) shall preclude the Corporation from submitting at any time or from time to time, but in no case less than 28 days before commencing the execution of any such works, a new plan, section and description thereof in lieu of the plan, section and description previously submitted, and thereupon the provisions of sub-paragraph (11)(b) shall apply to and in respect of such new plan, section and description;

(c) The Corporation shall not be required to comply with sub-paragraph (11)(a) above in a case of emergency but in such a case they shall give to the undertakers notice as soon as reasonably practicable and a plan, section and description of the works as soon as reasonably practicable thereafter and shall comply with sub-paragraph (11)(b) above so far as reasonably practicable in the circumstances:

(12) Where, in consequence of this Act, any part of any highway in which any apparatus is situate ceases to be part of a highway the undertakers may exercise the same rights of access to such apparatus as they enjoyed immediately before the passing of this Act, but nothing in this sub-paragraph shall prejudice or affect any right of the Corporation or of the undertakers to require removal of such apparatus under this paragraph or the power of the Corporation to execute works in accordance with sub-paragraph (11) above:

(13) Subject to sub-paragraph (14) below the Corporation shall pay to the undertakers the costs, charges and expenses reasonably incurred by the undertakers in or in connection with the inspection, removal, alteration or protection of any apparatus or the construction of any new apparatus which may be required in consequence of the execution of any such works as are referred to in sub-paragraph (7) above, less the value of any apparatus removed under the provisions of this paragraph (such value being calculated after removal) and shall also make compensation to the undertakers—

(a) for any damage caused to any apparatus (other than apparatus the repair of which is not reasonably necessary in view of its intended removal in accordance with the provisions of this paragraph); and

(b) for any other expenses, loss, damages, penalty or costs incurred by the undertakers;

in consequence of the execution, maintenance, use or failure of any such works or otherwise in consequence of the exercise by the Corporation of the powers of this Act:

(14) If in pursuance of the provisions of this paragraph—

(a) alternative apparatus of better type, or greater capacity or of greater dimensions is placed in substitution for existing apparatus of worse type, or smaller capacity or of smaller dimensions, except where this has been solely due to using the nearest currently available type, capacity or dimension, or

(b) apparatus (whether existing apparatus or alternative apparatus) is placed at a depth greater than the depth at which the existing apparatus was,

and the placing of apparatus of that type or capacity or of those dimensions or the placing of apparatus at that depth, as the case may be, is not agreed by the Corporation, or, in default of agreement, is not determined by arbitration to be necessary, then, if it involves cost in the execution of works under sub-paragraphs (8) and (9) exceeding that which would have been involved if the apparatus placed had been of the existing type, capacity or dimensions, or at the existing depth, as the case may be, the amount which apart from this sub-paragraph would be payable to the undertakers by virtue of sub-paragraph (13) above shall be reduced by the amount of that excess:

(15) For the purposes of sub-paragraph (14) above—

(a) an extension of apparatus to a length greater than the length of existing apparatus shall not be treated as a placing of apparatus of greater dimensions than those of the existing apparatus, and

(b) where the provision of a joint in a cable is agreed, or is determined to be necessary, the consequential provision of a jointing chamber or of a manhole shall be treated as if it also had been agreed or had been so determined:

(16) An amount which apart from this sub-paragraph would be payable to the undertakers in respect of works by virtue of sub-paragraph (13) above (and having regard, where relevant, to sub-paragraph (14) above) shall, if the works include the placing of apparatus provided in substitution for apparatus placed more than 7½ years earlier so as to confer on the undertakers any financial benefit by deferment of the time for renewal of the apparatus in the ordinary course, be reduced by the amount which represents that benefit as calculated in accordance with the Code of Practice entitled "Measures Necessary Where Apparatus is Affected by Major Works (Diversionary Works)" and dated June 1992, and approved by the Secretary of State on 30th June 1992 as revised and reissued from time to time:

(17) Where, in consequence of the stopping up of any highway under the powers of this Act, any apparatus belonging to the undertakers and laid or placed in such highway or elsewhere is rendered derelict or unnecessary, the Corporation shall pay to the undertakers the then value of such apparatus (which shall thereupon become the property of the Corporation) and the reasonable costs of and incidental to the cutting off of such apparatus from any other apparatus, and of and incidental to the execution or doing of any works or things rendered necessary or expedient by reason of such apparatus being so rendered derelict or unnecessary:

Provided that the Corporation shall not under the provisions of this sub-paragraph be required to pay to the undertakers the value of any apparatus rendered derelict or unnecessary if, to the reasonable satisfaction of the undertakers, other apparatus has at the expense of the Corporation been provided and laid and made ready for use in substitution for the apparatus so rendered derelict or unnecessary:

(18) Any difference arising between the Corporation and the undertakers under this paragraph shall be determined by arbitration:

(19) Nothing in this paragraph shall be deemed to prejudice or affect the provisions of any enactment or agreement regulating the relations between the Corporation and the undertakers in respect of any apparatus laid or erected in land belonging to the Corporation at the date of the passing of this Act:

(20) Nothing in this paragraph shall apply—

(a) in relation to street works (within the meaning of Part III of the New Roads and Street Works Act 1991) executed by the Corporation; or

(b) in relation to apparatus in respect of which the relations between the Corporation and the undertakers are regulated by that Part of that Act.

FOR PROTECTION OF THAMES WATER UTILITIES LIMITED

3. For the protection of Thames Water Utilities Limited (hereinafter called "the sewerage undertakers") the following provisions shall, unless otherwise agreed in writing between the Corporation and the sewerage undertakers, have effect:—

(1) In this paragraph—

"construction" includes execution, placing and altering and, in relation to temporary works, includes removal and "construct" and "constructed" shall be construed accordingly;

"new, altered or substituted works" includes any works required for the protection of any sewer;

"sewer" means a sewer or part of a sewer, including a public sewer, within the meaning of the Water Industry Act 1991 and includes any manholes, ventilating shafts, pumps or other accessories belonging to or forming part of a sewer;

"specified work" means so much of the authorised works and of any work (whether temporary or permanent) forming part of, or constructed in connection with, the authorised works, or any of them, as will or may be situated over or within 15 metres measured in any direction of, or (wherever situated) impose any load directly upon, any sewer, and includes the construction, maintenance or renewal of any such works:

(2) The Corporation shall not commence any specified work until they shall have given to the sewerage undertakers 56 days' previous notice in writing of their intention to commence the same, by leaving such notice at the principal office of the sewerage undertakers with plans as described in sub-paragraph (7) below (in this paragraph referred to as "the said plans"), and until the sewerage undertakers shall have signified their approval of the said plans:

Provided that such approval shall not be unreasonably withheld and if, within 56 days after the submission of the said plans, the sewerage undertakers have not approved or disapproved them, they shall be deemed to have approved the said plans:

(3) The Corporation shall comply with and conform to all reasonable orders, directions and regulations of the sewerage undertakers in the construction of any specified work and shall provide new, altered or substituted works in such manner as the sewerage undertakers shall reasonably require for the proper protection of, and for preventing injury or impediment to, a sewer of the sewerage undertakers by reason of any specified work and shall save harmless the sewerage undertakers against all expenses to be occasioned thereby:

(4) The specified works and all such new, altered or substituted works shall be constructed by or under the direction, superintendence and control of an officer of the sewerage undertakers duly appointed for the purpose at the cost, charge and expense in all respects of the Corporation; and all reasonable costs, charges and expenses to which the sewerage undertakers may be put by reason of such works, whether in the execution thereof, in the preparation or examination of plans or designs or in such direction, superintendence or control as aforesaid shall be paid to the sewerage undertakers by the Corporation on demand:

(5) When any such new, altered or substituted works or any work of defence connected therewith shall be completed by or at the cost of the Corporation under the provisions of this paragraph, the same shall thereafter be as fully and completely under the direction, jurisdiction and control of the sewerage undertakers as any sewers or works now or hereafter may be:

(6) Nothing in this Act shall extend to prejudice, diminish, alter or take away any of the rights, powers or authorities vested or to be vested in the sewerage undertakers in relation to sewers but all such rights, powers and authorities shall be as valid and effectual as if this Act had not been passed:

(7) The plans to be submitted to the sewerage undertakers for the purposes of this paragraph shall be detailed plans, drawings, sections and specifications which shall describe the exact position and manner in which, and the level at which, any specified work is proposed to be constructed and shall accurately describe the position of all sewers of the sewerage undertakers within the limits of deviation (for which purpose the sewerage undertakers shall allow the Corporation access to plans in their possession and, under their supervision, to any of their sewers, in order to enable the Corporation to obtain reliable information) and shall comprise detailed drawings of every alteration which the Corporation may propose to make in any such sewers:

(8) The sewerage undertakers may require such modifications to be made in the said plans as may be reasonably necessary to secure the sewerage system of the sewerage undertakers against interference or risk of damage and to provide and secure a proper and convenient means of access to the sewers of the sewerage undertakers:

(9) The Corporation shall indemnify the sewerage undertakers against all claims, demands, costs, expenses, damages or loss which may be made on or against the sewerage undertakers or which the sewerage undertakers may incur or have to pay or which they may sustain in consequence of the construction, maintenance or renewal of a specified work or

of the failure or want of repair thereof or any subsidence caused by the construction of any specified work or in consequence of any act or omission of the Corporation, their contractors, agents, workmen or servants, whilst engaged upon the specified work:

Provided that—

(i) the sewerage undertakers shall give to the Corporation reasonable notice of any such claim or demand as aforesaid and no settlement or compromise thereof shall be made without the agreement of the Corporation; and

(ii) nothing in this sub-paragraph shall impose any liability on the Corporation with respect to any claim, demand, costs, expenses, damage or loss which is attributable to the act, neglect or default of the sewerage undertakers or their agents, contractors, employees or workmen:

(10) If, in the construction of any specified work, or any new, altered or substituted works, or any work of defence connected therewith provided in accordance with this paragraph, the Corporation damage or, without the consent of the sewerage undertakers, in any way interfere with any sewer of the sewerage undertakers, the Corporation shall—

(a) pay to the sewerage undertakers a capitalised sum representing any additional expense which may be expected to be reasonably incurred by the sewerage undertakers in the maintenance, management or renewal of any new, altered or substituted work which may be necessary in consequence of the said construction taking into account any betterment; and

(b) give to the sewerage undertakers full, free and uninterrupted access at all times to any such new, altered or substituted work or to any such sewer and every reasonable facility for the inspection, maintenance, alteration and repair thereof:

(11) Notwithstanding the temporary stopping up or diversion of any street under the powers of section 18 (Temporary stoppage of streets) of this Act, the sewerage undertakers shall be at liberty at all times to execute and do all such works and things in, upon or under any such street as may be reasonably necessary or desirable to enable them to inspect, repair, maintain, renew, remove or use any sewer which at the time of the stopping up or diversion was in that street:

(12) In the exercise of the powers of section 23 (Underpinning of houses near works) of this Act, the Corporation shall not, so far as reasonably practicable, obstruct or render less convenient the access to any sewer of the sewerage undertakers and, if by reason or in consequence of the exercise of those powers any damage to any sewer (other than a sewer the repair of which is not reasonably necessary in view of its intended removal or abandonment) shall be caused, the Corporation shall bear and pay the cost reasonably incurred by the sewerage undertakers in making good such damage and shall—

(a) make reasonable compensation to the sewerage undertakers for any loss sustained by them; and

(b) indemnify the sewerage undertakers against all claims, demands, proceedings, costs, damages and expenses which may be made or taken against or recovered from or incurred by the sewerage undertakers;

by reason or in consequence of any such damage:

Provided that—

(i) nothing in this sub-paragraph shall impose any liability on the Corporation with respect to any damage to the extent that such damage may be attributable to the act, neglect or default of the sewerage undertakers or their agents, contractors, employees or workmen;

(ii) the sewerage undertakers shall give to the Corporation reasonable notice of any claim or demand as aforesaid and no settlement or compromise thereof shall be made without the prior consent of the Corporation:

(13) (a) If in the construction of any new, altered or substituted works under this paragraph—

(i) a sewer of better type or greater capacity is placed in substitution for an existing sewer of worse type or smaller capacity, except where this has been solely due to using the nearest currently available type or capacity, or

(ii) a sewer (whether an existing sewer or a sewer substituted for an existing sewer) is placed at a depth greater than the depth at which the existing sewer was,

and the placing of a sewer of that type or capacity or the placing of a sewer at that depth, as the case may be, is not agreed by the Corporation, or, in default of agreement, is not determined by arbitration to be necessary, then, if it involves cost in the construction of the new, altered or substituted works exceeding that which would have been involved if the apparatus placed had been of the existing type or capacity, or at the existing depth, as the case may be, the amount which apart from this sub-paragraph would be payable to the sewerage undertakers by virtue of sub-paragraphs (4) and (10) above shall be reduced by the amount of that excess:

(b) For the purposes of sub-paragraph (13)(a) above an extension of a sewer to a length greater than the length of an existing sewer shall not be treated as a placing of a sewer of greater dimensions than those of the existing sewer:

(c) An amount which apart from this sub-paragraph would be payable to the sewerage undertakers in respect of any new, altered or substituted works by virtue of sub-paragraphs (4) and (10) above (and having regard, where relevant, to sub-paragraph (13)(a) above) shall, if the works include the placing of a sewer provided in substitution for a sewer placed more than 7½ years earlier so as to confer on the sewerage undertakers any financial benefit by deferment of the time for renewal of the sewer in the ordinary course, be reduced by the amount which represents that benefit as calculated in accordance with the Code of Practice entitled "Measures Necessary Where Apparatus is Affected by Major Works (Diversionary Works)" and dated June 1992, and approved by the Secretary of State on 30th June 1992 as revised and reissued from time to time:

(14) It shall be lawful for an officer of the sewerage undertakers duly appointed for the purpose at any reasonable time and, if required by the Corporation, under their supervision to enter upon and inspect any specified work or any other works constructed under the powers of this Act, for which purpose the Corporation shall allow to any such officer access over any other works or land of the Corporation:

(15) The fact that any specified work has been constructed in accordance with a plan approved or not objected to by the sewerage undertakers or to their satisfaction or in accordance with any directions or award of an arbitrator shall not relieve the Corporation from any liability under the provisions of this paragraph:

(16) As soon as reasonably practicable after the completion of the construction of a specified work the Corporation shall deliver to the sewerage undertakers a plan and section showing the position and level of that work as constructed and all new, altered or substituted works provided under this paragraph:

(17) Any difference arising between the Corporation and the sewerage undertakers under this paragraph shall be referred to and settled by arbitration but the Corporation and the sewerage undertakers shall use their best endeavours to ensure that proceedings before an arbitrator commence in every case within seven days of the Corporation or the sewerage undertakers registering a failure to agree:

(18) Nothing in this paragraph shall apply—
> (a) in relation to street works (within the meaning of Part III of the New Roads and Street Works Act 1991) executed by the Corporation; or
> (b) in relation to apparatus in respect of which the relations between the Corporation and the sewerage undertakers are regulated by that Part of that Act.

FOR PROTECTION OF TELECOMMUNICATIONS OPERATORS

4. For the protection of telecommunications operators the following provisions shall, unless otherwise agreed in writing between the Corporation and the telecommunications operator concerned, have effect:—

(1) In this paragraph unless the contrary intention appears expressions defined in the Telecommunications Act 1984 have the same meanings as in that Act and—
> "apparatus" has the same meaning as in Part III of the New Roads and Street Works Act 1991; and
> "relocation works" means works executed, or apparatus provided, under sub-paragraph (5) below:

(2) The temporary stopping up or diversion of any street under section 18 (Temporary stoppage of streets) of this Act shall not affect any right of a telecommunications operator under paragraph 9 of the telecommunications code (contained in Schedule 2 to the Telecommunications Act 1984) to inspect, maintain, adjust, repair or alter any apparatus which, at the time of the stopping up or diversion, is in that street:

(3) Where a street is stopped up, diverted or substituted under section 19 (Stopping up streets without providing substitute) or section 20 (Stopping up streets in case of diversion or substitution) of this Act any telecommunications operator whose apparatus is under, in, upon, over, along or across the street shall have the same powers and rights in respect of that apparatus, subject to the provisions of this paragraph, as if this Act had not been passed:

(4) The Corporation shall give not less than 28 days' notice in writing of their intention to stop up, divert or substitute any street under section 19 (Stopping up streets without providing substitute) or section 20 (Stopping up streets in case of diversion or substitution) of this Act to any telecommunications operator whose apparatus is under, in, upon, over, along or across the street:

(5) Where a notice under sub-paragraph (4) above has been given, the telecommunications operator may, and if reasonably requested so to do by the Corporation in the notice, shall, as soon as reasonably practicable from the service of the notice—

　(a) remove the apparatus and place it or other apparatus provided in substitution for it in such other position as the telecommunications operator may reasonably determine and have power to place it, or

　(b) provide other apparatus in substitution for the existing apparatus and place it in such position as aforesaid:

(6) Subject to the following provisions of this paragraph, the Corporation shall pay to any telecommunications operator an amount equal to the cost reasonably incurred by the telecommunications operator in or in connection with—

　(a) the execution of relocation works required in consequence of the stopping up, diversion or substitution of the street, and

　(b) the doing of any other work or thing rendered necessary by the execution of relocation works:

(7) If in the course of the execution of relocation works under sub-paragraph (5) above—

　(a) apparatus of better type, or greater capacity or of greater dimensions is placed in substitution for existing apparatus of worse type, or smaller capacity or of smaller dimensions, except where this has been solely due to using the nearest currently available type, capacity or dimension, or

　(b) apparatus (whether existing apparatus or apparatus substituted for existing apparatus) is placed at a depth greater than the depth at which the existing apparatus was,

and the placing of apparatus of that type or capacity or of those dimensions or the placing of apparatus at that depth, as the case may be, is not agreed by the Corporation, or, in default of agreement, is not determined by arbitration to be necessary, then, if it involves cost in the execution of the relocation works exceeding that which would have been involved if the apparatus placed had been of the existing type, capacity or dimensions, or at the existing depth, as the case may be, the amount which apart from this paragraph would be payable to the telecommunications operator by virtue of sub-paragraph (6) above shall be reduced by the amount of that excess.

(8) For the purposes of sub-paragraph (7) above—

　(a) an extension of apparatus to a length greater than the length of existing apparatus shall not be treated as placing of apparatus of greater dimensions than those of the existing apparatus, and

　(b) where the provision of a joint in a cable is agreed, or is determined to be necessary, the consequential provision of a jointing chamber or of a manhole shall be treated as if it also had been agreed or had been so determined:

(9) An amount which apart from this sub-paragraph would be payable to a telecommunications operator in respect of works by virtue of sub-paragraph (6) above (and having regard, where relevant, to sub-paragraph (7) above) shall, if the works include the placing of apparatus provided in substitution for apparatus placed more than 7½ years earlier so as to confer on the telecommunications operator any financial benefit by deferment of the time for renewal of the apparatus in the ordinary course, be reduced by the amount which represents that benefit as calculated in accordance with the Code of Practice entitled "Measures Necessary Where Apparatus is Affected by Major Works (Diversionary Works)" and dated June 1992, and approved by the Secretary of State on 30th June 1992 as revised and reissued from time to time.

(10) Sub-paragraphs (6) to (9) above shall not apply where the authorised works constitute major transport works for the purposes of Part III of the New Roads and Street Works Act 1991, but instead—

　(a) the allowable costs of the relocation works shall be determined in accordance with section 85 of that Act (sharing of costs of necessary measures) and any regulations for the time being having effect under that section, and

　(b) the allowable costs shall be borne by the Corporation and the telecommunications operator in such proportions as may be prescribed by any such regulations.

FOR PROTECTION OF NATIONAL RIVERS AUTHORITY

5. For the protection of the National Rivers Authority (in this paragraph referred to as "the rivers authority") the following provisions shall, unless otherwise agreed in writing between the Corporation and the rivers authority, have effect:—

　(1) In this paragraph—

"construction" includes execution, placing and altering and, in relation to temporary works, includes removal; and "construct" and "constructed" have corresponding meanings;

"drainage work" means any watercourse and includes any land used for providing flood storage capacity for any watercourse and any bank, wall, embankment or other structure or appliance constructed or used for defence against water;

"plans" includes sections, drawings, specifications and method statements;

"specified work" means so much of any permanent or temporary work or operation authorised by this Act (other than works required in an emergency) as is situated in, on, under, over or within 8 metres of a drainage work; and

"watercourse" has the meaning given in section 72 of the Land Drainage Act 1991:

(2) (a) Before beginning to construct any specified work, the Corporation shall submit to the rivers authority plans of the work and such further particulars available to them as the rivers authority may reasonably require;

(b) Any such specified work shall not be constructed except in accordance with such plans as may be approved in writing by the rivers authority, or settled in accordance with sub-paragraph (10) below;

(c) Any approval of the rivers authority required under this paragraph—

(i) shall not be unreasonably withheld;

(ii) shall be deemed to have been given if it is neither given nor refused in writing and with a statement of the grounds for refusal within two months of the submission of plans for approval;

(iii) may be given subject to such reasonable requirements as the rivers authority may impose for the protection of any drainage work or water resources for the prevention of flooding and water pollution and in the discharge of its environmental and recreational duties:

(3) Without prejudice to the generality of sub-paragraph (2) above, the requirements which the rivers authority may impose under that sub-paragraph include conditions requiring the Corporation at their own expense to construct such protective works whether temporary or permanent during the construction of the specified works (including the provision of flood banks, walls or embankments and other new works and the strengthening, repair or renewal of existing banks, walls or embankments) as are reasonably necessary to safeguard any drainage work against damage or to secure that its efficiency for flood defence purposes is not impaired and that the risk of flooding is not otherwise increased by reason of any specified work:

(4) Any specified work, and all protective works required by the rivers authority under sub-paragraph (2) above, shall be constructed to the reasonable satisfaction of the rivers authority and the rivers authority shall be entitled by its officer to watch and inspect the construction of such works:

(5) If by reason of the construction of any specified work the efficiency of any drainage work for flood defence purposes is impaired or that work is damaged, such impairment or damage shall be made good by the Corporation to the reasonable satisfaction of the rivers authority and, if the Corporation fail to do so, the rivers authority may make good the same and recover from the Corporation the expense reasonably incurred by it in so doing:

(6) The Corporation shall indemnify the rivers authority in respect of all reasonable costs, charges and expenses which the rivers authority may reasonably incur or have to pay or which it may sustain—

(a) in the examination or approval of plans under this paragraph;

(b) in the inspection of the construction of the specified works or any protective works required by the rivers authority under this paragraph:

(7) (a) Without prejudice to the other provisions of this paragraph the Corporation shall indemnify the rivers authority from all claims, demands, proceedings, costs, damages or expenses or loss which may be made or taken against, or recovered from or incurred by, the rivers authority by reason of—

(i) any damage to any drainage work so as to impair its efficiency for the purposes of flood defence; or

(ii) any raising of the water table in land adjoining the works or any sewers, drains and watercourses; or

(iii) any flooding or increased flooding of any such lands; or

(iv) inadequate water quality in any watercourse or other surface waters or in groundwater;

which is caused by the construction of any of the works or any act or omission of the Corporation, their contractors, agents, workmen or servants whilst engaged upon any such work;

(b) The rivers authority shall give to the Corporation reasonable notice of any such claim or demand and no settlement or compromise thereof shall be made without the agreement of the Corporation:

(8) The fact that any work or thing has been executed or done in accordance with a plan approved or deemed to be approved by the rivers authority, or to its satisfaction, or in accordance with any directions or award of an arbitrator, shall not relieve the Corporation from any liability under the provisions of this paragraph:

    Provided that this sub-paragraph shall not apply to the extent that such liability arises from a failure by the rivers authority properly to perform its functions:

(9) For the purposes of section 109 of the Water Resources Act 1991 (as to structures in, over or under watercourses) as applying to the construction of any authorised work, any consent or approval given or deemed to be given by the rivers authority under this paragraph with respect to such construction shall be deemed also to constitute a consent or approval under that section:

(10) Any difference arising between the Corporation and the rivers authority under this paragraph (other than a difference as to its meaning or construction) shall be referred to and settled by arbitration.

FOR PROTECTION OF CERTAIN PROPERTIES AT GRAVEL HILL

6. The Corporation may enter into agreements to purchase any land pursuant to any direction of, or any undertaking given to, a Parliamentary Committee during the passage through Parliament of the Bill for this Act; and any such agreement may provide for the purchase price payable for that land to be equal to the amount of the compensation that would have been payable if the Corporation had been authorised to acquire the land compulsorily under Part III of this Act and had served a notice to treat in respect of that land.

FOR PROTECTION OF CERTAIN PROPERTIES AT WADDON NEW ROAD

7. The Council may enter into agreements to purchase any land pursuant to any direction of, or any undertaking given to, a Parliamentary Committee during the passage through Parliament of the Bill for this Act; and any such agreement may provide for the purchase price payable for that land to be equal to the amount of the compensation that would have been payable if the Council had been authorised to acquire the land compulsorily under Part III of this Act and had served a notice to treat in respect of that land.

INDEX

References are to sections and Schedules

LONDON LOCAL AUTHORITIES ACT 1994

(1994 c. xii)

ARRANGEMENT OF SECTIONS

An Act to confer further powers upon local authorities in London; and for other purposes.   [21st July 1994]

PARLIAMENTARY DEBATES

The Bill's progress through Parliament was as follows:

House of Lords: First Reading, January 13, 1992; Second Reading, March 5, 1992; Bill Committed, March 5, 1992; Suspended, March 12, 1992; Opposed Bill Committee, July 13–14, 1992; Unopposed Bill Committee, February 11–17, 1993; Third Reading, April 1, 1993; Commons' Amendments, July 12, 1994.

House of Commons: First Reading, April 1, 1993; Second Reading, July 22, 1993; Bill Committed, July 22, 1993; Suspended, November 2, 1993; Opposed Bill Committee, May 10–June 28, 1994; Bill as amended Considered, July 6, 1994; Third Reading, July 12, 1994.

INTRODUCTION

This Act makes various provisions to improve and develop local government services in London, making the necessary amendments to the powers of London borough councils. The Act covers: distribution of free literature; night café licensing; street trading; fee for hypnotism authorisation; dangerous structure fees; application of the London Local Authorities Act 1990 to Camden Borough Council; liability of directors.

WHEREAS—

(1) It is expedient that further and better provision should be made for the improvement and development of local government services in London and for the benefit of persons residing therein and that the powers of London borough councils should be extended and amended as provided in this Act:

(2) In relation to the promotion of the Bill for this Act the Westminster City Council have complied with the requirements of section 239 of the Local Government Act 1972 and the other London borough councils, all of whom are participating in the promotion of the Bill, have complied with the requirements of section 87 of the Local Government Act 1985:

(3) It is expedient that the other provisions contained in this Act should be enacted:

(4) The purposes of this Act cannot be effected without the authority of Parliament:

May it therefore please Your Majesty that it may be enacted, and be it enacted, by the Queen's most Excellent Majesty, by and with the advice and consent of the Lords Spiritual and Temporal, and Commons, in this present Parliament assembled, and by the authority of the same, as follows, that is to say:—

Short title and commencement

1. This Act may be cited as the London Local Authorities Act 1994 and except section 5 (Night café licensing) of this Act shall come into operation at the end of the period of two months beginning with the date on which it is passed.

Interpretation

2. In this Act, except as otherwise expressly provided or unless the context otherwise requires—

"the Act of 1990" means the London Local Authorities Act 1990;

"authorised officer" means an officer of a borough council authorised by the council in writing to act in relation to the relevant provision of this Act;

"borough council" means London borough council but does not include the Common Council of the City of London; and "borough" shall be construed accordingly.

Appointed day

3.—(1) In this Act "the appointed day" means such day as may be fixed in relation to a borough by resolution of the borough council, subject to and in accordance with the provisions of this section.

(2) Different days may be fixed under this section for the purpose of the application of different provisions of this Act to a borough.

(3) The borough council shall cause to be published in a local newspaper circulating in the borough notice—

(a) of the passing of any such resolution and of the day fixed thereby; and

(b) of the general effect of the provisions of this Act coming into operation as from that day;

and the day so fixed shall not be earlier than the expiration of three months from the publication of the said notice.

(4) Either a photostatic or other reproduction certified by the officer appointed for that purpose by the borough council to be a true reproduction of a page or part of a page of any such newspaper bearing the date of its publication and containing any such notice shall be evidence of the publication of the notice, and of the date of publication.

Distribution of free literature

4.—(1) A borough council may designate, in accordance with subsection (9) below, any of the following places, or any part of such places, in the borough as places to which this section applies:—

(a) (i) a public off-street car park;

(ii) a recreation ground, garden, park, pleasure ground or open space under the management or control of a local authority; or

(b) a street or way to which the public commonly have access, whether or not as of right.

(2) Any person who distributes free literature in a place designated under subsection (1) above without the consent of the borough council or in breach of any condition subject to which the council's consent is given or causes or permits any person so to do shall be guilty of an offence and liable on summary conviction to a fine not exceeding level 2 on the standard scale.

(3)(a) The reference in subsection (2) above to a person who distributes free literature in a place designated under subsection (1) above shall be deemed to include a reference to a person who distributes free literature on or from land within 7 metres of any designated street who is not—

    (i) the owner of that land; or

    (ii) the person liable to be assessed to the uniform business rate in respect thereof; or

    (iii) on that land with the consent in writing of either of the persons mentioned in sub-paragraphs (i) and (ii) above.

(b) Where in any proceedings under this section it is shown that any free literature was distributed by a person on or from land within 7 metres of any street or designated street the burden of proof shall lie on that person to show to the satisfaction of the court that at the relevant time he was a person referred to in sub-paragraph (i) or (ii) of the foregoing paragraph or had the consent referred to in sub-paragraph (iii) thereof.

(4) Where a person is distributing free literature in a place designated under subsection (1) above without the consent of the borough council an authorised officer may seize any supply of that literature which the person has at or near that place.

(5)(a) The following provisions of this subsection shall have effect where any literature is seized under subsection (4) above and references in those provisions to proceedings are to proceedings in respect of the alleged offence in relation to which the literature is seized.

(b) Subject to paragraph (c) below, at the conclusion of the proceedings the literature shall be returned to the person from whom it was seized unless the court orders it to be forfeited under any enactment.

(c) If no proceedings are instituted before the expiration of a period of 28 days beginning with the date of seizure, or any proceedings instituted within that period are discontinued, at the expiration of that period or, as the case may be, on the discontinuance of the proceedings, the literature shall be returned to the person from whom it was seized unless it has not proved possible, after diligent enquiry, to identify that person and ascertain his address.

(d) Where the literature is not returned because it has not proved possible to identify the person from whom it was seized and ascertain his address the council may apply to a magistrates' court for an order as to the manner in which they should deal with it.

(6) The conditions of consent referred to in subsection (2) above include, without prejudice to the generality of the power to impose conditions, conditions as to the times or period for which the consent is valid, conditions for the prevention of detriment to the amenities of the area, a condition requiring the person distributing free literature to produce on demand to an authorised officer of the borough council or to a constable documentary evidence of the consent, conditions as to the part of the place designated under subsection (1) above where the consent is to apply and conditions as to the payment for the consent of such reasonable fee to cover the expense of the borough council in dealing with applications for such consents as the borough council may by resolution prescribe; and any such consent may be revoked by notice to the person to whom the consent was given.

(7) The grounds upon which a borough council may withhold consent under subsection (2) above, and may revoke a consent under subsection (6) above are that—

    (a) the applicant is unsuitable by reason of misconduct;

    (b) the applicant has within the previous five years been convicted of an offence under this section;

    (c) there is already a sufficiency of persons to whom consent has been given under this section, carrying out in the designated place the activity in respect of which the consent is requested;

    (d) there would be a risk of danger or unreasonable inconvenience to users of any highway if the consent is given, or, as the case may be, not revoked;

(e) (in the case of a revocation) the applicant has failed to avail himself, or to avail himself to a reasonable extent, of his consent.

(8) A person aggrieved by—

(a) the withholding by the borough council of consent referred to in subsection (2) above;

(b) the conditions subject to which the borough council give such consent; or

(c) the revocation of such consent under subsection (6) above; may appeal to a magistrates' court by way of complaint for an order and on such an appeal the court may dismiss or allow the appeal or may vary any conditions imposed by the borough council.

(9)(a) Before designating any place under subsection (1) above the borough council shall give notice of their proposal by advertisement in a local newspaper circulating in the borough, and by posting a copy of the notice in the places to which it relates, stating that objections to the proposal may be made to the proper officer of the borough council within a time, not less than 28 days after the giving of the notice, specified in the notice.

(b) After taking into consideration any objections made in accordance with paragraph (a) above, the borough council may by resolution designate, as places to which this section applies for the purposes of subsection (2) above, all or any, or any part, of the places specified in the notice given under that paragraph.

(10) A resolution under subsection (9)(b) above shall come into force on such day as shall be specified by a notice given in the same manner as a notice given under subsection (9)(a) above, being a day not less than 28 days after the day on which notice is given under this subsection.

(11) Any resolution under subsection (9)(b) above may be rescinded, or varied by the deletion of any place or part of a place, by a subsequent resolution of the borough council.

(12) In proceedings for an offence under section 9 of the Metropolitan Streets Act 1867, it shall be a defence for the accused to show that he was acting with the consent of a borough council under this section and in compliance with any conditions subject to which that consent was given.

(13) This section does not apply to the distribution of free literature—

(a) by a charity within the meaning of the Charities Act 1960 where that literature relates to or is for the benefit of that body;

(b) by or on behalf of a political organisation;

(c) where the person who distributes it does so by putting it into a building or letterbox; or

(d) by London Regional Transport, any of its subsidiaries or any other person who provides a service pursuant to an agreement made in accordance with section 3 of the London Regional Transport Act 1984 where that literature relates to services provided by any of those persons.

(14) In this section—

"distribute" means to offer or make available, and includes the placing of free literature on, or affixing it to, a vehicle;

"free literature" means any newspaper, document, card or other literature for which no charge is made to the recipient and which advertises, or contains or comprises an advertisement, for commercial gain.

Night café licensing

5. As from the appointed day in a borough section 14 (Appeals) of the Act of 1990 is hereby amended—

(1) by the substitution for subsection (1) of—
"(1) Any of the following persons, that is to say:—
(a) an applicant for the grant, renewal or transfer of a night café licence whose application is refused;
(b) an applicant for the grant, renewal or transfer of a night café licence who is aggrieved by any term, condition or restriction on or subject to which the night café licence is granted, renewed or transferred;
(c) an applicant for the variation of the terms, conditions or restrictions on or subject to which a night café licence is held whose application is refused;
(d) an applicant for the variation of the terms, conditions or restrictions on or subject to which a night café licence is held who is aggrieved by any term, condition or restriction contained in a further variation made consequent on the variation applied for;
(e) the holder of a night café licence which is revoked under section 15 (Enforcement) of this Act;
may at any time before the expiration of the period of 21 days beginning with the relevant date appeal to the magistrates' court acting for the petty sessions area in which the premises are situated by way of complaint for an order.";
(2) by the substitution for subsections (7) and (8) of—
"(7) Where the holder of a night café licence makes an application under section 12 (Variation of night café licences) of this Act and the borough council make the variation applied for together with a further variation, then the night café licence shall continue as it was before the application—
(a) until the time for bringing an appeal under this section against any term, condition or restriction contained in the further variation has expired; and
(b) where any such appeal is brought, until the determination or abandonment of the appeal.".

Street trading

6.—(1) Section 21(2)(j) (Interpretation of Part III) of the Act of 1990 is hereby amended by the insertion after "offer for sale", of the words "of articles".

(2) Section 24(1) (Designation of licence streets) of the Act of 1990 is hereby amended by the substitution for the proviso of—
"Provided that a borough council shall—
(a) before passing a designating resolution, consult with the Commissioner of Police of the Metropolis on their proposal; and
(b) before rescinding or varying a designating resolution, consult with the licence holders trading in the street in question, or a body or bodies representative of them, on their proposal.".

(3) Section 27(6) (Conditions of street trading licences) of the Act of 1990 is hereby amended by the addition, at the end of the subsection, of "and shall notify the licence holders or a body or bodies representative of them of the making of such regulations.".

(4) In section 30(1) (Part III appeals) of the Act of 1990, the following paragraph shall be inserted after the words "Any person aggrieved":—
"(aa) by the refusal of a borough council to renew a licence because they are not satisfied as mentioned in subsection (4)(b) of section 25 (Application for street trading licences) of this Act.".

(5) In section 30(1)(d) (Part III appeals) of the Act of 1990, the words, "where that decision is based on any of the grounds mentioned in subsection (1)(d) to (h) of the said section 28" shall cease to have effect.

(6) Section 30(2)(a) (Part III appeals) of the Act of 1990 is hereby amended by the addition after "paragraph" of "(aa),".

(7) Section 30 (Part III appeals) of the Act of 1990 is hereby amended by the addition, after subsection (11) of the following subsection:—

"(12) An appeal under subsection (11) above may be brought—

(a) in the case of an appeal under paragraph (a) or (b) of that subsection, at any time before the expiration of the period of three months beginning with the date on which notice of the passing of the resolution is published for the second time in accordance with subsection (10) of section 24 (Designation of licence streets) of this Act;

(b) in the case of an appeal under paragraph (c) of that subsection, at any time before the expiration of the period of three months beginning with the date upon which the licence holders or a body or bodies representative of them were notified of the making of the regulations;

(c) in the case of an appeal under paragraph (d) of that subsection—

(i) if it relates to the amount of a fee payable under subsection (1) of section 32 (Fees and charges) of this Act, at any time before the expiration of the period of three months beginning with the date on which the fee payable is notified to the licence holders or a body or bodies representative of them;

(ii) if it relates to the amount of a charge under subsection (2) of section 32 (Fees and charges) of this Act, at any time before the expiration of the period of three months beginning with the date on which notice of the determination of the charge has been given to the licence holders or a body or bodies representative of them.".

(8) Section 32 (Fees and charges) of the Act of 1990 is hereby amended—

(a) (i) by the deletion in subsection (5), of "grant or" and "as aforesaid"; and

(ii) by the addition in that subsection after "any" of the word "such";

(b) by the substitution, in subsection (7) for "or varying the amount of such charges" of the words "(whether originally or by way of variation of charges previously determined)";

(c) by the addition after subsection (7) of the following subsection:—

"(7A) A notice under subsection (7)(a) above shall be accompanied by a statement showing how the proposed charges have been computed; and any body representative of licence holders may request the borough council to supply such further information or explanation with regard to the proposed charges as the body may reasonably require in order to ascertain whether the proposed charges are reasonable and have been computed in accordance with the provisions of this section.";

(d) by the addition in subsection (9)—

(i) after the first "to" of "(a)"; and

(ii) at the end, of the words "and (b) comply with any request made under subsection (7A) above;

and where any such request is made the period so specified, if still current, shall be treated as extended by the number of days in the period beginning with the day on which the request is made and ending with that on which it is complied with.";

(e) by the substitution for subsection (10) of—

"(10) When a borough council have determined fees under subsection (1) above or charges under subsection (2) above (whether originally or by way of variation of fees or charges previously determined) they shall give notice of the fees or charges so determined and of the date on which those fees or charges are to be brought into effect, in the manner prescribed in subsection (7) above.".

(9) Section 34 (Offences) of the Act of 1990 is hereby amended by the addition, at the beginning of paragraph (1) of the words "without reasonable excuse".

(10) Section 37 (Ice cream trading) of the Act of 1990 is hereby amended by the addition, in subsection (2) after "prohibited street" of the words "and in the case of any London borough except the City of Westminster and the Royal Borough of Kensington and Chelsea may so designate it for such days or for such parts of days as are specified in the resolution,".

(11) Section 38 (Unlicensed street trading) of the Act of 1990 is hereby amended—

(a) by the substitution for subsection (1) of—

"(1) A person who—

(a) is not the holder of a street trading licence or a temporary licence and who engages in street trading in a borough; or

(b) is the holder of a temporary licence and who engages in street trading in a borough on a day or in a place not specified in that temporary licence;

shall be guilty of an offence and shall be liable on summary conviction to a fine not exceeding level 3 on the standard scale.";

(b) by the addition, in subsection (4) after "of that offence" of the words "or may be the subject of forfeiture under subsection (5) below";

(c) by the addition, after subsection (4) of the following subsection:—

"(4A)(a) The following provisions of this subsection shall have effect where any article or thing (including any receptacle) is seized under subsection (4) above and references in those provisions to proceedings are to proceedings in respect of the alleged offence in relation to which the article or thing is seized.

(b) Subject to paragraph (e) below, at the conclusion of the proceedings the article or thing shall be returned to the person from whom it was seized unless the court orders it to be forfeited under subsection (5) below.

(c) Subject to paragraph (d) below, where a receptacle seized under subsection (4) above is a motor vehicle used for ice cream trading, the borough council or the Commissioner of Police of the Metropolis (as the case may be) shall, within three days of the receipt of an application in writing by the owner or registered keeper of the vehicle, permit him to remove it.

(d) Paragraph (c) above shall not apply where—

(i) the owner or registered keeper of the vehicle has been convicted of an offence under this Part of this Act; or

(ii) the owner or registered keeper of the vehicle is being prosecuted for a previous alleged offence under this Part of this Act; or

(iii) the vehicle has been used in the commission of such an offence or previous alleged offence;

if the offence or previous alleged offence was committed or is alleged to have been committed no more than three years before the seizure and (in the case of an alleged offence) the proceedings are continuing.

(e) If no proceedings are instituted before the expiration of a period of 28 days beginning with the date of seizure, or any proceedings instituted within that period are discontinued, at the expiration of that period or, as the case may be, on the discontinuance of the proceedings, the article or thing shall be returned to the person from whom it was seized unless it has not proved possible, after diligent enquiry, to identify that person and ascertain his address.

(f) Where the article or thing is not returned because it has not proved possible to identify the person from whom it was seized and ascertain his address the borough council (whether the article or thing was seized by a constable or by an authorised officer) may apply to a magistrates' court for an order as to the manner in which it should be dealt with.";

(d) by the addition, in subsection (6) at the end, of—

"and in considering whether to make such an order a court shall have regard—

    (i) to the value of the property; and

    (ii) to the likely financial and other effects on the offender of the making of the order (taken together with any other order that the court contemplates making).";

(e) by the substitution, in subsection (7) for "the article or thing" of the word "anything";

(f) by the addition, after subsection (7) of the following subsection:—

"(8)(a) This subsection shall have effect where—

    (i) an article, thing or receptacle is seized under subsection (4) above; and

    (ii) (A) not less than six months have passed since the date of the seizure and no information has been laid against any person for an offence under this section in respect of the acts or circumstances which occasioned the seizure; or

        (B) proceedings for such an offence have been brought and either the person charged has been acquitted (whether or not on appeal) and the time for appealing against or challenging the acquittal (where applicable) has expired without an appeal or challenge being brought, or the proceedings (including any appeal) have been withdrawn by, or have failed for want of prosecution by, the person by whom the original proceedings were brought.

(b) When this subsection has effect a person who has or at the time of seizure had a legal interest in the article, thing or receptacle seized may recover compensation from the borough council or (where it is seized by a constable) the Commissioner of Police of the Metropolis by civil action in the County Court in respect of any loss suffered by him as a result of the seizure.

(c) The court may not make an order for compensation under paragraph (b) above unless it is satisfied that seizure was not lawful under subsection (4) above.".

(12) Part III of the Act of 1990, as amended by this Act, is set out in the Schedule to this Act.

Fee for hypnotism authorisation

7.—(1) The Hypnotism Act 1952 is hereby amended by the addition, after section 2, of the following section:—

    "**Fee**

    2A. The person making an application to a controlling authority, being the council of a London borough, for an authorisation under section 2 of this Act shall on making the application pay to the council such reasonable fee as the council may determine.".

(2) If any regulations are made under section 150 of the Local Government and Housing Act 1989 whereby a borough council may impose a charge in

connection with the granting of an authorisation under section 2 of the Hypnotism Act 1952, then upon the coming into force of those regulations this section shall cease to have effect.

(3) For the purposes of subsection (1)(c) of the said section 150, the power conferred on a borough council by virtue of subsection (1) above shall be disregarded.

Dangerous structure fees

8.—(1) A borough council to which the London Building Acts apply may make regulations with respect to the amount of the fees payable to them under the London Building Acts in connection with any dangerous or neglected structure.

(2) Regulations made under this section may amend or repeal any of the provisions of the First Schedule to the Act of 1939 and may repeal any byelaws made under section 11 (Power to Council to make byelaws as to fees) of the London County Council (General Powers) Act 1955, and any references in the London Building Acts to any of those provisions shall be construed as references to those provisions as so amended and, where any such provisions are repealed by those regulations, to the provisions of those regulations corresponding to the provisions so repealed.

(3) Any regulations made under this section shall be printed and a copy of any such regulations in force shall be kept at the principal office of the borough council and a copy shall be supplied at all reasonable hours without payment to any applicant for the same.

(4) Section 11 of the London County Council (General Powers) Act 1955 shall cease to have effect except in the City of London, but any byelaws made thereunder shall continue in force until repealed under subsection (2) above.

(5) In this section—

"the Act of 1939" means the London Building Acts (Amendment) Act 1939; and

"the London Building Acts" means the London Building Acts 1930 to 1939 as amended by the London County Council (General Powers) Act 1952 and by the London County Council (General Powers) Act 1954.

Application of Act of 1990 to Camden

9. Schedule 1 (Participating councils) to the Act of 1990 shall be amended by the insertion, after "Bromley Borough Council" of "Camden Borough Council".

Liability of directors, etc.

10.—(1) Where an offence under this Act committed by a body corporate is proved to have been committed with the consent or connivance of, or to be attributable to any neglect on the part of, a director, manager, secretary or other similar officer of the body corporate or any person who was purporting to act in any such capacity, he, as well as the body corporate, shall be guilty of the offence.

(2) Where the affairs of a body corporate are managed by its members, subsection (1) above shall apply to the acts and defaults of a member in connection with his functions of management as if he were a director of the body corporate.

SCHEDULE

LONDON LOCAL AUTHORITIES ACT 1990 PART III AS HAVING
EFFECT IN ACCORDANCE WITH SECTION 6 (STREET TRADING) OF THIS ACT

PART III

STREET TRADING

Interpretation of Part III

21.—(1) In this Part of this Act—

"grant", unless the context otherwise requires, includes renew and renewal, and cognate words shall be construed accordingly;

"ice cream trading" means the selling, exposing or offering for sale of goods consisting wholly or mainly of ice cream, frozen confectionery or other similar commodities from a vehicle;

"itinerant ice cream trading" means ice cream trading from a vehicle which goes from place to place remaining in any one location in the course of trading for short periods only;

"licence street" means a street designated under section 24 (Designation of licence streets) of this Act;

"receptacle" includes a vehicle or stall and any basket, bag, box, vessel, stand, easel, board, tray or thing which is used (whether or not constructed or adapted for such use) as a container for or for the display of any article or thing or equipment used in the provision of any service;

"street" includes—

    (a) any road or footway;

    (b) any other area, not being within permanently enclosed premises, within 7 metres of any road or footway, to which the public have access without payment;

    (c) any part of such road, footway or area;

    (d) any part of any housing development provided or maintained by a local authority under Part II of the Housing Act 1985;

"street trading" means subject to subsection (2) below the selling or exposing or the offering for sale of any article (including a living thing) or the supplying or offering to supply any service in a street for gain or reward;

"street trading licence" means a licence granted under this Part of this Act and valid for the period specified therein being not less than six months and not more than three years;

"temporary licence" means a licence granted under this Part of this Act valid for a single day or for such period as may be specified in the licence not exceeding six months.

(2) The following are not street trading for the purposes of this Part of this Act:—

(a) trading by a person acting as a pedlar under the authority of a Pedlar's Certificate granted under the Pedlars Act 1871;

(b) anything done in a market or fair the right to hold which was acquired by virtue of a grant (including a presumed grant) or acquired or established by virtue of any enactment or order;

(c) trading in a trunk road picnic area provided by the Secretary of State under section 112 of the Highways Act 1980;

(d) trading as a news-vendor provided that the only articles sold or exposed or offered for sale are newspapers or periodicals and they are sold or exposed or offered for sale without a receptacle for them or, if with a receptacle for them such receptacle does not—

    (i) exceed 1 metre in length or width or 2 metres in height; or

    (ii) occupy a ground area exceeding 0.25 square metre; or

    (iii) stand on the carriageway of a street; or

    (iv) cause undue interference or inconvenience to persons using the street;

(e) selling articles or things to occupiers of premises adjoining any street, or offering or exposing them for sale from a vehicle which is used only for the regular delivery of milk or other perishable goods to those persons;

(f) the use for trading under Part VIIA of the Highways Act 1980 of any object or structure placed on, in or over a highway;

(g) the operation of facilities for recreation or refreshment under Part VIIA of the Highways Act 1980;

(h) the doing of anything authorised by regulations made under section 5 of the Police, Factories, &c. (Miscellaneous Provisions) Act 1916;

(i) trading in a highway in relation to which a control order under section 7 of the Local Government (Miscellaneous Provisions) Act 1976 is in force, other than trading to which the control order does not apply; and

(j) the sale, exposure or offer for sale of articles or offer or provision of services on any land comprised in a street (not being part of a highway) within the meaning of subsection (1) above by the owner or occupier of the land or by a bona fide employee of the owner or occupier of the land.

Application of Part III

22. This Part of this Act applies to the borough of a participating council as from the appointed day.

Licensing of street traders

23.—(1) Subject to the provisions of this Part of this Act it shall be unlawful for any person to engage in street trading (whether or not in or from a stationary position) in any licence street within a borough unless that person is authorised to do so by a street trading licence or a temporary licence.

(2) For the purposes of this Part of this Act a person shall be deemed to engage in street trading whether or not he regularly carries on the business of street trading.

Designation of licence streets

24.—(1) If a borough council consider that street trading should be licensed in their area they may from time to time pass any of the following resolutions:—

(a) a resolution (in this Part of this Act referred to as a "designating resolution") designating any street within the borough as a "licence street";

(b) a resolution specifying in relation to any such street or any part of a street any class or classes of articles, things or services which they will, or other than which they will not, prescribe in any street trading licence granted by them in respect of that street;

and may from time to time by subsequent resolution rescind or vary any such resolution:

*   *   *   *   *

Provided that a borough council shall—

(a) before passing a designating resolution, consult with the Commissioner of Police of the Metropolis on their proposal; and

(b) before rescinding or varying a designating resolution, consult with the licence holders trading in the street in question, or a body or bodies representative of them, on their proposal.

(2) At the appointed day for the purposes of this Part of this Act in a borough, the streets prescribed by any licences granted by the council of the borough in pursuance of powers contained in any of the enactments referred to in column (2) of Schedule 2 to this Act and then in force shall be deemed to have been designated as licence streets under a designating resolution.

(3) If a borough council pass a designating resolution the designation of the street shall take effect on the day specified in the resolution (which must not be before the expiration of the period of one month beginning with the day on which the resolution is passed).

(4) A borough council shall not pass a resolution or rescind or vary a resolution under this section unless—

(a) they have published notice of their intention to do so in a local newspaper circulating in their area;

(b) they have served a copy of the notice on the highway authority for that street (unless they are that highway authority); and

(c) where subsection (5) below applies, they have obtained the necessary consent.

(5) This subsection applies—

(a) where the resolution relates to a street which is owned or maintainable by a relevant corporation; and

(b) where the resolution designates as a licence street any street maintained by a highway authority;

and in subsection (4) above "necessary consent" means—

(i) in the case mentioned in paragraph (a) above, the consent of the relevant corporation; and

(ii) in the case mentioned in paragraph (b) above, the consent of the highway authority.

(6) The following are relevant corporations for the purposes of this section:—

(a) British Railways Board;

(b) London Regional Transport; and

(c) an urban development corporation established under the Local Government, Planning and Land Act 1980.

(7) The notice referred to in subsection (4) above shall—

(a) contain a draft of the resolution to which it relates; and

(b) state that representations relating to it may be made in writing to the borough council within such period, not less than 28 days after the publication of the notice, as may be specified in the notice.

(8) As soon as practicable after the expiry of the period specified under subsection (7) above, the borough council shall consider any representations relating to the proposed resolution which they have received before the expiry of that period.

(9) After the borough council have considered those representations, they may if they think fit, pass such a resolution relating to the street as is mentioned in subsection (1) above.

(10) The borough council shall publish notice of the passing of such a resolution in a local newspaper circulating in their area on two consecutive weeks.

(11) The first publication shall not be later than 28 days before the day specified in the resolution for the coming into force of the designation.

Application for street trading licences

25.—(1) An application for a street trading licence or renewal of such a licence shall be made in writing to the borough council, and in the case of an application for the renewal of a licence shall be made not later than two months or earlier than three months before the date on which that licence unless revoked or surrendered will cease to be valid:

Provided that nothing in this section shall prevent a borough council from renewing a licence, other than a temporary licence notwithstanding that application has been made for such renewal at a later date than aforesaid if they consider it reasonable in the circumstances so to do.

(2) In the application, the applicant shall state—

(a) in the case of an application by an individual, his full name and address and date of birth;

(b) in the case of an application for a licence to carry on ice cream trading—

(i) by a company incorporated under the Companies Acts, the name of the company and its registered office;

(ii) by a partnership, the names of its members and the address of its principal office;

(c) the licence street in which, the days on which and the times between which he desires to trade;

(d) the description of articles, things or services in which he desires to trade; and

(e) such other particulars, relevant to street trading, as the borough council may reasonably require;

and may in the case of an individual specify the name and address of a relative of his who is associated with, or dependent upon, the business of street trading in respect of which the application is made and to whom he desires the licence to be granted in any of the events specified in subsection (1)(a) of section 26 (Succession) of this Act.

(3) No later than the date on which he submits his application, the applicant shall hand to an authorised officer two identical full-face photographs of himself, taken within the preceding 12 months, signed by the applicant on the reverse except where the application is made by a company incorporated under the Companies Acts, or by a partnership, for a licence to carry on ice cream trading.

(4) A street trading licence—

(a) shall not be granted—

(i) to a person under the age of 17 years; or

(ii) except where the application is made by a company incorporated under the Companies Acts, or by a partnership, for a licence to carry on ice cream trading to a person, on a corresponding day, days or time, who holds a street trading licence in any other licence street granted under this Part of this Act but nothing in this paragraph shall prevent the renewal of such a licence; or

(iii) except where the application is made by a company incorporated under the Companies Acts, or by a partnership, for a licence to carry on ice cream trading to a body corporate or to an unincorporated association; or

(iv) in respect of an application for a licence which is not a temporary licence to trade in a street which is not a licence street; or

(v) where the street to which the application relates is a street in respect of which the borough council have by resolution passed under subsection (1)(b) of section 24 (Designation of licence streets) of this Act specified a class of articles or things, or services which they will not prescribe in any street trading licence and the grant of the licence would be contrary to any of the terms of that resolution;

(b) shall not be granted unless the borough council are satisfied that there is enough space in the street for the applicant to engage in the trading in which he desires to engage without causing undue interference or inconvenience to persons or vehicular traffic using the street.

(5) Subject to subsection (4) above, the borough council shall grant an application for a street trading licence unless they consider that the application ought to be refused on one or more of the grounds specified in subsection (6) below.

(6) Subject to subsection (8) below the council may refuse an application on any of the following grounds:—

(a) that there are enough traders trading in the street or in any street adjoining the street in respect of which the application is made in the goods in which the applicant desires to trade;

(b) that the applicant is on account of misconduct or for any other sufficient reason unsuitable to hold the licence;

(c) that the applicant is an individual who has without reasonable excuse failed personally to avail himself fully of a previous street trading licence;

(d) that the applicant has at any time been granted a street trading licence by the borough council which was revoked or could have been revoked on the grounds that he had refused or neglected to pay fees or other charges due to them in respect of the licence;

(e) that the applicant has failed to provide or to identify suitable or adequate premises for the storage of any receptacles or perishable goods in which he proposes to trade when street trading is not taking place;

(f) that—

(i) the application is for the grant (but not the renewal) of a street trading licence; and

(ii) the only available position is in that part of the street which is contiguous with the frontage of a shop; and

(iii) the articles, things or services mentioned in the application are sold or provided at the shop;

(g) that—

(i) the application is for the grant (but not the renewal) of a street trading licence; and

(ii) the only available position in the street is within the curtilage of a shop; and

(iii) the applicant is not the owner or occupier of the premises comprising the shop.

(7) If the borough council consider that grounds for refusal exist under subsection (6)(a) or (c) above they may grant the applicant a licence which permits him—

(a) to trade on fewer days or during a shorter period in each day than is specified in the application; or

(b) to trade only in one or more of the descriptions of goods specified in the application.

(8) Subject to subsection (4) above if—

(a) a person is at the appointed day licensed to trade in a street under the provisions of any local enactment; and

(b) the street becomes a licence street under this Part of this Act; and

(c) he was trading from a fixed position in the street immediately before it became a licence street; and

(d) within two months from the appointed day he applies for a street trading licence to trade in the street;

his application shall not be refused.

(9) Subject to subsections (4), (6) and (8) above a borough council when considering applications for licences to trade in licence streets under this Part of this Act shall give preference to applications from persons who immediately before the appointed day were under the provisions of any local enactment authorised to trade in a street in the borough which is not a licence street.

(10) A borough council when considering applications for licences to carry on ice cream trading in a licence street shall treat all applicants, whether companies, partnerships or individuals, on an equal footing and in particular—

(a) shall not treat individuals less favourably than companies or partnerships; and

(b) as between applicants who are companies or partnerships, shall not treat any particular company or partnership more favourably than others.

(11) A licence holder may at any time surrender his licence to the borough council and it shall then cease to be valid.

Succession

26.—(1)(a) When the holder of a licence who is an individual has specified the name and address of a relative to whom he desires the licence to be granted—
  (i) dies; or
  (ii) retires having reached the normal age for retirement; or
  (iii) notifies the borough council that owing to ill-health he is unable to continue to engage in the street trading permitted by the licence, and submits evidence to satisfy the borough council as to his ill-health;
the borough council shall not (except as provided in paragraph (b) of this subsection) grant a licence in respect of the position or place in a street at which the former licensee was entitled to engage in street trading under the authority of his licence until the expiration of 28 days from the date of the death of the licensee or his retirement or receiving the notification, as the case may be;
  (b) If during the said period of 28 days the person specified by the holder of the licence, when making application for the licence, as the relative to whom he desired the licence to be granted in any of the events mentioned in paragraph (a) above makes application for the grant of a licence in respect of the position or place available in the street the borough council shall, save as provided by paragraphs (b) to (e) of subsection (6) of section 25 (Application for street trading licences) of this Act grant a licence to that person.
(2) For the purposes of this section a person shall be treated as being related to another if the latter is the wife, husband, father, mother, grandfather, grandmother, stepfather, stepmother, son, daughter, grandson, granddaughter, stepson, stepdaughter, brother, sister, half-brother or half-sister of the former and shall be deemed to be so related notwithstanding that he is so related only through an illegitimacy or in consequence of an adoption.

Conditions of street trading licences

27.—(1) A licence granted under section 25 (Application for street trading licences) of this Act, shall—
  (a) unless it is revoked or surrendered, be valid for a period of three years from the date on which it is granted, or for such shorter period as the borough council may determine;
  (b) specify the conditions; and
  (c) in the case of an individual incorporate one of the photographs of the licence holder submitted under subsection (3) of the said section 25;
and on any occasion of the renewal of a licence, or at 1st January in any year during the currency thereof, (whether on application by the licence holder or otherwise) or at any time on application by the licence holder, the borough council may vary the conditions.
(2) Where a licence is granted to a company incorporated under the Companies Acts or to a partnership to carry on ice cream trading, any individual carrying on ice cream trading in accordance with that licence shall at all times while he is so trading carry with him a recent photograph of him authenticated by the company or on behalf of the partnership, as the case may be, which holds the licence.
(3) The borough council may make regulations prescribing standard conditions which they may attach to the licence on the occasion of its grant or renewal.
(4) Before making regulations under subsection (3) above, the borough council shall—
  (a) publish notice of their intention to do so in a local newspaper circulating in their area, and such notice shall—
      (i) contain a draft of the resolution to which it relates; and
      (ii) state that representations relating to it may be made in writing to the borough council within such period, not less than 28 days after the publication of the notice, as may be specified in the notice; and
  (b) consult the licence holders or a body or bodies representative of them.
(5) As soon as practicable after the expiry of the period specified under subsection (4) above, the borough council shall consider any representations relating to the proposed regulations which they have received before the expiry of that period.
(6) After the borough council have considered those representations they may if they think fit make regulations as mentioned in subsection (3) above and shall notify the licence holders or a body or bodies representative of them of the making of such regulations.

(7) Without prejudice to the generality of subsection (3) above the standard conditions shall include such conditions as may be reasonable—

   (a) identifying the street or streets in which and the position or place in any such street at which the licence holder may sell or expose or offer for sale articles or things, or offer or provide services under the authority of the licence;

   (b) identifying the class or classes of articles, things or services which the licence holder may so sell or expose or offer for sale or provide;

   (c) identifying the day or days on which and the time during which the licence holder may sell or expose or offer for sale articles, things or services as aforesaid;

   (d) identifying the nature and type of any receptacle which may be used by the licence holder or in connection with any sale or exposure or offer for sale or provision of services and the number of any such receptacles which may be so used;

   (e) requiring that any receptacle so used shall carry the name of the licence holder and the number of his licence;

   (f) regulating the storage of receptacles or perishable goods;

   (g) regulating the deposit and removal of refuse and the containers to be used for the deposit of such refuse and their location pending its removal;

   (h) requiring that the licence holder shall commence trading or exercising his rights under the licence by a certain time on any day or forfeit his right to trade or exercise his rights under the licence on that day from the fixed position to which his licence refers.

(8) Without prejudice to the standard conditions, the borough council may in addition attach to a licence such further conditions as appear to them to be reasonable in any individual case.

(9) When granting a licence a borough council shall give to the licence holder a copy of the licence which, in the case of an individual, shall bear his photograph.

Revocation or variation of licences under Part III

28.—(1) Subject to the provisions of this Part of this Act a borough council may at any time revoke a street trading licence if they are satisfied that—

   (a) owing to circumstances which have arisen since the grant or renewal of the licence, there is not enough space in the street in which the licence holder trades for him to engage in the trading permitted by the licence without causing undue interference or inconvenience to persons or vehicular traffic using the street; or

   (b) the licence holder is trading in a class of articles, things or services which the borough council have resolved under subsection (1)(b) of section 24 (Designation of licence streets) of this Act not to prescribe in licences granted for the licence street in which the licence holder trades; or

   (c) the licence holder is an individual who has without reasonable excuse personally failed fully to avail himself of his licence; or

   (d) the licence holder is on account of misconduct or for any other sufficient reason unsuitable to hold the licence; or

   (e) that since the grant or renewal of the licence, the licence holder has for a period of four weeks or more failed to pay fees or charges due to the borough council in connection with the street trading licence or has failed to pay any charges due from him for accommodation provided in pursuance of subsection (2) of section 33 (Receptacles and containers) of this Act; or

   (f) that since the grant or renewal of the licence, the licence holder has failed to make provision for the suitable and adequate storage of the receptacles used by him for trading or for any perishable goods in which he trades when trading is not taking place; or

   (g) that since the grant or renewal of the licence, the licence holder has persistently failed to remove to a place of storage the receptacles used by him for trading; or

   (h) that the licence holder has persistently failed to comply with any condition of his licence.

(2) If a borough council consider that a licence could be revoked on any of the grounds mentioned in paragraphs (a) to (c) of subsection (1) above they may instead of revoking it, vary its conditions by attaching further conditions—

   (a) reducing the number of days in any week or the period in any one day during which the licence holder is permitted to trade; or

   (b) specifying a different licence street or position or place in any such street at which the licence holder may sell or expose or offer for sale articles or things or offer or provide services; or

   (c) restricting the description of articles, things or services in which the licence holder is permitted to trade.

Further provisions relating to grant, renewal or revocation of street trading licences

29.—(1) A borough council shall not—
  (a) refuse to grant or renew a licence on any of the grounds mentioned in subsection (6) of section 25 (Application for street trading licences) of this Act; or
  (b) revoke or vary a licence under section 28 (Revocation or variation of licences under Part III) of this Act; or
  (c) vary a licence under subsection (1) of section 27 (Conditions of street trading licences) of this Act;
unless they shall have given to the applicant or licence holder not less than 21 days' previous notice in writing that objection has been or will be taken to such grant or renewal or that such revocation or variation is proposed, specifying the ground or grounds on which their decision would be based and giving him an opportunity to appear before the committee, sub-committee or officer determining the matter.

(2) A borough council shall not proceed to determine any of the matters referred to in subsection (1) above until after the expiry of the period specified in the notice given under that subsection; and in determining any of the matters referred to, they shall consider any representations made by an applicant or licence holder in respect of that matter.

(3) A borough council shall not refuse to grant or renew and shall not revoke a licence on the ground only that the applicant or licensee, being an individual, does not reside in the borough.

(4) If the borough council refuse to grant or renew a licence or decide to revoke or vary a licence—
  (a) they shall notify the applicant or licence holder in writing of their decision and of the ground or grounds for such refusal, revocation or variation; and
  (b) they shall notify the applicant or licence holder of his rights of appeal (if any) specified in the next following section.

Part III appeals

30.—(1) Any person aggrieved—
  (aa) by the refusal of a borough council to renew a licence because they are not satisfied as mentioned in subsection (4)(b) of section 25 (Application for street trading licences) of this Act;
  (a) by the refusal of a borough council to grant or renew a licence on any of the grounds mentioned in subsection (6)(a) to (e) of section 25 (Application for street trading licences); or
  (b) by a decision of a borough council under subsection (7) of the said section 25 to grant him a licence either on terms mentioned in that subsection different from those on the licence which he previously held or different from those for which he applied; or
  (c) by any further condition attached by a borough council under subsection (8) of section 27 (Conditions of street trading licences) of this Act in addition to the standard conditions; or
  (d) by a decision of the borough council either—
        (i) to vary the conditions of a licence under subsection (2) of section 28 (Revocation or variation of licences under Part III) of this Act; or
        (ii) to revoke a licence under subsection (1) of the said section 28;

*   *   *   *   *; or

  (e) by a resolution of a borough council under section 37 (Ice cream trading) of this Act;
may appeal to a magistrates' court acting for the area in which the licence street is situated.
(2) An appeal under subsection (1) above may be brought—
  (a) in the case of an appeal under paragraph (aa), (a), (b), (c) or (d) of that subsection, at any time before the expiration of the period of 21 days beginning with the date upon which notification in writing is given of the refusal or decision;
  (b) in the case of an appeal under paragraph (e) of that subsection, at any time before the expiration of the period of 21 days beginning with the date of the second publication of the notice required by subsection (10) of section 24 (Designation of licence streets) as applied by the said section 37.
(3) A person desiring to appeal against such refusal or decision as is mentioned in subsection (1) above shall give a written notice to the magistrates' court and to the borough council specifying the refusal or decision against which he wishes to appeal and the grounds upon which such appeal is made.

(4) An appeal by either party against the decision of the magistrates' court under this section may be brought to the Crown Court.

(5) On an appeal to the magistrates' court or to the Crown Court under this section, the court may make such order as it thinks fit.

(6) Subject to subsections (7) to (9) below, it shall be the duty of the borough council to give effect to the order of the magistrates' court or the Crown Court.

(7) A borough council need not give effect to the order of the magistrates' court until the time for bringing an appeal under subsection (4) above has expired and, if such an appeal is duly brought, until the determination or abandonment of the appeal.

(8) Where a licence holder applies for renewal of his licence, his existing licence shall remain valid—

    (a) until the grant by the borough council of a new licence with the same conditions; or

    (b) if the borough council refuse renewal of the licence or decide to grant a licence with conditions different from those of the existing licence and he has a right of appeal under this section, until the time for bringing an appeal has expired or where an appeal is duly brought, until the determination or abandonment of the appeal; or

    (c) if he has no right of appeal under this section until the borough council either grant him a new licence with conditions different from those of the existing licence or notify him of their decision to refuse his application.

(9) Where—

    (a) a borough council decide—

        (i) to vary the conditions of a licence under subsection (2) of the said section 28; or

        (ii) to revoke a licence under subsection (1) of the said section 28; and

    (b) a right of appeal is available to the licence holder under this section;

the variation or revocation shall not take effect until the time for bringing an appeal has expired or where an appeal is duly brought, until the determination or abandonment of the appeal.

(10) For the avoidance of doubt, it is hereby declared that an application under section 31 of the Supreme Court Act 1981 (application for judicial review) or under the Rules of the Supreme Court 1965 in respect of any matter which is or could be the subject of an appeal to the magistrates' court or to the Crown Court under this section shall not be treated as an appeal for the purposes of subsection (8) or (9) above.

(11) Any person aggrieved—

    (a) by a resolution rescinding or varying a designating resolution;

    (b) by a resolution under subsection (1)(b) of section 24 (Designation of licence streets) of this Act;

    (c) by a standard condition prescribed by regulations under subsection (3) of section 27 (Conditions of street trading licences) of this Act; or

    (d) by the amount of a fee or charge under section 32 (Fees and charges) of this Act;

may appeal to the Secretary of State whose decision shall be final.

(12) An appeal under subsection (11) above may be brought—

    (a) in the case of an appeal under paragraph (a) or (b) of that subsection, at any time before the expiration of the period of three months beginning with the date on which notice of the passing of the resolution is published for the second time in accordance with subsection (10) of section 24 (Designation of licence streets) of this Act;

    (b) in the case of an appeal under paragraph (c) of that subsection, at any time before the expiration of the period of three months beginning with the date upon which the licence holders or a body or bodies representative of them were notified of the making of the regulations;

    (c) in the case of an appeal under paragraph (a) of that subsection—

        (i) if it relates to the amount of a fee payable under subsection (1) of section 32 (Fees and charges) of this Act, at any time before the expiration of the period of three months beginning with the date on which the fee payable is notified to the licence holders or a body or bodies representative of them;

        (ii) if it relates to the amount of a charge under subsection (2) of section 32 (Fees and charges) of this Act, at any time before the expiration of the period of three months beginning with the date on which notice of the determination of the charge has been given to the licence holders or a body or bodies representative of them.

Temporary licences

31.—(1) A borough council may if they think fit on the receipt from, any person of an application for that purpose and accompanied by the appropriate fee grant to that person a temporary licence.

(2) A temporary licence shall be valid only for the day or period specified in the licence and—

(a) shall be in the like form as a street trading licence with such modifications therein as the circumstances require; and

(b) shall prescribe such conditions as the borough council deem appropriate.

(3) Where the holder of a street trading licence is not for the time being exercising his rights under the licence, a temporary licence authorising street trading in the position or place prescribed by the street trading licence may be granted to any other person but shall be subject to the condition that it shall cease to be valid if during the currency thereof the holder of the licence desires to resume the exercise of his rights and gives the appropriate notice, and for the purposes of this subsection "the appropriate notice" means—

(a) in the case of a holder of a licence who has not exercised his rights under the licence for a period of at least 14 days, 7 days' notice;

(b) in any other case, 24 hours' notice.

(4) In this section "appropriate fee" means such fee as the borough council may have determined under section 32 (Fees and charges) of this Act.

Fees and charges

32.—(1) A borough council may charge such fees for the grant or renewal of a street trading licence under this Part of this Act, the grant of a temporary licence or for the variation at the request of the licence holder of the conditions of a street trading licence as they may determine and as may be sufficient in the aggregate to cover in whole or in part the reasonable administrative or other costs in connection with their functions under this Part of this Act, not otherwise recovered.

(2) A borough council may recover from licence holders such charges as may be sufficient in the aggregate taking one year with another to cover the reasonable costs, not otherwise recovered, of—

(a) the collection, removal and disposal of refuse or other services rendered by them to such holders; and

(b) the cleansing of streets in which street trading takes place in so far as that cleansing is attributable to such trading; and

(c) any reasonable administrative or other costs incurred in connection with the administration of this Part of this Act; and

(d) the cost of enforcing the provisions of this Part of this Act.

(3) A borough council may determine—

(a) that charges under subsection (2) above shall be included in a fee payable under subsection (1) above; or

(b) that they shall be separately recoverable.

(4) A borough council may—

(a) require that every application for a licence under this Part of this Act be accompanied by the whole or part of the fee determined under subsection (1) above; and

(b) determine that the fee may be paid by instalments.

(5) Where a borough council refuse to * * renew a licence they shall repay to the person who made the application therefor the amount of any such fee paid by him * *.

(6) A borough council may determine the fees to be charged on the grant of a temporary licence under section 31 (Temporary licences? of this Act, and in doing so they shall have regard to the matters specified in subsection (2) above and such fees shall be included in the computation for the purposes of determining the fees and charges under subsections (1) and (2) above.

(7) Before determining charges to be made under subsection (2) above * * (whether originally or by way of variation of charges previously determined) a borough council—

(a) shall give notice of the proposed charges to licence holders or to a body or bodies representative of them; and

(b) shall publish notice of the proposed charges in a newspaper circulating in the area in which the licence street or streets in respect of which the charges will be applied is situated.

(7A) A notice under subsection (7)(a) above shall be accompanied by a statement showing how the proposed charges have been computed; and any body representative of licence holders may request the borough council to supply such further information or explanation with regard to the proposed charges as the body may reasonably require in order to ascertain whether the proposed charges are reasonable and have been computed in accordance with the provisions of this section.

(8) A notice under subsection (7)(a) above shall specify a reasonable period being not less than 28 days from the date of publication of the newspaper referred to in subsection (7)(b) above within which written representations concerning the proposed charges may be made to the borough council.

(9) It shall be the duty of a borough council to—

(a) consider any such representations which are made to them within the period specified in the notice; and

(b) comply with any request made under subsection (7A) above;

and where any such request is made the period so specified, if still current, shall be treated as extended by the number of days in the period beginning with the day on which the request is made and ending with that on which it is complied with.

*   *   *   *   *

(10) When a borough council have determined fees under subsection (1) above or charges under subsection (2) above (whether originally or by way of variation of fees or charges previously determined) they shall give notice of the fees or charges so determined and of the date on which those fees or charges are to be brought into effect, in the manner prescribed in subsection (7) above.

(11) Where a licence is revoked under subsection (1)(a) or (b) of section 28 (Revocation or variation of licences under Part III) of this Act, the borough council shall refund the appropriate part of any fee paid for the grant or renewal of the licence.

(12) Where a licence is revoked otherwise than under subsection (1)(a) or (b) of section 28 (Revocation or variation of licences under Part III) or is surrendered, the borough council may remit or refund, as they consider appropriate, the whole or a part—

(a) of any fee paid for the grant or renewal of the licence; or

(b) of any charges recoverable under subsection (2) above.

Receptacles and containers

33.—(1) A borough council may sell or let on hire or otherwise provide to any person holding a street trading licence or a temporary licence under this Part of this Act receptacles for use by him in street trading.

(2) A borough council may provide and maintain accommodation for the storage of receptacles and containers for the deposit of refuse arising in the course of street trading and for that purpose may—

(a) adapt any premises or erect any buildings on any land belonging to them but not already appropriated for such purpose; and

(b) make such charges as they think fit for the use of such accommodation.

Offences

34. Any person who—

(1) without reasonable excuse contravenes any of the conditions of a street trading licence or a temporary licence; or

(2) in connection with an application for a street trading licence or a temporary licence makes a statement which he knows to be false in a material particular; or

(3) resists or intentionally obstructs any authorised officer of a borough council in the execution of his duties under this Part of this Act; or

(4) fails on demand without reasonable excuse in the case of an individual licence holder to produce his licence duly signed by him and bearing his photograph, and, in the case of an individual carrying on ice cream trading under a licence granted to a company incorporated under the Companies Acts or to a partnership, to produce the photograph required by subsection (2) of section 27 (Conditions of street trading licences) of this Act to an authorised officer of the borough council or to a constable;

shall be guilty of an offence and shall be liable on summary conviction to a fine not exceeding level 3 on the standard scale.

Power to remove receptacles

35.—(1) Where any receptacle used by a licence holder is not removed to a place of storage on the cessation of trading on any day it shall be lawful for the borough council to cause it to be removed to a place of storage and to recover from the licence holder the costs incurred by them in removing and storing the receptacle.

(2) Such charges as the borough council may fix as the cost of removing and storing a receptacle in pursuance of subsection (1) above, shall be payable by the licence holder before the return of the receptacle to him.

(3) The provisions of subsection (1) above are without prejudice to the power of the borough council to prosecute the licence holder for any breach of the conditions of his licence arising from the failure to remove the receptacle.

Employment of assistants

36. Subject to the provisions of this section a person holding a street trading licence may employ any other person to assist him in the conduct of street trading authorised by the licence but if any person employed by a licence holder during the temporary absence of the licence holder fails to comply with the conditions of the street trading licence held by his employer such failure shall be deemed to be a failure by the licence holder.

Ice cream trading

37.—(1) Nothing in this Part of this Act shall apply to itinerant ice cream trading in any street unless—
  (a) that street is a licence street; or
  (b) the street has been designated as a prohibited street under the following provisions of this section.
  (2) If at any time it is necessary to prohibit itinerant ice cream trading in any street in the area of a borough council which is not a licence street in the interests of preventing obstruction to traffic, or undue interference or inconvenience to persons using that street, the borough council may by resolution designate the street as a prohibited street and in the case of any London borough except the City of Westminster and the Royal Borough of Kensington and Chelsea may so designate it for such days or for such parts of days as are specified in the resolution, and may from time to time by subsequent resolution rescind or vary any such resolution.
  (3) Before passing a resolution under this section, a borough council shall consult the Commissioner of Police of the Metropolis and such bodies as appear to them to be representative of persons carrying on ice cream trading in the area of the borough council.
  (4) Subsections (3) to (11) of section 24 (Designation of licence streets) of this Act shall apply to a resolution under this section as they apply to a resolution under that section.

Unlicensed street trading

38.—(1) A person who—
  (a) is not the holder of a street trading licence or a temporary licence and who engages in street trading in a borough; or
  (b) is the holder of a temporary licence and who engages in street trading in a borough on a day or in a place not specified in that temporary licence;
shall be guilty of an offence and shall be liable on summary conviction to a fine not exceeding level 3 on the standard scale.

*   *   *   *   *

(2) In any proceedings for an offence under this section or for an offence of aiding, abetting, counselling or procuring the commission of an offence under this section where it is shown that—
  (a) any article or thing was displayed (whether or not in or on any receptacle) in any street; or
  (b) any receptacle or equipment used in the provision of any service was available in any street in such circumstances that a service was being offered;
the article or thing shall be presumed to have been exposed or offered for sale and the receptacle or equipment shall be presumed to have been available for the provision of a service at such time and in such position as it was displayed or available by the person having care or control or appearing to have care and control thereof unless in either case, it is shown to the satisfaction of the court that the article or thing or receptacle or equipment was brought into that street for some purpose other than for the purpose of selling it or exposing or offering it for sale or using it in the course of the provision of the service in a street.
  (3) Where an offence under this section committed by a body corporate is proved to have been committed with the consent or connivance of, or to be attributable to any neglect on the part of,

any director, manager, secretary or other similar officer of the body corporate, or any person who was purporting to act in any such capacity, he, as well as the body corporate, shall be guilty of the offence and liable to the same maximum penalty as the body corporate.

(4) If an authorised officer or a constable has reasonable grounds for suspecting that a person has committed an offence under this section he may seize any article or thing being offered or exposed for sale or receptacle being used by that person which may be required to be used in evidence in any proceedings in respect of that offence, or may be the subject of forfeiture under subsection (5) below, provided that no article or thing which is of a perishable nature shall be seized under the provisions of this subsection.

(4A)(a) The following provisions of this subsection shall have effect where any article or thing (including any receptacle) is seized under subsection (4) above and references in those provisions to proceedings are to proceedings in respect of the alleged offence in relation to which the article or thing is seized.

(b) Subject to paragraph (e) below, at the conclusion of the proceedings the article or thing shall be returned to the person from whom it was seized unless the court orders it to be forfeited under subsection (5) below.

(c) Subject to paragraph (a) below, where a receptacle seized under subsection (4) above is a motor vehicle used for ice cream trading, the borough council or the Commissioner of Police of the Metropolis (as the case may be) shall, within three days of the receipt of an application in writing by the owner or registered keeper of the vehicle, permit him to remove it.

(d) Paragraph (c) above shall not apply where—
  (i) the owner or registered keeper of the vehicle has been convicted of an offence under this Part of this Act; or
  (ii) the owner or registered keeper of the vehicle is being prosecuted for a previous alleged offence under this Part of this Act; or
  (iii) the vehicle has been used in the commission of such an offence or previous alleged offence;
if the offence or previous alleged offence was committed or is alleged to have been committed no more than three years before the seizure and (in the case of an alleged offence) the proceedings are continuing.

(e) If no proceedings are instituted before the expiration of a period of 28 days beginning with the date of seizure, or any proceedings instituted within that period are discontinued, at the expiration of that period or, as the case may be, on the discontinuance of the proceedings, the article or thing shall be returned to the person from whom it was seized unless it has not proved possible, after diligent enquiry, to identify that person and ascertain his address.

(f) Where the article or thing is not returned because it has not proved possible to identify the person from whom it was seized and ascertain his address the borough council (whether the article or thing was seized by a constable or by an authorised officer) may apply to a magistrates' court for an order as to the manner in which it should be dealt with.

(5) Subject to subsection (6) below the court by or before which a person is convicted of an offence under this section or for an offence of aiding, abetting, counselling or procuring the commission of an offence under this section may order anything produced to the court, and shown to the satisfaction of the court to relate to the offence, to be forfeited and dealt with in such manner as the court may order.

(6) The court shall not order anything to be forfeited under subsection (5) above where a person claiming to be the owner of or otherwise interested in it applies to be heard by the court, unless an opportunity has been given to him to show cause why the order should not be made and in considering whether to make such an order a court shall have regard—
  (i) to the value of the property; and
  (ii) to the likely financial and other effects on the offender of the making of the order (taken together with any other order that the court contemplates making).

(7) An authorised officer shall produce his authority if required to do so by the person having care or control of * * anything seized in pursuance of the powers in subsection (4) above.

(8)(a) This subsection shall have effect where—
  (i) an article, thing or receptacle is seized under subsection (4) above; and
  (ii) (A) not less than six months have passed since the date of the seizure and no information has been laid against any person for an offence under this section in respect of the acts or circumstances which occasioned the seizure; or
  (B) proceedings for such an offence have been brought and either the person charged has been acquitted (whether or not on appeal) and the time for appealing against or challenging the acquittal (where applicable) has expired without an appeal or challenge being brought, or the proceedings (including any appeal) have been withdrawn by, or have failed for want of prosecution by, the person by whom the original proceedings were brought.

(b) When this subsection has effect a person who has or at the time of seizure had a legal interest in the article, thing or receptacle seized may recover compensation from the borough council or (where it is seized by a constable) the Commissioner of Police of the Metropolis by civil action in the County Court in respect of any loss suffered by him as a result of the seizure.

(c) The court may not make an order for compensation under paragraph (b) above unless it is satisfied that seizure was not lawful under subsection (4) above.

Savings

39.—(1) Nothing in this Part of this Act shall affect—
(a) section 13 of the Markets and Fairs Clauses Act 1847 (prohibition of sales elsewhere than in a market or in shops etc.) as applied by any other Acts;
(b) section 56 of the Food Act 1984 (prohibition of certain sales during market hours);
(c) the sale or exposure or offer for sale by London Regional Transport or (as the case may be) a designated company (within the meaning of the Transport (London) Act 1969) of refreshments at any shelter or other accommodation provided by either of them under section 65 (Refreshment shelters etc.) of the London Passenger Transport Act 1938.

(2) Nothing in this Part of this Act shall afford a defence to a charge in respect of any offence at common law or under an enactment other than this Part of this Act.

Local enactments relating to street trading repealed

40.—(1) Subject to subsection (2) below, the enactments specified in column (2) of Schedule 2 to this Act, so far as they relate to any part of Greater London, shall cease to have effect in a borough as from the appointed day for that borough to the extent specified in column (3) of that Schedule.

(2) Notwithstanding the repeal of the enactments specified in column (2) of Schedule 2 to this Act, any licence granted by a borough council under any of those enactments which authorises street trading in the borough and which was in force immediately before the appointed day shall continue in force until three months after the appointed day or until the determination of any application made by the holder of the licence under section 25 (Application for street trading licences) of this Act, whichever is the later.

Saving for sales in legal markets or fairs

41. In the case of any market or fair held in pursuance of any statute, royal licence, royal charter or letters patent, or as of right from time immemorial, nothing in this Part of this Act shall affect the sale or exposure or offer for sale of goods in any such market or fair by any person who has paid a toll to, or is acting under the written authority of, a person holding or entitled to hold such market or fair or entitled to receive tolls in respect of sales made or stalls or stands occupied in such market or fair.

INDEX

References are to sections and Schedule

LONDON DOCKLANDS DEVELOPMENT CORPORATION ACT 1994

(1994 c. xiii)

ARRANGEMENT OF SECTIONS

PART I

PRELIMINARY

PART II

MANAGEMENT AND REGULATION OF CERTAIN LANDS AND WATERS

PART III

PROTECTIVE PROVISIONS

PART IV

MISCELLANEOUS AND GENERAL

An Act to confer powers on the London Docklands Development Corporation for the management and regulation of certain lands and waters within its area, together with other lands and waters; and for other purposes.   [21st July 1994]

PARLIAMENTARY DEBATES
   The Bill's progress through Parliament was as follows:
   House of Lords: First Reading, January 19, 1993; Second Reading, March 2, 1993; Bill Committed, March 2, 1993; Unopposed Bill Committee, October 25, 1993; Suspended, October 28, 1993; Third Reading, December 6, 1993; Commons Amendments, July 15, 1994.
   House of Commons: First Reading, December 6, 1993; Second Reading, March 14, 1994; Bill Committed, March 14, 1994; Unopposed Bill Committee, May 25, 1994; Bill as amended Considered, July 14, 1994; Third Reading, July 14, 1994.

INTRODUCTION
   The London Docklands Development Corporation is charged with effecting the regeneration of the land within its jurisdiction. An area of lands and waters, formerly consisting of operational docks of the Port of London Authority, is being used for aquatic sports and leisure activities and by recreational and other craft. The Corporation are seeking to manage and regulate such lands and waters; this Act empowers the Corporation to manage, regulate and improve the designated areas.

WHEREAS—
   (1) By virtue of the Local Government, Planning and Land Act 1980, the London Docklands Development Corporation (hereinafter referred to as "the Corporation") was established by the London Docklands Development Corporation (Area and Constitution) Order 1981 as the urban development corporation for an area designated by that order lying within Greater London and comprising parts of the London boroughs of Newham, Southwark and Tower Hamlets for the purpose of securing the regeneration of its area:
   (2) It is the view of the Corporation that the powers conferred by this Act will advance the securing of such regeneration:
   (3) There are within the area of the Corporation various lands and waters formerly consisting of operational docks of the Port of London Authority (of which certain waters are now no longer accessible for navigation) which are used for aquatic sports and leisure activities, and by recreational and other craft:
   (4) It is expedient that the Corporation should be empowered to manage and regulate such lands and waters, together with other areas:
   (5) It is expedient that the other provisions contained in this Act be enacted:
   (6) A map marked "Deposited Map" showing the limits of jurisdiction of the Corporation as proposed to be designated by this Act has been deposited in the office of the Clerk of the Parliaments and in the Private Bill Office of the House of Commons and with the proper officers of the councils of the London boroughs of Lewisham, Newham, Southwark and Tower Hamlets:
   (7) The objects of this Act cannot be effected without the authority of Parliament:
   May it therefore please Your Majesty that it may be enacted, and be it enacted, by the Queen's most Excellent Majesty, by and with the advice and consent of the Lords Spiritual and Temporal, and Commons, in this present Parliament assembled, and by the authority of the same, as follows:—

PART I

PRELIMINARY

Short title

1. This Act may be cited as the London Docklands Development Corporation Act 1994.

Interpretation

2. In this Act, unless the context or subject otherwise requires—

"the Act of 1980" means the Local Government, Planning and Land Act 1980;

"the city corporation" means the mayor and commonalty and citizens of the city of London acting by the common council;

"the Corporation" means the London Docklands Development Corporation;

"daily fine" means a fine for each day or part of a day on which an offence is continued after conviction thereof;

"the deposited map" means the map referred to in section 3 (Extent of Act) of this Act;

"the designated areas" means the harbours or former harbours, docks or former docks, waterways and other lands described in Schedule 1 to this Act, together with the jetties, all of which are designated by and situated within the limits of jurisdiction, but does not include the waters lying beneath Rotherhithe Street bridge in the London borough of Southwark;

"functions" includes powers and duties;

"the jetties" means the jetties and other works in the river Thames vested in or under the control of the Corporation situated within the limits of jurisdiction and described in Schedule 2 to this Act;

"the limits of jurisdiction" means the limits delineated by a red line on the deposited map;

"the manager" means the officer appointed by the Corporation to manage the designated areas or any part thereof and includes his authorised deputies and assistants and any person authorised by the Corporation to act in that capacity;

"the port authority" means the Port of London Authority;

"the river Thames" means so much of the river Thames, the Thames estuary, rivers, streams, creeks, watercourses and the sea as is within the limits of the Port of London as defined in the Port of London Act 1968, and does not include the waters enclosed in the docks and in the other areas described in Schedule 1 to this Act;

"vehicle" means a vehicle of any description and includes a trailer, caravan or machine of any kind drawn or propelled along or over land whether by animal or mechanical power, and includes a hovercraft within the meaning of the Hovercraft Act 1968 or any other amphibious vehicle;

"vessel" means a ship, boat or raft of any description and includes any other thing constructed or adapted for floating on or being submersed in water (whether permanently or temporarily); and includes a hovercraft within the meaning of the Hovercraft Act 1968 or any other amphibious vehicle or a seaplane; and

"the waterside" means the roads, bridges, docks, quays, stages, wharves, steps and river walls together with the jetties and all other works and lands (not being lands covered by water) within the designated areas.

Extent of Act

3.—(1) The limits within which the Corporation shall have and may exercise the functions conferred on it by this Act, and within which the powers of the manager may be exercised, shall comprise the designated areas.

(2) If there be any discrepancy between the deposited map and the descriptions in Schedules 1 and 2 to this Act, the deposited map shall prevail but, for the avoidance of doubt, the designated areas do not extend to any part of the bed of the river Thames below the level of mean high water from time to time, or the waters or airspace above any such part, except for the area occupied from time to time by the structures of the Jetties.

(3) Copies of the deposited map certified by the chief executive of the Corporation to be true shall be receivable in all civil or criminal proceedings and elsewhere as evidence of the contents of the deposited map.

PART II

MANAGEMENT AND REGULATION OF CERTAIN LANDS AND WATERS

General powers as to designated areas

4.—(1) Subject to the provisions of this Act, the Corporation may preserve, maintain, regulate, manage and improve the designated areas and provide services, and facilities afforded therein, or in connection therewith, as it considers necessary or desirable and take such action as it considers incidental to the preservation, maintenance, regulation, management and improvement of the designated areas and the provision of such services and facilities.

(2) Without prejudice to the generality of the foregoing, the Corporation shall have power to do all such things as in its opinion are necessary or desirable for the proper discharge of the functions conferred or imposed on it by or under this Act and in particular to carry out dredging within so much of the designated areas as is covered by water.

(3) Nothing in this section shall authorise the Corporation to do anything on any land without the agreement of the occupier of the land.

General duty as to designated areas

5.—(1) It shall be the duty of the Corporation, in formulating or considering any proposals relating to its functions under this Act, to have regard to the desirability of securing the use of the designated areas for a diversity of purposes which may include sporting, recreational, cultural, commercial, energy-related and navigational purposes.

(2) Subject to the need to ensure the proper management of the designated areas, the Corporation shall not unreasonably promote the use of the designated areas for any of the purposes mentioned in subsection (1) above to the serious disadvantage of the use thereof for any of the other purposes so mentioned.

(3) Subject to the need to ensure the proper management of the designated areas, the Secretary of State shall have regard to the duty of the Corporation set out in subsection (1) above before confirming any byelaw submitted to him in accordance with section 10 (Byelaws: procedural provisions) of this Act.

(4) No legal proceedings shall be brought, with regard to any byelaw made under this Act, in respect of any failure or alleged failure by the Corporation or the Secretary of State to comply with the duty imposed by subsection (2) or, as the case may be, subsection (3) above after the expiration of a period of 72 days beginning with the date upon which the byelaw is confirmed.

Duty to regulate and manage

6. It shall be the duty of the Corporation, so far as is reasonably practicable, to regulate and manage the designated areas in accordance with the provisions of this Act and any byelaw made under section 9 (Byelaws) of this Act.

Duty as to waterside

7. Subject to the provisions of this Act, it shall be the duty of the Corporation, in formulating or considering any proposals relating to its functions under this Act, to have regard to the desirability of securing and maintaining public access to the waterside.

Charges

8.—(1) The Corporation may make, demand and recover such reasonable charges for services and facilities provided by it at the designated areas as it may from time to time determine.

(2) The services and facilities referred to in subsection (1) above shall include the use by any vessel of any waters comprised in the designated areas.

(3) Nothing in subsection (1) above shall authorise the Corporation—

(a) to make any charge for the use of moorings situated within any part of the designated areas which is owned by or leased to any person other than the Corporation; or

(b) to make any charge for the use in any manner of any part of the waterside by any person by whom that part is owned or leased, other than a reasonable charge in respect of any consent to such use required by this Act or byelaws made under this Act; or

(c) to make any charge for the use of the waters comprised in the designated areas by any vessel used by members of a police force or officers of the fire authority whilst in the exercise of their duties as such.

Byelaws

9.—(1) The Corporation may make byelaws for the good rule and government of the designated areas and, without prejudice to the generality of the foregoing, for all or any of the purposes set out in Schedule 3 to this Act.

(2) Byelaws made under this section may be expressed to be applicable within all or any part of the designated areas.

(3) Before making byelaws under this section in respect of any part of the designated areas the Corporation shall consult—

(a) the London borough council for that part;

(b) the port authority;

(c) the city corporation as port health authority and as a market authority for Billingsgate Market; and

(d) the London Fire and Civil Defence Authority.

(4) Byelaws shall not be made under this section which relate to—

(a) land forming part of a highway maintainable at the public expense, without the consent of the highway authority; or

(b) land which is a walkway within the meaning of Part III of the Greater London Council (General Powers) Act 1969, without the consent of the borough council in whose area the walkway is situated.

Byelaws: procedural provisions

10.—(1) The provisions of sections 236 (3) to (8) and (11) and 238 of the Local Government Act 1972 shall apply to any byelaw made by the Corporation under this Act and the said section 238 shall have effect as if the expression "proper officer" referred to the chief executive of the Corporation.

(2) In its application to this section, subsection (7) of section 236 of the said Act of 1972 shall have effect as if, after the words "the confirming authority may confirm", there were inserted the words "with or without modifications" and as if, at the end of that subsection, there were added the following proviso:—

"Provided that where the Secretary of State proposes to make a modification to a byelaw which appears to him to be substantial he shall inform the Corporation and require it to take any steps which he considers to be necessary for informing persons likely to be concerned with the modification; and he shall not confirm the byelaw until such period has elapsed as he thinks reasonable for the consideration of, and comment upon, the proposed modification by the Corporation and by any other persons who have, or are likely to have, been informed of it.".

Penalties for offences under byelaws

11. Byelaws made under section 9 (Byelaws) of this Act may provide that a person contravening any such byelaw shall be liable on summary conviction to such fine as may be specified as respects that byelaw, being a fine not exceeding—

(a) level 3 on the standard scale in the case of an offence against a byelaw which is stated in the byelaws to be a byelaw to protect the safety of members of the public; and

(b) level 2 on the standard scale in the case of any offence against any other byelaw;

and in addition, in the case of a continuing offence, a daily fine not exceeding—

(i) in the case of byelaws such as are referred to in paragraph (a) above, one-tenth of level 3; or

(ii) in the case of byelaws such as are referred to in paragraph (b) above, one-tenth of level 2.

Control of craft in designated areas, etc.

12. The provisions of Schedule 4 to this Act for the control of craft in the designated areas, and related matters, shall have effect.

Regulation of placing things on waterside

13.—(1) Any person who, without lawful authority, places any structure or object so as to obstruct the free passage over any part of the waterside to which the public have access shall be guilty of an offence and liable on summary conviction to a fine not exceeding level 3 on the standard scale and in addition, in the case of a continuing offence, a daily fine not exceeding one-tenth of that level.

(2) Nothing in subsection (1) above shall apply to anything done on any land by or with the consent of the occupier of the land.

As to section 161 of Water Resources Act 1991

14. Section 161 of the Water Resources Act 1991 (anti-pollution works and operations) shall have effect in relation to the designated areas as though references to the Authority included references to the Corporation.

Obstruction of officers

15. Any person who—

(a) intentionally obstructs the manager or any other officer of the Corporation acting in pursuance of this Act, or of any byelaw made under or by virtue of this Act; or

(b) without reasonable excuse fails to comply with a requirement properly made by any such person so acting; or

(c) without reasonable cause fails to give to any such person so acting any information which he may reasonably require for the purpose of the performance of his functions; or

(d) in giving such information as aforesaid makes a statement which he knows to be false;

shall be guilty of an offence and liable on summary conviction to a fine not exceeding level 3 on the standard scale.

Defence of due diligence

16.—(1) In any proceedings for an offence under this Act or any byelaw made under this Act it shall be a defence for the person charged to prove—

(a) that he took all reasonable precautions and exercised all due diligence to avoid the commission of such an offence; or

(b) that he had a reasonable excuse for his act or failure to act.

(2) If, in any case, the defence provided by subsection (1)(a) above involves the allegation that the commission of the offence was due to the act or default of another person, the person charged shall not, without leave of the Court, be entitled to rely on that defence unless, not less than 7 clear days before the hearing, he has served on the prosecutor a notice in writing giving such information identifying, or assisting in the identification of, that person as was then in his possession.

Removal of offenders

17. If any person wilfully continues to breach any provision of this Act or of any byelaw made under this Act after being requested to desist from so doing by a police officer or by the manager or any other person authorised by the Corporation to enforce those provisions, it shall be lawful for the manager or any police officer to remove such person, together with any vehicle or vessel under his control, from the designated areas.

PART III

PROTECTIVE PROVISIONS

For mutual protection of port authority and Corporation

18.—(1) In this section—

"enactment" includes any provision of any order, byelaw, rule, regulation, scheme or other instrument having effect by virtue of an enactment;

"harbourmaster" has the meaning given by section 2 of the Port of London Act 1968; and

"subsidiary" has the meaning given by section 736 of the Companies Act 1985.

(2) The exercise in, under or over the river Thames by the Corporation or by any officer of the Corporation of any function conferred or imposed by or under this or any other Act shall be subject to—

(a) any enactment relating to or made by the port authority and the terms of any licence granted by the port authority under section 66 of the Port of London Act 1968; and

(b) the exercise by the port authority or their harbourmaster of any functions conferred or imposed on them or him by or under any enactment.

(3) The exercise within the designated areas (other than the jetties) by the port authority, or by any officer of the port authority, of any function conferred or imposed by or under any enactment shall be subject to—

(a) any enactment relating to or made by the Corporation, including this Act and any byelaw made under this Act; and

(b) the exercise by the Corporation or the manager of any functions conferred or imposed on it or him by or under any enactment including
this Act or any byelaw made under this Act.

(4) Subject to subsection (3) above, and to any order made under section
30 (Termination of jurisdiction of port authority) or 32 (Repeal, etc., of legislation of port authority, etc.) of this Act, but notwithstanding any other provision of this Act, the designated areas shall continue to be treated as falling
within the limits described in paragraph 2 of Schedule 1 to the Port of London
Act 1968.

(5)(a) Subject to paragraph (b) below, section 28 (Certain waters not to be
subject to public rights of navigation) of this Act shall not apply to any right
of navigation exercisable by the owners, lessees or occupiers of land which is,
at the date of the passing of this Act, owned or leased by the port authority or
any subsidiary of the port authority.

(b) Any right of navigation which, but for this subsection, would have been
extinguished by section 28 shall be deemed to be a private right of navigation
for the purposes of section 29 (Extinguishment of private rights of navigation) of this Act.

For protection of Canary Wharf Investments Limited and others

19.—(1) In this section "the company" means any of—
(a) Canary Wharf Investments Limited;
(b) Canary Wharf Limited; or
(c) Heron Quays Developments Limited;
and includes the successors in title to or assigns of the company for the time
being in respect of any land within the designated areas.

(2) The provisions of this Act and of any byelaw made under this Act shall
not apply to any land in which the company has as at the date of the passing of
this Act a freehold or leasehold interest, or an entitlement to such an interest,
without the consent in writing of the company.

(3) Subject to any consent given under subsection (2) above, nothing in this
Act or any order or byelaw made under this Act shall affect any rights, powers or privileges which are vested in, or enjoyed by, the company, or any
person deriving title from the company, and which are in existence at the date
of the passing of this Act, or any title to or over any lands held at that date by
the company or any such person.

For protection of The Telegraph plc and others

20.—(1) In this section "the company" means any of—
(a) The Telegraph plc;
(b) West Ferry Printers Limited; or
(c) Mercury Communications Limited;
and includes the successors in title, lessees, sub-lessees or tenants of the company as occupiers of any part of the designated areas.

(2) Byelaws made under this Act shall not be enforceable in respect of any
land which for the time being is in the occupation of the company without the
consent in writing of the company.

For protection of Clippers Quay (Millwall) Management Company Limited

21.—(1) In this section—
"the company" means Clippers Quay (Millwall) Management Company Limited and includes the successors in title, lessees, sub-
lessees or tenants of the company as occupiers of any part of the
company's area; and
"the company's area" means the waters controlled by the company
within the designated areas, the boundaries of which are shown
edged red on the plan marked "Clippers Quay", of which copies

have been signed on behalf of the Corporation by Robert Gerald Broomfield, the Corporation Solicitor, and on behalf of the company by Simon Raynaud, the company chairman, and deposited respectively in—

(a) the office of the Clerk of the Parliaments, House of Lords;

(b) the Private Bill Office of the House of Commons; and

(c) the Department of the Environment.

(2) Byelaws made under this Act shall not be enforceable in respect of the company's area without the consent in writing of the company.

For protection of telecommunications operators

22.—(1) In this section expressions defined in the Telecommunications Act 1984 have the same meanings as in that Act.

(2) Nothing in this Act or in any byelaw made under this Act shall affect any right of a telecommunications operator under paragraph 9 of the telecommunications code to inspect, maintain, adjust, repair or alter any telecommunications apparatus within the designated areas.

Saving for Billingsgate Market

23.—(1) In this section—

"the Act of 1979" means the City of London (Various Powers) Act 1979;

"the Billingsgate Market Acts" has the meaning given by section 10 of the Act of 1979;

"the false quays" means the quays forming part of or adjoining the market, the boundaries of which are shown edged red on the plan marked "False Quays", of which copies have been signed on behalf of the Corporation by Robert Gerald Broomfield, the Corporation Solicitor, and on behalf of the city corporation by Samuel Jones, the Town Clerk, and deposited respectively in—

(a) the office of the Clerk of the Parliaments, House of Lords;

(b) the Private Bill Office of the House of Commons;

(c) the Department of the Environment; and

(d) the office of the City Remembrancer at Guildhall in the city of London; and

"the market" means Billingsgate Market as established at Trafalgar Way, West India Dock in the London borough of Tower Hamlets pursuant to the Act of 1979 and to the Billingsgate Market Acts, the limits of the market as respects West India Dock aforesaid being shown on the signed plan referred to in section 10 of the Act of 1979.

(2) Byelaws made under this Act shall not be enforceable in respect of the market without the consent in writing of the city corporation:

Provided that this subsection shall not apply to—

(a) any land which after the passing of this Act ceases to be used for the purposes of the market; or

(b) the land (including the waters and airspace) beneath the false quays.

Saving for London City Airport

24. It shall be the duty of the Corporation, in exercising any power conferred on it by or under this Act, to have due regard to the safe operation of London City Airport and in particular to any requirements made by the Civil Aviation Authority in respect of the airport.

Saving for port health authority

25. Except insofar as this Act otherwise expressly provides, nothing in this Act or in any byelaw made under this Act shall prejudice, alter or affect the functions of the city corporation as port health authority.

Saving for fire authority

26. Notwithstanding the proviso to section 2(1) of the Petroleum (Consolidation) Act 1928, the local authority empowered to grant petroleum-spirit licences under that Act in the designated areas (other than the jetties) shall be the fire authority.

Crown rights

27.—(1) Nothing in this Act affects prejudicially any estate, right, power, privilege, authority or exemption of the Crown and, in particular and without prejudice to the generality of the foregoing, nothing in this Act authorises the Corporation to take, use, enter upon, or in any manner interfere with, any land or hereditaments or any rights of whatsoever description (including any portion of the shore or bed of the sea or of any river, channel, creek, bay or estuary)—

  (a) belonging to Her Majesty in right of Her Crown and under the management of the Crown Estate Commissioners, without the consent in writing of those commissioners; or

  (b) belonging to a government department, or held in trust for Her Majesty for the purposes of a government department, without the consent in writing of that government department.

(2) A consent under subsection (1) above may be given unconditionally or subject to such conditions and upon such terms as shall be considered necessary or appropriate.

PART IV

MISCELLANEOUS AND GENERAL

Certain waters not to be subject to public rights of navigation

28. Subject to section 18 (For mutual protection of port authority and Corporation) of this Act, but notwithstanding anything in any other enactment, agreement or rule of law, the waters comprised in the designated areas shall not be subject to any public rights of navigation.

Extinguishment of private rights of navigation

29.—(1) The Corporation may by notice in writing under this section extinguish any private rights of navigation over the waters comprised in the designated areas.

(2) A notice under this section—

  (a) shall specify the rights to which it relates;

  (b) shall be served on every person, being the owner or occupier of lands within or adjoining the designated areas, whom the Corporation believes to be—

      (i) a person entitled to exercise the rights to which the notice relates; or

      (ii) a person claiming to be entitled to such exercise;

  (c) shall state that the rights specified in the notice shall be extinguished with effect from a date so specified; and

  (d) shall draw attention to the entitlement to compensation created by subsection (5) below.

(3) Any private right of navigation specified in a notice under this section shall be extinguished with effect from the date specified in the notice.

(4) Section 220 of the Water Resources Act 1991 shall apply to notices under this section as it applies to documents required or authorised to be served by virtue of that Act.

(5) Any person who suffers loss by reason of the extinguishment, by virtue of a notice under this section, of any private right of navigation shall be

entitled to be paid by the Corporation compensation to be determined, in case of dispute, by the Lands Tribunal; and the tribunal shall in determining the compensation take into account any contractual right offered by the Corporation in substitution for the right which is extinguished.

(6) No claim shall be brought pursuant to subsection (5) above after three years from the date of the service of the notice.

Termination of jurisdiction of port authority

30.—(1) Subject to subsection (2) below, the Secretary of State may by order made under this section provide that the port authority shall, to the extent specified in the order, cease to exercise jurisdiction over the designated areas, or any part thereof, as conservancy or harbour authority with effect from such day as may be specified in the order.

(2) Nothing in any order made under this section shall apply to the jetties.

Alteration of limits of jurisdiction

31.—(1) In this section "the urban development area" means the area for which the Corporation is for the time being the urban development corporation.

(2) The Secretary of State may by order made under this section alter the designated areas, as defined in section 2 (Interpretation) of this Act, so as to—

(a) include within the designated areas for the purposes of this Act any area of land in the London borough of Newham, Southwark or Tower Hamlets which for the time being is—

(i) situated within, or adjacent to, the urban development area; or

(ii) adjacent to any land which, not being situated within or adjacent to the urban development area, is adjacent to any land for the time being comprised in the designated areas;

(b) remove from the designated areas any land for the time being comprised in those areas.

Repeal, etc., of legislation of port authority, etc.

32. If it appears to the Secretary of State that, in consequence of the vesting in the Corporation at any time (whether before or after the date of the passing of this Act) of any land in the designated areas which is or was formerly vested in the port authority–

(a) any enactment conferring functions on that authority with respect to that land should be amended or repealed; or

(b) any such functions with respect to that land should be transferred to the Corporation;

he may by order amend or repeal the enactment or vest those functions in the Corporation.

Transfer of functions of Corporation

33.—(1) Notwithstanding any other provision of this Act or any provision of the Act of 1980, the Secretary of State, on the application of the Corporation, may by order at any time transfer to any person ("the transferee") with the agreement of that person all or any of the functions conferred or imposed on the Corporation by or under this Act.

(2) Following any transfer under subsection (1) above, the transferee shall have all the rights, liabilities and obligations to which the Corporation is entitled or subject in relation to the functions transferred; and any agreement to which the Corporation is a party that relates wholly or partly to the functions transferred and is in force immediately before the date of the transfer

shall to the extent that it relates to those functions have effect on and after that date as though references in it to the Corporation were or, as the case may require, included references to the transferee.

Orders: procedural provisions

34.—(1) This section applies to any order made under the following sections of this Act:—

section 30 (Termination of jurisdiction of port authority);
section 31 (Alteration of limits of jurisdiction);
section 32 (Repeal, etc., of legislation of port authority, etc.); or
section 33 (Transfer of functions of Corporation).

(2) The power to make an order under the sections mentioned in subsection (1) above shall be exercisable by statutory instrument.

(3) An order made under any of the sections mentioned in subsection (1) above may contain such transitional, incidental, supplementary or consequential provisions as the Secretary of State considers necessary or expedient.

(4) No order shall be made—

(a) under section 30;
(b) under section 31 so as to include any area of land vested in the port authority; or
(c) under section 32;

except with the consent of the port authority.

(5)(a) No order shall be made under section 31 so as to include any land forming part of an inland waterway of the British Waterways Board, or any other land vested in that Board, except with the consent of the said Board.

(b) For the purposes of this subsection, "inland waterway" means any canal or inland navigation belonging to or under the control of the British Waterways Board and includes any works, lands or premises belonging to or under the control of that Board and held or used by them in connection with such canal or inland navigation.

(6) Before making an order under section 31, to include any land within the limits of jurisdiction, or under section 33, to transfer to any person all or any of the functions conferred or imposed on the Corporation by or under this Act, the Secretary of State shall consult the borough council for the area where that land is situated or to which those functions relate.

(7) An order under section 31 shall be subject to annulment in pursuance of a resolution of either House of Parliament.

(8) An order under section 33 shall not be made unless a draft of the order has been laid before Parliament and been approved by a resolution of each House of Parliament.

Management arrangements

35.—(1) The Corporation may enter into and carry into effect agreements with any person with respect to the discharge of all or any of the functions conferred or imposed on the Corporation by or under this Act.

(2) The exercise of the powers of any enactment by any person in pursuance of any agreement under subsection (1) above shall be subject to the same restrictions, liabilities and obligations as would apply under this Act if those powers were exercised by the Corporation.

Corporation's undertaking

36. The functions conferred or imposed on the Corporation by or under this Act shall form a part of the undertaking of the Corporation for the purposes of sections 165 and 166 of the Act of 1980 (which relate to the transfer of undertakings and dissolution of urban development corporations).

Annual reports

37. As soon as possible after the end of each calendar year and in any event not later than 6 months after the end of such year the Corporation shall prepare and publish a report on the discharge of its functions under this Act during that year and shall submit a copy of such report to the Secretary of State; and the Corporation shall make copies of such report available for purchase by members of the public at a reasonable charge.

Restriction on powers of Corporation

38. For the purposes of section 138 of the Act of 1980 (which permits restrictions to be imposed on the exercise of the powers of an urban development corporation under that Act) that section shall apply to the powers of the Corporation conferred by or by virtue of this Act as if they were powers under that Act.

Provisions as to dissolution of Corporation

39. For the purposes of section 166 of the Act of 1980 (which provides for the dissolution of an urban development corporation following the transfer of all of its property, rights and liabilities by one or more relevant instruments) any transfer under section 33 (Transfer of functions of Corporation) of this Act shall be deemed to be a transfer by a relevant instrument within the meaning of section 166.

Status of Corporation

40. The Corporation shall not be a navigation authority, harbour authority or conservancy authority for the purposes of the Water Resources Act 1991 or the Land Drainage Act 1991 or any byelaw made under either of those Acts and section 23 of the Land Drainage Act 1991 shall apply to any works carried out or maintained under or in pursuance of this Act or any byelaw made under this Act.

SCHEDULES

Sections 2 and 3   SCHEDULE 1

DESCRIPTION OF HARBOURS OR FORMER HARBOURS AND OTHER AREAS

1. Hermitage Basin.
2. Western Dock Canal system.
3. Shadwell Basin, including Brussels Wharf.
4. Surrey Water, Thames Link, Albion Canal, Albion Dry Dock and Canada Water.
5. Greenland Dock, Steelyard Cut and South Dock.
6. West India North Branch Dock, West India Centre Branch Dock and West India South Dock.
7. Blackwall Basin and Poplar Dock.
8. Millwall Inner Dock, Millwall Outer Dock and Millwall Cutting.
9. East India Dock Basin.
10. Royal Victoria Dock and Royal Victoria Pontoon Dock.
11. Royal Albert Dock.
12. King George V Dock.
13. Albert Basin.

Sections 2 and 3   SCHEDULE 2

DESCRIPTION OF JETTIES

1. Greenland pier and associated jetties.
2. Blackwall pier.
3. Two jetties on either side of entrance of lock leading to King George V Dock.
4. Two jetties on either side of site of former entrance to Albert Basin.
5. Jetty on north side of Gallion's Yacht Lock entrance.
6. Cory's jetty.

Section 9   SCHEDULE 3

PURPOSES FOR WHICH BYELAWS MAY BE MADE

1. For regulating the conduct of all persons in the designated areas, not being members of a police force or officers of the fire authority or officers or servants of the Crown or officers of the port authority whilst in the exercise of their duties as such.

2. For regulating the use of buildings, parking places and facilities provided by the Corporation.

3. To promote the safety of persons in the designated areas.

4. For preventing damage or injury to or interference with any part of the designated areas or any property within the designated areas.

5. For prevention of nuisances in the designated areas.

6. For prohibiting the buying or selling of goods or the carrying on of any other trading activity in the designated areas, either absolutely or except with the consent of the Corporation and in accordance with any conditions (including conditions as to payment) subject to which such consent is given.

7. For regulating the movement, use, speed and parking of vehicles within the designated areas.

8. For regulating the landing and taking off of helicopters within the designated areas.

9. For regulating the entry onto the waterside of horses, ponies, asses or mules and the riding thereon of such animals.

10. For requiring dogs to be under proper control on the waterside or on the jetties, and for the prevention of fouling of those areas by dogs.

11. For the protection of flora and fauna within the designated areas.

12. For prohibiting or regulating the placing of materials or the depositing of litter, rubbish or other substances in the designated areas and making provision for the removal from the designated areas of objects and substances left without lawful authority or abandoned.

13. For the control of noise in the designated areas.

14. For regulating the playing of games in the designated areas.

15. For regulating firework displays or the lighting of fireworks in the designated areas.

16. For regulating the holding of exhibitions, festivals, concerts, displays, regattas and other public events in the designated areas.

17. For regulating cycling, roller-skating, ice skating, or the use of bicycles, tricycles, scooters, toboggans, pedal cars, soap box carts or any other similar conveyances or devices on the waterside.

18. For regulating water skiing, rowing, canoeing, sailing, aqua-planing, wet-biking, windsurfing, kiting or parachute towing or other similar activities in the designated areas and for securing the protection of persons taking part in such activities.

19. For prohibiting or regulating diving, swimming and bathing, and for securing the protection of divers, swimmers and bathers, within the waters of the designated areas.

20. For regulating fishing for marine creatures of any type and by whatever means within the designated areas.

21. To prescribe parts of the designated areas—
   (a) where vessels or a specified class of vessels may not moor, anchor or be otherwise secured; or
   (b) which vessels of a specified class may not enter.

22. For regulating the use within the designated areas of any class of vessels for business or residential purposes.

23. For requiring the registration of, or of any class of, pleasure-vessels, for the renewal of registration, for revocation of registration in specified circumstances and for prohibiting the use for navigation of the waters of the designated areas by pleasure-vessels which are not registered with the Corporation.

24. For regulating the removal or disposal of rubbish (including ballast, earth or clay or other refuse) and sewage from vessels in the designated areas.

25. For regulating within the designated areas the placing, laying down, maintenance and use of moorings and in particular for prohibiting the placing, laying down, maintaining or using of any mooring otherwise than under the authority of a licence granted by the Corporation in accordance with the conditions subject to which it is so granted.

26. For controlling, preventing and removing obstructions or impediments within the designated areas.

27. For regulating the use in the designated areas of flammable or dangerous substances or of fires, lights or any other equipment, tools or appliances which the Corporation considers involves a risk of fire and for the prevention of smoking.

28. For requiring the masters of vessels within the designated areas to take fire precautions and measures to combat fires on or in respect of their vessels.

29. To prevent the taking of vessels in the designated areas by unauthorised persons.

30. For regulating the carrying out of repairs to vessels in the designated areas, the breaking of or other works on or in respect of vessels in the designated areas or the washing, cleansing or scraping of vessels within the designated areas.

31. For regulating vessels in the designated areas and their entry into and departure from the designated areas and, without prejudice to the generality of the foregoing, to prescribe rules for regulating the notice to be given to the manager of the arrival at, departure from, or movement within the designated areas of vessels, the speed and manner of navigation and the lights and signals (including sound signals) to be exhibited or made by, or for the benefit of, vessels using, navigating or mooring within the designated areas.

32. For requiring notification of, and details of, collisions, accidents and other mishaps involving vessels or vehicles within the designated areas to be given to the manager.

33. For prescribing safety precautions to be taken within the designated areas during the fuelling of vessels.

34. For requiring the display on vessels within the designated areas of the name or other means of identification thereof.

35. For prohibiting the abandonment of vessels in the designated areas and in particular—
    (a) for prescribing the circumstances in which vessels shall be deemed to be abandoned;
    (b) for making provision for the removal of vessels sunk, stranded or abandoned in the designated areas without lawful authority;
    (c) for providing for the recovery of expenses from the owner.

36. For requiring the placing and maintenance of buoys or other devices giving warning of the presence of obstructions within the designated areas.

Section 12 SCHEDULE 4

CONTROL OF CRAFT IN DESIGNATED AREAS, ETC.

Incorporation of Act of 1847

1.—(1) The Harbours, Docks and Piers Clauses Act 1847 (in this Schedule called "the Act of 1847"), except sections 6 to 27, 29 to 50, 66 to 68, 79 to 90 and 94 to 96, so far as applicable for the purposes of and not inconsistent with this Act is hereby incorporated with this Act.

(2) In construing the Act of 1847, as incorporated with this Act—
    (a) the expression "harbour, dock or pier" shall mean the designated areas;
    (b) the expression "the harbour master" shall mean the manager;
    (c) the prescribed limits shall be the limits of jurisdiction;
    (d) the meaning of the word "vessel" as defined by this Act shall be substituted for the meaning assigned to it by section 3 of the Act of 1847; and
    (e) the expression "the undertakers" shall mean the Corporation.

(3) Sections 9(2) and (3), 10 and 11 of this Act shall apply to byelaws made under section 83 of the Act of 1847, as incorporated with this Act, as they apply to byelaws made under section 9(1) of this Act.

(4) For the purposes of the Act of 1847, as so incorporated, the jetties shall be deemed not to be within the limits of jurisdiction or the designated areas.

Directions of manager

2. Section 52 of the Act of 1847, in its application to the Corporation and the manager—
    (1) shall extend to empower the manager to give directions prohibiting the mooring of vessels within the designated areas or any part or parts thereof;
    (2) shall not be construed to require the manager in emergency to give particular directions in the case of every vessel in respect of which it is desired to exercise any of the powers of that section, but in pursuance of that section for all or any of the purposes thereof the manager shall be entitled in emergency to give general directions applicable to all vessels or to particular classes of vessels.

Orders of manager need not be in writing

3. Section 53 of the Act of 1847, in its application to the Corporation and the manager, shall not be construed to require the manager to serve a notice in writing of his directions upon the master of a vessel and such directions may be given orally or otherwise communicated to the master.

Boarding of vessels

4.—(1) The manager may, on producing if so required his authority, enter a vessel in the designated areas and inspect the vessel or any part thereof or its cargo or any machinery, boats, equipment or articles on board the vessel for the purposes of any enactment relating to the Corporation, or of any direction lawfully given under any such enactment, including the enforcement thereof, and may take such steps as may be necessary to prevent or extinguish fire.

(2) Where the manager indicates his intention of entering and inspecting a vessel, the master of the vessel shall, by any practical means consistent with the safety of the vessel, facilitate the manager boarding and subsequently leaving the vessel.

(3) If the master of a vessel fails to comply with sub-paragraph (2) above, he shall be guilty of an offence and liable on summary conviction to a fine not exceeding level 3 on the standard scale.

(4) In this and the following paragraph "master" means any person for the time being having or taking the command, charge, possession or management of a vessel whether lawfully or wrongfully.

Power to obtain information as to vessels

5.—(1) In this paragraph—
"owner" means the owner of a vessel and any person having any interest in a vessel (whether as joint owner, lessee, mortgagee or otherwise) and includes a person letting a vessel for hire whether or not that person owns the vessel; and
"vessel" means any vessel named or identified in a notice under this paragraph.

(2) Where, with a view to performing a function conferred or imposed on it by or under any enactment, the Corporation considers that it ought to have information as to the master or the owner, as the case may be, of any vessel which is or has been in the designated areas, it may serve a notice on any person reasonably believed by it to be the master or owner, or to have been the master or owner at any date specified in the notice, requiring the recipient to furnish to the Corporation within a period specified in the notice (which shall not be less than 14 days beginning with the day on which the notice is served) the following information:—
(a) the name and address of any person whom the recipient of the notice believes to be the master or owner of the vessel, or to have been such master or owner at any date specified in the notice; or
(b) the capacity in which any person who is or has been or is believed by the recipient of the notice to be or have been the master has or takes command, charge, possession or management of the vessel, or had or took such command, charge, possession or management at any date specified in the notice; or
(c) the nature of the interest in or control over the vessel, at any date specified in the notice, of any person who is or has been or is believed by the recipient of the notice to be or have been the owner.

(3) A notice under this paragraph shall—
(a) name or otherwise identify the vessel in respect of which it is served;
(b) specify the function for the purpose of the performance of which the notice is served; and
(c) specify the enactment by or under which that function is to be performed.

(4) A person who—
(a) fails, without reasonable excuse, to comply with the requirements of a notice served on him under sub-paragraph (2) above; or
(b) in furnishing any information in compliance with such a notice makes a statement which he knows to be false in a material particular or recklessly makes a statement which is false in a material particular;
shall be guilty of an offence and liable on summary conviction to a fine not exceeding level 3 on the standard scale.

(5) A person shall not be guilty of an offence under sub-paragraph (4)(a) above if—
(a) he has never been the master or owner of the vessel in respect of which the notice is served; or
(b) he ceased to be the master or owner of the vessel more than 6 months before the date upon which the notice is served on him.

INDEX

References are to sections and Schedules

HILL SAMUEL BANK AND UNITED DOMINIONS TRUST ACT 1994

(1994 c. xiv)

ARRANGEMENT OF SECTIONS

An Act to provide for the transfer to and vesting in TSB Bank plc of parts of the undertakings of Hill Samuel Bank Limited and United Dominions Trust Limited; and for connected purposes. [21st July 1994]

PARLIAMENTARY DEBATES

The Bill's progress through Parliament was as follows:

House of Lords: First Reading, January 12, 1994; Second Reading, February 16, 1994; Bill Committed, February 24, 1994; Unopposed Bill Committee, May 5, 1994; Third Reading, May 23, 1994; Commons' Amendments, July 19, 1994.

House of Commons: First Reading, May 23, 1994; Second Reading, June 21, 1994; Bill Committed, June 21, 1994; Unopposed Bill Committee, July 7, 1994; Bill as amended Considered, July 12, 1994; Third Reading, July 19, 1994.

INTRODUCTION

Hill Samuel Bank Limited and United Dominions Trust Limited are both companies incorporated in England under the Companies Act 1929. TSB Bank plc is a public company and is the beneficial owner of all the shares issued in Hill Samuel and UDT. By a series of agreements between the three companies the risk and reward attributable to parts of the business of Hill Samuel and UDT have been transferred to TSB but the legal title to those parts remains vested in Hill Samuel or UDT. In order to consolidate the core businesses more effectively this Act facilitates the transfer to and vesting in TSB of parts of the undertakings of Hill Samuel and UDT.

WHEREAS Hill Samuel Bank Limited (hereinafter called "Hill Samuel") is a company incorporated in England under the Companies Act 1929 as a company limited by shares and carries on in the United Kingdom and elsewhere the business of banking and financial services:

And whereas United Dominions Trust Limited (hereinafter called "UDT") is a company incorporated in England under the Companies Acts 1908 to 1917 as a company limited by shares and carries on in the United Kingdom and elsewhere the business of banking and financial services:

And whereas TSB Bank plc (hereinafter called "TSB") is a company incorporated in England under the Companies Acts 1948 to 1967 as a public company limited by shares and carries on in the United Kingdom and elsewhere the business of banking and financial services:

And whereas TSB is the beneficial owner of all the issued shares in Hill Samuel and UDT:

And whereas for the better conduct of the business of Hill Samuel, UDT and TSB, the risk and reward attributable to parts of the businesses of Hill Samuel and UDT have, by a series of agreements between them, been transferred to TSB but the legal title to those parts remains vested in Hill Samuel or UDT:

And whereas for the more effective consolidation of the core businesses of TSB, Hill Samuel and UDT and the better conduct thereof it is expedient that provision be made for the transfer to and vesting in TSB of parts of the undertakings of Hill Samuel and UDT:

And whereas it is expedient that the said transfers and vesting should be effected without interference with the conduct and continuity of the businesses carried on by TSB, Hill Samuel or UDT:

And whereas it is expedient that the other provisions in this Act should be enacted:

And whereas the objects of this Act cannot be attained without the authority of Parliament:

May it therefore please Your Majesty that it may be enacted, and be it enacted, by the Queen's most Excellent Majesty, by and with the advice and consent of the Lords Spiritual and Temporal, and Commons, in this present Parliament assembled, and by the authority of the same, as follows:—

Short title

1. This Act may be cited as the Hill Samuel Bank and United Dominions Trust Act 1994.

Interpretation

2.—(1) In this Act, unless the subject or context otherwise requires—

"appointed day" in relation to a transfer scheme means such day as may be specified under section 3(2) of this Act as the appointed day for the scheme;

"customer" includes any person having a bank account or other dealing, transaction, agreement or arrangement with Hill Samuel or UDT;

"document" has the same meaning as in section 10 of the Civil Evidence Act 1968;

"enactment" means any enactment in this Act or in any general or local Act or in any order, rule or regulation made under any Act;

"existing" means existing, outstanding or in force immediately before the appointed day for a transfer scheme;

"the first appointed day" means the earliest day which is the appointed day for any transfer scheme;

"Hill Samuel" means Hill Samuel Bank Limited;

"liabilities" includes duties and obligations of every description;

"property" means property and assets of every description including property and assets held on trust or in a fiduciary capacity and rights, benefits and powers of every description;

"security" includes a mortgage or charge (whether legal or equitable), debenture, bill of exchange, promissory note, guarantee, lien, pledge (whether actual or constructive), hypothecation, assignment by way of security, indemnity, right of set-off, flawed asset arrangement, undertaking or other means of securing payment or discharge of a debt or liability;

"transfer scheme" means a scheme made under section 3 (Schemes for transfer to TSB of property, liabilities, trusteeships and other appointments) of this Act;

"trustee" includes a trustee or custodian trustee of any trust deed, settlement, covenant, agreement or will; executor of the will, or administrator of the estate, of a deceased person; judicial trustee appointed by order of any court; attorney for another person; or any other person acting in a fiduciary capacity;

"TSB" means TSB Bank plc;

"UDT" means United Dominions Trust Limited; and

"will" includes a codicil and any other testamentary writing.

(2) Any reference in this Act to property or liabilities of Hill Samuel or UDT is a reference to property or liabilities wherever such property or liabilities are situated or arise and whether or not capable of being transferred or assigned by Hill Samuel or UDT and whether it is entitled or subject to the

property or liabilities under the law of any part of the United Kingdom or under the law of any country or territory outside the United Kingdom.

Schemes for transfer to TSB of property, liabilities, trusteeships and other appointments

3.—(1) Within five years from the passing of this Act TSB may jointly with Hill Samuel or jointly with UDT make a scheme or schemes for—

(a) the transfer to TSB of any of the property and liabilities to which, immediately before the appointed day for any such scheme, Hill Samuel or UDT (as the case may be) is entitled or subject and which are not rights or liabilities relating to a person's employment;

(b) the substitution of TSB for Hill Samuel or UDT or of a director, officer, representative or employee of TSB for a director, officer, representative or employee of Hill Samuel or UDT (as the case may be), in any position held by it or by such person as a trustee; and

(c) the substitution of TSB for Hill Samuel or UDT, or of a director, officer, representative or employee of TSB for a director, officer, representative or employee of Hill Samuel or UDT (as the case may be), as the holder of any office or appointment other than of trustee.

(2) Transfers by a transfer scheme or the substitution of TSB for Hill Samuel or UDT or of a director, officer, representative or employee of TSB for a director, officer, representative or employee of Hill Samuel or UDT (as the case may be) under subsection (1) above shall take effect on such day as may be specified in the scheme as the appointed day for the scheme; and before the first appointed day TSB shall publish in the London Gazette, the Edinburgh Gazette and the Belfast Gazette notice of the earliest day which is the appointed day for any transfer scheme stating that it is the first appointed day under this Act.

(3) Not less than seven days before the appointed day for a transfer scheme Hill Samuel or UDT (as the case may be) shall notify by post every person having a bank account which is to be transferred by or in consequence of the scheme (or, in the case of a joint account, the first-named account holder) that the account is to become an account with TSB and of the appointed day for the scheme:

Provided that a failure by Hill Samuel or UDT so to notify an account holder shall not invalidate the scheme.

(4) On the appointed day for a transfer scheme any property and liabilities transferred by the scheme shall, by virtue of this Act and without further assurance, be transferred to and vested in TSB to the intent that TSB shall succeed to such property and liabilities as if for all purposes TSB were the same person in law as Hill Samuel or UDT as the case may be.

(5) Where the transfer of any property or liability to which a transfer scheme relates is governed by the law of any country or territory outside the United Kingdom, Hill Samuel or UDT, as the case may be, shall, if TSB so requires, take all necessary steps to secure that the transfer of the property or liability to TSB is fully effective under the law of that country or territory and pending such transfer any such property shall be held by Hill Samuel or UDT (as the case may be) in trust for TSB and TSB shall be liable to Hill Samuel or UDT (as the case may be) for any such liability.

Provisions as to trust and other property and liabilities

4.—(1) Where a transfer scheme transfers to TSB property or a liability to which immediately before the appointed day for the scheme Hill Samuel or UDT was then entitled or subject as a trustee or as the holder of any other office or appointment, whether alone or jointly with another person, it shall be held by TSB, or TSB shall be subject to it, on and from the appointed day, alone or, as the case may be, jointly with that other person, in that capacity upon the same trusts or terms and with and subject to the same powers and provisions as were applicable theretofore.

(2) Where TSB is substituted for Hill Samuel or UDT as a trustee or as the holder of any other office or appointment under paragraph (b) or (c) of section 3(1) above—

(a) any property to which Hill Samuel or UDT was then in that capacity entitled, whether alone or jointly with another person, shall, by virtue of this Act and without further assurance, be transferred to and held by TSB alone or, as the case may be, jointly with that other person, upon the same trusts or terms and with and subject to the same powers, provisions and liabilities as were applicable theretofore; and

(b) TSB shall, by virtue of this Act and without further assurance, in the same capacity and upon the same terms, become subject to any liability to which Hill Samuel or UDT was then in that capacity subject, whether alone or jointly with another person.

(3) Where a director, officer, representative or employee of TSB is substituted for a director, officer, representative or employee of Hill Samuel or UDT as a trustee or as the holder of any other office or appointment under paragraph (b) or (c) of section 3(1) above—

(a) any property to which that director, officer, representative or employee of Hill Samuel or UDT was then, as trustee or as the holder of that office or appointment, entitled, whether alone or jointly with another person, shall, by virtue of this Act and without further assurance, be transferred to and held by that director, officer, representative or employee of TSB alone or, as the case may be, jointly with that other person upon the same trusts or terms and with and subject to the same powers, provisions and liabilities as were applicable theretofore; and

(b) that director, officer, representative or employee of TSB shall, by virtue of this Act and without further assurance, as trustee or as the holder of the office or appointment aforesaid, and upon the same terms, become subject to any liability to which the director, officer, representative or employee of Hill Samuel or UDT whom he is replacing was then, as trustee or as the holder of that office or appointment, subject, whether alone or jointly with another person.

(4) Any instrument or order of any court under or by virtue of which any property has been or is to become vested in Hill Samuel or UDT as a trustee or as the holder of any other office or appointment, and any provision therein, or any agreement or arrangement for the payment to, or retention by, Hill Samuel or UDT of remuneration for its services as a trustee or as the holder of any other office or appointment, shall, if that property is transferred by or in consequence of a transfer scheme, on and from the appointed day, be construed and have effect, so far as the context permits, as if for any reference therein to Hill Samuel or UDT, other than a reference (however worded and whether express or implied) to terms and conditions of, or to a scale of fees of, Hill Samuel or UDT, there were substituted a reference to TSB.

Supplementary provisions as to schemes and transfers

5.—(1) Without prejudice to the generality of the foregoing provisions of this Act but subject to any provision of this Act to the contrary effect, the following provisions shall have effect in relation to a transfer scheme and any property or liability transferred by or in consequence of a transfer scheme.

(2) A transfer scheme may—

(a) contain supplementary and incidental provisions for the purpose of giving full effect to the transfer by or in consequence of the scheme of property and liabilities and to the substitution of TSB for Hill Samuel or UDT under paragraph (b) or (c) of section 3(1) above; and

(b) revoke or vary any provision of an earlier transfer scheme before the appointed day for that scheme.

(3) An agreement, transaction, or other thing (not contained in an enactment and not being a will) which has been made, effected or done by, to or in relation to, or with reference to, Hill Samuel or UDT and which—

(a) immediately before the appointed day for a transfer scheme is in force or effective; and

(b) relates to any property or liability to be transferred to TSB by or in consequence of the scheme or to any position in respect of which TSB is substituted for Hill Samuel or UDT under paragraph (b) or (c) of section 3(1) above,

shall on and after that day have effect as if made, effected or done by, to or in relation to, or with reference to, TSB.

(4) Where any agreement, transaction or other thing has effect in accordance with subsection (3) above—

(a) any reference to Hill Samuel or UDT in any document incorporating or otherwise connected with the agreement, transaction or other thing shall on and after the appointed day for the transfer scheme be construed as a reference to TSB; and

(b) any reference (however worded and whether express or implied) in the agreement, transaction or other thing to the directors, officers, representatives or employees (or to any director, officer, representative or employee) of Hill Samuel or UDT shall on and after the appointed day for the transfer scheme be construed as a reference to the directors, officers, representatives or employees of TSB or, as the case may require, to such director, officer, representative or employee of TSB, as TSB may nominate for that purpose or, in default of nomination, to the director, officer, representative or employee of TSB who corresponds as nearly as may be to the first-mentioned director, officer, representative or employee.

(5) Any agreement or transaction which relates to property or liabilities which are only partly transferred to TSB by or in consequence of a transfer scheme shall be construed as if the agreement or transaction, to the extent to which it is enforceable by and against Hill Samuel or UDT, constituted two separate agreements or transactions, one of which is enforceable by and against TSB as regards the part of the property or, as the case may be, liabilities so transferred to it and not as regards the other part, and the other of which is enforceable by and against Hill Samuel or UDT as regards the part of the property or, as the case may be, liabilities not so transferred to TSB and not as regards the other part.

(6) Any account between Hill Samuel or UDT and a customer which is transferred by or in consequence of a transfer scheme shall be deemed for all purposes to be a single continuing account and, subject to the provisions of subsections (3) and (4) above and subsections (7) and (8) below, shall be subject to the same terms and conditions as those which applied before the transfer.

(7) Nothing in subsection (6) above shall preclude the exercise of any right of TSB (in place of Hill Samuel or UDT) or of a customer to vary the terms and conditions subject to which the account of the customer is kept.

(8) Without prejudice to the generality of the foregoing, where by virtue of a transfer scheme and the operation of this Act TSB becomes a party to an agreement, transaction or other thing in place of Hill Samuel or UDT, any reference in that agreement, transaction or other thing to a rate of interest prescribed by Hill Samuel or UDT shall be construed on and from the appointed day for the scheme as a reference to the equivalent rate of interest prescribed by TSB.

(9) Any negotiable instrument, letter of credit or order for payment of money which is transferred by a transfer scheme and has been drawn on, or given to, or accepted or endorsed by, Hill Samuel or UDT, or is payable at a place of business of Hill Samuel or UDT, shall have the same effect as if it had been drawn on, or given to, or accepted or endorsed by, TSB or were payable at a place of business of TSB.

(10) The custody of any document or record, goods or other thing held by Hill Samuel or UDT as bailee in connection with any property or liabilities to be transferred by a transfer scheme shall pass to TSB on the appointed day for the scheme, and the rights and obligations of Hill Samuel or UDT under any contract of bailment relating to any such document or record, goods or thing shall on that day become rights and obligations of TSB.

(11)(a) Any security held immediately before the appointed day for a transfer scheme by Hill Samuel or UDT in connection with any property or liabilities to be transferred by or in consequence of the scheme, or by a nominee or agent of or trustee for Hill Samuel or UDT, shall, on and from that day, be held by, or as the case may require, by that nominee, agent or trustee for, TSB and be available to TSB (whether for its own benefit or, as the case may be, for the benefit of any other person);

(b) In relation to any security transferred to TSB by or in consequence of a transfer scheme and to any liabilities thereby secured, TSB shall be entitled to the same rights and priorities and be subject to the same obligations as those to which Hill Samuel or UDT would have been entitled or subject if it had continued to hold the security;

(c) Without prejudice to the generality of paragraph (b) above, in any case where any existing liability subsists between Hill Samuel or UDT and TSB in respect of which Hill Samuel or UDT or TSB, or a nominee or agent of or trustee for Hill Samuel or UDT or TSB, holds security, that liability shall, for the purpose of enforcing or realising that security, be deemed to continue in effect notwithstanding a transfer to TSB of the liability or the benefit of the liability by or in consequence of a transfer scheme;

(d) Any security referred to in the foregoing provisions of this subsection which extends to future advances, liabilities or indebtedness shall, on and from the appointed day for the transfer scheme, be available to TSB (whether for its own benefit or, as the case may be, for the benefit of any other person) as security for the payment or discharge of future advances, liabilities and indebtedness to the same extent and in the same manner in all respects as it extends to future advances, liabilities or indebtedness immediately before that day.

(12) On and from the appointed day for a transfer scheme, TSB and all other persons shall have the same rights, powers and remedies (and in particular the same rights and powers as to taking or resisting legal proceedings or making or resisting applications to any authority) for ascertaining, perfecting or enforcing the property or liability transferred by or in consequence of the scheme as if it had been property or a liability of TSB for the period before the appointed day for the scheme during which it had been the property or a liability of Hill Samuel or UDT; and any legal proceedings or applications to any authority pending immediately before the appointed day for the scheme by or against Hill Samuel or UDT may be continued by or against TSB.

(13) Any judgment, order or award obtained by or against Hill Samuel or UDT relating to property or a liability transferred by or in consequence of a transfer scheme or to any position in respect of which TSB is substituted for Hill Samuel or UDT under paragraph (b) or (c) of section 3(1) above and not fully satisfied before the appointed day for the scheme shall on and from that day, to the extent to which it was enforceable by or against Hill Samuel or UDT immediately before that day, be enforceable by or against TSB and no longer by or against Hill Samuel or UDT.

(14) In respect of—
(a) any data transferred to TSB by a transfer scheme, or
(b) any data relating to any property or a liability transferred to TSB by or in consequence of a transfer scheme,
the Data Protection Registrar may, on and from the appointed day for that transfer scheme, serve on TSB any notice under section 10 of the Data Protection Act 1984 which he could have served on Hill Samuel or UDT in respect of a breach of the data protection principles by Hill Samuel or UDT before that appointed day; but the transfer of property or liabilities to TSB by or in consequence of a transfer scheme and any disclosure to TSB of any information in contemplation or as a result thereof shall not amount to a breach of any duty of confidentiality to which Hill Samuel or UDT is or was subject immediately before the appointed day for the scheme or to a contravention by TSB or Hill Samuel or UDT of the data protection principles.

Evidence: books and documents

6. All books and other documents which would, before the appointed day for a transfer scheme, have been evidence for or against Hill Samuel or UDT in respect of any matter to which the scheme relates shall be admissible in evidence in respect of the same matter for or against TSB.

Application of Bankers' Books Evidence Act 1879

7.—(1) In this section "books" shall be construed in accordance with section 9(2) of the Bankers' Books Evidence Act 1879.
(2) On and from the appointed day for a transfer scheme the said Act of 1879 shall apply to those books of Hill Samuel or UDT which are transferred to TSB by the scheme, and to entries made in those books before that day, as if such books were the books of TSB.
(3) For the purposes of section 4 of the said Act of 1879, books so transferred to TSB shall be deemed to have been the ordinary books of TSB at the time of the making of any entry therein which purports to have been made before the appointed day for the scheme, and any such entry shall be deemed to have been made in the usual and ordinary course of business.

Evidence of transfer and vesting

8.—(1) In this section "convey" has the same meaning as in the Law of Property Act 1925.
(2) A certificate issued jointly by or on behalf of TSB and Hill Samuel or UDT that by or in consequence of a transfer scheme any property or liabilities specified in the certificate have been transferred to TSB shall be conclusive evidence for all purposes of that fact.
(3) A certificate issued under subsection (2) above, shall, in relation to any registered securities within the meaning of the Stock Transfer Act 1963 transferred to TSB by or in consequence of a transfer scheme, operate for all the purposes of the said Act of 1963 as a duly executed stock transfer in respect of the transfer of such securities from Hill Samuel or UDT to TSB.
(4) Without prejudice to subsection (2) above (but subject to that subsection)—
(a) any document made or executed on or after the first appointed day whereby TSB, whether alone or jointly with any other person, conveys or transfers, or purports to convey or transfer, to any person (whether for consideration or not), or applies to be registered as the holder or proprietor of, any property held by Hill Samuel or UDT immediately before that day, whether alone or jointly with any other person, shall be sufficient evidence that the interest of Hill Samuel or UDT in that property has been transferred to TSB by or in consequence of a transfer scheme; and

(b) where there is any other transaction by TSB on or after the first appointed day in connection with, or in relation to, any property or liability which immediately before that day is property or a liability of Hill Samuel or UDT, it shall be deemed in favour of any other party to the transaction, or any person claiming through or under him, that TSB has full power and authority for that transaction.

(5) Without prejudice to subsection (2) above (but subject to that subsection)—

(a) any document made or executed on or after the first appointed day whereby Hill Samuel or UDT, whether alone or jointly with any other person, conveys or transfers, or purports to convey or transfer, to any person (whether for consideration or not), or applies to be registered as the holder or proprietor of, any property held by it immediately before that day, whether alone or jointly with any other person, shall be sufficient evidence that its interest in that property has not been transferred to TSB by or in consequence of a transfer scheme; and

(b) where there is any other transaction by Hill Samuel or UDT on or after the first appointed day in connection with, or in relation to, any property or liability which immediately before that day is, or would but for this Act or a transfer scheme be, property or a liability of Hill Samuel or UDT, it shall be deemed in favour of any other party to the transaction, or any person claiming through or under him, that Hill Samuel or UDT, as the case may be, has full power and authority for that transaction.

(6) No person may rely upon the provisions of subsection (4) or (5) above if he has knowledge to the contrary and nothing in this section affects the liability of TSB, or of Hill Samuel or UDT, to the other of them in respect of anything done, or purported to have been done, by one of them in connection with, or in relation to, any property or liabilities transferred by or in consequence of a transfer scheme.

Savings in respect of transfers of property

9. The transfer of any property or of a liability by or in consequence of a transfer scheme or the substitution of TSB for Hill Samuel or UDT under paragraph (b) or (c) of section 3(1) above shall not—

(1) constitute a purchase or creation of an interest in land for the purposes of section 30(2) of the Landlord and Tenant Act 1954 or constitute a relevant disposal within the meaning of section 4 of the Landlord and Tenant Act 1987 for the purposes of that Act; or

(2) constitute an assignment, transfer, devolution, alienation, parting with possession or other disposition of property or of an interest in property for the purposes of any provision in any instrument, contract (whether in writing or not) or order of any court concerning that property or that interest; or

(3) give rise to any forfeiture; or

(4) invalidate or discharge any agreement, transaction, security or other thing; or

(5) require further registration in respect of any security transferred by or in consequence of the scheme; or

(6) cause the benefit of any agreement, licence or privilege enjoyed by Hill Samuel or UDT to be lost or surrendered or otherwise affected, or require the disposal by Hill Samuel or UDT of any interest, otherwise than as provided for in this Act; or

(7) relieve any person under an obligation to Hill Samuel or UDT of a corresponding obligation to TSB; or

(8) constitute a breach of, or default under, or require any obligation to be performed sooner or later than would have otherwise been the case under, any agreement or arrangement to which TSB, Hill Samuel or UDT is a party; or

(9) operate so as to merge any leasehold interest in the reversion expectant on it.

Application to Scotland and Northern Ireland

10.—(1) In the application of this Act to Scotland the following provisions shall have effect:—

  (a) in the construction of this Act—

    "assignment" includes an assignation;

    "bailee" includes a custodian or a holder on deposit or pledge and "contract of bailment" includes any other contract regulating custody of things;

    "convey" includes the execution of any deed or other instrument or document by which any property, or any estate, interest, security or other right in or over property, is constituted, completed, disponed, assigned, transmitted or discharged;

    "debenture" includes a floating charge or any instrument containing a floating charge;

    "freehold land" includes heritable property;

    "judgment" includes a decree;

    "judicial trustee" includes a judicial factor;

    "mortgage" includes a standard security, an assignation or disposition ex facie absolute and any agreement qualifying the same, a bond and disposition or assignation in security, a cash credit bond and disposition or assignation in security, an assignation in security and any real right or burden of whatever kind in the nature of a security whether or not constituted in respect of a heritable property; and

    "will" includes a trust disposition and settlement and any deed taking effect on the death of any person whereby any part of his estate is disposed of, or under which a succession thereto arises.

  (b) all standard securities and cash credit bonds and dispositions or assignations in security expressed to be in favour of Hill Samuel or UDT transferred to TSB by or in consequence of a transfer scheme shall, on and from the appointed day for the scheme, have the same effect in favour of TSB up to the maximum amounts stated therein respectively in all respects as if they had been originally granted in favour of TSB for such maximum amounts;

  (c) to enable TSB to complete a title, if thought fit, to any property transferred to it by or in consequence of a transfer scheme, by notice of title or otherwise, or to deduce title, the transfer scheme shall be deemed to be, and may be used as, a general disposition, conveyance or, as the case may be, assignation of such property in favour of TSB;

  (d) for the reference in subsection (1) of section 2 (Interpretation) of this Act to section 10 of the Civil Evidence Act 1968 there shall be substituted reference to section 17 of the Law Reform (Miscellaneous Provisions) (Scotland) Act 1968.

(2) In the application of this Act to Northern Ireland—

  (a) for the reference in subsection (1) of section 2 (Interpretation) of this Act to section 10 of the Civil Evidence Act 1968 there shall be substituted reference to section 6 of the Civil Evidence Act (Northern Ireland) 1971;

  (b) for the reference in subsection (1) of section 8 (Evidence of transfer and vesting) of this Act to the Law of Property Act 1925 there shall be substituted reference to the Conveyancing Act 1881;

   (c) the reference in subsection (3) of section 8 (Evidence of transfer and vesting) of this Act to the Stock Transfer Act 1963 shall include a reference to the Stock Transfer Act (Northern Ireland) 1963; and

   (d) for paragraph (1) of section 9 (Savings in respect of transfers of property) of this Act, there shall be substituted the following:—

      "(1) constitute a purchase or creation of an estate for the purposes of section 10(3) of the Business Tenancies Act (Northern Ireland) 1964; or".

Costs of Act

11. All costs, charges and expenses preliminary to, and of and incidental to, the preparing for, obtaining and passing of this Act, or otherwise in relation thereto, shall be paid by TSB.

INDEX

References are to sections

GREATER NOTTINGHAM LIGHT RAPID TRANSIT ACT 1994

(1994 c. xv)

ARRANGEMENT OF SECTIONS

PART I

PRELIMINARY

PART II

WORKS

PART III

LANDS

PART IV

PROTECTIVE PROVISIONS

An Act to confer on Nottinghamshire County Council and on Nottingham City Council powers for the development and operation of a light rail system of rapid passenger transport in the City of Nottingham and elsewhere in the County of Nottinghamshire; to authorise the construction of works and the acquisition of lands for those purposes; to authorise the said councils to transfer the undertaking established by this Act or any part thereof to Greater Nottingham Rapid Transit Limited or any other person; to confer further powers on the said councils; and for other purposes.   [21st July 1994]

PARLIAMENTARY DEBATES

The Bill's progress through Parliament was as follows:

House of Commons: First Reading, January 22, 1992; Second Reading, January 29, 1992; Suspended, March 12, 1992; Opposed Bill Committee, June 24, 1992–June 17, 1993; Bill as amended Considered, June 29, 1993; Third Reading, July 13, 1993; Lords' Amendments, July 20, 1993.

House of Lords: First Reading, July 13, 1993; Second Reading, October 19, 1993; Bill Committed, October 19, 1993; Suspended, October 28, 1993; Opposed Bill Committee, December 6, 1993–February 9, 1994; Unopposed Bill Committee, April 21, 1994; Third Reading, July 18, 1994; Commons' Amendments, July 20, 1994.

INTRODUCTION

Nottingham City Council and Nottingham County Council are responsible for the local government and management of the City of Nottingham and the County of Nottingham respectively. It has been identified that a light rail system would be of particular benefit to the public. This Act makes the provisions necessary to empower the County Council and City Council to undertake all works and acquire all lands necessary to undertake the works to develop the light rail system.

WHEREAS—

(1) The County of Nottinghamshire and the City of Nottingham are under the management and local government respectively of Nottinghamshire County Council (hereinafter referred to as "the County Council") and Nottingham City Council (hereinafter referred to as "the City Council"):

(2) The provision of a light rail system of rapid passenger transport in the City of Nottingham and elsewhere in the County of Nottinghamshire would be of public benefit:

(3) It is expedient that the County Council and the City Council should be empowered to construct the works authorised by this Act, and to acquire or use the lands referred to in this Act, for the provision of such a system (hereinafter referred to as "the LRT system"), and that the other powers in this Act should be conferred upon the County Council and on the City Council:

(4) The County Council and the City Council intend that the functions conferred on them by this Act shall be exercised by a joint committee appointed under the powers already available to the said Councils in that behalf:

(5) The said Councils and Nottingham Development Enterprise Limited (a company limited by guarantee established by the said Councils and the private sector to promote social, physical and economic regeneration of the County) have together formed a private company limited by shares under the name of Greater Nottingham Rapid Transit Limited (hereafter referred to as "the Company") to undertake the construction and operation of the LRT system in participation with the said Councils and the private sector:

(6) It is expedient that provision should be made to allow the said Councils to transfer the undertaking established by this Act or any part thereof to the Company or any other person and that the other provisions contained in this Act should be enacted:

(7) The purposes of this Act could not have been effected without the authority of Parliament when the Bill for this Act was deposited:

(8) Plans and sections showing the lines or situations and levels of the works to be constructed under this Act, and plans of the lands which the County Council and the City Council may acquire or use compulsorily under the powers of this Act, and a book of reference to such plans containing the names of the owners or reputed owners, lessees or reputed lessees and of the occupiers of all such lands have been deposited in the office of the Clerk of the Parliaments and in the Private Bill Office of the House of Commons and with the proper officer of the County Council which plans, sections and book of reference are in this Act referred to respectively as the deposited plans, the deposited sections and the deposited book of reference:

(9) Alteration having been required in the alignment of part of the works since plans and sections thereof were so deposited, a plan and sections showing the lines or situations and levels of the substituted works and a plan of the lands authorised to be acquired or used by this Act for the purposes of the substituted works, and a book of reference to such plan containing the names of the owners and lessees, or reputed owners and lessees, and of the occupiers of the said lands have been deposited in the office of the Clerk of the Parliaments and in the Private Bill Office of the House of Commons and with the proper officer of the County Council, which plan, sections and book of reference form part of the deposited plans, the deposited sections and the deposited book of reference:

(10) In relation to the promotion of the Bill for this Act the requirements of section 239 of the Local Government Act 1972 have been observed by the County Council and the City Council:

May it therefore please Your Majesty that it may be enacted, and be it enacted, by the Queen's most Excellent Majesty, by and with the advice and consent of the Lords Spiritual and Temporal, and Commons, in this present Parliament assembled, and by the authority of the same, as follows:—

PART I

PRELIMINARY

Short title

1. This Act may be cited as the Greater Nottingham Light Rapid Transit Act 1994.

Interpretation

2.—(1) In this Act, unless the context otherwise requires, the several words and expressions to which meanings are assigned by the Acts wholly or partly incorporated herewith have the same respective meanings, and—

"the Act of 1845" means the Railways Clauses Consolidation Act 1845;

"the Act of 1965" means the Compulsory Purchase Act 1965;

"the Act of 1991" means the New Roads and Street Works Act 1991;

"the Act of 1993" means the Railways Act 1993;

"the authorised railways" means the railways authorised by this Act, including, where the context so admits, any railway adapted for use as part of the LRT system under section 17 (Agreements with British Railways Board) of this Act;

"the authorised works" means the works (including railways) authorised by this Act;

"the City" means the City of Nottingham;

"the City Council" means the Nottingham City Council;

"the County Council" means Nottinghamshire County Council;

"enactment" means any enactment, whether public general or local, and includes any order, byelaw, rule, regulation, scheme or other instrument having effect by virtue of an enactment;

"existing" means existing at the commencement of this Act;

"land" includes land covered by water, any interest in land and any easement or right in, to or over land;

"the limits of deviation" mean the limits so shown on the deposited plans and, where, in the case of a work in any street, no such limits are shown for that work, the boundaries of the street (including any verge or roadside waste adjoining it);

"the LRT system" means the light rail transit system comprising the authorised railways including such railways designated as tramways, and all works and conveniences provided in connection with any of those railways, as that system is constructed, extended or altered from time to time;

"the railways board" means the British Railways Board or, as the case may require, any person who pursuant to the Act of 1993 succeeds (whether before or after the date of this Act) to any functions of the British Railways Board, or any other person who derives title to any property from the British Railways Board or such successor and holds that property for railway purposes;

"the rivers authority" means the National Rivers Authority;

"statutory undertakers" means any of the following, namely a licence holder within the meaning of Part I of the Electricity Act 1989, a public gas supplier within the meaning of Part I of the Gas Act 1986, a sewerage undertaker or a water undertaker;

"street" has the meaning given by section 329 of the Highways Act 1980 and in sections 19 to 22 of this Act includes a bridleway, cycle track or footpath as defined in the said section 329;

"telecommunication system" has the meaning given by section 4 of the Telecommunications Act 1984;

"traffic sign" has the meaning given by section 64 of the Road Traffic Regulation Act 1984;

"tramcar" means any vehicle (whether or not used for the carriage of passengers) carried on flanged wheels on any railway forming part of the LRT system;

"tramway" means any railway, or any part of a railway, authorised by this Act and thereby designated as a tramway;

"the tribunal" means the Lands Tribunal;

"the undertakers" means the County Council and the City Council or either of them.

(2) In the case of any street in relation to which an order made under section 249(2) of the Town and Country Planning Act 1990 (a pedestrian planning order) is in force, the kerbline of the street, where there is no kerb, shall be taken to be the edge of the part of the street on which the passage of vehicles is permitted.

(3) Unless the context otherwise requires, any reference in this Act to a work identified by the number of the work shall be construed as a reference to the work of that number authorised by this Act.

(4) References in this Act to points identified by letters, with or without numbers, shall be construed as references to the points so marked on the deposited plans.

(5)(a) Except as mentioned in paragraph (b) below, all distances and lengths stated in any description of works, powers or lands shall be construed as if the words "or thereabouts" were inserted after each such distance and length, and distances between points on a railway shall be taken to be measured along the railway.

(b) This subsection does not apply to distances or lengths stated in the following provisions of this Act:—

section 13 (Power to deviate);

section 15 (Gauge of railways and restrictions on working);

paragraph (7) of section 45 (For protection of certain statutory undertakers).

(6) Any reference in this Act to rights over land includes reference to the right to do, or to place and maintain, anything in, on or under the land, or in the air space above its surface.

(7) References in this Act to access to any place include egress from that place.

Incorporation and application of enactments relating to railways

3.—(1) The following enactments, so far as they are applicable for the purposes and are not inconsistent with or varied by the provisions of this Act, are incorporated with and form part of this Act, and this Act shall be deemed to be the special Act for the purposes of those enactments:—

the Act of 1845 (except sections 7 to 9, 11 to 15, 17, 19, 20, 22, 23, 47 to 62, 94, 95 and 115 to 124); and

section 4 of the Railways Clauses Act 1863.

(2) In the enactments incorporated by subsection (1) above—

(a) the expression "the company" means the undertakers; and

(b) sections 18 and 21 of the Act of 1845 shall not extend to regulate the relations between the undertakers and any other person in respect of any matter or thing concerning which those relations are regulated in any respect by—

(i) Part III of the Act of 1991; or

(ii) section 45 (For protection of certain statutory undertakers) of this Act;

(c) the reference in section 34 of the Act of 1845 to notice under section 33 of that Act shall include a notice under section 34 of this Act; and

(d) in section 4 of the said Act of 1863, the words "and subject to the limitations contained in sections eleven, twelve and fifteen of those Acts respectively," and the proviso shall be omitted.

(3) Notwithstanding anything in section 46 of the Act of 1845, as incorporated by subsection (1) above, or in any other enactment, the undertakers may carry any of the authorised railways, not being designated as a tramway, across and on the level of any footpath without obtaining the consent of two or more justices.

(4) The following enactments shall not apply to the LRT system:—

the Highway (Railway Crossings) Act 1839;

in the Railway Regulation Act 1842, sections 9 and 10;

in the Regulation of Railways Act 1868, section 22;

in the Regulation of Railways Act 1889, sections 1 to 4 and 8;

in the Road and Rail Traffic Act 1933, section 42.

Application of Street Works Acts and Road Traffic Regulation Act 1984

4.—(1) In relation to so much of the authorised works as would, if executed by the highway authority, be works for road purposes or major highway works within the meanings given by section 86 of the Act of 1991, Part III of that Act shall have effect as if the undertakers were the highway authority.

(2) Part III of the Act of 1991 shall not extend to regulate the relations between the undertakers and a highway authority in respect of any matter or thing concerning which those relations are regulated by section 39 (As to highways, traffic, etc.) of this Act.

(3) Section 45(17)(b) (betterment arising on provision of alternative apparatus for statutory undertakers) of this Act shall have effect notwithstanding the repeal by the Act of 1991 of the Public Utilities Street Works Act 1950.

(4) Section 14 of the Road Traffic Regulation Act 1984 (temporary restriction or prohibition of the use of roads by vehicles in certain circumstances) shall apply to tramcars used on tramways forming part of the LRT system.

(5) Section 65(1) of the Road Traffic Regulation Act 1984 (placing of traffic signs by highway authorities) shall have effect with respect to the erection and display of any traffic sign by the undertakers as if it were a traffic sign erected and displayed by the traffic authority.

Application of Part I of Compulsory Purchase Act 1965

5.—(1) Part I of the Act of 1965 (except section 4 and paragraph 3(3) of Schedule 3), in so far as it is applicable for the purposes and is not inconsistent with the provisions of this Act, shall apply to the compulsory acquisition of land under this Act as it applies to a compulsory purchase to which Part II of the Acquisition of Land Act 1981 applies and as if this Act were a compulsory purchase order under the said Act of 1981.

(2) Section 11(1) of the Act of 1965 (which relates to notice of entry) as so applied shall have effect as if for the word "fourteen" there were substituted, in respect of the lands over which rights only are required, the word "twenty-eight" and, in the case of any other lands, the word "ninety-one".

(3) The Lands Clauses Consolidation Act 1845 shall not apply to the acquisition of land under this Act.

PART II

WORKS

Power to make works

6.—(1) Subject to the provisions of this Act, the undertakers may, in the lines or situations shown on the deposited plans and according to the levels shown on the deposited sections, make and maintain the works specified in Part I of Schedule 1 to this Act, with all necessary works and conveniences connected therewith.

(2) Notwithstanding anything in this Act or shown on the deposited plans or the deposited sections, but without prejudice to the provisions of section 13 (Power to deviate) of this Act, the undertakers may, subject to the approval of the Secretary of State, construct the whole or part of so much of Work No. 9 as is to be situated to the west of Bagnall Road within the limits of deviation in accordance with dimensions and descriptions other than the dimensions and descriptions shown on the deposited plans and the deposited sections or specified in Part I of Schedule 1 to this Act.

Further works and powers

7.—(1) Subject to the provisions of this Act (and, in so far as the same are shown on the deposited plans and sections, in the lines or situations and according to the levels so shown), the undertakers may exercise the powers, and make and maintain the further works, described in Part II of Schedule 1 to this Act, with all necessary works and conveniences connected therewith.

(2) Without prejudice to the specific powers conferred by subsection (1) above, for the purposes of constructing or maintaining the authorised railways in or adjoining any street, the undertakers may, with the consent of the highway authority—

(a) increase the width of the carriageway of the street by reducing the width of any footway, cycle track or verge or other land within the boundary of the street;

(b) alter or interfere with the level of any kerb, footway, cycle track, verge or other land within the boundary of the street; or

(c) at any stopping place on a tramway reduce the width of the carriageway of the street by forming a reserved area in the street or by setting forward the kerbline of the street and providing access for vehicles to adjoining premises and a footway on the side of that kerbline nearest to those premises.

(3) Where the carriageway, or part of the carriageway, of any street in which a tramway is laid is of sufficient width to provide not less than 3 metres of width for vehicular traffic clear of the tramway path (as determined in accordance with the clearance required by the Secretary of State), the undertakers may, with the consent of the highway authority, carry out such works as may be required to deter, but not prevent, the passage of vehicular traffic along the tramway, whether by raising or lowering the level of the part of the carriageway occupied by the tramway path above or below the level of the adjoining carriageway or by placing a kerb or other obstruction along the edge of that adjoining carriageway.

(4)(a) Subject to the provisions of this Act, the undertakers may—
  (i) lay down double lines in lieu of single lines or single lines in lieu of double lines or interlacing lines in lieu of double or single lines on any of the tramways, either when constructing it or at any time thereafter, and construct or take up and reconstruct any such tramway or associated work in such position in the street or land in which it is authorised to be constructed as they think fit; and
  (ii) make, maintain, alter and remove such crossings, passing places, sidings, junctions and other works, in addition to those specified in and authorised by this Act, as they find necessary or convenient for the efficient working of the LRT system, for the purposes of the control of traffic or for providing access to any premises.

(b) The powers of paragraph (a) above shall not be exercised in any street which is a highway without the consent of the highway authority.

(5)(a) When, by reason of the carrying out of any work affecting any road along or across which any tramway is laid, it is, in the opinion of the undertakers, necessary or expedient temporarily to remove or discontinue the use of that tramway, or any part thereof, the undertakers may, with the consent of the highway authority, construct and maintain, in the same or any adjacent road, a temporary tramway in lieu of the length of tramway so removed or discontinued.

(b) If the undertakers alter the route of a tramway under paragraph (a) above, they shall, in accordance with section 8(2) of this Act, provide traffic signs to give warning of such alteration and any associated traffic arrangements.

(6) Notwithstanding anything in section 68 of the Act of 1845, where any part of a railway is constructed on any verge or roadside waste comprised in a road, the undertakers shall not be required to fence that part of that railway.

Provisions as to tramways

8.—(1) The tramways shall be so laid and maintained that—
  (a) except as provided in section 7(3) of this Act, the uppermost surface of the rails is level with the surrounding surfaces of the street in which they are laid; and
  (b) the distance between the sides of the widest tramcars to be used on the tramways when passing one another thereon shall not be less than 380 millimetres (15 inches).

(2)(a) On completion of any tramway the undertakers shall provide traffic signs to give warning to other traffic of the presence of the tramway.

(b) Subject to any directions and any other requirements given or imposed by the Secretary of State with respect to such a traffic sign, the places at which the traffic signs are displayed shall be such as may be approved by the highway authority.

(3)(a) Where a tramway has been constructed in a street in such manner that—

    (i) the uppermost surface of the rails is level with the surface of the street; or

    (ii) the level of the width of the carriageway occupied by the tramway path is altered as provided in section 7(3) of this Act;

works for the purpose, or having the effect, of altering the level of the part of the street in which the tramway is situated shall not be carried out without the consent of the undertakers.

(b) Consent under paragraph (a) above may be given subject to such reasonable terms and conditions as the undertakers may require, but shall not be unreasonably withheld, and any difference arising under this paragraph shall be determined by the Secretary of State.

Level crossings

9.—(1) The undertakers may, in the construction of the railways authorised by this Act, carry the same with a double line across and on the level of the streets, footpaths, cycleways and other ways specified in Schedule 2 to this Act.

(2) In the exercise of the powers of subsection (1) above, the undertakers may alter or interfere with the level of any footway or cycleway upon which any railway or associated work is to be laid.

Subsidiary works

10.—(1) Subject to the provisions of this Act the undertakers may, for the purposes of the LRT system and associated traffic control—

    (a) within the limits of deviation make, lay down, place, erect, repair, alter, renew, maintain, operate and use rails, rail fixings, plates, sleepers, channels, conduits, tubes, stations, platforms, islands, gates, junctions, points, turntables, turnouts, crossings, temporary or permanent cross-overs, passing places, pillars, posts, poles, brackets, wires, subways, manholes, shafts, engines, dynamos, substations, transformers, switchgear, cabling, signalling, monitoring and communications equipment, together with subsidiary and incidental machinery, apparatus, works and appliances;

    (b) in, or under any street in which it may be necessary or convenient, or in other land over which the undertakers have or obtain sufficient right, lay, place, erect, maintain, renew and repair electric wires, conductors, cables, brackets, posts, tubes, substations, boxes and other electrical apparatus for connecting the authorised railways and associated works with any electricity generating station or substations or for the purposes of signalling, monitoring and communication in connection with the LRT system; and

    (c) alter the position of mains, sewers, cables and other apparatus.

(2)(a) For the purposes of exercising their powers under subsection (1) above in relation to any apparatus or works, or of inspecting or removing apparatus or works, the undertakers may break open any road, and any sewer, drain or tunnel in or under any road, and may remove and use the soil or other materials in or under the road.

(b) In exercising their powers under this subsection the undertakers shall do as little damage as may be, and for any damage done shall (in so far as the matter of compensation is not governed by the provisions of Part III of the Act of 1991) pay compensation to be determined, in case of dispute, in accordance with Part I of the Land Compensation Act 1961.

Footpaths and cycleways at Cinderhill

11. Notwithstanding anything shown on the deposited plans and sections the undertakers, if they proceed with the construction of Work No. 9—

(a) shall not stop up and discontinue so much of the footpath and cycleway at Cinderhill in the City as is between the points marked H1 and H2 on the deposited plans, but shall lower the surface thereof between those points to such extent as will enable pedestrians and cyclists to use the said footpath and cycleway where it is crossed by the bridge over the river Leen comprised in Work No. 9;

(b) shall lay out the new footpath and cycleway authorised by section 7 (Further works and powers) of, and paragraph (33) of Part II of Schedule 1 to, this Act with convenient ramps for use by pedestrians and cyclists.

Provision of accommodation for apparatus

12. Where the undertakers lay down conduits for the accommodation of cables or other apparatus for the purposes of the LRT system or associated traffic control under section 10 above, they may, in pursuance of those powers, provide in, or in connection with, such conduits accommodation for the apparatus of any other person, and manholes and other facilities for access to such accommodation, and may permit the use of such conduits and facilities on such terms and conditions as may be agreed between the undertakers and such other person.

Power to deviate

13. In the execution of the authorised works the undertakers may, except as may be otherwise provided by this Act, deviate from the lines or situations thereof shown on the deposited plans to the extent of the limits of deviation and deviate vertically from the levels shown on the deposited sections to any extent not exceeding 3 metres upwards and to such extent downwards as may be found necessary or convenient.

Plans to be approved by Secretary of State before works commenced

14.—(1) Before constructing any of the authorised railways the undertakers shall submit to the Secretary of State for his approval plans, sections and particulars of their proposals concerning—

(a) permanent way, track or stations;

(b) signalling; and

(c) lighting.

(2) Any such works shall be constructed and maintained in accordance with such plans, sections and particulars approved by the Secretary of State.

Gauge of railways and restrictions on working

15.—(1) The railways shall be constructed on a gauge of 1,435 millimetres (4 feet 8½ inches) and the motive power to be used shall be electrical energy or such other motive power as the Secretary of State may approve.

(2) No part of the LRT system shall be used for, or in connection with, the conveyance of passengers without the written permission of the Secretary of State and the undertakers shall comply with the conditions (if any) which the Secretary of State may from time to time prescribe for the safety of persons using the LRT system.

(3) If, without reasonable excuse, the undertakers contravene the provisions of subsection (2) above they shall be guilty of an offence and liable on summary conviction to a fine not exceeding level 5 on the standard scale.

(4) Without prejudice to the generality of subsection (2) above, traction cables of the overhead line equipment of any tramway, and of so much of any

authorised railway as is comprised in any level crossing shall be erected at a height agreed by the Secretary of State and, if at any place a height of less than 5·63 metres (18 feet 6 inches) above the surface of the ground is so agreed for a cable, the undertakers shall, in accordance with section 8(2) of this Act, erect such traffic signs as may be directed by the Secretary of State to give warning of the cable.

Operation and use of tramways

16.—(1) Subject to subsection (3) below and to section 71 (Powers of disposal, agreements for operation, etc.) of this Act, the undertakers shall, for the purpose of operating the tramways, have the exclusive right to use the rails, foundations, cables, masts, overhead wires and other apparatus provided for their operation.

(2) Any person who, without the consent of the undertakers or other reasonable excuse, uses any tramway, or other apparatus mentioned in subsection (1) above, for the passage of vehicles having wheels suitable only for running on the rails of such tramways shall be guilty of an offence and liable on summary conviction to a fine not exceeding level 2 on the standard scale.

(3) Nothing in this section shall restrict the exercise of any public right of way over any part of a road in which a tramway, or other apparatus mentioned in subsection (1) above, is situated except to the extent to which the exercise of that right is constrained by—

(a) the presence of the tramway or such other apparatus; or

(b) the exercise of the powers of section 7(3) of this Act.

Agreements with British Railways Board

17.—(1) The undertakers and the railways board may enter into, and carry into effect, agreements for the transfer to, and vesting in, the undertakers of any or any part of the existing railways of the railways board within or adjoining the limits of deviation of the authorised works, together with all lands and other property held in connection with that railway and all rights and obligations of the railways board in relation to that railway.

(2) Where agreement is made for the transfer to, and vesting in, the undertakers of any existing railway of the railways board under subsection (1) above, or the undertakers otherwise acquire any such existing railway or sufficient rights therein, the undertakers may adapt for use, maintain, use and work that railway as part of the LRT system in accordance with the provisions of the Act of 1845 and the Railways Clauses Act 1863 incorporated with this Act and the provisions of the Railway Regulation Acts 1840 to 1889 applicable to the LRT system.

(3) Any enactment by which any such existing railway was authorised, including the enactments specified in Schedule 3 to this Act, shall have effect subject to the provisions of this Act.

(4) The provisions of sections 54 and 56 of the Transport Act 1962 (advance notice of discontinuance of certain services to be published and functions of transport consultative committees) and of sections 37 to 50 of, and Schedule 5 to, the Act of 1993 (closure of railway passenger services, passenger networks, etc.) shall not apply in respect of the discontinuance of any existing railway passenger services from any station or on any line or, as the case may be, the discontinuance of any railway passenger or goods services provided by the railways board, where such discontinuance is for the purposes of, or in connection with, the construction of the authorised works or the transfer of any parts of the existing railways to form part of the LRT system.

Temporary stoppage of highways

18.—(1) During and for the purpose of the execution of the authorised works, the undertakers may temporarily stop up and interfere with the whole or any part of any street to the extent of the limits of deviation, or, if different, the limits of land to be acquired or used shown on the deposited plans, and may for any reasonable time divert the traffic therefrom and prevent all persons, other than those bona fide going to or from any land, house or building abutting on the said part of the street, from passing along and using the same.

(2) The undertakers shall provide reasonable access for foot passengers bona fide going to or from any such land, house or building.

Stopping-up streets and footpaths without providing substitute

19.—(1) After the stopping up of any part of any street under this Act, other than under section 18 (Temporary stoppage of highways) of this Act, without the provision of a substitute, all rights of way over or along the street, or portion thereof, authorised to be stopped up shall be extinguished and the undertakers may, without making any payment therefor, but subject to the provisions of the Act of 1845 incorporated with this Act with respect to mines lying under or near the railways, appropriate and use for the purposes of their undertaking the site of the street or portion thereof, so stopped up.

(2) Any person who suffers loss by the extinguishment of any private right under this section shall be entitled to be paid by the undertakers compensation to be determined in case of dispute by the tribunal.

Stopping-up streets and footpaths in case of diversion or substitution

20.—(1) Except as provided in section 18 of this Act, where this Act authorises the making of a new street, either by way of diversion of, or in substitution for, an existing street and the stopping-up of the existing street or portion thereof, the stopping-up shall not, in either case, take place until the highway authority are satisfied that the new street has been completed in accordance with their reasonable requirements and is open for public use or, in the case of any difference between the undertakers and the highway authority as to whether the said requirements have been complied with or as to their reasonableness, until the matter in dispute has been determined by arbitration and the new street has been completed accordingly.

(2) Before referring the matter to arbitration under this section the undertakers shall give to the highway authority 7 days' notice in writing of their intention to do so.

(3) As from the completion of the new street to the satisfaction of the highway authority or, in the case of dispute, according to the decision of the arbitrator, all rights of way over or along the existing street, or portion thereof, authorised to be diverted or stopped-up shall be extinguished, and the undertakers may, without making any payment therefor, but subject to the provisions of the Act of 1845 incorporated with this Act with respect to mines lying under or near the railways, appropriate and use for the purposes of their undertaking the site of the street, or portion thereof, diverted or stopped-up so far as the same is bounded on both sides by lands in the possession of the undertakers.

(4) Any person who suffers loss by the extinguishment of any private right under subsection (3) of this section shall be entitled to be paid by the undertakers compensation to be determined in case of dispute by the tribunal.

Provisions as to repair of streets, footpaths, etc.

21.—(1) Any street, or portion thereof, made, diverted or altered under this Act shall, when completed, unless otherwise agreed, be maintained by and at the expense of the undertakers for a period of 12 months from its completion and at the expiration of that period shall be maintained by and at the expense of the highway authority.

(2) The undertakers shall not, by reason of the obligation to maintain any street under subsection (1) above, be taken to be the street authority in relation to that street for the purposes of Part III of the Act of 1991.

Underpinning of houses near works

22. The undertakers may, at their own expense, subject as hereinafter provided, underpin or otherwise strengthen any house or building within 30 metres of any of the authorised works, and for that purpose the following provisions shall have effect:—

(a) At least 28 days' notice shall (except in case of emergency) be given to the owner, lessee and occupier of the house or building intended to be so underpinned or otherwise strengthened:

(b) Each such notice shall be served in manner prescribed by section 6 of the Acquisition of Land Act 1981 as if required to be served under that Act:

(c) If any owner, lessee or occupier of any such house or building shall, within 21 days after the giving of such notice, give a counter-notice in writing that he disputes the necessity of such underpinning or strengthening, the question of the necessity shall be settled by arbitration:

(d) In any case in which any house or building shall have been underpinned or strengthened under the powers of this section the undertakers may, from time to time after the completion of such underpinning or strengthening, and during the execution of the authorised work in connection with which such underpinning or strengthening was done, or within five years after the opening for traffic of the authorised works, enter upon and survey such house or building and, after complying with the foregoing provisions of this section, do such further underpinning or strengthening as they may deem necessary or expedient:

(e) The undertakers shall be liable to compensate the owner, lessee and occupier of every such house or building for any loss or damage which they may suffer by reason of the exercise of the powers of this section:

(f) Nothing in this section shall affect liability to compensate under section 6 of the Act of 1845 or section 10(2) of the Act of 1965 as incorporated or applied by this Act, or under any other enactment, except in so far as compensation is payable under paragraph (e) above:

(g) Compensation payable under this section shall be determined, in case of dispute, in accordance with Part I of the Land Compensation Act 1961.

Use of sewers, etc., for removing water

23.—(1) The undertakers may use for the discharge of any water pumped or found during the construction of the authorised works any available stream or watercourse, or any sewer or drain of the relevant authority, and for that purpose may lay down, take up and alter conduits, pipes and other works and may make any convenient connections with any such stream, watercourse, sewer or drain.

(2)(a) The undertakers shall not—

(i) discharge any water into any sewer or drain vested in or under the control of the relevant authority except with the consent of that authority and subject to such terms and conditions as that authority may reasonably impose; or

(ii) make any opening into any such sewer or drain except in accordance with plans approved by, and under the superintendence (if given) of, the relevant authority.

(b) Consent to a discharge, or approval of plans submitted, under this subsection shall not be unreasonably withheld.

(3)(a) Section 85 of the Water Resources Act 1991 shall apply to, or to the consequence of, a discharge under this section into any controlled waters within the meaning given by section 104 of that Act as if this section were excluded from the reference to any local statutory provision mentioned in section 88(1)(f) of that Act.

(b) In the exercise of their powers under this section the undertakers shall not damage or interfere with the bed of any watercourse forming part of a main river of the rivers authority or the banks thereof within the meaning of section 72 of the Land Drainage Act 1991.

(4) The undertakers shall take all such steps as may be reasonably required to secure that any water discharged under this section shall be as free as may be reasonably practicable from any gravel, soil or other solid substance or matter in suspension.

(5) Any difference arising between the undertakers and the rivers authority, sewerage undertaker or local authority, as the case may be, under this section shall be determined by arbitration.

(6) In this section "the relevant authority" means the City Council or any sewerage undertaker.

Attachment of brackets, etc., to buildings for purposes of works

24.—(1) The undertakers may affix brackets, cables, wires and other apparatus required in connection with the LRT system to any building or structure: and for that purpose the provisions of subsections (2), (4) to (6), (8) and (9) of section 45 of the Public Health Act 1961 (affixing apparatus to buildings for street lighting) shall apply as if—

(a) the attachments therein mentioned included any such apparatus; and

(b) for the reference to the street lighting authority there were substituted reference to the undertakers.

(2) For the purpose of the provisions of the said section 45 applied by subsection (1) above, consent to the affixing of attachments to a building under subsection (2) of that section shall be deemed to have been withheld if no such consent is received by the undertakers before the expiration of the period of 56 days beginning on the date on which the undertakers serve on the owner of the building, in accordance with section 285 of the Public Health Act 1936, notice of an application for such consent.

Provisions as to use of electrical energy

25. The following provisions shall apply to the use of electrical energy for the purposes of the LRT system:—

(1) The undertakers shall employ either insulated returns or uninsulated metallic returns of low resistance.

(2) The undertakers shall take all reasonable precautions in designing, constructing, placing and maintaining their electric lines and circuits and other works of all descriptions and also in working the LRT system so as to minimise the discharge of electrical currents into the ground and not—

(a) injuriously to affect by fusion or electrolytic action any electric lines or any gas or water pipes, or other metallic pipes, structures or substances; or

(b) injuriously to interfere with, or with the working of—
    (i) any wire, line or apparatus from time to time used for the purpose of transmitting electrical energy or of any telecommunication system; or
    (ii) the currents in any such wire, line or apparatus.

(3) (a) The Secretary of State may make regulations under this section for regulating the use of electrical energy for the operation of the LRT system, and the design, voltage, testing and working of the overhead equipment and return circuits of the LRT system, including regulations—
    (i) for preventing injurious affection (by the discharge of electrical currents into the ground, fusion or electrolytic action) of electric lines or gas or water pipes or other metallic pipes, structures or substances; and
    (ii) for minimising, so far as is reasonably practicable, interference with, and with the working of, electric wires, lines and apparatus, whether such apparatus does or does not use the earth as a return.

(b) Before making regulations under this section the Secretary of State shall consult the undertakers and the statutory undertakers.

(4) The undertakers shall be deemed to take all reasonable and proper precautions against interference with, or with the working of, any wire, line or apparatus if and so long as they use, at the option of the undertakers, either such insulated returns, or such uninsulated metallic returns of low resistance and such other means of preventing injurious interference with, and with the working of, the electric wires, lines and apparatus, as may be prescribed by the regulations; and in prescribing such means the Secretary of State shall have regard to the expense involved in relation to the protection afforded.

(5) The provisions of this section shall not give any right of action in respect of injurious interference with, or with the working of, any electric wire, line or apparatus, or the currents therein, unless, in the construction, erection, maintaining and working of such wire, line and apparatus, all reasonable and proper precautions, including the use of an insulated return, have been taken to minimise injurious interference therewith, and with the currents therein, by or from other electric currents.

(6) If any difference arises between the undertakers and any other person with respect to anything in the foregoing provisions of this section, the difference shall, unless the parties otherwise agree, be determined by the Secretary of State, or, at his option by an arbitrator to be appointed by him, and the costs of such determination shall be in the discretion of the Secretary of State or the arbitrator as the case may be.

(7) The power to make regulations conferred on the Secretary of State by this section shall be exercisable by statutory instrument.

(8) In this section reference to an insulated return includes reference to a return by means of a combined neutral and earth cable which is covered by an insulated sheath suitable for protection against corrosion and is approved for use below ground by the Secretary of State for the purpose of any regulations relating to the supply of electricity.

PART III

LANDS

Power to acquire lands

26. Subject to the provisions of this Act, the undertakers may enter upon, take and use—

   (a) so much of the land delineated on the deposited plans and described in the deposited book of reference as they may require for the purposes of the authorised works or for any purpose connected with, or ancillary to, their undertaking including (without prejudice to the generality of the foregoing) the provision of parking facilities for road vehicles and means of access thereto; and

   (b) so much of any land specified in columns (2) and (3) of Schedule 4 to this Act shown on the deposited plans within the limits delineated by the line marked "limit of land to be acquired or used" as they may require for the purpose specified in relation to that land in column (1) of that Schedule.

Extinction of private rights of way

27.—(1) All private rights of way over any land that may be acquired compulsorily under this Act shall be extinguished on the acquisition of the land, whether compulsorily or by agreement, or on entry on the land in pursuance of section 11(1) of the Act of 1965 as applied by this Act, whichever is the sooner.

(2) All private rights of way over land owned by the undertakers which, being within the limits of deviation or the limits delineated on the deposited plans by the line marked "limit of land to be acquired or used", is required for the purposes of this Act shall be extinguished on the appropriation of the land for any of those purposes by the undertakers.

(3) Any person who suffers loss by the extinguishment of any right under this section shall be entitled to compensation to be determined, in case of dispute, in accordance with Part I of the Land Compensation Act 1961.

Power to acquire new rights

28.—(1) In this section references to the purchase by the undertakers of new rights are references to the purchase of rights to be created in favour of the undertakers.

(2) The undertakers may, for the purposes of constructing, maintaining, protecting, renewing and using any of the authorised works, purchase compulsorily such new rights as they may require over any of the lands that may be acquired compulsorily under this Act instead of acquiring those lands.

(3) The Act of 1965 as applied by this Act shall have effect with the modifications necessary to make it apply to the compulsory purchase of rights under subsection (2) above as it applies to the compulsory purchase of land so that, in appropriate contexts, references in that Act to land are read as referring, or as including references, to the rights or to land over which the rights are or are to be exercisable, according to the requirements of the context.

(4) Without prejudice to the generality of subsection (3) above, in relation to the purchase of rights under subsection (2) above—

   (a) Part I of the Act of 1965 shall have effect with the modifications specified in Schedule 5 to this Act; and

   (b) the enactments relating to compensation for the compulsory purchase of land shall apply with the necessary modifications as they apply to such compensation.

Acquisition of part only of certain properties

29.—(1) Where a copy of this section is endorsed on, or annexed to, a notice to treat served under the Act of 1965 as applied by this Act, the following provisions of this section shall apply to the land subject to the notice instead of section 8(1) of that Act.

(2) Where the land subject to the notice is part only of a house, building or factory, or part only of land consisting of a house together with any park or garden belonging thereto, then, if the person on whom the notice is served,

within 21 days after the day on which the notice is served on him, serves on the undertakers a counter-notice objecting to the sale of the part and stating that he is willing and able to sell the whole (hereafter in this section referred to as "the land subject to the counter-notice"), the question whether he shall be required to sell the part shall, unless the undertakers agree to take the land subject to the counter-notice, be referred to the tribunal.

(3) If the said person does not serve such a counter-notice as aforesaid within 21 days after the day on which the notice to treat is served on him, or if on such a reference to the tribunal the tribunal determine that the part subject to the notice to treat can be taken without material detriment to the remainder of the land subject to the counter-notice or, in the case of part of land consisting of a house together with a park or garden belonging thereto, without material detriment to the remainder of the land subject to the counter-notice and without seriously affecting the amenity and convenience of the house, the said person shall be required to sell the part.

(4) If, on such a reference to the tribunal, the tribunal determine that part only of the land subject to the notice to treat can be taken without material detriment to the remainder of the land subject to the counter-notice or, as the case may be, without material detriment to the remainder of the land subject to the counter-notice and without seriously affecting the amenity and convenience of the house, the notice to treat shall be deemed to be a notice to treat for that part.

(5) If, on such a reference to the tribunal, the tribunal determine that the land subject to the notice to treat cannot be taken without material detriment to the remainder of the land subject to the counter-notice but that the material detriment is confined to a part of the land subject to the counter-notice, the notice to treat shall be deemed to be a notice to treat for the land to which the material detriment is confined in addition to the land already subject to the notice, whether or not the additional land is land which the undertakers are authorised to acquire compulsorily under this Act.

(6) If the undertakers agree to take the land subject to the counter-notice, or if the tribunal determine that—

(a) none of the land subject to the notice to treat can be taken without material detriment to the remainder of the land subject to the counter-notice or, as the case may be, without material detriment to the remainder of the land subject to the counter-notice and without seriously affecting the amenity and convenience of the house; and

(b) the material detriment is not confined to a part of the land subject to the counter-notice;

the notice to treat shall be deemed to be a notice to treat for the land subject to the counter-notice, whether or not the whole of that land is land which the undertakers are authorised to acquire compulsorily under this Act.

(7) In any case where, by virtue of a determination by the tribunal under subsection (4), (5) or (6) above, a notice to treat is deemed to be a notice to treat for part of the land specified in the notice or for more land than is specified in the notice, the undertakers may, within six weeks after the tribunal make their determination, withdraw the notice to treat, and if they do so shall pay to the person on whom the notice was served compensation for any loss or expense occasioned to him by the giving and withdrawal of the notice, to be determined in default of agreement by the tribunal.

(8) For the purposes of subsection (7) above, the determination shall not be taken to have been made so long as—

(a) the time for requiring the tribunal to state a case with respect to the determination has not expired;

(b) any proceedings on points raised by a case stated have not been concluded; or

(c) any proceedings on appeal from any decision on points raised by a case stated have not been concluded.

(9) Where a person is required under this section to sell part only of a house, building or factory, or of land consisting of a house together with any park or garden belonging thereto, the undertakers shall pay him compensation for any loss sustained by him due to the severance of that part in addition to the value of his interest therein.

Disregard of recent improvements and interests

30. In determining a question with respect to compensation claimed in consequence of the compulsory acquisition of land (including rights) under this Act, the tribunal shall not take into account—

(a) any interest in land; or

(b) any enhancement of the value of any interest in land, by reason of any building erected, works executed or improvement or alteration made, whether on the land acquired, or, as the case may be, on the land over which rights are acquired, or on any other land with which the claimant is, or was, at the time of erection, executing or making of the building, works, improvement or alteration, directly or indirectly concerned;

if the tribunal are satisfied that the creation of the interest, the erection of the building, the execution of the works or the making of the improvement or alteration, as the case may be, was not reasonably necessary and was undertaken with a view to obtaining compensation or increased compensation.

Set-off for enhancement in value of retained land

31.—(1) In this section "relevant land" means any land or any new rights over any land purchased by the undertakers for the purposes of the authorised works.

(2) In assessing the compensation payable to any person on the acquisition or purchase by the undertakers from him of any relevant land, the tribunal shall set off against the value of the relevant land any increase in value of any contiguous or adjacent lands belonging to the same person in the same capacity, or of the land over which new rights are acquired, which will accrue to him by reason of the construction of any of the authorised works.

(3) The Land Compensation Act 1961 shall have effect subject to the provisions of this section.

Grant of rights by persons under disability

32.—(1) Any person empowered by the Act of 1965 as applied by this Act to sell and convey or release lands may, if he thinks fit, subject to the provisions of the Act of 1965, grant to the undertakers any right required for the purposes of this Act over the lands.

(2) Nothing in this section shall be construed as empowering persons to grant any right of water in which any other person has an interest, unless that other person concurs in the grant.

(3) The provisions of the Act of 1965 with respect to lands and rent-charges so far as they are applicable shall extend and apply to any such grant and to any such right as aforesaid.

Compensation in respect of depreciation in value of interest in land subject to mortgage

33. Where an interest in land is subject to a mortgage—

(a) any compensation which is payable under this Act in respect of the depreciation in value of that interest shall be calculated as if the interest were not subject to the mortgage;

(b) a claim for the payment of any such compensation may be made by any mortgagee of the interest under a mortgage made before the happening of the event giving rise to the compensation, but without prejudice to the making of a claim by any other person;

(c) a mortgagee shall not be entitled to claim any such compensation in respect of his interest as such; and

(d) any such compensation payable in respect of the interest subject to the mortgage shall be paid to the mortgagee or, where there is more than one mortgagee, to the first mortgagee, and shall in either case be applied by him as if it were proceeds of sale.

Temporary possession of land

34.—(1) In this section "the relevant land" means any of the lands in the City numbered 15, 16, 17, 18, 19, 21, 22, 107, 112, 113, 114 and 162 on the deposited plans, and any of the lands in the district of Ashfield numbered 19 on the deposited plans, shown on the deposited plans within the limits delineated by the line marked "limit of land to be acquired or used" and specified in Schedule 4 to this Act.

(2) Subject to the provisions of this section, the undertakers may take temporary possession of and use the relevant land for the provision of working sites and access for construction purposes, and for that purpose may remove any structures and vegetation on the land.

(3) Not less than 28 days before entering upon and taking temporary possession of the relevant land the undertakers shall give notice to the owners and occupiers of the land.

(4) All private rights of way over any land of which the undertakers take possession under this Act shall be suspended and unenforceable against the undertakers for so long as they shall remain in lawful possession of the land.

(5)(a) The undertakers shall not, without the agreement of the owners and occupiers, remain in possession of any part of the relevant land under the powers of this section after a period of 18 months from the completion of the work of construction for which possession was required.

(b) Before giving up possession of the relevant land, the undertakers shall remove all temporary works and, subject to any agreement to the contrary with the owners and occupiers of the land, restore the relevant land to the reasonable satisfaction of the owners and occupiers thereof.

(6)(a) The undertakers shall not be empowered to purchase compulsorily, or be required to purchase, any part of the relevant land of which they take possession under this section.

(b) The undertakers shall compensate the owners and occupiers of the relevant land for any loss or damage which may result to them by reason of the exercise of the powers of this section in relation to the relevant land.

(c) Nothing in this section shall relieve the undertakers from liability to compensate under section 6 or 43 of the Act of 1845 or section 10(2) of the Act of 1965 as incorporated or applied by this Act, or under any other enactment, in respect of loss or damage arising from the execution of any works, other than loss or damage for which compensation is payable under paragraph (b) above.

(7) Compensation payable under this section shall be determined, in case of dispute, in accordance with Part I of the Land Compensation Act 1961.

Correction of errors in deposited plans and book of reference

35.—(1) If the deposited plans or the deposited book of reference are inaccurate in their description of any land, or in their statement or description of the ownership or occupation of any land, the undertakers, after giving not less than 10 days' notice to the owner, lessee and occupier of the land in question, may apply to two justices having jurisdiction in the place where the land is situated for the correction thereof.

(2) If on any such application it appears to the justices that the misstatement or wrong description arose from mistake or inadvertence, the justices shall certify the fact accordingly and shall in their certificate state in what respect any matter is misstated or wrongly described.

(3) The certificate shall be deposited in the office of the Clerk of the Parliaments, and a copy thereof in the Private Bill Office, House of Commons, and with the proper officer of the district council for the area in which the land is situated and thereupon the deposited plans and the deposited book of reference shall be deemed to be corrected according to the certificate, and it shall be lawful for the undertakers to take the land or, as the case may be, a right over the land and execute the works in accordance with the certificate.

(4) A person with whom a copy of the certificate is deposited under this section shall keep it with the other documents to which it relates.

Period of compulsory purchase of lands or rights

36.—(1) The powers of the undertakers for the compulsory acquisition of the lands and rights which they are authorised to acquire by this Part of this Act shall not be exercised after the expiration of five years from the passing of this Act.

(2) The powers of the undertakers for the compulsory acquisition of the said lands and rights shall, for the purposes of this section, be deemed to have been exercised if notice to treat has been served in respect of those lands and rights.

Acquisition of land in advance of requirements

37. Without prejudice to the generality of their powers to acquire land by agreement under section 120 of the Local Government Act 1972 and section 26 of the Land Compensation Act 1973, the undertakers may acquire by agreement any land in their area which, in their opinion—

(a) is likely to be required for the development of a light rail transit network in their area; or

(b) by reason of published proposals indicating that it might be so required, is a hereditament in respect of which a valid blight notice could have been served on them under section 150 or 161 of the Town and Country Planning Act 1990 if it were land of the description specified in paragraph 21 of Schedule 13 to the said Act of 1990.

PART IV

PROTECTIVE PROVISIONS

Notice to police, etc.

38. Before breaking up or otherwise interfering with any street in connection with the construction of the LRT system the undertakers shall give not less than 14 days' notice to the chief officer of police and to the fire authority of their intention to do so, except in the case of emergency when such notice as is practicable shall be given.

As to highways, traffic, etc.

39. For the protection of highway authorities the following provisions shall, unless otherwise agreed in writing between the undertakers and the highway authority concerned, have effect:—

(1) In this section "highway" means a street vested in, or repairable or maintained by, the highway authority:

(2) Wherever in this section provision is made with respect to the approval or consent of the highway authority, that approval or consent shall be in writing and may be given subject to such reasonable terms and conditions as the highway authority may require, but shall not be unreasonably withheld:

(3) Before commencing to construct any part of the authorised works which will involve interference with a highway, or the traffic in any highway, or before temporarily stopping up any highway, the undertakers shall consult the highway authority as to—

    (a) the time when such part shall be commenced;

    (b) the extent of the surface of the highway which it may be reasonably necessary for the undertakers to occupy, or the nature of the interference which may be caused to that traffic in the construction of such part; or

    (c) the time during which, and the extent to which, such highway shall be stopped up; and

    (d) the conditions under which such part shall be constructed or the highway shall be stopped up;

so as to reduce so far as possible inconvenience to the public and to ensure the safety of the public; and

    (i) such part shall not be constructed and the surface of the highway shall not be occupied by the undertakers; or

    (ii) such highway shall not be stopped up and the interference with traffic shall not be caused by the undertakers;

except at such time, to such extent, and in accordance with such conditions, as may be agreed between the undertakers and the highway authority or determined by arbitration:

(4) At least 14 days before commencing to make any trial holes in any part of any highway in exercise of the powers of section 11(3) of the Act of 1965 as applied by this Act, the undertakers shall serve notice in writing on the highway authority of their intention to do so describing the place or places at which the trial holes are intended to be made, and, if within 14 days after the receipt of such notice any objection is made by the highway authority, the matter shall (unless otherwise agreed) be determined by arbitration before the making of any trial hole is commenced, but if no such objection is made the undertakers may proceed with the making of any trial hole of which notice has been so given:

(5) So much of the authorised works as is intended to become public highway, or part of any such highway, shall be completed in accordance with the reasonable requirements of the local highway authority or, in case of difference between the undertakers and the highway authority as to whether those requirements have been complied with or as to their reasonableness, in accordance with the determination of the Secretary of State upon any such difference:

(6) It shall be lawful for the proper officer of the highway authority at all reasonable times, on giving to the undertakers such notice as may in the circumstances be reasonable, to enter upon and inspect any part of the authorised works in any highway, or which may affect any highway or any property or work of the highway authority, during the execution thereof, and the undertakers shall give to such officer all reasonable facilities for such inspection:

(7) The undertakers shall not, except with the consent of the highway authority, alter, disturb or in any way interfere with any sanitary convenience, refuge, sewer, drain, lamp column, traffic sign, bollard, bin for refuse or road materials or apparatus connected therewith, or any other property or work belonging to, or under the jurisdiction or control of, the highway authority on or under any highway or repairable by them or the access thereto:

(8) If the highway authority, after giving to the undertakers not less than 28 days' notice (or in the case of emergency such other notice as is reasonably practicable) of their intention to do so, incur any extra expense in the signposting of traffic diversions or the taking of other measures in relation thereto, or in the repair of any highway, by reason of the diversion thereto of traffic from a road of a higher classification in consequence of the construction of the authorised works, the undertakers shall repay the amount of the expense reasonably so incurred by the highway authority:

(9) The undertakers shall not, except with the consent of the highway authority, deposit any soil or materials or stand any vehicle or plant on or over any highway so as to obstruct or render less safe the use of the highway by any person or, except with the like consent, deposit any soil or materials on any highway except within a hoarding:

(10) The undertakers shall, if reasonably so required by the highway authority, provide and maintain to the reasonable satisfaction of the highway authority, during such time as the undertakers may occupy any part of a highway for the purpose of the construction of any part of the authorised works, temporary bridges and temporary ramps for vehicular traffic or pedestrian traffic, or both, in such position as may be necessary to prevent undue interference with the flow of traffic in any highway:

(11) Where any part of any highway shall have been temporarily broken up or disturbed by the undertakers, the undertakers shall make good the subsoil foundations and surface of such part of the highway to the reasonable satisfaction of the highway authority and maintain the same to the reasonable satisfaction of the highway authority for such time as may be reasonably required for the permanent reinstatement of the highway:

    Provided that the reinstatement of such part of the highway shall in the first instance be of a temporary nature only and the permanent reinstatement shall be carried out by the highway authority as soon as reasonably practicable after the completion of the temporary reinstatement, and the costs, charges and expenses reasonably incurred by the highway authority in so doing shall be repaid by the undertakers:

(12) It shall not be lawful for the undertakers to place any hoardings on any part of any highway except for such period and in such manner as may be reasonably necessary, and the provisions of sections 172 and 173 of the Highways Act 1980 shall apply to any hoarding erected on any part of any highway, and, for the purposes of the said section 172, any such hoarding shall be deemed to have been erected in compliance with subsection (1) of that section:

(13) The undertakers shall make compensation to the highway authority for any subsidence of, or damage to, any highway or any sanitary convenience, refuge, sewer, drain, lamp column, traffic sign, bollard, bin for refuse or road materials or apparatus connected therewith or any other property or work belonging to, or under the jurisdiction or control of, the highway authority on or under any highway, or maintainable by them, which may be caused by, or in consequence of, any act or default of the undertakers, their contractors, servants or agents, whether such damage or subsidence shall happen during the construction of the authorised works or at any time thereafter:

(14) The highway authority may require that the authorised works, so far as they involve any serious interference with the movement of traffic in any highway, shall be carried on, so far as reasonably practicable, continuously by day and night, and the undertakers shall take all such

steps as may be reasonably necessary to reduce so far as possible the period of such interference:

(15) Except as provided in paragraph (5) above, any difference arising between the undertakers and the highway authority under this section (other than a difference as to its meaning or construction) shall be determined by arbitration.

Approval of plans by local authorities, etc.

40. The following provisions shall, unless otherwise agreed in writing between the undertakers and the council, have effect:—

(1) In this section—

"construction" includes placing, alteration and renewal;

"the council" means whichever of the City Council, the Broxtowe Borough Council or the Ashfield District Council are the local authority for the area where the specified works are constructed or authorised to be constructed;

"plans" includes sections, drawings, specifications, particulars and descriptions (including descriptions of methods of construction);

"the specified works" means any of the authorised works constructed or to be constructed in the area of the council:

(2) The undertakers shall, before commencing the construction of the specified works, supply to the council proper and sufficient plans thereof for their approval:

Provided that if within 56 days after such plans have been supplied to the council they have not notified their disapproval thereof and the grounds of their disapproval, they shall be deemed to have approved the plans as supplied:

(3) The council may approve the plans subject to such reasonable conditions as may be necessary to prevent unacceptable detriment to the environment or to the amenity of the area of the council:

(4) The undertakers shall not commence the specified works until plans thereof have been approved in writing by the council, or settled by arbitration in accordance with subsection (7) below:

(5) The construction of the specified works shall, when commenced, be carried out in accordance with the plans as approved by the council or deemed to have been so approved or settled by arbitration in accordance with subsection (7) below, and in constructing the specified works the undertakers shall comply with such conditions (if any) as may be so approved or settled:

(6) The council may not withhold their approval under this section except in respect of any detail of the plans which—

(a) in their reasonable opinion will cause unacceptable detriment to the environment or to the amenity of the area of the council; and

(b) is susceptible of a reasonable alternative which will not in their reasonable opinion cause such detriment:

(7) Any difference arising between the undertakers and the council under this section shall be referred to and settled by arbitration but the undertakers and the council shall use their best endeavours to ensure that proceedings before an arbitrator commence in every case within 7 days of the undertakers or the council registering such a difference.

For protection of British Railways Board

41. For the protection of the railways board the following provisions shall, unless otherwise agreed in writing between the undertakers and the railways board, have effect:—

(1) In this section—
   "construction" includes placing, alteration and renewal;
   "the engineer" means an engineer to be appointed by the railways board;
   "plans" includes sections, drawings, specifications and particulars (including descriptions of methods of construction);
   "railway property" means any railway of the railways board and any works connected therewith for the maintenance or operation of which the railways board are responsible and includes any land held or used by the railways board for the purposes of such railway or works, not being railway property acquired by the undertakers;
   "specified works" means so much of the authorised works as may be situated upon, across, under or over or within 15 metres of, or may in any way affect, any railway property:

(2) (a) The undertakers shall not under the powers of this Act acquire any land or other property of the railways board, or any right in such land or other property, without the consent of the railways board, which consent shall not be unreasonably withheld;

(b) Where any specified works are situated in land in respect of which easements or rights only in railway property are acquired, the undertakers shall fence off those works from that railway property to the reasonable satisfaction of the engineer where so required by him and shall thereafter be responsible for keeping in good repair the fencing so provided:

(3) In the exercise of the powers of section 18 (Temporary stoppage of highways) of this Act the undertakers shall at all times provide reasonable access, with or without vehicles, plant, machinery and materials, to any station or depot of the railways board or other railway property:

(4) The undertakers shall, before commencing the construction of the specified works, supply to the railways board proper and sufficient plans thereof for the approval of the engineer and shall not commence the construction of those works until such plans have been approved in writing by the engineer or settled by arbitration:
   Provided that approval of plans supplied under this paragraph shall not be unreasonably withheld and, if within 56 days after the plans have been supplied to the railways board the engineer shall not have intimated his disapproval of the plans and the grounds of his disapproval, he shall be deemed to have approved them:

(5) If, within 56 days after such plans have been supplied to the railways board, the railways board give notice to the undertakers that the railways board desire themselves to construct any part of the specified works which, in the opinion of the engineer, will or may affect the stability of any operational railway or the safe operation of traffic on the railways of the railways board then, if the undertakers desire such part of the specified works to be constructed, the railways board shall construct the same with all reasonable dispatch on behalf of, and to the reasonable satisfaction of, the undertakers in accordance with the plans approved or deemed to be approved or settled as aforesaid:

(6) Upon signifying his approval or disapproval of the plans the engineer may specify any protective works (whether temporary or permanent) which in his opinion should be carried out before commencement of the construction of the specified works to ensure the safety or stability of the railways of the railways board, and such protective works as may be reasonably necessary for those purposes shall be constructed by the railways board or by the undertakers, if the railways board so desire, with all reasonable dispatch, and the undertakers shall not commence the construction of the specified works until the engineer shall have notified them that the protective works have been completed to his reasonable satisfaction:

(7) (a) The undertakers shall give to the railways board notice in writing of their intention to commence the construction of any of the specified works in accordance with sub-paragraph (b) below and, except in case of emergency (when they shall give such notice as may be reasonably practicable), of their intention to carry out any works for the repair or maintenance of the specified works in so far as such works of repair or maintenance affect or interfere with railway property;

(b) The period of notice required under sub-paragraph (a) above shall be—

    (i) 6 months in any case where the engineer, upon signifying his approval or disapproval of plans supplied to the railways board under paragraph (4) above, has reasonably given his opinion that the construction or maintenance of the specified works will require the undertakers to have temporary occupation of the permanent way of any operational railway (including land lying within a distance of 2 metres from any outer rail of the railway) or will necessitate the imposition of speed restrictions, or the substitution, diversion or suspension of train services; and

    (ii) 28 days in all other cases:

(8) (a) When construction of any specified works is commenced the work shall be carried out—

    (i) with all reasonable dispatch in accordance with plans approved or deemed to have been approved or settled as aforesaid;

    (ii) under the supervision (if given) and to the reasonable satisfaction of the engineer;

    (iii) in such manner as to cause as little damage to railway property as may be; and

    (iv) so far as is reasonably practicable, so as not to interfere with or obstruct the free, uninterrupted and safe user of any railway of the railways board or the traffic thereon and the use by passengers of railway property;

(b) If any damage to railway property or any such interference or obstruction shall be caused or take place, the undertakers shall, notwithstanding any such approval as aforesaid, make good such damage and pay to the railways board all reasonable expenses to which they may be put and compensation for any loss which they may sustain by reason of any damage, interference or obstruction:

(9) Nothing in paragraph (8)(b) above shall impose any liability on the undertakers for any damage, cost, expense or loss which is attributable to the neglect or default of the railways board or their servants or agents:

(10) The undertakers shall—

    (a) at all times afford reasonable facilities to the engineer for access to the specified works during their construction; and

    (b) supply the engineer with all such information as he may reasonably require with regard to the specified works or the method of construction of those works:

(11) The railways board shall—

    (a) at all times afford reasonable facilities to the undertakers and their agents for access to any works carried out by the railways board under this section during their construction; and

    (b) supply the undertakers with such information as they may reasonably require with regard to such works or the method of construction of those works:

(12) If any alterations or additions (either permanent or temporary) to any operational railway of the railways board shall be reasonably necessary during the construction of the specified works, or during a period of 12 months after their completion, in consequence of the construc-

tion of the specified works, such alterations and additions may be made by the railways board and, if the railways board give to the undertakers reasonable notice of their intention to make such alterations or additions, the undertakers shall pay to the railways board the cost thereof as certified by the engineer, subject to the addition, in the case of permanent alterations and additions, of a capitalised sum representing the increased or additional cost of maintaining, working and, when necessary, renewing any such alterations or additions:

Provided that if the cost of maintaining, working or renewing railway property is reduced in consequence of any such alterations or additions, a capitalised sum representing such saving shall be set off against any sum payable by the undertakers to the railways board under this section:

(13) If the cost to the railways board of altering any existing railway within its boundaries or of maintaining or reconstructing any existing railway under any powers existing at the passing of this Act is increased by reason of the existence of the specified works any such additional expense which the railways board, after giving 56 days' notice to the undertakers, reasonably so incur shall be repayable by the undertakers to the railways board:

(14) The undertakers shall repay to the railways board all costs, charges and expenses reasonably incurred by the railways board—

(a) in constructing any part of the specified works on behalf of the undertakers as provided by paragraph (5) above, or in constructing any protective works under the provisions of paragraph (6) above, including, in respect of any permanent protective works, a capitalised sum representing the reasonable cost of maintaining and renewing those works;

(b) in respect of the employment of any inspectors, signalmen, watchmen and other persons whom it shall be reasonably necessary to appoint for inspecting, watching, lighting and signalling railways and for preventing interference, obstruction, danger or accident arising from the construction, maintenance, repair or failure of the specified works;

(c) in respect of any special traffic working resulting from any speed restrictions which may, in the opinion of the engineer, be necessary by reason of the construction, maintenance, repair or failure of the specified works or from the substitution, suspension or diversion of services which may be necessary for that reason;

(d) in respect of any additional temporary lighting of railways in the vicinity of the specified works, being lighting made reasonably necessary by reason of the specified works or the failure thereof;

(e) in respect of the approval by the engineer of plans supplied by the undertakers under paragraph (4) above and the supervision by him of the construction of the specified works:

(15) If at any time after the completion of the specified works, not being works vested in the railways board, the railways board give notice to the undertakers that the state of repair of the specified works appears to affect prejudicially any operational railway of the railways board, the undertakers shall, on receipt of such notice, take such steps as may be reasonably necessary to remedy any such defect:

(16) All temporary structures, erections, works, apparatus and appliances erected or placed by the undertakers under the powers of this Act upon, over or under any operational railway of the railways board shall, as soon as reasonably practicable, be removed by the undertakers at times to be agreed with, and to the reasonable satisfaction of, the engineer and in such a way as to cause as little damage to the railway and as little interference with, or delay or interruption to, the

traffic on the railways of the railways board as may be; and if any damage to railway property or such interference, delay or interruption shall be caused by any such failure to remove any such temporary structures, erections, works, apparatus or appliances, the undertakers shall make good such damage and pay to the railways board the reasonable costs and expenses to which they may be put, and reasonable compensation for any loss which they may sustain, by reason of such damage, interference, delay or interruption:

(17) Before providing any illumination or illuminated traffic sign on or in connection with the specified works, or otherwise in the vicinity of any railway of the railways board, the undertakers shall consult with the railways board and comply with their reasonable requirements with a view to ensuring that such illumination or illuminated sign could not be confused with any railway signal or other light used for controlling, directing or securing the safety of traffic on the railway:

(18) (a) The undertakers shall be responsible for and make good to the railways board all costs, charges, damages and expenses not otherwise provided for in this section which may be occasioned to, or reasonably incurred by, the railways board—

(i) by reason of the construction or repair of the specified works or the failure thereof; or

(ii) by reason of any act or omission of the undertakers or of any person in their employ or of their contractors or others whilst engaged upon the construction or repair of the specified works;

and the undertakers shall indemnify the railways board from and against all claims and demands arising out of, or in connection with, the construction or repair of the specified works or any such failure, act or omission as aforesaid;

(b) The fact that any act or thing may have been done by the railways board on behalf of the undertakers or in accordance with plans approved by the engineer or in accordance with any requirement of the engineer or under his supervision shall not (if it was done without neglect or default on the part of the railways board or of any person in their employ or of their contractors or agents) excuse the undertakers from any liability under this paragraph;

(c) The railways board shall give to the undertakers reasonable notice of any claim or demand as aforesaid and no settlement or compromise thereof shall be made without the prior consent of the undertakers:

(19) Any difference arising between the undertakers and the railways board under this section (other than a difference as to its meaning or construction) shall be determined by arbitration.

For protection of British Waterways Board

42. For the protection of the British Waterways Board (in this section referred to as "the waterways board") the following provisions shall, unless otherwise agreed in writing between the undertakers and the waterways board, have effect:—

(1) In this section—

"the canal" means any canal or inland waterway owned or managed by the waterways board, and any works connected therewith for the maintenance of which the waterways board are responsible, and includes any lands held or used by the waterways board for the purposes of any canal;

"construction" includes placing, alteration and renewal;

"the engineer" means an engineer to be appointed by the waterways board;

"plans" includes sections, drawings and particulars;

"the specified works" means so much of any of the authorised works as is situated over or upon or abuts on or in any way affects the canal:

(2) Notwithstanding anything in this Act or shown on the deposited plans, the undertakers shall not acquire compulsorily or occupy any land or other property of the waterways board but they may subject to the consent of the waterways board (which consent shall not unreasonably be withheld) in accordance with the provisions of section 28 (Power to acquire new rights) of this Act acquire such easements and rights as they may reasonably require for the purposes of the works in any such land or property delineated on the deposited plans:

(3) The undertakers shall not use any land or property of the waterways board (including the towing paths comprised in the canal) for the passage of vehicles, plant or machinery employed in the construction of the specified works other than—

    (a) with the consent in writing of the engineer, whose consent shall not be unreasonably withheld;

    (b) subject to compliance with such reasonable requirements as the engineer may from time to time specify—

        (i) for the prevention of damage to such land and property and of danger to persons thereon; and

        (ii) in order to avoid or reduce any inconvenience to the waterways board, their officers and agents and all other persons lawfully on such land or property.

(4) The undertakers shall, before commencing the construction of the specified works, supply to the waterways board proper and sufficient plans thereof for the approval of the engineer, and shall not commence the specified works until plans thereof have been approved in writing by the engineer or settled by arbitration:

Provided that approval of plans supplied under this paragraph shall not be unreasonably withheld and, if within 28 days after such plans have been supplied to the waterways board the engineer shall not have intimated his disapproval thereof and the grounds of his disapproval, he shall be deemed to have approved the plan as supplied:

(5) Upon signifying his approval or disapproval of the plans the engineer may specify any protective works, whether temporary or permanent, which in his opinion should be carried out before the commencement of the specified works to ensure the safety or stability of the canal, and such protective works as may be reasonably necessary for those purposes shall be constructed by the undertakers with all reasonable dispatch:

(6) The undertakers shall pay to the waterways board a capitalised sum representing the increased or additional cost of maintaining and, when necessary, renewing any permanent protective works provided under paragraph (5) above, but if the cost of maintaining the canal, or of works of renewal on the canal, is reduced in consequence of any such protective works, a capitalised sum representing such saving shall be set off against any sum payable by the undertakers to the waterways board under this section:

(7) The undertakers shall give to the engineer 28 days' notice of their intention to commence the construction or repair of any of the specified works, or, in the case of repair carried out in an emergency, such notice as may be reasonably practicable:

(8) The undertakers shall at all times afford reasonable facilities to the engineer for access to the specified works during their construction and shall supply him with all such information as he may reasonably

require with regard to the specified works or the method of construction thereof:

(9) When construction of any specified works is commenced the works shall be carried out—

(a) in accordance with the plans approved or deemed to be approved or settled as provided in paragraph (4) above;

(b) under the supervision (if given) and to the reasonable satisfaction of the engineer;

(c) so as not to interfere with or obstruct the use of the towing paths of the canal so far as is reasonably practicable; and

(d) so as not to interfere or obstruct the passage of vessels on the canal—

    (i) at any time in the period in each year beginning on 17th March and ending on 3rd November except in case of emergency; and

    (ii) at any other time so far as is reasonably practicable:

(10) Following the completion of the construction of the specified works the undertakers shall restore the canal to a condition no less satisfactory than its condition immediately prior to the commencement of those works:

(11) The undertakers shall not in the course of constructing or repairing the specified works do or permit anything which may result in the pollution of the canal or the deposit of materials therein and shall take such steps as the engineer may reasonably require to avoid such pollution:

(12) Nothing in section 23 (Use of sewers, etc., for removing water) of this Act shall authorise the undertakers—

(a) to discharge any water directly or indirectly into the canal except with the consent in writing of the waterways board; or

(b) to carry out any works to, or make any opening in, or otherwise interfere with the canal (including the banks and bed thereof) save in accordance with plans approved by, and under the supervision (if given), of the engineer:

(13) The consent of the waterways board under paragraph (12)(a) above and the approval of plans under paragraph (12)(b) above shall not be unreasonably withheld but may be given subject to reasonable conditions which (without prejudice to the generality of the foregoing) may include conditions—

(a) requiring the undertakers to make payments to the waterways board for the discharge of water in accordance with the said section 23 including payments in respect of the employment of persons in connection with such discharges and the cost to the waterways board of pumping water so discharged;

(b) providing for the charges so payable by the undertakers (other than any charge in respect of the employment of persons, or the provision or alteration of works or facilities for the accommodation and disposal of water) to be determined by reference to the volume of such discharges as recorded by metering devices of a design approved by the waterways board and supplied and maintained by them at the expense of the undertakers;

(c) specifying the maximum volume of water which may be discharged in any period;

(d) authorising the waterways board to require the undertakers to suspend the discharge of water or reduce the flow thereof where this is necessary by reason of any operational requirement of the waterways board.

(14) The undertakers shall pay to the waterways board all costs, charges and expenses reasonably incurred by them in respect of the approval by the engineer of plans supplied by the undertakers under paragraph

(4) above and the supervision by him of the construction of the specified works:

(15) If any damage to the canal or other land or property of the waterways board, any stoppage of the canal or any interference with the passage of vessels using the canal shall be caused by the carrying out of works for the construction of the specified works, the undertakers shall make good such damage and pay to the waterways board all reasonable expenses to which they may be put and compensation for any loss which they may sustain by reason of any such damage, stoppage or interference:

Provided that nothing in this paragraph shall impose any liability on the undertakers with respect to any damage, expenses or loss which is attributable to the act, neglect or default of the waterways board or their servants, contractors or agents:

(16) Nothing in this Act shall authorise the undertakers to make or maintain any permanent works in or over the canal so as to reduce the width thereof if such reduction in width would impede or prevent the passage of any vessel of a kind (as to its dimensions) for which the waterways board are required by section 105(1)(b) and (2) of the Transport Act 1968 to maintain the canal:

(17) (a) The undertakers shall be responsible for and make good to the waterways board all costs, charges, damages and expenses not otherwise provided for in this section which may be occasioned to, or reasonably incurred by, the waterways board—

(i) by reason of the construction or repair of the specified works or the failure thereof; or

(ii) by reason of any act or omission of the undertakers or of any person in their employ or of their contractors or others whilst engaged upon the construction or repair of the specified works;

and the undertakers shall indemnify the waterways board from and against all claims and demands arising out of, or in connection with, the construction or repair of the specified works or any such failure, act or omission as aforesaid;

(b) The fact that any act or thing has been done by the waterways board on behalf of the undertakers or in accordance with plans approved by the engineer or in accordance with any requirement of the engineer or under his supervision shall not (if it was done without neglect or default on the part of the waterways board or of any person in their employ or of their contractors or agents) excuse the undertakers from any liability under this paragraph;

(c) The waterways board shall give to the undertakers reasonable notice of any claim or demand as aforesaid and no settlement or compromise thereof shall be made without the prior consent of the undertakers:

(18) (a) The undertakers shall not exercise the powers of the sections of this Act mentioned in sub-paragraph (b) below in relation to the towing path forming part of the canal without the consent in writing of the waterways board;

(b) The sections to which sub-paragraph (a) above applies are—
   section 10 (Subsidiary works),
   section 18 (Temporary stoppage of highways);

(c) The consent of the waterways board under paragraph (a) above shall not be unreasonably withheld but may be given subject to reasonable conditions;

(d) Where the waterways board own the towing path in respect of which consent is given under sub-paragraph (a) above for the exercise of the powers of the said section 10, they may require the payment of such charges as would have been fair and reasonable if that consent had been given willingly;

(e) Nothing in this paragraph applies to anything done by the undertakers on the existing viaduct referred to in the description of Work No. 1:

(19) Any difference arising between the undertakers and the waterways board under this section (other than a difference as to its meaning or construction) shall be determined by arbitration.

For protection of National Rivers Authority

43. For the protection of the rivers authority the following provisions shall, unless otherwise agreed in writing between the undertakers and the rivers authority, have effect:—

(1) In this section—

"construction" includes execution, placing and altering and, in relation to temporary works, includes removal; and "construct" and "constructed" have corresponding meanings;

"drainage work" means any watercourse and includes any land used for providing flood storage capacity for any watercourse and any bank, wall, embankment or other structure or appliance constructed or used for defence against water;

"the fishery" means fish in the river Leen and the spawn, habitat or food of such fish;

"plans" includes sections, drawings, specifications and method statements and other such particulars;

"specified work" means so much of any work or operation authorised by this Act (other than works required in an emergency) as is in, on, under, over or within 16 metres of a drainage work or is otherwise likely to—

(a) affect any drainage work or the volumetric flow of water in or flowing to or from any drainage work;

(b) affect the purity or quality of water in any watercourse;

(c) cause obstruction to the free passage of fish in any watercourse; or

(d) affect the conservation, distribution or use of water resources; and

"watercourse" has the meaning given in section 221 of the Water Resources Act 1991;

(2) In the event that the undertakers commence to construct Work No. 7C or any other specified work the rivers authority may so far as is reasonably necessary for the protection of any drainage work or fishery or water resources or for the prevention of flooding and pollution require the undertakers to construct and complete the whole of that work and any other work required in the approval of that work under paragraph (3) below:

(3) (a) Before beginning to construct any specified work, the undertakers shall submit to the rivers authority plans of the work and such further particulars available to them as the rivers authority may reasonably require;

(b) Any such specified work shall not be constructed except in accordance with such plans as may be approved in writing by the rivers authority, or settled in accordance with paragraph (12) below;

(c) Any approval of the rivers authority required under this paragraph—

(i) shall not be unreasonably withheld;

(ii) shall be deemed to have been given if it is neither given nor refused in writing and with a statement of the grounds for refusal within two months of the submission of plans for approval;

(iii) may be given subject to such reasonable requirements as the rivers authority may impose for the protection of any drainage

work or the fishery or water resources, for the prevention of flooding and water pollution and in the discharge of its environmental
and recreational duties:

(4) Without prejudice to the generality of paragraph (3) above, the
requirements which the rivers authority may impose under that paragraph include—

(a) requirements as to the levels and alignments within the limits
of deviation for Work No. 7C;

(b) requirements as to sluices, gauges and other monitoring
devices to be constructed as part of or in connection with Work No.
7C;

(c) conditions as to the time at which and the manner in which
any work is to be carried out;

(d) conditions requiring the undertakers at their own expense—

(i) to provide or maintain means of access for the rivers
authority;

(ii) to undertake landscaping;

(iii) to construct such protective works whether temporary or
permanent during the construction of the specified works
(including the provision of flood banks, walls or embankments
and other new works and the strengthening, repair or renewal of
existing banks, walls or embankments) as are reasonably necessary to safeguard any drainage work against damage or to secure
that its efficiency for flood defence purposes is not impaired and
that the risk of flooding is not otherwise increased by reason of
any specified work:

(5) Any specified work, and all protective works required by the rivers
authority under paragraph (3) above, shall be constructed to the
reasonable satisfaction of the rivers authority and the rivers authority
shall be entitled by its officer to watch and inspect the construction of
such works:

(6) If by reason of the construction of any specified work the efficiency of
any drainage work for flood defence purposes is impaired or that work
is damaged, such impairment or damage shall be made good by the
undertakers to the reasonable satisfaction of the rivers authority and,
if the undertakers fail to do so, the rivers authority may make good the
same and recover from the undertakers the expense reasonably
incurred by it in so doing:

(7) (a) Without prejudice to the other provisions of this section, the
undertakers shall take all such measures as may be reasonably practicable to prevent any interruption in the passage of fish during the construction of any specified work;

(b) The undertakers shall be responsible for and make good to the rivers
authority all costs, charges, expenses and losses which may be
occasioned to, suffered by, or reasonably incurred by the rivers authority in taking action—

(i) after notice in writing to the undertakers to protect the fishery
against anticipated damage; or

(ii) to remedy any damage to that fishery;

being damage anticipated or suffered by reason or in consequence of
the execution of the authorised works, of the failure or want of repair
of the works, or in consequence of any act or omission of the undertakers, their contractors, agents, workmen or servants in connection
with those works:

(8) The undertakers shall indemnify the rivers authority in respect of all
costs, charges and expenses which the rivers authority may reasonably
incur or have to pay or which it may sustain—

    (a) in the examination or approval of plans under this section;

    (b) in the inspection of the construction of the specified works or any protective works required by the rivers authority under this section:

(9) (a) Without prejudice to the other provisions of this section the undertakers shall indemnify the rivers authority from all claims, demands, proceedings, costs, damages or expenses or loss which may be made or taken against, or recovered from or incurred by, the rivers authority by reason of—

      (i) any damage to any drainage work so as to impair its efficiency for the purposes of flood defence; or

      (ii) any damage to the fishery; or

      (iii) any raising of the water table in land adjoining the works or any sewers, drains and watercourses; or

      (iv) any flooding or increased flooding of any such lands; or

      (v) inadequate water quality in any watercourse or other surface waters or in groundwater;

which is caused by the construction of any of the works or any act or omission of the undertakers, their contractors, agents, workmen or servants whilst engaged upon any such work;

    (b) The rivers authority shall give to the undertakers reasonable notice of any such claim or demand and no settlement or compromise thereof shall be made without the agreement of the undertakers which agreement shall not be unreasonably withheld:

(10) The fact that any work or thing has been executed or done in accordance with a plan approved or deemed to be approved by the rivers authority, or to its satisfaction, or in accordance with any directions or award of an arbitrator, shall not relieve the undertakers from any liability under the provisions of this section:

    Provided that this paragraph shall not apply to the extent that such liability arises from a failure by the rivers authority properly to perform its functions.

(11) For the purposes of section 109 of the Water Resources Act 1991 (as to structures in, over or under watercourses) as applying to the construction of any authorised work, any consent or approval given or deemed to be given by the rivers authority under this section with respect to such construction shall be deemed also to constitute a consent or approval under that section:

(12) (a) Unless the parties agree to arbitration any difference arising between the undertakers and the rivers authority under paragraph (3) above shall be settled by the Minister of Agriculture, Fisheries and Food and the Secretary of State acting jointly on a reference to them by the undertakers or rivers authority after notice by one to the other;

    (b) Subject to sub-paragraph (a) above, any difference arising between the undertakers and the rivers authority under this section (other than a difference as to its meaning or construction) shall be referred to and settled by arbitration.

For protection of public sewers

44. For the protection of certain sewerage authorities the following provisions shall, unless otherwise agreed in writing between the undertakers and the sewerage authority concerned, have effect:—

    (1) In this section—

      "construction" includes placing and altering;

      "sewer" means a public sewer within the meaning of the Water Industry Act 1991 and includes a sludge main, disposal main (within the meaning of that Act) or sewer outfall and any manholes, ventilating shafts, pumps or other accessories forming part of any such public sewer, main or outfall not being, in any such case, apparatus in respect of which the relations between the undertakers and the sewerage authority are regulated by the provisions of Part III of the Act of 1991;

"sewerage authority" means a sewerage undertaker and any local authority which is a relevant authority for the purposes of section 97 of the Water Industry Act 1991;

"new, altered or substituted works" includes any works required for the protection of any public sewer of the sewerage authority;

"specified works" means any part of the authorised works which will or may be situated within 15 metres measured in any direction of any sewer vested in a sewerage authority:

(2) Wherever in this section provision is made with respect to the approval or consent of the sewerage authority such approval shall be in writing, but shall not be unreasonably withheld:

(3) The undertakers shall not commence the construction of the specified works until they have given to the sewerage authority not less than 56 days' notice in writing of their intention to do so with plans as described in paragraph (9) below (in this section referred to as "the said plans") for their approval:

Provided that approval of the said plans shall not be unreasonably withheld and, if within 56 days after the submission of the said plans the sewerage authority have not approved or disapproved them, they shall be deemed to have approved the plans as submitted:

(4) The undertakers shall comply with, and conform to, all reasonable orders, directions and regulations of the sewerage authority in the construction of the specified works and shall provide new, altered or substituted works in such manner as the sewerage authority shall reasonably require for the protection of, and for preventing injury or impediment to, or for securing access to, any existing sewer of the sewerage authority by reason of the specified works, and shall indemnify the sewerage authority against all expenses occasioned thereby:

(5) The specified works and all such new, altered or substituted works—

(a) shall be constructed in accordance with such plans as may be approved or deemed to be approved by the sewerage authority as aforesaid or settled by arbitration, subject however to any modification of those plans from time to time agreed upon between the undertakers and the sewerage authority; and

(b) shall be constructed to the reasonable satisfaction of the sewerage authority who shall be given reasonable notice of the date and time on and at which any new, altered or substituted works are to be commenced:

(6) All new, altered or substituted works shall, where so required by the sewerage authority, be constructed by the sewerage authority, or under the direction, superintendence and control of an officer of the sewerage authority duly appointed for the purpose, at the cost of the undertakers and all costs, charges and expenses reasonably incurred by the sewerage authority by reason of such works, whether in the execution thereof, or in the preparation or examination of plans or designs, or in such direction, superintendence or control as aforesaid, or otherwise, shall be paid to the sewerage authority by the undertakers:

(7) When any new, altered or substituted works shall be completed by, or at the cost of, the undertakers under the provisions of this section the same shall thereafter be as fully and completely under the direction, jurisdiction and control of the sewerage authority as any sewers or works now or hereafter may be:

(8) It shall not be lawful for the undertakers without the consent of the sewerage authority, in the exercise of the powers of section 11(3) of the Act of 1965 as applied by this Act, to make any trial holes which interfere with any sewer:

(9) The plans to be submitted to the sewerage authority for the purposes of this section shall be detailed plans, drawings, sections and specifications which shall describe the exact position and manner in which, and the level at which, the specified works are to be constructed and shall accurately describe the position of all sewers of the sewerage authority within the limits of deviation (for which purpose the sewerage authority shall allow the undertakers access to plans in their possession and to any of their sewers in order to enable the undertakers to obtain reliable information) and shall comprise detailed drawings of every alteration which the undertakers may propose to make in any such sewer:

(10) The undertakers shall be liable to make good, or, if the sewerage authority so decide, to repay any expense reasonably incurred by the sewerage authority in making good, damage caused by, or resulting from, the construction of the specified works to any sewers, drains or works vested in the sewerage authority whether or not identified at the commencement of the construction of the specified works:

(11) If the undertakers, in the construction of the specified works or any new, altered or substituted works provided in accordance with this section, damage, or, without the consent of the sewerage authority, alter or in any way interfere with, any existing sewer of the sewerage authority, the undertakers shall—

    (a) pay to the sewerage authority any additional expense which may be reasonably incurred by the sewerage authority in the maintenance, operation, management or renewal of any new, altered or substituted sewer which may be necessary in consequence of the said construction; and

    (b) give to the sewerage authority free and uninterrupted access at all times to any such new, altered or substituted sewer and reasonable facilities for the inspection, maintenance, alteration and repair thereof:

(12) It shall be lawful for the proper officer of the sewerage authority at any reasonable time, on giving to the undertakers such notice as may in the circumstances be reasonable, to enter upon and inspect the specified works or any other works constructed under the powers of this section:

(13) The approval by the sewerage authority of any plans, or the superintendence by them of any work, under the provisions of this section shall not exonerate the undertakers from any liability, or affect any claim for damages, under this section or otherwise:

(14) As soon as reasonably practicable after the completion of the construction of a specified work the undertakers shall deliver to the sewerage authority a plan and section showing the position and level of that work as constructed and all new, altered or substituted works of the sewerage authority provided under this section:

(15) If by reason or in consequence of the construction or failure of any of the LRT system or any subsidence resulting from the LRT system any damage shall be caused to any sewer or property of the sewerage authority (other than a sewer the repair of which is not reasonably necessary in view of its intended removal), the undertakers shall repay the cost reasonably incurred by the sewerage authority in making good such damage and shall—

    (a) make reasonable compensation to the sewerage authority for any loss sustained by them; and

(b) indemnify the sewerage authority against all claims, demands, proceedings, costs, damages and expenses which may be made or taken against or recovered from, or incurred by, the sewerage authority;

by reason or in consequence of any such damage:

Provided that—

(i) nothing in this paragraph shall impose any liability on the undertakers with respect to any damage to the extent that such damage is attributable to the act, neglect or default of the sewerage authority, their officers, servants, contractors or agents; and

(ii) the sewerage authority shall give to the undertakers reasonable notice of any claim or demand as aforesaid and no settlement or compromise thereof shall be made without the consent of the undertakers:

(16) Notwithstanding the temporary stopping up or diversion of any highway under the powers of section 18 (Temporary stoppage of highways) of this Act, the sewerage authority shall be at liberty at all times to construct and do all such works and things in, upon or under any such highway as may be reasonably necessary to enable them to inspect, repair, maintain, renew, alter, protect, remove or use any sewer which at the time of the stopping up or diversion was in that highway:

(17) Where, in consequence of this Act, any part of any street, bridleway or footpath in which any sewer is situate ceases to be part of the street, bridleway or footpath, the sewerage authority may exercise the same rights of access to such sewer as they enjoyed immediately before the passing of this Act, but nothing in this paragraph shall prejudice or affect any right of the undertakers or of the sewerage authority to require alteration of such sewer under this section:

(18) The undertakers shall, so far as is reasonably practicable, so exercise the powers conferred by section 22 (Underpinning of houses near works) of this Act as not to obstruct or render less convenient the access to any sewer:

(19) Any difference arising between the undertakers and the sewerage authority under this section (other than a difference as to its meaning or construction) shall be determined by arbitration.

For protection of certain statutory undertakers

45. For the protection of certain statutory undertakers the following provisions shall, unless otherwise agreed in writing between the undertakers and the undertakers concerned, apply and have effect:—

(1) In this section, unless the context otherwise requires—

"the company" means any of the following, namely a licence holder within the meaning of Part I of the Electricity Act 1989, a public gas supplier within the meaning of Part I of the Gas Act 1986 or a water undertaker;

"adequate alternative apparatus" means alternative apparatus adequate to enable the company to fulfil their statutory functions in a manner not less efficient than previously;

"apparatus" means—

(a) electric lines and works (as defined in Part I of the Electricity Act 1989) belonging to, or maintained by, a licence holder under that Part; or

(b) mains, pipes or other apparatus belonging to, or maintained by, a public gas supplier within the meaning of Part I of the Gas Act 1986; or

   (c) mains, pipes or other apparatus belonging to, or maintained
        by, a water undertaker for the purposes of water supply;
   (not being apparatus in respect of which the relations between the
   undertakers and the company are regulated by the provisions of
   Part III of the Act of 1991), and includes any structure for the lodging therein of apparatus;
        "construction" includes placing and altering;
        "in" in a context referring to apparatus includes under, over,
   across, along or upon:
(2) Notwithstanding anything in this Act or shown on the deposited plans
   the undertakers shall not acquire any apparatus under this Act otherwise than by agreement:
(3) If the undertakers in the exercise of the powers of this Act acquire any
   interest in any land in which any apparatus is placed, that apparatus
   shall not be removed under this section, nor shall any right of the company to use, maintain, repair, renew or inspect any apparatus in those
   lands be extinguished, until any necessary adequate alternative apparatus has been constructed and is in operation to the reasonable satisfaction of the company:
(4) (a) If the undertakers, for the purpose of constructing any of the authorised works in, on or under any lands (including lands forming part of
   any street) acquired, held or used under this Act, require the removal
   of any apparatus placed in those lands, and give to the company not
   less than 56 days' written notice of such requirement, together with a
   plan and section of the work proposed, and of the proposed position of
   the alternative apparatus to be provided or constructed so as to provide adequate alternative apparatus in lieu of the apparatus to be
   removed, or if, in consequence of the exercise of any of the powers of
   this Act, the company shall reasonably require to remove any apparatus, the undertakers shall, if it is practicable to do so, afford to the
   company the necessary facilities and rights for the construction of any
   necessary adequate alternative apparatus in other lands of the undertakers and thereafter for the maintenance, repair, renewal and inspection of such apparatus;
   (b) If the alternative apparatus, or any part thereof, is to be constructed
   elsewhere than in other lands of the undertakers, the company shall,
   on receipt of a written notice to that effect from the undertakers, as
   soon as reasonably practicable exercise their powers to lay alternative
   apparatus:
(5) (a) Subject, in the case of any alternative apparatus to be laid in a road,
   to any requirements imposed under Part III of the Act of 1991 any
   alternative apparatus to be constructed in pursuance of paragraph (4)
   above shall be constructed in such manner, and in such line or situation, as may be agreed between the company and the undertakers or,
   in default of agreement, determined by arbitration;
   (b) The company shall, after the manner of construction and the line and
   situation of any necessary alternative apparatus have been agreed or
   determined as aforesaid, proceed with all reasonable dispatch to construct and bring into operation the alternative apparatus and thereafter to remove any apparatus required by the undertakers to be
   removed under the provisions of this section:
(6) Notwithstanding anything in paragraph (5) above, if the undertakers
   give notice in writing to the company that they desire to carry out any
   part of so much of the work necessary in connection with the construction of the alternative apparatus, or the removal of the apparatus
   required to be removed, such work, instead of being carried out by the
   company, shall be carried out by the undertakers with all reasonable

dispatch under the superintendence (if given) and to the reasonable satisfaction of the company:

(7) Nothing in paragraph (6) above shall authorise the undertakers to carry out the actual placing, erection, installation, bedding, packing, removal, connection or disconnection of any apparatus or execute any filling around the apparatus (where the apparatus is laid in a trench, tunnel, heading or boring) within 600 millimetres (measured in any direction) of the apparatus:

(8) Where, in accordance with the provisions of this section, the undertakers afford to the company facilities and rights for the construction, maintenance, repair, renewal and inspection in lands of the undertakers of alternative apparatus in substitution for apparatus to be removed as aforesaid, those facilities and rights shall be granted upon such terms and conditions as may be agreed between the undertakers and the company or, in default of agreement, determined by arbitration:

(9) In determining such terms and conditions as mentioned in paragraph (8) above in respect of alternative apparatus to be constructed across or along the authorised works the arbitrator shall—

(a) give effect to all reasonable requirements of the undertakers for ensuring the safety and efficient operation of the authorised works and for securing any subsequent alterations or adaptations of the alternative apparatus which may be required to prevent interference with any such works; and

(b) so far as it may be reasonable and practicable to do so in the circumstances of the case, give effect to any terms and conditions applicable to the apparatus (if any) constructed across or along the authorised works for which the alternative apparatus is to be substituted:

(10) If the facilities and rights to be afforded by the undertakers in respect of any alternative apparatus under paragraph (8) above and the terms and conditions subject to which the same are to be granted are, in the opinion of the arbitrator, more or less favourable on the whole to the company than the facilities, rights, terms and conditions applying to the apparatus to be removed, the arbitrator shall make such provision for the payment of compensation to or by the undertakers by or to the company in respect thereof as shall appear to him to be reasonable having regard to all the circumstances of the case:

(11) (a) Not less than 56 days before commencing to construct any of the authorised works which are near to, or will or may affect, any apparatus the removal of which has not been required by the undertakers under paragraph (4) above, the undertakers shall submit to the company a plan, section and description of the works to be constructed;

(b) Such works shall be constructed only in accordance with the plan, section and description submitted as aforesaid and in accordance with such reasonable requirements as may be made by the company for the alteration or otherwise for the protection of the apparatus, or for securing access thereto, and the company shall be entitled by their officer to watch and inspect the construction of such works:

(12) If the company within 42 days after the submission to them of any plan, section and description under paragraph (11) above shall, in consequence of the works proposed by the undertakers, reasonably require the removal of any apparatus and give written notice to the undertakers of such requirement, the foregoing provisions of this section shall have effect as if the removal of such apparatus had been required by the undertakers under paragraph (4) above:

(13) Nothing in paragraph (11) or (12) above shall preclude the undertakers from submitting at any time, or from time to time, but in no case

less than 28 days before commencing the construction of any such works, a new plan, section and description thereof in lieu of the plan, section and description previously submitted, and thereupon the provisions of those paragraphs shall apply to, and in respect of, such new plan, section and description:

(14) The undertakers shall not be required to comply with paragraph (11)(a) above in a case of emergency but, in such a case, they shall give to the company notice so soon as reasonably practicable, and a plan, section and description of the works so soon as reasonably practicable thereafter, and shall comply with paragraph (11)(b) above so far as reasonably practicable in the circumstances:

(15) If in consequence of the exercise of the powers of this Act the access to any apparatus is materially obstructed the undertakers shall provide alternative means of access to such apparatus:

(16) The following provisions of this paragraph shall have effect for the provision by the undertakers, in the construction of the railways authorised by this Act, of accommodation or other facilities for the laying of apparatus under the railways:—

(a) Not less than six months before the undertakers commence the construction of any of the railways in any highway they shall give notice thereof in writing to each of the companies;

(b) If, within 56 days from the service on them of notice of the intended construction of any works under paragraph (a) above, the company give to the undertakers notice in writing that they desire such accommodation or other facilities to be provided, and such information as the undertakers may require to enable them to determine the extent and description of the accommodation or facilities to be provided and the means of access to apparatus laid therein, the undertakers shall, so far as it is reasonably practicable to do so, provide in the construction of the railway such accommodation or facilities for the laying of apparatus under the railway as may be agreed between them and the company, or in default of agreement, determined by arbitration;

(c) Subject to the provisions of this section, the company shall be entitled to use accommodation or other facilities and the means of access thereto provided by the undertakers for the laying and installing therein of the apparatus for which they were provided and for the purpose of inspecting, repairing, removing or renewing that apparatus;

(d) Except in case of emergency when they shall give such notice as they can in the circumstances, the company shall give the undertakers not less than 42 days' notice of their intention to lay and install or to repair, remove or renew apparatus in any such accommodation or facilities;

(e) In laying and installing apparatus in accommodation or other facilities provided by the undertakers the company shall conform with the reasonable requirements of the undertakers as to the times at which, and the manner in which, such company's works affecting the railways shall be carried out, and the undertakers shall be entitled to superintend the carrying out of such works;

(f) The company shall maintain in good repair and to the reasonable satisfaction of the undertakers any apparatus laid and installed in accommodation or facilities provided by the undertakers and shall take such precautions as the undertakers reasonably require to be taken for ensuring the safety of the railway and the traffic thereon;

(g) The accommodation or facilities provided by the undertakers shall be maintained by the undertakers to the reasonable satisfaction of the company;

(h) Except in case of emergency when they shall give such notice as they can, the undertakers shall give to the company not less than 42 days' notice in writing of their intention to carry out any works affecting any such accommodation or facilities and, in carrying out the same, shall take such measures as the company may reasonably require for the protection of, or for preventing interference with, their apparatus laid or installed therein:

(17) (a) The undertakers shall repay the reasonable expenses incurred by the company in, or in connection with—

(i) the removal and re-laying or replacing, alteration or protection of any apparatus or the provision and construction of any new apparatus under any of the provisions of this section; and

(ii) the cutting off of any apparatus from any other apparatus;

(b) Subsections (3) and (4) of section 23 of the Public Utilities Street Works Act 1950 shall, so far as material, apply to any payment to be made by the undertakers under sub-paragraph (a) above as if the works there mentioned were such undertakers' works as are referred to in the said subsection (3), and as if in that subsection for the words "specified as so necessary in a specification of the works settled under Part I of the Fourth Schedule to this Act or agreed so to be by the promoting authority" there were substituted the words "agreed or settled by arbitration under section 45 (For protection of certain statutory undertakers) of the Greater Nottingham Light Rapid Transit Act 1994":

(18) (a) If, by reason or in consequence of the construction or failure of any of the authorised works or any subsidence resulting from any of those works, any damage shall be caused to any apparatus (other than apparatus the repair of which is not reasonably necessary in view of its intended removal) or property of the company, or any interruption shall be caused in the supply of electricity, gas or, as the case may be, water by the company, the undertakers shall repay the cost reasonably incurred by the company in making good such damage, or restoring the supply, and shall—

(i) make reasonable compensation to the company for any loss sustained by them; and

(ii) indemnify the company against all claims, demands, proceedings, costs, damages and expenses which may be made or taken against or recovered from, or incurred by, the company;

by reason or in consequence of any such damage or interruption;

(b) Nothing in sub-paragraph (a) above shall impose any liability on the undertakers with respect to any damage or interruption to the extent that such damage or interruption is attributable to the neglect or default of the company, their officers, servants, contractors or other agents;

(c) The company shall give to the undertakers reasonable notice of any claim or demand as aforesaid and no settlement or compromise thereof shall be made without the consent of the undertakers:

(19) Where, in consequence of this Act, any part of any street, bridleway or footpath in which any apparatus is situate ceases to be part of the street, bridleway or footpath, the company may exercise the same rights of access to such apparatus as they enjoyed immediately before the passing of this Act, but nothing in this paragraph shall prejudice or affect any right of the undertakers or of the company to require removal of such apparatus under this section or the power of the undertakers to construct works in accordance with paragraph (11) above:

(20) Notwithstanding the temporary stopping-up or diversion of any highway under the powers of section 18 (Temporary stoppage of highways) of this Act, the company shall be at liberty at all times to carry out and do all such works and things in, upon or under any such highway as may be reasonably necessary to enable them to inspect, repair, maintain, renew, remove or use any apparatus which at the time of the stopping-up or diversion was in that highway:

(21) The undertakers shall, so far as is reasonably practicable, so exercise the powers conferred by section 22 (Underpinning of houses near works) of this Act as not to obstruct or render less convenient the access to any apparatus:

(22) (a) Any difference arising between the undertakers and the company under this section (other than a difference as to its meaning or construction) shall be determined by arbitration;

(b) In determining any difference under this section the arbitrator may, if he thinks fit, require the undertakers to construct any temporary or other works so as to avoid, so far as may be reasonably possible, interference with the use of any apparatus.

For protection of telecommunications operators

46. For the protection of telecommunications operators the following provisions shall, unless otherwise agreed in writing between the undertakers and the telecommunications operators concerned, apply and have effect:—

(1) In this section expressions defined in the Telecommunications Act 1984 have the same meanings as in that Act.

(2) The temporary stopping-up or diversion of any highway under section 18 (Temporary stoppage of highways) of this Act shall not affect any right of a telecommunications operator under paragraph 9 of the telecommunications code to inspect, maintain, adjust, repair or alter any apparatus which, at the time of the stopping-up or diversion, is in that highway.

Crown rights

47.—(1) Nothing in this Act affects prejudicially any estate, right, power, privilege or exemption of the Crown and, without prejudice to the generality of the foregoing, nothing in this Act authorises the undertakers to take, use or in any manner interfere with any land or hereditaments or any rights of whatsoever description—

(a) belonging to Her Majesty in right of Her Crown and under the management of the Crown Estate Commissioners, without the consent in writing of those commissioners; or

(b) belonging to Her Majesty in right of Her Crown and under the management (pursuant to any statute or otherwise) of the Secretary of State, without his consent in writing; or

(c) belonging to a government department or held in trust for Her Majesty for the purposes of a government department, without the consent in writing of that government department.

(2) A consent under subsection (1) above may be given unconditionally or subject to such conditions and upon such terms as may be considered necessary or appropriate.

(3) Nothing in this section shall prejudice or affect the exercise of statutory powers to carry out works in or affecting any highway vested in or maintained by the Secretary of State in relation to which the provisions of section 39 (As to highways, traffic, etc.) of this Act apply.

PART V

PENALTY FARES

Interpretation for Part V

48.—(1) In this Part of this Act, unless the context otherwise requires—
"authorised person" means, in relation to any purpose, a person authorised for that purpose by the undertakers;
"fare ticket" means a ticket authorising the person in respect of whom it is issued to travel on the LRT system;
"general travel authority" means any permit, other than a fare ticket, authorising the person in respect of whom it is issued to travel on the LRT system;
"LRT stop" means a station or other regular stopping place on the LRT system at which passengers may get on or off tramcars;
"penalty fare" means a penalty fare payable pursuant to section 50 of this Act;
"the penalty fare provisions" means sections 50 to 54 of this Act.

(2) Any reference in this Part to a person producing a fare ticket or general travel authority on being required to do so by an authorised person is a reference to producing, when so required, a fare ticket or general travel authority which, either by itself or together with any other document produced by that person at the same time, is valid for the journey he has made.

(3) For the purposes of subsection (2) above, a person who is on a tramcar shall be taken to have made a journey ending at the next scheduled LRT stop.

Operation of Part

49.—(1) The penalty fare provisions have effect in relation to travel on any tramcar if an order under subsection (2) below is for the time being in force.

(2) The Secretary of State may by order (referred to in subsections (3) to (5) below as an "activating order") provide that the penalty fare provisions shall have effect as from such day as may be specified in the order.

(3) The revocation by the Secretary of State of an activating order shall be without prejudice to the power of the Secretary of State to make further activating orders.

(4) Any activating order, and any order revoking an activating order, may contain such supplementary, incidental and consequential provisions (including transitional provisions) as may appear to the Secretary of State to be necessary or expedient.

(5) No activating order may be made except at the request of the undertakers.

Penalty fares

50.—(1) If a person travelling on a tramcar, on being required to do so by an authorised person, fails to produce a fare ticket or a general travel authority, he shall be liable to pay a penalty fare if required to do so by an authorised person.

(2)(a) A person shall not be liable to pay a penalty fare if at the LRT stop where, and the time when, he boarded the tramcar—
   (i) in the case of a person falling within paragraph (b) below, there were no facilities for making the required imprint on fare tickets; or

(ii) in the case of any other person, there were no facilities for the sale of the necessary fare ticket for his journey.

(b) A person falls within this paragraph if (pursuant to a requirement under subsection (1) above) he produces a fare ticket which is invalid only by reason of its not bearing the required imprint.

(3) Subsections (4) and (5) below have effect with respect to the burden of proof in any action for the recovery of a penalty fare under this section so far as concerns the question whether the facts of the case fall within subsection (2) above.

(4) In any case where the defendant has provided the plaintiff with a relevant statement in due time it shall be for the plaintiff to show that the facts of the case do not fall within subsection (2) above, and in any other case it shall be for the defendant to show that the facts of the case fall within that provision.

(5) For the purposes of subsection (4) above—

(a) a relevant statement is a statement giving an explanation of the defendant's failure to produce a fare ticket or general travel authority, together with any information as to his journey relevant to that explanation (including, in every case, an indication of the LRT stop where he boarded the tramcar); and

(b) a statement is provided in due time if it is provided when the defendant is required to produce a fare ticket or general travel authority, or at any later time before the expiration of the period of 21 days beginning with the day following the day on which the journey is completed.

(6) In this section "the required imprint" means an imprint signifying a date, time and stop (being the date and time when, and the LRT stop where, the imprint is made).

Amount of penalty fare

51.—(1) Subject to subsection (2) below, a penalty fare shall be £10 and shall be payable to the undertakers before the expiration of the period of 21 days beginning with the day following the day on which the journey in respect of which it is payable is completed.

(2) The Secretary of State may by order prescribe that the amount of the penalty fare shall be different (whether higher or lower), and any such order shall be subject to annulment in pursuance of a resolution of either House of Parliament.

Document to be issued in connection with penalty fare requirement

52.—(1) An authorised person who requires a person (referred to below as "the passenger") to pay a penalty fare shall give him either a receipt for the payment of the amount of the penalty (where the passenger makes that payment to the authorised person) or a notice stating that the requirement has been made.

(2) A receipt or notice given under subsection (1) above shall specify the passenger's destination on the tramcar on which he is travelling when required to pay the penalty fare, and shall operate as an authority to him to complete his journey to that destination.

(3) For the purposes of subsection (2) above, the passenger's destination shall (unless only one destination is possible in the circumstances) be taken to be the destination stated by the passenger or, in default of any statement by him for that purpose, such destination as may be specified by the authorised person.

Notice of penalty fare provisions

53.—(1) It shall be the duty of the undertakers to secure that a warning notice meeting the requirements of subsection (2) below shall be posted—

(a) at every LRT stop, in such a position as to be readily visible to prospective passengers; and

(b) in every tramcar for travel on which the penalty provisions have effect, in such a position as to be readily visible to passengers travelling on that tramcar.

(2) A warning notice posted pursuant to subsection (1) above shall (however expressed) indicate the circumstances (as provided in section 50 of this Act) in which persons travelling on a tramcar may be liable to pay a penalty fare and state the amount of the penalty fare.

Supplementary provisions

54.—(1) A person who is required to pay a penalty fare shall, unless he pays, immediately and in cash, the amount of the penalty fare to an authorised person requiring such payment, give to that authorised person, if that person requires him to do so, his name and address; and any person failing to do so shall be guilty of an offence and liable on summary conviction to a fine not exceeding level 2 on the standard scale.

(2) Where an authorised person requires any person to do anything pursuant to any provision of this Part of this Act he shall, if so requested by the person concerned, produce to that person a duly authenticated document showing his authority; and a requirement by an authorised person shall be of no effect if, as respects that requirement, he fails to comply with this subsection.

Exclusion of double liability

55.—(1) Where a person has become liable to pay a penalty fare in respect of any journey (referred to below as "the relevant journey"), no proceedings may be brought against him for any of the offences specified in subsection (2) below before the end of the period mentioned in section 51(1) of this Act; and no such proceedings may be brought after the end of that period if—

(a) he has paid the penalty fare to the undertakers before the end of that period; or

(b) an action has been brought against him for the recovery of that fare.

(2) The offences mentioned in subsection (1) above are—

(a) any offence under byelaws made under section 62 below involving a failure to obtain or produce a fare ticket or general travel authority for the relevant journey;

(b) any offence under section 25(3) of the Public Passenger Vehicles Act 1981 of contravening or failing to comply with any provision of regulations for the time being having effect by virtue of that section and section 63 (Tramcars on LRT system deemed public service vehicles) of this Act by failing to pay the fare properly payable for the relevant journey or any part of it; and

(c) any offence under section 5(3)(a) or (b) of the Regulation of Railways Act 1889 (travelling without paying the correct fare with intent to avoid payment) arising from the relevant journey.

(3) If proceedings are brought against any such person for any such offence he shall cease to be liable to pay the penalty fare and, if he has paid it, the undertakers shall be liable to repay to him an amount equal to the amount of that fare.

Orders under this Part

56. Any power to make an order conferred on the Secretary of State by this Part shall be exercisable by statutory instrument.

PART VI

MISCELLANEOUS AND GENERAL

Noise insulation

Insulation against noise

57.—(1) The undertakers shall make a scheme providing for the making of grants towards the cost of insulating buildings, or such classes of buildings as the undertakers may think fit, or any parts of any such buildings, against noise caused, or expected to be caused, by the use of the LRT system.

(2)(a) A scheme under subsection (1) above shall in particular require the undertakers to make grants towards the cost of insulating any habitable room comprised in a residential building if noise caused by the use of the LRT system and audible within that room habitually exceeds either of the levels specified in column (2) of the following table between the hours specified in relation to that level in column (1) of the table; but nothing in this paragraph shall preclude the undertakers from including in a scheme under subsection (1) above provisions authorising them to make grants at their discretion towards any other cost falling within that subsection.

TABLE

Hours (1)	Noise level (dB(A) – LAeq) (2)
Between 0700 hours and 2300 hours on any day	68
Between 2300 hours on any day and 0700 hours on the following day	63

(b) In this subsection "habitable room" means a room which could reasonably be lived in or slept in and includes a living room, a dining room, a kitchen and a bedroom, but excludes a bathroom, a water-closet, a staircase, corridor or landing, a cloakroom, a utility room and an outhouse.

(c) The following provisions of this section are without prejudice to this subsection and in particular, but without prejudice to the generality of the foregoing, an application for a grant for which provision is made by this subsection shall not be invalid by reason of the fact that it is not made on the date specified in accordance with subsection (4)(d) below if it is made during a period beginning with the opening to the public of the part of the LRT system to which the application relates and ending five years thereafter.

(3) The undertakers may make grants in accordance with a scheme made under subsection (1) above.

(4) A scheme under subsection (1) above—

(a) shall specify the areas in respect of which grants are payable;

(b) shall make provision as to the persons to whom, the expenditure in respect of which, and the rate at which the grants are to be paid;

(c) may make the payment of any grant dependent upon compliance with such conditions as may be specified in the scheme;

(d) shall specify a date, not less than two years after first publication of the notice referred to in subsection (6) below, for the submission of a valid application for a grant; and

(e) shall require the undertakers, in any case where application for a grant is refused, to give to the applicant at his request a written statement of their reasons for the refusal.

(5) A scheme under subsection (1) above may make different provisions with respect to different areas or different circumstances and may be varied or revoked by a subsequent scheme under subsection (1) above without affecting grants already made.

(6)(a) As soon as may be after the making of a scheme under this section the undertakers shall publish, once at least in each of two successive weeks in one or more newspapers circulating in the areas to which the scheme relates, a notice stating the general effect of the scheme and specifying a place or places in each such area where a copy of the scheme may be inspected by any person free of charge at all reasonable hours.

(b) A photostatic or other reproduction certified by the secretary of the undertakers or some other person authorised by the undertakers for that purpose to be a true reproduction of a page, or part of a page, of any newspaper bearing the date of its publication and containing a notice mentioned in this subsection shall be evidence of the publication of the notice and of the date of publication.

Orders for insulating new buildings

58.—(1) Where the undertakers have made a scheme under section 57 (Insulation against noise) of this Act in respect of any area or areas, they may apply to the Secretary of State for an order requiring provision for insulation against noise to be made in any building of a class to which the scheme applies which is erected after a date specified in the order, or in any extension of, or alteration to, any building of such class made after that date.

(2) The order shall define by reference to a map the areas to which it applies, which may comprise the whole or part of any areas to which the scheme relates.

(3) Application for an order under this section shall be accompanied by a draft of the order and a map defining the areas to which it relates.

(4) Before making application for an order under this section the undertakers shall publish, once at least in each of two successive weeks in one or more newspapers circulating in the areas to which the draft order applies, a notice—

(a) stating the general effect of the intended order;
(b) specifying a place in the said areas where a copy of the draft order and of the relevant map may be inspected by any person free of charge at all reasonable hours during a period of 28 days from the date of the first publication of the notice;
(c) stating that within that period any person may, by notice to the Secretary of State, object to the application.

(5) Any person claiming to be affected by the application may object to it by sending notice of his objection stating the grounds of objection to the Secretary of State within the period specified in the notice and a copy of the notice of objection to the undertakers.

(6) The Secretary of State may make the order in the terms of the draft or in those terms as modified in such manner as he thinks fit:

Provided that, if any objection is duly made by any person appearing to the Secretary of State to be affected by the application and is not withdrawn, the Secretary of State shall not make the order unless he has caused a public local inquiry to be held into the proposed order and has considered the report of the person who held the inquiry.

(7) If the Secretary of State makes an order under this section the undertakers shall publish notice of the making, and of the effect of the order, in one or more newspapers circulating in the areas to which the order relates.

(8) An order under this section shall be a local land charge.

(9) Where—

(a) plans are in accordance with building regulations deposited with a local authority; or

(b) an initial notice is given to a local authority under section 47 of the Building Act 1984;

for the erection, extension or alteration of a building in an area to which an order under this section relates, the local authority shall, notwithstanding anything in section 16 or 47 of the said Act, reject the plans or, as the case may be, the notice unless it is shown to them—

(i) that satisfactory provision will be made for insulating the building (or, as the case may be, the extension or alteration of the building) against noise; or

(ii) that in the case of an extension or alteration no such insulation is necessary.

(10) Section 16(6) to (8) and section 36(2) to (6) and section 48(2) of the Building Act 1984 (notice of rejection or passing of plans, enforcement of requirements and effect of initial notice) shall have effect as if this section were a section of that Act and specified in section 48(3) of that Act.

(11) The Secretary of State may cause such local inquiries to be held as he may consider necessary for the purpose of any of his functions under this section, and section 250(2) to (5) of the Local Government Act 1972 shall apply to any such inquiry.

Repeal of sections 57 and 58

59.—(1) If it appears to the Secretary of State that, as a result of the passing of any enactment after the date of this Act, it is appropriate that sections 57 (Insulation against noise) and 58 (Orders for insulating new buildings) of this Act should be repealed, he may make an order repealing those sections.

(2) An order under this section may contain such transitional, consequential and saving provisions as may be appropriate.

(3) Subsection (11) of section 58 (Orders for insulating new buildings) of this Act shall apply to the functions of the Secretary of State under this section as it applies to his functions under that section.

(4) An order under this section shall be made by statutory instrument and shall not be made except on application by the undertakers.

Prevention of obstacles

Removal of obstructions

60.—(1) If any obstruction to traffic on the LRT system is caused by—

(a) a vehicle on any tramway or at any level crossing waiting, loading, unloading or breaking down; or

(b) a load falling on any tramway or at any level crossing from a vehicle;

the person in charge of the vehicle shall forthwith remove the vehicle or the load so as to prevent the continuance of the obstruction and, if he fails to do so, the undertakers may remove the vehicle or load, taking all necessary steps for that purpose, and may recover from the person responsible the expenses reasonably incurred in doing so.

(2) In subsection (1) above "person responsible" means—

(a) in the case of a vehicle waiting, loading, unloading or breaking down—

(i) the owner of the vehicle at the time at which it became an obstruction to traffic on the LRT system unless he shows that he was not concerned in, or aware of, the vehicle being put or left in that place at that time; and

(ii) the person by whom the vehicle was put or left in the place in which it became an obstruction to traffic on the LRT system; and

(b) in the case of a load falling from a vehicle—
> (i) the owner of the vehicle at the time of that event unless he shows that he was not concerned in, or aware of, the vehicle being put or left, or as the case may be, being in the place at which the load fell from it; and
> (ii) the person in charge of the vehicle at the time when the load fell from it.

Power to lop trees overhanging railway

61.—(1) The undertakers may cut and lop any trees in or near any railway forming part of the LRT system which may in any way interfere with the construction or working of the railway or cables, wires or other apparatus, or with the clear and safe passage of tramcars and their passengers.

(2) In exercising the powers of this section the undertakers shall do no unnecessary damage to trees and shall pay compensation to any person who may sustain damage by reason of the exercise of the powers.

(3) Every case of compensation under subsection (2) above shall be ascertained in accordance with Part I of the Land Compensation Act 1961.

Public order

Byelaws relating to LRT system

62.—(1) The undertakers may make byelaws regulating the use of and, working of, and travel on, the LRT system, the maintenance of order on the LRT system and on the undertakers' premises or other facilities provided in connection with the LRT system and the conduct of all persons including officers and servants of the undertakers while on those premises.

(2) Without prejudice to the generality of subsection (1) above, byelaws under this section may contain provisions—
> (a) with respect to tickets issued for travel on the LRT system, the payment of fares and charges and the evasion of payment of fares and charges;
> (b) with respect to interference with, or obstruction of, the working of the LRT system or other facilities provided in connection with the LRT system;
> (c) for prohibiting or regulating the carriage of dangerous goods on the LRT system;
> (d) regulating the use of vehicles (other than tramcars) on any road along which a tramway is laid;
> (e) with respect to the use of tobacco or other substances and the prevention of nuisances;
> (f) for regulating the passage of bicycles and other vehicles on ways and other places intended for the use of persons on foot within railway premises of the undertakers, not being premises within the boundary of any street;
> (g) for the safe custody and re-delivery or disposal of property found in premises of the undertakers forming part of, or provided in connection with, the LRT system, or elsewhere on the LRT system and for fixing the charges which may be made in respect thereof; and
> (h) for prohibiting or restricting the placing or leaving of any vehicle without its driver on any authorised railway, or in premises of the undertakers forming part of the LRT system.

(3) Byelaws made under this section may provide that any person contravening them shall be liable on summary conviction to a fine not exceeding for each offence level 3 on the standard scale.

(4) Without prejudice to the taking of proceedings under subsection (3) above, if the contravention of any byelaw having effect under this section is

attended with danger or annoyance to the public, or hindrance to the undertakers in the conduct of the LRT system, it shall be lawful for the undertakers summarily to take action to obviate or remove the danger, annoyance or hindrance.

(5) In subsection (4) above the reference to action to obviate or remove danger, annoyance or hindrance includes, in the case of a vehicle parked in any part of any premises provided in connection with the LRT system which is not a public highway, in contravention of any byelaw having effect under this section, action to fix to the vehicle a device or appliance for the purpose of preventing it from being driven or put in motion, together with a notice specifying the steps to be taken to secure the release of the vehicle from the device or appliance.

(6) Subsections (5) to (11) of section 67 of the Transport Act 1962 (confirmation of byelaws) shall apply to any byelaws made by the undertakers under this section as if for references to the board, or to the board in question, there were substituted references to the undertakers.

Tramcars on LRT system deemed public service vehicles

63.—(1) On such day as may be appointed under subsection (2) below, regulations made, or having effect as if made, under sections 24, 25, 26 or 60(1)(j) or (k) of the Public Passenger Vehicles Act 1981 shall have effect as if the tramcars used on the LRT system were public service vehicles used in the provision of a local service within the meaning of the Transport Act 1985.

(2)(a) The undertakers may by resolution appoint a day for the purpose of any regulation mentioned in subsection (1) above, the day so appointed being fixed in accordance with paragraph (b) below.

(b) The undertakers shall publish in a newspaper circulating in their area, notice—

    (i) of the passing of any such resolution and of the day fixed thereby; and

    (ii) of the general effect of the enactments for the purposes of which the day has been fixed;

and the day so fixed shall not be earlier than the expiration of 28 days from the date of the publication of the notice.

(c) A photostatic or other reproduction certified by the secretary of the undertakers to be a true reproduction of a page, or part of a page, of any newspaper bearing the date of its publication and containing the notice mentioned in paragraph (b) above shall be evidence of the publication of the notice and of the date of publication.

Intentional obstruction of works or operation of tramways

64.—(1) Any person who, without reasonable excuse, intentionally obstructs another person in the laying out, construction, repair or renewal of any authorised work shall be guilty of an offence and liable on summary conviction to a fine not exceeding level 2 on the standard scale.

(2) Any person who, without reasonable excuse, intentionally—

    (a) removes or alters any part of a tramway;

    (b) operates, moves, or tampers with, any mechanical or electrical apparatus forming part of a tramway; or

    (c) places any obstruction on any part of a tramway or otherwise obstructs a tramcar on any tramway;

shall be guilty of an offence and liable on summary conviction to a fine not exceeding level 3 on the standard scale.

For better prevention of trespass on railways

65.—(1) Any person who trespasses upon any railway lines or sidings or in any tunnel or upon any viaduct, bridge embankment, cutting or similar work forming part of any railway of the LRT system which is not designated as a tramway and which is sufficiently fenced to deter trespass, or upon any other lands of the undertakers in dangerous proximity to any such lines or other works or to any electrical apparatus used for or in connection with the working of any such railway, shall be guilty of an offence and liable on summary conviction to a fine not exceeding level 3 on the standard scale.

(2) No person shall be convicted of an offence under this section unless it shall be proved to the satisfaction of the court before which complaint is laid that public warning has been given to persons not to trespass upon the railways of the LRT system by notice clearly exhibited and maintained at the station on the LRT system nearest to the place where the offence is alleged to have been committed.

Modification of railway regulation enactments

66.—(1) In their application to the undertakers and the LRT system the enactments specified in column (1) of the following table (which create the offences broadly described in column (2) of the table) shall each have effect as if the maximum fine which may be imposed on summary conviction of any offence specified in the enactment were, instead of that specified in column (3) of the table, a fine not exceeding the level specified in column (4) of the table.

THE TABLE

Enactment	Description of offence	Maximum fine otherwise applicable (level on standard scale)	Maximum fine (level on standard scale)
(1)	(2)	(3)	(4)
Section 16 of the Railway Regulation Act 1840.	Obstruction of officers of railway company or trespass upon railway.	Level 1.	Level 3.
Section 17 of the Railway Regulation Act 1842.	Misconduct of persons employed on railways.	Level 1.	Level 3.
In section 5 of the Regulation of Railways Act 1889—			
Subsection (1)	Failure to produce ticket, to pay fare or to give name and address.	Level 1.	Level 2.
Subsection (2)	Travel with intent to avoid payment of fare.	Level 2.	Level 3.

(2) In its application to the undertakers and the LRT system subsection (2) of section 5 of the said Act of 1889 (power to arrest passenger who fails to produce ticket and refuses to give his name and address) shall have effect as if in subsection (2) after the word "refuses" there were inserted the words "or fails".

Other provisions

Power to contract for police

67.—(1) The undertakers may from time to time make agreements with the chief officer of police and a police authority for the employment by the undertakers of any members of the police establishment of that police authority for police duty within railway premises of the undertakers or elsewhere upon the LRT system or any part of the LRT system.

(2) Any such agreement may contain such terms and conditions and provide for such payment or consideration as the undertakers may agree with the police authority.

(3) In this section "police authority" includes—

(a) a police authority within the meaning of the Police Act 1964; and

(b) the railways board.

Power to operate LRT system and charge

68.—(1) The undertakers may operate and use the LRT system for the carriage of passengers and goods.

(2) The undertakers may demand, take and recover such charges for the use of the LRT system and any services and facilities provided in connection therewith, and may make such use subject to such terms and conditions, as they think fit.

Arrangements with other operators

69.—(1) The undertakers may enter into and carry into effect agreements with other persons providing public passenger transport services with regard to the issue of travel cards and the making of through ticketing arrangements.

(2) In this section "public passenger transport service" has the meaning given by section 63(10)(a) of the Transport Act 1985.

Power to form companies, etc.

70. The undertakers may form and promote, or join with any other person in forming and promoting, a company for carrying on any activities which the undertakers have power to carry on under this Act.

Powers of disposal, agreements for operation, etc.

71.—(1) The undertakers may, with the consent of the Secretary of State, sell, lease, charge or otherwise dispose of, on such terms and conditions as they think fit, the whole or any part of the LRT system or the right to operate the LRT system under this Act, to any person, including Greater Nottingham Rapid Transit Limited or any company formed under section 70 (Power to form companies, etc.) of this Act.

(2) Without prejudice to the generality of subsection (1) above, the undertakers may enter into and carry into effect agreements with any person, including Greater Nottingham Rapid Transit Limited or any company formed under section 70 (Power to form companies, etc.) of this Act with respect to any of the following matters, namely, the construction, maintenance, use and operation of the LRT system, or any part or parts of that system, by any such person, and other matters incidental or subsidiary thereto or consequential thereon, and the defraying of, or the making of contributions towards, the cost of the matters aforesaid by the undertakers or any such person.

(3) Any agreement under subsection (2) above may provide (inter alia) for the exercise of the powers of the undertakers in respect of the LRT system or any part or parts thereof, and for the transfer to any person of the LRT system or any part or parts thereof together with the rights and obligations of the undertakers in relation thereto.

(4) The exercise of the powers of any enactment by any person in pursuance of any sale, lease, charge or disposal under subsection (1) above, or any agreement under subsection (2) above shall be subject to the same restrictions, liabilities and obligations as would apply under this Act, or under any agreement or undertaking concerning the exercise of the powers of this Act, if those powers were exercised by the undertakers.

(5) The railways board may enter into and carry into effect agreements with the undertakers under subsection (2) above.

Application of landlord and tenant law

72.—(1) This section applies to any agreement for leasing to any person the whole or any part of the LRT system or the right to operate the same under section 71(1) of this Act or any agreement entered into by the undertakers with any person for the construction, maintenance, use or operation of the LRT system, or any part of that system under section 71(2) of this Act, so far as any such agreement relates to the terms on which any land which is the subject of a lease granted by or under that agreement is to be provided for that person's use.

(2) No enactment or rule of law regulating the rights and obligations of landlords and tenants shall prejudice the operation of any agreement to which this section applies.

(3) Accordingly no such enactment or rule of law shall apply in relation to the rights and obligations of the parties to any lease granted by or under any such agreement so as to—

    (a) exclude or in any respect modify any of the rights and obligations of those parties under the terms of the lease, whether with respect to the termination of the tenancy or any other matter;

    (b) confer or impose on any such party any right or obligation arising out of or connected with anything done or omitted on or in relation to land which is the subject of the lease, in addition to any such right or obligation provided for by the terms of the lease; or

    (c) restrict the enforcement (whether by action for damages or otherwise) by any party to the lease of any obligation of any other party under the lease.

Substitute road services

73.—(1) The undertakers may provide or secure the provision by other persons of services for the carriage of passengers by road ("substitute services") where the LRT system has been temporarily interrupted, curtailed or discontinued.

(2) The route, frequency and stopping places of any substitute service need not correspond with the route of the interrupted, curtailed or discontinued service.

(3) Section 6 of the Transport Act 1985 shall not apply to any substitute services.

Advisory committee

74.—(1) The undertakers shall establish a committee to be known as the Greater Nottingham Light Rapid Transit Advisory Committee ("the advisory committee") to advise the undertakers as regards the construction and operation of the LRT system.

(2) Before making appointments to the advisory committee the undertakers shall consult the Rail Users' Consultative Committee for the time being established under section 2(2) of the Act of 1993 for the area where the LRT system is situated.

(3) It shall be the duty of the advisory committee to consider representations made to them as regards the construction and operation of the LRT system by members of the public.

Disapplication of enactment

75. Section 21 (For the protection of the Corporation of Nottingham) of the Manchester, Sheffield and Lincolnshire Railway (Extension to London &c.) Act 1893 shall not apply to any of the authorised works.

Forest Recreation Ground

76.—(1) In this section—

"the car park" means the interchange car park and associated facilities to be provided pursuant to section 26 of, and Schedule 4 to, this Act on the lands in the City numbered 192 on the deposited plans;

"the designated works" means so much of Works Nos. 2E, 3A and 3B as is situated on the relevant land;

"the particular purpose" means the provision of the car park; and

"the relevant land" means so much of the lands in the City numbered 192 on the deposited plans as is not required for Work No. 2J.

(2) Nothing in this Act shall authorise the undertakers to acquire any part of the relevant land for the particular purpose but the City Council may make the relevant land or any part thereof available to the undertakers for the particular purpose on the terms specified in subsection (3) of this section.

(3) The terms to which this subsection applies are such terms as the City Council considers appropriate and shall in particular include provisions such as are referred to in Schedule 6 to this Act.

(4) If at any time after the opening to traffic of the designated works the undertakers cease to operate any part of those works with the intention that that cessation shall be permanent, they shall as soon as reasonably practicable, unless otherwise agreed with the City Council—

(a) remove the rails and any other works, equipment and apparatus which have become redundant; and

(b) restore, to the reasonable satisfaction of the City Council, the relevant land to as good a condition as that in which it was before the making of the designated works.

(5) Following the completion of any restoration pursuant to subsection (4)(b) above so much of the relevant land as is so restored shall continue to be held by the City Council as though this Act had not been passed.

Fencing of railways

77. Nothing in this Act or any other enactment shall require the undertakers to fence—

(a) so much of the authorised railways as is constructed in or adjoining the Forest Recreation Ground; or

(b) any other portion of the authorised railways which, not being designated as a tramway, adjoins any public open space or other unenclosed land.

Level crossings at Basford Vernon

78.—(1) In this section—

"the additional David Lane crossing" means the level crossing authorised to be provided by the undertakers adjoining the existing David Lane crossing pursuant to section 9 of this Act, whereby Work No. 7 will be carried over David Lane, Basford Vernon;

"the board's new level crossing" means the new level crossing authorised to be provided by the railways board at Basford Vernon pursuant to the relevant section;

"the existing David Lane crossing" means the existing David Lane level crossing as defined in the relevant section;

"the new road" means the new road referred to in the relevant section;

"the northern crossings" means the board's new level crossing and the undertakers' new level crossing;

"the relevant section" means section 21 of the British Railways Act 1990;

"the southern crossings" means the additional David Lane crossing and the existing David Lane crossing;

"the undertakers' new level crossing" means the new level crossing authorised to be provided by the undertakers adjoining the board's new level crossing pursuant to section 9 of this Act, whereby Work No. 7 will be carried over the new road.

(2)(a) This subsection shall apply if, at the date when the undertakers are ready to carry Work No. 7 over David Lane by the additional David Lane crossing, the board's new level crossing has not been completed and opened for public use.

(b) If this subsection applies, then, notwithstanding anything in the relevant section, the extinguishment of all rights of way over the existing David Lane crossing pursuant to the relevant section shall not take effect until—

   (i) both the board's new level crossing and the undertakers' new level crossing have been completed and opened for public use; and

   (ii) the County Council determine that the existing David Lane crossing and the additional David Lane crossing shall be closed.

(c) Upon the extinguishment, as from the completion and opening for public use of the board's new level crossing, of all rights of way over the existing David Lane crossing pursuant to subsection (4) of the relevant section (as that section has effect subject to paragraph (b) above) all rights of way over the additional David Lane crossing shall also be extinguished.

(3)(a) This subsection shall apply if—

   (i) before the date when the undertakers are ready to carry Work No. 7 over David Lane, the board's new level crossing has been completed and opened for public use; and

   (ii) the County Council and the railways board have not entered into an agreement pursuant to subsection (4) below whereby both the northern crossings and the southern crossings shall be kept open for public use.

(b) If this subsection applies—

   (i) the undertakers shall not be required to provide the additional David Lane crossing; and

   (ii) all rights of way over so much of David Lane as is required for Work No. 7 shall be extinguished as from the completion and opening for public use of the board's new level crossing.

(4) Notwithstanding anything in the foregoing provision of this section or in the relevant sections the County Council and the railways board may enter into and carry into effect agreements whereby both the northern crossings and the southern crossings shall be kept open for public use.

Restoration of streets if tramway discontinued

79. If the undertakers cease to operate any tramway with the intention that that cessation shall be permanent, they shall as soon as reasonably practicable, unless otherwise agreed with the highway authority—

   (a) remove from the street in which that discontinued tramway is laid, the rails and any other works, equipment and apparatus which have become redundant; and

   (b) restore, to the reasonable satisfaction of the highway authority, the part of the street along which the discontinued tramway was laid, regard being had to the condition of the street before the tramway was laid.

Local inquiries

80.—(1) Subject to subsection (2) below, subsections (2) to (5) of section 250 of the Local Government Act 1972 (supplementary provisions with respect to local inquiries held in pursuance of that section) shall apply to local inquiries under this Act as they apply to inquiries under that section.

(2) Subsection (4) of the said section 250 shall apply in accordance with subsection (1) above, in relation to such local inquiries as are held with respect to any order under this Act as if the reference to a local authority in that subsection were a reference to the undertakers.

Arbitration

81. Where under this Act any difference (other than a difference to which the provisions of the Act of 1965 apply) is to be determined by arbitration, then, unless otherwise provided, the difference shall be referred to and settled by a single arbitrator to be agreed between the parties or, failing agreement, to be appointed, on the application of either party (after notice in writing to the other)—

(a) in the case of a difference under section 40 (Approval of plans by local authorities, etc.) relating to works in the Forest Recreation Ground, by the President of the Landscape Institute;

(b) in the case of any other difference arising under the said section 40, by the President of the Royal Town Planning Institute following consultation with the President of the Royal Institute of British Architects;

(c) in any other case, by the President of the Institution of Civil Engineers.

Planning permission

82.—(1) Subject to subsection (2) below, in its application to development authorised by this Act, the planning permission specified in subsection (3) below shall have effect as if the authority to develop given by this Act were limited to development begun within 10 years after the passing of this Act.

(2) Subsection (1) above shall not apply to the carrying out of any development consisting of the alteration, maintenance or repair of the authorised works or the substitution of new works therefor.

(3) The planning permission referred to in subsection (1) above is that granted for development permitted by article 3 of, and Class A in Part 11 of Schedule 2 to, the Town and Country Planning General Development Order 1988 (which permits development authorised by private Act designating specifically both the nature of the development thereby authorised and the land on which it may be carried out).

SCHEDULES

Section 6(1)   SCHEDULE 1

The authorised works

Part I

Description of works specifically authorised

In the City of Nottingham

Work No. 1—A railway (309 metres in length) commencing at a point on the existing viaduct of the former Great Central Railway 27 metres north-west of the junction of Station Street with Trent Street, passing northwards along the course of the said former railway over the Nottingham Canal and Canal Street, then by a new ramp from the said existing viaduct and terminating at a point on the eastern side of Middle Hill 85 metres north of its junction with Collin Street, including a new bridge over Canal Street and a new ramp linking the said existing viaduct with Middle Hill.

Work No. 1A—A footbridge over Station Street between a point on the existing footbridge over Nottingham Midland Station 15 metres south-west of the junction of Station Street with Trent Street and a point on the said existing viaduct of the former Great Central Railway 23 metres north-west of the said road junction.

Work No. 2—A railway (1,915 metres in length) commencing by a junction with Work No. 1 at its termination, forming double lines of tramway passing northwards along Middle Hill, Weekday Cross and Fletcher Gate, westwards along Victoria Street, Cheapside, Poultry South Parade, northwards along Beast Market Hill and Market Street, across Upper Parliament Street and Wollaton Street, along Goldsmith Street and Waverley Street and terminating at a point on Waverley Street 63 metres south of the junction of that street with Gedling Grove.

Work No. 2A—A widening on the south-western side of Goldsmith Street between a point 50 metres north-west of its junction with Chaucer Street and a point 30 metres south of its junction with Shakespeare Street.

Work No. 2B—A widening on the east side of Middle Hill between a point 35 metres south of its junction with Weekday Cross and a point 16 metres south of that junction.

Work No. 2C—A railway (257 metres in length) commencing by a junction with Work No. 2 at its termination, forming a single line of tramway passing north-westwards along the eastern side of Waverley Street and the northern side of Mount Hooton Road and terminating at a point on Mount Hooton Road 97 metres south-east of the junction of that street with Hardy Street including the alteration of the level of Waverley Street between a point 60 metres north-west of its junction with Arboretum Street and a point 40 metres south of its junction with Forest Road East.

Work No. 2D—A railway (250 metres in length) commencing by a junction with Work No. 2 at its termination, forming a single line of tramway passing north-westwards along the western side of Waverley Street and the southern side of Mount Hooton Road and terminating at a point on Mount Hooton Road 97 metres south-east of the junction of that street with Hardy Street together with a retaining wall on the south-western side of Waverley Street between a point 45 metres north-west of its junction with Arthur Street and a point 40 metres south of its junction with Forest Road West.

Work No. 2E—A railway (419 metres in length) commencing by a junction with Works Nos. 2C and 2D at their termination, forming double lines of tramway (331 metres in length) passing north-westwards and northwards along Mount Hooton Road and Noel Street to a point on the eastern side of Noel Street 100 metres north of its junction with Bentinck Road, then passing northwards through the Forest Recreation Ground and terminating at a point on the southern side of Gregory Boulevard at its junction with Noel Street.

Work No. 2F—A widening including alteration of the line of the carriageway on the north-eastern side of Waverley Street between a point 67 metres north of its junction with Arboretum Street and a point 35 metres south of its junction with Forest Road East.

Work No. 2G—A widening including alteration of the line of the carriageway on the northern side of Forest Road East and the north-eastern side of Mount Hooton Road between a point on Forest Road East 12 metres north-east of its junction with Waverley Street and a point on Mount Hooton Road 107 metres north-west of its junction with Forest Road East.

Work No. 2H—A widening on the north-eastern side of Mount Hooton Road and the southern side of the vehicular access road through the Forest Recreation Ground at the junction of those roads between a point on Mount Hooton Road 43 metres south-east of that junction and a point on the said vehicular access road 21 metres north-east of that junction.

Work No. 2J—A widening on the east side of Noel Street between its junction with the vehicular access road through the Forest Recreation Ground and a point 100 metres north of that junction.

Work No. 3A—A railway (123 metres in length) commencing by a junction with Work No. 2E at its termination, passing eastwards over land adjoining Gregory Boulevard and terminating at a point 20 metres south-east of the junction of Gregory Boulevard and Russell Road.

Work No. 3B—A railway (36 metres in length) commencing by a junction with Work No. 2E, 25 metres south-east of its termination, turning eastwards and terminating by a junction with Work No. 3A, 98 metres west of the termination of that work.

Work No. 4—A railway (115 metres in length) commencing by a junction with Work No. 2E at its termination and Work No. 3A at its commencement forming double lines of tramway passing across Gregory Boulevard, along Noel Street and terminating at a point in Noel Street at its junction with Terrace Street.

Work No. 5A—A railway (806 metres in length) commencing by a junction with Work No. 4 at its termination, forming a single line of tramway (619 metres in length) passing north-westwards along Noel Street and westwards along Gladstone Street to a point 18 metres west of the junction of Fisher Street with Gladstone Street, then passing north-westwards through land between Gladstone Street and Shipstone Street to a point in Shipstone Street 55 metres west of the junction of that street with Fisher Street, then forming a single line of tramway (132 metres in length) passing westwards along Shipstone Street and terminating at the junction of that street with Radford Road and Wilkinson Street (being the point of termination of Work No. 5B).

Work No. 5B—A railway (862 metres in length) commencing by a junction with Work No. 4 at its termination, forming a single line of tramway passing westwards along Terrace Street, north-westwards along Radford Road and terminating at the junction of that road with Shipstone Street (being the point of termination of Work No. 5A).

Work No. 5C—A widening on the southern side of Terrace Street from a point 90 metres west of its junction with Noel Street and a point 60 metres east of its junction with Radford Road.

Work No. 5D—A widening on the northern side of Terrace Street between a point 100 metres west of its junction with Noel Street and its junction with Radford Road.

Work No. 5E—A widening on the eastern side of Radford Road between a point 122 metres south of its junction with Berridge Road and a point 190 metres south of that junction.

Work No. 5F—A widening on the eastern side of Radford Road between a point 80 metres south of its junction with Berridge Road and a point 110 metres south of that junction.

Work No. 6—A railway (680 metres in length) commencing by a junction with Works Nos. 5A and 5B at their termination, forming double lines of tramway (370 metres in length) passing north-westwards along Wilkinson Street to a point on the north side of Wilkinson Street 42 metres west of the bridge carrying that street over the Nottingham to Hucknall railway of the railways board, then turning northwards through land to the west of the said Nottingham to Hucknall railway, then passing alongside that railway and terminating at a point 300 metres north of the bridge carrying Wilkinson Street over the railway of the railways board.

Work No. 6A—A widening on the southern side of Wilkinson Street and the western side of Radford Road between points 20 metres west and 57 metres south of the junction of those roads.

Work No. 6B—A railway (252 metres in length) commencing by a junction with Work No. 6 at a point 40 metres west of the bridge carrying Wilkinson Street over the river Leen forming double lines of tramway (27 metres in length) passing northwards through land adjoining Wilkinson Street and terminating at a point 235 metres north-east of the bridge carrying Wilkinson Street over the said Nottingham to Hucknall railway together with sidings comprising a depot for the LRT system.

In the City of Nottingham and the District of Ashfield, Nottinghamshire

Work No. 7—A railway (5,590 metres in length) commencing in the City by a junction with Work No. 6 at its termination passing northwards and north-westwards alongside the Nottingham to Hucknall railway of the railways board, over the river Leen, under the bridges carrying Western Boulevard and Church Street over the said railway, over the river Leen, across David Lane on the level, over the river Leen, under the bridge carrying Highbury Road over the railway, across Carey Road on the level, under the bridge carrying Moor Bridge over the railway, over the river Leen and terminating at a point in the district of Ashfield 125 metres north of Forge Mills (public footpath) level crossing including three bridges over the river Leen.

Work No. 7A—A footbridge in the City over Work No. 7 and the Nottingham to Hucknall railway of the railways board between Nottingham Road, Basford and Vernon Road.

Work No. 7B—A footbridge in the City over Work No. 7 and the Nottingham to Hucknall railway of the railways board between Lincoln Street, Basford and Vernon Road.

Work No. 7C—A diversion of the river Leen in the City at Old Basford between the western abutment of the bridge carrying the Nottingham to Hucknall railway of the railways board over the said river at a point 65 metres to north-west of that bridge.

Work No. 7D—A footbridge in the City over Work No. 7 and the Nottingham to Hucknall railway of the railways board between Deptford Crescent and Coventry Road, Bulwell.

Work No. 7E—A railway (767 metres in length), in the City forming a deviation of the Nottingham to Hucknall railway of the railways board, commencing at a point 265 metres north-east of the bridge carrying Highbury Road over the said railway passing northwards across Carey Road on the level and terminating at a point 397 metres north of Carey Road level crossing.

Work No. 7F—A footbridge in the City over Work No. 7 and Work No. 7E and the Nottingham to Hucknall railway of the railways board between Carey Road and Bestwood Road.

In the District of Ashfield, Nottinghamshire

Work No. 8—A railway (2,211 metres in length) commencing by a junction with Work No. 7 at its termination, passing north-westwards alongside the Nottingham to Hucknall railway of the railways board and terminating at Hucknall at a point one metre south of the southern parapet of the bridge carrying Station Road, Hucknall over the said railway.

Work No. 8A—A railway (1,195 metres in length), commencing by a junction with the existing Calverton Colliery branch railway at a point 297 metres north of the existing Forge Mills level crossing, passing north-westwards forming (as to part) a deviation of the Nottingham to Hucknall railway of the railways board and terminating by a junction with that railway at a point 85 metres north of Brickyard Drive level crossing.

Work No. 8B—A footbridge at Broomhill, Hucknall over Works Nos. 8 and 8A and the Nottingham to Hucknall railway of the railways board between the eastern and western sections of the Bestwood footpath.

In the City of Nottingham and the Borough of Broxtowe, Nottinghamshire

Work No. 9—A railway (1,850 metres in length) commencing in the City by a junction with Work No. 7 at a point 190 metres south-east of the footbridge carrying the footpath between Lauriston Drive and the open land adjoining the river Leen over the Nottingham to Hucknall railway of the railways board passing westwards on the formation of the dismantled Babbington branch railway, over the river Leen under the bridges carrying Bagnall Road and Cinderhill Road, and terminating at a point in the borough of Broxtowe, parish of Nuthall 710 metres north-west of the junction of Cinderhill Road with the Eastwood Bypass roundabout, including a new bridge over the river Leen at a point 55 metres south-east of the eastern end of Neston Drive.

PART II

Section 7(1)   *Description of further works and powers*

The undertakers may exercise the following powers and carry out the following works in the City of Nottingham:—

(1) set back the kerbline on the west side of Middle Hill between the points marked A1 and A2;

(2) set forward the kerbline on the east side of Weekday Cross between the points marked A3 and A4;

(3) alter the kerbline on—

    (a) the west side of Weekday Cross between the points marked A5 and A6; and

    (b) the east side of Weekday Cross between the points marked A7 and A8;

(4) set back the kerblines on—

    (a) the west side of Fletcher Gate between the points marked A9 and A10;

    (b) the east side of Fletcher Gate between the points marked A11 and A12;

    (c) the north side of Victoria Street between the points marked A13 and A14;

    (d) the south side of Victoria Street between the points marked A15 and A16; and

    (e) the south side of Poultry between the points marked A17 and A18;

(5) alter the carriageways and kerblines of so much of South Parade and Beast Market Hill and the junction of Market Street with Long Row West, Angel Row and Beast Market Hill between the points marked A19 and A20;

(6) set back the kerbline on—

    (a) the east side of Market Street between the points marked A21 and A22; and

    (b) the east side of the junction of Market Street and Upper Parliament Street between the points marked A23 and A24;

(7) form a kerbline on the north side of Upper Parliament Street at its junction with Wollaton Street between the points marked A25 and A26;

(8) stop up vehicular rights in so much of Wollaton Street between the points marked A27 and A28;

(9) alter the kerbline on the east side of Goldsmith Street between the points marked A29 and A30;

(10) set back—

    (a) the kerbline on the west side of Goldsmith Street between the points marked A31 and A32;

    (b) the footway and kerbline on the south-west side of Goldsmith Street between the points marked A33 and A34;

    (c) the kerbline on the east side of Waverley Street between the points marked A35 and A36;

      (d) the kerbline on the west side of Waverley Street between the points marked A37 and A38;

(11) set back the kerblines on the south-east side and the north-west side of Gedling Grove between the points marked J1 and J2 and J3 and J4 to form a turning-circle;

(12) stop up vehicular rights of access to Gedling Grove at its junction with Waverley Street and form a new footway and kerbline across Gedling Grove between the points marked J5 and J6;

(13) set back the footway and kerbline on the north-eastern side of Waverley Street between the points marked J7 and J8;

(14) set back and otherwise alter the footway and kerbline on the north-eastern side of Waverley Street between the points marked J9 and J10;

(15) set back the footway and kerbline on the north-eastern side of Mount Hooton Road between the points marked J11 and J12 and J13 and J14;

(16) set back the footway and kerbline on the eastern side of Noel Street between the points marked J15 and J16;

(17) set back the kerbline on—

      (a) the north-east side of Noel Street between the points marked C1 and C2; and

      (b) the southern side of the junction of Terrace Street and Noel Street between the points marked D1 and D2;

(18) alter the kerbline on the northern side of the junction of Terrace Street and Noel Street between the points marked D3 and D4;

(19) form a footway and kerbline on the western side of Noel Street between the points marked D5 and D6;

(20) alter the kerbline on—

      (a) the western side of Noel Street between the points marked D7 and D8; and

      (b) the eastern side of Noel Street between the points marked D9 and D10;

(21) set—

      (a) back the kerbline on the southern side of Shipstone Street between the points marked D11 and D12;

      (b) forward the kerbline on the northern side of Terrace Street between the points marked D13 and D14;

      (c) back the kerbline on the southern side of Terrace Street between the points marked D15 and D16 and create a footway between the points marked D15 and D17;

(22) alter—

      (a) the kerbline on the north-east side of Radford Road between the points marked D18 and D19; and

      (b) the footway and kerbline on the north-east side of Radford Road between the points marked D20 and D21;

(23) set back the kerbline on the south-west side of Radford Road between the points marked D22 and D23;

(24) alter—

      (a) the kerbline on the north-east side of Radford Road between the points marked D24 and D25;

      (b) the kerbline on the north side of Wilkinson Street between the points marked E1 and E2; and

      (c) the footway and kerbline on the west side of Radford Road and the south side of Wilkinson Street between its junctions with Gauntley Street and Radford Road between the points marked E3 and E4;

(25) set back the kerbline on the southern side of Wilkinson Street between the points marked E4 and E4A;

(26) set back the kerbline on the south side of Wilkinson Street between the points marked E5 and E6;

(27) form a new kerbline on the north side of Wilkinson Street between the points marked E7 and E8;

(28) set back the existing kerbline on the north side of Wilkinson Street between the points marked E9 and E10;

(29) stop up and discontinue so much of the footpath between Nottingham Road, Basford and Vernon Road as is between the points marked F1 and F2 substituting therefor a new footpath and footbridge (Work No. 7A) between the points marked F1, F3, F4 and F2;

(30) stop up and discontinue so much of Nottingham Road, Basford as is between the points marked F5 and F6;

(31) stop up and discontinue so much of the footpath between Lincoln Street, Basford and Vernon Road as is between the points marked F7 and F8 substituting therefor a new footpath and footbridge (Work No. 7B) between the points marked F9, F10, F11 and F12;

(32) stop up and discontinue so much of the footpath between Coventry Road and Deptford Crescent, Bulwell as is between the points marked F13 and F14 substituting therefor a new footpath and footbridge (Work No. 7D) between the points marked F13, F15 and F16;

(33) provide a new footpath and cycleway to the west of the river Leen at Cinderhill between the points marked H1, H3, H4 and H2.

The undertakers may exercise the following powers and carry out the following works in the district of Ashfield:—

(34) stop up and discontinue so much of the Bestwood footpath (F.P.13) at Broomhill, Hucknall as is between the points marked G1 and G2 substituting therefor a new footpath and footbridge (Work No. 8B) between points G1, G3, G4 and G2.

Section 9	SCHEDULE 2

LEVEL CROSSINGS

In the City

David Lane, Old Basford.
Intended road between Mill Street and Vernon Road, Old Basford.
Carey Road, Bulwell.
Footpath between Neston Drive and Greenwich Avenue, Cinderhill, and new cycleway on the route of that footpath.

In the district of Ashfield, Nottinghamshire

Footpath between Nottingham Road and Moor Road, Bestwood.
Brickyard, Butlers Hill.

Section 17	SCHEDULE 3

ENACTMENTS RELATING TO EXISTING RAILWAYS

Chapter	Title or short title
9 & 10 Vict. c. clxiii.	Midland Railways, Nottingham and Mansfield, Act 1846.
11 & 12 Vict. c. lxxxviii.	Midland Railway, Ripley Branches, Act 1848.
56 & 57 Vict. c. i.	Manchester, Sheffield and Lincolnshire Railway (Extension to London &c.) Act 1893.
10 & 11 Geo. 6 c. xxxv.	London Midland and Scottish Railway Act 1947.

Section 26	SCHEDULE 4

ADDITIONAL LANDS WHICH MAY BE ACQUIRED OR USED

Purpose (1)	Location (2)	Lands numbered on the deposited plans (3)
In the City of Nottingham		
For the provision of a working site and for access for construction purposes	Maltmill Lane	15, 16, 17, 18, 19, 21 and 22.
For the provision of a turning-circle	Gedling Grove	181.
For the provision of a working site and for access for construction purposes and thereafter for the provision of an interchange car park and associated facilities	Forest Recreation Ground	192.

Purpose (1)	Location (2)	Lands numbered on the deposited plans (3)
For the provision of a working site and for access for construction purposes	David Lane	107.
For the provision of a working site and for access for construction purposes	Mill Street	112, 113 and 114.
For the provision of a working site and for access for construction purposes	Carey Road	162.
For the provision of a working site and for access for construction purposes and thereafter for the provision of an interchange car park and associated facilities	Hucknall Lane	171 and 172.

In the District of Ashfield, Nottinghamshire

For the provision of a working site and for access for construction purposes	Station Terrace, Hucknall	19.

Section 28   SCHEDULE 5

ADAPTATION OF PART I OF THE COMPULSORY PURCHASE ACT 1965

1. For section 7 of the Act of 1965 (measure of compensation) there shall be substituted the following:—

"7. In assessing the compensation to be paid by the acquiring authority under this Act regard shall be had, not only to the extent (if any) to which the value of the land over which the right is to be acquired is depreciated by the acquisition of the right, but also to the damage (if any) to be sustained by the owner of the land by reason of its severance from other land of his, or injurious affection of that other land by the exercise of the powers conferred by this or the special Act.".

2. For section 8(1) of the Act of 1965 (protection for vendor against severance of house, garden, etc.) there shall be substituted the following:—

"(1) No person shall be required to grant any right over part only—

(a) of any house, building or factory; or

(b) of a park or garden belonging to a house;

if he is willing to sell the whole of the house, building, factory, park or garden, unless the Lands Tribunal determine that—

(i) in the case of a house, building or factory, the part over which the right is proposed to be acquired can be made subject to that right without material detriment to the house, building or factory; or

(ii) in the case of a park or garden, the part over which the right is proposed to be acquired can be made subject to that right without seriously affecting the amenity or convenience of the house;

and, if the Lands Tribunal so determine, the tribunal shall award compensation in respect of any loss due to the acquisition of the right, in addition to its value; and thereupon the party interested shall be required to grant to the acquiring authority that right over that part of the house, building, factory, park or garden.

(1A) In considering the extent of any material detriment to a house, building or factory, or any extent to which the amenity or convenience of a house is affected, the Lands Tribunal shall have regard not only to the right which is to be acquired over the land, but also to any adjoining or adjacent land belonging to the same owner and subject to compulsory purchase.".

3. The following provisions of the Act of 1965 (being provisions stating the effect of a deed poll executed in various circumstances where there is no conveyance by persons with interests in the land):—

section 9(4) (refusal by owners to convey);

Schedule 1, paragraph 10(3) (owners under incapacity);

Schedule 2, paragraph 2(3) (absent and untraced owners); and

Schedule 4, paragraphs 2(3) and 7(2) (common land);

shall be so modified as to secure that, as against persons with interests in the land which are expressed to be overridden by the deed, the right which is to be compulsorily acquired is vested absolutely in the acquiring authority.

4. Section 11 of the Act of 1965 (powers of entry) shall be so modified as to secure that, as from the date on which the acquiring authority have served notice to treat in respect of any right, they have power, exercisable in the like circumstances and subject to the like conditions, to enter for the purpose of exercising that right (which shall be deemed for this purpose to have been created on the date of service of the notice); and sections 12 (penalty for unauthorised entry) and 13 (entry on sheriff's warrant in the event of obstruction) shall be modified correspondingly.

Section 76   SCHEDULE 6

PROVISIONS TO BE INCLUDED IN TERMS FOR THE USE OF FOREST CAR PARK

1. A prohibition on the use of the car park for goods vehicles (as defined in section 192(1) of the Road Traffic Act 1988) other than those used—
   (a) for the purposes of the authorised works; or
   (b) by any statutory undertakers or by any local or highway authority; or
   (c) by the emergency services; or
   (d) in connection with the use of the Forest Recreation Ground for any purpose which would have been lawful if this Act had not been passed.
2. Provisions for the City Council to require the temporary closure of the car park to permit the use of the relevant land for any purpose which would have been lawful if this Act had not been passed.
3. Requirements that the undertakers maintain and keep clean the car park to the reasonable satisfaction of the City Council.

INDEX

UNIVERSITY OF LONDON ACT 1994

(1994 c. xvi)

An Act to make new provision for the making of statutes for the University of London; to repeal certain obsolete or unnecessary enactments; and for connected purposes.   [3rd November 1994]

PARLIAMENTARY DEBATES

The Bill's progress through Parliament was as follows:

House of Commons: First Reading, January 24, 1994; Second Reading, April 14, 1994; Bill Committed, April 14, 1994; Unopposed Bill Committee, June 22, 1994; Amended Bill considered, June 28, 1994; Third Reading, July 5, 1994; Lords Amendments considered, October 25, 1994.

House of Lords: First Reading, July 5, 1994; Second Reading, July 25, 1994; Bill Committed, July 25, 1994; Unopposed Bill Committee, October 12, 1994; Third Reading, October 19, 1994.

INTRODUCTION

In June 1989, the Joint Planning Committee of the University of London established a Strategic Issues Group to consider the strategy for the future organisation, operation and management of the University. The Group's report in April 1991 recommended changes including the replacement of the Senate and the Court of the University by a single governing and executive body; the "Council of the University". These recommendations were implemented and this Act makes fresh provision for the making of any subsequent statutes as a result of the replacement of the Senate and the Court.

Whereas—

(1) The University of London (hereinafter referred to as "the University") was incorporated by Royal Charter on 28th November 1836 and the University is at present incorporated by Royal Charter granted on 6th January 1863:

(2) The University of London Act 1898 provided for the making by Commissioners of new statutes for the University and such statutes were made in 1900:

(3) In 1926 the report of the Departmental Committee appointed by minute of the former Board of Education dated 8th October 1924 (hereinafter referred to as "the Hilton Young Report") recommended that the University should be accorded a substantial measure of financial control over the Schools of the University:

(4) By the University of London Act 1926 (hereinafter referred to as "the 1926 Act") Commissioners were appointed to make new statutes in general accordance with the recommendations of the Hilton Young Report:

(5) The effect of the 1926 Act was that the statutes for the University could not be altered except in general accordance with the recommendations of the Hilton Young Report with the result that the precise power to make new statutes was both uncertain and unduly restrictive:

(6) The University of London Act 1978 (hereinafter referred to as "the 1978 Act") removed those uncertainties and restrictions and made fresh provision for the making of statutes by the body known as the Senate of the University:

(7) Fundamental changes have since occurred in higher education in the United Kingdom. In June 1989 the Joint Planning Committee of the University established a Strategic Issues Group "to consider the strategy for the future organisation, operation and management of the University, with the objective of devolving, where appropriate, administrative processes to the Colleges (formerly known as Schools) of the University whilst retaining central management of functions which might most effectively be operated on a federal basis, including essential planning and resourcing functions":

(8) The Strategic Issues Group issued its report in April 1991, recommending changes designed to meet those objectives including the replacement of

the Senate and the Court of the University by a single governing and executive body to be known as the Council of the University:

(9) In accordance with section 5 of the 1978 Act statutes giving effect to the recommendations of the Strategic Issues Group have been made. These statutes were approved by Her Majesty in Council on 19th July 1994 and came into force on 1st September 1994:

(10) It is necessary to make fresh provision for the making of any subsequent statutes as a result of the replacement of the Senate and the Court and it is expedient to simplify the procedure at present contained in the 1978 Act for approval of such statutes:

(11) The remaining provisions of the 1978 Act are obsolete or otherwise unnecessary and it is therefore expedient that that Act should be repealed:

(12) It is expedient that the other provisions contained in this Act should be enacted:

(13) The purposes of this Act cannot be effected without the authority of Parliament:

May it therefore please Your Majesty that it may be enacted, and be it enacted, by the Queen's most Excellent Majesty, by and with the advice and consent of the Lords Spiritual and Temporal, and Commons, in this present Parliament assembled, and by the authority of the same, as follows:—

Short title

1. This Act may be cited as the University of London Act 1994.

Interpretation

2. In this Act, unless the context otherwise requires—
"the 1978 Act" means the University of London Act 1978;
"the charter" means the charter incorporating the University granted by Her late Majesty Queen Victoria on 6th January 1863;
"College" means an educational, academic or research institution having for the time being the status of a College under the statutes;
"College governing body" means the body for the time being charged with the administration of a College;
"Convocation" means the Convocation of the University;
"the Council" means the Council of the University or such other body as the statutes may from time to time designate as the governing and executive body of the University;
"the Court" means the Court of the University;
"Professor", "Reader", "Teacher" and "Student" mean respectively a person who is for the time being a Professor, Reader, Teacher or Student of the University for the purposes of the statutes;
"the Senate" means the Senate of the University;
"the statutes" means the statutes for the University;
"the University" means the University of London.

Power to make statutes

3.—(1) The Council may, in accordance with the following provisions of this section, make statutes for altering, revoking or adding to the statutes for the time being.

(2) A copy of any proposed statute which the Council is minded to make shall be sent to Convocation, to the College governing bodies and to any trade union recognised by the University, together with a written request that any representations should be submitted to the Council within four months beginning with the date on which the copy is sent to the body concerned.

(3) The Council shall take such other steps as are in its opinion best adapted for facilitating the making of representations regarding the proposed statute.

(4) The Council shall consider any representations regarding the proposed statute made by Convocation, by any College governing body, by any recognised trade union or by any Professor, Reader, Teacher, Member of Convocation or Student.

(5) After considering any representations referred to in subsection (4) above the Council may if it thinks fit modify the proposed statute.

(6) The Council may make a statute by means of a resolution which satisfies the requirements of subsections (7) to (10) below.

(7) The resolution shall be passed at one meeting of the Council and confirmed at a subsequent such meeting held not less than one month nor more than six months after the former meeting.

(8) Written notice of each meeting referred to in subsection (7) above and of the object of the meeting shall be given to each member of the Council not less than 15 clear days before the date fixed for the meeting.

(9) At each meeting referred to in subsection (7) above—

(a) not less than two-thirds of the members of the Council shall be present; and

(b) the resolution shall be passed or confirmed, as the case may be, by not less than two-thirds of those present and voting.

(10) At the subsequent meeting referred to in subsection (7) above the resolution shall not be confirmed unless—

(a) at least two-thirds in number of the College governing bodies have given their consent thereto; and

(b) in the case of a proposed statute which would alter the constitution or functions of Convocation, the consent of Convocation has been given to the making of that statute.

(11) No statute shall have the effect of amending the charter or other instrument of government of any College.

Approval of statutes

4.—(1) No statute or part of a statute made under section 3 (Power to make statutes) of this Act shall have effect until it has been approved by Her Majesty in Council.

(2) Within one month after making a statute the Council shall cause it to be submitted to Her Majesty in Council and notice of its having been so submitted and of the place where copies of it can be obtained shall be published in the London Gazette.

Construction of instruments

5. Any scheme, will, deed, contract, conveyance, transfer, lease, licence or other instrument (whether made or executed before or after the passing of this Act) shall (except where the context otherwise requires) have effect as if—

(a) for any reference (however worded) describing or otherwise referring to a body as a School of the University there were substituted a reference describing or otherwise referring to that body as a College; and

(b) for any reference (however worded) to the Senate or the Court there were substituted a reference to the Council.

Repeal of 1978 Act

6. The 1978 Act is repealed.

Savings

7.—(1) Nothing in this Act shall affect those provisions of the charter whereby the University is incorporated with perpetual succession and a common seal with power to sue and be sued and to purchase, take on lease, hold and dispose of land and other property.

(2) Notwithstanding the repeal by this Act of the 1978 Act any statutes confirmed by or made under that Act and in force immediately before the passing of this Act shall, subject to any alteration, revocation or addition made in accordance with the provisions of this Act, continue to have effect as the statutes for the time being.

INDEX

References are to sections

PASTORAL (AMENDMENT) MEASURE 1994

(1994 No. 1)

A Measure passed by the General Synod of the Church of England to amend the Pastoral Measure 1983, in so far as it relates to redundant buildings and land annexed or belonging thereto, in connection with financial matters, with the removal of the legal effects of consecration, with the discharge and modification of covenants and with the annual report of the Advisory Board for Redundant Churches; and to provide a new name for the Redundant Churches Fund.   [24th March 1994]

Annual report of the Advisory Board for Redundant Churches

1. In section 41 of the Pastoral Measure 1983 (appointment of Advisory Board for Redundant Churches) in subsection (8)—
   (a) for the word "calendar" there shall be substituted the word "reporting";
   (b) at the end there shall be inserted the words "; and in this subsection "reporting year" means the period of twelve months beginning on a date to be determined by the Board with the agreement of the Commissioners".

Redundant Churches Fund

2.—(1) Section 44 of the 1983 Measure (appointment of Redundant Churches Fund) shall be amended as follows.
   (2) In subsection (5)—
   (a) after paragraph (b) there shall be inserted—
   "(bb) to let any property vested in the Fund on such terms (including terms as to the purposes for which it may be used) as the Commissioners may approve, after consultation with the bishop and the Advisory Board, being terms which the Commissioners consider reasonable and proper having regard to all the circumstances;
   (bbb) in respect of any property which the Fund has let or is proposing to let under paragraph (bb), to carry out such works as the Fund considers desirable, after consultation with the Advisory Board;";
   (b) in paragraph (c) for the words "such property" there shall be substituted the words "property vested in the Fund";
   (c) after paragraph (c) there shall be inserted—

"(cc) to assist, on payment of a fee, in the management of any place of Christian religious worship (not being a church or part of a church) which is vested in any body entrusted with functions similar to those of the Fund;".

(3) In subsection (7) there shall be substituted—

"(7) The powers conferred on the Redundant Churches Fund by subsection 5(b) and (bb) may be exercised so as to permit the use of a church or part of a church vested in the Fund for such worship (including worship by persons belonging to other Christian Churches) as may be authorised by the bishop after consulting the incumbent or priest in charge of the benefice in the area of which the church is situated.".

(4) After subsection (7) there shall be inserted—

"(7A) The terms of a lease granted under subsection (5)(bb) in respect of any property may provide that the property shall not be subject to the legal effects of consecration during the currency of the lease, notwithstanding the provisions of section 61(2).

(7B) Where any such property has been let under subsection (5)(bb) and the terms of the lease provide to the effect that no alteration may be made thereto without the approval of the Redundant Churches Fund, its approval shall only be given after consultation with the Advisory Board.

(7C) A statement in a document signed by the secretary or other duly authorised officer of the Commissioners that the Commissioners have approved the terms of any lease granted under subsection (5)(bb) which is specified in the document shall be conclusive evidence that those terms have been so approved.

(7D) As a condition of giving their approval to the terms of any lease under subsection (5)(bb) the Commissioners may require the Redundant Churches Fund to include in the lease such provisions, if any, as appear to them to be necessary to give effect to those terms.".

(5) In subsection (9) the words from ", and the Fund" to the end shall be omitted.

(6) After subsection (9) there shall be inserted—

"(9A) The Redundant Churches Fund shall give to the Commissioners and to the Advisory Board such information and advice as the Commissioners or the Advisory Board may, from time to time, require about—

(a) the Fund's financial position generally; and

(b) the estimated cost of repairing and thereafter maintaining any church or part of a church which is proposed to be vested in the Fund or which the Commissioners consider is likely to be proposed for vesting in the Fund.".

(7) In subsection (10) for the words "five year period (calculated in accordance with section 52(2)" there shall be substituted the words "funding period".

(8) In subsection (11)—

(a) for the word "calendar" there shall be substituted the word "accounting";

(b) at the end there shall be inserted the words "; and in this subsection "accounting year" means the period of twelve months beginning on a date to be determined by the Fund with the agreement of the Commissioners".

(9) In subsection (12) the words "for the Home Department" shall be omitted.

Pastoral schemes

3. In section 47 of the 1983 Measure (other provision by pastoral scheme for redundant church) in subsection (2) for the words from "after consultation" to the end there shall be substituted—

"(a) after consultation with the Advisory Board that the building is of such historic and archaeological interest or architectural quality that it ought to be preserved in the interests of the nation and the Church of England; and

(b) that the Redundant Churches Fund will have the resources to meet the cost of repairing and maintaining it,

the scheme may provide for its care and maintenance by the Fund".

Redundancy schemes

4. In subsection (1) of section 51 of the 1983 Measure (contents of redundancy schemes) in paragraph (b) for the words from "after consultation" to the end there shall be substituted—

"(i) after consultation with the Advisory Board that the building is of such historic and archaeological interest or architectural quality that it ought to be preserved in the interests of the nation and the Church of England; and

(ii) that the Redundant Churches Fund will have the resources to meet the cost of repairing and maintaining it,

the scheme may provide for its care and maintenance by the Fund".

Proceeds of sales, etc.

5. In section 52 of the 1983 Measure (application of remainder of proceeds of sales and other disposals)—

(a) in subsection (1)—

(i) in paragraph (a) for the words "five year" there shall be substituted the word "funding";

(ii) after paragraph (a) there shall be inserted—

"(aa) so far as the said moneys exceed that figure in any funding period, but subject to an appropriate order made under section 53(1)(c), they may from time to time be allocated to the redundant churches temporary maintenance account in such amounts as the Commissioners may determine;";

(iii) for paragraph (b) there shall be substituted—

"(b) the balance of the said moneys remaining after the making of payments under paragraph (a) and allocations under paragraph (aa) shall from time to time be allocated to the diocesan pastoral accounts of such dioceses, in such amounts, as the Commissioners may determine";

(b) subsection (2) (which defines the expression "five year period") is hereby repealed.

Funding periods

6. In section 53 of the 1983 Measure (orders of Commissioners determining or varying payments to Redundant Churches Fund)—

(a) in subsection (1)—

(i) in paragraph (a) for the words "in respect for each five year" there shall be substituted the words "the funding periods for the purposes of this Part and in respect of each funding";

(ii) in paragraphs (b) and (c) for the words "five year" there shall be substituted in both places the word "funding";

(b) in subsection (5) at the end there shall be inserted the words "and the subsequent order may contain such transitional provisions as the Commissioners may consider necessary or expedient to give effect to the variation or revocation";

(c) after subsection (6) there shall be inserted—

"(6A) Where the Standing Committee of the General Synod determines that an order made under this section does not need to be debated by the General Synod, then, unless notice is given by a member of the General Synod in accordance with its Standing Orders that he wishes the order to be debated, the order shall for the purposes of subsection (6) be deemed to have been approved by the General Synod.".

Legal effects of consecration

7. In section 61 of the 1983 Measure (removal of legal effects of consecration of buildings and land)—
(a) in subsection (2) after the word "aforesaid" there shall be inserted the words "and subject to any terms included in a lease under section 44(7A)";
(b) in subsection (3) the words from the beginning to "Church of England, and" shall be omitted.

Covenants

8. In section 62 of the 1983 Measure (power to impose and enforce covenants) at the end there shall be inserted—
"(3) Section 84 (except subsection (2)) of the Law of Property Act 1925 (which enables the Lands Tribunal to discharge or modify restrictions affecting land) shall not apply in relation to conditions and requirements imposed under subsection (1).".

Diocesan pastoral accounts

9. In subsection (3) of section 78 of the 1983 Measure (payment of expenses from diocesan pastoral accounts, and application of other moneys therein) in paragraph (a) for the words "making of" there shall be substituted the words "coming into operation of arrangements under".

Temporary maintenance account

10. In the 1983 Measure after section 78 there shall be inserted—

"Temporary maintenance account
78A.—(1) The Commissioners shall hold an account to be called the redundant churches temporary maintenance account and shall transfer thereto any moneys which are payable to the said account under section 52.
(2) The Commissioners may apply moneys standing to the credit of the redundant churches temporary maintenance account by way of grant or loan to the repair and maintenance of any redundant building vested in a diocesan board of finance pending the coming into operation of arrangements under a redundancy scheme.".

Interpretation of 1983 Measure

11. In subsection (1) of section 87 of the 1983 Measure (general interpretation)—
(a) after the definition of "endowments" there shall be inserted—
""funding period" means a period determined as such by an order made under section 53(1);";
(b) after the definition of "redundant building" there shall be inserted—
""redundant churches temporary maintenance account" means the account referred to in section 78A;".

Crediting of moneys to temporary maintenance account

12. In paragraph 10 of Schedule 3 to the 1983 Measure (crediting of sums to and adjustment of funds and accounts by Commissioners)—
- (a) after the words "or a diocesan pastoral account" there shall be inserted the words "or the redundant churches temporary maintenance account";
- (b) at the end there shall be inserted the words "or the redundant churches temporary maintenance account".

Re-naming of Redundant Churches Fund

13.—(1) The body called the Redundant Churches Fund shall cease to be called by that name but shall continue to exist under a new name as follows.

(2) The said body shall be called the Churches Conservation Trust and accordingly the references to the Redundant Churches Fund in section 44 of the 1983 Measure and any reference to the Redundant Churches Fund in any other enactment or in any instrument or other document shall, unless the context otherwise requires, be construed as references to the Churches Conservation Trust.

Transitional provisions as to the funding period

14. For the purposes of any provision of the 1983 Measure relating to the application of the moneys mentioned in section 52(1) of that Measure, any reference to a funding period shall be construed as including a reference to any such period of five years commencing before the coming into operation of section 6 above as the Church Commissioners may determine by order made under their seal; and more than one period of five years may be so determined by the Church Commissioners.

Citation, commencement, extent and interpretation

15.—(1) This Measure may be cited as the Pastoral (Amendment) Measure 1994.

(2) This Measure shall come into operation on such date as the Archbishops of Canterbury and York may jointly appoint, and different dates may be appointed for different provisions.

(3) This Measure shall extend to the whole of the provinces of Canterbury and York except the Channel Islands and the Isle of Man, but the provisions thereof may be applied to the Channel Islands as defined in the Channel Islands (Church Legislation) Measures 1931 and 1957, or either of them, in accordance with those Measures, and if an Act of Tynwald or an instrument made under an Act of Tynwald so provides, shall extend to the Isle of Man subject to such exceptions, adaptations and modifications as may be specified in the Act of Tynwald or instrument.

(4) In this Measure "the 1983 Measure" means the Pastoral Measure 1983.

CARE OF CATHEDRALS (SUPPLEMENTARY PROVISIONS) MEASURE 1994

(1994 No. 2)

ARRANGEMENT OF SECTIONS

A Measure passed by the General Synod of the Church of England to make further provision in connection with the care and conservation of cathedral churches.   [21st July 1994]

Preliminary interview re. contravention of s.2 of 1990 Measure

1. Subject to section 3(1) below, where it appears to the bishop of a diocese, whether of his own motion or on the advice of the Cathedrals Fabric Commission or on the basis of an allegation made by another person, that the administrative body of the cathedral church of the diocese may have committed or be intending to commit an act in contravention of section 2 of the 1990 Measure, he shall, as soon as practicable and before taking any further action, afford to the members of the administrative body an opportunity of being interviewed in private by him with respect to the matter in question.

Power of bishop to order special visitation

2.—(1) Subject to subsection (2) below, where it appears to a bishop, after complying with section 1 above with respect to the members of an administrative body, that the administrative body has committed or is intending to commit an act as mentioned in that section, he shall within such period as may be prescribed order a special visitation under this section in respect of the cathedral church concerned for the purpose of inquiring into the matter in question; and, if he does so, he shall cause a written statement of his reasons for ordering the visitation to be sent to the administrative body.

(2) It shall not be necessary for a bishop to order a special visitation under this section in respect of any act if—

(a) he is satisfied that the administrative body concerned intends to make an application for approval of that act under the 1990 Measure; or

(b) the administrative body concerned has made such an application and the application has not been refused; or

(c) he considers that there are exceptional reasons for not doing so.

(3) Without prejudice to any rule of law as to the effect of episcopal visitations, where a special visitation under this section is ordered by a bishop in respect of a cathedral church, the administrative body of the cathedral church shall have no power to act as such with regard to the matter under inquiry without the prior approval in writing of the bishop.

(4) A special visitation under this section shall not be treated as an episcopal visitation for the purposes of any provision contained in the constitution and statutes of the cathedral church concerned restricting the ordering of such visitations.

Power of bishop to give directions

3.—(1) Where it appears to a bishop that an administrative body may have committed or be intending to commit an act in contravention of section 2 of the 1990 Measure and he is satisfied, having regard to the urgency of the matter, that there is insufficient time to comply with section 1 above he may from time to time give such interim directions with respect to the matter in question as he thinks fit to the administrative body before complying with that section.

(2) Where a bishop has ordered a special visitation he may from time to time give such directions with respect to the matter in question as he thinks fit to the administrative body concerned.

(3) Without prejudice to the generality of the powers to give directions under this section, such directions may require the administrative body—

    (a) to take such steps as the bishop may consider necessary for the purpose of avoiding a contravention of section 2 of the 1990 Measure;

    (b) to refrain from taking such steps as the bishop may consider likely to lead to such a contravention;

    (c) to take such steps as the bishop may consider necessary for the purpose of restoring the position so far as possible to that which existed before the act was committed.

(4) Before a bishop gives directions under this section which include a requirement of the kind mentioned in subsection (3)(c) above he shall seek the advice of the Cathedrals Fabric Commission.

(5) Directions given by a bishop under this section shall be in writing unless he is satisfied, having regard to the urgency of the matter, that there is insufficient time for them to be committed to writing; but if they are given orally he shall as soon as practicable commit them to writing.

(6) It shall be the duty of an administrative body to which directions are given under this section to comply with them.

Institution of proceedings for injunction or restoration order

4.—(1) Where a bishop has ordered a special visitation and he considers it necessary or expedient to take further steps in respect of any actual or intended contravention of section 2 of the 1990 Measure, he may authorise a person designated by him for the purposes of this Measure, either generally or in a particular case, to institute proceedings on his behalf against the administrative body of the cathedral church concerned for the purpose of obtaining an injunction or restoration order or both against the administrative body.

(2) Where a bishop proposes to authorise the institution of proceedings under subsection (1) above, he shall inform the Commissioners of the course he proposes to take and the Commissioners shall, as soon as practicable—

    (a) decide whether or not they would be prepared to pay, under section 58 of the Ecclesiastical Jurisdiction Measure 1963, any costs or expenses incurred in respect of the proceedings and, if so, to what extent; and

    (b) notify the bishop of their decision.

Jurisdiction and composition of Vicar-General's court

5.—(1) The Vicar-General's court of each of the provinces of Canterbury and York shall, in respect of every cathedral church in the province, have original jurisdiction to hear and determine proceedings instituted under section 4 above.

(2) Where, in any such proceedings—

    (a) The Vicar-General is for any reason unable to act; or

    (b) the cathedral church concerned is in a diocese of which the Vicar-General is the chancellor, the court shall be presided over by a chancellor appointed by the Archbishop of the province of Canterbury or York, as the case may be, to act as deputy Vicar-General; and a chancellor so appointed shall have all the powers and perform all the duties of the Vicar-General.

(3) Any such proceedings shall be instituted and conducted in such manner as the Vicars-General of Canterbury and York, acting jointly, may direct.

Powers of court

6.—(1) In any proceedings instituted under section 4 above against an administrative body the court may by way of special citation add as a further party to the proceedings any person who appears to the court to be or to have been concerned in furthering the alleged contravention of section 2 of the 1990 Measure.

(2) A special citation under subsection (1) above may require the person to whom it is issued to attend the court concerned at such time and place as may be specified in the citation.

(3) Where, in any such proceedings, it appears to the court that the administrative body concerned intends to commit or continue to commit any act in contravention of section 2 of the 1990 Measure, the court may issue an injunction restraining—

(a) the administrative body from committing or continuing to commit that act; or

(b) any other party to the proceedings from committing or continuing to commit any act in furtherance of the contravention.

(4) Where, in any such proceedings, it appears to the court that the administrative body against which the proceedings were instituted, has committed any act in contravention of the said section 2, the court may make an order (a "restoration order") requiring the administrative body or any other party to the proceedings to take such steps as the court may consider necessary, within such time as the court may specify, for the purpose of restoring the position so far as possible to that which existed before the act was committed.

(5) The court shall not make a restoration order in respect of any act unless the court is satisfied that less than six years have elapsed since the act was committed.

(6) The court shall seek the advice of the Cathedrals Fabric Commission before making a restoration order.

(7) Where proceedings for obtaining a restoration order are instituted on behalf of a bishop under section 4 above and any fact relevant to the institution of such proceedings has been deliberately concealed from him the period of six years mentioned in subsection (5) above shall not begin to run until the bishop has discovered the concealment or could with reasonable diligence have discovered it.

(8) For the purpose of subsection (7) above, deliberate commission of a breach of duty in circumstances in which it is unlikely to be discovered for some time amounts to deliberate concealment of the facts involved in that breach of duty.

(9) Failure to comply without reasonable excuse with any requirement of an injunction or restoration order shall be a contempt of the court.

(10) In any such proceedings the court may order that the special visitation from which the proceedings ensued shall continue on such terms as it considers just or shall cease and may make such further order in relation to the proceedings as it considers just.

Amendment of 1990 Measure

7.—(1) The 1990 Measure shall have effect subject to the following amendments.

(2) In section 2 (approval required for alteration to cathedrals) at the end there shall be inserted the following subsection—

"(3) Where a proposal has been implemented in contravention of this section, anything done in connection with such implementation may be approved under this Measure and, in that event, shall be deemed to have been done in compliance with this section.".

(3) In section 3 (the Cathedrals Fabric Commission for England) in subsection (2) after paragraph (a) there shall be inserted the following paragraph—

"(aa)   to give advice to bishops and to the Vicar-General's court when it is sought under the Care of Cathedrals (Supplementary Provisions) Measure 1994;".

(4) In section 6 (body to which application for approval to be made) after subsection (3) there shall be inserted the following subsection—

"(3A) Any application for approval in pursuance of section 2(3) above shall be made to the Commission.".

(5) In section 8 (applications for approval of Cathedrals Fabric Commission) at the end there shall be inserted the following subsection—

"(4) This section shall apply in relation to an application for approval in pursuance of section 2(3) above as it applies in relation to an application for approval of a proposal.".

(6) In section 10 (Commission of Review) in subsection (5) the words "to the proposal" shall be omitted.

Amendment of Ecclesiastical Jurisdiction Measure 1963

8. The Ecclesiastical Jurisdiction Measure 1963 shall have effect subject to the amendments specified in the Schedule to this Measure.

Rules

9. In section 26 of the Care of Churches and Ecclesiastical Jurisdiction Measure 1991 (functions of Rule Committee) in subsections (1)(d) and (2)(a) for the words "Care of Cathedrals Measure 1990" there shall be substituted in both places the words "Care of Cathedrals Measures 1990 and 1994".

Interpretation

10. In this Measure—

"the 1990 Measure" means the Care of Cathedrals Measure 1990;
"administrative body"—

(a) in relation to a cathedral church in respect of which there is a corporate body known as the dean and chapter, means the body by which administrative functions in relation to the cathedral church are performed by virtue of paragraph (b) of section 7 of the Cathedrals Measure 1963;

(b) in relation to any other cathedral church, means the body by which administrative functions in relation to the cathedral church are performed by virtue of paragraph (b) of section 8 of that Measure;

"cathedral church" means any cathedral church in the provinces of Canterbury and York, except—

(a) the Cathedral Church of Christ in Oxford;

(b) any cathedral church in the diocese of Sodor and Man or in the diocese in Europe; and

(c) any cathedral church to which the 1990 Measure does not, for the time being, apply by virtue of an order under section 18(1) of that Measure;

"Cathedrals Fabric Commission" means the Cathedrals Fabric Commission for England established under section 3 of the 1990 Measure;

"Commissioners" means the Church Commissioners;

"the court", in relation to proceedings instituted under section 4 above in respect of a cathedral church, means the Vicar-General's court of the province in which the cathedral church is situated;

"injunction" means an injunction under section 6(3) above;

"prescribed" means prescribed by rules made under section 26 of the Care of Churches and Ecclesiastical Jurisdiction Measure 1991;

"restoration order" means a restoration order under section 6(4) above;

"special visitation" means a special visitation under section 2 above.

Short title and commencement

11.—(1) This Measure may be cited as the Care of Cathedrals (Supplementary Provisions) Measure 1994, and this Measure may be cited with the 1990 Measure as the Care of Cathedrals Measures 1990 and 1994.

(2) This Measure shall come into force on such date as the Archbishops of Canterbury and York may jointly appoint.

SCHEDULE

AMENDMENT OF ECCLESIASTICAL JURISDICTION MEASURE 1963

1. The Ecclesiastical Jurisdiction Measure 1963 shall be amended as follows.

2. In section 7 (jurisdiction of Arches and Chancery Courts)—

(a) after subsection (1) there shall be inserted the following subsection—

"(1A) Each of the said Courts shall also have jurisdiction to hear and determine appeals from judgments, orders or decrees of the Vicar-General's court of the province of Canterbury or York, as the case may be.";

(b) in subsection (2) after the words "consistory court" there shall be inserted the words "or the Vicar-General's court, as the case may be,".

3. In section 58 (payment of costs of bishop and promoter by Commissioners) after paragraph (b) there shall be inserted the following paragraph—

"and

(c) any bishop or person designated by a bishop to act on his behalf for the purposes of the Care of Cathedrals (Supplementary Provisions) Measure 1994 in or in relation to or directly or indirectly arising out of legal proceedings authorised, taken or contemplated in the Vicar-General's court under section 4 of that Measure:".

4. In section 60 (powers of courts and commissions in regard to costs)—

(a) in subsection (1) after the words "under this Measure" there shall be inserted the words "and the Vicar-General's court of each of the provinces of Canterbury and York in proceedings instituted under section four of the Care of Cathedrals (Supplementary Provisions) Measure 1994";

(b) in subsection (2) after the word "court" there shall be inserted the words "(including a Vicar-General's court)".

5. In section 62 (payment of expenses of courts, etc. by Central Board) after the words "section fourteen thereof" there shall be inserted the words "and of the Vicar-General's court for the purpose of proceedings instituted under section four of the Care of Cathedrals (Supplementary Provisions) Measure 1994".

6. In section 63 (fees payable in or in connection with proceedings) after the words "under this Measure" there shall be inserted the words "or the Care of Cathedrals (Supplementary Provisions) Measure 1994".

7. In section 80 (place where courts, etc., are to sit) after the word "Measure" there shall be inserted the words "and the Vicar-General's court of each of the provinces of Canterbury and York".

8. In section 81 (evidence and general powers and rights of courts and commissions)—
- (a) in subsection (1) after the word "Measure" there shall be inserted the words "and the Vicar-General's Court of each of the provinces of Canterbury and York";
- (b) in subsection (2) after the words "such court or commission" there shall be inserted the words "or Vicar-General's court";
- (c) in subsection (4) for the words from "subsection (2)" to the end there shall be inserted the words "section 13(2) of the Care of Churches and Ecclesiastical Jurisdiction Measure 1991 or section 6(1) of the Care of Cathedrals (Supplementary Provisions) Measure 1994 and an injunction under section 13(4) of the former Measure or section 6(3) of the latter Measure".

CHURCH OF ENGLAND (LEGAL AID) MEASURE 1994

(1994 No. 3)

A Measure passed by the General Synod of the Church of England to consolidate with amendments the provisions concerning legal aid contained in the Church of England (Legal Aid and Miscellaneous Provisions) Measure 1988.   [21st July 1994]

Legal Aid Fund and Legal Aid Commission

1.—(1) The General Synod shall continue to maintain the Legal Aid Fund to which the General Synod and the Church Commissioners may contribute such sums as each shall from time to time decide.

(2) After every ordinary election to the General Synod the Standing Committee of the General Synod shall appoint a commission, to be known as the Legal Aid Commission, which shall be charged with the duty of administering the Legal Aid Fund.

(3) The Legal Aid Fund shall be held by the Central Board of Finance on behalf of the General Synod, and the Board may, subject to and in accordance with the provisions of this Measure, make such payments out of the Fund as may be authorised by a certificate in writing issued by the Legal Aid Commission under section 2 of this Measure.

(4) The members of the Legal Aid Commission shall be entitled to hold office until their successors, who may be the same persons, come into office; and if a member of the Commission dies, resigns or otherwise vacates his office, the Standing Committee shall appoint another person to hold office for the unexpired portion of the term of office of the person in whose place he is appointed.

Applications for legal aid

2.—(1) Where any proceedings mentioned in the first column of Schedule 1 to this Measure are taken or are proposed to be taken in the province of Canterbury or the province of York, any person mentioned in the second column of that Schedule in relation to those proceedings may apply to the Legal Aid Commission for financial assistance in respect of costs incurred in connection with those proceedings.

(2) On an application under subsection (1) above, the Commission may, subject to and in accordance with the provisions of this Measure, issue a cer-

tificate authorising the payment out of the Legal Aid Fund of the whole or part of the costs incurred by the applicant, after the date of the issue of the certificate, in or in relation to or directly or indirectly arising out of the proceedings concerned; and any payment made or authorised under this subsection is in this Measure referred to as "legal aid".

(3) The Commission may issue a certificate for the payment of the costs, or part of the costs, incurred by any person subject to such conditions specified in the certificate as the Commission thinks fit.

(4) Without prejudice to the generality of subsection (3) above, where on an application under subsection (1) above the Commission considers that legal aid should be granted in respect of some but not all of the costs incurred by the applicant, in or in relation to or directly or indirectly arising out of the proceedings concerned, the Commission may issue a certificate for—

   (a) the payment of a contribution towards those costs of an amount specified in the certificate, or

   (b) the payment of those costs subject to a contribution from the applicant of an amount so specified, or

   (c) the payment of such proportion of those costs as may be so specified, or

   (d) the payment of the costs of, or a specified proportion of the costs of, such part of the proceedings as may be so specified, whether by reference to issues in or stages of those proceedings.

(5) Before deciding whether to grant any legal aid under this section and, if so, to what extent, the Commission shall have regard to all the circumstances of the case and, in particular, shall consider the financial resources of the applicant (including the financial resources of the wife or husband of the applicant), and legal aid shall not be granted if it appears to the Commission that the applicant could afford to proceed without legal aid.

(6) Except as expressly provided by rules made under this Measure, the Commission shall not grant legal aid to any person in connection with any proceedings unless that person shows that he has reasonable grounds for taking or defending the proceedings or being a party thereto.

Supplementary provisions as to legal aid

3.—(1) Subject to the provisions of this Measure, where a certificate is issued under section 2 of this Measure for the payment out of the Legal Aid Fund of the costs or part of the costs of any person, that payment shall be made to the solicitor who has acted for that person.

(2) Where a certificate is issued under section 2 of this Measure for the payment of the costs, or part of the costs, incurred by any person, the solicitor who has acted for that person shall not be entitled to receive from, or on behalf of, that person more than the amount (if any) by which the total amount of those costs, as taxed or assessed in accordance with rules made under section 4 of this Measure, exceeds the amount payable to that solicitor out of the Legal Aid Fund under that certificate.

(3) Except as expressly provided by rules made under this Measure—

   (a) the fact that legal aid is granted in respect of the services of counsel or a solicitor shall not affect the relationship between or rights of counsel, solicitor and client or any privilege arising out of that relationship; and

   (b) the fact that any person is granted legal aid shall not affect the rights or liabilities of other parties to the proceedings or the principles on which the discretion of any court or tribunal is normally exercised.

Rules

4.—(1) The Standing Committee of the General Synod may make such rules as it considers necessary or desirable for giving effect to, or for preventing abuses of, this Measure, and rules made under this subsection may in particular—

(a) make provision as to the procedure to be observed in relation to an application for legal aid;

(b) make provision as to the information to be furnished by any person applying for or receiving legal aid and as to the provision of information by any solicitor or counsel acting for any such person;

(c) make provision for the circumstances in which the Legal Aid Commission may amend, revoke or discharge a certificate issued by the Commission and as to the effect of such amendment, revocation or discharge;

(d) make provision for regulating the procedure in proceedings in respect of which legal aid is granted and in particular make provision—

(i) as to the taxation of costs in respect of which legal aid is granted, including any such costs incurred in connection with proceedings not actually begun;

(ii) as to the assessment of those costs, without taxation, by such person as may be specified in the rules, but with a view to allowing as nearly as may be the same amount as on taxation;

(iii) as to the cases in which and the extent to which a person to whom legal aid is granted may be required to give security for costs, and the manner in which it may be given;

(e) make provision for the enforcement for the benefit of the Legal Aid Fund of any order or agreement for costs made in favour of a person to whom legal aid is granted;

(f) make provision enabling the chairman of the Commission or such officer of the Commission as may be specified in the rules, in such circumstances as may be so specified, to issue an interim certificate on behalf of the Commission for the payment of the costs, or part of the costs, incurred by any person before the determination by the Commission of that person's application for the grant of legal aid;

(g) make provision enabling the Commission to appoint committees to carry out such of its functions as may be specified in the rules.

(2) The Standing Committee of the General Synod may by rules vary the provisions of Schedule 1 to this Measure so as to add to or exclude from the proceedings therein mentioned any proceedings specified in the rules (being proceedings under a provision of a Measure of the General Synod or of any Canon, rules or regulations made under such a Measure), including this Measure, and any such rules may make any consequential changes in the second column of that Schedule; except that the provisions of that Schedule shall not be varied so as to enable legal aid to be granted in connection with proceedings before any court or tribunal before which persons have no right, and are not normally allowed, to be heard by counsel or solicitor.

(3) Any rules made under subsection (1) above may make different provision in relation to different proceedings.

(4) Any rules made under this section shall be laid before the General Synod and shall not come into force until they have been approved by the General Synod, whether with or without amendment.

(5) Where the Standing Committee determines that rules made under this section do not need to be debated by the General Synod then, unless—

(a) notice is given by a member of the General Synod in accordance with its Standing Orders that he wishes the rules to be debated, or

(b) notice is so given by any such member that he wishes to move an amendment to the rules,

the rules shall for the purposes of subsection (4) above be deemed to have been approved by the General Synod without amendment.

(6) The Statutory Instruments Act 1946 shall apply to any rules approved by the General Synod under this section as if they were a statutory instru-

ment and as if this Measure were an Act providing that any such rules shall be subject to annulment in pursuance of a resolution of either House of Parliament.

Transitional provisions

5.—(1) Where—

(a) any proceedings mentioned in the first column of Schedule 1 to the Church of England (Legal Aid and Miscellaneous Provisions) Measure 1988 have been taken; or

(b) in relation to any such proceedings proposed to be taken, a certificate under section 2 of that Measure has been issued,

before the coming into force of this Measure, Part I of the said Measure of 1988 shall have effect in relation to such proceedings or certificate as if this Measure had not been enacted.

(2) The Legal Aid Commission appointed under section 1 of the said Measure of 1988 and in existence immediately before the coming into force of this Measure shall continue to exist for the purposes of this Measure as if it had been appointed under section 1 of this Measure.

(3) Any rules made under section 4(1) of the said Measure of 1988 and in force immediately before the coming into force of this Measure shall continue to have effect as if made under section 4(1) of this Measure.

Extent

6. This Measure shall extend to the whole of the provinces of Canterbury and York except the Channel Islands and the Isle of Man, but the provisions thereof may be applied to the Channel Islands as defined in the Channel Islands (Church Legislation) Measures 1931 and 1957, or either of them, in accordance with those Measures and if an Act of Tynwald or an instrument made in pursuance of an Act of Tynwald so provides, shall extend to the Isle of Man subject to such exceptions, adaptations or modifications as may be specified in the Act of Tynwald or instrument.

Repeal and consequential amendments

7.—(1) Part I of and Schedule 1 to the Church of England (Legal Aid and Miscellaneous Provisions) Measure 1988 are hereby repealed.

(2) The enactments mentioned in Schedule 2 to this Measure shall have effect subject to the consequential amendments specified in that Schedule.

Short title and commencement

8.—(1) This Measure may be cited as the Church of England (Legal Aid) Measure 1994.

(2) This Measure shall come into force on such date as the Archbishops of Canterbury and York may jointly appoint.

SCHEDULES

Sections 2(1) and 4(2)   SCHEDULE 1

PROCEEDINGS FOR WHICH LEGAL AID MAY BE GIVEN

Description of proceedings	*Description of applicants*
1. Proceedings in any ecclesiastical court or before any commission, committee, bishop or examiner in respect of an offence under the Ecclesiastical Jurisdiction Measure 1963.	Any accused person.

Description of proceedings	Description of applicants
2. Proceedings on an enquiry under Part I of the Incumbents (Vacation of Benefices) Measure 1977 conducted by a provincial tribunal.	The incumbent concerned in the proceedings.
3. Proceedings under Schedule 4 to the Pastoral Measure 1983 (including any interview by a pastoral committee).	Any person having a right to compensation conferred by paragraphs 1, 2, 3 or 4 of the said Schedule 4.
4. Proceedings under Schedule 4 to the Pastoral Measure 1983 as extended by subsection (3) of section 13 of the Incumbents (Vacation of Benefices) Measure 1977 (including any interview by a pastoral committee).	Any incumbent having a right to compensation conferred by subsection (1) of the said section 13.
5. Proceedings on an appeal under any Canon made in pursuance of section 7 of the Church of England (Legal Aid and Miscellaneous Provisions) Measure 1988 against revocation of a licence granted to a minister, deaconess, lay worker or stipendiary reader.	The appellant.
6. Proceedings on an appeal under section 50 of the Ecclesiastical Jurisdiction Measure 1963 against an intended deposition of a priest or deacon from Holy Orders.	The appellant.

Section 7(2)   SCHEDULE 2

CONSEQUENTIAL AMENDMENTS

Ecclesiastical Jurisdiction Measure 1963

1. In section 60 of the Ecclesiastical Jurisdiction Measure 1963 (which relates to costs)—
  (a) in subsection (1) for the words "Part I of the Church of England (Legal Aid and Miscellaneous Provisions) Measure 1988" there shall be substituted the words "the Church of England (Legal Aid) Measure 1994";
  (b) in subsection (2) for the words "Part I of the Church of England (Legal Aid and Miscellaneous Provisions) Measure 1988" there shall be substituted the words "the Church of England (Legal Aid) Measure 1994".
  (c) in subsection (4) for the words "Church of England (Legal Aid and Miscellaneous Provisions) Measure 1988" there shall be substituted the words "Church of England (Legal Aid) Measure 1994".

Pastoral Measure 1983

2. In paragraph 16(1) of Schedule 4 to the Pastoral Measure 1983 (rules made by Church Commissioners) for the words "Part I of the Church of England (Legal Aid and Miscellaneous Provisions) Measure 1988" there shall be substituted the words "the Church of England (Legal Aid) Measure 1994".

Care of Churches and Ecclesiastical Jurisdiction Measure 1991

3. In section 26(2) of the Care of Churches and Ecclesiastical Jurisdiction Measure 1991 (functions of Rule Committee) for the words "Church of England (Legal Aid and Miscellaneous Provisions) Measure 1988" there shall be substituted the words "Church of England (Legal Aid) Measure 1994".

CURRENT LAW STATUTES 1994

COMMENCEMENT DIARY

This table notes alphabetically by statute the commencement of statutes from January 1994 as initiated by Orders released in 1993, 1994 and 1995 and by statutory provisions. This is up to date to **March 10, 1995**. The full texts of the Orders can be found in the Commencement Orders section of Current Law Statutes.

Notes

The Weights and Measures Act 1985 Commencement (Revocation) Order 1993 (S.I. 1993 No. 2698 (C.55)) revokes the Weights and Measures Act 1985 (Commencement) Order 1992 (S.I. 1992 No. 770) which appointed April 1, 1994 as the date on which s.43 of the Weights and Measures Act 1985 was to come into force.

The Road Traffic Act 1991 (Commencement No. 10 and Transitional Provisions) Order 1994 (S.I. 1994 No. 81 (C.2)) amended S.I. 1993 No. 3238 to extend the order to the London Borough of Richmond upon Thames and its council only and not Southwark as in the original text.

The Education Act 1993 (Commencement No. 2 and Transitional Provisions) (Amendment) Order 1994 (S.I. 1994 No. 436 (C.13)) amended S.I. 1993 No. 3106 (C.62) amending Sched. 2, para. 2(2) and adding a new sub-para. (8) to that paragraph (transitional provisions).

The Environmental Protection Act 1990 (Commencement No. 15) Order 1994 (S.I. 1994 No. 1096 (C.18)) provides for the commencement of certain provisions of that Act (as set out in arts. 2 and 3 of that Order) on May 1 and October 1, 1994. This was amended to April 1, 1995 by S.I. 1994 No. 3234 (C.81). These provisions are also deemed to come into force on certain other dates, not specified in the Order, but linked to certain other activities. Please see the full text of the Order for interpretation.

The Finance Act 1994, section 47, (Appointed Day) Order 1994 (S.I. 1994 No. 1234 (C.20)) was revoked by the Finance Act 1994, section 47, (Appointed Day) (No. 2) Order 1994 (S.I. 1994 No. 1253 (C.21)).

Act Affected	Provision Brought Into Force	Commencement Date	Authority
Appropriation Act 1994 (c. 24)	All provisions	July 21, 1994	Royal Assent
Bail (Amendment) Act 1993 (c. 26)	All remaining provisions	June 27, 1994	S.I. 1994 No. 1437 (C.24)
Charities Act 1992 (c. 41)	Pt. II (ss.58–64) [except that for the purposes of exercising the power to make regulations under ss.59 or 64 it shall come into force on November 28, 1994]	March 1, 1995	S.I. 1994 No. 3023 (C.69)
Chiropractors Act 1994 (c. 17)	s.42, Sched. 2	July 5, 1994	s.44(2)

Act Affected	Provision Brought Into Force	Commencement Date	Authority
Coal Industry Act 1994 (c. 21)	ss.7–9, 12–14, 17, 54, 62–66, 67(2)–(6), (8) (part), Scheds. 2, 11, Pt. I	July 5, 1994	s.68(6)
Coal Industry Act 1994 (c. 21)	ss.1, 4–6, 21, Scheds. 1, 4	September 19, 1994	S.I. 1994 No. 2189 (C.45)
Coal Industry Act 1994 (c. 21)	ss.2, 3, 15, 16, 19, 20, 22 (part), 25–30, 35, 37, 45–47, 56–61, 67(1) (8) (part) (7), Scheds. 3, 5, Sched. 9, paras. 8, 11(1) (2), 12 (all in part), Scheds. 10, 11, Pt. III (part)	October 31, 1994	S.I. 1994 No. 2552 (C.53)
Coal Industry Act 1994 (c. 21)	ss.10, 11, 18, 23, 31–34, 36, 38–44, 48–53, 55, 67(1) (8) (part), Scheds. 6, 7, 8, 9 (part), 11, Pt. II	October 31, 1994	s.68(2) and S.I. 1994 No. 2553
Coal Industry Act 1994 (c. 21)	Sched. 9, paras. 13(3), 39(2) (3), Sched. 11, Pt. III (part)	November 1, 1994	S.I. 1994 No. 2552 (C.53)
Coal Industry Act 1994 (c. 21)	Sched. 11, Pt. III (part)	December 24, 1994	S.I. 1994 No. 3063 (C.71)
Coal Industry Act 1994 (c. 21)	s.24	January 31, 1995	S.I. 1995 No. 159 (C.7)
Coal Industry Act 1994 (c. 21)	Sched. 11, Pt. III (part)	March 1, 1995	S.I. 1995 No. 273 (C.9)
Consolidated Fund Act 1994 (c. 4)	All provisions	March 24, 1994	Royal Assent
Consolidated Fund (No. 2) Act 1994 (c. 41)	All provisions	December 16, 1994	Royal Assent
Criminal Justice Act 1991 (c. 53)	ss.12, 13	January 9, 1995	S.I. 1994 No. 3191 (C.77)
Criminal Justice Act 1993 (c. 36)	ss.16, 17, 29–31, 33, 47, 49, 74, 78 (remainder), 79(13) (part) (14) (part), Sched. 5, para. 14, Sched. 6 (part)	February 15, 1994	S.I. 1994 No. 71 (C.1)
Criminal Justice Act 1993 (c. 36)	ss.52–64, 79(13) (part) (14) (part), Scheds. 1, 2, 5 (part), 6 (part)	March 1, 1994	S.I. 1994 No. 242 (C.7)

Act Affected	Provision Brought Into Force	Commencement Date	Authority
Criminal Justice Act 1993 (c. 36)	ss.18, 19, 26, 32, 48, 50, 51, 77, 79(13) (part), Sched. 4, Sched. 5 (part) [the commencement of ss.18, 19, 26, 32, Scheds. 4 and 5 is limited to certain jurisdictions—see Order]	April 1, 1994	S.I. 1994 No. 700 (C.12)
Criminal Justice Act 1993 (c. 36)	s.72	August 22, 1994	S.I. 1994 No. 1951 (C.36)
Criminal Justice Act 1993 (c. 36)	ss.24(12)–(15) (Scotland only), 27, 28 (both England & Wales only), 36–43 (all N.I. only), Sched. 5, paras. 3, 17(2) (3) (6) (7), Sched. 6, (part) (all N.I. only)	February 3, 1995	S.I. 1995 No. 43 (C.3)
Criminal Justice and Public Order Act 1994 (c. 33)	ss.5–15, 61, 63, 65, 68–71, 77–80, 81–83, 90, Pt. VIII, Chaps. I, IV, (ss.93–101, 126–128), ss.142–148, 150, 158(1) (3) (4), 166, 167, 171, 172, Scheds. 1, 2, 9, para. 46, Sched. 10 (part), Sched. 11 (part)	November 3, 1994	s.172
Criminal Justice and Public Order Act 1994 (c. 33)	s.159(1)(2)(4)	December 19, 1994	S.I. 1994 No. 2935 (C.66)
Criminal Justice and Public Order Act 1994 (c. 33)	ss.16, 151, 168 (part), Sched. 9, paras. 34, 41, Sched. 10, paras. 40, 64 (part), 69, Sched. 11 (part)	January 9, 1995	S.I. 1994 No. 3192 (C.78)
Criminal Justice and Public Order Act 1994 (c. 33)	s.52	January 11, 1995	S.I. 1994 No. 3258 (C.82)
Criminal Justice and Public Order Act 1994 (c. 33)	s.53	February 2, 1995	S.I. 1995 No. 24 (C.1)

Act Affected	Provision Brought Into Force	Commencement Date	Authority
Criminal Justice and Public Order Act 1994 (c. 33)	ss.17, 18, 23, 24, 31–33, 40–43, 46–51, 64(1)–(3) (in part), 66(6) (10)–(13), 67(3)–(5) (8) (9), 72–74, 84–88, 91, 92, 102–117, 129–133, 134(1) (2), (3) (part), (4)–(6), 135–141, 152–155, 157, 160–164, 168 (part), 169, 170, Scheds. 6, 8, 9 (part), 10 (part), 11 (part)	February 3, 1995	S.I. 1995 No. 127 (C.4)
Criminal Justice and Public Order Act 1994 (c. 33)	s.134(3) (remainder)	June 1, 1995	S.I. 1995 No. 127 (C.4)
Deregulation and Contracting Out Act 1994 (c. 40)	Pt. I, Chap. I (ss.1–6), 14, 18, 25–30, 32–34, 37, 39 (part), 40, 41, 54, 55, 57(1) (part), 81 (part), 82, Scheds. 11 (part), 13 (part), 17 (part)	November 3, 1994	s.82(3)
Deregulation and Contracting Out Act 1994 (c. 40)	ss.22, 23, 24, 81 (part), Sched. 17 (part)	December 1, 1994	S.I. 1994 No. 3037 (C.70)
Deregulation and Contracting Out Act 1994 (c. 40)	ss.8, 11, 19, 35, 36(1), 39 (part), 51, 58, 62, 64, 67, 68 (part), 81 (part), Scheds. 7, 10, 11, paras. 1 (part), 2 (part), Sched. 14, para. 1 (part), Sched. 17 (part)	January 3, 1995	S.I. 1994 No. 3188 (C.76)
Deregulation and Contracting Out Act 1994 (c. 40)	ss.7, 9, 10, 12, 15, 16, 17, 20, 21, 31, 39 (part), Pt. II (ss.69–79), 81 (part), Scheds. 2–4, 8, 9, 11 (part), 17 (part)	January 3, 1995	s.82(2)
Deregulation and Contracting Out Act 1994 (c. 40)	s.60	April 1, 1995	S.I. 1994 No. 3188 (C.76)
Drug Trafficking Act 1994 (c. 37)	All provisions	February 3, 1995	s.69(2)

Act Affected	Provision Brought Into Force	Commencement Date	Authority
Education Act 1993 (c. 35)	ss.22(1) (2)(a) (b) (part) (3), 23, 25–35, 36(1) (2), 37–46, 47(5)–(9), 55–67, 71–77, 79, 80, 92, 136(1) (3), 137, 152, 153(1) (2) (4), 155–158, 161(5), 177(2)–(6), 178, 179, 180(1) (2), 181, 182 (part), 213–216, 217(1), 218–223, 227, 228(1)–(3), 238, 239, 246, 266, 267, 268, 271, 274–276, 281, 287, 288, 290–292, 299, 300, Sched. 3, Pt. I, Scheds. 4–7, Sched. 11, para. 14, Scheds. 12, 13, 16, 17	January 1, 1994	S.I. 1993 No. 3106 (C.62)
Education Act 1993 (c. 35)	ss.172(1) (6), 182 (1)–(3) (part), 186(1) (2) (4), 187, 252, 278(1)–(5), 307(1) (part) (3) (part), Sched. 19 (part), Sched. 21 (part)	March 3, 1994	S.I. 1994 No. 507 (C.10)
Education Act 1993 (c. 35)	Pt. I (ss.1–21), Pt. II (ss.22–155) (all for remaining purposes), 159, 161(1)–(4), 162, 163, 166(4), 167(5) (part), 168(7) (part), 180(4), 182 (remainder), 183–185, 186(3), 188, 189, 191, 217(2), 229 (remainder), 230 (remainder), 231–237, 253–258, 272, 273, 278(6), 289, 295–297, 304, 307(1) (part) (2) (part) (3) (part), Sched. 1, Sched. 2, Sched. 3, Pt. II, Sched. 8, Sched. 9 (part), Sched. 10 (part), Sched. 11 (remainder), Sched. 15, Sched. 19 (part), Sched. 20 (part), Sched. 21 (part)	April 1, 1994	S.I. 1994 No. 507 (C.10)

Act Affected	Provision Brought Into Force	Commencement Date	Authority
Education Act 1993 (c. 35)	s.279 (part)	June 15, 1994	S.I. 1994 No. 1558 (C.28)
Education Act 1993 (c. 35)	ss.298(2) (part) (8) (part), 307(1) (part), Sched. 18, para. 3, Sched. 19, paras. 97(a) (part), 98(a)	August 1, 1994	S.I. 1994 No. 2038 (C.39)
Education Act 1993 (c. 35)	ss.160, 164, 165, 166(1)–(3) (5), 167(5) (remainder), 168(7) (remainder), 169, 170, 171, 172 (2)–(5), 173–176, 177(1), 180(3) (5) (6), 192 (6) (remainder) (7) (remainder), 196, 197(5), 241, 261, 262, 298(2) (remainder) (8) (remainder), 307(1) (part) (3) (part), Scheds. 9 (remainder), 10 (remainder), 18 (remainder), 19, paras. 16, 31(a), 44, 54(a), 74, 82 (remainder), 87(a) (c), 88, 95, 96, 97 (remainder), 98 (remainder), 101(a), 120, 121, 139 (remainder), 145 (remainder), 147, 148, 151, 154 (remainder), 160, Sched. 21 (part)	September 1, 1994	S.I. 1994 No. 2039 (C.39)
Education Act 1993 (c. 35)	ss.279 (remainder), 307(1) (part) (3) (part), Sched. 19, paras. 103, 104, 107 (part), Sched. 21	April 1, 1995	S.I. 1994 No. 1558 (C.28)
Education Act 1994 (c. 30)	All provisions save for s.22(3)–(5)	September 21, 1994	S.I. 1994 No. 2204 (C.46)
Education Act 1994 (c. 30)	s.22(3)–(5)	April 1, 1995	S.I. 1994 No. 2204 (C.46)
Education (Schools) Act 1992 (c. 38)	ss.15, 21(8) (part), Sched. 5 (part) (all in relation to schools other than secondary schools)	September 1, 1994	S.I. 1993 No. 1491 (C.30)

Act Affected	Provision Brought Into Force	Commencement Date	Authority
Environmental Protection Act 1990 (c. 43)	s.41 (remainder)	March 16, 1994	S.I. 1994 No. 780 (C.15)
Environmental Protection Act 1990 (c. 43)	ss.33 (remainder) (part), 35–40 (remainder) (part), 42–43 (remainder) (part), 44 (part), 54 (remainder), 57 (part), 58, 59, 60 (remainder), 64–67 (remainder), 73, 74, 162(1) (part) (2) (part)	May 1, 1994 [see notes above]	S.I. 1994 No. 1096 (C.18)
Environmental Protection Act 1990 (c. 43)	ss.33 (remainder) (part), 35–40 (remainder) (part), 42 (remainder) (part), 43 (remainder) (part), 44 (part), 57 (part), 162(1) (part) (2) (part)	April 1, 1995 [see notes above]	S.I. 1994 No. 1096 (C.18) as amended by S.I. 1994 Nos. 2487 (C.49) and 3234 (C.81)
Environmental Protection Act 1990 (c. 43)	s.162(2) (part)	December 1, 1994	S.I. 1994 No. 2854 (C.64)
European Communities (Finance) Act 1995 (c. 1)	All provisions	January 16, 1995	Royal Assent
European Parliamentary Elections Act 1993 (c. 41)	s.1	May 1, 1994	S.I. 1994 No. 1089 (C.17)
European Union (Accessions) Act 1994 (c. 38)	All provisions	November 3, 1994	Royal Assent
Finance Act 1989 (c. 26)	s.152	February 1, 1994	S.I. 1994 No. 87 (C.4)
Finance Act 1989 (c. 26)	s.165(2)	May 20, 1995	S.I. 1994 No. 2508 (C.50)
Finance Act 1993 (c. 34)	Chapter II (remainder), Sched. 23, Pt. I (part)	February 1, 1994	S.I. 1993 No. 2842 (C.61)
Finance Act 1993 (c. 34)	s.4(2)(b)(d)(3)	January 1, 1995	S.I. 1994 No. 2968 (C.67)
Finance Act 1993 (c. 34)	s.165	March 23, 1995	S.I. 1994 No. 3224 (C.79)

Act Affected	Provision Brought Into Force	Commencement Date	Authority
Finance Act 1994 (c. 9)	s.47 (part)	May 10, 1994	S.I. 1994 No. 1253 (C.21)
Finance Act 1994 (c. 9)	s.45 (part)	June 1, 1994	S.I. 1994 No. 1257 (C.22)
Finance Act 1994 (c. 9)	s.7 (except subs. (1)(b))	July 1, 1994	S.I. 1994 No. 1690 (C.31)
Finance Act 1994 (c. 9)	s.7(1)(b)	August 31, 1994	S.I. 1994 No. 2143 (C.43)
Finance Act 1994 (c. 9)	ss.59, 60	October 1, 1994	S.I. 1994 No. 1773 (C.32)
Finance Act 1994 (c. 9)	ss.8, 9(1)–(8), 10, 11, 12(1)–(6), (7) (part), (8), 13, 14(1) (part) (2)–(5), 15, 16(1)– (5), (6) (part), (7) (8), 17, 18(1) (2) (7) (8), Sched. 5, paras. 9, 10	November 1, 1994	S.I. 1994 No. 2679 (C.59)
Finance Act 1994 (c. 9)	Pt. I, Chap. II, (ss.7–19) Scheds. 4, 5, 26, Pt. III (all in remainder)	January 1, 1995	S.I. 1994 No. 2679 (C.59)
Finance Act 1994 (c. 9)	Pt. IV, Chap. II (ss.147–177)	March 23, 1995	S.I. 1994 No. 3225 (C.80)
Firearms (Amendment) Act 1994 (c. 31)	All provisions	September 21, 1994	s.4(2)
Friendly Societies Act 1992 (c. 40)	ss.27–30, 31 (part), 32(7), 44, 46–49, 55, 68–71, 72(2) (part), 73–79, 98 (part), 120(2) (part), Sched. 11, Sched. 12, Sched. 14 (except paras. 7(1)–(3), (5)–(7)), Sched. 18 (except para. 13), Sched. 22, Pt. I (part) [all provisions in remainder] ss.31 (part), 93(5)– (15), 95 (part), 100 (part), 120(2) (part), Sched. 14, para. 7 (remainder), Sched. 16 (part), Sched. 19, Pt. I (part), Sched. 22 (part)	January 1, 1994	S.I. 1993 No. 2213 (C.43)

Act Affected	Provision Brought Into Force	Commencement Date	Authority
Friendly Societies Act 1992 (c. 40)	ss.82(5), 95 (part), 96, 98 (remainder) (part), 100 (part), 120 (part), 124, Sched. 16 (part), Sched. 18, para. 13 (remainder), Sched. 19, Pt. II (part), Sched. 21, Pt. I (part), Sched. 22, (part)	January 1, 1994	S.I. 1993 No. 3226 (C.65)
Friendly Societies Act 1992 (c. 40)	s.31 (part)	November 1, 1994	S.I. 1994 No. 2543 (C.51)
Friendly Societies Act 1992 (c. 40)	s.120(2) (part), Sched. 22, Pt. I (part), Pt. II (part)	November 1, 1994	S.I. 1994 No. 2543 (C.51)
Friendly Societies Act 1992 (c. 40)	s.31 (part)	January 1, 1995	S.I. 1993 No. 3226 (C.65)
Friendly Societies Act 1992 (c. 40)	s.31 (remainder)	April 1, 1995	S.I. 1994 No. 2543 (C.51)
Gas (Exempt Supplies) Act 1993 (c. 1)	All provisions	October 31, 1994	S.I. 1994 No. 2568 (C.54)
Human Fertilisation and Embryology Act 1990 (c. 37)	s.30(9) (10), 48(1) (part)	July 5, 1994	S.I. 1994 No. 1776 (C.33)
Human Fertilisation and Embryology Act 1990 (c. 37)	ss.30 (remainder), 48(1) (part)	November 1, 1994	S.I. 1994 No. 1776 (C.33)
Immigration Act 1988 (c. 14)	s.7(1)	July 20, 1994	S.I. 1994 No. 1923 (C.35)
Inshore Fishing (Scotland) Act 1994 (c. 27)	All provisions	August 8, 1994	S.I. 1994 No. 2124 (C.41)
Insolvency Act 1994 (c. 7)	All provisions	March 24, 1994	Royal Assent
Insolvency (No. 2) Act 1994 (c. 12)	All provisions	July 26, 1994	s.6
Intelligence Services Act 1994 (c. 13)	All provisions (except that for the purposes of making any Order in Council under s.12(4), the Act is brought into force on November 2, 1994)	December 15, 1994	S.I. 1994 No. 2734 (C.60)

CLS Commencement Diary

Act Affected	Provision Brought Into Force	Commencement Date	Authority
Land Drainage Act 1994 (c. 25)	All provisions	September 21, 1994	s.3(2)
Land Registration (Scotland) Act 1979 (c. 33)	ss.2(1) (2), 3(3) [for the purposes of the County of Fife]	April 1, 1995	S.I. 1994 No. 2588 (C.56) (S.124)
Law of Property (Miscellaneous Provisions) Act 1994 (c. 36)	s.21(1) so far as it relates to Sched. 1, para. 2	February 15, 1995	S.I. 1995 No. 145 (C.6)
Law Reform (Miscellaneous Provisions) (Scotland) Act 1990 (c. 40)	ss.56–59 (remainder)	April 3, 1995	S.I. 1995 No. 364 (C.10) (S.14)
Leasehold Reform, Housing and Urban Development Act 1993 (c. 28)	s.122 (see Transitional Provisions)	February 1, 1994	S.I. 1993 No. 2762 (C.57)
Leasehold Reform, Housing and Urban Development Act 1993 (c. 28)	ss.146, 147, 152, 153	April 1, 1994	S.I. 1993 No. 2163 (C.42)
Leasehold Reform, Housing and Urban Development Act 1993 (c. 28)	ss.132 (remainder), 184, 187(2) (part)	April 1, 1994	S.I. 1994 No. 935 (C.16)
Local Government Act 1992 (c. 19)	s.11 (part), Sched. 1, para. 12 (part)	January 6, 1994	S.I. 1993 No. 3169 (C.64)
Local Government Act 1992 (c. 19)	s.11 (part), Sched. 1, paras. 2(1), (3)–(5), 9, 10	June 13, 1994	S.I. 1994 No. 1445 (C.25)
Local Government etc. (Scotland) Act 1994 (c. 39)	s.163	November 3, 1994	s.184(2)
Local Government etc. (Scotland) Act 1994 (c. 39)	ss.1, 5, 7, 12, 57, 61, 97(6), 125, 137(1) (part), 157, 177(1) (part) (3) (part), 178, 181(1)(2)(8)(9), 183(1), 184, Scheds. 1, 2	November 8, 1994	S.I. 1994 No. 2850 (C.63)
Local Government etc. (Scotland) Act 1994 (c. 39)	s.180(1) (part), Sched. 13, para. 176(1) (19)(b)	December 31, 1994	S.I. 1994 No. 3150 (C.74) (S.174)

Act Affected	Provision Brought Into Force	Commencement Date	Authority
Local Government etc. (Scotland) Act 1994 (c. 39)	ss.8–11, 13–17, 24, 34, 38, 40, 44, 47, 49, 50, 51(3), 60, 97 (remainder), 101, 104, 113–115, 124, 126, 137 (remainder), 141, 143, 146–151, 165–167, 170, 172, 173, 175, 179, 180 (part), 182, Scheds. 5, 13 (part), 14 (part)	January 4, 1995	S.I. 1994 No. 2850 (C.63)
Local Government etc. (Scotland) Act 1994 (c. 39)	ss.153, 160, 161, 180(2) (part), Sched. 14 (part)	January 4, 1995	S.I. 1994 No. 3150 (C.74) (S.174)
Local Government etc. (Scotland) Act 1994 (c. 39)	ss.152, 154, 155, 156, 158, 159, 162(1), 180 (part), Sched. 13, paras. 57, 60(4), 67(1) (2) (5), 100 (2) (4) (5), Sched. 14 (part)	April 1, 1995	S.I. 1994 No. 3150 (C.74) (S.174)
Local Government Finance Act 1992 (c. 14)	s.110(2)(3)	March 31, 1995	S.I. 1994 No. 3152 (C.75) (S.176)
Local Government Finance Act 1992 (c. 14)	Sched. 13, para. 37(1)	April 1, 1995	S.I. 1994 No. 3152 (C.75) (S.176)
Local Government (Wales) Act 1994 (c. 19)	ss.1(1) (2) (7), 3, 6, 7, 39, 40, 43, 46, 47, 48, 54, 55, 63, 64, 66(1)–(4) (9), Scheds. 1, 3, 13, 14, 17, paras. 1, 4, 6, 9	July 5, 1994	s.66(2)
Local Government (Wales) Act 1994 (c. 19)	ss.41, 52, 65	August 15, 1994	S.I. 1994 No. 2109 (C.40)
Local Government (Wales) Act 1994 (c. 19)	ss.1(3) (part) (4) (5) (6) (8), 66(5) (part) (8) (part), Sched. 2, paras. 4, 5, Sched. 15, paras. 1, 7, 8(5), 9(4)(b), 11(2), 12(b), 18, 19, 57, Sched. 18 (part)	October 24, 1994	S.I. 1994 No. 2790 (C.62)
Local Government (Wales) Act 1994 (c. 19)	s.39(1)	February 1, 1995	S.I. 1995 No. 103 (C.5)

Act Affected	Provision Brought Into Force	Commencement Date	Authority
Marriage Act 1994 (c. 34)	ss.2(1) (part), (2), 3	January 1, 1995	S.I. 1994 No. 3116 (C.73)
Marriage Act 1994 (c. 34)	s.1(2) (3), Sched. (all in part)	February 24, 1995	S.I. 1995 No. 424 (C.11)
Marriage Act 1994 (c. 34)	s.1(1) (2) (remainder), (3) (remainder), 2(1) (remainder), Sched. (remainder)	April 1, 1995	S.I. 1995 No. 424 (C.11)
Medicinal Products: Prescription by Nurses etc. Act 1992 (c. 28)	ss.1, 2	October 3, 1994	S.I. 1994 No. 2408 (C.48)
Mental Health (Amendment) Act 1994 (c. 6)	All provisions	April 14, 1994	s.2(3)
Merchant Shipping Act 1979 (c. 39)	ss.38(4), 50(4) (part), Sched. 7 (part)	November 22, 1994	S.I. 1994 No. 2789 (C.61)
Merchant Shipping Act 1988 (c. 12)	ss.48, 57, Scheds. 5, 7 (all in part)	June 1, 1994	S.I. 1994 No. 1201 (C.19)
Merchant Shipping (Registration, etc.) Act 1993 (c. 22)	ss.1–7, 8(1) (2) and (4) (part), 9, 10, Scheds. 1–3, 5, Pt. I	March 21, 1994	S.I. 1993 No. 3137 (C.63)
Merchant Shipping (Registration, etc.) Act 1993 (c. 22)	s.8(3) and (4) (part), Sched. 4 (part), Sched. 5, Pt. II (part)	May 1, 1994	S.I. 1993 No. 3137 (C.63)
Merchant Shipping (Salvage and Pollution) Act 1994 (c. 28)	ss.3, 9, 10(1) (2) (4) (5)	July 28, 1994	S.I. 1994 No. 1988 (C.37)
Merchant Shipping (Salvage and Pollution) Act 1994 (c. 28)	ss.6(1) (part) (2), 7, 8, 10(3) (part), Sched. 3, Pt. 1, Sched. 4 (part)	October 1, 1994	S.I. 1994 No. 1988 (C.37)
Merchant Shipping (Salvage and Pollution) Act 1994 (c. 28)	ss.1, 2, 4, 10(3) (part), Scheds. 1, 2, 4 (part)	January 1, 1995	S.I. 1994 No. 2971 (C.68)
National Health Service and Community Care Act 1990 (c. 19)	s.36(1) (part), Sched. 7, paras. 1 (part), 3(1) (part) (2)(d) (6)	October 24, 1994	S.I. 1994 No. 2658 (C.57) (S.136)

Act Affected	Provision Brought Into Force	Commencement Date	Authority
National Health Service and Community Care Act 1990 (c. 19)	s.36(1) (part), Sched. 7, paras. 1 (part), 2, 3(1) (part), 3(2)(a)–(c) (5), 13, 15	December 1, 1994	S.I. 1994 No. 2658 (C.57) (S.136)
National Health Service and Community Care Act 1990 (c. 19)	ss.36(1) (remainder), 66(2) (part), Scheds. 7 (remainder), 10 (part)	April 1, 1995	S.I. 1994 No. 2658 (C.57) (S.136)
National Lottery etc. Act 1993 (c. 39)	ss.48, 49, 51–55, 64 (remainder), Scheds. 7, 8, 10 (remainder)	May 3, 1994	S.I. 1994 No. 1055 (C.16)
National Lottery etc. Act 1993 (c. 39)	s.50, Sched. 9	October 3, 1994	S.I. 1994 No. 1055 (C.16)
National Lottery etc. Act 1993 (c. 39)	Pt. IV (ss.56–59)	November 14, 1994	S.I. 1994 No. 2659 (C.58)
New Towns (Amendment) Act 1994 (c. 5)	All provisions	March 24, 1994	Royal Assent
Non-Domestic Rating Act 1994 (c. 3)	All provisions	February 24, 1994	Royal Assent
Parliamentary Commissioner Act 1994 (c. 14)	All provisions	September 5, 1994	s.3(2)
Pension Schemes Act 1993 (c. 48)	All provisions except ss.188(1) (in relation to Sched. 5, Pt. II), 190 (in relation to Sched. 7), Scheds. 5, Pt. II, 7	February 7, 1994	S.I. 1994 No. 86 (C.3)
Planning and Compensation Act 1991 (c. 34)	ss.58, 61 (part), Sched. 13 (part)	March 7, 1994	S.I. 1994 No. 398 (C.8) (S.14)
Planning and Compensation Act 1991 (c. 34)	ss.44, 46, 61 (part), 84(6) (part), Scheds. 13 (part), 19 (part)	February 3, 1995	S.I. 1994 No. 3292 (C.84) (S.191)
Police and Magistrates' Courts Act 1994 (c. 29)	ss.3 (part), 13, 26 (part), 44 (part), 50, 60 (part), 63(4) (7)(a) (part), Sched. 2 (part), 5, paras. 17–20 (part)	July 21, 1994	s.94(3)

Act Affected	Provision Brought Into Force	Commencement Date	Authority
Police and Magistrates' Courts Act 1994 (c. 29)	ss.1 (part), 2 (part), 3 (part), 18 (part), 41, 44 (part), 46, 52 (part), 65, 93 (part), Sched. 1 (part), Sched. 5, Pt. 1 (part), Sched. 9 (part)	August 8, 1994	S.I. 1994 No. 2025 (C.38)
Police and Magistrates' Courts Act 1994 (c. 29)	Pt. III (ss.66–68), s.93 (part), Sched. 9, Pt. 1 (part)	August 23, 1994	S.I. 1994 No. 2151 (C.44)
Police and Magistrates' Courts Act 1994 (c. 29)	ss.4 (part), 8 (part), 10 (part), 11 (part), 14 (part), 15 (part), 16 (part), 22, 25, 31 (part), 32 (part), 33, 39 (part), 42, 43 (part), 44 (part), 45 (part), 93 (part), Sched. 4 (part), Sched. 5 (part), Sched. 9 (part)	October 1, 1994	S.I. 1994 No. 2025 (C.38)
Police and Magistrates' Courts Act 1994 (c. 29)	ss.17, 27, 28 (for the purposes of any financial year beginning on or after April 1, 1995)	November 1, 1994	S.I. 1994 No. 2025 (C.38)
Police and Magistrates' Courts Act 1994 (c. 29)	ss.69, 70 (part), 71 (part), 74, 78, 79 (part), 85, 86, 87, 88 (not (6)), 89, 90, 91(1) (part), 92, 93 (part), Sched. 8, Pt. I (part), Sched. 9, Pt. II (part)	November 1, 1994	S.I. 1994 No. 2594 (C.55)
Police and Magistrates' Courts Act 1994 (c. 29)	ss.44 (part), 93 (part), Sched. 5, paras. 1, 8, Sched. 9, Pt. I (part)	December 31, 1994	S.I. 1994 No. 3262 (C.83)
Police and Magistrates' Courts Act 1994 (c. 29)	ss.48 (part), 51 (part), 52(1)(3) (part), 53(1), 55(1) (part), 56, 57, 58, 59 (part), 62, 63(1)(6) (7)(b) (9)(b), 93 (part), Sched. 9, Pt. I (part)	January 1, 1995	S.I. 1994 No. 3075 (C.72) (S.163)
Police and Magistrates' Courts Act 1994 (c. 29)	Sched. 8, para. 19(1) (2)	February 3, 1995	S.I. 1995 No. 42 (C.2)

Act Affected	Provision Brought Into Force	Commencement Date	Authority
Police and Magistrates' Courts Act 1994 (c. 29)	ss.1–12, 14–16, 20, 21, 23, 24, 26, 29–31, 39(2)(3), 40, 43, 44 (part), 45, 93 (part), Scheds. 1, 2, 4, 5, paras. 2–7, 9, 10(2), 13, 14, 15, 17–20, 22, 23, 24(a), 29, 30, 35–38, Sched. 9, Pt. I (part)	April 1, 1995	S.I. 1994 No. 3262 (C.83)
Police and Magistrates' Courts Act 1994 (c. 29)	s.59 (remainder)	April 1, 1995	S.I. 1994 No. 3075 (C.72) (S.163)
Police and Magistrates' Courts Act 1994 (c. 29)	ss.47(2)(a), 48, 53(2), 59, 60, 63(2) (4) (5) (7) (all in remainder), 93 (part), Sched. 9, Pt. I (part)	April 1, 1995	S.I. 1995 No. 492 (C.12) (S.34)
Police and Magistrates' Courts Act 1994 (c. 29)	s.51 (remainder)	January 1, 1996	S.I. 1994 No. 3075 (C.72) (S.163)
Police and Magistrates' Courts Act 1994 (c. 29)	ss.47(1) (2) (3) (4) (5), 49, 54, 63(9), 64 (all in remainder), 93 (part), Sched. 9, Pt. I	April 1, 1996	S.I. 1995 No. 492 (C.12) (S.34)
Prisoners and Criminal Proceedings (Scotland) Act 1993 (c. 9)	ss.30, 33–35	January 1, 1994	S.I. 1993 No. 2050 (C.39)
Race Relations (Remedies) Act 1994 (c. 10)	All provisions	July 3, 1994	s.3
Railways Act 1993 (c. 43)	ss.6(2), 23(3) (4), 25(1) (part) (2) (part), 29(8), 83(1) (part), 84, 85, 87(1) (part) (2)–(5), 88–92, 93 (except subs. (3)(b)), 94–116, 126–128, 130, 131, 134(1) (part) (2) (3), 141 (except subs. (1)(a)), 151 (remainder), 152(1) (part) (3) (part), 153, Scheds. 8, 9, 11 (part), 12 (part), 14 (part)	January 6, 1994	S.I. 1993 No. 3237 (C.66)

Act Affected	Provision Brought Into Force	Commencement Date	Authority
Railways Act 1993 (c. 43)	s.117	February 2, 1994	S.I. 1994 No. 202 (C.6)
Railways Act 1993 (c. 43)	s.4(1)–(3) (5) (6) (all in part), 70, 83(1) (part)	February 22, 1994	S.I. 1994 No. 447 (C.9)
Railways Act 1993 (c. 43)	ss.118–121, 132(1)–(7) (8) (part) (9) (10), 133, 152(3) (part), Sched. 10 (part), Sched. 14 (part)	March 8, 1994	S.I. 1994 No. 571 (C.11)
Railways Act 1993 (c. 43)	ss.4 (remainder), 5, 52, 54(2) (part) (3) (part), 138	March 21, 1994	S.I. 1994 No. 571 (C.11)
Railways Act 1993 (c. 43)	s.152 (part), Sched. 14 (part)	March 31, 1994	S.I. 1994 No. 571 (C.11)
Railways Act 1993 (c. 43)	ss.2, 3, 6 (remainder), 7–16, 23 (remainder), 24, 25 (remainder), 26–28, 29 (remainder), 30, 31, 34–51, 53, 54 (remainder), 55–69, 71–80, 83 (remainder), 86, 87 (remainder), 93 (remainder), 122–125, 129, 135–137, 141 (remainder), 145 (remainder), 150 (remainder), 152 (part), Scheds. 2, 3, 5–7, 12 (except para. 32), 13, 14 (part)	April 1, 1994	S.I. 1994 No. 571 (C.11)
Railways Act 1993 (c. 43)	ss.17–22, Sched. 4	April 2, 1994	S.I. 1994 No. 571 (C.11)
Railways Act 1993 (c. 43)	ss.139, 140, 152(3) (part), Sched. 14 (part)	July 15, 1994	S.I. 1994 No. 1648 (C.29)
Railways Act 1993 (c. 43)	s.134(1) (remainder), Sched. 11 (remainder)	August 16, 1994	S.I. 1994 No. 2142 (C.42)

Act Affected	Provision Brought Into Force	Commencement Date	Authority
Road Traffic Act 1991 (c. 40)	ss.64 (remainder), 65, 66 (remainder), 67(4) (part) (6) (part), 68(2)(b) (part), 69, 81 (part), Sched. 7, para. 5 (remainder) [all provisions in relation to the London borough of Richmond upon Thames]	January 31, 1994	S.I. 1993 No. 3238 (C.67)
Road Traffic Act 1991 (c. 40)	ss.64 (remainder), 65, 66 (remainder), 67(4) (part) (6) (part), 68(2)(b) (part), 69, 81 (part), Sched. 7, para. 5 (part) [all in relation to the London borough of Southwark]	April 5, 1994	S.I. 1994 No. 81 (C.2)
Road Traffic Act 1991 (c. 40)	ss.64 (remainder), 65, 66 (remainder), 67 (part), 68 (part), 69, 81 (part), Sched. 7, para. 5 (part) [all in relation to the City of London and the boroughs named in the Schedule to this Order]	July 4, 1994	S.I. 1994 No. 1482 (C.26)
Road Traffic Act 1991 (c. 40)	ss.64 (remainder), 65, 66 (remainder), 81 (part), Sched. 7, para. 5 [all in relation to the London borough of Bexley]	July 4, 1994	S.I. 1994 No. 1484 (C.27)
Road Traffic Regulation (Special Events) Act 1994 (c. 11)	All provisions	May 3, 1994	Royal Assent
Sale and Supply of Goods Act 1994 (c. 35)	All provisions	January 3, 1995	s.8(2)
Sale of Goods (Amendment) Act 1994 (c. 32)	All provisions	January 3, 1995	s.3(3)

Act Affected	Provision Brought Into Force	Commencement Date	Authority
Social Security Act 1989 (c. 24)	Sched. 5, paras. 1 (part), 2 (part), 3 (part), 5 (except subpara. (2)(b)(c)), 6 (except subpara. (3)(b)(c)), 7 (part), 9 (part), 10 (part)	June 23, 1994	S.I. 1994 No. 1661 (C.30)
Social Security Contributions Act 1994 (c. 1)	s.3	July 23, 1987	s.3
Social Security Contributions Act 1994 (c. 1)	s.2	October 5, 1989	s.2
Social Security Contributions Act 1994 (c. 1)	ss.4, 5	February 10, 1994	Royal Assent
Social Security Contributions Act 1994 (c. 1)	s.1	April 6, 1994	s.1
Social Security (Incapacity for Work) Act 1994 (c. 18)	ss.14, 15, 16	July 5, 1994	s.16(2)
Social Security (Incapacity for Work) Act 1994 (c. 18)	ss.2(3)(7), 4, 7, 8(2), 9(4), 12	November 18, 1994	S.I. 1994 No. 2926 (C.65)
Social Security (Incapacity for Work) Act 1994 (c. 18)	ss.2(1)(5), 3(1), 5, 6, 9(1)(2)(3), 10(1) (3) [All only for the purposes of making regulations]	November 18, 1994	S.I. 1994 No. 2926 (C.65)
Social Security (Incapacity for Work) Act 1994 (c. 18)	s.8(1)(3)(4)	April 6, 1995	S.I. 1994 No. 2926 (C.65)
Social Security (Incapacity for Work) Act 1994 (c. 18)	ss.2(1)(5), 3(1), 5, 6, 9(1)(2)(3), 10(1)(3) [For all purposes other than the making of regulations]	April 13, 1995	S.I. 1994 No. 2926 (C.65)
Social Security (Incapacity for Work) Act 1994 (c. 18)	ss.1, 2(2) (4) (6), 3(2), 10(2), 11, 13, Scheds. 1, 2	April 13, 1995	S.I. 1994 No. 2926 (C.65)
Statutory Sick Pay Act 1994 (c. 2)	ss.2–5	February 10, 1994	s.5

Act Affected	Provision Brought Into Force	Commencement Date	Authority
Statutory Sick Pay Act 1994 (c. 2)	s.1	April 6, 1994	s.5
Sunday Trading Act 1994 (c. 20)	ss.1, 6–8, 9(1) (3) (4), Scheds. 1, 2	July 5, 1994	Royal Assent
Sunday Trading Act 1994 (c. 20)	ss.2–5, 9(2), Scheds. 3–5	August 26, 1994	S.I. 1994 No. 1841 (C.34)
Trade Marks Act 1994 (c. 26)	All provisions	October 31, 1994	S.I. 1994 No. 2550 (C.52)
Trade Union Reform and Employment Rights Act 1993 (c. 19)	ss.8, 9, 49(2) (part), 51 (part), Sched. 8 (part), Sched. 10 (part)	January 1, 1994	S.I. 1993 No. 1908 (C.34)
Trade Union Reform and Employment Rights Act 1993 (c. 19)	ss.45 (remainder), 46, 49(2) (part), 51 (part), Sched. 8, paras. 1, 3–5, 8, 9, 33, 34, Sched. 10 (part) [in relation to England and Scotland]	April 1, 1994	S.I. 1993 No. 2503 (C.52)
Trade Union Reform and Employment Rights Act 1993 (c. 19)	ss.23, 24 (remainder), 25, 49 (remainder), 51 (remainder), Scheds. 2, 3, 7 (remainder), 8 (remainder), 10 (part)	June 10, 1994	S.I. 1994 No. 1365 (C.23)
Trade Union Reform and Employment Rights Act 1993 (c. 19)	ss.45 (remainder), 46, 49(2) (part), 51 (part), Sched. 8, paras. 1, 3–5, 8, 9, 33, 34, Sched. 10 (part) [for all other purposes]	April 1, 1995	S.I. 1993 No. 2503 (C.52)
Trade Union Reform and Employment Rights Act 1993 (c. 19)	ss.7(2) (3), 51 (part), Sched. 10 (part)	April 1, 1996	S.I. 1993 No. 1908 (C.34)
Transport and Works Act 1992 (c. 42)	ss.65(1)(b) (part), 68(1) (part), Sched. 4, Pt. 1 (part)	April 5, 1994	S.I. 1994 No. 718 (C.14)
Transport Police (Jurisdiction) Act 1994 (c. 8)	All provisions	April 1, 1994	s.2(2)
Value Added Tax Act 1994 (c. 23)	All provisions	September 1, 1994	s.101

Act Affected	Provision Brought Into Force	Commencement Date	Authority
Vehicle Excise and Registration Act 1994 (c. 22)	All provisions (subject to transitional provisions in Sched. 4)	September 1, 1994	s.66
Welsh Language Act 1993 (c. 38)	s.30(1) (part) (6) (part)	January 25, 1994	S.I. 1994 No. 115 (C.5)
Welsh Language Act 1993 (c. 38)	ss.30 (remainder), 31, 35(1) (part) (2), Sched. 2	February 1, 1994	S.I. 1994 No. 115 (C.5)

CRIMINAL LAW, ENGLAND AND WALES
CRIMINAL LAW, SCOTLAND
CRIMINAL LAW, NORTHERN IRELAND

THE CRIMINAL JUSTICE ACT 1993 (COMMENCEMENT NO. 4) ORDER 1994

(S.I. 1994 No. 71 (C. 1))

Made - - - - - *14th January 1994*

INTRODUCTION

This Order brings into force certain provisions of the Criminal Justice Act 1993. Provisions relating to, *inter alia*, the acquisition, possession or use of the proceeds of drug trafficking, money laundering, amendments to the Northern Ireland (Emergency Provisions) Act 1991 and the Prevention of Terrorism (Temporary Provisions) Act 1989 and various miscellaneous provisions are brought into force on February 15, 1994. Article 3 specifies the extent of the Order.

In exercise of the powers conferred on me by section 78(3) and (4) of the Criminal Justice Act 1993 (c. 36), I hereby make the following Order:

1. This Order may be cited as the Criminal Justice Act 1993 (Commencement No. 4) Order 1994.

2. The provisions of the Criminal Justice Act 1993 ("the 1993 Act") referred to in the left-hand column of the Schedule to this Order (which relate to the matters described in the right-hand column of the Schedule) shall come into force on 15th February 1994.

3.—(1) So far as relating to the following provisions of the 1993 Act, namely—
  (a) sections 47, 49 and 78; and
  (b) so far as it relates to the Prevention of Terrorism (Temporary Provisions) Act 1989 (c. 4), the Criminal Justice (International Co-operation) Act 1990 (c. 5) and section 67(6) of the Northern Ireland (Emergency Provisions) Act 1991 (c. 24), Schedule 6,
this Order extends to the United Kingdom.
  (2) So far as relating to the following provisions of the 1993 Act, namely—
  (a) sections 29, 30 and 31; and
  (b) paragraph 14(2)(a) of Schedule 5,
this Order extends to Great Britain only.
  (3) So far as relating to the following provisions of the 1993 Act, namely—
  (a) sections 16 and 74; and
  (b) paragraph 14(1) of Schedule 5 and, so far as it relates to the Drug Trafficking Offences Act 1986 (c. 32) and to the Criminal Justice Act 1988 (c. 33), Schedule 6,
this Order extends to England and Wales only.
  (4) So far as relating to the following provisions of the 1993 Act, namely—
  (a) sections 17 and 33; and
  (b) paragraph 14(2)(b) of Schedule 5,
this Order extends to Scotland only.
  (5) So far as relating to the entry in Schedule 6 to the 1993 Act relating to section 50(2) of the Northern Ireland (Emergency Provisions) Act 1991, this Order extends to Northern Ireland only.

Home Office

Michael Howard
14th January 1994 One of Her Majesty's Principal Secretaries of State

Article 2   SCHEDULE

PROVISIONS OF THE CRIMINAL JUSTICE ACT 1993 COMING INTO FORCE ON
15TH FEBRUARY 1994

Provisions of the Act	*Subject matter of provisions*
Section 16	Acquisition, possession or use of proceeds of drug trafficking
Section 17	Acquisition, possession or use of proceeds of drug trafficking: Scotland
Section 29	Assisting another to retain the benefit of criminal conduct
Section 30	Acquisition, possession or use of proceeds of criminal conduct
Section 31	Concealing or transferring proceeds of criminal conduct
Section 33	Application to Scotland of sections 93A to 93D of 1988 Act
Section 47	Offences relating to proceeds of terrorist-related activities
Section 49	Financial assistance for terrorism
Section 74	Persons not eligible for early release
Section 78 to the extent that it is not already in force	Commencement etc.
Section 79(13) to the extent necessary to bring into force the provision of Schedule 5 specified below	Consequential amendments
Section 79(14) to the extent necessary to bring into force the provisions of Schedule 6 specified in the Appendix hereto	Repeals and revocations
Schedule 5, paragraph 14	Consequential amendments
So much of Schedule 6 as is specified in the Appendix hereto	Repeals and revocations

APPENDIX

PROVISIONS OF SCHEDULE 6 COMING INTO FORCE ON 15TH FEBRUARY 1994

So much of Part I as relates to the following enactments:
    Sections 1(5)(b)(iii) and 27(5) of the Drug Trafficking Offences Act 1986 (c. 32)
    The Criminal Justice Act 1988 (c. 33)
    The Prevention of Terrorism (Temporary Provisions) Act 1989 (c. 4)
    The Criminal Justice (International Co-operation) Act 1990 (c. 5)
    Sections 50(2) and 67(6) of the Northern Ireland (Emergency Provisions) Act 1991 (c. 24)

INDEX

References are to article number

ROAD TRAFFIC

THE ROAD TRAFFIC ACT 1991 (COMMENCEMENT NO. 10 AND TRANSITIONAL PROVISIONS) ORDER 1994

(S.I. 1994 No. 81 (C. 2))

Made - - - - - *18th January 1994*

Introduction

This Order brings into force certain provisions of Pt. II of the Road Traffic Act 1991 (Traffic in London: Parking) with effect in relation to the London Borough of Southwark; the provisions come into force on April 5, 1994. The Order also amends the Road Traffic Act 1991 (Commencement No. 9 and Transitional Provisions) Order 1993 (S.I. 1993 No. 3238), by removing references to the London Borough of Southwark from that Order.

The Secretary of State for Transport, in exercise of the powers conferred by section 84 of the Road Traffic Act 1991 (c. 40), hereby makes the following Order:

Citation and interpretation

1.—(1) This Order may be cited as the Road Traffic Act 1991 (Commencement No. 10 and Transitional Provisions) Order 1993.

(2) In this Order—
"the 1991 Act" means the Road Traffic Act 1991;
"the Commencement No. 9 Order" means the Road Traffic Act 1991 (Commencement No. 9 and Transitional Provisions) Order 1993 (S.I. 1993 No. 3238); and
"vehicle" has the meaning given by section 99(5) of the Road Traffic Regulation Act 1984 (c. 27).

Amendment of Commencement No. 9 Order

2.—(1) The Commencement No. 9 Order shall be amended as follows.

(2) In articles 2 and 3 for "the London boroughs of Richmond upon Thames and Southwark" in each place where those words occur there shall be substituted "the London borough of Richmond upon Thames".

(3) In article 4 for "the councils of the London Boroughs of Richmond upon Thames and Southwark" there shall be substituted "the council of the London borough of Richmond upon Thames".

(4) In article 5 "or Southwark", in both places where those words occur, shall be omitted.

Commencement and transitional provisions

3. The following provisions of the 1991 Act shall come into force on 5th April 1994 in respect of the London borough of Southwark—
(a) section 64, to the extent that it is not already in force;
(b) section 65;
(c) section 66, to the extent that it is not already in force;
(d) section 69;
(e) section 81, to the extent necessary for bringing into force the provisions of Schedule 7 brought into force by this article; and
(f) paragraph 5 of Schedule 7, to the extent that that paragraph is not already in force.

4. Subsections (4) and (6) of section 67 of the 1991 Act shall come into force on 5th April 1994 for the purpose of the application of the subsections thereby inserted in relation to vehicles found in the London borough of Southwark.

5. Subsection (2)(b) of section 68 of the 1991 Act shall come into force on 5th April 1994 for the purpose of the application of the subsection thereby inserted in relation to the council of the London borough of Southwark.

6.—(1) In relation to a vehicle that is stationary in a designated parking place in the London borough of Southwark immediately before 5th April 1994, section 66(2) of the 1991 Act shall have effect for so long as it remains in that parking place as if the words "on or after 5th April 1994" were inserted after—

(a) the word "left" in paragraph (a) of section 66(2),

(b) the word "payable" in paragraph (b) of that subsection, and

(c) the word "has" in paragraph (c) of that subsection.

(2) Where a vehicle found in the London borough of Southwark has pursuant to any enactment been removed before 5th April 1994, sections 67 and 68 of the 1991 Act shall not apply in relation to that removal or to any storage or disposal of the vehicle as a consequence of that removal.

Signed by authority of the Secretary of State for Transport

Steven Norris
Parliamentary Under Secretary of State,
18th January 1994
Department of Transport

INDEX

References are to article number

PENSIONS

THE PENSION SCHEMES ACT 1993 (COMMENCEMENT NO. 1) ORDER 1994

(S.I. 1994 No. 86 (C. 3))

Made -   -   -   -   -   *19th January 1994*

INTRODUCTION

This Order brings into force the Pension Schemes Act 1993 (with the exception of certain provisions specified in art. 2 of this Order) on February 7, 1994. The provisions excluded from the scope of this Order provide for prospective repeals.

The Secretary of State for Social Security, in exercise of the powers conferred on him by section 193(2) and (3) of the Pension Schemes Act 1993 (c. 48) and of all other powers enabling him in that behalf, hereby makes the following Order:

Citation and interpretation

1.—(1) This Order may be cited as the Pension Schemes Act 1993 (Commencement No. 1) Order 1994.

(2) In this Order, unless the context otherwise requires, references to sections and Schedules are references to sections of and Schedules to the Pension Schemes Act 1993.

Appointed day

2. Apart from—
   (a) Part II of Schedule 5 and section 188(1) so far as it relates to it (prospective repeal of equal access requirements); and
   (b) Schedule 7 and section 190 so far as it relates to it (re-enactment or amendment of certain provisions not yet in force),
the day appointed for the coming into force of the Pension Schemes Act 1993 is 7th February 1994.

Signed by authority of the Secretary of State for Social Security.

William Hague
Parliamentary Under-Secretary of State,
19th January 1994   Department of Social Security

INDEX

References are to article number

INCOME TAX

THE FINANCE ACT 1989, SECTION 152, (APPOINTED DAY) ORDER 1994

(S.I. 1994 No. 87 (C. 4))

Made -   -   -   -   -   *19th January 1994*

INTRODUCTION

This Order brings into force s.152 of the Finance Act 1989 on February 1, 1994. This section amends s.61 of the Taxes Management Act 1970 (distraint by collectors of tax).

The Treasury, in exercise of the powers conferred on them by section 152(7) of the Finance Act 1989 (c. 26), hereby make the following Order:

1. This Order may be cited as the Finance Act 1989, section 152, (Appointed Day) Order 1994.

2. The day appointed for the coming into force of section 152 of the Finance Act 1989 is 1st February 1994.

Tim Wood
Andrew Mackay
Two of the Lords Commissioners of
Her Majesty's Treasury

19th January 1994

INDEX

References are to article number

COMPANIES

THE WELSH LANGUAGE ACT 1993 (COMMENCEMENT) ORDER 1994

(S.I. 1994 No. 115 (C. 5))

Made -   -   -   -   -   *24th January 1994*

INTRODUCTION

The Welsh Language Act 1993 received Royal Assent on October 21, 1993; the majority of the provisions in the Act came into force two months after that date by virtue of s.36, with the exception of ss.30, 31 and 35(2) and the repeals made in the Companies Act 1985. This Order brings into force s.30(1) and (6) for specified purposes on January 25, 1994 and in remainder, along with ss.31, 35(2), and s.35(1) and Sched. 2 (both in relation to the Companies Act 1985) on February 1, 1994.

The Secretary of State, in exercise of his powers under section 36(2) of the Welsh Language Act 1993 (c. 38), hereby makes the following Order:

Citation and Interpretation

1.—(1) This Order may be cited as the Welsh Language Act 1993 (Commencement) Order 1994.

(2) In this Order, "the Act" means the Welsh Language Act 1993.

Provisions brought into force by the Order

2.—(1) Subsections (1) and (6) of section 30 of the Act shall come into force on 25th January 1994 in so far as necessary to enable:

(a) the prescription of descriptions of documents for the purpose of the new section 710B(3)(a) of the Companies Act 1985 (c. 6) inserted thereby; and

(b) the prescription of the manner in which a translation is to be certified for the purpose of the new section 710B(8) inserted thereby.

(2) Sections 30 (in so far as it is not commenced by paragraph (1) above), 31 and 35(2) of the Act, together with section 35(1) of, and Schedule 2 to, the Act in so far as they make repeals in the Companies Act 1985, shall come into force on 1st February 1994.

Neil Hamilton
Parliamentary Under-Secretary of State
for Corporate Affairs,
Department of Trade and Industry

24th January 1994

INDEX

References are to article number

TRANSPORT

THE RAILWAYS ACT 1993 (COMMENCEMENT NO. 2) ORDER 1994

(S.I. 1994 No. 202 (C. 6))

Made - - - - - *1st February 1994*

INTRODUCTION
This Order brings into force s.117 of the Railways Act 1993 on February 2, 1994. Section 117 provides for various safety, emergency and security considerations on railways and other guided transport systems, bringing certain, named statutory provisions from previous Acts within the ambit of Pt. I of the Health and Safety at Work etc. Act 1974.

The Secretary of State, in exercise of his powers under section 154(2) of the Railways Act 1993 (c. 43), hereby makes the following Order:

1. This Order may be cited as the Railways Act 1993 (Commencement No. 2) Order 1994.

2. Section 117 of the Railways Act 1993 shall come into force on 2nd February 1994.

Signed by authority of the
Secretary of State for Transport

Roger Freeman
Minister of State,
1st February 1994   Department of Transport

INDEX

References are to article number

CRIMINAL LAW, ENGLAND AND WALES
CRIMINAL LAW, SCOTLAND
CRIMINAL LAW, NORTHERN IRELAND

THE CRIMINAL JUSTICE ACT 1993 (COMMENCEMENT NO. 5) ORDER 1994

(S.I. 1994 No. 242 (C. 7))

Made - - - - -   *4th February 1994*

INTRODUCTION

This Order brings into force various provisions of the Criminal Justice Act 1993 on March 1, 1994. The provisions brought into force on that date, are, in the main, those provisions relating to insider dealing. A number of supplementary and miscellaneous provisions are also brought into force.

In exercise of the powers conferred on me by section 78(3) and (4) of the Criminal Justice Act 1993 (c. 36), I hereby make the following Order:

1. This Order may be cited as the Criminal Justice Act 1993 (Commencement No. 5) Order 1994.

2. The provisions of the Criminal Justice Act 1993 ("the 1993 Act") referred to in the left-hand column of the Schedule to this Order (which relate to the matters described in the right-hand column of the Schedule) shall come into force on 1st March 1994.

3.—(1) Subject to paragraphs (2) and (3) below, this Order extends to the United Kingdom.

(2) So far as relating to the following provisions of the 1993 Act, namely, paragraph 4 of Schedule 5 and, so far as relating to the Company Securities (Insider Dealing) Act 1985 (c. 8) and to the Companies Act 1989 (c. 40), Schedule 6, this Order extends to Great Britain only.

(3) So far as relating to the following provisions of the 1993 Act, namely, paragraphs 18 to 22 of Schedule 5 and Part II (save as applying to the Banking Coordination (Second Council Directive) Regulations 1992 (S.I. 1992 No. 3218)) of Schedule 6, this Order extends to Northern Ireland only.

Home Office   *Michael Howard*
4th February 1994   One of Her Majesty's Principal Secretaries of State

Article 2   SCHEDULE

PROVISIONS OF THE CRIMINAL JUSTICE ACT 1993 COMING INTO FORCE ON
1ST MARCH 1994

Provisions of the Act	*Subject matter of provisions*
Section 52	The offence
Section 53	Defences
Section 54	Securities to which Part V applies
Section 55	"Dealing" in securities
Section 56	"Inside information", etc.
Section 57	"Insiders"
Section 58	Information "made public"
Section 59	"Professional intermediary"
Section 60	Other interpretation provisions
Section 61	Penalties and prosecution
Section 62	Territorial scope of offence of insider dealing

Provisions of the Act	Subject matter of provisions
Section 63	Limits on section 52
Section 64	Orders
Section 79(13) to the extent necessary to bring into force the provisions of Schedule 5 specified below	Consequential amendments
Section 79(14) to the extent necessary to bring into force the provisions of Schedule 6 specified in the Appendix hereto	Repeals and revocations
Schedule 1	Special defences
Schedule 2	Securities
Schedule 5, paragraphs 4, 7 to 13, 16 and 18 to 22	Consequential amendments
So much of Schedule 6 as is specified in the Appendix hereto	Repeals and revocations

APPENDIX

PROVISIONS OF SCHEDULE 6 COMING INTO FORCE ON 1ST MARCH 1994

So much of Part I as relates to the following enactments:
  The Company Securities (Insider Dealing) Act 1985 (c. 8)
  The Financial Services Act 1986 (c. 60)
  The Banking Act 1987 (c. 22)
  The Criminal Justice Act 1987 (c. 38)
  The Companies Act 1989 (c. 40)
The whole of Part II.

INDEX

References are to article number

TOWN AND COUNTRY PLANNING, SCOTLAND

THE PLANNING AND COMPENSATION ACT 1991 (COMMENCE-MENT NO. 16) (SCOTLAND) ORDER 1994

(S.I. 1994 No. 398 (C. 8) (S.14))

Made - - - - -   *21st February 1994*

INTRODUCTION

This Order brings into force a number of the Scottish town and country planning provisions of the Planning and Compensation Act 1991 on March 7, 1994. Section 58 adds a new s.18A to the Town and Country Planning (Scotland) Act 1972, affecting the status of development plans. Section 61 gives effect to Sched. 13 to the 1991 Act (minor and consequential amendments) and is brought into force to the extent necessary to give effect to paras. 3 and 4 of that Schedule, which make minor amendments to the 1972 Act.

The Secretary of State, in exercise of the powers conferred on him by section 84(2) of the Planning and Compensation Act 1991 (c. 34) and of all other powers enabling him in that behalf, hereby makes the following Order:

Citation

1. This Order may be cited as the Planning and Compensation Act 1991 (Commencement No. 16) (Scotland) Order 1994.

Provisions coming into force on 7th March 1994

2. The following provisions of the Planning and Compensation Act 1991 shall come into force on 7th March 1994:

> section 61 in so far as it relates to the provisions of Schedule 13 referred to below;
> section 58;
> Schedule 13 in so far as it relates to paragraphs 3 and 4.

Allan Stewart

St Andrew's House, Edinburgh   Parliamentary Under Secretary of State,
21st February 1994   Scottish Office

INDEX

References are to article number

TRANSPORT

THE RAILWAYS ACT 1993 (COMMENCEMENT NO. 3) ORDER 1994

(S.I. 1994 No. 447 (C. 9))

Madę -   -   -   -   -   *21st February 1994*

INTRODUCTION

This Order brings into force various provisions of the Railways Act 1993 on February 22, 1994. Section 70, which provides for the preparation of a code of practice for the protection of the interests of disabled rail users, is brought into force in full; s.4(1)–(3), (5) and (6), which sets out the general duties of the Secretary of State and the Regulator, is brought into force for the purposes of the Regulator as set out in s.70. Related definitions in s.83 (interpretation of Pt. 1) as specified in art. 2 of this Order are also brought into force on that date.

The Secretary of State, in exercise of his powers under section 154(2) of the Railways Act 1993 (c. 43), hereby makes the following Order:

1. This Order may be cited as the Railways Act 1993 (Commencement No. 3) Order 1994.

2. The following provisions of the Railways Act 1993 shall come into force on 22nd February 1994:

 in section 4, subsections (1) to (3), (5) and (6) for the purposes of the functions of the Regulator under section 70;

 section 70;

 in section 83, subsection (1) for the purposes of the definitions of "network licence" and "railway facility".

Signed by authority of the
Secretary of State for Transport

Roger Freeman
Minister of State,
Department of Transport

21st February 1994

INDEX

References are to article number

EDUCATION, ENGLAND AND WALES

EDUCATION ACT 1993 (COMMENCEMENT NO. 3 AND TRANSITIONAL PROVISIONS) ORDER 1994

(S.I. 1994 No. 507 (C. 10))

Made -　-　-　-　-　　　　　*1st March 1994*

INTRODUCTION

This Order provides for the commencement of various provisions of the Education Act 1993.

The provisions specified in art. 2 of and Sched. 1 to the Order came into force on March 3, 1994. Along with various miscellaneous provisions these contain certain provisions relating to education for children with special educational needs.

Part I (ss.1–21) (responsibility for education) and Pt. II (ss.22–155) (grant-maintained schools) were brought into force for all remaining purposes on April 1, 1994. A number of provisions from Pt. III (children with special educational needs), Pt. IV (school attendance), Pt. V (standards of education) and certain miscellaneous provisions from Pt. VI were also brought into force on that date.

In exercise of the powers conferred on the Secretary of State by sections 301(6) and 308(3) of, and paragraph 2 of Schedule 20 to, the Education Act 1993 (c. 35) the Secretary of State for Education hereby makes the following order:

Citation and interpretation

1.—(1) This Order may be cited as the Education Act 1993 (Commencement No. 3 and Transitional Provisions) Order 1994.

(2) In this Order "the Act" means the Education Act 1993.

Commencement of certain provisions of Part III and sections 252 and 278 of the Act

2.—(1) The provisions of the Act specified in the first column of Schedule 1 to this Order (which relate to the matters mentioned in the second column thereof) shall come into force on 3rd March 1994; and, save as otherwise provided in the first column of Schedule 1, they shall come into force on that date for all purposes.

(2) Notwithstanding the repeal on 3rd March 1994 of section 7(10) of the Education Act 1981 (c. 60), under which regulation 9 of the Education (Special Educational Needs) Regulations 1983 (S.I. 1983 No. 29) was made, that regulation shall, subject to sub-paragraph (3) below, continue in force on and after that date.

(3) Regulation 9 of the Education (Special Educational Needs) Regulations 1983, as so continued in force, shall have effect as if made under section 172(1) of the Act and may be amended or revoked thereunder.

Commencement of Parts I and II of the Act

3.—(1) Part I (responsibility for education) and Part II (grant-maintained schools) of the Act, to the extent that they are not already in force on that date, shall come into force on 1st April 1994 for all remaining purposes.

(2) Part I of Schedule 3 to this Order shall have effect for the purpose of making transitional provisions in connection with the provisions brought into force by this Article.

Commencement of other provisions of the Act

4.—(1) The provisions of the Act specified in the first column of Schedule 2 to this Order (which relate to the matters mentioned in the second column thereof) shall come into force on 1st April 1994; and, save as otherwise provided in the first column of Schedule 2, they shall come into force on that date for all purposes.

(2) Part II of Schedule 3 to this Order shall have effect for the purpose of making transitional provisions in connection with the provisions brought into force by this Article and Schedule 2 to this Order.

Article 2   SCHEDULE 1

PROVISIONS COMING INTO FORCE ON 3RD MARCH 1994

Provisions of the Act	Subject matter of provisions
Section 172(1) and (6).	Power to make regulations with respect to the frequency of assessments under section 167 of the Act, and with respect to reviews of statements of special educational needs.
Section 182(1) to (3) (for the purpose of defining the expressions "special school", "maintained special school" and "grant-maintained special school" in relation to regulations made under Part III and section 228 of the Act).	Meaning of the expressions "special school", "maintained special school" and "grant-maintained special school".
Section 186(1), (2) and (4).	Power to make regulations providing for maintained special schools to become grant-maintained special schools.
Section 187.	Power to make regulations enabling groups of schools to include grant-maintained special schools.
Section 252.	Transfer in relation to Wales of functions of the School Curriculum and Assessment Authority.
Section 278(1) to (5).	Grants for education support and training.
Paragraph 82 (for the purpose of omitting section 7(10) of the Education Act 1981), and paragraph 125(a) of Schedule 19, and section 307(1) so far as it relates thereto.	Minor and consequential amendments.
Schedule 21, in so far as it relates to the repeals set out in the Appendix to this Schedule, and section 307(3) so far as it relates thereto.	Repeals.

Appendix to Schedule 1

REPEALS TAKING EFFECT FROM 3RD MARCH 1994

Chapter	Short title	Extent of repeal
1981 c. 60.	The Education Act 1981.	Section 7(10).
1984 c. 11.	The Education (Grants and Awards) Act 1984.	In section 1(3)(b), "not exceeding 70 per cent. of the expenditure so approved". In section 3, subsections (2) and (5) and, in subsection (3), the words "not being regulations to which subsection (2) above applies".

SCHEDULE 2

PROVISIONS COMING INTO FORCE ON 1ST APRIL 1994

Provisions of the Act	*Subject matter of provisions*
Section 159.	Duty of local education authorities to review arrangements for special educational provision.
Section 161(1) to (4).	Duties of governing bodies etc. in relation to pupils with special educational needs.
Section 162.	Provision of goods and services in connection with special educational needs.
Section 163.	Special educational provision otherwise than in schools.
Section 166(4).	Power to make regulations in connection with the duty imposed on District Health Authorities and local authorities under that section.
Section 180(4).	Power to make regulations with respect to the proceedings of the Special Educational Needs Tribunal.
Section 182 (for all remaining purposes).	Special schools.
Section 183.	Establishment, etc. of maintained or grant-maintained special schools.
Section 184.	Procedure for dealing with proposals under section 183 of the Act.
Section 185.	Approval of premises of maintained or grant-maintained special schools.
Section 186(3).	Incorporation of the governing body of a school approved to become a grant-maintained special school.
Section 188.	Approval of special schools.
Section 189.	Approval of independent schools as suitable for the admission of children with statements of special educational needs.
Section 191.	Variation of trust deeds etc. by order of the Secretary of State.
Section 217(2).	Prohibition on a maintained special school becoming a grant-maintained special school.
Section 229 (for all remaining purposes).	Amendments to section 12 of the Education Act 1980 (c. 20) (establishment and alteration of county schools by local education authorities).
Section 230 (for all remaining purposes).	Amendments to section 13 of the Education Act 1980 (establishment and alteration of county schools by local education authorities).
Section 231.	Nursery education in grant-maintained schools.
Section 232.	Power of Secretary of State to direct that proposals be brought forward to remedy excessive provision in schools.
Section 233.	Power of Secretary of State to direct that proposals be brought forward for additional provision in maintained schools.
Section 234.	Publication of proposals by the Secretary of State.
Section 235.	Public inquiry into proposals.
Section 236.	Adoption of proposals by the Secretary of State and approval of related proposals.
Section 237.	Provisions supplementary to sections 232 to 236 of the Act.

C10

Provisions of the Act	Subject matter of provisions
Section 253.	Change of name of the Curriculum Council for Wales.
Section 254.	Duty to reconvene conference on agreed syllabus of religious education.
Section 255.	Duty of local education authorities to constitute a new standing advisory council on religious education.
Section 256.	Reconsideration of agreed syllabus.
Section 257.	Power of Secretary of State to direct standing advisory councils on religious education to revoke a determination or discharge a duty.
Section 258.	Access to documents and meetings of standing advisory councils on religious education and conferences on agreed syllabus of religious education.
Section 272.	Power of governing bodies of county schools to propose change of character etc.
Section 273.	Power to make and deal with proposals in the case of schools eligible for grant-maintained status.
Section 278(6).	Grants for teacher training etc.
Section 289.	Teachers' pay and conditions: special provisions for teachers on transfer of employment to maintained and grant-maintained schools.
Section 295.	Provision by local education authorities of goods and services to grant-maintained and grant-maintained special schools.
Section 296.	Abolition of requirement to establish education committees.
Section 297.	Power of Secretary of State to direct appointment of members of committees of local authorities.
Section 304.	Meaning of "school" in the Education Acts.
Schedule 1.	Supplementary provisions relating to the funding authorities established under Part I of the Act.
Schedule 2.	Distribution of functions where an order is made under section 12 of the Act.
Part II of Schedule 3.	Proposals for the establishment of new grant-maintained schools.
Schedule 8.	Core governors for groups of grant-maintained schools.
Paragraph 3 of Schedule 9, and section 167(5) so far as it relates thereto.	Power to make regulations as to the manner and timing of assessments under section 167 of the Act.
Paragraphs 5(3), 7 and 8(5) of Schedule 10, and section 168(7) so far as it relates thereto.	Power to make regulations relating statements under section 168 of the Act.
Schedule 11 (for all remaining purposes).	Government and conduct of grant-maintained special schools.
Schedule 15.	Amendments consequential on section 253 of the Act.
Paragraphs 6, 9, 12, 13, 18, 19, 20(b), 21, 23(b), 26, 27, 34 (for all remaining purposes), 38, 46, 47, 48, 49, 50, 51, 52, 55(a), 57, 59, 61, 62, 64, 65, 66, 70, 73, 76, 77(b), 79, 81, 82 (for the purpose of omitting sections 2(4) to (7), 3, 11(2) and (3), 12, 13 and 14 of, and paragraphs	Minor and consequential amendments.

Provisions of the Act	Subject matter of provisions
1(3) and 4 of Schedule 1 and paragraphs 1, 2, 10 and 13 of Schedule 3 to, the Education Act 1981 (c. 61)), 85, 86, 87(b), 89, 90 (for all remaining purposes), 91, 92, 93, 94, 99, 100, 101(b), 102, 105, 106, 108, 109(b)(ii), (c) and (d), 110, 111, 113(a), 114, 115, 116, 117, 125(b), 126 (for all remaining purposes), 127, 128, 129, 130 (for all remaining purposes), 136, 137 (for all remaining purposes), 138 (for all remaining purposes), 140, 142, 145 (for the purpose of omitting paragraphs 26 and 33 of Schedule 12 to the Education Reform Act 1988 (c. 40)), 156, 157, 158, 159, 161, 163(b), 167(a), 168, 169, 171, 172 and 173(1)(a) of Schedule 19, and section 307(1) so far as it relates thereto.	
Paragraphs 2 and 4 of Schedule 20, and section 307(2) so far as it relates thereto.	Transitional provisions and savings.
Schedule 21, in so far as it relates to the repeals set out in the Appendix to this Schedule, and section 307(3) so far as it relates thereto.	Repeals.

Appendix to Schedule 2

REPEALS TAKING EFFECT FROM 1ST APRIL 1994

Chapter	Short title	Extent of repeal
1944 c. 31.	The Education Act 1944.	Section 9(5). In section 50(1), "by them". In paragraph (a) of the proviso to section 52(1), "by the authority". Parts I and II of the First Schedule. In paragraph 13(4) of the Fifth Schedule, "either".
1972 c. 70.	The Local Government Act 1972.	Section 101(9)(a).
1973 c. 16.	The Education Act 1973.	Section 1(2)(b).
1980 c. 20.	The Education Act 1980.	In section 12(3), "voluntary". In section 13(1), "after consultation with the authority". In section 13(3), "voluntary". Section 14(4). In paragraph 1 of Schedule 2, in sub-paragraph (3) "or of any education committee of the authority" in each place where it occurs, and in sub-paragraph (4) "or of any education committee of the authority" in each place in which it occurs and "by more than one". In Schedule 3, paragraphs 4 and 13.
1981 c. 60.	The Education Act 1981.	Sections 2(4) to (7), 3, 11(2) and (3), 12, 13 and 14. In Schedule 1, paragraphs 1(3) and 4 and, in Schedule 3, paragraphs 1, 2, 10 and 13.
1986 c. 61.	The Education (No. 2) Act 1986.	In section 5(4)(b), the words after "by the authority".

Chapter	Short title	Extent of repeal
		In section 9(5), the "or" at the end of paragraph (a)(ii), and paragraph (b).
		In section 11, the "or" at the end of subsection (2)(a)(ii), subsection (2)(b), "or (b)" in subsection (2)(c) and subsection (7).
		Section 12(3).
		In section 13(2), "or (b)".
		In section 38, in subsection (4)(c) the words after "to the post" and, in subsection (6)(b), "or (4)(c)(ii)".
		In section 50, in subsection (3)(c) the words "local education authorities, and other", and subsection (4).
		Section 54(12)(f).
		In section 65(1), the definition of "the 1981 Act".
		In Schedule 2, paragraph 2(2)(b), in paragraph 5(2)(b) the words after "proposal", and in paragraph 7(7) the words after "by the authority".
1988 c. 9.	The Local Government Act 1988.	Section 1(1)(j).
		In Schedule 2, the words from "A joint education committee" to "1944".
1988 c. 40.	The Education Reform Act 1988.	Sections 52(1) and (2), 57, 73 and 79 to 101.
		In section 104, paragraphs (c), (d), (e), (i) and (j) of subsection (1), subsection (3) (other than the definition of "incorporation date"), and subsection (4).
		In section 111, subsection (4) and, in subsection (5)(b), the words "provided under arrangements made by the authority".
		In section 119(2), "89 or 92".
		In section 230, in subsection (1) "section 95(4)" and "section 96(2)", subsections (2), (3) and (4)(b).
		In section 232(2), "53(2)" and "91, 94".
		In Schedule 1, paragraph 9.
		In Schedule 2, paragraph 9 and in paragraph 10(5) the words from "and accordingly" to the end.
		In Schedule 12, paragraphs 26 and 33.
1989 c. 42.	The Local Government and Housing Act 1989.	In section 13, subsections (2)(b) and (6).
		In paragraph 4 of Schedule 1, in sub-paragraph (1) the definition of "education committee" and, in paragraph (a) of the definition of "ordinary committee", "education committee, their" and in sub-paragraph (2), in paragraph (a) of the definition of "ordinary committee", "education committee or".
		In Schedule 11, paragraphs 4 and 98.
1990 c. 11.	The Planning (Consequential Provisions) Act 1990.	In Schedule 2, paragraph 78.
1992 c. 13.	The Further and Higher Education Act 1992.	Section 13.
		Section 59(5).
		In Schedule 8, paragraphs 18 and 29.
1992 c. 14.	The Local Government Finance Act 1992.	In Schedule 13, paragraph 58.

       SCHEDULE 3

TRANSITIONAL PROVISIONS

PART I

TRANSITIONAL PROVISIONS CONSEQUENTIAL ON THE COMMENCEMENT OF PARTS I AND II OF THE ACT

1.—(1) The requirement, imposed on the governing body of a grant-maintained school under section 96(3) of the Act, to have regard to any guidance given by the Secretary of State in determining the persons whom it is appropriate to consult before publishing proposals, shall not apply in relation to any proposals published under that section before 1st July 1994.

(2) Section 96(6)(a) of the Act shall not apply in relation to any proposals published before 1st April 1994 under section 89 of the Education Reform Act 1988 which have not been determined before that date.

2.—(1) Sub-paragraph (2) below applies where before 1st April 1994—

(a) proposals have been published by the governing body of a grant-maintained school in England in accordance with section 89 of the Education Reform Act 1988; and

(b) the Secretary of State has in accordance with section 90 of that Act directed the governing body to submit to him particulars of the premises or proposed premises of the school; but

(c) he has not approved those particulars in accordance with that section.

(2) Any particulars so submitted in accordance with section 90 of the Education Reform Act 1988 shall be treated on and after 1st April 1994 as having been submitted to the funding authority in accordance with section 99(1) of the Act; and the Secretary of State shall as soon as reasonably practicable after that date send copies of those particulars to the funding authority.

3. The requirement, imposed on the governing body of a grant-maintained school under section 104(2) of the Act, to have regard to any guidance given by the Secretary of State in determining the persons whom it is appropriate to consult before passing a resolution under section 104(1)(a) of the Act, shall not apply in relation to any such resolution passed before 1st July 1994.

4. The amendment to section 11(3)(b) of the Education Reform Act 1988 made by section 147(1) of the Act shall not affect a person's appointment to a standing advisory council on religious education where that appointment was made under section 11(3)(b) of the Education Reform Act 1988 before 1st April 1994.

PART II

TRANSITIONAL PROVISIONS CONSEQUENTIAL ON THE COMMENCEMENT OF OTHER PROVISIONS OF THE ACT ON 1ST APRIL 1994

5.—(1) Where—

(a) before 1st April 1994 a local education authority apply to the Secretary of State for his approval under section 9(5) of the Education Act 1944 (c. 31; s.9(5) was substituted by s.11(1) of the Education Act 1981 (c. 60)) for a school, proposed to be maintained by them, to be a special school within the meaning of that section; but

(b) the application is not determined by the Secretary of State before that date,

the application shall be treated on and after that date as if made in accordance with section 183(2)(a) and (6) and 184(1) to (3) of the Act; and sections 184(4) to (6) and 185 of the Act shall have effect accordingly.

(2) Where—

(a) before 1st April 1994 a local education authority apply to the Secretary of State for his approval for the making of a change in the arrangements which are required to apply to a special school maintained by them in accordance with regulations made under section 12(1)(b) and (2) of the 1981 Act (see the Education (Approval of Special Schools) Regulations 1983 (S.I. 1983 No. 1499)); but

(b) the application is not determined by the Secretary of State before that date,

the application shall be treated on and after that date as if made in accordance with sections 183(2)(b) and (6) and 184(1) to (3) of the Act; and sections 184(4) to (6) and 185 of the Act shall have effect accordingly.

6.—(1) The requirement imposed by sections 12(1A) and 13(1B) of the Education Act 1980 (c. 20) (as amended respectively by sections 229(1) and 230(1) of the Act), to have regard to any guidance given by the Secretary of State in determining the persons whom it is appropriate to consult before publishing proposals, shall not apply in relation to any proposals published under section 12 or 13 of the Education Act 1980 before 1st July 1994.

(2) The amendments to sections 12(3) and 13(3) of the Education Act 1980 made respectively by sections 229(2) and 230(2) of the Act shall not apply in relation to any proposals published before 1st April 1994 under section 12 or 13 of the Education Act 1980.

7.—(1) Sub-paragraph (2) below shall have effect notwithstanding the amendments made to section 50(1) of the Education (No. 2) Act 1986 by section 278(6) of the Act and the repeal in section 50(3)(c) of that Act of the words "local education authorities".

(2) The Education (Training Grants) Regulations 1993 (S.I. 1993 No. 72), which were made under section 50 of the Education (No. 2) Act 1986 (c. 40), shall continue to have effect on and after 1st April 1994 in so far as they relate to the payment of grant on and after that date, or grant paid before that date, in respect of expenditure incurred on or before 31st March 1994.

8. Notwithstanding the repeal of section 6(2) of, and Part II of the First Schedule to, the Education Act 1944, in relation to any joint education committee constituted immediately before 1st April 1994—

(a) that section and that Schedule, other than paragraphs 1 and 7 thereof, shall continue to have effect; and

(b) the repeal of, or (in the case of paragraphs (ii) and (v) below) the amendments made to—
    (i) section 101(9)(a) of the Local Government Act 1972 (c. 70) by paragraph 49 of Schedule 19 and Part II of Schedule 21 to the Act;
    (ii) section 104(2)(a) of the Local Government Act 1972 by paragraph 50 of Schedule 19 to the Act;
    (iii) section 1(1)(j) of the Local Government Act 1988 (c. 9) by paragraph 110 of Schedule 19 and Part II of Schedule 21 to the Act;
    (iv) the words from "A joint education committee" to "1944" in paragraph 2 of Schedule 2 to the Local Government Act 1988 by paragraph 111 of Schedule 19 and Part II of Schedule 21 to the Act;
    (v) section 13 of the Local Government and Housing Act 1989 (c. 42) by paragraph 156(a), (b) and (d) of that Schedule; and
    (vi) paragraph 4 of Schedule 11 to the Local Government and Housing Act 1989 by Part II of Schedule 21 to the Act,
shall not have effect.

9.—(1) Notwithstanding the repeal on 1st April 1994 of paragraph 4 of Schedule 1 to the Education Act 1981, under which regulation 12 of the Education (Special Educational Needs) Regulations 1983 (S.I. 1983 No. 29; reg. 12 was amended by S.I. 1988 No. 1067) was made, that regulation shall, subject to sub-paragraph (2) below, continue in force on and after that date.

(2) Regulation 12 of the Education (Special Educational Needs) Regulations 1983, as so continued in force, shall have effect as if made under section paragraph 7(2) of Schedule 10 to the Act and may be amended or revoked thereunder.

10.—(1) Notwithstanding the repeal on 1st April 1994 of sections 79 and 80 of the Education Reform Act 1988, the old grants code shall continue to have effect on and after that date in relation to—

(a) any payments of maintenance grant under section 79(1) of that Act in respect of any financial year ending before that date; and

(b) any payments of capital and special purpose grants under section 79(3) of that Act made before that date.

(2) The functions conferred on the Secretary of State by or under the old grants code (as it has effect by virtue of sub-paragraph (1) above) shall, so far as relating to any amounts which—

(a) fall or may fall to be paid in any financial year beginning on or after 1st April 1994; or

(b) have been paid by the Secretary of State before that date,
in respect of any grant under that code, be exercisable by the funding authority.

(3) In this paragraph, "the old grants code" means sections 79 and 80 of the Education Reform Act 1988 as they apply in relation to England.

11. Notwithstanding the repeal on 1st April 1994 of section 81 of the Education Reform Act 1988 (section 81 was amended by para. 98 of Sched. 11 to the Local Government and Housing Act 1989 (c. 42) and para. 58 of Sched. 13 to the Local Government Finance Act 1992 (c. 14)), that section shall continue to have effect on and after that date in relation to any sums recoverable by the Secretary of State under section 81(1) of that Act for any financial year ending before that date.

12.—(1) Notwithstanding the repeal on 1st April of sections 79 and 81 of the Education Reform Act 1988 under which the Education (Grant-maintained Schools) (Finance) Regulations 1990 (S.I. 1990 No. 549, amended by S.I. 1990 No. 2279, 1991 No. 353) ("the 1990 Regulations") were made, those Regulations shall, subject to sub-paragraphs (2) to (5) below, continue in force on and after that date.

(2) The 1990 Regulations, as so continued in force, shall have effect as if made under sections 81(2), 82(2), 83(2), 88, 89, 90 and 94 of the Act and may be amended or revoked.

(3) The 1990 Regulations, as so continued in force, shall not apply in relation to any school which is established as a grant-maintained school under Chapter IV of Part II of the Act.

(4) In the 1990 Regulations, as so continued in force, any reference to the incorporation date in respect of any school, shall be read as a reference to the date of implementation of the proposals in respect of the school (within the meaning of section 37(2) of the Act).

(5) In the 1990 Regulations, as so continued in force, any reference to the former maintaining authority shall be read as a reference to the local education authority named in a determination under section 93 of the Act applying that section in relation to the school (or that school and other schools) and financial year in question.

John Patten
1st March 1994 Secretary of State for Education

INDEX

References are to article and Schedule number

TRANSPORT

THE RAILWAYS ACT 1993
(COMMENCEMENT NO. 4 AND TRANSITIONAL PROVISION)
ORDER 1994

(S.I. 1994 No. 571 (C. 11))

Made -   -   -   -   -   *7th March 1994*

INTRODUCTION

This Order brings into force a large number of the remaining provisions of the Railways Act 1993.

Certain miscellaneous and supplemental provisions in Pt. III are brought into force on March 8, 1994; provisions relating to the duties of the Secretary of State, the Regulator and the Franchising Director and certain financial provisions are brought into force on March 21, 1994. The repeals relating to the Transport Act 1981, set out in Sched. 14 to the 1993 Act are brought into force on March 31, 1994. The majority of the provisions in Pts. I and II, which have not yet been brought into force, are commenced on April 1 and 2, 1994.

The Secretary of State, in exercise of the powers under sections 143(3) and 154(2) of the Railways Act 1993 (c. 43), hereby makes the following Order:

Citation

1.—(1) This Order may be cited as the Railways Act 1993 (Commencement No. 4 and Transitional Provision) Order 1994.

(2) In this Order, "the Act" means the Railways Act 1993.

Provisions coming into force

2. The following provisions of the Act shall come into force on 8th March 1994:

sections 118 to 121;

in section 132, subsections (1) to (7), subsection (8) for the purpose of bringing into force the provisions of Schedule 10 referred to in this article, and subsections (9) and (10);

section 133;

section 152(3) for the purpose of bringing into force the provisions of Schedule 14 referred to in this article;

in Schedule 10, paragraphs 1 and 2, and paragraph 3(1) for the purpose of providing for sections 69 and 71 of the Transport Act 1962 (c. 46) to cease to have effect, and paragraph 3(2) and (3);

in Schedule 14, the repeals relating to sections 54(1)(b) and (2), 69 and 71 of the Transport Act 1962.

3. The following provisions of the Act shall come into force on 21st March 1994:

section 4, so far as not already in force;

section 5;

section 52;

in section 54, subsection (2), and subsection (3) for the purposes of the definitions of "franchising functions", in relation to the Franchising Director, and "railway investment";

section 138.

4. The following provisions of the Act shall come into force on 31st March 1994:

section 152(3) for the purpose of bringing into force the provisions of Schedule 14 referred to in this article;

in Schedule 14, the repeals relating to Part I of, and Schedule 1 to, the Transport Act 1981 (c. 56).

5. The following provisions of the Act shall come into force on 1st April 1994:

> section 2;
> section 3;
> section 6, so far as not already in force;
> sections 7 to 16;
> section 23, so far as not already in force;
> section 24;
> section 25, so far as not already in force;
> sections 26 to 28;
> section 29, so far as not already in force;
> section 30;
> section 31;
> sections 34 to 51;
> section 53;
> section 54, so far as not already in force;
> sections 55 to 69;
> sections 71 to 80;
> section 83, so far as not already in force;
> section 86;
> section 87, so far as not already in force;
> section 93, so far as not already in force;
> sections 122 to 125;
> section 129;
> sections 135 to 137;
> section 141, so far as not already in force;
> section 145, so far as not already in force;
> section 150, so far as not already in force;
> in section 152, subsection (1) for the purpose of bringing into force the provisions of Schedule 12 referred to in this article, subsection (2) for the purpose of bringing into force the provisions of Schedule 13, and subsection (3) for the purpose of bringing into force the provisions of Schedule 14 referred to in this article;
> Schedule 2;
> Schedule 3;
> Schedules 5 to 7;
> in Schedule 12, all paragraphs so far as not already in force except paragraph 32;
> Schedule 13;
> in Schedule 14, all repeals so far as not already in force except the repeals relating to:
>> section 70 of the Transport Act 1962;
>> section 8 of the Railways Act 1974 (c. 48);
>> section 36 of the Transport Act 1981.

6. Sections 17 to 22 of, and Schedule 4 to, the Act shall come into force on 2nd April 1994.

Transitional provision

7. Without prejudice to section 17(2) of the Interpretation Act 1978 (c. 30), any person who, immediately prior to the coming into force of the amendments made to section 53 of the British Transport Commission Act 1949 (c. xxix. In its application to England and Wales, s.53 has been amended by the British Transport Commission Act 1962 (c. xlii), s.43; the Transport Act 1962, s.70; and the British Railways Act 1978 (c. xxi), s.25. In its application to Scotland, s.53 is as set out in para. 3 of the Provisional Order contained in the Schedule to the British Railways Order Confirmation Act 1980 (c. xxviii)) by Schedule 10 to the Railways Act 1993, is or is deemed to have been appointed to act as a constable throughout England and Wales or, as the case may be, in

Scotland under the said section 53 shall be deemed thereafter to have been appointed so to act under the said section 53 as amended by the said Schedule 10.

Signed by authority of the
Secretary of State for Transport

Roger Freeman

7th March 1994
Minister of State, Department of Transport

INDEX

References are to article number

CRIMINAL LAW, ENGLAND AND WALES
CRIMINAL LAW, SCOTLAND
CRIMINAL LAW, NORTHERN IRELAND

THE CRIMINAL JUSTICE ACT 1993 (COMMENCEMENT NO. 6) ORDER 1994

(S.I. 1994 No. 700 (C. 12))

Made -   -   -   -   -   *10th March 1994*

INTRODUCTION

This Commencement Order brings into force on March 10, 1994 various provisions of the Criminal Justice Act 1993, as specified in the Schedule to this Order. Sections 18 and 19 deal with offences in connection with laundering money from drug trafficking. Section 26 exempts disclosure of information received in certain privileged circumstances. Section 32 relates to "tipping-off" offences. Section 48 relates to failure to disclose knowledge or suspicion relating to proceeds of terrorist-related activities. Sections 50 and 51 deal with investigation of terrorist activities and failure to disclose knowledge or suspicion of financial assistance for terrorism. Section 77 activates the power to extend certain offences to Crown servants and to exempt regulators. Other provisions introduce certain consequential amendments and extensions and exemptions.

In exercise of the powers conferred on me by section 78(3) and (4) of the Criminal Justice Act 1993 (c. 36), I hereby make the following Order:

1. This Order may be cited as the Criminal Justice Act 1993 (Commencement No. 6) Order 1994.

2. The provisions of the Criminal Justice Act 1993 ("the 1993 Act") referred to in the left-hand column of the Schedule to this Order (which relate to the matters described in the right-hand column of the Schedule) shall come into force on 1st April 1994.

3.—(1) So far as relating to the following provisions of the 1993 Act, namely—
  (a) sections 48, 50, 51 and 77; and
  (b) paragraphs 4 to 6 of Schedule 4 and paragraphs 15 and 17(4) of Schedule 5,
this Order extends to the United Kingdom.
  (2) So far as relating to the following provisions of the 1993 Act, namely—
  (a) section 32; and
  (b) paragraph 3 of Schedule 4,
this Order extends to Great Britain only.
  (3) So far as relating to the following provisions of the 1993 Act, namely—
  (a) sections 18 and 26(1); and
  (b) paragraph 1 of Schedule 4,
this Order extends to England and Wales only.
  (4) So far as relating to the following provisions of the 1993 Act, namely—
  (a) sections 19 and 26(2); and
  (b) paragraph 2 of Schedule 4,
this Order extends to Scotland only.

(5) So far as relating to the following provisions of the 1993 Act, namely, paragraphs 17(1) and 17(5) of Schedule 5, this Order extends to Northern Ireland only.

Home Office   *Michael Howard*
10th March 1994   One of Her Majesty's Principal Secretaries of State

Article 2   SCHEDULE

Provisions of the Criminal Justice Act 1993 coming into force on 1st April 1994

Provisions of the Act	*Subject matter of provisions*
Section 18	Offences in connection with laundering money from drug trafficking
Section 19	Offences in connection with laundering money from drug trafficking: Scotland
Section 26	Disclosure of information etc. received in privileged circumstances
Section 32	Tipping-off
Section 48	Failure to disclose knowledge or suspicion relating to proceeds of terrorist-related activities
Section 50	Investigation of terrorist activities
Section 51	Failure to disclose knowledge or suspicion of financial assistance for terrorism
Section 77	Power to extend certain offences to Crown servants and to exempt regulators etc.
Section 79(13) to the extent necessary to bring into force the provisions of Schedule 5 specified below	Consequential amendments
Schedule 4	Extensions and exemptions
Schedule 5, paragraphs 15, 17(1), 17(4) and 17(5)	Consequential amendments

TABLE A

PROVISIONS OF THE ACT BROUGHT INTO FORCE FOR ENGLAND AND WALES
ONLY BY S.I. 1993/1968, 1993/2734 AND 1994/71

Provision of the Act	*Date of coming into force*
Section 66	16th August 1993
Section 67	16th August 1993
Section 65	20th September 1993
Section 79(14) (partially)	20th September 1993
Schedule 3	20th September 1993
Schedule 6 (partially)	20th September 1993
Section 20(1)	1st December 1993
Section 21(2)	1st December 1993
Section 21(3)(a), (b) and (g)	1st December 1993
Section 22(1)	1st December 1993
Section 16	15th February 1994
Section 74	15th February 1994
Schedule 5 (partially)	15th February 1994
Schedule 6 (partially)	15th February 1994

TABLE B

PROVISIONS OF THE ACT BROUGHT INTO FORCE FOR SCOTLAND ONLY BY
S.I. 1993/2035, 1993/2734 AND 1994/71

Provision of the Act	*Date of coming into force*
Section 67(1)	16th August 1993
Section 20(2)	1st December 1993
Section 21(3)(c) and (d)	1st December 1993
Section 22(2)	1st December 1993
Section 17	15th February 1994
Section 33	15th February 1994
Schedule 5 (partially)	15th February 1994

TABLE C

PROVISIONS OF THE ACT BROUGHT INTO FORCE FOR THE UNITED KINGDOM
BY S.I. 1993/2734, 1994/71 AND 1994/242

Provision of the Act	*Date of coming into force*
Section 21(1)	1st December 1993
Section 21(3)(h)	1st December 1993
Section 23	1st December 1993
Section 45	1st December 1993
Section 46	1st December 1993
Section 47	15th February 1994
Section 49	15th February 1994
Section 78	15th February 1994
Section 79(13) (partially)	15th February 1994
Section 79(14) (partially)	15th February 1994
Schedule 6 (partially)	15th February 1994
Section 52	1st March 1994
Section 53	1st March 1994
Section 54	1st March 1994
Section 55	1st March 1994
Section 56	1st March 1994
Section 57	1st March 1994
Section 58	1st March 1994
Section 59	1st March 1994
Section 60	1st March 1994
Section 61	1st March 1994
Section 62	1st March 1994
Section 63	1st March 1994
Section 64	1st March 1994
Section 79(13) (partially)	1st March 1994
Section 79(14) (partially)	1st March 1994
Schedule 1	1st March 1994
Schedule 2	1st March 1994
Schedule 5 (partially)	1st March 1994
Schedule 6 (partially)	1st March 1994

TABLE D

PROVISIONS OF THE ACT BROUGHT INTO FORCE FOR GREAT BRITAIN ONLY
BY S.I. 1993/2734, 1994/71 AND 1994/242

Provision of the Act	Date of coming into force
Section 21(3)(e)	1st December 1993
Section 34(1)	1st December 1993
Section 35	1st December 1993
Section 73	1st December 1993
Section 29	15th February 1994
Section 30	15th February 1994
Section 31	15th February 1994
Schedule 5 (partially)	15th February 1994
Schedule 5 (partially)	1st March 1994
Schedule 6 (partially)	1st March 1994

TABLE E

PROVISIONS OF THE ACT BROUGHT INTO FORCE FOR SCOTLAND AND
NORTHERN IRELAND ONLY BY S.I. 1993/2734

Provision of the Act	Date of coming into force
Section 21(3)(f)	1st December 1993
Section 34(2)	1st December 1993

TABLE F

PROVISIONS OF THE ACT BROUGHT INTO FORCE FOR NORTHERN IRELAND
ONLY BY S.I. 1993/2734, 1994/71 AND 1994/242

Provision of the Act	Date of coming into force
Section 44	1st December 1993
Schedule 6 (partially)	15th February 1994
Schedule 5 (partially)	1st March 1994
Schedule 6 (partially)	1st March 1994

INDEX

References are to article number

EDUCATION, ENGLAND AND WALES

EDUCATION ACT 1993 (COMMENCEMENT NO. 2 AND TRANSITIONAL PROVISIONS) (AMENDMENT) ORDER 1994

(S.I. 1994 No. 436 (C. 13))

Made	-	-	-	-	*18th February 1994*

INTRODUCTION

This Order amends the Education Act 1993 (Commencement No. 2 and Transitional Provisions) Order 1993 (S.I. 1993 No. 3106 (C. 62)), inserting a new sub-para. (8) in para. 2 of Sched. 2 to that Order. Schedule 2 to that Order sets out transitional provisions consequential on the commencement of the provisions in Pt. II, Chaps. I, II and III of the 1993 Act. This Order adds a further transitional measure relating to the balloting of parents vis-à-vis the grant-maintained status of a school.

In exercise of the powers conferred on the Secretary of State by sections 301(6) and 308(3) of the Education Act 1993 (c. 35) the Secretary of State for Education hereby makes the following Order:

Citation

1. This Order may be cited as the Education Act 1993 (Commencement No. 2 and Transitional Provisions) (Amendment) Order 1994.

Amendment of Order

2.—(1) Paragraph 2 of Schedule 2 to the Education Act 1993 (Commencement No. 2 and Transitional Provisions) Order 1993 (S.I. 1993 No. 3106 (C. 62)) is amended as follows.

(2) In sub-paragraph (2), at the beginning, there are inserted the words "Subject to sub-paragraph (8) below,".

(3) After sub-paragraph (7), there is inserted the following sub-paragraph—

"(8) Where in the case of any school to which this paragraph applies the Secretary of State, in exercise of his powers under section 61(11) of the 1988 Act, declares void the ballot required to be held in relation to the school by that section or section 60 of that Act, section 31(3) of the Act shall have effect—

(a) as if the references therein to subsection (2) of that section and section 29(1) of the Act were references to, respectively, sections 61(11) and 61(14) of the 1988 Act; and

(b) as if for the words " "registered" " to the end there were substituted the words "for the words "immediately following the end of the period of fourteen days beginning with the date on which the relevant resolution or request was passed or received by the governing body" there were substituted the words "specified for the purposes of section 31(3)(b) of the Education Act 1993"."."

John Patten
18th February 1994   Secretary of State for Education

INDEX

References are to article number

TRANSPORT

THE TRANSPORT AND WORKS ACT 1992 (COMMENCEMENT NO. 5 AND TRANSITIONAL PROVISIONS) ORDER 1994

(S.I. 1994 No. 718 (C. 14))

Made -   -   -   -   -   *10th March 1994*

INTRODUCTION

This Commencement Order brings into force on March 10, 1994 provisions repealing parts of the Tramway Act 1870, the Road and Rail Traffic Act 1933 and the Transport Act 1968. It also contains transitional provisions.

The Secretary of State for Transport, in exercise of the powers conferred on him by section 70(1) and (2) of the Transport and Works Act 1992 (c. 42), hereby makes the following Order:

Citation and interpretation

1.—(1) This Order may be cited as the Transport and Works Act 1992 (Commencement No. 5 and Transitional Provisions) Order 1994.

(2) In this Order "the Act" means the Transport and Works Act 1992.

Provisions coming into force

2. The provisions of the Act specified in the first column of the Schedule to this Order (which relate to matters specified in the second column of that Schedule) shall come into force on 5th April 1994.

Transitional provisions

3.—(1) The repeal of the provisions of section 25 of the Tramways Act 1870 (c. 78) effected by this Order shall not affect the operation of those provisions in relation to a tramway in respect of which notice of intention to open it, or a portion of it, pursuant to rule XXV of the Board of Trade Rules (S.R. & O. Rev. XXIII p.263) dated January 1892, with respect to Provisional Orders and other Matters under the Tramways Act 1870, has been received by the Secretary of State prior to 5th April 1994.

(2) The repeal of section 41 of the Road and Rail Traffic Act 1933 (c. 53) shall not affect the operation of that section in relation to an application made pursuant to subsection (1) thereof for approval of any proposal to which that subsection relates, where the application has been received by the Secretary of State prior to 5th April 1994.

Signed by authority of the
Secretary of State for Transport

Roger Freeman
Minister of State,
Department of Transport

10th March 1994

Article 2   SCHEDULE

PROVISIONS OF THE ACT COMING INTO FORCE

Provisions of the Act	*Subject matter of provisions*
In section 65(1)(b), the words 'in section 25, the words "and shall not be opened" onwards,'.	Enactment to cease to have effect.
Section 68(1) in so far as it relates to the entries in Schedule 4 referred to below.	Repeal of enactments.

In Part I of Schedule 4—
    in the entry relating to the Tramways Act 1870, the words 'In section 25, the words "and shall not be opened" onwards.';
    the entry relating to section 41 of the Road and Rail Traffic Act 1933;
    the entry relating to section 125(4) of the Transport Act 1968 (c. 73).
	Repeal of enactments.

INDEX

References are to article number

ENVIRONMENTAL PROTECTION

THE ENVIRONMENTAL PROTECTION ACT 1990 (COMMENCEMENT NO. 14) ORDER 1994

(S.I. 1994 No. 780 (C. 15))

Made -   -   -   -   -   *15th March 1994*

INTRODUCTION

This Order provides for the commencement of the remainder of s.41 of the Environmental Protection Act 1990 on March 16, 1994. Section 41 deals with the fees and charges payable for waste management licences.

The Secretary of State, in exercise of his powers under section 164(3) of the Environmental Protection Act 1990 (c. 43), hereby makes the following Order:

Citation

1. This Order may be cited as the Environmental Protection Act 1990 (Commencement No. 14) Order 1994.

Provisions coming into force on 16th March 1994

2. Section 41 of the Environmental Protection Act 1990 (in so far as not already in force) shall come into force on 16th March 1994.

Department of the Environment

John Selwyn Gummer
15th March 1994   One of Her Majesty's Principal Secretaries of State

INDEX

References are to article number

NATIONAL LOTTERY
BETTING, GAMING AND LOTTERIES

THE NATIONAL LOTTERY ETC. ACT 1993 (COMMENCEMENT NO. 2 AND TRANSITIONAL PROVISIONS) ORDER 1994

(S.I. 1994 No. 1055 (C. 16))

Made - - - - - *10th April 1994*

INTRODUCTION

This Order brings into force certain of the provisions of the National Lottery etc. Act 1993.

The provisions from Pt. II of the Act dealing with societies' lotteries and local lotteries are brought into force on May 3, 1994, with the exception of s.50 (lottery managers). Certain repeals are also brought into force on that date. Section 50 is brought into force on October 3, 1994 as are the amendments to the Lotteries and Amusements Act 1976 set out in Sched. 9.

This Order has been allocated the C. number 16 as has S.I. 1994 No. 935. This Order will be corrected in accordance with any correction slip issued subsequently.

The Secretary of State, in exercise of the powers conferred on him by section 65 together with section 60(5) of the National Lottery etc. Act 1993 (c. 39), hereby makes the following Order:

Citation and interpretation

1.—(1) This Order may be cited as the National Lottery etc. Act 1993 (Commencement No. 2 and Transitional Provisions) Order 1994.

(2) In this Order "the Act" means the National Lottery etc. Act 1993.

Provisions coming into force on 3rd May 1994

2. The following provisions of the Act shall come into force on 3rd May 1994:

sections 48 and 49,
sections 51 to 55,
section 64 so far as not yet in force,
Schedules 7 and 8,
Schedule 10 so far as not yet in force.

Provisions coming into force on 3rd October 1994

3. The following provisions of the Act shall come into force on 3rd October 1994:

section 50,
Schedule 9.

Transitional provisions

4. For the purposes of determining whether section 5(3C) or (3D) of the Lotteries and Amusements Act 1976 (c. 32) ("the 1976 Act") (which was inserted by section 48(3) of the Act) applies to a lottery, any earlier lottery (within the meaning of section 5 of the 1976 Act) shall be disregarded if the date of the lottery fell before 3rd May 1994.

5. The following provisions of the Lotteries and Amusements Act 1976, namely—

(a) section 11(4A) (which was inserted by section 52(4) of the Act);
(b) section 11(14) (which was inserted by section 52(8) of the Act);
(c) paragraph 11(cc) of Schedule 1 (which was inserted by paragraph 7 of Part I of Schedule 7 to the Act);

shall not have effect in relation to any lottery in respect of which any tickets or chances have been sold before 3rd May 1994.

6. The amendments made to section 11(13) of the Lotteries and Amusements Act 1976 (c. 32) ("the 1976 Act") by section 52(7) of the Act shall not have effect in relation to any lottery in respect of which any tickets or chances have been sold before 3rd May 1994 but section 11(13) of the 1976 Act shall apply to any such lotteries as if it had not been amended.

Home Office

Michael Howard

10th April 1994   One of Her Majesty's Principal Secretaries of State

INDEX

References are to article number

REPRESENTATION OF THE PEOPLE

THE EUROPEAN PARLIAMENTARY ELECTIONS ACT 1993 (COMMENCEMENT) ORDER 1994

(S.I. 1994 No. 1089 (C. 17))

Made - - - - - *15th April 1994*

INTRODUCTION

The European Parliamentary Elections Act 1993 gives effect to the Decision of the Council of the European Communities, 93/81 Euratom, ECSC, EEC of February 1, 1993. This increases the number of U.K. representatives to be elected to the European Parliament.

The Act, save for s.1, came into force on November 5, 1993, with Royal Assent. This Order brought into force s.1 on May 1, 1994.

In exercise of the powers conferred upon me by section 3(3) of the European Parliamentary Elections Act 1993 (c. 41), I hereby make the following Order:

1. This Order may be cited as the European Parliamentary Elections Act 1993 (Commencement) Order 1994.

2. Section 1 of the European Parliamentary Elections Act 1993 shall come into force for all purposes on 1st May 1994.

Home Office   *Michael Howard*
15th April 1994   One of Her Majesty's Principal Secretaries of State

INDEX

References are to article number

ENVIRONMENTAL PROTECTION

THE ENVIRONMENTAL PROTECTION ACT 1990 (COMMENCEMENT NO. 15) ORDER 1994

(S.I. 1994 No. 1096 (C. 18))

Made - - - - - *14th April 1994*

INTRODUCTION

This Order provides for the commencement of various provisions of the Environmental Protection Act 1990 (c. 43) relating to waste management licensing. Article 2 names May 1, 1994 as the commencement date for the majority of the provisions for specified purposes. Article 3 specifies October 1, 1994 as the commencement date for certain of the same provisions for other purposes. Article 3 also provides that in specified circumstances the provisions will come into force on another date, linked to the nature of the activity in question and the date of application for a licence or an appeal.

The correction in art. 2 was inserted by a correction slip issued in May 1994.

S.I. 1994 No. 2487 (C. 49) amended the date given in each of sub-paragraphs (a), (b) and (c) of art. 3(2) to January 1, 1995 and S.I. 1994 No. 3234 (C. 81) amended those dates, again, to April 1, 1995.

The Secretary of State, in exercise of his powers under section 164(3) of the Environmental Protection Act 1990 (c. 43), hereby makes the following Order:

Citation and interpretation

1.—(1) This Order may be cited as the Environmental Protection Act 1990 (Commencement No. 15) Order 1994.

(2) In this Order—

"appropriate date", in relation to an appeal, means the date on which—

(a) the period for appealing expires without an appeal being made; or

(b) any appeal is withdrawn or finally determined;

"authorisation" has the meaning given in section 1(9) of the Environmental Protection Act 1990;

"existing process" and "prescribed date" have the same meaning as in Schedule 3 to the Environmental Protection (Prescribed Processes and Substances) Regulations 1991 (S.I. 1991 No. 472, amended by S.I.s 1991 No. 836, 1992 No. 614, 1993 Nos. 1749, 2405);

"relevant date", in relation to an application for a licence, means the date on which the licence applied for is granted or, if the application is (or is deemed to be) rejected, the date on which—

(a) the period for appealing expires without an appeal being made; or

(b) any appeal is withdrawn or finally determined;

and

"scrap metal" has the same meaning as in the Scrap Metal Dealers Act 1964 (c. 69; see s.9(2)).

Provisions coming into force on 1st May 1994

2.—(1) The following provisions of the Environmental Protection Act 1990 shall come into force on 1st May 199[4]—

section 54 (insofar as not already in force);

sections 58 and 59;

section 60 (insofar as not already in force);

sections 64 to 67 (insofar as not already in force);

sections 73 and 74 (insofar as not already in force);

section 162(1) insofar as it relates to paragraph 27 of Schedule 15;

section 162(2) insofar as it relates to the following repeals in Part II of Schedule 16—

the repeal of section 1 of the Control of Pollution Act 1974 (c. 40); in relation to Scotland only, the repeal of section 11 of the Control of Pollution Act 1974.

(2) The provisions of the Environmental Protection Act 1990 set out in paragraph (3) below shall come into force on 1st May 1994, save for the purposes of their application to the following activities—

(a) an activity which on that date is the subject of a pending application for a disposal licence under Part I of the Control of Pollution Act 1974;

(b) an activity in respect of which on that date an appeal in pursuance of section 10(1)(d) of the Control of Pollution Act 1974 (appeals to Secretary of State where a disposal licence is revoked) is pending or where the period for making such an appeal has not expired;

(c) an activity which involves treating, keeping or disposing of scrap metal or motor vehicles which are to be dismantled;

(d) an activity—
   (i) which on that date is the subject of a disposal licence under Part I of the Control of Pollution Act 1974;
   (ii) which is or forms part of an existing process for which no authorisation has been granted; and
   (iii) to which, if an authorisation were granted, section 33(1)(a) and (b) of the Environmental Protection Act 1990 would not apply by virtue of the Waste Management Licensing Regulations 1994 (S.I. 1994 No. 1056; see regs. 16 and 17, and Sched. 3).

(3) The provisions referred to in paragraph (2) are—
section 33 (insofar as not already in force);
sections 35 to 40 (insofar as not already in force);
sections 42 and 43 (insofar as not already in force);
section 44;
section 57;
section 162(1) insofar as it relates to paragraph 26 of Schedule 15;
section 162(2) insofar as it relates to the following repeals in Part II of Schedule 16—
   the repeal of sections 3 to 10, 18 and 27 of the Control of Pollution Act 1974.

Provisions coming into force after 1st May 1994

3.—(1) Subject to paragraphs (2) and (3) below, the provisions of the Environmental Protection Act 1990 set out in article 2(3) ("the relevant provisions") shall come into force—

(a) for the purposes of their application to an activity falling within article 2(2)(a), on the day immediately following the relevant date in relation to the application in question;

(b) for the purposes of their application to an activity falling within article 2(2)(b), on the day immediately following the appropriate date in relation to the appeal in question.

(2) Subject to paragraph (3) below, where an activity falls within article 2(2)(c) (whether or not it also falls within article 2(2)(a) or (b)), the relevant provisions shall come into force for the purposes of their application to that activity—

(a) if on [1st April 1995] that activity is the subject of a pending application for a disposal licence under Part I of the Control of Pollution Act 1974, on the day immediately following the relevant date in relation to the application in question;

(b) if on [1st April 1995] an appeal in pursuance of section 10(1)(d) of the Control of Pollution Act 1974 (appeals to Secretary of State where a disposal licence is revoked) is pending in respect of that activity or the period for making such an appeal has not expired, on the day immediately following the appropriate date in relation to that appeal;

(c) in any other case, on [1st April 1995].

(3) Where an activity falls within article 2(2)(d) (whether or not it also falls within any other sub-paragraph of article 2(2)), the relevant provisions shall come into force for the purposes of their application to that activity on the day immediately following the prescribed date in relation to the process in question.

Department of the Environment

John Selwyn Gummer

14th April 1994   One of Her Majesty's Principal Secretaries of State

INDEX

References are to article number

MERCHANT SHIPPING

THE MERCHANT SHIPPING ACT 1988 (COMMENCEMENT NO. 4) ORDER 1994

(S.I. 1994 No. 1201 (C. 19))

Made - - - - - *28th April 1994*

INTRODUCTION

This Order brings into force ss.48 and 57 of the Merchant Shipping Act 1988, to the extent that those sections effect the amendment of certain provisions of the Merchant Shipping Act 1970 and the repeal of ss.73 and 89 of that Act as set out in Scheds. 5 and 7 to the 1988 Act. These provisions will come into force on June 1, 1994.

The Secretary of State for Transport, in exercise of the powers conferred on him by section 58(2) of the Merchant Shipping Act 1988 (c. 12), hereby makes the following Order:

1. This Order may be cited as the Merchant Shipping Act 1988 (Commencement No. 4) Order 1994.

2. The provisions of the Merchant Shipping Act 1988 specified in the first column of the Schedule to this Order (which relate to the matters specified in the second column of that Schedule) shall come into force on 1st June 1994.

Signed by authority of the
Secretary of State for Transport

Mackay of Ardbrecknish
Parliamentary Under Secretary for State,
28th April 1994 Department of Transport

Article 2 SCHEDULE

PROVISIONS COMING INTO FORCE ON 1ST JUNE 1994

Provisions of Merchant Shipping Act 1988	Subject matter of provisions
Section 48, to the extent that it relates to the provisions of Schedule 5 specified below.	Miscellaneous amendments of the Merchant Shipping Acts.
Section 57, subsection (5) to the extent that it relates to the provisions of Schedule 7 specified below.	Repeals.
In Schedule 5, paragraph 7 of the amendments of the Merchant Shipping Act 1970 (c. 36)	Omission of section 89 (return of deserters under reciprocal arrangements).
In Schedule 7, the repeal of sections 73 and 89 of the Merchant Shipping Act 1970, and the repeal in section 95(1) of that Act.	Repeals.

INDEX

References are to article number

VALUE ADDED TAX

THE FINANCE ACT 1994, SECTION 47, (APPOINTED DAY) ORDER 1994

(S.I. 1994 No. 1234 (C. 20))

This Order was revoked by the Finance Act 1994, Section 47, (Appointed Day) (No. 2) Order 1994 (S.I. 1994 No. 1253 (C. 21)) and, consequently, the text is not reproduced here.

VALUE ADDED TAX

THE FINANCE ACT 1994, SECTION 47, (APPOINTED DAY) (NO. 2) ORDER 1994

(S.I. 1994 No. 1253 (C. 21))

Made - - - - - *9th May 1994*

INTRODUCTION

This Order gives effect to s.47 of the Finance Act 1994 in relation to s.21(1)(a) of the Finance Act 1988 to the extent specified in art. 2 of this Order. Section 47 of the 1994 Act inserts a new subs. (2) into s.21 of the 1988 Act, relating to set-off credits. This Order also revokes the Finance Act 1994, Section 47, (Appointed Day) Order 1994 (S.I. 1994 No. 1234 (C.20)).

The Commissioners of Customs and Excise, in the exercise of the powers conferred on them by section 47 of the Finance Act 1994 (c. 9), and of all other powers enabling them in that behalf, hereby make the following Order:

1. This Order may be cited as the Finance Act 1994, section 47, (Appointed Day) (No. 2) Order 1994.

2. Section 47 of the Finance Act 1994 shall have effect in relation to amounts mentioned in section 21(1)(a) of the Finance Act 1988 (c. 39) which become due on or after 10th May 1994.

3. The Finance Act 1994, section 47, (Appointed Day) Order 1994 (S.I. 1994 No. 1234 (C. 20)) is hereby revoked.

New King's Beam House
22 Upper Ground
London SE1 9PJ

E. Woods
9th May 1994 Commissioner of Customs and Excise

INDEX

References are to article number

VALUE ADDED TAX

THE FINANCE ACT 1994, SECTION 45, (APPOINTED DAY) ORDER 1994

(S.I. 1994 No. 1257 (C. 22))

Made - - - - -   *9th May 1994*

INTRODUCTION

This Order specifies June 1, 1994 as the date on which s.45 of the Finance Act 1994 shall have effect in relation to any prescribed accounting period beginning on or after June 1, 1994. Section 45 of the 1994 Act relates to misdeclaration of VAT and provides for the amendment of s.14 of the Finance Act 1985 (misdeclaration penalty).

The Treasury, in exercise of the powers conferred on them by section 45(4) of the Finance Act 1994 (c. 9) and of all other powers enabling them in that behalf, hereby make the following Order:

1. This Order may be cited as the Finance Act 1994, section 45, (Appointed Day) Order 1994.

2. Section 45 of the Finance Act 1994 shall have effect in relation to any prescribed accounting period beginning on or after 1st June 1994.

Tim Wood
Andrew Mackay
Two of the Lords Commissioners
of Her Majesty's Treasury

9th May 1994

INDEX

References are to article number

TRADE UNIONS
TERMS AND CONDITIONS OF EMPLOYMENT

THE TRADE UNION REFORM AND EMPLOYMENT RIGHTS ACT 1993 (COMMENCEMENT NO. 3 AND TRANSITIONAL PROVISIONS) ORDER 1994

(S.I. 1994 No. 1365 (C. 23))

Made - - - - - *19th May 1994*

INTRODUCTION

This Order brings into force, on June 10, 1994, the majority of the remaining provisions of the Trade Union Reform and Employment Rights Act 1993, with the exception of s.31 and certain parts of Sched. 10. Note the transitional provisions set out in art. 3. See Orders S.I. 1993 No. 1908 and S.I. 1993 No. 2503 for the commencement of previous provisions.

The Secretary of State, in exercise of the powers conferred on him by section 52 of, and paragraph 1 of Schedule 9 to, the Trade Union Reform and Employment Rights Act 1993 (c. 19), hereby makes the following Order:

Citation and interpretation

1.—(1) This Order may be cited as the Trade Union Reform and Employment Rights Act 1993 (Commencement No. 3 and Transitional Provisions) Order 1994.

(2) In this Order—
(i) "the 1978 Act" means the Employment Protection (Consolidation) Act 1978 (c. 44),
(ii) "the 1993 Act" means the Trade Union Reform and Employment Rights Act 1993, and
(iii) "expected week of childbirth" and "effective date of termination" have the same meanings as in the 1978 Act.

Commencement

2. The provisions of the 1993 Act which are specified in the Schedule to this Order shall come into force on 10th June 1994.

Transitional provisions

3.—(1) The amendments and repeals made by the provisions of the 1993 Act which are specified in the Schedule to this Order shall have effect only in relation to women whose expected week of childbirth begins on or after 16th October 1994.

(2) The amendments to the 1978 Act made by section 24 of the 1993 Act and brought into force by this Order shall apply to any dismissal where the effective date of termination in relation to that dismissal falls on or after 10th June 1994.

Signed by order of the
Secretary of State

Michael Forsyth
19th May 1994   Minister of State, Department of Employment

C23

SCHEDULE

Provision	Subject matter of Provision
Section 23	Right to maternity leave and right to return to work
Section 24, so far as it is not already in force	Dismissal rights
Section 25	Rights on suspension on maternity grounds
Section 49, so far as it is not already in force	Miscellaneous and consequential amendments
Section 51, so far as it is not already in force	Repeals
Schedule 2	Right to return to work
Schedule 3	Suspension on maternity grounds
Schedule 7, so far as it is not already in force	Miscellaneous amendments
Schedule 8, so far as it is not already in force	Consequential amendments
Schedule 10, so far as it is not already in force except the repeal of the words "subject to sub-sections (3) to (5)" in section 138 of the 1978 Act so far as they relate to subsection (3)	Repeals

INDEX

References are to article number

CRIMINAL LAW, ENGLAND AND WALES

THE BAIL (AMENDMENT) ACT 1993 (COMMENCEMENT) ORDER 1994

(S.I. 1994 No. 1437 (C. 24))

Made -   -   ˙ -   -   -   *25th May 1994*

INTRODUCTION

The Bail (Amendment) Act 1993 received Royal Assent on July 20, 1993 and provided for new rights of appeal against decisions to grant bail. Section 2 of the Act came into force with the passing of the Act; this Order brings into force all remaining provisions on June 27, 1994.

In exercise of the power conferred upon me by section 2(2) of the Bail (Amendment) Act 1993 (c. 26), I hereby make the following Order:

1. This Order may be cited as the Bail (Amendment) Act 1993 (Commencement) Order 1994.

2. 27th June 1994 is the day appointed for the coming into force of the provisions of the Bail (Amendment) Act 1993 apart from section 2 (s. 2 came into force on the passing of the Act).

Home Office   *Michael Howard*
25th May 1994   One of Her Majesty's Principal Secretaries of State

INDEX

References are to article number

LOCAL GOVERNMENT, ENGLAND AND WALES
LOCAL GOVERNMENT, SCOTLAND

THE LOCAL GOVERNMENT ACT 1992 (COMMENCEMENT NO. 4) ORDER 1994

(S.I. 1994 No. 1445 (C. 25))

Made - - - - -   *1st June 1994*

INTRODUCTION

This Act brings into force various parts of the Local Government Act 1992 giving effect to the amendments to the Local Government, Planning and Land Act 1980 and the Local Government Act 1988 specified in art. 2 of this Order. The provisions amended relate to the competitive activities of local authorities.

The Secretary of State, in exercise of the powers conferred on him by section 30(3) of the Local Government Act 1992 (c. 19), and all other powers enabling him in that behalf, hereby makes the following Order:

Citation and interpretation

1.—(1) This Order may be cited as the Local Government Act 1992 (Commencement No. 4) Order 1994.

(2) In this Order "the 1992 Act" means the Local Government Act 1992.

Provisions of the 1992 Act coming into force on 13th June 1994

2. Section 11 of the 1992 Act so far as it relates to paragraphs 2(1), 3, 4, 5, 9 and 10 of Schedule 1, and those paragraphs, shall come into force on 13th June 1994.

Signed by authority of the Secretary of State.

David Curry
Minister of State,
1st June 1994   Department of the Environment

INDEX

References are to article number

ROAD TRAFFIC

THE ROAD TRAFFIC ACT 1991
(COMMENCEMENT NO. 11 AND TRANSITIONAL PROVISIONS) ORDER 1994

(S.I. 1994 No. 1482 (C. 26))

Made -　　-　　-　　-　　-　　　　　　*3rd June 1994*

INTRODUCTION
This Order brings into force certain of the provisions of the Road Traffic Act 1991 relating to parking in London. The provisions are brought into force on July 4, 1994 only in relation to the City of London and those London boroughs listed in the Schedule to this Order.

The Secretary of State for Transport, in exercise of the powers conferred by section 84 of the Road Traffic Act 1991 (c. 40), hereby makes the following Order:

Citation and interpretation

1.—(1) This Order may be cited as the Road Traffic Act 1991 (Commencement No. 11 and Transitional Provisions) Order 1994.
(2) In this Order—
"the 1991 Act" means the Road Traffic Act 1991;
"the scheduled boroughs" means the City of London and the London boroughs whose names are included in the Schedule to this Order and a reference to the councils of the Scheduled boroughs includes, in relation to the City of London, the Common Council of the City of London;
"vehicle" has the meaning given by section 99(5) of the Road Traffic Regulation Act 1984 (c. 27).

Commencement and transitional provisions

2. The following provisions of the 1991 Act shall come into force on 4th July 1994 in respect of each of the scheduled boroughs—
(a) section 64, to the extent that it is not already in force;
(b) section 65;
(c) section 66, to the extent that it is not already in force;
(d) section 69;
(e) section 81, to the extent necessary for bringing into force the provisions of Schedule 7 brought into force by this article; and
(f) paragraph 5 of Schedule 7, to the extent that that paragraph is not already in force.

3. Subsections (4) and (6) of section 67 of the 1991 Act shall come into force on 4th July 1994 for the purpose of the application of the subsections thereby inserted in relation to vehicles found in any of the scheduled boroughs.

4. Subsection (2)(b) of section 68 of the 1991 Act shall come into force on 4th July 1994 for the purpose of the application of the subsection thereby inserted in relation to the councils of the scheduled boroughs.

5.—(1) In relation to a vehicle that is stationary in a designated parking place in one of the scheduled boroughs immediately before 4th July 1994, section 66(2) of the 1991 Act shall have effect for so long as it remains in that parking place as if the words "on or after 4th July 1994" were inserted after—
(a) the word "left" in paragraph (a) of section 66(2),
(b) the word "payable" in paragraph (b) of that subsection, and
(c) the word "has" in paragraph (c) of that subsection.

(2) Where a vehicle found in one of the scheduled boroughs has, pursuant to any enactment, been removed before 4th July 1994, sections 67 and 68 of the 1991 Act shall not apply in relation to that removal or to any storage or disposal of the vehicle as a consequence of that removal.

Signed by authority of the
Secretary of State for Transport

Steven Norris
Parliamentary Under Secretary of State,
3rd June 1994
Department of Transport

Article 1(2)

SCHEDULE

THE SCHEDULED BOROUGHS

Barking and Dagenham
Barnet
Brent
Croydon
Ealing
Enfield
Greenwich
Haringey
Harrow
Havering
Hillingdon
Islington
Royal borough of Kensington and Chelsea
Royal borough of Kingston upon Thames
Lambeth
Merton
Newham
Redbridge
Sutton
Tower Hamlets
Waltham Forest
City of Westminster

INDEX

References are to article number

ROAD TRAFFIC

**THE ROAD TRAFFIC ACT 1991
(COMMENCEMENT NO. 12 AND TRANSITIONAL PROVISIONS)
ORDER 1994**

(S.I. 1994 No. 1484 (C. 27))

Made - - - - - *3rd June 1994*

INTRODUCTION
    This Order brings into force certain of the provisions of the Road Traffic Act 1991 relating to parking in London. The provisions are brought into force on July 4, 1994 only in relation to the London borough of Bexley.

The Secretary of State for Transport, in exercise of the powers conferred by section 84 of the Road Traffic Act 1991 (c. 40), hereby makes the following Order:

Citation and interpretation

1.—(1) This Order may be cited as the Road Traffic Act 1991 (Commencement No. 12 and Transitional Provisions) Order 1994.
    (2) In this Order—
        "the 1991 Act" means the Road Traffic Act 1991; and
        "vehicle" has the meaning given by section 99(5) of the Road Traffic Regulation Act 1984 (c. 27).

Commencement and transitional provisions

2. The following provisions of the 1991 Act shall come into force on 4th July 1994 in respect of the London borough of Bexley—
    (a) section 64, to the extent that it is not already in force;
    (b) section 65;
    (c) section 66, to the extent that it is not already in force;
    (d) section 81, to the extent necessary for bringing into force the provisions of Schedule 7 brought into force by this article; and
    (e) paragraph 5 of Schedule 7, to the extent that that paragraph is not already in force.

3. In relation to a vehicle that is stationary in a designated parking place in the London borough of Bexley immediately before 4th July 1994, section 66(2) of the 1991 Act shall have effect for so long as it remains in that parking place as if the words "on or after 4th July 1994" were inserted after—
    (a) the word "left" in paragraph (a) of section 66(2),
    (b) the word "payable" in paragraph (b) of that subsection, and
    (c) the word "has" in paragraph (c) of that subsection.

Signed by authority of the   *Steven Norris*
Secretary of State for Transport   Parliamentary Under Secretary of State,
3rd June 1994   Department of Transport

INDEX

References are to article number

EDUCATION, ENGLAND AND WALES

EDUCATION ACT 1993 (COMMENCEMENT NO. 4) ORDER 1994

(S.I. 1994 No. 1558 (C. 28))

Made - - - - - *14th June 1994*

INTRODUCTION

This Order brings into force various provisions of the Education Act 1993.

Section 279, which amends s.51 of the Education (No. 2) Act 1986 (recoupment) so as to enable a local education authority which provides education to a child to recoup all or part of the cost from the LEA in whose area the child lives, comes into force on June 15, 1994 for the purposes of enabling regulations to be made under s.51(1)–(4) of the 1986 Act.

The remainder of s.279 and Scheds. 19, paras. 103, 104 and 107 (and s.307(1) so far as it relates to those provisions) and 21 (repeals set out in the Appendix to the Schedule to this Order) (and s.307(3) so far as it relates to it) come into force on April 1, 1995. These provisions effect amendments to ss.51 and 52 of the 1986 Act.

In exercise of the powers conferred on the Secretary of State by section 308(3) of the Education Act 1993 (c. 35) the Secretary of State for Education hereby makes the following order:

1.—(1) This Order may be cited as the Education Act 1993 (Commencement No. 4) Order 1994.

(2) In this Order, "the Act" means the Education Act 1993.

2. Section 279 of the Act (inter-authority recoupment) shall come into force on 15th June 1994 for the purposes of enabling regulations to be made under section 51(1) to (4) of the Education (No. 2) Act 1986 (as substituted by that section).

3. The provisions of the Act specified in the first column of the Schedule to this Order (which relate to the matters mentioned in the second column thereof) shall come into force on 1st April 1995; and, save as otherwise provided in the first column of that Schedule, they shall come into force on that date for all purposes.

SCHEDULE

Provisions of the Act	Subject matter of provisions
Section 279 (for all remaining purposes).	Inter-authority recoupment.
Paragraphs 103, 104 and 107 of Schedule 19, and section 307(1) so far as it relates thereto.	Consequential amendments.
Schedule 21, in so far as it relates to the repeals set out in the Appendix to this Schedule, and section 307(3) so far as it relates thereto.	Repeals.

Appendix to the Schedule

Chapter	Short title	Extent of repeal
1986 c.61.	The Education (No. 2) Act 1986.	Section 51(9) and (13). Section 63(4).

14th June 1994

John Patten
Secretary of State for Education

INDEX

References are to article number

TRANSPORT

THE RAILWAYS ACT 1993
(COMMENCEMENT NO. 5 AND TRANSITIONAL PROVISIONS)
ORDER 1994

(S.I. 1994 No. 1648 (C. 29))

Made - - - - - *22nd June 1994*

INTRODUCTION

This Order brings into force various provisions of the Railways Act 1993 on July 15, 1994. The provisions brought into force make provision for the payment of grants to assist the provision of facilities for freight haulage by railway and by inland waterway (ss.139 and 140) and give effect to the repeal of corresponding provisions in the Railways Act 1974 and the Transport Act 1981 (subject to the transitional provisions contained in art. 3).

The Secretary of State, in exercise of the powers conferred on him by sections 143(3) and 154(2) of the Railways Act 1993 (c. 43), hereby makes the following Order:—

Citation

1. This Order may be cited as the Railways Act 1993 (Commencement No. 5 and Transitional Provisions) Order 1994.

Provisions coming into force

2. Subject to article 3 below, the following provisions of the Railways Act 1993 shall come into force on 15th July 1994:
sections 139 and 140;
section 152(3) for the purpose of bringing into force the provisions of Schedule 14 referred to in this article;
in Schedule 14, the repeals relating to section 8 of the Railways Act 1974 (c. 48) and section 36 of the Transport Act 1981 (c. 56).

Transitional provisions

3.—(1) The repeal of section 8 of the Railways Act 1974 shall not affect the operation of that section in relation to any application for grant made pursuant to that section before 15th July 1994 but in respect of which no decision has been made by the Secretary of State before that date.

(2) The repeal of section 36 of the Transport Act 1981 shall not affect the operation of that section in relation to any application for grant made pursuant to that section before 15th July 1994 but in respect of which no decision has been made by the Secretary of State before that date.

Signed by authority of the
Secretary of State for Transport

Roger Freeman
Minister of State,
22nd June 1994   Department of Transport

INDEX

References are to article number

SOCIAL SECURITY

THE SOCIAL SECURITY ACT 1989 (COMMENCEMENT NO. 5) ORDER 1994

(S.I. 1994 No. 1661 (C. 30))

Made - - - - -   *22nd June 1994*

INTRODUCTION

This Order brings into force various parts of Sched. 5 to the Social Security Act 1989, which deals with equal treatment of men and women in employment-related schemes for pensions, on June 23, 1994. Schedule 5, paras. 1, 2(1)(2)(4)(c)(5)(9), 3 (except subpara. (2)), 7 (except subpara. (d)), 9 and 10 are brought into force only to the extent necessary to give effect to Sched. 5, paras. 5 (except subpara. (2)(b) and (c)) and 6 (except subpara. (3)(b) and (c)) which cover unfair maternity and unfair family leave provisions respectively.

The Secretary of State for Social Security, in exercise of powers conferred upon him by section 33(2) of the Social Security Act 1989 (c. 24) and of all other powers enabling him in that behalf, hereby makes the following Order:

Citation and interpretation

1.—(1) This Order may be cited as the Social Security Act 1989 (Commencement No. 5) Order 1994.

(2) In this Order references to "the Act" are references to the Social Security Act 1989.

Appointed day

2. The day appointed for the coming into force of—

(a) the provisions of the Act specified in Part I of the Schedule to this Order, for the purposes only of giving effect to the provisions of the Act specified in Part II of that Schedule;

(b) the provisions of the Act specified in Part II of the Schedule to this Order; and

(c) section 23 of the Act in so far as it relates to the provisions specified in the Schedule to this Order,

is 23rd June 1994.

Signed by authority of the Secretary of State for Social Security.

William Hague
Parliamentary Under-Secretary of State,
22nd June 1994   Department of Social Security

Article 2   SCHEDULE

PART I

PROVISIONS OF THE ACT COMING INTO FORCE FOR LIMITED PURPOSES ON 23RD JUNE 1994

Provision	*Subject matter*
Schedule 5, paragraph 1	Compliance with equal treatment
Schedule 5, paragraph 2(1), (2), (4)(c), (5) and (9)	Principle of equal treatment
Schedule 5, paragraph 3 (except sub-paragraph (2))	Compulsory levelling up
Schedule 5, paragraph 7 (except sub-paragraph (d))	Definitions
Schedule 5, paragraph 9	Jurisdiction
Schedule 5, paragraph 10	Interpretation

PART II

PROVISIONS OF THE ACT COMING INTO FORCE ON 23RD JUNE 1994

Provision	Subject matter
Schedule 5, paragraph 5 (except sub-paragraph (2)(b) and (c))	Unfair maternity provisions
Schedule 5, paragraph 6 (except sub-paragraph 3(b) and (c))	Unfair family leave provisions

INDEX

References are to article number

CUSTOMS AND EXCISE

THE FINANCE ACT 1994, SECTION 7, (APPOINTED DAY) ORDER 1994

(S.I. 1994 No. 1690 (C. 31))

Made -   -   -   -   -   *27th June 1994*

INTRODUCTION

    This Order appoints July 1, 1994 as the date on which s.7 of the Finance Act 1994 comes into force (with the exception of subs. (1)(b)). Section 7 makes various provisions relating to the duties and jurisdiction of the tribunals established under Sched. 8 to the Value Added Tax Act 1983. The jurisdiction of the tribunals (to be known as the VAT and duties tribunal) is extended to matters relating to Customs and Excise as conferred by Pt. I, chap. II of the 1994 Act.

The Commissioners of Customs and Excise, in exercise of the powers conferred on them by section 19 of the Finance Act 1994 (c. 9; s.17(1) applies the definition of "the Commissioners" in s.1(1) of the Customs and Excise Management Act 1979 (c. 2)) and of all other powers enabling them in that behalf, hereby make the following Order:

    1. This Order may be cited as the Finance Act 1994, section 7, (Appointed Day) Order 1994.

    2. The day appointed as the day on which section 7 of the Finance Act 1994 comes into force (with the exception of paragraph (b) of subsection (1) of that section) is 1st July 1994.

New King's Beam House
22 Upper Ground
London
SE1 9PJ

Leonard Harris
Commissioner of Customs and Excise

27th June 1994

INDEX

References are to article number

INSURANCE PREMIUM TAX

THE FINANCE ACT 1994 (APPOINTED DAY) ORDER 1994

(S.I. 1994 No. 1773 (C. 32))

Made -   -   -   -   -   *6th July 1994*

INTRODUCTION

This Order appoints October 1, 1994 as the date on which ss.59 and 60 of the Finance Act 1994 come into force. Sections 59 and 60 make provisions relating to insurance premium tax, setting out the procedure for reviewing and appealing a Commissioner's decision.

The Commissioners of Customs and Excise, in exercise of the powers conferred on them by sections 61 and 74(1) of the Finance Act 1994 (c. 9; s.73(1) defines "the Commissioners" as meaning the Commissioners of Customs and Excise) and of all other powers enabling them in that behalf, hereby make the following Order:

1. This Order may be cited as the Finance Act 1994 (Appointed Day) Order 1994.

2. The day appointed as the day on which sections 59 and 60 of the Finance Act 1994 come into force is 1st October 1994.

New King's Beam House
22 Upper Ground
London
SE1 9PJ

Leonard Harris
6th July 1994   Commissioner of Customs and Excise

INDEX

References are to article number

HUMAN FERTILISATION AND EMBRYOLOGY

THE HUMAN FERTILISATION AND EMBRYOLOGY ACT 1990 (COMMENCEMENT NO. 5) ORDER 1994

(S.I. 1994 No. 1776 (C. 33))

Made -   -   -   -   -   *4th July 1994*

INTRODUCTION

This Order appoints July 5, 1994 and November 1, 1994 as the dates on which s.30 of the Human Fertilisation and Embryology Act 1990 comes into force. Section 48(1) (extension of certain provisions to Northern Ireland), so far as it relates to s.30, is also brought into force on those dates.

Section 30(9) and (10), which deals with the application and interpretation of s.30 is brought into force on July 5, 1994. The remaining provisions of s.30 (parental orders in favour of gamete donors) are brought into force on November 1, 1994.

The year in art. 2(1) was added by a correction slip issued in August 1994.

The Secretary of State for Health, in exercise of powers conferred by section 49(2) of the Human Fertilisation and Embryology Act 1990 (c. 37) and of all other powers enabling her in that behalf, hereby makes the following Order:

Citation and interpretation

1.—(1) This Order may be cited as the Human Fertilisation and Embryology Act 1990 (Commencement No. 5) Order 1994.

(2) In this Order "the Act" means the Human Fertilisation and Embryology Act 1990.

Appointed days

2.—(1) 5th July [1994] is the day appointed for the coming into force of subsections (9) and (10) of section 30 of the Act (parental orders in favour of gamete donors) and of section 48(1) of the Act (extent) so far as it relates to those subsections.

(2) 1st November 1994 is the day appointed for the coming into force of the remaining provisions of section 30 of the Act (parental orders in favour of gamete donors) and section 48(1) of the Act (extent) so far as it relates to those provisions.

Signed by authority of the Secretary of State for Health

Tom Sackville
Parliamentary Under Secretary of State
Department of Health

4th July 1994

INDEX

References are to article number

SHOPS AND OFFICES

THE SUNDAY TRADING ACT 1994 APPOINTED DAY ORDER 1994

(S.I. 1994 No. 1841 (C. 34))

Made -   -   -   -   -   *11th July 1994*

INTRODUCTION

The Sunday Trading Act 1994 makes provision for the reform of the law relating to Sunday trading. Sections 1, 6–8, 9(1), (3), (4) and Scheds. 1 and 2 came into force on July 5, 1994 (Royal Assent). This Order appoints August 26 as the date on which all remaining provisions of the Act shall come into force.

In exercise of the power conferred upon me by section 1 of the Sunday Trading Act 1994 (c. 20), I hereby make the following Order:

1. This Order may be cited as the Sunday Trading Act 1994 Appointed Day Order 1994.

2. 26th August 1994 shall be the appointed day for the purposes of section 1 of the Sunday Trading Act 1994.

Home Office   *Michael Howard*

11th July 1994   One of Her Majesty's Principal Secretaries of State

INDEX

References are to article number

APPOINTED DAY, 2

CITATION, 1
COMMENCEMENT, 2

IMMIGRATION

THE IMMIGRATION ACT 1988 (COMMENCEMENT NO. 3) ORDER 1994

(S.I. 1994 No. 1923 (C. 35))

Made -   -   -   -   -   *16th July 1994*

INTRODUCTION

This Order brings into force s.7(1) of the Immigration Act 1988 (c. 14) on July 20, 1994. Section 7(1) relates to persons exercising Community rights and nationals of Member States and is aimed at bringing domestic immigration law into line with the law of the European Union. Under this section leave to enter or remain in the U.K. will not be required in any case in which the person entitled to do so by virtue of an enforceable Community right or of any provision made under s.2(2) of the European Communities Act 1972 (c. 68).

In exercise of the power conferred upon me by section 12(4) of the Immigration Act 1988 (c. 14), I hereby make the following Order:

1. This Order may be cited as the Immigration Act 1988 (Commencement No. 3) Order 1994.

2. Section 7(1) of the Immigration Act 1988 shall come into force on 20th July 1994.

Home Office   *Michael Howard*
16th July 1994   One of Her Majesty's Principal Secretaries of State

INDEX

References are to article number

**CRIMINAL LAW, ENGLAND AND WALES
CRIMINAL LAW, SCOTLAND
CRIMINAL LAW, NORTHER IRELAND**

**THE CRIMINAL JUSTICE ACT 1993 (COMMENCEMENT NO. 7)
ORDER 1994**

(S.I. 1994 No. 1951 (C. 36))

Made - - - - - *20th July 1994*

INTRODUCTION

This Order brings into force s.72 of the Criminal Justice Act 1993 (c. 36) on August 22, 1994. Section 72 relates to safeguards of the backing of warrants and provides for the amendment of the Backing of Warrants (Republic of Ireland) Act 1965 (c. 45). The Act as amended also the Secretary of State to introduce a statutory speciality rule into the backing of warrants arrangements with the Republic of Ireland.

In exercise of the power conferred upon me by section 78(3) and (4) of the Criminal Justice Act 1993 (c. 36), I hereby make the following Order:

1. This Order may be cited as the Criminal Justice Act 1993 (Commencement No. 7) Order 1994.

2. Section 72 of the Criminal Justice Act 1993 (Backing of Warrants: Safeguards) shall come into force on 22nd August 1994.

Home Office   *Michael Howard*
20th July 1994   One of Her Majesty's Principal Secretaries of State

INDEX

References are to article number

MERCHANT SHIPPING

THE MERCHANT SHIPPING (SALVAGE AND POLLUTION) ACT 1994 (COMMENCEMENT NO. 1) ORDER 1994

(S.I. 1994 No. 1988 (C. 37))

Made -   -   -   -   -   *26th July 1994*

INTRODUCTION

This Order provides for the commencement of various provisions of the Merchant Shipping (Salvage and Pollution) Act 1994. The provisions brought into force on July 28, 1994 are mainly general provisions relating to expenses and the citation, construction and extent of the Act. Section 3 is also brought into force on that date and amends the powers to implement international conventions relating to pollution from ships, as set out in s.20 of the Merchant Shipping Act 1979.

Further provisions relating to marine pollution (ss.6 (part), 7 and 8) are brought into force on October 1, 1994 along with other general provisions.

The Secretary of State for Transport, in exercise of the powers conferred on him by section 10(4) of the Merchant Shipping (Salvage and Pollution) Act 1994 (c. 28), hereby makes the following Order:

1. This Order may be cited as the Merchant Shipping (Salvage and Pollution) Act 1994 (Commencement No. 1) Order 1994.

2. The provisions of the Merchant Shipping (Salvage and Pollution) Act 1994 specified in the first column of Schedule 1 to this Order (which relate to the matters specified in the second column of that Schedule) shall come into force on 28th July 1994.

3. The provisions of the Merchant Shipping (Salvage and Pollution) Act 1994 specified in the first column of Schedule 2 to this Order (which relate to the matters specified in the second column of that Schedule) shall come into force on 1st October 1994.

Signed by authority of the
Secretary of State for Transport

Goschen
Parliamentary Under Secretary of State,
Department of Transport

26th July 1994

Article 2   SCHEDULE 1

Provisions coming into force on 28th July 1994

Provisions of Merchant Shipping (Salvage and Pollution) Act 1994	*Subject matter of provisions*
Section 3	Amendments as to powers of implementation
Section 9	Expenses
Section 10, subsections (1), (2), (4) and (5)	Short title, citation, construction, commencement and extent

Article 3   SCHEDULE 2

Provisions coming into force on 1st October 1994

Provisions of Merchant Shipping (Salvage and Pollution) Act 1994	*Subject matter of provisions*
Section 6, subsection (1), so far as it relates to Part I of Schedule 3, and (2)	Extension of strict liability for oil pollution by ships
Section 7	Extension of rights of Fund by subrogation
Section 8	Functions of Secretary of State in relation to marine pollution
Section 10, subsection (3), to the extent that it relates to the repeals in Schedule 4 specified below	Repeals
Schedule 3, Part I	Extension of strict liability for oil pollution by ships
In Schedule 4, the repeals in: Merchant Shipping (Oil Pollution) Act 1971 (c. 59) Prevention of Oil Pollution Act 1971 (c. 60) Merchant Shipping Act 1974 (c. 43)	Repeals

INDEX

References are to article number

POLICE

THE POLICE AND MAGISTRATES' COURTS ACT 1994 (COMMENCEMENT NO. 1 AND TRANSITIONAL PROVISIONS) ORDER 1994

(S.I. 1994 No. 2025 (C. 38))

Made - - - - -	*1st August 1994*
Laid before Parliament - -	*5th August 1994*
Coming into force - - -	*8th August 1994*

INTRODUCTION

This Order provides for the commencement of various provisions of the Police and Magistrates' Courts Act 1994 on August 8, October 1 and November 1, 1994. The provisions are in the main from Pt. I of the Act, relating to policing in England and Wales, and include provisions for the financing of the new police authorities.

In exercise of the powers conferred upon me by section 94(1), (4), (5) and (6) of the Police and Magistrates' Courts Act 1994 (c. 29), I hereby make the following Order:

Citation and commencement

1.—(1) This Order may be cited as the Police and Magistrates' Courts Act 1994 (Commencement No. 1 and Transitional Provisions) Order 1994.

(2) This Order shall come into force on 8th August 1994.

Interpretation

2.—(1) In this Order—

"the 1964 Act" means the Police Act 1964 (c. 48);

"the 1994 Act" means the Police and Magistrates' Courts Act 1994, and

"the new police authorities" means the police authorities to be established under section 3 of the 1964 Act (as substituted by section 2 of the 1994 Act) and "the old police authorities" means the police authorities which they are to supersede.

(2) In this Order the period of co-existence of an old and new police authority is the period—

(a) beginning with the date on which a new police authority comes into existence or 1st October 1994, whichever is the later, and

(b) ending immediately before 1st April 1995.

(3) For the purposes of this Order, a new police authority shall be deemed to come into existence when appointments to it have been made under paragraph 5 of Schedule 1B to the 1964 Act (Schedule 1B was inserted by s.3(2) of, and Sched. 2 to, the 1994 Act).

Commencement on 8th August 1994

3.—(1) The provisions of the 1994 Act which are listed in paragraph (2) below shall come into force on 8th August 1994.

(2) The provisions referred to in paragraph (1) above are—

(a) section 18 (regulations for police forces), except to the extent that subsection (3) inserts a new subsection (3) into section 33 of the 1964 Act;

(b) section 41 (metropolitan police: assistant commissioners);

(c) section 46 (interpretation of Part I);

(d) section 52(1) and (3) (regulations for police forces) to the extent only that those subsections insert a new subsection (2B) in section 26 of the Police (Scotland) Act 1967 (c. 77);

(e) section 65 (interpretation of Part II);
(f) section 93 (repeals) so far as it relates to the entries referred to in sub-paragraph (g) below, and
(g) in Part I of Schedule 9 (repeals: police), the entries in respect of—
    (i) the Metropolitan Police Act 1856 (19 & 20 Vict. c. 2);
    (ii) section 33(5) of the 1964 Act; and
    (iii) the Drug Trafficking Offences Act 1986 (c. 32).

Commencement on 8th August 1994 for certain purposes only

4.—(1) Subject to the modifications set out in paragraphs (3) to (6) below, the provisions of the 1994 Act which are listed in paragraph (2) below shall come into force on 8th August 1994 for the purposes of—
(a) the appointment, as soon as practicable thereafter, of members of the new police authorities, and
(b) any provision which applies (by virtue of articles 5 to 7 below) to a new police authority which has come into existence.
(2) The provisions referred to in paragraph (1) above are—
(a) section 1 (police areas);
(b) section 2 (police forces and police authorities), to the extent only that it substitutes a new section 3 of the 1964 Act;
(c) section 3 (membership of police authorities);
(d) section 44 (minor and consequential amendments), so far as it relates to paragraphs 5 and 15 of Schedule 5;
(e) section 93 (repeals) so far as it relates to the entry referred to in sub-paragraph (h) below;
(f) Schedules 1 (Schedule to be inserted in 1964 Act: police areas) and 2 (Schedules to be inserted in 1964 Act: police authorities);
(g) paragraphs 5 and 15 of Part I of Schedule 5 (minor and consequential amendments to the 1964 Act), and
(h) in Part I of Schedule 9 (repeals), the entry in respect of section 25(5) of the 1964 Act.
(3) Nothing in paragraph (1) above shall prejudice the continued operation of the enactments amended by the provisions listed in paragraph (2) above as respects the old police authorities at any time before the expiry of the period of co-existence.
(4) In determining the period of a term of years for the purpose of paragraph 17 (term of appointment of members of a police authority) of Schedule 1B to the 1964 Act (Schedule 1B was inserted by s.3(2) of, and Sched. 2 to, the 1994 Act), any period as a member of a new police authority prior to 1st April 1995 shall be disregarded.
(5) The functions conferred by—
(a) paragraph 26 (reimbursement of expenses and allowances) of Schedule 1B to the 1964 Act, and
(b) paragraph 7 (reimbursement of expenses and allowances) of Schedule 1C to the 1964 Act (Schedule 1C was inserted by s.3(2) of, and Sched. 2 to, the 1994 Act),
shall, during the period before the new police authorities come into existence, be performed by the old police authorities; but a new police authority shall, as soon as practicable after it comes into existence, reimburse the old police authority in respect of the payments made under paragraph 26(1) of Schedule 1B to the 1964 Act and paragraph 7(1) of Schedule 1C to that Act (as modified by this paragraph) and such reasonable expenses as were necessarily incurred by the old police authority under paragraph 7(2) of Schedule 1C (as so modified).
(6) Schedule 1B to the 1964 Act shall have effect as if there was inserted after paragraph 24 the following:

"**24A.**—(1) The first meeting of a police authority shall be—

(a) held within twenty-one days after appointments to it have been made under paragraph 5 of this Schedule, and

(b) treated as being the annual meeting of the authority in the year in which it is held.

(2) The provisions of article 8 of the Police and Magistrates' Courts Act 1994 (Commencement No. 1 and Transitional Provisions) Order 1994 shall have effect in relation to the first meeting of a police authority.".

Commencement on 1st October 1994

5.—(1) Subject to paragraph (3) below, the provisions of the 1994 Act which are listed in paragraph (2) below shall come into force on 1st October 1994.

(2) The provisions referred to in paragraph (1) above are—

(a) section 14 (alteration of police areas) in so far as it substitutes new sections 21A and 21C in the 1964 Act;

(b) section 22 (assistant inspectors and staff officers);

(c) section 25 (acceptance of gifts and loans);

(d) section 32 (initial financing of new police authorities);

(e) section 33 (validation of past grants);

(f) section 39 (police areas in England: alterations under Local Government Act 1992), except subsections (2) and (3);

(g) section 42 (application of Firearms Act 1968 to civilian staff);

(h) section 44 (minor and consequential amendments), so far as it relates to paragraphs 10(1) and (3), 16 and 21 of Schedule 5;

(i) section 93 (repeals) so far as it relates to the entries referred to in sub-paragraph (m) below;

(j) paragraph 10(1) and (3) (amendment of section 43 of the 1964 Act) of Schedule 5;

(k) paragraph 16 (amendment of section 90 of the Offices, Shops and Railway Premises Act 1963 (c. 41)) of Schedule 5;

(l) paragraph 21 (amendment of section 1 of the Police Negotiating Board Act 1980 (c. 10)) of Schedule 5, and

(m) in Part I of Schedule 9 (repeals) the entries in respect of—

(i) the Licensing Act 1902 (2 Edw. 7 c. 28)

(ii) the Police Negotiating Board Act 1980, and

(iii) section 30(2) of the Local Government Act 1985 (c. 51).

(3) The coming into force of section 32 of the 1994 Act shall have effect only in respect of new police authorities which have come into existence.

Commencement on 1st October 1994 for certain purposes only

6.—(1) Subject to the modifications set out in paragraphs (3) to (6) below, the provisions of the 1994 Act which are listed in paragraph (2) below shall come into force on 1st October 1994 for the purpose of the exercise, during the period of co-existence, of the functions conferred by those provisions (as so modified)—

(a) by any new police authority which has come into existence, and

(b) by the Secretary of State in relation to any such police authority.

(2) The provisions referred to in paragraph (1) above are—

(a) section 4 (functions of police authorities), except to the extent that it substitutes a new section 4(1) of the 1964 Act and inserts a new section 4C of that Act;

(b) sections 8 (police fund), 10 (civilian employees) and 11 (appointment of officers);

(c) section 15 (functions of Secretary of State), except to the extent that it substitutes a new section 28D of the 1964 Act;

(d) sections 16 (reports from police authorities) and 31 (financial administration);

(e) section 43 (application to police authorities of enactments relating to local authorities etc.), except in so far as it relates to paragraphs 1 to 4, 15(2) and 42 of Schedule 4;

(f) section 45 (application of certain provisions to new police authorities), and

(g) Schedule 4 (application to police authorities of enactments relating to local authorities etc.) except paragraphs 1 to 4, 15(2) and 42.

(3) Section 4A(3)(b) of the 1964 Act, as substituted by section 4 of the 1994 Act, shall have effect as if it referred to the views obtained under section 106 of the Police and Criminal Evidence Act 1984 (c. 60) by the old police authority.

(4) Section 28A(2) of the 1964 Act, as inserted by section 15 of the 1994 Act, shall not apply.

(5) In the amendment made by paragraph 38 of Schedule 4 to the 1994 Act to section 21 of the Local Government and Housing Act 1989 (c. 42) (interpretation of Part I of that Act) before the words "a police authority" there shall be inserted "except in section 20 above".

(6) Nothing in paragraph (1) above shall prejudice the continued operation of the enactments amended by the provisions listed in paragraph (2) above as respects the old police authorities at any time before the expiry of the period of co-existence.

Commencement of financial provisions on 1st November 1994

7.—(1) Subject to paragraphs (3) and (4) below, the provisions of the 1994 Act which are listed in paragraph (2) below shall come into force on 1st November 1994 for the purposes of any financial year beginning on or after 1st April 1995.

(2) The provisions referred to in paragraph (1) above are—

(a) section 17 (police grant and other grants);

(b) section 27 (precepts); and

(c) section 28 (approval of decisions about precepts).

(3) In section 39(1)(b) of the Local Government Finance Act 1992 (c. 14), as amended by section 27 of the 1994 Act, the reference to "a police authority established under section 3 of the Police Act 1964" shall apply only to a new police authority which has come into existence.

(4) For the purposes of any financial year beginning on or after 1st April 1995, the functions conferred by Chapter IV of Part I of the Local Government Finance Act 1992 shall not be exercised by an old police authority.

First meeting of new authorities

8.—(1) The first meeting of a new police authority shall be convened, and held at a place appointed, by the proper officer of the old police authority.

(2) Notice of the meeting shall be published at the place where the meeting is to be held and summonses to attend the meeting shall be signed by the proper officer of the old police authority.

(3) Until completion of the election of a chairman at the meeting, the functions falling to be exercised by the chairman shall be exercised by a member of the new police authority chosen by the members of that authority present at the meeting.

(4) At the meeting the proper officer of the old police authority shall exercise any functions falling to be exercised by the proper officer of the new police authority in relation to the meeting.

(5) The standing orders for the regulation of the proceedings and business of the old police authority shall, as far as practicable, apply at the meeting.

(6) The new police authority shall, as soon as practicable after the expenses were incurred, reimburse the old police authority in respect of such reasonable expenses as were necessarily incurred by the old police authority under this article.

(7) In this article references to the proper officer of the old police authority are references to the officer whose duty it is to summon meetings of that authority.

Home Office   *John Redwood*
1st August 1994   One of Her Majesty's Principal Secretaries of State

INDEX

References are to article number

EDUCATION, ENGLAND AND WALES

THE EDUCATION ACT 1993 (COMMENCEMENT NO. 5 AND TRANSITIONAL PROVISIONS) ORDER 1994

(S.I. 1994 No. 2038 (C. 39))

Made - - - - -   *28th July 1994*

INTRODUCTION

This Order brings into force, on August 1, 1994 provisions of the Education Act 1993 which relate to pupil referral units and also partially brings into force on that date paras. 97(a) and 98(a) of Sched. 19 to the 1993 Act which amend ss.24 and 25 of the Education (No. 2) Act 1986. The remaining provisions of Pts. III and IV of the 1993 Act are brought into force on September 1, 1994 as are ss.241 (sex education), 261 and 262 (exclusion of pupils) and, for all remaining purposes, s.298 and Sched. 18 (duty of local educational authorities to make exceptional provision of education in school or elsewhere, and pupil referral units). Sections 224 to 226 and 228(4) (relating to education associations) come into force on December 1, 1994. The Order also includes transitional provisions consequential on the commencement of the provisions of Pts. III and IV of the 1993 Act. Due to defects this Order was published jointly with correcting S.I. 1994 No. 2248.

In exercise of the powers conferred on the Secretary of State by sections 301(6) and 308(3) of the Education Act 1993 (1993 c. 35) the Secretary of State for Education hereby makes the following order:

Citation and interpretation

1.—(1) This Order may be cited as the Education Act 1993 (Commencement No. 5 and Transitional Provisions) Order 1994.

(2) In this Order "the Act" means the Education Act 1993.

2. The provisions of the Act specified in the first column of Schedule 1 to this Order (which relate to the matters mentioned in the second column thereof) shall come into force on 1st August 1994; and, save as otherwise provided in the first column of Schedule 1, they shall come into force on that date for all purposes.

3.—(1) The provisions of the Act specified in the first column of Schedule 2 to this Order (which relate to the matters mentioned in the second column thereof) shall come into force on 1st September 1994; and, save as otherwise provided in the first column of Schedule 2, they shall come into force on that date for all purposes.

(2) Schedule 4 to this Order shall have effect for the purpose of making transitional provisions in connection with the provisions brought into force by this Article and Schedule 2 to this Order.

4. The provisions of the Act specified in the first column of Schedule 3 to this Order (which relate to the matters mentioned in the second column thereof) shall come into force for all purposes on 1st December 1994.

Article 2   SCHEDULE 1

PROVISIONS COMING INTO FORCE ON 1ST AUGUST 1994

Provisions of the Act	*Subject matter of provisions*
Section 298(2) (for the purposes of defining the expression "pupil referral unit" in relation to regulations made under paragraph 3 of Schedule 18 to the Act).	Definition of "pupil referral unit".
Paragraph 3 of Schedule 18, and section 298(8) so far as it relates thereto.	Power to make regulations with respect to pupil referral units.

Provisions of the Act	*Subject matter of provisions*
Paragraph 97(a) of Schedule 19 (for the purposes of prescribing the period within which, under the articles of government for county, voluntary controlled and maintained special schools, the governing body are to be required to express their views to the local education authority as to the reinstatement of a permanently excluded pupil), and section 307(1) so far as it relates thereto.	Reinstatement of permanently excluded pupils: county, voluntary controlled and maintained special schools.
Paragraph 98(a) of Schedule 19 (for the purposes of prescribing the period within which, under the articles of government for voluntary aided and special agreement schools, the governing body are to be required to express their views to the local education authority as to the reinstatement of a pupil excluded for a fixed period), and section 307(1) so far as it relates thereto.	Reinstatement of pupils excluded for a fixed period: voluntary aided and special agreement schools.

Article 3   SCHEDULE 2

PROVISIONS COMING INTO FORCE ON 1ST SEPTEMBER 1994

Provisions of the Act	*Subject matter of provisions*
Section 160.	Qualified duty to secure education of children with special educational needs in ordinary schools.
Section 164.	Provision outside England and Wales for children with statements of special educational needs.
Section 165.	Duty of local education authorities to identify children with special educational needs.
Section 166(1) to (3) and (5).	Duty of District Health Authority or local authority to help a local education authority in the exercise of their functions.
Section 167 (subsection (5) of that section for all remaining purposes).	Assessment of special educational needs.
Section 168 (subsection (7) of that section for all remaining purposes).	Statements of special educational needs.
Section 169.	Appeals against decision not to make a statement of special educational needs.
Section 170.	Appeals against contents of statements.
Section 171.	Access for local education authorities to certain schools.
Section 172(2) to (5).	Reviews of educational needs of children with statements.
Section 173.	Assessment of a child's educational needs at request of the parent.
Section 174.	Assessment of a child's educational needs at the request of the governing body of a grant-maintained school.
Section 175.	Assessment of educational needs of children under the age of two years.
Section 176.	Duties of District Health Authorities and National Health Service trusts in respect of children under the age of five years.

Provisions of the Act	*Subject matter of provisions*
Section 177(1).	Establishment of the Special Educational Needs Tribunal.
Section 180(3), (5) and (6).	Procedure of the Special Educational Needs Tribunal.
Section 192(6) and (7) (for all remaining purposes).	School Attendance Orders.
Section 196.	Choice of school to be specified in a school attendance order: child with statement of special educational needs.
Section 197(5).	Revocation of a school attendance order in respect of a child with a statement of special educational needs under section 168 of the Act.
Section 241.	Sex education.
Section 261.	Restrictions on power to exclude pupils.
Section 262.	Exclusion of pupils: funding.
Section 298 (subsections (2) and (8) for all remaining purposes).	Duty of local education authorities to make exceptional provision of education in school or elsewhere.
Schedule 9 (for all remaining purposes).	Making of assessments under section 167 of the Act.
Schedule 10 (for all remaining purposes).	Making and maintenance of statements under section 168 of the Act.
Schedule 18 (for all remaining purposes).	Pupil referral units.
Paragraphs 16, 31(a), 44, 54(a), 74, 82 (for all remaining purposes), 87(a) and (c), 88, 95, 96, 97 (for all remaining purposes), 98 (for all remaining purposes), 101(a), 120, 121, 139 (for all remaining purposes), 145 (for all remaining purposes), 147, 148, 151, 154 (for all remaining purposes) and 160 of Schedule 19, and section 307(1) so far as it relates thereto.	Minor and consequential amendments.
Schedule 21, in so far as it relates to the repeals set out in the Appendix to this Schedule, and section 307(3) so far as it relates thereto.	Repeals.

APPENDIX TO SCHEDULE 2

REPEALS TAKING EFFECT ON 1ST SEPTEMBER 1994

Chapter	*Short title*	*Extent of repeal*
1944 c. 31.	The Education Act 1944.	Section 56.
1981 c. 60.	The Education Act 1981.	Sections 2(2) and (3), 3A, 4, 5, 6, 7(1) to (9) and (11), 8, 9, 10, 15, 16, 18, 19 and 20(1) (other than the definition of "principal Act").
		Paragraphs 1(1) and (2), 2, 3, and 5 to 7 of Schedule 1, paragraphs 2 to 8 of Schedule 2 and paragraphs 8(2)(a) and (c), 9, 15 and 16 of Schedule 3.
1986 c. 61.	The Education (No. 2) Act 1986.	In section 23(a)(ii) and (b) "or indefinite".
		Section 24(c) and (e) and, in paragraph (f), "or (c)".
		Section 25(d), (e) and (f).

Chapter	Short title	Extent of repeal
1988 c. 40.	The Education Reform Act 1988.	In section 235(1), the definition of "the 1981 Act". In Schedule 12, paragraphs 27, 28 and 83 to 85.
1989 c. 41.	The Children Act 1989.	Section 27(4). In Schedule 12, paragraph 36.
1990 c. 19.	The National Health Service and Community Care Act 1990.	In Schedule 9, paragraph 22.

Article 4   SCHEDULE 3

PROVISIONS COMING INTO FORCE ON 1ST DECEMBER 1994

Provisions of the Act	Subject matter of provisions
Section 224.	School conducted by education association acquiring grant-maintained status.
Section 225.	Discontinuance of school conducted by an education association.
Section 226.	Winding-up of an education association.
Section 228(4).	Application of sections 186 and 224 of the Act in relation to former maintained special schools being conducted by education associations.

Article 3   SCHEDULE 4

TRANSITIONAL PROVISIONS

1. In this Schedule, "the 1981 Act" means the Education Act 1981 (1981 c. 60).

2.—(1) This paragraph applies in any case where—
  (a) before 1st September 1994 a local education authority serve notice under section 5(5) of the 1981 Act of their intention to carry out an assessment under that section, and
  (b) by a time immediately before that date the local education authority have not served on the parent of the child concerned a notice under section 5(7) of that Act or a copy of a proposed statement under section 7(3) of that Act.

(2) Subject to sub-paragraph (4) below, in any case to which this paragraph applies sections 5(6), (7) and (10) and 7(1) and (3) to (8) of, and paragraphs 1, 2 and 3 of Schedule 1 to, the 1981 Act shall continue to have effect on and after 1st September 1994 in relation to—
  (a) the making of an assessment of the child's special educational needs in pursuance of the notice under section 5(5) of the 1981 Act, and
  (b) (where it is decided in the light of that assessment that the local education authority should determine the special educational provision which is to be made for the child) the making of a statement of special educational needs in pursuance of that decision.

(3) Where section 5(6) of the 1981 Act has effect by virtue of sub-paragraph (2) above, that section shall have effect as if for "in writing to the Secretary of State" there were substituted "to the Special Educational Needs Tribunal".

(4) Sub-paragraph (2) above shall cease to apply in any case where the local education authority have failed before 1st January 1995 either—
  (a) to serve notice on the parent of the child in accordance with section 5(7) of the 1981 Act, or
  (b) to serve on the parent in accordance with section 7(3) of that Act a copy of the child's proposed statement of educational needs.

(5) In any case to which sub-paragraph (2) above applies—
  (a) sections 167(6), 168(1) to (4) and 169(1) and (2) of, and Schedule 9 and paragraphs 2 to 5 of Schedule 10 to, the Act shall not apply, and
  (b) section 169(3) shall have effect as if the reference to an appeal under that section included a reference to an appeal under section 5(6) of the 1981 Act (as if it has effect by virtue of this paragraph).

(6) An appeal under section 5(6) of the 1981 Act (as it has effect by virtue of this paragraph) shall be treated for the purposes of Part III of the Act as if made under section 169(2) of the Act.

(7) Any assessment or any statement of special educational needs made under section 5 or 7 of the 1981 Act by virtue of sub-paragraph (2) above shall have effect as if made (as the case may be) under section 167 or 168 of the Act; and any reference, whether express or implied, in any enactment, instrument or document to an assessment under section 167 of the Act, or a statement under section 168 of the Act, is to be read so far as the nature of the reference permits as including a reference to any assessment or any statement so made.

3.—(1) This paragraph applies where before 1st September 1994 a local education authority give notice under section 5(7) of the 1981 Act to the parent of a child who has been assessed in accordance with that section.

(2) In any case to which this paragraph applies—

(a) section 5(6) and (8) of the 1981 Act shall continue to have effect on and after 1st September 1994, and

(b) section 169 of the Act shall not apply,

in relation to the decision of the local education authority to which the notice under section 5(7) of the 1981 Act relates.

4.—(1) This paragraph applies where before 1st September 1994 a local education authority serve on the parent of a child in accordance with section 7(3) of the 1981 Act a copy of a proposed statement of special educational needs for that child.

(2) In any case to which this paragraph applies—

(a) section 7(1) and (4) to (8) of, and paragraph 3 of Schedule 1 to, the 1981 Act shall continue to have effect on and after 1st September 1994,

(b) section 168(1) to (4) of, and paragraphs 3 to 5 of Schedule 10 to, the Act shall not apply,

in relation to a statement of special educational needs made pursuant to the proposed statement served under section 7(3) of the 1981 Act.

(3) Any statement of special educational needs made under section 7 of the 1981 Act by virtue of sub-paragraph (2) above shall have effect as if made under section 168 of the Act; and any reference, whether express or implied, in any enactment, instrument or document to a statement under section 168 of the Act, is to be read so far as the nature of the reference permits as including a reference to any statement so made.

5.—(1) This paragraph applies where before 1st September 1994 a local education authority serve on the parent of a child in accordance with section 7(9) of the 1981 Act a copy of the statement of special educational needs made for that child under that section.

(2) In any case to which this paragraph applies—

(a) section 8 of the 1981 Act shall continue to have effect on and after 1st September 1994, and

(b) section 170 of the Act shall not apply,

with respect to any appeal against the special educational provision specified in the statement served under section 7(9) of the 1981 Act.

6.—(1) This paragraph applies where—

(a) before 1st September 1994 a local education authority, in accordance with paragraph 6 of Schedule 1 to the 1981 Act, serve notice on the parent of a child, for whom they maintain a statement of special educational needs, of their proposal to amend or to cease to maintain that statement; and

(b) by a time immediately before that date the local education authority have not informed the parent of their decision on the proposal in accordance with paragraph 6(3) of that Schedule.

(2) In any case to which this paragraph applies—

(a) paragraph 6 of Schedule 1 to the 1981 Act shall continue to have effect on and after 1st September 1994, and

(b) paragraphs 9 to 11 of Schedule 10 to the 1981 Act shall not apply,

in relation to any determination of the local education authority to amend or to cease to maintain the statement made in pursuance of that proposal.

(3) Where paragraph 6(4) of Schedule 1 to the 1981 Act has effect by virtue of sub-paragraph (2) above, that paragraph shall have effect as if for the words from "section 8(1)" to the end of that paragraph there were substituted—

"section 170(1) of the Education Act 1993 to appeal against the description in the statement of the authority's assessment of the child's special educational needs, the special educational provision specified in the statement or, if no school is named in the statement, that fact".

(4) For the purposes of any determination under paragraph 6(3) of Schedule 1 to the 1981 Act (as it has effect by virtue of sub-paragraph (2) above), or any appeal under section 170(1) of the Act against any such determination, the local education authority shall be treated as if they were under a duty to maintain the statement, to which the determination relates, by virtue of section 7(1) of the 1981 Act instead of section 168(1) of the Act.

7.—(1) This paragraph applies where before 1st September 1994 a local education authority, in accordance with paragraph 6(4) of Schedule 1 to the 1981 Act, inform the parent of a child, for whom they maintain a statement of special educational needs, of his right to appeal in consequence of any amendment made by them to the child's statement.

(2) In any case to which this paragraph applies—

(a) section 8 of the 1981 Act shall continue to have effect on or after 1st September 1994, and

(b) section 170 of, and paragraph 10(4) of Schedule 10 to, the Act shall not apply,

with respect to any appeal made by the parent in consequence of the amendment made to his child's statement of special educational needs by the local education authority.

8. Where on 1st September 1994 no decision has been made by a local education authority in relation to a request for an assessment made by a parent under section 9(1) of the 1981 Act, that request shall have effect on and after that date as if it had been made under section 173(1) of the Act.

9.—(1) This paragraph applies where before 1st September 1994 a local education authority have served a notice on the parent of a child under section 15(2) of the 1981 Act with respect to the naming of a school in a school attendance order, and immediately before that date no determination has been made in accordance with that section as to which school is to be named in the order.

(2) In any case to which this paragraph applies—

(a) section 15(1) to (5) of the 1981 Act shall continue to have effect on and after 1st September 1994,

(b) section 196(1) to (3) of the Act shall not apply, and

(c) paragraph 9 of Schedule 10 shall have effect as if the reference to section 197 included a reference to section 15 of the 1981 Act,

for the purpose of determining the school to be named in the school attendance order, and for the purpose of making any consequential amendments to the child's statement of special educational needs.

10.—(1) This paragraph applies in any case where before 1st September 1994 a parent has requested the local education authority in accordance with section 16(2) of the 1981 Act to amend or revoke the school attendance order relating to his child, and immediately before that date either—

(a) no determination has been made by the local education authority with respect to the parent's request, or

(b) where the authority have refused to amend the order in compliance with the parent's request, the matter has been referred to the Secretary of State and he has yet to determine the matter.

(2) In relation to any request, to which this paragraph applies, for the school attendance order to be amended—

(a) section 16(1) to (4) shall continue to have effect on and after 1st September 1994,

(b) section 196(4) of the Act shall not apply, and

(c) paragraph 9 of Schedule 10 shall have effect as if the reference to section 197 included a reference to section 16 of the 1981 Act.

(3) In relation to any request, to which this paragraph applies, for the school attendance order to be revoked, section 197(5) of the Act shall have effect as if paragraph (a), and in paragraph (b) the words "in any other case", were omitted.

Gillian Shephard
Secretary of State for Education

28th July 1994

INDEX

References are to article and Schedule number

LOCAL GOVERNMENT, ENGLAND AND WALES

WALES

THE LOCAL GOVERNMENT (WALES) ACT 1994 (COMMENCEMENT NO. 1) ORDER 1994

(S.I. 1994 No. 2109 (C. 40))

Made -   -   -   -   -   *6th August 1994*

INTRODUCTION

The Local Government (Wales) Act 1994 received Royal Assent on July 5, 1994. This Order brings into force s.41 (which relates to the continuity of employment in certain cases of voluntary transfer), s.52 (which provides that certain parts of the Local Government Act 1988 apply during the transitional period) and s.65 (which makes provision for the payment of certain expenses incurred whilst carrying out duties under the 1994 Act) on August 15, 1994.

The Secretary of State for Wales, in exercise of the powers conferred upon him by section 66(3) of the Local Government (Wales) Act 1994 (c. 19), hereby makes the following Order:

1. This Order may be cited as the Local Government (Wales) Act 1994 (Commencement No. 1) Order 1994.

2. The date appointed for the coming into force of the following provisions of the Local Government (Wales) Act 1994 is 15th August 1994—

Section 41 (continuity of employment in certain cases of voluntary transfer);

Section 52 (application of Part I of the Local Government Act 1988 (c. 9) during transitional period);

Section 65 (expenses).

6th August 1994

John Redwood
Secretary of State for Wales

INDEX

References are to article number

SEA FISHERIES

THE INSHORE FISHING (SCOTLAND) ACT 1994 (COMMENCEMENT) ORDER 1994

(S.I. 1994 No. 2124 (C. 41) (S.110))

Made -   -   -   -   -   *3rd August 1994*

INTRODUCTION

The Inshore Fishing (Scotland) Act 1994 received Royal Assent on July 21, 1994 and makes provision for the amendment of the Inshore Fishing (Scotland) Act 1984 extending the power to prohibit sea fishing in certain areas. This Order brings all of the provisions of the Act into force on August 8, 1994.

The Secretary of State, in exercise of the powers conferred on him by section 5(1) of the Inshore Fishing (Scotland) Act 1994 (c. 27) and of all other powers enabling him in that behalf, hereby makes the following Order:

Citation

1. This Order may be cited as the Inshore Fishing (Scotland) Act 1994 (Commencement) Order 1994.

Appointed day

2. The Inshore Fishing (Scotland) Act 1994 shall come into force on 8th August 1994.

Hector Monro

St Andrew's House, Edinburgh   Parliamentary Under Secretary of State,
3rd August 1994   Scottish Office

INDEX

References are to article number

TRANSPORT

THE RAILWAYS ACT 1993 (COMMENCEMENT NO. 6) ORDER 1994

(S.I. 1994 No. 2142 (C. 42))

Made -   -   -   -   -   *15th August 1994*

INTRODUCTION

This Order brings into force various provisions of the Railways Act 1993. The remainder of s.134(1), which gives effect to Sched. 11, and the remainder of Sched. 11 are brought into force on August 16, 1994. Schedule 11 makes provision in relation to pensions, amending and modifying the application of existing statutes.

The Secretary of State, in exercise of the powers conferred on him by section 154(2) of the Railways Act 1993 (c. 43), hereby makes the following Order:—

1. This Order may be cited as the Railways Act 1993 (Commencement No. 6) Order 1994.

2. The following provisions of the Railways Act 1993 shall come into force on 16th August 1994:
in section 134, subsection (1), so far as not already in force; and
Schedule 11, so far as not already in force.

Signed by authority of the
Secretary of State for Transport

John Watts
Minister of State,
15th August 1994   Department of Transport

INDEX

References are to article number

CUSTOMS AND EXCISE

THE FINANCE ACT 1994, SECTION 7, (APPOINTED DAY) (NO. 2) ORDER 1994

(S.I. 1994 No. 2143 (C. 43))

Made -   -   -   -   -   *15th August 1994*

INTRODUCTION

Section 7(1)(b) of the Finance Act 1994 extends the jurisdiction of VAT and duties tribunals to matters relating to customs and excise. This Order appoints August 31, 1994 as the date on which that provision comes into force.

The Commissioners of Customs and Excise, in exercise of the powers conferred on them by section 19 of the Finance Act 1994 (c. 9; s.17(1) applies the definition of "the Commissioners" in s.1(1) of the Customs and Excise Management Act 1979 (c. 2)) and of all other powers enabling them in that behalf, hereby make the following Order:

1. This Order may be cited as the Finance Act 1994, section 7, (Appointed Day) (No. 2) Order 1994.

2. The day appointed as the day on which section 7(1)(b) of the Finance Act 1994 comes into force is 31st August 1994.

New King's Beam House
22 Upper Ground
LONDON
SE1 9PJ

Leonard Harris
15th August 1994   Commissioner of Customs and Excise

INDEX

References are to article number

NORTHERN IRELAND

THE POLICE AND MAGISTRATES' COURTS ACT 1994 (COMMENCEMENT NO. 2) ORDER 1994

(S.I. 1994 No. 2151 (C. 44))

Made - - - - - *15th August 1994*

INTRODUCTION

This Order brings into force various provisions of the Police and Magistrates' Courts Act 1994. Part III (ss.66–68) which makes provision in relation to the policing of Northern Ireland is brought into force on August 23, 1994. Section 93, which gives effect to Sched. 9 (repeals) is brought into force to the extent necessary to give effect to the entries in that Schedule which relate to the Police Act (Northern Ireland) 1970 (ss.10(5), 25(5), 26(3)).

In exercise of the powers conferred upon me by section 94(1) and (4) of the Police and Magistrates' Courts Act 1994 (c. 29), I hereby make the following Order:

1. This Order may be cited as the Police and Magistrates' Courts Act 1994 (Commencement No. 2) Order 1994.

2.—(1) The provisions of the Police and Magistrates' Courts Act 1994 which are listed in paragraph (2) below shall come into force on 23rd August 1994.

(2) The provisions referred to in paragraph (1) above are—

(a) Part III (Police (Northern Ireland));

(b) section 93 (repeals) so far as it relates to the entries referred to in sub-paragraph (c) below; and

(c) in Part I of Schedule 9 (repeals), the entries in respect of the Police Act (Northern Ireland) 1970 (c. 9 (N.I.)).

Northern Ireland Office

Malcolm Rifkind
15th August 1994　　　　One of Her Majesty's Principal Secretaries of State

INDEX

References are to article number

COAL INDUSTRY

THE COAL INDUSTRY ACT 1994
(COMMENCEMENT NO. 1) ORDER 1994

(S.I. 1994 No. 2189 (C. 45))

Made - - - - - *21st August 1994*

INTRODUCTION

This Order brings into force various provisions of the Coal Industry Act 1994 on September 19, 1994. The provisions brought into force relate to the reorganisation of the coal industry, in particular the establishment of the Coal Authority, and the taxation effects of that restructuring.

The Secretary of State, in exercise of the powers conferred on him by section 68(4) and (5) of the Coal Industry Act 1994 (c. 21), and of all other powers enabling him in that behalf, hereby makes the following Order:

Citation and interpretation

1.—(1) This Order may be cited as the Coal Industry Act 1994 (Commencement No. 1) Order 1994.

(2) In this Order "the Act" means the Coal Industry Act 1994.

Coming into force of certain provisions of Act

2. The provisions of the Act specified in the first column of the Schedule to this Order (which relate to the matters specified in the second column thereof) shall come into force on 19th September 1994.

Tim Eggar
Minister for Industry and Energy
Department of Trade and Industry

21st August 1994

SCHEDULE

PROVISIONS COMING INTO FORCE ON 19TH SEPTEMBER 1994

Provisions of the Act	Subject matter of provisions
Section 1	Establishment of the Coal Authority.
Section 4	Duty of the Authority with respect to safety.
Section 5	General powers of Authority.
Section 6	Directions to the Authority by the Secretary of State.
Section 21	Taxation effects of restructuring.
Schedule 1	The Coal Authority.
Schedule 4	Taxation provisions.

INDEX

References are to article number

EDUCATION, ENGLAND AND WALES
EDUCATION, SCOTLAND

THE EDUCATION ACT 1994 (COMMENCEMENT) ORDER 1994

(S.I. 1994 No. 2204 (C. 46))

Made - - - - - *23rd August 1994*

INTRODUCTION

The Education Act 1994 makes provision for the reorganisation of teacher training and the conduct of students' unions. This Order brings the majority of the provisions of that Act, with the exception of s.22(3)–(5) (requirements to be observed in relation to students' unions), into force on September 21, 1994. The remaining provisions are brought into force on April 1, 1995.

The Secretary of State, in exercise of the powers conferred by section 26 of the Education Act 1994 (c. 30), hereby makes the following order:

1.—(1) This Order may be cited as the Education Act 1994 (Commencement) Order 1994.

(2) In this Order "the Act" means the Education Act 1994.

2.—(1) All the provisions of the Act, except for those mentioned in paragraph (2) below, shall come into force on 21st September 1994.

(2) Subsections (3), (4) and (5) of section 22 of the Act shall come into force on 1st April 1995.

Gillian Shephard
One of Her Majesty's Principal
23rd August 1994   Secretaries of State

INDEX

References are to article number

EDUCATION, ENGLAND AND WALES

THE EDUCATION ACT 1993 (COMMENCEMENT NO. 5 AND TRANSITIONAL PROVISIONS) (AMENDMENT) ORDER 1994

(S.I. 1994 No. 2248 (C. 47))

Made - - - - - *25th August 1994*

INTRODUCTION

This Order was made in consequence of defects in S.I. 1994 No. 2038. It amends Sched. 4 to that Order which contains transitional provisions consequential on the commencement of provisions of Pts. III and IV of the Education Act 1993.

In exercise of the powers conferred on the Secretary of State by sections 301(6) and 308(3) of the Education Act 1993 (1993 c. 35), the Secretary of State for Education hereby makes the following Order:

Citation

1. This Order may be cited as the Education Act 1993 (Commencement No. 5 and Transitional Provisions) (Amendment) Order 1994.

Amendment of Order

2. In Schedule 4 to the Education Act 1993 (Commencement No. 5 and Transitional Provisions) Order 1994 (S.I. 1994 No. 2038)—

(a) in paragraph 2(4)(b), after "statement of" there shall be inserted "special";

(b) in paragraph 6(2)(b), "1981" shall be omitted; and

(c) for paragraph 7(1) there shall be substituted—

"**7.**—(1) This paragraph applies where before 1st September 1994 a local education authority inform the parent of a child for whom they maintain a statement of special educational needs—

(a) in pursuance of section 8(5) of the 1981 Act, of any decision to amend the statement in the light of an appeal committee's observations, or

(b) in accordance with paragraph 6(4) of Schedule 1 to the 1981 Act, of the parent's right to appeal in consequence of any amendment made by them to the statement.".

Eric Forth
Minister of State
Department for Education

25th August 1994

INDEX

References are to article number

MEDICINES

NATIONAL HEALTH SERVICE, ENGLAND AND WALES

THE MEDICINAL PRODUCTS: PRESCRIPTION BY NURSES ETC. ACT 1992 (COMMENCEMENT NO. 1) ORDER 1994

(S.I. 1994 No. 2408 (C. 48))

Made - - - - -   *12th September 1994*

INTRODUCTION
This Order appoints October 3, 1994 as the day on which ss.1 and 2 of the Medicinal Products: Prescription by Nurses etc. Act 1992 come into force.

The Secretary of State, in exercise of powers conferred by section 6(2) of the Medicinal Products: Prescription by Nurses etc. Act 1992 (1992 c. 28) and of all other powers enabling her in that behalf, hereby makes the following Order:

Citation

1. This Order may be cited as the Medicinal Products: Prescription by Nurses etc. Act 1992 (Commencement No. 1) Order 1994.

Appointed Day

2. 3rd October 1994 is the day appointed for the coming into force of sections 1 and 2 of the Medicinal Products: Prescription by Nurses etc. Act 1992.

Virginia Bottomley
One of Her Majesty's
Principal Secretaries of State
(Department of Health)

12th September 1994

INDEX

References are to article number

ENVIRONMENTAL PROTECTION

THE ENVIRONMENTAL PROTECTION ACT 1990 (COMMENCEMENT NO. 15) (AMENDMENT) ORDER 1994

(S.I. 1994 No. 2487 (C. 49))

Made - - - - - *19th September 1994*

INTRODUCTION

This Order amends art. 3(2) of S.I. 1994 No. 1096 (C. 18), which makes provision for determining the date upon which certain provisions of the Environmental Protection Act 1990 (c. 43) (relating to waste management licensing) come into force for the purposes of their application to activities involving the treatment, keeping or disposal of scrap metal or motor vehicles which are to be dismantled. As respects any such activity, that date is now by this Order determined according to the state of affairs on January 1, 1995.

S.I. 1994 No. 3234 (C. 81) amended this date, again, to April 1, 1995.

The Secretary of State, in exercise of his powers under section 164(3) of the Environmental Protection Act 1990 (1990 c. 43), hereby makes the following Order:

Citation

1. This Order may be cited as the Environmental Protection Act 1990 (Commencement No. 15) (Amendment) Order 1994.

Amendment of the Environmental Protection Act 1990 (Commencement No. 15) Order 1994

2. In each of sub-paragraphs (a), (b) and (c) of article 3(2) of the Environmental Protection Act 1990 (Commencement No. 15) Order 1994 (S.I. 1994/1096), for the words "1st October 1994" there shall be substituted the words "1st January 1995".

Signed by authority of the Secretary of State

Robert Atkins
Minister of State,
Department of the Environment

19th September 1994

INDEX

References are to article number

INCOME TAX

THE FINANCE ACT 1989, SECTION 165(2), (APPOINTED DAY) ORDER 1994

(S.I. 1994 No. 2508 (C. 50))

Made - - - - - *23rd September 1994*

INTRODUCTION

This Order appoints May 20, 1995 as the appointed day for the purposes of s.165(2) of the Finance Act 1989 (determination of penalties for failure to make a return within a 12-month period), this being the first day on which there will be a failure to make a return in accordance with the Income Tax (Employments) Regulations 1993 (S.I. 1993 No. 744) and the Income Tax (Sub-Contractors in the Construction Industry) Regulations 1993 (S.I. 1993 No. 743) for the year of assessment 1994–1995.

The Treasury, in exercise of the powers conferred on them by section 165(2) of the Finance Act 1989 (1989 c. 26), hereby make the following Order:

1. This Order may be cited as the Finance Act 1989, section 165(2), (Appointed Day) Order 1994.

2. The day appointed for the purposes of section 165(2) of the Finance Act 1989 is 20th May 1995.

Tim Wood
Kenneth Clarke
Two of the Lords Commissioners
of Her Majesty's Treasury

23rd September 1994

INDEX

References are to article number

FRIENDLY SOCIETIES

THE FRIENDLY SOCIETIES ACT 1992 (COMMENCEMENT NO. 8) ORDER 1994

(S.I. 1994 No. 2543 (C. 51))

Made -   -   -   -   -   *28th September 1994*

INTRODUCTION

This Order brings into force s.31 of the Friendly Societies Act 1992 (c. 40) in relation to registered friendly societies conducting insurance business or non-insurance business, other than societies to which that section already applies. Previous commencement orders are S.I. 1992 Nos. 1325 and 3117, S.I. 1993 Nos. 16, 197, 1186, 2213 and 3226.

The Treasury, in exercise of the powers conferred on them by section 126(2) of the Friendly Societies Act 1992 (1992 c. 40) and of all other powers enabling them in that behalf, hereby make the following Order:

Citation and interpretation

1.—(1) This Order may be cited as the Friendly Societies Act 1992 (Commencement No. 8) Order 1994.

(2) In this Order—

"the 1923 Act" means the Industrial Assurance Act 1923 (13 and 14 Geo. 5 c. 8);

"the 1979 Order" means the Industrial Assurance (Northern Ireland) Order 1979 (S.I. 1979 No. 1574 (N.I. 13);

"the 1992 Act" means the Friendly Societies Act 1992.

Days appointed

2.—(1) Section 31 of the 1992 Act shall come into force on 1st November 1994 in relation to the carrying on of any insurance business or non-insurance business by a registered friendly society (other than a registered society to which article 2(2), 2(3) or 2(4) of the Friendly Societies Act 1992 (Commencement No. 6 and Transitional Provisions) Order 1993 (S.I. 1993 No. 2213 (C. 43)) applies) which does not duly apply to the Commission before 1st November 1994 under section 32 or 33 of the 1992 Act for authorisation to carry on or to continue to carry on any class or part of a class of insurance business or any description of non-insurance business.

(2) Section 31 of the 1992 Act shall come into force on 1st April 1995 for all remaining purposes.

(3) The following provisions of the 1992 Act shall come into force on 1st November 1994:

(a) section 120(2), to the extent necessary to bring into force the provisions of Parts I and II of Schedule 22 to the 1992 Act specified in the following sub-paragraphs;

(b) in Part I of Schedule 22 the repeal of:

(i) that part of section 2(1) of the 1923 Act which has not already been brought into force (the provision in Part I of Schedule 22 repealing section 2 of the Industrial Assurance Act 1923 was commenced in part by Schedule 3 to S.I. 1993/16 (C.1); and

(ii) section 2(2) of the 1923 Act; and

(c) in Part II of Schedule 22, the repeal of:
  (i) that part of article 4(1) of the 1979 Order which has not already been brought into force (the provision in Part II of Schedule 22 repealing article 4(1) of the Industrial Assurance (Northern Ireland) Order 1979 was commenced in part by S.I. 1993 No. 3226 (C. 65)); and
  (ii) article 4(3) of the 1979 Order.

Derek Conway
Tim Wood
Two of the Lords Commissioners
of Her Majesty's Treasury

28th September 1994

INDEX

References are to article number

TRADE MARKS

THE TRADE MARKS ACT 1994 (COMMENCEMENT) ORDER 1994

(S.I. 1994 No. 2550 (C. 52))

Made -   -   -   -   -   *29th September 1994*

INTRODUCTION

This Order brings into force all the provisions of the Trade Marks Act 1994 on October 31, 1994 and for the purpose of enabling subordinate legislation to be made under the provisions of the Act specified in the Schedule to the Order, to come into force on that date, the Order brings into force forthwith those provisions. It also brings into force forthwith ss.66(1) and 80(1), (3) to enable the registrar to exercise his powers.

The Secretary of State, in exercise of the powers conferred upon him by section 109 of the Trade Marks Act 1994 (1994 c. 26), hereby makes the following Order:

1. This Order may be cited as the Trade Marks Act 1994 (Commencement) Order 1994.

2. All the provisions of the Trade Marks Act 1994 ("the Act") shall come into force on 31st October 1994; and, accordingly, for the purposes of subsection (2) of the said section 109, that date shall be the date of commencement in respect of the references to commencement of the Act in Schedules 3 and 4 to the Act (transitional provisions and consequential amendments).

3.—(1) The provisions of the Act specified in the Schedule to this Order shall come into force forthwith for the purpose only of enabling the making of subordinate legislation thereunder, by the authority shown in relation to those provisions, expressed to come into force on 31st October 1994.

(2) Section 66(1) (power of registrar to require use of forms and give directions as to their use) and section 80(1) and (3) (power of the registrar to give directions as to the hours of business and business days) of the Act shall come into force forthwith for the purpose of enabling the registrar to exercise his powers thereunder, the same being effective on 31st October 1994.

Ian Taylor
Parliamentary Under-Secretary of State
for Trade and Technology
29th September 1994   Department of Trade and Industry

SCHEDULE

Provision and Authority	*Subject-matter*
Rules by the Secretary of State under the following provisions, as read with (except in the case of items (u) and (cc)(i) and (iv) below) paragraph (a) or (b), or both, as appropriate, of subsection (1) of section 78 (section 78(1)(a) and (b) empowers the Secretary of State to make rules for the purposes of any provision of the Act authorising the making of rules with respect to any matter and for prescribing anything authorised or required by any provision of the Act to be prescribed)—	
(a) section 4(4)	Prohibiting the registration of a trade mark which consists of arms to which a person is

Provision and Authority	Subject-matter
	entitled by virtue of a grant of arms by the Crown.
(b) section 13(2)	Providing for the publication and entry in the register of a disclaimer or limitation with respect to the registration of a trade mark.
(c) section 25(1), (5) and (6)	Prescribing the particulars of transactions affecting registered trade marks to be entered in the register; providing for amendments to, or removal of registered particulars relating to licences or to a security interest.
(d) section 34(1)	Prescribing the system of classification of trade marks.
(e) section 35(5)	Providing for the manner of claiming a right to priority on the basis of a Convention application.
(f) section 38(1) and (2)	Prescribing the manner of publication of an application for registration, the time within which, and the manner in which, notice of opposition to the registration must be given.
(g) section 39(3)	Providing for the publication of amendments of applications for registration.
(h) section 40(4)	Prescribing the manner of publication of the registration of a trade mark.
(i) section 41(1) and (3)	Providing as to division or merging of an application for registration and the registration of a series of trade marks.
(j) section 43(2), (3), (5) and (6)	Providing for informing the proprietor of the date of expiry of the registration; prescribing the period for the payment of the renewal fee; providing for the restoration of a trade mark to the register and the manner of publication of the renewal or restoration of the registration.
(k) section 44(3)	Providing for the publication of any alteration of a registered trade mark and for the making of objections thereto by persons affected.
(l) section 45(2)	Providing for the manner of surrender of a registered trade mark and for protecting interests of other persons having a right therein.
(m) section 63(2) and (3)	Prescribing the particulars of registrable transactions to be entered in the register and the manner in which the register shall be kept; providing for public inspection of the register and the supply of copies of entries therein.
(n) section 64(4)	Prescribing the manner in which a request may be made for a change in the name or address of the proprietor as recorded in the register.
(o) section 65(1), (3), (4) and (5)	Providing for the adaptation of entries to new classification; prescribing the time within which a proposal for amendment may be filed and the manner in which such proposal shall be advertised and opposed.
(p) section 66(2)	Prescribing the manner of publication of the forms required by the registrar and his directions as to their use.
(q) section 67(1) and (2)	Prescribing restrictions with regard to information about applications and the manner of requesting information.

Provision and Authority	Subject-matter
(r) section 68(1) and (3)	Providing for the registrar to award costs and direct how and by what parties they are to be paid and for him to require a party to give security for costs.
(s) section 69	Providing for the giving of evidence by affidavit or statutory declaration in proceedings before the registrar, conferring on him the powers of an official referee of the Supreme Court and applying the rules applicable to the attendance of witnesses.
(t) section 76(1)	Providing for decisions of the registrar from which no appeal lies.
(u) section 78	Providing for rules for the purposes of any provision of the Act authorising rules or for prescribing anything required to be prescribed by any provision of the Act, and generally for regulating practice and procedure and for other matters.
(v) section 79	Prescribing fees in respect of applications and registration and other matters; providing for the payment of a single fee in respect of two or more matters and the circumstances in which a fee may be repaid or remitted.
(w) section 80(3)	Prescribing the manner of publication of the registrar's directions on hours of business and business days of the Office.
(x) section 81	Providing for the publication of a journal.
(y) section 82	Providing for the recognition of persons authorised to act as agents.
(z) section 88	Providing for the registrar to refuse to deal with certain agents.
(aa) Schedule 1, paragraph 6(2)	Prescribing the period during which the applicant for a collective mark must file the regulations.
(bb) Schedule 2, paragraph 7(2)	Prescribing the period during which the applicant for a certification mark must file the regulations.
(cc) Schedule 3—	
(i) paragraph 10(2)	In relation to an application for registration pending on the commencement of the Act, the exercise of powers under section 78 of the Act.
(ii) paragraph 11(2)	Prescribing the form of the notice claiming to have the registrability of the mark determined in accordance with the provisions of the Act.
(iii) paragraph 12	Providing for the exercise by the registrar of his powers under section 65 of the Act (adaptation of entries to new classification).
(iv) paragraph 14(5)	Providing as to the manner of claiming a right to priority on the basis of a relevant overseas application under section 39A of the Trade Marks Act 1938.
Regulations by the Commissioners of Customs and Excise under section 90	Prescribing the form in which notice is to be given under section 89 of the Act and requiring security or indemnity from a person giving such a notice.

INDEX

References are to article and Schedule number

COAL INDUSTRY

THE COAL INDUSTRY ACT 1994 (COMMENCEMENT NO. 2 AND TRANSITIONAL PROVISION) ORDER 1994

(S.I. 1994 No. 2552 (C. 53))

Made	-	-	-	*29th September 1994*
Laid before Parliament	-	-	*5th October 1994*
Coming into force	-	-	-	*31st October 1994*

INTRODUCTION

This Order brings into force all the provisions of the Coal Industry Act 1994 not brought into force directly by the Act, by S.I. 1994 No. 2189 (C. 45) or by virtue of the making of the Coal Industry (Restructuring Date) Order 1994 (S.I. 1994 No. 2553), except for s.22(2) (repeal of the Miners' Welfare Act 1952) and s.24 (abolition of the Domestic Coal Consumers' Council), the provisions of the Act specified in s.68(3) and the repeal of certain of the statutory provisions specified in Pt. III of Sched. 11 to the Act. All provisions (apart from those concerning town and country planning legislation, which are specified in Sched. 2 to the Order, and are brought into force on November 1, 1994) are brought into force on October 31, 1994. Transitional amendments are also made to s.56 of the Coal Industry Nationalisation Act 1946.

The Secretary of State, in exercise of the powers conferred on him by section 68(4) and (5) of the Coal Industry Act 1994 (1994 c. 21), and of all other powers enabling him in that behalf, hereby makes the following Order:

Citation, commencement and interpretation

1.—(1) This Order may be cited as the Coal Industry Act 1994 (Commencement No. 2 and Transitional Provision) Order 1994 and shall come into force on 31st October 1994.

(2) In this Order—

"the Act" means the Coal Industry Act 1994; and

"the 1946 Act" means the Coal Industry Nationalisation Act 1946 (1946 c. 59).

Provisions coming into force on 31st October 1994

2. The provisions of the Act specified in column 1 of Schedule 1 to this Order (which relate to the matters specified in column 2 thereof) shall come into force on 31st October 1994.

Provisions coming into force on 1st November 1994

3. The provisions of the Act specified in column 1 of Schedule 2 to this Order (which relate to the matters specified in column 2 thereof) shall come into force on 1st November 1994.

Transitional provision

4.—(1) This article shall have effect until the coming into force of the repeal by the Act (see section 68(4) and Schedule 11, Part III) of section 56 of the 1946 Act.

(2) Section 56 of the 1946 Act shall have effect with the following modifications—

(a) the insertion after the words "this Act" in the second place in which they occur in subsection (1) and in the first place in which they occur in subsection (2) of the words "or the Coal Industry Act 1994"; and

(b) the substitution for the words "this Act" in the third place in which they occur in subsection (1) and in the second place in which they occur in subsection (2) of the words "those Acts".

Tim Eggar
Minister for Industry and Energy,
Department of Trade and Industry

29th September 1994

Article 2   SCHEDULE 1

PROVISIONS COMING INTO FORCE ON 31ST OCTOBER 1994

(1) *Provisions of the Act*	(2) *Subject matter of provisions*
Section 2	Duties of the Authority with respect to licensing.
Section 3	Duties of the Authority with respect to property.
Section 15	Financial structure of successor companies.
Section 16	Target investment limit for Government holding in successor companies.
Section 19	Concessionary coal.
Section 20	Extinguishment of loans to the Corporation.
Section 22, except subsection (2)	Pensions and miners' welfare organisations.
Section 25	Coal-mining operations to be licensed.
Section 26	Grant of licences.
Section 27	Authorisation contained in licence.
Section 28	Conditions of licence: general.
Section 29	Conditions for the provision of security.
Section 30	Publication of licensing arrangements.
Section 35	Register of licences and orders.
Section 37	Areas of responsibility.
Section 45	Information to be provided by responsible persons.
Section 46	The subsidence adviser.
Section 47	Disputes etc. as to subsidence matters.
Section 56	Registration of rights.
Section 57	Public access to information held by the Authority.
Section 58	Liability for inaccurate information furnished to the Authority.
Section 59	Information to be kept confidential by the Authority.
Section 60	Annual report of the Authority.
Section 61	Report on financial assistance for coal-mining museums.
Section 67(1) and (8), so far as it relates to provisions coming into force by virtue of this Order. Section 67(7)	Amendments, transitional provisions, savings and repeals.
Schedule 3	Financial structure of successor companies.
Schedule 5	Pensions provision in respect of restructuring.

(1) *Provisions of the Act*	(2) *Subject matter of provisions*
In Schedule 9, paragraphs 8, 11(1) and (2) and 12 except in so far as they relate to provisions coming into force on the restructuring date by virtue of section 68(2)(d)	Minor and consequential amendments.
Schedule 10	Transitional provisions and savings.
Schedule 11, Part III, so far as it relates to the repeals set out in the Appendix to this Schedule	Repeals.

APPENDIX TO SCHEDULE 1

REPEALS TAKING EFFECT ON 31ST OCTOBER 1994

Chapter	Short title	Extent of repeal
1 & 2 Geo. 6. c. 52.	The Coal Act 1938.	Sections 52 to 55. Section 58.
6 & 7 Geo. 6. c. 38.	The Coal Act 1943.	Section 14. Sections 17 and 18.
9 & 10 Geo. 6. c. 59.	The Coal Industry Nationalisation Act 1946.	Section 52. Sections 57 and 58. In section 63, subsection (2).
6 & 7 Eliz. 2. c. 69.	The Opencast Coal Act 1958.	Section 17(4). Sections 19 and 20. In Schedule 6, paragraphs 3, 7, 12 and 22.
1967 c. 1.	The Land Commission Act 1967.	In section 14, subsection (5). In section 15, subsection (5).
1989 c. 29.	The Electricity Act 1989.	In section 57(2), the word "or" at the end of paragraph (b)(ix).

Article 3   SCHEDULE 2

PROVISIONS COMING INTO FORCE ON 1ST NOVEMBER 1994

(1) *Provisions of the Act*	(2) *Subject matter of provisions*
In Schedule 9, paragraphs 13(3) and 39(2) and (3).	Minor and consequential amendments.
Schedule 11, Part III, so far as it relates to the repeals set out in the Appendix to this Schedule.	Repeals.

APPENDIX TO SCHEDULE 2

REPEALS TAKING EFFECT ON 1ST NOVEMBER 1994

Chapter	Short title	Extent of repeal
1972 c. 52.	The Town and Country Planning (Scotland) Act 1972.	Section 251(3)(b). Section 259.
1990 c. 8.	The Town and Country Planning Act 1990.	In section 315(4), paragraph (b) and the word "or" immediately preceding it. Section 317.

INDEX

References are to article and Schedule number

GAS

THE GAS (EXEMPT SUPPLIES) ACT 1993 (COMMENCEMENT) ORDER 1994

(S.I. 1994 No. 2568 (C. 54))

Made -   -   -   -   -   *1st October 1994*

INTRODUCTION

This Order appoints October 31, 1994 as the day for bringing into force the Gas (Exempt Supplies) Act 1993 for the purposes of s.4(2) of that Act.

The Secretary of State, in exercise of the powers conferred on him by section 4(2) of the Gas (Exempt Supplies) Act 1993 (1993 c. 1) hereby makes the following Order:

1. This Order may be cited as the Gas (Exempt Supplies) Act 1993 (Commencement) Order 1994.

2. The Gas (Exempt Supplies) Act 1993 shall come into force on 31st October 1994.

Tim Eggar
Minister for Industry and Energy,
1st October 1994   Department of Trade and Industry

INDEX

References are to article number

MAGISTRATES' COURTS

THE POLICE AND MAGISTRATES' COURTS ACT 1994 (COMMENCEMENT NO. 3 AND TRANSITIONAL PROVISIONS) ORDER 1994

(S.I. 1994 No. 2594 (C. 55))

Made - - - - - -	*8th October 1994*
Laid before Parliament - - -	*10th October 1994*
Coming into force - - - -	*1st November 1994*

INTRODUCTION

This Order brings into force on November 1, 1994 various sections of Pt. IV, which relates to magistrates' courts, of the Police and Magistrates' Courts Act 1994 (c. 29) and certain provisions of the Act in Pt. I of Sched. 8 (minor and consequential amendments) and Pt. II of Sched. 9 (repeals). Section 79 of the Act is brought into force only for the purpose of constituting a magistrates' courts committee for the inner London area. Previous commencement orders, S.I. 1994 Nos. 2025 (C. 38) and 2151 (C. 44) brought into force provisions relating to policing in England and Wales and Northern Ireland.

The Lord Chancellor, in exercise of the powers conferred on him by section 94(2), (4), (5) and (7) of the Police and Magistrates' Courts Act 1994 (1994 c. 29), hereby makes the following Order:

Citation and Commencement

1.—(1) This Order may be cited as the Police and Magistrates' Courts Act 1994 (Commencement No. 3 and Transitional Provisions) Order 1994.

(2) This Order shall come into force on 1st November 1994.

Interpretation

2. In this Order—

"the 1979 Act" means the Justices of the Peace Act 1979 (1979 c. 55);

"the 1994 Act" means the Police and Magistrates' Courts Act 1994.

3. Subject to article 5, the following provisions of the 1994 Act shall come into force by virtue of this Order—

(a) section 69 (alteration of magistrates' courts committee areas);

(b) section 70 (constitution of magistrates' courts committees);

(c) section 71 (regulations as to constitution etc. of magistrates' courts committees);

(d) section 74 (reports and plans);

(e) section 78 (independence of justices' clerk and staff in relation to legal functions);

(f) section 85 (regulations as to accounts and audit);

(g) section 86 (inspectors of the magistrates' courts service);

(h) section 87 (powers of inspectors);

(i) section 88 (default powers), except for subsection (6);

(j) section 89 (studies by Audit Commission);

(k) section 90 (regulations under the 1979 Act);

(l) section 91(1) (magistrates' courts: minor and consequential amendments), so far as it relates to the entries in Part 1 of Schedule 8 referred to in article 6 below;

(m) section 92 (interpretation of Part IV);

(n) section 93 (repeals), so far as it relates to the entries in Part II of Schedule 9 (magistrates' courts: repeals) referred to in article 7 below.

4. Section 79 of the 1994 Act (inner London area) and section 93, so far as it relates to the entry in Part II of Schedule 9 in respect of section 35 of the 1979

Act, shall come into force for the purpose only of enabling a magistrates' courts committee for the inner London area to be constituted in accordance with regulations made under section 21 of the 1979 Act as amended by section 71 of the 1994 Act.

5.—(1) Sections 70 and 71 of the 1994 Act shall come into force subject to the transitional provisions specified below.

(2) Notwithstanding the substitution by section 70 of a new section 20 ("the new section 20") for the old section 20 ("the old section 20") of the 1979 Act—

(a) the old section 20 shall continue to apply in relation to magistrates' courts committees constituted in accordance with the Magistrates' Courts Committees (Constitution) Regulations 1973 (S.I. 1973/1522 as amended by S.I. 1980 No. 1258, S.I. 1985 No. 1258 and S.I. 1992 No. 2047) as if the new section 20 had not been so substituted;

(b) the new section 20 shall come into force only in relation to magistrates' courts committees constituted in accordance with regulations made under section 21 of the 1979 Act as amended by section 71 of the 1994 Act;

(c) notwithstanding the amendments made by section 71(1), (2) and (3) to section 21 of the 1979 Act, section 21 of that Act shall continue to apply in relation to magistrates' courts committees constituted in accordance with the Magistrates' Courts Committees (Constitution) Regulations 1973 as if those amendments had not been made.

Magistrates' courts: minor and consequential amendments of the 1979 Act

6. The entries in Part 1 of Schedule 8 (amendments of the 1979 Act) referred to in paragraph (1) of article 3 above are—

(a) paragraph 2(1) and (2) (amendment of section 17(1));
(b) paragraph 2(1), (3) and (4) (amendment of section 17(2) and insertion of new section 17(2A));
(c) paragraph 3 (amendment of section 18);
(d) paragraph 4 (amendment of section 19);
(e) paragraph 6 (amendment of section 23);
(f) paragraph 7 (amendment of section 24);
(g) paragraph 8 (amendment of section 24A);
(h) paragraph 9 (amendment of section 24B);
(i) paragraph 17 (amendment of section 42);
(j) paragraph 22 (substitution of new definition of "magistrate" and insertion of definition of "magistrates' courts committee area" in section 70), except that the former definition of "magistrate" in section 70 shall continue to apply for the purposes of interpretation of the old section 20 (as defined in paragraph (2) of article 5 above).

Repeals

7. The entries in Part II of Schedule 9 (repeals: magistrates' courts) referred to in paragraph (n) of article 3 above are—

(a) section 12(7) of the 1979 Act;
(b) section 18(2) of the 1979 Act;
(c) section 19(3) and (4) of the 1979 Act;
(d) section 21(1) of the 1979 Act;
(e) section 23(1) of the 1979 Act;
(f) section 24(1)(a), (2) and (5) of the 1979 Act;
(g) section 24A(1) of the 1979 Act;
(h) the definition of "joint committee area" in section 70 of the 1979 Act.

Dated 8th October 1994   *Mackay of Clashfern, C*

INDEX

References are to article number

LAND REGISTRATION, SCOTLAND

THE LAND REGISTRATION (SCOTLAND) ACT 1979 (COMMENCEMENT NO. 8) ORDER 1994

(S.I. 1994 No. 2588 (C. 56) (S. 124))

Made - - - - - *29th September 1994*

INTRODUCTION

This Order brings into force, on April 1, 1995, in the area of the County of Fife, s.2(1) and (2) of the Land Registration (Scotland) Act 1979 (c. 33) which provides for the circumstances in which an interest in land shall be registrable, and s.3(3) which provides that certain persons are to obtain a real right only by registration.

The Secretary of State, in exercise of the powers conferred on him by section 30(2) of the Land Registration (Scotland) Act 1979 (1979 c. 33) and of all other powers enabling him in that behalf, hereby makes the following Order:

1. This Order may be cited as the Land Registration (Scotland) Act 1979 (Commencement No. 8) Order 1994.

2. Sections 2(1) and (2) and 3(3) of the Land Registration (Scotland) Act 1979 shall come into force on 1st April 1995 in the area, for the purpose of registration of writs, of the County of Fife.

St Andrew's House, Edinburgh
29th September 1994

Fraser of Carmyllie
Minister of State,
Scottish Office

INDEX

References are to article number

NATIONAL HEALTH SERVICE, SCOTLAND

THE NATIONAL HEALTH SERVICE AND COMMUNITY CARE ACT 1990 (COMMENCEMENT NO. 11) (SCOTLAND) ORDER 1994

(S.I. 1994 No. 2658 (C. 57) (S. 136))

Made - - - - - *10th October 1994*

INTRODUCTION
This Order brings into force provisions of the National Health Service and Community Care Act 1990 (c. 19), concerned with the transfer of responsibility for auditing the accounts of certain health service bodies in Scotland to the Commission for Local Authority Accounts in Scotland (which is renamed the Accounts Commission for Scotland). Transfer of that responsibility takes effect as at April 1, 1995.

The Secretary of State, in exercise of the powers conferred on him by section 67(2) of the National Health Service and Community Care Act 1990 (1990 c. 19) and of all other powers enabling him in that behalf, hereby makes the following Order:

Citation and interpretation

1.—(1) This Order may be cited as the National Health Service and Community Care Act 1990 (Commencement No. 11) (Scotland) Order 1994.

(2) In this Order, "the Act" means the National Health Service and Community Care Act 1990.

Days appointed

2. 24th October 1994 is appointed as the day for the coming into force of—
  (a) section 36(1) of the Act (accounts and audit of NHS trusts and fund-holding practices), so far as it relates to the provisions of Schedule 7 to the Act specified in paragraphs (b) and (c) below;
  (b) paragraph 1 of Schedule 7 to the Act (amendments relating to audit of accounts of Scottish health service bodies), so far as it relates to the provisions specified in paragraph (c) below; and
  (c) sub-paragraphs (2)(d) and (6) of paragraph 3 of that Schedule, and sub-paragraph (1) of that paragraph so far as it relates to those sub-paragraphs.

3. 1st December 1994 is appointed as the day for the coming into force of—
  (a) section 36(1) of the Act, so far as it relates to the provisions of Schedule 7 to the Act specified in paragraphs (b) to (e) below;
  (b) paragraph 1 of Schedule 7 to the Act, so far as it relates to the provisions specified in paragraphs (c) to (e) below;
  (c) paragraph 2 of that Schedule;
  (d) sub-paragraphs (2)(a) to (c) and (5) of paragraph 3 of that Schedule, and sub-paragraph (1) of that paragraph so far as it relates to those sub-paragraphs; and
  (e) paragraphs 13 and 15 of that Schedule.

4. 1st April 1995 is appointed as the day for the coming into force of—

(a) section 36(1) of, and Schedule 7 to, the Act (so far as not then in force);

(b) section 66(2) of the Act, so far as it relates to the provisions on Schedule 10 to the Act specified in paragraph (c) below; and

(c) in Schedule 10 to the Act (repeals), the repeals of—

    (i) section 86(2) of the National Health Service (Scotland) Act 1978 (1978 c. 29); and

    (ii) section 36(5) of the Act.

J Allan Stewart
St Andrew's House, Edinburgh   Parliamentary Under Secretary of State,
10th October 1994   Scottish Office

INDEX

References are to article number

NATIONAL LOTTERY
BETTING, GAMING AND LOTTERIES

THE NATIONAL LOTTERY ETC. ACT 1993
(COMMENCEMENT NO. 3) ORDER 1994

(S.I. 1994 No. 2659 (C. 58))

Made -   -   -   -   -   *10th October 1994*

INTRODUCTION

This Order brings into force on November 14, 1994, Pt. IV of the National Lottery etc. Act 1993 (c. 39). The provisions of Pt. IV relate to pool betting and make amendments to the Betting, Gaming and Lotteries Act 1963 (c. 2). Previous commencement orders are S.I. 1993 No. 2632 and S.I. 1994 No. 1055.

The Secretary of State, in exercise of the powers conferred on him by section 65 of the National Lottery etc. Act 1993 (1993 c. 39), hereby makes the following Order:

1. This Order may be cited as the National Lottery etc. Act 1993 (Commencement No. 3) Order 1994.

2. Part IV of the National Lottery etc. Act 1993 shall come into force on 14th November 1994.

Home Office

Michael Howard
One of Her Majesty's Principal
10th October 1994   Secretaries of State

INDEX

References are to article number

CUSTOMS AND EXCISE

THE FINANCE ACT 1994, PART I, (APPOINTED DAY ETC.) ORDER 1994

(S.I. 1994 No. 2679 (C. 59))

Made - - - - -   *17th October 1994*

INTRODUCTION

This Order appoints November 1, 1994 as the day on which, for the purposes of air passenger duty, the appeals and penalties provisions set out in Chap. II of Pt. I of, and Sched. 5 to, the Finance Act 1994 (c. 9) come into force. It also appoints January 1, 1995 as the day on which, for all other purposes, the appeals and penalties provisions set out in Chap. II of Pt. I of, and Scheds. 4 and 5 and Pt. III of Sched. 26 to, the Act come into force. The Order also makes some transitional provisions.

The Commissioners of Customs and Excise, in exercise of the powers conferred on them by section 19 of the Finance Act 1994 (1994 c. 9; section 17(1) applies the definition of "the Commissioners" in section 1(1) of the Customs and Excise Management Act 1979 (c. 2); section 17(2) defines "the Management Act") and of all other powers enabling them in that behalf, hereby make the following Order:

Citation

1. This Order may be cited as the Finance Act 1994, Part I, (Appointed Day etc.) Order 1994.

Commencement for the purpose of air passenger duty

2. For the purpose of air passenger duty (air passenger duty is charged in accordance with the provisions of Chapter IV of Part I of, and Schedule 6 to, the Act), the day appointed as the day on which the provisions of the Finance Act 1994 ("the Act") specified in the first column of the Schedule to this Order come into force is 1st November 1994.

Commencement for other purposes

3. The day appointed as the day on which Chapter II of Part I of, and Schedule 4, Schedule 5 and Part III of Schedule 26 to, the Act come into force (insofar as they are not then already in force) is 1st January 1995.

Transitional provisions

4.—(1) Paragraphs (2) to (4) below shall have effect without prejudice to the operation of section 16 of the Interpretation Act 1978 (1978 c. 30).

(2) Where at a time prior to the coming into force of section 18(3) of the Act a referee was appointed under section 127 of the Management Act, such appointment and any arbitration that referee conducts shall not be affected by any provision of the Act brought into force by this Order.

(3) None of the provisions of the Act brought into force by this Order shall affect the liability of any person to be prosecuted for any offence in respect of conduct which occurred before 1st January 1995.

(4) From 1st January 1995 section 12 of the Act shall apply to duty which appears to have become due before that date as it applies to duty which is due after 31st December 1994.

New King's Beam House
22 Upper Ground
London SE1 9PJ

Leonard Harris
17th October 1994   Commissioner of Customs and Excise

Article 2   SCHEDULE

Provisions of the Act	*Subject matter of provisions*
section 8	Penalty for evasion of excise duty
section 9(1) to (8)	Penalties for contraventions of statutory requirements
sections 10 and 11	Exceptions and breaches of walking possession agreements
section 12(1) to (6), (7) (with the exception of, in paragraph (a) the references to sections 100(3), 136(1), 159(6), 170(1) and (2) and 170B(1) of the Management Act, and paragraphs (b) and (c)) and (8)	Assessments to excise duty
section 13	Assessments to penalties
section 14(1) (with the exception of paragraph (a)) and (2) to (5)	Requirement for review of a decision
section 15	Review procedure
section 16(1) to (5), (6) (with the exception of paragraphs (b) and (c)), (7) and (8)	Appeals to a tribunal
section 17	Interpretation
section 18(1), (2), (7) and (8)	Consequential modifications of enactments
paragraphs 9 and 10 of Schedule 5	Decisions concerning air passenger duty subject to review and appeal and interpretation of Schedule

INDEX

References are to article number and the Schedule

INTELLIGENCE SERVICES

THE INTELLIGENCE SERVICES ACT 1994 (COMMENCEMENT) ORDER 1994

(S.I. 1994 No. 2734 (C. 60))

Made   -   -   -   -   -   *15th October 1994*

INTRODUCTION

This Order brings into force on December 15, 1994 the provisions of the Intelligence Services Act 1994 (c. 13), except that for the purposes of making any Order in Council under s.12(4) it is brought into force on November 2, 1994.

In exercise of the powers conferred upon me by section 12(2) of the Intelligence Services Act 1994 (1994 c. 13), I hereby make the following Order:

1. This Order may be cited as the Intelligence Services Act 1994 (Commencement) Order 1994.

2. The Intelligence Services Act 1994 shall come into force on 15th December 1994 except that for the purposes of making any Order in Council under section 12(4) thereof it shall come into force on 2nd November 1994.

Douglas Hurd
Her Majesty's Principal Secretary of
State for Foreign and Commonwealth Affairs

15th October 1994

INDEX

References are to article number

MERCHANT SHIPPING

THE MERCHANT SHIPPING ACT 1979 (COMMENCEMENT NO. 14) ORDER 1994

(S.I. 1994 No. 2789 (C. 61))

Made - - - - - *2nd November 1994*

INTRODUCTION

This Order brings into force, on November 22, 1994, s.38(4) of the Merchant Shipping Act 1979 (c. 39), which substitutes special drawing rights for gold francs in certain sections of the Merchant Shipping Act 1974 (c. 43). The Order also brings into force consequential repeals in the 1974 Act.

The Secretary of State for Transport, in exercise of the powers conferred by section 52(2) of the Merchant Shipping Act 1979 (c. 39), hereby makes the following Order:—

1. This Order may be cited as the Merchant Shipping Act 1979 (Commencement No. 14) Order 1994.

2. The provisions of the Act specified in the first column of the Schedule to this Order (which relate to the matters specified in the second column) shall come into force on 22nd November 1994, immediately after the Coming into force of the Merchant Shipping (Sterling Equivalents) (Revocation) Order 1994 (S.I. 1994 No. 2788).

Signed by authority of the
Secretary of State for Transport

Goschen
Parliamentary Under Secretary of State,
Department of Transport

2nd November 1994

Article 2   SCHEDULE

PROVISIONS COMING INTO FORCE ON 22ND NOVEMBER 1994

Provisions of Merchant Shipping Act 1979	*Subject matter of provisions*
Section 38(4).	Replacement of gold francs by special drawing rights for certain purposes of the Merchant Shipping Act 1974.
Section 50(4) so far as it relates to the provisions of Schedule 7 set out below.	Repeals.
In Schedule 7, the repeal of section 1(6) and (7) of the Merchant Shipping Act 1974.	Enactment repealed.

INDEX

References are to article number and Schedule

LOCAL GOVERNMENT, ENGLAND AND WALES

WALES

THE LOCAL GOVERNMENT (WALES) ACT 1994 (COMMENCEMENT NO. 2) ORDER 1994

(S.I. 1994 No. 2790 (C. 62))

Made - - - - - *19th October 1994*

INTRODUCTION

This Order brings into force, on October 24, 1994, some definition provisions of the Local Government (Wales) Act 1994 (c. 19) which have effect only for the interpretation of Pt. IV of the Local Government Act 1972 (c. 70), provisions in relation to the Local Government Boundary Commission for Wales and related matters and consequential repeals.

The Secretary of State for Wales, in exercise of the powers conferred upon him by sections 63(5) and 66(3) of the Local Government (Wales) Act 1994 (c. 19), hereby makes the following Order:—

1.—(1) This Order may be cited as the Local Government (Wales) Act 1994 (Commencement No. 2) Order 1994.

(2) In this Order—

"the 1994 Act" means the Local Government (Wales) Act 1994;

"the 1972 Act" means the Local Government Act 1972 (c. 70).

2.—(1) Subject to paragraphs (2) and (3) below, the provisions of the 1994 Act which are specified in the Schedule to this Order shall come into force on 24th October 1994.

(2) The provisions of section 1(5), (6) and (8) of the 1994 Act brought into force by this Order shall have effect only for the interpretation of Part IV of the 1972 Act as amended in consequence of this Order.

(3) The provisions of sections 54, 55(5), 56(1) and (5), 58(4), 59(2), 72, 73, and 270(1) of the 1972 Act in force immediately prior to the commencement of this Order shall continue to have effect in relation to the administration of local government in Wales before 1st April 1996.

John Redwood

19th October 1994   Secretary of State for Wales

Article 2(1)   SCHEDULE

PROVISIONS OF THE 1994 ACT COMING INTO FORCE ON 24TH OCTOBER 1994

Provision of the 1994 Act	*Subject matter of provision*
Section 1(4)	Definitions — introductory.
Section 1(5)	Definition of "local authority".
Section 1(6)	Definition of "local government area".
Section 1(8)	Definition of "principal area".
Paragraphs 4 and 5 of Schedule 2 and section 1(3) so far as it relates thereto	The Local Government Boundary Commission for Wales and related matters.
Paragraphs 1, 7, 8(5), 9(4)(b), 11(2), 12(b), 18, 19 and 57 of Schedule 15 and section 66(5) so far as it relates thereto	As above.
In Schedule 18, the repeals to sections 55(5)(a), 59(2) and 72(2) of the 1972 Act and section 66(8) so far as it relates thereto	Consequential repeals.

INDEX

References are to article number and Schedule

LOCAL GOVERNMENT, SCOTLAND
WATER SUPPLY, SCOTLAND

THE LOCAL GOVERNMENT ETC. (SCOTLAND) ACT 1994 (COMMENCEMENT No. 1) ORDER 1994

(S.I. 1994 No. 2850 (C. 63) (S. 145))

Made - - - - - *7th November 1994*

INTRODUCTION

This Order brings into force various provisions, specified in Scheds. 1, 2 and 3, of the Local Government etc. (Scotland) Act 1994 (c. 39) on November 8, 1994 and January 4, 1995. It also modifies certain provisions of the Sewerage (Scotland) Act 1968 (c. 47) and the Control of Pollution Act 1974 (c. 40) (which provisions are amended or added by provisions of the 1994 Act brought into force by art. 3 of this Order) in their application in the period from January 4, 1995 to April 1, 1996. The provisions in art. 4 are modified by the substitution of references to "local" authorities for the references to "sewerage" authorities.

Article 3(c)(xiii) was amended by S.I. 1994 No. 3150 (C. 74) (S. 174).

The Secretary of State, in exercise of the powers conferred on him by sections 182(2) and 184(2) of the Local Government etc. (Scotland) Act 1994 (c. 39) and of all other powers enabling him in that behalf, hereby makes the following Order:

Citation and interpretation

1.—(1) This Order may be cited as the Local Government etc. (Scotland) Act 1994 (Commencement No. 1) Order 1994.

(2) In this Order, "the Act" means the Local Government etc. (Scotland) Act 1994.

Days appointed

2. 8th November 1994 is the day appointed for the coming into force of the provisions of the Act specified in column 1 of Schedule 1 to this Order (which relate to the matters specified in column 2 of that Schedule).

3. 4th January 1995 is the day appointed for the coming into force of—

(a) the provisions of the Act specified in column 1 of Schedule 2 to this Order (which relate to the matters specified in column 2 of that Schedule);

(b) section 180 of the Act, so far as it relates to the provisions of Schedules 13 and 14 to the Act specified in paragraphs (c) and (d) below;

(c) in Schedule 13 to the Act (minor and consequential amendments)—

    (i) paragraph 3;

    (ii) paragraph 4(1) and (3);

    (iii) paragraph 27(1), (2) and (3)(a)(i);

    (iv) paragraph 60(1) and (3)(a) to (c);

    (v) paragraph 71(1) and (6);

    (vi) paragraph 75(1), (2)(b), (d) and (e), (13)(a)(ii), (14), (17)(d), (18)(c), (19)(b), (20) and (24);

    (vii) paragraph 92(1), (20), (22), (26), (27), (60) and (70);

    (viii) paragraph 95(1) and (2)(a), (b) and (d);

    (ix) paragraph 100(1) and (9)(f) and (g);

    (x) paragraph 119(1), (5)(d), (7)(c)(ii), (34), (36), (42) to (45), (46) (so far as that sub-paragraph relates to the definition of "wholesome" in section 76L(1) of the Water (Scotland) Act 1980 (c. 45; section 76L(1) was added by the Water Act 1989 (c. 15), Schedule 22, paragraph 1)), (51) and (53)(a)(iv) and (vi);

    (xi) paragraph 129(1) and (20)(b);

    (xii) paragraph 156(1), (3) and (4);

    (xiii) paragraph 176 [...] (19)(c) and (d); and

(xiv) paragraph 177; and

(d) the repeals in Schedule 14 to the Act specified in Schedule 3 to this Order.

Modifications

4.—(1) The relevant provisions (being provisions amended or as the case may be added by provisions in the Act brought into force by article 3 of this Order) shall in the period from 4th January 1995 until 1st April 1996 apply as if modified by the substitution of the word "local" for the word "sewerage" in each place where that word appears in the relevant provisions (those modifications being such as appear to the Secretary of State requisite having regard to the fact that other provisions of Part II of, and Schedule 13 to, the Act are not for the time being in effect).

(2) In paragraph (1) above, "the relevant provisions" means—

(a) sections 1(2) and (4), 3A, 16A, 20(5), 22(2A), 23 and 48 of the Sewerage (Scotland) Act 1968 (c. 47; the provisions listed are amended or added by way of section 101 of, and paragraph 75(2), (14), (17), (19), (20) and (24) of Schedule 13 to, the Act); and

(b) section 32(2) of the Control of Pollution Act 1974 (c. 40; section 32(2)) is substituted by paragraph 95(2)(b) of Schedule 13 to the Act.

St Andrew's House, Edinburgh

7th November 1994

Ian Lang
One of Her Majesty's Principal Secretaries of State

Article 2   SCHEDULE 1

PROVISIONS OF THE ACT COMING INTO FORCE ON 8TH NOVEMBER 1994

Column 1 *Provision of the Act*	*Column 2* *Subject matter*
Section 1	Local government areas in Scotland
Section 5	Elections and term of office of councillors
Section 7	Establishment of new local authorities and supplementary provisions
Section 12	Staff commission
Section 57	Power and duty of existing local authorities to assist new authorities
Section 61	Interpretation of Part I
Section 97(6)	Extension of staff commission functions
Section 125	Interpretation of Part II
Section 137(1) (so far as it applies section 12 of the Act)	Extension of staff commission functions
Section 157	Certain orders relating to valuation not to be treated as hybrid
Section 177(1) and (3) (so far as those subsections relate to the entry in Part III of the House of Commons Disqualification Act 1975 (c. 24) concerning any member of the staff commission)	Parliamentary disqualification
Section 178	Financial provisions
Section 181(1), (2), (8) and (9)	Consequential and supplementary provisions
Section 183(1)	Interpretation
Section 184	Short title, commencement and extent
Schedule 1	New local government areas
Schedule 2	Establishment of new local authorities

Article 3(a) SCHEDULE 2

PROVISIONS OF THE ACT COMING INTO FORCE ON 4TH JANUARY 1995

Column 1 Provision of the Act	*Column 2* Subject matter
Section 8	Transfer of employees
Section 9	Effect of section 8 on contracts of employment
Section 10	Continuity of employment
Section 11	Remuneration of employees of local authorities
Section 13	Compensation for loss of office or diminution of emoluments
Section 14	Employment by new authorities
Section 15	Transfer of property
Section 16	Property held on trust
Section 17	Educational endowments
Section 24	Transitional provisions: finance
Section 34	Reorganisation of police areas
Section 38	Roads
Section 40	Establishment etc. of Strathclyde Passenger Transport Authority
Section 44	Restriction on order-making powers of existing authorities
Section 47	Proceedings in district courts: transitional provisions
Section 49	Justice of the peace
Section 50	Stipendiary magistrates
Section 51(3)	Registration offices
Section 60	Applications to sheriff in cases of difficulty
Section 97 (so far as not already in force)	Staff: application of Chapter 2 of Part I etc.
Section 101	Authorisation of construction of certain private sewers etc.
Section 104	Disapplication of restrictions on disclosure of information
Section 113	Actings of Secretary of State on default of water authority
Section 114	Publication and provision of information as respects quality of private supplies of water
Section 115	Regulations as to certain procedures
Section 124	Cancellation of obligation to contribute towards certain expenses incurred as respects sewerage, or disposal of sewage, in rural localities
Section 126	Orders under Part II
Section 137 (so far as not already in force)	Staff: application of Chapter 2 of Part I
Section 141	Byelaws under section 121 of the Civic Government (Scotland) Act 1982 (c. 45)
Section 143	Self-governing schools: certain proposals under the Education (Scotland) Act 1980 (c. 44)
Section 146	Definition of "road"
Section 147	Provisions consequential on making of special road order
Section 148	Toll orders
Section 149	Road works register
Section 150	Traffic signs
Section 151	Exclusion from valuation roll of shootings, deer forests, fishings and fish counters
Section 165	Powers of authorities to borrow and lend money
Section 166	Grants in relation to ethnic minorities
Section 167	Special grants
Section 170	Effective use of resources

Column 1 *Provision of the Act*	Column 2 *Subject matter*
Section 172	Duty of Secretary of State to establish area tourist boards
Section 173	Power of Secretary of State to amend and revoke schemes
Section 175	Provision of assistance to boards by old authorities
Section 179	Savings
Section 182	Further transitional provisions
Schedule 5	Strathclyde Passenger Transport Authority

Article 3(d) SCHEDULE 3

REPEALS IN SCHEDULE 14 TO THE ACT COMING INTO FORCE ON 4TH JANUARY 1995

Chapter	*Short title*	*Extent of repeal*
18 & 19 Vict. c. 68	The Burial Grounds (Scotland) Act 1855	In section 10, the words "any of the Lords Ordinary of" and the words from "And provided" to "such dwelling house". In section 11, the words from "but no ground" to the end.
10 & 11 Geo. 6 c. 41	The Fire Services Act 1947	In section 15(2), the proviso. In section 36, in subsection (2), the words "and thirty-six" and "and twenty-three".
1973 c. 65	The Local Government (Scotland) Act 1973	In section 84, subsections (2) and (4).
1980 c. 45	The Water (Scotland) Act 1980	Sections 64 to 67. In section 76H(8), the words from "; and section 65" to the end. In section 76L(1), the definition of "wholesome". In section 109, in subsection (1), in the definition of "owner", the words ", save in sections 64 to 67,".
1982 c. 45	The Civic Government (Scotland) Act 1982	In section 121, in subsection (6), the words from "and of" to "that proposal" and, in subsection (7), the words from "but the" to "his consent" and the word "nevertheless".

INDEX

References are to article numbers and Schedules

ENVIRONMENTAL PROTECTION

THE ENVIRONMENTAL PROTECTION ACT 1990 (COMMENCEMENT No. 16) ORDER 1994

(S.I. 1994 No. 2854 (C. 64))

Made - - - - - *6th November 1994*

INTRODUCTION

This Order brings s.162(2) of the Environmental Protection Act 1990 (c. 43) into force so far as it relates to the repeal of the Alkali, &c. Works Regulation Act 1906 (c. 14).

The Secretary of State, in exercise of his powers under section 164(3) of the Environmental Protection Act 1990 (c. 43), hereby makes the following Order:

Citation

1. This Order may be cited as the Environmental Protection Act 1990 (Commencement No. 16) Order 1994.

Provision coming into force on or after 1st December 1994

2.—(1) Section 162(2) of the Environmental Protection Act 1990, insofar as it relates to the repeal of the Alkali, &c. Works Regulation Act 1906 (c. 14) ("the 1906 Act") in Part I of Schedule 16, shall come into force, for the purposes of the application of the 1906 Act to activities which fall within a description of a process which has been but has ceased to be a prescribed process—

(a) on 1st December 1994; or, if later,

(b) on the date on which that description of process ceases to be a prescribed process.

(2) In this article "prescribed process" has the meaning given in section 1 of the Environmental Protection Act 1990.

Signed by authority of the Secretary of State

Paul Beresford
Parliamentary Under Secretary of State,
6th November 1994   Department of the Environment

INDEX

References are to article number

SOCIAL SECURITY

THE SOCIAL SECURITY (INCAPACITY FOR WORK) ACT 1994 (COMMENCEMENT) ORDER 1994

(S.I. 1994 No. 2926 (C. 65))

Made - - - - -   *17th November 1994*

INTRODUCTION

This Order brings into force provisions of the Social Security (Incapacity for Work) Act 1994 (c. 18). For the purposes of the rate of statutory sick pay, the commencement date is April 6, 1995, for the purposes of up-rating the rate of incapacity benefit, statutory sick pay and severe disablement allowance and enabling regulations to be made, the commencement date is November 18, 1994 and for all remaining purposes the commencement date is April 13, 1995.

The Secretary of State for Social Security, in exercise of the powers conferred by section 16(3) of the Social Security (Incapacity for Work) Act 1994 (c. 18) and of all other powers enabling him in that behalf, hereby makes the following Order:

Citation and interpretation

1.—(1) This Order may be cited as the Social Security (Incapacity for Work) Act 1994 (Commencement) Order 1994.

(2) In this Order, unless the context otherwise requires, references to sections and Schedules are references to sections of and Schedules to the Social Security (Incapacity for Work) Act 1994.

Appointed days

2.—(1) The day appointed for the coming into force of the sections specified in Part I of the Schedule to this Order is 18th November 1994.

(2) The day appointed for the coming into force of the sections specified in Part II of the Schedule to this Order—

(a) for the purpose only of authorising the making of regulations expressed to come into force on 13th April 1995, is 18th November 1994; and

(b) for all other purposes, is 13th April 1995.

(3) The day appointed for the coming into force of the section specified in Part III of the Schedule to this Order is 6th April 1995.

(4) The day appointed for the coming into force of the sections and Schedules specified in Part IV of the Schedule to this Order is 13th April 1995.

Signed by authority of the Secretary of State for Social Security.

William Hague
Minister of State,
Department of Social Security

17th November 1994

Article 2   SCHEDULE

PART I

PROVISIONS COMING INTO FORCE ON 18TH NOVEMBER 1994

Provisions of the Social Security (Incapacity for Work) Act 1994	Subject Matter
Section 2(3) and (7)	Up-rating of incapacity benefit.
Section 4	Power to provide for the transition to incapacity benefit.
Section 7	Power to provide for the transition to the new test of incapacity for work.
Section 8(2)	Up-rating of statutory sick pay.
Section 9(4)	Up-rating of severe disablement allowance.
Section 12	General power to make transitional and consequential provisions.

PART II

PROVISIONS COMING INTO FORCE ON 18TH NOVEMBER 1994
FOR THE PURPOSES ONLY OF THE MAKING OF REGULATIONS AND FOR ALL OTHER PURPOSES ON 13TH APRIL 1995

Provisions of the Social Security (Incapacity for Work) Act 1994	Subject Matter
Section 2(1) and (5)	Rate of incapacity benefit.
Section 3(1)	Supplementary provisions relating to incapacity benefit.
Section 5	Test of incapacity for work.
Section 6	Supplementary provisions and adjudication relating to test of incapacity for work.
Section 9(1), (2) and (3)	Severe disablement allowance.
Section 10(1) and (3)	Disability working allowance.

PART III

PROVISIONS COMING INTO FORCE ON 6TH APRIL 1995

Provisions of the Social Security (Incapacity for Work) Act 1994	Subject Matter
Section 8(1), (3) and (4)	Rate of statutory sick pay.

PART IV

PROVISIONS COMING INTO FORCE ON 13TH APRIL 1995

Provisions of the Social Security (Incapacity for Work) Act 1994	*Subject Matter*
Section 1	Entitlement to incapacity benefit.
Section 2(2), (4) and (6)	Rate of incapacity benefit.
Section 3(2)	Amendment of Schedule 3 to the Social Security Contributions and Benefits Act 1992 (c. 4) (contribution conditions).
Section 10(2)	Amendment of section 129(1) of the Social Security Contributions and Benefits Act 1992 (disability working allowance).
Section 11 and Schedules 1 and 2	Consequential amendments and repeals.
Section 13	Saving for existing enactments.

INDEX

References are to article number and Schedule

CRIMINAL LAW, ENGLAND AND WALES
CRIMINAL LAW, SCOTLAND
CRIMINAL LAW, NORTHERN IRELAND

THE CRIMINAL JUSTICE AND PUBLIC ORDER ACT 1994 (COMMENCEMENT No. 1) ORDER 1994

(S.I. 1994 No. 2935 (C. 66))

Made -   -   -   -   -   *19th November 1994*

INTRODUCTION

This Order is the first commencement order to be made in respect of the Criminal Justice and Public Order Act 1994 (c. 33) and it brings into force two amendments to the Backing of Warrants (Republic of Ireland) Act 1965 (c. 45) on December 19, 1994.

In exercise of the powers conferred on me by section 172(2) of the Criminal Justice and Public Order Act 1994 (c. 33), I hereby make the following Order:

1. This Order may be cited as the Criminal Justice and Public Order Act 1994 (Commencement No. 1) Order 1994 and extends to the United Kingdom and to the Channel Islands and the Isle of Man.

2. Section 159(1), (2) and (4) of the Criminal Justice and Public Order Act 1994 (Backing of Warrants: Republic of Ireland) shall come into force on 19th December 1994.

Home Office   *Michael Howard*
19th November 1994   One of Her Majesty's Principal Secretaries of State

INDEX

References are to article number

CUSTOMS AND EXCISE

THE FINANCE ACT 1993, SECTION 4, (APPOINTED DAY) ORDER 1994

(S.I. 1994 No. 2968 (C. 67))

Made - - - - - *23rd November 1994*

INTRODUCTION

This Order brings into force on January 1, 1995 subss. 4(2)(b)(d) and (3) of the Finance Act 1993 (c. 34), which relate to the removal of specific reference to the Isle of Man in the provisions for drawback made in s.42 of the Alcoholic Liquor Duties Act 1979 (c. 4).

The Commissioners of Customs and Excise, in exercise of the powers conferred upon them by section 4(8) of the Finance Act 1993 (c. 34) and of all other powers enabling them in that behalf, hereby make the following Order.

1. This Order may be cited as the Finance Act 1993, section 4, (Appointed Day) Order 1994.

2. The day appointed as the day on which section 4(2)(b) and (d) and (3) comes into force is 1st January 1995.

New King's Beam House
22 Upper Ground
London
SE1 9PJ

Leonard Harris
23rd November 1994 Commissioner of Customs and Excise

INDEX

References are to article number

MERCHANT SHIPPING

SAFETY

THE MERCHANT SHIPPING (SALVAGE AND POLLUTION) ACT 1994 (COMMENCEMENT No. 2) ORDER 1994

(S.I. 1994 No. 2926 (C. 68))

Made - - - - - *22nd November 1994*

INTRODUCTION

This Order brings provisions of the Merchant Shipping (Salvage and Pollution) Act 1994 (c. 28) into force on January 1, 1995. *Inter alia*, it brings into force provisions giving the Salvage Convention, 1989 the force of law in the U.K. and makes possible the implementation of the International Convention on Oil Pollution Preparedness, Response and Co-operation, 1990.

The Secretary of State for Transport, in exercise of the powers conferred on him by section 10(4) of the Merchant Shipping (Salvage and Pollution) Act 1994 (c. 28), hereby makes the following Order:

1. This Order may be cited as the Merchant Shipping (Salvage and Pollution) Act 1994 (Commencement No. 2) Order 1994.

2. The provisions of the Merchant Shipping (Salvage and Pollution) Act 1994 specified in the first column of the Schedule to this Order (which relate to the matters specified in the second column of that Schedule) shall come into force on 1st January 1995.

Signed by authority of the
Secretary of State for Transport

Goschen
Parliamentary Under Secretary of State,
22nd November 1994   Department of Transport

Article 2   SCHEDULE

PROVISIONS COMING INTO FORCE ON 1ST JANUARY 1995

Provision of Merchant Shipping (Salvage and Pollution) Act 1994	*Subject matter*
Section 1.	Salvage Convention, 1989 to have force of law.
Section 2.	Power to implement 1990 OPRC Convention.
Section 4.	Prevention of pollution from ships: further power to implement international agreements.
Section 10, subsection (3), so far as it relates to the repeals in Schedule 4 specified below.	Repeals.
Schedule 1.	International Convention on Salvage, 1989.
Schedule 2.	Salvage: Consequential and Related Amendments.

Provision of Merchant Shipping (Salvage and Pollution) Act 1994	Subject matter
In Schedule 4, the repeals in: Merchant Shipping Act 1894(**a**); Maritime Conventions Act 1911(**b**); Crown Proceedings Act 1947(**c**); Merchant Shipping (Safety Convention) Act 1949(**d**); Administration of Justice Act 1956(**e**); Merchant Shipping Act 1988(**f**), except the repeal of paragraph 12 Schedule 4; Merchant Shipping (Registration, etc.) Act 1993(**g**), except the repeal of paragraph 18 Schedule 4.	Repeals.

(**a**)   1894 c. 60.
(**b**)   1911 c. 57.
(**c**)   1947 c. 44.
(**d**)   1949 c. 43.
(**e**)   1956 c. 46.
(**f**)   1988 c. 12.
(**g**)   1993 c. 22.

INDEX

References are to article number and Schedule

CHARITIES

THE CHARITIES ACT 1992
(COMMENCEMENT NO. 2) ORDER 1994

(S.I. 1994 No. 3023 (C. 69))

Made -   -   -   -   -   *27th November 1994*

INTRODUCTION

  This Order brings into force on March 1, 1995, Pt. II of the Charities Act 1992 (c. 41), which concerns the control of fund-raising for charitable institutions. However, for the purposes of exercising power to make regulations under that Part, the date of commencement is November 28, 1994. This Order was preceded by the Charities Act 1992 (Commencement No. 1 and Transitional Provisions) Order 1992 (S.I. 1992 No. 1900).

The Secretary of State in exercise of the powers conferred upon him by sections 77(3) and 79(2) of the Charities Act 1992 (c. 41; sections 77 and 79 were repealed in part by Schedule 7 to the Charities Act 1993 (c. 10)), hereby makes the following Order:

  1. This Order may be cited as the Charities Act 1992 (Commencement No. 2) Order 1994.

  2. Part II of the Charities Act 1992 (sections 58 and 63 were amended by sections 25 and 26 respectively of the Deregulation and Contracting Out Act 1994 (c. 40)) (control of fund-raising for charitable institutions) shall come into force on 1st March 1995, except that for the purposes of exercising the power to make regulations under section 59 or 64 thereof it shall come into force on the day after the day on which this Order is made.

Home Office   *Blatch*
27th November 1994   Minister of State

INDEX

References are to article number

DEREGULATION

THE DEREGULATION AND CONTRACTING OUT ACT 1994 (COMMENCEMENT NO. 1) ORDER 1994

(S.I. 1994 No. 3037 (C. 70))

Made - - - - -   *28th November 1994*

INTRODUCTION

This Order brings into force, on December 1, 1994, provisions of the Deregulation and Contracting Out Act 1994 (c. 40) which relate to Sunday opening of licensed premises in Scotland and the repeal of the Shops Act 1950 (c. 28), and provisions in other enactments relating to the 1950 Act.

The Secretary of State, in exercise of the powers conferred on him by section 82(4) of the Deregulation and Contracting Out Act 1994 (c. 40) and of all other powers enabling him in that behalf, hereby makes the following Order:

1. This Order may be cited as the Deregulation and Contracting Out Act 1994 (Commencement No. 1) Order 1994.

2. The provisions of the Deregulation and Contracting Out Act 1994 specified in article 3 below shall come into force on 1st December 1994.

3. The provisions referred to in article 2 above are—
(a) section 22 (Sunday opening of certain licensed premises in Scotland);
(b) section 23 (repeal of Part I of the Shops Act 1950);
(c) section 24 (repeal of remainder of the Shops Act 1950);
(d) section 81 (repeals) so far as relating to the entries referred to in paragraph (e) below; and
(e) in Schedule 17 (repeals), the entries in respect of—
   (i) the Shops Act 1950 (c. 28);
   (ii) the Shops (Airports) Act 1962 (c. 35);
   (iii) the Shops (Early Closing Days) Act 1965 (c. 35);
   (iv) the Local Government Act 1972 (c. 70);
   (v) the Local Government (Scotland) Act 1973 (c. 65);
   (vi) the Cinemas Act 1985 (c. 13);
   (vii) the Employment Act 1989 (c. 38); and
   (viii) the Sunday Trading Act 1994 (c. 20).

Fraser of Carmyllie
Minister of State,
St Andrew's House, Edinburgh   Scottish Office
28th November 1994

INDEX

References are to article numbers

COAL INDUSTRY

THE COAL INDUSTRY ACT 1994
(COMMENCEMENT NO. 3) ORDER 1994

(S.I. 1994 No. 3063 (C. 71))

Made - - - - - *1st December 1994*

INTRODUCTION

This Order brings into force on December 24, 1994 repeals specified in Sched. 11, Pt. III to the Coal Industry Act 1994 (c. 21) relating to the Coal Industry Nationalisation Act 1946 (c. 59), the Housing and Planning Act 1986 (c. 63) and the Coal Industry Act 1987 (c. 3).

The Secretary of State, in exercise of the powers conferred on him by section 68(4) and (5) of the Coal Industry Act 1994 (c. 21), and of all other powers enabling him in that behalf, hereby makes the following Order:

Citation and interpretation

1.—(1) This Order may be cited as the Coal Industry Act 1994 (Commencement No. 3) Order 1994.

(2) In this Order "the Act" means the Coal Industry Act 1994.

Provision coming into force on 24th December 1994

2. Part III of Schedule 11 to the Act shall, so far as it relates to the repeals set out in the Schedule to this Order, come into force on 24th December 1994.

Charles Wardle
Parliamentary Under Secretary
for Industry and Energy,
1st December 1994   Department of Trade and Industry

SCHEDULE

REPEALS TAKING EFFECT ON 24TH DECEMBER 1994

Chapter	Short title	Extent of repeal
9 & 10 Geo. 6. c. 59.	The Coal Industry Nationalisation Act 1946.	Section 45, for the purposes specified in subsection (1) of that section.
1986 c. 63.	The Housing and Planning Act 1986.	In Schedule 8, paragraph 8.
1987 c. 3.	The Coal Industry Act 1987.	In Schedule 1, paragraphs 9, 17 and, so far as unrepealed, paragraph 20.

INDEX

References are to articles and Schedule

POLICE

THE POLICE AND MAGISTRATES' COURTS ACT 1994 (COMMENCEMENT NO. 4 AND TRANSITIONAL PROVISIONS) (SCOTLAND) ORDER 1994

(S.I. 1994 No. 3075 (C. 72) (S.163))

Made - - - - -	*2nd December 1994*
Laid before Parliament - - -	*9th December 1994*
Coming into force - - - -	*1st January 1995*

INTRODUCTION

This Order brings into force on January 1, 1995, April 1, 1995 and January 1, 1996, for specified purposes, various provisions of Pt. II, concerning the arrangements for policing in Scotland, of the Police and Magistrates' Courts Act 1994 (c. 29).

The Secretary of State, in exercise of the powers conferred on him by section 94(1), (4) and (5) of the Police and Magistrates' Courts Act 1994 (c. 29) and of all other powers enabling him in that behalf, hereby makes the following Order:

Citation, commencement and interpretation

1.—(1) This Order may be cited as the Police and Magistrates' Courts Act 1994 (Commencement No. 4 and Transitional Provisions) (Scotland) Order 1994.

(2) This Order shall come into force on 1st January 1995.

(3) In this Order—

"the 1967 Act" means the Police (Scotland) Act 1967 (c. 77); and

"the 1994 Act" means the Police and Magistrates' Courts Act 1994.

Provisions of the 1994 Act coming into force on 1st January 1995

2. The provisions of the 1994 Act which are specified in column 1 of the Schedule to this Order, and described by reference to the subject matter in column 2 of that Schedule, shall, insofar as not then in force, come into force on 1st January 1995 but, where a particular purpose is specified in relation to any provision in column 3 of that Schedule, that provision shall come into force on that day only for that purpose.

Provision of the 1994 Act coming into force on 1st April 1995

3. Section 59 of the 1994 Act shall, insofar as not then in force, come into force on 1st April 1995.

Provision of the 1994 Act coming into force on 1st January 1996 and transitional provision

4.—(1) Section 51 of the 1994 Act shall, insofar as not then in force, come into force on 1st January 1996.

(2) Notwithstanding the amendments to section 15(1) of the 1967 Act made by section 51(a) and (c) of the 1994 Act brought into force by virtue of paragraph (1) above, the chief constable of a police force shall also include, in the report which he is required by section 15(1) of the 1967 Act to submit before 31st July 1996 as respects policing during the twelve months ending on 31st March in that year, a general report in writing on such matters as may have been prescribed by the Secretary of State under section 15(1) of the

1967 Act as respects, and generally as respects, the policing, during the period commencing on 1st January 1995 and ending on 31st March 1995, of the area for which the police force is maintained.

St Andrew's House, Edinburgh
2nd December 1994

Fraser of Carmyllie
Minister of State,
Scottish Office

Article 2 SCHEDULE

PROVISIONS OF THE 1994 ACT WHICH COME INTO FORCE ON 1st JANUARY 1995

Column 1 Provision	Column 2 Subject matter	Column 3 Extent of commencement
Section 48	Assistant chief constables	Only for the purpose of enabling regulations to be made under Part II of the 1967 Act with respect to appointments and promotions to the rank of assistant chief constable.
Section 51	Chief constables' annual reports	Only for the purpose of bringing into force the substitution made by paragraph (b).
Section 52(1)	Regulations for police forces	
Section 52(3)	Regulations for police forces	Only for the purpose of bringing into force the power to make regulations under section 26 of the 1967 Act for the purposes mentioned in subsections (2A) and (2C) inserted by section 52(3) of the 1994 Act.
Section 53(1)	Fixed term appointments etc.	
Section 55(1)	Appeals against dismissal etc.	Only for the purpose of bringing into force the power to make rules under section 30(3), (4) and (6) of the 1967 Act as substituted by section 55(1) of the 1994 Act.
Section 56	Expenditure in safeguarding national security	
Section 57	Duty of inspectors of constabulary	
Section 58	Assistant inspectors of constabulary and staff officers to inspectors of constabulary	
Section 59	Common services	Only for the purposes of bringing into force the provisions of section 36(1) of the 1967 Act as substituted by section 59 in relation to consultation by the Secretary of State with the Joint Central Committee and such bodies or associations as appear to the Secretary of State to be representative of police authorities or of chief constables or superintendents and the power to make regulations or an order under section 36 of the 1967 Act as so substituted.
Section 62	Transmission of criminal statistics	
Section 63(1), (6), (7)(b) and (9)(b)	Other amendments of 1967 Act	

Column 1 *Provision*	Column 2 *Subject matter*	Column 3 *Extent of commencement*
Section 93	Repeals	Only so far as it relates to the entries in Schedule 9, Part I specified below.
Schedule 9, Part I	Repeals	The following entries in respect of the 1967 Act:– In section 24(3) the words from "and the expression" onwards. Section 38(1) to (3). In section 38(5), the words from ""police regulations"" onwards. In Schedule 4, the entry relating to the Police (Overseas Service) Act 1945.

INDEX

References are to article and Schedule

MARRIAGE

THE MARRIAGE ACT 1994
(COMMENCEMENT NO. 1) ORDER 1994

(S.I. 1994 No. 3116 (C. 73))

Made   -   -   -   -   -   *7th December 1994*

INTRODUCTION

This Order brings into force on January 1, 1995 those provisions of the Marriage Act 1994 (c. 34) which amend the Marriage Act 1949 (c. 76) to permit marriage in a registry office outside the couple's district(s) of residence.

In exercise of the powers conferred by section 3(2) of the Marriage Act 1994 (c. 34), I hereby make the following Order:

Citation

1. This Order may be cited as the Marriage Act 1994 (Commencement No. 1) Order 1994.

Appointed day

2. 1st January 1995 is the day appointed for the coming into force of the following provisions of the Marriage Act 1994—
  (a) section 2(1) (registration districts in which marriages may be solemnised), so far as it inserts subsection (2A) in section 35 of the Marriage Act 1949 (c. 76);
  (b) section 2(2) (superintendent registrar not normally to issue licences for marriages in registered buildings outside his district); and
  (c) section 3 (short title and commencement).

Virginia Bottomley
One of Her Majesty's
Principal Secretaries of State

7th December 1994

INDEX

References are to article number

RATING AND VALUATION

THE LOCAL GOVERNMENT ETC. (SCOTLAND) ACT 1994 (COMMENCEMENT NO. 2) ORDER 1994

(S.I. 1994 No. 3150 (C. 74) (S. 174))

Made -   -   -   -   -   *7th December 1994*

INTRODUCTION
   This Order brings into force various provisions, principally concerned with rating and valuation matters, of the Local Government etc. (Scotland) Act 1994, on December 31, 1994, January 4, 1995 and April 1, 1995. This Order also amends the Local Government etc. (Scotland) Act 1994 (Commencement No. 1) Order 1994 (S.I. 1994 No. 2850).

The Secretary of State, in exercise of the powers conferred on him by section 184 of the Local Government etc. (Scotland) Act 1994 (c. 39) and of all other powers enabling him in that behalf, hereby makes the following Order:

Citation and interpretation

1.—(1) This Order may be cited as the Local Government etc. (Scotland) Act 1994 (Commencement No. 2) Order 1994.

(2) In this Order, "the Act" means the Local Government etc. (Scotland) Act 1994.

Days appointed

2. 31st December 1994 is the day appointed for the coming into force of—
   (a) paragraph 176(1) and (19)(b) of Schedule 13 to the Act (minor and consequential amendments); and
   (b) section 180(1) of the Act (minor and consequential amendments), so far as it relates to those provisions.

3. 4th January 1995 is the day appointed for the coming into force of the following provisions of the Act:—
   (a) section 153 (power of Secretary of State to prescribe amount of non-domestic rate);
   (b) section 160 (further provision as to valuation by formula);
   (c) section 161 (power of Secretary of State to combine and divide lands and heritages);
   (d) section 180(2) (repeals), so far as it relates to the provisions specified in paragraph (e) below; and
   (e) in Schedule 14 (repeals), the repeals of—
      (i) section 116(6) of the Local Government (Scotland) Act 1973 (c. 65);
      (ii) paragraphs 41 and 42 of Schedule 2 to the Local Government (Miscellaneous Provisions) (Scotland) Act 1981 (c. 23); and
      (iii) paragraph 60(2) of Schedule 25 to the Water Act 1989 (c. 15).

4. 1st April 1995 is the day appointed for the coming into force of—
   (a) the provisions of the Act specified in column 1 of Schedule 1 to this Order (which relate to the matters specified in column 2 of that Schedule);
   (b) section 180 of the Act, so far as it relates to the provisions of Schedules 13 and 14 to the Act specified in paragraphs (c) and (d) below;
   (c) in Schedule 13 to the Act—
      (i) paragraph 57;

C74

    (ii) paragraph 60(4);
    (iii) paragraph 67(1), (2) and (5); and
    (iv) paragraph 100(2), (4) and (5); and
 (d) the repeals in Schedule 14 to the Act specified in Schedule 2 to this Order.

Transitional provision

5. The amendments of paragraph 10(3)(a) of Schedule 12 to the Local Government Finance Act 1992 (c. 14) brought into force by article 2 of this Order shall not affect the continuing operation of regulations made under that paragraph (*see* S.I. 1992/3061, as amended by S.I. 1993/3059) in relation to a financial year (within the meaning of that Act) beginning before 1st April 1995.

Amendment of earlier Order

6. Article 3(c)(xiii) of the Local Government etc. (Scotland) Act 1994 (Commencement No. 1) Order 1994 (S.I. 1994/2850) is hereby amended by deleting the words "(1) and".

St Andrew's House, Edinburgh
7th December 1994

Allan Stewart
Parliamentary Under Secretary of State,
Scottish Office

Article 4(a)   SCHEDULE 1

PROVISIONS OF THE ACT COMING INTO FORCE ON 1ST APRIL 1995

Column 1 Provision of the Act	Column 2 Subject matter
Section 152	Amendment of definition of "lands and heritages"
Section 154	Rating of unoccupied lands and heritages
Section 155	Rating of lands and heritages partly unoccupied for a short time
Section 156	Remission of rates on account of hardship
Section 158	Grants in respect of certain rate rebates
Section 159	Rating of enterprise zone
Section 162(1)	Abolition of Scottish Valuation Advisory Council

Article 4(d)   SCHEDULE 2

REPEALS IN SCHEDULE 14 TO THE ACT COMING INTO FORCE ON 1ST APRIL 1995

Chapter	Short title	Extent of repeal
49 & 50 Vict. c. 15	The Sporting Lands Rating (Scotland) Act 1886	The whole Act.
10 & 11 Geo. 6 c. 43	The Local Government (Scotland) Act 1947	Sections 243, 243A, 243B and 244.
4 & 5 Eliz. 2 c. 60	The Valuation and Rating (Scotland) Act 1956	Section 22A.
6 & 7 Eliz. 2 c. 64	The Local Government and Miscellaneous Financial Provisions (Scotland) Act 1958	Section 7.

Chapter	Short title	Extent of repeal
1966 c. 51	The Local Government (Scotland) Act 1966	Section 17. Section 20. In section 25, in subsection (1), the words "the determination of rateable values," and subsections (3), (4) and (5). In section 46(1), the definition of "rate". In Schedule 3, paragraph 1, in paragraph 3(1), the words from "and that" to "heritages", in paragraph 5, the word "relevant", in both places where it occurs, paragraphs 6 and 7, in paragraph 8, the words from ""relevant lands" to "Act" and the words from "included" to "heritages", where it second occurs. In Schedule 5, paragraph 3.
1972 c. 52	The Town and Country Planning (Scotland) Act 1972	In Part II of Schedule 21, the words from "In section 25(3)(c)" to the end of the paragraph.
1973 c. 65	The Local Government (Scotland) Act 1973	In Schedule 9, paragraph 11.
1975 c. 30	The Local Government (Scotland) Act 1975	In Part II of Schedule 6, paragraphs 6, 13 and 34.
1980 c. 65	The Local Government, Planning and Land Act 1980	In Schedule 32, in paragraph 33, in sub-paragraph (2), head (a), sub-paragraph (3) and, in sub-paragraph (4), the definitions of "private garage" and "private storage premises".
1981 c. 23	The Local Government (Miscellaneous Provisions) (Scotland) Act 1981	Section 6. In Schedule 3, paragraph 26.
1982 c. 43	The Local Government and Planning (Scotland) Act 1982	Section 4.
1984 c. 31	The Rating and Valuation (Amendment) (Scotland) Act 1984	Sections 6 and 7. In Schedule 2, paragraph 7.
1988 c. 41	The Local Government Finance Act 1988	Section 128. In Part II of Schedule 12, paragraph 6.
1989 c. 15	The Water Act 1989	In Schedule 25, paragraph 22.
1989 c. 42	The Local Government and Housing Act 1989	In Schedule 6, paragraph 7.
1992 c. 14	The Local Government Finance Act 1992	In Schedule 13, paragraph 75.

INDEX

References are to article number and Schedules

RATING AND VALUATION

THE LOCAL GOVERNMENT FINANCE ACT 1992 (COMMENCEMENT NO. 9 AND TRANSITIONAL PROVISION) ORDER 1994

(S.I. 1994 No. 3152 (C. 75) (S.176))

Made -   -   -   -   -   *7th December 1994*

INTRODUCTION

This Order brings into force on March 31, 1995, s.110(2) (3) of the Local Government Finance Act 1992 (c. 14) and on April 1, 1995, Sched. 13, para. 37(1) of that Act. These provisions relate to the insertion in the Local Government (Scotland) Act 1975 (c. 30) of a new s.7B to enable the Secretary of State to prescribe a single non-domestic rate for the whole of Scotland with effect from financial year 1995–1996.

The Secretary of State, in exercise of the powers conferred on him by sections 113(2) and 119(2) of the Local Government Finance Act 1992 (c. 14) and of all other powers enabling him in that behalf, hereby makes the following Order:

Citation and interpretation

1.—(1) This Order may be cited as the Local Government Finance Act 1992 (Commencement No. 9 and Transitional Provision) Order 1994.

(2) In this Order, "the Act" means the Local Government Finance Act 1992.

Commencement of provisions

2. Subsections (2) and (3) of section 110 of the Act shall come into force on 31st March 1995.

3. Sub-paragraph (1) of paragraph 37 of Schedule 13 to the Act shall come into force on 1st April 1995.

Transitional provision

4. Nothing in this Order shall affect the operation of section 7A of the Local Government (Scotland) Act 1975 (c. 30: section 7A was inserted by section 110(1) of the Act), or of any order made under that section, in relation to any financial year beginning before 1st April 1995.

Allan Stewart
St Andrew's House, Edinburgh   Parliamentary Under Secretary of State,
7th December 1994   Scottish Office

INDEX

References are to article number

DEREGULATION
ROAD TRAFFIC
PUBLIC PASSENGER TRANSPORT

THE DEREGULATION AND CONTRACTING OUT ACT 1994 (COMMENCEMENT NO. 2) ORDER 1994

(S.I. 1994 No. 3188 (C. 76))

Made - - - - - *9th December 1994*

INTRODUCTION

This Order brings into force on January 3, 1995 various provisions of the Deregulation and Contracting Out Act 1994 (c. 40) and on April 1, 1995, provisions relating to objections to applications of public service vehicle licences. It also makes transitional provisions.

The Secretary of State, in exercise of the powers conferred on him by section 82(4) of the Deregulation and Contracting Out Act 1994 (c. 40) and of all other powers enabling him in that behalf, hereby makes the following Order:

1. This Order may be cited as the Deregulation and Contracting Out Act 1994 (Commencement No. 2) Order 1994.

2. The provisions of the Deregulation and Contracting Out Act 1994 ("the Act") specified in article 3 below shall come into force on 3rd January 1995.

3. The provisions referred to in article 2 above are—
(a) section 8 (Newspaper mergers: meaning of "newspaper proprietor" etc.)
(b) section 11 (Restrictive trade practices: registration of commercially sensitive information)
(c) section 19 (Bars in licensed premises in England and Wales: children's certificates)
(d) section 35 (Employment Agencies etc.: replacement of licensing)
(e) section 36(1) (Unfair dismissal: selection for redundancy)
(f) section 39 so far as relating to the Licensing Act 1964 (c. 26) and to section 77 of the Fair Trading Act 1973 (c. 41)
(g) section 51 (Assessors)
(h) section 58 (The 1981 Act)
(j) section 62 (Suspension of licences)
(k) section 64 (Repeal of section 27 of the 1981 Act)
(l) section 67 (Disqualification of PSV operators)
(m) section 68 (Chapter IV: minor and consequential amendments) so far as relating to the entries referred to in paragraph (r) below
(n) section 81 (repeals) so far as relating to the entries referred to in paragraph (s) below
(o) Schedule 7 (Children's Certificates: Supplementary Provisions)
(p) Schedule 10 (Employment Agencies etc.: Replacement of Licensing)
(q) in Schedule 11 (Miscellaneous Deregulatory Provisions: Consequential Amendments) paragraph 1 and paragraph 2 so far as relating to section 77 of the Fair Trading Act 1973
(r) in Schedule 14 (PSV Operator Licensing etc: Minor and Consequential amendments) paragraph 1 so far as relating to the following paragraphs and paragraphs 3 and 5(2)(b)
(s) in Schedule 17 (Repeals) the entries in respect of
    (i) The Merchant Shipping Act 1894 (57 and 58 Vict. c. 60)
    (ii) The Licensing Act 1964
    (iii) The Employment Agencies Act 1973 (c. 35)
    (iv) The House of Commons Disqualification Act 1975 (c. 24)
    (v) The Employment Protection Act 1975 (c. 71)

   (vi) The Employment Protection (Consolidation) Act 1978 (c. 44)
  (vii) The Merchant Shipping Act 1979 (c. 39)
(viii) The Public Passenger Vehicles Act 1981 (c. 14) so far as relating to sections 14A(3), 17(2)(b) and 27 of that Act
  (ix) The Employment (Miscellaneous Provisions) (Northern Ireland) Order 1981 (S.I. 1981 No. 839 (N.I. 20))
   (x) The Income and Corporation Taxes Act 1988 (c. 1)

4. Section 60 of the Act shall come into force on 1st April 1995.

5. The transitional provisions set out in Article 6(1) and (2) below shall have effect in connection with the coming into force of section 36(1) and section 60 of the Act respectively.

6.—(1) The omission of paragraph (b) from section 59(1) of the Employment Protection (Consolidation) Act 1978 ("the 1978 Act") effected by section 36(1) of the Act shall have effect in relation to any dismissal where the effective date of termination (as defined by section 55(4) of the 1978 Act) falls on or after 3 January 1995, other than a dismissal in respect of which notice was required to be given before that date (whether or not it was so given) in order to terminate the contract of employment on the effective date of termination by notice duly given in compliance with the contract of employment of the employee or with section 49 of the 1978 Act.

(2) The insertion of subsection (2A) in section 14A of the Public Passenger Vehicles Act 1981 effected by section 60 of the Act shall have effect in relation to any application for a PSV operators' licence made on or after 1st April 1995.

Jonathan Evans
Parliamentary Under Secretary of State
Department of Trade and Industry

9th December 1994

INDEX

References are to article number

CRIMINAL LAW, ENGLAND AND WALES

THE CRIMINAL JUSTICE ACT 1991 (COMMENCEMENT NO. 4) ORDER 1994

(S.I. 1994 No. 3191 (C. 77))

Made - - - - -   *11th December 1994*

INTRODUCTION

   This Order brings into force on January 9, 1995, ss.12 and 13 of the Criminal Justice Act 1991 (c. 53) which provide for the making of curfew orders and the electronic monitoring of such orders.

In exercise of the powers conferred on me by section 102(2) of the Criminal Justice Act 1991 (c. 53), I hereby make the following Order:

1. This Order may be cited as the Criminal Justice Act 1991 (Commencement No. 4) Order 1994.

2. Sections 12 and 13 of the Criminal Justice Act 1991 (section 12 is amended by paragraph 41 of Schedule 9 to the Criminal Justice and Public Order Act 1994 (c. 33)) shall come into force on 9th January 1995.

Home Office   *Michael Howard*
11th December 1994   One of Her Majesty's Principal Secretaries of State

INDEX

References are to article number

CRIMINAL LAW, ENGLAND AND WALES
CRIMINAL LAW, SCOTLAND

THE CRIMINAL JUSTICE AND PUBLIC ORDER ACT 1994 (COMMENCEMENT NO. 2) ORDER 1994

(S.I. 1994 No. 3192 (C. 78))

Made - - - - -   *11th December 1994*

INTRODUCTION

This Order brings into force on January 9, 1995, various provisions of the Criminal Justice and Public Order Act 1994 (c. 33), relating to, *inter alia*, curfew orders and electronic monitoring of curfew orders, on which matters see also the Criminal Justice Act 1991 (Commencement No. 4) Order 1994 (S.I. 1994 No. 3191).

In exercise of the powers conferred on me by section 172(2) of the Criminal Justice and Public Order Act 1994 (c. 33), I hereby make the following Order:

1. This Order may be cited as the Criminal Justice and Public Order Act (Commencement No. 2) Order 1994.

2. The provisions of the Criminal Justice and Public Order Act 1994 referred to in the left-hand column of the Schedule to this Order (which relate to the matters described in the right-hand column of that Schedule) shall come into force on 9th January 1995.

Home Office   *Michael Howard*
11th December 1994   One of Her Majesty's Principal Secretaries of State

Article 2   SCHEDULE

PROVISIONS OF THE CRIMINAL JUSTICE AND PUBLIC ORDER ACT 1994 COMING INTO FORCE ON 9TH JANUARY 1995

Provisions of the Act	*Subject matter of provisions*
Section 16	Long term detention of young offenders
Section 151	Power to test prisoners for drugs
Section 168, to the extent necessary to bring into force respectively the provisions of Schedules 9, 10 and 11 specified below	Minor and consequential amendments and repeals
Schedule 9, paragraph 34	Reviews of sentencing
Schedule 9, paragraph 41	Curfew orders
Schedule 10, paragraph 40	Procedure for young offenders in cases of grave crimes
Schedule 10, paragraph 64, to the extent that, in section 19(4) of the Prisons (Scotland) Act 1989 (1989 c. 45), it substitutes for the reference to section 41 of that Act references to sections 41 and 41B of that Act	Young offenders: power to test for drugs
Schedule 10, paragraph 69	Testing prisoners for drugs: director's functions
Schedule 11, the entry relating to section 24 of the Magistrates' Courts Act 1980 (c. 43)	Trial of young persons for indictable offences

Provisions of the Act	*Subject matter of provisions*
Schedule 11, the entry relating to section 126 of the Criminal Justice Act 1988 (c. 33)	Amendment of section 53(2) of Children and Young Persons Act 1933 (c. 12)
Schedule 11, the entry relating to section 64 of the Criminal Justice Act 1991 (c. 53)	Custodial sentences under the Children and Young Persons Act 1933 (c. 12)
Schedule 11, the entry relating to section 67(2) of the Criminal Justice Act 1993 (c. 36)	Penalty for causing death by dangerous driving or by careless driving

INDEX

References are to article number and Schedule

INCOME TAX

THE FINANCE ACT 1993, SECTION 165, (APPOINTED DAY) ORDER 1994

(S.I. 1994 No. 3224 (C. 79))

Made - - - - - *15th December 1994*

INTRODUCTION

This Order appoints March 23, 1995 as the appointed day for the purposes of s.165 of the Finance Act 1993 (c. 34). Subsection (1) of that section makes provision regarding Chap. II of the Act which makes provision in connection with exchange gains and losses and subs. (7) makes provision regarding a company's commencement day.

The Treasury, in exercise of the powers conferred on them by sections 165(7)(b) and 167(1) of the Finance Act 1993 (c. 34), hereby make the following Order:

1. This Order may be cited as the Finance Act 1993, section 165, (Appointed Day) Order 1994.

2. The day appointed for the purposes of section 165 of the Finance Act 1993 is 23rd March 1995.

Derek Conway
Andrew Mitchell
Two of the Lords Commissioners of
15th December 1994   Her Majesty's Treasury

INDEX

References are to article number

INCOME TAX

THE FINANCE ACT 1994, CHAPTER II OF PART IV, (APPOINTED DAY) ORDER 1994

(S.I. 1994 No. 3225 (C. 80))

Made -   -   -   -   -   *15th December 1994*

INTRODUCTION

   This Order appoints March 23, 1995 as the appointed day for the purposes of ss.147–177 of the Finance Act 1994 (c. 9), which concern interest rate and currency contracts.

The Treasury, in exercise of the powers conferred on them by section 147(4)(b) of the Finance Act 1994 (c. 9), hereby make the following Order:

1. This Order may be cited as the Finance Act 1994, Chapter II of Part IV, (Appointed Day) Order 1994.

2. The day appointed for the purposes of the provisions of Chapter II of Part IV of the Finance Act 1994 is 23rd March 1995.

Derek Conway
Andrew Mitchell
Two of the Lords Commissioners of
Her Majesty's Treasury

15th December 1994

INDEX

References are to article number

ENVIRONMENTAL PROTECTION

THE ENVIRONMENTAL PROTECTION ACT 1990 (COMMENCEMENT NO. 15) (AMENDMENT NO. 2) ORDER 1994

(S.I. 1994 No. 3234 (C. 81))

Made - - - - - *6th December 1994*

INTRODUCTION

This Order amends art. 3(2) of S.I. 1994 No. 1096 (C. 18) (already amended once by S.I. 1994 No. 2487 (C. 49)), which makes provision for determining the date upon which certain provisions of the Environmental Protection Act 1990 (c. 43) (relating to waste management licensing) come into force for the purposes of their application to activities involving the treatment, keeping or disposal of scrap metal or motorvehicles which are to be dismantled. As respects any such activity, that date is now by this Order determined according to the state of affairs on April 1, 1995.

The Secretary of State, in exercise of his powers under section 164(3) of the Environmental Protection Act 1990 (c. 43), hereby makes the following Order:

Citation

1. This Order may be cited as the Environmental Protection Act 1990 (Commencement No. 15) (Amendment No. 2) Order 1994.

Amendment of the Environmental Protection Act 1990 (Commencement No. 15) Order 1994

2. In each of sub-paragraphs (a), (b) and (c) of article 3(2) of the Environmental Protection Act 1990 (Commencement No. 15) Order 1994 (S.I. 1994/1096; the words "1st January 1995" in each of sub-paragraphs (a), (b) and (c) of article 3(2) were substituted by S.I. 1994/2487), for the words "1st January 1995" there shall be substituted the words "1st April 1995".

Signed by authority of the Secretary of State

Robert Atkins
Minister of State,
Department of the Environment

6th December 1994

INDEX

References are to article number

SUPREME COURT OF ENGLAND AND WALES
COMPOSITION OF THE COURT OF APPEAL

THE CRIMINAL JUSTICE AND PUBLIC ORDER ACT 1994
(COMMENCEMENT NO. 3) ORDER 1994

(S.I. 1994 No. 3258 (C. 82))

Made - - - - - *15th December 1994*

INTRODUCTION

This Order brings into force on January 11, 1995, s.52 of the Criminal Justice and Public Order Act 1994 (c. 33) which makes amendments to the Supreme Court Act 1981 (c. 54) enabling circuit judges to act as judges of the criminal division of the Court of Appeal.

The Lord Chancellor, in exercise of the powers conferred on him by section 172(2) of the Criminal Justice and Public Order Act 1994 (c. 33), hereby makes the following Order:

1. This Order may be cited as the Criminal Justice and Public Order Act 1994 (Commencement No. 3) Order 1994.

2. Section 52 of the Criminal Justice and Public Order Act 1994 (Circuit judges to act as judges of criminal division of Court of Appeal) shall come into force on 11th January 1995.

Dated 15th December 1994   *Mackay of Clashfern,* C

INDEX

References are to article number

POLICE

THE POLICE AND MAGISTRATES' COURTS ACT 1994 (COMMENCEMENT NO. 5 AND TRANSITIONAL PROVISIONS) ORDER 1994

(S.I. 1994 No. 3262 (C. 83))

Made - - - - -	*14th December 1994*
Laid before Parliament - -	*22nd December 1994*
Coming into force: - - -	
articles 1 to 3 - - - -	*31st December 1994*
remainder of the Order - -	*15th January 1995*

INTRODUCTION

This Order brings into force on December 31, 1994 and April 1, 1995 most of those provisions in Pt. I of the Police and Magistrates' Courts Act 1994 (c. 29), concerning the arrangements for policing in England and Wales, which are not currently in force. Provisions concerning police discipline are not included in this Order.

The words in square brackets in arts. 4 and 11 were substituted by S.I. 1995 No. 246 (C.8) which came into force on March 14, 1995.

The Secretary of State, in exercise of the powers conferred upon him by section 94(1), (4), (5) and (6) of the Police and Magistrates' Courts Act 1994 (c. 29), hereby makes the following Order:

Citation and commencement

1.—(1) This Order may be cited as the Police and Magistrates' Courts Act 1994 (Commencement No. 5 and Transitional Provisions) Order 1994.

(2) This article and articles 2 and 3 of this Order shall come into force on 31st December 1994 and the remainder of this Order shall come into force on 15th January 1995.

Interpretation

2. In this Order—

"the 1964 Act" means the Police Act 1964 (c. 48);

"the 1994 Act" means the Police and Magistrates' Courts Act 1994;

"joint police authority" means—

(a) a metropolitan county police authority constituted in accordance with the provisions of Part IV of the Local Government Act 1985 (c. 51), or

(b) the Northumbria Police Authority;

"new police authority" means the police authority to be established under section 3 of the 1964 Act (as substituted by section 2 of the 1994 Act) for a police area and "old police authority" means the police authority for that area which it is to supersede;

"nominated person" means a person nominated and appointed under article 6(4) or, as the case may be, article 8(5) below; and

"property" includes money and all other property, real or personal.

Commencement of provisions on 31st December 1994

3.—(1) Subject to paragraph (2) below, the following provisions of the 1994 Act, namely—

(a) paragraphs 1 and 8 of Schedule 5 (amendment of provisions relating to report of chief constables);

(b) section 44 so far as it relates to those paragraphs;

(c) the entries in Part I of Schedule 9 (repeals, police) in respect of section 12 of the 1964 Act; and

(d) section 93 so far as it relates to those entries,
shall come into force on 31st December 1994.

(2) As respects the first report which is required to be made under section 12(1) of the 1964 Act or submitted to the Secretary of State under section 30(2) of that Act after the amendments made by paragraphs 1(2)(a) and 8(3) of Schedule 5 to the 1994 Act have come into force, those sections shall have effect as if, for any reference to the financial year, there was substituted a reference to the period of fifteen months ending with 31st March 1995.

Commencement of provisions on 1st April 1995

4.—(1) Subject to paragraphs (2) to (8) and article 5 below, the provisions of the 1994 Act which are listed in the Schedule to this Order shall come into force for all purposes (or, as the case may be, all remaining purposes) on 1st April 1995.

(2) Section 4C of the 1964 Act, as inserted by section 4 of the 1994 Act, shall not apply in respect of the financial year ending on 31st [March 1995].

(3) Any person who on 1st April 1995 would hold the rank of deputy chief constable in a police force maintained under section 2 of the 1964 Act (as substituted by section 2 of the 1994 Act) but for the commencement by this Order of the provisions of the 1994 Act abolishing that rank shall hold the rank of assistant chief constable in that force.

(4) For the purposes of any financial year ending before 1st April 1995, section 8 of the 1964 Act shall continue to have effect in the form in which it has effect immediately before the commencement by this article of section 8 of the 1994 Act.

(5) The provision inserted by section 21 of the 1994 Act shall not apply to a report received by the Secretary of State under section 38(2) of the 1964 Act before 1st April 1995.

(6) For the purposes of the issue of a basic credit approval under section 53 of the Local Government and Housing Act 1989 (c. 42) to a new police authority in respect of the financial year beginning on 1st April 1995, section 30 of the 1994 Act (which amends the definition of "local authority" for purposes including that of the said section 53) shall come into force on 15th March 1995.

(7) Without prejudice to the generality of articles 7 and 8 below, any duty on an old police authority in relation to any person exercising functions of a public nature (such as the Audit Commission under Part I of the Local Government Act 1992 (c. 19)) which has not been discharged on 31st March 1995 shall, so far as is practicable, be discharged by the new police authority.

(8) For the purposes of a direction under section 1 of the Local Government Act 1992, paragraph 25 of Schedule 4 to the 1994 Act (which amends section 12 of the Local Government Finance Act 1982 (c. 32) and thereby brings the new police authorities within section 1(7)(a) of the Local Government Act 1992) shall come into force on 15th January 1995 and (notwithstanding section 2(4) of the Local Government Act 1992) any such direction may be given to a new police authority in respect of the financial year beginning on 1st April 1995 not later than 31st January 1995.

Transitional provision about budget requirement

5.—(1) For the purposes of section 54(1) of the Local Government Finance Act 1992 (c. 14) and the financial year beginning on 1st April 1995 only—

(a) a new police authority shall be regarded as the same authority as the police authority which it supersedes (the relevant old police authority), and

(b) the budget requirement of the relevant old police authority shall be regarded as being the budget requirement of the new police authority.

(2) In paragraph (1) above, "budget requirement of the relevant old police authority" means—
  (a) where the relevant old police authority is a joint police authority, the budget requirement of that authority;
  (b) where the relevant old police authority is a committee of the council of a county constituted in accordance with section 2 of the 1964 Act, the portion of the budget requirement of that county attributable to the functions of that committee;
  (c) where the relevant old police authority is for a combined area constituted in accordance with section 3 of the 1964 Act, the sum of the portions of the budget requirements of the constituent councils of that authority attributable to the functions of that authority.

Transfer of civilian employees

6.—(1) Every person who—
  (a) immediately before 1st April 1995 is employed by an old police authority (whether or not that old police authority is a body corporate separate from a county council), and
  (b) but for the provisions of this Order, would continue to be so employed,
shall, on that date, transfer to, and become an employee of, the new police authority.
  (2) Every person who—
  (a) during the period of two months ending with 31st March 1995 is employed by the council of a county in an undertaking that is provided wholly for police purposes, and
  (b) but for the provisions of this Order, would continue to be so employed,
shall, on the relevant date, transfer to, and become an employee of, the new police authority whose police area as listed in Schedule 1A to the 1964 Act (Schedule 1A was inserted by Schedule 1 to the 1994 Act) consists of or includes the county of the council by which the person is so employed.
  (3) Every person who—
  (a) immediately before 1st April 1995 is employed for police purposes by the council of a county, and
  (b) but for the provisions of this Order, would continue to be so employed,
shall, on that date, transfer to, and become an employee of, the new police authority whose police area as listed in Schedule 1A to the 1964 Act consists of or includes the county of the council by which the person is so employed where, prior to that date, the council of the county and the new police authority agree to the transfer.
  (4) Where there is a dispute between the council of a county and the relevant new police authority as to whether a person falls within paragraph (2) above—
  (a) the council and the authority may nominate and appoint a person to determine the dispute in accordance with article 10(3) below, or
  (b) if the council and the authority are unable to agree that the dispute should be so determined or on the person to be nominated, either of them may require the Secretary of State to nominate and appoint such a person.
  (5) The contract of employment between a person who is transferred by virtue of this article or a determination under article 10(3) below shall be deemed to have effect from the relevant date as if originally made between him and the new police authority.
  (6) In this article "the relevant date" means—
  (a) 1st April 1995, or
  (b) where there is a dispute between the council of a county and the relevant new police authority as to whether any person falls within paragraph (2) above and the nominated person determines under article 10(3) below that the person does so fall, the date of his determination.

Transfer of property etc. from joint police authorities and most combined police authorities

7.—(1) This article applies to an old police authority which is—

(a) a joint police authority, or

(b) the police authority for a combined area constituted in accordance with section 3 of the 1964 Act other than section 3(4).

(2) This article shall have effect to transfer on 1st April 1995 from an old police authority to which this article applies to the new police authority and to vest in the latter all the property, rights and liabilities (including rights and liabilities relating to property and in connection with any pending legal proceedings) of the former.

Agreements to transfer property etc. from certain local authorities

8.—(1) As soon as practicable after 15th January 1995, every relevant authority and every appropriate new police authority shall use their best endeavours—

(a) to determine which transfers (if any) of property, rights and liabilities from a relevant authority to the appropriate new police authority it is fair and reasonable to make, and

(b) to make an agreement in writing specifying which of those transfers are to take effect under article 9 below on 1st April 1995 and which of those transfers are to take effect on such later date as may be so specified.

(2) An agreement under this article may—

(a) indicate that there are matters specified therein about which agreement is still to be reached, or

(b) provide for a variation in the transfer of property, rights or liabilities in circumstances specified in the agreement (where, for example, there is a change of circumstances as a result of the auditing of a relevant authority's accounts).

(3) Subject to paragraph (4) below as soon as practicable after 1st April 1995 every relevant authority and every appropriate new police authority shall use their best endeavours—

(a) to determine whether it is fair and reasonable to make any transfer of property, rights and liabilities (other than a loan attributable to the relevant authority's functions as a police authority) from a relevant authority to the appropriate new police authority in addition to any transfer in an agreement under paragraph (1) above, and

(b) to make an agreement in writing specifying any such transfers and the date or dates on which they are to take effect under article 9 below.

(4) A relevant authority and an appropriate new police authority may agree to delay an agreement under paragraph (3) above pending the outcome of some future event; but paragraph (3) above shall have effect after that event has taken place as if, for the reference therein to 1st April 1995, there were substituted a reference to the event.

(5) Subject to paragraph (6) below, where it has become apparent that a relevant authority and an appropriate new police authority are unable to agree about whether a transfer of property, rights and liabilities should be made—

(a) those authorities may nominate and appoint a person to determine the dispute in accordance with article 10(1) below, or

(b) if those authorities are unable to agree either that the dispute should be so determined or on the person to be nominated, either authority may require the Secretary of State to nominate and appoint such a person.

(6) Paragraph (5) above shall not apply where—
(a) the relevant authority falls within sub-paragraph (a) of the definition "relevant authority" in paragraph (8) below, and
(b) the transfer about which that authority and the appropriate new police authority are unable to agree concerns any loan attributable to the relevant authority's police authority functions.

(7) In this article and article 10 below, references to the transfer of property, rights and liabilities mean—
(a) the transfer from a relevant authority to an appropriate new police authority or apportionment between them of any property and rights and liabilities relating to it;
(b) such transfer or apportionment of any other rights and liabilities (including rights and liabilities in connection with any pending legal proceedings); and
(c) the creation of any rights and liabilities between them.

(8) In this article and articles 9 and 10 below—
"appropriate new police authority" means the new police authority whose police area as listed in Schedule 1A to the 1964 Act (Schedule 1A was inserted by Schedule 1 to the 1994 Act) includes the county of which the relevant authority is the council; and
"relevant authority" means—
(a) the council of a county where the old police authority is a committee of that council constituted in accordance with section 2 or 3(4) of the 1964 Act;
(b) the council of any constituent county where the old police authority is a combined police authority constituted in accordance with section 3 of the 1964 Act (other than section 3(4)).

Transfer of property etc. from certain local authorities

9.—(1) This article shall have effect to—
(a) transfer from a relevant authority to the appropriate new police authority and to vest in the latter—
  (i) such property;
  (ii) such rights and liabilities relating thereto, and
  (iii) such other rights and liabilities (including rights and liabilities in connection with any pending legal proceedings),
as may be specified in a written agreement between them under article 8 above or in an instrument giving effect to the decision of a nominated person under article 10(2) below;
(b) apportion between them—
  (i) such property;
  (ii) such rights and liabilities relating thereto, and
  (iii) such other rights and liabilities (including rights and liabilities in connection with pending legal proceedings),
as may be so specified;
(c) create between them such rights and liabilities as may be so specified;
on 1st April 1995 or such other later date, or dates, as may be so specified.

(2) In this article "appropriate new police authority" and "relevant authority" have the same meanings as in article 8 above.

Determinations by nominated person

10.—(1) Where a nominated person has been appointed under article 8(5) above, he shall (as soon as practicable after his appointment) proceed to determine in accordance with paragraphs (4) to (9) below a dispute as to which (if any) transfers of property, rights and liabilities from a relevant authority to an appropriate new police authority it is fair and reasonable to make.

(2) Where a nominated person appointed under article 8(5) above determines that a transfer shall be made, he shall draw up an instrument to give effect to his determination; and any such instrument shall specify the date or dates on which it is to take effect.

(3) Where a nominated person has been appointed under article 6(4) above to determine a dispute as to whether a person falls within article 6(2), he shall (as soon as practicable after his appointment) proceed to determine in accordance with paragraphs (4) to (9) below whether the person who is the subject of the dispute falls within article 6(2) and set out his determination in writing.

(4) A nominated person shall not determine a dispute unless both parties to it have been afforded an opportunity to make written or, if either so requests, oral representations and any such representations have been considered.

(5) Any oral representations shall be made at a hearing on a date appointed by the nominated person after consultation with the parties to a dispute.

(6) The parties shall have the right to appear by counsel, a solicitor or by the clerk or other officer of either of the parties.

(7) The nominated person shall be paid such remuneration and reimbursed for such expenses as—
(a) the parties to the dispute may determine before he is appointed; or
(b) in the absence of such agreement, may be determined by the Secretary of State.

(8) The nominated person shall make such order as to which of the parties to the dispute shall pay the costs incurred under this article, including the costs incurred under paragraphs (6) and (7) above, as may appear to him to be fair and reasonable.

(9) Any order under paragraph (8) above may apportion the costs between the parties.

(10) In this article "appropriate new police authority", "relevant authority" and "transfer of property, rights and liabilities" have the same meaning as in article 8 above.

Liability of certain new police authorities in respect of loan debts

11.—(1) In this article—
(a) "the 1989 Act" means the Local Government and Housing Act 1989 (c. 42);
(b) any expression used in this article which is defined for the purposes of Part IV of the 1989 Act (revenue accounts and capital finance of local authorities) shall have the same meaning as it has for those purposes;
(c) "relevant council" means the council of a county where the old police authority is a committee of that council constituted in accordance with section 2 or 3(4) of the 1964 Act; and
(d) "relevant new police authority" means such an authority replacing a relevant council as police authority.

(2) Where a relevant council and a relevant new police authority are unable to agree before 1st April 1995 under article 8 above to the transfer of all loans attributable to the council's police authority functions, a relevant new police authority shall be deemed to have borrowed from the relevant council an amount (in this article referred to as "the principal") equal to the police amount for that council for 31st March 1995 less the amount of any loan that the relevant council and the relevant new police authority have agreed before 1st April 1995 under article 8 above to transfer.

(3) For the purposes of this article—
(a) the police amount for a relevant council for 31st March in any of the years 1991 to 1995 shall be determined—
  (i) by adding to the police amount for that council for 31st March in the immediately preceding year the amount of the police increase for that council for the financial year following it; and
  (ii) by subtracting from the resulting amount the amount of the police decrease for that council for that financial year; and
(b) the police amount for a relevant council for 31st March 1990 shall be an amount equal to the portion of that council's initial credit ceiling attributable to the police authority functions of that council.

(4) For the purposes of paragraph (3) above, the amount of the police increase for any relevant council for any financial year is the total of the amounts of all the supplementary credit approvals [used by the council and] issued—
(a) to [a local authority] in respect of its police authority functions by the Secretary of State for the Home Department under Part IV of the 1989 Act;
(b) in the case of—
  (i) a financial year ending on 31st March in the years 1991 to 1994, for a period beginning in that financial year;
  (ii) the financial year ending on 31st March 1995, on or before 31st December 1994 and for a period beginning in that financial year,
less an amount equal to the total of the amounts by which the credit ceiling of the [relevant] council was increased in that year as respects credit arrangements entered into in that year by the council in respect of [its police authority functions].

(5) For the purposes of paragraph (3) above, the amount of the police decrease for any relevant council for any financial year is the total of the following amounts—
(a) four per cent. of the police amount for the council for 31st March in the financial year immediately preceding the financial year in question;
(b) the total of any amounts set aside by the council as provision to meet credit liabilities from the reserved part of any capital receipts in respect of a disposal or repayment attributable to police authority functions or, in relation to consideration to which section 61(4) of the 1989 Act applies, from the amount which would be the reserved part of a notional capital receipt in respect of such a disposal or repayment;
(c) the total of any amounts set aside by the council from its revenue account or from the usable part of its capital receipts as provision to meet credit liabilities in respect of its police excluded credit arrangements; and
(d) the total of any amounts shown in the accounts of the council as being set aside from its revenue account as provision for credit liabilities in respect of its police authority functions in excess of the amounts referred to in sub-paragraph (a) above, and the amount of any usable part of the council's capital receipts shown in its accounts as being applied as such provision in respect of its police authority functions.

(6) In paragraph (5) above "police excluded credit arrangements" means any credit arrangements excluded by regulations made under paragraph 11(2) of Schedule 3 to the 1989 Act entered into in respect of land, goods or services held or used for police authority functions.

(7) Subject to paragraph (9) below, a relevant new police authority which by virtue of this article is deemed to have borrowed from a relevant council shall discharge its liability to that council by—
(a) making annual repayment of the principal to that council in 25 equal instalments over a period of 25 years, with the first such repayment falling due on 1st October 1995, and
(b) in each financial year in which any part of the principal remains out-

standing, paying that council interest calculated in accordance with paragraph (8) below.

(8) The interest to be paid by a relevant new police authority on its deemed borrowing shall be paid on 31st March in each year beginning with 1996 and shall be calculated in respect of each financial year by applying the formula of X divided by Y and multiplied by Z where—

X is determined by dividing by 12 the total of the sums which equal the amount of principal which remains unpaid on the first day of each month of the financial year in question;

Y is determined by dividing by 12 the total of the sums which equal the amount of the outstanding borrowing of the relevant council on the first day of each month of the financial year in question;

Z is the amount of interest payable by the relevant council for the financial year in question in respect of its outstanding borrowing in that year.

(9) A relevant new police authority may repay the whole or any part of the principal outstanding in respect of its deemed borrowing at any time before it is repaid in full after giving to the relevant council not less than thirty days' notice of its intention to do so.

Home Office   *David Maclean*
14th December 1994   Minister of State

Article 4   SCHEDULE

PROVISIONS OF THE 1994 ACT COMING INTO FORCE ON 1ST APRIL 1995

Provisions of the Act	*Subject matter of provisions*
Section 1	Police areas
Section 2	Police forces and police authorities
Section 3	Membership of police authorities etc.
Section 4	Functions of police authorities
Section 5	Chief constables
Section 6	Deputy and assistant chief constables
Section 7	Other members of police forces
Section 8	Police fund
Section 9	Supply of goods and services
Section 10	Civilian employees
Section 11	Appointment of officers
Section 12	Questions by local councillors
Section 14	Alteration of police areas
Section 15	Functions of Secretary of State
Section 16	Reports from police authorities
Section 20	Inspectors of constabulary
Section 21	Reports from inspectors of constabulary
Section 23	Common services
Section 24	Grants by local authorities
Section 26	Police officers employed on service outside their force
Section 29	Directions as to minimum budget
Section 30	Revenue accounts and capital finance
Section 31	Financial administration
In section 39, subsections (2) and (3)	Police areas in England: alterations under the Local Government Act 1992
Section 40	Police areas in Wales: alterations under the Local Government Act 1972
Section 43	Application to police authorities of enactments relating to local authorities etc.
Section 44	Minor and consequential amendments, so far as it relates to the paragraphs of Schedule 5 specified below

Provisions of the Act	Subject matter of provisions
Section 45	Application of certain provisions to new authorities
Section 93	Repeals, so far as it relates to the entries in Part I of Schedule 9 specified below
Schedule 1	Schedule to be inserted in Police Act 1964: Police areas
Schedule 2	Schedules to be inserted in Police Act 1964: Police authorities
Schedule 4	Application to police authorities of enactments relating to local authorities
In Part I of Schedule 5, paragraphs 2 to 7, 9, 10(2), 13, 14 and 15	Minor and consequential amendments of the 1964 Act
In Part II of Schedule 5, paragraphs 17 to 20, 22, 23, 24(a), 29, 30, 35, 36, 37 and 38	Police: minor and consequential amendments of other enactments
In Part I of Schedule 9, all of the entries so far as they relate to enactments as they apply in England and Wales except those in respect of the following enactments— the Metropolitan Police Act 1856 (19 & 20 Vict. c. 2); the Licensing Act 1902 (2 Edw. 7 c. 28); sections 12, 33(5), 53(1) and 60 of the 1964 Act; the Police Negotiating Board Act 1980 (c. 10); sections 67(8), 85(8), 90(3), (4), (6) and (8), 91, 92, 94, 97(4), 99(2), 101, 103, 104(1) and (2) and 105 of, and Schedule 4 to, the Police and Criminal Evidence Act 1984 (c. 60); section 30(2) of the Local Government Act 1985 (c. 51); the Drug Trafficking Offences Act 1986 (c. 32); the Courts and Legal Services Act 1990 (c. 41); and the Police Act (Northern Ireland) 1970 (c. 9) (N.I.).	Repeals: police

INDEX

References are to article number and Schedule

TOWN AND COUNTRY PLANNING, SCOTLAND

THE PLANNING AND COMPENSATION ACT 1991 (COMMENCEMENT NO. 17 AND TRANSITIONAL PROVISION) (SCOTLAND) ORDER 1994

(S.I. 1994 No. 3292 (C. 84) (S. 191))

Made - - - - - *15th December 1994*

INTRODUCTION

This Order brings into force on February 3, 1995 various provisions of the Planning and Compensation Act 1991 (c. 34) relating to the demolition of buildings, notice of applications to owners and agricultural tenants, also certain minor and consequential amendments and a repeal.

The Secretary of State, in exercise of the powers conferred on him by section 84(2) and (3) of the Planning and Compensation Act 1991 (c. 34) and of all other powers enabling him in that behalf, hereby makes the following Order:

Citation

1. This Order may be cited as the Planning and Compensation Act 1991 (Commencement No. 17 and Transitional Provision) (Scotland) Order 1994.

Interpretation

2. In this Order—
"the 1972 Act" means the Town and Country Planning (Scotland) Act 1972 (c. 52);
"the 1991 Act" means the Planning and Compensation Act 1991.

Provisions coming into force on 3rd February 1995

3. The following provisions of the 1991 Act shall come into force on 3rd February 1995:—
section 44;
section 46;
section 61 insofar as it relates to the provisions of Schedule 13 referred to below;
section 84(6) insofar as it gives effect to the repeal in Part IV of Schedule 19 referred to below;
in Schedule 13 paragraphs 7(a)(i), 10(a) (insofar as not already in force) and (b), 11(b)(i), (ii) and (iv), 15, 40(1)(b) and (c), 41(3) and (4) and 42; and
in Part IV of Schedule 19 the entry in respect of section 28(1) of the 1972 Act.

Transitional provision

4. Section 44 of, and paragraph 40(1)(c) of Schedule 13 to, the 1991 Act shall not have effect so far as they relate to the demolition of a building on land in a case where, before 3rd February 1995 planning permission has been granted under Part III of the 1972 Act (except under article 3 of, and Schedule 1 to, the Town and Country Planning (General Permitted Development) (Scotland) Order 1992 (S.I. 1992/223; to which there are amendments not relevant for the purposes of this Order)), or has been deemed to be granted under that Part of that Act, for the redevelopment of the land.

Allan Stewart
St Andrew's House, Edinburgh   Parliamentary Under Secretary of State
15th December 1994   Scottish Office

INDEX

References are to article number

CURRENT LAW STATUTES

NUMERICAL TABLE OF STATUTORY INSTRUMENTS 1994

This table details in numerical order Statutory Instruments released in 1994. The table is up to date to **March 10, 1995**. For brief digests of Statutory Instruments see the Current Law Monthly Digest.

110................A18 Trunk Road (Junction 5, M180 Motorway) (Detrunking) Order 1994

111 (S. 4) .....Salmon (Definition of Methods of Net Fishing and Construction of Nets) (Scotland) Amendment Regulations 1994

115 (C. 5).....Welsh Language Act 1993 (Commencement) Order 1994
Deddf Iaith Gymraeg 1993 Gorchymyn (Cychwyn) 1994

116................Driving Licences (Designation of Relevant External Law) Order 1994

117................Companies (Welsh Language Forms and Documents) Regulations 1994
Rheoliadau (Furflenni a Dogfenni Cymreag) Cwmniau 1994

118................Control of Industrial Major Accident Hazards (Amendment) Regulations 1994

119................Criminal Justice Act 1988 (Reviews of Sentencing) Order 1994

129................Fertilisers (Sampling and Analysis) (Amendment) Regulations 1994

130................Cardiff and Vale of Glamorgan (Areas) Order 1994

131................National Health Service (Optical Charges and Payments) Amendment Regulations 1994

132................Friendly Societies (Auditors) Order 1994

133................Secure Tenants of Local Housing Authorities (Right to Repair) Regulations 1994

134................A23 Trunk Road (Brighton Road, Croydon) (Prohibition of Right Turn and U-Turn) Order 1994

135................Council Tax (Transitional Reduction Scheme) (England) Regulations 1994

141................European Communities (Iron and Steel Employees Re-adaptation Benefits Scheme) (No. 2) (Scheme Termination) Regulations 1994

142................Vale of Glamorgan (Barry and Dinas Powys Communities) Order 1994

143................Free Zone (Prestwick Airport) Designation (Variation) Order 1994

144................Free Zone (Humberside) Designation Order 1994

145 (S. 5) .....National Health Service (Optical Charges and Payments) (Scotland) Amendment Regulations 1994

156................Education (Grant) (Henrietta Barnett School) Regulations 1994

157................Railways and Other Transport Systems (Approval of Works, Plant and Equipment) Regulations 1994

158................Industrial Training Levy (Engineering Construction Board) Order 1994

159................Industrial Training Levy (Construction Board) Order 1994

160................Dairy Product Quotas (Amendment) Regulations 1994

161................South Manchester University Hospital National Health Service Trust (Establishment) Order 1994

162................Dudley Priority Health National Health Service Trust (Establishment) Order 1994

163................Kent and Sussex Weald National Health Service Trust (Establishment) Order 1994

164................Salford Hospitals National Health Service Trust (Establishment) Order 1994

165................Mid-Sussex National Health Service Trust (Establishment) Order 1994

166................Royal West Sussex National Health Service Trust (Establishment) Order 1994

167................Dorset Community National Health Service Trust (Establishment) Order 1994

9

570................Channel Tunnel (Security) Order 1994
571 (C. 11)...Railways Act 1993 (Commencement No. 4 and Transitional Provision) Order 1994
572................Railways (Licence Application) Regulations 1994
573................Railways (London Regional Transport) (Exemptions) Order 1994
574................Railways (Heathrow Express) (Exemptions) Order 1994
575................Railways (Registers) Order 1994
576................Railways (Penalty Fares) Regulations 1994
577................British Railways (Penalty Fares) Act 1989 (Revocation of Activating Orders) Order 1994
578................Housing Benefit and Council Tax Benefit (Miscellaneous Amendments) Order 1994
579................Housing Benefit (Permitted Totals) Order 1994
580................Education (London Residuary Body) (Transfer of Property etc.) Order 1994
581................Education (Middle Schools) (Amendment) Regulations 1994
582 (S. 25)...Rent Officers (Additional Functions) (Scotland) Amendment Order 1994
586................National Board for Nursing, Midwifery and Health Visiting for England (Constitution and Administration) Amendment Order 1994
589................National Blood Authority (Establishment and Constitution) Amendment Order 1994
590................National Health Service Functions (Directions to Authorities and Administration Arrangements) Amendment Regulations 1994
592................Statutory Maternity Pay (Compensation of Employers) Amendment Regulations 1994
595................Wireless Telegraphy (Television Licence Fees) (Amendment) Regulations 1994
599................Medicines (Veterinary Drugs) (Pharmacy and Merchants' List) (Amendment) Order 1994
600................Crown Office Fees Order 1994
601 (L. 2).....Enrolment of Deeds (Fees) Regulations 1994
602................Microbiological Research Authority Regulations 1994
603................Microbiological Research Authority (Establishment and Constitution) Order 1994
604 (L. 3).....Enrolment of Deeds (Change of Name) Regulations 1994
606................Railways (Class and Miscellaneous Exemptions) Order 1994
607................Railways (Alternative Closure Procedure) Order 1994
608................Railways (Amendment) Regulations 1994
609................British Transport Police Force Scheme 1963 (Amendment) Order 1994
610................Education (Grant-maintained Schools) (Finance) (Wales) Regulations 1994
611................Research Councils (Transfer of Property etc.) Order 1994
612................Education (Grants for Education Support and Training) Regulations 1994
613................Secure Tenants of Local Authorities (Compensation for Improvements) Regulations 1994
615................Local Authorities (Members' Allowances) (Amendment) Regulations 1994
617................Motor Vehicles (EC Type Approval) (Amendment) Regulations 1994
619................Thanet Health Care National Health Service Trust (Transfer of Trust Property) Order 1994

620................Canterbury and Thanet Community Health Care National Health Service Trust (Transfer of Trust Property) Order 1994

621................West Lindsey National Health Service Trust (Transfer of Trust Property) Order 1994

622................Mancunian Community Health National Health Service Trust (Transfer of Trust Property) Order 1994

623................Hillingdon Hospital National Health Service Trust (Transfer of Trust Property) Order 1994

624................Andover District Community Health Care National Health Service Trust (Transfer of Trust Property) Order 1994

625................South Tees Community and Mental Health National Health Service Trust (Transfer of Trust Property) Order 1994

626 (S. 26) ...Council Tax (Discounts) (Scotland) Amendment Order 1994

627................Housing (Right to Manage) Regulations 1994

628 (S. 27) ...Council Tax (Exempt Dwellings) (Scotland) Amendment Order 1994

629 (S. 28) ...Council Tax (Discounts) (Scotland) Amendment Regulations 1994

630 (S. 29) ...Local Government etc. (Allowances) (Scotland) Amendment Regulations 1994

631................Parliament: Resolution of the House of Commons, dated March 4, 1994, passed in pursuance of the House of Commons Members' Fund Act 1948, s.3 (11 & 12 Geo. 6 c.36) & the House of Commons Members' Fund and Parliamentary Pensions Act 1981, s.2 (1981 c.7)

632 (S. 30) ...Secure Tenants (Compensation for Improvements) (Scotland) Regulations 1994

633................National Health Service (General Medical Services) Amendment Regulations 1994

634................National Health Service (Service Committees and Tribunal) Amendment Regulations 1994

635 (S. 31) ...National Health Service (Optical Charges and Payments) (Scotland) Amendment (No. 2) Regulations 1994

636 (S. 32) ...National Health Service (Dental Charges) (Scotland) Amendment Regulations 1994

637................Home Energy Efficiency Grants (Amendment) Regulations 1994

638................Motor Vehicles (Driving Licences) (Amendment) Regulations 1994

639................Motor Vehicles (Driving Licences) (Large Goods and Passenger-Carrying Vehicles) (Amendment) Regulations 1994

640................National Health Service (Fund-Holding Practices) Amendment Regulations 1994

641................Police Pensions (Amendment) Regulations 1994

642................Fees for Inquiries (Standard Daily Amount) Regulations 1994

643................Insurance (Fees) Regulations 1994

644................Partnerships (Unrestricted Size) (No. 11) Regulations 1994

645................Education (School Curriculum and Assessment Authority) (Transfer of Functions) Order 1994

646................Education (National Curriculum) (Assessment Arrangements for English, Welsh, Mathematics and Science) (Key Stage 1) (Wales) (Amendment) Order 1994

647................Education (National Curriculum) (Assessment Arrangements for English, Welsh, Mathematics and Science) (Key Stage 3) (Wales) (Amendment) Order 1994

648................Housing Renovation etc. Grants (Reduction of Grant) Regulations 1994

681...............National Health Service (Determination of Districts) Order 1994

682...............National Health Service (Regional and District Health Authorities) (Miscellaneous Amendments) Regulations 1994

683...............National Health Service (Determination of Regions) Order 1994

684...............National Health Service (Regional Health Authorities) Order 1994

685 (S. 33)...Milk Marketing Schemes (Substitution of Date of Revocation) (Scotland) Order 1994

686...............Value Added Tax (Tax Free Shops) Order 1994

687...............Value Added Tax (Sport, Physical Education and Fund-Raising Events) Order 1994

689...............Road Traffic (Special Parking Areas) (London Boroughs of Bromley, Hammersmith and Fulham and Lewisham) (Amendment) Order 1994

690...............National Health Service (Charges for Drugs and Appliances) Amendment Regulations 1994

691...............Bowes Extension Light Railway Order 1994

692...............Education (No. 2) Act 1986 (Amendment) Order 1994

693...............Housing Renovation etc. Grants (Prescribed Forms and Particulars) (Welsh Forms and Particulars) Regulations 1994

694...............Hydrocarbon Oil (Amendment) (No. 2) Regulations 1994

695...............Tower Hamlets Housing Action Trust (Transfer of Property) Order 1994

696...............Medicines (Products of Human Use—Fees) Amendment Regulations 1994

697 (S. 34)...National Health Service (Charges for Drugs and Appliances) (Scotland) Amendment Regulations 1994

700 (C. 12)...Criminal Justice Act 1993 (Commencement No. 6) Order 1994

701...............Greater Manchester (Light Rapid Transit System) (Modification) Order 1994

702...............London Regional Transport (Penalty Fares) Act 1992 (Activating No. 1) Order 1994

703...............Incumbents (Vacation of Benefices) Rules 1994

704...............Social Security Pensions (Home Responsibilities) Regulations 1994

706...............Civil Courts (Amendment) Order 1994

707...............Environmentally Sensitive Areas (Blackdown Hills) Designation Order 1994

708...............Environmentally Sensitive Areas (Cotswold Hills) Designation Order 1994

709...............Environmentally Sensitive Areas (Shropshire Hills) Designation Order 1994

710...............Environmentally Sensitive Areas (Dartmoor) Designation Order 1994

711...............Environmentally Sensitive Areas (Essex Coast) Designation Order 1994

712...............Environmentally Sensitive Areas (Upper Thames Tributaries) Designation Order 1994

714...............Public Trustee (Fees) (Amendment) Order 1994

715...............Personal Injuries (Civilians) Amendment Scheme 1994

717...............Education (Registered Inspectors of Schools Appeal Tribunal) (Procedure) Regulations 1994

718 (C. 14)...Transport and Works Act 1992 (Commencement No. 5 and Transitional Provisions) Order 1994

723...............National Rivers Authority (Alteration of Boundaries of the South Holland Internal Drainage District) Order 1994

770...............Double Taxation Relief (Taxes on Income) (Uzbekistan) Order 1994
771...............Home Guard (Amendment) Order 1994
772...............Naval, Military and Air Force etc. (Disablement and Death) Service Pensions Amendment Order 1994
773...............Ulster Defence Regiment (Amendment) Order 1994
774...............Merchant Shipping (Modification of Enactments) (Bareboat Charter Ships) Order 1994
775...............Income Tax (Employments) (Amendment) Regulations 1994
776...............Pensions Increase (Review) Order 1994
777...............Income Tax (Car Benefits) (Replacement Accessories) Regulations 1994
778...............Income Tax (Replacement Cars) Regulations 1994
779...............Education (Groups including Grant-Maintained Special Schools) Regulations 1994
780 (C. 15)...Environmental Protection Act 1990 (Commencement No. 14) Order 1994
781...............Housing Benefit and Council Tax Benefit (Subsidy) Regulations 1994
782...............European Parliamentary Elections (Northern Ireland) (Amendment) Regulations 1994
787...............Medicines (Control of Substances for Manufacture and Exportation of Specified Products for Human Use) Amendment Order 1994
791...............Merchant Shipping (Seaman's Wages and Accounts) (Amendment) Regulations 1994
797...............North Kent Healthcare National Health Service Trust (Establishment) Amendment Order 1994
798...............South Birmingham Community Health Service Trust (Change of Name) Order 1994
799...............A564 Trunk Road (Stoke–Derby Route) (Derby Southern Bypass and Slip Road) (No. 3) Order 1994
800...............(M1) Motorway (Lockington) Connecting Roads Scheme 1994
801...............A564 Trunk Road (Stoke–Derby Route) (Derby Southern Bypass, Derby Spur and Slip Roads) Amendment Order 1994
802...............A564 Trunk Road (Stoke–Derby Route) (Derby Southern Bypass) (Detrunking) (No. 2) Order 1994
803...............Value Added Tax (Accounting and Records) (Amendment) Regulations 1994
804...............Food Labelling (Amendment) Regulations 1994
805...............Legal Advice and Assistance (Amendment) Regulations 1994
806...............Civil Legal Aid (Assessment of Resources) (Amendment) Regulations 1994
807...............Legal Aid in Criminal and Care Proceedings (General) (Amendment) Regulations 1994
808 (L. 4).....Family Proceedings (Amendment) Rules 1994
809 (L. 5).....Family Proceedings Court (Miscellaneous Amendments) Rules 1994
810 (S. 35)...Borders Regional Council (Galashiels Mill Lade) (Amendment) Water Order 1994
818...............Tees and Hartlepool Port Authority (Dissolution) Order 1994
825...............National Assistance (Assessment of Resources) (Amendment) Regulations 1994
826...............National Assistance (Sums for Personal Requirements) Regulations 1994

875................Public Telecommunications System Designation (Encom Cable TV & Telecommunications Limited) (Epping Forest) Order 1994

876................Public Telecommunications System Designation (NYNEX CableComms Oldham and Tameside) Order 1994

884 (S. 36) ...National Health Service (General Medical and Pharmaceutical Services) (Scotland) Amendment Regulations 1994

894................European Parliamentary Elections (Returning Officers) (England and Wales) Order 1994

895................Occupational Pension Schemes (Deficiency on Winding Up etc.) Regulations 1994

896................Dorset Ambulance National Health Service Trust (Transfer of Trust Property) Order 1994

898................B4260 Trunk Road (De-Trunking at Ross-on-Wye) Order 1994

899................Medicines (Homeopathic Medicinal Products for Human Use) Amendment Regulations 1994

902................Local Government Act 1988 (Defined Activities) (Exemption) (Broxtowe Borough Council and Harrogate Borough Council) Order 1994

903................Telecommunications Industry (Rateable Values) (Amendment) Order 1994

909................Nuclear Installations (Increase of Operators' Limits of Liability) Order 1994

910................Education (Schools Teachers' Pay and Conditions) Order 1994

911 (S. 37) ...Football Grounds (Rateable Values) (Scotland) Order 1994

912 (S. 38) ...Mines and Quarries (Rateable Values) (Scotland) Order 1994

913 (S. 39) ...Industrial and Freight Transport (Rateable Values) (Scotland) Order 1994

918................Environmentally Sensitive Areas (North Kent Marshes) (Amendment) Order 1994

919................Environmentally Sensitive Areas (Test Valley) Designation (Amendment) Order 1994

920................Environmentally Sensitive Areas (Suffolk River Valleys) Designation (Amendment) Order 1994

921................Environmentally Sensitive Areas (Clun) Designation (Amendment) Order 1994

922................Environmentally Sensitive Areas (North Peak) Designation (Amendment) Order 1994

923................Environmentally Sensitive Areas (Breckland) Designation (Amendment) Order 1994

924................Environmentally Sensitive Areas (South Wessex Downs) Designation (Amendment) Order 1994

925................Environmentally Sensitive Areas (Lake District) Designation (Amendment) Order 1994

926................Environmentally Sensitive Areas (South West Peak) Designation (Amendment) Order 1994

927................Environmentally Sensitive Areas (Avon Valley) Designation (Amendment) Order 1994

928................Environmentally Sensitive Areas (Exmoor) Designation (Amendment) Order 1994

929................Environmentally Sensitive Areas (The Broads) Designation (Amendment) (No. 2) Order 1994

930................Environmentally Sensitive Areas (Pennine Dales) Designation (Amendment) (No. 2) Order 1994

931................Environmentally Sensitive Areas (South Downs) Designation (Amendment) (No. 2) Order 1994

990...............East Berkshire Community Health National Health Service Trust (Transfer of Trust Property) Order 1994

991...............Heatherwood and Wexham Park Hospitals' National Health Service Trust (Transfer of Trust Property) Order 1994

992...............East Berkshire National Health Service Trust for People with Learning Disabilities (Transfer of Trust Property) Order 1994

993...............East Surrey Hospital and Community Healthcare Service National Health Service Trust (Transfer of Trust Property) Order 1994

994...............Southend Health Care Services National Health Service Trust (Transfer of Trust Property) Order 1994

995...............Southend Community Care Services National Health Service Trust (Transfer of Trust Property) Order 1994

997 (S. 41)...Advice and Assistance (Financial Conditions) (Scotland) Regulations 1994

998 (S. 42)...Civil Legal Aid (Financial Conditions) (Scotland) Regulations 1994

999...............Railways (Rateable Values) (Amendment) Order 1994

1000 (S. 43)...Advice and Assistance (Assistance by Way of Representation) (Scotland) Amendment Regulations 1994

1001 (S. 44)...Criminal Legal Aid (Scotland) (Prescribed Proceedings) Regulations 1994

1002...............Highways (Assessment of Environmental Effects) Regulations 1994

1003...............Housing Benefit (General) Amendment Regulations 1994

1004...............Income Support (General) Amendment Regulations 1994

1005...............Development Board for Rural Wales (Transfer of Housing Stock) (Amendment) Regulations 1994

1006...............Public Telecommunication System Designation (Insight Communications Guildford Limited) Order 1994

1007...............Public Telecommunication System Designation (Insight Communications Cardiff Limited) Order 1994

1008...............Public Telecommunication System Designation (NORWEB plc) Order 1994

1009...............A30 Trunk Road (Honiton to Exeter Improvement and Slip Roads) (Detrunking) Order 1994

1010...............A30 Trunk Road (Honiton to Exeter Improvement) (Detrunking) Order 1994

1011...............M5 Motorway (Junction 29 and the A30 Trunk Road Honiton to Exeter Improvement) (Slip Roads Special Roads) Scheme 1994

1012...............Injuries in War (Shore Employments) Compensation (Amendment) Scheme 1994

1013 (S. 45)...Crofting Counties Agricultural Grants (Scotland) Amendment Scheme 1994

1014 (S. 46)...Crofters etc. Livestock Purchase Loans (Scotland) Revocation Scheme 1994

1015 (S. 47)...Civil Legal Aid (Scotland) (Fees) Amendment Regulations 1994

1016 (S. 48)...Legal Aid in Contempt of Court Proceedings (Scotland) Amendment Regulations 1994

1017 (S. 49)...Legal Aid (Scotland) (Children) Amendment Regulations 1994

1018 (S. 50)...Legal Aid in Contempt of Court Proceedings (Scotland) (Fees) Amendment Regulations 1994

1019 (S. 51)...Criminal Legal Aid (Scotland) (Fees) Amendment Regulations 1994

1261................National Health Service (Determination of Districts) (No. 2) Order 1994
1262................Regional and District Health Authorities (Membership and Procedure) Amendment Regulations 1994
1263................Collective Enfranchisement and Tenants' Audit (Qualified Surveyors) Regulations 1994
1265................Motor Vehicles (Type Approval and Approval Marks) (Fees) Regulations 1994
1266 (S. 65)...Building Standards (Scotland) Amendment Regulations 1994
1268................Surrey Ambulance National Health Service Trust (Change of Name) Order 1994
1269................Salford Hospitals National Health Service Trust (Change of Name) Order 1994
1270................Education (National Curriculum) (Exceptions in Welsh at Key Stage 4) Regulations 1994
1271................Environmental Protection (Prescribed Processes and Substances Etc.) (Amendment) Regulations 1994
1288 (L. 7).....County Court (Amendment No. 2) Rules 1994
1289 (L. 8).....County Court (Forms) (Amendment) Rules 1994
1291................Habitat (Water Fringe) Regulations 1994
1292................Habitat (Former Set-Aside Land) Regulations 1994
1293................Habitat (Salt-Marsh) Regulations 1994
1294................Two Shires Ambulance National Health Service Trust (Transfer of Trust Property) (No. 2) Order 1994
1295................West Berkshire Priority Care Service National Health Service Trust (Transfer of Trust Property) Order 1994
1296................Royal Cornwall Hospitals National Health Service Trust (Transfer of Trust Property) Order 1994
1297................Royal Berkshire and Battle Hospitals National Health Service Trust (Transfer of Trust Property) Order 1994
1298................Royal Berkshire Ambulance National Health Service Trust (Transfer of Trust Property) Order 1994
1299................Grimsby Health National Health Service Trust (Transfer of Trust Property) Order 1994
1300................East Hertfordshire National Health Service Trust (Transfer of Trust Property) Order 1994
1301................Countess of Chester Hospital National Health Service Trust (Transfer of Trust Property) Order 1994
1302................Farm and Conservation Grant (Variation) Scheme 1994
1303................Education (Lay Members of Appeal Committees) Regulations 1994
1304................Religious Education (Meetings of Local Conferences and Councils) 1994
1307................Taxes (Interest Rate) (Amendment) Regulations 1994
1308................Police (Amendment) Regulations 1994
1309................Airedale National Health Service Trust (Transfer of Trust Property) Order 1994
1310................Avon Ambulance Service National Health Service Trust (Transfer of Trust Property) Order 1994
1311................Barnet Community Healthcare National Health Service Trust (Transfer of Trust Property) Order 1994
1312................Chase Farm Hospitals National Health Service Trust (Transfer of Trust Property) Order 1994
1313................Chorley and South Ribble National Health Service Trust (Transfer of Trust Property) Order 1994
1314................Community Health Services, Southern Derbyshire National Health Service Trust (Transfer of Trust Property) Order 1994

1495................Road Traffic (Special Parking Area) (London Borough of Greenwich) Order 1994
1496................Road Traffic (Special Parking Area) (London Borough of Enfield) Order 1994
1497................Road Traffic (Special Parking Area) (London Borough of Kingston upon Thames) Order 1994
1498................Road Traffic (Special Parking Area) (Royal Borough of Kensington and Chelsea) Order 1994
1499................Road Traffic (Special Parking Area) (London Borough of Islington) Order
1500................Road Traffic (Special Parking Area) (London Borough of Hillingdon) Order 1994
1501................Road Traffic (Special Parking Area) (London Borough of Waltham Forest) Order 1994
1502................Road Traffic (Special Parking Area) (London Borough of Brent) Order 1994
1503................Removal and Disposal of Vehicles (Amendment) Regulations 1994
1504................Road Traffic (Special Parking Area) (City of Westminster) Order 1994
1505................Road Traffic (Special Parking Area) (London Borough of Barnet) Order 1994
1506................Road Traffic (Special Parking Area) (London Borough of Newham) Order 1994
1507................Road Traffic (Special Parking Area) (London Borough of Sutton) Order 1994
1508................Road Traffic (Special Parking Area) (London Borough of Lambeth) Order 1994
1509................Road Traffic (Special Parking Area) (London Borough of Redbridge) Order 1994
1510................Road Traffic (Special Parking Area) (London Borough of Merton) Order 1994
1511................Children's Homes Amendment Regulations 1994
1515................Insurance Companies (Accounts and Statements) (Amendment) Regulations 1994
1516................Insurance Companies Regulations 1994
1517................Financial Services Act 1986 (Miscellaneous Exemptions) Order 1994
1518................Private Medical Insurance (Disentitlement to Tax Relief and Approved Benefits) Regulations 1994
1519................Traffic Signs Regulations and General Directions 1994
1520................Education (National Curriculum) (Attainment Targets and Programmes of Study in Science) (Amendment) Order 1994
1527................Private Medical Insurance (Tax Relief) (Amendment) Regulations 1994
1528................Suckler Cow Premium (Amendment) Regulations 1994
1529................Cosmetic Products (Safety) (Amendment) Regulations 1994
1531................Medicines (Medicated Animal Feeding Stuffs) (Amendment) Regulations 1994
1532................Railtrack (Marsh Lane, Leeds, Footbridge) Order 1994
1533................Reservoirs (Panels of Civil Engineers) (Application Fees) (Amendment) Regulations 1994
1534................West Lindsey National Health Service Trust (Establishment) Amendment Order 1994
1535................National Health Service (Charges to Overseas Visitors) (Amendment) Regulations 1994
1536................Civil Courts (Amendment No. 2) Order 1994
1542................Combined Probation Areas (Gloucestershire) Order 1994

1613................Road Traffic (Special Parking Area) (London Borough of Tower Hamlets) Order 1994

1614................London-Fishguard Trunk Road (A40) (Whitland By-pass) Order 1994

1623................Industrial Tribunals Extension of Jurisdiction (England and Wales) Order 1994

1624................Industrial Tribunals Extension of Jurisdiction (Scotland) Order 1994

1632................Export of Goods (Control) Order 1994 (Amendment) Order 1994

1633................Education (Chief Inspector of Schools in England) Order 1994

1634................British Nationality (South Africa) Order 1994

1635................Criminal Justice (International Co-operation) (Anguilla) Order 1994

1636................South Africa (United Nations Arms Embargo) (Prohibited Transactions) Revocations Order 1994

1637................United Nations Arms Embargoes (Amendment) (Rwanda) Order 1994

1638................Virgin Islands (Constitution) (Amendment) Order 1994

1639................Criminal Justice Act 1988 (Designated Countries and Territories) (Amendment) Order 1994

1640................Criminal Justice (International Co-operation) Act 1990 (Enforcement of Overseas Forfeiture Orders) (Amendment) Order 1994

1641................Drug Trafficking Offences Act 1986 (Designated Countries and Territories) (Amendment) Order 1994

1642................International Headquarters and Defence Organisations (Designation and Privileges) (Amendment) Order 1994

1643................Visiting Forces and International Headquarters (Application of Law) (Amendment) Order 1994

1644 (S. 72) ...Confiscation of the Proceeds of Drug Trafficking (Designated Countries and Territories) (Scotland) Amendment Order 1994

1645 (S. 73) ...Criminal Justice (International Co-operation) Act 1990 (Enforcement of Overseas Forfeiture Orders) (Scotland) Amendment Order 1994

1646................Social Security (Cyprus) Order 1994

1647................Lancaster Port Commission Harbour Revision Order 1994

1648 (C. 29)...Railways Act 1993 (Commencement No. 5 and Transitional Provisions) Order 1994

1649................Railways Act 1993 (Consequential Modifications) (No. 2) Order 1994

1650................Bournemouth and West Hampshire Water (Amendment of Local Enactments etc.) Order 1994

1661 (C. 30)...Social Security Act 1989 (Commencement No. 5) Order 1994

1662................European Parliamentary (United Kingdom Representatives) Pensions (Consolidation and Amendment) Order 1994

1663................European Parliament (Pay and Pensions) Act 1979 (Section 3 (Amendment)) Order 1994

1666................Football Spectators (Seating) Order 1994

1667................Channel Tunnel (Application of Road Traffic Enactments) (No. 2) Order 1994

1671................Local Government Act 1988 (Competition) (Defined Activities) (Housing Management) Order 1994

1673................Education (School Teachers' Pay and Conditions) (No. 2) Order 1994

1675 (S. 74) ...Mental Health (Class of Nurse) (Scotland) Order 1994

1744................Education (National Curriculum) (Attainment Targets and Programmes of Study in Geography) (Wales) (Amendment) Order 1994

1746................Council Tax (Alteration of Lists and Appeals) (Amendment) Regulations 1994

1747................Council Tax (Situation and Valuation of Dwellings) (Amendment) Regulations 1994

1748................Race Relations (Interest on Awards) Regulations 1994

1751................Protected Rights (Transfer Payment) Amendment Regulations 1994

1753................River Humber (Upper Burcom Cooling Works) Order 1994

1754................Epsom School of Art and Design (Dissolution) Order 1994

1755................Cleveland College of Further Education and Sir William Turners' Sixth Form College, Redcar (Dissolution) Order 1994

1756................Criminal Justice (International Co-operation) Act 1990 (Crown Servants) Regulations 1994

1757................Drug Trafficking Offences Act 1986 (Crown Servants and Regulators etc.) Regulations 1994

1758................Prevention of Terrorism (Temporary Provisions) Act 1989 (Crown Servants and Regulators etc.) Regulations 1994

1759................Criminal Justice Act 1988 (Crown Servants) Regulations 1994

1760................Northern Ireland (Emergency Provisions) Act 1991 (Crown Servants and Regulators etc.) Regulations 1994

1761................Wirral Tramway Light Railway Order 1994

1762................Housing (Right to Buy) (Priority of Charges) Order 1994

1763................Mortgage Indemnities (Recognised Bodies) Order 1994

1768................Plugs and Sockets etc. (Safety) Regulations 1994

1769 (S. 78)...Act of Adjournal (Consolidation Amendment) (Miscellaneous) 1994

1770 (S. 79)...National Health Service (Charges to Overseas Visitors) (Scotland) Amendment Regulations 1994

1771................Ecclesiastical Exemption (Listed Buildings and Conservation Areas) Order 1994

1772................Northern Ireland Act 1974 (Interim Period Extension) Order 1994

1773 (C. 32)...Finance Act 1994 (Appointed Day) Order 1994

1774................Insurance Premium Tax Regulations 1994

1776 (C. 33)...Human Fertilisation and Embryology Act 1990 (Commencement No. 5) Order 1994

1777................Severn Bridge (Amendment) Regulations 1994

1778................Lerwick Harbour Revision Order 1994

1779................Social Security (Attendance Allowance and Disability Living Allowance) (Amendment) Regulations 1994

1780................A20 Trunk Road (Sidcup Road, Greenwich) (Prohibition of Use of Gaps in Central Reservation) Order 1994

1803................Chinnor and Princes Risborough Railway Order 1994

1806................Notification of Existing Substances (Enforcement) Regulations 1994

1807................Income-related Benefits Schemes (Miscellaneous Amendments) (No. 3) Regulations 1994

1808 (S. 80)...Criminal Justice (Scotland) Act 1987 (Crown Servants and Regulators Etc.) Regulations 1994

1809................Non-Domestic Rating (Alteration of Lists and Appeals) (Amendment) Regulations 1994

1811................Special Commissioners (Jurisdiction and Procedure) Regulations 1994

1812...............General Commissioners (Jurisdiction and Procedure) Regulations 1994
1813...............General and Special Commissioners (Amendment of Enactments) Regulations 1994
1814...............Education (National Curriculum) (Foundation Subjects at Key Stage 4) Order 1994
1815...............Education (National Curriculum (Attainment Targets and Programmes of Study in Modern Foreign Languages and Technology at Key Stage 4) (England) (Amendment) Order 1994
1816...............Education (National Curriculum) (Attainment Targets and Programmes of Study in History) (England) (Amendment) Order 1994
1817...............Education (National Curriculum) (Attainment Targets and Programmes of Study in Geography) (England) (Amendment) Order 1994
1818...............Education (National Curriculum) (Modern Foreign Languages) (Amendment) Order 1994
1819...............Insurance Premium Tax (Prescribed Rates of Interest) Order 1994
1820...............Air Passenger Duty (Prescribed Rates of Interest) Order 1994
1821...............Air Passenger Duty (Connected Flights) Order 1994
1822...,...........Civil Legal Aid (General) (Amendment) (No. 2) Regulations 1994
1823...............Legal Advice and Assistance (Amendment) (No. 2) Regulations 1994
1824...............Legal Advice and Assistance at Police Stations (Remuneration) (Amendment) Regulations 1994
1825...............Legal Aid in Criminal and Care Proceedings (Costs) (Amendment) (No. 2) Regulations 1994
1826 (S. 81)...St Mary's Music School (Aided Places) Amendment Regulations 1994
1827 (S. 82)...Education (Assisted Places) (Scotland) Amendment Regulations 1994
1828 (S. 83)...Inshore Fishing (Prohibition of Fishing for Cockles) (Scotland) Order 1994
1830...............Lincolnshire College of Art and Design and Lincolnshire College of Agriculture and Horticulture (Dissolution) Order 1994
1831...............Authorities for London Post-Graduate Teaching Hospitals (Abolition) Order 1994
1832...............Social Security Benefit (Persons Abroad) Amendment (No. 2) Regulations 1994
1836...............Offshore Installations (Safety Zones) (No. 2) Order 1994
1837...............Social Security (Credits) Amendment Regulations 1994
1838...............Passenger and Goods Vehicles (Recording Equipment) Regulations 1994
1841 (C. 34)...Sunday Trading Act 1994 Appointed Day Order 1994
1842...............Protection of Wrecks (Designation No. 1) Order 1994
1850...............Building Regulations (Amendment) Regulations 1994
1851...............Weights and Measures (Metrication Amendments) Regulations 1994
1852...............Weights and Measures (Packaged Goods and Quantity Marking and Abbreviations of Units) (Amendment) Regulations 1994
1853...............Price Marking (Amendment) Order 1994
1859 (S. 84)...Seed Potatoes (Fees) (Scotland) Order 1994

1916................Leicester General Hospital National Health Trust (Transfer of Trust Property) Order 1994

1917................Glenfield Hospital National Health Service Trust (Transfer of Trust Property) Order 1994

1918................Leicester Royal Infirmary National Health Service Trust (Transfer of Trust Property) Order 1994

1919................Milton Keynes Community Health National Trust (Transfer of Trust Property) Order 1994

1920................Milton Keynes General National Health Service Trust (Transfer of Trust Property) Order 1994

1921................South West Durham Mental Health National Health Service Trust (Transfer of Trust Property) Order 1994

1922................Monopoly References (Alteration of Exclusions) Order 1994

1923 (C. 35)...Immigration Act 1988 (Commencement No. 3) Order 1994

1924................Income-Related Benefits Schemes (Miscellaneous Amendments) (No. 4) Regulations 1994

1925................Housing Benefit (Supply of Information) and Council Tax Benefit (General) Amendment Regulations 1994

1931 (S. 85)...Prisons and Young Offenders Institutions (Scotland) Rules 1994

1932................Medicines (Advertising) Regulations 1994

1933................Medicines (Monitoring of Advertising) Regulations 1994

1934................Fair Trading Act (Amendment) (Merger Prenotification) Regulations 1994

1935................Companies Act 1985 (Audit Exemption) Regulations 1994

1936 (L. 9).....County Court Fees (Amendment) Order 1994

1946 (S. 86)...Loch Ewe, West Ross, Scallops Fishery Order 1994

1948................Registration of Births and Deaths (Amendment) Regulations 1994

1949 (S. 87)...River Clyde Catchment Area (Part) Protection Order 1994

1950................Food Protection (Emergency Prohibitions) (Paralytic Shellfish Poisoning) Order 1994

1951 (C. 36)...Criminal Justice Act 1993 (Commencement No. 7) Order 1994

1952................Backing of Warrants (Republic of Ireland) (Rule of Speciality) Order 1994

1953 (S. 88)...Police (Promotion) (Scotland) Amendment Regulations 1994

1972................London–Holyhead Trunk Road (A5) (Bangor Bypass Section) (Eastbound on Slip Road from A4087 Caernarfon Road) Order 1994

1974................Land Registration Fees Order 1994

1975 (L. 10)...Rules of the Supreme Court (Amendment) 1994

1976 (S. 89)...Scottish Development Agency Dissolution Order 1994

1977................Food Protection (Emergency Prohibitions) (Paralytic Shellfish Poisoning) (No. 2) Order 1994

1978................Value Added Tax Tribunals Appeals (Northern Ireland) Order 1994

1980 (S. 90)...University of Abertay Dundee (Scotland) Order 1994

1981................Friendly Societies (Insurance Business) Regulations 1994

1982................Friendly Societies (Authorisation) Regulations 1994

1983................Friendly Societies (Accounts and Related Provisions) Order 1994

1984................Friendly Societies Act 1992 (Amendment) Regulations 1994

1985................Pesticides (Maximum Residue Levels in Crops, Food and Feeding Stuffs) Regulations 1994

1986................Race Relations (Prescribed Public Bodies) (No. 2) Regulations 1994

1987................Stonebridge Housing Action Trust (Area and Constitution) Order 1994

1988 (C. 37)...Merchant Shipping (Salvage and Pollution) Act 1994 (Commencement No. 1) Order 1994
1989................Environmentally Sensitive Areas Designation (Radnor) (Welsh Language Provisions) Order 1994
1990................Environmentally Sensitive Areas Designation (Ynys Môn) (Welsh Language Provisions) Order 1994
1993................Remand (Temporary Provisions) (Northern Ireland) Order 1994
1994................Lazy Acres Natural Gas Pipe-Lines Order 1994
2003................Education (Initial Government of Grant-maintained Special Schools) Regulations 1994
2004................Welfare Food Amendment Regulations 1994
2005................Railway Pensions (Transfers and Miscellaneous Provisions) Order 1994
2009................Ecclesiastical Judges and Legal Officers (Fees) Order 1994
2010................Legal Officers (Annual Fees) Order 1994
2011................Parochial Fees Order 1994
2012 (S. 91)...Environmental Assessment (Scotland) Amendment Regulations 1994
2013................Merchant Shipping (Accident Reporting and Investigation) Regulations 1994
2014................Merchant Shipping (Safety Officials and Reporting of Accidents and Dangerous Occurrences) (Amendment) Regulations 1994
2016................Education (Bursaries for Teacher Training) Regulations 1994
2017................Education (Norwich School of Art and Design Further Education Corporation) (Transfer to the Higher Education Sector) Order 1994
2018................Education (Northern School of Contemporary Dance, Leeds Further Education Corporation) (Transfer to the Higher Education Sector) Order 1994
2019................Education (Writtle Agricultural College Further Education Corporation) (Transfer to the Higher Education Sector) Order 1994
2020................Building (Prescribed Fees) Regulations 1994
2021................Personal Injuries (Civilians) Amendment (No. 2) Scheme 1994
2022................General Medical Council (Constitution of Fitness to Practise Committees) (Amendment) Rules Order of Council 1994
2023................Police Authorities (Selection Panel) Regulations 1994
2024................Police (Number of Members of Police Authorities) Order 1994
2025 (C. 38)...Police and Magistrates' Courts Act 1994 (Commencement No. 1 and Transitional Provisions) Order 1994
2026................Gipsy Encampments (Rushmoor and Hart) Order 1994
2029................Food Protection (Emergency Prohibitions) (Paralytic Shellfish Poisoning) (No. 3) Order 1994
2030 (S. 92)...Local Authorities (Recognised Bodies for Heritable Securities Indemnities) (Scotland) Order 1994
2031................Dartford–Thurrock Crossing Regulations 1994
2032................Railway Heritage Scheme Order 1994
2033................Dartford–Thurrock Crossing Tolls Order 1994
2034................Education (Assisted Places) (Amendment) Regulations 1994
2035................Education (Assisted Places) (Incidental Expenses) (Amendment) Regulations 1994
2036................Education (Grants) (Music and Ballet Schools) (Amendment) Regulations 1994

2038 (C. 39)...Education Act 1993 (Commencement No. 5 and Transitional Provisions) Order 1994

2040................York City Council (Foss Bank Bridge) Scheme 1993 Confirmation Instrument 1994

2041................York City Council (Peasholme Green Bridge) Scheme 1993 Confirmation Instrument 1994

2042................Buckinghamshire County Council (Marsh Drive Great Linford) (Canal Footbridge) Scheme 1993 Confirmation Instrument 1994

2063................Supply of Machinery (Safety) (Amendment) Regulations 1994

2064................Tees and Hartlepool Harbour Revision Order 1994

2068 (S. 93)...Alcan Aluminium UK Ltd (Rateable Values) (Scotland) Order 1994

2069 (S. 94)...British Gas Plc (Rateable Values) (Scotland) Order 1994

2070 (S. 95)...Railways (Rateable Values) (Scotland) Order 1994

2071 (S. 96)...British Telecommunications plc (Rateable Values) (Scotland) Order 1994

2072 (S. 97)...Electricity Generators (Rateable Values) (Scotland) Order 1994

2073 (S. 98)...Glasgow Underground (Rateable Values) (Scotland) Order 1994

2074 (S. 99)...Lochaber Power Company (Rateable Values) (Scotland) Order 1994

2075 (S. 100).Mercury Communications Ltd (Rateable Values) (Scotland) Order 1994

2076 (S. 101).Scottish Hydro-Electric plc (Rateable Values) (Scotland) Order 1994

2077 (S. 102).Scottish Nuclear Limited (Rateable Values) (Scotland) Order 1994

2078 (S. 103).Scottish Power plc (Rateable Values) (Scotland) Order 1994

2079 (S. 104).Water Undertakings (Rateable Values) (Scotland) Order 1994

2080 (S. 105).Caledonian MacBrayne Limited (Rateable Values) (Scotland) Order 1994

2081 (S. 106).Forth Ports plc (Rateable Values) (Scotland) Order 1994

2082................Merchant Shipping (IBC Code) (Amendment) Regulations 1994

2083................Merchant Shipping (Control of Pollution by Noxious Liquid Substances in Bulk) (Amendment) Regulations 1994

2084................Merchant Shipping (BCH Code) (Amendment) Regulations 1994

2085................Merchant Shipping (Prevention of Oil Pollution) (Amendment) Regulations 1994

2086................County Council of Norfolk (Reconstruction of Three Holes Bridge—Temporary Bridge) Scheme 1993 Confirmation Instrument 1994

2087................County Council of Norfolk (Reconstruction of Three Holes Bridge) Scheme 1993 Confirmation Instrument 1994

2092................Education (No. 2) Act 1986 (Amendment) Order 1994

2093................Education (Exclusions from Schools) (Prescribed Periods) Regulations 1994

2094................Education (Grant-maintained Schools) (Initial Governing Instruments) (Amendment) Regulations 1994

2095 (S. 107).Police (Scotland) Amendment Regulations 1994

2096 (S. 108).Police Cadets (Scotland) Amendment Regulations 1994

2097 (S. 109).Right to Purchase (Prescribed Persons) (Scotland) Amendment Order 1994

2099...............Education (National Curriculum) (Assessment Arrangements for the Core Subjects) (Key Stage 1) (Amendment) Order 1994
2100...............Education (National Curriculum) (Assessment Arrangements for the Core Subjects) (Key Stage 2) (England) Order 1994
2101...............Education (National Curriculum) (Assessment Arrangements for the Core Subjects) (Key Stage 3) (England) Order 1994
2102...............Education (Grant) (Amendment) Regulations 1994
2103...............Education (Pupil Referral Units) (Application of Enactments) Regulations 1994
2104...............Education (Grant-maintained Special Schools) (Initial Governing Instruments) Regulations 1994
2109 (C. 40)...Local Government (Wales) Act 1994 (Commencement No. 1) Order 1994
2110 (L. 11)...County Court (Forms) (Amendment No. 2) Rules 1994
2111...............Education (Grant-maintained Special Schools) (Finance) Regulations 1994
2112...............Education (National Curriculum Exceptions) Regulations 1994
2124 (C. 41) (S. 110) Inshore Fishing (Scotland) Act 1994 (Commencement) Order 1994
2126...............Welfare of Livestock Regulations 1994
2127...............Preserved Tuna and Bonito (Marketing Standards) Regulations 1994
2128...............Pupils' Registration (Amendment) Regulations 1994
2129...............M4 Motorway (Heathrow Airport Spur) (Speed Limit) Regulations 1994
2136...............Motor Vehicles (Tests) (Amendment) Regulations 1994
2137...............Housing Benefit and Council Tax Benefit (Miscellaneous Amendments) (No. 2) Regulations 1994
2138...............Council Tax Benefit (Permitted Total) Order 1994
2139...............Income-related Benefits Schemes (Miscellaneous Amendments) (No. 5) Regulations 1994
2141...............M27 South Coast Motorway (Ower–Chilworth Section) Connecting Roads Scheme 1970 (Variation) Scheme 1994
2142 (C. 42)...Railways Act 1993 (Commencement No. 6) Order 1994
2143 (C. 43)...Finance Act 1994, section 7, (Appointed Day) (No. 2) Order 1994
2144...............Food Protection (Emergency Prohibitions) (Paralytic Shellfish Poisoning) (No. 2) Order 1994
2145...............Compulsory Purchase of Land Regulations 1994
2150...............Railways Pensions Guarantee (Prescribed Persons) Order 1994
2151 (C. 44)...Police and Magistrates' Courts Act 1994 (Commencement No. 2) Order 1994
2152...............A1033 Trunk Road (Hedon Road Improvement) Order 1994
2153...............A1033 Trunk Road (Hedon Road) (Detrunking) Order 1994
2154...............Local Government Act 1988 (Defined Activities) (Exemption) (Gillingham Borough Council) Order 1994
2155...............Pig Carcase (Grading) Regulations 1994
2156...............Education (Payment for Special Educational Needs Supplies) (Amendment) Regulations 1994
2157...............Medicines (Veterinary Medicinal Products) (Applications for Product Licences) (Amendment) Regulations 1994
2158...............A47 Trunk Road (Allexton–Belton in Rutland Improvement) Order 1994

2371 (S. 114).Queen Margaret College, Edinburgh (Scotland) Order of Council 1994
2372................Protection of Wrecks (MV Braer) (Revocation) Order 1994
2386................National Assistance (Assessment of Resources) (Amendment) Regulations 1994
2387................Education (School Information) (England) (Amendment) Regulations 1994
2388................Railway Pensions (Substitution) Order 1994
2390................A628/A616 Trunk Road (Flouch Junction Improvement and Detrunking) Order 1994
2402................National Health Service (Pharmaceutical Services and Charges for Drugs and Appliances) Amendment Regulations 1994
2403 (L. 15)...County Court (Amendment No. 3) Rules 1994
2404................Potato Marketing Scheme (Amendment) Order 1994
2405................A550 and A5117 Trunk Roads (Improvement Between Deeside Park and Ledsham) and Connecting Roads Order 1994
2406................A550 Trunk Road (Improvement between Deeside Park and Ledsham) (Detrunking) Order 1994
2408 (C. 48)...Medicinal Products: Prescription by Nurses etc. Act 1992 (Commencement No. 1) Order 1994
2409................Medicines (Pharmacy and General Sales—Exemption) Amendment Order 1994
2410................Medicines (Products Other than Veterinary Drugs) (General Sale List) (Amendment) Order 1994
2411................Medicines (Sale or Supply) (Miscellaneous Provisions) Amendment Regulations 1994
2412................Bridgend and District National Health Service Trust (Transfer of Trust Property) Order 1994
2413................M606 Motorway (Staygate Extension) Scheme 1994
2414................A417 Trunk Road (North of Stratton to Nettleton Improvement) Order 1994
2415................A417 Trunk Road (North of Stratton to Nettleton Improvement) (Detrunking) Order 1994
2416................A417 Trunk Road (Daglingworth Quarry Junction) Order 1994
2417................A417 Trunk Road (Daglingworth Quarry Junction) (Detrunking) Order 1994
2418................A419/A417 Trunk Road (Cirencester and Stratton Bypass and Slip Roads) Order 1994
2419................A419/A417 Trunk Road (Cirencester and Stratton Bypass and Slip Roads) Order 1994
2420................Consumer Credit (Exempt Agreements) (Amendment) Order 1994
2421................Insolvent Partnerships Order 1994
2422................Local Government (Publication of Manpower Information) (England) (Revocation) Regulations 1994
2446................Education (Grants for Education Support and Training) (Amendment) Regulations 1994
2448................Dairy Produce Quotas (Amendment) Regulations 1994
2457................Building Societies (Designation of Qualifying Bodies) (Amendment) Order 1994
2458................Building Societies (Aggregation) (Amendment) Rules 1994
2459................Building Societies (Accounts and Related Provisions) (Amendment) Regulations 1994
2460................Milk Marketing Board Scheme of Reorganisation (Third Party Rights) Regulations 1994

2594 (C. 55)...Police and Magistrates' Courts Act 1994 (Commencement No. 3 and Transitional Provisions) Order 1994

2595................Town and Country Planning General Development (Amendment) (No. 2) Order 1994

2613 (S. 128).Inshore Fishing (Prohibition of Fishing for Cockles) (Scotland) (No. 2) Order 1994

2614................Firearms (Period of Certificate) Order 1994

2615................Firearms (Variation of Fees) Order 1994

2616................Solicitors' (Non-Contentious Business) Remuneration Order 1994

2617................Value Added Tax Tribunals (Amendments) Rules 1994

2618 (S. 129).Dumfries and Galloway College of Technology (Change of Name) (Scotland) Order 1994

2619................National Health Service (Optical Charges and Payments) Amendment (No. 3) Regulations 1994

2620................National Health Service (General Medical Services) Amendment (No. 2) Regulations 1994

2621 (S. 130).Rivers Tweed and Eye Protection (Renewal) Order 1991 Variation Order 1994

2622 (S. 131).River Luncan Catchment Area Protection (Renewal) Order 1991 Variation Order 1994

2623 (S. 132).River Tummel Catchment Area Protection (Renewal) Order 1991 Variation Order 1994

2624 (S. 133).National Health Service (General Medical and Pharmaceutical Services) (Scotland) Amendment (No. 2) Regulations 1994

2625................Trade Marks (Customs) Regulations 1994

2626................Civil Courts (Amendment No. 3) Order 1994

2627................Spongiform Encephalopathy (Miscellaneous Amendments) Order 1994

2628................Bovine Offal (Prohibition) (Amendment) Regulations 1994

2651................A12 Trunk Road (Lowestoft Eastern Relief Road) (Trunking and Detrunking) Order 1994

2652 (S. 134).Firearms (Variation of Fees) (Scotland) Order 1994

2653 (S. 135).Motor Vehicles (Competitions and Trials) (Scotland) Amendment Regulations 1994

2654................Public Telecommunication System Designation (Comment Cablevision Wearside Partnership) Order 1994

2655................Public Telecommunication System Designation (Racal Network Services Limited) Order 1994

2656................Capital Gains Tax (Gilt-edged Securities) Order 1994

2657................Taxes (Interest Rate) (Amendment No. 3) Regulations 1994

2658 (S. 136).National Health Service and Community Care Act 1990 (Commencement No. 11) (Scotland) Order 1990

2659 (C. 58)...National Lottery etc. Act 1993 (Commencement No. 3) Order 1994

2660................Cardiff-Glan Conway Trunk Road (A470) (Nant Crew Improvement) Order 1994

2673................Former Yugoslavia (United Nations Sanctions) (Dependent Territories) Order 1994

2674................Former Yugoslavia (United Nations Sanctions) (Dependent Territories) Order 1994

2675................Former Yugoslavia (United Nations Sanctions) (Channel Islands) Order 1994

2676................Former Yugoslavia (United Nations Sanctions) (Isle of Man) Order 1994

2677................Local Government (Publication of Manpower Information) (Wales) (Revocation) Regulations 1994

2678................Police (Secretary of State's Objectives) Order 1994

2679 (C. 59)...Finance Act 1994, Part I, (Appointed Day etc.) Order 1994

2680................Valuations for Rating (Plant and Machinery) Regulations 1994

2686................Social Security (Adjudication) Amendment (No. 2) Regulations 1994

2687................Addenbrookes's National Health Service Trust (Transfer of Trust Property) Order 1994

2688................Crawley Horsham National Health Service Trust (Transfer of Trust Property) Order 1994

2690................East Birmingham Hospital National Health Service Trust (Establishment) Amendment Order 1994

2691................Hinchingbroke Health Care National Health Service Trust (Transfer of Trust Property) Order 1994

2692................Kingston and District Community National Health Service Trust (Transfer of Trust Property) Order 1994

2693................Lincoln District Healthcare National Health Service Trust (Transfer of Trust Property) Order 1994

2694................Louth and District Healthcare National Health Service Trust (Transfer of Trust Property) Order 1994

2695................Community Health Care Service (North Derbyshire) National Health Service Trust (Transfer of Trust Property) Order 1994

2696................Northwick Park and St. Mark's National Health Service Trust (Transfer of Trust Property) Order 1994

2697................Papworth Hospital National Health Service Trust (Transfer of Trust Property) Order 1994

2698................St. George's Healthcare National Health Service Trust (Transfer of Trust Property) Order 1994

2699 (S. 137).Teacher's Superannuation (Scotland) Amendment Regulations 1994

2708................Harrow and Hillingdon Healthcare National Health Service Trust (Transfer of Trust Property) (No. 2) Order 1994

2709................Papworth Hospital National Health Service Trust (Transfer of Trust Property) (No. 2) Order 1994

2710 (S. 138).Habitats (Scotland) Regulations 1994

2711................Export of Goods (Control) Order 1994 (Amendment No. 3) 1994

2716................Conservation (Natural Habitats, &c.) Regulations 1994

2731................Apple Orchard Grubbing Up (Amendment) Regulations 1994

2732................Education (No. 2) Act 1986 (Amendment) (No. 3) Order 1994

2733................Portsmouth Mile End Quay (Continental Ferry Port Phase 7) Harbour Revision Order 1994

2734................Intelligence Services Act 1994 (Commencement) Order 1994

2735................Road Vehicles (Registration and Licensing) (Amendment) Regulations 1994

2736................Welsh Language (Names for Police Authorities in Wales) Order 1994

2740................Hill Livestock (Compensatory Allowances) Regulations 1994

2741................Sheep Annual Premium (Amendment) Regulations 1994

2744................Local Government Act 1988 (Defined Activities) (Exemption) (Gateshead Borough Council) Order 1994

2758 (S. 139).Shetland Islands Council (Laxa Burn, Mid Yell) (Amendment) Water Order 1994

2759................Milk Marketing Board (Residuary Functions) Regulations 1994

2762................Brucellosis (England and Wales) (Amendment) Order 1994

2765................Housing Renovation etc. Grants (Prescribed Forms and Particulars) (Amendment) Regulations 1994

2767................Parental Orders (Human Fertilisation and Embryology) Regulations 1994

2768................Legal Aid (Scope) Regulations 1994

2770 (S. 140) .Brucellosis (Scotland) Amendment Order 1994

2773................Isles of Scilly (National Health Service) Order 1994

2774................Teachers' Superannuation (Amendment) (No. 2) Regulations 1994

2782................Food Safety (Live Bivalve Molluscs and Other Shellfish) (Import Conditions and Miscellaneous Amendments) Regulations 1994

2783................Food Safety (Fishery Products) (Import Conditions and Miscellaneous Amendments) Regulations 1994

2784................Liverpool Obstetric and Gynaecology Services National Health Service Trust (Change of Name) Order 1994

2785................Road Traffic (Special Parking Areas) (London Borough of Barnet) (Amendment) Order 1994

2786................Road Traffic (Special Parking Areas) (London Borough of Wandsworth) (Amendment) Order 1994

2787................London North Circular Trunk Road (A406) (Barnet, Brent and Ealing) (Speed Limits) Order 1994

2788................Merchant Shipping (Sterling Equivalents) (Revocation) Order 1994

2789 (C. 61)...Merchant Shipping Act 1979 (Commencement No. 14) Order 1994

2790 (C. 62)...Local Government (Wales) Act 1994 (Commencement No. 2) Order 1994

2791................European Communities (Designation) (No. 4) Order 1994

2792................Child Abduction and Custody (Parties to Conventions) (Amendment) (No. 5) Order 1994

2793................Consular Fees Order 1994

2794................Extradition (Drug Trafficking) (Certain Territories) Order 1994

2795 (NI 15)..Criminal Justice (Northern Ireland) Order 1994

2796................European Convention on Extradition (Bulgaria) (Amendment) Order 1994

2797................Former Yugoslavia (United Nations Sanctions) (Channel Islands) (Amendment) Order 1994

2798................Summer Time Ends Order 1994

2799................Child Abduction and Custody Act 1985 (Isle of Man) Order 1994

2800................Family Law Act 1986 (Dependent Territories) (Amendment) Order 1994

2801................A19 Trunk Road (Portrack Roundabout) (Trunking) Order 1994

2802................Social Security (Jersey and Guernsey) Order 1994

2803................Trade Marks (Claims to Priority from Relevant Countries) Order 1994

2804 (S. 141) .Parental Orders (Human Fertilisation and Embryology) (Scotland) Regulations 1994

2805 (S. 142) .Act of Sederunt (Sheriff Court Parental Orders (Human Fertilisation and Embryology) Rules) 1994

2806 (S. 143) .Act of Sederunt (Rules of the Court of Session 1994 Amendment No. 2) (Human Fertilisation and Embryology) (Parental Orders) 1994

2809................Ports (Northern Ireland) Order 1994

2810................Ports (Northern Ireland Consequential Provisions) Order 1994
2811................Magistrates' Courts Committees (Constitution) Regulations 1994
2812................Local Government (Magistrates' Courts etc.) (Amendment) Order 1994
2813................Sea Fishing (Licences and Notices) Regulations 1994
2825................Local Government Changes for England (Finance) Regulations 1994
2826................Local Government Changes for England (Calculation of Council Tax Base) Regulations 1994
2841................Urban Waste Water Treatment (England and Wales) Regulations 1994
2842 (S. 144).Urban Waste Water Treatment (Scotland) Regulations 1994
2843................Welsh Principal Councils (Day of Election) Order 1994
2844................Dangerous Substances and Preparations (Safety) (Consolidation) Regulations 1994
2846................Shetland Islands Council Harbour Revision Order 1994
2847................Environmental Protection (Authorisation of Processes) (Determination Periods) (Amendment) Order 1994
2848................Education (Special Schools Conducted by Education Associations) (Amendment) Regulations 1994
2849................Education (Schools Conducted by Education Associations) (Initial Articles of Government) Regulations 1994
2850 (C. 63) (S. 145) Local Government etc. (Scotland) Act 1994 (Commencement No. 1) Order 1994
2851................Reconstitution of the Buckingham Internal Drainage Board Order 1994
2852................Medicines (Standard Provisions for Manufacturer's Licences for Veterinary Medicinal Products) Regulations 1994
2853................Beef Carcase (Classification) (Amendment) Regulations 1994
2854 (C. 64)...Environmental Protection Act 1990 (Commencement No. 16) Order 1994
2865................Management of Health and Safety at Work (Amendment) Regulations 1994
2866................Weights and Measures Act 1985 (Metrication) (Amendment) Order 1984
2867................Units of Measurement Regulations 1994
2868................Weights and Measures (Metrication) (Miscellaneous Goods) (Amendment) Order 1994
2876................Teachers' Superannuation (Amendment) (No. 3) Regulations 1994
2877................Merger Reference (Thomas Cook Group Limited and Barclays Bank plc) Order 1994
2879................Companies Act 1985 (Audit Exemption) (Amendment) Regulations 1994
2880................Commonwealth Development Corporation (Additional Enterprises) Order 1994
2884................Local Government Act 1988 (Competition) (Defined Activities) Order 1994
2887................A13 Trunk Road (Tower Hamlets) (Bus Lanes) Traffic Order 1994
2888................Local Government Act 1988 (Competition) (Defined Activities) (Construction and Property Services) Order 1994
2889................Alternative names in Welsh Order 1994
2890 (L. 17)...Family Proceedings (Amendment) (No. 3) Rules 1994
2891................Occupational Pensions (Revaluation) Order 1994
2893................Civil Courts (Amendment No. 4) Order 1994

2950...............Blackpool, Wyre and Fylde Community National Health Service Trust (Transfer of Trust Property) (No. 2) Order 1994
2952...............Parkside National Health Service Trust (Transfer of Trust Property) (No. 2) Order 1994
2953...............Merger Reference (Thomas Cook Group Limited and Barclays Bank plc) (No. 2) Order 1994
2954...............Health Service Commissioner for England (National Blood Authority) Order 1994
2955...............Intelligence Services Act 1994 (Channel Islands) Regulations 1994
2956...............Exempt Charities Order (No. 2) 1994
2957...............Education (Chief Inspector of Schools in Wales) Order 1994
2958 (S. 148).Local Government Staff Commission (Scotland) Order 1994
2964...............Local Authorities (Funds) (Wales) (Amendment) Regulations 1994
2965...............Diseases of Animals (Approved Disinfectants) (Amendment) Order 1994
2967...............Bingo Duty (Exemptions) Order 1994
2968 (C. 67)...Finance Act 1993, section 4 (Appointed Day) Order 1994
2696...............Value Added Tax (Education) (No. 2) Order 1994
2971 (C. 68)...Merchant Shipping (Salvage and Pollution) Act 1994 (Commencement No. 2) Order 1994
2972...............Export of Goods (Control) (Croation and Bosnian Territories) (Revocation) Order 1994
2973...............Industry-Wide Coal Staff Superannuation Scheme Regulations 1994
2974...............Industry-Wide Mineworkers' Pension Scheme Regulations 1994
2975...............Social Security (Medical Evidence) Amendment Regulations 1994
2976...............Retention of Registration Marks (Amendment) Regulations 1994
2977...............Sale of Registration Marks (Amendment) Regulations 1994
2978...............Suppression of Terrorism Act 1978 (Designation of Countries) Order 1994
2979...............Margaret Danyers College (Incorporation) Order 1994
2981...............Forms of Entry for Parental Orders Regulations 1994
2986...............Medicines (Veterinary Medicinal Products) (Veterinary Surgeons from Other EEA States) Regulations 1994
2987...............Medicines (Restrictions on the Administration of Veterinary Products) Regulations 1994
2988...............Aintree Hospitals National Health Service Trust (Transfer of Property) (No. 2) Order 1994
2989...............Hartlepool Community Care National Health Service Trust (Transfer of Trust Property) Order 1994
2990...............Hartlepool and Peterlee Hospitals National Health Service Trust (Transfer of Trust Property) Order 1994
2991...............South Lincolnshire Community and Mental Health Service Trust (Transfer of Trust Property) Order 1994
2993...............Police (Amendment) (No. 4) Regulations 1994
2994 (S. 149).Scottish Ambulance Service National Health Service Trust (Establishment) Order 1994
2995 (S. 150).Glasgow Dental Hospital and School National Health Service Trust (Establishment) Order 1994
2996 (S. 151).Argyll and Bute National Health Service Trust (Establishment) Order 1994
2997 (S. 152).Borders Community Health Service Trust (Establishment) Order 1994

2998 (S. 153).Borders General Hospital National Health Service Trust (Establishment) Order 1994

2999 (S. 154).Dumfries and Galloway Community Health National Health Service Trust (Establishment) Order 1994

3000 (S. 155).Lanarkshire Healthcare National Health Service Trust (Establishment) Order 1994

3001 (S. 156).Lomond Healthcare National Health Service Trust (Establishment) Order 1994

3002...............Farm and Conservation Grant (Variation) (No. 2) Scheme 1994

3003...............Farm and Conservation Grant (Amendment) Regulations 1994

3004...............A1 Trunk Road (Haringey) Red Route Traffic Order 1993 Variation Order 1994

3005...............A1 Trunk Road (Haringey) (Bus Lanes) Red Route Traffic Order 1993 Variation Order 1994

3006...............A1 Trunk Road (Islington) Red Route Traffic Order 1993 Variation Order 1994

3007...............A1 Trunk Road (Islington) (Bus Lanes) Red Route Traffic Order 1993 Variation Order 1994

3008...............Capital Gains Tax (Annual Exempt Amount) Order 1994

3009...............Retirement Benefits Schemes (Indexation of Earnings Cap) Order 1994

3010...............Income Tax (Cash Equivalents of Car Fuel Benefits) Order 1994

3011...............Inheritance Tax (Indexation) Order 1994

3013...............Value Added Tax (Buildings and Land) Order 1994

3014...............Value Added Tax (Transport) Order 1994

3015...............Value Added Tax (General) (Amendment) Regulations 1994

3016...............Medicines (Products Other Than Veterinary Drugs) (Prescription only) Amendment (No. 2) Order 1994

3017...............Medical Devices Regulations 1994

3018...............Accounts and Audit (Amendment) Regulations 1994

3021...............Electricity Supply (Amendment) (No. 2) Regulations 1994

3022...............Firearms (Amendment) Rules 1994

3023...............Charities Act 1992 (Commencement No. 2) Order 1994

3024...............Charitable Institutions (Fund-Raising) Regulations 1994

3025...............Local Government (Compensation for Redundancy) Regulations 1994

3026...............Local Government Superannuation (Amendment) Regulations 1994

3037 (C. 70)...Deregulation and Contracting Out Act 1994 (Commencement No. 1) Order 1994

3040...............Rent Officers (Additional Functions) (Amendment No. 2) Order 1994

3041...............Excise Duty (Amendment of the Isle of Man Act 1979) Order 1994

3042...............Education (Fees and Awards) Regulations 1994

3043...............Education (Mandatory Awards) (Amendment) (No. 2) Regulations 1994

3044...............Education (Mandatory Awards) Regulations 1994

3045...............Education (Student Loans) Regulations 1994

3049...............Merchant Shipping (Liability of Shipowners and Others) (Rate of Interest) Order 1994

3050...............Medicines (Products Other Than Veterinary Drugs) (Prescription Only) Amendment (No. 3) Order 1994

3051................Construction Products (Amendment) Regulations 1994
3053 (S. 159).Water Byelaws (Loch an Sgoltaire) Extension Order 1994
3054................Local Government Changes for England (Non-Domestic Rating) (Contributions) Regulations 1994
3056................Cambridgeshire County Council (River Nene B1040 Dog-in-a-Doublet Bridge) Scheme 1994 Confirmation Instrument 1994
3061................Income-related Benefits Schemes (Miscellaneous Amendments) (No. 6) Regulations 1994
3062................Doncaster Area Drainage Act 1929 (Amendment) Order 1994
3063 (C. 71)...Coal Industry Act 1994 (Commencement No. 3) Order 1994
3064................Coal Mining Subsidence (Land Drainage) Regulations 1994
3065................Aire and Calder Navigation Act 1992 (Amendment) Order 1994
3067 (S. 161).Environmentally Sensitive Areas (Scotland) Orders Amendment Order 1994
3068 (S. 162).Local Government (Compensation for Redundancy) (Scotland) Regulations 1994
3069................Insurance Brokers Registration Council (Registration and Enrolment) (Amendment) Rules Approval Order 1994
3070................Coal Industry (Protected Persons) Pensions Regulations 1994
3075 (C. 72) (S. 163) Police and Magistrates' Courts Act 1994 (Commencement No. 4 and Transitional Provisions) (Scotland) Order 1994
3078................Education (London Residuary Body) (Property Transfer) (Amendment) Order 1994
3079................District Probate Registries (Amendment No. 2) Order 1994
3080................Electromagnetic Compatibility (Amendment) Regulations 1994
3081................Coal Industry Act 1994 (Consequential Modifications of Local Acts) Order 1994
3082................Meat Products (Hygiene) Regulations 1994
3084 (S. 164).Local Government Act 1988 (Defined Activities) (Exemption) (Livingston Development Corporation) Order 1994
3085 (S. 165).Set-Aside Access (Scotland) Regulations 1994
3086 (S. 166).Act of Sederunt (Proceedings in the Sheriff Court under the Debtors (Scotland) Act 1987) (Amendment) 1994
3093................Treatment of Spruce Bark (Amendment) Order 1994
3094................Plant Health (Forestry) (Great Britain) (Amendment) Order 1994
3095................Vehicle Licences (Duration of First Licences and Rate of Duty) (Amendment) Order 1994
3096 (S. 167).Highlands and Islands Agricultural Programme Regulations 1994
3098................Simple Pressure Vessels (Safety) (Amendment) Regulations 1994
3099................Habitat (Broadleaved Woodland) (Wales) Regulations 1994
3100................Habitat (Water Fringe) (Wales) Regulations 1994
3101................Habitat (Coastal Belt) (Wales) Regulations 1994
3102................Habitat (Species-Rich Grassland) (Wales) Regulations 1994
3103................Licensing (Fees) (Amendment) Order 1994
3105................Education (London Residuary Body) (Property Transfer) (Amendment) (No. 2) Order 1994
3106................Education (University Commissioners) Order 1994
3107 (S. 168).Local Government Act 1988 (Supervision of Parking) (Exemption) (Scotland) Order 1994

3108 (S. 169) .Rent Officers (Additional Functions) (Scotland) Amendment (No. 2) Order 1994

3115...............Local Government Changes for England (Collection Fund Surpluses and Deficits) Regulations 1994

3116 (C. 73)...Marriage Act 1994 (Commencement No. 1) Order 1994

3117...............Motor Vehicles Tyres (Safety) Regulations 1994

3118...............Church Representation Rules (Amendment) Resolution 1994

3119...............Medical Devices (Consequential Amendments—Medicines) Regulations 1994

3120...............Medicines (Committee on Dental and Surgical Materials) (Revocation) Order 1994

3121...............Central Rating Lists Regulations 1994

3122...............Non-Domestic Rating (Miscellaneous Provisions) (No. 2) (Amendment) Regulations 1994

3123...............Non-Domestic Rating (Railways, Telecommunications and Canals) Regulations 1994

3124...............Local Government Reorganisation (Wales) (Transitional Provisions) Order 1994

3125...............Non-Domestic Rating Contributions (Wales) (Amendment) No. 3) Regulations 1994

3128...............Value Added Tax (Means of Transport) Order 1994

3129...............Telecommunications Terminal Equipment (Amendment and Extension) Regulations 1994

3130...............Vocational Training for General Medical Practice (European Requirements) Regulations 1994

3131...............Beef Special Premium (Amendment) Regulations 1994

3132...............Insurance Companies (Amendment) Regulations 1994

3133...............Insurance Companies (Amendment No. 2) Regulations 1994

3134...............A69 Trunk Road (Haltwhistle Bypass) Order 1994

3135...............A69 Trunk Road (Haltwhistle Bypass) (Detrunking) Order 1994

3136...............Legal Aid in Criminal and Care Proceedings (General) (Amendment) (No. 2) Regulations 1994

3138...............Children (Allocation of Proceedings) (Amendment) (No. 2) Order 1994

3139...............Non-Domestic Rating Contributions (England) (Amendment No. 3) Regulations 1994

3140...............Construction (Design and Management) Regulations 1994

3141...............Diseases of Poultry Order 1994

3142...............Marketing Authorisations for Veterinary Medicinal Products Regulations 1994

3143...............Medicines (Veterinary Drugs) (Renewal Applications for Licences and Animal Test Certificates) Regulations 1994

3144...............Medicines for Human Use (Marketing Authorisations Etc.) Regulations 1994

3146 (S. 170) .Non-Domestic Rating Contributions (Scotland) Amendment Regulations 1994

3147 (S. 171) .Parental Order Register (Form of Entry) (Scotland) Regulations 1994

3148 (S. 172) .Education (European Community Enlargement) (Scotland) Regulations 1994

3149 (S. 173) .Self-Governing Schools (Suspension of Proposals) (Scotland) Order 1994

3150 (C. 74) (S. 174) Local Government etc. (Scotland) Act 1994 (Commencement No. 2) Order 1994

3151 (S. 175) .Registration of Births, Still-Births, Deaths and Marriages (Prescription of Forms) (Scotland) Amendment Regulations 1994

3152 (C. 75) (S. 176) Local Government Finance Act 1992 (Commencement No. 9 and Transitional Provision) Order 1994
3153 (L. 19)...Crown Court (Amendment) (No. 2) Rules 1994
3154 (L. 20)...Magistrates' Courts (Miscellaneous Amendments) Rules 1994
3155 (L. 21)...Family Proceedings (Amendment) (No. 4) Rules 1994
3156 (L. 22)...Family Proceedings Courts (Children Act 1989) (Amendment) (No. 2) Rules 1994
3157................Parental Responsibility Agreement (Amendment) Regulations 1994
3158................Severn Bridges Tolls Order 1994
3159................Unfair Terms in Consumer Contracts Regulations 1994
3161................Local Government Act 1988 (Defined Activities) (Exemption) (Hastings Borough Council, Worthing Borough Council and Barnet London Borough Council) Order 1994
3162................Gloucester Harbour Revision Order 1994
3163................Telecommunications Meters (Approval Fees) (BABT) (Amendment) Order 1994
3164................Local Government Act 1988 (Competition) (Legal Services) (England) Regulations 1994
3165................Local Government Act 1988 (Defined Activities) (Competition) (Supervision of Parking, Management of Vehicles and Security Work) (England) Regulations 1994
3166................Local Government Act 1988 (Competition) (Construction and Property Services) (England) Regulations 1994
3167................Local Government Changes for England (Direct Labour and Service Organisations) Regulations 1994
3168................Ogwr (Ogmore Valley and Garw Valley Communities) Order 1994
3169................Medicines (Veterinary Drugs) (Pharmacy and Merchants' List) (Amendment No. 2) Order 1994
3170 (S. 177).Council Tax (Reduction of Liability) (Scotland) Regulations 1994
3172................Broadcasting (Unlicensed Television Services) Exemption Order 1994
3173................Bournewood Community and Mental Health National Health Service Trust (Establishment) Order 1994
3174................Manchester Children's Hospital National Health Service Trust (Establishment) Order 1994
3175................Grantham and District Hospital National Health Service Trust (Establishment) Order 1994
3176................Sussex Ambulance Service National Health Service Trust (Establishment) Order 1994
3177................Black Country Mental Health National Health Service Trust (Establishment) Order 1994
3178................Pathfinder National Health Service Trust (Establishment) Order 1994
3179................Princess Alexandra Hospital National Health Service Trust (Establishment) Order 1994
3180................Essex and Herts Community National Health Service Trust (Establishment) Order 1994
3181................Homerton Hospital National Health Service Trust (Establishment) Order 1994
3182................Birmingham Children's Hospital National Health Service Trust (Establishment) Order 1994
3183................St. James's and Seacroft University Hospitals National Health Service Trust (Establishment) Order 1994
3184................Royal Liverpool and Broadgreen University Hospitals National Health Service Trust (Establishment) Order 1994

3185................Fosse Health, Leicestershire Community National Health Service Trust (Establishment) Order 1994

3186................United Leeds Teaching Hospitals National Health Service Trust (Establishment) Order 1994

3187................Air Navigation (Dangerous Goods) Regulations 1994

3188 (C. 76)...Deregulation and Contracting Out Act 1994 (Commencement No. 2) Order 1994

3189................Local Government Act 1988 (Defined Activities) (Exemption) (South Norfolk District Council) Order 1994

3190................Local Government Act 1988 (Defined Activities) (Exemption) (Southwark London Borough Council) Order 1994

3191................Criminal Justice Act 1991 (Commencement No. 4) Order 1994

3192 (C. 78)...Criminal Justice and Public Order Act 1994 (Commencement No. 2) Order 1994

3193................Criminal Justice Act 1991 (Suspension of Prisoner Custody Officer Certificate) (Amendment) Regulations 1994

3194................Young Offender Institution (Amendment) Rules 1994

3195................Prison (Amendment) Rules 1994

3196................Social Security (Claims and Payments) Amendment (No. 4) Regulations 1994

3197................Wolverhampton Health Care National Health Service Trust (Establishment) Order 1994

3198 (S. 178).Firearms (Scotland) Amendment Rules 1994

3199 (S. 179).Valuation for Rating (Plant and Machinery) (Scotland) Regulations 1994

3200................Non-Domestic Rating (Unoccupied Property) (Scotland) Regulations 1994

3201................Child Abduction and Custody (Parties to Conventions) (Amendment) (No. 6) Order 1994

3202................Consular Fees (Amendment) Order 1994

3203................European Convention on Extradition (Amendment) Order 1994

3204 (NI 17)..Firearms (Amendment) (Northern Ireland) Order 1994

3205................Food and Environment Protection Act 1985 (Isle of Man) (Revocation) Order 1994

3206................Ministerial and Other Salaries Order 1994

3207................Double Taxation Relief (Taxes on Income) (Estonia) Order 1994

3208................Double Taxation Relief (Taxes on Income) (Isle of Man) Order 1994

3209................Double Taxation Relief (Taxes on Income) (Guernsey) Order 1994

3210................Double Taxation Relief (Taxes on Income) (Jersey) Order 1994

3211................Double Taxation Relief (Taxes on Income) (Kazakhstan) Order 1994

3212................Double Taxation Relief (Taxes on Income) (Mexico) Order 1994

3213................Double Taxation Relief (Taxes on Income) (Russian Federation) Order 1994

3214................Double Taxation Relief (Taxes on Estates of Deceased Persons and Inheritances) (Switzerland) Order 1994

3215................Double Taxation Relief (Taxes on Income) (Switzerland) Order 1994

3216................Double Taxation Relief (Taxes on Income) (Vietnam) Order 1994

3217................Maximum Number of Judges Order 1994

3264................Compulsory Purchase by Ministers (Inquiries Procedure) Rules 1994

3265 (S. 185).Court of Session etc. Fees Amendment Order 1994

3266 (S. 186).High Court of Justiciary Fees Amendment Order 1994

3267 (S. 187).Act of Sederunt (Fees of Sheriff Officers) (No. 2) 1994

3268 (S. 188).Act of Sederunt (Fees of Messengers-at-Arms) (No. 2) 1994

3269 (S. 189).Town and Country Planning (Fees for Applications and Deemed Applications) (Scotland) Amendment Regulations 1994

3270................Road Vehicles (Construction and Use) (Amendment) (No. 3) Regulations 1994

3271................Public Service Vehicles (Registration of Local Services) (Amendment) Regulations 1994

3272................Public Service Vehicles (Traffic Regulation Conditions) (Amendment) Regulations 1994

3275 (S. 190).Electricity (Non-Fossil Fuel Sources) (Scotland) Order 1994

3276................Sex Discrimination Act 1975 (Application to Armed Forces etc.) Regulations 1994

3277................National Savings Stock Register (Amendment) Regulations 1994

3278................Overseas Life Assurance Fund (Amendment) Order 1994

3279................Non-Domestic Rating (Chargeable Amounts) Regulations 1994

3280................Docks and Harbours (Rateable Values) (Amendment) Order 1994

3281................British Waterways Board and Telecommunications Industry (Rateable Values) Revocations Order 1994

3282................Electricity Supply Industry (Rateable Values) Order 1994

3283................British Gas plc (Rateable Values) Order 1994

3284................Railways (Rateable Values) Order 1994

3285................Water Undertakers (Rateable Values) Order 1994

3286................Channel Tunnel (Sunday Trading Act 1994) (Disapplication) Order 1994

3292 (C. 84) (S. 191) Planning and Compensation Act 1991 (Commencement No. 17 and Transitional Provision) (Scotland) Order 1994

3293 (S. 190).Town and Country Planning (General Development Procedure) (Scotland) Amendment (No. 2) Order 1994

3294 (S. 193).Town and Country Planning (General Permitted Development) (Scotland) Amendment (No. 3) Order 1994

3296................Road Vehicles (Registration and Licensing) (Amendment) (No. 3) Regulations 1994

3297................Road Vehicles (Registration and Licensing) (Amendment) (No. 2) Regulations (Northern Ireland) 1994

3298................General Medical Council Preliminary Proceedings Committee and Professional Conduct Committee (Procedure) (Amendment) Rules Order of Council 1994

3301................Employers' Liability (Compulsory Insurance) General (Amendment) Regulations 1994

3302 (S. 194).North West Sutherland Protection Order 1994

3303................Legal Advice and Assistance at Police Stations (Remuneration) (Amendment) (No. 2) Regulations 1994

3307................A630 Trunk Road (Doncaster) (Detrunking) Order 1994

3308 (S. 195).Strathclyde Regional Council (Loch Assapol) Water Order 1994

3309 (S. 196).Strathclyde Regional Council (Ayr Burgh Act 1885) (Amendment) Water Order 1994

3313................Combined Probation Areas (Derbyshire) Order 1994

NUMERICAL TABLE OF STATUTORY INSTRUMENTS 1995

This table details in numerical order Statutory Instruments released in 1995. The table is up to date to **March 10, 1995.** For brief digests of Statutory Instruments see the Current Law Monthly Digest.

1 (S. 1).....National Health Service (Optical Charges and Payments) (Scotland) Amendment Regulations 1995
2................Plymouth Hospitals National Health Service Trust (Transfer of Trust Property) Order 1995
10................Criminal Justice Act 1988 (Reviews of Sentencing) Order 1995
11................Pigs (Records, Identification and Movement) Order 1995
12................Bovine Animals (Records, Identification and Movement) Order 1995
13................Enzootic Bovine Leukosis (Amendment) Order 1995
14................Beef Special Premium (Amendment) Regulations 1995
15................Suckler Cow Premium (Amendment) Regulations 1995
16................Fertilisers (Amendment) Regulations 1995
17................A23 Trunk Road (Brighton Road, Croydon) (Prohibition of Right Turn and U-Turn) Order 1995
21................Community Charges (Administration and Enforcement) (Amendment) Regulations 1995
22................Council Tax (Administration and Enforcement) (Amendment) Regulations 1995
24 (C. 1).....Criminal Justice and Public Order Act 1994 (Commencement No. 4) Order 1995
23................Local Government Changes for England (Council Tax and Non-Domestic Rating, Demand Notices) Regulations 1995
31................Employment Protection (Part-time Employees) Regulations 1995
33................Borough of Trafford (Eastern Spine Canal Bridge) Scheme 1993 Confirmation Instrument 1995
38................Borough of Trafford (A5063 Trafford/White City Gyratory System Canal Bridges) Scheme 1993 Confirmation Instrument 1995
39................Food Protection (Emergency Prohibitions) (Radioactivity in Sheep) (England) (Partial Revocation) Order 1995
40................Apple Orchard Grubbing Up (Amendment) Regulations 1995
41................Justices of the Peace Act 1949 (Compensation) (Variation) Regulations 1995
42 (C. 2).....Police and Magistrates' Courts Act 1994 (Commencement No. 6 and Transitional Provisions) Order 1995
43 (C. 3).....Criminal Justice Act 1993 (Commencement No. 8) Order 1995
45................Education (Special Educational Needs) (Prescribed Forms) (Welsh Forms) Regulations 1995
48................Food Protection (Emergency Prohibitions) (Radioactivity in Sheep) Partial Revocation Order 1995
49................Home Energy Efficiency Grants (Amendment) Regulations 1995
51................Education (National Curriculum) (Attainment Targets and Programmes of Study in English) Order 1995
52................Education (National Curriculum) (Attainment Targets and Programmes of Study Mathematics) Order 1995

476...............Environmental Protection (Waste Recycling Payments) (Amendment) Regulations 1995
477...............Broadgreen Hospital National Health Service Trust Dissolution Order 1995
478...............Fosse Health, Leicestershire Community National Health Service Trust Dissolution Order 1995
479...............Royal Liverpool University Hospital National Health Service Trust Dissolution Order 1995
480...............St James's University Hospital National Health Service Trust Dissolution Order 1995
481...............Weybourne Community National Health Service Trust Dissolution Order 1995
482...............Disability Working Allowance and Income Support (General) Amendment Regulations 1995
484 (S. 33) ...Spirit Drinks (Scotland) Amendment Regulations 1995
485...............A5 Trunk Road (Priorslee–Gailey) (Detrunking) Order 1995
490...............Antarctic Regulations 1995
493...............Avon (Structural Change) Order 1995
495...............Port of Folkstone Licensing (Liquor) Order 1995
496...............Port of Ramsgate Licensing (Liquor) Order 1995
497...............Civil Aviation (Navigation Services Charges) Regulations 1995
501...............Education (Grants for Education Support and Training) (Wales) Regulations 1995
502...............Carmarthen and District National Health Service Trust (Transfer of Trust Property) Order 1995
503...............Derwen National Health Service Trust (Transfer of Trust Property) Order 1995
504...............Ceredigion and Mid Wales National Health Service Trust (Transfer of Trust Property) Order 1995
505...............Llanelli Dinefwr National Health Service Trust (Transfer of Trust Property) Order 1995
506...............Misuse of Drugs (Licence Fees) (Amendment) Regulations 1995
510...............Marriages (Approved Premises) Regulations 1995
512...............Statutory Sick Pay Percentage Threshold Order 1995
513...............Statutory Sick Pay Percentage Threshold Order 1995 (Consequential) Regulations 1995
514...............Social Security (Contributions) Amendment Regulations 1995
515...............Guaranteed Minimum Pensions Increase Order 1995
520...............Local Government Changes for England (Staff) Regulations 1995
522...............Education (Individual Pupils' Achievements) (Information) (Wales) (Amendment) Regulations 1995
524...............Occupational and Personal Pension Schemes (Levy) Regulations 1995
525...............Merchant Shipping (Light Dues) (Amendment) Regulations 1995
531...............Local Government Changes for England (Housing Benefit and Council Tax Benefit) Regulations 1995
532...............Education (School Financial Statements) (Prescribed Particulars, etc.) (Amendment) Regulations 1995
533...............National Health Service (Determination of Districts) (No. 2) Order 1995
534...............National Health Service (District Health Authorities) (No. 2) Order 1995

535................Local Authorities (Capital Finance) (Rate of Discount for 1995/96) Regulations 1995

536................Greater London and Surrey (County and London Borough Boundaries) (Variation) Order 1995

539................Fresh Meat (Hygiene and Inspection) Regulations 1995

540................Poultry, Farmed Game Bird Meat and Rabbit Meat (Hygiene and Inspection) Regulations 1995

541................Medicines (Homeopathic Medicinal Products for Human Use) Amendment Regulations 1995

549................Non-Domestic Rating (Unoccupied Property) (Amendment) Regulations 1995

553................Local Authorities (Members' Allowances) (Amendment) Regulations 1995

556................Local Government (Promotion of Economic Development) (Amendment) Regulations 1995

ALPHABETICAL TABLE OF STATUTES

This is an alphabetical table of statutes from 1700–1994. It comprises a listing of Acts printed in the edition of the Record Commissioners known as Statutes of the Realm so far as it extends (1713), the Acts printed in Ruffhead's Edition so far as it extends (1785) and thereafter all Acts printed by the King's or Queen's Printer as Public Acts or (since 1797) Public General Acts. It should be noted that from 1797 Public Acts were divided into two series, Public General and Public Local and Personal Acts, prior to that date Acts which might now be classified as local were included in the definition Public Acts. Such Acts are therefore included in this list. For 1995 statutes see the most recent table in the Contents section of the Service File.

Abandonment of Animals Act 1960 (c.43)
Abandonment of Railways Act 1850 (c.83)
Abandonment of Railways Act 1869 (c.114)
Aberbrothock Beer Duties Act 1737 (c.4)
Aberbrothock Beer Duties Act 1763 (c.28)
Aberbrothock Beer Duties Act 1787 (c.46)
Aberdare Canal Act 1793 (c.95)
Aberdeen Beer Duties Act 1730 (c.13)
Aberdeen Commissary Court Records Act 1721 (c.28)
Aberdeen Harbour Act 1772 (c.29)
Aberdeen Harbour Act 1795 (c.41)
Aberdeen Harbour Act 1796 (c.68)
Aberdeen: Harbour Improvement Act 1797 (c.101)
Aberdeen Improvements Act 1795 (c.76)
Aberdeen Records Act 1722 (c.25)
Aberdeen Roads Act 1795 (c.161)
Abergavenny: Improvement Act 1794 (c.106)
Abergele and Rhydlan: Drainage Act 1794 (c.110)
Aberystwyth Harbour Act 1780 (c.26)
Abingdon: Improvement Act 1794 (c.89)
Abingdon to Swinford Roads Act 1768 (c.61)
Abingdon to Trowbridge Canal Act 1795 (c.52)
Abnormal Importations (Customs Duties) Act 1931 (c.1)
Abolition of Domestic Rates Etc. (Scotland) Act 1987 (c.47)
Abolition of Offices in Courts of Law Act 1845 (c.78)
Abolition of Slave Trade Act 1807 (c.36)
Abolition of Slavery Act 1836 (c.5)
Abolition of Slavery Act 1836 (c.16)
Abolition of Slavery Act 1836 (c.82)
Abolition of Slavery Act 1837 (c.3)
Abolition of Slavery Act 1838 (c.19)
Abolition of Slavery Act 1841 (c.18)
Abortion Act 1967 (c.87)
Absconding Debtors Act 1870 (c.76)
Access to Health Records Act 1990 (c.23)
Access to Medical Reports Act 1988 (c.28)
Access to Mountains Act 1939 (c.30)
Access to Neighbouring Land Act 1992 (c.23)
Access to Personal Files Act 1987 (c.37)
Accession Declaration Act 1910 (c.29)
Accessories and Abettors Act 1861 (c.94)

Accommodation Agencies Act 1953 (c.23)
Account of Civil List Revenues Act 1815 (c.15)
Accountant General in Chancery Act 1804 (c.82)
Accountant General of Court of Chancery Act 1813 (c.14)
Accounting for Certain Debentures Act 1706 (c.33)
Accounts, etc., of Barrack Master General Act 1807 (c.13)
Accounts of Barrack Office Act 1808 (c.89)
Accounts of Colonial Revenues Act 1814 (c.184)
Accounts of Expenditure in France Act 1814 (c.98)
Accounts of Expenditure in West Indies Act 1808 (c.91)
Accounts of Paymaster General Act 1808 (c.49)
Accumulations Act 1800 (c.98)
Accumulations Act 1892 (c.58)
Achurch Parish Church 1778 (c.9)
Acknowledgement of Deeds by Married Women Act 1854 (c.75)
Acknowledgement of Deeds by Married Women (Ireland) Act 1878 (c.23)
Acquisition of Land Act 1981 (c.67)
Acquisition of Land (Assessment of Compensation) Act 1919 (c.57)
Acquisition of Land (Assessment of Compensation) (Scotland) Act 1931 (c.11)
Acquisition of Land (Authorisation Procedure) Act 1946 (c.49)
Acquisition of Land (Authorisation Procedure) (Scotland) Act 1947 (c.42)
Act of Marriage 1929 (c.36)
Act of Settlement 1700 (c.2)
Act of Uniformity 1662 (c.4)
Act of Uniformity Amendment Act 1872 (c.35)
Actions Against Certain Spiritual Persons Act 1803 (c.34)
Actions Against Spiritual Persons Act 1813 (c.6)
Actions, etc., for Buying Oak Bark, etc. Act 1806 (c.152)
Actions for Gaming Act 1844 (c.3)
Actions for Gaming Act 1844 (c.58)

1

Acts of Common Council, London Act 1745 (c.8)

Acts of Parliament (Commencement) Act 1793 (c.13)

Acts of Parliament (Expiration) 1808 (c.106)

Acts of Parliament (Mistaken References) Act 1837 (c.60)

Acts of Parliament Numbering and Citation Act 1962 (c.34)

Adam Buildings Act 1772 (c.75)

Aden, Perim and Kuria Muria Islands Act 1967 (c.71)

Addenbrooke's Hospital, Cambridge Act 1767 (c.99)

Adderbury and Oxford Road Act 1797 (c.170)

Addingham to Black Lane End Road Act 1781 (c.99)

Additional Income Tax Act 1884 (c.1)

Additional Taxes Act 1795 (c.14)

Admeasurement of Coals Act 1780 (c.34)

Administration Act 1868 (c.90)

Administration of Estates Act 1798 (c.87)

Administration of Estates Act 1869 (c.46)

Administration of Estates Act 1925 (c.23)

Administration of Estates Act 1971 (c.25)

Administration of Estates (Probate) Act 1800 (c.72)

Administration of Estates (Small Payments) Act 1965 (c.32)

Administration of Intestates' Estates Act 1856 (c.94)

Administration of Justice Act 1705 (c.3)

Administration of Justice Act 1813 (c.24)

Administration of Justice Act 1920 (c.81)

Administration of Justice Act 1925 (c.28)

Administration of Justice Act 1928 (c.26)

Administration of Justice Act 1932 (c.55)

Administration of Justice Act 1956 (c.46)

Administration of Justice Act 1960 (c.65)

Administration of Justice Act 1964 (c.42)

Administration of Justice Act 1965 (c.2)

Administration of Justice Act 1968 (c.5)

Administration of Justice Act 1969 (c.58)

Administration of Justice Act 1970 (c.31)

Administration of Justice Act 1973 (c.15)

Administration of Justice Act 1977 (c.38)

Administration of Justice Act 1982 (c.53)

Administration of Justice Act 1985 (c.61)

Administration of Justice (Appeals) Act 1934 (c.40)

Administration of Justice (Emergency Provisions) Act 1939 (c.78)

Administration of Justice (Emergency Provisions) Act 1939 (c.105)

Administration of Justice (Emergency Provisions) (Scotland) Act 1939 (c.79)

Administration of Justice (Emergency Provisions) (Scotland) Act 1979 (c.19)

Administration of Justice in Certain Boroughs Act 1836 (c.105)

Administration of Justice (Judges and Pensions) Act 1960 (c.3)

Administration of Justice (Miscellaneous Provisions) Act 1933 (c.36)

Administration of Justice (Miscellaneous Provisions) Act 1938 (c.63)

Administration of Justice, New South Wales, etc. Act 1838 (c.50)

Administration of Justice (Pensions) Act 1950 (c.11)

Administration of Justice (Scotland) Act 1809 (c.119)

Administration of Justice (Scotland) Act 1933 (c.41)

Administration of Justice (Scotland) Act 1948 (c.10)

Administration of Justice (Scotland) Act 1972 (c.59)

Administration of Justice, West Indies Act 1836 (c.17)

Admiralty and Prize Courts Act 1810 (c.118)

Admiralty and War Office Regulation Act 1878 (c.53)

Admiralty Court Act 1840 (c.65)

Admiralty Court Act 1861 (c.10)

Admiralty, etc. Acts Repeal Act 1865 (c.112)

Admiralty, etc., Courts, (Scotland) Act 1786 (c.47)

Admiralty Jurisdiction (Indian) Act 1860 (c.88)

Admiralty Lands Act 1843 (c.58)

Admiralty Lands and Works Act 1864 (c.57)

Admiralty Offences Act 1826 (c.38)

Admiralty Offences Act 1844 (c.2)

Admiralty Offences (Colonial) Act 1849 (c.96)

Admiralty Offences (Colonial) Act 1860 (c.122)

Admiralty Pensions Act 1921 (c.39)

Admiralty Powers etc. Act 1865 (c.124)

Admiralty Suits Act 1868 (c.78)

Admission of Vassals (Scotland) Act 1751 (c.20)

Adoption Act 1950 (c.26)

Adoption Act 1958 (c.5)

Adoption Act 1960 (c.59)

Adoption Act 1964 (c.57)

Adoption Act 1968 (c.53)

Adoption Act 1976 (c.36)

Adoption of Children Act 1926 (c.29)

Adoption of Children Act 1949 (c.98)

Adoption of Children (Regulation) Act 1939 (c.27)

Adoption of Children (Scotland) Act 1930 (c.37)

Adoption of Children (Workmen's Compensation) Act 1934 (c.34)

Adoption (Scotland) Act 1978 (c.28)

Adulteration of Coffee Act 1718 (c.11)

Adulteration of Food and Drugs Act 1872 (c.74)

Adulteration of Hops Act 1733 (c.19)

Adulteration of Seeds Act 1869 (c.112)

Adulteration of Seeds Act 1878 (c.17)

Adulteration of Tea Act 1730 (c.14)

Adulteration of Tea Act 1776 (c.29)

Adulteration of Tea and Coffee Act 1724 (c.30)

Advance by Bank of England Act 1781 (c.60)
Advance by Bank of England Act 1816 (c.7)
Advance by Bank of England Act 1816 (c.14)
Advance from Bank of England Act 1808 (c.3)
Advance of Money to Foreign States Act 1729 (c.5)
Advance of Unclaimed Dividends, etc. Act 1808 (c.4)
Advance of Unclaimed Dividends, etc. Act 1816 (c.97)
Advance Petroleum Revenue Tax Act 1986 (c.68)
Advance to Boyed, Benfield and Co. Act 1805 (c.78)
Advances by Bank of Ireland Act 1811 (c.35)
Advances for Public Works Act 1837 (c.51)
Advances for Public Works Act 1838 (c.88)
Advances for Public Works Act 1840 (c.10)
Advances for Public Works Act 1842 (c.9)
Advances for Public Works Act 1861 (c.80)
Advances for Public Works Act 1862 (c.30)
Advances for Railways (Ireland) Act 1847 (c.73)
Advances to County of Mayo Acts 1854 (c.110)
Advertisements (Hire Purchase) Act 1957 (c.41)
Advertisements (Hire-Purchase) Act 1967 (c.42)
Advertisements Regulation Act 1907 (c.27)
Advertisements Regulation Act 1925 (c.52)
Advertising Stations (Rating) Act 1889 (c.27)
Advowsons Act 1707 (c.18)
Aerial Navigation Act 1911 (c.4)
Aerial Navigation Act 1913 (c.22)
Affidavits in County of Durham Act 1763 (c.21)
Affidavits in County of Lancaster Act 1743 (c.7)
Affiliation Orders Act 1914 (c.6)
Affiliation Orders Act 1952 (c.41)
Affiliation Orders (Increase of Maximum Payment) Act 1918 (c.49)
Affiliation Proceedings Act 1957 (c.55)
Affiliation Proceedings (Amendment) Act 1972 (c.49)
Affirmation by Quakers Act 1701 (c.4)
Affirmations Act 1861 (c.66)
Affirmations by Quakers etc. Act 1859 (c.10)
Affirmations (Scotland) Act 1855 (c.25)
Affirmations (Scotland) Act 1865 (c.9)
African Company Act 1711 (c.34)
African Company Act 1750 (c.49)
African Company Act 1751 (c.40)
African Company Act 1783 (c.65)
African Slave Trade Act 1862 (c.40)
African Slave Trade Act 1862 (c.90)
African Slave Trade Treaty Act 1863 (c.34)
Age of Legal Capacity (Scotland) Act 1991 (c.50)
Age of Majority (Scotland) Act 1969 (c.39)
Age of Marriage Act 1929 (c.36)
Agent General for Volunteers, etc. Act 1812 (c.152)

Agent General for Volunteers, etc. Act 1815 (c.170)
Aggravated Vehicle-Taking Act 1992 (c.11)
Agricultural and Technical Instruction (Ireland) - Northern Irish Act 1899 (c.50)
Agricultural and Forestry Associations Act 1962 (c.29)
Agricultural and Forestry (Financial Provisions) Act 1991 (c.33)
Agricultural Children Act 1873 (c.67)
Agricultural Credits Act 1923 (c.34)
Agricultural Credits Act 1928 (c.43)
Agricultural Credits Act 1931 (c.35)
Agricultural Credits (Scotland) Act 1929 (c.13)
Agricultural Development Act 1939 (c.48)
Agricultural Development (Ploughing up of Land) Act 1946 (c.32)
Agricultural Gangs Act 1867 (c.130)
Agricultural Holdings Act 1900 (c.50)
Agricultural Holdings Act 1906 (c.56)
Agricultural Holdings Act 1908 (c.28)
Agricultural Holdings Act 1913 (c.21)
Agricultural Holdings Act 1914 (c.7)
Agricultural Holdings Act 1923 (c.9)
Agricultural Holdings Act 1948 (c.63)
Agricultural Holdings Act 1984 (c.41)
Agricultural Holdings Act 1986 (c.5)
Agricultural Holdings (Amendment) Act 1990 (c.15)
Agricultural Holdings (Amendment) (Scotland) Act 1983 (c.46)
Agricultural Holdings (England) Act 1875 (c.92)
Agricultural Holdings (England) Act (1875) Amendment Act 1876 (c.74)
Agricultural Holdings (England) Act 1883 (c.61)
Agricultural Holdings (Notices to Quit) Act 1977 (c.12)
Agricultural Holdings (Scotland) Act 1883 (c.62)
Agricultural Holdings (Scotland) Act 1889 (c.20)
Agricultural Holdings (Scotland) Act 1908 (c.64)
Agricultural Holdings (Scotland) Act 1923 (c.10)
Agricultural Holdings (Scotland) Act 1949 (c.75)
Agricultural Holdings (Scotland) Amendment Act 1910 (c.30)
Agricultural Improvement Grants Act 1959 (c.31)
Agricultural Land (Removal of Surface Soil) Act 1953 (c.10)
Agricultural Land Sales (Restriction of Notice to Quit) Act 1919 (c.63)
Agricultural Land (Utilisation) Act 1931 (c.41)
Agricultural Marketing Act 1931 (c.42)
Agricultural Marketing Act 1933 (c.31)
Agricultural Marketing Act 1949 (c.38)
Agricultural Marketing Act 1958 (c.47)

Agricultural Marketing Act 1983 (c.3)

Agricultural Marketing (No. 2) Act 1933 (c.1)

Agricultural (Miscellaneous Provisions) Act 1949 (c.37)

Agricultural (Miscellaneous Provisions) Act 1950 (c.17)

Agricultural Mortgage Corporation Act 1956 (c.38)

Agricultural Mortgage Corporation Act 1958 (c.2)

Agricultural Produce (Grading and Marking) Act 1928 (c.19)

Agricultural Produce (Grading and Marking) Amendment Act 1931 (c.40)

Agricultural Rates Act 1896 (c.16)

Agricultural Rates Act, 1896, etc., Continuance Act 1901 (c.13)

Agricultural Rates Act, 1896, etc., Continuance Act 1905 (c.8)

Agricultural Rates Act 1923 (c.39)

Agricultural Rates Act 1929 (c.26)

Agricultural Rates (Additional Grant) Continuance Act 1925 (c.10)

Agricultural Rates, Congested Districts, and Burgh Land Tax Relief (Scotland) 1896 (c.37)

Agricultural Research Act 1955 (c.28)

Agricultural Research etc. (Pensions) Act 1961 (c.9)

Agricultural Returns Act 1925 (c.39)

Agricultural Statistics Act 1979 (c.13)

Agricultural Training Board Act 1982 (c.9)

Agricultural Training Board Act 1985 (c.36)

Agricultural Training Board Act 1987 (c.29)

Agricultural Wages Act 1948 (c.47)

Agricultural Wages (Regulation) Act 1924 (c.37)

Agricultural Wages (Regulation) Act 1947 (c.15)

Agricultural Wages (Regulation) Amendment Act 1939 (c.17)

Agricultural Wages (Regulation) (Scotland) Act 1937 (c.53)

Agricultural Wages (Regulation) (Scotland) Act 1939 (c.27)

Agricultural Wages (Scotland) Act 1949 (c.30)

Agriculture Act 1920 (c.76)

Agriculture Act 1937 (c.70)

Agriculture Act 1947 (c.48)

Agriculture Act 1957 (c.57)

Agriculture Act 1958 (c.71)

Agriculture Act 1967 (c.22)

Agriculture Act 1970 (c.40)

Agriculture Act 1986 (c.49)

Agriculture Act 1993 (c.37)

Agriculture (Amendment) Act 1921 (c.17)

Agriculture (Amendment) Act 1923 (c.25)

Agriculture (Amendment) Act 1984 (c.20)

Agriculture and Horticulture Act 1964 (c.28)

Agriculture and Technical Instruction (Ireland) Act 1902 (c.3)

Agriculture and Technical Instruction (Ireland) (No. 2) Act 1902 (c.33)

Agriculture (Artificial Insemination) Act 1946 (c.29)

Agriculture (Calf Subsidies) Act 1952 (c.62)

Agriculture (Emergency Payments) Act 1947 (c.32)

Agriculture (Fertilisers) Act 1952 (c.15)

Agriculture (Improvement of Roads) Act 1955 (c.20)

Agriculture (Miscellaneous Provisions) Act 1940 (c.14)

Agriculture (Miscellaneous Provisions) Act 1941 (c.50)

Agriculture (Miscellaneous Provisions) Act 1943 (c.16)

Agriculture (Miscellaneous Provisions) Act 1944 (c.28)

Agriculture (Miscellaneous Provisions) Act 1949 (c.37)

Agriculture (Miscellaneous Provisions) Act 1950 (c.17)

Agriculture (Miscellaneous Provisions) Act 1954 (c.39)

Agriculture (Miscellaneous Provisions) Act 1963 (c.11)

Agriculture (Miscellaneous Provisions) Act 1968 (c.34)

Agriculture (Miscellaneous Provisions) Act 1972 (c.62)

Agriculture (Miscellaneous Provisions) Act 1976 (c.55)

Agriculture (Miscellaneous War Provisions) Act 1940 (c.14)

Agriculture (Miscellaneous War Provisions) (No.2) Act 1940 (c.50)

Agriculture Mortgage Corporation Act 1956 (c.38)

Agriculture (Ploughing Grants) Act 1952 (c.35)

Agriculture (Poisonous Substances) Act 1952 (c.60)

Agriculture (Safety, Health and Welfare Provisions) Act 1956 (c.49)

Agriculture (Scotland) Act 1948 (c.45)

Agriculture (Small Farmers) Act 1959 (c.12)

Agriculture (Spring Traps) (Scotland) Act 1969 (c.26)

Agriculture and Horticulture Act 1964 (c.28)

Aid to Government of France Act 1794 (c.9)

Aid to Russia, etc. Act 1813 (c.13)

AIDS Control Act 1987 (c.33)

Air Corporations Act 1949 (c.91)

Air Corporations Act 1960 (c.13)

Air Corporations Act 1962 (c.5)

Air Corporations Act 1966 (c.11)

Air Corporations Act 1967 (c.33)

Air Corporations Act 1968 (c.30)

Air Corporations Act 1969 (c.43)

Air Corporations Act 1971 (c.5)

Air Force Act 1955 (c.19)

Air Force (Constitution) Act 1917 (c.51)

Air Force Reserve Act 1950 (c.33)

Air Force Reserve (Pilots and Observers) Act 1934 (c.5)

Air Guns and Shot Guns, etc. Act 1962 (c.49)

Air Ministry (Heston and Kenley Aerodromes Extension) Act 1939 (c.59)

Air Ministry (Kenley Common Acquisition) Act 1922 (c.40)

Air Navigation Act 1919 (c.3)

Air Navigation Act 1920 (c.80)

Air Navigation Act 1936 (c.44)

Air Navigation Act 1947 (c.18)

Air Navigation (Financial Provisions) Act 1938 (c.33)

Air Raid Precaution (Postponement of Financial Investigations) Act 1941 (c.10)

Air Raid Precautions Act 1937 (c.6)

Air Transport (Subsidy Agreements) Act 1930 (c.30)

Air Travel Reserve Fund Act 1975 (c.36)

Aircraft and Shipbuilding Industries Act 1977 (c.3)

Aire and Calder, Navigation Act 1774 (c.96)

Airports Act 1986 (c.31)

Airport Authority Act 1965 (c.16)

Airports Authority Act 1972 (c.8)

Airports Authority Act 1975 (c.78)

Airways Corporations Act 1949 (c.57)

Alcoholic Liquor Duties Act 1979 (c.4)

Alderney Harbour (Transfer) Act 1874 (c.92)

Alderney (Transfer of Property etc.) Act 1923 (c.15)

Alford to Cowbridge Road Act 1784 (c.62)

Aldwork Bridge, Ure Act 1772 (c.87)

Alehouses Act 1753 (c.31)

Alehouses Act 1756 (c.12)

Alexander Wilson (Provost of Edinburgh) Act 1736 (c.34)

Alice Holt Forest Act 1812 (c.72)

Aliens Act 1746 (c.44)

Aliens Act 1793 (c.4)

Aliens Act 1794 (c.82)

Aliens Act 1795 (c.24)

Aliens Act 1796 (c.109)

Aliens Act 1797 (c.92)

Aliens Act 1798 (c.50)

Aliens Act 1798 (c.77)

Aliens Act 1800 (c.24)

Aliens Act 1802 (c.92)

Aliens Act 1803 (c.155)

Aliens Act 1814 (c.155)

Aliens Act 1815 (c.54)

Aliens Act 1816 (c.86)

Aliens Act 1844 (c.66)

Aliens Act 1847 (c.83)

Aliens Act 1848 (c.20)

Aliens Act 1905 (c.13)

Aliens' Employment Act 1955 (c.18)

Aliens Restriction Act 1914 (c.12)

Aliens Restriction (Amendment) Act 1919 (c.92)

Alkali Act 1863 (c.124)

Alkali Act 1874 (c.43)

Alkali Act Perpetuation Act 1868 (c.36)

Alkali, etc., Works Regulation Act 1881 (c.37)

Alkali, etc., Works Regulation Act 1892 (c.30)

Alkali, etc., Works Regulation Act 1906 (c.14)

Alkali, etc., Works Regulation (Scotland) Act 1951 (c.21)

All Saints' Church, Newcastle Act 1786 (c.117)

All Saints' Church, Southampton Act 1791 (c.71)

All Saints' Church, Southampton Act 1793 (c.101)

Allied Forces Act 1939 (c.51)

Allied Powers (Maritime Courts) Act 1941 (c.21)

Allied Powers (War Service) Act 1942 (c.29)

Alloa Beer Duties Act 1754 (c.35)

Alloa Harbour Act 1786 (c.13)

Allotments Act 1887 (c.48)

Allotments Act 1890 (c.65)

Allotments Act 1922 (c.51)

Allotments Act 1925 (c.61)

Allotments Act 1950 (c.31)

Allotments and Cottage Gardens Compensation for Crops Act 1887 (c.26)

Allotments Extension Act 1882 (c.80)

Allotments Rating Exemption Act 1891 (c.33)

Allotments (Scotland) Act 1892 (c.54)

Allotments (Scotland) Act 1922 (c.52)

Allotments (Scotland) Act 1926 (c.5)

Allotments (Scotland) Act 1950 (c.38)

Allowance for Mint Prosecutions Act 1772 (c.52)

Allowance of Duty to Meux & Co. Act 1815 (c.189)

Allowance to Brewers Act 1785 (c.73)

Allowance to Distillers (Scotland) Act 1790 (c.39)

Allowances to Foreign Officers Act 1815 (c.126)

Allowing Time for First Meetings Act 1757 (c.13)

Alteration of Terms in Scotland Act 1708 (c.15)

Altrincham and Warrington Roads Act 1796 (c.145)

Alvingham, Lincoln, Navigation Act 1763 (c.39)

Amendment of c.10 of this Session Act 1800 (c.19)

Amendment of cc.26, 28 of this Session Act 1808 (c.71)

Amendment of c.29 of this Session Act 1793 (c.51)

American and European Payments (Financial Provisions) Act 1949 (c.17)

American Colonies Act 1766 (c.12)

American Loan Act 1915 (c.81)

American Loyalists Act 1783 (c.80)

American Loyalists Act 1785 (c.76)

American Loyalists Act 1786 (c.68)

American Loyalists Act 1787 (c.39)

American Loyalists Act 1788 (c.44)

American Loyalists Act 1789 (c.62)

American Loyalists Act 1790 (c.34)

American Prizes Act 1813 (c.63)

American Rebellion Act 1774 (c.39)
American Rebellion Act 1774 (c.45)
American Rebellion Act 1778 (c.13)
American Treaty Commissioners Act 1803 (c.135)
Amlwch Harbour Act 1793 (c.125)
Anatomy Act 1832 (c.75)
Anatomy Act 1871 (c.16)
Anatomy Act 1984 (c.14)
Anchors and Chain Cables Act 1899 (c.23)
Ancient Monument Act 1931 (c.16)
Ancient Monuments and Archaeological Areas Act 1979 (c.46)
Ancient Monuments Consolidation and Amendment Act 1913 (c.32)
Ancient Monuments Protection Act 1882 (c.73)
Ancient Monuments Protection Act 1900 (c.34)
Ancient Monuments Protection Act 1910 (c.3)
Ancient Monuments Protection (Ireland) Act 1892 (c.46)
Andover Canal Act 1789 (c.72)
Anglesey: Drainage, etc. Act 1788 (c.71)
Anglesey: Drainage Act 1790 (c.59)
Anglesey Roads Act 1765 (c.56)
Anglo-French Convention Act 1904 (c.33)
Anglo-French Treaty (Defence of France) Act 1919 (c.34)
Anglo-German Agreement Act 1890 (c.32)
Anglo-Italian Treaty (East African Territories) Act 1925 (c.9)
Anglo-Persian Oil Company (Acquisition of Capital) Act 1914 (c.37)
Anglo-Persian Oil Company (Acquisition of Capital) (Amendment) Act 1919 (c.86)
Anglo-Persian Oil Company (Payment of Calls) Act 1922 (c.26)
Anglo-Portuguese Commercial Treaty Act 1914 (c.1)
Anglo-Portuguese Commercial Treaty Act 1916 (c.39)
Anglo-Turkish (Armaments Credit) Agreement 1938 (c.60)
Anglo-Venezuelan Treaty (Island of Patos) Act 1942 (c.17)
Anguilla Act 1971 (c.63)
Anguilla Act 1980 (c.67)
Animal Boarding Establishments Act 1963 (c.43)
Animal Health Act 1981 (c.22)
Animal Health and Welfare Act 1984 (c.40)
Animals Act 1948 (c.35)
Animals Act 1971 (c.22)
Animals (Anaesthetics) Act 1919 (c.54)
Animals (Cruel Poisons) Act 1962 (c.26)
Animals (Restriction of Importation) Act 1964 (c.61)
Animals (Scientific Procedures) Act 1986 (c.14)
Animals (Scotland) Act 1987 (c.9.)
Annoyance Jurors, Westminster Acts 1861 (c.78)

Annual Revision of Rateable Property (Ireland) Amendment Act 1860 (c.4)
Annual Turnpike Acts Continuance Act 1850 (c.79)
Annual Turnpike Acts Continuance Act 1851 (c.37)
Annual Turnpike Acts Continuance Act 1853 (c.135)
Annual Turnpike Acts Continuance Act 1854 (c.58)
Annual Turnpike Acts Continuance Act 1859 (c.51)
Annual Turnpike Acts Continuance Act 1860 (c.73)
Annual Turnpike Acts Continuance Act 1861 (c.64)
Annual Turnpike Acts Continuance Act 1862 (c.72)
Annual Turnpike Acts Continuance Act 1863 (c.94)
Annual Turnpike Acts Continuance Act 1864 (c.75)
Annual Turnpike Acts Continuance Act 1865 (c.107)
Annual Turnpike Acts Continuance Act 1866 (c.105)
Annual Turnpike Acts Continuance Act 1867 (c.121)
Annual Turnpike Acts Continuance Act 1867 (c.129)
Annual Turnpike Acts Continuance Act 1868 (c.99)
Annual Turnpike Acts Continuance Act 1869 (c.90)
Annual Turnpike Acts Continuance Act 1870 (c.73)
Annual Turnpike Acts Continuance Act 1871 (c.115)
Annual Turnpike Acts Continuance Act 1872 (c.85)
Annual Turnpike Acts Continuance Act 1873 (c.90)
Annual Turnpike Acts Continuance Act 1874 (c.95)
Annual Turnpike Acts Continuance Act 1876 (c.39)
Annual Turnpike Acts Continuance Act 1877 (c.64)
Annual Turnpike Acts Continuance Act 1878 (c.62)
Annual Turnpike Acts Continuance Act 1879 (c.46)
Annual Turnpike Acts Continuance Act 1880 (c.12)
Annual Turnpike Acts Continuance Act 1881 (c.31)
Annual Turnpike Acts Continuance Act 1882 (c.52)
Annual Turnpike Acts Continuance Act 1883 (c.21)
Annual Turnpike Acts Continuance Act 1884 (c.52)
Annual Turnpike Acts Continuance Act 1885 (c.37)

Annuities Act 1704 (c.2)
Annuities Act 1799 (c.29)
Annuities Act 1799 (c.30)
Annuities, etc. Act 1702 (c.14)
Annuities, etc. Act 1704 (c.14)
Annuities (Ireland) Act 1807 (c.21)
Annuities (Prince of Wales, etc.) Act 1863 (c.1)
Annuities to Branches of Royal Family Act 1807 (c.39)
Annuities to Duke and Princess Mary of Cambridge Act 1850 (c.77)
Annuities to Duke, etc., of York 1792 (c.13)
Annuities to Duke of Sussex etc. Act 1802 (c.48)
Annuities to Lady Abercromby, etc. Act 1801 (c.59)
Annuities to Princesses Act 1812 (c.57)
Annuities to Retired Judges (Scotland) Act 1814 (c.94)
Annuities to Royal Family Act 1806 (c.145)
Annuity, Duchess of Mecklenburgh Strelitz Act 1843 (c.25)
Annuity, Duke of Albany Act 1882 (c.5)
Annuity, Duke of Edinburgh Act 1866 (c.8)
Annuity, Duke of Marlborough; Pension Act 1706 (c.6)
Annuity, etc., to Duke of Wellington Act 1814 (c.161)
Annuity (Heirs of Sir T. Clarges) Act 1799 (c.84)
Annuity, Lady Mayo Act 1872 (c.56)
Annuity (Lady of Havelock) Act 1858 (c.2)
Annuity (Lord Amherst) Act 1803 (c.159)
Annuity (Lord and Lady Raglan) Act 1855 (c.64)
Annuity, Lord Exmouth Act 1814 (c.164)
Annuity, Lord Gough Act 1846 (c.32)
Annuity Lord Hardinge Act 1846 (c.31)
Annuity (Lord Napier) Act 1868 (c.91)
Annuity (Lord Rodney) Act 1793 (c.77)
Annuity (Penn's Descendants) Act 1790 (c.46)
Annuity, Princess Beatrice Act 1885 (c.24)
Annuity, Princess Helena Act 1866 (c.7)
Annuity, Princess Mary of Cambridge Act 1866 (c.48)
Annuity, Princess Royal Act 1857 (c.2)
Annuity (Sir H. Brand) Act 1884 (c.1)
Annuity Tax in Edinburgh and Montrose Act 1860 (c.50)
Annuity Tax in Edinburgh and Montrose, etc. Act 1870 (c.87)
Annuity to Admiral Duckworth Act 1806 (c.40)
Annuity to Admiral Saumanez Act 1803 (c.37)
Annuity to Brook Watson, Esq. Act 1786 (c.93)
Annuity to Brook Watson, Esq. Act 1788 (c.43)
Annuity to Dr. Willis Act 1790 (c.44)
Annuity to Duchess of Brunswick Wolfenbuttel Act 1808 (c.59)
Annuity to Duke and Duchess of Edinburgh Act 1873 (c.80)

Annuity to Duke of Atholl, etc. Act 1805 (c.123)
Annuity to Duke of Brunswick Act 1810 (c.37)
Annuity to Duke of Clarence Act 1791 (c.34)
Annuity to Duke of Connaught Act 1871 (c.64)
Annuity to Duke of Gloucester Act 1785 (c.53)
Annuity to Duke of St. Albans Act 1788 (c.41)
Annuity to Duke of Wellington, etc. Act 1810 (c.8)
Annuity to Duke of Wellington, etc. Act 1812 (c.37)
Annuity to Family of Lord Kilwarden Act 1804 (c.76)
Annuity to Family of Sir G. Carlton Act 1788 (c.42)
Annuity to Lady Elgin Act 1864 (c.31)
Annuity to Lady Maria Carlton Act 1786 (c.88)
Annuity to Lady Nelson Act 1806 (c.4)
Annuity to Lord Beresford, etc. Act 1814 (c.162)
Annuity to Lord Camperdown Act 1797 (c.22)
Annuity to Lord Collingwood, etc. Act 1806 (c.13)
Annuity to Lord Combermere, etc. Act 1814 (c.163)
Annuity to Lord Hill Act 1814 (c.165)
Annuity to Lord Hutchinson, etc. Act 1802 (c.113)
Annuity to Lord Keane, etc. Act 1841 (c.1)
Annuity to Lord Lynedoch Act 1814 (c.166)
Annuity to Lord Nelson, etc. Act 1798 (c.1)
Annuity to Lord Rodney Act 1783 (c.86)
Annuity to Lord Rodney Act 1806 (c.147)
Annuity to Lord St. Vincent Act 1797 (c.21)
Annuity to Lord St. Vincent Act 1806 (c.50)
Annuity to Lord Walsingham Act 1815 (c.18)
Annuity to Major-Gen. Sir J. Stuart Act 1807 (c.4)
Annuity to Prince Leopold Act 1874 (c.65)
Annuity to Prince of Wales, etc. Act 1803 (c.26)
Annuity to Princess Alice Act 1861 (c.15)
Annuity to Princess Louise Act 1871 (c.1)
Annuity to Princess of Wales Act 1814 (c.160)
Annuity to Right Hon. Charles Shaw Lefevre Act 1857 (c.9)
Annuity to Sir G.A. Elliott Act 1783 (c.85)
Annuity to Sir J. Marriott Act (c.58)
Annuity to Sir J. Skynner Act 1787 (c.12)
Annuity to Sir R. Strachan Act 1806 (c.5)
Annuity to Sir Sidney Smith Act 1801 (c.5)
Annuity to Sir W.F. Williams Act 1856 (c.30)
Annuity to Viscount Lake, etc. Act 1808 (c.13)
Anstruther Easter Beer Duties Act 1748 (c.10)
Anstruther Easter Beer Duties Act 1775 (c.48)
Anstruther Union Harbour Act 1860 (c.39)
Antarctic Act 1994 (c.15)
Antarctic Minerals Act 1989 (c.21)
Antarctic Treaty Act 1967 (c.65)
Anthrax Prevention Act 1919 (c.23)

Antigua and Barbuda Act 1859 (c.13)
Anwick: Inclosure Act 1791 (c.93)
"Anzac" (Restriction on Trade Use of Word) Act 1916 (c.51)
Apothecaries Act 1702 (c.5)
Apothecaries Act 1815 (c.194)
Apothecaries Act Amendment Act 1874 (c.34)
Appeal (Forma Pauperis) Act 1893 (c.22)
Appeal in Revenue Cases (Ireland) Act 1812 (c.78)
Appeals on Civil Bills, Dublin Act 1848 (c.34)
Appellate Jurisdiction Act 1876 (c.59)
Appellate Jurisdiction Act 1887 (c.70)
Appellate Jurisdiction Act 1908 (c.51)
Appellate Jurisdiction Act 1913 (c.21)
Appellate Jurisdiction Act 1929 (c.8)
Appellate Jurisdiction Act 1947 (c.11)
Application of Bounties on Linen, etc. Act 1812 (c.96)
Application of Highway Rates to Turnpikes Act 1841 (c.59)
Appointment Act 1834 (c.22)
Appointment of a Judge at Bombay Act 1864 (c.16)
Appointment of Judges in Vacation Act 1799 (c.113)
Appointment of Revising Barristers Act 1872 (c.84)
Appointment of Superintending Magistrates, etc. Act 1814 (c.131)
Appointment of Vice-Chancellor Act 1851 (c.4)
Appointments in Cathedral Churches Act 1839 (c.14)
Apportionment Act 1820 (c.108)
Apportionment Act 1834 (c.22)
Apportionment Act 1870 (c.35)
Appraisers Licences Act 1806 (c.43)
Apprehension of Certain Offenders Act 1853 (c.118)
Apprehension of Endorsed Warrants Act 1750 (c.55)
Apprehension of Housebreakers Act 1706 (c.31)
Apprehension of Offenders Act 1804 (c.92)
Apprehension of Offenders Act 1814 (c.186)
Apprehension of Offenders Act 1843 (c.34)
Apprentices Act 1814 (c.96)
Apprentices (Settlement) Act 1757 (c.11)
Apprenticeship Indentures Act 1801 (c.22)
Appropriation Act 1775 (c.12)
Appropriation Act 1775 (c.42)
Appropriation Act 1776 (c.47)
Appropriation Act 1776 (c.49)
Appropriation Act 1778 (c.54)
Appropriation Act 1779 (c.71)
Appropriation Act 1780 (c.62)
Appropriation Act 1781 (c.57)
Appropriation Act 1782 (c.67)
Appropriation Act 1783 (c.78)
Appropriation Act 1784 (c.44)
Appropriation Act 1786 (c.61)

Appropriation Act 1787 (c.33)
Appropriation Act 1788 (c.26)
Appropriation Act 1789 (c.61)
Appropriation Act 1790 (c.32)
Appropriation Act 1791 (c.41)
Appropriation Act 1792 (c.35)
Appropriation Act 1793 (c.72)
Appropriation Act 1794 (c.49)
Appropriation Act 1795 (c.120)
Appropriation Act 1796 (c.126)
Appropriation Act 1797 (c.144)
Appropriation Act 1798 (c.90)
Appropriation Act 1799 (c.114)
Appropriation Act 1800 (c.14)
Appropriation Act 1802 (c.120)
Appropriation Act 1803 (c.162)
Appropriation Act 1804 (c.110)
Appropriation Act 1805 (c.129)
Appropriation Act 1806 (c.149)
Appropriation Act 1807 (c.76)
Appropriation Act 1808 (c.148)
Appropriation Act 1809 (c.128)
Appropriation Act 1810 (c.115)
Appropriation Act 1811 (c.117)
Appropriation Act 1812 (c.154)
Appropriation Act 1813 (c.136)
Appropriation Act 1814 (c.167)
Appropriation Act 1815 (c.187)
Appropriation Act 1835 (c.80)
Appropriation Act 1836 (c.98)
Appropriation Act 1837 (c.79)
Appropriation Act 1838 (c.111)
Appropriation Act 1839 (c.89)
Appropriation Act 1840 (c.112)
Appropriation Act 1841 (c.11)
Appropriation Act 1841 (c.53)
Appropriation Act 1842 (c.121)
Appropriation Act 1843 (c.99)
Appropriation Act 1844 (c.104)
Appropriation Act 1845 (c.130)
Appropriation Act 1846 (c.116)
Appropriation Act 1848 (c.126)
Appropriation Act 1849 (c.98)
Appropriation Act 1850 (c.107)
Appropriation Act 1851 (c.101)
Appropriation Act 1852 (c.82)
Appropriation Act 1853 (c.110)
Appropriation Act 1854 (c.121)
Appropriation Act 1855 (c.129)
Appropriation Act 1856 (c.105)
Appropriation Act 1857 (c.20)
Appropriation Act 1857 (c.69)
Appropriation Act 1858 (c.107)
Appropriation Act 1859 (c.23)
Appropriation Act 1859 (c.55)
Appropriation Act 1860 (c.131)
Appropriation Act 1861 (c.103)
Appropriation Act 1862 (c.71)
Appropriation Act 1863 (c.99)
Appropriation Act 1865 (c.123)
Appropriation Act 1866 (c.91)
Appropriation Act 1867 (c.120)
Appropriation Act 1868 (c.85)

Appropriation Act 1869 (c.93)
Appropriation Act 1870 (c.96)
Appropriation Act 1871 (c.89)
Appropriation Act 1872 (c.87)
Appropriation Act 1873 (c.79)
Appropriation Act 1874 (c.56)
Appropriation Act 1875 (c.78)
Appropriation Act 1876 (c.60)
Appropriation Act 1877 (c.61)
Appropriation Act 1878 (c.65)
Appropriation Act 1879 (c.51)
Appropriation Act 1880 (c.13)
Appropriation Act 1881 (c.56)
Appropriation Act 1882 (c.71)
Appropriation Act 1883 (c.50)
Appropriation Act 1884 (c.73)
Appropriation Act 1885 (c 64)
Appropriation Act 1886 (c.26)
Appropriation Act 1887 (c.50)
Appropriation Act 1888 (c.61)
Appropriation Act 1889 (c.70)
Appropriation Act 1890 (c.72)
Appropriation Act 1891 (c.55)
Appropriation Act 1892 (c.33)
Appropriation Act 1893 (c.60)
Appropriation Act 1894 (c.59)
Appropriation Act 1895 (c.6)
Appropriation Act 1895 (c.31)
Appropriation Act 1896 (c.46)
Appropriation Act 1897 (c.67)
Appropriation Act 1898 (c.61)
Appropriation Act 1899 (c.1)
Appropriation Act 1899 (c.49)
Appropriation Act 1900 (c.2)
Appropriation Act 1900 (c.57)
Appropriation Act 1901 (c.21)
Appropriation Act 1902 (c.27)
Appropriation Act 1903 (c.32)
Appropriation Act 1904 (c.17)
Appropriation Act 1905 (c.17)
Appropriation Act 1906 (c.26)
Appropriation Act 1907 (c.20)
Appropriation Act 1908 (c.30)
Appropriation Act 1909 (c.5)
Appropriation Act 1910 (c.14)
Appropriation Act 1911 (c.15)
Appropriation Act 1912 (c.7)
Appropriation Act 1913 (c.27)
Appropriation Act 1913 (c.35)
Appropriation Act 1914 (c.24)
Appropriation Act 1915 (c.77)
Appropriation Act 1916 (c.71)
Appropriation Act 1917 (c.52)
Appropriation Act 1918 (c.56)
Appropriation Act 1919 (c.88)
Appropriation Act 1921 (c.46)
Appropriation Act 1922 (c.3)
Appropriation Act 1922 (c.32)
Appropriation Act 1923 (c.35)
Appropriation Act 1924 (c.31)
Appropriation Act 1925 (c.57)
Appropriation Act 1926 (c.23)
Appropriation Act 1927 (c.11)

Appropriation Act 1928 (c.18)
Appropriation Act 1929 (c.22)
Appropriation Act 1930 (c.27)
Appropriation Act 1931 (c.29)
Appropriation Act 1931 (c.50)
Appropriation Act 1933 (c.34)
Appropriation Act 1934 (c.44)
Appropriation Act 1935 (c.28)
Appropriation Act 1936 (c.37)
Appropriation Act 1937 (c.55)
Appropriation Act 1938 (c.47)
Appropriation Act 1939 (c.46)
Appropriation Act 1939 (c.52)
Appropriation Act 1941 (c.38)
Appropriation Act 1942 (c.27)
Appropriation Act 1943 (c.31)
Appropriation Act 1944 (c.25)
Appropriation Act 1944 (c.30)
Appropriation Act 1946 (c.65)
Appropriation Act 1947 (c.52)
Appropriation Act 1948 (c.50)
Appropriation Act 1949 (c.48)
Appropriation Act 1950 (c.16)
Appropriation Act 1951 (c.44)
Appropriation Act 1952 (c.38)
Appropriation Act 1953 (c.35)
Appropriation Act 1954 (c.45)
Appropriation Act 1955 (c.16)
Appropriation Act 1956 (c.55)
Appropriation Act 1957 (c.63)
Appropriation Act 1959 (c.59)
Appropriation Act 1960 (c.45)
Appropriation Act 1961 (c.59)
Appropriation Act 1962 (c.45)
Appropriation Act 1963 (c.26)
Appropriation Act 1964 (c.62)
Appropriation Act 1965 (c.23)
Appropriation Act 1966 (c.3)
Appropriation Act 1967 (c.59)
Appropriation Act 1968 (c.43)
Appropriation Act 1969 (c.31)
Appropriation Act 1970 (c.25)
Appropriation Act 1971 (c.67)
Appropriation Act 1972 (c.56)
Appropriation Act 1973 (c.40)
Appropriation Act 1974 (c.2)
Appropriation Act 1975 (c.44)
Appropriation Act 1976 (c.43)
Appropriation Act 1977 (c.35)
Appropriation Act 1978 (c.57)
Appropriation Act 1979 (c.24)
Appropriation Act 1980 (c.54)
Appropriation Act 1981 (c.51)
Appropriation Act 1982 (c.40)
Appropriation Act 1983 (c.27)
Appropriation Act 1983 (c.48)
Appropriation Act 1984 (c.44)
Appropriation Act 1985 (c.55)
Appropriation Act 1986 (c.42)
Appropriation Act 1987 (c.17)
Appropriation Act 1988 (c.38)
Appropriation Act 1989 (c.25)
Appropriation Act 1990 (c.28)

Appropriation Act 1991 (c.32)
Appropriation Act 1992 (c.22)
Appropriation Act 1993 (c.33)
Appropriation Act 1994 (c.24)
Appropriation Acts Amendment Act 1842 (c.1)
Appropriation, etc. Act 1785 (c.60)
Appropriation, etc. Act 1801 (c.84)
Appropriation (No. 2) Act 1902 (c.30)
Appropriation (No. 2) Act 1910 (c.38)
Appropriation (No. 2) Act 1915 (c.86)
Appropriation (No. 2) Act 1921 (c.63)
Appropriation (No. 2) Act 1925 (c.78)
Appropriation (No. 2) Act 1926 (c.33)
Appropriation (No. 2) Act 1927 (c.25)
Appropriation (No. 2) Act 1931 (c.50)
Appropriation (No. 2) Act 1939 (c.63)
Appropriation (No. 2) Act 1941 (c.43)
Appropriation (No. 2) Act 1942 (c.33)
Appropriation (No. 2) Act 1943 (c.41)
Appropriation (No. 2) Act 1944 (c.37)
Appropriation (No. 2) Act 1955 (c.3)
Appropriation (No. 2) Act 1966 (c.26)
Appropriation (No. 2) Act 1970 (c.48)
Appropriation (No. 2) Act 1974 (c.31)
Appropriation (No. 2) Act 1979 (c.51)
Appropriation (No. 2) Act 1983 (c.48)
Appropriation (No. 2) Act 1987 (c.50)
Appropriation (No. 2) Act 1992 (c.47)
Appropriation (No. 3) Act 1942 (c.34)
Appropriation of Certain Duties Act 1799 (c.11)
Appropriation of Revenue Act 1700 (c.12)
Appropriation (Session 2) Act 1880 (c.40)
Appropriation (Session 2) Act 1886 (c.1)
Arbitration Act 1889 (c.49)
Arbitration Act 1934 (c.14)
Arbitration Act 1950 (c.27)
Arbitration Act 1975 (c.3)
Arbitration Act 1979 (c.42)
Arbitration Clauses (Protocol) Act 1924 (c.39)
Arbitration (Foreign Awards) Act 1930 (c.15)
Arbitration (International Investment Disputes) Act 1966 (c.41)
Arbitration (Masters and Workmen) Act 1872 (c.46)
Arbitration (Scotland) Act 1894 (c.13)
Arbitrations Act 1844 (c.93)
Archbishops' etc., House of Residence Act 1839 (c.18)
Archbishops' Palace, Dublin Act 1804 (c.63)
Archdeaconries and Rural Deaneries Act 1874 (c.63)
Archdeaconry of Cornwall Act 1897 (c.9)
Archdeaconry of London (Additional Endowment) Act 1897 (c.45)
Archdeaconry of Rochester Act 1861 (c.131)
Architects Registration Act 1938 (c.54)
Architects (Registration) Act 1931 (c.33)
Architects (Registration) Act 1934 (c.38)
Argentine Treaty Act 1842 (c.40)
Argyll Roads and Bridges Act 1775 (c.63)
Argyllshire Valuation Act 1748 (c.29)

Architects Registration (Amendment) Act 1969 (c.42)
Argyllshire Valuation Act 1748 (c.29)
Arklow Harbour Act 1882 (c.13)
Armed Forces Act 1966 (c.45)
Armed Forces Act 1971 (c.33)
Armed Forces Act 1976 (c.52)
Armed Forces Act 1981 (c.55)
Armed Forces Act 1986 (c.21)
Armed Forces Act 1991 (c.62)
Armed Forces (Conditions of Service) Act 1939 (c.68)
Armed Forces (Housing Loans) Act 1949 (c.77)
Armed Forces (Housing Loans) Act 1953 (c.3)
Armed Forces (Housing Loans) Act 1958 (c.1)
Armed Forces (Housing Loans) Act 1965 (c.9)
Armorial Bearings Act 1798 (c.53)
Armorial Bearings Act 1799 (c.8)
Arms and Gunpowder (Ireland) Act 1807 (c.8)
Arms and Gunpowder (Ireland) Act 1836 (c.39)
Arms and Gunpowder (Ireland) Act 1838 (c.71)
Arms Control and Disarmament (Inspections) Act 1991 (c.41)
Arms Control and Disarmament (Privileges and Immunities) Act 1988 (c.2)
Arms, etc. (Ireland) Act 1843 (c.74)
Arms (Ireland) Act 1810 (c.109)
Arms (Ireland) Act 1813 (c.78)
Army Act 1774 (c.54)
Army Act 1811 (c.106)
Army Act 1812 (c.27)
Army Act 1812 (c.120)
Army Act 1881 (c.58)
Army Act 1955 (c.18)
Army Act 1992 (c.39)
Army (Amendment) Act 1915 (c.26)
Army (Amendment) No. 2 Act 1915 (c.58)
Army and Air Force Act 1961 (c.52)
Army and Air Force (Annual) Act 1921 (c.9)
Army and Air Force (Annual) Act 1922 (c.6)
Army and Air Force (Annual) Act 1923 (c.3)
Army and Air Force (Annual) Act 1924 (c.5)
Army and Air Force (Annual) Act 1925 (c.25)
Army and Air Force (Annual) Act 1926 (c.6)
Army and Air Force (Annual) Act 1927 (c.7)
Army and Air Force (Annual) Act 1928 (c.7)
Army and Air Force (Annual) Act 1929 (c.20)
Army and Air Force (Annual) Act 1930 (c.22)
Army and Air Force (Annual) Act 1931 (c.14)
Army and Air Force (Annual) Act 1932 (c.22)
Army and Air Force (Annual) Act 1933 (c.11)
Army and Air Force (Annual) Act 1934 (c.11)
Army and Air Force (Annual) Act 1935 (c.17)
Army and Air Force (Annual) Act 1936 (c.14)
Army and Air Force (Annual) Act 1937 (c.26)
Army and Air Force (Annual) Act 1938 (c.20)
Army and Air Force (Annual) Act 1939 (c.17)

Army and Air Force (Annual) Act 1940 (c.18)
Army and Air Force (Annual) Act 1941 (c.17)
Army and Air Force (Annual) Act 1942 (c.15)
Army and Air Force (Annual) Act 1943 (c.15)
Army and Air Force (Annual) Act 1944 (c.18)
Army and Air Force (Annual) Act 1945 (c.22)
Army and Air Force (Annual) Act 1946 (c.47)
Army and Air Force (Annual) Act 1947 (c.25)
Army and Air Force (Annual) Act 1948 (c.28)
Army and Air Force (Annual) Act 1949 (c.28)
Army and Air Force (Annual) Act 1950 (c.3)
Army and Air Force (Annual) Act 1951 (c.24)
Army and Air Force (Annual) Act 1952 (c.24)
Army and Air Force (Annual) Act 1953 (c.31)
Army and Air Force (Annual) Act 1954 (c.35)
Army and Air Force (Women's Service) Act 1948 (c.21)
Army and Navy Act 1797 (c.6)
Army and Navy Act 1798 (c.4)
Army and Navy Act 1800 (c.16)
Army and Navy Act 1800 (c.29)
Army and Navy Act 1800 (c.100)
Army and Navy Act 1807 (c.15)
Army and Navy Audit Act 1889 (c.31)
Army (Annual) Act 1882 (c.7)
Army (Annual) Act 1883 (c.6)
Army (Annual) Act 1884 (c.8)
Army (Annual) Act 1885 (c.8)
Army (Annual) Act 1886 (c.8)
Army (Annual) Act 1887 (c.2)
Army (Annual) Act 1888 (c.4)
Army (Annual) Act 1889 (c.3)
Army (Annual) Act 1890 (c.4)
Army (Annual) Act 1891 (c.5)
Army (Annual) Act 1892 (c.2)
Army (Annual) Act 1893 (c.4)
Army (Annual) Act 1894 (c.3)
Army (Annual) Act 1895 (c.7)
Army (Annual) Act 1896 (c.2)
Army (Annual) Act 1897 (c.3)
Army (Annual) Act 1898 (c.1)
Army (Annual) Act 1899 (c.3)
Army (Annual) Act 1900 (c.5)
Army (Annual) Act 1901 (c.2)
Army (Annual) Act 1902 (c.2)
Army (Annual) Act 1903 (c.4)
Army (Annual) Act 1904 (c.5)
Army (Annual) Act 1905 (c.2)
Army (Annual) Act 1906 (c.2)
Army (Annual) Act 1907 (c.2)
Army (Annual) Act 1908 (c.2)
Army (Annual) Act 1909 (c.3)
Army (Annual) Act 1910 (c.6)
Army (Annual) Act 1911 (c.3)
Army (Annual) Act 1912 (c.5)
Army (Annual) Act 1913 (c.2)
Army (Annual) Act 1914 (c.2)
Army (Annual) Act 1915 (c.25)
Army (Annual) Act 1916 (c.5)
Army (Annual) Act (1916) Amendment 1917 (c.10)
Army (Annual) Act 1917 (c.9)
Army (Annual) Act 1918 (c.6)

Army (Annual) Act 1919 (c.11)
Army Chaplains Act 1868 (c.83)
Army (Conditions of Enlistment) Act 1957 (c.50)
Army (Courts of Inquiry) Act 1916 (c.33)
Army Discipline and Regulation Act 1879 (c.33)
Army Discipline and Regulation (Annual) Act 1880 (c.9)
Army Discipline and Regulation (Annual) Act 1881 (c.9)
Army Enlistment Act 1849 (c.73)
Army Enlistment Act 1855 (c.4)
Army Enlistment Act 1858 (c.55)
Army Enlistment Act 1867 (c.34)
Army in Ireland Act 1768 (c.13)
Army Pensions Act 1830 (c.41)
Army Pensions Act 1914 (c.83)
Army Prize Money Act 1814 (c.86)
Army Prize Money Act 1848 (c.103)
Army Prize (Shares of Deceased) Act 1864 (c.36)
Army Reserve Act 1950 (c.32)
Army Reserve Act 1962 (c.10)
Army Reserve Act 1969 (c.23)
Army Schools Act 1891 (c.16)
Army (Supply of Food, Forage and Stores) Act 1914 (c.26)
Army (Suspension of Sentences) Act 1915 (c.23)
Army (Suspension of Sentences) Amendment Act 1916 (c.103)
Army (Transfer) Act 1915 (c.43)
Arrangements Between Debtors and Creditors Act 1844 (c.70)
Arranmore Polling District Act 1878 (c.75)
Arrears of Crown, etc., Rents (Ireland) Act 1816 (c.71)
Arrears of Crown Rents (Ireland) Act 1811 (c.91)
Arrears of Rent (Ireland) Act 1882 (c.47)
Arrest for Debtors Act 1851 (c.52)
Arrest in Personal Actions (Ireland) Act 1841 (c.17)
Arsenic Act 1851 (c.13)
Art Act 1866 (c.16)
Art Unions Act 1846 (c.48)
Art Unions Indemnity Act 1844 (c.109)
Art Unions Indemnity Act 1845 (c.57)
Arthur Jenkins Indemnity Act 1941 (c.1)
Articles of Commerce (Returns, &c.) Act 1914 (c.65)
Artificers Act 1718 (c.27)
Artificers etc. Act 1749 (c.13)
Artificial Cream Act 1929 (c.32)
Artillery and Rifle Ranges Act 1885 (c.36)
Artillery Corps, etc. Act 1795 (c.83)
Artizans and Labourers Dwellings Act 1868 (c.130)
Artizans and Labourers Dwellings Act (1868) Amendment 1879 (c.64)
Artizans' and Labourers' Dwellings Improvement Act 1875 (c.36)

Artizans and Labourers Dwellings Improvement Act 1879 (c.63)

Artizans and Labourers Dwellings Improvement (Scotland) Act 1875 (c.49)

Artizans and Labourers Dwellings Improvement (Scotland) Act 1880 (c.2)

Artizans' Dwellings Act (1868) Amendment Act (1879) Amendment 1880 (c.8)

Artizans Dwellings Act 1882 (c.54)

Arun, Sussex: Navigation Act 1785 (c.100)

Arundel: Improvement Act 1785 (c.90)

Ascertaining of Strength of Spirits Act 1791 (c.44)

Ashburton Roads Act 1776 (c.79)

Assaulting a Privy Counsellor Act 1710 (c.21)

Assaults (Ireland) Act 1814 (c.181)

Assaults (Ireland) Act 1815 (c.88)

Assaults (Ireland) Act 1839 (c.77)

Assaults (Ireland) Act 1844 (c.23)

Assaults (Ireland) Act 1849 (c.38)

Assaults with Intent to Rob Act 1733 (c.21)

Assay of Imported Watch-Cases (Existing Stocks Exemption) Act 1907 (c.8)

Assay of Plate Act 1702 (c.3)

Assessed Rates Act 1879 (c.10)

Assessed Taxes Act 1791 (c.5)

Assessed Taxes Act 1805 (c.13)

Assessed Taxes Act 1805 (c.105)

Assessed Taxes Act 1806 (c.78)

Assessed Taxes Act 1810 (c.104)

Assessed Taxes Act 1811 (c.72)

Assessed Taxes Act 1812 (c.93)

Assessed Taxes Act 1812 (c.147)

Assessed Taxes Act 1816 (c.66)

Assessed Taxes Act 1837 (c.61)

Assessed Taxes Act 1840 (c.38)

Assessed Taxes Act 1841 (c.26)

Assessed Taxes Act 1845 (c.36)

Assessed Taxes Act 1851 (c.33)

Assessed Taxes Act 1854 (c.1)

Assessed Taxes Composition Act 1850 (c.96)

Assessed Taxes and Income Tax Act 1846 (c.56)

Assessed Taxes, etc. Act 1839 (c.35)

Assessed Taxes, etc. (Ireland) Act 1807 (c.11)

Assessed Taxes, etc. (Ireland) Act 1816 (c.57)

Assessed Taxes (Ireland) Act 1807 (c.21)

Assessed Taxes (Ireland) Act 1808 (c.42)

Assessed Taxes (Ireland) Act 1815 (c.61)

Assessed Taxes (Ireland) Act 1815 (c.67)

Assessed Taxes (Ireland) Act 1815 (c.140)

Assessed Taxes, Property Tax and Duty on Pensions and Offices of Profit Act 1844 (c.46)

Assessionable Manors Award Act 1848 (c.83)

Assessment of Taxes Act 1808 (c.141)

Assessments in Edinburgh Act 1861 (c.27)

Assessor of Public Undertakings (Scotland) Act 1934 (c.22)

Assise and Making of Bread, London Act 1797 (c.98)

Assise of Bread Act 1798 (c.62)

Assise of Fuel Act 1710 (c.20)

Assise of Fuel Act 1711 (c.5)

Assistant Postmaster-General Act 1909 (c.14)

Assizes Act 1839 (c.72)

Assizes and Quarter Sessions Act 1908 (c.41)

Assizes for Cornwall Act 1715 (c.45)

Assizes (Ireland) Act 1825 (c.51)

Assizes (Ireland) Act 1835 (c.26)

Assizes (Ireland) Act 1850 (c.85)

Assizes (Ireland) Act 1850 (c.88)

Assizes Relief Act 1889 (c.12)

Association of County Councils (Scotland) Act 1946 (c.77)

Assurance Companies Act 1909 (c.49)

Assurance Companies Act 1946 (c.28)

Assurance Companies (Winding Up) Act 1933 (c.9)

Assurance Companies (Winding Up) Act 1935 (c.45)

Assurance on French Ships Act 1747 (c.4)

Asthall to Buckland Road Act 1777 (c.105)

Asylum and Immigration Appeals Act 1993 (c.23)

Asylums and Certified Institutions (Officers Pensions) Act 1918 (c.33)

Asylums' Officers Superannuation Act 1909 (c.48)

Atomic Energy Act 1946 (c.80)

Atomic Energy Act 1989 (c.7)

Atomic Energy Authority Act 1954 (c.32)

Atomic Energy Authority Act 1959 (c.5)

Atomic Energy Authority Act 1971 (c.11)

Atomic Energy Authority Act 1986 (c.3)

Atomic Energy Authority (Special Constables) Act 1976 (c.23)

Atomic Energy Authority (Weapons Group) Act 1973 (c.4)

Atomic Energy (Miscellaneous Provisions) Act 1981 (c.48)

Atomic Weapons Establishment Act 1991 (c.46)

Attachment of Earnings Act 1971 (c.32)

Attachment of Goods (Ireland) Act 1850 (c.73)

Attainder of Bishop of Rochester Act 1722 (c.17)

Attainder of David Ogilvy: Disabilities Removed on Pardon Act 1783 (c.34)

Attainder of Duke of Ormonde Act 1714 (c.17)

Attainder of Earl of Kellie and Others Act 1745 (c.26)

Attainder of Earl of Mar and Others Act 1715 (c.32)

Attainder of Earl of Marischal and Others Act 1715 (c.42)

Attainder of George Kelley Act 1722 (c.16)

Attainder of John Plunket Act 1722 (c.15)

Attainder of Thomas Forster and Others Act 1715 (c.53)

Attainder of Viscount Bolingbroke Act 1714 (c.16)

Attempted Rape Act 1948 (c.19)

Attendance of Witnesses Act 1854 (c.34)

Attorneys Act 1809 (c.28)

Attorneys and Solicitors Act 1728 (c.23)

Attorneys and Solicitors Act 1732 (c.27)

Attorneys and Solicitors Act (1860) Amendment 1872 (c.81)

Attorneys and Solicitors Act 1870 (c.28)

Attorneys and Solicitors Act 1874 (c.68)

Attorneys and Solicitors (Ireland) Act 1866 (c.84)

Auction Duties Act 1815 (c.142)

Auction Duties, etc. Act 1779 (c.56)

Auction Duties (Ireland) Act 1807 (c.17)

Auction Duties (Ireland) Act 1814 (c.82)

Auction Duty Act 1792 (c.41)

Auction Duty Act 1807 (c.65)

Auction Duty Act 1812 (c.53)

Auction Duty, etc. Act 1790 (c.26)

Auctioneers Act 1845 (c.15)

Auctioneers' Licences Act 1776 (c.50)

Auctions (Bidding Agreements) Act 1927 (c.12)

Auctions (Bidding Agreements) Act 1969 (c.56)

Auctions Duties (Ireland) Act 1809 (c.100)

Audit (Local Authorities) Act 1927 (c.31)

Audit (Local Authorities etc.) Act 1922 (c.14)

Audit of Accounts Act 1813 (c.100)

Audit of Accounts, etc. Act 1813 (c.150)

Audit of Military Accounts (Ireland) Act 1812 (c.51)

Audit of Public Accounts Act 1780 (c.40)

Audit of Public Accounts Act 1780 (c.45)

Audit of Public Accounts Act 1780 (c.54)

Audit of Public Accounts Act 1782 (c.50)

Audit of Public Accounts Act 1784 (c.13)

Audit of Public Accounts Act 1785 (c.52)

Audit of Public Accounts Act 1785 (c.68)

Audit of Public Accounts Act 1786 (c.67)

Audit of Public Accounts Act 1794 (c.59)

Audit of Public Accounts Act 1805 (c.55)

Audit of Public Accounts Act 1806 (c.141)

Audit of Public Accounts (Ireland) Act 1812 (c.52)

Auditing of Public Accounts Act 1805 (c.91)

Auditing of Public Accounts Act 1809 (c.95)

Auditing of the Public Accounts Act 1783 (c.68)

Auditor of the Exchequer Act (1806) (c.1)

Auditors of Land Revenue Act 1799 (c.83)

Augmentation of Benefices Act 1854 (c.84)

Augmentation of 60th Regiment Act 1797 (c.13)

Augmentation of 60th Regiment Act 1799 (c.104)

Augmentation of 60th Regiment Act 1813 (c.12)

Australia Act 1986 (c.2)

Australian Colonies Act 1801 (c.44)

Australian Colonies Duties Act 1873 (c.22)

Australian Colonies Duties Act 1895 (c.3)

Australian Colonies, Waste Lands Act 1842 (c.36)

Australian Constitution (Public Record Copy) Act 1990 (c.17)

Australian Constitutions Act 1842 (c.76)

Australian Constitutions Act 1844 (c.74)

Australian Constitutions Act 1850 (c.59)

Australian Constitutions Act 1862 (c.11)

Australian Passengers Act 1861 (c.52)

Australian States Constitution Act 1907 (c.7)

Australian Waste Lands Act 1855 (c.56)

Austrian Loan Guarantee Act 1931 (c.5)

Austrian State Treaty Act 1955 (c.1)

Auxiliary Air Force and Air Force Reserve Act 1924 (c.15)

Auxiliary and Reserve Forces Act 1949 (c.96)

Auxiliary Forces Act 1953 (c.50)

Average Price of Brown Sugar Act 1809 (c.43)

Aviation and Maritime Security Act 1990 (c.31)

Aviation Security Act 1982 (c.36)

Axminster Roads Act 1754 (c.32)

Aylesbury Gaol and Shire Hall: Rate in Buckinghamshire Act 1736 (c.10)

Aylesbury to West Wycombe Road Act 1795 (c.149)

Ayre and Lamark Roads Act 1771 (c.90)

Ayr Bridge Act 1785 (c.37)

Ayr (County) Roads Act 1797 (c.162)

Ayr Harbour Act 1772 (c.22)

Ayr Harbour Act 1794 (c.99)

Ayr Roads Act 1757 (c.57)

Ayr Roads Act 1767 (c.106)

Ayr Roads Act 1774 (c.109)

Ayr Roads Act 1789 (c.79)

Ayr Roads Act 1791 (c.95)

Ayr Roads Act 1791 (c.107)

Ayr Roads Act 1792 (c.121)

Backing of Warrants (Republic of Ireland) Act 1965 (c.45)

Bacon Industry Act 1938 (c.71)

Bacon Industry (Amendment) Act 1939 (c.10)

Badgers Act 1973 (c.57)

Badgers Act 1991 (c.36)

Badgers (Further Protection) Act 1991 (c.35)

Badgers (Protection) Act 1992 (c.51)

Bagshot to Hertford Bridge Hill Road Act 1777 (c.84)

Bagshot to Winchester Road Act 1773 (c.88)

Bahama Islands (Constitution) Act 1963 (c.56)

Bahama Islands Trade Act 1812 (c.99)

Bahamas Independence Act 1973 (c.27)

Bail Act 1898 (c.7)

Bail Act 1976 (c.63)

Bail (Amendment) Act 1993 (c.26)

Bail Bonds Act 1808 (c.58)

Bail etc. (Scotland) Act 1980 (c.4)

Bail in Cases of Forgery, etc. (Scotland) Act 1835 (c.73)

Bail in Criminal Cases (Scotland) Act 1724 (c.26)
Bail in Criminal Cases (Scotland) Act 1799 (c.49)
Bail in Error Act 1845 (c.68)
Bail in Error Act 1853 (c.32)
Bail (Scotland) Act 1888 (c.36)
Bails Act 1869 (c.38)
Bakehouse Regulation Act 1863 (c.40)
Baking Industry (Hours of Work) Act 1938 (c.41)
Baking Industry (Hours of Work) Act 1954 (c.57)
Baking Trade Act 1810 (c.73)
Baking Trade, Dublin Act 1802 (c.8)
Balby to Worksop Road Act 1765 (c.67)
Balby to Worksop Road Act 1787 (c.84)
Bale and Dolgelly Roads Act 1796 (c.147)
Ballot Act 1872 (c.33)
Banbury Church Act 1790 (c.72)
Banbury Road Act 1780 (c.67)
Banbury to Lutterworth Road Act 1785 (c.128)
Bancroft's Patent Act 1785 (c.38)
Bangladesh Act 1973 (c.49)
Bank Act 1892 (c.48)
Bank Charter Act 1844 (c.32)
Bank Holiday (Ireland) Act 1903 (c.1)
Bank Holidays Act 1871 (c.17)
Bank Notes (Scotland) Act 1765 (c.49)
Bank Notes Act 1833 (c.83)
Bank Notes Act 1841 (c.50)
Bank Notes Act 1852 (c.2)
Bank Notes Act 1853 (c.2)
Bank Notes Forgery Act 1801 (c.57)
Bank Notes (Forgery) Act 1805 (c.89)
Bank Notes Forgery (Scotland) Act 1820 (c.92)
Bank Notes (Ireland) Act 1864 (c.78)
Bank Notes (Scotland) Act 1765 (c.49)
Bank Notes (Scotland) Act 1845 (c.38)
Bank of Ayr Act 1774 (c.21)
Bank of Bombay Failure Commissioners Act 1868 (c.63)
Bank of England Act 1694 (c.20)
Bank of England Act 1696 (c.20)
Bank of England Act 1707 (c.59)
Bank of England Act 1708 (c.30)
Bank of England Act 1709 (c.1)
Bank of England Act 1710 (c.7)
Bank of England Act 1716 (c.8)
Bank of England Act 1727 (c.8)
Bank of England Act 1728 (c.3)
Bank of England Act 1741 (c.13)
Bank of England Act 1745 (c.6)
Bank of England Act 1750 (c.4)
Bank of England Act 1784 (c.32)
Bank of England Act 1785 (c.83)
Bank of England Act 1791 (c.33)
Bank of England Act 1800 (c.28)
Bank of England Act 1833 (c.98)
Bank of England Act 1854 (c.1)
Bank of England Act 1861 (c.3)

Bank of England Act 1946 (c.27)
Bank of England (Advance) Act 1816 (c.96)
Bank of England Buildings Act 1764 (c.49)
Bank of England: Buildings Act 1766 (c.76)
Bank of England (Election of Directors) Act 1872 (c.34)
Bank of England Notes Act 1773 (c.79)
Bank of England Notes Act 1797 (c.28)
Bank of England Site Act 1793 (c.15)
Bank of England Stock Act 1796 (c.90)
Bank of Ireland Act 1808 (c.103)
Bank of Ireland Act 1860 (c.31)
Bank of Ireland Act 1865 (c.16)
Bank of Ireland Advances Act 1837 (c.59)
Bank of Ireland Advances Act 1838 (c.81)
Bank of Ireland Advances Act 1839 (c.91)
Bank of Ireland Charter Act 1872 (c.5)
Bank of Ireland, Transfer of Stocks Act 1862 (c.21)
Bank of Scotland Act 1774 (c.32)
Bank of Scotland Act 1784 (c.12)
Bank of Scotland Act 1792 (c.25)
Bank of Scotland Act 1794 (c.19)
Bank Post Bills Composition (Ireland) Act
Bank (Scotland) Act 1797 (c.40)
Bank (Scotland) Act 1797 (c.137)
Bankers' Books Evidence Act 1876 (c.48)
Bankers' Books Evidence Act 1879 (c.11)
Bankers' Composition Act 1856 (c.20)
Bankers' Composition (Scotland) Act 1853 (c.63)
Bankers' (Scotland) Act 1854 (c.73)
Bankers' Debt Act 1703 (c.9)
Bankers (Ireland) Act 1845 (c.37)
Bankers (Northern Ireland) Act 1928 (c.15)
Banking Act 1979 (c.37)
Banking Act 1987 (c.22)
Banking and Financial Dealings Act 1971 (c.80)
Banking Companies' (Shares) Act 1867 (c.29)
Banking Copartnerships Act 1864 (c.32)
Bankrupt and Insolvent Act 1857 (c.60)
Bankruptcy Act 1621 (c.18)
Bankruptcy Act 1716 (c.12)
Bankruptcy Act 1836 (c.27)
Bankruptcy Act 1839 (c.29)
Bankruptcy Act 1839 (c.86)
Bankruptcy Act 1842 (c.122)
Bankruptcy Act 1845 (c.48)
Bankruptcy Act 1852 (c.77)
Bankruptcy Act 1854 (c.119)
Bankruptcy Act 1861 (c.134)
Bankruptcy Act 1862 (c.99)
Bankruptcy Act 1869 (c.71)
Bankruptcy Act 1883 (c.52)
Bankruptcy Act 1890 (c.71)
Bankruptcy Act 1914 (c.59)
Bankruptcy (Agricultural Labourers' Wages) Act 1886 (c.28)
Bankruptcy Amendment Act 1868 (c.104)
Bankruptcy (Amendment) Act 1926 (c.7)
Bankruptcy and Cessio (Scotland) Act 1881 (c.22)

Bankruptcy and Deeds of Arrangement Act 1913 (c.34)
Bankruptcy and Real Securities (Scotland) Act 1857 (c.19)
Bankruptcy Appeals (County Courts) Act 1884 (c.9)
Bankruptcy Court Act 1853 (c.81)
Bankruptcy (Discharge and Closure) Act 1887 (c.66)
Bankruptcy Disqualification Act 1871 (c.50)
Bankruptcy, etc. Act 1847 (c.102)
Bankruptcy, etc. (Ireland) Act 1859 (c.62)
Bankruptcy Frauds and Disabilities (Scotland) Act 1884 (c.16)
Bankruptcy (Ireland) Act 1836 (c.14)
Bankruptcy (Ireland) Act 1837 (c.48)
Bankruptcy (Ireland) Act 1849 (c.107)
Bankruptcy (Ireland) Amendment Act 1872 (c.58)
Bankruptcy Law Consolidation Act 1849 (c.106)
Bankruptcy (Office Accommodation) Act 1885 (c.47)
Bankruptcy (Office Accommodation) Act 1886 (c.12)
Bankruptcy Repeal and Insolvent Court Act 1869 (c.83)
Bankruptcy (Scotland) Act 1839 (c.41)
Bankruptcy (Scotland) Act 1853 (c.53)
Bankruptcy (Scotland) Act 1856 (c.79)
Bankruptcy (Scotland) Act 1875 (c.26)
Bankruptcy (Scotland) Act 1913 (c.20)
Bankruptcy (Scotland) Act 1985 (c.66)
Bankruptcy (Scotland) Act 1993 (c.6)
Bankruptcy (Scotland) Amendment Act 1860 (c.33)
Bankrupts Act 1705 (c.4)
Bankrupts Act 1706 (c.22)
Bankrupts Act 1711 (c.25)
Bankrupts Act 1718 (c.24)
Bankrupts Act 1720 (c.19)
Bankrupts Act 1720 (c.31)
Bankrupts Act 1731 (c.30)
Bankrupts Act 1742 (c.27)
Bankrupts Act 1745 (c.32)
Bankrupts Act 1763 (c.33)
Bankrupts Act 1772 (c.47)
Bankrupts Act 1794 (c.57)
Bankrupts Act 1797 (c.124)
Bankrupts Act 1806 (c.135)
Bankrupts (England) and (Ireland) Act 1809 (c.121)
Bankrupts, etc. Act 1763 (c.36)
Bankrupts Release Act 1848 (c.86)
Banks (Scotland) Act 1797 (c.62)
Baptismal Fees Abolition Act 1872 (c.36)
Barbados Independence Act 1966 (c.37)
Barbed Wire Act 1893 (c.32)
Barking Act 1786 (c.115)
Barmouth Harbour Act 1797 (c.50)
Barnsley Canal Act 1793 (c.110)
Barnsley Canal Act 1793 (c.115)
Barnstaple Roads Act 1763 (c.35)

Barnstaple Roads Act 1783 (c.31)
Barrack Lane, Windsor Act 1867 (c.109)
Barracks Act 1890 (c.25)
Barristers Admission (Ireland) Act 1885 (c.20)
Barristers Admission, Stamp Duty Act 1874 (c.19)
Barristers (Qualifications for Office) Act 1961 (c.44)
Barthomley Church, Chester Act 1789 (c.11)
Basingstoke Canal Act 1778 (c.75)
Basingstoke Canal Act 1793 (c.16)
Basingstoke Roads Act 1797 (c.169)
Basingstoke to Winchester Road Act 1795 (c.162)
Basses Lights Act 1869 (c.77)
Basses Lights Act 1872 (c.55)
Bastard Children Act 1732 (c.31)
Bastard Children Act 1839 (c.85)
Bastards Act 1810 (c.51)
Bastards (Scotland) Act 1836 (c.22)
Bastardy Act 1809 (c.68)
Bastardy Act 1845 (c.10)
Bastardy Act 1923 (c.23)
Bastardy (Ireland) Act 1863 (c.21)
Bastardy Laws Act Amendment 1872 (c.65)
Bastardy Laws Amendment Act 1873 (c.9)
Bastardy Orders Act 1880 (c.32)
Bastardy (Witness Process) Act 1929 (c.38)
Bath City Prison Act 1871 (c.46)
Bath Highway, Streets, etc. Act 1707 (c.42)
Bath Highway, Streets, etc. Act 1720 (c.19)
Bath Hospital Act 1738 (c.31)
Bath Hospital Act 1779 (c.23)
Bath: Improvement Act 1766 (c.70)
Bath: Improvement Act 1789 (c.73)
Bath Roads Act 1757 (c.67)
Bath Roads Act 1758 (c.51)
Bath Roads Act 1760 (c.31)
Bath Roads Act 1793 (c.144)
Bath Roads, Streets, etc. Act 1738 (c.20)
Bath (Streets, Buildings, Watch etc.) 1757 (c.65)
Baths and Washhouses Act 1846 (c.74)
Baths and Washhouses Act 1847 (c.61)
Baths and Washhouses Act 1878 (c.14)
Baths and Washhouses Act 1882 (c.30)
Baths and Washhouses Act 1896 (c.59)
Baths and Washhouses Act 1899 (c.29)
Baths and Washhouses (Ireland) Act 1846 (c.87)
Bathwick Roads and Bridges, etc. Act 1769 (c.95)
Battersea Bridge Act 1766 (c.66)
Battersea Bridge and Embankment, etc. Act 1846 (c.39)
Battersea Parish Church Act 1774 (c.95)
Battersea Park Act 1846 (c.38)
Battersea Park Act 1851 (c.77)
Battersea Park Act 1853 (c.47)
Battle-axe Guards (Ireland) Act 1813 (c.54)
Bawtry to Markham Road Act 1793 (c.136)
Bawtry by Selby Road Act 1793 (c.166)

Beaconsfield and Redhill Road Act 1750 (c.32)

Beaconsfield and Stokenchurch Road Act 1759 (c.37)

Beaconsfield to Stokenchurch Road Act 1775 (c.70)

Beaconsfield to Stokenchurch Road Act 1794 (c.142)

Beccles: Improvement Act 1796 (c.51)

Bedford and Buckingham Highways Act 1708 (c.25)

Bedford and Buckingham Highways Act 1709 (c.25)

Bedford and Buckingham Roads Act 1727 (c.10)

Bedford and Buckingham Roads Act 1754 (c.21)

Bedford and Buckingham Roads Act 1754 (c.34)

Bedford and Buckingham Roads Act 1780 (c.68)

Bedford and Buckingham Roads Act 1790 (c.114)

Bedford and Hertford Roads Act 1742 (c.42)

Bedford and Hertford Roads Act 1775 (c.72)

Bedford and Hertford Roads Act 1786 (c.130)

Bedford and Hertford Roads Act 1795 (c.163)

Bedford and Hunts. Roads Act 1770 (c.83)

Bedford and Hunts. Roads Act 1791 (c.96)

Bedford and Northants Roads Act 1754 (c.33)

Bedford and Woburn Road Act 1796 (c.151)

Bedford Level Act 1754 (c.19)

Bedford Level Act 1756 (c.9)

Bedford Level Act 1772 (c.9)

Bedford Level Act 1780 (c.25)

Bedford Level Act 1783 (c.25)

Bedford Level Act 1789 (c.22)

Bedford Level Act 1796 (c.73)

Bedford Level and Swaffham Drainage Act 1767 (c.53)

Bedford Level: Drainage Act 1757 (c.18)

Bedford Level: Drainage Act 1771 (c.78)

Bedford Level: Drainage Act 1772 (c.40)

Bedford Level: Drainage Act 1772 (c.45)

Bedford Level: Drainage Act 1772 (c.49)

Bedford Level: Drainage Act 1775 (c.12)

Bedford Level: Drainage Act 1777 (c.65)

Bedford Level: Drainage Act 1779 (c.24)

Bedford Level: Drainage Act 1796 (c.33)

Bedford Roads Act 1731 (c.26)

Bedford Roads Act 1772 (c.89)

Bedford Roads Act 1772 (c.107)

Bedford Roads Act 1777 (c.94)

Bedford Roads Act 1793 (c.178)

Bedford: Poor Relief Act 1794 (c.98)

Bedford to Kimbolton Road Act 1795 (c.148)

Bedfordshire and Buckinghamshire Roads Act 1706 (c.4)

Bedfordshire and Buckinghamshire Roads Act 1739 (c.9)

Bedfordshire and Hertfordshire Roads Act 1763 (c.27)

Bedfordshire Highways Act 1706 (c.13)

Bedfordshire Roads Act 1724 (c.20)

Bedfordshire Roads Act 1736 (c.24)

Bedfordshire Roads Act 1753 (c.41)

Bee Pest Prevention (Ireland) Act 1908 (c.34)

Beef and Veal Customs Duties Act 1937 (c.8)

Beer Act 1761 (c.14)

Beer Act 1816 (c.58)

Beer and Malt (Ireland) Act 1809 (c.57)

Beer Dealers Retail Licences Act 1880 (c.6)

Beer Dealers, Retail Licences (Amendment) Act 1882 (c.34)

Beer, Devon, Harbour Act 1792 (c.92)

Beer Duties, Borrowstoness Act 1743 (c.21)

Beer Duties, Borrowstoness Act 1767 (c.90)

Beer Duties: Borrowstoness Act 1794 (c.91)

Beer, etc., Licences (Great Britain) Act 1816 (c.113)

Beer Licences Regulation (Ireland) Act 1877 (c.4)

Beer Retailers etc., Retail Licences (Ireland) Act 1900 (c.30)

Beerhouse Act 1840 (c.61)

Beerhouse Act 1870 (c.111)

Beerhouses (Ireland) Act 1864 (c.35)

Beerhouses (Ireland) Act (1864) Amendment 1871 (c.111)

Bees Act 1980 (c.12)

Behring Sea Award Act 1894 (c.2)

Belfast Borough Extension Act 1853 (c.114)

Belfast Commission Act 1886 (c.4)

Belfast Constabulary Act 1866 (c.46)

Belfast Custom House Act 1852 (c.30)

Belize Act 1981 (c.52)

Benefice (Ireland) Act 1865 (c.82)

Benefices Act 1807 (c.75)

Benefices Act 1808 (c.5)

Benefices Act 1898 (c.48)

Benefices (England) Act 1803 (c.84)

Benefices (England) Act 1803 (c.109)

Benefices (Ireland) Act 1808 (c.66)

Benefices (Ireland) Act 1860 (c.72)

Benefices (Scotland) Act 1843 (c.61)

Benefit Building Societies Act 1836 (c.32)

Benthall Bridge, Severn Act 1776 (c.17)

Berkshire Act 1751 (c.21)

Berkshire and Oxford Roads Act 1765 (c.55)

Berkshire and Southampton Roads Act 1772 (c.78)

Berkshire and Southampton Roads Act 1794 (c.141)

Berkshire and Wiltshire Roads Act 1770 (c.100)

Berkshire and Wiltshire Roads Act 1771 (c.97)

Berkshire and Wiltshire Roads Act 1781 (c.91)

Berkshire and Wiltshire Roads Act 1781 (c.101)

Berkshire and Wiltshire Roads Act 1793 (c.138)

Berkshire Highways Act 1713 (c.28)

Berkshire, Oxford, Buckinghamshire and Hertford Roads Act 1787 (c.81)

16

Berkshire Roads Act 1732 (c.16)
Berkshire Roads Act 1738 (c.11)
Berkshire Roads Act 1746 (c.6)
Berkshire Roads Act 1751 (c.21)
Berkshire Roads Act 1756 (c.77)
Berkshire Roads Act 1756 (c.81)
Berkshire Roads Act 1771 (c.70)
Berkshire Roads Act 1772 (c.104)
Berkshire Roads Act 1778 (c.99)
Berkshire Roads Act 1783 (c.100)
Berkshire Roads Act 1790 (c.106)
Berkshire Roads Act 1791 (c.105)
Berkshire Roads Act 1794 (c.132)
Bermuda Constitution Act 1967 (c.63)
Bermondsey, etc.: Streets Act 1785 (c.23)
Bermondsey (Poor Relief) Act 1757 (c.45)
Bermondsey: Poor Relief Act 1791 (c.19)
Bermuda Trade Act 1813 (c.50)
Berwick and Durham Roads Act 1793 (c.185)
Berwick-on-Tweed Act 1836 (c.103)
Berwick Roads Act 1753 (c.82)
Berwick Roads Act 1766 (c.73)
Berwick Roads Act 1772 (c.97)
Berwick Roads Act 1779 (c.79)
Berwick Roads Act 1781 (c.91)
Berwick Roads Act 1787 (c.89)
Berwick Roads Act 1792 (c.149)
Berwickshire County Town Act 1903 (c.5)
Berwickshire Courts Act 1853 (c.27)
Bethnal Green and Shoreditch: Improvement Act 1793 (c.88)
Bethnal Green: Completion of Church and Poor Relief Act 1745 (c.15)
Bethnal Green: Parish Act 1742 (c.28)
Bethnal Green: Poor Relief Act 1763 (c.40)
Bethnal Green: Poor Relief Act 1772 (c.53)
Bethnal Green Road Act 1756 (c.43)
Bethnal Green Road Act 1767 (c.105)
Betting Act 1853 (c.119)
Betting Act 1874 (c.15)
Betting and Gaming Act 1960 (c.60)
Betting and Gaming Duties Act 1972 (c.25)
Betting and Gaming Duties Act 1981 (c.63)
Betting and Loans (Infants) Act 1892 (c.4)
Betting and Lotteries Act 1934 (c.58)
Betting Duties Act 1963 (c.3)
Betting, Gaming and Lotteries Act 1963 (c.2)
Betting, Gaming and Lotteries Act 1964 (c.78)
Betting, Gaming and Lotteries (Amendment) Act 1969 (c.17)
Betting, Gaming and Lotteries (Amendment) Act 1971 (c.26)
Betting, Gaming and Lotteries (Amendment) Act 1980 (c.18)
Betting, Gaming and Lotteries (Amendment) Act 1984 (c.25)
Betting, Gaming and Lotteries (Amendment) Act 1985 (c.18)
Betting (Juvenile Messengers) (Scotland) Act 1928 (c.27)
Betting Levy Act 1961 (c.17)
Beverley and Kexby Bridge Road Act 1764 (c.76)

Beverley Improvement Act 1726 (c.4)
Beverley Improvement Act 1744 (c.13)
Beverley to Kexby Bridge Road Act 1785 (c.110)
Bewdley Bridge Act 1795 (c.78)
Bewdley Roads Act 1753 (c.39)
Bewdley Roads Act 1774 (c.112)
Bicester and Aylesbury Road Act 1770 (c.72)
Bicester Roads Act 1793 (c.180)
Bicester to Aylesbury Road Act 1791 (c.101)
Bicester to Aynho Road Act 1791 (c.103)
Bideford Roads Act 1764 (c.87)
Bideford Roads Act 1785 (c.119)
Bigamy Act 1795 (c.67)
Billiards (Abolition of Restrictions) Act 1987 (c.19)
Bill Chamber Procedure Act 1857 (c.18)
Bill of Exchange Act 1702 (c.8)
Bill of Exchange Act 1704 (c.8)
Bill of Exchange Act 1776 (c.30)
Bill of Exchange Act 1800 (c.42)
Bill of Exchange Act 1808 (c.88)
Bill of Exchange (Scotland) Act 1772 (c.72)
Bill of Sale Act 1891 (c.35)
Billeting of Civilians Act 1917 (c.20)
Bills and Notes Metropolis Act 1852 (c.1)
Bills and Notes Metropolis Act 1863 (c.2)
Bills Confirming Provisional Orders Act 1870 (c.1)
Bills of Exchange Act 1836 (c.58)
Bills of Exchange Act 1871 (c.74)
Bills of Exchange Act 1878 (c.13)
Bills of Exchange Act 1882 (c.61)
Bills of Exchange Act 1914 (c.82)
Bills of Exchange Act (1882) Amendment Act 1932 (c.44)
Bills of Exchange (Crossed Cheques) Act 1906 (c.17)
Bills of Exchange, etc. Act 1783 (c.7)
Bills of Exchange (Ireland) Act 1828 (c.24)
Bills of Exchange (Ireland) Act 1862 (c.23)
Bills of Exchange (Ireland) Act 1864 (c.7)
Bills of Exchange (Scotland) Act 1772 (c.72)
Bills of Exchange (Time of Noting) Act 1917 (c.48)
Bills of Lading Act 1855 (c.111)
Bills of Sale Act 1854 (c.36)
Bills of Sale (Ireland) Act 1854 (c.55)
Bills of Sale Act 1866 (c.96)
Bills of Sale Act 1878 (c.31)
Bills of Sale Act (1878) Amendment Act 1882 (c.43)
Bills of Sale Act 1890 (c.53)
Bills of Sale (Ireland) Act 1879 (c.50)
Bills of Sale (Ireland) Act (1879) Amendment Act 1883 (c.7)
Bingo Act 1992 (c.10)
Biological Standards Act 1975 (c.4)
Biological Weapons Act 1974 (c.6)
Birkenhead Enfranchisement Act 1861 (c.112)
Birmingham and Chesterfield Roads Act 1786 (c.149)

17

Birmingham and Stratford Roads Act 1825 (c.6)

Birmingham and Wednesbury Roads Act 1726 (c.14)

Birmingham Canal Act 1769 (c.53)

Birmingham Canal, Navigation Act 1768 (c.38)

Birmingham Canal, Navigation Act 1771 (c.67)

Birmingham Canal, Navigation Act 1783 (c.92)

Birmingham Canal, Navigation Act 1784 (c.4)

Birmingham Canal: Navigation Act 1785 (c.99)

Birmingham Canal: Navigation Act 1792 (c.81)

Birmingham Canal: Navigation Act 1794 (c.25)

Birmingham Canal: Navigation Act 1794 (c.87)

Birmingham Chapels Act 1772 (c.64)

Birmingham: Improvement Act 1769 (c.83)

Birmingham: Improvement Act 1772 (c.36)

Birmingham Police Act 1839 (c.88)

Birmingham: Poor Relief Act 1783 (c.54)

Birmingham to Edghill Road Act 1757 (c.58)

Birmingham to Stratford Roads Act 1725 (c.6)

Birmingham to Stratford Road Act 1771 (c.74)

Birmingham and Wednesbury Roads Act 1726 (c.14)

Birmingham Canal, Navigation Act 1784 (c.4)

Birstall to Huddersfield Roads Act 1786 (c.140)

Births and Deaths Registration Act 1836 (c.86)

Births and Deaths Registration Act 1837 (c.22)

Births and Deaths Registration Act 1858 (c.25)

Births and Deaths Registration Act 1874 (c.88)

Births and Deaths Registration Act 1901 (c.26)

Births and Deaths Registration Act 1926 (c.48)

Births and Deaths Registration Act 1947 (c.12)

Births and Deaths Registration Act 1953 (c.20)

Births and Deaths Registration (Ireland) Act 1880 (c.13)

Bishop of Calcutta Act 1874 (c.13)

Bishop of Quebec Act 1852 (c.53)

Bishopric of Bristol Act 1884 (c.66)

Bishopric of Bristol Amendment Act 1894 (c.21)

Bishopric of Bristol Amendment Act 1896 (c.29)

Bishopric of Christ Church, New Zealand Act 1852 (c.88)

Bishopric of St. Albans Act 1875 (c.34)

Bishopric of Southwark and Birmingham Act 1904 (c.30)

Bishopric of Truro Act 1876 (c.54)

Bishoprics Act 1878 (c.68)

Bishoprics, etc., in West Indies Act 1842 (c.4)

Bishoprics of Bradford and Coventry Act 1918 (c.57)

Bishoprics of Sheffield, Chelmsford and for the County of Suffolk Act 1913 (c.36)

Bishoprics of Southwark and Birmingham Act 1904 (c.30)

Bishops in Foreign Countries Act 1841 (c.6)

Bishops of London and Durham Act 1856 (c.115)

Bishops Trusts Substitution Act 1858 (c.71)

Bishops Resignation Act 1869 (c.111)

Bishops Resignation Act 1875 (c.19)

Bishops Resignation Act Continuance 1872 (c.40)

Bishopsgate: Poor Relief Act 1795 (c.61)

Black Game in Somerset and Devon Act 1810 (c.67)

Blackburn and Addingham Road Act 1796 (c.137)

Blackburn Roads Act 1776 (c.75)

Blackburn Roads Act 1796 (c.144)

Blackburn to Burscough Bridge Road Act 1793 (c.134)

Blackfriars Bridge Act 1756 (c.86)

Blackfriars Bridge Act 1756 (c.86)

Blackfriars Bridge (Sunday Tolls) Act 1786 (c.37)

Blackfriars Sewer Act 1795 (c.131)

Blackheath, etc., Small Debts Act 1770 (c.29)

Blackwater Bridge Act 1867 (c.57)

Blackwater Bridge Act 1873 (c.46)

Blackwater Bridge Debt Act 1873 (c.47)

Blandford Forum (Rebuilding after the Fire) Act 1731 (c.16)

Bleaching and Dyeing Works Act 1860 (c.78)

Bleaching and Dyeing Works Act Amendment Act 1863 (c.38)

Bleaching and Dyeing Works Act Ext. 1864 (c.98)

Bleaching Powder Act 1815 (c.38)

Bleaching Works Act 1862 (c.8)

Blind Persons Act 1938 (c.11)

Blind Voters Act 1933 (c.27)

Bloomsbury Churches Act 1730 (c.19)

Bloomsbury: Poor Relief Act 1774 (c.62)

Bloomsbury: Poor Relief Act 1774 (c.108)

Blything, Suffolk: Poor Relief, etc. Act 1764 (c.56)

Blything, Suffolk (Poor Relief, Guardians, etc.) Act 1793 (c.126)

Board of Agriculture Act 1889 (c.30)

Board of Agriculture and Fisheries Act 1903 (c.31)

Board of Agriculture and Fisheries Act 1909 (c.15)

Board of Education Act 1899 (c.33)

Board of Education (Scotland) Act 1877 (c.38)

Board of Trade Act 1909 (c.23)

Board of Trade Arbitrations etc. Act 1874 (c.40)

Boards of Guardians (Default) Act 1926 (c.20)

Boards of Management of Poor Law District Schools (Ireland) Act 1892 (c.41)

Bodies Corporate (Joint Tenancy) Act 1899 (c.20)

Bodmin Canal Act 1797 (c.29)

Bodmin Gaol Act 1778 (c.17)

Bodmin Roads Act 1769 (c.69)

Bodmin Roads Act 1786 (c.129)

Bogs (Ireland) Act 1811 (c.122)

Bogs (Ireland) Act 1812 (c.74)

Boiler Explosions Act 1882 (c.22)

Boiler Explosions Act 1890 (c.35)

Bolton and Nightingale's Road Act 1763 (c.31)

Bolton and Nightingale's Road Act 1763 (c.40)

Bolton and St. Helens Road Act 1796 (c.149)

Bolton, Blackburn and Twisey Roads Act 1797 (c.173)

Bolton Grammar School Act 1788 (c.81)

Bolton Police Act 1839 (c.95)

Bombay Civil Fund Act 1882 (c.45)

Bonded Corn Act 1842 (c.92)

Bonded Corn Act 1845 (c.103)

Bonded Warehouses Act 1805 (c.87)

Bonded Warehouses Act 1848 (c.122)

Bonding of Coffee, etc. Act 1807 (c.48)

Bonding of Spirits Act 1806 (c.27)

Bonding of Spirits (Ireland) Act 1804 (c.104)

Bonding of Sugar Act 1804 (c.36)

Bonding of Wine Act 1803 (c.103)

Bonding of Wines Act 1803 (c.14)

Bonding Warehouses Act 1806 (c.137)

Bonding Warehouses (Ireland) Act 1808 (c.32)

Bonded Warehouses (Ireland) Act 1810 (c.38)

Bonds of East India Company Act 1803 (c.3)

Booth's Charity, Salford Act 1776 (c.55)

Booth's Patent Act 1792 (c.73)

Borders Rivers (Prevention of Pollution) Act 1951 (c.7)

Borough and Local Courts of Record Act 1872 (c.86)

Borough and Watch Rates Act 1845 (c.110)

Borough Charters Confirmation Act 1842 (c.111)

Borough Clerks of the Peace (Ireland) Act 1868 (c.98)

Borough Constables Act 1883 (c.44)

Borough Coroners (Ireland) Act 1860 (c.74)

Borough Councillors (Alteration of Number) Act 1925 (c.11)

Borough Courts (England) Act 1839 (c.27)

Borough Electors Act 1868 (c.41)

Borough Fund in Certain Boroughs Act 1836 (c.104)

Borough Funds Act 1872 (c.91)

Borough Funds Act 1903 (c.14)

Borough Funds (Ireland) Act 1888 (c.53)

Borough Justices Act 1850 (c.91)

Borough of Hanley Act 1857 (c.10)

Borough Police Act 1848 (c.14)

Borough Quarter Sessions Act 1877 (c.17)

Borough Rates (England) Act 1854 (c.71)

Borough Recorders' Deputies Act 1869 (c.23)

Borough Watch Rates Act 1839 (c.28)

Boroughbridge and Darlington Road Act 1744 (c.8)

Boroughs, Relief from County Expenditure Act 1849 (c.82)

Borrowing (Control and Guarantees) Act 1946 (c.58)

Borrowstoness Canal Act 1783 (c.5)

Bosmere and Claydon, Suffolk (Poor Relief) Act 1764 (c.57)

Boston: Improvement Act 1792 (c.80)

Boston Pilotage Act 1776 (c.23)

Boston Pilotage Act 1792 (c.79)

Boston: Streets Act 1776 (c.25)

Boston Water Supply Act 1711 (c.44)

Botswana Independence Act 1966 (c.23)

Boundaries of Burghs Extension (Scotland) Act 1857 (c.70)

Boundaries of Burghs Extension (Scotland) Act 1861 (c.36)

Boundary Act 1868 (c.46)

Boundary Commissions Act 1992 (c.55)

Boundary Survey (Ireland) Act 1854 (c.17)

Boundary Survey (Ireland) Act 1857 (c.45)

Boundary Survey (Ireland) Act 1859 (c.8)

Bounties Act 1779 (c.27)

Bounties Act 1780 (c.40)

Bounties Act 1783 (c.21)

Bounties Act 1795 (c.21)

Bounties Act 1796 (c.56)

Bounties Act 1801 (c.13)

Bounties Act 1801 (c.34)

Bounties Act 1801 (c.92)

Bounties Act 1802 (c.59)

Bounties and Drawbacks Act 1805 (c.24)

Bounties and Drawbacks Act 1808 (cc.16, 17)

Bounties, etc., on Sugar Act 1809 (cc.10, 11)

Bounties, etc., on Sugar Act 1812 (c.15)

Bounties, etc., on Sugar Act 1813 (c.24)

Bounties for Destroying Spanish Ships Act 1785 (c.29)

Bounties for Destroying Spanish Ships Act 1786 (c.35)

Bounties (Great Britain) Act 1807 (c.29)

Bounties on Exportation Act 1744 (c.25)

Bounties on Importation Act 1800 (c.10)

Bounties on Importation Act 1800 (c.29)

Bounties on Pilchards Act 1812 (c.42)

Bounties on Sugar Act 1807 (c.22)

Bounties on Sugar Act 1808 (c.12)

Bounty for Taking L'Amazone Act 1784 (c.28)

Bounty of Exportation Act 1766 (c.45)

Bounty of Raw Sugar Act 1810 (c.9)

Bounty on British Calicoes Act 1807 (c.64)

Bounty on British Sail Cloth Exported Act 1797 (c.30)

Bounty on Certain Linens Exported Act 1799 (c.28)
Bounty on Cordage Exported Act 1786 (c.85)
Bounty on Corn Act 1780 (c.31)
Bounty on Corn, etc. Act 1750 (c.56)
Bounty on Exportation Act 1797 (c.76)
Bounty on Exportation Act 1806 (c.99)
Bounty on Exportation Act 1810 (c.40)
Bounty on Hemp Act 1779 (c.37)
Bounty on Importation Act 1800 (c.35)
Bounty on Pilchards Act 1797 (c.94)
Bounty on Pilchards Act 1799 (c.65)
Bounty on Pilchards Act 1808 (c.68)
Bounty on Rye Act 1800 (c.53)
Bounty on Silk Manufactures Act 1806 (c.110)
Bounty on Sugar Act 1816 (c.19)
Bounty on Sugar, etc. Act 1806 (c.109)
Bounty to Garrison of Gibraltar Act 1783 (c.16)
Bounty upon Importation Act 1763 (c.26)
Board of Trade (Parliamentary Secretary) Act 1867 (c.72)
Beurn, Lincs.: Navigation Act 1780 (c.22)
Bradford and Wakefield Road Act 1753 (c.83)
Bradford-on-Avon (Additional Overseer) Act 1783 (c.20)
Bradford to Idle Canal Act 1771 (c.89)
Bradford, Yorks: Water Supply Act 1790 (c.63)
Branding of Herrings (Northumberland) Act 1891 (c.28)
Brandon and Sams Cut Drain: Drainage Act 1757 (c.35)
Brandon and Waveney: Navigation Act 1750 (c.12)
Brazilian Slave Trade Repeal Act 1869 (c.2)
Bread Act 1762 (c.6)
Bread Act 1762 (c.11)
Bread Act 1772 (c.62)
Bread Act 1793 (c.37)
Bread Act 1836 (c.37)
Bread Acts Amendment Act 1922 (c.28)
Bread (Ireland) Act 1838 (c.28)
Brecknock and Abergavenny Canal Act 1793 (c.96)
Brecknock Forest Act 1815 (c.190)
Brecknock Water Supply Act 1776 (c.56)
Brecon Roads Act 1767 (c.60)
Brecon Roads Act 1772 (c.105)
Brecon Roads Act 1787 (c.75)
Brecon Roads Act 1793 (c.154)
Breeding of Dogs Act 1973 (c.60)
Breeding of Dogs Act 1991 (c.64)
Brent Bridge to Plymouth Road Act 1777 (c.81)
Brentford Road Act 1791 (c.124)
Bretton Woods Agreements Act 1945 (c.19)
Brewers' Licensing Act 1850 (c.67)
Brewn Roads Act 1772 (c.105)
Bribery at Elections Act 1842 (c.102)
Brick Duties Repeal Act 1850 (c.9)
Brick Making Act 1725 (c.35)

Brickmaking Act 1728 (c.15)
Brickmaking Act 1730 (c.22)
Bricks and Tiles Act 1770 (c.49)
Bricks and Tiles Act 1776 (c.42)
Bridewell Hospital Act 1780 (c.27)
Bridgeford Lane, Notts. to Kettering Road 1754 (c.39)
Bridges Act 1670 (c.12)
Bridges Act 1702 (c.12)
Bridges Act 1740 (c.33)
Bridges Act 1803 (c.59)
Bridges Act 1812 (c.110)
Bridges Act 1814 (c.90)
Bridges Act 1815 (c.143)
Bridges Act 1850 (c.64)
Bridges Act 1929 (c.33)
Bridges (Ireland) Act 1843 (c.42)
Bridges (Ireland) Act 1850 (c.4)
Bridges (Ireland) Act 1851 (c.21)
Bridges (Ireland) Act 1867 (c.50)
Bridges (Ireland) Act 1875 (c.46)
Bridges (Ireland) Act 1813 (c.77)
Bridges (Scotland) Act 1813 (c.117)
Bridgewell Hospital Act 1783 (c.27)
Bridgnorth Bridge Act 1797 (c.58)
Bridgnorth Church Act 1792 (c.30)
Bridgwater and Beverly Disfranchisement Act 1870 (c.21)
Bridgwater Canal Act 1795 (c.44)
Bridgwater Markets Act 1779 (c.36)
Bridgwater: Navigation Act 1794 (c.105)
Bridgwater Roads Act 1730 (c.34)
Bridgwater Roads Act 1779 (c.100)
Bridlington Pier Act 1715 (c.49)
Bridlington Pier Act 1718 (c.10)
Bridlington Pier Act 1789 (c.23)
Bridlington Piers Act 1720 (c.16)
Bridlington Piers Act 1753 (c.10)
Bridlington Roads Act 1767 (c.89)
Bridport, Dorset, Harbour Act 1721 (c.11)
Bridport: Improvement Act 1785 (c.91)
Brighton: Streets Act 1772 (c.34)
Brine Pumping (Compensation for Subsidence) Act 1891 (c.40)
Bringing of Coals, etc., to London, etc. Act 1805 (c.128)
Bringing of Coals, etc., to London Act 1807 (c.34)
Bringing of Coals, etc., to London, etc. Act 1808 (c.95)
Bringing of Coals, etc., to London, etc. Act 1810 (c.110)
Bringing of Coals, etc., to London Act 1811 (c.29)
Bringing of Coals, etc., to London, etc. Act 1817 (c.114)
Bringing of Coals to London, etc. Act 1806 (c.104)
Bringing of Coals to London, etc. Act 1813 (c.135)
Bringing of Coals to London, etc. 1815 (c.175)
Bringing of Coals to London, etc. Act 1816 (c.124)

Bristol and Exeter Railway Act 1836 (c.36)
Bristol Bridge Act 1759 (c.52)
Bristol Bridge Act 1786 (c.111)
Bristol: Building Act 1788 (c.66)
Bristol Charities Act 1858 (c.30)
Bristol Charities Act 1858 (c.31)
Bristol Churches Act 1750 (c.37)
Bristol Dock Act 1776 (c.33)
Bristol Gaol Act 1792 (c.82)
Bristol Guildhall, etc. Act 1788 (c.67)
Bristol Hospitals Act 1744 (c.38)
Bristol: Improvement Act 1788 (c.65)
Bristol Museum Act 1766 (c.18)
Bristol (Nightly Watch) Act 1755 (c.32)
Bristol, Paving, etc. Act 1748 (c.20)
Bristol, Poor Relief Act 1713 (c.32)
Bristol (Poor Relief) Act 1757 (c.56)
Bristol Roads Act 1726 (c.12)
Bristol Roads Act 1730 (c.22)
Bristol Roads Act 1748 (c.28)
Bristol Roads Act 1779 (c.117)
Bristol Roads Act 1797 (c.178)
Bristol Streets Act 1766 (c.34)
Bristol Theatre Act 1778 (c.8)
Bristol Watch Act 1756 (c.47)
British Aerospace Act 1980 (c.26)
British Airways Board Act 1977 (c.13)
British Calicoes Act 1811 (c.33)
British Caribbean Federation Act 1956 (c.63)
British Coal and British Rail (Transfer Proposals) Act 1993 (c.2)
British Columbia Act 1866 (c.67)
British Columbia Boundaries Act 1863 (c.83)
British Columbia Government Act 1858 (c.99)
British Columbia Government Act 1870 (c.66)
British Columbia (Loan) Act 1892 (c.52)
British Council and Commonwealth Institute Superannuation Act 1986 (c.51)
British Empire Exhibition (Amendment) Act 1922 (c.25)
British Empire Exhibition (Guarantee) Act 1920 (c.74)
British Empire Exhibition (Guarantee) Act 1925 (c.26)
British Ferries Society Act 1799 (c.100)
British Film Institute Act 1949 (c.35)
British Fisheries Act 1795 (c.56)
British Fisheries Act 1798 (c.58)
British Fisheries Act 1800 (c.85)
British Fisheries Act 1804 (c.86)
British Fisheries Act 1806 (c.34)
British Fisheries Act 1806 (c.156)
British Fisheries Act 1807 (c.51)
British Fisheries Act 1808 (c.86)
British Fisheries Act 1810 (c.54)
British Fisheries, etc. Act 1802 (c.79)
British Fisheries Society Act 1786 (c.106)
British Fishing Boats Act 1983 (c.8)
British Forces in India Act 1862 (c.27)
British Guiana Act 1928 (c.5)
British Honduras (Court of Appeal) Act 1881 (c.36)
British Hydrocarbon Oils Production Act 1934 (c.4)

British Industries Fair (Guarantees and Grants) Act 1954 (c.26)
British Kaffrania Act 1865 (c.5)
British Law Ascertainment Act 1859 (c.63)
British Leyland Act 1975 (c.43)
British Library Act 1972 (c.54)
British Mercantile Marine Uniform Act 1919 (c.62)
British Museum Act 1700 (c.7)
British Museum Act 1706 (c.30)
British Museum Act 1753 (c.22)
British Museum Act 1766 (c.18)
British Museum Act 1805 (c.127)
British Museum Act 1807 (c.36)
British Museum Act 1816 (c.99)
British Museum Act 1839 (c.10)
British Museum Act 1878 (c.55)
British Museum Act 1902 (c.12)
British Museum Act 1924 (c.23)
British Museum Act 1930 (c.46)
British Museum Act 1931 (c.34)
British Museum Act 1932 (c.34)
British Museum Act 1938 (c.62)
British Museum Act 1946 (c.56)
British Museum Act 1955 (c.23)
British Museum Act 1962 (c.18)
British Museum Act 1963 (c.24)
British Museum (Purchase of Land) Act 1894 (c.34)
British Nationality Act 1730 (c.21)
British Nationality Act 1772 (c.21)
British Nationality Act 1948 (c.56)
British Nationality Act 1958 (c.10)
British Nationality Act 1964 (c.22)
British Nationality Act 1965 (c.34)
British Nationality Act 1981 (c.61)
British Nationality and Status of Aliens Act 1918 (c.38)
British Nationality and Status of Aliens Act 1922 (c.44)
British Nationality and Status of Aliens Act 1933 (c.49)
British Nationality and Status of Aliens Act 1943 (c.14)
British Nationality (Falkland Islands) Act 1983 (c.6)
British Nationality (Hong Kong) Act 1990 (c.34)
British Nationality (No. 2) Act 1964 (c.54)
British North America Act 1840 (c.35)
British North America Act 1867 (c.3)
British North America Act 1870 (c.28)
British North America Act 1871 (c.28)
British North America Act 1886 (c.35)
British North America Act 1907 (c.11)
British North America Act 1915 (c.45)
British North America Act 1916 (c.19)
British North America Act 1930 (c.26)
British North America Act 1939 (c.36)
British North America Act 1940 (c.36)
British North America Act 1943 (c.30)
British North America Act 1946 (c.63)
British North America Act 1949 (c.22)

British North America Act 1951 (c.32)
British North America Act 1960 (c.2)
British North America Act 1964 (c.73)
British North America (No. 2) Act 1949 (c.81)
British North America (Quebec) Act 1774 (c.83)
British Overseas Airways Act 1939 (c.61)
British Railways Board (Finance) Act 1991 (c.63)
British Sailcloth, etc. Act 1793 (c.49)
British Settlements Act 1887 (c.54)
British Settlements Act 1945 (c.7)
British Settlements in Africa, etc. Act 1764 (c.44)
British Shipbuilders Act 1983 (c.15)
British Shipbuilders (Borrowing Powers) Act 1983 (c.58)
British Shipbuilders (Borrowing Powers) Act 1986 (c.19)
British Shipbuilders (Borrowing Powers) Act 1987 (c.52)
British Shipping (Assistance) Act 1935 (c.7)
British Shipping (Continuance of Subsidy) Act 1936 (c.12)
British Shipping (Continuance of Subsidy) Act 1937 (c.21)
British Ships Act 1772 (c.26)
British Ships Captured by the Enemy Act 1808 (c.70)
British Ships (Transfer Restriction) Act 1915 (c.21)
British Ships (Transfer Restriction) Act 1916 (c.42)
British Standard Time Act 1968 (c.45)
British Steel Act 1988 (c.35)
Btitish Subjects Act 1751 (c.39)
British Subjects in China Act 1843 (c.80)
British Sugar Industry (Assistance) Act 1931 (c.35)
British Sugar (Subsidy) Act 1925 (c.12)
British Sugar (Subsidy) Act 1934 (c.39)
British Sugar (Subsidy) Act 1935 (c.37)
British Technology Group Act 1991 (c.66)
British Telecommunications Act 1981 (c.38)
British White Herring Fishery Act 1811 (c.101)
British White Herring Fishery Act 1812 (c.153)
British White Herring Fishery Act 1814 (c.102)
Brixton: Small Debts Act 1757 (c.23)
Broadcasting Act 1980 (c.64)
Broadcasting Act 1981 (c.68)
Broadcasting Act 1987 (c.10)
Broadcasting Act 1990 (c.42)
Broadstairs Pier Act 1792 (c.86)
Brokers, Bristol Act 1730 (c.31)
Bromsgrove and Birmingham Roads Act 1776 (c.15)
Bromsgrove to Birmingham Road Act 1790 (c.101)
Brown Linen Manufacture (Ireland) Act 1815 (c.25)

Brunei and Maldives Act 1985 (c.3)
Brunei Appeals Act 1989 (c.36)
Bruntisland Beer Duties Act 1746 (c.26)
Bruntisland Beer Duties Act 1776 (c.20)
Bruntisland Beer Duties Act 1794 (c.8)
Bruton Roads Act 1756 (c.50)
Bubble Schemes, Colonies Act 1740 (c.37)
Bubwith Bridge Act 1793 (c.106)
Buckingham and Hanwell Road Act 1792 (c.134)
Buckingham and Middlesex Roads Act 1779 (c.83)
Buckingham and Oxford Roads Act 1770 (c.58)
Buckingham and Oxford Roads Act 1785 (c.127)
Buckingham to Banbury Road Act 1791 (c.133)
Buckingham to Hanwell Road Act 1769 (c.52)
Buckingham to Warmington Road Act 1743 (c.43)
Buckinghamshire and Oxford Roads Act 1769 (c.88)
Buckinghamshire and Oxford Roads Act 1791 (c.136)
Buckinghamshire Assizes Act 1747 (c.12)
Buckinghamshire Assizes Act 1849 (c.6)
Buckinghamshire Highways Act 1722 (c.13)
Buckinghamshire Roads Act 1720 (c.24)
Buckinghamshire Roads Act 1735 (c.11)
Buckinghamshire Roads Act 1735 (c.21)
Buckinghamshire Roads Act 1741 (c.5)
Buckinghamshire Roads Act 1741 (c.6)
Buckinghamshire Roads Act 1759 (c.43)
Buckinghamshire Roads Act 1767 (c.61)
Buckinghamshire Roads Act 1777 (c.82)
Bude Canal Act 1774 (c.53)
Building Act 1984 (c.55)
Building Control Act 1966 (c.27)
Building Materials and Housing Act 1945 (c.20)
Building of Churches, etc. (Ireland) Act 1809
Building of Churches, London and Westminster Act 1714 (c.23)
Building Restrictions (War-Time Contraventions) Act 1946 (c.35)
Building (Scotland) Act 1959 (c.24)
Building (Scotland) Act 1970 (c.38)
Building Sites for Religious and Other Purposes Act 1868 (c.44)
Building Societies Act 1874 (c.42)
Building Societies Act 1875 (c.9)
Building Societies Act 1877 (c.63)
Building Societies Act 1884 (c.41)
Building Societies Act 1894 (c.47)
Building Societies Act 1939 (c.55)
Building Societies Act 1960 (c.64)
Building Societies Act 1962 (c.37)
Building Societies Act 1986 (c.53)
Bunhill Fields Burial Ground Act 1867 (c.38)
Burford Charities Act 1861 (c.22)
Burford to Preston Road Act 1780 (c.76)
Burgesses Qualification (Scotland) Act 1876 (c.12)

Burgesses (Scotland) Act 1860 (c.47)
Burgh Council Elections (Scotland) Act 1853 (c.26)
Burgh Customs (Scotland) Act 1870 (c.42)
Burgh Gas Supply (Scotland) Amendment Act 1918 (c.45)
Burgh Harbours (Scotland) Act 1853 (c.93)
Burgh Police (Amendment) (Scotland) Act 1964 (c.33)
Burgh Police, etc. (Scotland) Act 1847 (c.39)
Burgh Police (Scotland) Act 1892 (c.55)
Burgh Police (Scotland) Act 1892, Amendment 1894 (c.18)
Burgh Police (Scotland) Act 1893 (c.25)
Burgh Police (Scotland) Act 1903 (c.33)
Burgh Police (Scotland) Amendment Act 1911 (c.51)
Burgh Registers (Scotland) Act 1926 (c.50)
Burgh, Scotland (Petty Customs) Act 1879 (c.13)
Burgh Sewerage, Drainage and Water Supply (Scotland) Act 1901 (c.24)
Burgh Trading Act 1846 (c.17)
Burgh Voters' Registration (Scotland) Act 1856 (c.58)
Burgh Wards (Scotland) Act 1876 (c.25)
Burghs Gas Supply (Scotland) Act 1876 (c.49)
Burghs Gas Supply (Scotland) Act 1893 (c.52)
Burghs of Barony (Scotland) Act 1795 (c.122)
Burghs (Scotland) Act 1852 (c.33)
Burglaries, etc. Act 1706 (c.9)
Burglary Act 1837 (c.86)
Burglary Act 1896 (c.57)
Burial Act 1852 (c.85)
Burial Act 1853 (c.134)
Burial Act 1854 (c.87)
Burial Act 1855 (c.128)
Burial Act 1857 (c.81)
Burial Act 1859 (c.1)
Burial Act 1860 (c.64)
Burial Act 1862 (c.100)
Burial Act 1871 (c.33)
Burial Act 1900 (c.15)
Burial Act 1906 (c.44)
Burial and Registration Acts (Doubts Removal) Act 1881 (c.2)
Burial Boards (Contested Elections) Act 1885 (c.21)
Burial Grounds (Ireland) Act 1856 (c.98)
Burial Grounds (Ireland) Act 1860 (c.76)
Burial Grounds (Scotland) Act 1855 (c.68)
Burial Grounds (Scotland) Act, 1855, Amendment Act 1881 (c.27)
Burial Grounds (Scotland) Act 1857 (c.42)
Burial Grounds (Scotland) Amendment Act 1886 (c.21)
Burial in Burghs (Scotland) Act 1866 (c.46)
Burial (Ireland) Act 1868 (c.103)
Burial Laws Amendment Act 1880 (c.41)
Burial of Drowned Persons Act 1808 (c.75)
Burial of Drowned Persons Act 1886 (c.20)

Burma Independence Act 1947 (c.3)
Burma Legislature Act 1946 (c.57)
Burning of Buildings, etc. Act 1837 (c.89)
Burning of Farm Buildings Act 1844 (c.62)
Burning of Houses (Dublin) Act 1841 (c.10)
Burning of Land (Ireland) Act 1814 (c.115)
Burnley Roads Act 1795 (c.146)
Burnt Fen (Northampton): Drainage Act 1797 (c.89)
Bursledon Bridge, Southampton Act 1797 (c.131)
Burton-upon-Trent and Derby Road Act 1753 (c.59)
Burton-upon-Trent and Derby Road Act 1764 (c.51)
Burton-upon-Trent: Improvement Act 1779 (c.39)
Burtry Ford to Burnstone Road 1794 (c.125)
Bury and Bolton Roads Act 1797 (c.174)
Bury and Stratton Road Act 1755 (c.35)
Bury St. Edmunds (Poor Relief) Act 1749 (c.21)
Bury to Church Kirk Canal Act 1794 (c.77)
Burying in Woollen Act 1814 (c.108)
Bus Fuel Grants Act 1966 (c.46)
Bushey Heath to Aylesbury Road Act 1783 (c.93)
Business Names Act 1985 (c.7)
Butter and Cheese Trade Act 1844 (c.48)
Butter and Margarine Act 1907 (c.21)
Butter Trade (Ireland) Act 1812 (c.134)
Butter Trade (Ireland) Act 1813 (c.46)
Buxton and Manchester Road Act 1753 (c.53)
Buxton to Manchester Road Act 1729 (c.4)
Buxton to Manchester Road Act 1748 (c.12)
Byron's Shorthand Act 1741 (c.23)

Cable and Broadcasting Act 1984 (c.46)
Cable and Wireless Act 1946 (c.82)
Caddington Church Act 1740 (c.26)
Caithness Roads Act 1793 (c.120)
Calder and Hebb: Navigation Act 1769 (c.71)
Calder Canal Act 1774 (c.13)
Calder Navigation Act 1757 (c.72)
Caldey Island Act 1990 (c.44)
Caldon Canal Act 1797 (c.36)
Caledonian and Crinan Canals Amendment Act 1860 (c.46)
Caledonian Canal Act 1803 (c.102)
Caledonian Canal Act 1804 (c.62)
Caledonian Canal Act 1840 (c.41)
Caledonian Canal Act 1848 (c.54)
Caledonian Canal Act 1857 (c.27)
Calendar Act 1750 (c.30)
Calendar (New Style) Act 1750 (c.23)
Callington Roads Act 1764 (c.48)
Camberwell and Peckham: Streets Act 1776 (c.26)
Camberwell, Bristol and Nottingham Elections (Validation) Act 1946 (c.43)
Camberwell: Streets Act 1787 (c.52)

Cambrics Act 1744 (c.36)
Cambrics Act 1747 (c.26)
Cambridge and Arrington Roads Act 1797 (c.179)
Cambridge and Ely Roads Act 1763 (c.36)
Cambridge and Newmarket Road Act 1763 (c.30)
Cambridge and Norfolk Roads Act 1770 (c.97)
Cambridge Commissioners Act 1873 (c.73)
Cambridge: Improvement Act 1788 (c.64)
Cambridge: Improvement Act 1794 (c.104)
Cambridge Roads Act 1723 (c.12)
Cambridge Roads Act 1724 (c.14)
Cambridge Roads Act 1730 (c.37)
Cambridge Roads Act 1755 (c.36)
Cambridge Roads Act 1765 (c.74)
Cambridge Roads Act 1765 (c.76)
Cambridge Roads Act 1765 (c.79)
Cambridge Roads Act 1766 (c.84)
Cambridge Roads Act 1773 (c.110)
Cambridge Roads Act 1790 (c.94)
Cambridge Roads Act 1792 (c.129)
Cambridge to Royston Road Act 1793 (c.130)
Cambridge University Act 1856 (c.88)
Cambridge University Act 1858 (c.11)
Cambridge University, etc. Act 1859 (c.34)
Cambridgeshire Roads Act 1730 (c.24)
Cambridgeshire Roads Act 1741 (c.16)
Camps Act 1939 (c.22)
Camps Act 1945 (c.26)
Canada Act 1775 (c.40)
Canada Act 1982 (c.11)
Canada Civil List Act 1847 (c.71)
Canada Company's Amendment Act 1856 (c.23)
Canada Copyright Act 1875 (c.53)
Canada Defences Loan Act 1870 (c.82)
Canada Loan Guarantee Act 1842 (c.118)
Canada (Ontario Boundary) Act 1889 (c.28)
Canada (Public Works) Loan Act 1873 (c.45)
Canada Railway Loan Act 1867 (c.16)
Canada (Rupert's Land) Loan Act 1869 (c.101)
Canada Union Act 1848 (c.56)
Canadian Speaker (Appointment of Deputy) Act 1895 (c.3)
Canadian Stock Stamp Act 1874 (c.26)
Canal Boats Act 1877 (c.60)
Canal Boats Act 1884 (c.75)
Canal, Carmarthen Act 1766 (c.55)
Canal Carriers Act 1845 (c.42)
Canal (Carriers) Act 1847 (c.94)
Canal Tolls Act 1845 (c.28)
Canals (Continuance of Charging Powers) Act 1922 (c.27)
Canals (Continuance of Charging Powers) Act 1924 (c.2)
Canals, etc. (Scotland) Act 1806 (c.155)
Canals (Ireland) Act 1816 (c.55)
Canals (Offences) Act 1840 (c.50)
Canals Protection (London) Act 1898 (c.16)
Canals: Trent and Mersey Act 1797 (c.81)

Cancer Act 1939 (c.13)
Canterbury Association (New Zealand) Act 1850 (c.70)
Canterbury Association (New Zealand) Act 1851 (c.84)
Canterbury: Church of St. Andrew Act 1763 (c.49)
Canterbury: Poor Relief Act 1727 (c.20)
Canterbury: Streets Act 1787 (c.14)
Canterbury to Whitstable Road Act 1783 (c.97)
Canvey Island, Sea Defences Act 1792 (c.23)
Cape of Good Hope (Advance) Act 1885 (c.7)
Cape of Good Hope Trade Act 1796 (c.21)
Cape of Good Hope Trade Act 1806 (c.30)
Cape of Good Hope Trade Act 1807 (c.11)
Cape of Good Hope Trade Act 1808 (c.105)
Cape of Good Hope Trade Act 1809 (c.17)
Cape of Good Hope Trade Act 1816 (c.8)
Cape Race Lighthouse Act 1886 (c.13)
Cape Rock Lighthouse (Scotland) Act 1806 (c.132)
Capital Allowances Act 1968 (c.3)
Capital Allowances Act 1990 (c.1)
Capital Expenditure (Money) Act 1904 (c.21)
Capital Gains Tax Act 1979 (c.14)
Capital Punishment, etc. Act 1823 (c.46)
Capital Punishment Abolition Act 1835 (c.81)
Capital Punishment Abolition Act 1836 (c.4)
Capital Punishment Amendment Act 1868 (c.24)
Capital Punishment (Ireland) Act 1842 (c.28)
Capital Transfer Tax Act 1984 (c.51)
Captive Birds Shooting (Prohibition) Act 1921 (c.13)
Captures Act 1776 (c.40)
Car Tax (Abolition) Act 1992 (c.58)
Car Tax Act 1983 (c.53)
Caravan Sites Act 1968 (c.52)
Caravan Sites and Control of Development Act 1960 (c.62)
Caravans (Standard Community Charge and Rating) Act 1991 (c.2)
Cardiff Bay Barrage Act 1993 (c.42)
Cardiff: Improvement Act 1774 (c.9)
Cardigan Roads Act 1770 (c.55)
Cardigan Roads Act 1791 (c.97)
Care and Treatment of Lunatics Act 1853 (c.96)
Care, etc., of Lunatics Act 1841 (c.4)
Care of King During His Illness, etc. Act 1811 (c.1)
Care of King's Estate During His Illness Act 1812 (c.14)
Carlford, Suffolk: Poor Relief Act 1756 (c.79)
Carlford, Suffolk (Poor Relief) Act 1764 (c.58)
Carlisle and Eamont Bridge Road Act 1753 (c.40)
Carlisle and Newcastle Road Act 1750 (c.25)
Carlton Bridge, Yorks. Act 1774 (c.63)
Carmarthen and Pembroke Roads Act 1763 (c.34)
Carmarthen: Improvement Act 1792 (c.104)

Carmarthen Roads Act 1765 (c.76)
Carmarthen Roads Act 1779 (c.102)
Carmarthen Roads Act 1779 (c.103)
Carmarthen Roads Act 1783 (c.33)
Carmarthen Roads Act 1786 (c.150)
Carmarthen Roads Act 1788 (c.109)
Carmarthen Roads Act 1792 (c.156)
Carnarvon Harbour Act 1793 (c.123)
Carnarvon Roads Act 1769 (c.77)
Carnarvon Roads Act 1795 (c.143)
Carriage and Deposit of Dangerous Goods Act 1866 (c.69)
Carriage by Air Act 1931 (c.36)
Carriage by Air Act 1961 (c.27)
Carriage by Air and Road Act 1979 (c.28)
Carriage by Air (Supplementary Provisions) Act 1962 (c.43)
Carriage by Railway Act 1972 (c.33)
Carriage Duties Act 1795 (c.109)
Carriage of Corn, etc. Act 1702 (c.20)
Carriage of Goods by Road Act 1965 (c.37)
Carriage of Goods by Sea Act 1924 (c.22)
Carriage of Goods by Sea Act 1971 (c.19)
Carriage of Goods by Sea Act 1992 (c.50)
Carriage of Gunpowder (Great Britain) Act 1814 (c.152)
Carriage of Passengers by Road Act 1974 (c.35)
Carriers Act 1830 (c.68)
Carriers Act Amendment Act 1865 (c.94)
Carrying of Knives etc. (Scotland) Act 1993 (c.13)
Carts on Highways Act 1744 (c.33)
Casting Away of Vessels, etc. Act 1803 (c.113)
Castle Stewart and Nairn Road Assessment Act 1860 (c.37)
Casual Poor Act 1882 (c.36)
Catering Wages Act 1943 (c.24)
Cathedral Acts Amendment Act 1873 (c.39)
Cathedral Churches, etc. Act 1853 (c.35)
Cathedral Statutes Act 1707 (c.75)
Cathedrals Act 1864 (c.70)
Catterick Bridge to Durham Road Act 1788 (c.90)
Cattle Assurance Act 1866 (c.34)
Cattle Disease Act 1866 (c.15)
Cattle Disease (Ireland) Act 1866 (c.4)
Cattle Disease (Ireland) Act 1876 (c.51)
Cattle Disease (Ireland) Acts Amendment 1874 (c.6)
Cattle Disease (Ireland) Amendment Act 1872 (c.16)
Cattle Diseases (Ireland) Amendment Act 1870 (c.36)
Cattle Disease Prevention Amendment Act 1866 (c.110)
Cattle Diseases Prevention Act 1866 (c.2)
Cattle Distemper, Vagrancy, Marshalsea Prison Act 1753 (c.34)
Cattle Industry Act 1936 (c.46)
Cattle Industry (Emergency Provisions) Act 1934 (c.54)

Cattle Industry (Emergency Provisions) Act 1935 (c.12)
Cattle Industry (Emergency Provisions) (No. 2) Act 1935 (c.39)
Cattle sheds in Burghs (Scotland) Act 1866 (c.17)
Cattle Stealing Act 1740 (c.6)
Cattle Stealing Act 1741 (c.34)
Cattle Theft (Scotland) Act 1747 (c.34)
Catwater Harbour and Sutton Pool, Plymouth Act 1709 (c.4 (b))
Causey, Yarmouth to Caistor Act 1723 (c.8)
Cawdle Fen. etc. Drainage Act 1737 (c.34)
Cayman Islands Act 1863 (c.31)
Cayman Islands and Turks and Caicos Islands Act 1958 (c.13)
Celluloid and Cinematograph Film Act 1922 (c.35)
Cemeteries Clauses Act 1847 (c.65)
Census Act 1800 (c.15)
Census Act 1841 (c.7)
Census Act 1841 (c.9)
Census Act 1860 (cc.61, 62)
Census Act 1880 (c.37)
Census Act 1920 (c.41)
Census (Confidentiality) Act 1991 (c.6)
Census (England) Act 1870 (c.107)
Census (England and Wales) Act 1890 (c.61)
Census (Great Britain) Act 1811 (c.6)
Census (Great Britain) Act 1840 (c.99)
Census, Great Britain Act 1850 (c.53)
Census (Great Britain) Act 1900 (c.4)
Census (Great Britain) Act 1910 (c.27)
Census (Ireland) Act 1812 (c.133)
Census (Ireland) Act 1815 (c.120)
Census (Ireland) Act 1840 (c.100)
Census (Ireland) Act 1850 (c.44)
Census (Ireland) Act 1870 (c.80)
Census (Ireland) Act 1880 (c.28)
Census (Ireland) Act 1890 (c.46)
Census (Ireland) Act 1900 (c.6)
Census (Ireland) Act 1910 (c.11)
Census of Production Act 1906 (c.49)
Census of Production Act 1917 (c.2)
Census of Production Act 1939 (c.15)
Census (Scotland) Act 1860 (c.98)
Census (Scotland) Act 1870 (c.108)
Census (Scotland) Act 1880 (c.38)
Census (Scotland) Act 1890 (c.38)
Central Criminal Court Act 1837 (c.77)
Central Criminal Court Act 1846 (c.24)
Central Criminal Court Act 1856 (c.16)
Central Criminal Court (Prisons) Act 1881 (c.64)
Central Criminal Lunatic Asylum (Ireland) Act 1845 (c.107)
Cereals Marketing Act 1965 (c.14)
Certain Export Duties Repeal Act 1845 (c.7)
Certain Mutinous Crews Act 1797 (c.71)
Certain Parliamentary Grants Act 1801 (c.73)
Certificates for Killing Hares Act 1791 (c.21)
Certificates of Attorneys, etc. Act 1804 (c.59)
Cessio (Scotland) Act 1836 (c.56)

Cestui que Vie Act 1707 (c.72)

Ceylon Independence Act 1947 (c.7)

Chaff-Cutting Machines (Accidents) Act 1897 (c.60)

Chain Cable and Anchor Act 1864 (c.27)

Chain Cable and Anchor Act 1871 (c.101)

Chain Cable and Anchor Act 1872 (c.30)

Chain Cables and Anchors Act 1874 (c.51)

Chairman of District Councils Act 1896 (c.22)

Chairman of Quarter Sessions (Ireland) Act 1858 (c.88)

Chairman of Quarter Sessions (Ireland) Jurisdiction Act 1876 (c.71)

Chairman of Traffic Commissioners etc. (Tenure of Office) Act 1937 (c.52)

Chancel Repairs Act 1931 (c.20)

Chancery Amendment Act 1858 (c.27)

Chancery and Common Law Offices (Ireland) Act 1867 (c.129)

Chancery Appeal Court (Ireland) Act 1856 (c.92)

Chancery Court Act 1838 (c.54)

Chancery (Ireland) Act 1834 (c.78)

Chancery (Ireland) Act 1835 (c.16)

Chancery (Ireland) Act 1851 (c.15)

Chancery (Ireland) Act 1867 (c.44)

Chancery of Lancaster Act 1890 (c.23)

Chancery Receivers (Ireland) Act 1856 (c.77)

Chancery Regulation Act 1862 (c.42)

Chancery Regulation (Ireland) Act 1862 (c.46)

Chancery Rules and Orders Act 1860 (c.128)

Chancery Taxing Master (Ireland) Act 1845 (c.115)

Channel Tunnel Act 1987 (c.53)

Channel Tunnel (Initial Finance) Act 1973 (c.66)

Chapel of Ease, Yarmouth Act 1713 (c.16(d))

Chapels of Ease Act 1836 (c.31)

Chapels of Ease, etc. (Ireland) Act 1849 (c.99)

Chaplains in Gaols, etc. (England) Act 1815 (c.48)

Chaplains in the Navy (1820) (c.106)

Charge of Certain Annuities Act 1813 (c.156)

Charge of Loan Act 1807 (c.55)

Charge of Loan Act 1811 (c.61)

Charges of Loan, etc., of Present Session Act 1810 (c.71)

Charge of Loans Act 1809 (c.92)

Charging Orders Act 1979 (c.53)

Charitable Corporation Act 1732 (c.2)

Charitable Corporation (Arrangements with Creditors) Act 1732 (c.36)

Charitable Corporation (Claims and Disputes) Act 1731 (c.31)

Charitable Corporation Frauds Act 1731 (c.3)

Charitable Corporation Lottery Act 1733 (c.11)

Charitable Corporation Lottery Act 1734 (c.14)

Charitable Donations and Bequest (Ireland) Act 1867 (c.54)

Charitable Donations and Bequests (Ireland) Act 1844 (c.97)

Charitable Donations and Bequests (Ireland) Act 1871 (c.102)

Charitable Donations Registration Act 1812 (c.102)

Charitable Funds Investment Act 1870 (c.34)

Charitable Loan Societies (Ireland) Act 1844 (c.38)

Charitable Loan Societies (Ireland) Act 1900 (c.25)

Charitable Loan Societies (Ireland) Act 1906 (c.23)

Charitable Pawn Offices (Ireland) Act 1842 (c.75)

Charitable Trust (Recovery) Act 1891 (c.17)

Charitable Trustees Incorporation Act 1872 (c.24)

Charitable Trusts Act 1853 (c.137)

Charitable Trusts Act 1860 (c.136)

Charitable Trusts Act 1862 (c.112)

Charitable Trusts Act 1869 (c.110)

Charitable Trusts Act 1887 (c.49)

Charitable Trusts Act 1914 (c.56)

Charitable Trusts Act 1925 (c.27)

Charitable Trusts Amendment Act 1855 (c.124)

Charitable Trusts Deeds Enrolment Act 1866 (c.57)

Charitable Trusts (Places of Religious Worship) Amendment Act 1894 (c.35)

Charitable Trusts (Validation) Act 1954 (c.58)

Charitable Uses Act 1735 (c.36)

Charitable Uses Act 1861 (c.9)

Charitable Uses Act 1862 (c.17)

Charities Act 1960 (c.58)

Charities Act 1985 (c.20)

Charities Act 1992 (c.41)

Charities Act 1993 (c.10)

Charities (Enrolment of Deeds) Act 1864 (c.13)

Charities (Fuel Allotments) Act 1939 (c.26)

Charities Inquiries Commission Expenses Act 1837 (c.4)

Charities Inquiries (England) Act 1835 (c.71)

Charities of John Pierrepont Act 1708 (c.10)

Charities of Thomas Guy Act 1724 (c.12)

Charities Procedure Act 1812 (c.101)

Charities (Service of Notice) Act 1851 (c.56)

Charity Inquiries Expenses Act 1892 (c.15)

Charity Lands Act 1863 (c.106)

Charles Beattie Indemnity Act 1956 (c.27)

Charles Radcliffe's Estates Act 1788 (c.63)

Charlwood and Horley Act 1974 (c.11)

Charter Trustees Act 1985 (c.45)

Chartered and Other Bodies (Resumption of Elections) Act 1945 (c.6)

Chartered and Other Bodies (Temporary Provisions) Act 1939 (c.119)

Chartered and Other Bodies (Temporary Provisions) Act 1941 (c.19)

Chartered Associations (Protection of Names and Uniforms) Act 1926 (c.26)

Chartered Companies Act 1837 (c.73)
Chartered Companies Act 1884 (c.56)
Charterhouse Governors (Quorum) Act 1721 (c.29)
Charterhouse Square: Rates Act 1742 (c.6)
Chatham and Sheerness Stipendiary Magistrate Act 1867 (c.63)
Chatham and Sheerness Stipendiary Magistrate Act 1929 (c.30)
Chatham Dockyard Act 1861 (c.41)
Chatham Fortifications Act 1780 (c.49)
Chatham: Improvement Act 1776 (c.58)
Chatham Lands Purchase Act 1857 (c.30)
Chatham Roads Act 1797 (c.155)
Chatham: Streets Act 1772 (c.18)
Cheap Trains Act 1883 (c.34)
Cheap Trains and Canal Carriers Act 1858 (c.75)
Checkweighing in Various Industries Act 1919 (c.51)
Chelmsford and Blackwater Canal Act 1793 (c.93)
Chelmsford Gaol Act 1770 (c.28)
Chelmsford: Improvement Act 1789 (c.44)
Chelmsford Roads Act 1794 (c.137)
Chelsea and Greenwich Out-Pensioners Act 1847 (c.54)
Chelsea and Greenwich Out-Pensioners, etc. Act 1848 (c.84)
Chelsea and Kilmainham Hospitals Act 1826 (c.16)
Chelsea Bridge Act 1858 (c.66)
Chelsea Hospital Act 1755 (c.1)
Chelsea Hospital Act 1812 (c.109)
Chelsea Hospital Act 1815 (c.125)
Chelsea Hospital Act 1843 (c.31)
Chelsea Hospital Act 1858 (c.18)
Chelsea Hospital Act 1876 (c.14)
Chelsea Hospital Out-Pensioners Act 1842 (c.70)
Chelsea Hospital Out-Pensioners Act 1843 (c.95)
Chelsea Hospital Purchase Act 1855 (c.21)
Chelsea and Greenwich Hospitals Act 1815 (c.133)
Chelsea Pensions (Abolition of Poundage) Act 1847 (c.4)
Cheltenham Roads Act 1785 (c.125)
Cheltenham: Streets Act 1786 (c.116)
Chequers Estate Act 1917 (c.55)
Chequers Estate Act 1958 (c.60)
Cheques Act 1957 (c.36)
Cheques Act 1992 (c.32)
Cheshire Roads Act 1730 (c.3)
Cheshire Roads Act 1753 (c.62)
Cheshire Roads Act 1774 (c.100)
Cheshire Roads Act 1781 (c.82)
Cheshire Roads Act 1786 (c.139)
Chest of Greenwich Act 1806 (c.101)
Chester and Derby Roads Act 1770 (c.97)
Chester and Derby Roads Act 1789 (c.93)
Chester and Derby Roads Act 1790 (c.88)
Chester and Lancaster Roads Act 1770 (c.89)

Chester and Stafford Roads Act 1783 (c.101)
Chester and Stafford Roads Act 1788 (c.104)
Chester and Whitchurch Roads Act 1778 (c.86)
Chester Courts Act 1867 (c.36)
Chester Highways Act 1705 (c.26)
Chester: Improvement Act 1788 (c.82)
Chester, Lancaster and Yorks. Roads Act 1765 (c.100)
Chester Lighthouse Act 1776 (c.61)
Chester–Nantwich Canal Act 1772 (c.75)
Chester (Poor Relief, etc.) Act 1762 (c.45)
Chester Roads Act 1753 (c.84)
Chester Roads Act 1765 (c.98)
Chester Roads Act 1769 (c.65)
Chester Roads Act 1777 (c.76)
Chester Roads Act 1779 (c.113)
Chester Roads Act 1787 (c.93)
Chester Roads Act 1788 (c.111)
Chester Roads Act 1789 (c.99)
Chester Roads Act 1791 (c.125)
Chester Theatre Act 1776 (c.14)
Chester to Birmingham Road Act 1759 (c.51)
Chesterfield to Stockwith (Trent) Canal Act 1771 (c.75)
Chesterfield to Worksop Road Act 1786 (c.152)
Chevening Estate Act 1959 (c.49)
Chevening Estate Act 1987 (c.20)
Chichester Paving and Improvement Act 1791 (c.63)
Chichester: Poor Relief, etc. Act 1753 (c.100)
Chief Justice's Salary Act 1851 (c.41)
Chief Superintendent in China Act 1859 (c.9)
Child Abduction Act 1984 (c.37)
Child Abduction and Custody Act 1985 (c.60)
Child Benefit Act 1975 (c.61)
Child Care Act 1980 (c.5)
Child Stealing Act 1814 (c.101)
Child Support Act 1991 (c.48)
Children Act 1908 (c.67)
Children Act 1921 (c.4)
Children Act 1948 (c.43)
Children Act 1958 (c.65)
Children Act 1972 (c.44)
Children Act 1975 (c.72)
Children Act 1989 (c.41)
Children Act (1908) Amendment Act 1910 (c.25)
Children and Young Persons Act 1931 (c.46)
Children and Young Persons Act 1932 (c.46)
Children and Young Persons Act 1933 (c.12)
Children and Young Persons Act 1938 (c.40)
Children and Young Persons Act 1956 (c.24)
Children and Young Persons Act 1963 (c.37)
Children and Young Persons Act 1969 (c.54)
Children and Young Persons Act 1952 (c.50)
Children and Young Persons (Amendment) Act 1986 (c.28)
Children and Young Persons (Harmful Publications) Act 1955 (c.28)
Children and Young Persons (Protection from Tobacco) Act 1991 (c.23)

Children and Young Persons (Scotland) Act 1931 (c.47)

Children and Young Persons (Scotland) Act 1937 (c.37)

Children (Employment Abroad) Act 1913 (c.7)

Children's Dangerous Performances Act 1879 (c.34)

Children's (Employment Abroad) Act 1930 (c.21)

Children's Homes Act 1982 (c.20)

Chimney Sweepers Act 1788 (c.48)

Chimney Sweepers Act 1875 (c.70)

Chimney Sweepers Act 1894 (c.51)

Chimney Sweepers Acts (Repeal) Act 1938 (c.58)

Chimney Sweepers and Chimneys Regulation Act 1840 (c.85)

Chimney Sweepers Regulations Act 1864 (c.37)

China (Currency Stabilisation) Act 1939 (c.14)

China Indemnity (Application) Act 1925 (c.41)

China Indemnity (Application) Act 1931 (c.7)

Chinese Passengers Act 1855 (c.104)

Chippenham Roads Act 1726 (c.13)

Chiropractors Act 1994 (c.17)

Cholera, etc. Protection (Ireland) Act 1884 (c.69)

Cholera Hospitals (Ireland) Act 1883 (c.48)

Cholera Hospitals (Ireland) Act 1884 (c.59)

Cholera Hospitals (Ireland) Act 1885 (c.39)

Cholera Hospitals (Ireland) Act 1893 (c.13)

Chorley and Rufford Chapels, Lancaster Act 1793 (c.24)

Christ Church, Oxford Act 1867 (c.76)

Christ Church, Surrey Act 1737 (c.21)

Christ College of Brecknock Act 1853 (c.82)

Christchurch, Middlesex Act 1772 (c.38)

Christchurch, Middlesex: Improvement Act 1788 (c.60)

Christchurch, Middlesex: Light and Watch Act 1737 (c.35)

Christchurch, Stepney: Poor Relief Act 1753 (c.98)

Christchurch, Stepney: Poor Relief Act 1778 (c.74)

Christchurch, Surrey: Improvement Act 1791 (c.61)

Christchurch, Surrey, Streets Act 1793 (c.90)

Christmas Islands Act 1958 (c.25)

Chronically Sick and Disabled Persons Act 1970 (c.44)

Chronically Sick and Disabled Persons (Amendment) Act 1976 (c.49)

Chronically Sick and Disabled Persons (Northern Ireland) Act 1978 (c.53)

Chronically Sick and Disabled Persons (Scotland) Act 1972 (c.51)

Church at Coventry Act 1733 (c.27)

Church at Gravesend Act 1730 (c.20)

Church at Limerick Act 1844 (c.89)

Church at Woolwich Act 1731 (c.4)

Church, Buckingham Act 1776 (c.32)

Church Building Act 1818 (c.45)

Church Building Act 1819 (c.134)

Church Building Act 1822 (c.72)

Church Building Act 1824 (c.103)

Church Building Act 1827 (c.72)

Church Building Act 1831 (c.38)

Church Building Act 1832 (c.61)

Church Building Act 1837 (c.75)

Church Building Act 1838 (c.107)

Church Building Act 1839 (c.49)

Church Building Act 1840 (c.60)

Church Building Act 1845 (c.70)

Church Building Act 1848 (c.37)

Church Building Act 1851 (c.97)

Church Building Act 1854 (c.32)

Church Building Acts Amendment Act 1871 (c.82)

Church Building (Banns and Marriages) Act 1844 (c.56)

Church Building (Burial Service in Chapels) Act 1846 (c.68)

Church Building Commission Act 1848 (c.71)

Church Building Commission Act 1854 (c.14)

Church Building Commissioners (Transfer of Powers) Act 1856 (c.55)

Church Building etc. (Ireland) Act 1808 (c.65)

Church Building (Ireland) Act 1814 (c.117)

Church Discipline Act 1840 (c.86)

Church in Sheffield Act 1739 (c.12)

Church in Strand on Maypole Site: Stepney Advowsons Act 1712 (c.17)

Church, Macclesfield Act 1779 (c.7)

Church of Abthorpe and Foxcoate, Northants Act 1736 (c.21)

Church of Allhallows, City Act 1765 (c.65)

Church of Allhallows, City Act 1766 (c.75)

Church of All Saints, Worcester Act 1737 (c.5)

Church of England 1706 (c.8)

Church of England Act 1966 (c.2)

Church of England Assembly (Powers) Act 1919 (c.76)

Church of Ireland Act 1858 (c.59)

Church of Ireland Act 1863 (c.123)

Church of Ireland Acts Repeal Act 1851 (c.71)

Church of Ireland Act 1851 (c.72)

Church of Scotland Act 1921 (c.29)

Church of Scotland, etc. Act 1748 (c.21)

Church of Scotland Courts Act 1863 (c.47)

Church of Scotland (Property and Endowments) Act 1925 (c.33)

Church of Scotland (Property and Endowments) Amendment Act 1933 (c.44)

Church of St. George, Southwark Act 1732 (c.8)

Church of St. John, Wapping Act 1756 (c.89)

Church of St. Leonard, Shoreditch Act 1734 (c.27)

Church of St. Olave, Southwark Act 1736 (c.18)

Church of Scotland, etc. Act 1743 (c.11)

Church of Scotland (Property and Endowments) Act 1925 (c.33)

Church of Scotland (Property and Endowments) Act 1957 (c.30)

Church of Scotland (Property and Endowments) Amendment Act 1933 (c.44)

Church Patronage Act 1737 (c.17)

Church Patronage Act 1846 (c.88)

Church Patronage Act 1870 (c.39)

Church Patronage (Scotland) Act 1711 (c.21)

Church Patronage (Scotland) Act 1718 (c.29)

Church Patronage (Scotland) Act 1874 (c.82)

Church Seats Act 1872 (c.49)

Church Services (Wales) Act 1863 (c.82)

Church Temporalities Act 1854 (c.11)

Church Temporalities Act 1860 (c.150)

Church Temporalities (Ireland) Act 1836 (c.99)

Church Temporalities (Ireland) Act 1840 (c.101)

Church Temporalities (Ireland) Act 1867 (c.137)

Churches in London and Westminster Act 1711 (c.20 (c))

Churches (Scotland) Act 1905 (c.12)

Cider and Perry Act 1763 (c.7)

Cinemas Act 1985 (c.13)

Cinematograph Act 1909 (c.30)

Cinematograph Act 1952 (c.68)

Cinematograph (Amendment) Act 1982 (c.33)

Cinematograph Films Act 1927 (c.29)

Cinematograph Films Act 1937 (c.17)

Cinematograph Films Act 1948 (c.23)

Cinematograph Films Act 1957 (c.21)

Cinematograph Films Act 1960 (c.14)

Cinematograph Films Act 1975 (c.73)

Cinematograph Films (Animals) Act 1937 (c.59)

Cinematograph Film Production (Special Loans) Act 1949 (c.20)

Cinematograph Film Production (Special Loans) Act 1950 (c.18)

Cinematograph Film Production (Special Loans) Act 1952 (c.20)

Cinematograph Film Production (Special Loans) Act 1954 (c.15)

Cinque Ports Act 1811 (c.36)

Cinque Ports Act 1855 (c.48)

Cinque Ports Act 1857 (c.1)

Cinque Ports Act 1869 (c.53)

Cinque Ports Pilots Act 1813 (c.140)

Circulation of Notes, etc., Issued in France Act 1793 (c.1)

Circuit Clerks (Scotland) Act 1898 (c.40)

Circuit Courts and Criminal Procedure (Scotland) Act 1925 (c.81)

Circuit Courts (Scotland) Act 1828 (c.29)

Circuit Courts (Scotland) Act 1709 (c.16)

Circuits Courts Act 1711 (c.40)

Cirencester Roads Act 1726 (c.11)

Cirencester to Birdlip Hill Road Act 1795 (c.141)

Cirencester to Cricklade Road Act 1779 (c.116)

Citation Amendment (Scotland) Act 1871 (c.42)

Citation Amendment (Scotland) Act 1882 (c.77)

Citations (Scotland) Act 1846 (c.67)

City of London Burial Act 1857 (c.35)

City of London Elections Act 1724 (c.18)

City of London (Garbling of Spices and Admission of Brokers) Act 1707 (c.68)

City of London: Improvement Act 1759 (c.38)

City of London: Improvement Act 1765 (c.91)

City of London: Improvement Act 1785 (c.97)

City of London Militia Act 1662 (c.3)

City of London Militia Act 1813 (c.17)

City of London Militia Act 1813 (c.38)

City of London Parochial Charities Act 1883 (c.36)

City of London Sewerage Act 1771 (c.29)

City Streets Act 1783 (c.46)

Civic Amenities Act 1967 (c.69)

Civic Government (Scotland) Act 1982 (c.45)

Civic Restaurants Act 1947 (c.22)

Civil Aviation Act 1946 (c.70)

Civil Aviation Act 1949 (c.67)

Civil Aviation Act 1968 (c.61)

Civil Aviation Act 1971 (c.75)

Civil Aviation Act 1978 (c.8)

Civil Aviation Act 1980 (c.60)

Civil Aviation Act 1982 (c.16)

Civil Aviation (Air Navigation Charges) Act 1989 (c.9)

Civil Aviation (Amendment) Act 1982 (c.1)

Civil Aviation Authority (Borrowing Powers) Act 1990 (c.2)

Civil Aviation (Declaratory Provisions) Act 1971 (c.6)

Civil Aviation (Eurocontrol) Act 1962 (c.8)

Civil Aviation (Eurocontrol) Act 1983 (c.11)

Civil Aviation (Licensing) Act 1960 (c.38)

Civil Bill Court (Ireland) Act 1865 (c.1)

Civil Bill Courts (Ireland) Act 1836 (c.75)

Civil Bill Courts (Ireland) Act 1851 (c.57)

Civil Bill Courts (Ireland) Act 1874 (c.66)

Civil Bill Courts Procedure Amendment (Ireland) Act 1864 (c.99)

Civil Bill Courts Procedure Amendment (Ireland) Act 1871 (c.99)

Civil Bill Decrees (Ireland) Act 1842 (c.33)

Civil Contingencies Fund Act 1919 (c.6)

Civil Contingencies Fund Act 1952 (c.2)

Civil Defence Act 1939 (c.31)

Civil Defence Act 1948 (c.6)

Civil Defence Act 1949 (c.5)

Civil Defence (Armed Forces) Act 1954 (c.66)

Civil Defence (Electricity Undertakings) Act 1954 (c.19)

Civil Defence (Suspension of Powers) Act 1945 (c.12)

Civil Evidence Act 1968 (c.64)

Civil Evidence Act 1972 (c.30)

Civil Evidence (Scotland) Act 1988 (c.32)

Civil Imprisonment (Scotland) Act 1882 (c.42)

Civil Jurisdiction and Judgments Act 1982 (c.27)

Coal Loading: Newcastle and Sunderland Act 1772 (c.22)

Coal Measurement, London Act 1776 (c.13)

Coal Metage, etc., London Act 1766 (c.23)

Coal Mines Act 1855 (c.107)

Coal Mines Act 1862 (c.79)

Coal Mines Act 1886 (c.40)

Coal Mines Act 1911 (c.50)

Coal Mines Act 1914 (c.22)

Coal Mines Act 1919 (c.48)

Coal Mines Act 1926 (c.17)

Coal Mines Act 1930 (c.34)

Coal Mines Act 1931 (c.27)

Coal Mines Act 1932 (c.29)

Coal Mines (Check Weigher) Act 1894 (c.52)

Coal Mines Control Agreement (Confirmation) Act 1918 (c.56)

Coal Mines (Decontrol) Act 1921 (c.6)

Coal Mines (Employment of Boys) Act 1937 (c.62)

Coal Mines Inspection Act 1850 (c.100)

Coal Mines (Minimum Wage) Act 1912 (c.2)

Coal Mines Regulation Act 1872 (c.76)

Coal Mines Regulation Act 1887 (c.58)

Coal Mines Regulation Act (1887) Amendment 1903 (c.7)

Coal Mines Regulation Act 1896 (c.43)

Coal Mines Regulation Act 1908 (c.57)

Coal Mines Regulation (Amendment) Act 1917 (c.8)

Coal Mines (Weighing of Minerals) Act 1905 (c.9)

Coal Mining (Subsidence) Act 1950 (c.23)

Coal Mining (Subsidence) Act 1957 (c.59)

Coal Mining Subsidence Act 1991 (c.45)

Coal (Registration of Ownership) Act 1937 (c.56)

Coal Trade Act 1710 (c.30)

Coal Trade Act 1730 (c.26)

Coal Trade Act 1730 (c.30)

Coal Trade Act 1788 (c.53)

Coal Trade Act 1836 (c.109)

Coal Trade, London Act 1745 (c.35)

Coal Trade, London Act 1758 (c.27)

Coal Trade, London Act 1786 (c.83)

Coal Trade, London Act 1796 (c.61)

Coal Trade: Westminster Act 1766 (c.35)

Coal Trade, Westminster Act 1786 (c.108)

Coal Vendors Act 1843 (c.2)

Coalport Bridge over Severn (Tolls, etc.) Act 1776 (c.12)

Coals Act 1743 (c.35)

Coals, Newcastle Act 1782 (c.32)

Coalwhippers, London Act 1851 (c.78)

Coalwhippers, Port of London Act 1846 (c.36)

Coast Protection Act 1939 (c.39)

Coast Protection Act 1949 (c.74)

Coast Trade Act 1792 (c.50)

Coastal Flooding (Emergency Provisions) Act 1953 (c.18)

Coastguard Act 1925 (c.88)

Coastguard Service Act 1856 (c.83)

Coasting Trade Act 1805 (c.81)

Coasting Trade Act 1854 (c.5)

Coatbridge and Springburn Elections (Validation) Act 1945 (c.3)

Cobham, Leatherhead and Godalming Bridges Act 1782 (c.17)

Cockburnspath Bridge, Berwick Act 1789 (c.42)

Cockermouth and Workington Road Act 1779 (c.105)

Cockerton Bridge to Staindrop Road Act 1793 (c.146)

Cockfighting Act 1952 (c.59)

Cocos Islands Act 1955 (c.5)

Codbreck Brook, Navigation Act 1767 (c.95)

Coffee and Cocoa-Nuts Act 1783 (c.79)

Coffee, etc. Act 1812 (c.149)

Coffee, etc. Act 1814 (c.47)

Coin Act 1732 (c.26)

Coin Act 1774 (c.70)

Coin Act 1816 (c.68)

Coin Act 1849 (c.41)

Coinage Act 1708 (c.24)

Coinage Act 1859 (c.30)

Coinage Act 1870 (c.10)

Coinage Act 1889 (c.58)

Coinage Act 1891 (c.72)

Coinage Act 1893 (c.1)

Coinage Act 1946 (c.74)

Coinage Act 1971 (c.24)

Coinage (Colonial Offences) Act 1853 (c.48)

Coinage Duties Act 1730 (c.12)

Coinage Duties Act 1738 (c.5)

Coinage Duties Act 1745 (c.14)

Coinage Duties Act 1760 (c.16)

Coinage Duties Act 1769 (c.25)

Coinage Duties, etc. Act 1754 (c.11)

Coinage in American Plantations Act 1707 (c.57)

Coinage Offences Act 1861 (c.99)

Coinage Offences Act 1936 (c.16)

Colewort Barracks, Portsmouth Act 1860 (c.49)

Collecting Societies and Industrial Assurance Companies Act 1896 (c.26)

Collection of Charity Money Act 1705 (c.25)

Collection of Malt Duties, etc. Act 1805 (c.53)

Collection of Revenue, etc. (Ireland) Act 1803 (c.98)

Collection of Revenue (Ireland) Act 1803 (c.43)

Collection of Revenue (Ireland) Act 1803 (c.97)

Collection of Revenue (Ireland) Act 1804 (c.105)

Collection of Revenues (Ireland) Act 1802 (c.36)

College Charter Act 1871 (c.63)

College of Physicians (Ireland) Act 1862 (c.15)

Collegiate Church of Manchester Act 1728 (c.29)

Collieries and Mines Act 1800 (c.77)

Collieries (Ireland) Act 1807 (c.45)

Colliers Act 1775 (c.28)
Colliers (Scotland) Act 1799 (c.56)
Collingham to York Road Act 1792 (c.142)
Colneis and Carlford Hundreds, Suffolk: Poor Relief Act 1790 (c.22)
Colne Oyster Fishery Act 1757 (c.71)
Colne River, Essex: Navigation Act 1718 (c.31)
Colonial Acts Confirmation Act 1863 (c.84)
Colonial Acts Confirmation Act 1894 (c.72)
Colonial Acts Confirmation Act 1901 (c.29)
Colonial Affidavits Act 1859 (c.12)
Colonial and Other Territories (Divorce Jurisdiction) Act 1950 (c.20)
Colonial Attorneys Relief Act 1857 (c.39)
Colonial Attorneys Relief Act 1874 (c.41)
Colonial Attorneys Relief Amendment Act 1884 (c.24)
Colonial Bishops Act 1852 (c.52)
Colonial Bishops Act 1853 (c.49)
Colonial Boundaries Act 1895 (c.34)
Colonial Branch Mint Act 1866 (c.65)
Colonial Clergy Act 1874 (c.77)
Colonial Copyright Act 1847 (c.95)
Colonial Courts of Admiralty Act 1890 (c.27)
Colonial Development Act 1929 (c.5)
Colonial Development and Welfare Act 1939 (c.40)
Colonial Development and Welfare Act 1944 (c.20)
Colonial Development and Welfare Act 1949 (c.49)
Colonial Development and Welfare Act 1950 (c.4)
Colonial Development and Welfare Act 1955 (c.6)
Colonial Development and Welfare Act 1959 (c.71)
Colonial Docks Loans Act 1865 (c.106)
Colonial Duties Act 1842 (c.49)
Colonial Fortifications Act 1877 (c.23)
Colonial Governors (Pensions) Act 1865 (c.113)
Colonial Governors (Pensions) Act 1872 (c.29)
Colonial Inland Post Office Act 1849 (c.66)
Colonial Laws Validity Act 1865 (c.63)
Colonial Leave of Absence Act 1782 (c.75)
Colonial Letters Patent Act 1863 (c.76)
Colonial Loans Act 1899 (c.36)
Colonial Loans Act 1949 (c.50)
Colonial Loans Act 1952 (c.1)
Colonial Loans Act 1962 (c.41)
Colonial Marriages Act 1865 (c.64)
Colonial Marriages (Deceased Wife's Sister) Act 1906 (c.30)
Colonial Naval Defence Act 1865 (c.14)
Colonial Naval Defence Act 1909 (c.19)
Colonial Naval Defence Act 1931 (c.9)
Colonial Naval Defence Act 1949 (c.18)
Colonial Officers (Leave of Absence) Act 1894 (c.17)
Colonial Offices Act 1830 (c.4)

Colonial Prisoners Removal Act 1869 (c.10)
Colonial Prisoners Removal Act 1884 (c.31)
Colonial Probates Act 1892 (c.6)
Colonial Probates (Protected States and Mandated Territories) Act 1927 (c.43)
Colonial Shipping Act 1868 (c.129)
Colonial Solicitors Act 1900 (c.14)
Colonial Stock Act 1877 (c.59)
Colonial Stock Act 1892 (c.35)
Colonial Stock Act 1900 (c.62)
Colonial Stock Act 1934 (c.47)
Colonial Stock Act 1948 (c.1)
Colonial Trade Act 1730 (c.28)
Colonial Trade Act 1734 (c.19)
Colonial Trade Act 1738 (c.30)
Colonial Trade Act 1760 (c.9)
Colonial Trade Act 1763 (c.27)
Colonial Trade Act 1768 (c.22)
Colonial Trade Act 1769 (c.27)
Colonial Trade Act 1812 (c.98)
Colonial War Risks Insurance (Guarantees) Act 1941 (c.35)
(Colonies) Evidence Act 1843 (c.22)
Colony of New York Act 1770 (c.35)
Colouring of Porter Act 1811 (c.87)
Combination of Workmen Act 1796 (c.111)
Combinations of Workmen Act 1825 (c.38)
Combination of Workmen Act 1859 (c.34)
Commerce with Certain Countries Act 1721 (c.8)
Commerce with Spain Act 1739 (c.27)
Commerce with Sweden Act 1716 (c.1)
Commerce with United States Act 1816 (c.15)
Commerce with United States Act 1816 (c.51)
Commercial Treaty with Portugal Act 1811 (c.47)
Commissariat Accounts Act 1821 (c.121)
Commissary Court of Edinburgh Act 1815 (c.97)
Commissary Court of Edinburgh, etc. Act 1836 (c.41)
Commissioners Clauses Act 1847 (c.16)
Commissioners for Oaths Act 1853 (c.78)
Commissioners for Oaths Act 1855 (c.42)
Commissioners for Oaths Act 1889 (c.10)
Commissioners for Oaths Act 1891 (c.50)
Commissioners for Oaths Amendment Act 1890 (c.7)
Commissioners for Oaths, Bail in Error, etc. Act 1859
Commissioners for Oaths, Bail in Error, etc. Act 1859 (c.16)
Commissioners for Oaths (Ireland) Act 1872 (c.75)
Commissioners for Oaths (Prize Proceedings) Act 1907 (c.25)
Commissioners of Customs Act 1845 (c.85)
Commissioners of Sewers (City of London) Act 1708 (c.32)
Commissioners of Supply Meetings (Scotland) Act 1865 (c.38)

Commissioners of Supply (Scotland) Act 1856 (c.93)
Commissioners of Supply (Scotland) Act 1857 (c.11)
Commissioners of the Treasury Act 1807 (c.20)
Commissioners of Woods (Audit) Act 1844 (c.89)
Commissioners of Woods (Thames Piers) Act 1879 (c.73)
Commissioners of Works Act 1852 (c.28)
Commissioners of Works Act 1894 (c.23)
Commissions of Sewers Act 1708 (c.33)
Commissions of the Peace Continuance Act 1837 (c.1)
Commissions to Foreign Protestants Act 1756 (c.5)
Commissions and Salaries of Judges Act 1760 (c.23)
Commission of Assize in County Palatine of Lancaster Act 1855 (c.45)
Common Informers Act 1951 (c.39)
Common Land (Rectification of Registers) Act 1989 (c.18)
Common Law Chambers Act 1867 (c.68)
Common Law Courts Act 1852 (c.73)
Common Law Courts (Fees) Act 1865 (c.45)
Common Law Courts (Fees and Salaries) Act 1866 (c.101)
Common Law Courts (Ireland) Act 1851 (c.17)
Common Law Offices (Ireland) Act 1844 (c.107)
Common Law Procedure Act 1838 (c.45)
Common Law Procedure Act 1852 (c.76)
Common Law Procedure Act 1854 (c.125)
Common Law Procedure Act 1860 (c.126)
Common Law Procedure Act 1864 (c.28)
Common Law Procedure Amendment (Ireland) Act 1853 (c.113)
Common Law Procedure Amendment (Ireland) Act 1856 (c.102)
Common Law Procedure Amendment (Ireland) Act 1870 (c.109)
Common Law Procedure (Ireland) Act 1855 (c.7)
Common Law Procedure (Ireland) Act 1860 (c.82)
Common Lodging House Act 1853 (c.41)
Common Lodging Houses Act 1851 (c.28)
Common Lodging Houses (Ireland) Act 1860 (c.26)
Common Pleas of Lancaster Act 1794 (c.46)
Common Pleas of Lancaster Act 1800 (c.105)
Common Pleas at Lancaster Amendment Act 1869 (c.37)
Common Recoveries, etc. Act 1740 (c.20)
Commonable Rights Compensation Act 1882 (c.15)
Commons Act 1876 (c.56)
Commons Act 1879 (c.37)
Commons Act 1899 (c.30)
Commons Act 1908 (c.44)

Commons (Expenses) Act 1878 (c.56)
Commons Registration Act 1965 (c.64)
Commonwealth Development Act 1963 (c.40)
Commonwealth Development Corporation Act 1978 (c.2)
Commonwealth Development Corporation Act 1982 (c.54)
Commonwealth Development Corporation Act 1986 (c.25)
Commonwealth Immigrants Act 1962 (c.21)
Commonwealth Immigration Act 1968 (c.9)
Commonwealth (India (Consequential) Provisions) Act 1949 (c.92)
Commonwealth Institute Act 1958 (c.16)
Commonwealth of Australia Constitution Act 1900 (c.12)
Commonwealth Scholarships Act 1959 (c.6)
Commonwealth Scholarships (Amendment) Act 1963 (c.6)
Commonwealth Secretariat Act 1966 (c.10)
Commonwealth Settlement Act 1957 (c.8)
Commonwealth Settlement Act 1962 (c.17)
Commonwealth Settlement Act 1967 (c.31)
Commonwealth Teachers Act 1960 (c.40)
Commonwealth Telecommunications Act 1968 (c.24)
Commonwealth Telegraphs Act 1949 (c.39)
Communications from Marylebone to Charing Cross Act 1813 (c.121)
Community Care (Residential Accommodation) Act 1992 (c.49)
Community Charges (General Reduction) Act 1991 (c.9)
Community Charges (Substitute Setting) Act 1991 (c.8)
Community Health Councils (Access to Information) Act 1988 (c.24)
Community Land Act 1975 (c.77)
Community Service by Offenders (Scotland) Act 1978 (c.49)
Companies Act 1862 (c.89)
Companies Act 1867 (c.131)
Companies Act 1877 (c.26)
Companies Act 1879 (c.76)
Companies Act 1880 (c.19)
Companies Act 1883 (c.28)
Companies Act 1886 (c.23)
Companies Act 1898 (c.26)
Companies Act 1900 (c.48)
Companies Act 1907 (c.50)
Companies Act 1908 (c.12)
Companies Act 1913 (c.25)
Companies Act 1928 (c.45)
Companies Act 1929 (c.23)
Companies Act 1947 (c.47)
Companies Act 1948 (c.38)
Companies Act 1967 (c.81)
Companies Act 1976 (c.69)
Companies Act 1980 (c.22)
Companies Act 1981 (c.62)
Companies Act 1985 (c.6)
Companies Act 1989 (c.40)

Companies (Beneficial Interests) Act 1983 (c.50)

Companies Clauses Act 1863 (c.118)

Companies Clauses Act 1869 (c.48)

Companies Clauses Consolidation Act 1845 (c.16)

Companies Clauses Consolidation Act 1888 (c.48)

Companies Clauses Consolidation Act 1889 (c.37)

Companies Clauses Consolidation (Scotland) Act 1845 (c.17)

Companies (Colonial Registers) Act 1883 (c.30)

Companies (Consolidation) Act 1908 (c.69)

Companies Consolidation (Consequential Provisions) Act 1985 (c.9)

Companies (Converted Societies) Act 1910 (c.23)

Companies (Defence) Act 1939 (c.75)

Companies (Floating Charges and Receivers) (Scotland) Act 1972 (c.67)

Companies (Floating Charges) (Scotland) Act 1961 (c.46)

Companies (Foreign Interests) Act 1917 (c.18)

Companies (Memorandum of Association) Act 1890 (c.62)

Companies (Particulars as to Directors) Act 1917 (c.28)

Companies (Winding-up) Act 1890 (c.63)

Companies (Winding-up) Act 1893 (c.58)

Company Directors (Disqualification) Act 1986 (c.46)

Company Seals Act 1864 (c.19)

Company Securities (Insider Dealing) Act 1985 (c.8)

Compassionate List of the Navy, etc. Act 1809 (c.45)

Compensation (Defence) Act 1939 (c.75)

Compensation for Injuries to Mills etc. Act 1801 (c.24)

Compensation for Works at Portsmouth Act 1815 (c.123)

Compensation of Displaced Officers (War Service) Act 1945 (c.10)

Compensation to American Loyalists, etc. Act 1788 (c.40)

Compensation to Patentee Officers (Ireland) Act 1808 (c.108)

Competency of Witnesses Act 1787 (c.29)

Competition Act 1980 (c.21)

Competition and Service (Utilities) Act 1992 (c.43)

Completing St. Paul's, etc. Act 1702 (c.12)

Completion of Somerset House Act 1780 (c.40)

Composition for a Certain Crown Debt Act 1770 (c.12)

Composition for a Crown Debt Act 1774 (c.35)

Composition for a Crown Debt Act 1775 (c.19)

Composition for a Crown Debt Act 1776 (c.31)

Composition for a Crown Debt Act 1776 (c.49)

Composition for a Crown Debt Act 1779 (c.77)

Composition for a Crown Debt Act 1784 (c.14)

Composition for a Crown Debt Act 1801 (c.60)

Compound Householders Act 1851 (c.14)

Comptroller of the Exchequer, etc. Act 1865 (c.93)

Compulsory Church Date Abolition 1868 (c.109)

Compulsory Purchase Act 1965 (c.56)

Compulsory Purchase (Vesting Declarations) Act 1981 (c.66)

Computer Misuse Act 1990 (c.18)

Concealment of Birth (Scotland) Act 1809 (c.14)

Concessionary Travel for Handicapped Persons (Scotland) Act 1980 (c.29)

Conciliation Act 1896 (c.30)

Concorde Aircraft Act 1973 (c.7)

Confirmation and Probate Amendment Act 1859 (c.30)

Confirmation of Certain Marriages Act 1781 (c.53)

Confirmation of Certain Marriages Act 1858 (c.46)

Confirmation of Certain Marriages Act 1889 (c.38)

Confirmation of Certain Proceedings Act 1842 (c.43)

Confirmation of Executors (Scotland) Act 1823 (c.98)

Confirmation of Executors (Scotland) Act 1858 (c.56)

Confirmation of Executors (War Service) (Scotland) Act 1917 (c.27)

Confirmation of Executors (War Service) (Scotland) Act 1939 (c.41)

Confirmation of Executors (War Service) (Scotland) Act 1940 (c.41)

Confirmation of Marriages Act 1853 (c.122)

Confirmation of Marriages Act 1854 (c.88)

Confirmation of Marriages Act 1855 (c.66)

Confirmation of Marriages Act 1856 (c.70)

Confirmation of Marriages Act 1857 (c.29)

Confirmation of Marriages Act 1859 (c.24)

Confirmation of Marriages Act 1859 (c.64)

Confirmation of Marriages Act 1860 (c.1)

Confirmation of Marriages Act 1861 (c.16)

Confirmation of Marriages, Blakedown Chapel Act 1868 (c.113)

Confirmation of Marriages (Cove Chapel) Act 1873 (c.1)

Confirmation of Marriages on Her Majesty's Ships Act 1879 (c.29)

Confirmation of Provision Order (Land Drainage) Act 1867 (c.22)

Confirmation of Provisional Orders, Turnpike Trusts Act 1867 (c.66)

Confirmation of Sales etc., by Trustees Act 1862 (c.108)
Confirmation to Small Estates (Scotland) Act 1979 (c.22)
Congenital Disabilities (Civil Liability) Act 1976 (c.28)
Congested Districts Board (Ireland) Act 1893 (c.35)
Congested Districts Board (Ireland) Act 1894 (c.50)
Congested Districts Board (Ireland) Act 1899 (c.18)
Congested Districts Board (Ireland) Act 1901 (c.34)
Congested Districts (Scotland) Act 1897 (c.53)
Conjugal Rights (Scotland) Amendment Act 1861 (c.86)
Conjugal Rights (Scotland) Amendment Act 1874 (c.31)
Consecration of Bishops Abroad Act 1786 (c.84)
Consecration of Churchyards Act 1867 (c.133)
Consecration of Churchyards Act 1868 (c.47)
Conservation of Seals Act 1970 (c.30)
Conservation of Wild Creatures and Wild Plants Act 1975 (c.48)
Consolidated Annuities (Ireland) Act 1853 (c.75)
Consolidated Fund Act 1806 (c.44)
Consolidated Fund Act 1816 (c.98)
Consolidated Fund Act 1947 (c.17)
Consolidated Fund Act 1950 (c.1)
Consolidated Fund Act 1951 (c.12)
Consolidated Fund Act 1952 (c.16)
Consolidated Fund Act 1953 (c.6)
Consolidated Fund Act 1954 (c.22)
Consolidated Fund Act 1955 (c.3)
Consolidated Fund Act 1956 (c.32)
Consolidated Fund Act 1957 (c.7)
Consolidated Fund Act 1958 (c.7)
Consolidated Fund Act 1960 (c.10)
Consolidated Fund Act 1963 (c.1)
Consolidated Fund Act 1965 (c.1)
Consolidated Fund Act 1966 (c.1)
Consolidated Fund Act 1968 (c.1)
Consolidated Fund Act 1969 (c.3)
Consolidated Fund Act 1970 (c.1)
Consolidated Fund Act 1971 (c.1)
Consolidated Fund Act 1972 (c.13)
Consolidated Fund Act 1973 (c.1)
Consolidated Fund Act 1974 (c.1)
Consolidated Fund Act 1975 (c.1)
Consolidated Fund Act 1976 (c.2)
Consolidated Fund Act 1977 (c.1)
Consolidated Fund Act 1978 (c.7)
Consolidated Fund Act 1979 (c.20)
Consolidated Fund Act 1980 (c.14)
Consolidated Fund Act 1981 (c.4)
Consolidated Fund Act 1982 (c.8)
Consolidated Fund Act 1983 (c.1)
Consolidated Fund Act 1984 (c.1)

Consolidated Fund Act 1985 (c.1)
Consolidated Fund Act 1986 (c.4)
Consolidated Fund Act 1987 (c.8)
Consolidated Fund Act 1988 (c.6)
Consolidated Fund Act 1989 (c.2)
Consolidated Fund Act 1990 (c.4)
Consolidated Fund Act 1991 (c.7)
Consolidated Fund Act 1992 (c.1)
Consolidated Fund Act 1993 (c.4)
Consolidated Fund Act 1994 (c.4)
Consolidated Fund (Civil List Provisions) Act 1951 (c.50)
Consolidated Fund (No. 1) Act 1879 (c.2)
Consolidated Fund (No. 1) Act 1880 (c.5)
Consolidated Fund (No. 1) Act 1881 (c.1)
Consolidated Fund (No. 1) Act 1882 (c.1)
Consolidated Fund (No. 1) Act 1883 (c.2)
Consolidated Fund (No. 1) Act 1884 (c.2)
Consolidated Fund (No. 1) Act 1884 (c.4)
Consolidated Fund (No. 1) Act 1886 (c.4)
Consolidated Fund (No. 1) Act 1887 (c.1)
Consolidated Fund (No. 1) Act 1888 (c.1)
Consolidated Fund (No. 1) Act 1889 (c.1)
Consolidated Fund (No. 1) Act 1890 (c.1)
Consolidated Fund (No. 1) Act 1891 (c.6)
Consolidated Fund (No. 1) Act 1892 (c.3)
Consolidated Fund (No. 1) Act 1893 (c.3)
Consolidated Fund (No. 1) Act 1894 (c.1)
Consolidated Fund (No. 1) Act 1895 (c.4)
Consolidated Fund (No. 1) Act 1896 (c.3)
Consolidated Fund (No. 1) Act 1897 (c.4)
Consolidated Fund (No. 1) Act 1898 (c.3)
Consolidated Fund (No. 1) Act 1899 (c.2)
Consolidated Fund (No. 1) Act 1900 (c.1)
Consolidated Fund (No. 1) Act 1901 (c.1)
Consolidated Fund (No. 1) Act 1902 (c.1)
Consolidated Fund (No. 1) Act 1903 (c.3)
Consolidated Fund (No. 1) Act 1904 (c.1)
Consolidated Fund (No. 1) Act 1905 (c.1)
Consolidated Fund (No. 1) Act 1906 (c.1)
Consolidated Fund (No. 1) Act 1907 (c.1)
Consolidated Fund (No. 1) Act 1908 (c.1)
Consolidated Fund (No. 1) Act 1909 (c.1)
Consolidated Fund (No. 1) Act 1910 (c.4)
Consolidated Fund (No. 1) Act 1911 (c.1)
Consolidated Fund (No. 1) Act 1912 (c.1)
Consolidated Fund (No. 1) Act 1913 (c.1)
Consolidated Fund (No. 1) Act 1914 (c.1)
Consolidated Fund (No. 1) Act 1916 (c.1)
Consolidated Fund (No. 1) Act 1917 (c.1)
Consolidated Fund (No. 1) Act 1918 (c.1)
Consolidated Fund (No. 1) Act 1919 (c.5)
Consolidated Fund (No. 1) Act 1921 (c.2)
Consolidated Fund (No. 1) Act 1922 (c.1)
Consolidated Fund (No. 1) Act 1923 (c.1)
Consolidated Fund (No. 1) Act 1924 (c.2)
Consolidated Fund (No. 1) Act 1925 (c.8)
Consolidated Fund (No. 1) Act 1926 (c.1)
Consolidated Fund (No. 1) Act 1927 (c.2)
Consolidated Fund (No. 1) Act 1928 (c.1)
Consolidated Fund (No. 1) Act 1928 (c.2)
Consolidated Fund (No. 1) Act 1929 (c.10)
Consolidated Fund (No. 1) Act 1932 (c.1)

Consolidated Fund (No. 1) Act 1932 (c.14)
Consolidated Fund (No. 1) Act 1934 (c.3)
Consolidated Fund (No. 1) Act 1935 (c.4)
Consolidated Fund (No. 1) Act 1936 (c.8)
Consolidated Fund (No. 1) Act 1937 (c.7)
Consolidated Fund (No. 1) Act 1938 (c.9)
Consolidated Fund (No. 1) Act 1939 (c.12)
Consolidated Fund (No. 1) Act 1940 (c.11)
Consolidated Fund (No. 1) Act 1941 (c.6)
Consolidated Fund (No. 1) Act 1943 (c.4)
Consolidated Fund (No. 1) Act 1944 (c.1)
Consolidated Fund (No. 1) Act 1944 (c.4)
Consolidated Fund (No. 1) Act 1945 (c.4)
Consolidated Fund (No. 1) Act 1946 (c.33)
Consolidated Fund (No. 1) Act 1948 (c.18)
Consolidated Fund (No. 1) Act 1949 (c.24)
Consolidated Fund (No. 1) (Session 2) Act
  1880 (c.3)
Consolidated Fund (No. 1) (Session 2) Act
  1914 (c.6)
Consolidated Fund (No. 1) (Session 2) Act
  1931 (c.1)
Consolidated Fund (No. 1) (Session 2) Act
  1941 (c.2)
Consolidated Fund (No. 2) Act 1879 (c.7)
Consolidated Fund (No. 2) Act 1881 (c.8)
Consolidated Fund (No. 2) Act 1882 (c.4)
Consolidated Fund (No. 2) Act 1883 (c.5)
Consolidated Fund (No. 2) Act 1884 (c.15)
Consolidated Fund (No. 2) Act 1885 (c.6)
Consolidated Fund (No. 2) Act 1886 (c.7)
Consolidated Fund (No. 2) Act 1887 (c.14)
Consolidated Fund (No. 2) Act 1888 (c.16)
Consolidated Fund (No. 2) Act 1889 (c.2)
Consolidated Fund (No. 2) Act 1890 (c.28)
Consolidated Fund (No. 2) Act 1891 (c.27)
Consolidated Fund (No. 2) Act 1892 (c.20)
Consolidated Fund (No. 2) Act 1893 (c.16)
Consolidated Fund (No. 2) Act 1894 (c.7)
Consolidated Fund (No. 2) Act 1895 (c.15)
Consolidated Fund (No. 2) Act 1896 (c.7)
Consolidated Fund (No. 2) Act 1898 (c.32)
Consolidated Fund (No. 2) Act 1900 (c.3)
Consolidated Fund (No. 2) Act 1901 (c.6)
Consolidated Fund (No. 2) Act 1905 (c.6)
Consolidated Fund (No. 2) Act 1909 (c.2)
Consolidated Fund (No. 2) Act 1910 (c.9(a))
Consolidated Fund (No. 2) Act 1911 (c.5)
Consolidated Fund (No. 2) Act 1913 (c.5)
Consolidated Fund (No. 2) Act 1915 (c.33)
Consolidated Fund (No. 2) Act 1916 (c.3)
Consolidated Fund (No. 2) Act 1917 (c.7)
Consolidated Fund (No. 2) Act 1918 (c.11)
Consolidated Fund (No. 2) Act 1919 (c.49)
Consolidated Fund (No. 2) Act 1921 (c.3)
Consolidated Fund (No. 2) Act 1922 (c.3)
Consolidated Fund (No. 2) Act 1924 (c.4)
Consolidated Fund (No. 2) Act 1929 (c.10)
Consolidated Fund (No. 2) Act 1930 (c.14)
Consolidated Fund (No. 2) Act 1931 (c.10)
Consolidated Fund (No. 2) Act 1933 (c.3)
Consolidated Fund (No. 2) Act 1935 (c.10)
Consolidated Fund (No. 2) Act 1936 (c.11)

Consolidated Fund (No. 2) Act 1937 (c.20)
Consolidated Fund (No. 2) Act 1939 (c.39)
Consolidated Fund (No. 2) Act 1941 (c.9)
Consolidated Fund (No. 2) Act 1942 (c.12)
Consolidated Fund (No. 2) Act 1943 (c.11)
Consolidated Fund (No. 2) Act 1944 (c.17)
Consolidated Fund (No. 2) Act 1945 (c.4)
Consolidated Fund (No. 2) Act 1957 (c.10)
Consolidated Fund (No. 2) Act 1958 (c.18)
Consolidated Fund (No. 2) Act 1961 (c.12)
Consolidated Fund (No. 2) Act 1962 (c.11)
Consolidated Fund (No. 2) Act 1963 (c.8)
Consolidated Fund (No. 2) Act 1964 (c.17)
Consolidated Fund (No. 2) Act 1965 (c.8)
Consolidated Fund (No. 2) Act 1967 (c.6)
Consolidated Fund (No. 2) Act 1968 (c.15)
Consolidated Fund (No. 2) Act 1969 (c.9)
Consolidated Fund (No. 2) Act 1970 (c.12)
Consolidated Fund (No. 2) Act 1971 (c.14)
Consolidated Fund (No. 2) Act 1972 (c.23)
Consolidated Fund (No. 2) Act 1973 (c.10)
Consolidated Fund (No. 2) Act 1974 (c.12)
Consolidated Fund (No. 2) Act 1975 (c.12)
Consolidated Fund (No. 2) Act 1976 (c.84)
Consolidated Fund (No. 2) Act 1977 (c.52)
Consolidated Fund (No. 2) Act 1978 (c.59)
Consolidated Fund (No. 2) Act 1979 (c.56)
Consolidated Fund (No. 2) Act 1980 (c.68)
Consolidated Fund (No. 2) Act 1981 (c.70)
Consolidated Fund (No. 2) Act 1983 (c.5)
Consolidated Fund (No. 2) Act 1984 (c.61)
Consolidated Fund (No. 2) Act 1985 (c.11)
Consolidated Fund (No. 2) Act 1986 (c.67)
Consolidated Fund (No. 2) Act 1987 (c.54)
Consolidated Fund (No. 2) Act 1988 (c.55)
Consolidated Fund (No. 2) Act 1989 (c.46)
Consolidated Fund (No. 2) Act 1990 (c.46)
Consolidated Fund (No. 2) Act 1991 (c.10)
Consolidated Fund (No. 2) Act 1992 (c.21)
Consolidated Fund (No. 2) Act 1993 (c.7)
Consolidated Fund (No. 2) Act 1994 (c.41)
Consolidated Fund (No. 2) (Session 2) Act
  1880 (c.30)
Consolidated Fund (No. 3) Act 1879 (c.14)
Consolidated Fund (No. 3) Act 1881 (c.15)
Consolidated Fund (No. 3) Act 1882 (c.8)
Consolidated Fund (No. 3) Act 1883 (c.13)
Consolidated Fund (No. 3) Act 1885 (c.14)
Consolidated Fund (No. 3) Act 1888 (c.26)
Consolidated Fund (No. 3) Act 1889 (c.15)
Consolidated Fund (No. 3) Act 1893 (c.28)
Consolidated Fund (No. 3) Act 1894 (c.29)
Consolidated Fund (No. 3) Act 1915 (c.53)
Consolidated Fund (No. 3) Act 1916 (c.16)
Consolidated Fund (No. 3) Act 1917 (c.17)
Consolidated Fund (No. 3) Act 1918 (c.37)
Consolidated Fund (No. 3) Act 1930 (c.18)
Consolidated Fund (No. 3) Act 1939 (c.52)
Consolidated Fund (No. 3) Act 1941 (c.26)
Consolidated Fund (No. 3) Act 1942 (c.22)
Consolidated Fund (No. 3) Act 1943 (c.20)
Consolidated Fund (No. 3) Act 1944 (c.20)
Consolidated Fund (No. 3) Act 1945 (c.13)

Consolidated Fund (No. 3) Act 1951 (c.1)
Consolidated Fund (No. 3) Act 1953 (c.2)
Consolidated Fund (No. 3) Act 1971 (c.79)
Consolidated Fund (No. 3) Act 1972 (c.78)
Consolidated Fund (No. 3) Act 1974 (c.15)
Consolidated Fund (No. 3) Act 1975 (c.79)
Consolidated Fund (No. 3) Act 1983 (c.57)
Consolidated Fund (No. 3) Act 1985 (c.74)
Consolidated Fund (No. 3) Act 1987 (c.55)
Consolidated Fund (No. 3) Act 1991 (c.68)
Consolidated Fund (No. 3) Act 1992 (c.59)
Consolidated Fund (No. 3) Act 1993 (c.52)
Consolidated Fund (No. 4) Act 1879 (c.20)
Consolidated Fund (No. 4) Act 1881 (c.50)
Consolidated Fund (No. 4) Act 1882 (c.28)
Consolidated Fund (No. 4) Act 1883 (c.23)
Consolidated Fund (No. 4) Act 1893 (c.46)
Consolidated Fund (No. 4) Act 1915 (c.80)
Consolidated Fund (No. 4) Act 1916 (c.30)
Consolidated Fund (No. 4) Act 1917 (c.33)
Consolidated Fund (No. 4) Act 1974 (c.57)
Consolidated Fund (No. 5) Act 1916 (c.48)
Consolidated Fund (No. 5) Act 1917 (c.49)
Consolidated Fund (Permanent Charges Redemption) Act 1873 (c.57)
Consolidated Fund (Permanent Charges Redemption) Act 1883 (c.1)
Consolidation of Enactments (Procedure) Act 1949 (c.33)
Conspiracy and Protection of Property Act 1875 (c.86)
Constables Expenses Act 1801 (c.78)
Constables Near Public Works (Scotland) Act 1845 (c.3)
Constables Protection Act 1750 (c.44)
Constables (Scotland) Act 1875 (c.47)
Constabulary and Police (Ireland) Act 1883 (c.14)
Constabulary and Police (Ireland) Act 1914 (c.54)
Constabulary and Police (Ireland) Act 1916 (c.59)
Constabulary and Police (Ireland) Act 1918 (c.53)
Constabulary and Police (Ireland) Act 1919 (c.68)
Constabulary (Ireland) Act 1836 (c.13)
Constabulary (Ireland) Act 1846 (c.97)
Constabulary (Ireland) Act 1848 (c.72)
Constabulary (Ireland) Act 1851 (c.85)
Constabulary (Ireland) Act 1857 (c.17)
Constabulary (Ireland) Act 1859 (c.22)
Constabulary (Ireland) Act 1866 (c.103)
Constabulary (Ireland) Act 1875 (c.44)
Constabulary (Ireland) Act 1877 (c.20)
Constabulary (Ireland) Act 1897 (c.64)
Constabulary (Ireland) Act 1908 (c.60)
Constabulary (Ireland) Act 1922 (c.55)
Constabulary (Ireland) Amendment Act 1865 (c.70)
Constabulary (Ireland) Amendment) Act 1870 (c.83)
Constabulary (Ireland) Amendment Act 1882 (c.63)

Constabulary (Ireland) (Consular Advances) Act 1825 (c.87)
Constabulary (Ireland) (No. 2) Act 1836 (c.36)
Constabulary (Ireland) Redistribution Act 1885 (c.12)
Consular Conventions Act 1949 (c.29)
Consular Fees Act 1980 (c.23)
Consular Marriage Act 1868 (c.61)
Consular Marriages Act 1849 (c.68)
Consular Relations Act 1968 (c.18)
Consular Salaries and Fees Act 1891 (c.36)
Consuls in Ottoman Dominions Act 1836 (c.78)
Consumer Arbitration Agreements Act 1988 (c.21)
Consumer Credit Act 1974 (c.39)
Consumer Protection Act 1961 (c.40)
Consumer Protection Act 1971 (c.15)
Consumer Protection Act 1987 (c.43)
Consumer Safety Act 1978 (c.38)
Consumer Safety (Amendment) Act 1986 (c.29)
Consumption of Malt Liquors (Ireland) Act 1810 (c.46)
Contagious Diseases Act 1866 (c.35)
Contagious Diseases Act 1869 (c.96)
Contagious Diseases Acts Repeal 1886 (c.10)
Contagious Diseases (Animals) Act 1853 (c.62)
Contagious Diseases, Animals Act 1856 (c.101)
Contagious Diseases (Animals) Act 1867 (c.125)
Contagious Diseases (Animals) Act 1869 (c.70)
Contagious Diseases (Animals) Act 1878 (c.74)
Contagious Diseases (Animals) Act 1884 (c.13)
Contagious Diseases (Animals) Act 1886 (c.32)
Contagious Diseases (Animals) Act 1892 (c.47)
Contagious Diseases (Animals) Act 1893 (c.43)
Contagious Diseases (Animals) (Pleuro pneumonia) Act 1890 (c.14)
Contagious Diseases (Animals) (Scotland) Act 1875 (c.75)
Contagious Diseases (Animals) Transfer of Parts of Districts Act 1884 (c.47)
Contagious Diseases (Ireland) Amendment Act 1868 (c.80)
Contagious Diseases of Sheep Act 1858 (c.62)
Contagious Diseases Prevention Act 1864 (c.85)
Contagious Disorders (Sheep), etc. Act 1848 (c.107)
Contempt of Court Act 1981 (c.49)
Continental Shelf Act 1964 (c.29)

Conveyance of Real Property Act 1845 (c.119)
Conveyancers (Ireland) Act 1864 (c.8)
Conveyancing Act 1881 (c.41)
Conveyancing Act 1882 (c.39)
Conveyancing Act 1911 (c.37)
Conveyancing Amendment (Scotland) Act 1938 (c.24)
Conveyancing and Feudal Reform (Scotland) Act 1970 (c.35)
Conveyancing and Law of Property Act 1892 (c.13)
Conveyancing (Scotland) Act 1874 (c.94)
Conveyancing (Scotland) Act, 1874, Amendment 1879 (c.40)
Conveyancing (Scotland) Act 1924 (c.27)
Conveyancing (Scotland) Acts (1874 and 1879) Amendment 1887 (c.69)
Convict Prisons Act 1850 (c.39)
Convict Prisons Act 1853 (c.121)
Convict Prisons Abroad Act 1859 (c.25)
Convict Prisons Act 1854 (c.76)
Convict Prisons Returns Act 1876 (c.42)
Convicted Prisoners Removal, etc. Act 1853
Conway's Patent Kiln Act 1795 (c.68)
Conwy Tunnel (Supplementary Powers) Act 1983 (c.7)
Co-operative Development Agency 1978 (c.21)
Co-operative Development Agency and Industrial Development Act 1984 (c.57)
Copyhold Act 1843 (c.23)
Copyhold Act 1852 (c.51)
Copyhold Act 1887 (c.73)
Copyhold Act 1894 (c.46)
Copyhold Commission Act 1846 (c.53)
Copyhold Commission Act 1847 (c.101)
Copyhold Commission Act 1858 (c.53)
Copyhold Commission Cont. Act 1860 (c.81)
Copyhold, etc., Commission Act 1853 (c.124)
Copyhold, etc., Commission Act 1855 (c.52)
Copyhold, etc., Commission Act 1857 (c.8)
Copyhold, etc., Commission Cont. Act 1862 (c.73)
Copyhold Lands Act 1844 (c.55)
Copyholds Act 1722 (c.29)
Copyholds Act 1853 (c.57)
Copyholds Act 1858 (c.94)
Copyright Act 1709 (c.21(i))
Copyright Act 1775 (c.53)
Copyright Act 1798 (c.71)
Copyright Act 1801 (c.107)
Copyright Act 1814 (c.156)
Copyright Act 1836 (c.110)
Copyright Act 1842 (c.45)
Copyright Act 1911 (c.46)
Copyright Act 1956 (c.74)
Copyright Act 1956 (Amendment) Act 1982 (c.35)
Copyright (Amendment) Act 1983 (c.42)
Copyright (British Museum) Act 1915 (c.38)
Copyright (Computer Software) Amendment Act 1985 (c.41)

Copyright, Designs and Patents Act 1988 (c.48)
Copyright (Musical Compositions) Act 1882 (c.40)
Copyright (Musical Compositions) Act 1888 (c.17)
Copyright of Designs Act 1839 (c.13)
Copyright of Designs Act 1839 (c.17)
Copyright of Designs Act 1842 (c.100)
Copyright of Designs Act 1843 (c.65)
Copyright of Designs Act 1850 (c.104)
Copyright of Designs Act 1858 (c.70)
Copyright of Designs Act 1861 (c.73)
Copyright of Designs Act 1875 (c.93)
Cordage for Shipping Act 1785 (c.56)
Cork Infirmary Act 1861 (c.29)
Corn Act 1731 (c.12)
Corn Act 1766 (c.17)
Corn Act 1770 (c.39)
Corn Act 1774 (c.64)
Corn Act 1780 (c.50)
Corn Accounts and Returns Act 1864 (c.87)
Corn Duties Act 1847 (c.1)
Corn, etc. Act 1801 (c.13)
Corn Exportation Act 1737 (c.22)
Corn Production Act 1917 (c.46)
Corn Production Acts (Repeal) Act 1921 (c.48)
Corn Production (Amendment) Act 1918 (c.36)
Corn Rents Act 1963 (c.14)
Corn Returns Act 1882 (c.37)
Corn Sales Act 1921 (c.35)
Corneal Grafting Act 1952 (c.28)
Corneal Tissue Act 1986 (c.18)
Cornwall and Devon Roads Act 1770 (c.87)
Cornwall and Devon Roads Act 1777 (c.79)
Cornwall Duchy Act 1760 (c.11)
Cornwall Duchy Act 1793 (c.78)
Cornwall Duchy Act 1810 (c.6)
Cornwall Roads Act 1759 (c.42)
Cornwall Roads Act 1760 (c.27)
Cornwall Roads Act 1760 (c.32)
Cornwall Roads Act 1762 (c.46)
Cornwall Roads Act 1763 (c.52)
Cornwall Roads Act 1781 (c.78)
Cornwall Roads Act 1781 (c.90)
Cornwall Roads Act 1782 (c.104)
Cornwall Roads Act 1783 (c.27)
Cornwall Roads Act 1785 (c.108)
Cornwall Roads Act 1785 (c.114)
Cornwall Submarine Mines Act 1858 (c.109)
Coroners Act 1751 (c.29)
Coroners Act 1836 (c.89)
Coroners Act 1843 (c.12)
Coroners Act 1843 (c.83)
Coroners Act 1844 (c.92)
Coroners Act 1887 (c.71)
Coroners Act 1892 (c.56)
Coroners Act 1921 (c.30)
Coroners Act 1954 (c.31)
Coroners Act 1980 (c.38)
Coroners Act 1988 (c.13)

Coroners (Amendment) Act 1926 (c.59)

Coroners (Emergency Provisions) Act 1917 (c.19)

Coroners (Emergency Provisions Continuance) Act 1922 (c.2)

Coroners' Inquests, Bail Act 1859 (c.33)

Coroners' Inquests Expenses Act 1837 (c.68)

Coroners (Ireland) Act 1846 (c.37)

Coroners (Ireland) Act 1881 (c.35)

Coroners (Ireland) Act 1908 (c.37)

Coroners' Juries Act 1983 (c.31)

Corporate Bodies' Contracts Act 1960 (c.46)

Corporation of Dublin Act 1850 (c.55)

Corporations Act 1718 (c.6)

Correspondence with Enemies Act 1704 (c.13)

Correspondence with Enemies Act 1793 (c.27)

Correspondence with Foreign Parts Act 1801 (c.11)

Correspondence with James the Pretender (High Treason) Act 1701 (c.3)

Corrupt and Illegal Practices Prevention Act 1883 (c.51)

Corrupt and Illegal Practices Prevention Act 1895 (c.40)

Corrupt Practice (Municipal Elections) Act 1872 (c.60)

Corrupt Practices Act 1856 (c.84)

Corrupt Practices Act 1858 (c.87)

Corrupt Practices Act 1859 (c.48)

Corrupt Practices Act 1861 (c.122)

Corrupt Practices Act 1862 (c.109)

Corrupt Practices 1854 Act, Continuation Act 1860 (c.99)

Corrupt Practices at Elections Act 1735 (c.38)

Corrupt Practice Commission Expenses Act 1869 (c.21)

Corrupt Practices at Parliamentary Elections Act 1728 (c.24)

Corrupt Practices, Dublin City 1869 (c.65)

Corrupt Practices Prevention Act 1854 (c.102)

Corrupt Practices Prevention Act 1863 (c.29)

Corrupt Practices (Suspension of Election) Act 1882 (c.68)

Corrupt Practices (Suspension of Elections) Act 1881 (c.42)

Corrupt Practices (Suspension of Elections) Act 1883 (c.46)

Corrupt Practices (Suspension of Elections) Act 1884 (c.78)

Corruption of Blood Act 1814 (c.145)

Corsham to Bath Easton Bridge Road Act 1779 (c.112)

Cosford, Suffolk: Poor Relief Act 1779 (c.30)

Cosham to Chichester Road Act 1762 (c.84)

Cosham to Chichester Road Act 1783 (c.32)

Costs Act 1803 (c.46)

Costs in Criminal Cases Act 1952 (c.48)

Costs in Criminal Cases Act 1908 (c.15)

Costs in Criminal Cases Act 1973 (c.14)

Costs of Action of Trespass Act 1840 (c.24)

Costs of Leases Act 1958 (c.52)

Cottier Tenant (Ireland) Act 1856 (c.65)

Cottingham, Yorks: Inclosure Act 1791 (c.20)

Cotton Act 1954 (c.24)

Cotton Association (Emergency Action) Act 1915 (c.69)

Cotton (Centralised Buying) Act 1947 (c.26)

Cotton Cloth Factories Act 1889 (c.62)

Cotton Cloth Factories Act 1897 (c.58)

Cotton Industry Act 1923 (c.22)

Cotton Industry Act 1928 (c.11)

Cotton Industry Act 1933 (c.30)

Cotton Industry Act 1938 (c.15)

Cotton Industry Act 1939 (c.9)

Cotton Industry Act 1959 (c.48)

Cotton Industry (Reorganisation) Act 1939 (c.54)

Cotton Industry (Reorganisation) (Postponement) Act 1939 (c.116)

Cotton Manufacture (Scotland) Act 1803 (c.151)

Cotton Manufacturing Industry (Temporary Provisions) Act 1934 (c.30)

Cotton Spinning Industry Act 1936 (c.21)

Cotton Spinning (Re-equipment Subsidy) Act 1948 (c.31)

Cotton Statistics Act 1868 (c.33)

Cotton Trade (Ireland) Act 1813 (c.75)

Council of India Act 1876 (c.7)

Council of India Act 1907 (c.35)

Council of India Reduction Act 1889 (c.65)

Councils of Conciliation Act 1867 (c.105)

Counter Inflation Act 1973 (c.9)

Counter Inflation (Temporary Provisions) Act 1972 (c.74)

Counterfeit Currency (Convention) Act 1935 (c.25)

Counterfeit Dollars and Tokens Act 1804 (c.71)

Counterfeit Medal Act 1883 (c.45)

Counterfeiting Act 1702 (c.3)

Counterfeiting Bank of England Tokens Act 1811 (c.110)

Counterfeiting Bank of Ireland Silver Tokens, etc. Act 1805 (c.42)

Counterfeiting Coin Act 1741 (c.28)

Counterfeiting Coin Act 1797 (c.126)

Counterfeiting, etc., of Gold Coin Act 1772 (c.71)

Counterfeiting of Bank of Ireland Tokens Act 1813 (c.106)

Counterfeiting of Copper Coin Act 1771 (c.40)

Counterfeiting of Tokens, etc. Act 1808 (c.31)

Counterfeiting of Tokens, etc. Act 1812 (c.138)

Countervailing Duties Act 1802 (c.27)

Countervailing Duties Act 1804 (c.27)

Countervailing Duties (Ireland) Act 1807 (c.18)

Countervailing Duties on Spirit Mixtures, etc. Act 1836 (c.72)

Countervailing Duty Act 1803 (c.154)

Counties and Boroughs (Ireland) Act 1840 (c.109)
Counties (Detached Parts) Act 1839 (c.82)
Counties (Detached Parts) Act 1844 (c.61)
Counties of Cities Act 1798 (c.52)
Counties of Cities Act 1811 (c.100)
Counties of Drogheda and Meath Act 1845 (c.121)
Countryside Act 1968 (c.41)
Countryside (Scotland) Act 1967 (c.86)
Countryside (Scotland) Act 1981 (c.44)
County and Borough Councils (Qualification) Act 1914 (c.21)
County and Borough Police Act 1856 (c.69)
County and Borough Police Act 1859 (c.32)
County and Borough Police Act 1919 (c.84)
County and City of Dublin Grand Juries Act 1873 (c.65)
County Boundaries (Ireland) Act 1872 (c.48)
County Bridges Act 1841 (c.49)
County Bridges Loans Extension Act 1880 (c.5)
County Buildings Act 1837 (c.24)
County Buildings Act 1847 (c.28)
County Buildings (Loans) Act 1872 (c.7)
County Cessation (Ireland) Act 1848 (c.32)
County Cessation (Ireland) Act 1849 (c.36)
County Cessation (Ireland) Act 1850 (c.1)
County Cessation (Ireland) Act 1859 (c.23)
County Cessation (Ireland) Act 1861 (c.58)
County Common Juries Act 1910 (c.17)
County Contributions to Prisons, etc. Act 1861 (c.12)
County Coroners Act 1860 (c.116)
County Council Association Expenses (Amendment) Act 1937 (c.27)
County Council (Elections) Act 1891 (c.68)
County Councils Association Expenses Act 1890 (c.3)
County Councils Association Expenses (Amendment) Act 1947 (c.13)
County Councils Association (Scotland) Expenses Act 1894 (c.5)
County Councils (Bills in Parliament) Act 1903 (c.9)
County Councils (Elections) Amendment Act 1900 (c.13)
County Councils Mortgages Act 1909 (c.38)
County Court Amendment (Ireland) Act 1882 (c.29)
County Court Appeals (Ireland) Act 1889 (c.48)
County Court (Buildings) Act 1870 (c.15)
County Court (Costs and Salaries) Act 1882 (c.57)
County Court Districts (England) Act 1858 (c.74)
County Court Judges Act 1859 (c.57)
County Court Judges (Retirement Pensions and Deputies) Act 1919 (c.70)
County Court Jurisdiction in Lunacy (Ireland) Act 1880 (c.39)
County Court (Penalties for Contempt) Act 1983 (c.45)

County Courts Act 1849 (c.101)
County Courts Act 1850 (c.61)
County Courts Act 1852 (c.54)
County Courts Act 1854 (c.16)
County Courts Act 1856 (c.108)
County Courts Act 1857 (c.36)
County Courts Act 1866 (c.14)
County Courts Act 1867 (c.142)
County Courts Act 1875 (c.50)
County Courts Act 1888 (c.43)
County Courts Act 1903 (c.42)
County Courts Act 1919 (c.73)
County Courts Act 1924 (c.17)
County Courts Act 1934 (c.53)
County Courts Act 1955 (c.8)
County Courts Act 1959 (c.22)
County Courts Act 1984 (c.28)
County Courts Admiralty Jurisdiction Act 1868 (c.71)
County Courts Admiralty Jurisdiction Amendment Act 1869 (c.51)
County Courts (Amendment) Act 1934 (c.17)
County Courts (Equity Jurisdiction) Act 1865 (c.99)
County Courts (Expenses) Act 1887 (c.3)
County Courts (Investment) Act 1900 (c.47)
County Courts (Jurisdiction) Act 1963 (c.5)
County Courts Westminster and Southwark Act 1859 (c.8)
County Debentures Act 1873 (c.35)
County Dublin Baronies Act 1838 (c.115)
County Dublin Grand Jury Act 1844 (c.106)
County Dublin Surveyors Act 1897 (c.2)
County Elections Act 1788 (c.36)
County Elections Act 1789 (c.13)
County Elections Act 1789 (c.18)
County Elections (Ireland) Act 1862 (c.62)
County Elections (Scotland) Act 1853 (c.28)
County Electors Act 1888 (c.10)
County Fermanagh Baronies Act 1837 (c.82)
County General Assessment (Scotland) Act 1868 (c.82)
County Infirmaries (Ireland) Act 1805 (c.111)
County Infirmaries (Ireland) Act 1807 (c.50)
County Infirmaries (Ireland) Act 1814 (c.62)
County Institutions (Ireland) Act 1838 (c.116)
County Law Procedure Act 1848 (c.31)
County of Clare Treasurer Act 1838 (c.104)
County of Dublin Jurors and Voters' Revision Act 1884 (c.35)
County of Durham Coroners Act 1837 (c.64)
County of Hertford Act 1878 (c.50)
County of Hertford and Liberty of St. Albans Act 1874 (c.45)
County of Roscommon Act 1840 (c.76)
County of Sussex Act 1865 (c.37)
County Officers and Courts (Ireland) Act 1877 (c.56)
County Officers and Courts (Ireland) Amendment Act 1885 (c.71)
County Palatine of Chester Act 1787 (c.43)
County Police Act 1839 (c.93)
County Police Act 1840 (c.88)

County Police Act 1856 (c.2)
County Property Act 1858 (c.92)
County Property Act 1871 (c.14)
County Rate Act 1866 (c.78)
County Rates Act 1815 (c.51)
County Rates Act 1816 (c.49)
County Rates Act 1844 (c.33)
County Rates Act 1845 (c.111)
County Rates Act 1852 (c.81)
County Rates (England) Act 1858 (c.33)
County Rates Within Boroughs Act 1849 (c.65)
County Surveyors, etc. (Ireland) Act 1861 (c.63)
County Surveyors (Ireland) Act 1862 (c.106)
County Surveyors (Ireland) Act 1893 (c.49)
County Surveyors (Ireland) Act 1900 (c.18)
County Surveyors Superannuation (Ireland) - Northern Irish Act 1875 (c.56)
County, Town and Parish Councils (Qualification) (Scotland) Act 1914 (c.39)
County Treasurers (Ireland) Act 1837 (c.54)
County Treasurers (Ireland) Act 1838 (c.53)
County Treasurers (Ireland) Act 1867 (c.46)
County Voters Registration Act 1865 (c.36)
County Votes Registration (Scotland) Act 1861 (c.83)
County Works (Ireland) Act 1846 (c.2)
County Works (Ireland) Act 1846 (c.78)
Court Funds Act 1829 (c.13)
Court House (Ireland) Act 1813 (c.131)
Court Houses (Ireland) Act 1815 (c.89)
Court Houses (Ireland) Act 1840 (c.102)
Court Houses (Ireland) Act 1841 (c.31)
Court-martial on Admiral Keppel Act 1779 (c.6)
Court of Admiralty Act 1854 (c.78)
Court of Admiralty (Ireland) Act 1867 (c.114)
Court of Admiralty (Ireland) Amendment Act 1876 (c.28)
Court of Appeal in Chancery Act 1867 (c.64)
Court of Appeal in Chancery Act 1868 (c.11)
Court of Bankruptcy (Ireland) Officers and Clerks Act 1881 (c.23)
Court of Chancery Act 1738 (c.24)
Court of Chancery Act 1763 (c.32)
Court of Chancery Act 1765 (c.28)
Court of Chancery Act 1769 (c.19)
Court of Chancery Act 1774 (c.43)
Court of Chancery Act 1806 (c.129)
Court of Chancery Act 1840 (c.94)
Court of Chancery Act 1841 (c.5)
Court of Chancery Act 1841 (c.52)
Court of Chancery Act 1842 (c.103)
Court of Chancery Act 1845 (c.105)
Court of Chancery Act 1848 (c.10)
Court of Chancery Act 1851 (c.83)
Court of Chancery Act 1852 (c.87(a))
Court of Chancery Act 1854 (c.100)
Court of Chancery Act 1855 (c.134)
Court of Chancery Act 1860 (c.149)
Court of Chancery and Exchequer Funds (Ireland) Act 1868 (c.88)

Court of Chancery Act 1852 (c.80)
Court of Chancery (England) Act 1850 (c.35)
Court of Chancery (England) Act 1853 (c.98)
Court of Chancery Examiners Act 1853 (c.22)
Court of Chancery (Funds) Act 1872 (c.44)
Court of Chancery (Ireland) Act 1823 (c.61)
Court of Chancery (Ireland) Act 1836 (c.74)
Court of Chancery (Ireland) Reg. Act 1850 (c.89)
Court of Chancery of Lancaster Act 1850 (c.43)
Court of Chancery of Lancaster Act 1854 (c.82)
Court of Chancery of Lancaster Act 1952 (c.49)
Court of Chancery of Lancaster (Amendment) Act 1961 (c.38)
Court of Chancery (Officers) Act 1867 (c.87)
Court of Chancery Offices Act 1848 (c.94)
Court of Chancery Procedure Act 1852 (c.86)
Court of Common Pleas Act 1850 (c.75)
Court of Common Pleas Act 1862 (c.96)
Court of Exchequer Chamber (Ireland) Act 1857 (c.6)
Court of Exchequer, Equity Side Act 1836 (c.112)
Court of Exchequer (Ireland) Act 1816 (c.122)
Court of Exchequer (Ireland) Act 1855 (c.50)
Court of Exchequer (Scotland) Act 1806 (c.154)
Court of Exchequer (Scotland) Act 1836 (c.73)
Court of Justice Act Act 1866 (c.63)
Court of Justiciary (Scotland) Act 1864 (c.30)
Court of Justiciary (Scotland) Act 1868 (c.95)
Court of Pleas of Durham Act 1839 (c.16)
Court of Probate Act 1857 (c.77)
Court of Probate Act 1858 (c.95)
Court of Probate Act (Ireland) 1859 (c.31)
Court of Probate (Ireland) Act 1861 (c.111)
Court of Queen's Bench Act 1843 (c.20)
Court of Session Act 1723 (c.19)
Court of Session Act 1808 (c.151)
Court of Session Act 1810 (c.112)
Court of Session Act 1813 (c.64)
Court of Session Act 1821 (c.38)
Court of Session Act 1825 (c.120)
Court of Session Act 1830 (c.69)
Court of Session Act 1838 (c.86)
Court of Session Act 1839 (c.36)
Court of Session Act 1850 (c.36)
Court of Session Act 1857 (c.56)
Court of Session Act 1868 (c.100)
Court of Session Act 1988 (c.36)
Court of Session Adjournment Act 1762 (c.27)
Court of Session Consignations (Scotland) Act 1895 (c.19)
Court of Session (Extracts) Act 1916 (c.49)
Court of Session (No. 2) Act 1838 (c.118)
Court of Session (Records) Act 1815 (c.70)
Court of Session (Scotland) Act 1745 (c.7)
Courts Act 1672 (c.40)

Courts Act 1971 (c.23)
Courts and Legal Services Act 1990 (c.41)
Courts Baron of High Peak and Castleton Act 1759 (c.31)
Courts Baron, Sheffield Act 1756 (c.37)
Courts (Colonial) Jurisdiction Act 1874 (c.27)
Courts (Emergency Powers) Act 1914 (c.78)
Courts (Emergency Powers) Act 1917 (c.25)
Courts (Emergency Powers) Act 1919 (c.64)
Courts (Emergency Powers) Act 1939 (c.67)
Courts (Emergency Powers) Act 1940 (c.37)
Courts (Emergency Powers) Act 1943 (c.19)
Courts (Emergency Powers) (Amendment) Act 1916 (c.13)
Courts (Emergency Powers) Amendment Act 1942 (c.36)
Courts (Emergency Powers) (Ireland) Act 1914 (c.19)
Courts (Emergency Power) (No. 2) Act 1916 (c.18)
Courts (Emergency Powers) (Scotland) Act 1939 (c.113)
Courts (Emergency Powers) (Scotland) Act 1944 (c.6)
Courts in Prince of Wales Island and India Act 1855 (c.93)
Courts in Wales and Chester Act 1732 (c.14)
Courts-Martial (Appeals) Act 1951 (c.46)
Courts-Martial (Appeals) Act 1968 (c.20)
Courts-Martial, East Indies Act 1760 (c.14)
Courts-Martial in India Act 1844 (c.18)
Courts-Martial on Troops of East India Company Act 1810 (c.87)
Courts, Newfoundland Act 1791 (c.29)
Courts, Newfoundland Act 1792 (c.46)
Courts, Newfoundland Act 1793 (c.76)
Courts, Newfoundland Act 1795 (c.25)
Courts, Newfoundland Act 1796 (c.37)
Courts, Newfoundland Act 1799 (c.16)
Courts, Newfoundland, etc. Act 1794 (c.44)
Courts of Common Law, Sittings Act 1838 (c.32)
Courts of Exchequer Act 1799 (c.67)
Courts of Judicature, India Act 1839·(c.34)
Courts of Justice (Additional Site) Act 1871 (c.57)
Courts of Justice Building Act 1865 (c.48)
Courts of Justice Building Amendment Act 1880 (c.29)
Courts of Justice, Canada Act 1803 (c.138)
Courts of Justice Concentration (Site) Act 1865 (c.49)
Courts of Justice (Salaries and Funds) Act 1869 (c.91)
Courts of Law Fees Act 1867 (c.122)
Courts of Law Fees (Scotland) Act 1868 (c.55)
Courts of Law Fees (Scotland) Act 1895 (c.14)
Covent Garden Market Act 1961 (c.49)
Covent Garden Market (Financial Provisions) Act 1977 (c.2)
Coventry Act 1842 (c.110)

Coventry Canal Act 1768 (c.36)
Coventry Canal Act 1786 (c.20)
Coventry Canal Act 1786 (c.30)
Coventry Freemen, etc. Act 1781 (c.54)
Coventry Gaol Act 1768 (c.40)
Coventry Grammar School Act 1864 (c.41)
Coventry Improvement Act 1763 (c.41)
Coventry–Oxford Canal Act 1775 (c.9)
Coventry Roads Act 1796 (c.133)
Coventry: Streets Act 1790 (c.77)
Coventry to Oxford Canal Act 1769 (c.70)
Coventry to Oxford Canal Act 1794 (c.103)
Coventry to Ticknall Canal Act 1794 (c.93)
Cowgil Parish; Marriages Confirmation, Park Gate Chapel Act 1869 (c.30)
Cowley's Charity Act 1858 (c.81)
Cran Measures Act 1908 (c.17)
Cranbourne Street Act 1864 (c.111)
Cranford and Maidenhead Road Act 1726 (c.31)
Credit-Sale Agreements (Scotland) Act 1961 (c.56)
Credit Unions Act 1979 (c.34)
Cremation Act 1902 (c.8)
Cremation Act 1952 (c.31)
Crew of a Certain Foreign Vessel Act 1786 (c.8)
Crewkerne Roads Act 1765 (c.61)
Crewkerne Roads Act 1786 (c.123)
Crime and Outrage (Ireland) Act 1850 (c.106)
Crime and Outrage (Ireland) Act 1852 (c.66)
Crime and Outrage (Ireland) Act 1853 (c.72)
Crime and Outrage (Ireland) Act 1854 (c.92)
Crimes and Outrage (Ireland) Act 1855 (c.112)
Criminal and Dangerous Lunatics (Scotland) Amendment Act 1871 (c.55)
Criminal Appeal Act 1907 (c.23)
Criminal Appeal Act 1964 (c.43)
Criminal Appeal Act 1966 (c.31)
Criminal Appeal Act 1968 (c.19)
Criminal Appeal (Amendment) Act 1908 (c.46)
Criminal Appeal (Northern Ireland) Act 1930 (c.45)
Criminal Appeal (Northern Ireland) Act 1968 (c.21)
Criminal Appeal (Northern Ireland) Act 1980 (c.47)
Criminal Appeal (Scotland) Act 1926 (c.15)
Criminal Appeal (Scotland) Act 1927 (c.26)
Criminal Attempts Act 1981 (c.47)
Criminal Costs (Dublin) Act 1815 (c.91)
Criminal Court, Norfolk Island Act 1794 (c.45)
Criminal Court, Norfolk Island Act 1795 (c.18)
Criminal Damage Act 1971 (c.48)
Criminal Evidence Act 1898 (c.36)
Criminal Evidence Act 1965 (c.20)
Criminal Evidence Act 1979 (c.16)
Criminal Injuries (Ireland) Act 1919 (c.14)
Criminal Jurisdiction Act 1802 (c.85)
Criminal Jurisdiction Act 1975 (c.59)
Criminal Justice Act 1855 (c.126)

Criminal Justice Act 1856 (c.118)
Criminal Justice Act 1925 (c.86)
Criminal Justice Act 1948 (c.58)
Criminal Justice Act 1961 (c.39)
Criminal Justice Act 1965 (c.26)
Criminal Justice Act 1967 (c.80)
Criminal Justice Act 1972 (c.71)
Criminal Justice Act 1982 (c.48)
Criminal Justice Act 1987 (c.38)
Criminal Justice Act 1988 (c.33)
Criminal Justice Act 1991 (c.53)
Criminal Justice Act 1993 (c.36)
Criminal Justice Administration Act 1851 (c.55)
Criminal Justice Administration Act 1914 (c.58)
Criminal Justice Administration Act 1956 (c.34)
Criminal Justice Administration Act 1962 (c.15)
Criminal Justice Administration (Amendment) Act 1959 (c.41)
Criminal Justice Administration (Postponement) Act 1914 (c.9)
Criminal Justice (Amendment) Act 1925 (c.13)
Criminal Justice (Amendment) Act 1981 (c.27)
Criminal Justice and Public Order Act 1994 (c.33)
Criminal Justice (International Co-operation) Act 1990 (c.5)
Criminal Justice (Scotland) Act 1949 (c.94)
Criminal Justice (Scotland) Act 1963 (c.39)
Criminal Justice (Scotland) Act 1980 (c.62)
Criminal Justice (Scotland) Act 1987 (c.41)
Criminal Law Act 1722 (c.22)
Criminal Law Act 1772 (c.31)
Criminal Law Act 1776 (c.43)
Criminal Law Act 1778 (c.62)
Criminal Law Act 1779 (c.54)
Criminal Law Act 1781 (cc.68, 69)
Criminal Law Act 1782 (c.40)
Criminal Law Act 1782 (c.58)·
Criminal Law Act 1826 (c.64)
Criminal Law Act 1967 (c.58)
Criminal Law Act 1977 (c.45)
Criminal Law Amendment Act 1867 (c.35)
Criminal Law Amendment Act 1871 (c.32)
Criminal Law Amendment Act 1880 (c.45)
Criminal Law Amendment Act 1885 (c.69)
Criminal Law Amendment Act 1912 (c.20)
Criminal Law Amendment Act 1922 (c.56)
Criminal Law Amendment Act 1928 (c.42)
Criminal Law Amendment Act 1951 (c.36)
Criminal Law and Procedure (Ireland) Act 1887 (c.20)
Criminal Law (Ireland) Act 1828 (c.54)
Criminal Law (Scotland) Act 1829 (c.38)
Criminal Law (Scotland) Act 1830 (c.37)
Criminal Lunatic Asylums Act 1860 (c.75)
Criminal Lunatics Act 1800 (c.94)
Criminal Lunatics Act 1838 (c.14)

Criminal Lunatics Act 1867 (c.12)
Criminal Lunatics Act 1869 (c.78)
Criminal Lunatics Act 1884 (c.64)
Criminal Lunatics (Ireland) Act 1838 (c.27)
Criminal Lunatics (Scotland) Act 1935 (c.32)
Criminal Procedure Act 1694 (c.43)
Criminal Procedure Act 1701 (c.6)
Criminal Procedure Act 1848 (c.46)
Criminal Procedure Act 1851 (c.100)
Criminal Procedure Act 1853 (c.30)
Criminal Procedure Act 1865 (c.18)
Criminal Procedure (Attendance of Witnesses) Act 1965 (c.69)
Criminal Procedure (Insanity) Act 1964 (c.84)
Criminal Procedure (Insanity and Unfitness to Plead) Act 1991 (c.25)
Criminal Procedure (Right of Reply) Act 1964 (c.34)
Criminal Procedure (Scotland) Act 1887 (c.35)
Criminal Procedure (Scotland) Act 1921 (c.50)
Criminal Procedure (Scotland) Act 1938 (c.48)
Criminal Procedure (Scotland) Act 1965 (c.39)
Criminal Procedure (Scotland) Act 1975 (c.21)
Criminal Prosecutions Fees (Ireland) Act 1809 (c.101)
Criminal Statutes Repeal Act 1861 (c.95)
Crinan Canal Act 1793 (c.104)
Crinan Canal Act 1805 (c.85)
Cripplegate: Church Building Act 1732 (c.21)
Crofter Forestry (Scotland) Act 1991 (c.18)
Crofters Commission (Delegation of Powers) Act 1888 (c.63)
Crofters Common Grazings Regulation Act 1891 (c.41)
Crofters Common Grazings Regulation Act 1908 (c.50)
Crofters Holdings (Scotland) Act 1886 (c.29)
Crofters Holdings (Scotland) Act 1887 (c.24)
Crofters (Scotland) Act 1955 (c.21)
Crofters (Scotland) Act 1961 (c.58)
Crofters (Scotland) Act 1993 (c.44)
Crofting Reform (Scotland) Act 1976 (c.21)
Cromarty Harbour Act 1785 (c.39)
Cromford Bridge to Langley Mill Road Act 1786 (c.124)
Cromford Canal Act 1789 (c.74)
Crossbows Act 1987 (c.32)
Crossed Cheques Act 1876 (c.81)
Crossford Bridge and Altrincham Road Act 1796 (c.143)
Crown Agents Act 1979 (c.43)
Crown Agents (Amendment) Act 1986 (c.43)
Crown Appointments, Colonies Act 1846 (c.91)
Crown Cases Act 1848 (c.78)
Crown Debt from Late Right Hon. R. Rigby Act 1794 (c.66)
Crown Debt of Abraham Goldsmid, etc. Act 1812 (c.75)

Crown Debtors Act 1785 (c.35)
Crown Debts Act 1541 (c.39)
Crown Debts Act 1801 (c.90)
Crown Debts Act 1824 (c.111)
Crown Debts and Judgments Act 1860 (c.115)
Crown Estate Act 1956 (c.73)
Crown Estate Act 1961 (c.55)
Crown Land, Revenues Act 1854 (c.68)
Crown Lands Act 1702 (c.1)
Crown Lands Act 1775 (c.33)
Crown Lands Act 1784 (c.57)
Crown Lands Act 1800 (c.78)
Crown Lands Act 1806 (c.151)
Crown Lands Act 1810 (c.65)
Crown Lands Act 1814 (c.70)
Crown Lands Act 1841 (c.1)
Crown Lands Act 1845 (c.99)
Crown Lands Act 1848 (c.102)
Crown Lands Act 1851 (c.42)
Crown Lands Act 1852 (c.62)
Crown Lands Act 1853 (c.56)
Crown Lands Act 1855 (c.16)
Crown Lands Act 1866 (c.62)
Crown Lands Act 1873 (c.36)
Crown Lands Act 1885 (c.79)
Crown Lands Act 1894 (c.43)
Crown Lands Act 1906 (c.28)
Crown Lands Act 1913 (c.8)
Crown Lands Act 1927 (c.23)
Crown Lands Act 1936 (c.47)
Crown Lands Act 1943 (c.7)
Crown Lands at Byfleet, Weybridge, etc., Surrey Act 1804 (c.25)
Crown Lands at Catterick and Tunstall, Yorkshire Act 1790 (c.51)
Crown Lands at Egham, Exchange King and David Jebb Act 1807 (c.77)
Crown Lands at Enfield, Middlesex Act 1776 (c.17)
Crown Lands at North Scotland Yard, Middlesex Act 1785 (c.98)
Crown Lands at Richmond, Surrey Act 1772 (c.35)
Crown Lands at Richmond, Surrey Act 1772 (c.59)
Crown Lands at Shilston Bay, Devon Act 1805 (c.116)
Crown Lands (Copyholds) Act 1851 (c.46)
Crown Lands, Escheats Act 1807 (c.24)
Crown Lands (Forfeited Estates) Act 1715 (c.50)
Crown Lands—Forfeited Estates Act 1717 (c.8)
Crown Lands—Forfeited Estates Act 1718 (c.22)
Crown Lands—Forfeited Estates Act 1719 (c.24)
Crown Lands—Forfeited Estates Act 1720 (c.22)
Crown Lands—Forfeited Estates Act 1726 (c.28)
Crown Lands—Forfeited Estates Act 1727 (c.21)

Crown Lands—Forfeited Estates Act 1728 (c.33)
Crown Lands—Forfeited Estates Act 1744 (c.37)
Crown Lands—Forfeited Estates Act 1746 (c.41)
Crown Lands—Forfeited Estates Act 1748 (c.52)
Crown Lands—Forfeited Estates Act 1751 (c.41)
Crown Lands, Forfeited Estates Act 1757 (c.16)
Crown Lands, Forfeited Estates Act 1762 (c.17)
Crown Lands—Forfeited Estates Act 1774 (c.22)
Crown Lands—Forfeited Estates Act 1794 (c.101)
Crown Lands—Forfeited Estates Act 1795 (c.69)
Crown Lands (Forfeited Estates): Greenwich Hospital Act 1737 (c.30)
Crown Lands, Forfeited Estates in Ireland Act 1793 (c.46)
Crown Lands, Forfeited Estates (Ireland) Act 1702 (c.18(a))
Crown Lands, Forfeited Estates (Ireland) Act 1702 (c.25)
Crown Lands, Forfeited Estates (Ireland) Act 1706 (c.25)
Crown Lands, Forfeited Estates (Ireland) Act 1778 (c.61)
Crown Lands Grant to Jame's Archbald Stuart Act 1772 (c.44)
Crown Lands—Greenwich Hospital Act 1778 (c.29)
Crown Lands in Fenchurch Street London Act 1772 (c.19)
Crown Lands in Holborn, London Act 1772 (c.43)
Crown Lands in Meath to Vest in Gerald Fitzgerald Act 1771 (c.56)
Crown Lands in Northamptonshire, Grant to Earl of Exeter Act 1796 (c.63)
Crown Lands in Northamptonshire, Grant to Earl of Upper Ossory Act 1795 (c.40)
Crown Lands in Northamptonshire, Grant to Earl of Westmorland Act 1796 (c.62)
Crown Lands in Privy Garden, Westminster Act 1792 (c.24)
Crown Lands (Ireland) Act 1822 (c.63)
Crown Lands - New Forest Act 1800 (c.86)
Crown Land Revenues, etc. Act 1786 (c.87)
Crown Lands, Savoy Act 1771 (c.4)
Crown Lands (Scotland) Act 1833 (c.69)
Crown Lands: Taxation Act 1801 (c.47)
Crown Lessees (Protection of Sub-Tenants) Act 1952 (c.40)
Crown Office Act 1860 (c.54)
Crown Office Act 1877 (c.41)
Crown Office Act 1890 (c.2)
Crown Pensioners Disqualification Act 1715 (c.56)

Crown Pre-Emption of Lead Ore Act 1815 (c.134)
Crown Private Estate Act 1800 (c.88)
Crown Private Estates Act 1862 (c.37)
Crown Private Estates Act 1873 (c.61)
Crown Proceedings Act 1947 (c.44)
Crown Proceedings (Armed Forces) Act 1987 (c.25)
Crown Land Revenues Act 1794 (c.75)
Crown Revenues (Colonies) Act 1852 (c.39)
Crown Suits Act 1769 (c.16)
Crown Suits Act 1855 (c.90)
Crown Suits Act 1861 (c.62)
Crown Suits, etc. Act 1865 (c.104)
Crown Suits (Isle of Man) Act 1862 (c.14)
Crown Suits (Scotland) Act 1857 (c.44)
Croydon Parish Church Act 1760 (c.38)
Cruelty to Animals Act 1849 (c.92)
Cruelty to Animals Act 1854 (c.60)
Cruelty to Animals Act 1876 (c.77)
Cruelty to Animals (Ireland) Act 1837 (c.66)
Cruelty to Animals (Scotland) Act 1850 (c.92)
Cruelty to Animals (Scotland) Act 1895 (c.13)
Cultivation, etc. of Trees Act 1766 (c.36)
Cultivation of Madder Act 1765 (c.18)
Cumberland and Westmorland Roads Act 1762 (c.81)
Cumberland and Westmorland Roads Act 1783 (c.108)
Cumberland Roads Act 1749 (c.40)
Cumberland Roads Act 1753 (c.37)
Cumberland Roads Act 1753 (c.49)
Cumberland Roads Act 1767 (c.83)
Cumberland Roads Act 1778 (c.108)
Cumberland Roads Act 1779 (c.97)
Cumberland Roads Act 1789 (c.97)
Cumberland Roads Act 1794 (c.143)
Cunard Agreement (Money) Act 1904 (c.22)
Cunard (Insurance) Agreement Act 1931 (c.2)
Curates, etc. Act 1796 (c.83)
Curragh of Kildare Act 1868 (c.60)
Curragh of Kildare Act 1870 (c.74)
Currency Act 1982 (c.3)
Currency Act 1983 (c.9)
Currency and Bank Notes Act 1914 (c.14)
Currency and Bank Notes Act 1928 (c.13)
Currency and Bank Notes Act 1939 (c.7)
Currency and Bank Notes Act 1954 (c.12)
Currency and Bank Notes (Amendment) Act 1914 (c.72)
Currency (Defence) Act 1939 (c.64)
Curriers, etc. Act 1738 (c.25)
Cursitor Baron of the Exchequer Act 1856 (c.86)
Custody of Children Act 1891 (c.3)
Custody of Children (Scotland) Act 1939 (c.4)
Custody of Infants Act 1839 (c.54)
Custody of Infants Act 1873 (c.12)
Custody of Insane Persons Act 1816 (c.117)
Custody of Napoleon Buonaparte Act 1816 (c.22)
Customs Act 1719 (c.12)

Customs Act 1722 (c.21)
Customs Act 1772 (c.50)
Customs Act 1772 (c.60)
Customs Act 1724 (c.7)
Customs Act 1736 (c.30)
Customs Act 1753 (c.12)
Customs Act 1763 (c.9)
Customs Act 1763 (c.22)
Customs Act 1766 (c.20)
Customs Act 1766 (c.28)
Customs Act 1766 (c.41)
Customs Act 1766 (c.45)
Customs Act 1766 (c.50)
Customs Act 1767 (c.58)
Customs Act 1768 (c.23)
Customs Act 1770 (c.17)
Customs Act 1770 (c.30)
Customs Act 1770 (c.43)
Customs Act 1775 (c.34)
Customs Act 1775 (c.35)
Customs Act 1775 (c.37)
Customs Act 1776 (c.12)
Customs Act 1776 (c.27)
Customs Act 1776 (c.41)
Customs Act 1776 (c.42)
Customs Act 1776 (c.43)
Customs Act 1776 (c.48)
Customs Act 1778 (c.4)
Customs Act 1778 (cc.24, 25)
Customs Act 1778 (c.27)
Customs Act 1778 (c.40)
Customs Act 1778 (c.58)
Customs Act 1779 (c.29)
Customs Act 1779 (c.41)
Customs Act 1779 (c.62)
Customs Act 1780 (c.7)
Customs Act 1780 (c.16)
Customs Act 1780 (c.25)
Customs Act 1780 (c.30)
Customs Act 1780 (c.32)
Customs Act 1782 (c.20)
Customs Act 1782 (c.21)
Customs Act 1782 (c.28)
Customs Act 1782 (c.49)
Customs Act 1782 (c.61)
Customs Act 1783 (c.11)
Customs Act 1783 (c.56)
Customs Act 1783 (c.74)
Customs Act 1784 (c.9)
Customs Act 1784 (c.16)
Customs Act 1784 (c.49)
Customs Act 1785 (c.25)
Customs Act 1785 (c.69)
Customs Act 1786 (c.42)
Customs Act 1786 (c.104)
Customs Act 1788 (c.27)
Customs Act 1788 (c.33)
Customs Act 1789 (c.59)
Customs Act 1789 (c.60)
Customs Act 1789 (c.64)
Customs Act 1790 (c.4)
Customs Act 1791 (c.15)
Customs Act 1791 (c.26)

Customs Act 1792 (c.32)
Customs Act 1792 (c.43)
Customs Act 1792 (c.54)
Customs Act 1793 (c.48)
Customs Act 1793 (c.70)
Customs Act 1793 (c.81)
Customs Act 1794 (c.51)
Customs Act 1794 (c.70)
Customs Act 1795 (c.20)
Customs Act 1796 (c.15)
Customs Act 1796 (cc.78, 79)
Customs Act 1796 (c.110)
Customs Act 1797 (c.110)
Customs Act 1798 (c.86)
Customs Act 1799 (c.61)
Customs Act 1800 (c.51)
Customs Act 1800 (c.59)
Customs Act 1800 (c.60)
Customs Act 1801 (c.87)
Customs Act 1801 (c.89)
Customs Act 1801 (c.94)
Customs Act 1802 (c.95)
Customs Act 1803 (c.68)
Customs Act 1803 (c.70)
Customs Act 1803 (c.128)
Customs Act 1803 (c.131)
Customs Act 1804 (c.53)
Customs Act 1805 (c.18)
Customs Act 1805 (c.29)
Customs Act 1805 (cc.44, 45)
Customs Act 1805 (c.88)
Customs Act 1805 (c.103)
Customs Act 1806 (c.150)
Customs Act 1807 (c.51)
Customs Act 1807 (c.61)
Customs Act 1808 (c.9)
Customs Act 1808 (c.26)
Customs Act 1808 (c.28)
Customs Act 1808 (cc.56, 57)
Customs Act 1808 (c.67)
Customs Act 1809 (c.46)
Customs Act 1809 (c.65)
Customs Act 1809 (c.98)
Customs Act 1810 (c.77)
Customs Act 1811 (c.52)
Customs Act 1811 (c.55)
Customs Act 1811 (c.71)
Customs Act 1811 (c.96)
Customs Act 1812 (c.2)
Customs Act 1812 (c.60)
Customs Act 1812 (c.89)
Customs Act 1812 (c.117)
Customs Act 1812 (c.141)
Customs Act 1813 (cc.26, 27)
Customs Act 1813 (c.29)
Customs Act 1813 (c.33)
Customs Act 1813 (c.47)
Customs Act 1813 (c.104)
Customs Act 1813 (c.105)
Customs Act 1814 (c.14)
Customs Act 1814 (c.50)
Customs Act 1814 (cc.64–66)
Customs Act 1814 (c.69)

Customs Act 1814 (c.77)
Customs Act 1814 (c.103)
Customs Act 1814 (c.122)
Customs Act 1815 (cc.22, 23)
Customs Act 1815 (c.24)
Customs Act 1815 (cc.32, 33)
Customs Act 1815 (c.36)
Customs Act 1815 (c.52)
Customs Act 1815 (c.95)
Customs Act 1815 (c.135)
Customs Act 1815 (c.163)
Customs Act 1815 (c.174)
Customs Act 1815 (c.181)
Customs Act 1816 (c.77)
Customs Act 1816 (c.93)
Customs Act 1835 (c.66)
Customs Act 1836 (c.60)
Customs Act 1838 (c.113)
Customs Act 1840 (c.19)
Customs Act 1840 (c.95)
Customs Act 1842 (c.47)
Customs Act 1843 (c.84)
Customs Act 1844 (c.16)
Customs Act 1844 (c.43)
Customs Act 1844 (c.73)
Customs Act 1845 (c.12)
Customs Act 1845 (c.84)
Customs Act 1845 (c.86)
Customs Act 1845 (c.92)
Customs Act 1846 (c.24)
Customs Act 1846 (c.58)
Customs Act 1846 (c.94)
Customs Act 1846 (c.102)
Customs Act 1847 (c.24)
Customs Act 1849 (c.90)
Customs Act 1850 (c.95)
Customs Act 1851 (c.62)
Customs Act 1853 (c.54)
Customs Act 1853 (c.106)
Customs Act 1854 (cc.28, 29)
Customs Act 1854 (c.122)
Customs Act 1855 (c.21)
Customs Act 1856 (c.75)
Customs Act 1857 (c.15)
Customs Act 1857 (c.62)
Customs Act 1858 (c.12)
Customs Act 1858 (c.16)
Customs Act 1859 (c.37)
Customs Act 1860 (c.22)
Customs Act 1860 (c.36)
Customs Act 1867 (c.82)
Customs Amendment Act 1842 (c.56)
Customs Amendment Act 1886 (c.41)
Customs and Excise Act 1711 (c.19)
Customs and Excise Act 1782 (c.66)
Customs and Excise Act 1787 (c.13)
Customs and Excise Act 1804 (c.67)
Customs and Excise Act 1806 (c.38)
Customs and Excise Act 1809 (c.116)
Customs and Excise Act 1814 (cc.120, 121)
Customs and Excise Act 1815 (c.118)
Customs and Excise Act 1816 (c.85)
Customs and Excise Act 1857 (c.61)

Customs and Excise Act 1952 (c.44)

Customs and Excise Duties (General Reliefs) Act 1979 (c.3)

Customs and Excise (Ireland) Act 1804 (c.103)

Customs and Excise (Ireland) Act 1805 (c.108)

Customs and Excise (Ireland) Act 1806 (c.58)

Customs and Excise (Ireland) Act 1807 (c.48)

Customs and Excise (Ireland) Act 1808 (c.62)

Customs and Excise (Ireland) Act 1816 (c.20)

Customs and Excise Management Act 1979 (c.2)

Customs and Excise Warehousing Act 1869 (c.103)

Customs and Income Tax Act 1871 (c.21)

Customs and Inland Revenue Act 1861 (c.20)

Customs and Inland Revenue Act 1863 (c.22)

Customs and Inland Revenue Act 1867 (c.23)

Customs and Inland Revenue Act 1870 (c.32)

Customs and Inland Revenue Act 1872 (c.20)

Customs and Inland Revenue Act 1873 (c.18)

Customs and Inland Revenue Act 1874 (c.16)

Customs and Inland Revenue Act 1875 (c.23)

Customs and Inland Revenue Act 1876 (c.16)

Customs and Inland Revenue Act 1878 (c.15)

Customs and Inland Revenue Act 1879 (c.21)

Customs and Inland Revenue Act 1880 (c.14)

Customs and Inland Revenue Act 1881 (c.12)

Customs and Inland Revenue Act 1882 (c.41)

Customs and Inland Revenue Act 1883 (c.10)

Customs and Inland Revenue Act 1884 (c.25)

Customs and Inland Revenue Act 1885 (c.51)

Customs and Inland Revenue Act 1886 (c.18)

Customs and Inland Revenue Act 1887 (c.15)

Customs and Inland Revenue Act 1888 (c.8)

Customs and Inland Revenue Act 1889 (c.7)

Customs and Inland Revenue Act 1890 (c.8)

Customs and Inland Revenue Act 1891 (c.25)

Customs and Inland Revenue Act 1892 (c.16)

Customs and Inland Revenue Act 1893 (c.7)

Customs and Inland Revenue Amendment Act 1877 (c.10)

Customs and Inland Revenue Buildings (Ireland) - Northern Irish Act 1882 (c.17)

Customs Buildings Act 1879 (c.36)

Customs Consolidation Act 1853 (c.107)

Customs Consolidation Act 1860 (c.110)

Customs Consolidation Act 1876 (c.36)

Customs Consolidation Act, 1876, Amendment 1887 (c.7)

Customs Consolidation Act, 1876, Amendment 1890 (c.56)

Customs Duties Act 1811 (cc.67, 68)

Customs Duties (Dumping and Subsidies) Act 1957 (c.18)

Customs Duties (Dumping and Subsidies) Act 1969 (c.16)

Customs Duties (Dumping and Subsidies) Amendment Act 1968 (c.33)

Customs Duties, etc. Act 1763 (c.15)

Customs, etc. Act 1721 (c.18)

Customs, etc. Act 1727 (c.17)

Customs, etc. Act 1728 (c.18)

Customs, etc. Act 1736 (c.27)

Customs, etc. Act 1765 (cc.29–32)

Customs, etc. Act 1765 (c.45)

Customs, etc. Act 1766 (cc.46, 47)

Customs, etc. Act 1766 (c.52)

Customs, etc. Act 1769 (c.35)

Customs, etc. Act 1769 (c.41)

Customs, etc. Act 1784 (c.7)

Customs, etc. Act 1798 (c.76)

Customs, etc. Act 1813 (c.36)

Customs, etc. Act 1814 (c.171)

Customs, etc. Act 1815 (cc.82, 83)

Customs, etc. Act 1816 (c.29)

Customs, etc. (Ireland) Act 1812 (c.76)

Customs, etc., Revenues Act 1725 (c.28)

Customs, etc., Revenues Act 1765 (c.43)

Customs, Excise and Taxes Act 1804 (c.26)

Customs (Exportation Prohibition) Act 1914 (c.64)

Customs (Exportation Restriction) Act 1914 (c.2)

Customs (Exportation Restriction) Act 1915 (c.52)

Customs (Import Deposits) Act 1968 (c.74)

Customs (Import Deposits) Act 1969 (c.64)

Customs, Inland Revenue, and Savings Banks Act 1877 (c.13)

Customs (Ireland) Act 1806 (c.87)

Customs (Ireland) Act 1807 (c.12)

Customs (Ireland) Act 1808 (c.80)

Customs (Isle of Man) Act 1870 (c.12)

Customs (Isle of Man) Tariff Act 1874 (c.46)

Customs (Manchester Bonding) Act 1850 (c.84)

Customs (Officers) Act 1881 (c.30)

Customs Refined Sugar Duties, Isle of Man Act 1870 (c.43)

Customs Rotulorum (Ireland) Act 1831 (c.17)

Customs Seizures Act 1790 (c.43)

Customs Sugar Duties (Isle of Man) Act 1873 (c.29)

Customs Tariff Act 1855 (c.97)

Customs Tariff Act 1876 (c.35)

Customs (War Powers) Act 1915 (c.31)

Customs (War Powers) Act 1916 (c.102)

Customs (War Powers) (No. 2) Act 1915 (c.71)

Customs (Wine Duty) Act 1888 (c.14)

Cutlery Trade Act 1819 (c.7)

Cycle Tracks Act 1984 (c.38)

Cyprus Act 1960 (c.52)

Czecho-Slovakia (Financial Assistance) Act 1939 (c.6)

Czecho-Slovakia (Financial Claims and Refugees) Act 1940 (c.4)

Czecho-Slovakia (Restrictions on Banking Accounts etc.) Act 1939 (c.11)

Dalkeith Beer Duties Act 1759 (c.53)

Dalkeith Beer Duties Act 1782 (c.18)

Damages (Scotland) Act 1976 (c.13)

Damages (Scotland) Act 1993 (c.5)
Damaging of Hides Act 1801 (c.53)
Dangerous Dogs Act 1989 (c.30)
Dangerous Dogs Act 1991 (c.65)
Dangerous Drugs Act 1925 (c.74)
Dangerous Drugs Act 1931 (c.14)
Dangerous Drugs Act 1951 (c.48)
Dangerous Drugs Act 1964 (c.36)
Dangerous Drugs Act 1965 (c.15)
Dangerous Drugs Act 1967 (c.82)
Dangerous Drugs (Amendment) Act 1950 (c.7)
Dangerous Drugs and Poisons (Amendment) Act 1923 (c.5)
Dangerous Litter Act 1971 (c.35)
Dangerous Performances Act 1897 (c.52)
Dangerous Vessels Act 1985 (c.22)
Dangerous Wild Animals Act 1976 (c.38)
Danube Works Loan Act 1868 (c.126)
Darby Court, Westminster Act 1845 (c.104)
Dartford and Strood Road Act 1760 (c.40)
Dartford Roads Act 1766 (c.98)
Dartford Roads Act 1788 (c.84)
Dartford–Thurrock Crossing Act 1988 (c.20)
Data Protection Act 1984 (c.35)
Day Industrial Schools (Scotland) Act 1893 (c.12)
Deal Act 1711 (c.43)
Deal Chapel of Ease Act 1711 (c.43)
Deal: Improvement Act 1791 (c.64)
Deal: Improvement Act 1796 (c.45)
Dealers in Excisable Articles Act 1805 (c.52)
Dean and Chapter Act 1868 (c.19)
Dean and New Forests Act 1808 (c.72)
Dean Forest (Encroachments) Act 1838 (cc.39–41)
Dean Forest Act 1861 (c.40)
Dean Forest (Mines) Act 1838 (c.43)
Dean Forest (Mines) Act 1871 (c.85)
Dean Forest (Mines) Act 1871 (c.85)
Dean Forest Roads Act 1796 (c.131)
Deanery of Manchester Act 1906 (c.19)
Deans and Canons Resignation Act 1872 (c.8)
Dean's Yard, Westminster Act 1755 (c.54)
Death Duties (Killed in War) Act 1914 (c.76)
Debenture Stock Act 1871 (c.27)
Debt of City of Edinburgh, etc. Act 1838 (c.55)
Debtors Act 1869 (c.62)
Debtors Act 1878 (c.54)
Debtors and Creditors Act 1860 (c.147)
Debtors and Imprisonment Act 1758 (c.28)
Debtors Imprisonment Act 1758 (c.28)
Debtors (Ireland) Act 1840 (c.105)
Debtors (Ireland) Act 1872 (c.57)
Debtors, Middlesex Act 1785 (c.45)
Debtors' Prison, Devonshire Act 1753 (c.57)
Debtors Relief Act 1793 (c.5)
Debtors Relief Act 1801 (c.64)
Debtors Relief Act 1812 (c.34)
Debtors (Scotland) Act 1838 (c.114)
Debtors (Scotland) Act 1880 (c.34)
Debtors (Scotland) Act 1987 (c.18)

Debts Clearing Offices Act 1948 (c.2)
Debts Clearing Offices and Import Restrictions Act 1934 (c.31)
Debts Due to Swiss Government Act 1798 (c.45)
Debts Due to the Army Act 1702 (c.24)
Debts Due to the Army Act 1711 (c.38)
Debts Due to the Army Act 1714 (c.24)
Debts Due to the Army Act 1715 (c.35)
Debts Due to the Army Act 1716 (c.17)
Debts Due to the Army Act 1720 (c.30)
Debts Due to the Army, etc. Act 1701 (c.1)
Debts Due to the Army, etc. Act 1717 (c.9)
Debts Due to the Army, etc. Act 1718 (c.14)
Debts Due to the Army, etc. Act 1719 (c.17)
Debts Due to the United Provinces, etc. Act 1797 (c.28)
Debts of East India Company Act 1812 (c.121)
Debts of Traders Act 1807 (c.74)
Debts Recovery Act 1839 (c.60)
Debts Recovery Act 1848 (c.87)
Debts Recovery (Scotland) Act 1867 (c.96)
Debts Securities (Scotland) Act 1856 (c.91)
Deceased Brother's Widow's Marriage Act 1921 (c.24)
Deceased Wife's Sister's Marriage Act 1907 (c.47)
Decimal Currency Act 1967 (c.47)
Decimal Currency Act 1969 (c.19)
Declaration by Quakers, etc. Act 1837 (c.5)
Declaration of Title Act 1862 (c.67)
Declarations by Quakers, etc. on Acceptance of Offices Act 1838 (c.15)
Declarations Before Taking Office Act 1866 (c.22)
Deeds of Arrangement Act 1887 (c.57)
Deeds of Arrangement Act 1914 (c.47)
Deeds of Arrangement Amendment Act 1890 (c.24)
Deep Sea Mining (Temporary Provisions) Act 1981 (c.53)
Deeping Fen Drainage Act 1737 (c.39)
Deeping Fens Act 1774 (c.23)
Deer Act 1963 (c.36)
Deer Act 1980 (c.49)
Deer Act 1987 (c.28)
Deer Act 1991 (c.54)
Deer (Amendment) (Scotland) Act 1967 (c.37)
Deer (Amendment) (Scotland) Act 1982 (c.19)
Deer (Scotland) Act 1959 (c.40)
Deer Stealers Act 1718 (c.15)
Deer Stealing (England) Act 1802 (c.107)
Deer Stealing (England) Act 1811 (c.120)
Defacing the Coin Act 1853 (c.102)
Defamation Act 1952 (c.66)
Defective Premises Act 1972 (c.35)
Defence Act 1842 (c.94)
Defence Act 1854 (c.67)
Defence Act 1859 (c.12)
Defence Act 1860 (c.112)

Defence Act 1865 (c.65)
Defence Act Amendment Act 1864 (c.89)
Defence Acts Amendment Act 1873 (c.72)
Defence (Barracks) Act 1935 (c.26)
Defence Contracts Act 1958 (c.38)
Defence Loans Act 1937 (c.13)
Defence Loans Act 1939 (c.8)
Defence of the Realm Act 1797 (c.27)
Defence of the Realm Act 1803 (c.55)
Defence of the Realm Act 1803 (c.120)
Defence of the Realm Act 1803 (c.125)
Defence of the Realm Act 1804 (c.95)
Defence of the Realm Act 1806 (c.90)
Defence of the Realm Act 1808 (c.107)
Defence of the Realm Act 1914 (c.29)
Defence of the Realm (Acquisition of Land) Act 1916 (c.63)
Defence of the Realm (Acquisition of Land) Act 1920 (c.79)
Defence of the Realm (Amendment) Act 1915 (c.34)
Defence of the Realm (Amendment) (No. 2) Act 1915 (c.37)
Defence of the Realm (Amendment) (No. 3) Act 1915 (c.42)
Defence of the Realm (Beans, Peas and Pulse Orders) Act 1918 (c.12)
Defence of the Realm Consolidation Act 1914 (c.8)
Defence of the Realm (Employment Exchanges) Act 1918 (c.58)
Defence of the Realm (England) Act 1803 (c.82)
Defence of the Realm (England) Act 1803 (c.123)
Defence of the Realm, etc. Act 1803 (c.96)
Defence of the Realm, etc. Act 1804 (c.56)
Defence of the Realm, etc. Act 1804 (c.66)
Defence of the Realm, etc. Act 1804 (c.74)
Defence of the Realm (Food Profits) Act 1918 (c.9)
Defence of the Realm (Ireland) Act 1803 (c.85)
Defence of the Realm (Ireland) Act 1806 (c.63)
Defence of the Realm, London Act 1803 (c.101)
Defence of the Realm, London Act 1804 (c.96)
Defence of the Realm, London Act 1806 (c.144)
Defence of the Realm (No. 2) Act 1914 (c.63)
Defence of the Realm (Scotland) Act 1803 (c.83)
Defence of the Realm (Scotland) Act 1803 (c.124)
Defence (Transfer of Functions) Act 1964 (c.15)
Defranchisement of Sudbury Act 1844 (c.53)
Delamere Forest Act 1856 (c.13)
Delay Act 1387 (c.10)
Delay of Cause After Issue Joined Act 1740 (c.17)

Demise of Parts of Rolls Estate Act 1836 (c.49)
Demise of the Crown Act 1727 (c.5)
Demise of the Crown Act 1830 (c.43)
Demise of the Crown Act 1837 (c.31)
Demise of the Crown Act 1901 (c.5)
Denbigh and Carnarvon Roads Act 1757 (c.69)
Denbigh and Flint Roads Act 1769 (c.45)
Denbigh and Flint Roads Act 1790 (c.110)
Denbigh, Flint and Carnarvon Roads Act 1758 (c.55)
Denbigh, Flint and Carnarvon Roads Act 1779 (c.109)
Denbigh, Flint and Carnarvon Roads Act 1780 (c.97)
Denbigh, Flint, Salop. and Chester Roads Act 1767 (c.104)
Denbigh Roads Act 1756 (c.68)
Denbigh Roads Act 1762 (c.77)
Denbigh Roads Act 1763 (c.43)
Denbigh Roads Act 1777 (c.111)
Denbigh Roads Act 1788 (c.112)
Denbigh to Rutland Road Act 1781 (c.80)
Dentists Act 1878 (c.33)
Dentists Act 1921 (c.21)
Dentists Act 1923 (c.36)
Dentists Act 1956 (c.29)
Dentists Act 1957 (c.28)
Dentists Act 1983 (c.38)
Dentists Act 1984 (c.24)
Dentists (Amendment) Act 1973 (c.31)
Denver, etc., Drainage, Norfolk Act 1771 (c.72)
Denver, etc. (Norfolk and Cambridge) Drainage Act 1748 (c.16)
Deodands Act 1846 (c.62)
Department of Science and Art Act 1875 (c.68)
Department of Scientific and Industrial Research Act 1956 (c.58)
Department of Technical Co-operation Act 1961 (c.30)
Dependency of Ireland on Great Britain Act 1719 (c.5)
Deposit of Poisonous Waste Act 1972 (c.21)
Depredations on the Thames Act 1800 (c.87)
Depredations on the Thames Act 1807 (c.37)
Depredations on the Thames Act 1814 (c.187)
Deputy Lieutenants Act 1918 (c.19)
Deputy Speaker Act 1855 (c.84)
Derby and Cheshire Roads Act 1792 (c.128)
Derby and Chester Roads Act 1782 (c.107)
Derby and Leicester Roads Act 1794 (c.120)
Derby and Nottinghamshire Roads Act 1757 (c.60)
Derby and Nottinghamshire Roads Act 1764 (c.67)
Derby and Nottinghamshire Roads Act 1780 (c.74)
Derby and Nottinghamshire Roads Act 1790 (c.113)

Dindings Agreement (Approval) Act 1934 (c.55)

Diocesan Boundaries Act 1871 (c.14)

Diocesan Boundaries Act 1872 (c.14)

Diocese of Norwich Act 1848 (c.61)

Diplomatic and Consular Premises Act 1987 (c.46)

Diplomatic and Other Privileges Act 1971 (c.64)

Diplomatic Immunities (Commonwealth Countries and Republic of Ireland) Act 1951 (c.18)

Diplomatic Immunities (Conferences with Commonwealth Countries and Republic of Ireland) Act 1961 (c.11)

Diplomatic Immunities Restriction Act 1955 (c.22)

Diplomatic Privileges Act 1708 (c.12)

Diplomatic Privileges Act 1964 (c.81)

Diplomatic Privileges (Extension) Act 1941 (c.7)

Diplomatic Privileges (Extension) Act 1944 (c.44)

Diplomatic Privileges (Extension) Act 1946 (c.66)

Diplomatic Privileges (Extension) Act 1950 (c.7)

Diplomatic Relations with See of Rome Act 1848 (c.108)

Diplomatic Salaries, etc. Act 1869 (c.43)

Directors' Liability Act 1890 (c.64)

Disability (Grants) Act 1993 (c.14)

Disability Living Allowance and Disability Working Allowance Act 1991 (c.21)

Disabled Men (Facilities for Employment) (Master and Servant) Act 1919 (c.22)

Disabled Persons Act 1981 (c.43)

Disabled Persons Act 1986 (c.33)

Disabled Persons (Employment) Act 1944 (c.10)

Disabled Persons (Employment) Act 1958 (c.33)

Disabled Persons (Northern Ireland) Act 1989 (c.10)

Disarming the Highlands, etc. Act 1745 (c.39)

Disarming the Highlands, etc. Act 1753 (c.29)

Discharge of a Crown Debt Act 1788 (c.32)

Discharge of Certain Imprisoned Debtors Act 1808 (c.123)

Discharge to Lady A. Jekyll's Executors Act 1772 (c.53)

Discharged Prisoners Act 1774 (c.20)

Discharged Prisoners' Aid Act 1862 (c.44)

Discharged Soldiers, etc. Act 1748 (c.44)

Discontinuance of Duties Act 1757 (c.7)

Discontinuance of Duties Act 1757 (c.14)

Discontinuance of Duties Act 1758 (c.12)

Discontinuance of Duties Act 1770 (c.8)

Discontinuance of Portsdown Fair, Southampton Act 1862 (c.34)

Discount on Newspapers Act 1809 (c.50)

Discovery of Longitude at Sea Act 1713 (c.14)

Discovery of Longitude at Sea Act 1762 (c.14)

Discovery of Longitude at Sea Act 1762 (c.18)

Discovery of Longitude at Sea Act 1765 (c.11)

Discovery of Longitude at Sea Act 1765 (c.20)

Discovery of Longitude at Sea Act 1770 (c.34)

Discovery of Longitude at Sea Act 1774 (c.66)

Discovery of Longitude at Sea Act 1790 (c.14)

Discovery of Longitude at Sea Act 1815 (c.75)

Discovery of Longitude at Sea, etc. Act 1803 (c.118)

Discovery of Longitude at Sea, etc. Act 1806 (c.77)

Discovery of Longitude at Seas Act 1753 (c.25)

Discovery of North-West Passage Act 1744 (c.17)

Discovery of Northern Passage Act 1776 (c.6)

Disease Among Cattle Act 1772 (c.51)

Diseased Sheep, etc. Act 1798 (c.65)

Diseases of Animals Act 1894 (c.57)

Diseases of Animals Act 1896 (c.15)

Diseases of Animals Act 1903 (c.43)

Diseases of Animals Act 1909 (c.26)

Diseases of Animals Act 1910 (c.20)

Diseases of Animals Act 1922 (c.8)

Diseases of Animals Act 1923 (c.3)

Diseases of Animals Act 1925 (c.63)

Diseases of Animals Act 1927 (c.13)

Diseases of Animals Act 1935 (c.31)

Diseases of Animals Act 1950 (c.36)

Diseases of Animals Act 1975 (c.40)

Diseases of Animals (Ireland) Act 1914 (c.40)

Diseases of Fish Act 1937 (c.33)

Diseases of Fish Act 1983 (c.30)

Diseases Prevention Act 1855 (c.116)

Diseases Prevention (Metropolis) Act 1883 (c.35)

Disfranchisement of Freemen, Great Yarmouth Act 1848 (c.24)

Disfranchisement of St. Alban's Act 1852 (c.9)

Disorderly Houses Act 1751 (c.36)

Dispensary Committees (Ireland) Act 1896 (c.10)

Dispensary Houses (Ireland) Act 1879 (c.25)

Disposal of Ulysses Fitzmaurice's Intestate Estate Act 1774 (c.40)

Disposal of Uncollected Goods Act 1952 (c.43)

Disposition of Copyhold Estates by Will Act 1815 (c.192)

Disputes Between Masters and Workmen Act 1800 (c.90)

Dissolved Boards of Management and Guardians Act 1870 (c.2)

Distemper Amongst Cattle Act 1745 (c.5)
Distemper Amongst Cattle Act 1746 (c.4)
Distemper Amongst Cattle Act 1749 (c.23)
Distemper Amongst Cattle Act 1750 (c.31)
Distemper Amongst Cattle Act 1754 (c.14)
Distemper Amongst Cattle Act 1755 (c.18)
Distemper Amongst Cattle Act 1757 (c.20)
Distemper Amongst Cattle Act 1770 (c.4)
Distemper Amongst Cattle Act 1770 (c.45)
Distillation Act 1757 (c.10)
Distillation Act 1757 (c.15)
Distillation Act 1759 (c.9)
Distillation, etc. Act 1702 (c.14)
Distillation, etc. Act 1774 (c.73)
Distillation, etc. of Spirits (Ireland) Act 1813 (c.52)
Distillation from Corn, etc. Act 1812 (c.118)
Distillation from Corn Prohibition, etc. Act 1812 (c.7)
Distillation from Wheat, etc. Act 1799 (c.7)
Distillation from Wheat, etc. Act 1800 (c.21)
Distillation from Wheat, etc., Prohibition Act 1795 (c.20)
Distillation from Wheat (Ireland) Act 1801 (c.15)
Distillation (Ireland) Act 1812 (c.47)
Distillation of Spirits Act 1803 (c.11)
Distillation of Spirits Act 1805 (c.100)
Distillation of Spirits Act 1808 (c.118)
Distillation of Spirits Act 1809 (c.7)
Distillation of Spirits Act 1809 (c.24)
Distillation of Spirits Act 1810 (c.5)
Distillation of Spirits Act 1812 (c.3)
Distillation of Spirits from Sugar Act 1847 (c.6)
Distillation of Spirits from Sugar, etc. Act 1848 (c.100)
Distillation of Spirits (Ireland) Act 1813 (c.145)
Distillation of Spirits (Ireland) Act 1813 (c.148)
Distillation of Spirits (Ireland) Act 1814 (c.150)
Distillation of Spirits (Ireland) Act 1815 (c.151)
Distillation of Spirits (Ireland) Act 1816 (c.112)
Distillation of Spirits (Scotland) Act 1808 (c.10)
Distillation of Spirits (Scotland) Act 1810 (c.79)
Distillation of Spirits (Scotland) Act 1813 (c.9)
Distilleries, etc. Act 1793 (c.61)
Distillers Act 1746 (c.39)
Distillers Act 1779 (c.50)
Distillers of Spirits Act 1811 (c.42)
Distress (Costs) Act 1817 (c.93)
Distress for Rates Act 1849 (c.14)
Distress for Rent Act 1737 (c.19)
Distress for Rent Act 1960 (c.12)
Distressed Unions Advances (Ireland) Act 1850 (c.14)
Distressed Unions (Ireland) Act 1852 (c.68)

Distresses Under Justices' Warrants Act 1754 (c.20)
Distribution of Certain Monies Act 1803 (c.39)
Distribution of Industry Act 1944 (c.36)
Distribution of Industry (Industrial Finance) Act 1958 (c.41)
District Auditors Act 1879 (c.6)
District Church Tithes Act 1865 (c.42)
District Councillors and Guardians (Term of Office) Act 1900 (c.16)
District Councils (Water Supply Facilities) Act 1897 (c.44)
District Courts and Prisons Act 1842 (c.53)
District Courts and Prisons Act 1844 (c.50)
District Courts (Scotland) Act 1975 (c.20)
Distribution of Germany Enemy Property Act 1949 (c.85)
Distribution of Industry Act 1950 (c.8)
Disused Burial Grounds Act 1884 (c.72)
Disused Burial Grounds (Amendment) Act 1981 (c.18)
Disused Public Buildings (Ireland) Act 1808 (c.113)
Divided Parishes and Poor Law Amendment Act 1876 (c.61)
Divided Parishes and Poor Law Amendment Act 1882 (c.58)
Dividends Act 1978 (c.54)
Dividends and Stock Act 1869 (c.104)
Dividends and Stock Act 1870 (c.47)
Division of Deanery of St. Burian Act 1850 (c.76)
Divorce Amendment Act 1868 (c.77)
Divorce (Insanity and Desertion) Act 1958 (c.54)
Divorce Jurisdiction, Court Fees and Legal Aid (Scotland) Act 1983 (c.12)
Divorce Reform Act 1969 (c.55)
Divorce (Scotland) Act 1938 (c.50)
Divorce (Scotland) Act 1964 (c.91)
Divorce (Scotland) Act 1976 (c.39)
Dock Work Regulation Act 1976 (c.79)
Dock Workers (Pensions) Act 1960 (c.39)
Dock Workers (Regulation of Employment) Act 1946 (c.22)
Docking and Nicking of Horses Act 1949 (c.70)
Docks and Harbours Act 1966 (c.28)
Docks and Ordnance Service Act 1804 (c.79)
Docks, etc., at Chatham, etc. Act 1806 (c.130)
Dockyard Act 1865 (c.25)
Dockyard Ports Regulation Act 1865 (c.125)
Dockyard Services Act 1986 (c.52)
Dockyards, etc., Protection Act 1772 (c.24)
Dockyards Protection Act Amendment Act 1863 (c.30)
Doctrine of the Trinity Act 1813 (c.160)
Documentary Evidence Act 1868 (c.37)
Documentary Evidence Act 1882 (c.9)
Documentary Evidence Act 1895 (c.9)
Dog Licences Act 1959 (c.55)
Dog Licences Act 1867 (c.5)

Dog Racecourse Betting (Temporary Provisions) Act 1947 (c.20)
Dog Stealing Act 1770 (c.18)
Dog Stealing Act 1845 (c.47)
Dogs Act 1865 (c.60)
Dogs Act 1871 (c.56)
Dogs Act 1906 (c.32)
Dogs (Amendment) Act 1928 (c.21)
Dogs Amendment Act 1938 (c.21)
Dogs (Ireland) Act 1862 (c.59)
Dogs (Ireland) Act 1867 (c.116)
Dogs (Protection of Livestock) Act 1953 (c.28)
Dogs Regulation (Ireland) Act 1865 (c.50)
Dogs Regulation (Ireland) Act 1919 (c.81)
Dogs (Scotland) Act 1863 (c.100)
Domestic and Appellate Proceedings (Restriction of Publicity) Act 1968 (c.63)
Domestic Proceedings and Magistrates' Courts Act 1978 (c.22)
Domestic Violence and Matrimonial Proceedings Act 1976 (c.50)
Domicile Act 1861 (c.121)
Domicile and Matrimonial Proceedings Act 1973 (c.45)
Dominica Act 1938 (c.10)
Dominica Loan Act 1860 (c.57)
Dominica Loan Act 1867 (c.91)
Doncaster and Tadcaster Road Act 1740 (c.28)
Doncaster Road and Bridges Act 1795 (c.158)
Doncaster Roads Act 1785 (c.104)
Doncaster: Small Debts, Lighting, etc. Act 1763 (c.40)
Doncaster to Bawtry Road Act 1776 (c.71)
Doncaster to Chester Road Act 1789 (c.98)
Donnington to Southall Canal Act 1788 (c.73)
Dorchester Bridge and Causeway Act 1745 (c.24)
Dorchester: Streets Act 1776 (c.27)
Dorset and Devon Roads Act 1757 (c.43)
Dorset and Devon Roads Act 1765 (c.75)
Dorset and Somerset Roads Act 1765 (c.102)
Dorset and Somerset Roads Act 1767 (c.82)
Dorset and Wilts: Canal Act 1796 (c.47)
Dorset, Devon and Somerset Roads Act 1777 (c.89)
Dorset, etc., Roads Act 1762 (c.61)
Dorset Roads Act 1758 (c.50)
Dorset Roads Act 1760 (c.24)
Dorset Roads Act 1766 (c.68)
Dorset Roads Act 1766 (c.92)
Dorset Roads Act 1769 (c.47)
Dorset Roads Act 1777 (c.103)
Dorset Roads Act 1782 (c.101)
Dorset Roads Act 1788 (c.91)
Dorset Roads Act 1790 (c.95)
Dover and Rye Harbours Act 1764 (c.72)
Dover, Deal and Sandwich Road Act 1797 (c.156)
Dover Harbour Act 1703 (c.7)
Dover Harbour Act 1717 (c.13)

Dover Harbour Act 1722 (c.30)
Dover Harbour Act 1737 (c.7)
Dover Harbour Act 1757 (c.8)
Dover Harbour Act 1786 (c.11)
Dover Harbour Act 1794 (c.112)
Dover Streets Act 1778 (c.76)
Doveridge Roads, Derby Act 1769 (c.59)
Downpatrick Election Committee Act 1815 (c.98)
Drafts on Bankers Act 1856 (c.25)
Drafts on Bankers Act 1858 (c.79)
Drainage and Improvement of Land (Ireland) Act 1866 (c.40)
Drainage and Improvement of Land (Ireland) Act 1892 (c.65)
Drainage and Improvement of Land, Supplemental (Ireland) Act 1865 (c.13)
Drainage and Improvement of Land, Supplemental (Ireland) Act 1865 (c.50)
Drainage and Improvement of Land, Supplemental (Ireland) Act 1867 (c.43)
Drainage and Improvement of Lands Amendment (Ireland) Act 1865 (c.52)
Drainage and Improvement of Lands Amendment (Ireland) Act 1869 (c.72)
Drainage and Improvement of Lands Amendment (Ireland) Act 1872 (c.31)
Drainage and Improvement of Lands Amendment (Ireland) Act 1874 (c.32)
Drainage and Improvement of Lands (Ireland) Act 1853 (c.130)
Drainage and Improvement of Lands (Ireland) Act 1855 (c.110)
Drainage and Improvement of Lands (Ireland) Act 1863 (c.88)
Drainage and Improvement of Lands (Ireland) Act 1864 (c.72)
Drainage and Improvement of Lands (Ireland) Act 1878 (c.59)
Drainage and Improvement of Lands (Ireland) Act 1880 (c.27)
Drainage and Improvement of Lands Supplemental Act 1866 (c.61)
Drainage and Improvement of Lands, Supplemental (Ireland) Act 1864 (c.107)
Drainage and Improvement of Lands, Supplemental (Ireland) Act 1867 (c.139)
Drainage: Cambridge, Isle of Ely Act 1772 (c.26)
Drainage, etc. (Ireland) Act 1847 (c.106)
Drainage (Ireland) Act 1842 (c.89)
Drainage (Ireland) Act 1846 (c.4)
Drainage (Ireland) Act 1847 (c.79)
Drainage (Ireland) Act 1856 (c.62)
Drainage: Isle of Ely Act 1772 (c.27)
Drainage Haddenham Level Act 1726 (c.18)
Drainage Maintenance Act 1866 (c.49)
Drainage of Bogs, etc. (Ireland) Act 1809 (c.102)
Drainage of Lands Act 1849 (c.100)
Drainage Rates Act 1958 (c.37)
Drainage Rates Act 1962 (c.39)
Drainage Rates Act 1963 (c.10)

Drainage Rates (Disabled Persons) Act 1986 (c.17)
Dramatic and Musical Performers' Protection Act 1925 (c.46)
Dramatic and Musical Performers' Protection Act 1958 (c.44)
Dramatic and Musical Performers' Protection Act 1972 (c.32)
Drawback Act 1795 (c.98)
Drawback Act 1795 (c.110)
Drawback Act 1796 (c.106)
Drawback Act 1806 (c.114)
Drawback Act 1807 (c.49)
Drawback, etc. on Glass Act 1812 (c.77)
Drawback of Duties Act 1795 (c.39)
Drawback of Duty on Coals Act 1811 (c.83)
Drawback on Chocolate Act 1812 (c.11)
Drawback on Coals Act 1813 (c.18)
Drawback on Linens Act 1805 (c.98)
Drawback on Paper Act 1814 (c.153)
Drawback on Wines Act 1813 (c.44)
Drawbacks Act 1802 (c.17)
Drawbacks Act 1802 (c.60)
Drawbacks Act 1803 (c.5)
Drawbacks Act 1803 (c.10)
Drawbacks Act 1807 (c.20)
Drawbacks Act 1807 (c.62)
Drawbacks Act 1808 (c.43)
Drawbacks and Bounties Act 1795 (c.18)
Drawbacks and Bounties Act 1802 (c.11)
Drawbacks and Bounties Act 1805 (c.93)
Drawbacks, etc. Act 1798 (c.61)
Drawbacks, etc. (Ireland) Act 1805 (c.23)
Drawbacks, etc., on Sugar Act 1811 (c.12)
Drawbacks, etc. on Tobacco, etc. Act 1815 (c.129)
Drawbacks (Ireland) Act 1806 (c.14)
Drawbacks (Ireland) Act 1807 (c.19)
Drawbacks on Paper Act 1814 (c.106)
Drawbacks on Spirits Act 1811 (c.121)
Drawbacks upon Sugar Act 1806 (c.10)
Drayton and Edgehill Road Act 1753 (c.78)
Drill Grounds Act 1886 (c.5)
Driving of Cattle, Metropolis Act 1774 (c.87)
Driving of Cattle, Metropolis Act 1781 (c.67)
Droitwich Roads Act 1768 (c.39)
Drought Act 1976 (c.44)
Drouly Fund Act 1838 (c.89)
Drugging of Animals Act 1876 (c.13)
Drugs (Prevention of Misuse) Act 1964 (c.64)
Drug Trafficking Act 1994 (c.37)
Drug Trafficking Offences Act 1986 (c.32)
Drury Lane Theatre Act 1776 (c.13)
Dublin Amended Carriage Act 1854 (c.45)
Dublin Amended Carriage Act 1855 (c.65)
Dublin and Other Roads Turnpikes Abolition Act 1855 (c.69)
Dublin Baronies Act 1842 (c.96)
Dublin Carriage Act 1853 (c.112)
Dublin, Collection of Rates Act 1849 (c.91)
Dublin Collector-General of Rates Act 1870 (c.11)
Dublin Corporation Act 1849 (c.85)

Dublin Corporation Act 1850 (c.81)
Dublin Foundling Hospital 1814 (c.128)
Dublin, Four Courts Act 1858 (c.84)
Dublin General Post Office Act 1808 (c.48)
Dublin General Post Office Act 1809 (c.70)
Dublin Grand Jury Act 1845 (c.81)
Dublin Harbour Act 1815 (c.191)
Dublin Harbour Act 1816 (c.62)
Dublin Hospitals Act 1856 (c.110)
Dublin, Hotels and Restaurants Act 1910 (c.33)
Dublin Improvement Act 1849 (c.97)
Dublin Improvement Act 1861 (c.26)
Dublin Justices Act 1840 (c.103)
Dublin Justices Act 1875 (c.20)
Dublin National Gallery Act 1865 (c.71)
Dublin Parliamentary Revising Act 1853 (c.58)
Dublin Paying, etc., Inquiry Act 1806 (c.68)
Dublin, Phoenix Park Act 1860 (c.42)
Dublin Police Act 1836 (c.29)
Dublin Police Act 1837 (c.25)
Dublin Police Act 1839 (c.78)
Dublin Police Act 1842 (c.24)
Dublin Police Act 1848 (c.113)
Dublin Police Act 1859 (c.52)
Dublin Police District Act 1838 (c.63)
Dublin Police Magistrates Act 1808 (c.140)
Dublin, Public Offices Site Act 1903 (c.16)
Dublin, Purchase of Land Act 1841 (c.16)
Dublin Reconstruction Act 1916 (c.66)
Dublin Record Office Act 1814 (c.63)
Dublin Revising Barristers Act 1857 (c.68)
Dublin Revising Barristers Act 1861 (c.56)
Dublin, Sale of Game Act 1865 (c.2)
Dublin, Sale of Property Act 1842 (c.62)
Dublin Science and Art Museum Act 1884 (c.6)
Dublin, Site of Record Office Act 1814 (c.113)
Dublin Tramways Act 1876 (c.65)
Dublin Voters Disfranchisement Act 1870 (c.54)
Duchess of Kent's Annuity Act 1838 (c.8)
Duchies of Lancaster and Cornwall (Accounts) Act 1838 (c.101)
Duchy of Cornwall Act 1700 (c.13)
Duchy of Cornwall Act 1707 (c.52)
Duchy of Cornwall Act 1713 (c.25)
Duchy of Cornwall Act 1715 (c.37)
Duchy of Cornwall Act 1750 (c.50)
Duchy of Cornwall Act 1759 (c.10)
Duchy of Cornwall Act 1768 (c.26)
Duchy of Cornwall Act 1776 (c.10)
Duchy of Cornwall Act 1812 (c.123)
Duchy of Cornwall Act 1844 (c.65)
Duchy of Cornwall Act 1860 (c.53)
Duchy of Cornwall Lands Act 1862 (c.49)
Duchy of Cornwall Leases, etc. Act 1842 (c.2)
Duchy of Cornwall (Limitation of Actions, etc.) Act 1860 (c.53)
Duchy of Cornwall Management Act 1863 (c.49)
Duchy of Cornwall Management Act 1868 (c.35)

Duchy of Cornwall Management Act 1893 (c.20)

Duchy of Cornwall Management Act 1982 (c.47)

Duchy of Cornwall (No. 2) Act 1844 (c.105)

Duchy of Cornwall Office Act 1854 (c.93)

Duchy of Lancaster Lands Act 1855 (c.58)

Duchy of Lancaster Act 1779 (c.45)

Duchy of Lancaster Act 1787 (c.34)

Duchy of Lancaster Act 1796 (c.97)

Duchy of Lancaster Act 1808 (c.73)

Duchy of Lancaster Act 1812 (c.161)

Duchy of Lancaster Act 1920 (c.51)

Duchy of Lancaster Act 1988 (c.10)

Duchy of Lancaster (Application of Capital Moneys) Act 1921 (c.45)

Duchy of Lancaster (Precinct of Savoy) Act 1772 (c.42)

Dudley Canal Act 1776 (c.66)

Dudley Canal Act 1785 (c.87)

Dudley Canal Act 1796 (c.13)

Dudley: Improvement Act 1791 (c.79)

Duke of Connaught, Annuity Act 1878 (c.46)

Duke of Connaught's Leave Act 1887 (c.10)

Duke of Grafton's Annuity Act 1806 (c.79)

Duke of Marlborough; Pension Act 1706 (c.7)

Duke of Marlborough's Annuity Act 1839 (c.94)

Duke of Richmond's Annuity Act 1800 (c.43)

Duke of Wellington, Purchase of Estate for Act 1815 (c.186)

Duke of York's School (Chapel) Act 1910 (c.16)

Dulwich College Act 1857 (c.84)

Dunbar Beer Duties Act 1718 (c.16)

Dumbarton Road and Bridges Act 1786 (c.21)

Dumfries and Roxburgh Roads Act 1764 (c.85)

Dumfries Beer Duties Act 1716 (c.6)

Dumfries Beer Duties Act 1736 (c.7)

Dumfries Beer Duties Act 1762 (c.55)

Dumfries Beer Duties Act 1787 (c.57)

Dumfries Roads Act 1777 (c.107)

Dumfries Roads Act 1785 (c.120)

Dumfries Roads Act 1788 (c.114)

Dumfries Roads Act 1789 (c.87)

Dumping at Sea Act 1974 (c.20)

Dunbar Beer Duties Act 1736 (c.4)

Dunbar Beer Duties Act 1764 (c.46)

Dunbar Harbour Loan Act 1857 (c.63)

Dunbar Water Supply Act 1768 (c.57)

Dunchurch to Southam Road Act 1794 (c.128)

Dunchurch to Stone Bridge Road Act 1770 (c.90)

Dundee Beer Duties Act 1730 (c.11)

Dundee Beer Duties Act 1746 (c.17)

Dundee Beer Duties Act 1776 (c.16)

Dunstable Highways Act 1710 (c.34)

Dunstable Highways Act 1713 (c.29)

Dunstable Roads Act 1722 (c.11)

Dunstable to Hockliffe Road Act 1792 (c.159)

Durham and Northumberland Roads Act 1792 (c.113)

Durham and Tyne Bridge Road Act 1753 (c.48)

Durham Chancery Act 1869 (c.84)

Durham (County Palatine) Act 1836 (c.19)

Durham County Palatine Act 1858 (c.45)

Durham Roads Act 1747 (c.5)

Durham Roads Act 1749 (c.27)

Durham Roads Act 1750 (c.30)

Durham Roads Act 1754 (c.29)

Durham Roads Act 1756 (c.70)

Durham Roads Act 1759 (c.56)

Durham Roads Act 1773 (c.99)

Durham Roads Act 1777 (c.110)

Durham Roads Act 1789 (c.81)

Durham Roads Act 1792 (c.127)

Durham Roads Act 1793 (c.148)

Durham Roads Act 1793 (c.161)

Durham Roads Act 1795 (c.139)

Durham: Streets Act 1790 (c.67)

Durham to Tyne Bridge Road Act 1746 (c.12)

Duties and Drawbacks Act 1799 (c.12)

Duties and Drawbacks (Ireland) Act 1806 (c.12)

Duties and Drawbacks (Ireland) Act 1806 (c.62)

Duties, Bounties, etc. (Ireland) Act 1806 (c.120)

Duties Continuance Act 1801 (c.17)

Duties Continuance Act 1802 (c.31)

Duties Continuance Act 1803 (c.24)

Duties, Drawbacks, etc. (Ireland) Act 1809 (c.74)

Duties, etc. Act 1743 (c.31)

Duties, etc., India Act 1814 (c.105)

Duties, etc. (Ireland) Act 1803 (c.92)

Duties, etc., on Coffee, etc. Act 1802 (c.83)

Duties, etc., on Foreign Liquors, etc. Act 1812 (c.159)

Duties, etc., on Glass, etc. Act 1815 (c.113)

Duties, etc., on Glass (Ireland) Act 1814 (c.87)

Duties, etc., on Malt, etc. (Ireland) Act 1807 (c.40)

Duties, etc., on Soap Act 1816 (c.44)

Duties, etc., on Sugar, etc. Act 1803 (c.42)

Duties, etc., on Tobacco (Ireland) Act 1813 (c.73)

Duties in American Colonies Act 1765 (c.12)

Duties in American Colonies Act 1766 (c.11)

Duties (Logwood, etc.) Act 1766 (c.47)

Duties of Customs Act 1845 (c.90)

Duties of Customs and Tonnage Act 1802 (c.43)

Duties of Prisage and Butlerage (Ireland) Act (c.94)

Duties on Auctioneers, etc. Act 1803 (c.130)

Duties on Auctions (Ireland) Act 1808 (c.63)

Duties on Beer, etc. Act 1802 (c.38)

Duties on Beetroot Sugar Act 1837 (c.57)

Duties on Bricks Act 1839 (c.24)

Duties on Bricks and Tiles Act 1784 (c.24)

Duties on Bricks and Tiles Act 1785 (c.66)

Duties on Bricks and Tiles Act 1794 (c.15)

Duties on Buckwheat, etc. Act 1847 (c.3)

Duties on Calicoes, etc. Act 1807 (c.47)

Duties on Candles Act 1784 (c.36)

Duties on Candles Act 1792 (c.7)

Duties on Cape Wines Act 1813 (c.84)

Duties on Carriages, etc. (Ireland) Act 1813 (c.59)

Duties on Certain Goods Act 1806 (c.42)

Duties on Certain Licences Act 1784 (c.41)

Duties on Certain Licences Act 1808 (c.143)

Duties on Certain Woods, etc. Act 1811 (c.43)

Duties on Cider, etc. Act 1766 (c.14)

Duties on Cinnamon, etc. Act 1798 (c.68)

Duties on Cinnamon, etc. Act 1802 (c.24)

Duties on Cinnamon, etc. Act 1808 (c.18)

Duties on Clocks and Watches Act 1797 (c.108)

Duties on Coach Makers' Licences, etc. 1785 (c.49)

Duties on Coals, etc. Act 1785 (c.54)

Duties on Coals, etc. Act 1812 (c.9)

Duties on Copper and Lead Act 1848 (c.127)

Duties on Corn Act 1842 (c.14)

Duties on Corn, etc. Act 1847 (c.64)

Duties on Distillation Act 1800 (c.73)

Duties on Distilleries Act 1797 (c.11)

Duties on Distilleries Act 1797 (c.31)

Duties on Distilleries Act 1799 (c.31)

Duties on Distilleries (Scotland) Act 1799 (c.78)

Duties on Distilleries (Scotland), etc. Act 1796 (c.17)

Duties on Dogs Act 1796 (c.124)

Duties on East India Goods Act 1707 (c.37)

Duties on Epsom Salts Act 1815 (c.162)

Duties on Foreign Cambrics, etc. Act 1741 (c.29)

Duties on Foreign Hops Act 1800 (c.82)

Duties on Foreign Packets Act 1816 (c.9)

Duties on Game Certificates Act 1803 (c.23)

Duties on Glass Act 1795 (c.114)

Duties on Glass Act 1805 (c.122)·

Duties on Glass Act 1811 (c.69)

Duties on Glass Act 1812 (c.54)

Duties on Glass Act 1813 (c.109)

Duties on Glass Act 1839 (c.25)

Duties on Glass Act 1840 (c.22)

Duties on Glass, etc. Act 1800 (c.45)

Duties on Glass, etc. (Ireland) Act 1814 (c.7)

Duties on Glass (Great Britain) Act 1814 (c.97)

Duties on Glass (Great Britain) Act 1816 (c.1)

Duties on Hair Powder, etc. Act 1800 (c.32)

Duties on Hats, etc., Repeal (Ireland) Act 1811 (c.60)

Duties on Hides, etc. Act 1815 (c.105)

Duties on Hides, etc. (Ireland) Act 1813 (c.60)

Duties on Hops Act 1800 (c.4)

Duties on Horse Dealers' Licences Act 1795 (c.17)

Duties on Horses Act 1784 (c.31)

Duties on Horses Act 1795 (cc.15, 16)

Duties on Horses Act 1797 (c.106)

Duties on Horses and Carriage Act 1789 (c.49)

Duties on Horses, etc. Act 1802 (c.100)

Duties on Horses Let for Hire Act 1853 (c.88)

Duties on Houses, etc. Act 1779 (c.59)

Duties on Houses, etc. Act 1786 (c.79)

Duties on Importation, etc. Act 1791 (c.42)

Duties on Income Act 1799 (c.13)

Duties on Income Act 1799 (c.22)

Duties on Income Act 1799 (c.42)

Duties on Income Act 1799 (c.72)

Duties on Income Act 1800 (c.49)

Duties on Income Act 1800 (c.96)

Duties on Kid Skins Act 1800 (c.63)

Duties on Killing Game Act 1814 (c.141)

Duties on Leather Act 1815 (c.102)

Duties on Linens Act 1784 (c.40)

Duties on Linens Act 1785 (c.72)

Duties on Madder Act 1816 (c.69)

Duties on Mahogany, etc. Act 1812 (c.36)

Duties on Malt Act 1803 (c.16)

Duties on Malt Act 1805 (c.1)

Duties on Malt Act 1806 (c.2)

Duties on Malt Act 1807 (c.3)

Duties on Malt, etc. Act 1780 (c.35)

Duties on Malt, etc. Act 1795 (c.1)

Duties on Malt, etc. Act 1796 (c.1)

Duties on Malt, etc. Act 1797 (c.4)

Duties on Malt, etc. Act 1801 (c.1)

Duties on Malt, etc. Act 1802 (c.3)

Duties on Malt, etc. Act 1805 (c.22)

Duties on Malt, etc. Act 1808 (c.2)

Duties on Malt, etc. Act 1809 (c.1)

Duties on Malt, etc. Act 1810 (c.1)

Duties on Malt, etc. Act 1811 (c.2)

Duties on Malt, etc. Act 1812 (c.1)

Duties on Malt, etc. Act 1812 (c.15)

Duties on Malt, etc. Act 1813 (c.2)

Duties on Malt, etc. Act 1814 (c.3)

Duties on Malt, etc. Act 1816 (c.3)

Duties on Malt, etc. Act 1816 (c.43)

Duties on Malt (Ireland) Act 1815 (c.99)

Duties on Norway Timber Act 1811 (c.93)

Duties on Offices and Pensions Act 1836 (c.97)

Duties on Paper Act 1805 (c.106)

Duties on Paper Act 1839 (c.23)

Duties on Paper (Ireland) Act 1815 (c.112)

Duties on Paper (Ireland) Act 1816 (c.78)

Duties on Pensions, etc. Act 1798 (c.3)

Duties on Pensions, etc. Act 1799 (c.3)

Duties on Pensions, etc. Act 1801 (c.2)

Duties on Pensions, etc. Act 1802 (c.4)

Duties on Pensions, etc. Act 1803 (c.17)

Duties on Pensions, etc. Act 1805 (c.2)

Duties on Pensions, etc. Act 1806 (c.3)

Duties on Pensions, etc. Act 1807 (c.4)

Duties on Plate Act 1797 (c.24)

Duties on Post Horses, etc. Act 1785 (c.51)

Duties on Property, etc. Act 1816 (c.65)

Duties on Property, etc. (Great Britain) Act 1815 (c.53)

Duties on Rape Seed, etc. Act 1816 (c.75)
Duties on Rape Seed, etc. Act 1816 (c.79)
Duties on Rum, etc. Act 1802 (c.20)
Duties on Rum, etc. Act 1841 (c.8)
Duties on Salt Act 1703 (c.16)
Duties on Salt Act 1795 (c.19)
Duties on Salt Act 1798 (c.43)
Duties on Salt, etc. Act 1706 (c.29)
Duties on Scotch Distilleries Act 1795 (c.59)
Duties on Servants Act 1780 (c.31)
Duties on Servants Act 1785 (c.43)
Duties on Servants Act 1785 (c.70)
Duties on Servants Act 1791 (c.3)
Duties on Servants Act 1797 (c.107)
Duties on Servants Act 1798 (c.80)
Duties on Servants, etc. Act 1797 (c.41)
Duties on Servants, etc. Act 1802 (c.37)
Duties on Shops Act 1785 (c.30)
Duties on Shops Act 1786 (c.9)
Duties on Shops Act 1789 (c.9)
Duties on Smalts, etc. Act 1783 (c.75)
Duties on Soap Act 1839 (c.63)
Duties on Soap Act 1840 (c.49)
Duties on Soap, etc. Act 1776 (c.52)
Duties on Spanish Red Wine Act 1805 (c.67)
Duties on Spirit Licences Act 1787 (c.30)
Duties on Spirit Mixtures, etc. Act 1842 (c.25)
Duties on Spirits Act 1784 (c.46)
Duties on Spirits Act 1795 (c.89)
Duties on Spirits Act 1799 (c.8)
Duties on Spirits Act 1808 (c.115)
Duties on Spirits Act 1808 (c.119)
Duties on Spirits Act 1811 (c.59)
Duties on Spirits Act 1843 (c.49)
Duties on Spirits Act 1845 (c.65)
Duties on Spirits Act 1848 (c.60)
Duties on Spirits and Coffee Act 1808 (cc.121, 122)
Duties on Spirits, etc. Act 1794 (cc.3, 4)
Duties on Spirits, etc. Act 1842 (c.15)
Duties on Spirits, etc. Act 1853 (c.37)
Duties on Spirits, etc. (Scotland) Act 1815 (c.155)
Duties on Spirits, etc. (Scotland) Act 1816 (c.106)
Duties on Spirits (Great Britain) Act 1813 (c.147)
Duties on Spirits (Ireland) Act 1806 (c.56)
Duties on Spirits (Ireland) Act 1806 (c.88)
Duties on Spirits (Ireland) Act 1807 (c.17)
Duties on Spirits (Ireland) Act 1808 (c.81)
Duties on Spirits (Ireland) Act 1809 (c.73)
Duties on Spirits (Ireland) Act 1810 (c.15)
Duties on Spirits (Ireland) Act 1812 (c.46)
Duties on Spirits (Ireland) Act 1812 (c.48)
Duties on Spirits (Ireland) Act 1814 (c.88)
Duties on Spirits (Ireland) Act 1815 (c.111)
Duties on Spirits (Ireland) Act 1816 (c.111)
Duties on Spirits (Scotland) Act 1814 (c.172)
Duties on Spirituous Liquors (Ireland) Act 1805 (c.104)
Duties on Starch Act 1779 (c.40)
Duties on Starch Act 1786 (c.51)

Duties on Starch and Soap Act 1784 (c.48)
Duties on Stills, etc. (Scotland) Act 1806 (c.102)
Duties on Stone Bottles Act 1812 (c.139)
Duties on Sugar Act 1813 (c.62)
Duties on Sugar Act 1845 (c.13)
Duties on Sugar Act 1865 (c.95)
Duties on Sugar Act 1867 (c.10)
Duties on Sugar, etc. Act 1799 (c.63)
Duties on Sugar, etc. Act 1800 (c.48)
Duties on Sugar, etc. Act 1802 (c.47)
Duties on Sweets, etc. (Ireland) Act 1815 (c.110)
Duties on Tea, etc. (American Plantations) Act 1766 (c.46)
Duties on Tobacco Act 1785 (c.81)
Duties on Tobacco Act 1811 (c.56)
Duties on Tobacco and Snuff Act 1789 (c.68)
Duties on Waggons, etc. Act 1783 (c.66)
Duties on Wagons, etc. Act 1792 (c.4)
Duties on Wash Made From Sugar Act 1800 (c.61)
Duties on Wheat, etc. Act 1843 (c.29)
Duties on Windows, etc. Act 1802 (c.34)
Duties on Wines, etc. Act 1783 (c.76)
Duties on Wines, etc. Act 1796 (c.123)
Duties on Worts or Wash Act 1808 (c.152)
Duties on Worts, Spirits, etc. Act 1791 (c.1)
Duties on Worts, Wash, etc. Act 1794 (c.2)
Duties upon Candles Act 1784 (c.11)
Duties upon East India Goods Act 1814 (c.10)
Duties upon Malt, etc. Act 1798 (c.2)
Duties upon Malt, etc. Act 1799 (c.2)
Duties upon Silks Act 1808 (c.117)
Duty of Spirits, Newfoundland Act 1812 (c.106)
Duty on Almanacks Act 1781 (c.56)
Duty on Coffee, etc., Warehoused Act 1807 (c.52)
Duty on Copper Act 1811 (c.31)
Duty on Corks Act 1816 (c.34)
Duty on Cotton Stuffs, etc. Act 1774 (c.72)
Duty on Foreign Spirits Act 1815 (c.164)
Duty on Hair Powder Act 1795 (c.49)
Duty on Hats Act 1796 (c.125)
Duty on Hats, etc., Repeal (Great Britain) Act 1811 (c.70)
Duty on Hawkers, etc. Act 1789 (c.26)
Duty on Hops Act 1805 (c.94)
Duty on Horses Act 1797 (c.134)
Duty on Horses Act 1801 (c.9)
Duty on Houses Act 1806 (c.36)
Duty on Lead (Great Britain) Act 1816 (c.18)
Duty on Linen Act 1811 (c.44)
Duty on Malt Act 1812 (c.9)
Duty on Malt (Ireland) Act 1804 (c.28)
Duty on Malt (Ireland) Act 1813 (c.74)
Duty on Malt (Ireland) Act 1816 (c.59)
Duty on Oil, etc. Act 1816 (c.118)
Duty on Paper Act 1816 (c.103)
Duty on Paper Hangings, etc. (Ireland) Act 1815 (c.106)
Duty on Pensions, etc. Act 1800 (c.8)

Duty on Pensions, etc. Act 1800 (c.31)
Duty on Racehorses Act 1856 (c.82)
Duty on Racehorses Act 1857 (c.16)
Duty on Rice Act 1812 (c.10)
Duty on Salt Act 1812 (c.107)
Duty on Salt Act 1813 (c.21)
Duty on Servants Act 1778 (c.30)
Duty on Silk Handkerchiefs Act 1815 (c.93)
Duty on Spanish Red Wines Act 1805 (c.107)
Duty on Spirits Act 1788 (c.4)
Duty on Spirits (Ireland) Act 1813 (c.94)
Duty on Spirits (Ireland) Act 1815 (c.139)
Duty on Stage Carriages Act 1839 (c.66)
Duty on Sugar Act 1809 (c.61)
Duty on Sugar, etc. Act 1810 (c.61)
Duty on Taxed Carts Act 1798 (c.93)
Duty on Tiles Act 1815 (c.176)
Duty on Tobacco Act 1794 (c.55)
Duty on Tobacco and Snuff Act 1790 (c.40)
Duty on Woollen Goods Act 1805 (c.82)
Duty on Worts, etc. Act 1801 (c.5)
Dwelling-houses for the Working Classes (Scotland) Act 1855 (c.88)
Dyeing Trade Act 1726 (c.24)
Dyeing Trade (Frauds) Act 1783 (c.15)
Dyers Act 1776 (c.33)
Dyestuffs (Import Regulations) Act 1920 (c.77)
Dyestuffs (Import Regulations) Act 1934 (c.6)
Dygart Beer Duties Act 1753 (c.44)

Ealing Church Act 1738 (c.7)
Ealing Roads Act 1767 (c.75)
Earl of Clanriccard's Estates Act 1708 (c.29)
Earldom of Mar Act 1885 (c.48)
East Africa Loans Act 1926 (c.62)
East Africa Loans (Amendment) Act 1931 (c.21)
East African Protectorates (Loans) Act 1914 (c.38)
East and West Flegg: Poor Relief Act 1775 (c.13)
East Greenwich Church: Burial Act 1751 (c.11)
East Grinstead Church Act 1790 (c.79)
East India Act 1797 (c.142)
East India Annuity Funds Act 1874 (c.12)
East India Company Act 1707 (c.71)
East India Company Act 1711 (c.35)
East India Company Act 1730 (c.14)
East India Company Act 1767 (c.49)
East India Company Act 1767 (c.57)
East India Company Act 1768 (c.11)
East India Company Act 1769 (c.24)
East India Company Act 1770 (c.47)
East India Company Act 1772 (c.7)
East India Company Act 1772 (c.9)
East India Company Act 1772 (c.63)
East India Company Act 1772 (c.64)
East India Company Act 1775 (c.44)
East India Company Act 1776 (c.8)
East India Company Act 1776 (c.51)

East India Company Act 1779 (c.61)
East India Company Act 1780 (c.56)
East India Company Act 1780 (c.58)
East India Company Act 1780 (c.70)
East India Company Act 1781 (c.65)
East India Company Act 1782 (c.51)
East India Company Act 1783 (c.2)
East India Company Act 1783 (c.3)
East India Company Act 1783 (c.36)
East India Company Act 1783 (c.83)
East India Company Act 1784 (c.25)
East India Company Act 1784 (c.34)
East India Company Act 1786 (c.16)
East India Company Act 1786 (c.57)
East India Company Act 1788 (c.8)
East India Company Act 1788 (c.29)
East India Company Act 1793 (c.52)
East India Company Act 1796 (c.120)
East India Company Act 1797 (c.31)
East India Company Act 1797 (c.74)
East India Company Act 1799 (c.89)
East India Company Act 1803 (c.48)
East India Company Act 1803 (c.63)
East India Company Act 1803 (c.137)
East India Company Act 1806 (c.85)
East India Company Act 1807 (c.41)
East India Company Act 1810 (c.86)
East India Company Act 1811 (c.75)
East India Company Act 1812 (c.10)
East India Company Act 1812 (c.135)
East India Company Act 1813 (c.155)
East India Company Act 1815 (c.64)
East India Company Bonds Act 1811 (c.64)
East India Company (Money) Act 1794 (c.41)
East India Company Stock Act 1786 (c.62)
East India Company Stock Act 1789 (c.65)
East India Company (Stock) Act 1791 (c.11)
East India Company (Stock) Act 1793 (c.47)
East India Company, Warehouses Act 1787 (c.48)
East India Company's Officers Superannuation Act 1897 (c.10)
East India Contracts Act 1870 (c.59)
East India Irrigation and Canal Act 1869 (c.7)
East India Unclaimed Stock Act 1885 (c.25)
East India Loan Act 1859 (c.11)
East India Loan Act 1860 (c.130)
East India Loan Act 1861 (c.25)
East India Loan Act 1861 (c.118)
East India Loan Act 1869 (c.106)
East India Loan Act 1873 (c.32)
East India Loan Act 1874 (c.3)
East India Loan Act 1877 (c.51)
East India Loan Act 1879 (c.60)
East India Loan Act 1885 (c.28)
East India Loan Act 1893 (c.70)
East India Loan Act 1898 (c.13)
East India Loan (East Indian Railway Debentures) Act 1880 (c.10)
East India Loan (Great Indian Peninsular Railway Debentures) Act 1901 (c.25)
East India Loan (No. 2) Act 1859 (c.39)
East India Loans Act 1858 (c.3)

East India Loans Act 1908 (c.54)
East India Loans Act 1923 (c.31)
East India Loans Act 1937 (c.14)
East India Loans (Railway and Irrigation) Act 1922 (c.9)
East India Loans (Railways) Act 1905 (c.19)
East India Loans (Railways and Irrigation) Act 1910 (c.5)
East India Merchants: Land for Warehouses etc. Act 1796 (c.127)
East India Merchants: Purchase of Land in City, etc. Act 1796 (c.119)
East India Prize Goods Act 1804 (c.72)
East India Stock Act 1860 (c.102)
East India Stock Dividend Redemption Act 1873 (c.17)
East India Trade Act 1774 (c.34)
East India Trade Act 1813 (c.34)
East India Trade Act 1813 (c.35)
East India Trade Act 1840 (c.56)
East India Trade, etc. Act 1814 (c.134)
East India Unclaimed Stock Act 1885 (c.25)
East Indian Loan (Annuities) Act 1879 (c.61)
East Indian Railway (Redemption of Annuities) Act 1879 (c.43)
East Indian Railway (Redemption of Annuities) Act 1881 (c.53)
East Indies Act 1791 (c.40)
East Kent: Drainage Act 1776 (c.62)
East Stonehouse Chapel Act 1787 (c.17)
East Tarbet Harbour Act 1707 (c.79(b))
Easter Act 1928 (c.35)
Eccles, Appointments Suspension Act 1836 (c.67)
Ecclesiastical Appointments Suspension Act 1838 (c.108)
Ecclesiastical Assessments (Scotland) Act 1900 (c.20)
Ecclesiastical Buildings and Glebes (Scotland) Act 1868 (c.96)
Ecclesiastical Commissioners Act 1836 (c.77)
Ecclesiastical Commissioners Act 1840 (c.113)
Ecclesiastical Commissioners Act 1840, Amendment 1885 (c.55)
Ecclesiastical Commissioners Act 1841 (c.39)
Ecclesiastical Commissioners Act 1847 (c.108)
Ecclesiastical Commissioners Act 1850 (c.94)
Ecclesiastical Commissioners Act 1860 (c.124)
Ecclesiastical Commissioners Act 1866 (c.111)
Ecclesiastical Commissioners Act 1868 (c.114)
Ecclesiastical Commissioners Act 1873 (c.64)
Ecclesiastical Commissioners Act 1875 (c.71)
Ecclesiastical Commissioners Act 1885 (c.31)

Ecclesiastical Commissioners (Exchange of Patronage) Act 1853 (c.50)
Ecclesiastical Commissioners (Superannuation) Act 1865 (c.68)
Ecclesiastical Commissioners (Takenhill Rectory) Act 1885 (c.31)
Ecclesiastical Courts Act 1813 (c.127)
Ecclesiastical Courts Act 1840 (c.93)
Ecclesiastical Courts Act 1844 (c.68)
Ecclesiastical Courts Act 1854 (c.47)
Ecclesiastical Courts Act 1855 (c.41)
Ecclesiastical Courts and Registries (Ireland) Act 1864 (c.54)
Ecclesiastical Courts Jurisdiction Act 1860 (c.32)
Ecclesiastical Dilapidations Act 1871 (c.43)
Ecclesiastical Dilapidations Act 1872 (c.96)
Ecclesiastical Districts in Forest of Dean Act 1842 (c.65)
Ecclesiastical Fees Act 1867 (c.135)
Ecclesiastical Fees Act 1875 (c.76)
Ecclesiastical Houses of Residence Act 1842 (c.26)
Ecclesiastical Jurisdiction Act 1842 (c.58)
Ecclesiastical Jurisdiction Act 1843 (c.60)
Ecclesiastical Jurisdiction Act 1847 (c.98)
Ecclesiastical Jurisdiction Act 1848 (c.67)
Ecclesiastical Jurisdiction Act 1849 (c.39)
Ecclesiastical Jurisdiction Act 1850 (c.47)
Ecclesiastical Jurisdiction Act 1851 (c.29)
Ecclesiastical Jurisdiction Act 1852 (c.17)
Ecclesiastical Jurisdiction Act 1853 (c.108)
Ecclesiastical Jurisdiction Act 1854 (c.65)
Ecclesiastical Jurisdiction Act 1855 (c.75)
Ecclesiastical Jurisdiction Act 1857 (c.10)
Ecclesiastical Jurisdiction Act 1858 (c.50)
Ecclesiastical Jurisdiction Act 1859 (c.45)
Ecclesiastical Leases Act 1800 (c.41)
Ecclesiastical Leases Act 1836 (c.20)
Ecclesiastical Leases Act 1842 (c.27)
Ecclesiastical Leases Act 1861 (c.104)
Ecclesiastical Leases Act 1862 (c.52)
Ecclesiastical Leases Act 1865 (c.57)
Ecclesiastical Leases Act 1765 (c.17)
Ecclesiastical Leases (Amendment) Act 1836 (c.64)
Ecclesiastical Leases (Isle of Man) Act 1866 (c.81)
Ecclesiastical Leasing Act 1842 (c.108)
Ecclesiastical Leasing Act 1858 (c.57)
Ecclesiastical Patronage (Ireland) Act 1845 (c.51)
Ecclesiastical Patronage (Ireland) Act 1848 (c.78)
Ecclesiastical Patronage (Ireland) Act 1848 (c.67)
Ecclesiastical Preferments (England) Act 1839 (c.55)
Ecclesiastical Proctors (Ireland) Act 1814 (c.68)
Ecclesiastical Property (Ireland) Act 1855 (c.28)
Ecclesiastical Property Valuation (Ireland) Act 1851 (c.74)

Ecclesiastical Services (Omission of Account on War) Act 1917 (c.5)

Ecclesiastical Suits Act 1787 (c.44)

Ecclesiastical Tithe Rentcharges (Rates) Act 1922 (c.58)

Ecclesiastical Titles Act 1851 (c.60)

Ecclesiastical Titles Act 1871 (c.53)

Ecclesiastical Unions, etc. (Ireland) Act 1848 (c.41)

Economy (Miscellaneous Provisions) Act 1926 (c.9)

Eddystone Lighthouse Act 1705 (c.7)

Eddystone Lighthouse Act 1709 (c.17)

Eden River, Cumberland (Temporary Tolls for Improvement) Act 1721 (c.14)

Edinburgh and Glasgow Roads Act 1757 (c.55)

Edinburgh and Leith Road Act 1750 (c.35)

Edinburgh and Linlithgow Roads Act 1764 (c.86)

Edinburgh Beer Duties Act 1716 (c.5)

Edinburgh Beer Duties Act 1722 (c.14)

Edinburgh Beer Duties Act 1727 (c.22)

Edinburgh Beer Duties Act 1751 (c.9)

Edinburgh Bridewell Act 1791 (c.57)

Edinburgh Bridges and Highways Act 1713 (c.30)

Edinburgh Buildings Act 1753 (c.36)

Edinburgh College of Surgeons Act 1787 (c.65)

Edinburgh Debt Act 1844 (c.20)

Edinburgh, etc., Roads Act 1795 (c.150)

Edinburgh General Register House Act 1896 (c.24)

Edinburgh: Improvement Act 1772 (c.15)

Edinburgh: Improvement Act 1786 (c.113)

Edinburgh: Improvement Act 1787 (c.51)

Edinburgh: Improvements Act 1766 (c.27)

Edinburgh, Linlithgow and Lanark Roads, etc. Act 1792 (c.120)

Edinburgh Roads Act 1755 (c.39)

Edinburgh Roads Act 1783 (c.18)

Edinburgh Roads Act 1789 (c.105)

Edinburgh (Slaughter of Animals) Act 1782 (c.52)

Edinburgh: Streets Act 1771 (c.36)

Edinburgh: Streets Act 1785 (c.28)

Edinburgh University Property Arrangement Act 1861 (c.90)

Edinburgh University (Transfer of Patronage) Act 1897 (c.13)

Edinburgh Water Act 1756 (c.74)

Edington, Somerset Drainage, etc. Act 1790 (c.58)

Education Act 1901 (c.11)

Education Act 1901 (Renewal) 1902 (c.19)

Education Act 1902 (c.42)

Education Act 1918 (c.39)

Education Act 1921 (c.51)

Education Act 1936 (c.41)

Education Act 1944 (c.31)

Education Act 1946 (c.50)

Education Act 1959 (c.60)

Education Act 1962 (c.12)

Education Act 1964 (c.82)

Education Act 1967 (c.3)

Education Act 1968 (c.17)

Education Act 1973 (c.16)

Education Act 1975 (c.2)

Education Act 1976 (c.81)

Education Act 1979 (c.49)

Education Act 1980 (c.20)

Education Act 1981 (c.60)

Education Act 1986 (c.40)

Education Act 1993 (c.35)

Education Act 1994 (c.30)

Education (Administrative Provisions) Act 1907 (c.43)

Education (Administrative Provisions) Act 1909 (c.29)

Education (Administrative Provisions) Act 1911 (c.32)

Education (Amendment) Act 1986 (c.1)

Education (Amendment) (Scotland) Act 1984 (c.6)

Education and Local Taxation Account (Scotland) Act 1892 (c.51)

Education (Choice of Employment) Act 1910 (c.37)

Education Code (1890) (c.22)

Education (Compliance with Conditions of Grants) Act 1919 (c.41)

Education (Deaf Children) Act 1937 (c.25)

Education Department Act 1856 (c.116)

Education (Emergency) Act 1939 (c.111)

Education (Emergency) (Scotland) Act 1939 (c.112)

Education Endowments (Scotland) Act 1931 (c.5)

Education (Exemptions) (Scotland) Act 1947 (c.36)

Education (Fees and Awards) Act 1983 (c.40)

Education (Grants and Awards) Act 1984 (c.11)

Education (Handicapped Children) Act 1970 (c.52)

Education (Institution Children) Act 1923 (c.38)

Education (Ireland) Act 1806 (c.122)

Education (Local Authorities) Act 1931 (c.6)

Education (Local Authority Default) Act 1904 (c.18)

Education (London) Act 1903 (c.24)

Education (Mentally Handicapped Children) (Scotland) Act 1974 (c.27)

Education (Milk) Act 1971 (c.74)

Education (Miscellaneous Provisions) Act 1948 (c.40)

Education (Miscellaneous Provisions) Act 1953 (c.33)

Education (Necessity of Schools) Act 1933 (c.29)

Education (Northern Ireland) Act 1978 (c.13)

Education (No. 2) Act 1968 (c.37)

Education (No. 2) Act 1986 (c.61)

Education of Blind and Deaf Children (Scotland) Act 1890 (c.43)

Education of Defective Children (Scotland) Act 1906 (c.10)

Education of Pauper Children Act 1855 (c.34)

Education (Provision of Meals) Act 1906 (c.57)

Education (Provision of Meals) Act 1914 (c.20)

Education (Provision of Meals) (Ireland) Act 1914 (c.35)

Education (Provision of Meals) (Ireland) Act 1916 (c.10)

Education (Provision of Meals) (Ireland) Act 1917 (c.53)

Education (Provision of the Working Balances) Act 1903 (c.10)

Education Reform Act 1988 (c.40)

Education (School-Leaving Dates) Act 1976 (c.5)

Education (School Milk) Act 1970 (c.14)

Education (Schools) Act 1992 (c.38)

Education (Scotland) Act 1872 (c.62)

Education (Scotland) Act 1878 (c.78)

Education (Scotland) Act 1883 (c.56)

Education (Scotland) Act 1897 (c.62)

Education (Scotland) Act 1901 (c.9)

Education (Scotland) Act 1908 (c.63)

Education (Scotland) Act 1913 (c.12)

Education (Scotland) Act 1918 (c.48)

Education (Scotland) Act 1925 (c.89)

Education (Scotland) Act 1928 (c.28)

Education (Scotland) Act 1930 (c.36)

Education (Scotland) Act 1936 (c.42)

Education (Scotland) Act 1942 (c.5)

Education (Scotland) Act 1944 (c.37)

Education (Scotland) Act 1945 (c.37)

Education (Scotland) Act 1946 (c.72)

Education (Scotland) Act 1949 (c.19)

Education (Scotland) Act 1956 (c.75)

Education (Scotland) Act 1962 (c.47)

Education (Scotland) Act 1963 (c.21)

Education (Scotland) Act 1965 (c.7)

Education (Scotland) Act 1969 (c.49)

Education (Scotland) Act 1971 (c.42)

Education (Scotland) Act 1973 (c.59)

Education (Scotland) Act 1976 (c.20)

Education (Scotland) Act 1980 (c.44)

Education (Scotland) Act 1981 (c.58)

Education (Scotland) (Glasgow Electoral Division) Act 1913 (c.13)

Education (Scotland) (Provision of Meals) Act 1914 (c.68)

Education (Scotland) (Superannuation) Act 1919 (c.17)

Education (Scotland) (Superannuation) Act 1922 (c.48)

Education (Scotland) (Superannuation) Act 1924 (c.13)

Education (Scotland) (Superannuation) Act 1925 (c.55)

Education (Scotland) (War Service Superannuation) Act 1914 (c.67)

Education (Scotland) (War Service Superannuation) Act 1939 (c.96)

Education (Small Population Grants) Act 1915 (c.95)

Education (Student Loans) Act 1990 (c.6)

Education (Work Experience) Act 1973 (c.23)

Educational Endowments (Ireland) Act 1885 (c.78)

Educational Endowments (Scotland) Act 1882 (c.59)

Educational Endowments (Scotland) Act 1928 (c.30)

Educational Endowments (Scotland) Act 1935 (c.5)

Edw. Whitaker, Public Accountant Act 1702 (c.16)

Effects of Residents in France Act 1794 (c.79)

Egham and Bagshot Roads Act 1727 (c.6)

Egham and Bagshot Road Act 1738 (c.16)

Egham and Bagshot Road Act 1763 (c.47)

Egyptian Loan Act 1885 (c.11)

Egyptians Act 1783 (c.51)

Eire (Confirmation of Agreements) Act 1938 (c.25)

Eisteddfod Act 1959 (c.32)

Ejectment and Distress (Ireland) Act 1846 (c.111)

Elders Widows' Fund (India) Act 1878 (c.47)

Elected Authorities (Northern Ireland) Act 1989 (c.3)

Election Commissioners Act 1852 (c.57)

Election Commissioners Act 1949 (c.90)

Election Commissioners Expenses Act 1871 (c.61)

Election (Hours of Poll) Act 1884 (c.34)

Election in the Recess Act 1863 (c.20)

Election (Ireland) Act 1862 (c.92)

Election of Members During Recess Act 1858 (c.110)

Election of Members for Cheshire Act 1846 (c.44)

Election of Representative Peers (Ireland) Act 1882 (c.26)

Election Petitions Act 1794 (c.83)

Election Petitions Act 1839 (c.38)

Election Petitions Act 1848 (c.98)

Election Petitions Act 1865 (c.8)

Election Recognizances Act 1848 (c.18)

Elections and Jurors Act 1945 (c.21)

Elections and Registration Act 1915 (c.76)

Elections (Fraudulent Conveyance) Act 1711 (c.31)

Elections (Hours of Poll) Act 1885 (c.10)

Elections in Recess Act 1863 (c.20)

Elections (Northern Ireland) Act 1985 (c.2)

Elections (Scotland) (Corrupt and Illegal Practices) Act 1890 (c.55)

Elections (Welsh Forms) Act 1964 (c.31)

Electoral Disabilities (Military Service) Removal Act 1900 (c.8)

Electoral Disabilities (Naval and Military Service) Removal Act 1914 (c.25)

Electoral Disabilities Removal Act 1891 (c.11)

Electoral Registers Act 1949 (c.86)

Electoral Registers Act 1953 (c.8)
Electric Lighting Act 1882 (c.56)
Electric Lighting Act 1888 (c.12)
Electric Lighting Act 1909 (c.34)
Electric Lighting (Clauses) Act 1899 (c.19)
Electric Lighting (Scotland) Act 1890 (c.13)
Electric Lighting (Scotland) Act 1902 (c.35)
Electricity Act 1947 (c.54)
Electricity Act 1957 (c.48)
Electricity Act 1972 (c.17)
Electricity Act 1989 (c.29)
Electricity (Amendment) Act 1961 (c.8)
Electricity and Gas Act 1963 (c.59)
Electricity (Borrowing Powers) Act 1959 (c.20)
Electricity (Borrowing Powers) (Scotland) Act 1962 (c.7)
Electricity (Financial Provisions) Act 1982 (c.56)
Electricity (Financial Provisions) (Scotland) Act 1976 (c.61)
Electricity (Financial Provisions) (Scotland) Act 1982 (c.56)
Electricity (Financial Provisions) (Scotland) Act 1988 (c.37)
Electricity Reorganisation (Scotland) Act 1954 (c.60)
Electricity (Scotland) Act 1969 (c.1)
Electricity (Scotland) Act 1979 (c.11)
Electricity (Supply) Act 1919 (c.100)
Electricity (Supply) Act 1922 (c.46)
Electricity (Supply) Act 1926 (c.51)
Electricity (Supply) Act 1928 (c.4)
Electricity (Supply) Act 1933 (c.46)
Electricity Supply Act 1935 (c.3)
Electricity Supply (Meters) Act 1936 (c.20)
Electricity Supply (Meters) Act 1952 (c.32)
Elementary Education Act 1870 (c.75)
Elementary Education Act 1873 (c.86)
Elementary Education Act 1876 (c.79)
Elementary Education Act 1880 (c.23)
Elementary Education Act 1891 (c.56)
Elementary Education Act 1897 (c.16)
Elementary Education Act 1900 (c.53)
Elementary Education Act Amendment Act 1872 (c.27)
Elementary Education Amendment Act 1903 (c.13)
Elementary Education (Blind and Deaf Children) Act 1893 (c.42)
Elementary Education (Defective and Epileptic Children) Act 1899 (c.32)
Elementary Education (Defective and Epileptic Children) Act 1914 (c.45)
Elementary Education (Election) Act 1871 (c.94)
Elementary Education (Elections) Act 1872 (c.59)
Elementary Education (Fee Grant) Act 1916 (c.35)
Elementary Education (Industrial Schools) Act 1879 (c.48)
Elementary Education (Orders) Act 1874 (c.90)

Elementary Education (School Attendance) Act 1893 (c.51)
Elementary Education (School Attendance) Act (1893) Amendment 1899 (c.13)
Elementary Education (Wenlock) Act 1874 (c.39)
Elementary School Teachers (Superannuation) Act 1898 (c.57)
Elementary School Teachers (Superannuation) Act 1912 (c.12)
Elementary School Teachers Superannuation (Isle of Man) Act 1900 (c.38)
Elementary School Teachers Superannuation (Jersey) Act 1900 (c.40)
Elementary School Teachers (War Service Superannuation) Act 1914 (c.66)
Elgin Beer Duties Act 1721 (c.7)
Elizabeth Taylor's Patent Act 1776 (c.18)
Elland and Leeds Road Act 1753 (c.61)
Elland to Leeds Road Act 1777 (c.87)
Elland to Leeds Road Act 1795 (c.159)
Elland to Leeds Road Act 1740 (c.25)
Ellesmere and Chester Canal Act 1793 (c.91)
Ellesmere and Chester Canal Act 1796 (c.71)
Ellesmere and Chester Canal Act 1796 (c.96)
Ellesmere, Salop: Poor Relief Act 1791 (c.78)
Elloe, Lincoln: Small Debts Act 1775 (c.64)
Elver Fishing Act 1876 (c.34)
Ely Roads Act 1740 (c.14)
Embezzlement Act 1799 Act (c.85)
Embezzlement Act 1814 (c.60)
Embezzlement by Bankers, etc. Act 1812 (c.63)
Embezzlement by Collectors Act 1810 (c.59)
Embezzlement (Ireland) Act 1811 (c.38)
Embezzlement of Naval, etc., Stores Act 1812 (c.12)
Embezzlement of Public Stores Act 1800 (c.89)
Embezzlement of Public Stores Act (c.126)
Embezzlement of Public Stores Act 1815 (c.127)
Emergency Laws (Miscellaneous Provisions) Act 1947 (c.10)
Emergency Laws (Miscellaneous Provisions) Act 1953 (c.47)
Emergency Laws (Re-enactments and Repeals) Act 1964 (c.60)
Emergency Laws (Repeal) Act 1959 (c.19)
Emergency Laws (Transitional Provisions) Act 1946 (c.26)
Emergency Powers Act 1920 (c.55)
Emergency Powers Act 1964 (c.38)
Emergency Powers (Defence) Act 1939 (c.20)
Emergency Powers (Defence) Act 1939 (c.62)
Emergency Powers (Defence) Act 1944 (c.31)
Emergency Powers (Defence) (No. 2) Act 1939 (c.45)
Emergency Powers (Isle of Man—Defence) Act 1943 (c.36)

Emigration from Scotland Act 1851 (c.91)

Empire Settlement Act 1922 (c.13)

Empire Settlement Act 1937 (c.18)

Empire Settlement Act 1952 (c.26)

Employers and Workmen Act 1875 (c.90)

Employers' Liability Act 1880 (c.42)

Employers' Liability Act 1888 (c.58)

Employers' Liability (Compulsory Insurance) Act 1969 (c.57)

Employers' Liability (Defective Equipment) Act 1969 (c.37)

Employers' Liability Insurance Companies Act 1907 (c.46)

Employment Act 1980 (c.42)

Employment Act 1982 (c.46)

Employment Act 1988 (c.19)

Employment Act 1989 (c.38)

Employment Act 1990 (c.38)

Employment Agencies Act 1973 (c.35)

Employment and Training Act 1948 (c.46)

Employment and Training Act 1973 (c.50)

Employment and Training Act 1981 (c.57)

Employment (Continental Shelf) Act 1978 (c.46)

Employment Medical Advisory Service Act 1972 (c.28)

Employment of Children Act 1903 (c.45)

Employment of Children Act 1973 (c.24)

Employment of Poor Act 1847 (c.87)

Employment of Poor, etc. (I.) Act 1847 (c.80)

Employment of Women Act 1907 (c.10)

Employment of Women and Young Persons Act 1936 (c.24)

Employment of Women, Young Persons and Children Act 1920 (c.65)

Employment Protection Act 1975 (c.71)

Employment Protection (Consolidation) Act 1978 (c.44)

Employment Subsidies Act 1978 (c.6)

Encouragement of Manufacturers Act 1723 (c.11)

Encouragement of Seamen, etc. Act 1803 (c.160)

Endangered Species (Import and Export) Act 1976 (c.72)

Endowed Institutions (Scotland) Act 1869 (c.39)

Endowed Institutions (Scotland) Act 1878 (c.48)

Endowed School Acts Continuance 1879 (c.66)

Endowed Schools Act 1813 (c.107)

Endowed Schools Act 1860 (c.11)

Endowed Schools Act 1869 (c.56)

Endowed Schools Act 1868 (c.32)

Endowed Schools Act 1869 (c.56)

Endowed Schools Act 1873 (c.87)

Endowed Schools Act 1874 (c.87)

Endowed Schools Inquiries (Ireland) Act 1855 (c.59)

Endowed Schools (Ireland) Act 1813 (c.107)

Endowed Schools (Masters) Act 1908 (c.39)

Endowed Schools (Time of Address) Act 1873 (c.7)

Endowed Schools (Vested Interests) Act Continued 1875 (c.29)

Enduring Power of Attorney Act 1985 (c.29)

Enemy Property Act 1953 (c.52)

Energy Act 1976 (c.76)

Energy Act 1983 (c.25)

Energy Conservation Act 1981 (c.17)

Enfranchisement of Copyholds Act 1841 (c.35)

English Industrial Estates Corporation Act 1981 (c.13)

Engraving Copyright Act 1734 (c.13)

Engraving Copyright Act 1766 (c.38)

Enlargement of Time for First Meetings Act 1757 (c.34)

Enlargement of Time for First Meetings Act 1759 (c.14)

Enlargement of Times for Executing Acts Act 1757 (c.37)

Enlargement of Times for Executing Acts Act 1765 (c.15)

Enlistment Act 1794 (c.43)

Enlistment of Foreigners Act 1804 (c.75)

Enlistment of Foreigners Act 1806 (c.23)

Enlistment of Foreigners Act 1815 (c.85)

Enlistment of Foreigners Act 1837 (c.29)

Enlistment of Foreigners Act 1855 (c.2)

Enlistment of Persons Transferred from the Indian Forces Act 1861 (c.74)

Enlistment in Foreign Service Act 1713 (c.10)

Entail Act 1838 (c.70)

Entail Amendment Act 1848 (c.36)

Entail Amendment Act 1853 (c.94)

Entail Amendment (Scotland) Act 1868 (c.84)

Entail Amendment (Scotland) Act 1875 (c.61)

Entail Amendment (Scotland) Act 1878 (c.28)

Entail Cottages Act 1860 (c.95)

Entail Improvement Act 1770 (c.51)

Entail Powers Act 1836 (c.42)

Entail (Scotland) Act 1882 (c.53)

Entail (Scotland) Act 1914 (c.43)

Entail Sites Act 1840 (c.48)

Entailed Estates Act 1800 (c.56)

Entailed Lands, etc. (Scotland) Act 1841 (c.24)

Enterprise and New Towns (Scotland) Act 1990 (c.35)

Entertainments Duty Act 1958 (c.9)

Entertainments (Increased Penalties) Act 1990 (c.20)

Environment and Safety Information Act 1988 (c.30)

Environmental Protection Act 1990 (c.43)

Epidemic and Other Diseases Prevention Act 1883 (c.59)

Episcopal and Capitular Estates Act 1851 (c.104)

Episcopal and Capitular Estates Act 1854 (c.116)

Episcopal and Capitular Estates Act 1857 (c.74)

Episcopal and Capitular Estates Act 1859 (c.46)

Exchequer Bills Act 1852 (c.10)
Exchequer Bills Act 1853 (c.25)
Exchequer Bills Act 1854 (c.3)
Exchequer Bills Act 1854 (c.12)
Exchequer Bills Act 1855 (c.8)
Exchequer Bills Act 1856 (c.19)
Exchequer Bills Act 1857 (c.17)
Exchequer Bills Act 1858 (c.13)
Exchequer Bills Act 1859 (c.22)
Exchequer Bills Act 1860 (c.20)
Exchequer Bills Act 1861 (c.5)
Exchequer Bills Act 1862 (c.3)
Exchequer Bills and Bonds Act 1855 (c.130)
Exchequer Bills and Bonds Act 1856 (c.44)
Exchequer Bills and Bonds Act 1866 (c.25)
Exchequer Bills and Bonds Act 1877 (c.5)
Exchequer Bills and Bonds Act 1878 (c.2)
Exchequer Bills and Bonds Act 1879 (c.62)
Exchequer Bills and Bonds Act 1880 (c.16)
Exchequer Bills and Bonds (Session 2) Act 1880 (c.21)
Exchequer Bills (Great Britain) Act 1815 (c.196)
Exchequer Bonds Act 1858 (c.14)
Exchequer Bonds Act 1862 (c.13)
Exchequer Bonds Act 1863 (c.16)
Exchequer Bonds Act 1864 (c.74)
Exchequer Bonds Act 1865 (c.29)
Exchequer Bonds Act 1867 (c.31)
Exchequer Bonds Act 1868 (c.27)
Exchequer Bonds Act 1869 (c.22)
Exchequer Bonds Act 1870 (c.41)
Exchequer Bonds Act 1871 (c.52)
Exchequer Bonds Act 1873 (c.54)
Exchequer Bonds Act 1876 (c.1)
Exchequer Bonds Act 1878 (c.7)
Exchequer Bonds and Bills Act 1854 (c.23)
Exchequer Bonds and Bills Act 1860 (c.132)
Exchequer Bonds and Bills (No. 2) Act 1878 (c.64)
Exchequer Bonds (No. 1) Act 1879 (c.3)
Exchequer Bonds (No. 2) Act 1878 (c.22)
Exchequer Court (Ireland) Act 1843 (c.55)
Exchequer Court (Ireland) Act 1843 (c.78)
Exchequer Court (Scotland) Act 1707 (c.53)
Exchequer Court (Scotland) Act 1779 (c.38)
Exchequer Court (Scotland) Act 1837 (c.65)
Exchequer Court (Scotland) Act 1856 (c.56)
Exchequer Equitable Jurisdiction (Ireland) Act 1850 (c.51)
Exchequer, etc., Courts (Scotland) Act 1790 (c.17)
Exchequer Extra Receipts Act 1868 (c.9)
Exchequer (Ireland) Act 1814 (c.83)
Excisable Goods on the Thames Act 1803 (c.115)
Excisable Liquors (Scotland) Act 1804 (c.55)
Excise Act 1719 (c.21)
Excise Act 1758 (c.29)
Excise Act 1772 (c.46)
Excise Act 1781 (c.55)
Excise Act 1781 (c.64)
Excise Act 1783 (c.70)

Excise Act 1785 (c.22)
Excise Act 1785 (c.47)
Excise Act 1785 (c.74)
Excise Act 1786 (c.59)
Excise Act 1786 (c.64)
Excise Act 1786 (cc.73, 74)
Excise Act 1786 (c.77)
Excise Act 1788 (c.37)
Excise Act 1788 (c.46)
Excise Act 1789 (c.63)
Excise Act 1790 (c.37)
Excise Act 1793 (c.59)
Excise Act 1795 (cc.10–13)
Excise Act 1795 (c.13)
Excise Act 1795 (c.97)
Excise Act 1795 (c.116)
Excise Act 1796 (c.14)
Excise Act 1798 (c.42)
Excise Act 1798 (c.54)
Excise Act 1800 (c.23)
Excise Act 1801 (c.91)
Excise Act 1802 (c.93)
Excise Act 1802 (c.96)
Excise Act 1803 (c.69)
Excise Act 1803 (c.81)
Excise Act 1803 (c.129)
Excise Act 1804 (c.49)
Excise Act 1805 (c.30)
Excise Act 1806 (c.39)
Excise Act 1806 (c.75)
Excise Act 1806 (c.112)
Excise Act 1806 (cc.138, 139)
Excise Act 1807 (c.27)
Excise Act 1807 (c.37)
Excise Act 1809 (c.63)
Excise Act 1809 (c.77)
Excise Act 1809 (c.80)
Excise Act 1809 (c.81)
Excise Act 1811 (c.32)
Excise Act 1812 (c.58)
Excise Act 1812 (c.61)
Excise Act 1812 (c.94)
Excise Act 1812 (c.128)
Excise Act 1813 (cc.56, 57)
Excise Act 1813 (c.88)
Excise Act 1813 (c.103)
Excise Act 1814 (c.73)
Excise Act 1814 (c.148)
Excise Act 1814 (c.183)
Excise Act 1815 (c.27)
Excise Act 1815 (c.30)
Excise Act 1815 (c.35)
Excise Act 1815 (c.62)
Excise Act 1815 (c.63)
Excise Act 1816 (c.17)
Excise Act 1816 (c.104)
Excise Act 1816 (c.108)
Excise Act 1836 (c.52)
Excise Act 1840 (c.17)
Excise Act 1848 (c.118)
Excise Act 1854 (c.27)
Excise Act 1855 (c.94)
Excise Act 1858 (c.15)

Excise Act 1860 (c.113)
Excise and Customs Act 1815 (c.66)
Excise and Stamps Act 1808 (c.41)
Excise and Stamps (Ireland) Act 1807 (c.14)
Excise and Taxes (Ireland) Act 1805 (c.19)
Excise Duties Act 1780 (c.17)
Excise Duties Act 1789 (c.45)
Excise Duties Act 1794 (c.33)
Excise Duties Act 1855 (c.22)
Excise Duties Act 1856 (c.34)
Excise Duties Act 1862 (c.84)
Excise Duties and Drawbacks Act 1807 (c.63)
Excise Duties and Licences (Ireland) Act 1815 (c.19)
Excise Duties and Taxes (Ireland) Act 1807 (c.18)
Excise Duties (Surcharges or Rebates) Act 1979 (c.8)
Excise Duty on Malt Act 1863 (c.3)
Excise Duty on Malt Act 1865 (c.66)
Excise, etc. Act 1811 (c.95)
Excise, etc. (Great Britain) Act 1807 (c.30)
Excise, etc. Act 1816 (c.30)
Excise (Great Britain) Act 1809 (c.117)
Excise (Ireland) Act 1807 (c.35)
Excise (Ireland) Act 1808 (c.82)
Excise (Ireland) Act 1809 (c.33)
Excise Incorporation (Scotland) Act 1835 (c.72)
Excise Laws, Glass Act 1792 (c.40)
Excise Management Act 1841 (c.20)
Excise Officers Act 1810 (c.44)
Excise Officers Allowance Act 1812 (c.81)
Excise on Spirits Act 1860 (c.129)
Excise (Scotland) Act 1793 (c.69)
Exclusive Trading (Ireland) Act 1846 (c.76)
Execution Act 1844 (c.96)
Execution (Ireland) Act 1848 (c.28)
Execution of Diligence (Scotland) Act 1926 (c.16)
Execution of Sentences (Scotland) Act 1730 (c.32)
Execution of Trusts (Emergency Provisions) Act 1939 (c.114)
Execution of Trusts (War Facilities) Act 1914 (c.13)
Execution of Trusts (War Facilities) Amendment Act 1915 (c.70)
Executions for Murder Act 1836 (c.30)
Executors (Scotland) Act 1900 (c.55)
Exemption from Coal Duty Act 1787 (c.21)
Exemption from Duties Act 1809 (c.44)
Exemption from Impressment Act 1739 (c.17)
Exemption from Toll Act 1812 (c.145)
Exemption of Bankers from Penalties Act 1813 (c.139)
Exercise Act 1723 (c.10)
Exercise Act 1727 (c.16)
Exercise of Trade by Soldiers Act 1784 (c.6)
Exercise of Trade by Soldiers, etc. Act 1802 (c.69)
Exercise of Trades by Soldiers, etc. Act 1816 (c.67)

Exercises of Trades Act 1712 (c.14)
Exercising Ground, Chatham Act 1808 (c.101)
Exeter: Lighting, etc. Act 1760 (c.28)
Exeter (Poor Relief) Act 1757 (c.53)
Exeter: Poor Relief Act 1774 (c.61)
Exeter: Poor Relief Act 1785 (c.21)
Exeter: Poor Relief Act 1788 (c.76)
Exeter Roads Act 1753 (c.74)
Exeter Roads Act 1756 (c.55)
Exeter Roads Act 1769 (c.93)
Exeter Roads Act 1770 (c.73)
Exeter Roads, etc. Act 1773 (c.109)
Exeter: Small Debts Act 1772 (c.27)
Exhibition Medals Act 1863 (c.119)
Exmoor Forest Act 1815 (c.138)
Ex-Officio Justice of the Peace (Scotland) Act 1898 (c.20)
Expenditure, etc., of Office of Works, etc. Act 1812 (c.41)
Expenditure in the West Indies Act 1800 (c.22)
Expenses of Fortifications for Protecting Royal Arsenals (No. 1) Act 1867 (c.24)
Expenses of Fortifications for Protecting Royal Arsenals (No. 2) Act 1867 (c.145)
Expenses of H.M. Forces, India Act 1791 (c.10)
Expenses of Prince Regent Act 1812 (c.7)
Expiring Laws Act 1922 (c.50)
Expiring Laws Act 1925 (c.76)
Expiring Laws Act 1931 (c.2)
Expiring Laws Act 1969 (c.61)
Expiring Laws Continuance Act 1841 (c.7)
Expiring Laws Continuance Act 1863 (c.95)
Expiring Laws Continuance Act 1864 (c.84)
Expiring Laws Continuance Act 1865 (c.119)
Expiring Laws Continuance Act 1866 (c.102)
Expiring Laws Continuance Act 1867 (c.143)
Expiring Laws Continuance Act 1868 (c.111)
Expiring Laws Continuance Act 1869 (c.85)
Expiring Laws Continuance Act 1870 (c.103)
Expiring Laws Continuance Act 1871 (c.95)
Expiring Laws Continuance Act 1872 (c.88)
Expiring Laws Continuance Act 1873 (c.75)
Expiring Laws Continuance Act 1874 (c.76)
Expiring Laws Continuance Act 1875 (c.72)
Expiring Laws Continuance Act 1876 (c.69)
Expiring Laws Continuance Act 1877 (c.67)
Expiring Laws Continuance Act 1878 (c.70)
Expiring Laws Continuance Act 1879 (c.67)
Expiring Laws Continuance Act 1880 (c.48)
Expiring Laws Continuance Act 1881 (c.70)
Expiring Laws Continuance Act 1882 (c.64)
Expiring Laws Continuance Act 1883 (c.40)
Expiring Laws Continuance Act 1884 (c.53)
Expiring Laws Continuance Act 1885 (c.59)
Expiring Laws Continuance Act 1886 (c.5)
Expiring Laws Continuance Act 1887 (c.63)
Expiring Laws Continuance Act 1888 (c.38)
Expiring Laws Continuance Act 1889 (c.67)
Expiring Laws Continuance Act 1890 (c.49)
Expiring Laws Continuance Act 1891 (c.60)

Expiring Laws Continuance Act 1892 (c.60)
Expiring Laws Continuance Act 1893 (c.59)
Expiring Laws Continuance Act 1894 (c.48)
Expiring Laws Continuance Act 1895 (c.1)
Expiring Laws Continuance Act 1896 (c.39)
Expiring Laws Continuance Act 1897 (c.54)
Expiring Laws Continuance Act 1898 (c.47)
Expiring Laws Continuance Act 1899 (c.34)
Expiring Laws Continuance Act 1900 (c.37)
Expiring Laws Continuance Act 1901 (c.33)
Expiring Laws Continuance Act 1902 (c.32)
Expiring Laws Continuance Act 1903 (c.40)
Expiring Laws Continuance Act 1904 (c.29)
Expiring Laws Continuance Act 1905 (c.21)
Expiring Laws Continuance Act 1906 (c.51)
Expiring Laws Continuance Act 1907 (c.34)
Expiring Laws Continuance Act 1908 (c.18)
Expiring Laws Continuance Act 1909 (c.46)
Expiring Laws Continuance Act 1910 (c.36)
Expiring Laws Continuance Act 1911 (c.22)
Expiring Laws Continuance Act 1912 (c.18)
Expiring Laws Continuance Act 1913 (c.15)
Expiring Laws Continuance Act 1914 (c.23)
Expiring Laws Continuance Act 1915 (c.63)
Expiring Laws Continuance Act 1916 (c.29)
Expiring Laws Continuance Act 1917 (c.38)
Expiring Laws Continuance Act 1918 (c.21)
Expiring Laws Continuance Act 1919 (c.39)
Expiring Laws Continuance Act 1920 (c.73)
Expiring Laws Continuance Act 1921 (c.53)
Expiring Laws Continuance Act 1923 (c.37)
Expiring Laws Continuance Act 1924 (c.1)
Expiring Laws Continuance Act 1926 (c.49)
Expiring Laws Continuance Act 1927 (c.34)
Expiring Laws Continuance Act 1928 (c.3)
Expiring Laws Continuance Act 1929 (c.12)
Expiring Laws Continuance Act 1931 (c.4)
Expiring Laws Continuance Act 1932 (c.2)
Expiring Laws Continuance Act 1933 (c.48)
Expiring Laws Continuance Act 1934 (c.57)
Expiring Laws Continuance Act 1935 (c.4)
Expiring Laws Continuance Act 1936 (c.4)
Expiring Laws Continuance Act 1937 (c.1)
Expiring Laws Continuance Act 1938 (c.1)
Expiring Laws Continuance Act 1939 (c.1)
Expiring Laws Continuance Act 1941 (c.3)
Expiring Laws Continuance Act 1942 (c.1)
Expiring Laws Continuance Act 1943 (c.1)
Expiring Laws Continuance Act 1944 (c.2)
Expiring Laws Continuance Act 1945 (c.9)
Expiring Laws Continuance Act 1947 (c.1)
Expiring Laws Continuance Act 1948 (c.3)
Expiring Laws Continuance Act 1949 (c.71)
Expiring Laws Continuance Act 1950 (c.1)
Expiring Laws Continuance Act 1951 (c.3)
Expiring Laws Continuance Act 1952 (c.5)
Expiring Laws Continuance Act 1953 (c.9)
Expiring Laws Continuance Act 1954 (c.69)
Expiring Laws Continuance Act 1955 (c.22)
Expiring Laws Continuance Act 1957 (c.2)
Expiring Laws Continuance Act 1958 (c.4)
Expiring Laws Continuance Act 1959 (c.4)
Expiring Laws Continuance Act 1960 (c.4)

Expiring Laws Continuance Act 1961 (c.4)
Expiring Laws Continuance Act 1962 (c.3)
Expiring Laws Continuance Act 1963 (c.58)
Expiring Laws Continuance Act 1964 (c.94)
Expiring Laws Continuance Act 1965 (c.77)
Expiring Laws Continuance Act 1966 (c.40)
Expiring Laws Continuance Act 1967 (c.89)
Expiring Laws Continuance Act 1968 (c.76)
Expiring Laws Continuance Act 1970 (c.58)
Explosive Substances Act 1883 (c.3)
Explosives Act 1875 (c.17)
Explosives Act 1923 (c.17)
Explosives (Age of Purchase) Act 1976 (c.26)
Export and Investment Guarantees Act 1991 (c.67)
Export Duty Act 1804 (c.57)
Export Guarantees Act 1937 (c.61)
Export Guarantees Act 1939 (c.5)
Export Guarantees Act 1944 (c.9)
Export Guarantees Act 1948 (c.54)
Export Guarantees Act 1949 (c.14)
Export Guarantees Act 1952 (c.21)
Export Guarantees Act 1957 (c.23)
Export Guarantees Act 1959 (c.63)
Export Guarantees Act 1967 (c.11)
Export Guarantees Act 1968 (c.26)
Export Guarantees Act 1975 (c.38)
Export Guarantees Amendment Act 1975 (c.19)
Export Guarantees and Overseas Investment Act 1978 (c.18)
Export Guarantees and Payments Act 1970 (c.14)
Export Guarantees and Payments Act 1970 (c.15)
Export of Salted Beef, etc. (Ireland) Act 1807 (c.10)
Exportation Act 1705 (c.19)
Exportation Act 1707 (c.44)
Exportation Act 1709 (c.2)
Exportation Act 1709 (c.7)
Exportation Act 1730 (c.29)
Exportation Act 1740 (c.3)
Exportation Act 1753 (c.11)
Exportation Act 1753 (c.15)
Exportation Act 1756 (cc.15, 16)
Exportation Act 1757 (c.1)
Exportation Act 1757 (c.9)
Exportation Act 1757 (c.37)
Exportation Act 1758 (c.8)
Exportation Act 1759 (c.15)
Exportation Act 1759 (c.28)
Exportation Act 1768 (c.24)
Exportation Act 1769 (c.1)
Exportation Act 1770 (c.1)
Exportation Act 1770 (c.10)
Exportation Act 1770 (c.31)
Exportation Act 1770 (c.38)
Exportation Act 1771 (c.37)
Exportation Act 1771 (c.39)
Exportation Act 1772 (cc.1, 2)
Exportation Act 1774 (c.5)
Exportation Act 1774 (c.10)

Exportation Act 1774 (c.11)
Exportation Act 1774 (c.26)
Exportation Act 1774 (c.71)
Exportation Act 1775 (c.5)
Exportation Act 1776 (c.28)
Exportation Act 1776 (c.37)
Exportation Act 1778 (c.16)
Exportation Act 1780 (c.37)
Exportation Act 1780 (c.46)
Exportation Act 1783 (c.14)
Exportation Act 1783 (c.81)
Exportation Act 1785 (c.5)
Exportation Act 1785 (c.62)
Exportation Act 1785 (c.67)
Exportation Act 1786 (c.2)
Exportation Act 1786 (c.76)
Exportation Act 1786 (c.89)
Exportation Act 1788 (c.16)
Exportation Act 1788 (c.38)
Exportation Act 1788 (c.45)
Exportation Act 1792 (c.2)
Exportation Act 1792 (c.9)
Exportation Act 1793 (c.3)
Exportation Act 1794 (c.34)
Exportation Act 1795 (c.5)
Exportation Act 1796 (c.53)
Exportation Act 1797 (c.10)
Exportation Act 1797 (c.29)
Exportation Act 1797 (c.125)
Exportation Act 1798 (c.67)
Exportation Act 1799 (c.26)
Exportation Act 1799 (c.96)
Exportation Act 1800 (c.1)
Exportation Act 1800 (c.2)
Exportation Act 1800 (c.91)
Exportation Act 1801 (c.21)
Exportation Act 1803 (c.49)
Exportation Act 1803 (c.105)
Exportation Act 1804 (c.22)
Exportation Act 1804 (c.70)
Exportation Act 1804 (c.101)
Exportation Act 1806 (c.11)
Exportation Act 1806 (c.17)
Exportation Act 1806 (c.115)
Exportation Act 1806 (c.116)
Exportation Act 1807 (c.9)
Exportation Act 1807 (c.30)
Exportation Act 1807 (c.49)
Exportation Act 1808 (c.29)
Exportation Act 1808 (cc.33–35)
Exportation Act 1808 (c.44)
Exportation Act 1808 (c.69)
Exportation Act 1809 (c.23)
Exportation Act 1809 (cc.30, 31)
Exportation Act 1810 (c.26)
Exportation Act 1810 (c.34)
Exportation Act 1810 (c.60)
Exportation Act 1810 (c.63)
Exportation Act 1810 (c.64)
Exportation Act 1811 (c.50)
Exportation Act 1811 (c.57)
Exportation Act 1812 (c.25)
Exportation Act 1812 (c.45)

Exportation Act 1812 (c.140)
Exportation Act 1813 (c.7)
Exportation Act 1813 (c.30)
Exportation Act 1813 (cc.31, 32)
Exportation Act 1813 (c.38)
Exportation Act 1813 (c.40)
Exportation Act 1813 (c.45)
Exportation Act 1813 (c.98)
Exportation Act 1813 (c.125)
Exportation Act 1814 (c.57)
Exportation Act 1814 (c.100)
Exportation Act 1814 (c.127)
Exportation Act 1814 (c.142)
Exportation Act 1814 (c.185)
Exportation Act 1815 (c.180)
Exportation Act 1815 (c.183)
Exportation Act 1816 (c.76)
Exportation Act 1816 (c.92)
Exportation Act 1816 (c.109)
Exportation Act 1816 (c.127)
Exportation and Importation Act 1768 (cc.1–3)
Exportation and Importation Act 1795 (c.3)
Exportation and Importation Act 1795 (c.4)
Exportation and Importation Act 1796 (c.7)
Exportation and Importation Act 1797 (c.83)
Exportation and Importation Act 1803 (c.12)
Exportation and Importation Act 1804 (c.65)
Exportation and Importation Act 1805 (c.33)
Exportation and Importation Act 1808 (c.27)
Exportation and Importation Act 1811 (c.14)
Exportation and Importation Act 1811 (c.86)
Exportation and Importation Act 1813 (c.67)
Exportation and Importation Act 1815 (c.31)
Exportation and Importation Act 1815 (c.37)
Exportation and Importation (Great Britain) Act 1810 (cc.18, 19)
Exportation and Importation (Ireland) Act 1810 (cc.16, 17)
Exportation, etc. Act 1716 (c.21)
Exportation, etc. Act 1749 (c.14)
Exportation, etc. Act 1758 (c.2)
Exportation, etc. Act 1769 (c.28)
Exportation etc. Act 1771 (c.1)
Exportation, etc. Act 1778 (c.55)
Exportation, etc. Act 1784 (c.50)
Exportation, etc. Act 1801 (c.36)
Exportation, etc. Act 1808 (c.22)
Exportation (Ireland) Act 1807 (c.58)
Exportation (Ireland) Act 1809 (c.76)
Exportation of Arms Act 1900 (c.44)
Exportation of Army Clothing Act 1775 (c.45)
Exportation of Gunpowder Act 1803 (c.52)
Exportation of Horses Act 1914 (c.15)
Exportation of Horses Act 1937 (c.42)
Exportations, etc. Act 1704 (c.7)
Exportations, etc. Act 1780 (c.59)
Exportations, etc. Act 1802 (cc.12, 13)
Exports Act 1786 (c.40)
Exports Act 1787 (c.31)
Extension of Polling Hours Act 1913 (c.6)
Extradition Act 1843 (cc.75, 76)
Extradition Act 1845 (c.120)

Extradition Act 1862 (c.70)
Extradition Act 1866 (c.121)
Extradition Act 1870 (c.52)
Extradition Act 1873 (c.60)
Extradition Act 1895 (c.33)
Extradition Act 1906 (c.15)
Extradition Act 1931 (c.39)
Extradition Act 1932 (c.39)
Extradition Act 1989 (c.33)
Extraordinary Tithe Act 1897 (c.23)
Extraordinary Tithe Redemption Act 1886 (c.54)
Extra-Parochial Places Act 1857 (c.19)
Eyemouth Harbour Act 1797 (c.49)
Eynsham Bridge Act 1767 (c.68)

Fabrics (Misdescription) Act 1913 (c.17)
Factories Act 1802 (c.73)
Factories Act 1937 (c.67)
Factories Act 1844 (c.15)
Factories Act 1847 (c.29)
Factories Act 1850 (c.54)
Factories Act 1853 (c.104)
Factories Act 1856 (c.38)
Factories Act 1948 (c.55)
Factories Act 1959 (c.67)
Factories Act 1961 (c.34)
Factors Act 1842 (c.39)
Factors Act 1889 (c.45)
Factors Acts Amendment 1877 (c.39)
Factors (Scotland) Act 1890 (c.40)
Factory Act 1874 (c.44)
Factory Acts Extension Act 1864 (c.48)
Factory Acts Extension Act 1867 (c.103)
Factory and Workshop Act 1870 (c.62)
Factory and Workshop Act 1871 (c.104)
Factory and Workshop Act 1878 (c.16)
Factory and Workshop Act 1883 (c.53)
Factory and Workshop Act 1891 (c.75)
Factory and Workshop Act 1895 (c.37)
Factory and Workshop Act 1901 (c.22)
Factory and Workshop Act 1907 (c.39)
Factory and Workshop Amendment (Scotland) Act 1888 (c.22)
Factory and Workshop (Cotton Cloth Factories) Act 1911 (c.21)
Factory and Workshop (Cotton Cloth Factories) Act 1929 (c.15)
Failure of Corn Crop Act 1783 (c.53)
Fair Employment (Northern Ireland) Act 1976 (c.25)
Fair Employment (Northern Ireland) Act 1989 (c.32)
Fair Trading Act 1973 (c.41)
Fairs Act 1868 (c.51)
Fairs Act 1871 (c.12)
Fairs Act 1873 (c.37)
Fairs and Market Act 1850 (c.23)
Fairs (Ireland) Act 1868 (c.12)
Falmouth Gaol Act 1865 (c.103)
False Alarms of Fire Act 1895 (c.28)
False Oaths (Scotland) Act 1933 (c.20)

False Personation Act 1874 (c.36)
False Weights and Scales Act 1770 (c.44)
Falsification of Accounts Act 1875 (c.24)
Families of Militiamen Act 1793 (c.8)
Families of Militiamen Act 1795 (c.81)
Families of Militiamen, etc. Act 1794 (c.47)
Families of Militiamen, etc. Act 1796 (c.114)
Family Allowances Act 1944 (c.41)
Family Allowances Act 1965 (c.53)
Family Allowances and National Insurance Act 1952 (c.29)
Family Allowances and National Insurance Act 1956 (c.50)
Family Allowances and National Insurance Act 1959 (c.18)
Family Allowances and National Insurance Act 1961 (c.6)
Family Allowances and National Insurance Act 1963 (c.10)
Family Allowances and National Insurance Act 1967 (c.90)
Family Allowances and National Insurance Act 1968 (c.40)
Family Income Supplements Act 1970 (c.55)
Family Law Act 1986 (c.55)
Family Law Reform Act 1969 (c.46)
Family Law Reform Act 1987 (c.42)
Family Law (Scotland) Act 1985 (c.37)
Family of Rt. Hon. S. Perceval Act 1812 (c.67)
Family Provision Act 1966 (c.35)
Farm and Garden Chemicals Act 1967 (c.50)
Farm Land and Rural Development Act 1988 (c.16)
Farnborough and Seven Oaks Road Act 1796 (c.128)
Farnborough to Seven Oaks Road Act 1773 (c.92)
Farnhurst, Chichester and Delkey Road Act 1797 (c.148)
Farriers (Registration) Act 1975 (c.35)
Farriers (Registration) (Amendment) Act 1977 (c.31)
Farringdon to Burford Road 1771 (c.84)
Fatal Accidents Act 1846 (c.93)
Fatal Accidents Act 1864 (c.95)
Fatal Accidents Act 1959 (c.65)
Fatal Accidents Act 1976 (c.30)
Fatal Accidents and Sudden Deaths Inquiry (Scotland) Act 1906 (c.35)
Fatal Accidents and Sudden Deaths Inquiry (Scotland) Act 1976 (c.14)
Fatal Accidents (Damages) Act 1908 (c.7)
Fatal Accidents Inquiry (Scotland) Act 1895 (c.36)
Faversham (Improvement) Act 1789 (c.69)
Faversham, Portsmouth, Plymouth Fortifications Act 1786 (c.94)
Federal Council of Australasia Act 1885 (c.60)
Federation of Malaya Independence Act 1957 (c.60)
Fee-Farm Rents (Ireland) Act 1851 (c.20)
Fees, etc., in Public Offices (Ireland) Act 1807 (c.41)

Fees etc., in Public Offices, etc. (Ireland) Act 1811 (c.81)
Fees for Pardons Act 1818 (c.29)
Fees in Public Offices, etc. Act 1809 (c.51)
Fees in Public Offices, etc. (Ireland) Act 1810 (c.81)
Fees in Public Offices, etc. (Ireland) Act 1812 (c.92)
Fees (Increase) Act 1923 (c.4)
Fees of Coroners (Ireland) Act 1810 (c.30)
Fees, Officers of the Exchequer Act 1786 (c.99)
Fees, Port of London, etc. Act 1806 (c.82)
Felony Act 1819 (c.27)
Felony Act 1841 (c.22)
Felony and Piracy Act 1772 (c.20)
Fencibles Act 1793 (c.36)
Fen Drainage Act 1749 (c.18)
Fen Drainage Act 1758 (c.13)
Fen Drainage Act 1774 (c.16)
Fen Drainage Act 1775 (c.65)
Fen Drainage Act 1776 (c.64)
Ferries (Acquisition by Local Authorities) Act 1919 (c.75)
Ferrybridge and Boroughbridge Road Act 1753 (c.77)
Fertilisers and Feeding Stuffs Act 1893 (c.56)
Fertilisers and Feeding Stuffs Act 1906 (c.27)
Fertilisers and Feeding Stuffs Act 1926 (c.45)
Festival of Britain (Additional Loans) Act 1951 (c.47)
Festival of Britain (Sunday Opening) Act 1951 (c.14)
Festival of Britain (Supplementary Provisions) Act (c.102)
Festival Pleasure Gardens 1952 (c.13)
Feudal Casualties (Scotland) Act 1914 (c.48)
Fever (Ireland) Act 1846 (c.6)
Fever (Ireland) Act 1847 (c.22)
Fever (Ireland) Act 1848 (c.131)
Field Monuments Act 1972 (c.43)
Fife (Country) Roads Act 1797 (c.180)
Fife Roads Act 1772 (c.83)
Fife Roads Act 1790 (c.93)
Fife Roads and Bridges Act 1774 (c.31)
Fifield, St. John's and Newbridge Road Act 1763 (c.29)
Fiji Independence Act 1970 (c.50)
Fiji Marriage Act 1878 (c.61)
Film Levy Finance Act 1981 (c.16)
Films Act 1960 (c.57)
Films Act 1964 (c.52)
Films Act 1966 (c.48)
Films Act 1970 (c.26)
Films Act 1979 (c.9)
Films Act 1980 (c.41)
Films Act 1985 (c.21)
Finance Act 1894 (c.30)
Finance Act 1895 (c.16)
Finance Act 1896 (c.28)
Finance Act 1897 (c.24)
Finance Act 1898 (c.10)
Finance Act 1899 (c.9)

Finance Act 1900 (c.7)
Finance Act 1901 (c.7)
Finance Act 1902 (c.7)
Finance Act 1903 (c.8)
Finance Act 1904 (c.7)
Finance Act 1905 (c.4)
Finance Act 1906 (c.8)
Finance Act 1907 (c.13)
Finance Act 1908 (c.16)
Finance (1909–10) Act 1910 (c.8)
Finance Act 1910 (c.35)
Finance Act 1911 (c.48)
Finance Act 1912 (c.8)
Finance Act 1913 (c.30)
Finance Act 1914 (c.10)
Finance Act 1915 (c.62)
Finance Act 1916 (c.24)
Finance Act 1917 (c.31)
Finance Act 1918 (c.15)
Finance Act 1919 (c.32)
Finance Act 1920 (c.18)
Finance Act 1921 (c.32)
Finance Act 1922 (c.17)
Finance Act 1923 (c.14)
Finance Act 1924 (c.21)
Finance Act 1925 (c.36)
Finance Act 1926 (c.22)
Finance Act 1927 (c.10)
Finance Act 1928 (c.17)
Finance Act 1929 (c.21)
Finance Act 1930 (c.28)
Finance Act 1931 (c.25)
Finance Act 1931 (c.28)
Finance Act 1932 (c.25)
Finance Act 1933 (c.19)
Finance Act 1934 (c.32)
Finance Act 1935 (c.24)
Finance Act 1936 (c.34)
Finance Act 1937 (c.54)
Finance Act 1938 (c.46)
Finance Act 1939 (c.41)
Finance Act 1940 (c.29)
Finance Act 1941 (c.30)
Finance Act 1942 (c.21)
Finance Act 1943 (c.28)
Finance Act 1944 (c.23)
Finance Act 1945 (c.24)
Finance Act 1946 (c.64)
Finance Act 1947 (c.35)
Finance Act 1948 (c.49)
Finance Act 1949 (c.47)
Finance Act 1950 (c.15)
Finance Act 1951 (c.43)
Finance Act 1952 (c.33)
Finance Act 1953 (c.34)
Finance Act 1954 (c.44)
Finance Act 1955 (c.15)
Finance Act 1956 (c.54)
Finance Act 1957 (c.49)
Finance Act 1958 (c.56)
Finance Act 1959 (c.58)
Finance Act 1960 (c.44)
Finance Act 1961 (c.36)

Finance Act 1962 (c.44)
Finance Act 1963 (c.25)
Finance Act 1964 (c.49)
Finance Act 1965 (c.25)
Finance Act 1966 (c.18)
Finance Act 1967 (c.54)
Finance Act 1968 (c.44)
Finance Act 1969 (c.32)
Finance Act 1970 (c.24)
Finance Act 1971 (c.68)
Finance Act 1972 (c.41)
Finance Act 1973 (c.51)
Finance Act 1974 (c.30)
Finance Act 1975 (c.7)
Finance Act 1976 (c.40)
Finance Act 1977 (c.36)
Finance Act 1978 (c.42)
Finance Act 1979 (c.25)
Finance Act 1980 (c.48)
Finance Act 1981 (c.35)
Finance Act 1982 (c.39)
Finance Act 1983 (c.28)
Finance Act 1984 (c.43)
Finance Act 1985 (c.54)
Finance Act 1986 (c.41)
Finance Act 1987 (c.16)
Finance Act 1988 (c.39)
Finance Act 1989 (c.26)
Finance Act 1990 (c.29)
Finance Act 1991 (c.31)
Finance Act 1992 (c.20)
Finance Act 1993 (c.34)
Finance Act 1994 (c.9)
Finance (Exchequer Bonds) Amendment Act 1916 (c.36)
Finance (Income Tax Reliefs) Act 1977 (c.53)
Finance (New Duties) Act 1916 (c.11)
Finance (No. 2) Act 1915 (c.89)
Finance (No. 2) Act 1931 (c.49)
Finance (No. 2) Act 1939 (c.109)
Finance (No. 2) Act 1940 (c.48)
Finance (No. 2) Act 1945 (c.13)
Finance (No. 2) Act 1947 (c.9)
Finance (No. 2) Act 1955 (c.17)
Finance (No. 2) Act 1964 (c.92)
Finance (No. 2) Act 1975 (c.45)
Finance (No. 2) Act 1979 (c.47)
Finance (No. 2) Act 1983 (c.49)
Finance (No. 2) Act 1987 (c.51)
Finance (No. 2) Act 1992 (c.48)
Finance (Session 2) Act 1914 (c.7)
Financial Emergency Enactments (Cont.) Act 1931 (c.13)
Financial Powers (U.S.A. Securities) Act 1941 (c.36)
Financial Services Act 1986 (c.60)
Findhorn Harbour Act 1778 (c.70)
Finding of the Longitude at Sea Act 1776 (c.48)
Finding of the Longitude at Sea Act 1780 (c.52)
Finding of the Longitude at Sea Act 1780 (c.61)

Fine Arts Copyright Act 1862 (c.68)
Fine or Imprisonment (Scotland and Ireland) Act 1899 (c.11)
Fines Act 1833 (c.99)
Fines Act (Ireland) 1851 (c.90)
Fines Act (Ireland) 1851, Amendment Act 1874 (c.72)
Fines Act (Ireland) 1874 (c.72)
Fines and Penalties (Ireland) Act 1839 (c.92)
Fines and Recoveries Act 1833 (c.74)
Fines and Recoveries Act 1842 (c.32)
Fines and Recoveries Act 1848 (c.70)
Fines and Recoveries (Ireland) Act 1834 (c.82)
Fines by Justices Act 1801 (c.85)
Fines, etc. (Ireland) Act 1838 (c.99)
Fines, etc. (Ireland) Act 1843 (c.56)
Fines (Ireland) Act 1851 (c.90)
Fines on Stills Act 1810 (c.100)
Finsbury Square Act 1791 (c.90)
Finsbury Square (Paving, Watching, etc.) Act 1795 (c.45)
Fire Brigade Pensions Act 1925 (c.47)
Fire Brigade Pensions Act 1929 (c.35)
Fire Brigades Act 1938 (c.72)
Fire Insurance Duty Act 1782 (c.48)
Fire Precautions Act 1971 (c.40)
Fire Precautions (Loans) Act 1973 (c.11)
Fire Prevention (Metropolis) Act 1774 (c.78)
Fire Safety and Safety of Places of Sport Act 1987 (c.27)
Fire Service College Board (Abolition) Act 1982 (c.13)
Fire Services Act 1947 (c.41)
Fire Services Act 1951 (c.27)
Fire Services Act 1959 (c.44)
Fire Services (Emergency Provisions) Act 1941 (c.22)
Firearms Act 1813 (c.115)
Firearms Act 1815 (c.59)
Firearms Act 1934 (c.16)
Firearms Act 1937 (c.12)
Firearms Act 1965 (c.44)
Firearms Act 1968 (c.27)
Firearms Act 1982 (c.31)
Firearms (Amendment) Act 1936 (c.39)
Firearms (Amendment) Act 1988 (c.45)
Firearms (Amendment) Act 1992 (c.31)
Firearms (Amendment) Act 1994 (c.31)
Firearms and Imitation Firearms (Criminal Use) Act 1933 (c.50)
Fires Prevention Act 1785 (c.77)
Fires Prevention Act 1838 (c.75)
Fireworks Act 1951 (c.58)
Fireworks Act 1964 (c.23)
First Meetings of Certain Commissioners Act 1786 (c.95)
First Meetings of Commissioners Act 1808 (c.133)
First Meetings of Commissioners, etc. Act 1776 (c.36)
First Meetings of Commissioners, etc. Act 1779 (c.55)

First Meetings of Commissioners, etc. Act 1782 (c.74)

First Offenders Act 1958 (c.31)

First Offenders (Scotland) Act 1960 (c.23)

First Public Health Supplemental Act 1852 (c.41)

Fish Act 1705 (c.8)

Fish Act 1714 (c.18)

Fish Act 1756 (c.39)

Fish Act 1759 (c.27)

Fish Act 1796 (c.118)

Fish Act 1801 (c.3)

Fish Act 1801 (c.99)

Fish Carriage Act 1762 (c.15)

Fish Market, Westminster Act 1748 (c.49)

Fish, Newfoundland, etc. Act 1801 (c.77)

Fish Teinds (Scotland) Act 1864 (c.33)

Fisheries Act 1780 (c.60)

Fisheries Act 1785 (c.65)

Fisheries Act 1786 (c.41)

Fisheries Act 1786 (c.81)

Fisheries Act 1787 (c.10)

Fisheries Act 1891 (c.37)

Fisheries Act 1955 (c.7)

Fisheries Act 1981 (c.29)

Fisheries Close Season (Ireland) Act 1895 (c.29)

Fisheries, Continuance of Laws Act 1801 (c.97)

Fisheries, Convention with France Act 1839 (c.96)

Fisheries, Convention with France Act 1840 (c.69)

Fisheries, Convention with France Act 1842 (c.63)

Fisheries (Dynamite) Act 1877 (c.65)

Fisheries in Greenland Seas, etc. Act 1799 (c.101)

Fisheries (Ireland) Act 1807 (c.22)

Fisheries (Ireland) Act 1842 (c.106)

Fisheries (Ireland) Act 1844 (c.108)

Fisheries (Ireland) Act 1845 (c.108)

Fisheries (Ireland) Act 1846 (c.3)

Fisheries (Ireland) Act 1846 (c.114)

Fisheries (Ireland) Act 1848 (c.92)

Fisheries (Ireland) Act 1850 (c.88)

Fisheries (Ireland) Act 1869 (c.92)

Fisheries (Ireland) Act 1901 (c.38)

Fisheries (Ireland) Act 1909 (c.25)

Fisheries (Norfolk and Suffolk) Act 1896 (c.18)

Fisheries (Oyster, Crab and Lobster) Act 1877 (c.42)

Fisheries (Oyster, Crab and Lobster) Act (1877) Amendment 1884 (c.26)

Fisheries (Scotland) Act 1726 (c.30)

Fisheries (Scotland) Act 1756 (c.23)

Fisheries (Severn and Verniew) Act 1778 (c.33)

Fishery Act 1791 (c.22)

Fishery Act 1794 (c.22)

Fishery Board (Scotland) Act 1882 (c.78)

Fishery Boards (Scotland) Extension of Powers Act 1894 (c.14)

Fishery Convention with France Act 1855 (c.101)

Fishery Harbours Act 1915 (c.48)

Fishery Harbours (Continuance of Powers) Act 1917 (c.39)

Fishery (Ireland) Act 1888 (c.30)

Fishery Limits Act 1964 (c.72)

Fishery Limits Act 1976 (c.86)

Fishery Treaty with United States Act 1855 (c.3)

Fishguard Roads Act 1791 (c.106)

Fishhouse Bridge Lancashire Act 1750 (c.36)

Fishing Vessel Grants Act 1967 (c.35)

Fishing Vessels (Safety Provisions) Act 1970 (c.27)

Flax and Cotton Manufactures Act 1789 (c.54)

Flax and Hemp Seed (Ireland) Act 1810 (c.82)

Flax Companies (Financial Assistance) Act 1918 (c.24)

Flax, etc., Manufacture Act 1783 (c.77)

Flax, etc. Manufacture (Great Britain) Act 1815 (c.178)

Flax Seed (Ireland) Act 1809 (c.29)

Fleet Ditch Act 1732 (c.22)

Flint and Carnarvon Roads Act 1779 (c.107)

Flint Canal Act 1788 (c.72)

Flint Roads Act 1769 (c.45)

Flint Roads Act 1771 (c.69)

Flint Roads Act 1788 (c.101)

Flintshire Roads Act 1763 (c.44)

Flood Prevention (Scotland) Act 1961 (c.41)

Folkestone: Improvement Act 1796 (c.49)

Folkestone Parish Church Act 1766 (c.63)

Food Act 1984 (c.30)

Food and Drugs Act 1938 (c.56)

Food and Drugs Act 1955 (c.16)

Food and Drugs (Amendment) Act 1954 (c.67)

Food and Drugs (Amendment) Act 1981 (c.26)

Food and Drugs (Amendment) Act 1982 (c.26)

Food and Drugs (Control of Food Premises) Act 1976 (c.37)

Food and Drugs (Milk) Act 1970 (c.3)

Food and Drugs (Milk and Dairies) Act 1944 (c.29)

Food and Drugs (Milk and Dairies and Artificial Cream) Act 1950 (c.35)

Food and Drugs (Scotland) Act 1956 (c.30)

Food and Environment Protection Act 1985 (c.48)

Food Safety Act 1990 (c.16)

Foods and Drugs (Adulteration) Act 1928 (c.31)

Foodstuffs (Prevention of Exploitation) Act 1931 (c.51)

Football (Offences) Act 1991 (c.19)

Football Spectators Act 1989 (c.37)

Forces Act 1922 (c.11)

Forces of East India Company Act 1799 (c.109)

Forces of East India Company Act 1805 (c.36)

Forces of East India Company Act 1812 (c.122)

Forcible Entry Act 1381 (c.7)

Forcible Entry Act 1429 (c.9)

Forcible Entry Act 1588 (c.1588)

Forcible Entry Act 1623 (c.15)

Forcible Entry (Ireland) Act 1786 (c.24)

Forehoe, Norfolk (Borrowing Powers of Guardians) Act 1783 (c.29)

Forehoe, Norfolk (Guardians' Borrowing Powers) Act 1789 (c.4)

Forehoe, Norfolk: Poor Relief Act 1776 (c.9)

Foreign and Protestants Naturalization Act 1708 (c.5)

Foreign Compensation Act 1950 (c.12)

Foreign Compensation Act 1962 (c.4)

Foreign Compensation Act 1969 (c.20)

Foreign Compensation (Amendment) Act 1993 (c.16)

Foreign Corporations Act 1991 (c.44)

Foreign Deserters Act 1852 (c.26)

Foreign Enlistment Act 1735 (c.30)

Foreign Enlistment Act 1756 (c.17)

Foreign Enlistment Act 1870 (c.90)

Foreign Judgments (Reciprocal Enforcement) Act 1933 (c.13)

Foreign Jurisdiction Act 1844 (c.94)

Foreign Jurisdiction Act 1875 (c.85)

Foreign Jurisdiction Act 1878 (c.67)

Foreign Jurisdiction Act 1890 (c.37)

Foreign Jurisdiction Act 1913 (c.16)

Foreign Jurisdiction Act Amendment Act 1865 (c.16)

Foreign Jurisdiction Act Amendment Act 1866 (c.87)

Foreign Jurisdiction Act Foreign Law Ascertainment Act 1861 (c.11)

Foreign Law Ascertainment Act 1861 (c.11)

Foreign Limitation Periods Act 1984 (c.16)

Foreign Marriage Act 1891 (c.74)

Foreign Marriage Act 1892 (c.23)

Foreign Marriage Act 1947 (c.33)

Foreign Marriage (Amendment) Act 1988 (c.44)

Foreign Prison-Made Goods Act 1897 (c.63)

Foreign Protestants Naturalization Act 1714 (c.29)

Foreign Service Act 1943 (c.35)

Foreign Service Act 1960 (c.11)

Foreign Ships Act 1797 (c.63)

Foreign Ships, etc. Act 1805 (c.32)

Foreign Tribunals Evidence Act 1856 (c.113)

Forest of Dean Act 1836 (c.3)

Forest of Dean Act 1844 (c.13)

Forest of Dean (Poor Relief) Act 1842 (c.48)

Forestalling, Regrating, etc. Act 1844 (c.24)

Forestry Act 1919 (c.58)

Forestry Act 1921 (c.61)

Forestry Act 1927 (c.6)

Forestry Act 1944 (c.35)

Forestry Act 1947 (c.21)

Forestry Act 1951 (c.61)

Forestry Act 1967 (c.10)

Forestry Act 1979 (c.21)

Forestry Act 1981 (c.39)

Forestry Act 1986 (c.30)

Forestry Act 1991 (c.43)

Forestry (Sale of Land) (Scotland) Act 1963 (c.23)

Forestry (Transfer of Woods) Act 1923 (c.21)

Forfar Roads Act 1789 (c.20)

Forfar Roads Act 1794 (c.100)

Forfeited and Unclaimed Prize Money Act 1811 (c.104)

Forfeited Estates Act 1703 (c.61)

Forfeited Estates—Derwentwater Estate Act 1731 (c.23)

Forfeited Estates, etc. Act 1718 (c.23)

Forfeited Estates—Greenwich Hospital Act 1734 (c.29)

Forfeited Estates (Ireland) Act 1705 (c.11)

Forfeited Estates (Ireland) Act 1703 (c.19)

Forfeited Estates (Ireland) etc. Act 1703 (c.21)

Forfeited Estates (Scotland) Act 1774 (c.65)

Forfeited Estates, Scotland Act 1786 (c.27)

Forfeited Estates (Time for Claims) Act 1716 (c.20)

Forfeiture Act 1870 (c.23)

Forfeiture Act 1982 (c.34)

Forfeiture upon Attainder of Treason Act 1799 (c.93)

Forged Exchequer Bills Act 1842 (c.11)

Forged Exchequer Bills Act 1843 (c.1)

Forged Transfers Act 1891 (c.43)

Forged Transfers Act 1892 (c.36)

Forgeries and Frauds in Bank Transfers Act 1793 (c.30)

Forgery Act 1733 (c.22)

Forgery Act 1778 (c.18)

Forgery Act 1797 (c.122)

Forgery Act 1830 (c.66)

Forgery Act 1837 (c.84)

Forgery Act 1861 (c.98)

Forgery Act 1870 (c.58)

Forgery Act 1913 (c.27)

Forgery and Counterfeiting Act 1981 (c.45)

Forgery of Bank of Ireland Notes, etc. Act 1809 (c.13)

Forgery of Banknotes Act 1801 (c.39)

Forgery of Foreign Bills Act 1803 (c.139)

Form of Deeds Act (Scotland) 1856 (c.89)

Former Enemy Aliens (Disabilities Removal) Act 1925 (c.43)

Forms of Pleading Act 1838 (c.100)

Forms of Pleading in High Court Act 1855 (c.26)

Forsyth's Indemnity Act 1866 (c.20)

Fort Marlborough in India Act 1802 (c.29)

Fort of Senegal Act 1763 (c.20)

Fort William in Bengal Act 1786 (c.25)

Fort William Pulp and Paper Mills Act 1963 (c.15)

Forth and Clyde and Monkland Canal Act 1790 (c.73)

Forth and Clyde Canal (Extinguishment of Rights of Navigation) Act 1962 (c.16)

Forth and Clyde Navigation Act 1768 (c.63)

Forth and Clyde, Navigation Act 1771 (c.62)

Forth and Clyde, Navigation Act 1773 (c.104)

Forth and Clyde: Navigation Act 1784 (c.59)

Forth and Clyde: Navigation Act 1787 (c.20)

Forth and Clyde: Navigation Act 1787 (c.55)

Fortifications Act 1708 (c.26)

Fortifications Act 1709 (c.23)

Fortifications Act 1757 (cc.38, 39)

Fortifications (Expenses) Act 1869 (c.76)

Fortifications for Royal Arsenals, etc. Act 1863 (c.80)

Fortifications for Royal Arsenals, etc. Act 1864 (c.109)

Fortifications - Portsmouth Act 1722 (c.32)

Fortifications - Portsmouth and Dover Act 1806 (c.105)

Fortifications, Portsmouth and Dover Act 1809 (c.39)

Fortifications, Royal Arsenals, etc. Act 1865 (c.61)

Fosdyke Bridge Act 1984 (c.17)

Foss, York: Navigation Act 1793 (c.99)

Foster Children Act 1980 (c.6)

Foster Children (Scotland) Act 1984 (c.56)

Foston Bridge and Witham Common Road Act 1725 (c.16)

Founding Hospital Act 1739 (c.29)

Foundling Hospital, Dublin Act 1801 (c.50)

Four and a Half Per Cent, Duties Repeal Act 1838 (c.92)

Four Courts Library Act 1894 (c.4)

Four Courts Marshalsea Discontinuance Act 1874 (c.21)

Four Courts Marshalsea (Ireland) Act 1842 (c.95)

Foyle College Act 1874 (c.79)

Frame Work Knitters Act 1766 (c.29)

Frampton Mansel Marriage Act 1868 (c.23)

Franchise Prisons Abolition Act 1858 (c.22)

Frauds by Boatmen and Others, etc. Act 1809 (c.122)

Frauds by Boatmen, etc. Act 1813 (c.87)

Frauds by Boatmen in Cinque Ports, etc. Act 1808 (c.130)

Frauds by Journeymen Shoemakers Act 1722 (c.27)

Frauds by Workmen Act 1748 (c.27)

Frauds by Workmen Act 1777 (c.56)

Frauds, etc., in Woollen Manufacturers Act 1774 (c.25)

Frauds in Excise Revenue Act 1791 (c.21)

Frauds in Excise Revenue Act 1792 (c.8)

Frauds in Manufacture of Clocks, etc. Act 1754 (c.7)

Frauds in Manufacture of Sweets Act 1815 (c.177)

Frauds in the Public Revenues, etc. Act 1738 (c.72)

Frauds of Workmen Act 1739 (c.8)

Frauds on Exportation Act 1810 (c.53)

Fraudulent Bankrupts (Scotland) Act 1827 (c.20)

Fraudulent Mediums Act 1951 (c.33)

Free Fishers of Whitstable Act 1793 (c.42)

Free Ports Act 1796 (c.55)

Free Ports Act 1797 (c.77)

Free Ports Act 1800 (c.23)

Free Ports, Jamaica Act 1774 (c.41)

Free Ports, West Indies, etc. Act 1766 (c.49)

Freeman (Admission) Act 1763 (c.15)

Freshwater and Salmon Fisheries (Scotland) Act 1976 (c.22)

Freshwater Fish (Scotland) Act 1902 (c.29)

Freshwater Fisheries Act 1878 (c.39)

Freshwater Fisheries Act 1884 (c.11)

Freshwater Fisheries Act 1886 (c.2)

Friendly and Industrial and Provident Societies Act 1968 (c.55)

Friendly Societies Act 1793 (c.54)

Friendly Societies Act 1795 (c.111)

Friendly Societies Act 1803 (c.111)

Friendly Societies Act 1809 (c.125)

Friendly Societies Act 1840 (c.73)

Friendly Societies Act 1846 (c.27)

Friendly Societies Act 1850 (c.115)

Friendly Societies Act 1852 (c.65)

Friendly Societies Act 1854 (c.101)

Friendly Societies Act 1855 (c.63)

Friendly Societies Act 1858 (c.101)

Friendly Societies Act 1860 (c.13)

Friendly Societies Act 1860 (c.58)

Friendly Societies Act 1875 (c.60)

Friendly Societies Act 1879 (c.9)

Friendly Societies Act 1887 (c.56)

Friendly Societies Act 1888 (c.66)

Friendly Societies Act 1889 (c.22)

Friendly Societies Act 1893 (c.30)

Friendly Societies Act 1895 (c.26)

Friendly Societies Act 1896 (c.25)

Friendly Societies Act 1908 (c.32)

Friendly Societies Act 1916 (c.54)

Friendly Societies Act 1924 (c.11)

Friendly Societies Act 1955 (c.19)

Friendly Societies Act 1971 (c.66)

Friendly Societies Act 1974 (c.46)

Friendly Societies Act 1981 (c.50)

Friendly Societies Act 1984 (c.62)

Friendly Societies Act 1992 (c.40)

Friendly Societies Amendment Act 1876 (c.32)

Friendly Society Amendment Act 1885 (c.27)

Friendly Societies Discharge Act 1854 (c.56)

Friendly Societies (Ireland) Act 1809 (c.58)

Friendly Societies (Quinquennial Returns) Act 1882 (c.35)

Frivolous Arrests Act 1725 (c.29)

Frivolous Arrests Act 1811 (c.124)

Frivolous Suits Act 1772 (c.51)

Frivolous Suits Act 1841 (c.28)

Frogmore House Act 1841 (c.2)

Frome Roads Act 1757 (c.39)

Frome Roads Act 1772 (c.94)

Frome Roads Act 1797 (c.175)

Fuel and Electricity (Control) Act 1973 (c.67)
Fugitive Offenders Act 1881 (c.69)
Fugitive Offenders Act 1967 (c.68)
Fugitive Offenders (Protected States) Act 1915 (c.39)
Fulbourne Church Act 1775 (c.49)
Fulham and Putney Bridge Act 1725 (c.36)
Fulham Bridge Act 1727 (c.18)
Fulham Roads Act 1730 (c.34)
Fulham Roads Act 1749 (c.16)
Fund for Fire Victims in Edinburgh Act 1727 (c.22)
Furnished Houses (Rent Control) Act 1946 (c.34)
Furnished Lettings (Rent Allowances) Act 1973 (c.6)
Further and Higher Education Act 1992 (c.13)
Further and Higher Education (Scotland) Act 1992 (c.37)
Further Education Act 1985 (c.47)

Gainsborough Bridge Act 1787 (c.15)
Gainsborough Church Act 1735 (c.22)
Gainsborough Church Act 1740 (c.15)
Gainsborough: Improvement Act 1769 (c.21)
Gainsborough: Inclosure Act 1796 (c.101)
Gainsborough Inclosure, etc. Act 1795 (c.82)
Galashiels Act 1867 (c.85)
Galashiels and Selkirk Act 1872 (c.47)
Galway Harbour Act 1859 (c.28)
Galway Harbour Act 1867 (c.56)
Gambia Independence Act 1964 (c.93)
Game Act 1706 (c.16)
Game Act 1710 (c.27)
Game Act 1716 (c.11)
Game Act 1721 (c.19)
Game Act 1755 (c.12)
Game Act 1762 (c.19)
Game Act 1766 (c.21)
Game Act 1770 (c.19)
Game Act 1773 (c.80)
Game Act 1796 (c.39)
Game Act 1796 (c.54)
Game Act 1831 (c.32)
Game Act 1970 (c.13)
Game Birds (Ireland) Act 1874 (c.11)
Game Certificates Act 1784 (c.43)
Game Certificates Act 1785 (c.50)
Game Certificates (Ireland) Act 1842 (c.81)
Game (England) Act 1772 (c.55)
Game Laws (Amendment) Act 1960 (c.36)
Game Laws Amendment (Scotland) Act 1877 (c.28)
Game Laws (England); Local Taxes, etc. (Scotland) Act 1836 (c.65)
Game Licences Act 1860 (c.90)
Game (Scotland) Act 1750 (c.34)
Game (Scotland) Act 1772 (c.54)
Game Trespass (Ireland) Act 1864 (c.67)
Gamekeepers Act 1808 (c.93)
Gaming Act 1710 (c.19)
Gaming Act 1738 (c.28)

Gaming Act 1739 (c.19)
Gaming Act 1744 (c.34)
Gaming Act 1802 (c.119)
Gaming Act 1845 (c.109)
Gaming Act 1892 (c.9)
Gaming Act 1922 (c.19)
Gaming Act 1968 (c.65)
Gaming Act (Northern Ireland) 1845 (c.109)
Gaming (Amendment) Act 1973 (c.12)
Gaming (Amendment) Act 1982 (c.22)
Gaming (Amendment) Act 1980 (c.8)
Gaming (Amendment) Act 1986 (c.11)
Gaming (Amendment) Act 1987 (c.11)
Gaming (Amendment) Act 1990 (c.26)
Gaming (Bingo) Act 1985 (c.35)
Gaming Houses Act 1854 (c.38)
Gaming Machines (Scotland) Act 1917 (c.23)
Gaming Transactions Act 1844 (c.7)
Gaol Fees Abolition Act 1815 (c.50)
Gaol Fees Abolition Act 1845 (c.114)
Gaols Act 1772 (c.58)
Gaols Act 1784 (c.54)
Gaols Act 1789 (c.67)
Gaols Act 1791 (c.46)
Garrotters Act 1863 (c.44)
Gas Act 1948 (c.67)
Gas Act 1960 (c.27)
Gas Act 1965 (c.36)
Gas Act 1972 (c.60)
Gas Act 1980 (c.37)
Gas Act 1986 (c.44)
Gas and Electricity Act 1968 (c.39)
Gas and Electricity (Borrowing Powers) Act 1954 (c.52)
Gas and Steam Vehicles (Excise Duties) Act 1939 (c.6)
Gas and Water Works Facilities Act 1870 (c.70)
Gas and Water Works Facilities Act, 1870, Amendment 1873 (c.89)
Gas (Borrowing Powers) Act 1965 (c.60)
Gas (Exempt Supplies) Act 1993 (c.1)
Gas Levy Act 1981 (c.3)
Gas (Standard of Calorific Power) Act 1916 (c.25)
Gas Undertakings Act 1929 (c.24)
Gas Undertakings Act 1931 (c.40)
Gas Undertakings Act 1934 (c.28)
Gasworks Clauses Act 1847 (c.15)
Gasworks Clauses Act 1871 (c.41)
General Board of Health Act 1856 (c.85)
General Board of Health Act 1857 (c.38)
General Board of Health Continuance Act 1855 (c.115)
General de Lancey (Crown Claims) Act 1807 (c.69)
General de Lancey (Estates and Crown Claims) Act 1811 (c.102)
General Dealers (Ireland) Act 1903 (c.44)
General Pardon Act (c.19)
General Pardon Act 1707 (c.22)
General Pardon Act 1720 (c.29)
General Pardon Act 1746 (c.52)

General Pier and Harbour Act 1861 (c.45)

General Pier and Harbour Act, 1861, Amendment Act 1862 (c.19)

General Police and Improvement (Scotland) Act 1862 (c.101)

General Police and Improvement (Scotland) Act, 1862, Amendment Act 1877 (c.22)

General Police and Improvement (Scotland) Act, 1862, Amendment Act 1889 (c.51)

General Police and Improvement (Scotland) Act 1865 (c.7)

General Police and Improvement (Scotland) Act 1882 (c.6)

General Police and Improvement (Scotland) Amendment Act 1878 (c.30)

General Police and Improvement (Scotland) Supplemental Act 1863

General Police and Improvement (Scotland) Supplemental Act 1865 (c.7)

General Police and Improvement (Scotland) Supplemental Act 1866 (c.93)

General Police and Improvement (Scotland) Supplemental Act 1867 (c.79)

General Prisons (Ireland) Act 1877 (c.49)

General Rate Act 1967 (c.9)

General Rate Act 1970 (c.19)

General Rate Act 1975 (c.5)

General Rate (Public Utilities) Act 1977 (c.11)

General Register House, Edinburgh Act 1847 (c.20)

General Register Office Act 1852 (c.25)

Geneva Convention Act 1911 (c.20)

Geneva Convention Act 1937 (c.15)

Geneva Conventions Act 1957 (c.52)

Genocide Act 1969 (c.12)

Geological Survey Act 1845 (c.63)

German Conventions Act 1955 (c.2)

German Reparation (Recovery) Act 1921 (c.5)

Ghana (Consequential Provisions) Act 1960 (c.41)

Ghana Independence Act 1957 (c.6)

Gibraltar Lighthouse, etc. Act 1838 (c.66)

Gifts for Churches Act 1803 (c.108)

Gifts for Churches Act 1811 (c.115)

Glamorgan, Llansamlett–Llangevelach Bridge, River Tawey Act 1778 (c.68)

Glamorgan Roads Act 1764 (c.88)

Glamorgan Roads Act 1771 (c.77)

Glamorgan Roads Act 1779 (c.110)

Glamorgan Roads Act 1785 (c.122)

Glamorgan Roads Act 1793 (c.133)

Glamorganshire Canal Act 1796 (c.69)

Glamorganshire Election Act 1815 (c.72)

Glasgow and Dumbarton Roads Act 1772 (c.106)

Glasgow and Renfrew Road Act 1797 (c.161)

Glasgow and Renfrew Roads Act 1794 (c.140)

Glasgow and Shotts Road Act 1753 (c.81)

Glasgow Beer Duties Act 1715 (c.44)

Glasgow Beer Duties Act 1725 (c.27)

Glasgow Beer Duties Act 1735 (c.31)

Glasgow Beer Duties Act 1755 (c.29)

Glasgow Boundaries Act 1871 (c.68)

Glasgow (Improvement) Act 1768 (c.16)

Glasgow: Improvement Act 1793 (c.124)

Glasgow Parliamentary Divisions Act 1896 (c.17)

Glasgow Roads Act 1753 (c.90)

Glasgow Roads Act 1754 (c.27)

Glasgow Roads Act 1766 (c.82)

Glasgow Roads Act 1774 (c.102)

Glasgow Roads Act 1774 (c.105)

Glasgow Roads Act 1788 (c.92)

Glasgow Roads Act 1792 (c.152)

Glasgow Roads Act 1792 (c.154)

Glasgow Roads Act 1793 (c.160)

Glasgow Roads Act 1793 (c.174)

Glasgow Roads Act 1795 (c.155)

Glass Duties Act 1787 (c.28)

Glass Duties Act 1794 (c.27)

Glass Duties Act 1835 (c.77)

Glass Duties Act 1838 (c.44)

Glass Duties Repeal Act 1845 (c.6)

Glass, etc., Duties Act 1813 (c.70)

Glebe Exchange Act 1815 (c.147)

Glebe Exchange Act 1816 (c.52)

Glebe Houses (Ireland) Act 1803 (c.158)

Glebe (Ireland) Act 1851 (c.73)

Glebe Lands Act 1888 (c.20)

Glebe Lands Leasing Powers (Ireland) Act 1857 (c.47)

Glebe Lands, Representative Church Body, Ireland, Act 1875 (c.42)

Glebe Lands (Scotland) Act 1866 (c.71)

Glebe Loan Act 1870 (c.112)

Glebe Loan Act 1871 (c.100)

Glebe Loan (Ireland) Acts Amendment 1880 (c.2)

Glebe Loan (Ireland) Acts Amendment 1883 (c.8)

Glebe Loan (Ireland) Acts Amendment 1886 (c.6)

Glebe Loan (Ireland) Amendment Act 1875 (c.30)

Glebe Loan (Ireland) Amendment Act 1878 (c.6)

Glebe Loan (Ireland) Amendments Act 1871 (c.100)

Gloucester and Berkeley Canal Act 1793 (c.97)

Gloucester and Berkeley Canal Act 1797 (c.54)

Gloucester and Crickley Hull Road Act 1760 (c.30)

Gloucester and Hereford Roads Act 1746 (c.31)

Gloucester and Hereford Roads Act 1759 (c.34)

Gloucester and Hereford Roads Act 1769 (c.50)

Gloucester and Oxford Road Act 1750 (c.28)

Gloucester and Oxford Roads Act 1768 (c.41)

Gloucester and Oxford Roads Act 1787 (c.77)

Gloucester and Warwick Roads Act 1755 (c.47)

Gloucester and Wiltshire Roads Act 1756 (c.56)

Gloucester and Wiltshire Roads Act 1757 (c.61)

Gloucester and Wiltshire Roads Act 1762 (c.74)

Gloucester and Wiltshire Roads Act 1779 (c.118)

Gloucester and Wiltshire Roads Act 1792 (c.153)

Gloucester and Worcester Roads Act 1764 (c.79)

Gloucester and Worcester Roads Act 1794 (c.135)

Gloucester Gaol Act 1781 (c.74)

Gloucester Gaol Act 1785 (c.10)

Gloucester (Poor Relief, etc.) Act 1764 (c.60)

Gloucester Roads Act 1742 (c.21)

Gloucester Roads Act 1742 (c.22)

Gloucester Roads Act 1745 (c.18)

Gloucester Roads Act 1746 (c.23)

Gloucester Roads Act 1751 (c.13)

Gloucester Roads Act 1756 (c.58)

Gloucester Roads Act 1770 (c.74)

Gloucester Roads Act 1778 (c.102)

Gloucester Roads Act 1779 (c.93)

Gloucester Roads Act 1779 (c.115)

Gloucester Roads Act 1780 (c.70)

Gloucester Roads Act 1780 (c.84)

Gloucester Roads Act 1780 (c.93)

Gloucester Roads Act 1783 (c.104)

Gloucester Roads Act 1787 (c.68)

Gloucester Roads Act 1787 (c.78)

Gloucester Roads Act 1792 (c.146)

Gloucester Roads Act 1795 (c.140)

Gloucester Streets Act 1749 (c.15)

Gloucester to Stroud Road Act 1778 (c.98)

Gloucester Water Supply Act 1740 (c.11)

Gloucestershire Highways Act 1722 (c.31)

Gloucestershire Roads Act 1725 (c.24)

Gloucestershire Roads Act 1741 (c.15)

Gloucestershire Roads Act 1756 (c.51)

Gloucestershire Roads Act 1757 (c.54)

Gloucestershire Roads Act 1757 (c.64)

Gloucestershire Roads Act 1757 (c.65)

Gloucestershire Roads Act 1757 (c.70)

Gloucestershire Roads Act 1769 (c.58)

Gloucestershire Roads Act 1774 (c.111)

Gloucestershire Roads Act 1783 (c.106)

Gloucestershire: Small Debts Act 1792 (c.77)

Glove Duties Act 1785 (c.55)

Godmanchester to Cambridge Road Act 1793 (c.156)

Godstone to Highgate Road Act 1766 (c.58)

Gold and Silver (Export Control, etc.) Act 1920 (c.70)

Gold and Silver Thread Act 1702 (c.11)

Gold and Silver Thread Act 1741 (c.20)

Gold and Silver Thread Act 1788 (c.7)

Gold and Silver Wares Act 1844 (c.22)

Gold and Silver Wares Act 1854 (c.96)

Gold Currency Act 1812 (c.5)

Gold Currency Act 1814 (c.52)

Gold Currency and Bank Notes Act 1811 (c.127)

Gold Currency, etc. Act 1812 (c.50)

Gold Plate (Standard) Act 1798 (c.69)

Gold Standard Act 1925 (c.29)

Gold Standard (Amendment) Act 1931 (c.46)

Golden Square (Rates) Act 1750 (c.27)

Goodman's Fields Act 1778 (c.50)

Goods and Services (Price Control) Act 1941 (c.31)

Goods in Neutral Ships Act 1802 (c.80)

Gordon Memorial College at Khartoum Act 1899 (c.16)

Gosport: Improvement Act 1763 (c.56)

Goswell St., Middlesex Act 1780 (c.48)

Government and Other Stocks (Emergency Provisions) Act 1939 (c.100)

Government Annuities Act 1838 (c.49)

Government Annuities Act 1853 (c.45)

Government Annuities Act 1873 (c.44)

Government Annuities Act 1882 (c.51)

Government Annuities Act 1929 (c.29)

Government Annuities (Investments) Act 1864 (c.46)

Government Contractors Act 1815 (c.195)

Government of Burma Act 1935 (c.3)

Government of Burma (Temporary Provisions) Act 1944 (c.30)

Government of India Act 1800 (c.79)

Government of India Act 1833 (c.85)

Government of India Act 1853 (c.95)

Government of India Act 1854 (c.77)

Government of India Act 1858 (c.106)

Government of India Act 1859 (c.41)

Government of India Act 1865 (c.17)

Government of India Act 1869 (c.97)

Government of India Act 1870 (c.3)

Government of India Act 1912 (c.6)

Government of India Act 1915 (c.61)

Government of India Act 1919 (c.101)

Government of India Act 1935 (c.2)

Government of India Act 1935 (c.42)

Government of India (Aden) Act 1929 (c.2)

Government of India Amendment Act 1911 (c.25)

Government of India Amendment Act 1916 (c.37)

Government of India Amendment Act 1933 (c.23)

Government of India (Amendment) Act 1939 (c.66)

Government of India (Civil Services) Act 1925 (c.83)

Government of India (Indian Navy) Act 1927 (c.8)

Government of India (Leave of Absence) Act 1924 (c.28)

Government of India (Reprinting) Act 1935 (c.1)

Government of India (Statutory Commission) Act 1927 (c.24)

Government of Ireland Act 1914 (c.90)
Government of Ireland Act 1920 (c.67)
Government of New South Wales and Van Diemen's Land Act 1866 (c.74)
Government of New Zealand Act 1846 (c.103)
Government of Newfoundland Act 1847 (c.44)
Government of Northern Ireland (Loan Guarantee) Act 1922 (c.24)
Government of Soudan Loan Act 1919 (c.43)
Government of the Soudan Loan Act 1913 (c.10)
Government of the Soudan Loan Act 1914 (c.9)
Government of the Soudan Loan (Amendment) Act 1922 (c.15)
Government of New Zealand Act 1848 (c.5)
Government Offices Security Act 1810 (c.85)
Government Offices Security Act 1836 (c.28)
Government Offices Security Act 1838 (c.61)
Government Offices (Security) Act 1875 (c.64)
Government Trading Act 1990 (c.30)
Government Trading Funds Act 1973 (c.63)
Government War Obligations Act 1914 (c.11)
Government War Obligations Act 1915 (c.96)
Government War Obligations Act 1916 (c.70)
Government War Obligations Act 1918 (c.28)
Government War Obligations Act 1919 (c.44)
Governors, etc., of West Indies Islands Act 1794 (c.35)
Governors' Pension Act 1956 (c.64)
Governors' Pensions Act 1957 (c.62)
Grain Between Great Britain and Ireland Act 1806 (c.97)
Grammar Schools Act 1840 (c.77)
Grand Canal Branches (Ireland) Act 1844 (c.98)
Grand Canal (Ireland) Act 1813 (c.143)
Grand Junction Canal Act 1793 (c.80)
Grand Junction Canal Act 1794 (c.24)
Grand Junction Canal (No. 1) Act 1795 (c.8)
Grand Junction Canal (No. 2) Act 1795 (c.43)
Grand Junction Canal (No. 3) Act 1795 (c.85)
Grand Junction Canal (No. 4) Act 1795 (c.25)
Grand Juries Act 1856 (c.54)
Grand Juries (Ireland) Act 1843 (c.32)
Grand Juries (Suspension) Act 1917 (c.4)
Grand Jury Cess. Act 1846 (c.60)
Grand Jury Cess. Dublin Act 1838 (c.51)
Grand Jury Cess. (Dublin) Act 1851 (c.65)
Grand Jury Cess. (Ireland) Act 1848 (c.26)
Grand Jury Cess. (Ireland) Act 1849 (c.32)
Grand Jury Cess. (Ireland) Act 1850 (c.82)
Grand Jury Cess. (Ireland) Act 1853 (c.13)
Grand Jury Cess. (Ireland) Act 1857 (c.7)
Grand Jury (Ireland) Act 1816 (c.87)
Grand Jury (Ireland) Act 1836 Amendment 1908 (c.29)
Grand Jury (Ireland) Act 1836 (c.116)
Grand Jury (Ireland) Act 1837 (c.2)
Grand Jury (Ireland) Act 1838 (c.37)

Grand Jury (Ireland) Act 1853 (c.136)
Grand Jury (Ireland) Act 1856 (c.63)
Grand Jury (Ireland) Act 1857 (c.15)
Grand Jury (Ireland) Act 1872 (c.42)
Grand Jury (Ireland) Act 1873 (c.34)
Grand Jury (Ireland) Act 1895 (c.8)
Grand Jury Presentments (Ireland) Act 1842 (c.77)
Grand Jury Presentments (Ireland) Act 1843 (c.71)
Grant of Administration (Bonds) Act 1919 (c.26)
Grant of Feu Duties to John Francis Erskine Act 1815 (c.188)
Grant of Frogmore, etc. Act 1807 (c.45)
Grant of Manor of Corsham to Paul Methuen Act 1770 (c.13)
Grant of Military, etc. Commissions Act 1857 (c.4)
Grant to Duke of Marlborough Act 1704 (c.4)
Grant to J. Palmer, Esq. (Post Office Services) Act 1813 (c.157)
Grant to the House of Orange Act 1803 (c.149)
Grantham Canal Act 1793 (c.94)
Grantham Canal Act 1797 (c.30)
Grantham Town Hall Act 1787 (c.61)
Grants for Glebe Houses (I.) Act 1807 (c.23)
Grants of Life Annuities Act 1776 (c.26)
Grants of Officers Act 1812 (c.40)
Grants of Offices in Reversion, etc. Act 1808 (c.50)
Grants of Pensions Act 1811 (c.21)
Grants to George Keith Act 1760 (c.15)
Graves End: Streets Act 1772 (c.15)
Grease Butter from Ireland Act 1763 (c.20)
Great and Little Botton: Improvement Act 1792 (c.71)
Great Farringdon to Burford Road Act 1792 (c.150)
Great Grimsby (Lincoln) Harbour Act 1796 (c.98)
Great Marlow to Stokenchurch Road Act 1791 (c.135)
Great Seal Act 1851 (c.82)
Great Seal Act 1880 (c.10)
Great Seal Act 1884 (c.30)
Great Seal (Offices) Act 1874 (c.81)
Great Sessions in Wales Act 1768 (c.14)
Great Torrington Roads Act 1765 (c.58)
Great Torrington Roads Act 1786 (c.128)
Great Tower Hill: Improvement, etc. Act 1797 (c.87)
Great Yarmouth Haven Act 1749 (c.6)
Great Yarmouth: Improvement Act 1772 (c.14)
Great Yarmouth: Improvement Act 1785 (c.36)
Great Yarmouth Pier Act (c.10)
Greek Loan Act 1864 (c.40)
Greek Loan Act 1898 (c.4)
Greek Loan Guarantee Act 1836 (c.94)
Greek Marriages Act 1884 (c.20)

Greenland and Whale Fishery Act 1771 (c.38)
Greenland, etc., Fishery Act 1782 (c.19)
Greenland Fishery Act 1723 (c.16)
Greenland Fishery Act 1731 (c.78)
Greenland Fishery Act 1804 (c.23)
Greenland Trade Act 1702 (c.10)
Greenland Whale Fisheries Act 1802 (c.22)
Greenland Whale Fisheries Act 1815 (c.39)
Greenland Whale Fisheries, etc. Act (c.20)
Greenland Whale Fishery Act 1803 (c.32)
Greenland Whale Fishery Act 1805 (c.9)
Greenland Whale Fishery Act 1806 (c.9)
Greenland Whale Fishery Act 1810 (c.11)
Greenock Beer Duties Act 1750 (c.38)
Greenock: Improvement Act 1789 (c.43)
Greenock: Water Supply, etc. Act 1772 (c.28)
Greenwich Hospital Act 1728 (c.7)
Greenwich Hospital Act 1744 (c.31)
Greenwich Hospital Act 1751 (c.42)
Greenwich Hospital Act 1776 (c.24)
Greenwich Hospital Act 1806 (c.100)
Greenwich Hospital Act 1807 (c.52)
Greenwich Hospital Act 1814 (c.110)
Greenwich Hospital Act 1815 (c.56)
Greenwich Hospital Act 1829 (c.25)
Greenwich Hospital Act 1850 (c.24)
Greenwich Hospital Act 1865 (c.89)
Greenwich Hospital Act 1869 (c.44)
Greenwich Hospital Act 1870 (c.100)
Greenwich Hospital Act 1872 (c.67)
Greenwich Hospital Act 1883 (c.32)
Greenwich Hospital Act 1885 (c.42)
Greenwich Hospital Act 1898 (c.24)
Greenwich Hospital Act 1921 (c.41)
Greenwich Hospital Act 1942 (c.35)
Greenwich Hospital Act 1947 (c.5)
Greenwich Hospital Act 1967 (c.74)
Greenwich Hospital Act 1990 (c.13)
Greenwich Hospital (Disused Burial Ground) Act 1925 (c.58)
Greenwich Hospital, etc. Act 1711 (c.27)
Greenwich Hospital (Provision for Widows) Act 1863 (c.67)
Greenwich Markets Act 1849 (c.28)
Greenwich Out-Pensioners Act 1763 (c.16)
Grenada and St. Vincent Traders Act (c.11)
Grenada and St. Vincent Traders Act 1800 (c.27)
Grenada and St. Vincent Traders Act 1803 (c.40)
Grenada and St. Vincent Traders Act 1803 (c.104)
Grenada and St. Vincent Traders Act 1808 (c.135)
Gresham College, etc. Act 1768 (c.32)
Grey Seals Protection Act 1914 (c.3)
Grey Seals Protection Act 1931 (c.23)
Grosvenor Square: Paving, etc. Act 1774 (c.52)
Ground Game Act 1880 (c.47)
Ground Game (Amendment) Act 1906 (c.21)
Groundhurst Roads Act 1768 (c.35)

Growth of Coffee Act 1731 (c.24)
Growth of Coffee Act 1745 (c.23)
Growth of Coffee, etc. Act 1750 (c.35)
Growth of Hemp and Flax Act 1781 (c.58)
Growth of Raw Silk Act 1749 (c.20)
Guarantee by Companies Act 1867 (c.108)
Guard Dogs Act 1975 (c.50)
Guardians (Ireland) Act 1849 (c.4)
Guardianship Act 1973 (c.29)
Guardianship and Maintenance of Infants Act 1951 (c.56)
Guardianship of Infants Act 1886 (c.27)
Guardianship of Infants Act 1925 (c.45)
Guardianship of Minors Act 1971 (c.3)
Guardianship (Refugee Children) Act 1944 (c.8)
Guildford and Arundel Road Act 1757 (c.60)
Guildford and Farnham Road Act 1757 (c.78)
Guildford Hospital Act 1861 (c.32)
Guildford Streets Act 1758 (c.58)
Guildford to Farnham Road Act 1780 (c.96)
Gun Barrel Proof Act 1978 (c.9)
Gun Licence Act 1870 (c.57)
Gunpowder Act 1772 (c.61)
Gunpowder Act Amendment Act 1862 (c.98)
Gunpowder and Fireworks Act 1860 (c.139)
Gunpowder and Fireworks Act 1861 (c.130)
Gunpowder in Mersey Act 1851 (c.67)
Gunpowder Mill, Tonbridge Act 1772 (c.13)
Guyana Independence Act 1966 (c.14)
Guyana Republic Act 1970 (c.18)

Habeas Corpus Act 1679 (c.2)
Habeas Corpus Act 1803 (c.140)
Habeas Corpus Act 1804 (c.102)
Habeas Corpus Act 1816 (c.100)
Habeas Corpus Act 1862 (c.20)
Habeas Corpus (Ireland) Act 1868 (c.7)
Habeas Corpus Suspension Act 1707 (c.67)
Habeas Corpus Suspension Act 1715 (c.30)
Habeas Corpus Suspension Act 1722 (c.1)
Habeas Corpus Suspension Act 1743 (c.6)
Habeas Corpus Suspension Act 1745 (c.1)
Habeas Corpus Suspension Act 1745 (c.17)
Habeas Corpus Suspension Act 1746 (c.1)
Habeas Corpus Suspension Act 1776 (c.9)
Habeas Corpus Suspension Act 1778 (c.1)
Habeas Corpus Suspension Act 1779 (c.1)
Habeas Corpus Suspension Act 1780 (c.2)
Habeas Corpus Suspension Act 1782 (c.1)
Habeas Corpus Suspension Act 1794 (c.54)
Habeas Corpus Suspension Act 1795 (c.3)
Habeas Corpus Suspension Act 1797 (c.36)
Habeas Corpus Suspension Act 1799 (c.15)
Habeas Corpus Suspension Act 1799 (c.44)
Habeas Corpus Suspension Act 1800 (c.20)
Habeas Corpus Suspension Act 1800 (c.32)
Habeas Corpus Suspension Act 1801 (c.26)
Habeas Corpus Suspension, etc. Act 1714 (c.8)
Habeas Corpus Suspension (Ireland) Act 1803 (c.8)

Habeas Corpus Suspension (Ireland) Act 1801 (c.15)

Habeas Corpus Suspension (Ireland) Act 1803 (c.116)

Habeas Corpus Suspension (Ireland) Act 1805 (c.4)

Habeas Corpus Suspension (Ireland) Act 1848 (c.35)

Habeas Corpus Suspension (Ireland) Act 1849 (c.2)

Habeas Corpus Suspension (Ireland) Act 1866 (c.1)

Habeas Corpus Suspension (Ireland) Act 1866 (c.119)

Habeas Corpus Suspension (Ireland) Act 1867 (c.1)

Habeas Corpus Suspension (Ireland) Act 1867 (c.25)

Habitual Criminals Act 1869 (c.99)

Habitual Drunkards Act 1879 (c.19)

Hackney Carriages Act 1815 (c.159)

Hackney Carriages, Metropolis Act 1838 (c.79)

Hackney Chairs Act 1712 (c.15)

Hackney Chairs, etc. Act 1759 (c.25)

Hackney Coach Fares Act 1808 (c.87)

Hackney Coaches Act 1771 (c.24)

Hackney Coaches Act 1772 (c.49)

Hackney Coaches Act 1784 (c.27)

Hackney Coaches Act 1786 (c.72)

Hackney Coaches Act 1792 (c.47)

Hackney Coaches Act 1804 (c.88)

Hackney Coaches Act 1814 (c.147)

Hackney Coaches, etc. Act 1715 (c.57)

Hackney Coaches, etc., London Act 1800 (c.47)

Hackney Coaches, Metropolis Act 1802 (c.78)

Hackney Coachmen Act 1771 (c.28)

Hackney (Poor Relief etc.) Act 1764 (c.43)

Haddington County Roads Act 1749 (c.17)

Haddington Roads Act 1769 (c.74)

Haddington Roads Act 1793 (c.163)

Hagley and Birmingham Road Act 1753 (c.47)

Haileybury College Act 1838 (c.22)

Haileybury College Act 1855 (c.52)

Hainault Forest Act 1851 (c.43)

Hainault Forest (Allotment of Commons) Act 1858 (c.37)

Hair Powder Certificates, etc. Act 1795 (c.112)

Hairdressers' and Barbers' Shops (Sunday Closing) Act 1930 (c.35)

Hairdressers (Registration) Act 1964 (c.89)

Half-Pay and Pensions Act 1807 (c.25)

Half Pay of Officers, etc. 1815 (c.131)

Halifax and Sheffield Road Act 1797 (c.160)

Halifax Church Act 1795 Act (c.71)

Halifax to Manchester Canal Act 1794 (c.78)

Halifax to Sheffield Road Act 1777 (c.106)

Halifax to Sheffield Road Act 1793 (c.142)

Halifax: Water Supply Act 1762 (c.40)

Halifax: (Water Supply, etc.) Act 1768 (c.44)

Hallamshire Cutlers Act 1791 (c.58)

Halliwell and Finsbury Drainage Act 1778 (c.66)

Hallmarking Act 1973 (c.43)

Hall-marking of Foreign Plate Act 1904 (c.6)

Hall-marking of Foreign Plate Act 1939 (c.36)

Hamilton Bridge Act 1770 (c.93)

Hampshire and Berkshire Roads Act 1766 (c.86)

Hampshire and Dorset Roads Act 1762 (c.57)

Hampshire and Dorset Roads Act 1780 (c.92)

Hampshire and Wiltshire Fisheries Act 1797 (c.95)

Hampshire and Wiltshire Roads Act 1774 (c.104)

Hampshire, Kent, Sussex—Fortifications Act 1762 (c.37)

Hampshire, Kent, Sussex—Fortifications Act 1763 (c.35)

Hampshire Roads Act 1741 (c.14)

Hampshire Roads Act 1757 (c.73)

Hampshire Roads Act 1757 (c.74)

Hampshire Roads Act 1765 (c.95)

Hampstead Roads Act 1753 (c.80)

Hampstead: Streets Act 1775 (c.58)

Hampton Court Bridge Act 1749 (c.37)

Hampton to Staines Road Act 1773 (c.105)

Hampton to Staines Road Act 1793 (c.135)

Hanbury Church Act 1793 (c.45)

Hanley Chapel, Stafford Act 1787 (c.62)

Hans Town, Chelsea: Improvement Act 1790 (c.76)

Happing and Tunstead, Norfolk: Poor Relief Act 1785 (c.27)

Harbour Loans Act 1866 (c.30)

Harbour of Colombo Loan Act 1874 (c.24)

Harbour of Galle Loan Act 1869 (c.105)

Harbour of Howth Act 1805 (c.113)

Harbour of Leith Act 1800 (c.57)

Harbour of Leith Act 1805 (c.114)

Harbour Transfer Act 1865 (c.100)

Harbours Act 1745 (c.22)

Harbours Act 1814 (c.159)

Harbours Act 1964 (c.40)

Harbours (Amendment) Act 1970 (c.53)

Harbours and Passing Tolls etc. Act 1861 (c.47)

Harbours Development (Scotland) Act 1972 (c.64)

Harbours, Docks and Piers Clauses Act 1847 (c.27)

Harbours, Docks and Piers (Temporary Increase of Charges) Act 1922 (c.23)

Harbours (Ireland) Act 1805 (c.64)

Harbours (Loans) Act 1972 (c.16)

Harbours, Piers and Ferries (Scotland) Act 1937 (c.28)

Harbours, Piers and Ferries (Scotland) Act 1953 (c.11)

Harbours, Piers and Ferries (Scotland) Act 1972 (c.29)

Harbours (Scotland) Act 1982 (c.17)

Harbours Transfer Act 1862 (c.69)

Hardington and Old Stratford Road Act 1768 (c.52)

Hares Act 1848 (c.29)

Hares Preservation Act 1892 (c.8)

Hares Preservation (Ireland) Act 1879 (c.23)

Hares (Scotland) Act 1848 (c.30)

Harrogate to Ripon Road Act 1794 (c.121)

Hartlepool Pilotage Order Confirmation Act 1864 (c.58)

Hartley's Patent (Fire Prevention) Act 1776 (c.6)

Hartsmere, etc., Suffolk: Poor Relief Act 1779 (c.13)

Harvey's Charity, Folkestone Act 1858 (c.29)

Harwich, etc., Election Act 1842 (c.31)

Harwich Harbour Act 1863 (c.71)

Harwich Harbour Act 1864 (c.102)

Harwich Harbour Act 1865 (c.120)

Hastings: Improvement Act 1789 (c.27)

Hat Duties Act 1803 (c.22)

Hat Duties, etc. Act 1784 (c.51)

Hat Manufacture Act 1731 (c.22)

Hat Manufacture Act 1784 (c.21)

Hatfield Chase Act 1783 (c.13)

Hatfield Chase: Drainage Act 1787 (c.53)

Hawford–Droitwich Canal Act 1768 (c.37)

Hawkers Act 1717 (c.6)

Hawkers Act 1785 (c.78)

Hawkers Act 1810 (c.41)

Hawkers Act 1812 (c.108)

Hawkers Act 1888 (c.33)

Hawkers and Pedlars Act 1795 (c.91)

Hawkers (Scotland) Act 1815 (c.71)

Hay and Straw Act 1796 (c.88)

Hay and Straw Act 1856 (c.114)

Hay Bridge Over Wye Act 1756 (c.73)

Haydon, Chapel, Northumberland Act 1795 (c.47)

Heage to Duffield Road Act 1793 (c.177)

Health and Medicines Act 1988 (c.49)

Health and Safety at Work etc. Act 1974 (c.37)

Health and Social Security Act 1984 (c.48)

Health and Social Services and Social Security Adjudications Act 1983 (c.41)

Health of Prisoners Act 1774 (c.59)

Health Resorts and Watering Places Act 1921 (c.27)

Health Resorts and Watering Places Act 1936 (c.48)

Health Resorts, etc. (Ireland) Act 1909 (c.32)

Health Service Commissioners Act 1993 (c.46)

Health Service Joint Consultative Committees (Access to Information) Act 1986 (c.24)

Health Services Act 1976 (c.83)

Health Services Act 1980 (c.53)

Health Services and Public Health Act 1968 (c.46)

Health Visiting and Social Work (Training) Act 1962 (c.33)

Hearing Aid Council Act 1968 (c.50)

Hearing Aid Council (Amendment) Act 1989 (c.12)

Hearing Aid Council (Extension) Act 1975 (c.39)

Heather Burning (Scotland) Act 1926 (c.30)

Heating Appliances (Fireguards) Act 1952 (c.42)

Heavy Commercial Vehicles (Controls and Regulations) Act 1973 (c.44)

Hedon Haven Act 1774 (c.106)

Heir Apparent's Establishment Act 1795 (c.125)

Hemingbrough to Market Weighton Road Act 1793 (c.159)

Hemlingford Riots Act 1793 (c.39)

Hemp and Flax Act 1770 (c.40)

Hemp and Flax Act 1786 (c.43)

Henley Grammar School Act 1778 (c.41)

Henley Improvement Act 1795 (c.79)

Henley to Oxford Road Act 1781 (c.97)

Henley-upon-Thames Bridge Act 1780 (c.33)

Hereditary Revenues Act 1856 (c.43)

Hereford and Bedford Roads Act 1769 (c.64)

Hereford and Gloucester Roads Act 1764 (c.62)

Hereford and Gloucester Roads Act 1789 (c.104)

Hereford and Salop Roads Act 1758 (c.66)

Hereford and Worcester Roads Act 1782 (c.100)

Hereford Cathedral Act 1792 (c.87)

Hereford (City) Roads Act 1730 (c.18)

Hereford, Radnor and Salop Roads Act 1778 (c.111)

Hereford Roads Act 1748 (c.15)

Hereford Roads Act 1748 (c.18)

Hereford Roads Act 1748 (c.26)

Hereford Roads Act 1751 (c.56)

Hereford Roads Act 1756 (c.65)

Hereford Roads Act 1770 (c.91)

Hereford Roads Act 1773 (c.95)

Hereford Roads Act 1773 (c.96)

Hereford Roads Act 1767 (c.67)

Hereford Roads Act 1769 (c.90)

Hereford Roads Act 1781 (c.105)

Hereford Roads Act 1782 (c.108)

Hereford Roads Act 1782 (c.112)

Hereford Roads Act 1784 (c.69)

Hereford Roads Act 1789 (c.108)

Hereford Roads Act 1791 (c.114)

Hereford Roads Act 1791 (c.130)

Hereford Roads Act 1794 (c.119)

Hereford Roads, etc. Act 1759 (c.58)

Hereford Streets Act 1774 (c.38)

Herefordshire and Gloucestershire Canal Act 1791 (c.89)

Herefordshire Roads Act 1740 (c.13)

Herefordshire Roads Act 1741 (c.17)

Heritable Jurisdictions (Scotland) Act 1746 (c.43)

Heritable Securities (Scotland) Act 1845 (c.31)

Heritable Securities (Scotland) Act 1847 (c.50)
Heritable Securities (Scotland) Act 1854 (c.62)
Heritable Securities (Scotland) Act 1860 (c.80)
Heritable Securities (Scotland) Act 1894 (c.44)
Herring Fisheries (Scotland) Act 1858 (c.69)
Herring Fisheries (Scotland) Act 1860 (c.92)
Herring Fisheries (Scotland) Act 1865 (c.22)
Herring Fisheries (Scotland) Act 1867 (c.52)
Herring Fishery Act 1749 (c.24)
Herring Fishery Act 1753 (c.9)
Herring Fishery Act 1755 (c.14)
Herring Fishery Act 1757 (c.30)
Herring Fishery Act 1765 (c.22)
Herring Fishery Act 1772 (c.58)
Herring Fishery Act 1851 (c.26)
Herring Fishery Barrels Act 1874 (c.25)
Herring Fishery (Scotland) Act 1808 (c.110)
Herring Fishery (Scotland) Act 1815 (c.94)
Herring Fishery (Scotland) Act 1889 (c.23)
Herring Fishery (Scotland) Act Amendment 1890 (c.10)
Herring Fishing (Branding) Act 1913 (c.9)
Herring Industry Act 1935 (c.9)
Herring Industry Act 1938 (c.42)
Herring Industry Act 1944 (c.32)
Hertford and Bedford Roads Act 1757 (c.43)
Hertford and Bedford Roads Act 1769 (c.87)
Hertford and Bedford Roads Act 1790 (c.115)
Hertford and Broadwater Road Act 1757 (c.45)
Hertford and Bucks. Roads Act 1762 (c.63)
Hertford and Cambridge Roads Act 1769 (c.86)
Hertford and Middlesex Roads Act 1791 (c.108)
Hertford and Ware Roads Act 1732 (c.15)
Hertford and Ware Roads Act 1753 (c.56)
Hertford Church Act 1765 (c.94)
Hertford College Act 1874 (c.55)
Hertford Highways Act 1721 (c.9)
Hertford: Improvement Act 1788 (c.75)
Hertford Prison Act 1775 (c.25)
Hertford Roads Act 1762 (c.48)
Hertford Roads Act 1771 (c.57)
Hertford Roads Act 1778 (c.90)
Hertford Roads Act 1778 (c.94)
Hertford Roads Act 1782 (c.91)
Hertford Roads Act 1783 (c.25)
Hertford Shire-House Act 1768 (c.58)
Hertfordshire and Gloucestershire Canal Act 1793 (c.119)
Hertfordshire and Huntingdonshire Highways Act 1713 (c.33)
Hertfordshire and Huntingdonshire Roads Act 1765 (c.77)
Hertfordshire and Huntingdonshire Roads Act 1790 (c.89)
Hertfordshire and Middlesex Roads Act 1770 (c.107)

Hertfordshire Highways Act 1706 (c.14)
Hertfordshire Highways Act 1710 (c.14)
Hertfordshire Highways Act 1719 (c.20)
Hertfordshire Roads Act 1724 (c.11)
Hertfordshire Roads Act 1725 (c.10)
Hertfordshire Roads Act 1726 (c.32)
Hertfordshire Roads Act 1731 (c.10)
Hertfordshire Roads Act 1732 (c.24)
Hertfordshire Roads Act 1742 (c.16)
Hertfordshire Roads Act 1763 (c.26)
Hexham Bridge Act 1778 (c.44)
Hexham: Inclosure Act 1792 (c.110)
Hexham to Alston Road Act 1778 (c.116)
Hides and Skins Act 1769 (c.39)
High Constables Act 1869 (c.47)
High Court and County Court (Judges) Act 1950 (c.4)
High Court of Admiralty Act 1859 (c.6)
High Court of Admiralty (E.) Act 1840 (c.66)
High Court of Justiciary (Scotland) Act 1892 (c.21)
High Highlands Act 1823 (c.79)
High Peak Mining Customs and Mineral Courts. Act 1851 (c.94)
Highgate and Chipping Barnet Road Act 1720 (c.18)
Highgate and Chipping Barnet Road Act 1763 (c.37)
Highgate and Hampstead Highways Act 1721 (c.5)
Highgate and Hampstead Roads Act 1734 (c.28)
Highgate and Hampstead Roads Act 1756 (c.88)
Highgate and Hampstead Roads Act 1776 (c.76)
Highgate and Hampstead Roads Act 1780 (c.78)
Highgate: Streets Act 1775 (c.43)
Highland Road and Bridges (Scotland) Act (c.43)
Highland Roads and Bridges Act 1851 (c.66)
Highland Roads and Bridges Act 1862 (c.105)
Highland Schools Act 1838 (c.87)
Highland Schools Act 1873 (c.53)
Highland Services Act 1715 (c.54)
Highlands and Islands Air Services (Scotland) Act 1980 (c.19)
Highlands and Islands Development (Scotland) Act 1965 (c.46)
Highlands and Islands Development (Scotland) Act 1968 (c.51)
Highlands and Islands (Medical Service) Additional Grant Act 1929 (c.13)
Highlands and Islands (Medical Service) Grant Act 1913 (c.26)
Highlands and Islands Shipping Services Act 1960 (c.31)
Highland Roads and Bridges Act 1862 (c.105)
Highland Services Act 1715 (c.54)
Highway Accounts Returns Act 1879 (c.39)

Highway Act 1794 (c.64)
Highway Act 1835 (c.50)
Highway Act 1841 (c.51)
Highway Act 1845 (c.71)
Highway Act 1863 (c.61)
Highway Act 1864 (c.101)
Highway Act Amendment 1885 (c.13)
Highway (Railway Crossing) Act 1839 (c.45)
Highway Rate Assessment and Expenditure Act 1882 (c.27)
Highway Rates Act 1836 (c.63)
Highway Rates Act 1839 (c.81)
Highway Rates Act 1840 (c.98)
Highway Rates Act 1843 (c.59)
Highway Rates Act 1845 (c.59)
Highway Rates Act 1846 (c.49)
Highway Rates Act 1847 (c.93)
Highway Rates Act 1848 (c.66)
Highway Rates Act 1849 (c.54)
Highway Rates Act 1850 (c.58)
Highway Rates Act 1851 (c.30)
Highway Rates Act 1852 (c.19)
Highway Rates Act 1853 (c.66)
Highway Rates Act 1854 (c.52)
Highway Rates Act 1860 (c.67)
Highway (Scotland) Act 1718 (c.30)
Highway (Scotland) Act 1771 (c.53)
Highway (Scotland) Act 1803 (c.80)
Highways Act 1707 (c.56)
Highways Act 1710 (c.23)
Highways Act 1714 (c.11)
Highways Act 1715 (c.52)
Highways Act 1718 (c.12)
Highways Act 1733 (c.9)
Highways Act 1742 (c.29)
Highways Act 1749 (c.28)
Highways Act 1750 (c.43)
Highways Act 1753 (c.28)
Highways Act 1765 (c.38)
Highways Act 1766 (c.42)
Highways Act 1766 (c.43)
Highways Act 1768 (c.5)
Highways Act 1773 (c.78)
Highways Act 1794 (c.74)
Highways Act 1839 (c.40)
Highways Act 1854 (c.69)
Highways Act 1862 (c.61)
Highways Act 1959 (c.25)
Highways Act 1971 (c.41)
Highways Act 1980 (c.66)
Highways (Amendment) Act 1965 (c.30)
Highways (Amendment) Act 1986 (c.13)
Highways and Bridges Act 1891 (c.63)
Highways and Locomotives (Amendment) Act 1878 (c.77)
Highways and Turnpike Roads Act 1753 (c.30)
Highways and Turnpike Roads Act 1755 (c.17)
Highways and Turnpike Roads Act 1757 (cc.27, 28)
Highways (England) Act 1814 (c.109)
Highways, etc. (England) Act 1815 (c.68)

Highways, etc. (Scotland) Act 1845 (c.41)
Highways (Ireland) Act 1805 (c.43)
Highways (Ireland) Act 1805 (c.96)
Highways (Ireland) Act 1806 (c.134)
Highways (Ireland) Act 1809 (c.84)
Highways (Ireland) Act 1810 (c.29)
Highways (Ireland) Act 1811 (c.40)
Highways (Ireland) Act 1811 (c.92)
Highways (Ireland) Act 1813 (c.76)
Highways (Ireland) Act 1813 (c.146)
Highways (Ireland) Act 1814 (c.135)
Highways (Isle of Wight) Act 1881 (c.72)
Highways (Miscellaneous Provisions) Act 1961 (c.63)
Highways, Old Stratford to Dunchurch Act 1757 (c.77)
Highways (Provision of Cattle Grids) Act 1950 (c.24)
Highways Returns Act 1849 (c.35)
Highways, South Wales Act 1851 (c.16)
Highways, South Wales Act 1854 (c.7)
Highworth, Wiltshire (Workhouse and Additional Overseer) Act 1789 (c.29)
Hijacking Act 1971 (c.70)
Hill Farming Act 1946 (c.73)
Hill Farming Act 1954 (c.23)
Hill Farming Act 1956 (c.72)
Hill Farming Act 1985 (c.32)
Hill to Lyde Way Road Act 1782 (c.109)
Hinckley and Coventry Road Act 1756 (c.66)
Hinckley and Coventry Road Act 1762 (c.69)
Hinckley to Melbourne Common Road Act 1774 (c.110)
Hire-Purchase Act 1938 (c.53)
Hire-Purchase Act 1954 (c.51)
Hire-Purchase Act 1964 (c.53)
Hire-Purchase Act 1965 (c.66)
Hire-Purchase (Scotland) Act 1965 (c.67)
Historic Buildings and Ancient Monuments Act 1953 (c.49)
Hockliffe to Stony Stratford Road Act 1786 (c.143)
Holborn: Improvement Act 1766 (c.100)
Holborn: Poor Relief Act 1770 (c.79)
Holborn: Poor Relief Act 1770 (c.80)
Holderness: Drainage Act 1774 (c.107)
Holderness to Beverley Road Act 1782 (c.90)
Holdings of County Courts Act 1732 (c.23)
Holidays Extension Act 1875 (c.13)
Holidays With Pay Act 1938 (c.70)
Holloway Prison Act 1852 (c.70)
Holy Island: Inclosure Act 1791 (c.92)
Holy Trinity Church, Bristol Act 1785 (c.95)
Holyhead Banks (Ireland) Act 1850 (c.111)
Holyhead Harbour Act 1810 (c.93)
Holyhead Harbour Act 1816 (c.84)
Holyhead Harbour Act 1847 (c.76)
Holyhead Harbour Railway Act 1859 (c.60)
Holyhead Harbours Act 1854 (c.44)
Holyhead Old Harbour Road Act 1874 (c.30)
Holyhead Road Act 1861 (c.28)
Holyhead Roads Act 1775 (c.69)
Holyhead Roads Act 1815 (c.152)

Holyhead Roads Act 1840 (c.104)
Home Counties (Music and Dancing) Licensing Act 1926 (c.31)
Home Guard Act 1951 (c.8)
Home Purchase Assistance and Housing Corporation Guarantee Act 1978 (c.27)
Home Safety Act 1961 (c.20)
Homes Insulation Act 1978 (c.48)
Homicide Act 1957 (c.11)
Honiton: Improvement Act 1790 (c.25)
Honorary Freedom of Boroughs Act 1885 (c.29)
Honourable Lady Hylton-Foster's Annuity Act 1965 (c.70)
Hong Kong Act 1985 (c.15)
Hop (Prevention of Frauds) Act 1866 (c.37)
Hop Trade Act 1800 (c.81)
Hop Trade Act 1814 (c.123)
Hops Act 1774 (c.68)
Hops Act 1808 (c.134)
Hops Marketing Act 1982 (c.5)
Horse Breeding Act 1918 (c.13)
Horse Breeding Act 1958 (c.43)
Horse Duty Act 1811 (c.76)
Horse Patrol, Metropolis Act 1836 (c.50)
Horse Racing Act 1840 (c.5)
Horserace Betting Levy Act 1969 (c.14)
Horserace Betting Levy Act 1981 (c.30)
Horserace Totalisator and Betting Levy Boards Act 1972 (c.69)
Horses (Protective Headgear for Young Riders) Act 1990 (c.25)
Horsham Roads Act 1792 (c.115)
Horsleytown Parish Act 1732 (c.11)
Horticultural Produce Act 1986 (c.20)
Horticultural Products (Emergency Customs Duties) Act 1931 (c.3)
Horticultural Produce (Sales on Commission) Act 1926 (c.39)
Horticulture Act 1960 (c.22)
Horticulture (Special Payments) Act 1974 (c.5)
Hosiery Act 1845 (c.77)
Hosiery Manufacture (Wages) ˙Act 1874 (c.48)
Hospital Complaints Procedure Act 1985 (c.42)
Hospital Endowments (Scotland) Act 1953 (c.41)
Hospital Endowments (Scotland) Act 1971 (c.8)
Hospitals and Infirmaries (Ireland) Act 1806 (c.95)
Hospitals (Ireland) Act 1807 (c.44)
Hospitals (Ireland) Act 1809 (c.36)
Hospitals (Ireland) Act 1814 (c.112)
Hotel Proprietors Act 1956 (c.62)
Hours of Employment (Conventions) Act 1936 (c.22)
House and Window Duties Act 1766 (c.38)
House Duties Act (c.105)
House Duty Act 1778 (c.26)
House Duty (Ireland) Act 1814 (c.132)

House Letting and Rating (Scotland) Act 1911 (c.53)
House Letting and Rating (Scotland) Act 1920 (c.8)
House Occupiers Disqualification Removal Act 1878 (c.3)
House Occupiers Disqualification Removal (Scotland) Act 1878 (c.5)
House Occupiers in Counties Disqualification Removal (Scotland) Act 1880 (c.6)
House of Commons Act 1800 (c.92)
House of Commons Act 1855 (c.10)
House of Commons Act 1859 (c.5)
House of Commons (Administration) Act 1978 (c.36)
House of Commons (Clergy Disqualification) Act 1801 (c.63)
House of Commons (Commissions in H.M.'s Forces) Act 1914 (c.3)
House of Commons Cost Taxation Act 1847 (c.69)
House of Commons Costs Taxation Act 1879 (c.17)
House of Commons Disqualification Act 1741 (c.22)
House of Commons (Disqualification) Act 1782 (c.45)
House of Commons Disqualification Act 1957 (c.20)
House of Commons Disqualification Act 1975 (c.24)
House of Commons Disqualification (Declaration of Law) Act 1931 (c.13)
House of Commons Disqualification (Declaration of Law) Act 1935 (c.38)
House of Commons Disqualification (Temporary Provisions) Act 1941 (c.8)
House of Commons Disqualifications (Temporary Provisions) Act 1943 (c.10)
House of Commons Disqualification (Temporary Provisions) Act 1944 (c.11)
House of Commons (Disqualifications) Act 1801 (c.52)
House of Commons (Disqualifications) Act 1813 (c.16)
House of Commons (Electors) Act 1786 (c.100)
House of Commons (Indemnification of Certain Members) Act 1949 (c.46)
House of Commons Members' Fund Act 1939 (c.49)
House of Commons Members' Fund Act 1948 (c.36)
House of Commons Members' Fund Act 1957 (c.24)
House of Commons Members' Fund Act 1960 (c.50)
House of Commons Members' Fund Act 1962 (c.53)
House of Commons Members' Fund and Parliamentary Pensions Act 1981 (c.7)
House of Commons Officers Act 1834 (c.70)
House of Commons (Offices) Act 1812 (c.11)

House of Commons Offices Act 1846 (c.77)
House of Commons Offices Act 1849 (c.72)
House of Commons Offices Act 1856 (c.1)
House of Commons Qualification Act 1838 (c.48)
House of Commons (Redistribution of Seats) Act 1944 (c.41)
House of Commons (Redistribution of Seats) Act 1947 (c.10)
House of Commons (Redistribution of Seats) Act 1949 (c.66)
House of Commons (Redistribution of Seats) Act 1958 (c.26)
House of Commons (Redistribution of Seats) Act 1979 (c.15)
House of Commons (Service in His Majesty's Forces) Act 1939 (c.85)
House of Commons (Speaker) Act 1832 (c.105)
House of Correction Act (1852) (c.70)
House of Lords Costs Taxation Act 1849 (c.78)
House of Lords Oath Act 1843 (c.6)
House Purchase and Housing Act 1959 (c.33)
House Purchase Assistance and Housing Corporation Guarantee Act 1978 (c.27)
House Tax Act 1803 (c.161)
House Tax Act 1808 (c.55)
House Tax Act 1851 (c.36)
House Tax Act 1871 (c.103)
House to House Collections Act 1939 (c.44)
Houses of Correction Act 1782 (c.64)
Houses of Correction Act 1784 (c.55)
Houses of Industry, etc. (I.) Act 1841 (c.41)
Houses of Parliament Act 1806 (c.89)
Houses of Parliament Act 1810 (c.119)
Houses of Parliament Act 1837 (c.7)
Houses of Parliament Act 1867 (c.40)
Housing Act 1914 (c.31)
Housing Act 1921 (c.19)
Housing Act 1925 (c.14)
Housing Act 1930 (c.39)
Housing Act 1935 (c.40)
Housing Act 1936 (c.51)
Housing Act 1949 (c.60)
Housing Act 1952 (c.53)
Housing Act 1957 (c.56)
Housing Act 1961 (c.65)
Housing Act 1964 (c.56)
Housing Act 1969 (c.33)
Housing Act 1971 (c.76)
Housing Act 1974 (c.44)
Housing Act 1980 (c.51)
Housing Act 1985 (c.68)
Housing Act 1988 (c.50)
Housing (Agricultural Population) (Scotland) Act 1938 (c.38)
Housing (Agricultural Population) (Scotland) Act 1943 (c.22)
Housing (Amendment) Act 1973 (c.5)
Housing (Amendment) (Scotland) Act 1965 (c.40)

Housing (Amendment) (Scotland) Act 1970 (c.5)
Housing (Amendment) (Scotland) Act 1976 (c.11)
Housing (Amendment) (Scotland) Act 1981 (c.72)
Housing and Building Control Act 1984 (c.29)
Housing and Planning Act 1986 (c.63)
Housing and Town and Development (Scotland) Act 1957 (c.38)
Housing Associations Act 1985 (c.69)
Housing (Consequential Provisions) Act 1985 (c.71)
Housing Defects Act 1984 (c.50)
Housing (Emergency Powers) Act 1939 (c.73)
Housing, etc. Act 1923 (c.24)
Housing Finance Act 1972 (c.47)
Housing Finance (Special Provisions) Act 1975 (c.67)
Housing (Financial and Miscellaneous Provisions) Act 1946 (c.48)
Housing (Financial Provisions) Act 1924 (c.35)
Housing (Financial Provisions) Act 1933 (c.15)
Housing (Financial Provisions) Act 1938 (c.16)
Housing (Financial Provisions) Act 1958 (c.42)
Housing (Financial Provisions) (Scotland) Act 1933 (c.16)
Housing (Financial Provisions) (Scotland) Act 1946 (c.54)
Housing (Financial Provisions) (Scotland) Act 1967 (c.20)
Housing (Financial Provisions) (Scotland) Act 1968 (c.31)
Housing (Financial Provisions) (Scotland) Act 1972 (c.46)
Housing (Financial Provisions) (Scotland) Act 1978 (c.14)
Housing (Homeless Persons) Act 1977 (c.48)
Housing (Ireland) Act 1919 (c.45)
Housing (No. 2) Act 1914 (c.52)
Housing (No. 2) (Amendment) Act 1914 (c.71)
Housing of the Working Classes Act 1885 (c.72)
Housing of the Working Classes Act 1890 (c.70)
Housing of the Working Classes Act, 1890, Amendment (Scotland) 1892 (c.22)
Housing of the Working Classes Act, 1890, Amendment (Scotland) 1896 (c.31)
Housing of the Working Classes Act 1894 (c.55)
Housing of the Working Classes Act 1900 (c.59)
Housing of the Working Classes Act 1903 (c.39)
Housing of the Working Classes Act 1908 (c.61)

Housing of the Working Classes (Ireland) Act 1893 (c.33)
Housing of the Working Classes (Ireland) Act 1896 (c.11)
Housing of the Working Classes (Ireland) Act 1908 (c.61)
Housing Rents and Subsidies Act 1975 (c.6)
Housing Rents and Subsidies (Scotland) Act 1975 (c.28)
Housing Repairs and Rents Act 1954 (c.53)
Housing (Repairs and Rents) (Scotland) Act 1954 (c.50)
Housing (Revision of Contributions) Act 1929 (c.6)
Housing (Rosyth Dockyard) Act 1915 (c.49)
Housing (Rural Authorities) Act 1931 (c.39)
Housing (Rural Workers) Act 1926 (c.56)
Housing (Rural Workers) Act 1942 (c.32)
Housing (Rural Workers) Amendment Act 1931 (c.22)
Housing (Rural Workers) Amendment Act 1938 (c.35)
Housing (Scotland) Act 1920 (c.71)
Housing (Scotland) Act 1921 (c.33)
Housing (Scotland) Act 1925 (c.15)
Housing (Scotland) Act 1930 (c.40)
Housing (Scotland) Act 1935 (c.41)
Housing (Scotland) Act 1944 (c.39)
Housing (Scotland) Act 1949 (c.61)
Housing (Scotland) Act 1950 (c.34)
Housing (Scotland) Act 1952 (c.63)
Housing (Scotland) Act 1962 (c.28)
Housing (Scotland) Act 1966 (c.49)
Housing (Scotland) Act 1969 (c.34)
Housing (Scotland) Act 1974 (c.45)
Housing (Scotland) Act 1986 (c.65)
Housing (Scotland) Act 1987 (c.26)
Housing (Scotland) Act 1988 (c.43)
Housing (Slum Clearance Compensation) Act 1965 (c.81)
Housing Subsidies Act 1956 (c.33)
Housing Subsidies Act 1967 (c.29)
Housing (Temporary Accommodation) Act 1944 (c.36)
Housing (Temporary Accommodation) Act 1945 (c.39)
Housing (Temporary Accommodation) Act 1947 (c.6)
Housing (Temporary Provisions) Act 1944 (c.33)
Housing, Town Planning etc. Act 1919 (c.35)
Housing, Town Planning, etc. Act 1909 (c.44)
Housing, Town Planning, etc. (Scotland) Act 1919 (c.60)
Housing (Underground Rooms) Act 1959 (c.34)
Hovercraft Act 1968 (c.59)
Howth Harbour Act 1810 (c.72)
Howth Harbour Act 1863 (c.72)
Hubberston and Pill, Pembroke: Docks and Piers Act 1790 (c.55)
Huddersfield Burial Ground Act 1852 (c.41)
Huddersfield Burial Ground Act 1855 (c.89)

Huddersfield Roads Act 1788 (c.103)
Huddersfield to Ashton-under-Lyne Canal Act 1794 (c.53)
Hudson's Bay Company Act 1868 (c.105)
Hue and Cry Act 1734 (c.16)
Hue and Cry Act 1748 (c.24)
Hull: Drainage Act 1792 (c.109)
Hull: Improvement Act 1795 (c.46)
Hull, Poor Relief Act 1741 (c.10)
Hulmes Chapel and Chelpord Road Act 1797 (c.157)
Human Fertilisation and Embryology Act 1990 (c.37)
Human Fertilisation and Embryology (Disclosure of Information) Act 1992 (c.54)
Human Organ Transplants Act 1989 (c.31)
Human Tissue Act 1961 (c.54)
Hundred Foot River and Ouse: Bedford Level Act 1756 (c.22)
Hungerford to Leckford Road Act 1793 (c.168)
Huntingdon Clergy Charity Act 1775 (c.24)
Huntingdon: Drainage Act 1772 (c.39)
Huntingdon: Improvement Act 1785 (c.9)
Huntingdon Roads Act 1755 (c.26)
Huntingdon Roads Act 1765 (c.51)
Huntingdonshire and Cambridgeshire Roads Act 1744 (c.23)
Huntingdonshire and Northamptonshire Roads Act 1750 (c.59)
Huntingdonshire and Northamptonshire Roads Act 1771 (c.80)
Huntingdonshire Roads Act 1727 (c.4)
Huntingdonshire Roads Act 1757 (c.51)
Huntingdonshire Roads Act 1774 (c.118)
Huntingdonshire Roads Act 1779 (c.86)
Huntingdonshire Roads Act 1790 (c.103)
Hyde Park Act 1842 (c.19)
Hyde Park (Underground Parking) Act 1961 (c.26)
Hydrocarbon Oil (Customs and Excise) Act 1971 (c.12)
Hydrocarbon Oil Duties Act 1979 (c.5)
Hydrocarbon Oil Duties (Temporary Increase) Act 1956 (c.2)
Hydro-Electric Development (Scotland) Act 1943 (c.32)
Hydro-Electric Undertaking (Valuation for Rating) (Scotland) Act 1944 (c.34)
Hydro-Electricity Development (Scotland) Act 1952 (c.22)
Hydrogen Cyanide (Fumigation) Act 1937 (c.45)
Hypnotism Act 1952 (c.46)
Hypothec Abolition (Scotland) Act 1880 (c.12)
Hypothec Amendment (Scotland) Act 1867 (c.42)

Idiots Act 1886 (c.25)
Ilfracombe Harbour Act 1730 (c.19)
Illegal Trawling (Scotland) Act 1934 (c.18)

Illegitimate Children (Scotland) Act 1930 (c.33)
Illicit Distillation (Ireland) Act 1813 (c.32)
Illicit Distillation (Ireland) Act 1831 (c.55)
Illicit Distillation (Ireland) Act 1857 (c.40)
Immature Spirits (Restriction) Act 1915 (c.46)
Immigration Act 1971 (c.77)
Immigration Act 1988 (c.14)
Immigration Appeals Act 1969 (c.21)
Immigration (Carriers' Liability) Act 1987 (c.24)
Immoral Traffic (Scotland) Act 1902 (c.11)
Imperial Defence Act 1888 (c.32)
Imperial Institute (Management) Act 1916 (c.8)
Imperial Telegraphs Act 1929 (c.7)
Imperial Telegraphs Act 1938 (c.57)
Imperial War Graves Endowment Fund Act 1926 (c.14)
Imperial War Museum Act 1920 (c.16)
Imperial War Museum Act 1955 (c.14)
Import and Export Control Act 1990 (c.45)
Import and Export Duties Act 1802 (c.117)
Import Duties Act 1931 (c.8)
Import Duties Act 1958 (c.6)
Import Duties (Emergency Provisions) Act 1939 (c.97)
Import Duty Act 1804 (c.85)
Import, Export and Customs Powers (Defence) Act 1939 (c.69)
Import of Live Fish (England and Wales) Act 1980 (c.27)
Import of Live Fish (Scotland) Act 1978 (c.35)
Importation Act 1702 (c.8)
Importation Act 1702 (cc. 21, 22)
Importation Act 1703 (c.15)
Importation Act 1704 (c.9)
Importation Act 1706 (c.19)
Importation Act 1707 (c.60)
Importation Act 1711 (c.36)
Importation Act 1712 (c.9)
Importation Act 1714 (c.15)
Importation Act 1715 (c.40)
Importation Act 1719 (c.14)
Importation Act 1721 (c.12)
Importation Act 1726 (c.5)
Importation Act 1726 (c.25)
Importation Act 1728 (c.9)
Importation Act 1730 (c.12)
Importation Act 1730 (c.15)
Importation Act 1731 (c.9)
Importation Act 1732 (c.7)
Importation Act 1738 (c.36)
Importation Act 1740 (c.36)
Importation Act 1743 (c.36)
Importation Act 1753 (c.8)
Importation Act 1755 (c.21)
Importation Act 1757 (c.3)
Importation Act 1763 (c.6)
Importation Act 1763 (c.28)
Importation Act 1765 (c.1)
Importation Act 1765 (c.3)
Importation Act 1765 (c.10)

Importation Act 1765 (c.48)
Importation Act 1766 (cc.11, 12)
Importation Act 1766 (c.13)
Importation Act 1766 (c.19)
Importation Act 1766 (c.22)
Importation Act 1766 (c.30)
Importation Act 1766 (c.43)
Importation Act 1768 (c.9)
Importation Act 1769 (c.4)
Importation Act 1769 (c.9)
Importation Act 1770 (c.2)
Importation Act 1771 (c.8)
Importation Act 1771 (c.41)
Importation Act 1771 (cc.49, 50)
Importation Act 1772 (c.7)
Importation Act 1772 (cc.32, 33)
Importation Act 1772 (c.67)
Importation Act 1774 (c.9)
Importation Act 1774 (c.74)
Importation Act 1775 (c.1)
Importation Act 1775 (c.7)
Importation Act 1776 (c.8)
Importation Act 1776 (c.35)
Importation Act 1776 (c.41)
Importation Act 1778 (c.56)
Importation Act 1779 (c.28)
Importation Act 1780 (c.6)
Importation Act 1781 (c.62)
Importation Act 1782 (c.7)
Importation Act 1782 (c.30)
Importation Act 1782 (c.38)
Importation Act 1782 (c.72)
Importation Act 1782 (c.78)
Importation Act 1783 (c.1)
Importation Act 1783 (cc.9, 10)
Importation Act 1783 (c.14)
Importation Act 1788 (c.39)
Importation Act 1789 (c.16)
Importation Act 1790 (c.28)
Importation Act 1790 (c.41)
Importation Act 1791 (c.37)
Importation Act 1791 (c.38)
Importation Act 1792 (c.49)
Importation Act 1793 (c.63)
Importation Act 1794 (c.50)
Importation Act 1795 (c.4)
Importation Act 1795 (c.15)
Importation Act 1795 (c.100)
Importation Act 1795 (c.115)
Importation Act 1795 (c.117)
Importation Act 1796 (c.8)
Importation Act 1796 (c.81)
Importation Act 1796 (c.113)
Importation Act 1797 (c.3)
Importation Act 1797 (c.25)
Importation Act 1797 (c.72)
Importation Act 1797 (c.84)
Importation Act 1799 (c.27)
Importation Act 1799 (c.75)
Importation Act 1799 (c.87)
Importation Act 1799 (c.95)
Importation Act 1799 (c.98)
Importation Act 1799 (c.111)

Importation Act 1799 (c.112)
Importation Act 1800 (c.11)
Importation Act 1800 (c.18)
Importation Act 1800 (c.25)
Importation Act 1800 (c.83)
Importation Act 1800 (c.107)
Importation Act 1801 (c.7)
Importation Act 1801 (c.16)
Importation Act 1801 (c.37)
Importation Act 1801 (c.41)
Importation Act 1801 (c.93)
Importation Act 1802 (c.44)
Importation Act 1804 (cc.29, 30)
Importation Act 1806 (c.74)
Importation Act 1806 (c.103)
Importation Act 1806 (c.113)
Importation Act 1806 (c.117)
Importation Act 1806 (c.121)
Importation Act 1807 (c.24)
Importation Act 1807 (cc.25, 26)
Importation Act 1807 (c.27)
Importation Act 1807 (c.67)
Importation Act 1808 (c.11)
Importation Act 1808 (c.19)
Importation Act 1808 (cc.23, 24)
Importation Act 1808 (c.125)
Importation Act 1809 (c.9)
Importation Act 1809 (c.16)
Importation Act 1809 (cc.25, 26)
Importation Act 1809 (c.60)
Importation Act 1809 (c.105)
Importation Act 1810 (c.55)
Importation Act 1810 (c.80)
Importation Act 1811 (c.48)
Importation Act 1811 (c.58)
Importation Act 1811 (c.62)
Importation Act 1812 (c.18)
Importation Act 1812 (c.33)
Importation Act 1812 (c.119)
Importation Act 1813 (c.34)
Importation Act 1813 (c.37)
Importation Act 1813 (c.41)
Importation Act 1814 (c.51)
Importation Act 1814 (c.124)
Importation Act 1814 (c.125)
Importation Act 1815 (c.26)
Importation Act 1815 (c.34)
Importation Act 1815 (c.86)
Importation Act 1816 (c.2)
Importation Act 1816 (cc.25, 26)
Importation Act 1816 (c.36)
Importation Act 1816 (c.37)
Importation Act 1840 (c.32)
Importation Act 1844 (c.100)
Importation Act 1847 (c.2)
Importation Act 1847 (c.86)
Importation and Exportation Act 1766 (cc.1–5)
Importation and Exportation Act 1772 (cc. 1–5)
Importation and Exportation Act 1772 (cc.69, 70)
Importation and Exportation Act 1772 (cc.72, 73)

Importation and Exportation Act 1787 (c.27)
Importation and Exportation Act 1789 (c.58)
Importation and Exportation Act 1790 (c.1)
Importation and Exportation Act 1790 (c.29)
Importation and Exportation Act 1790 (c.42)
Importation and Exportation Act 1791 (c.4)
Importation and Exportation Act 1791 (c.30)
Importation and Exportation Act 1791 (c.47)
Importation and Exportation Act 1792 (c.37)
Importation and Exportation Act 1793 (c.50)
Importation and Exportation Act 1793 (c.65)
Importation and Exportation Act 1797 (c.39)
Importation and Exportation Act 1799 (c.88)
Importation and Exportation Act 1800 (c.58)
Importation and Exportation Act 1804 (c.109)
Importation and Exportation Act 1805 (c.57)
Importation and Exportation Act 1805 (c.86)
Importation and Exportation Act 1807 (c.34)
Importation and Exportation Act 1810 (cc.12, 13)
Importation and Exportation Act 1810 (c.21)
Importation and Exportation Act 1812 (c.8)
Importation and Exportation Act 1812 (c.69)
Importation and Exportation Act 1812 (c.79)
Importation and Exportation Act 1813 (c.55)
Importation and Exportation Act 1814 (c.81)
Importation and Exportation Act 1814 (c.129)
Importation and Exportation Act 1815 (c.117)
Importation and Exportation (Ireland) Act 1807 (c.1)
Importation and Exportation (Ireland) Act 1807 (c.16)
Importation and Exportation (Ireland) Act 1810 (c.97)
Importation, etc. Act 1750 (c.32)
Importation, etc. Act 1766 (c.28)
Importation, etc. Act 1766 (c.36)
Importation, etc. Act 1780 (c.45)
Importation, etc. Act 1801 (c.68)
Importation, etc. Act 1804 (c.35)
Importation, etc. Act 1804 (c.89)
Importation, etc. Act 1806 (c.53)
Importation, etc. Act 1809 (c.18)
Importation, etc. Act 1809 (c.22)
Importation, etc. Act 1812 (c.2)
Importation, etc. Act 1812 (c.20)
Importation, etc. Act 1814 (cc.8, 9)
Importation, etc. Act 1814 (c.111)
Importation, Exportation, etc. Act 1805 (c.26)
Importation in Neutral Vessel, etc. Act 1803 (c.153)
Importation into Isle of Man Act 1813 (c.110)
Importation into Quebec Act 1763 (c.19)
Importation into Quebec Act 1766 (c.42)
Importation into Scotland Act 1740 (c.7)
Importation (Ireland) Act 1807 (c.31)
Importation of Animals Act 1922 (c.5)
Importation of Arms, etc. (Ireland) Act 1841 (c.25)
Importation of Milk Act 1983 (c.37)
Importation of Pedigree Animals Act 1925 (c.30)
Importation of Plumage (Prohibition) Act 1921 (c.16)

Indemnity Act 1728 (c.31)
Indemnity Act 1730 (c.6)
Indemnity Act 1732 (c.4)
Indemnity Act 1733 (c.10)
Indemnity Act 1734 (c.4)
Indemnity Act 1734 (c.17)
Indemnity Act 1735 (c.6)
Indemnity Act 1736 (c.13)
Indemnity Act 1737 (c.31)
Indemnity Act 1738 (c.6)
Indemnity Act 1739 (c.6)
Indemnity Act 1740 (c.18)
Indemnity Act 1742 (c.30)
Indemnity Act 1754 (c.13)
Indemnity Act 1755 (c.3)
Indemnity Act 1755 (c.24)
Indemnity Act 1757 (c.9)
Indemnity Act 1763 (c.31)
Indemnity Act 1765 (c.4)
Indemnity Act 1766 (c.7)
Indemnity Act 1766 (c.31)
Indemnity Act 1766 (c.51)
Indemnity Act 1768 (c.6)
Indemnity Act 1769 (c.12)
Indemnity Act 1770 (c.42)
Indemnity Act 1771 (c.18)
Indemnity Act 1772 (c.12)
Indemnity Act 1772 (c.31)
Indemnity Act 1772 (c.76)
Indemnity Act 1774 (c.47)
Indemnity Act 1775 (c.17)
Indemnity Act 1776 (c.37)
Indemnity Act 1776 (c.50)
Indemnity Act 1778 (c.39)
Indemnity Act 1779 (c.47)
Indemnity Act 1780 (c.47)
Indemnity Act 1782 (c.55)
Indemnity Act 1783 (c.30)
Indemnity Act 1784 (c.58)
Indemnity Act 1785 (c.82)
Indemnity Act 1786 (c.98)
Indemnity Act 1787 (c.40)
Indemnity Act 1788 (c.22)
Indemnity Act 1789 (c.40)
Indemnity Act 1790 (c.12)
Indemnity Act 1791 (c.8)
Indemnity Act 1791 (c.27)
Indemnity Act 1793 (c.12)
Indemnity Act 1794 (c.12)
Indemnity Act 1795 (c.50)
Indemnity Act 1796 (c.11)
Indemnity Act 1796 (c.57)
Indemnity Act 1797 (c.14)
Indemnity Act 1797 (c.93)
Indemnity Act 1799 (c.17)
Indemnity Act 1800 (c.19)
Indemnity Act 1800 (c.31)
Indemnity Act 1801 (c.66)
Indemnity Act 1802 (c.6)
Indemnity Act 1802 (c.23)
Indemnity Act 1803 (c.7)
Indemnity Act 1805 (c.6)
Indemnity Act 1806 (c.7)

Indemnity Act 1807 (c.5)
Indemnity Act 1807 (c.3)
Indemnity Act 1807 (c.35)
Indemnity Act 1808 (c.40)
Indemnity Act 1809 (c.15)
Indemnity Act 1810 (c.4)
Indemnity Act 1811 (cc.17, 18)
Indemnity Act 1811 (c.98)
Indemnity Act 1812 (c.26)
Indemnity Act 1813 (c.5)
Indemnity Act 1815 (c.17)
Indemnity Act 1816 (c.33)
Indemnity Act 1836 (c.7)
Indemnity Act 1837 (c.12)
Indemnity Act 1838 (c.16)
Indemnity Act 1840 (c.16)
Indemnity Act 1841 (c.11)
Indemnity Act 1842 (c.10)
Indemnity Act 1843 (c.9)
Indemnity Act 1844 (c.10)
Indemnity Act 1845 (c.24)
Indemnity Act 1846 (c.13)
Indemnity Act 1847 (c.18)
Indemnity Act 1866 (c.116)
Indemnity Act 1867 (c.88)
Indemnity as to Certain Books Act 1809 (c.69)
Indemnity, etc. Act 1735 (c.26)
Indemnity for Certain Acts Act 1801 (c.46)
Indemnity for Certain Orders of Council Act
    1805 (c.97)
Indemnity (Ireland) Act 1801 (c.49)
Indemnity (Ireland) Act 1802 (c.53)
Indemnity (Ireland) Act 1803 (c.77)
Indemnity, Masters in Chancery Act 1724
    (c.2)
Indemnity (O. in C., West Indies Importation)
    Act 1812 (c.12)
Indemnity of Innkeepers Act 1774 (c.60)
Indemnity, Suppression of Riots Act 1780
    (c.63)
Indemnity to Certain Governors Act 1836
    (c.48)
Indemnity to Certain Governors, etc. Act
    1795 (c.57)
Indemnity to Certain Persons Act 1838
    (c.112)
Indemnity to Certain Printers Act 1801 (c.80)
Indemnity to Governor of Surinam Act 1800
    (c.108)
Indemnity to Governors of West Indies Act
    1796 (c.32)
Indemnity to Governors of West Indies Act
    1797 (c.64)
Indemnity to Governors of West Indies Act
    1798 (c.72)
Indemnity to Governors of West Indies Act
    1799 (c.57)
Indemnity to Printers Act 1800 (c.95)
Indemnity to Proprietors, etc., of Newspapers
    Act 1792 (c.61)
Indemnity, West Indies Act 1800 (c.76)
Independent Broadcasting Authority Act
    1973 (c.19)

Inquiry into Military Expenditure, etc. Act 1811 (c.19)
Inquiry into Naval Departments Act 1805 (c.46)
Inquiry into Public Expenditure Act 1805 (c.70)
Inquiry into Public Offices (Ireland) Act 1804 (c.106)
Inquiry into Public Offices (Ireland) Act (c.65)
Inquiry into Public Offices (Ireland) Act 1813 (c.130)
Inrolment of Grants of Annuities Act (c.141)
Insane Prisoners Act 1840 (c.54)
Inshore Fishing Industry Act 1945 (c.11)
Inshore Fishing (Scotland) Act 1984 (c.26)
Inshore Fishing (Scotland) Act 1994 (c.27)
Insolvency Act 1976 (c.60)
Insolvency Act 1985 (c.65)
Insolvency Act 1986 (c.45)
Insolvency Act 1994 (c.7)
Insolvency (No. 2) Act 1994 (c.12)
Insolvency Services (Accounting and Investment) Act 1970 (c.8)
Insolvent Act 1812 (c.163)
Insolvent Debtors Act 1839 (c.39)
Insolvent Debtors Act 1842 (c.116)
Insolvent Debtor's Discharge Act 1794 (c.69)
Insolvent Debtor's Discharge Act 1795 (c.88)
Insolvent Debtors, East Indies Act 1836 (c.47)
Insolvent Debtors (England) Act 1813 (c.23)
Insolvent Debtors (England) Act 1813 (c.102)
Insolvent Debtors (England) Act 1816 (c.102)
Insolvent Debtors (England) Act 1836 (c.44)
Insolvent Debtors, etc., Relief Act 1774 (c.77)
Insolvent Debtors, India Act 1840 (c.80)
Insolvent Debtors, India Act 1846 (c.14)
Insolvent Debtors (Ireland) Act 1810 (c.47)
Insolvent Debtors (Ireland) Act 1813 (c.138)
Insolvent Debtors (Ireland) Act 1814 (c.114)
Insolvent Debtors (Ireland) Act 1816 (c.126)
Insolvent Debtors (Ireland) Act 1836 (c.23)
Insolvent Debtors (Ireland) Act 1840 (c.14)
Insolvent Debtors (Ireland) Act 1840 (c.107)
Insolvent Debtors (Ireland) Act 1841 (c.47)
Insolvent Debtors Relief Act 1702 (c.19)
Insolvent Debtors Relief Act 1703 (c.10)
Insolvent Debtors' Relief Act 1711 (c.29)
Insolvent Debtors' Relief Act 1724 (c.21)
Insolvent Debtors' Relief Act 1728 (c.20)
Insolvent Debtors' Relief Act 1730 (c.27)
Insolvent Debtors' Relief Act 1737 (c.9)
Insolvent Debtors' Relief Act 1755 (c.13)
Insolvent Debtors' Relief Act 1765 (c.41)
Insolvent Debtors' Relief Act 1769 (c.26)
Insolvent Debtors Relief Act 1776 (c.38)
Insolvent Debtors Relief Act 1781 (c.63)
Insolvent Debtors Relief Act 1801 (c.70)
Insolvent Debtors Relief Act 1804 (c.108)
Insolvent Debtors Relief Act 1805 (c.3)
Insolvent Debtors Relief Act 1806 (c.108)
Insolvent Debtors Relief Act 1809 (c.54)
Insolvent Debtors Relief Act 1809 (c.115)

Insolvent Debtors Relief Act 1812 (c.13)
Insolvent Debtors Relief Act 1812 (c.165)
Insolvent Debtors Relief (England) Act 1811 (c.125)
Insolvent Debtors Relief (England) Act 1812 (c.6)
Insolvent Debtors Relief (England) Act 1813 (c.28)
Insolvent Debtors' Relief, etc. Act 1719 (c.22)
Insolvent Debtors Relief, etc. Act 1778 (c.52)
Insolvent Debtors Relief (Ireland) Act 1811 (c.123)
Insurance Brokers (Registration) Act 1977 (c.46)
Insurance Companies Act 1958 (c.72)
Insurance Companies Act 1974 (c.49)
Insurance Companies Act 1980 (c.25)
Insurance Companies Act 1981 (c.31)
Insurance Companies Act 1982 (c.50)
Insurance Companies Amendment Act 1973 (c.58)
Insurance Contracts (War Settlement) Act 1952 (c.56)
Insurance (Fees) Act 1985 (c.46)
Insurances on Ships, etc. Act 1785 (c.44)
Insurrection and Disturbances (Ireland) Act 1807 (c.13)
Intelligence Services Act 1994 (c.13)
Interception of Communications Act 1985 (c.56)
Interchange of Grain Between Great Britain and Ireland Act 1807 (c.7)
Intercourse Between Jamaica and St. Domingo Act 1812 (c.3)
Intercourse with St. Helena Act 1816 (c.23)
Interest on Damages (Scotland) Act 1958 (c.61)
Interest on Damages (Scotland) Act 1971 (c.31)
Intermediate Education (Ireland) Act 1878 (c.66)
Intermediate Education (Ireland) Act 1882 (c.69)
Intermediate Education (Ireland) Act 1900 (c.43)
Intermediate Education (Ireland) Act 1913 (c.29)
Intermediate Education (Ireland) Act 1914 (c.41)
Interments (Felo de se) Act 1882 (c.19)
International Bank and Monetary Fund Act 1959 (c.17)
International Carriage of Perishable Foodstuffs Act 1976 (c.58)
International Cocoa Agreement Act 1973 (c.46)
International Copyright Act 1838 (c.59)
International Copyright Act 1844 (c.12)
International Copyright Act 1875 (c.12)
International Copyright Act 1886 (c.33)
International Development Association Act 1960 (c.35)
International Development Association Act 1964 (c.13)

International Finance Corporation Act 1955 (c.5)

International Finance, Trade and Aid Act 1977 (c.6)

International Headquarters and Defence Organisations Act 1964 (c.5)

International Monetary Arrangements Act 1983 (c.51)

International Monetary Fund Act 1962 (c.20)

International Monetary Fund Act 1968 (c.58)

International Monetary Fund Act 1970 (c.49)

International Monetary Fund Act 1979 (c.29)

International Organisations Act 1968 (c.48)

International Organisations Act 1981 (c.9)

International Organisations (Immunities and Privileges) Act 1950 (c.14)

International Parliamentary Organisations (Registration) Act 1989 (c.19)

International Road Haulage Permits Act 1975 (c.46)

International Sugar Organisation Act 1973 (c.68)

International Transport Conventions Act 1983 (c.14)

Internationally Protected Persons Act 1978 (c.17)

Interpleader (Ireland) Act 1846 (c.64)

Interpretation Act 1889 (c.63)

Interpretation Act 1978 (c.30)

Interpretation of Terms Act 1837 (c.39)

Intestate Husband's Estate (Scotland) Act 1911 (c.10)

Intestate Husband's Estate (Scotland) Act 1919 (c.9)

Intestate Husband's Estate (Scotland) Act 1959 (c.21)

Intestate Moveable Succession (Scotland) Act 1919 (c.61)

Intestates Act 1873 (c.52)

Intestates Act 1875 (c.27)

Intestates' Estates Act 1884 (c.71)

Intestates' Estates Act 1890 (c.29)

Intestates' Estates Act 1952 (c.64)

Intestates' Widows and Children (Scotland) Act 1875 (c.41)

Institute of Management (Customs) Act 1951 (c.51)

Intoxicating Liquor (Sales to Persons Under Eighteen) Act 1923 (c.28)

Intoxicating Liquor (Temporary Restriction) Act 1914 (c.77)

Intoxicating Liquors (Ireland) Act 1906 (c.39)

Intoxicating Liquors (Licences Suspension) Act 1871 (c.88)

Intoxicating Liquors (Sale to Children) Act 1886 (c.56)

Intoxicating Liquors (Sale to Children) Act 1901 (c.27)

Intoxicating Substances (Supply) Act 1985 (c.26)

Inventories (Scotland) Act 1816 (c.107)

Inverness and Elgin County Boundaries Act 1870 (c.16)

Inverness Beer Duties Act 1718 (c.17)

Inverness Beer Duties Act 1737 (c.16)

Inverness Gaol Act 1788 (c.69)

Inverness Roads Act 1793 (c.118)

Investment and Building Grants Act 1971 (c.51)

Investment of Certain Money Act 1808 (c.21)

Investments of Trust Funds Act 1867 (c.132)

Ionian Islands Commissioners Act 1868 (c.128)

Ipswich and Stowmarket Navigation Act 1790 (c.57)

Ipswich and Stowmarket Navigation Act 1793 (c.20)

Ipswich and Yaxley Roads Act 1793 (c.128)

Ipswich: Improvement Act 1793 (c.92)

Ipswich: Improvement, etc. Act 1797 (c.44)

Iran (Temporary Powers) Act 1980 (c.28)

Ireland Act 1949 (c.41)

Ireland (Confirmation of Agreement) Act 1925 (c.77)

Ireland Development Grant Act 1903 (c.23)

Irish and Scotch Paupers Removal Act 1837 (c.10)

Irish Appeals Act 1780 (c.28)

Irish Appeals Act 1783 (c.28)

Irish Bankrupt and Insolvent Act 1857 (c.60)

Irish Charges Act 1801 (c.32)

Irish Church Act 1869 (c.42)

Irish Church Act Amendment Act 1881 (c.71)

Irish Church Act (1869) Amendment Act 1872 (c.90)

Irish Church Amendment Act 1872 (c.13)

Irish Constabulary Act 1874 (c.80)

Irish Education Act 1892 (c.42)

Irish Education Act 1893 (c.41)

Irish Free State (Agreement) Act 1922 (c.4)

Irish Free State (Confirmation of Agreement) Act 1924 (c.41)

Irish Free State (Confirmation of Agreement) Act 1929 (c.4)

Irish Free State (Consequential Provisions) Act 1922 (c.2)

Irish Free State Constitution Act 1922 (c.1)

Irish Free State Land Purchase (Loan Guarantee) Act 1924 (c.3)

Irish Free State (Special Duties) Act 1931 (c.30)

Irish Handloom Weavers Act 1909 (c.21)

Irish Land Act 1903 (c.37)

Irish Land Act 1904 (c.34)

Irish Land Act 1907 (c.38)

Irish Land Act 1909 (c.42)

Irish Land (Provisions for Sailors and Soldiers) Act 1919 (c.82)

Irish Lighthouses Act 1811 (c.66)

Irish Loans Act 1880 (c.44)

Irish Mariners, etc. Act 1802 (c.61)

Irish Militia Act 1805 (c.38)

Irish Militia Act 1806 (c.124)

Irish Militia Act 1807 (c.6)

Irish Police Constables (Naval and Military Service) Act 1914 (c.84)

Irish Police (Naval and Military Service) Act 1915 (c.32)
Irish Presbyterian Church Act 1871 (c.24)
Irish Railways (Confirmation of Agreement) Act 1919 (c.78)
Irish Reformatory Schools Act 1868 (c.59)
Irish Reproductive Loan Fund Act 1883 (c.33)
Irish Reproductive Loan Fund Amendment Act 1882 (c.16)
Irish Sailors and Soldiers Land Trust Act 1952 (c.58)
Irish Sailors and Soldiers Land Trust Act 1967 (c.67)
Irish Sailors and Soldiers Land Trust Act 1987 (c.48)
Irish Tobacco Act 1907 (c.3)
Irish Universities Act 1908 (c.38)
Iron and Steel Act 1949 (c.72)
Iron and Steel Act 1953 (c.15)
Iron and Steel Act 1967 (c.17)
Iron and Steel Act 1969 (c.45)
Iron and Steel Act 1972 (c.12)
Iron and Steel Act 1975 (c.64)
Iron and Steel Act 1981 (c.46)
Iron and Steel Act 1982 (c.25)
Iron and Steel (Amendment) Act 1976 (c.41)
Iron and Steel (Amendment) Act 1978 (c.41)
Iron and Steel (Borrowing Powers) Act 1981 (c.2)
Iron and Steel (Financial Provisions) Act 1960 (c.26)
Irvine Beer Duties Act 1735 (c.27)
Island of Rockall Act 1972 (c.2)
Isle of Axholme: Inclosure, etc. Act 1795 (c.107)
Isle of Ely and Norfolk Roads Act 1767 (c.100)
Isle of Ely: Drainage Act 1757 (c.19)
Isle of Ely: Drainage Act 1772 (c.20)
Isle of Ely: Drainage Act 1791 (c.81)
Isle of Ely: Drainage Act 1792 (c.108)
Isle of Ely: Drainage Act 1795 (c.48)
Isle of Ely: Drainage Act 1797 (c.96)
Isle of Ely, etc.: Drainage Act 1772 (c.19)
Isle of Ely, etc.: Drainage Act 1772 (c.60)
Isle of Ely, etc.: Drainage Act 1775 (c.66)
Isle of Ely: Small Debts Act 1778 (c.36)
Isle of Ely to Ramsey Road Act 1794 (c.127)
Isle of Man Act 1780 (c.42)
Isle of Man 1865 (c.28)
Isle of Man Act 1958 (c.11)
Isle of Man Act 1979 (c.58)
Isle of Man (Church Building and New Parishes) Act 1897 (c.33)
Isle of Man (Customs) Act 1810 (c.42)
Isle of Man (Customs) Act 1887 (c.5)
Isle of Man (Customs) Act 1888 (c.7)
Isle of Man (Customs) Act 1892 (c.28)
Isle of Man (Customs) Act 1895 (c.38)
Isle of Man (Customs) Act 1898 (c.27)
Isle of Man (Customs) Act 1899 (c.39)
Isle of Man (Customs) Act 1900 (c.31)
Isle of Man (Customs) Act 1901 (c.32)
Isle of Man (Customs) Act 1902 (c.23)

Isle of Man (Customs) Act 1903 (c.35)
Isle of Man (Customs) Act 1904 (c.25)
Isle of Man (Customs) Act 1905 (c.16)
Isle of Man (Customs) Act 1906 (c.18)
Isle of Man (Customs) Act 1907 (c.26)
Isle of Man (Customs) Act 1908 (c.9)
Isle of Man (Customs) Act 1909 (c.45)
Isle of Man (Customs) Act 1910 (c.18)
Isle of Man (Customs) Act 1911 (c.14)
Isle of Man (Customs) Act 1912 (c.9)
Isle of Man (Customs) Act 1913 (c.18)
Isle of Man (Customs) Act 1914 (c.19)
Isle of Man (Customs) Act 1915 (c.67)
Isle of Man (Customs) Act 1916 (c.27)
Isle of Man (Customs) Act 1917 (c.35)
Isle of Man (Customs) Act 1918 (c.41)
Isle of Man (Customs) Act 1919 (c.74)
Isle of Man (Customs) Act 1921 (c.40)
Isle of Man (Customs) Act 1922 (c.36)
Isle of Man (Customs) Act 1923 (c.26)
Isle of Man (Customs) Act 1924 (c.24)
Isle of Man (Customs) Act 1925 (c.56)
Isle of Man (Customs) Act 1926 (c.27)
Isle of Man (Customs) Act 1927 (c.20)
Isle of Man (Customs) Act 1928 (c.38)
Isle of Man (Customs) Act 1929 (c.1)
Isle of Man (Customs) Act 1930 (c.42)
Isle of Man (Customs) Act 1931 (c.16)
Isle of Man (Customs) Act 1931 (c.34)
Isle of Man (Customs) Act 1931 (c.41)
Isle of Man (Customs) Act 1933 (c.40)
Isle of Man (Customs) Act 1934 (c.46)
Isle of Man (Customs) Act 1935 (c.34)
Isle of Man (Customs) Act 1936 (c.45)
Isle of Man (Customs) Act 1937 (c.64)
Isle of Man (Customs) Act 1938 (c.68)
Isle of Man (Customs) Act 1939 (c.49)
Isle of Man (Customs) Act 1939 (c.53)
Isle of Man (Customs) Act 1941 (c.32)
Isle of Man (Customs) Act 1942 (c.25)
Isle of Man (Customs) Act 1943 (c.37)
Isle of Man (Customs) Act 1944 (c.27)
Isle of Man (Customs) Act 1945 (c.14)
Isle of Man (Customs) Act 1946 (c.69)
Isle of Man (Customs) Act 1947 (c.50)
Isle of Man (Customs) Act 1948 (c.61)
Isle of Man (Customs) Act 1949 (c.58)
Isle of Man (Customs) Act 1950 (c.19)
Isle of Man (Customs) Act 1952 (c.51)
Isle of Man (Customs) Act 1953 (c.44)
Isle of Man (Customs) Act 1954 (c.54)
Isle of Man (Customs) Act 1955 (c.17)
Isle of Man Customs Duties Act 1867 (c.86)
Isle of Man (Detention) Act 1941 (c.16)
Isle of Man Harbours Act 1771 (c.52)
Isle of Man Harbours Act 1814 (c.143)
Isle of Man Harbours Act 1840 (c.63)
Isle of Man Harbours Act 1872 (c.23)
Isle of Man Harbours Act 1874 (c.8)
Isle of Man Harbours Act 1883 (c.9)
Isle of Man Harbours Act 1884 (c.7)
Isle of Man Harbours Act 1911 (c.33)
Isle of Man (Harbours) Act 1947

Judicial Committee Act 1845 (c.30)
Judicial Committee Act 1871 (c.91)
Judicial Committee Act 1881 (c.3)
Judicial Committee Act 1915 (c.92)
Judicial Committee Amendment Act 1895 (c.44)
Judicial Factors Act 1849 (c.51)
Judicial Factors (Scotland) Act 1880 (c.4)
Judicial Factors (Scotland) Act 1889 (c.39)
Judicial Offices (Salaries and Pensions) Act 1957 (c.46)
Judicial Officers (Salaries, etc.) Act 1952 (c.12)
Judicial Pensions Act 1959 (c.9)
Judicial Pensions Act 1981 (c.20)
Judicial Pensions and Retirement Act 1993 (c.8)
Judicial Proceedings (Regulation of Reports) Act 1926 (c.61)
Judicial Ratifications (Scotland) Act 1836 (c.43)
Judicial Statistics (Scotland) Act 1869 (c.33)
Judicial Trustees Act 1896 (c.35)
Juries Act 1730 (c.7)
Juries Act 1730 (c.25)
Juries Act 1756 (c.19)
Juries Act 1825 (c.50)
Juries Act 1862 (c.107)
Juries Act 1870 (c.77)
Juries Act 1871 (c.2)
Juries Act 1871 (c.65)
Juries Act 1918 (c.23)
Juries Act 1922 (c.11)
Juries Act 1949 (c.27)
Juries Act 1954 (c.41)
Juries Act 1974 (c.23)
Juries Detention Act 1897 (c.18)
Juries (Disqualification) Act 1984 (c.34)
Juries (Emergency Provisions) Act 1920 (c.78)
Juries (Emergency Provisions) (Renewal) Act 1921 (c.36)
Juries, etc. Act 1750 (c.18)
Juries (Ireland) Act 1839 (c.48)
Juries (Ireland) Act 1845 (c.67)
Juries (Ireland) Act 1868 (c.75)
Juries (Ireland) Act 1871 (c.65)
Juries (Ireland) Act 1872 (c.25)
Juries (Ireland) Act 1873 (c.27)
Juries (Ireland) Act 1874 (c.28)
Juries (Ireland) Act 1875 (c.37)
Juries (Lighthouse Keepers' Exemption) Act 1869 (c.36)
Juries Procedure (Ireland) Act 1876 (c.78)
Juries (Scotland) Act 1826 (c.8)
Jurisdiction in Homicides Act 1862 (c.65)
Jurisdiction in Rating Act 1877 (c.11)
Jurisdiction in Siam Act 1857 (c.75)
Jurors Act 1587 (c.54)
Jurors Affirmation (Scotland) Act 1868 (c.39)
Jurors (Enrolment of Women) (Scotland) Act 1920 (c.53)
Jurors (Ireland) Amendment Act 1894 (c.49)

Jurors Prize Money Act 1868 (c.38)
Jurors Qualification (Ireland) Act 1876 (c.21)
Jurors (Scotland) Act 1745 (c.9)
Jurors (Scotland) Act 1825 (c.22)
Jury Trials Amendment (Scotland) Act 1910 (c.31)
Jury Trials (Scotland) Act 1815 (c.42)
Jury Trials (Scotland) Act 1819 (c.35)
Jury Trials (Scotland) Act 1837 (c.14)
Jury Trials (Scotland) Act 1854 (c.59)
Jury Trials (Scotland) Act 1859 (c.7)
Justice of Assize Act 1809 (c.91)
Justice of Assizes Act 1850 (c.25)
Justice of the Peace Act 1906 (c.16)
Justice of the Peace, Metropolis Act 1811 (c.119)
Justice of the Peace, the Metropolis Act 1792 (c.53)
Justices Act 1753 (c.27)
Justices' Clerks Act 1877 (c.43)
Justices' Clerks' Fees Act 1753 (c.14)
Justices' Clerks' Fees (Middlesex) Act 1754 (c.16)
Justices Commitment Act 1741 (c.24)
Justices Commitment Act 1743 (c.5)
Justices (Ireland) Act 1842 (c.46)
Justices (Ireland) Act 1843 (c.8)
Justices Jurisdiction Act 1742 (c.18)
Justices Jurisdiction Act 1852 (c.38)
Justices of Assize Act 1738 (c.27)
Justices of Assize Act 1839 (c.22)
Justices of the Peace Act 1361 (c.1)
Justices of the Peace Act 1661 (c.38)
Justices of the Peace Act 1788 (c.49)
Justices of the Peace Act 1867 (c.115)
Justices of the Peace Act 1906 (c.16)
Justices of the Peace Act 1949 (c.101)
Justices of the Peace Act 1965 (c.28)
Justices of the Peace Act 1968 (c.69)
Justices of the Peace Act 1979 (c.55)
Justices of the Peace in Metropolis Act 1837 (c.37)
Justices of the Peace, Nottingham Act 1803 (c.45)
Justices of the Peace Small Debt (Scotland) Act 1825 (c.48)
Justices of the Peace Small Debt (Scotland) Act 1849 (c.34)
Justices Oaths Act 1766 (c.9)
Justices Proceedings Confirmation (Sussex) Act 1864 (c.100)
Justices Protection Act 1803 (c.141)
Justices Protection Act 1848 (c.44)
Justices Protection (Ireland) Act 1849 (c.16)
Justices Qualification Act 1731 (c.18)
Justices Qualification Act 1744 (c.20)
Justices' Qualification Act 1760 (c.13)
Justices Qualification Act 1871 (c.18)
Justices Qualification Act 1875 (c.54)
Justices Quorum Act 1766 (c.21)
Justices (Scotland) Act 1856 (c.48)
Justices (Supplement List) Act 1941 (c.27)
Justiciary and Circuit Courts (Scotland) Act 1783 (c.45)

Justiciary Court (Scotland) Act 1868 (c.95)
Justiciary Courts (Scotland) Act 1814 (c.67)
Justiciary (Scotland) Act 1848 (c.79)
Juvenile Convict Prison (Ireland) Act 1856 (c.24)
Juvenile Courts (Metropolis) Act 1920 (c.68)
Juvenile Offenders Act 1847 (c.82)
Juvenile Offenders (Ireland) Act 1848 (c.59)

Keeper of Holyrood Park, etc. Act 1843 (c.64)
Keeping, etc., of Gunpowder Act 1748 (c.38)
Keeping, etc., of Gunpowder Act 1771 (c.35)
Keeping of Gunpowder Act 1718 (c.26)
Keeping of Gunpowder Act 1724 (c.23)
Keeping of Gunpowder Act 1741 (c.32)
Keighley to Bradford Road Act 1795 (c.135)
Keighley to Halifax Road Act 1795 (c.151)
Keighley to Kirby Kendal Road Act 1778 (c.113)
Kelso Beer Duties Act 1758 (c.56)
Kelso Beer Duties Act 1780 (c.11)
Kennet and Avon: Canal Act 1796 (c.44)
Kennington Common Act 1852 (c.29)
Kensington, Chelsea and Fulham: Improvements Act 1767 (c.101)
Kensington, Chelsea and Fulham Roads (Toll Continuation) Act 1740 (c.16)
Kensington, Chelsea and Fulham Roads (Tolls) Act 1725 (c.37)
Kensington: Improvement Act 1795 (c.74)
Kensington: Poor Relief Act 1777 (c.64)
Kensington Road Act 1795 (c.142)
Kensington Station and North and South London Junction Railway Act 1872 (c.80)
Kent and Surrey Roads Act 1765 (c.68)
Kent and Surrey Roads Act 1770 (c.62)
Kent and Surrey Roads Act 1781 (c.100)
Kent and Surrey Roads Act 1787 (c.70)
Kent and Surrey Roads Act 1792 (c.151)
Kent and Sussex Roads Act 1740 (c.12)
Kent and Sussex Roads Act 1762 (c.67)
Kent and Sussex Roads Act 1766 (c.56)
Kent and Sussex Roads Act 1767 (c.84)
Kent and Sussex Roads Act 1767 (c.86)
Kent and Sussex Roads Act 1770 (c.108)
Kent and Sussex Roads Act 1772 (c.92)
Kent and Sussex Roads Act 1787 (c.80)
Kent and Sussex Roads Act 1788 (c.85)
Kent and Sussex Roads Act 1789 (c.85)
Kent, Devon Fortifications Act 1794 (c.76)
Kent Fortifications Act 1797 (c.66)
Kent Roads Act 1724 (c.5)
Kent Roads Act 1724 (c.15)
Kent Roads Act 1730 (c.15)
Kent Roads Act 1735 (c.7)
Kent Roads Act 1737 (c.37)
Kent Roads Act 1743 (c.4)
Kent Roads Act 1748 (c.4)
Kent Roads Act 1748 (c.8)
Kent Roads Act 1751 (c.8)
Kent Roads Act 1753 (c.68)
Kent Roads Act 1754 (c.26)

Kent Roads Act 1759 (c.40)
Kent Roads Act 1762 (c.65)
Kent Roads Act 1762 (c.76)
Kent Roads Act 1764 (c.78)
Kent Roads Act 1765 (c.63)
Kent Roads Act 1765 (c.71)
Kent Roads Act 1766 (c.91)
Kent Roads Act 1766 (c.93)
Kent Roads Act 1767 (c.91)
Kent Roads Act 1767 (c.103)
Kent Roads Act 1769 (c.43)
Kent Roads Act 1769 (c.49)
Kent Roads Act 1769 (c.76)
Kent Roads Act 1769 (c.78)
Kent Roads Act 1769 (c.92)
Kent Roads Act 1773 (c.98)
Kent Roads Act 1773 (c.114)
Kent Roads Act 1776 (c.69)
Kent Roads Act 1782 (c.98)
Kent Roads Act 1782 (c.102)
Kent Roads Act 1785 (c.103)
Kent Roads Act 1785 (c.112)
Kent Roads Act 1786 (c.132)
Kent Roads Act 1786 (c.134)
Kent Roads Act 1786 (c.145)
Kent Roads Act 1788 (c.93)
Kent Roads Act 1789 (c.84)
Kent Roads Act 1789 (c.100)
Kent Roads Act 1790 (c.90)
Kent Roads Act 1791 (c.94)
Kent Roads Act 1792 (c.117)
Kent Roads Act 1793 (c.162)
Kent Roads Act 1793 (c.183)
Kent Roads Act 1795 (c.165)
Kent: Small Debts Act 1783 (c.8)
Kent: Small Debts Act 1786 (c.18)
Kent: Small Debts Act 1786 (c.22)
Kent: Small Debts Act 1786 (c.118)
Kent, Sussex Fortifications Act 1780 (c.10)
Kentish Town: Footpath Act 1771 (c.59)
Kenya Divorces (Validity) Act 1922 (c.10)
Kenya Independence Act 1963 (c.54)
Kenya Republic Act 1965 (c.5)
Kettering and Newport Pagnell Road Act 1754 (c.31)
Kettering to Newport Pagnell Roads Act 1773 (c.92)
Kettering to Newport Pagnell Road Act 1781 (c.103)
Kew Bridge (Building and Tolls) Act 1782 (c.42)
Kidderminster Church Act 1785 (c.94)
Kidderminster Roads Act 1777 (c.75)
Kidderminster: Small Debts Act 1772 (c.66)
Kilburn Road Act 1779 (c.120)
Kilmainham Hospital Act 1815 (c. 136)
Kilmainham Hospital Pensions Act 1807 (c.5)
Kilmainham Hospital (Pensions Commutation) Act 1813 (c.154)
Kimbolton Road Act 1755 (c.33)
Kincardine (County) Roads Act 1796 (c.132)
Kinghorn Beer Duties Act 1748 (c.13)
Kinghorn Beer Duties Act 1774 (c.28)

King's Bench Prison Act 1754 (c.17)
King's Bench Prison: Poor Relief Act 1783 (c.23)
King's Lynn: Pilotage Act 1772 (c.30)
King's Lynn: Small Debts Act 1770 (c.20)
Kingsholm District Act 1871 (c.54)
Kingston to Sheetbridge Road Act 1792 (c.119)
Kingston-upon-Hull: Improvement Act 1755 (c.27)
Kingston-upon-Hull: Improvement Act 1762 (c.70)
Kingston-upon-Hull: Improvement Act 1764 (c.74)
Kingston-upon-Hull: Improvement Act 1783 (c.55)
Kingston-upon-Hull Port Act 1774 (c.56)
Kingston-upon-Hull Roads Act 1744 (c.4)
Kingston-upon-Hull Roads Act 1767 (c.70)
Kingston-upon-Hull Roads Act 1788 (c.95)
Kingston-upon-Hull: Small Debts Act 1762 (c.38)
Kingston-upon-Thames: Streets Act 1772 (c.61)
Kingston-upon-Thames to Street Bride Road Act 1768 (c.56)
Kingstown and Dublin Harbours Act 1838 (c.36)
Kingstown Harbour Act 1836 (c.117)
Kingstown Harbour Act 1865 (c.67)
Kingstown Township Act 1898 (c.52)
Kinross and Alloa Road Act 1797 (c.171)
Kirby Kendal and Kirkby Ireleth Road Act 1763 (c.33)
Kirby Kendal to Kirkby Ireleth Road Act 1783 (c.23)
Kirby, Westmorland: Small Debts Act 1764 (c.41)
Kiribati Act 1979 (c.27)
Kirkby Lonsdale and Milnthorpe Road Act 1797 (c.165)
Kirkcaldy Beer Duties Act 1741 (c.8)
Kirkcaldy Beer Duties Act 1757 (c.69)
Kirkcaldy Beer Duties Act 1791 (c.82)
Kirkcudbright Roads Act 1780 (c.24)
Kirkcudbright Roads Act (c.153)
Knackers Act 1786 (c.71)
Knackers Act 1844 (c.87)
Knaresborough and Greenhammerton Road Act 1771 (c.65)
Knaresborough Inclosure Act 1789 (c.76)
Knaresborough: Water Supply Act 1764 (c.93)

L.C.C. (Money) Act 1890 (c.41)
L.C.C. (Money) Act 1891 (c.62)
Labour Bureaux (London) Act 1902 (c.13)
Labour Exchange Act 1909 (c.7)
Labourers' Cottages and Allotments (Ireland) Act 1882 (c.60)
Labourers (Ireland) Act 1883 (c.60)
Labourers (Ireland) Act 1885 (c.77)

Labourers (Ireland) Act 1886 (c.59)
Labourers (Ireland) Act 1891 (c.71)
Labourers (Ireland) Act 1892 (c.7)
Labourers (Ireland) Act 1896 (c.53)
Labourers (Ireland) Act 1906 (c.37)
Labourers (Ireland) Act 1911 (c.19)
Labourers (Ireland) Act 1914 (c.32)
Labourers (Ireland) Act 1918 (c.20)
Labourers (Ireland) Act 1919 (c.55)
Labouring Classes Lodging Houses and Dwellings (Ireland) Act 1866 (c.44)
Lairy Embankment (Plymouth) Act 1802 (c.32)
Lambeth Water Works Act 1785 (c.89)
Lanark and Hamilton Roads Act 1792 (c.122)
Lanark and Renfrew Roads Act 1789 (c.92)
Lanark Prisons Act 1868 (c.50)
Lanark Roads Act 1772 (c.82)
Lanark Roads Act 1792 (c.124)
Lancashire Roads Act 1730 (c.31)
Lancashire Roads Act 1774 (c.99)
Lancashire Roads Act 1784 (c.68)
Lancaster and Westmorland Roads Act 1782 (c.88)
Lancaster Bridge Act 1782 (c.57)
Lancaster Canal Act 1793 (c.107)
Lancaster County Clerk Act 1871 (c.73)
Lancaster: Drainage Act 1779 (c.33)
Lancaster Marsh: Drainage Act 1795 (c.11)
Lancaster Palatine Courts Act 1794 (c.58)
Lancaster Roads Act 1771 (c.91)
Lancaster Roads Act 1785 (c.106)
Lancaster Roads Act 1789 (c.107)
Lancaster Roads Act 1789 (c.110)
Lancaster Roads Act 1792 (c.139)
Lancaster Roads Act 1793 (c.181)
Lancaster Roads Act 1795 (c.144)
Land at Snaith Yorks. Act 1773 (c.85)
Land Charges Act 1900 (c.26)
Land Charges Act 1925 (c.22)
Land Charges Act 1972 (c.61)
Land Charges Registration and Searches Act 1888 (c.51)
Land Clauses Consolidation Act 1845 (c.18)
Land Clauses Consolidation Acts Amendment Act 1860 (c.106)
Land Clauses (Umpire) Act 1883 (c.15)
Land Commisssion Act 1967 (c.1)
Land Commission (Dissolution) Act 1971 (c.18)
Land Commissioners (Ireland) Salaries Act 1892 (c.45)
Land Compensation Act 1961 (c.33)
Land Compensation Act 1967 (c.1)
Land Compensation Act 1973 (c.26)
Land Compensation (Scotland) Act 1963 (c.51)
Land Compensation (Scotland) Act 1973 (c.56)
Land Drainage Act 1845 (c.56)
Land Drainage Act 1914 (c.4)
Land Drainage Act 1918 (c.17)
Land Drainage Act 1926 (c.24)

Land Drainage Act 1929 (c.8)
Land Drainage Act 1930 (c.44)
Land Drainage Act 1961 (c.48)
Land Drainage Act 1976 (c.70)
Land Drainage Act 1991 (c.59)
Land Drainage Act 1994 (c.25)
Land Drainage (Amendment) Act 1976 (c.17)
Land Drainage (Rating) Act 1743 (c.37)
Land Drainage (Scotland) Act 1930 (c.20)
Land Drainage (Scotland) Act 1935 (c.19)
Land Drainage (Scotland) Act 1941 (c.13)
Land Drainage (Scotland) Act 1958 (c.24)
Land Drainage Supplemental (No. 2) Act 1866 (c.80)
Land Drained at Great Carlton, Lincolnshire Act 1792 (c.91)
Land for Ordnance Services Act 1803 (cc. 65, 66)
Land for Prisons (Ireland) Act 1847 (c.26)
Land Law (Ireland) Act 1881 (c.49)
Land Law (Ireland) Act 1887 (c.33)
Land Law (Ireland) Act 1888 (c.13)
Land Law (Ireland) Act, 1888, Amendment 1889 (c.59)
Land Law (Ireland) Act 1896 (c.47)
Land Law (Ireland) Act 1881 (c.49)
Land Law (Ireland) Act 1887 (c.33)
Land Powers (Defence) Act 1958 (c.30)
Land Registers (Scotland) Act 1868 (c.64)
Land Registration Act 1925 (c.21)
Land Registration Act 1936 (c.26)
Land Registration Act 1966 (c.39)
Land Registration Act 1986 (c.26)
Land Registration Act 1988 (c.3)
Land Registration and Land Charges Act 1971 (c.54)
Land Registration (Scotland) Act 1979 (c.33)
Land Registry Act 1862 (c.53)
Land Registry Act 1886 (c.1)
Land Registry (Middlesex Deeds) Act 1891 (c.64)
Land Registry (New Buildings) Act 1900 (c.19)
Land Revenue of the Crown Act 1815 (c.55)
Land Revenues of the Crown Act 1790 (c.50)
Land Settlement Amendment Act 1921 (c.43)
Land Settlement (Facilities) Act 1919 (c.59)
Land Settlement (Facilities) Amendment Act 1925 (c.85)
Land Settlement (Scotland) Act 1919 (c.97)
Land Settlement (Scotland) Act 1934 (c.35)
Land Tax Act 1702 (c.1)
Land Tax Act 1704 (c.1)
Land Tax Act 1705 (c.1)
Land Tax Act 1707 (c.35)
Land Tax Act 1708 (c.1)
Land Tax Act 1710 (c.1)
Land Tax Act 1711 (c.1)
Land Tax Act 1712 (c.1)
Land Tax Act 1713 (c.1)
Land Tax Act 1714 (c.1)
Land Tax Act 1715 (c.31)
Land Tax Act 1717 (c.1)

Land Tax Act 1718 (c.1)
Land Tax Act 1719 (c.1)
Land Tax Act 1720 (c.4)
Land Tax Act 1721 (c.1)
Land Tax Act 1723 (c.1)
Land Tax Act 1724 (c.1)
Land Tax Act 1725 (c.1)
Land Tax Act 1726 (c.1)
Land Tax Act 1727 (c.5)
Land Tax Act 1728 (c.4)
Land Tax Act 1729 (c.1)
Land Tax Act 1730 (c.4)
Land Tax Act 1732 (c.10)
Land Tax Act 1733 (c.7)
Land Tax Act 1734 (c.23)
Land Tax Act 1735 (c.3)
Land Tax Act 1736 (c.3)
Land Tax Act 1737 (c.14)
Land Tax Act 1746 (c.2)
Land Tax Act 1757 (c.4)
Land Tax Act 1757 (c.7)
Land Tax Act 1771 (c.5)
Land Tax Act 1772 (c.3)
Land Tax Act 1772 (c.8)
Land Tax Act 1774 (c.1)
Land Tax Act 1774 (c.17)
Land Tax Act 1775 (c.3)
Land Tax Act 1775 (c.26)
Land Tax Act 1776 (c.1)
Land Tax Act 1776 (c.4)
Land Tax Act 1776 (c.14)
Land Tax Act 1778 (c.2)
Land Tax Act 1778 (c.23)
Land Tax Act 1780 (c.2)
Land Tax Act 1780 (c.3)
Land Tax Act 1780 (c.23)
Land Tax Act 1782 (c.2)
Land Tax Act 1782 (c.9)
Land Tax Act 1783 (c.3)
Land Tax Act 1783 (c.4)
Land Tax Act 1783 (c.10)
Land Tax Act 1785 (c.4)
Land Tax Act 1785 (c.20)
Land Tax Act 1786 (c.3)
Land Tax Act 1786 (c.54)
Land Tax Act 1786 (c.103)
Land Tax Act 1786 (c.105)
Land Tax Act 1786 (c.121)
Land Tax Act 1787 (c.5)
Land Tax Act 1787 (c.47)
Land Tax Act 1788 (c.2)
Land Tax Act 1789 (c.6)
Land Tax Act 1790 (c.2)
Land Tax Act 1790 (c.13)
Land Tax Act 1791 (c.6)
Land Tax Act 1791 (c.14)
Land Tax Act 1792 (c.5)
Land Tax Act 1792 (c.23)
Land Tax Act 1793 (c.7)
Land Tax Act 1794 (c.8)
Land Tax Act 1795 (c.2)
Land Tax Act 1795 (c.17)
Land Tax Act 1796 (c.2)

Land Tax Act 1796 (c.89)
Land Tax Act 1797 (c.5)
Land Tax Act 1797 (c.26)
Land Tax Act 1797 (c.35)
Land Tax Act 1797 (c.128)
Land Tax Act 1800 (c.68)
Land Tax Act 1805 (c.48)
Land Tax Act 1808 (c.102)
Land Tax Act 1809 (c.55)
Land Tax Act 1809 (c.67)
Land Tax Act 1813 (c.142)
Land Tax Act 1814 (c.190)
Land Tax Act 1842 (c.37)
Land Tax, Assessed Tax, and Income Tax Act 1843 (c.24)
Land Tax Certificates Forgery Act 1812 (c.143)
Land Tax Commissioners Act 1798 (c.48)
Land Tax Commissioners Act 1844 (c.79)
Land Tax Commissioners Act 1867 (c.51)
Land Tax Commissioners Act 1906 (c.52)
Land Tax Commissioners Act 1927 (c.16)
Land Tax Commissioners Act 1937 (c.18)
Land Tax Commissioners (Appointment) Act 1836 (c.80)
Land Tax Commissioners (Appointment) Act 1838 (c.57)
Land Tax Commissioners (Appointment) Act 1866 (c.59)
Land Tax Commissioners (Appointment) Act 1869 (c.64)
Land Tax Commissioners (Appointment) Act 1874 (c.18)
Land Tax Commissioners (Names) Act 1879 (c.52)
Land Tax Commissioners (Names) Act 1881 (c.16)
Land Tax Commissioners Names Act 1886 (c.47)
Land Tax Commissioners Names Act 1893 (c.27)
Land Tax Commissioners Names Act 1899 (c.25)
Land, Tax, etc. Act 1806 (c.107)
Land, Tax, etc. Act 1815 (c.150)
Land Tax, Forfeited Estates, etc. Act 1702 (c.6)
Land Tax Perpetuation Act 1798 (c.60)
Land Tax Redemption Act 1799 (c.10)
Land Tax Redemption Act 1799 (c.21)
Land Tax Redemption Act 1799 (c.40)
Land Tax Redemption Act 1799 (c.43)
Land Tax Redemption Act 1799 (c.108)
Land Tax Redemption Act 1800 (c.28)
Land Tax Redemption Act 1800 (c.30)
Land Tax Redemption Act 1801 (c.72)
Land Tax Redemption Act 1802 (c.116)
Land Tax Redemption Act 1803 (c.51)
Land Tax Redemption Act 1805 (c.77)
Land Tax Redemption Act 1806 (c.133)
Land Tax Redemption Act 1810 (c.58)
Land Tax Redemption Act 1812 (c.80)
Land Tax Redemption Act 1813 (c.123)

Land Tax Redemption Act 1814 (c.173)
Land Tax Redemption Act 1837 (c.17)
Land Tax Redemption Act 1838 (c.58)
Land Tax Redemption, etc. Act 1798 (c.6)
Land Tenure Reform (Scotland) Act 1974 (c.38)
Land Transfer Act 1875 (c.87)
Land Transfer Act 1897 (c.65)
Landed Estates Court (Ireland) Act 1858 (c.72)
Landed Estates Court (Ireland) Act 1866 (c.99)
Landed Property Improvement (Ireland) Act 1847 (c.32)
Landing of Merchandise Act 1796 (c.82)
Landlord and Tenant Act 1709 (c.18(i))
Landlord and Tenant Act 1730 (c.28)
Landlord and Tenant Act 1871 (c.92)
Landlord and Tenant Act 1927 (c.36)
Landlord and Tenant Act 1954 (c.56)
Landlord and Tenant Act 1959 (c.64)
Landlord and Tenant Act 1962 (c.50)
Landlord and Tenant Act 1985 (c.70)
Landlord and Tenant Act 1987 (c.31)
Landlord and Tenant Act 1988 (c.26)
Landlord and Tenant (Ireland) Act 1870 (c.46)
Landlord and Tenant (Ireland) Act 1871 (c.92)
Landlord and Tenant (Ireland) Act 1872 (c.32)
Landlord and Tenant Law Amendment Act Ireland 1860 (c.154)
Landlord and Tenant (Licensed Premises) Act 1990 (c.39)
Landlord and Tenant (Rent Control) Act 1949 (c.40)
Landlord and Tenant (Requisitioned Land) Act 1942 (c.13)
Landlord and Tenant (Requisitioned Land) Act 1944 (c.5)
Landlord and Tenant (Temporary Provisions) Act 1958 (c.68)
Landlord and Tenant (War Damage) Act 1939 (c.72)
Landlord and Tenant (War Damage) (Amendment) Act 1941 (c.41)
Lands at Sheerness and Chatham Act 1816 (c.74)
Lands Clauses Consolidation Act 1845 (c.18)
Lands Clauses Consolidation Act 1869 (c.18)
Lands Clauses Consolidation (Scotland) Act 1845 (c.19)
Lands Clauses (Taxation of Costs) Act 1895 (c.11)
Lands for Ordnance Services, Woolwich Act 1802 (c.89)
Lands for Ordnance Services, Woolwich Act 1803 (c.35)
Lands for the Defence of the Realm Act 1809 (c.112)
Lands of Earl of Pembroke Act 1783 (c.61)
Lands Tribunal Act 1949 (c.42)

Lands Valuation Amendment (Scotland) Act 1982 (c.57)

Lands Valuation (Scotland) Act 1854 (c.91)

Lands Valuation (Scotland) Act 1857 (c.58)

Lands Valuation (Scotland) Amendment Act 1895 (c.41)

Lands Valuation (Scotland) Amendment Act 1902 (c.25)

Lane End Chapel, Stoke upon Trent 1792 (c.88)

Langbaurgh Coroners Act 1873 (c.81)

Lapworth to Kingswood Canal Act 1795 (c.72)

Larceny Act 1808 (c.129)

Larceny Act 1868 (c.116)

Larceny Act 1896 (c.52)

Larceny Act 1901 (c.10)

Larceny Act 1916 (c.50)

Larceny (Advertisements) Act 1870 (c.65)

Late Earl of Seaforth Act 1734 (c.22)

Late Night Refreshment Houses Act 1969 (c.53)

Latent Damage Act 1986 (c.37)

Launceston: Poor Relief Act 1784 (c.17)

Launceston Roads Act 1781 (c.86)

Law Agents and Notaries Public (Scotland) Act 1891 (c.30)

Law Agents Apprenticeship (War Service) (Scotland) Act 1914 (c.20)

Law Agents Apprenticeship (War Service) (Scotland) Act 1919 (c.24)

Law Agents (Scotland) Act 1873 (c.63)

Law Agents (Scotland) Act Amendment 1896 (c.49)

Law and Procedure (Emergency Provisions) (Ireland) Act 1916 (c.46)

Law Commissions Act 1965 (c.22)

Law Costs (Ireland) Act 1823 (c.89)

Law of Commons Amendment Act 1893 (c.57)

Law of Distress Amendment Act 1888 (c.21)

Law of Distress Amendment Act 1895 (c.24)

Law of Distress Amendment Act 1908 (c.53)

Law of Distress and Small Debts (Ireland) Act 1888 (c.47)

Law of Distress and Small Debts (Ireland) Act 1893 (c.36)

Law of Libel Amendment Act 1888 (c.64)

Law of Property Act 1922 (c.16)

Law of Property Act 1925 (c.20)

Law of Property Act 1969 (c.59)

Law of Property Act (Postponement) Act 1924 (c.4)

Law of Property Amendment Act 1859 (c.35)

Law of Property Amendment Act 1860 (c.38)

Law of Property (Amendment) Act 1924 (c.5)

Law of Property (Amendment) Act 1926 (c.11)

Law of Property (Amendment) Act 1926 (c.14)

Law of Property (Amendment) Act 1929 (c.9)

Law of Property (Entailed Interests) Act 1931 (c.27)

Law of Property (Joint Tenants) Act 1964 (c.63)

Law of Property (Miscellaneous Provisions) Act 1989 (c.34)

Law of Property (Miscellaneous Provisions) Act 1994 (c.36)

Law Officers Act 1944 (c.25)

Law Officers' Fees Act 1872 (c.70)

Law Reform (Contributory Negligence) Act 1945 (c.28)

Law Reform (Damages and Solatium) (Scotland) Act 1962 (c.42)

Law Reform (Diligence) (Scotland) Act 1973 (c.22)

Law Reform (Enforcement of Contracts) Act 1954 (c.34)

Law Reform (Frustrated Contracts) Act 1943 (c.40)

Law Reform (Husband and Wife) Act 1962 (c.48)

Law Reform (Husband and Wife) (Scotland) Act 1984 (c.15)

Law Reform (Jurisdiction in Delict) (Scotland) Act 1971 (c.55)

Law Reform (Limitation of Actions etc.) Act 1954 (c.36)

Law Reform (Married Women and Tortfeasors) Act 1935 (c.30)

Law Reform (Miscellaneous Provisions) Act 1934 (c.41)

Law Reform (Miscellaneous Provisions) Act 1949 (c.100)

Law Reform (Miscellaneous Provisions) Act 1970 (c.33)

Law Reform (Miscellaneous Provisions) Act 1971 (c.43)

Law Reform (Miscellaneous Provisions) (Scotland) Act 1940 (c.42)

Law Reform (Miscellaneous Provisions) (Scotland) Act 1966 (c.19)

Law Reform (Miscellaneous Provisions) (Scotland) Act 1968 (c.70)

Law Reform (Miscellaneous Provisions) (Scotland) Act 1980 (c.55)

Law Reform (Miscellaneous Provisions) (Scotland) Act 1985 (c.73)

Law Reform (Miscellaneous Provisions) (Scotland) Act 1990 (c.40)

Law Reform (Parent and Child) (Scotland) Act 1986 (c.9)

Law Reform (Personal Injuries) Act 1948 (c.41)

Law Reform (Personal Injuries) Amendment Act 1948 (c.7)

Law Reform (Personal Injuries) Amendment Act 1953 (c.7)

Laws Continuation, etc. Act 1739 (c.18)

Laws in Wales Act 1542 (c.39)

Laying of Documents before Parliament (Interpretation) Act 1948 (c.59)

Lazarets Act 1772 (c.57)

Lead Paint (Protection Against Poisoning) Act 1926 (c.37)

Lease of Exeter Castle Act 1710 (c.24)

Leasehold Property Act and Long Leases (Scotland) Act Extension Act 1953 (c.12)

Leasehold Property (Repairs) Act 1938 (c.34)

Leasehold Property (Temporary Provisions) Act 1951 (c.38)

Leasehold Reform Act 1967 (c.88)

Leasehold Reform Act 1979 (c.44)

Leasehold Reform, Housing and Urban Development Act 1993 (c.28)

Leases and Sales of Settled Estates Amendment Act 1874 (c.33)

Leases for Schools (Ireland) Act 1881 (c.65)

Leases (Ireland) Act 1846 (c.112)

Leases of Episcopal Lands (Ireland) Act 1813 (c.92)

Leasing-making, etc. (Scotland) Act 1837 (c.5)

Leasing-making (Scotland) Act 1825 (c.47)

Leasing Powers Amendment Act for Religious Purposes in Ireland Act 1875 (c.11)

Leasing Powers for Religious Worship in Ireland Act 1855 (c.39)

Leatherhead and Guildford Road Act 1757 (c.77)

Lecturers and Parish Clerks Act 1844 (c.59)

Lectures Copyright Act 1835 (c.65)

Ledbury Highways Act 1720 (c.23)

Ledbury Roads Act 1793 (c.132)

Leddon and Clavering, Norfolk: Poor Relief Act 1764 (c.90)

Leeds and Blackburn Roads Act 1781 (c.102)

Leeds and Halifax Roads Act 1740 (c.32)

Leeds and Halifax Roads Act 1751 (c.55)

Leeds and Halifax Roads Act 1783 (c.94)

Leeds and Harrogate Road Act 1796 (c.138)

Leeds and Liverpool Canal Act 1770 (c.114)

Leeds and Liverpool Canal Act 1783 (c.47)

Leeds and Wakefield Road Act 1770 (c.61)

Leeds Bridge Act 1759 (c.54)

Leeds Church Act 1792 (c.89)

Leeds Coal Supply Act 1779 (c.11)

Leeds Coal Supply Act 1793 (c.86)

Leeds Corporation (Consolidation) Act 1905 (c.1)

Leeds: Lighting, etc. Act 1755 (c.41)

Leeds to Liverpool Canal Act 1790 (c.65)

Leeds to Liverpool Canal Act 1794 (c.94)

Leeds to Otley Road Act 1781 (c.98)

Leeds to Sheffield Road Act 1760 (c.33)

Leeds to Wakefield Road Act 1792 (c.131)

Leeds University Act 1904 (c.12)

Leeds: Water Supply Act 1790 (c.68)

Leeward Islands Act 1871 (c.107)

Leeward Islands Act 1956 (c.23)

Legacy Duty Act 1796 (c.52)

Legacy Duty Act 1797 Act (c.135)

Legacy Duty Act 1799 (c.73)

Legacy Duty Act 1805 (c.28)

Legal Advice and Assistance Act 1972 (c.50)

Legal Aid Act 1960 (c.28)

Legal Aid Act 1964 (c.30)

Legal Aid Act 1974 (c.4)

Legal Aid Act 1979 (c.26)

Legal Aid Act 1982 (c.44)

Legal Aid Act 1988 (c.34)

Legal Aid and Advice Act 1949 (c.51)

Legal Aid and Solicitors (Scotland) Act 1949 (c.63)

Legal Aid (Scotland) Act 1967 (c.43)

Legal Aid (Scotland) Act 1986 (c.47)

Legal Practitioners Act 1875 (c.79)

Legal Practitioners Act 1876 (c.66)

Legal Practitioners (Ireland) Act 1876 (c.44)

Legal Proceedings Against Enemies Act 1915 (c.36)

Legal Rate of Interest Act 1774 (c.79)

Legislative Council for Canada Act 1854 (c.118)

Legislative Council of Canada Act 1859 (c.10)

Legislative Council, New Zealand Act 1868 (c.57)

Legitimacy Act 1926 (c.60)

Legitimacy Act 1959 (c.73)

Legitimacy Act 1976 (c.31)

Legitimacy Declaration Act 1858 (c.93)

Legitimacy Declaration Act (Ireland) 1868 (c.20)

Legitimation (Re-registration of Births) Act 1957 (c.39)

Legitimation (Scotland) Act 1968 (c.22)

Leicester and Derby Roads Act 1759 (c.46)

Leicester and Notts. Roads Act 1762 (c.82)

Leicester and Stafford Roads Act 1753 (c.85)

Leicester and Stafford Roads Act 1779 (c.85)

Leicester and Warwick Roads Act 1754 (c.42)

Leicester and Warwick Roads Act 1781 (c.85)

Leicester Navigation Act 1791 (c.65)

Leicester Navigation Act 1797 (c.51)

Leicester Road Act 1725 (c.5)

Leicester Roads Act 1745 (c.10)

Leicester Roads Act 1753 (c.46)

Leicester Roads Act 1757 (c.44)

Leicester Roads Act 1759 (c.41)

Leicester Roads Act 1764 (c.84)

Leicester Roads Act 1769 (c.91)

Leicester Roads Act 1776 (c.81)

Leicester Roads Act 1777 (c.108)

Leicester Roads Act 1779 (c.90)

Leicester Roads Act 1781 (c.89)

Leicester Roads Act 1783 (c.107)

Leicester Roads Act 1785 (c.113)

Leicester Roads Act 1788 (c.100)

Leicester Roads Act 1790 (c.92)

Leicester to Peterborough Road Act 1754 (c.30)

Leicester, Warwick and Coventry Roads Act 1762 (c.80)

Leicestershire and Northamptonshire Union Canal Act 1793 (c.98)

Leicestershire Roads Act 1757 (c.49)

Leicestershire Roads Act 1762 (c.54)

Leicestershire Roads Act 1771 (c.88)
Leigh and Deerhurst Canal Act 1792 (c.83)
Leith and Bruntisland Ferries, etc. Act 1792 (c.93)
Leith Harbour Act 1754 (c.8)
Leith Harbour Act 1788 (c.58)
Leith Harbour and Docks Act 1847 (c.114)
Leith Harbour and Docks Act 1860 (c.48)
Leominster Canal Act 1791 (c.69)
Leominster Canal Act 1796 (c.70)
Leominster Roads Act 1728 (c.13)
Leominster Roads Act 1777 (c.85)
Leominster Roads Act 1797 (c.176)
Lesotho Independence Act 1966 (c.24)
Letter Stealing (Scotland) Act 1836 (c.21)
Letters of Marque Act 1801 (c.76)
Letters Patent for Inventions Act 1835 (c.83)
Levant Trade Act 1753 (c.18)
Level Crossings Act 1983 (c.16)
Lewes and Brighton Road Act 1770 (c.64)
Lewes and Eastbourne Road Act 1758 (c.67)
Lewes: Improvement Act 1791 (c.86)
Lewes to Brighton Road Act 1791 (c.115)
Lewis (Estates and Crown Claims) Act 1806 (c.131)
Lewisham Church Act 1774 (c.93)
Liabilities (War-Time Adjustment) Act 1941 (c.24)
Liabilities (War-Time Adjustment) Act 1944 (c.40)
Liabilities (War-Time Adjustment) (Scotland) Act 1944 (c.29)
Liability for War Damage (Miscellaneous Provisions) Act 1939 (c.102)
Liardet's Cement Patent Act 1776 (c.29)
Libel Act 1792 (c.60)
Libel Act 1843 (c.96)
Libel Act 1845 (c.75)
Libel (Ireland) Act 1868 (c.69)
Liberties Act 1836 (c.87)
Liberties Act 1850 (c.105)
Liberty of Ely Act 1837 (c.53)
Liberty of Religious Worship Act 1855 (c.86)
Libraries Offences Act 1898 (c.53)
Licences for Retailing Beer, etc. Act 1784 (c.30)
Licence to J. Porter etc. to Import Silk Act 1740 (c.4)
Licensed Premises (Exclusion of Certain Persons) Act 1980 (c.32)
Licensed Premises in New Towns 1952 (c.65)
Licensing (Abolition of State Management) Act 1971 (c.65)
Licensing Act 1842 (c.44)
Licensing Act 1872 (c.94)
Licensing Act 1874 (c.49)
Licensing Act 1902 (c.28)
Licensing Act 1904 (c.23)
Licensing Act 1906 (c.42)
Licensing Act 1921 (c.42)
Licensing Act 1949 (c.59)
Licensing Act 1953 (c.46)

Licensing Act 1961 (c.61)
Licensing Act 1964 (c.26)
Licensing Act 1988 (c.17)
Licensing (Airports) Act 1956 (c.37)
Licensing (Alcohol Education and Research) Act 1981 (c.28)
Licensing (Amendment) Act 1967 (c.51)
Licensing (Amendment) Act 1976 (c.18)
Licensing (Amendment) Act 1977 (c.26)
Licensing (Amendment) Act 1980 (c.40)
Licensing (Amendment) Act 1981 (c.40)
Licensing (Amendment) Act 1985 (c.40)
Licensing (Amendment) Act 1989 (c.20)
Licensing Amendment (Scotland) Act 1897 (c.50)
Licensing (Amendment) (Scotland) Act 1992 (c.18)
Licensing (Amendment) (Scotland) Act 1993 (c.20)
Licensing (Certificates in Suspense) (Scotland) Act 1967 (c.14)
Licensing (Consolidation) Act 1910 (c.24)
Licensing (Evidence) Act 1884 (c.29)
Licensing (Ireland) Act 1836 (c.38)
Licensing (Ireland) Act 1855 (c.62)
Licensing (Ireland) Act 1860 (c.35)
Licensing (Ireland) Act 1874 (c.69)
Licensing (Ireland) Act 1902 (c.18)
Licensing (Ireland) Act 1905 (c.3)
Licensing (Low Alcohol Drinks) Act 1990 (c.21)
Licensing (Occasional Permissions) Act 1983 (c.24)
Licensing of Alehouses Act 1792 (c.59)
Licensing (Permitted Hours) Act 1934 (c.26)
Licensing Planning (Temporary Provisions) Act 1944 (c.15)
Licensing Planning (Temporary Provisions) Act 1946 (c.53)
Licensing (Restaurant Meals) Act 1987 (c.2)
Licensing (Retail Sales) Act 1988 (c.25)
Licensing (Scotland) Act 1903 (c.25)
Licensing (Scotland) Act 1959 (c.51)
Licensing (Scotland) Act 1962 (c.51)
Licensing (Scotland) Act 1969 (c.13)
Licensing (Scotland) Act 1976 (c.66)
Licensing (Seamen's Canteens) Act 1954 (c.11)
Lichfield Roads Act 1728 (c.5)
Lieutenancy Clerks Allowances Act 1887 (c.36)
Life Annuities Act 1808 (c.142)
Life Annuities Act 1809 (c.104)
Life Assurance Act 1774 (c.48)
Life Assurance Companies Act 1870 (c.61)
Life Assurance Companies Act 1871 (c.58)
Life Assurance Companies Act 1872 (c.41)
Life Insurance Companies (Payment into Court) Act 1896 (c.8)
Life Insurance (Ireland) Act 1866 (c.42)
Life Peerages Act 1958 (c.21)
Light Locomotives (Ireland) Act 1903 (c.2)
Light Railways Act 1896 (c.48)

Light Railways Act 1912 (c.19)
Light Railways Commissioners (Salaries) Act 1901 (c.36)
Light Railways (Ireland) Act 1889 (c.66)
Light Railways (Ireland) Act 1893 (c.50)
Light Silver Coin Act 1774 (c.42)
Lighthouses Act 1836 (c.79)
Lighthouses (Ireland) Act 1810 (c.95)
Lighting, etc., of Cities (Ireland) Act 1807 (c.42)
Lighting of Towns (Ireland) Act 1857 (c.12)
Lights on Vehicles Act 1907 (c.45)
Limehouse, Stepney Parish Act 1730 (c.17)
Limehouse, Stepney: Streets Act 1782 (c.87)
Limerick Harbour Act 1867 (c.53)
Limitation Act 1939 (c.21)
Limitation Act 1963 (c.47)
Limitation Act 1975 (c.54)
Limitation Act 1980 (c.58)
Limitation Amendment Act 1980 (c.24)
Limitation (Enemies and War Prisoners) Act 1945 (c.16)
Limitation of Action Act 1843 (c.54)
Limitation of Time (Ireland) (Canal Companies) Act 1815 (c.90)
Limitations of Actions and Costs Act 1842 (c.97)
Limited Liability Act 1855 (c.133)
Limited Owners Reservoirs and Water Supply Further Facilities Act 1877 (c.31)
Limited Owners Residence Act 1870 (c.56)
Limited Owners Residences Act (1870) Amendment Act 1871 (c.84)
Limited Partnerships Act 1907 (c.24)
Limited Penalties Act 1864 (c.110)
Lincoln and Northampton Roads Act 1757 (c.68)
Lincoln and Northamptonshire Roads Act 1765 (c.106)
Lincoln and Nottinghamshire Roads Act 1758 (c.57)
Lincoln and Nottinghamshire Roads Act 1766 (c.83)
Lincoln and Nottinghamshire Roads Act 1767 (c.78)
Lincoln and Nottinghamshire Roads Act 1767 (c.79)
Lincoln and Nottinghamshire Roads Act 1780 (c.73)
Lincoln and Nottinghamshire Roads Act 1782 (c.94)
Lincoln and Nottinghamshire Roads Act 1787 (c.71)
Lincoln and Peterborough Roads Act 1756 (c.85)
Lincoln and Rutland Roads Act 1762 (c.73)
Lincoln and Rutland Roads Act 1786 (c.159)
Lincoln (City) Roads Act 1738 (c.10)
Lincoln (City) Roads Act 1797 (c.168)
Lincoln: Drainage Act 1777 (c.70)
Lincoln: Drainage Act 1785 (c.14)
Lincoln: Drainage Act 1787 (c.66)
Lincoln: Drainage Act 1789 (c.32)

Lincoln: Drainage Act 1789 (c.70)
Lincoln: Drainage Act 1793 (c.116)
Lincoln: Drainage Act 1797 (c.67)
Lincoln: Drainage, etc. Act 1794 (c.102)
Lincoln: Improvement Act 1791 (c.80)
Lincoln: Poor Relief Act 1796 (c.102)
Lincoln Roads Act 1738 (c.8)
Lincoln Roads Act 1756 (c.84)
Lincoln Roads Act 1758 (c.44)
Lincoln Roads Act 1764 (c.53)
Lincoln Roads Act 1764 (c.80)
Lincoln Roads Act 1765 (c.73)
Lincoln Roads Act 1765 (c.88)
Lincoln Roads Act 1765 (c.96)
Lincoln Roads Act 1777 (c.109)
Lincoln Roads Act 1778 (c.104)
Lincoln Roads Act 1780 (c.75)
Lincoln Roads Act 1783 (c.34)
Lincoln Roads Act 1785 (c.123)
Lincoln Roads Act 1786 (c.137)
Lincoln Roads Act 1786 (c.138)
Lincoln Roads Act 1786 (c.141)
Lincoln Roads Act 1786 (c.146)
Lincoln Roads Act 1793 (c.150)
Lincoln: Small Debts Act 1778 (c.43)
Lincoln's Inn Fields Rate Act 1734 (c.26)
Lincolnshire Coroners Act 1899 (c.48)
Lincolnshire: Small Debts Act 1777 (c.62)
Lincolnshire: Small Debts Act 1778 (c.34)
Lincolnshire: Small Debts Act 1779 (c.43)
Linen and Hemp Manufacturers Act 1750 (c.31)
Linen and Hempen Manufacturers (Scotland) Act 1726 (c.26)
Linen, etc., Manufacturers (Ireland) Act 1850 (c.48)
Linen, etc., Manufacturers (Ireland) Act 1852 (c.13)
Linen, etc., Manufacturers (Ireland) Act 1853 (c.103)
Linen, etc., Manufacturers (Ireland) Act 1854 (c.46)
Linen, etc., Manufacturers (Ireland) Act 1859 (c.25)
Linen Manufacture (Ireland) Act 1802 (c.75)
Linen Manufacture (Ireland) Act 1804 (c.42)
Linen Manufacture (Ireland) Act 1804 (c.69)
Linen Manufacture, (Scotland) Act (c.23)
Linen Manufacture (Scotland) Act 1753 (c.20)
Linen Manufacturers, etc. (Ireland) Act 1838 (c.52)
Linen Manufacturers (Ireland) Act 1844 (c.47)
Linen (Trade Marks) Act 1743 (c.30)
Linen (Trade Marks) Act 1744 (c.24)
Linens, etc. Act 1794 (c.23)
Linlithgow and Stirling Roads Act 1790 (c.108)
Linlithgow Beer Duties Act 1732 (c.18)
Linlithgow Roads Act 1771 (c.79)
Linlithgow Roads Act 1781 (c.79)
Linlithgow Roads Act 1790 (c.105)

Linlithgow Roads and Bridges Act 1779 (c.12)
Liqueur Act 1848 (c.121)
Liquidation Act 1868 (c.68)
Lis. Pendens Act 1867 (c.47)
Liston, Essex Roads Act 1790 (c.84)
Litchfield Roads Act 1743 (c.24)
Literary and Scientific Institution Act 1854 (c.112)
Literary Copyright Act 1842 (c.45)
Litigants in Person (Costs and Expenses) Act 1975 (c.47)
Litter Act 1958 (c.34)
Litter Act 1983 (c.35)
Little Bowden to Rockingham Road Act 1793 (c.143)
Little Cumbrae Lighthouse Act 1756 (c.20)
Littlehampton Harbour Act 1732 (c.12)
Littlehampton Harbour Act 1793 (c.100)
Liverpool, Admiralty District Registrar Act 1970 (c.45)
Liverpool and Prescot Road Act 1725 (c.21)
Liverpool and Preston Road Act 1771 (c.93)
Liverpool Church Act 1792 (c.76)
Liverpool Churches Act 1767 (c.80)
Liverpool Court of Passage Act 1896 (c.21)
Liverpool Courts of Passage Act 1893 (c.37)
Liverpool Dock Act 1737 (c.32)
Liverpool Docks Act 1709 (c.8)
Liverpool Harbour Act 1762 (c.86)
Liverpool Harbour Act 1785 (c.15)
Liverpool, Improvement Act 1749 (c.24)
Liverpool: Improvement Act 1762 (c.68)
Liverpool: Improvement Act 1786 (c.12)
Liverpool: Improvement Act 1788 (c.13)
Liverpool Note Issue Act 1793 (c.31)
Liverpool Rectory Act 1786 (c.15)
Liverpool Theatre Act 1771 (c.16)
Liverpool to Preston Road Act 1786 (c.126)
Livestock Industry Act 1937 (c.50)
Livestock Rearing Act 1951 (c.18)
Llandilo Rhynws Bridge Act 1784 (c.66)
Llandovery Bridge Act 1773 (c.111)
Llanfyllin Market House Act 1789 (c.24)
Llangollen International Musical Eisteddfod Act 1967 (c.49)
Llanyblodwell to Newtown Canal Act 1794 (c.39)
Lloyd's Signal Stations Act 1888 (c.29)
Loan Act 1901 (c.12)
Loan Act 1902 (c.4)
Loan from Bank of England Act 1815 (c.16)
Loan Societies Act 1840 (c.110)
Loan Societies Act 1841 (c.55)
Loan Societies Act 1842 (c.5)
Loan Societies Act 1843 (c.41)
Loan Societies Act 1844 (c.54)
Loan Societies Act 1845 (c.60)
Loan Societies Act 1846 (c.52)
Loan Societies Act 1848 (c.64)
Loan Societies Act 1849 (c.37)
Loan Societies Act 1850 (c.45)
Loan Societies Act 1851 (c.31)

Loan Societies Act 1852 (c.15)
Loan Societies Act 1853 (c.109)
Loan Societies Act 1857 (c.41)
Loan Societies Act 1858 (c.19)
Loan Societies Act 1863 (c.56)
Loan Societies (Ireland) Act 1836 (c.55)
Loan Societies (Ireland) Act 1838 (c.78)
Loan Societies (Ireland) Act 1843 Amendment Act 1872 (c.17)
Loan to Emperor of Germany Act 1795 (c.93)
Loan to Emperor of Germany Act 1797 (c.59)
Loan to South Australia Act 1841 (c.13)
Loans for Erection of Workhouses Act 1802 (c.74)
Loans for Erection of Workhouses Act 1803 (c.110)
Loans for Parsonages, etc. (Ireland) Act 1803 (c.106)
Loans for Public Works (Ireland) Act 1846 (c.85)
Loans for Public Works (Ireland) Act 1846 (c.108)
Loans for Public Works (Ireland) Act 1851 (c.51)
Loans for Relief of Certain Merchants Act 1799 (c.5)
Loans for Schools, etc. (Ireland) Act 1884 (c.22)
Loans (Incumbents of Benefices) Amendment Act 1918 (c.42)
Loans of Exchequer Bills Act 1771 (c.25)
Loans of Exchequer Bills Act 1792 (cc.15, 16)
Loans of Exchequer Bills Act 1798 (cc.82–84)
Loans of Exchequer Bills Act 1799 (cc.68–71)
Loans or Exchequer Bills Act 1793 (cc.17, 18)
Loans or Exchequer Bills Act 1774 (c.69)
Loans or Exchequer Bills Act 1775 (c.38)
Loans or Exchequer Bills Act 1776 (c.35)
Loans or Exchequer Bills Act 1776 (c.38)
Loans or Exchequer Bills Act 1776 (c.45)
Loans or Exchequer Bills Act 1776 (c.51)
Loans or Exchequer Bills Act 1778 (c.38)
Loans or Exchequer Bills Act 1778 (c.57)
Loans or Exchequer Bills Act 1778 (c.64)
Loans or Exchequer Bills Act 1779 (cc.63, 64)
Loans or Exchequer Bills Act 1779 (c.73)
Loans or Exchequer Bills Act 1780 (cc.41, 42)
Loans or Exchequer Bills Act 1780 (c.43)
Loans or Exchequer Bills Act 1780 (c.53)
Loans or Exchequer Bills Act 1780 (c.57)
Loans or Exchequer Bills Act 1781 (c.59)
Loans or Exchequer Bills Act 1782 (c.36)
Loans or Exchequer Bills Act 1782 (c.76)
Loans or Exchequer Bills Act 1783 (c.12)
Loans or Exchequer Bills Act 1783 (c.72)
Loans or Exchequer Bills Act 1783 (c.84)
Loans or Exchequer Bills Act 1784 (c.33)
Loans or Exchequer Bills Act 1784 (c.52)
Loans or Exchequer Bills Act 1785 (cc.11, 12)
Loans or Exchequer Bills Act 1785 (c.33)
Loans or Exchequer Bills Act 1786 (cc.32, 33)
Loans or Exchequer Bills Act 1786 (c.24)
Loans or Exchequer Bills Act 1787 (c.24)
Loans or Exchequer Bills Act 1788 (cc.18, 19)

Loans or Exchequer Bills Act 1789 (cc.34, 35)

Loans or Exchequer Bills Act 1790 (cc.15, 16)

Loans or Exchequer Bills Act 1790 (c.24)

Loans or Exchequer Bills Act 1791 (cc.48–50)

Loans or Exchequer Bills Act 1794 (cc.28, 29)

Loans or Exchequer Bills Act 1794 (c.62)

Loans or Exchequer Bills Act 1795 (cc.21, 22)

Loans or Exchequer Bills Act 1795 (c.37)

Loans or Exchequer Bills Act 1796 (c.31)

Loans or Exchequer Bills Act 1797 (c.8)

Loans or Exchequer Bills Act 1797 (c.20)

Loans or Exchequer Bills Act 1797 (c.114)

Loans or Exchequer Bills Act 1799 (c.4)

Loans or Exchequer Bills Act 1799 (c.18)

Loans or Exchequer Bills Act 1799 (c.33)

Loans or Exchequer Bills Act 1799 (c.41)

Loans or Exchequer Bills Act 1800 (cc.102–104)

Loans or Exchequer Bills Act 1801 (c.9)

Loans or Exchequer Bills Act 1801 (cc.81–83)

Loans or Exchequer Bills Act 1802 (c.5)

Loans or Exchequer Bills Act 1802 (c.17)

Loans or Exchequer Bills Act 1802 (c.21)

Loans or Exchequer Bills Act 1802 (cc.110, 111)

Loans or Exchequer Bills Act 1803 (c.15)

Loans or Exchequer Bills Act 1803 (c.36)

Loans or Exchequer Bills Act 1803 (c.93)

Loans or Exchequer Bills Act 1803 (cc.146, 147)

Loans or Exchequer Bills Act 1804 (c.31)

Loans or Exchequer Bills Act 1804 (cc.45, 46)

Loans or Exchequer Bills Act 1804 (c.81)

Loans or Exchequer Bills Act 1805 (c.7)

Loans or Exchequer Bills Act 1806 (c.6)

Loans or Exchequer Bills Act 1806 (cc.25, 26)

Loans or Exchequer Bills Act 1806 (c.41)

Loans or Exchequer Bills Act 1807 (c.2)

Loans or Exchequer Bills Act 1807 (cc.6, 7)

Loans or Exchequer Bills Act 1807 (c.73)

Loans or Exchequer Bills Act 1812 (c.137)

Loans or Exchequer Bills, etc. Act 1805 (cc.118–120)

Loans to A. Houston and Co., etc. Act 1800 (c.101)

Loans to Grenada and St. Vincent Traders Act 1796 (c.27)

Loans to Grenada and St. Vincent Traders Act 1799 (c.13)

Lobsters (Scotland) Act 1735 (c.33)

Local Acts, Preliminary Inquiries Act 1846 (c.106)

Local Acts, Preliminary Inquiries Act 1848 (c.129)

Local and Personal (Durham University) Act 1861 (c.82)

Local and Personal (Inverness Bridge (Treasury Grant)) Act 1855 (c.113)

Local and Personal (River Suck Drainage) Act 1890 (c.12)

Local Authorities (Admission of the Press to Meetings) Act 1908 (c.43)

Local Authorities (Disqualification Relief) Act 1914 (c.10)

Local Authorities (Emergency Provisions) Act 1923 (c.6)

Local Authorities (Emergency Provisions) Act 1924 (c.29)

Local Authorities (Emergency Provisions) Act 1926 (c.10)

Local Authorities (Emergency Provisions) Act 1928 (c.9)

Local Authorities (Expenditure on Special Purposes) (Scotland) Act 1961 (c.32)

Local Authorities (Expenditure Powers) Act 1983 (c.52)

Local Authorities (Expenses) Act 1887 (c.72)

Local Authorities (Expenses) Act 1956 (c.36)

Local Authorities (Financial Provisions) Act 1921 (c.67)

Local Authorities (Goods and Services) Act 1970 (c.39)

Local Authorities (Historic Buildings) Act 1962 (c.36)

Local Authorities (Ireland) (etc.) Act 1911 (c.35)

Local Authorities (Land) Act 1963 (c.29)

Local Authorities Loans Act 1945 (c.18)

Local Authorities Loans (Scotland) Act 1891 (c.34)

Local Authorities Loans (Scotland) Act, 1891, Amendment 1893 (c.8)

Local Authorities Loans (Scotland) Act 1924 (c.36)

Local Authorities' Mutual Investment Trust Act 1968 (c.25)

Local Authorities (Publicity) Act 1931 (c.17)

Local Authorities (Qualification of Members) Act 1971 (c.7)

Local Authorities (Restoration of Works Powers) Act 1977 (c.47)

Local Authorities (Treasury Powers) Act 1906 (c.33)

Local Authority Social Services Act 1970 (c.42)

Local Bankruptcy (Ireland) Act 1888 (c.44)

Local Commissioners Relief Act 1838 (c.65)

Local Education Authorities (Medical Treatment) Act 1909 (c.13)

Local Elections and Register of Electors (Temporary Provisions) Act 1939 (c.115)

Local Elections and Register of Electors (Temporary Provisions) Act 1940 (c.3)

Local Elections and Register of Electors (Temporary Provisions) Act 1941 (c.3)

Local Elections and Register of Electors (Temporary Provisions) Act 1941 (c.49)

Local Elections and Register of Electors (Temporary Provisions) Act 1942 (c.38)

Local Elections and Register of Electors (Temporary Provisions) Act 1943 (c.2)

Local Elections and Register of Electors (Temporary Provisions) Act 1944 (c.3)

Local Elections (Expenses) Act 1919 (c.13)

Local Elections (Service Abroad) Act 1945 (c.1)

Local Employment Act 1960 (c.18)
Local Employment Act 1963 (c.19)
Local Employment Act 1970 (c.7)
Local Employment Act 1972 (c.5)
Local (Forfeited Estates: Scotland) Act 1789 (c.28)
Local Government Act 1858 (c.98)
Local Government Act 1888 (c.41)
Local Government Act 1894 (c.73)
Local Government Act 1897 (c.1)
Local Government Act 1929 (c.17)
Local Government Act 1933 (c.51)
Local Government Act 1948 (c.26)
Local Government Act 1958 (c.55)
Local Government Act 1966 (c.42)
Local Government Act 1972 (c.70)
Local Government Act 1974 (c.7)
Local Government Act 1978 (c.39)
Local Government Act 1985 (c.51)
Local Government Act 1986 (c.10)
Local Government Act 1987 (c.44)
Local Government Act 1988 (c.9)
Local Government Act 1992 (c.19)
Local Government (Access to Information) Act 1985 (c.43)
Local Government (Adjustments) Act 1913 (c.19)
Local Government (Adjustments) (Scotland) Act 1914 (c.74)
Local Government (Allotments and Land Cultivation) (Ireland) Act 1917 (c.30)
Local Government (Amendment) Act 1863 (c.17)
Local Government (Amendment) Act 1993 (c.27)
Local Government and Housing Act 1989 (c.42)
Local Government and Miscellaneous Financial Provisions (Scotland) Act 1958 (c.64)
Local Government and Other Officers' Superannuation Act 1922 (c.59)
Local Government and Other Officers Superannuation (Temporary Provisions) Act 1933 (c.43)
Local Government and Planning (Amendment) Act 1981 (c.41)
Local Government and Planning (Scotland) Act 1982 (c.43)
Local Government Board Act 1871 (c.70)
Local Government Board (Ireland) Act 1872 (c.69)
Local Government Board (Ireland) Amendment Act 1881 (c.28)
Local Government Boundaries Act 1871 (c.70)
Local Government (Boundaries) Act 1887 (c.61)
Local Government (Boundary Commission) Act 1944 (c.38)
Local Government Boundary Commission (Dissolution) Act 1949 (c.83)
Local Government (Clerks) Act 1931 (c.45)
Local Government (County Boroughs and Adjustments) Act 1926 (c.38)

Local Government (Determination of Differences) Act 1896 (c.9)
Local Government (Development and Finance) (Scotland) Act 1964 (c.67)
Local Government (Elections) Act 1896 (c.1)
Local Government Elections Act 1956 (c.43)
Local Government (Elections) (No. 2) Act 1896 (c.4)
Local Government (Emergency Provisions) Act 1916 (c.12)
Local Government Emergency Provisions (No. 2) Act 1916 (c.55)
Local Government etc. (Scotland) Act 1994 (c.39)
Local Government Finance Act 1982 (c.32)
Local Government Finance Act 1987 (c.6)
Local Government Finance Act 1988 (c.41)
Local Government Finance Act 1992 (c.14)
Local Government Finance and Valuation Act 1991 (c.51)
Local Government Finance (Publicity for Auditors' Reports) Act 1991 (c.15)
Local Government (Financial Provisions) Act 1937 (c.22)
Local Government (Financial Provisions) Act 1941 (c.33)
Local Government (Financial Provisions) Act 1946 (c.24)
Local Government (Financial Provisions) Act 1963 (c.46)
Local Government (Financial Provisions) (Scotland) Act 1937 (c.29)
Local Government (Financial Provisions) (Scotland) Act 1941 (c.45)
Local Government (Financial Provisions) (Scotland) Act 1946 (c.25)
Local Government (Financial Provisions) (Scotland) Act 1954 (c.13)
Local Government (Financial Provisions) (Scotland) Act 1963 (c.12)
Local Government (Financial Provisions etc.) (Scotland) Act 1962 (c.9)
Local Government (Footpath and Open Spaces) (Scotland) Act 1970 (c.28)
Local Government (General Exchequer Contributions) Act 1933 (c.8)
Local Government Grants (Social Need) Act 1969 (c.2)
Local Government (Hours of Poll) Act 1938 (c.59)
Local Government (Interim Provisions) Act 1984 (c.53)
Local Government (Ireland) Act 1871 (c.109)
Local Government (Ireland) Act 1898 (c.37)
Local Government (Ireland) Act (1898) Amendment 1906 (c.31)
Local Government (Ireland) Act 1900 (c.63)
Local Government (Ireland) Act 1901 (c.28)
Local Government (Ireland) Act 1902 (c.38)
Local Government (Ireland) Act 1919 (c.19)
Local Government (Ireland) (No. 2) Act 1900 (c.41)
Local Government (Joint Committees) Act 1897 (c.40)

Local Government (Members' Travelling Expenses) Act 1937 (c.36)

Local Government (Miscellaneous Provisions) Act 1953 (c.26)

Local Government (Miscellaneous Provisions) Act 1976 (c.57)

Local Government (Miscellaneous Provisions) Act 1982 (c.30)

Local Government (Miscellaneous Provisions) (Scotland) Act 1981 (c.23)

Local Government Act 1898 (c.37)

Local Government (Omnibus Shelters and Queue Barriers) (Scotland) Act 1958 (c.50)

Local Government (Overseas Assistance) Act 1993 (c.25)

Local Government (Pecuniary Interests) Act 1964 (c.77)

Local Government (Pecuniary Interests) (Scotland) Act 1966 (c.7)

Local Government, Planning and Land Act 1980 (c.65)

Local Government (Records) Act 1962 (c.56)

Local Government (Scotland) Act 1889 (c.50)

Local Government (Scotland) Act 1894 (c.58)

Local Government (Scotland) Act, 1894, Amendment 1895 (c.1)

Local Government (Scotland) Act 1908 (c.62)

Local Government (Scotland) Act 1929 (c.25)

Local Government (Scotland) Act 1939 (c.28)

Local Government (Scotland) Act 1947 (c.43)

Local Government (Scotland) Act 1951 (c.15)

Local Government (Scotland) Act 1965 (c.41)

Local Government (Scotland) Act 1966 (c.51)

Local Government (Scotland) Act 1973 (c.65)

Local Government (Scotland) Act 1975 (c.30)

Local Government (Scotland) Act 1978 (c.4)

Local Government (Scotland) Act 1947 (Amendment) Act 1965 (c.41)

Local Government Staffs (War Service) Act 1939 (c.94)

Local Government (Stock Transfer) Act 1895 (c.32)

Local Government (Street Works) (Scotland) (Amendment) Act 1956 (c.40)

Local Government Superannuation Act 1937 (c.68)

Local Government Superannuation Act 1939 (c.18)

Local Government Superannuation Act 1953 (c.25)

Local Government Superannuation (Scotland) Act 1937 (c.69)

Local Government Supplemental Act 1859 (c.31)

Local Government Supplemental Act 1860 (c.44)

Local Government Supplemental Act 1861 (c.39)

Local Government Supplemental Act 1862 (c.25)

Local Government Supplemental Act 1863 (c.32)

Local Government Supplemental Act 1864 (c.26)

Local Government Supplemental Act 1865 (c.24)

Local Government Supplemental Act 1866 (c.24)

Local Government Supplemental Act 1867 (c.21)

Local Government Supplemental (No. 2) Act 1859 (c.11)

Local Government Supplemental (No. 2) Act 1860 (c.118)

Local Government Supplemental (No. 2) Act 1861 (c.128)

Local Government Supplemental (No. 2) Act 1863 (c.64)

Local Government Supplemental (No. 2) Act 1864 (c.83)

Local Government Supplemental (No. 2) Act 1865 (c.25)

Local Government Supplemental (No. 2) Act 1866 (c.79)

Local Government Supplemental (No. 3) Act 1865 (c.41)

Local Government Supplemental (No. 3) Act 1866 (c.106)

Local Government Supplemental (No. 3) Act 1867 (c.49)

Local Government Supplemental (No. 4) Act 1865 (c.110)

Local Government Supplemental (No. 4) Act 1866 (c.107)

Local Government Supplemental (No. 5) Act 1865 (c.108)

Local Government Supplemental (No. 5) Act 1867 (c.83)

Local Government Supplemental (No. 6) Act 1867 (c.123)

Local Government (Termination of Reviews) Act 1967 (c.18)

Local Government (Transfer of Powers) Act 1903 (c.15)

Local Government (Wales) Act 1994 (c.19)

Local Land Charges Act 1975 (c.76)

Local Light Dues Reduction Act 1876 (c.27)

Local Loans Act 1875 (c.83)

Local Loans Sinking Funds Act 1885 (c.30)

Local Militia Ballot Suspension Act 1816 (c.38)

Local Militia (England) Act 1808 (c.111)

Local Militia (England) Act 1809 (c.40)

Local Militia (England) Act 1812 (c.38)

Local Militia (England) Act 1813 (c.28)

Local Militia (Exemption) Act 1812 (c.116)

Local Militia (Great Britain) Act 1809 (c.82)

Local Militia (Great Britain) Act 1813 (c.19)

Local Militia (Great Britain) Act 1815 (c.76)

Local Militia (Ireland) Act 1813 (c.48)

Local Militia Pay (Great Britain) Act 1814 (c.176)

Local Militia Pay (Great Britain) Act 1815 (c.166)

Local Militia Pay (Great Britain) Act 1816 (c.45)

Local Militia (Scotland) Act 1808 (c.150)

Local Militia (Scotland) Act 1809 (c.48)
Local Militia (Scotland) Act 1812 (c.68)
Local Officers Superannuation (Ireland) Act 1869 (c.79)
Local (Redstone Bridge, Severn) Act 1773 (c.113)
Local Registration of Title (Ireland) Act 1891 (c.66)
Local Registration of Title (Ireland) Act 1909 (c.36)
Local Registration of Title (Ireland) Amendment Act 1908 (c.58)
Local (Rutland Roads) Act 1773 (c.108)
Local Stamp Act 1869 (c.49)
Local Tax Act 1731 (c.5)
Local Taxation Account (Scotland) Act 1898 (c.56)
Local Taxation (Customs and Excise) Act 1890 (c.60)
Local Taxation (Ireland) Estate Duty Act 1896 (c.41)
Local Taxation Returns Act 1860 (c.51)
Local Taxation Returns Act 1877 (c.66)
Local Taxation Returns (Scotland) Act 1881 (c.6)
Local (Westminster Streets) Act 1765 (c.13)
Locomotive Act 1861 (c.70)
Locomotive Threshing Engines Act 1894 (c.37)
Locomotives Act 1865 (c.83)
Locomotives Act 1898 (c.29)
Locomotives Amendment (Scotland) Act 1878 (c.58)
Locomotives on Highways Act 1896 (c.36)
Lodgers' Goods Protection Act 1871 (c.79)
Lodgers' Goods Protection Societies Act 1871 (c.80)
Lodging Houses Act 1851 (c.34)
Lodgings of Justices of Assize Act 1799 (c.46)
Loes and Wilford, Suffolk: Poor Relief Act 1791 (c.72)
Lombs's Silk Engines Act 1731 (c.8)
London Act 1532 (c.16)
London and Hertford Hospitals Act 1795 (c.104)
London and Holyhead Road Act 1836 (c.35)
London Assurance Act 1796 (c.27)
London Barbers and Surgeons Act 1744 (c.15)
London Bridge Act 1756 (c.40)
London Bridge Act 1757 (c.20)
London Bridge Act 1762 (c.30)
London Bridge Act 1771 (c.26)
London Bridge Act 1842 (c.64)
London Bridge Approaches Act 1848 (c.124)
London Bridge Approaches Act 1850 (c.103)
London Bridge Approaches Fund Act 1847 (c.115)
London Brokers Relief Act 1870 (c.60)
London Brokers Relief Act 1884 (c.3)
London Cab Act 1896 (c.27)
London Cab Act 1968 (c.7)

London Cab Act 1973 (c.20)
London Cab and Stage Carriage Act 1907 (c.55)
London, City Road Act 1760 (c.26)
London, City Road Act 1783 (c.102)
London Coal and Wine Duties Cont. Act 1863 (c.46)
London Coal and Wine Duties Cont. Act 1868 (c.17)
London Coal Duties Abolition Act 1889 (c.17)
London: Coal Trade Act 1786 (c.14)
London Council (Money) Act 1889 (c.61)
London County Council Electors Qualification Act 1900 (c.29)
London County Council (General Powers) Act 1947 (c.45)
London County Council (Improvements) Act 1962 (c.49)
London Diocese Act 1863 (c.36)
London Docks (Warehousing of Goods) Act (c.100)
London Electric Lighting Areas Act 1904 (c.13)
London Electric Lighting Areas Act 1904 (c.13)
London (Equalization of Rates) Act 1894 (c.53)
London Flour Company Act 1800 (c.97)
London Government Act 1899 (c.14)
London Government Act 1939 (c.40)
London Government Act 1950 (c.22)
London Government Act 1963 (c.33)
London Government Act 1967 (c.5)
London Hackney Carriage Act 1831 (c.22)
London Hackney Carriage Act 1853 (c.33)
London Hackney Carriage (No. 2) Act 1853 (c.127)
London Hackney Carriages Act 1843 (c.86)
London Hackney Carriages Act 1850 (c.7)
London Hospitals Act 1782 (c.77)
London Institution (Transfer) Act 1912 (c.13)
London Militia Act 1795 (c.27)
London Militia Act 1796 (c.91)
London Museum Site Act 1868 (c.8)
London Naval Treaty Act 1930 (c.48)
London Naval Treaty Act 1937 (c.65)
London Park and Works Act 1887 (c.34)
London Passenger Transport Act 1933 (c.14)
London Paving and Lighting Act 1766 (c.26)
London Regional Transport Act 1984 (c.32)
London Regional Transport (Amendment) Act 1985 (c.10)
London Roads Act 1839 (c.80)
London Street Lighting Act 1743 (c.29)
London Streets Act 1762 (c.21)
London: Streets Act 1771 (c.54)
London: Streets Act 1772 (c.17)
London Streets Act 1772 (c.69)
London: Streets Act 1775 (c.54)
London: Streets Act 1776 (c.22)
London: Streets Act 1776 (c.23)
London: Streets Act 1778 (c.71)
London: Streets Act 1778 (c.73)

London: Streets Act 1782 (c.84)
London (Streets and Sewers) Act 1793 (c.75)
London Streets, City Act 1759 (c.30)
London: Thames Embankment Act 1771 (c.34)
London Traffic Act 1924 (c.34)
London Widening of Passages etc. Act 1766 (c.27)
Londonderry School Act 1808 (c.77)
Long Leases (Scotland) Act 1954 (c.49)
Long Leases (Temporary Provisions) (Scotland) Act 1951 (c.28)
Longitude and Latitude Act 1740 (c.39)
Longitude at Sea Act 1796 (c.107)
Lord Alcester's Grant Act 1883 (c.16)
Lord Blessington's Will Act 1772 (c.17)
Lord Chancellor of Ireland Act 1802 (c.105)
Lord Chancellor (Tenure of Office and Discharge of Ecclesiastical Functions) Act 1974 (c.25)
Lord Chancellor's Augmentation Act 1863 (c.120)
Lord Chancellor's Pension Act 1832 (c.111)
Lord Clerk Register (Scotland) Act 1861 (c.81)
Lord Clerk Register (Scotland) Act 1879 (c.44)
Lord Dundonald's Patent (Tar, Pitch, etc.) Act 1785 (c.42)
Lord High Commission (Church of Scotland) Act 1959 (c.8)
Lord High Commissioner (Church of Scotland) Act 1948 (c.30)
Lord High Commissioner (Church of Scotland) Act 1974 (c.19)
Lord Napier Act 1869 (c.3)
Lord Napier's Salary Act 1869 (c.3)
Lord Nelson, Purchase of Estate for Act 1815 (c.96)
Lord Powerscourt's Mansion Act 1807 (c.78)
Lord Wolseley's Grant Act 1883 (c.17)
Lords Justices Act 1837 (c.72)
Losses During Rebellion in Ireland Act 1805 (c.79)
Losses from Cession of East Florida Act 1786 (c.75)
Losses from Cession of East Florida Act 1788 (c.31)
Lost Property (Scotland) Act 1965 (c.27)
Lotteries Act 1710 (c.6)
Lotteries Act 1721 (c.2)
Lotteries Act 1787 (c.41)
Lotteries Act 1790 (c.30)
Lotteries Act 1802 (c.54)
Lotteries Act 1803 (c.91)
Lotteries Act 1804 (c.93)
Lotteries Act 1805 (c.74)
Lotteries Act 1806 (c.148)
Lotteries Act 1807 (c.9)
Lotteries Act 1808 (c.139)
Lotteries Act 1809 (c.94)
Lotteries Act 1810 (c.94)
Lotteries Act 1811 (c.113)

Lotteries Act 1812 (c.19)
Lotteries Act 1812 (c.125)
Lotteries Act 1813 (c.93)
Lotteries Act 1814 (c.74)
Lotteries Act 1815 (c.73)
Lotteries Act 1816 (c.61)
Lotteries Act 1836 (c.66)
Lotteries Act 1845 (c.74)
Lotteries Act 1975 (c.58)
Lotteries (Amendment) Act 1984 (c.9)
Lotteries and Amusements Act 1976 (c.32)
Lotteries and Gaming Act 1962 (c.55)
Lotteries (Ireland) Act 1780 (c.14)
Lottery Act 1771 (c.47)
Lottery Act 1785 (c.59)
Lottery Act 1786 (c.65)
Lottery Act 1787 (c.1)
Lottery Act 1788 (c.21)
Lottery Act 1789 (c.33)
Lottery Act 1791 (c.53)
Lottery Act 1792 (c.28)
Lottery Act 1793 (c.62)
Lottery Act 1794 (c.40)
Lottery Act 1795 (c.36)
Lottery Act 1796 (c.104)
Lottery Act 1797 (c.113)
Lottery Act 1798 (c.75)
Lottery Act 1799 (c.91)
Lottery Act 1800 (c.52)
Lottery Act 1801 (c.6)
Lottery Act 1801 (c.27)
Lottery Office Keepers Act 1779 (c.21)
Lottery Office Keepers Act 1782 (c.47)
Lottery Regulations Act 1802 (c.104)
Lough Corrib Act 1850 (c.112)
Lough Corrib Navigation Act 1874 (c.71)
Loughborough: Navigation Act 1766 (c.94)
Loughborough Navigation Act 1776 (c.65)
Louth, Lincoln, Roads Act 1770 (c.109)
Louth Roads Act 1780 (c.94)
Lower Canada Government Act 1838 (c.9)
Lower Canada Government Act 1839 (c.53)
Lower Ouse: Navigation Act 1791 (c.76)
Ludlow and Monk's Bridge Road Act 1750 (c.29)
Ludlow Roads Act 1756 (c.59)
Ludlow Roads Act 1779 (c.114)
Ludlow, Salop: Improvement Act 1793 (c.25)
Lunacy Act 1771 (c.20)
Lunacy Act 1842 (c.84)
Lunacy Act 1855 (c.13)
Lunacy Act 1890 (c.5)
Lunacy Act 1891 (c.65)
Lunacy Act 1908 (c.47)
Lunacy Act 1911 (c.40)
Lunacy Act 1922 (c.60)
Lunacy Act Amendment Act 1865 (c.80)
Lunacy Acts Amendment 1885 (c.52)
Lunacy Acts Amendment 1889 (c.41)
Lunacy Acts Amendments Act 1826 (c.111)
Lunacy Acts Amendments Act 1862 (c.111)
Lunacy Board (Scotland) Act 1864 (c.59)
Lunacy Board (Scotland) Salaries and Clerks Act 1900 (c.54)

Lunacy Districts (Scotland) Act 1887 (c.39)
Lunacy (Ireland) Act 1867 (c.118)
Lunacy (Ireland) Act 1901 (c.17)
Lunacy Regulation Act 1853 (c.70)
Lunacy Regulation Act 1855 (c.105)
Lunacy Regulation Act 1862 (c.86)
Lunacy Regulation Act 1871 (c.22)
Lunacy Regulation Amendment Act 1882 (c.82)
Lunacy Regulation (Ireland) Act 1871 (c.22)
Lunacy (Scotland) Act 1857 (c.71)
Lunacy (Scotland) Act 1862 (c.54)
Lunacy (Scotland) Act 1866 (c.51)
Lunacy (Vacating of Seats) Act 1886 (c.16)
Lunatic Asylums Act 1842 (c.87)
Lunatic Asylums Act 1853 (c.97)
Lunatic Asylums Act 1856 (c.87)
Lunatic Asylums, etc. Act 1846 (c.84)
Lunatic Asylums (Ireland) Act 1846 (c.79)
Lunatic Asylums (Ireland) Act 1846 (c.115)
Lunatic Asylums (Ireland) Act 1849 (c.56)
Lunatic Asylums (Ireland) Act 1851 (c.45)
Lunatic Asylums (Ireland) Act 1875 (c.67)
Lunatic Asylums (Ireland) Accounts Audit Act 1868 (c.97)
Lunatic Asylums Loans (Ireland) Act 1878 (c.24)
Lunatic Asylums Repayment of Advances (Ireland) Act 1855 (c.109)
Lunatic Asylums, Superannuations (Ireland) Act 1856 (c.99)
Lunatic Paupers or Criminals Act 1808 (c.96)
Lunatic Paupers, etc. (England) Act 1811 (c.79)
Lunatics Act 1730 (c.10)
Lunatics Act 1838 (c.73)
Lunatics Act 1845 (c.100)
Lunatics Act 1845 (c.126)
Lunatics Removal (India) Act 1851 (c.81)
Lunatics (Scotland) Act 1858 (c.89)
Lunatics (Scotland) Act 1867 (c.55)
Luton and St. Albans Road Act 1726 (c.17)
Luton and St. Albans Road Act 1742 (c.23)
Lying-in Hospitals Act 1773 (c.82)
Lyme Regis Roads Act 1770 (c.59)
Lymington Roads Act 1765 (c.59)
Lymington Roads Act 1786 (c.156)
Lyon King of Arms Act 1867 (c.17)

Macclesfield and Buxton Road Act 1958 (c.41)
Macclesfield to Buxton Road Act 1780 (c.91)
Macclesfield Grammar School Act 1774 (c.51)
Madder Act 1957 (c.12)
Madhouses Act 1774 (c.49)
Madhouses Act 1779 (c.15)
Madhouses Act 1786 (c.91)
Magdalen Hospital, London Act 1769 (c.31)
Magistrates' Courts Act 1952 (c.55)
Magistrates' Courts Act 1957 (c.29)
Magistrates' Courts Act 1980 (c.43)

Magistrates' Courts (Appeals from Binding Over Orders) Act 1956 (c.44)
Maidenhead and Reading, etc. Roads Act 1727 (c.3)
Maidenhead Bridge Act 1772 (c.41)
Maidenhead, Reading etc. Roads Act 1763 (c.46)
Maidenhead Road Act 1743 (c.19)
Maidenhead Roads Act 1779 (c.84)
Maidstone Gaol, Kent (Expenses) Act 1735 (c.12)
Maidstone, Kent: Improvement Act 1791 (c.62)
Maidstone: Poor Relief Act 1780 (c.22)
Maidstone to Ashford Road Act 1973 (c.173)
Maidstone to Cranbrook Road Act 1759 (c.57)
Maidstone to Cranbrook Road Act 1768 (c.43)
Mail to Spain Act 1793 (c.60)
Mail Ships Act 1902 (c.36)
Maintenance Agreements Act 1957 (c.35)
Maintenance Enforcement Act 1991 (c.17)
Maintenance of Church of England Act 1706 (c.8)
Maintenance of Live Stock Act 1915 (c.65)
Maintenance Orders Act 1950 (c.37)
Maintenance Orders Act 1958 (c.39)
Maintenance Orders Act 1968 (c.36)
Maintenance Orders (Facilities for Enforcement) Act 1920 (c.33)
Maintenance Orders (Reciprocal Enforcement) Act 1972 (c.18)
Maintenance Orders (Reciprocal Enforcement) Act 1992 (c.56)
Making of Bread Act 1957 (c.29)
Making of Indigo Act 1755 (c.25)
Making of indigo, etc. 1770 (c.37)
Making of Sail Cloth Act 1741 (c.35)
Malawi Independence 1964 (c.46)
Malaysia Act 1963 (c.35)
Malaysian Act 1963 (c.60)
Malicious Communications Act 1988 (c.27)
Malicious Damage Act 1812 (c.130)
Malicious Damage Act 1861 (c.97)
Malicious Damage Act 1964 (c.76)
Malicious Damage (Scotland) Act 1816 (c.125)
Malicious Injury Act 1769 (c.29)
Mall Approach (Improvement) Act 1914 (c.28)
Malmesbury Roads Act 1778 (c.114)
Malt Duties, etc. Act 1714 (c.2)
Malt Duties, etc. Act 1725 (c.4)
Malt Duties, etc. Act 1759 (c.7)
Malt Duties Act 1762 (c.13)
Malt Duties Act 1762 (c.2)
Malt Duties Act 1766 (c.6)
Malt Duties Act 1768 (c.4)
Malt Duties Act 1769 (c.2)
Malt Duties Act 1770 (c.5)
Malt Duties Act 1772 (c.6)
Malt Duties Act 1772 (c.6)

Malt Duties Act 1837 (c.49)
Malt Duties Act 1971 (c.2)
Malt Duties Act 1774 (c.2)
Malt Duties Act 1775 (c.2)
Malt Duties Act 1776 (c.1)
Malt Duties Act 1776 (c.2)
Malt Duties Act 1778 (c.3)
Malt Duties Act 1779 (c.3)
Malt Duties Act 1780 (c.3)
Malt Duties Act 1780 (c.4)
Malt Duties Act 1782 (c.3)
Malt Duties Act 1782 (c.4)
Malt Duties Act 1783 (c.64)
Malt Duties Act 1783 (c.1)
Malt Duties Act 1785 (c.2)
Malt Duties Act 1786 (c.6)
Malt Duties Act 1788 (c.1)
Malt Duties Act 1789 (c.10)
Malt Duties Act 1790 (c.3)
Malt Duties Act 1791 (c.2)
Malt Duties Act 1791 (c.7)
Malt Duties Act 1791 (c.6)
Malt Duties Act 1791 (c.18)
Malt Duties Act 1793 (c.11)
Malt Duties Act 1794 (c.7)
Malt, etc. Duties Act 1765 (c.2)
Malta Constitution Act 1932 (c.43)
Malta Independence Act 1964 (c.86)
Malta (Letters Patent) Act 1936 (c.29)
Malta (Reconstruction) Act 1947 (c.9)
Malta Republic Act 1975 (c.31)
Malton and Pickering Road Act 1765 (c.108)
Manchester and Oldham Canal Act 1792 (c.84)
Manchester-Oldham Canal Act 1974 (c.26)
Manchester and Salford: Improvement Act 1792 (c.69)
Manchester and Stockport Canal Act 1793 (c.21)
Manchester, Bolton and Bury Canal Act 1791 (c.68)
Manchester Canal Act 1794 (c.37)
Manchester Church Act 1753 (c.45)
Manchester Church Act 1769 (c.60)
Manchester, Church Building 1708 (c.28)
Manchester General Improvement Act 1851 (c.119)
Manchester Improvement Act 1765 (c.81)
Manchester: Poor Relief Act 1790 (c.81)
Manchester Roads Act 1731 (c.10)
Manchester Roads Act 1749 (c.5)
Manchester Roads Act 1771 (c.82)
Manchester Roads Act 1772 (c.88)
Manchester, School Mills Act 1758 (c.61)
Manchester Square: Improvement Act 1789 (c.5)
Manchester: Streets Act 1776 (c.63)
Manchester Theatre Act 1775 (c.47)
Manchester to Buxton Road Act 1793 (c.171)
Manchester to Chester Roads Act 1793 (c.139)
Manchester to Wilmslow Road Act 1793 (c.170)

Mandated and Trust Territories Act 1947 (c.8)
Manning of the Navy, etc. Act 1793 (c.66)
Manning of the Navy Act 1795 (c.5)
Manning of the Navy Act 1795 (c.9)
Manning of the Navy Act 1795 (c.19)
Manning of the Navy Act 1795 (c.29)
Manoeuvres Act 1958 (c.7)
Mansfield and Chesterfield Road Act 1958 (c.37)
Mansfield to Chesterfield Road Act 1780 (c.72)
Manufacture of Cambrics 1763 (c.37)
Manufacture of Hats Act 1776 (c.55)
Manufacture of Leather Act 1784 (c.19)
Manufacture of Ounce Thread Act 1788 (c.17)
Manufacture of Sail Cloth Act 1730 (c.27)
Manufacture of Sail Cloth Act 1735 (c.37)
Manufacture of Serges, etc. Act 1719 (c.13)
Manufacture of Serges, etc. Act 1723 (c.18)
Maplin Development Act 1973 (c.64)
Maplin Development Authority (Dissolution) Act 1976 (c.51)
Mar Peerage Restoration Act 1824 (c.59)
March, Cambridge, Isle of Ely: Drainage Act 1957 (c.36)
Margate Pier Act 1724 (c.3)
Margate Theatre Act 1786 (c.29)
Marine and Aviation Insurance (War Risks) Act 1952 (c.57)
Marine Duty Act 1791 (c.17)
Marine, etc. Broadcasting Offences Act 1967 (c.41)
Marine Insurance Act 1745 (c.37)
Marine Insurance Act 1788 (c.56)
Marine Insurance Act 1906 (c.41)
Marine Insurance (Gambling Policies) Act 1909 (c.12)
Marine Mutiny Act 1755 (c.11)
Marine Mutiny Act 1757 (c.11)
Marine Mutiny Act 1757 (c.6)
Marine Mutiny Act 1757 (c.9)
Marine Mutiny Act 1759 (c.8)
Marine Mutiny Act 1760 (c.8)
Marine Mutiny Act 1761 (c.12)
Marine Mutiny Act 1762 (c.3)
Marine Mutiny Act 1763 (c.8)
Marine Mutiny Act 1765 (c.6)
Marine Mutiny Act 1766 (c.10)
Marine Mutiny Act 1766 (c.13)
Marine Mutiny Act 1768 (c.12)
Marine Mutiny Act 1769 (c.7)
Marine Mutiny Act 1770 (c.7)
Marine Mutiny Act 1771 (c.7)
Marine Mutiny Act 1772 (c.5)
Marine Mutiny Act 1772 (c.11)
Marine Mutiny Act 1774 (c.4)
Marine Mutiny Act 1775 (c.4)
Marine Mutiny Act 1776 (c.7)
Marine Mutiny Act 1776 (c.4)
Marine Mutiny Act 1778 (c.5)
Marine Mutiny Act 1779 (c.8)
Marine Mutiny Act 1780 (c.13)

Marine Mutiny Act 1780 (c.9)
Marine Mutiny Act 1782 (c.5)
Marine Mutiny Act 1782 (c.7)
Marine Mutiny Act 1783 (c.17)
Marine Mutiny Act 1785 (c.3)
Marine Mutiny Act 1786 (c.7)
Marine Mutiny Act 1788 (c.3)
Marine Mutiny Act 1789 (c.3)
Marine Mutiny Act 1790 (c.7)
Marine Mutiny Act 1791 (c.9)
Marine Mutiny Act 1793 (c.6)
Marine Mutiny Act 1794 (c.6)
Marine Mutiny Act 1795 (c.7)
Marine Mutiny Act 1840 (c.8)
Marine Society Act 1772 (c.67)
Marine Works (Ireland) Act 1902 (c.24)
Marines Act 1792 (c.67)
Maritime Conventions Act 1911 (c.57)
Market Harborough and Brampton Road Act 1751 (c.57)
Market Harborough and Brampton Road Act 1754 (c.28)
Market Harborough and Brampton Road Act 1759 (c.38)
Market Harborough to Coventry Road Act 1755 (c.40)
Market Harborough to Coventry Road Act 1779 (c.82)
Market Harborough to Loughborough Road Act 1793 (c.176)
Market Weighton Act 1772 (c.37)
Markets and Fairs Clauses Act 1847 (c.14)
Markets and Fairs (Weighing of Cattle) Act 1887 (c.27)
Markets and Fairs (Weighing of Cattle) Act 1891 (c.70)
Markets and Fairs (Weighing of Cattle) Act 1926 (c.21)
Marriage Act 1939 (c.33)
Marriage Act 1949 (c.76)
Marriage Act 1983 (c.32)
Marriage Act 1949 (Amendment) 1954 (c.47)
Marriage Act 1994 (c.34)
Marriage Acts Amendment Act 1958 (c.29)
Marriage Confirmation Act 1830 (c.18)
Marriage (Enabling) Act 1960 (c.29)
Marriage (Extension of Hours) Act 1934 (c.13)
Marriage Law (Ireland) Amendment Act 1873 (c.16)
Marriage (Members of His Majesty's Forces) Act 1941 (c.47)
Marriage (Naval, Military and Air Force Chapels) Act 1932 (c.31)
Marriage Notice (Scotland) Act 1878 (c.43)
Marriage of British Subjects (Facilities) Act 1915 (c.40)
Marriage of British Subjects (Facilities) Amendment 1916 (c.21)
Marriage of Lunatics Act 1941 (c.30)
Marriage (Prohibited Degrees of Relationship) Act 1931 (c.31)
Marriage (Prohibited Degrees of Relationship) Act 1986 (c.16)

Marriage (Registrar General's Licence Act 1970 (c.34)
Marriage (Registration of Buildings) Act 1990 (c.33)
Marriage (Scotland) Act 1834 (c.28)
Marriage (Scotland) Act 1916 (c.7)
Marriage (Scotland) Act 1939 (c.34)
Marriage (Scotland) Act 1942 (c.20)
Marriage (Scotland) Act 1956 (c.70)
Marriage (Scotland) Act 1977 (c.15)
Marriage (Scotland) Emergency Provisions Act 1940 (c.30)
Marriage (Secretaries of Synagogues) Act 1959 (c.13)
Marriage (Wales) Act 1986 (c.7)
Marriage (Wales and Monmouthshire) Act 1962 (c.32)
Marriage with Foreigners Act 1906 (c.40)
Marriages (Confirmation) Act 1804 (c.77)
Marriages (Confirmation) Act 1808 (c.127)
Marriages (Confirmation) Act 1825 (c.92)
Marriages in Japan (Validity) Act 1912 (c.15)
Marriages (Ireland) Act 1844 (c.81)
Marriages (Ireland) Act 1846 (c.72)
Marriages (Ireland) Act 1918 (c.2)
Marriages Legalisation Act 1901 (c.23)
Marriages Legalisation Act 1903 (c.26)
Marriages (Validity) Act 1939 (c.35)
Marriages Validity (Provisional Orders) Act 1924 (c.20)
Married Women (Maintenance) Act 1920 (c.63)
Married Women (Restraint Upon Anticipation) Act 1949 (c.78)
Married Women's Policies of Assurance Act 1880 (c.26)
Married Women's Policies of Assurance (Scotland) (Amendment) Act 1980 (c.56)
Married Women's Property Act 1882 (c.75)
Married Women's Property Act 1907 (c.18)
Married Women's Property Act 1908 (c.27)
Married Women's Property Act 1964 (c.19)
Married Women's Property (Scotland) Act 1881 (c.21)
Married Women's Property (Scotland) Act 1920 (c.64)
Married Women's Reversionary Interests Act 1857 (c.57)
Marshall Aid Commemoration Act 1953 (c.39)
Marshall Scholarships Act 1959 (c.3)
Marylebone Act 1783 (c.110)
Marylebone: Improvement Act 1768 (c.46)
Marylebone Road Act 1720 (c.26)
Marylebone Road Act 1734 (c.8)
Maryport Harbour Act 1748 (c.6)
Maryport Harbour Act 1756 (c.57)
Maryport Harbour Act 1791 (c.23)
Master and Servant Act 1889 (c.24)
Matches and Mechanical Lighters Duties Act 1979 (c.6)
Maternity and Child Welfare Act 1918 (c.29)
Maternity Services (Scotland) Act 1937 (c.30)

Matrimonial and Family Proceedings Act 1984 (c.42)
Matrimonial Causes Act 1907 (c.12)
Matrimonial Causes Act 1923 (c.19)
Matrimonial Causes Act 1937 (c.57)
Matrimonial Causes Act 1950 (c.25)
Matrimonial Causes Act 1963 (c.45)
Matrimonial Causes Act 1965 (c.72)
Matrimonial Causes Act 1967 (c.56)
Matrimonial Causes Act 1973 (c.18)
Matrimonial Causes and Marriage Law (Ireland) Amendment Act 1871 (c.49)
Matrimonial Causes (Dominions Troops) Act 1919 (c.28)
Matrimonial Causes (Property and Maintenance) Act 1958 (c.35)
Matrimonial Causes (War Marriages) Act (c.43)
Matrimonial Homes Act 1967 (c.75)
Matrimonial Homes Act 1983 (c.19)
Matrimonial Homes and Property Act 1981 (c.24)
Matrimonial Homes (Family Protection) (Scotland) 1981 (c.59)
Matrimonial Proceedings and Property Act 1970 (c.45)
Matrimonial Proceedings (Children) Act 1958 (c.40)
Matrimonial Proceedings (Magistrates' Courts) Act 1960 (c.48)
Matrimonial Proceedings (Polygamous Marriages) Act 1972 (c.38)
Matrimonial Proceedings (Transfers) Act 1988 (c.18)
Mauritius Independence Act 1968 (c.8)
Mauritius Loan (Guarantee) Act 1931 (c.26)
Mauritius Republic Act 1992 (c.45)
Measurement of Coal Wagons, etc. Act 1775 (c.27)
Medical Act 1858 (c.90)
Medical Act 1860 (c.66)
Medical Act 1876 (c.41)
Medical Act 1886 (c.48)
Medical Act 1950 (c.29)
Medical Act 1956 (c.76)
Medical Act 1969 (c.40)
Medical Act 1978 (c.12)
Medical Act 1983 (c.54)
Medical Act (1886) Amendment 1904 (c.14)
Medical Act 1956 (Amendment) Act 1958 (c.58)
Medical Act (Royal College of Surgeons of England) 1875 (c.43)
Medical Act (University of London) 1873 (c.55)
Medical and Dentists Acts Amendment Act 1927 (c.39)
Medical Practitioners and Pharmacists Act 1947 (c.11)
Medical Qualifications (Amendment) Act 1991 (c.38)
Medicinal Products: Prescription by Nurses, etc. Act 1992 (c.28)

Medicine Duties Act 1785 (c.79)
Medicines Act 1968 (c.67)
Medicines Act 1971 (c.69)
Mediterranean Passes Act 1730 (c.18)
Medway Fisheries Act 1757 (c.21)
Medway: Navigation Act 1792 (c.105)
Medway Oyster Fishery Act 1728 (c.19)
Melton Mowbray to Grantham Road Act 1780 (c.95)
Members of Local Authorities Relief Act 1900 (c.46)
Memorials of Grants of Annuities Act 1822 (c.92)
Mental Deficiency Act 1913 (c.28)
Mental Deficiency Act 1927 (c.33)
Mental Deficiency Act 1938 (c.43)
Mental Deficiency (Amendment) Act 1925 (c.53)
Mental Deficiency and Lunacy (Amendment) Act 1919 (c.85)
Mental Deficiency (Scotland) Act 1940 (c.8)
Mental Health Act 1959 (c.72)
Mental Health Act 1983 (c.20)
Mental Health (Amendment) Act 1975 (c.29)
Mental Health (Amendment) Act 1982 (c.51)
Mental Health (Amendment) Act 1994 (c.6)
Mental Health (Amendment) (Scotland) Act 1983 (c.39)
Mental Health (Detention) (Scotland) Act 1991 (c.47)
Mental Health (Scotland) Act 1960 (c.61)
Mental Health (Scotland) Act 1984 (c.36)
Mental Treatment Act 1930 (c.23)
Mercantile Law Amendment Act 1856 (c.97)
Mercantile Law Amendment (Scotland) Act 1856 (c.60)
Mercers Company, London Act 1751 (c.7)
Mercers Company, London Act 1764 (c.50)
Mercers, London Act 1747 (c.32)
Merchandise Marks Act 1911 (c.31)
Merchandise Marks Act 1926 (c.53)
Merchandise Marks Act 1953 (c.48)
Merchandise Marks (Ireland) Act 1909 (c.24)
Merchant Seamen Act 1728 (c.36)
Merchant Seamen Act 1746 (c.38)
Merchant Seamen Act 1762 (c.31)
Merchant Seamen (Payment of Wages and Rating) Act 1880 (c.16)
Merchant Shipping Act 1786 (c.86)
Merchant Shipping Act 1791 (c.39)
Merchant Shipping Act 1794 (c.68)
Merchant Shipping Act 1872 (c.73)
Merchant Shipping Act 1894 (c.60)
Merchant Shipping Act 1906 (c.48)
Merchant Shipping Act 1907 (c.52)
Merchant Shipping Act 1911 (c.42)
Merchant Shipping Act 1921 (c.28)
Merchant Shipping Act 1937 (c.23)
Merchant Shipping Act 1948 (c.44)
Merchant Shipping Act 1950 (c.9)
Merchant Shipping Act 1952 (c.14)
Merchant Shipping Act 1954 (c.18)
Merchant Shipping Act 1964 (c.47)

Merchant Shipping Act 1965 (c.47)
Merchant Shipping Act 1967 (c.26)
Merchant Shipping Act 1970 (c.36)
Merchant Shipping Act 1974 (c.43)
Merchant Shipping Act 1979 (c.39)
Merchant Shipping Act 1981 (c.11)
Merchant Shipping Act 1983 (c.13)
Merchant Shipping Act 1984 (c.5)
Merchant Shipping Act 1988 (c.12)
Merchant Shipping Acts (Amendment) 1923 (c.40)
Merchant Shipping (Amendment) Act 1920 (c.2)
Merchant Shipping (Carriage of Munitions to Spain) Act 1936 (c.1)
Merchant Shipping (Certificates) Act 1914 (c.42)
Merchant Shipping (Convention) Act 1914 (c.50)
Merchant Shipping (Equivalent Provisions) Act 1925 (c.37)
Merchant Shipping (International Labour Convention) Act 1925 (c.42)
Merchant Shipping (Liability of Shipowners and Others) Act 1900 (c.32)
Merchant Shipping (Liability of Shipowners and Others) Act 1958 (c.62)
Merchant Shipping (Line-throwing Appliances) Act 1928 (c.40)
Merchant Shipping (Liner Conferences) Act 1982 (c.37)
Merchant Shipping (Load Lines) Act 1967 (c.27)
Merchant Shipping (Mercantile Marine Fund) Act 1898 (c.44)
Merchant Shipping (Minicoy Lighthouse) 1960 (c.42)
Merchant Shipping (Oil Pollution) Act 1971 (c.59)
Merchant Shipping (Registration, etc.) Act 1993 (c.22)
Merchant Shipping (Safety and Load Line Conventions) Act 1932 (c.9)
Merchant Shipping (Safety Convention) Act 1949 (c.43)
Merchant Shipping (Safety Convention) Act 1977 (c.24)
Merchant Shipping (Salvage and Pollution) Act 1994 (c.28)
Merchant Shipping (Scottish Fishing Boats) Act 1920 (c.39)
Merchant Shipping (Seamen's Allotment) Act 1911 (c.8)
Merchant Shipping (Salvage) Act 1916 (c.41)
Merchant Shipping (Salvage) Act 1940 (c.43)
Merchant Shipping (Spanish Frontiers Observation) Act 1937 (c.19)
Merchant Shipping (Stevedores and Trimmers) Act 1911 (c.41)
Merchant Shipping (Superannuation Contributions) Act 1937 (c.4)
Merchant Shipping (Wireless Telegraphy) Act 1919 (c.38)

Merioneth Roads Act 1777 (c.96)
Merioneth Roads Act 1969 (c.56)
Mersey Canal Act 1775 (c.20)
Methylated Spirits (Sale by Retail) (Scotland) Act 1937 (c.48)
Metropolis Gas Act 1860 (c.125)
Metropolis Gas Act 1861 (c.79)
Metropolis Water Act 1899 (c.41)
Metropolis Water Act 1902 (c.41)
Metropolitan Ambulances Act 1909 (c.17)
Metropolitan Board of Works (Money) Act 1884 (c.50)
Metropolitan Board of Works (Money) Act 1886 (c.44)
Metropolitan Buildings Act 1772 (c.73)
Metropolitan Improvements (Funds) Act 1904 (c.2)
Metropolitan Magistrates' Courts Act 1959 (c.45)
Metropolitan Police Act 1829 (c.44)
Metropolitan Police Act 1838 (c.47)
Metropolitan Police Act 1839 (c.47)
Metropolitan Police Act 1856 (c.2)
Metropolitan Police Act 1860 (c.135)
Metropolitan Police Act 1884 (c.17)
Metropolitan Police Act 1886 (c.22)
Metropolitan Police Act 1912 (c.4)
Metropolitan Police Act 1918 (c.61)
Metropolitan Police Act 1933 (c.33)
Metropolitan Police Act 1958 (c.48)
Metropolitan Police (Borrowing Powers) Act 1935 (c.16)
Metropolitan Police (Borrowing Powers) Act 1952 (c.19)
Metropolitan Police (Commission) Act 1906 (c.6)
Metropolitan Police (Courts) Act 1839 (c.71)
Metropolitan Police (Courts) Act 1897 (c.26)
Metropolitan Police (Employment in Scotland) Act (c.44)
Metropolitan Police (Receiver) Act 1867 (c.39)
Metropolitan Police (Staff Superannuation and Police Fund) Act 1931 (c.12)
Metropolitan Streets Act 1903 (c.17)
Mevagissey Pier, Cornwall Act 1775 (c.62)
Michaelmas Term Act 1750 (c.48)
Middlesex and Essex Roads Act 1785 (c.124)
Middlesex and Hertford Highways Act 1711 (c.3)
Middlesex and Hertford Roads Act 1730) (c.10)
Middlesex and Hertford Roads Act 1743 (c.14)
Middlesex and Hertford Roads Act 1770 (c.71)
Middlesex and Hertford Roads Act 1772 (c.84)
Middlesex and Hertfordshire Roads Act 1748 (c.14)
Middlesex and Surrey Roads Act 1791 (c.134)
Middlesex Deeds Act 1940 (c.34)

Middlesex Gaol Act 1786 (c.55)
Middlesex Highways Act 1711 (c.4)
Middlesex Highways Act 1723 (c.6)
Middlesex Registry Act 1708 (c.20)
Middlesex (Registry of Deeds) Act 1751 (c.4)
Middlesex Road Act 1767 (c.88)
Middlesex Roads Act 1733 (c.26)
Middlesex Roads Act 1741 (c.9)
Middlesex Roads Act 1767 (c.102)
Middlesex Roads Act 1778 (c.84)
Middlesex Roads Act 1789 (c.96)
Middlesex Roads Act 1794 (c.131)
Middlesex Roads Act 1937 (c.6)
Middlesex Sessions Act 1792 (c.48)
Middlesex Sessions House Act 1778 (c.67)
Midwives Act 1902 (c.17)
Midwives Act 1918 (c.43)
Midwives Act 1926 (c.32)
Midwives Act 1936 (c.40)
Midwives Act 1951 (c.53)
Midwives (Amendment) Act (c.13)
Midwives (Ireland) Act 1918 (c.59)
Midwives (Scotland) Act 1915 (c.91)
Midwives (Scotland) Act 1927 (c.17)
Midwives (Scotland) Act 1951 (c.54)
Milbank New Church Act 1728 (c.15)
Mile End Night Watch Act 1777 (c.66)
Milford Fortifications Act 1758 (c.26)
Milford Haven Conservancy Act 1958 (c.23)
Milford to Portsmouth Road Act 1764 (c.63)
Milford to Portsmouth Road Act 1787 (c.95)
Milk (Special Designations) Act (c.34)
Military Aircraft (Loans) Act 1966 (c.15)
Military and Air Forces (Prolongation of Service) Act 1939 (c.90)
Military Lands Act 1900 (c.56)
Military Lands Act 1903 (c.47)
Military Manoeuvres Act 1911 (c.44)
Military Service Act 1916 (c.104)
Military Service Act 1918 (c.66)
Military Service (No. 2) Act 1918 (c.5)
Military Service (Review of Exceptions) Act 1917 (c.12)
Military Service (Session 2) 1916 (c.15)
Military Training Act 1939 (c.25)
Military Tramways Act 1887 (c.65)
Military Works Act 1901 (c.40)
Military Works Act 1903 (c.29)
Militia Act 1700 (c.8)
Militia Act 1701 (c.17)
Militia Act 1702 (c.15(d))
Militia Act 1703 (c.14(e))
Militia Act 1704 (c.15(l))
Militia Act 1705 (c.10)
Militia Act 1706 (c.28)
Militia Act 1707 (c.63)
Militia Act 1708 (c.23)
Militia Act 1709 (c.22)
Militia Act 1710 (c.31)
Militia Act 1712 (c.8)
Militia Act 1766 (c.15)
Militia Act 1786 (c.107)
Militia Act 1714 (c.14)

Militia Act 1733 (c.23)
Militia Act 1745 (c.2)
Militia Act 1757 (c.25)
Militia Act 1757 (c.26)
Militia Act 1758 (c.20)
Militia Act 1759 (c.2)
Militia Act 1759 (c.2)
Militia Act 1762 (c.20)
Militia Act 1763 (c.17)
Militia Act 1765 (c.36)
Militia Act 1769 (c.40)
Militia Act 1771 (c.32)
Militia Act 1776 (c.3)
Militia Act 1778 (c.14)
Militia Act 1779 (c.76)
Militia Act 1780 (c.8)
Militia Act 1780 (c.44)
Militia Act 1780 (c.7)
Militia Act 1780 (c.18)
Militia Act 1782 (c.6)
Militia Act 1782 (c.62)
Militia Act 1794 (c.81)
Militia Act 1802 (c.90)
Militia Act 1882 (c.49)
Militia and Yeomanry Act 1901 (c.14)
Militia and Yeomanry Act 1902 (c.39)
Militia (City of London) Act 1820 (c.100)
Militia, Derbyshire Act 1795 (c.16)
Militia, etc. Act 1711 (c.33)
Militia, etc. Act 1713 (c.9(c))
Militia, etc. Act 1778 (c.59)
Militia, etc. Act 1779 (c.72)
Militia Pay Act 1757 (c.30)
Militia Pay Act 1758 (c.21)
Militia Pay Act 1759 (c.24)
Militia Pay Act 1760 (c.22)
Militia Pay Act 1762 (c.35)
Militia Pay Act 1762 (c.10)
Militia Pay Act 1763 (c.30)
Militia Pay Act 1765 (c.34)
Militia Pay Act 1768 (c.20)
Militia Pay Act 1770 (c.9)
Militia Pay Act 1772 (c.13)
Militia Pay Act 1772 (c.23)
Militia Pay Act 1774 (c.18)
Militia Pay Act 1775 (c.8)
Militia Pay Act 1776 (c.19)
Militia Pay Act 1776 (c.10)
Militia Pay Act 1779 (c.19)
Militia Pay Act 1780 (c.13)
Militia Pay Act 1780 (c.21)
Militia Pay Act 1782 (c.24)
Militia Pay Act 1783 (c.35)
Militia Pay Act 1785 (c.8)
Militia Pay Act 1786 (c.69)
Militia Pay Act 1788 (c.11)
Militia Pay Act 1789 (c.15)
Militia Pay Act 1790 (c.9)
Militia Pay Act 1791 (c.16)
Militia Pay Act 1791 (c.26)
Militia Pay Act 1793 (c.19)
Militia Pay Act 1794 (c.16)
Militia Pay Act 1794 (c.30)

Militia Pay, etc. Act 1766 (c.30)
Militia Pay, etc. Act 1766 (c.17)
Militia Pay, etc. Act 1783 (c.13)
Militia (Scotland) Act 1802 (c.91)
Militia (Storehouse) Act 1882 (c.12)
Militia, Sussex Act 1793 (c.79)
Milk Act 1934 (c.51)
Milk (Amendment) 1937 (c.66)
Milk and Dairies Act 1914 (c.49)
Milk and Dairies Act Postponement Act 1915 (c.59)
Milk and Dairies (Amendment) 1922 (c.54)
Milk and Dairies (Consolidation) Act 1915 (c.66)
Milk and Dairies (Scotland) Act 1914 (c.46)
Milk (Cessation of Production) Act 1985 (c.4)
Milk (Extension and Amendment) 1938 (c.61)
Milk (Extension of Temporary Provisions) Act 1936 (c.9)
Milk Industry Act 1939 (c.46)
Milk (Special Designations) Act 1949 (c.34)
Mine Adventurers of England Act (c.26(d))
Minehead Harbour Act 1700 (c.9)
Minehead Harbour Act 1711 (c.32)
Minehead Harbour Act 1770 (c.26)
Minehead Harbour Act 1937 (c.8)
Minehead Roads Act 1786 (c.136)
Mineral Exploration and Investment Grants Act 1972 (c.9)
Mineral Workings Act 1951 (c.60)
Mineral Workings Act 1971 (c.71)
Mineral Workings Act 1985 (c.12)
Mineral Workings (Offshore Installations) Act 1971 (c.61)
Miners Welfare Act 1952 (c.23)
Mines Accidents (Rescue and Aid) Act 1910 (c.15)
Mines and Quarries Act 1954 (c.70)
Mines and Quarries Act 1969 (c.10)
Mines and Quarries (Tips) Act 1969 (c.10)
Mines Management Act 1971 (c.20)
Mines (Prohibition of Child Labour Underground) Act 1900 (c.21)
Mines (Working Facilities) Act 1934 (c.27)
Mines (Working Facilities and Support) Act 1923 (c.20)
Mines (Working Facilities and Support) Act 1966 (c.4)
Mines (Working Facilities and Support) Act 1974 (c.36)
Mining Industry Act 1920 (c.50)
Mining Industry Act 1926 (c.28)
Mining Industry (Amendment) Act 1939 (c.45)
Mining Industry (Welfare Fund) Act 1925 (c.80)
Mining Industry (Welfare Fund) Act 1931 (c.23)
Mining Industry (Welfare Fund) Act 1934 (c.9)
Mining Industry (Welfare Fund) Act 1939 (c.9)
Mining Industry (Welfare Fund) Act 1943 (c.3)
Minister of Agriculture and Fisheries Act 1919 (c.91)

Minister of Food (Continuance) Act 1920 (c.47)
Minister of Health Act 1919 (c.21)
Minister of Pensions 1916 (c.65)
Minister of the Crown Act 1964 (c.98)
Minister of Transport Act 1919 (c.50)
Ministerial and Other Pensions and Salaries Act 1991 (c.5)
Ministerial and other Salaries Act 1971 (c.3)
Ministerial and other Salaries Act 1975 (c.27)
Ministerial Salaries Act 1946 (c.55)
Ministerial Salaries Act 1957 (c.47)
Ministerial Salaries and Members' Pensions Act 1965 (c.11)
Ministerial Salaries Consolidation 1965 (c.58)
Ministeries of Munitions and Shipping (Cessation) Act 1921 (c.8)
Ministers of the Crown Act 1951 (c.9)
Ministers of the Crown Act 1964 (c.98)
Ministers of the Crown Act 1974 (c.21)
Ministers of the Crown Act 1975 (c.26)
Ministers of the Crown (Parliamentary Secretaries) Act 1960 (c.6)
Ministers of the Crown (Parliamentary Under-Secretaries) Act 1951 (c.9)
Ministers of the Crown (Transfer of Functions) Act 1964 (c.31)
Ministers Widows Fund (Scotland) Act 1779 (c.20)
Ministry of Civil Aviation Act 1945 (c.21)
Ministry of Defence Police Act 1987 (c.4)
Ministry of Food (Financial Powers) Act 1949 (c.15)
Ministry of Fuel and Power Act 1945 (c.19)
Ministry of Materials Act 1951 (c.42)
Ministry of Munitions Act 1915 (c.51)
Ministry of Munitions Act 1918 (c.60)
Ministry of National Insurance Act 1944 (c.46)
Ministry of National Service Act 1917 (c.6)
Ministry of Religion (Removal of Disqualifications) Act 1925 (c.54)
Ministry of Social Security Act 1966 (c.20)
Ministry of Supply Act 1939 (c.38)
Ministry of the Crown Act 1937 (c.38)
Ministry of the Crown and House of Commons Disqualification Act 1942 (c.11)
Ministry of the Crown (Emergency Appointments) Act 1939 (c.77)
Ministry of the Crown (Transfer of Functions) Act 1946 (c.31)
Ministry of the Crown (Treasury Secretaries) Act 1947 (c.5)
Ministry of Town and Country Planning Act 1943 (c.5)
Ministry of Transport Act 1919 (c.50)
Ministry of Works Act 1942 (c.23)
Minority of Heir to the Crown Act 1765 (c.27)
Minority of Successor to Crown Act 1750 (c.24)
Minors' Contracts Act 1987 (c.13)
Mint Prosecutions Expenses Act 1776 (c.46)
Miscellaneous Financial Provisions Act 1946 (c.40)

Miscellaneous Financial Provisions Act 1950 (c.21)

Miscellaneous Financial Provisions Act 1955 (c.6)

Miscellaneous Financial Provisions Act 1968 (c.75)

Miscellaneous Financial Provisions Act 1983 (c.29)

Mischief by Fire 1724 (c.28)

Mischiefs by Fire 1708 (c.17)

Mischiefs from Fire 1707 (c.58)

Misrepresentation Act 1967 (c.7)

Misuse of Drugs Act 1971 (c.38)

Mitford and Launditch, Norfolk: Poor Relief Act 1775 (c.59)

Mobile Homes Act 1975 (c.49)

Mobile Homes Act 1983 (c.34)

Mock Auctions Act 1961 (c.47)

Money Payments (Justices Procedure) Act 1935 (c.46)

Moneylenders Act 1900 (c.51)

Moneylenders Act 1911 (c.38)

Moneylenders Act 1927 (c.21)

Moneylenders (Crown Agents) Act 1975 (c.81)

Monkland, Glasgow: Navigation, etc. Act 1770 (c.105)

Monmouth and Gloucester Roads Act 1757 (c.44)

Monmouth Roads Act 1755 (c.31)

Monmouth Roads Act 1770 (c.106)

Monmouth Roads Act 1777 (c.96)

Monmouth Roads Act 1793 (c.169)

Monmouthshire Canal: Navigation Act 1792 (c.102)

Monopolies and Mergers Act 1965 (c.50)

Monopolies and Restrictive Practices Commission (Inquiry and Control) Act 1948 (c.66)

Monopolies and Restrictive Practices Commission Act 1953 (c.51)

Montgomery: Poor Relief Act 1792 (c.96)

Montgomery, Salop and Denbigh Roads Act 1788 (c.96)

Montrose Beer Duties Act 1719 (c.7)

Montrose Beer Duties Act 1732 (c.5)

Montrose Beer Duties Act 1769 (c.57)

Montrose Bridge Act 1792 (c.38)

Morden College Kent Act 1771 (c.10)

Morpeth and Elsdon Road Act 1751 (c.33)

Morpeth to Elsdon Road Act 1778 (c.107)

Morrison's Haven and Fort, East Lothian (repair) 1708 (c.27)

Mortmain and Charitable Uses Act 1888 (c.42)

Mortgage Act 1733 (c.20)

Mortuaries (Bangor, etc.) Abolition Act 1713 (c.6)

Mortuaries (Chester) Act 1755 (c.6)

Moss Troopers Act 1700 (c.6)

Moss Troopers Act 1712 (c.10)

Motor Car Act 1903 (c.36)

Motor Car (International Circulation) Act 1909 (c.37)

Motor-Cycle Crash-Helmets (Religious Exemption) Act 1976 (c.62)

Motor-Cycle Crash-Helmets (Restriction of Liability) Act 1985 (c.28)

Motor-Cycle Noise Act 1987 (c.34)

Motor Spirit (Regulations) Act 1948 (c.34)

Motor Vehicles (International Circulation) Act 1952 (c.39)

Motor Vehicles (Passenger Insurance) Act 1971 (c.36)

Motor Vehicles (Safety Equipment for Children) Act 1991 (c.14)

Motor Vehicles (Wearing of Rear Seat Belts by Children) Act 1988 (c.23)

Mr Speaker Clifton Brown's Retirement Act 1951 (c.2)

Mr Speaker King's Retirement Act 1970 (c.13)

Mr Speaker Morrison's Retirement Act 1959 (c.1)

Mr Speaker's Retirement Act 1904 (c.5)

Mr Speaker's Retirement Act 1921 (c.10)

Mr Speaker's Retirement Act 1928 (c.16)

Much Wenlock Roads Act 1756 (c.60)

Much Wenlock Roads Act 1778 (c.89)

Multilateral Investment Guarantee Agency Act 1988 (c.8)

Municipal Corporations Act 1882 (c.50)

Municipal Corporations Act 1883 (c.18)

Municipal Corporations Amendment 1906 (c.12)

Municipal Corporations Amendment 1910 (c.19)

Municipal Corporations (Audit) Act 1933 (c.28)

Municipal Corporations (Ireland) Act 1840 (c.108)

Municipal Corporations (Mandamus) Act 1772 (c.21)

Municipal Elections Act 1924 (c.4)

Municipal Elections (Corrupt and Illegal Practices) Act 1884 (c.70)

Municipal Elections (Corrupt and Illegal Practices) Act 1911 (c.7)

Municipal Offices Act 1710 (c.25)

Municipal Rate (Edinburgh) Act 1868 (c.42)

Municipal Savings Banks (War Loan Investment) Act 1916 (c.47)

Munitions (Liability for Explosion) Act 1916 (c.61)

Munitions of War Act 1915 (c.54)

Munitions of War Act 1917 (c.45)

Munitions of War Amendment 1916 (c.99)

Murder (Abolition of Death Penalty) Act 1965 (c.71)

Murder Act 1728 (c.21)

Murder Act 1751 (c.37)

Murders Abroad Act 1817 (c.53)

Murderers of Captain Porteous Act 1735 (c.35)

Museums and Galleries Admission Charges Act 1972 (c.73)

Museums and Gymnasiums Act 1891 (c.22)

Museum of London Act 1965 (c.17)
Museum of London Act 1986 (c.8)
Museums and Galleries Act 1992 (c.44)
Musical Copyright Act 1906 (c.36)
Musical (Summary Proceedings) Copyright Act 1902 (c.15)
Mutford and Lothingland, Suffolk (Poor Relief) Act 1764 (c.89)
Mutiny Act 1701 (c.2)
Mutiny Act 1702 (c.20)
Mutiny Act 1703 (c.17)
Mutiny Act 1704 (c.5)
Mutiny Act 1705 (c.22)
Mutiny Act 1706 (c.18)
Mutiny Act 1707 (c.74)
Mutiny Act 1708 (c.4)
Mutiny Act 1709 (c.6)
Mutiny Act 1710 (c.9)
Mutiny Act 1711 (c.13)
Mutiny Act 1712 (c.13)
Mutiny Act 1713 (c.4)
Mutiny Act 1714 (c.3)
Mutiny Act 1714 (c.9)
Mutiny Act 1715 (c.34)
Mutiny Act 1716 (c.2)
Mutiny Act 1717 (c.4)
Mutiny Act 1718 (c.5)
Mutiny Act 1719 (c.3)
Mutiny Act 1720 (c.6)
Mutiny Act 1721 (c.3)
Mutiny Act 1722 (c.4)
Mutiny Act 1723 (c.3)
Mutiny Act 1724 (c.6)
Mutiny Act 1725 (c.3)
Mutiny Act 1726 (c.2)
Mutiny Act 1727 (c.2)
Mutiny Act 1728 (c.2)
Mutiny Act 1729 (c.2)
Mutiny Act 1730 (c.2)
Mutiny Act 1731 (c.2)
Mutiny Act 1732 (c.3)
Mutiny Act 1733 (c.2)
Mutiny Act 1734 (c.2)
Mutiny Act 1735 (c.2)
Mutiny Act 1736 (c.2)
Mutiny Act 1737 (c.2)
Mutiny Act 1738 (c.2)
Mutiny Act 1739 (c.10)
Mutiny Act 1740 (c.9)
Mutiny Act 1741 (c.4)
Mutiny Act 1742 (c.14)
Mutiny Act 1743 (c.16)
Mutiny Act 1744 (c.7)
Mutiny Act 1745 (c.11)
Mutiny Act 1746 (c.11)
Mutiny Act 1747 (c.6)
Mutiny Act 1747 (c.13)
Mutiny Act 1748 (c.5)
Mutiny Act 1749 (c.4)
Mutiny Act 1750 (c.6)
Mutiny Act 1751 (c.2)
Mutiny Act 1753 (c.5)
Mutiny Act 1754 (c.5)

Mutiny Act 1755 (c.4)
Mutiny Act 1756 (c.3)
Mutiny Act 1757 (c.6)
Mutiny Act 1757 (c.5)
Mutiny Act 1758 (c.5)
Mutiny Act 1759 (c.6)
Mutiny Act 1760 (c.6)
Mutiny Act 1761 (c.11)
Mutiny Act 1762 (c.7)
Mutiny Act 1763 (c.3)
Mutiny Act 1765 (c.7)
Mutiny Act 1766 (c.8)
Mutiny Act 1766 (c.10)
Mutiny Act 1768 (c.7)
Mutiny Act 1769 (c.7)
Mutiny Act 1770 (c.3)
Mutiny Act 1770 (c.15)
Mutiny Act 1771 (c.6)
Mutiny Act 1772 (c.4)
Mutiny Act 1772 (c.10)
Mutiny Act 1774 (c.3)
Mutiny Act 1775 (c.6)
Mutiny Act 1776 (c.2)
Mutiny Act 1776 (c.3)
Mutiny Act 1778 (c.4)
Mutiny Act 1779 (c.16)
Mutiny Act 1780 (c.12)
Mutiny Act 1782 (c.4)
Mutiny Act 1783 (c.17)
Mutiny Act 1783 (c.24)
Mutiny Act 1783 (c.52)
Mutiny Act 1783 (c.11)
Mutiny Act 1785 (c.6)
Mutiny Act 1786 (c.10)
Mutiny Act 1788 (c.12)
Mutiny Act 1789 (c.2)
Mutiny Act 1790 (c.6)
Mutiny Act 1791 (c.13)
Mutiny Act 1791 (c.19)
Mutiny Act 1793 (c.9)
Mutiny Act 1794 (c.13)
Mutiny Act 1795 (c.6)
Mutiny, America Act 1765 (c.33)
Mutiny, America Act 1768 (c.19)
Mutiny, East Indies Act 1754 (c.9)
Mutiny in America Act 1766 (c.18)
Mutiny in America Act 1767 (c.55)
Mutiny in America Act 1769 (c.18)
Mutiny in America Act 1771 (c.11)
Mutiny in America Act 1772 (c.12)
Mutiny in America Act 1773 (c.24)
Mutiny in America Act 1774 (c.6)
Mutiny in America Act 1775 (c.15)
Mutiny in America Act 1776 (c.11)

Namibia Act 1991 (c.4)
Nantwich Canal Act 1777 (c.67)
Nantwich Canal Act 1778 (c.21)
Nantwich to Chester Road Act 1789 (c.91)
Nar: Navigation Act 1750 (c.19)
National Assistance Act 1948 (c.29)
National Assistance Act 1948 (Amendment) Act 1962 (c.24)

National Assistance Act 1959 (c.52)
National Assistance (Amendment) Act 1951 (c.57)
National Assistance (Amendment) Act 1959 (c.30)
National Audit Act 1983 (c.44)
National Coal Board (Additional Powers) Act 1966 (c.47)
National Coal Board (Finance) Act 1976 (c.1)
National Debt Act 1714 (c.2)
National Debt Act 1714 (c.12)
National Debt Act 1714 (c.19)
National Debt Act 1714 (c.21)
National Debt Act 1716 (c.7)
National Debt Act 1716 (c.9)
National Debt Act 1717 (c.10)
National Debt Act 1718 (c.3)
National Debt Act 1718 (c.9)
National Debt Act 1718 (c.19)
National Debt Act 1719 (c.4)
National Debt Act 1719 (c.10)
National Debt Act 1720 (c.5)
National Debt Act 1721 (c.1)
National Debt Act 1721 (c.20)
National Debt Act 1721 (c.22)
National Debt Act 1722 (cc.5, 6)
National Debt Act 1722 (c.12)
National Debt Act 1723 (c.5)
National Debt Act 1724 (c.17)
National Debt Act 1726 (c.3)
National Debt Act 1726 (c.21)
National Debt Act 1730 (c.16)
National Debt Act 1730 (c.5)
National Debt Act 1730 (c.9)
National Debt Act 1731 (c.17)
National Debt Act 1732 (c.28)
National Debt Act 1735 (c.34)
National Debt Act 1736 (c.17)
National Debt Act 1737 (c.27)
National Debt Act 1741 (c.19)
National Debt Act 1742 (cc.12, 13)
National Debt Act 1743 (c.18)
National Debt Act 1744 (c.9)
National Debt Act 1745 (c.12)
National Debt Act 1746 (c.3)
National Debt Act 1746 (c.10)
National Debt Act 1747 (c.2)
National Debt Act 1748 (c.23)
National Debt Act 1749 (c.1)
National Debt Act 1749 (c.16)
National Debt Act 1750 (c.2)
National Debt Act 1750 (c.11)
National Debt Act 1751 (c.25)
National Debt Act 1751 (c.27)
National Debt Act 1753 (c.1)
National Debt Act 1753 (c.23)
National Debt Act 1755 (c.15)
National Debt Act 1756 (c.7)
National Debt Act 1757 (c.19)
National Debt Act 1758 (c.22)
National Debt Act 1759 (c.12)
National Debt Act 1760 (c.7)
National Debt Act 1761 (cc.9, 10)

National Debt Act 1762 (c.9)
National Debt Act 1762 (c.12)
National Debt Act 1763 (c.18)
National Debt Act 1763 (c.25)
National Debt Act 1765 (c.16)
National Debt Act 1765 (c.23)
National Debt Act 1765 (c.42)
National Debt Act 1766 (c.21)
National Debt Act 1766 (c.39)
National Debt Act 1766 (cc.24–26)
National Debt Act 1768 (c.29)
National Debt Act 1768 (c.31)
National Debt Act 1770 (c.36)
National Debt Act 1770 (c.46)
National Debt Act 1772 (c.63)
National Debt Act 1774 (c.76)
National Debt Act 1775 (c.41)
National Debt Act 1776 (c.46)
National Debt Act 1778 (c.22)
National Debt Act 1779 (c.18)
National Debt Act 1782 (c.8)
National Debt Act 1782 (c.34)
National Debt Act 1783 (c.35)
National Debt Act 1784 (c.10)
National Debt Act 1784 (c.37)
National Debt Act 1784 (c.39)
National Debt Act 1785 (c.32)
National Debt Act 1785 (c.71)
National Debt Act 1786 (c.34)
National Debt Act 1789 (c.37)
National Debt Act 1793 (c.28)
National Debt Act 1793 (c.32)
National Debt Act 1794 (c.1)
National Debt Act 1794 (c.21)
National Debt Act 1795 (c.14)
National Debt Act 1795 (c.23)
National Debt Act 1795 (c.32)
National Debt Act 1958 (c.6)
National Debt Act 1972 (c.65)
National Debt (Conversion of Stock) Act 1884 (c.23)
National Debt (No. 2) Act 1749 (c.22)
National Debt Reduction Act 1724 (c.9)
National Debt Reduction Act 1786 (c.31)
National Economy Act 1931 (c.48)
National Film Finance Corporation Act 1981 (c.15)
National Fire Service Regulations (Indemnity) Act 1944 (c.35)
National Galleries of Scotland Act 1906 (c.50)
National Galleries of Scotland Act 1959 (c.61)
National Gallery and St. James's Park Act 1911 (c.23)
National Gallery and Tate Gallery Act 1954 (c.65)
National Gallery Enlargement Act 1866 (c.83)
National Gallery Enlargement Act 1867 (c.41)
National Gallery (Overseas Loans) Act 1935 (c.18)
National Gallery (Purchase of Adjacent Land) Act 1901 (c.16)
National Health (Hospital Boards) Act 1964 (c.32)

National Health Insurance Act 1918 (c.62)
National Health Insurance Act 1919 (c.36)
National Health Insurance Act 1920 (c.10)
National Health Insurance Act 1921 (c.25)
National Health Insurance Act 1922 (c.38)
National Health Insurance Act 1924 (c.38)
National Health Insurance Act 1928 (c.14)
National Health Insurance Act 1936 (c.32)
National Health Insurance (Amendment) Act 1937 (c.24)
National Health Insurance (Amendment) Act 1938 (c.14)
National Health Insurance and Contributory Pensions Act 1932 (c.52)
National Health Insurance and Contributory Pensions Act 1935 (c.44)
National Health Insurance and Contributory Pensions (Emergency Provisions) Act 1939 (c.84)
National Health Insurance, Contributory Pensions and Workmen's Compensation Act 1941 (c.39)
National Health Insurance (Cost of Medical Benefit) Act 1924 (c.10)
National Health Insurance (Juvenile Contributors and Young Persons) Act 1937 (c.3)
National Health Insurance (Prolongation of Insurance) Act 1921 (c.66)
National Health Insurance (Prolongation of Insurance) Act 1931 (c.5)
National Health Insurance (Prolongation of Insurance) Act 1932 (c.6)
National Health Service Act 1946 (c.81)
National Health Service Act 1951 (c.31)
National Health Service Act 1952 (c.25)
National Health Service Act 1961 (c.19)
National Health Service Act 1966 (c.8)
National Health Service Act 1977 (c.49)
National Health Service (Amendment) Act 1949 (c.93)
National Health Service (Amendment) Act 1957 (c.44)
National Health Service (Amendment) Act 1986 (c.66)
National Health Service and Community Care Act 1990 (c.19)
National Health Service Contributions Act 1957 (c.34)
National Health Service Contributions Act 1961 (c.13)
National Health Service Contributions Act 1965 (c.54)
National Health Service Contributions Act 1970 (c.16)
National Health Service (Family Planning) Act 1967 (c.39)
National Health Service (Family Planning) Amendment Act 1972 (c.72)
National Health Service (Hospital Boards) Act 1964 (c.32)
National Health Service (Invalid Direction) Act 1980 (c.15)

National Health Service Reorganisation Act 1973 (c.32)
National Health Service (Scotland) Act 1947 (c.27)
National Health Service (Scotland) Act 1972 (c.58)
National Health Service (Scotland) Act 1978 (c.29)
National Health Service (Vocational Training) Act 1976 (c.59)
National Heritage Act 1980 (c.17)
National Heritage Act 1983 (c.47)
National Heritage (Scotland) Act 1985 (c.16)
National Insurance Act 1911 (c.55)
National Insurance Act 1913 (c.37)
National Insurance Act 1946 (c.67)
National Insurance Act 1947 (c.37)
National Insurance Act 1949 (c.56)
National Insurance Act 1951 (c.34)
National Insurance Act 1953 (c.29)
National Insurance Act 1955 (c.29)
National Insurance Act 1956 (c.47)
National Insurance Act 1957 (c.26)
National Insurance Act 1959 (c.47)
National Insurance Act 1960 (c.5)
National Insurance Act 1963 (c.7)
National Insurance Act 1965 (c.51)
National Insurance Act 1966 (c.6)
National Insurance Act 1967 (c.73)
National Insurance Act 1969 (c.4)
National Insurance Act 1969 (c.44)
National Insurance Act 1971 (c.50)
National Insurance Act 1972 (c.57)
National Insurance Act 1974 (c.14)
National Insurance &c Act 1964 (c.96)
National Insurance and Supplementary Benefit Act 1973 (c.42)
National Insurance (Amendment) Act 1972 (c.36)
National Insurance, etc. Act 1969 (c.4)
National Insurance (Industrial) Act 1953 (c.43)
National Insurance (Industrial Injuries) Act 1946 (c.62)
National Insurance (Industrial Injuries) Act 1948 (c.42)
National Insurance (Industrial Injuries) Act 1965 (c.52)
National Insurance (Industrial Injuries) (Amendment) Act 1967 (c.25)
National Insurance Land Purchase (Winding-up) Act 1935 (c.21)
National Insurance (Miscellaneous Provisions) Act 1928 (c.24)
National Insurance (Miscellaneous Provisions) Act 1932 (c.11)
National Insurance (Miscellaneous Provisions) Act 1945 (c.12)
National Insurance (Navy and Army) Act (c.81)
National Insurance (Navy and Army) (Session 2) Act 1914 (c.15)
National Insurance (No. 2) Act 1957 (c.1)

National Insurance (Old Persons' and Widows' Pensions and Attendance Allowance) Act 1970 (c.51)

National Insurance (Pt. I Amendment) Act 1915 (c.29)

National Insurance (Pt. I Amendment) Act 1917 (c.15)

National Insurance (Pt. II Amendment) Act 1914 (c.57)

National Insurance (Pt. II Amendment) Act 1914 (c.27)

National Insurance (Pt. II) (Munition Workers) Act 1916 (c.20)

National Insurance Regulations (Validation) Act 1972 (c.4)

National Insurance Surcharge Act 1976 (c.85)

National Insurance Surcharge Act 1982 (c.55)

National Insurance (Temporary Employment in Agriculture) Act 1916 (c.53)

National Insurance (Unemployment) Act 1918 (c.63)

National Insurance (Unemployment) Act 1919 (c.77)

National Library of Scotland Act 1925 (c.73)

National Loans Act 1939 (c.117)

National Loans Act 1940 (c.3)

National Loans Act 1941 (c.18)

National Loans Act 1942 (c.14)

National Loans Act 1943 (c.13)

National Loans Act 1944 (c.19)

National Loans Act 1945 (c.23)

National Loans Act 1968 (c.13)

National Loans (No. 2) Act 1940 (c.23)

National Lottery etc. Act 1993 (c.39)

National Maritime Museum Act 1934 (c.43)

National Maritime Museum Act 1989 (c.8)

National Mod (Scotland) Act 1969 (c.41)

National Museum of Antiquities of Scotland Act 1954 (c.14)

National Parks and Access to the Countryside Act 1949 (c.97)

National Portrait Gallery Act 1889 (c.25)

National Registration Act 1915 (c.60)

National Registration Act 1939 (c.91)

National Registration (Amendment) Act 1918 (c.60)

National Savings Bank Act 1971 (c.29)

National Service Act 1941 (c.15)

National Service Act 1942 (c.3)

National Service Act 1947 (c.31)

National Service Act 1948 (c.64)

National Service Act 1950 (c.30)

National Service Act 1955 (c.11)

National Service (Amendment) Act 1948 (c.6)

National Service (Armed Forces) Act 1939 (c.81)

National Service (Armed Forces) Act 1940 (c.22)

National Service (Channel Islands) Act 1940 (c.24)

National Service (Foreign Countries) Act 1942 (c.30)

National Service (No. 2) Act 1941 (c.4)

National Service (Release of Conscientious Objectors) Act 1946 (c.38)

National Theatre Act 1949 (c.16)

National Theatre Act 1969 (c.11)

National Theatre Act 1974 (c.55)

National Theatre and Museum of London Act 1973 (c.2)

Nationalised Industries Loans Act 1958 (c.19)

Natural Heritage (Scotland) Act 1991 (c.28)

Natural-born Children of Aliens Act 1776 (c.52)

Naturalisation Act 1711 (c.9)

Naturalisation Act 1714 (c.4)

Naturalisation Act 1739 (c.7)

Naturalisation Act 1762 (c.25)

Naturalisation Act 1763 (c.4)

Naturalisation Act 1772 (c.25)

Naturalisation Act 1774 (c.84)

Naturalisation of Jews Act 1753 (c.26)

Naturalisation of Jews Act 1754 (c.1)

Nature Conservancy Council Act 1973 (c.54)

Naval Agency and Distribution Act 1864 (c.24)

Naval and Marine Forces (Temporary Release from Service) Act 1941 (c.4)

Naval and Marine Pay and Pensions Act 1865 (c.73)

Naval and Marine Reserves Pay Act 1957 (c.32)

Naval and Military War Pensions, etc. Act 1915 (c.83)

Naval and Military War Pensions, etc. (Admin. Expenses) Act 1917 (c.14)

Naval and Military War Pension, etc. (Committees) Act 1917 (c.54)

Naval and Military War Pensions, etc. (Expenses) Act 1916 (c.4)

Naval and Military War Pensions, etc. (Transfer of Powers) Act 1917 (c.37)

Naval Billeting, etc. Act 1914 (c. 70)

Naval Courts-Martial Act 1779 (c.17)

Naval Discipline Act 1909 (c.41)

Naval Discipline Act 1915 (c.30)

Naval Discipline Act 1917 (c.34)

Naval Discipline Act 1922 (c.37)

Naval Discipline Act 1957 (c.53)

Naval Discipline (Amendment) Act 1938 (c.64)

Naval Discipline (Amendment) Act 1941 (c.29)

Naval Discipline (Delegation of Powers) Act 1916 (c.17)

Naval Discipline (Delegation of Powers) Act 1917 (c.11)

Naval Discipline (Dominion Naval Forces) Act 1911 (c.47)

Naval Discipline (No. 2) Act 1915 (c.73)

Naval Enlistment Act 1884 (c.46)

Naval Establishments in British Possessions Act 1909 (c.18)

Naval Forces Act 1903 (c.6)

Naval Forces (Enforcement of Maintenance Liabilities) Act (c.24)
Naval Forces (Extension of Services) Act 1944 (c.13)
Naval Forces (Service on Shore) Act 1916 (c.101)
Naval Knights of Windsor (Dissolution) Act 1892 (c.34)
Naval Lands (Volunteers) Act 1908 (c.25)
Naval Marriages Act 1908 (c.26)
Naval Marriages Act 1915 (c.35)
Naval Medical Compassionate Fund Act 1915 (c.28)
Naval, Military and Air Force Service Act 1919 (c.15)
Naval Pensions Act 1884 (c.44)
Naval Prize Act 1739 (c.4)
Naval Prize Act 1743 (c.34)
Naval Prize Act 1746 (c.24)
Naval Prize Act 1758 (c.25)
Naval Prize Act 1772 (c.25)
Naval Prize Act 1864 (c.25)
Naval Prize Act 1918 (c.30)
Naval Prize Act 1928 (c.36)
Naval Prize etc. Act 1756 (c.34)
Naval Prize Money Act 1820 (c.85)
Naval Prize (Procedure) Act 1916 (c.2)
Naval Reserve Act 1900 (c.52)
Naval Reserve (Mobilisation) Act 1900 (c.17)
Naval Reserve (Officers) Act 1926 (c.41)
Naval Stores Act 1745 (c.36)
Naval Volunteers Act 1853 (c.73)
Naval Works Act 1901 (c.39)
Naval Works Act 1903 (c.22)
Naval Works Act 1904 (c.20)
Navigation Act 1703 (c.6)
Navigation Act 1755 (c.16)
Navigation Act 1756 (c.11)
Navigation Act 1776 (c.20)
Navigation Act 1776 (c.34)
Navigation Act 1778 (c.6)
Navigation Act 1779 (c.14)
Navigation Act 1780 (c.19)
Navigation Act 1782 (c.16)
Navigation, Norfolk Act 1754 (c.12)
Navru Island Agreement Act 1920 (c.27)
Navy Act 1705 (c.6)
Navy Act 1727 (c.14)
Navy Act 1740 (c.38)
Navy Act 1744 (c.35)
Navy Act 1747 (c.11)
Navy Act 1748 (c.33)
Navy Act 1756 (c.27)
Navy Act 1756 (c.10)
Navy Act 1762 (c.16)
Navy Act 1769 (c.30)
Navy Act 1779 (c.67)
Navy Act 1779 (c.75)
Navy Act 1780 (c.23)
Navy Act 1780 (c.15)
Navy Act 1786 (c.63)
Navy Act 1791 (c.33)
Navy Act 1791 (c.34)

Navy and Marines Act 1795 (c.28)
Navy and Marines (Wills) Act 1914 (c.17)
Navy and Marines (Wills) Act 1930 (c.38)
Navy and Marines (Wills) Act 1939 (c.87)
Navy and Marines (Wills) Act 1953 (c.24)
Navy and Victualling Bills Act 1794 (c.56)
Navy, Army and Air Force Reserves Act 1954 (c.10)
Navy, Army and Air Force Reserves Act 1959 (c.10)
Navy, Army and Air Force Reserves Act 1964 (c.11)
Navy, etc. Act 1714 (c.25)
Navy, etc. Act 1780 (c.11)
Navy (Pledging of Certificates, etc.) Act 1914 (c.89)
Neath Canal Act 1791 (c.85)
Negotiations of Certain Bonds Act 1782 (c.11)
Negotiations of Notes and Bills 1775 (c.51)
Negotiations of Notes and Bills Act 1802 (c.1)
Nether Knutsford Church Act 1740 (c.5)
New Forest Act 1949 (c.69)
New Forest Act 1964 (c.83)
New Forest Act 1970 (c.21)
Newfoundland (Consequential Provisions) Act 1949 (c.5)
New Hebrides Act 1980 (c.16)
New Malton, Yorks. (Searching, Sealing, etc. of Butter) Act 1743 (c.8)
New Method of Tanning Act 1794 (c.63)
New Ministries Act 1917 (c.44)
New Ministries and Secretaries Act 1916 (c.68)
New Office of Excise Act 1770 (c.32)
New Palace Yard, Westminster 1706 (c.15)
New Parishes Act 1843 (c.37)
New Parishes Act 1844 (c.94)
New Parishes Act 1856 (c.104)
New Parishes Acts and Church Building Acts Amendment Act 1869 (c.94)
New Parishes Acts and Church Building Acts Amendment Act 1884 (c.65)
New Roads and Street Works Act 1991 (c.22)
New Sarum: Poor Relief Act 1770 (c.81)
New Shoreham Harbour Act 1759 (c.35)
New Shoreham Harbour Act 1789 (c.21)
New Streets Act 1951 (c.40)
New Streets Act 1951 (Amendment) Act 1957 (c.33)
New Towns Act 1946 (c.68)
New Towns Act 1952 (c.27)
New Towns Act 1953 (c.38)
New Towns Act 1955 (c.4)
New Towns Act 1958 (c.12)
New Towns Act 1959 (c.62)
New Towns Act 1965 (c.59)
New Towns Act 1966 (c.44)
New Towns Act 1969 (c.5)
New Towns Act 1971 (c.81)
New Towns Act 1975 (c.42)
New Towns Act 1977 (c.23)
New Towns Act 1980 (c.36)

New Towns Act 1981 (c.64)
New Towns Act 1982 (c.7)
New Towns (No. 2) Act 1964 (c.68)
New Towns (Amendment) Act 1976 (c.68)
New Towns (Amendment) Act 1994 (c.5)
New Towns and Urban Development Corporations Act 1985 (c.5)
New Towns (Scotland) Act 1968 (c.16)
New Towns (Scotland) Act 1977 (c.16)
New Valuation Lists (Postponement) Act 1952 (c.4)
New Woodstock, Kiddington, etc. Roads Act 1757 (c.48)
New Zealand Constitution (Amendment) 1947 (c.4)
Newbury and Marlborough Roads Act 1744 (c.12)
Newbury to Bath Canal Act 1794 (c.90)
Newbury to Marlborough Road Act 1725 (c.8)
Newcastle and Gateshead Bridge Act 1788 (c.78)
Newcastle and Sunderland: Coals Act 1790 (c.78)
Newcastle: Improvement Act 1763 (c.55)
Newcastle (Sale of Coal by Measured Keel) Act 1791 (c.36)
Newcastle: Streets Act 1786 (c.39)
Newcastle to Buckton Burn Road Act 1794 (c.130)
Newcastle to Carlisle Road Act 1786 (c.160)
Newfoundland Act 1933 (c.2)
Newfoundland (Consequential Provisions) Act 1950 (c.5)
Newfoundland Fisheries Act 1775 (c.31)
Newfoundland Fisheries Act 1786 (c.26)
Newfoundland Fisheries Act 1788 (c.35)
Newgate Gaol Delivery Act 1785 (c.18)
Newgate Gaol and Session House Act 1778 (c.48)
Newhaven Bridge Act 1783 (c.21)
Newhaven Harbour Act 1730 (c.17)
Newmarket and Cambridge Road Act 1763 (c.32)
Newmarket to Cambridge Road Act 1775 (c.68)
Newspaper Duty Act 1772 (c.65)
Newspaper Libel and Registration Act 1881 (c.60)
Newspapers, Printers and Reading Rooms Repeal Act 1869 (c.24)
Newport, Isle of Wight: Improvement Act 1786 (c.119)
Niall Macpherson Indemnity 1954 (c.29)
Nigeria Independence Act 1960 (c.55)
Nigeria (Remission of Payments) Act 1937 (c.63)
Nigeria Republic Act 1963 (c.57)
Night Poaching Act 1828 (c.69)
Night Watch Westminster Act (c.15)
Nisi Prius, Middlesex Act 1725 (c.31)
Nith Fisheries Act 1792 (c.94)
Noise Abatement Act 1960 (c.68)
Noise and Statutory Nuisance Act 1993 (c.40)

Nonconformist Relief Act 1779 (c.44)
Non-Domestic Rating Act 1992 (c.46)
Non-Domestic Rating Act 1993 (c.17)
Non-Domestic Rating Act 1994 (c.3)
Non-Ferrous Metal Industry Act 1917 (c.67)
Norfolk and Suffolk Broads Act 1988 (c.4)
Norfolk: Drainage Act 1783 (c,9)
Norfolk Highways Act 1708 (c.8)
Norfolk: Improvement Act 1725 (c.15)
Norfolk Roads Act 1765 (c.83)
Norfolk Roads Act 1765 (c.101)
Norfolk Roads Act 1767 (c.76)
Norfolk Roads Act 1770 (c.54)
Norfolk Roads Act 1770 (c.85)
Norfolk Roads Act 1770 (c.86)
Norfolk Roads Act 1786 (c.127)
Norfolk Roads Act 1790 (c.87)
Norfolk Roads Act 1790 (c.104)
Norfolk Roads Act 1791 (c.100)
Norfolk Roads Act 1791 (c.112)
Norfolk Roads Act 1791 (c.113)
Norfolk Roads Act 1792 (c.148)
Norfolk Roads Act 1792 (c.158)
Norfolk Roads Act 1794 (c.114)
North American Fisheries Act 1819 (c.38)
North Atlantic Shipping Act 1934 (c.10)
North Kyme Drainage Act 1788 (c.14)
North River, Norfolk: Navigation Act 1772 (c.37)
North Shields to Newcastle Road Act 1774 (c.115)
North Shields: Water Supply Act 1786 (c.110)
Northampton and Lincoln Roads Act 1756 (c.76)
Northampton and Lincoln Roads Act 1776 (c.72)
Northampton and Oxford Roads Act 1778 (c.87)
Northampton and Warwick Roads Act 1724 (c.25)
Northampton Highways Act (c.9)
Northampton: Improvement Act 1778 (c.79)
Northampton Roads Act 1748 (c.17)
Northampton Roads Act 1749 (c.8)
Northampton Roads Act 1753 (c.88)
Northampton Roads Act 1754 (c.23)
Northampton Roads Act 1778 (c.112)
Northampton Roads Act 1781 (c.94)
Northampton Roads Act 1783 (c.28)
Northampton Roads Act 1794 (c.126)
Northern Ireland Act 1929 (c.14)
Northern Ireland Act 1947 (c.37)
Northern Ireland Act 1955 (c.8)
Northern Ireland Act 1962 (c.30)
Northern Ireland Act 1972 (c.10)
Northern Ireland Act 1974 (c.28)
Northern Ireland Act 1982 (c.38)
Northern Ireland Assembly Act 1973 (c.17)
Northern Ireland Assembly Disqualifications Act 1975 (c.25)
Northern Ireland (Border Poll) Act 1972 (c.77)
Northern Ireland Compensation (for Compulsory Purchase) Act 1957 (c.14)

Northern Ireland Constitution Act 1973 (c.36)
Northern Ireland Constitution (Amendment) Act 1973 (c.69)
Northern Ireland (Emergency Provisions) Act 1973 (c.53)
Northern Ireland (Emergency Provisions) Act 1978 (c.5)
Northern Ireland (Emergency Provisions) Act 1987 (c.30)
Northern Ireland (Emergency Provisions) Act 1991 (c.24)
Northern Ireland (Emergency Provisions) Amendment Act 1975 (c.62)
Northern Ireland (Emergency Provisions) (Amendment) Act 1977 (c.34)
Northern Ireland (Financial Provisions) Act 1972 (c.76)
Northern Ireland (Foyle Fisheries) Act 1952 (c.11)
Northern Ireland Land Act 1925 (c.34)
Northern Ireland Land Act 1929 (c.14)
Northern Ireland Land Purchase (Winding Up) Act 1935 (c.21)
Northern Ireland (Loans) Act 1975 (c.83)
Northern Ireland (Loans) Act 1985 (c.76)
Northern Ireland (Miscellaneous Provisions) Act 1928 (c.24)
Northern Ireland (Miscellaneous Provisions) Act 1932 (c.11)
Northern Ireland (Miscellaneous Provisions) Act 1945 (c.12)
Northern Ireland (Temporary Provisions) Act 1972 (c.22)
Northern Ireland (Young Persons) Act 1974 (c.33)
Northern Roads, London Act 1735 (c.39)
Northumberland Fishery Act 1789 (c.25)
Northumberland and Durham Roads Act 1792 (c.145)
Northumberland Roads Act 1746 (c.9)
Northumberland Roads Act 1748 (c.7)
Northumberland Roads Act 1748 (c.9)
Northumberland Roads Act 1751 (c.18)
Northumberland Roads Act 1751 (c.46)
Northumberland Roads Act 1751 (c.48)
Northumberland Roads Act 1757 (c.52)
Northumberland Roads Act 1776 (c.68)
Northumberland Roads Act 1776 (c.83)
Northumberland Roads Act 1778 (c.83)
Northumberland Roads Act 1778 (c.115)
Northumberland Roads Act 1779 (c.95)
Norton Folley, Middlesex, Lighting etc. Act 1758 (c.49)
Norwich Assizes Act 1746 (c.21)
Norwich and Swaffham Road Act 1770 (c.67)
Norwich and Thetford Road Act 1725 (c.22)
Norwich and Thetford Road Act 1746 (c.16)
Norwich and Watton Road Act 1770 (c.77)
Norwich Mayors, Sheriffs, etc. 1922 (c.9)
Norwich Roads Act 1790 (c.86)
Norwich to Bixley Roads Act 1790 (c.85)
Norwich to New Buckingham Road Act 1772 (c.95)

Norwich to Scole Bridge Road Act 1969 (c.66)
Norwich to Scole Bridge Road Act 1772 (c.76)
Norwich to Thetford Road Act 1792 (c.111)
Norwich to Swaffham Road Act 1792 (c.112)
Norwich to Yarmouth Road Act 1969 (c.68)
Norwich Water Act 1790 (c.21)
Norwich Workhouse Act 1711 (c.15)
Notice of Accidents Act 1906 (c.53)
Notification of Births Act 1907 (c.40)
Notification of Births (Extension) Act 1915 (c.64)
Nottingham Roads Act 1770 (c.92)
Nottingham Roads Act 1774 (c.101)
Nottingham Roads Act 1785 (c.107)
Nottingham and Derby Road Act 1758 (c.38)
Nottingham and Derby Roads Act 1764 (c.83)
Nottingham and Derby Roads Act 1765 (c.90)
Nottingham and Derby Roads Act 1783 (c.24)
Nottingham and Derby Roads Act 1788 (c.87)
Nottingham and Derby Roads Act 1788 (c.99)
Nottingham and Leicester Highways Act 1721 (c.13)
Nottingham and Leicester Roads Act 1737 (c.3)
Nottingham and Leicester Roads Act 1754 (c.22)
Nottingham and Lincoln Roads Act 1765 (c.85)
Nottingham Canal Act 1792 (c.100)
Nottingham, Leicester, Rutland and Northampton Roads Act 1780 (c.81)
Nottingham: Lighting etc. Act 1762 (c.47)
Nottingham Roads Act 1765 (c.54)
Nottingham Roads Act 1791 (c.131)
Nottingham Roads Act 1791 (c.132)
Nottingham, Shire Hall Act 1769 (c.62)
Nottingham to Mansfield Road Act 1787 (c.76)
Nuclear Industry (Finance) Act 1977 (c.7)
Nuclear Industry (Finance) Act 1981 (c.71)
Nuclear Installations Act 1959 (c.46)
Nuclear Installations Act 1965 (c.57)
Nuclear Installations Act 1969 (c.18)
Nuclear Installations (Amendment) Act 1965 (c.6)
Nuclear Materials (Offences) Act 1983 (c.18)
Nuclear Safeguards and Electricity (Finance) Act 1978 (c.25)
Nuisances Removal (Scotland) Act 1856 (c.103)
Nullity of Marriage Act 1971 (c.44)
Nurseries and Child Minders Regulation Act 1948 (c.53)
Nurses Act 1943 (c.17)
Nurses Act 1945 (c.6)
Nurses Act 1949 (c.73)
Nurses Act 1957 (c.15)
Nurses Act 1964 (c.44)
Nurses Act 1969 (c.47)
Nurses Registration Act 1919 (c.94)
Nurses Registration (Ireland) Act 1919 (c.96)
Nurses Registration (Scotland) Act 1919 (c.95)

Nurses (Scotland) Act 1943 (c.33)
Nurses (Scotland) Act 1949 (c.95)
Nurses (Scotland) Act (c.55)
Nurses Agencies Act 1957 (c.16)
Nurses (Amendment) Act 1961 (c.14)
Nurses, Midwives and Health Visitors Act 1979 (c.36)
Nurses, Midwives and Health Visitors Act 1992 (c.16)
Nurses (Scotland) Act 1951 (c.55)
Nursing Homes Act 1963 (c.13)
Nursing Homes Act 1975 (c.37)
Nursing Homes Registration Act 1927 (c.38)
Nursing Homes Registration (Scotland) Act 1938 (c.73)

OECD Support Fund Act 1975 (c.80)
Oakham Canal Act 1793 (c.103)
Oakhampton Roads Act 1782 (c.92)
Oaths, etc. Act 1714 (c.3)
Oaths Act 1775 (c.39)
Oaths Act 1838 (c.105)
Oaths Act 1888 (c.46)
Oaths Act 1909 (c.39)
Oaths Act 1961 (c.21)
Oaths Act 1978 (c.19)
Oaths and Evidence (Overseas Authorities) (Land) Act 1963 (c.27)
Oaths at Parliamentary Elections Act 1794 (c.84)
Oaths of Justices of the Peace Act 1745 (c.13)
Obscene Publications Act 1857 (c.83)
Obscene Publications Act 1959 (c.66)
Obscene Publications Act 1964 (c.74)
Observance of Lord's Day by Bakers Act 1794 (c.61)
Obtaining Money by False Pretences, etc. Act 1757 (c.24)
Occasional Licences and Young Persons 1956 (c.42)
Occupiers' Liability Act 1957 (c.31)
Occupiers' Liability Act 1984 (c.3)
Occupier's Liability (Scotland) Act 1960 (c.30)
Odiham to Farnham Roads Act 1789 (c.89)
Offences Against Customs and Excise Laws Act 1935 (c.35)
Offences Against Customs or Excise Act 1745 (c.34)
Offences Against Excise Laws Act 1758 (c.17)
Offences Against Excise Laws Act 1791 (c.10)
Offences Against the Person Act 1861 (c.100)
Offences Against Persons and Property Act 1936 (c.32)
Offences at Sea Act 1806 (c.54)
Offenders (Conveyance) Act 1753 (c.3)
Offices Act 1960 (c.47)
Office and Oath Act 1867 (c.75)

Offices of Court of Chancery Act 1792 (c.42)
Offices, Shops and Railway Premises Act 1963 (c.41)
Officers of Inland Revenue Act (1849) (c.58)
Officer of Late Wine Licences Office Act 1791 (c.28)
Officers of the Royal Naval Reserve Act 1863 (c.69)
Official Secrets Act 1911 (c.28)
Official Secrets Act 1920 (c.75)
Official Secrets Act 1939 (c.121)
Official Secrets Act 1989 (c.6)
Official Solicitor Act 1919 (c.30)
Offshore Petroleum Development (Scotland) Act 1975 (c.8)
Offshore Safety Act 1992 (c.15)
Offshore Safety (Protection against Victimisation) Act 1992 (c.24)
Oil and Gas (Enterprise) Act 1982 (c.23)
Oil and Pipelines Act 1985 (c.62)
Oil in Navigable Waters Act 1922 (c.39)
Oil Burners (Standards) Act 1960 (c.53)
Oil in Navigable Waters Act 1963 (c.28)
Oil in Navigable Waters Act 1955 (c.25)
Oil in Navigable Waters Act 1971 (c.21)
Oil in Tobacco Act 1900 (c.35)
Oil Taxation Act 1975 (c.22)
Oil Taxation Act 1983 (c.56)
Okehampton Roads Act 1759 (c.36)
Old Age and Widows Pensions Act 1940 (c.13)
Old Age Pensions Act 1908 (c.40)
Old Age Pensions Act 1911 (c.16)
Old Age Pensions Act 1919 (c.102)
Old Age Pensions Act 1924 (c.33)
Old Age Pensions Act 1936 (c.31)
Old Age and Widows' Pensions Act 1940 (c.13)
Old Brentford Bridge Act 1757 (c.63)
Old Brentford Bridge Act 1757 (c.46)
Old Palace Yard Act 1966 (c.32)
Old Shoreham, Bridge, Sussex Act 1780 (c.35)
Old Stratford to Dunchurch Road Act 1757 (c.57)
Old Stratford to Dunchurch Road Act 1775 (c.73)
Old Street Road Act 1753 (c.87)
Old Street Road Act 1756 (c.44)
Old Street Road Act 1772 (c.99)
Old Street Road Act 1789 (c.82)
Old Swineford: Small Debts Act 1776 (c.19)
Oldham to Alton Road Act 1793 (c.182)
Opencast Coal Act 1958 (c.69)
Open Spaces Act 1887 (c.32)
Open Spaces Act 1906 (c.25)
Open Space Act 1986 (c.38)
Opticians Act 1958 (c.32)
Opticians Act 1989 (c.44)
Orders, etc. of the Master of the Rolls Act 1730 (c.30)
Ordination of Aliens Act 1783 (c.35)
Ordnance Board Transfer Act 1855 (c.117)

Paper Duties Act 1786 (c.78)
Paper Duties Act 1794 (c.20)
Papists Act 1715 (c.55)
Papists Act 1716 (c.18)
Papists Act 1722 (c.24)
Papists Act 1723 (c.4)
Papists Act 1732 (c.5)
Papists Act 1734 (c.25)
Papists Act 1737 (c.11)
Papists Act 1738 (c.14)
Papists Act 1740 (c.21)
Papists Act 1745 (c.16)
Papists Act 1753 (c.24)
Papists Act 1755 (c.10)
Papists Act 1757 (c.21)
Papists Act 1759 (c.13)
Papists Act 1762 (c.26)
Papists Act 1763 (c.38)
Papists Act 1766 (c.34)
Papists Act 1772 (c.10)
Papists Act 1774 (c.37)
Papists Act 1776 (c.45)
Papists Act 1778 (c.46)
Papists Act 1778 (c.60)
Papists Act 1780 (c.51)
Papists Act 1782 (c.23)
Papists Act 1783 (c.22)
Papists Act 1783 (c.16)
Papists Act 1787 (c.42)
Papists Act 1788 (c.47)
Papists Act 1789 (c.36)
Papists Act 1790 (c.19)
Papua New Guinea, Western Samoa and Nauru (Miscellaneous Provisions) Act 1980 (c.2)
Parish Apprentices Act 1778 (c.47)
Parish Apprentices Act 1792 (c.57)
Parish Church of St. Marylebone Act 1770 (c.112)
Parish Councils Act 1957 (c.42)
Parish Councils and Burial Authorities (Miscellaneous Provisions) Act 1970 (c.29)
Parish of The Trinity, Coventry Act 1779 (c.57)
Parish Officers Act 1793 (c.55)
Parish: Spittlefields, Stepney Act 1727 (c.10)
Park Lane Improvement Act 1958 (c.63)
Parking·Act 1989 (c.16)
Parks Regulation Act 1872 (c.15)
Parks Regulation (Amendment) Act 1926 (c.36)
Parks Regulation (Amendment) Act 1974 (c.29)
Parliament Act 1710 (c.5)
Parliament Act 1712 (cc.5,6)
Parliament Act 1712 (c.16)
Parliament Act 1775 (c.36)
Parliament Act 1780 (c.1)
Parliament Act 1780 (c.50)
Parliament Act 1780 (c.43)
Parliament Act 1782 (c.29)
Parliament Act 1782 (c.41)
Parliament Act 1911 (c.13)

Parliament Act 1949 (c.103)
Parliament of Canada Act 1875 (c.38)
Parliament and Local Elections Act 1916 (c.44)
Parliament and Local Elections Act 1917 (c.13)
Parliament and Local Elections Act 1918 (c.22)
Parliament and Local Elections (No.2) Act 1917 (c.50)
Parliament and Registration Act 1916 (c.100)
Parliament (Elections and Meeting) Act 1943 (c.48)
Parliament (Qualification of Women) Act 1918 (c.47)
Parliamentary and Health Service Commissioners Act 1987 (c.39)
Parliamentary and Other Pensions Act 1972 (c.48)
Parliamentary and Other Pensions Act 1987 (c.45)
Parliamentary and Other Pensions and Salaries Act 1976 (c.48)
Parliamentary Commissioner Act 1967 (c.13)
Parliamentary Commissioner Act 1994 (c.14)
Parliamentary Commissioner (Consular Complaints) Act 1981 (c.11)
Parliamentary Constituencies Act 1986 (c.56)
Parliamentary Corporate Bodies Act 1992 (c.27)
Parliamentary Documents Deposit Act 1837 (c.83)
Parliamentary Elections Act 1734 (c.30)
Parliamentary Elections Act 1742 (c.11)
Parliamentary Elections Act 1744 (c.18)
Parliamentary Elections Act 1745 (c.28)
Parliamentary Elections Act 1757 (c.14)
Parliamentary Elections Act 1763 (c.24)
Parliamentary Elections Act 1770 (c.16)
Parliamentary Elections Act 1770 (c.41)
Parliamentary Elections Act 1771 (c.42)
Parliamentary Elections Act 1774 (c.15)
Parliamentary Elections Act 1774 (c.58)
Parliamentary Elections Act 1774 (c.81)
Parliamentary Elections Act 1780 (c.17)
Parliamentary Elections Act 1785 (c.84)
Parliamentary Elections Act 1790 (c.35)
Parliamentary Elections Act 1793 (c.64)
Parliamentary Elections Act 1795 (c.65)
Parliamentary Elections Act 1868 (c.125)
Parliamentary Elections, Cricklade Act 1782 (c.31)
Parliamentary Elections (Fraudulent Conveyances) Act 1739 (c.20)
Parliamentary Elections, New Shoreham Act 1771 (c.55)
Parliamentary Elections, Norwich 1730 (c.8)
Parliamentary Elections (Returning Officers) Act (1875) Amendment Act 1886 (c.57)
Parliamentary Elections Corrupt Practices Act 1879 (c.75)
Parliamentary Elections (Scotland) Act (c.16)

Parliamentary Elections (Soldiers) Act 1919 (c.10)
Parliamentary Electors (War-time Registration) Act 1944 (c.24)
Parliamentary Papers Act 1840 (c.9)
Parliamentary Pensions Act 1978 (c.56)
Parliamentary Pensions etc. Act 1984 (c.52)
Parliamentary Privilege Act 1770 (c.50)
Parliamentary Privilege Act 1937 (c.24)
Parliamentary Witnesses Act 1858 (c.78)
Parliamentary Witnesses Oaths Act 1871 (c.83)
Parochial Libraries Act 1708 (c.14)
Parochial Registers Act 1812 (c.146)
Parsonages Act 1838 (c.23)
Parsonages Act 1911 (c.29)
Participation Agreements Act 1978 (c.1)
Partition Act 1868 (c.40)
Partnership Act 1890 (c.39)
Parton, Cumberland, Harbour Act 1724 (c.16)
Parton Harbour, Cumberland Act 1731 (c.13)
Partridges Act 1799 (c.34)
Party Processions (Ireland) Act 1832 (c.118)
Party Processions (Ireland) Act 1844 (c.63)
Passage from Charing Cross Act 1757 (c.36)
Passenger Ships Act 1845 (c.14)
Passenger Vehicles (Experimental Areas) Act 1977 (c.21)
Patent Law Amendment Act 1852 (c.83)
Patents Act 1901 (c.18)
Patents Act 1902 (c.34)
Patents Act 1949 (c.87)
Patents Act 1957 (c.13)
Patents Act 1977 (c.37)
Patents and Designs Act 1907 (c.29)
Patents and Designs Act 1908 (c.4)
Patents and Designs Act 1914 (c.18)
Patents and Designs Act 1919 (c.80)
Patents and Designs Act 1927 (c.3)
Patents and Designs Act 1932 (c.32)
Patents and Designs Act 1942 (c.6)
Patents and Designs Act 1946 (c.44)
Patents and Designs Act 1949 (c.62)
Patents and Designs (Amendment) Act 1907 (c.28)
Patents and Designs (Limits of Time) Act 1939 (c.32)
Patents and Designs (Partial Suspension) Act 1915 (c.85)
Patents and Designs (Renewals, Extensions and Fees) Act 1961 (c.25)
Patents, Designs and Marks Act 1986 (c.39)
Patents, Designs and Trade Marks Act 1883 (c.57)
Patents, Designs and Trade Marks (Temporary Rules) Act 1914 (c.27)
Patents, Designs and Trade Marks (Temporary Rules) Amendment 1914 (c.73)
Patents, Designs, Copyright and Trade Marks (Emergency) Act 1939 (c.107)
Patents etc. (International Conventions) Act 1938 (c.29)

Patriotic Fund Act 1866 (c.120)
Patriotic Fund Reorganisation Act 1903 (c.20)
Pauper Children (Ireland) Act 1902 (c.16)
Paving, etc. of London Act 1768 (c.21)
Pawnbrokers Act 1784 (c.42)
Pawnbrokers Act 1785 (c.48)
Pawnbrokers Act 1787 (c.37)
Pawnbrokers Act 1788 (c.50)
Pawnbrokers Act 1789 (c.57)
Pawnbrokers Act 1791 (c.52)
Pawnbrokers Act 1793 (c.53)
Pawnbrokers Act 1872 (c.93)
Pawnbrokers Act 1922 (c.5)
Pawnbrokers Act 1960 (c.24)
Paymaster General Act 1782 (c.81)
Paymaster General Act 1783 (c.50)
Paymaster General Act 1835 (c.35)
Paymaster General Act 1848 (c.55)
Paymaster General, Balance, etc. Act 1780 (c.48)
Payment of Certain Regiments Act 1705 (c.12)
Payment of Charges of Constables Act 1778 (c.19)
Payment of Creditors (Scotland) Act 1780 (c.41)
Payment of Creditors (Scotland) Act 1783 (c.18)
Payment of Creditors (Scotland) Act 1789 (c.5)
Payment of Creditors (Scotland) Act 1793 (c.74)
Payment of Creditors (Scotland) Act 1804 (c.24)
Payment of Creditors (Scotland) Act 1813 (c.65)
Payment of Lace Makers' Wages Act 1779 (c.49)
Payment of Wages Act 1960 (c.37)
Pedlars Act 1871 (c.96)
Peebles Road Act 1753 (c.93)
Peebles Road Act 1771 (c.85)
Peebles Road Act 1775 (c.71)
Peebles Roads Act 1792 (c.123)
Peerage Act 1963 (c.48)
Pembroke Gaol Act 1779 (c.46)
Pembroke Road Act 1771 (c.96)
Pembroke Roads Act 1788 (c.102)
Pembroke Roads Act 1790 (c.91)
Pembroke Roads Act 1791 (c.102)
Pembroke Roads Act 1791 (c.109)
Pembroke Roads Act 1791 (c.126)
Penal Servitude Act 1891 (c.69)
Penal Servitude Act 1926 (c.58)
Penalties for Drunkenness Act 1962 (c.52)
Penicillin Act 1947 (c.29)
Penicillin (Merchant Ships) 1951 (c.13)
Penitentiary for Convicts Act 1794 (c.84)
Penny Post Act 1794 (c.17)
Pension Duties Act 1720 (c.27)
Pension Duties Act 1725 (c.2)
Pension Duties Act 1757 (c.22)

Pension Duties Act 1758 (c.33)

Pension Schemes Act 1993 (c.48)

Pension Schemes (Northern Ireland) Act 1993 (c.49)

Pensioners and Family Income Supplement Payments Act 1972 (c.75)

Pensioners' Payments Act 1974 (c.54)

Pensioners Payments Act 1977 (c.51)

Pensioners Payments Act 1978 (c.58)

Pensioners' Payments and National Insurance Act 1973 (c.61)

Pensioners' Payments and National Insurance Contributions Act 1972 (c.80)

Pensioners' Payments and Social Security Act 1979 (c.48)

Pensions Act 1839 (c.51)

Pensions and Determination of Needs Act 1943 (c.27)

Pensions and Yeomanry Pay Act 1884 (c.55)

Pensions Appeal Tribunals Act 1943 (c.39)

Pensions Appeal Tribunals Act 1949 (c.12)

Pensions Commutation Act 1871 (c.36)

Pensions Commutation Act 1882 (c.44)

Pensions Commutation Act 1984 (c.7)

Pensions (Governors of Dominions, etc.) Act 1911 (c.24)

Pensions (Governors of Dominions, etc.) Act 1929 (c.16)

Pensions (Governors of Dominions, etc.) Act 1936 (c.25)

Pensions (Governors of Dominions, etc.) Act 1947 (c.12)

Pensions (Governors of Dominions, etc.) Amendment 1913 (c.26)

Pensions (Increase) Act 1920 (c.36)

Pensions (Increase) Act 1924 (c.32)

Pensions (Increase) Act 1944 (c.21)

Pensions (Increase) Act 1946 (c.7)

Pensions (Increase) Act 1952 (c.45)

Pensions (Increase) Act 1954 (c.25)

Pensions (Increase) Act 1956 (c.39)

Pensions (Increase) Act 1962 (c.2)

Pensions (Increase) Act 1965 (c.78)

Pensions (Increase) Act 1969 (c.7)

Pensions (Increase) Act 1971 (c.56)

Pensions (Increase) Act 1974 (c.9)

Pensions (India, Pakistan and Burma) Act 1955 (c.22)

Pensions (Mercantile Marine) Act 1942 (c.26)

Pensions (Miscellaneous Provisions) Act 1990 (c.7)

Pensions (Navy, Army, Air Force and Mercantile Marine) Act 1939 (c.83)

Pensions to Seamen, etc. Act 1814 (c.1)

Performers' Protection Act 1963 (c.53)

Performers' Protection Act 1972 (c.32)

Performing Animals (Regulation) Act 1925 (c.38)

Perjury Act 1727 (c.25)

Perjury Act 1911 (c.6)

Perpetuation and Amendment of Acts 1904 (c.16)

Perpetuation, etc. of Acts 1708 (c.25)

Perpetuation of Acts, etc. Act 1719 (c.19)

Perpetuation of Testimony Act 1842 (c.69)

Perpetuation of Various Laws Act 1732 (c.37)

Perpetuities and Accumulations Act 1964 (c.55)

Persons Going Armed or Disguised Act 1758 (c.18)

Persons Going Armed and Disguised Act 1754 (c.15)

Personal Injuries (Emergency Provisions) Act 1939 (c.82)

Persuading Soldiers to Desert, etc. Act 1715 (c.47)

Perth: Highways and Bridge Act 1785 (c.13)

Perth Roads Act 1753 (c.91)

Perth Roads Act 1765 (c.89)

Perth Roads Act 1789 (c.17)

Perth Roads Act 1793 (c.158)

Pesticides (Fees and Enforcement) Act 1989 (c.27)

Pests Act 1954 (c.68)

Pet Animals Act 1951 (c.35)

Pet Animals Act 1951 (Amendment) Act 1983 (c.26)

Peterborough: Streets Act 1790 (c.66)

Petersham: Streets Act 1772 (c.42)

Petersfield Highways Act 1710 (c.33(f))

Petersfield to Portsmouth Road Act 1725 (c.19)

Petroleum Act 1879 (c.47)

Petroleum Act 1926 (c.25)

Petroleum Act 1975 (c.74)

Petroleum Act 1987 (c.12)

Petroleum (Amendment) 1928 (c.21)

Petroleum and Submarine Pipelines Act 1975 (c.74)

Petroleum (Consolidation) Act 1928 (c.32)

Petroleum (Production) Act 1918 (c.52)

Petroleum (Production) Act 1934 (c.36)

Petroleum Revenue Tax Act 1980 (c.1)

Petroleum Royalties (Relief) Act 1983 (c.59)

Petroleum Royalties (Relief) and Continental Shelf Act 1989 (c.1)

Petroleum Royalties (Relief) Act 1983 (c.59)

Petroleum (Transfer of Licences) Act 1936 (c.27)

Petty Sessions Act 1849 (c.18)

Petty Sessions Clerks and Fines (Ireland) Act 1878 (c.69)

Petty Sessions (Ireland) Act 1851 (c.93)

Petty Sessions Clerk (Ireland) (Amendment) Act 1901 (c.22)

Pharmacy Act 1929 (c.31)

Pharmacy Act 1953 (c.19)

Pharmacy Act 1954 (c.61)

Pharmacy and Medicines Act 1941 (c.42)

Pharmacy and Poisons Act 1933 (c.25)

Pharmacy and Poisons (Amendment) Act 1964 (c.35)

Physical Training and Recreation Act 1937 (c.46)

Physical Training and Recreation Act 1958 (c.36)

Piccadilly Act 1844 (c.88)
Piccadilly; Watering Act 1775 (c.57)
Pig Industry Levy Act 1983 (c.4)
Pilchard Fisheries Act 1791 (c.45)
Pilchard Fishery Act 1785 (c.58)
Pilchard Fishery Act 1786 (c.45)
Pilchard Fishery, Cornwall Act 1776 (c.36)
Pillory Abolition Act 1816 (c.138)
Pilotage Act 1716 (c.13)
Pilotage Act 1731 (c.20)
Pilotage Act 1913 (c.31)
Pilotage Act 1983 (c.21)
Pilotage Act 1987 (c.21)
Pilotage Authorities (Limitation of Liability) Act 1936 (c.36)
Pipelines Act 1962 (c.58)
Piracy Act 1717 (c.11)
Piracy Act 1721 (c.24)
Piracy Act 1744 (c.30)
Piracy Act 1837 (c.88)
Pistols Act 1903 (c.18)
Pittenweem Beer Duties Act 1719 (c.9)
Places of Religious Worship Act 1812 (c.155)
Places of Worship (Enfranchisement) Act 1920 (c.56)
Places of Worship Registration Act 1855 (c.81)
Planning and Compensation Act 1991 (c.34)
Planning (Consequential Provisions) Act 1990 (c.11)
Planning (Hazardous Substances) Act 1990 (c.10)
Planning Inquiries (Attendance of Public) Act 1982 (c.21)
Planning (Listed Buildings and Conservation Areas) Act 1990 (c.9)
Plant Health Act 1967 (c.8)
Plant Varieties Act 1983 (c.17)
Plant Varieties and Seeds Act 1964 (c.14)
Plantation Trade etc., Act 1741 (c.31)
Plate Act 1696 (c.8)
Plate Assay Act 1700 (c.3)
Plate Assay (Sheffield) Act 1784 (c.20)
Plate Assay (Sheffield and Birmingham) Act 1772 (c.52)
Plate Duties Act 1784 (c.53)
Plate (Duties, Drawbacks) Act 1785 (c.64)
Plate Duty Act 1719 (c.11)
Plate (Duty on Dealer's Licence) Act 1757 (c.32)
Plate (Duty on Dealer's Licence) Act 1757 (c.24)
Plate Glass Manufacture Act 1772 (c.38)
Plate (Offences) Act 1738 (c.26)
Plate (Offences) Act 1772 (c.59)
Plate (Scotland) Act 1836 (c.69)
Plays and Wine Licences 1736 (c.28)
Pleading Act 1711 (c.28)
Pleading in Misdemeanour Act 1819 (c.4)
Pluralities Act 1838 (c.106)
Pluralities Act 1850 (c.98)
Pluralities Act 1887 (c.68)
Pluralities of Living Act 1801 (c.102)

Plymouth and Portsmouth Fortifications Act 1758 (c.30)
Plymouth Dock Act 1766 (c.102)
Plymouth Dock to Torpoint: Ferry Act 1790 (c.61)
Plymouth: Fortifications Act 1774 (c.50)
Plymouth Fortifications Act 1781 (c.61)
Plymouth Fortifications Act 1782 (c.12)
Plymouth Improvement Act 1770 (c.14)
Plymouth Improvement Act 1772 (c.8)
Plymouth: Poor Relief Act 1758 (c.59)
Plymouth: Poor Relief Act 1786 (c.19)
Plymouth: Poor Relief etc, Act 1781 (c.72)
Plymouth, Sheerness, Gravesend, Tilbury- Fortifications Act 1780 (c.38)
Plymouth: Streets Act 1774 (c.8)
Plymouth Water Supply Act 1793 (c.85)
Plymouth Workhouse 1707 (c.46(d))
Pneumoconiosis and Byssinosis Benefit Act 1951 (c.4)
Pneumoconiosis etc. (Workers' Compensation) Act 1979 (c.41)
Poaching Prevention Act 1862 (c.114)
Poisons Act 1972 (c.66)
Poisons and Pharmacy Act 1908 (c.55)
Polehampton Estates Act 1885 (c.40)
Police Act 1909 (c.40)
Police Act 1919 (c.46)
Police Act 1964 (c.48)
Police Act 1969 (c.63)
Police Act 1972 (c.39)
Police Act 1976 (c.46)
Police and Criminal Evidence Act 1984 (c.60)
Police and Firemen (War Service) Act 1939 (c.103)
Police and Firemen (War Service) Act 1944 (c.22)
Police and Magistrates' Courts Act 1994 (c.29)
Police (Appeals) Act 1927 (c.19)
Police (Appeals) Act 1943 (c.8)
Police Army Act 1946 (c.46)
Police Constables (Naval and Military Service) Act 1914 (c.80)
Police Constables (Naval and Military Service) Act 1917 (c.36)
Police (Emergency Provisions) Act 1915 (c.41)
Police Factories, etc. (Miscellaneous Provisions) Act 1916 (c.31)
Police Federation Act 1959 (c.38)
Police Federations Act 1962 (c.25)
Police Federation Act 1961 (c.51)
Police, Fire and Probation Officers' Remuneration Act 1956 (c.1)
Police (His Majesty's Inspectors of Constabulary) Act 1945 (c.11)
Police (Liverpool Inquiry) Act 1909 (c.35)
Police Magistrates (Superannuation) Act 1915 (c.74)
Police Magistrates Superannuation Amendment Act 1929 (c.37)
Police Negotiating Board Act 1980 (c.10)

Police Officers (Central Service) Act 1989 (c.11)

Police (Overseas Service) Act 1945 (c.17)

Police (Pensions) Act 1918 (c.51)

Police (Pensions) Act 1921 (c.31)

Police Pensions Act 1926 (c.34)

Police Pensions Act 1948 (c.24)

Police Pensions Act 1961 (c.35)

Police Pensions Act 1976 (c.35)

Police (Property) Act 1897 (c.30)

Police Revenue and Consolidated Fund Charges Act 1854 (c.94)

Police (Scotland) Act 1857 (c.72)

Police (Scotland) Act 1856 (c.26)

Police (Scotland) Act 1890 (c.67)

Police (Scotland) Act 1946 (c.71)

Police (Scotland) Act 1966 (c.52)

Police (Scotland) Act 1967 (c.77)

Police (Scotland) Act (1890) Amendment Act 1910 (c.10)

Police (Scotland) (Limit of Age) Act 1914 (c.69)

Police Reservists Act 1902 (c.10)

Police Reservists (Allowances) Act 1900 (c.9)

Police Reservists (Allowances) Act 1914 (c.34)

Police (Superannuation) Act 1906 (c.7)

Police (Superannuation) Act 1908 (c.5)

Police (Weekly Rest Day) Act 1910 (c.13)

Police (Weekly Rest Day) (Scotland) Act 1914 (c.8)

Policing of Airports Act 1974 (c.41)

Policyholders Protection Act 1975 (c.75)

Polish Resettlement Act 1947 (c.19)

Polling Arrangements (Parliamentary Boroughs) Act 1908 (c.14)

Polling Districts (County Councils) Act 1908 (c.13)

Polling Districts and Registration of Voters (Ireland) Act 1908 (c.35)

Ponies Act 1969 (c.28)

Pool Betting Act 1954 (c.33)

Pool Competitions Act 1971 (c.57)

Pool Harbour Act 1756 (c.10)

Poole Roads Act 1756 (c.52)

Poole Roads Act 1757 (c.52)

Poole Roads Act 1757 (c.66)

Poole Roads Act 1777 (c.104)

Poole to Blandford Road Act 1777 (c.86)

Poor Act 1762 (c.22)

Poor Act 1766 (c.39)

Poor Act 1776 (c.40)

Poor Act 1793 (c.35)

Poor Act 1912 (c.18)

Poor Apprentices Act 1780 (c.36)

Poor Law Act 1927 (c.14)

Poor Law Act 1930 (c.17)

Poor Law Act 1934 (c.59)

Poor Law Amendment Act 1844 (c.101)

Poor Law (Amendment) Act 1938 (c.23)

Poor Law Authorities (Transfer of Property) Act 1904 (c.20)

Poor Law (Dissolution of School Districts and Adjustments) Act 1903 (c.19)

Poor Law Emergency Provisions (Scotland) Act 1921 (c.64)

Poor Law Emergency Provisions (Scotland) Act 1927 (c.3)

Poor Law Emergency Provisions Continuance (Scotland) Act 1924 (c.9)

Poor Law Emergency Provisions Continuance (Scotland) Act 1925 (c.35)

Poor Law, Hull Act 1709 (c.24)

Poor Law Officers' Superannuation Act 1896 (c.50)

Poor Law (Scotland) Act 1934 (c.52)

Poor Persons 1495 (c.12)

Poor Prisoners' Defence Act 1903 (c.38)

Poor Prisoners' Defence Act 1930 (c.32)

Poor Prisoners Relief Act 1737 (c.20)

Poor Prisoners (Scotland) Act 1825 (c.62)

Poor Rate Act 1743 (c.3)

Poor Rate Exemption Act 1833 (c.30)

Poor Relief Act 1722 (c.7)

Poor Relief Act 1743 (c.38)

Poor Relief Act 1769 (c.37)

Poor Relief (Deserted Wives and Children) Act 1718 (c.8)

Poor Relief: Gloucester Act 1726 (c.19)

Poor Relief (Ireland) Act 1838 (c.56)

Poor Relief (Ireland) Act 1849 (c.104)

Poor Relief (Ireland) Act 1900 (c.45)

Poor Relief (Ireland) Act 1914 (c.14)

Poor Removal Act 1900 (c.23)

Poor, Staffordshire Act 1791 (c.20)

Population (Statistics) Act 1938 (c.13)

Population (Statistics) Act 1960 (c.32)

Porcelain Patent Act 1775 (c.52)

Port Glasgow Harbour Act 1772 (c.16)

Port of Liverpool Act 1766 (c.61)

Port of London (Financial Assistance) Act 1980 (c.31)

Portman Square: Improvement Act 1782 (c.85)

Ports Act 1991 (c.52)

Ports (Finance) Act 1985 (c.30)

Ports (Financial Assistance) Act 1981 (c.21)

Ports (Reduction of Debt) Act 1983 (c.22)

Portsea Chapel Act 1787 (c.64)

Portsea Common Chapel Act 1753 (c.58)

Portsea: Improvement Act 1792 (c.103)

Portsmouth, Chatham Fortifications Act 1782 (c.80)

Portsmouth, Chatham Fortifications Act 1783 (c.71)

Portsmouth, Faversham Fortifications Act 1783 (c.87)

Portsmouth Improvement Act 1768 (c.62)

Portsmouth, Plymouth Fortifications Act 1784 (c.29)

Portsmouth: Streets Act 1776 (c.59)

Portsmouth Water Supply (Farlington) Act 1740 (c.43)

Possession of Mortgaged Land (Emergency Provisions) Act 1939 (c.108)

Postage Act 1730 (c.33)
Postage Act 1763 (c.24)
Postage Act 1765 (c.25)
Postage Act 1782 (c.70)
Postage Act 1783 (c.69)
Postage Act 1784 (c.8)
Postage Act 1787 (c.9)
Postage Act 1794 (c.18)
Postage Act 1796 (c.18)
Postage Act 1805 (c.11)
Postage Act 1805 (c.21)
Post Fines Act 1758 (c.14)
Post Horse Duties Act 1787 (c.26)
Post Horse Duties Act 1790 (c.23)
Post Horse Duties Act 1793 (c.71)
Post Horse Duties Act 1796 (c.84)
Post Office Act 1748 (c.25)
Post Office Act 1904 (c.14)
Post Office Act 1908 (c.48)
Post Office Act 1913 (c.11)
Post Office Act 1918 (c.10)
Post Office Act 1953 (c.36)
Post Office Act 1961 (c.15)
Post Office Act 1969 (c.48)
Post Office Act 1977 (c.44)
Post Office (Amendment) Act 1935 (c.15)
Post Office and Telegraph Act 1915 (c.82)
Post Office and Telegraph Act 1920 (c.40)
Post Office and Telegraph Act 1940 (c.25)
Post Office and Telegraph (Money) Act 1928 (c.37)
Post Office and Telegraph (Money) Act 1931 (c.20)
Post Office and Telegraph (Money) Act 1935 (c.14)
Post Office and Telegraph (Money) Act 1937 (c.51)
Post Office and Telegraph (Money) Act 1939 (c.42)
Post Office and Telegraph (Money) Act 1942 (c.24)
Post Office and Telegraph (Money) Act 1946 (c.51)
Post Office and Telegraph (Money) Act 1947 (c.16)
Post Office and Telegraph (Money) Act 1950 (c.2)
Post Office and Telegraph (Money) Act 1952 (c.34)
Post Office and Telegraph (Money) Act 1953 (c.4)
Post Office and Telegraph (Money) Act 1955 (c.14)
Post Office and Telegraph (Money) Act 1957 (c.5)
Post Office and Telegraph (Money) Act 1950 (c.2)
Post Office (Banking Services) Act 1976 (c.10)
Post Office (Borrowing Powers) Act 1967 (c.15)
Post Office (Borrowing Powers) Act 1972 (c.79)

Post Office (Data Processing Service) Act 1967 (c.62)
Post Office (Literature for the Blind) Act 1906 (c.22)
Post Office (Money Orders) Act 1903 (c.12)
Post Office (Money Orders) Act 1906 (c.4)
Post Office Offences and Isle of Man Postage Act 1767 (c.50)
Post Office (Parcels) Act 1922 (c.49)
Post Office (Pneumatic Tubes Acquisition) Act 1922 (c.43)
Post Office (Protection) Act 1884 (c.76)
Post Office (Revenues) Act 1710 (c.11(p))
Post Office Savings Bank Act 1908 (c.8)
Post Office Savings Bank Act 1954 (c.62)
Post Office Savings Bank Act 1965 (c.12)
Post Office Savings Bank (Public Trustee) Act 1908 (c.52)
Post Office (Subway) Act 1966 (c.25)
Post Office Works Act 1959 (c.43)
Post Roads in Scotland Act 1951 (c.28)
Post Works Loans Act 1957 (c.4)
Postponement of Enactments (Miscellaneous Provisions) Act 1939 (c.2)
Postponement of Payments Act 1914 (c.11)
Postponement of Polling Day Act 1945 (c.40)
Pot and Pearl Ashes Act 1750 (c.51)
Poultry Act 1911 (c.11)
Powers of Attorney Act 1971 (c.27)
Powers of Criminal Courts Act 1973 (c.62)
Prescription Act 1832 (c.71)
Prescription and Limitation (Scotland) Act 1973 (c.52)
Prescription and Limitation (Scotland) Act 1984 (c.45)
Prescription (Scotland) Act 1987 (c.36)
Presentation of Benefices Act 1713 (c.13)
Preservation of Fish and Conies Act 1965 (c.14)
Preservation of House Doves, etc. Act 1762 (c.29)
Preservation of Roads Act 1740 (c.42)
Preservation of Timber Act 1772 (c.33)
Preservation of Timber Trees Act 1715 (c.48)
Preservation of Timber Trees Act 1766 (c.48)
Preservation of Timber Trees (Scotland) Act 1719 (c.16)
Preservation of Trees, America Act 1710 (c.22)
Preservation of Woods, America Act 1728 (c.35)
President of the Board of Trade 1932 (c.21)
Presteigne Road Act 1756 (c.94)
Preston Bridge Act 1757 (c.55)
Prestonpans Beer Duties Act 1753 (c.79)
Prestonpans Beer Duties Act 1757 (c.52)
Presumption of Death (Scotland) Act 1977 (c.27)
Presumption of Life Limitation (Scotland) Act 1891 (c.29)
Prevention and Treatment of Blindness (Scotland) Act 1938 (c.32)
Prevention of Corruption Act 1906 (c.34)

Prevention of Corruption Act 1916 (c.64)
Prevention of Crimes Act 1871 (c.112)
Prevention of Crime Act 1908 (c.59)
Prevention of Crime Act 1953 (c.14)
Prevention of Cruelty to Children Act 1904 (c.15)
Prevention of Damage by Pests Act 1949 (c.55)
Prevention of Damage by Rabbits 1939 (c.43)
Prevention of Eviction Act 1924 (c.18)
Prevention of Fraud (Investments) Act 1939 (c.16)
Prevention of Fraud (Investments) Act 1958 (c.45)
Prevention of Offences Act 1851 (c.19)
Prevention of Oil Pollution Act 1971 (c.60)
Prevention of Oil Pollution Act 1986 (c.6)
Prevention of Terrorism (Temporary Provisions) Act 1974 (c.55)
Prevention of Terrorism (Temporary Provisions) Act 1976 (c.8)
Prevention of Terrorism (Temporary Provisions Act 1984 (c.8)
Prevention of Terrorism (Temporary Provisions) Act 1989 (c.4)
Prevention of Violence (Temporary Provisions) Act 1939 (c.50)
Previous Conviction Act 1836 (c.111)
Price Commission Act 1977 (c.33)
Price Commission (Amendment) Act 1979 (c.1)
Price Control and Other Orders (Indemnity) Act 1951 (c.59)
Price Control (Regulation of Disposal of Stocks) Act 1943 (c.47)
Price of Coal (Limitation) Act 1915 (c.75)
Prices Act 1974 (c.24)
Prices Act 1975 (c.32)
Prices and Incomes Act 1966 (c.33)
Prices and Incomes Act 1967 (c.53)
Prices and Incomes Act 1968 (c.42)
Prices of Goods Act 1939 (c.118)
Princess Elizabeth's and Duke of Edinburgh's Annuities Act 1947 (c.14)
Printer's Imprint Act 1961 (c.31)
Prison Act 1952 (c.52)
Prison Officers (Pensions) Act (c.9)
Prison Security Act 1992 (c.25)
Prisoners and Criminal Proceedings (Scotland) Act 1993 (c.9)
Prisoners of War (Escape) Act 1812 (c.156)
Prisoners (Temporary Discharge for Ill-Health) Act 1913 (c.4)
Prisons (Ireland) Act 1819 (c.100)
Prisons (Ireland) Act 1907 (c.19)
Prisons (Scotland) Act 1839 (c.42)
Prisons (Scotland) Act 1844 (c.34)
Prisons (Scotland) Act 1904 (c.35)
Prisons (Scotland) Act 1909 (c.27)
Prisons (Scotland) Act 1926 (c.57)
Prisons (Scotland) Act 1952 (c.61)
Prisons (Scotland) Act 1989 (c.45)

Private Legislation Procedure (Scotland) Act 1933 (c.37)
Private Legislation Procedure (Scotland) Act 1936 (c.52)
Private Place of Entertainment (Licensing) Act 1967 (c.19)
Private Street Works Act 1961 (c.24)
Prize Act 1939 (c.65)
Prize Act 1948 (c.9)
Prize Causes Act 1797 (c.38)
Prize Courts Act 1915 (c.57)
Prize Courts (Procedure) Act 1914 (c.13)
Prize Goods Act 1803 (c.134)
Prize Salvage Act 1943 (c.7)
Prize Salvage Act 1944 (c.7)
Probate and Legacy Duties Act 1808 (c.149)
Probate and Legacy Duties (Ireland) Act 1814 (c.92)
Probate Duty Act 1801 (c.86)
Probate Duty Act 1859 (c.36)
Probate Duty Act 1860 (c.15)
Probate Duty Act 1861 (c.92)
Probate Duty (Ireland) Act 1816 (c.56)
Probates and Letters of Administration Act (Ireland) 1857 (c.79)
Probation of Offenders Act 1907 (c.17)
Probation of Offenders (Scotland) Act 1931 (c.30)
Probation Officers (Superannuation) Act 1947 (c.38)
Probation Service Act 1993 (c.47)
Proceedings Against Estates Act 1970 (c.17)
Professional Cavalry Act 1796 (c.23)
Professions Supplementary to Medicine Act 1960 (c.66)
Profiteering Act 1919 (c.66)
Profiteering Amendment Act 1920 (c.13)
Profiteering (Cont.) Act 1919 (c.87)
Profits Tax Act 1949 (c.64)
Prohibition of Female Circumcision Act 1985 (c.38)
Prolongation of Parliament Act 1940 (c.53)
Prolongation of Parliament Act 1941 (c.48)
Prolongation of Parliament Act 1942 (c.37)
Prolongation of Parliament Act 1943 (c.46)
Prolongation of Parliament Act 1944 (c.45)
Promissory Oaths Act 1868 (c.72)
Promissory Oaths Act 1871 (c.48)
Property Misdescriptions Act 1991 (c.29)
Property Services Agency and Crown Suppliers Act 1990 (c.12)
Prosecution of Offences Act 1879 (c.22)
Prosecution of Offences Act 1884 (c.58)
Prosecution of Offences Act 1908 (c.3)
Prosecution of Offences Act 1979 (c.31)
Prosecution of Offences Act 1985 (c.23)
Protection Against Cruel Tethering Act 1988 (c.31)
Protection from Eviction Act 1964 (c.97)
Protection from Eviction Act 1977 (c.43)
Protection of Aircraft Act 1973 (c.47)
Protection of Animals Act 1911 (c.27)
Protection of Animals Act 1934 (c.21)

Protection of Animals Act (1911) Amendment 1921 (c.14)

Protection of Animals (Amendment) 1927 (c.27)

Protection of Animals (Amendment) Act 1954 (c.40)

Protection of Animals (Amendment) Act 1988 (c.29)

Protection of Animals (Anaesthetics) Act 1954 (c.46)

Protection of Animals (Anaesthetics) Act 1964 (c.39)

Protection of Animals (Cruelty to Dogs) Act 1933 (c.17)

Protection of Animals (Cruelty to Dogs) (Scotland) Act 1934 (c.25)

Protection of Animals (Penalties) Act 1987 (c.35)

Protection of Animals (Scotland) Act 1912 (c.14)

Protection of Animals (Scotland) Act, 1912, Amendment Act 1921 (c.22)

Protection of Animals (Scotland) Act 1993 (c.15)

Protection of Birds Act 1925 (c.31)

Protection of Birds Act 1933 (c.52)

Protection of Birds Act 1954 (c.30)

Protection of Birds Act 1967 (c.46)

Protection of Birds Act 1954 (Amendment) Act 1964 (c.59)

Protection of Birds (Amendment) Act 1976 (c.42)

Protection of Children Act 1978 (c.37)

Protection of Children (Tobacco) Act 1986 (c.34)

Protection of Depositors Act 1963 (c.16)

Protection of Lapwings Act 1928 (c.2)

Protection of Military Remains Act 1986 (c.35)

Protection of Trading Interests Act 1980 (c.11)

Protection of Wrecks Act 1973 (c.33)

Provident Nominations and Small Intestacies Act 1883 (c.47)

Provisional Collection of Taxes 1913 (c.3)

Provisional Collection of Taxes Act 1968 (c.2)

Provisional Order Confirmation (Turnpikes) Act 1854 (c.51)

Provisional Order Confirmation (Turnpikes) Act 1855 (c.102)

Provisional Order Confirmation (Turnpikes) Act 1857 (c.9)

Provisional Order Confirmation (Turnpikes) Act 1858 (c.80)

Provisional Order Confirmation (Turnpikes) Act 1859 (c.33)

Provisional Order Confirmation (Turnpikes) Act 1860 (c.70)

Provisional Orders Confirmation (Turnpikes) Act 1862 (c.69)

Provisional Order Confirmation (Turnpikes) Act 1863 (c.98)

Provisional Order Confirmation (Turnpikes) Act 1864 (c.79)

Provisional Order (Marriages) Act 1904 (c.23)

Public Accounts Act 1804 (c.58)

Public Accounts and Charges Act 1891 (c.24)

Public and Other Schools (War Conditions) Act 1941 (c.20)

Public Authorities (Allowances) Act 1961 (c.43)

Public Authorities and Bodies (Loans) Act 1916 (c.69)

Public Bodies (Admission to Meetings) Act 1960 (c.67)

Public Bodies Corrupt Practices Act 1889 (c.69)

Public Buildings Expenses Act 1903 (c.41)

Public Buildings Expenses Act 1913 (c.14)

Public Entertainment Act 1875 (c.21)

Public Expenditure and Receipts Act 1968 (c.14)

Public Health Act 1875 (c.55)

Public Health Act 1904 (c.16)

Public Health Act 1908 (c.6)

Public Health Act 1925 (c.71)

Public Health Act 1936 (c.49)

Public Health Act (London) Act 1936 (c.50)

Public Health Act 1961 (c.64)

Public Health Acts Amendment Act 1890 (c.59)

Public Health Acts Amendment Act 1907 (c.53)

Public Health (Borrowing Powers) (Ireland) Act (c.35)

Public Health (Cleansing of Shellfish) Act 1932 (c.28)

Public Health (Coal Mine Refuse) Act 1939 (c.58)

Public Health (Coal Mine Refuse) (Scotland) Act 1939 (c.23)

Public Health (Confirmation of Byelaws) Act 1884 (c.12)

Public Health (Control of Disease) Act 1984 (c.22)

Public Health (Drainage of Trade Premises) Act 1937 (c.40)

Public Health (Interments) Act 1879 (c.31)

Public Health (Ireland) Act 1878 (c.52)

Public Health (Ireland) Act 1896 (c.54)

Public Health (Ireland) Act 1900 (c.10)

Public Health (Ireland) Act 1911 (c.12)

Public Health (Laboratory Service) Act 1960 (c.49)

Public Health (Laboratory Service) Act 1979 (c.23)

Public Health (London) Act 1936 (c.50)

Public Health (Medical Treatment, etc.) (Ireland) Act 1919 (c.16)

Public Health (Notification of Births) Act 1965 (c.42)

Public Health (Officers) Act 1921 (c.23)

Public Health Officers (Deputies) Act 1957 (c.19)

Public Health (Prevention and Treatment of Disease) Act 1913 (c.23)

Public Health (Prevention, etc. of Disease) (Ireland) Act 1917 (c.40)
Public Health (Recurring Nuisances) Act 1969 (c.25)
Public Health (Regulations as to Food) Act 1907 (c.32)
Public Health (Scotland) Act 1897 (c.38)
Public Health (Scotland) Amendment Act 1907 (c.30)
Public Health (Scotland) Act (1897) Amendment 1911 (c.30)
Public Health (Scotland) Amendment 1925 (c.75)
Public Health (Scotland) Act 1945 (c.15)
Public Health (Smoke Abatement) Act 1926 (c.43)
Public Health (Tuberculosis) Act 1921 (c.12)
Public Health (Water and Sewerage) (Scotland) Act 1935 (c.36)
Public Lavatories (Turnstiles) Act 1963 (c.32)
Public Lending Right Act 1979 (c.10)
Public Libraries Act 1884 (c.37)
Public Libraries Act 1901 (c.19)
Public Libraries Act 1919 (c.93)
Public Libraries (etc.) Act (Ireland) Act 1911 (c.9)
Public Libraries Act (Ireland) 1855 (c.40)
Public Libraries and Museums Act 1964 (c.75)
Public Libraries Consolidation (Scotland) Act 1887 (c.42)
Public Libraries (Ireland) Amendment Act 1877 (c.15)
Public Libraries (Ireland) Act 1894 (c.38)
Public Libraries (Ireland) Act 1902 (c.20)
Public Libraries (Ireland) Act 1920 (c.25)
Public Libraries (Scotland) Act 1894 (c.20)
Public Libraries (Scotland) Act 1899 (c.5)
Public Libraries (Scotland) Act 1920 (c.45)
Public Libraries (Scotland) Act 1955 (c.27)
Public Meeting Act 1908 (c.66)
Public Notaries (Articled Clerks) Act 1919 (c.25)
Public Notaries (Ireland) Act 1821 (c.36)
Public Notaries (War Service of Articled Clerks) Act 1946 (c.79)
Public Officers Protection (Ireland) Act 1803 (c.143)
Public Offices Fees Act 1879 (c.58)
Public Offices (Site) Act 1947 (c.45)
Public Order Act 1936 (c.6)
Public Order Act 1963 (c.52)
Public Order Act 1986 (c.64)
Public Parks (Scotland) Act 1878 (c.8)
Public Passenger Vehicles Act 1981 (c.14)
Public Records Act 1958 (c.51)
Public Records Act 1967 (c.44)
Public Records (Scotland) Act 1937 (c.43)
Public Registers and Records (Scotland) Act 1948 (c.57)
Public Registers and Records (Scotland) Act 1949 (c.11)
Public Roads (Ireland) Act 1911 (c.45)

Public Schools Act 1868 (c.118)
Public Schools (Eton College Property) Act 1873 (c.62)
Public Service Vehicles (Arrest of Offenders) Act 1975 (c.53)
Public Service Vehicles (Travel Concessions) Act 1955 (c.26)
Public Stores Act 1875 (c.25)
Public Trustee Act 1906 (c.55)
Public Trustee and Administration of Funds Act 1986 (c.57)
Public Trustee (Fees) Act 1957 (c.12)
Public Trustee (General Deposit Fund) Act 1939 (c.51)
Public Utilities Street Works Act 1950 (c.39)
Public Utility Companies (Capital Issues) Act 1920 (c.9)
Public Utility Transfers and Water Charges Act 1988 (c.15)
Public Works Facilities Act 1930 (c.50)
Public Works (Festival of Britain) Act 1949 (c.26)
Public Works Loans Act 1900 (c.36)
Public Works Loans Act 1901 (c.35)
Public Works Loans Act 1902 (c.22)
Public Works Loans Act 1903 (c.28)
Public Works Loans Act 1904 (c.22)
Public Works Loans Act 1904 (c.36)
Public Works Loans Act 1906 (c.29)
Public Works Loans Act 1907 (c.36)
Public Works Loans Act 1908 (c.23)
Public Works Loans Act 1909 (c.6)
Public Works Loans Act 1910 (c.21)
Public Works Loans Act 1911 (c.17)
Public Works Loans Act 1912 (c.11)
Public Works Loans Act 1913 (c.22)
Public Works Loans Act 1914 (c.33)
Public Works Loans Act 1915 (c.68)
Public Works Loans Act 1916 (c.28)
Public Works Loans Act 1917 (c.32)
Public Works Loans Act 1918 (c.27)
Public Works Loans Act 1919 (c.52)
Public Works Loans Act 1920 (c.61)
Public Works Loans Act 1921 (c.54)
Public Works Loans Act 1922 (c.33)
Public Works Loans Act 1923 (c.29)
Public Works Loans Act 1924 (c.26)
Public Works Loans Act 1925 (c.62)
Public Works Loans Act 1926 (c.2)
Public Works Loans Act 1927 (c.1)
Public Works Loans Act 1928 (c.5)
Public Works Loans Act 1930 (c.49)
Public Works Loans Act 1931 (c.47)
Public Works Loans Act 1932 (c.42)
Public Works Loans Act 1934 (c.48)
Public Works Loans Act 1935 (c.5)
Public Works Loans Act 1937 (c.11)
Public Works Loans Act 1939 (c.2)
Public Works Loans Act 1941 (c.14)
Public Works Loans Act 1944 (c.16)
Public Works Loans Act 1946 (c.41)
Public Works Loans Act 1947 (c.13)
Public Works Loans Act 1948 (c.48)

Public Works Loans Act 1949 (c.82)
Public Works Loans Act 1950 (c.5)
Public Works Loans Act 1951 (c.5)
Public Works Loans Act 1952 (c.3)
Public Works Loans Act 1953 (c.6)
Public Works Loans Act 1955 (c.11)
Public Works Loans Act 1956 (c.65)
Public Works Loans Act 1964 (c.9)
Public Works Loans Act 1965 (c.63)
Public Works Loans Act 1966 (c.16)
Public Works Loans Act 1967 (c.61)
Public Works Loans (No. 2) Act 1927 (c.28)
Public Works Loans (No. 2) Act 1937 (c.7)
Punishment of Incest Act 1908 (c.45)
Purchase of Land (Ireland) Act 1885 (c.73)
Purchase of Land (Ireland) Act 1891 (c.48)
Purchase of Land (Ireland) Act 1901 (c.3)
Purchase of Land (Ireland) (No. 2) Act 1901 (c.30)
Purchase Tax Act 1963 (c.9)

Quail Protection Act 1937 (c.5)
Quakers and Moravians Act 1833 (c.49)
Quakers and Moravians Act 1838 (c.77)
Qualification of Women (County and Borough Councils) Act 1907 (c.33)
Qualification of Women (County and Town Councils) Act 1907 (c.48)
Quarantine Act 1797 (c.33)
Quarantine Act 1800 (c.80)
Quarantine Act 1805 (c.10)
Quarantine Act 1810 (c.20)
Quarantine Act 1811 (c.46)
Quarantine Act 1825 (c.78)
Quarantine Act (Great Britain) Act 1806 (c.98)
Quarantine, etc., Act 1800 (c.30)
Quarries Act 1894 (c.42)
Quarry (Fencing) Act 1887 (c.19)
Quarter Sessions Act 1814 (c.84)
Quarter Sessions Act 1837 (c.4)
Quarter Sessions Act 1842 (c.38)
Quarter Sessions Act 1849 (c.45)
Quarter Sessions Act 1894 (c.6)
Quarter Sessions (Ireland) Act 1845 (c.80)
Quarter Sessions Jurors (Ireland) Act 1897 (c.20)
Quarter Sessions (London) Act 1896 (c.55)
Quartering of Soldiers Act 1795 (c.64)
Quartering of Soldiers Act 1796 (c.36)
Quartering of Soldiers Act 1797 (c.32)
Quartering of Soldiers Act 1797 (c.41)
Quartering of Soldiers Act 1799 (c.36)
Quartering of Soldiers Act 1800 (c.39)
Quartering of Soldiers Act 1801 (c.35)
Quartering of Soldiers Act 1802 (c.108)
Quartering of Soldiers Act 1803 (c.41)
Quartering of Soldiers Act 1804 (c.38)
Quartering of Soldiers Act 1805 (c.37)
Quartering of Soldiers Act 1806 (c.126)
Quartering of Soldiers Act 1807 (c.54)
Quartering of Soldiers Act 1808 (c.39)

Quartering of Soldiers Act 1809 (c.37)
Quartering of Soldiers Act 1810 (c.28)
Quartering of Soldiers Act 1810 (c.96)
Quartering of Soldiers Act 1811 (c.28)
Quartering of Soldiers Act 1812 (c.43)
Quartering of Soldiers Act 1813 (c.43)
Quartering of Soldiers Act 1814 (c.55)
Quartering of Soldiers Act 1815 (c.154)
Quartering of Soldiers Act 1816 (c.32)
Quartering of Soldiers Act 1817 (c.78)
Quartering of Soldiers Act 1818 (c.22)
Quartering of Soldiers Act 1819 (c.26)
Quartering of Soldiers Act 1820 (c.38)
Quartering of Soldiers Act 1821 (c.25)
Quartering of Soldiers Act 1822 (c.20)
Quartering of Soldiers Act 1823 (c.20)
Quartering of Soldiers Act 1824 (c.31)
Quartering of Soldiers Act 1825 (c.20)
Quartering of Soldiers Act 1826 (c.14)
Quartering of Soldiers Act 1826 (c.24)
Quartering of Soldiers Act 1828 (c.8)
Quartering of Soldiers Act 1828 (c.9)
Quays, etc. Between Tower and London Bridge Act 1832 (c.66)
Quebec Act 1774 (c.88)
Quebec Act 1852 (c.53)
Quebec Civil Government Charges Act 1831 (c.23)
Queen Anne's Bounty Act 1714 (c.10)
Queen Anne's Bounty Act 1803 (c.107)
Queen Anne's Bounty Act 1805 (c.84)
Queen Anne's Bounty Act 1838 (c.20)
Queen Anne's Bounty Act 1840 (c.20)
Queen Anne's Bounty (Superannuation) Act 1870 (c.89)
Queen's Bench (Ireland) Procedure Act 1872 (c.28)
Queen Caroline's Servants' Pension Act 1822 (c.98)
Queen's Colleges (Ireland) Act 1845 (c.66)
Queen's Prison Act 1842 (c.22)
Queen's Prison Act 1848 (c.7)
Queen's Prison Act 1860 (c.60)
Queen's Prison Discontinuance Act 1862 (c.104)
Queen's Remembrance Act 1859 (c.21)
Queensferry, Firth of Forth: Finance Act 1814 (c.138)

Rabies Act 1974 (c.17)
Race Relations Act 1965 (c.73)
Race Relations Act 1968 (c.71)
Race Relations Act 1976 (c.74)
Race Relations (Remedies) Act 1994 (c.10)
Racecourse Betting Act 1928 (c.41)
Racecourse Licensing Act 1879 (c.18)
Radioactive Material (Road Transport) Act 1991 (c.27)
Radioactive Substances Act 1948 (c.37)
Radioactive Substances Act 1960 (c.34)
Radioactive Substances Act 1993 (c.12)
Radiological Protection Act 1970 (c.46)

Rag Flock Act 1911 (c.52)

Rag Flock Act (1911) Amendment Act 1928 (c.39)

Rag Flock and Other Filling Materials Act 1951 (c.63)

Railways Act 1848 (c.3)

Railways Act 1974 (c.48)

Railway and Canal Commission (Abolition) Act 1949 (c.11)

Railway and Canal Commission (Consents) Act 1922 (c.47)

Railway and Canal Traffic Act 1854 (c.31)

Railway and Canal Traffic Act 1888 (c.25)

Railway and Canal Traffic Act 1892 (c.44)

Railway and Canal Traffic Act 1894 (c.54)

Railway and Canal Traffic Act 1913 (c.29)

Railway and Canal Traffic (Provisional Orders) Amendment Act 1891 (c.12)

Railway Assessors (Scotland) Superannuation Act 1897 (c.12)

Railway Clauses Act 1863 (c.92)

Railway Companies Act 1867 (c.127)

Railway Companies Act 1868 (c.79)

Railway Companies Act 1875 (c.31)

Railway Companies (Accounts and Returns) Act 1911 (c.34)

Railway Companies Arbitration Act 1859 (c.59)

Railway Companies (Ireland) Act 1867 (c.138)

Railway Companies (Ireland) Temporary Advances Act 1866 (c.95)

Railway Companies (Ireland) Temporary Advances Act 1868 (c.94)

Railway Companies Meetings Act 1869 (c.6)

Railway Companies Mortgage Trans. (Scotland) Act 1861 (c.50)

Railway Companies' Powers Act 1864 (c.120)

Railway Companies (Scotland) Act 1867 (c.126)

Railway Companies Securities Act 1866 (c.108)

Railway Employment (Prevention of Accidents) Act 1900 (c.27)

Railway Fires Act 1904 (c.11)

Railway Freight Rebates Act 1936 (c.2)

Railway Freight Rebates Act 1943 (c.23)

Railway Passenger Duty Act 1917 (c.3)

Railway Regulation Act 1851 (c.64)

Railway Regulation Act 1893 (c.29)

Railway Regulation Act (Returns of Signal Arrangements, Working &c.) Act 1873 (c.76)

Railway Returns (Continuous Brakes) Act 1878 (c.20)

Railways Act 1921 (c.55)

Railways Act 1993 (c.43)

Railways (Agreement) Act 1935 (c.6)

Railways Agreement (Powers) Act 1941 (c.5)

Railways and Canals Act 1860 (c.41)

Railways (Authorisation of Works) Act 1923 (c.30)

Railways Clauses Act 1863 (c.92)

Railways Clauses Consolidation Act 1845 (c.20)

Railways Clauses Consolidation (Scotland) Act 1845 (c.33)

Railways Commission Act 1846 (c.105)

Railway Companies Dissolution 1846 (c.28)

Railways Construction Amendment (Ireland) Act 1880 (c.31)

Railways Construction Facilities Act 1864 (c.121)

Railways (Conveyance of Mails) Act 1838 (c.98)

Railways (Electrical Power) Act 1903 (c.30)

Railways Employment (Prevention of Accidents) Act 1900 (c.27)

Railways (Extension of Time) Act 1868 (c.18)

Railway Fires Act 1905 (c.11)

Railway Fires Act (1905) Amendment Act 1923 (c.27)

Railways (Ireland) Act 1856 (c.72)

Railways (Ireland) Act 1858 (c.34)

Railways (Ireland) Act 1864 (c.71)

Railways (Ireland) Act 1867 (c.104)

Railways (Ireland) Act 1890 (c.52)

Railways (Ireland) Act 1896 (c.34)

Railway Passenger Duty Act 1842 (c.79)

Railway Passenger Duty Act 1847 (c.42)

Railways (Powers and Construction) Acts, 1864, Amendment Act 1870 (c.19)

Railways (Private Sidings) Act 1904 (c.19)

Railway Regulation Act 1840 (c.97)

Railway Regulation Act 1842 (c.55)

Railway Regulation Act 1844 (c.85)

Railway Regulation (Gauge) Act 1846 (c.57)

Railway Rolling Stock Protection Act 1872 (c.50)

Railway (Sales and Leases) Act 1845 (c.96)

Railways Act 1921 (c.55)

Railways Act (Ireland) 1851 (c.70)

Railways Act (Ireland) 1860 (c.97)

Railways (Private Sidings) Act 1904 (c.19)

Railways (Settlement of Claims) Act 1921 (c.59)

Railways Traverse Act 1868 (c.70)

Railways (Valuation for Rating) Act 1930 (c.24)

Railways (Valuation for Rating) Act 1946 (c.61)

Ramsey (Huntingdonshire): Drainage, etc. Act 1796 (c.72)

Ramsgate Harbour Act 1797 (c.86)

Ramsgate: Improvement Act 1796 (c.43)

Ranges Act 1891 (c.54)

Rate in Aid of Distressed Unions Act 1849 (c.24)

Rate Rebate Act 1973 (c.28)

Rate of Interest Act 1821 (c.51)

Rate of Interest Act 1822 (c.47)

Rate Support Grants Act 1986 (c.54)

Rate Support Grants Act 1987 (c.5)

Rate Support Grants Act 1988 (c.51)

Rateable Property (Ireland) Act 1846 (c.110)

Rates Act 1984 (c.33)
Rates of Carriage of Goods Act 1827 (c.39)
Rates (Proceedings for Recovery) Act 1914 (c.85)
Rating Act 1874 (c.54)
Rating Act 1966 (c.9)
Rating Act 1971 (c.39)
Rating and Valuation Act 1925 (c.90)
Rating and Valuation Act 1928 (c.8)
Rating and Valuation Act 1932 (c.18)
Rating and Valuation Act 1937 (c.60)
Rating and Valuation Act 1957 (c.17)
Rating and Valuation Act 1959 (c.36)
Rating and Valuation Act 1961 (c.45)
Rating and Valuation (Air-Raid Works) Act 1938 (c.65)
Rating and Valuation (Air-Raid Works) (Scotland) Act 1938 (c.66)
Rating and Valuation (Amendment) (Scotland) Act 1984 (c.31)
Rating and Valuation (Apportionment) Act 1928 (c.44)
Rating and Valuation (Miscellaneous Provisions) Act 1955 (c.9)
Rating and Valuation (No. 2) Act 1932 (c.33)
Rating and Valuation (Postponement of Valuations) Act 1938 (c.19)
Rating and Valuation (Postponement of Valuations) Act 1940 (c.12)
Rating and Valuation (Scotland) Act 1952 (c.47)
Rating (Caravan Sites) Act 1976 (c.15)
Rating (Charity Shops) Act 1976 (c.45)
Rating (Disabled Persons) Act 1978 (c.40)
Rating Exemption (Scotland) Act 1874 (c.20)
Rating (Interim Relief) Act 1964 (c.18)
Rating of Small Tenements Act 1850 (c.99)
Rating of Small Tenements Act 1851 (c.39)
Rating (Revaluation Rebates) (Scotland) Act 1985 (c.33)
Rating (Scotland) Act 1926 (c.47)
Rating (Scotland) Amendment Act 1928 (c.6)
Rating (War Damage Insurance) Act 1941 (c.25)
Rating (War Damages) (Scotland) Act 1941 (c.25)
Rats and Mice (Destruction) Act 1919 (c.72)
Reading Charities Act 1861 (c.23)
Ready Money Football Betting Act 1920 (c.52)
Real Estate Charges Act 1854 (c.113)
Real Estate Charges Act 1867 (c.69)
Real Etate Charges Act 1877 (c.34)
Real Property Act 1845 (c.106)
Real Property Limitation Act 1833 (c.27)
Real Property Limitation Act 1837 (c.28)
Real Property Limitation Act 1874 (c.57)
Real Rights Act 1693 (c.22)
Rebuilding of London Bridge Act 1823 (c.50)
Recall of Army and Air Force Pensions Act 1948 (c.8)
Recaptured British-built Ships Act 1809 (c.41)

Receipt and Remittance of Taxes, etc. Act 1831 (c.18)
Receipt Stamps Act 1828 (c.27)
Receiver General of Stamps Act 1806 (c.76)
Receivers of Crown Rents Act 1816 (c.16)
Receivers of Stolen Goods, etc., Act 1822 (c.24)
Recess Elections Act 1784 (c.26)
Recess Elections Act 1975 (c.66)
Reclamation of Lands, etc. Act 1842 (c.105)
Reclamation of Lands, etc. (Ireland) Act 1831 (c.57)
Recognition of Divorces and Legal Separations Act 1971 (c.53)
Recognition of Trusts Act 1987 (c.14)
Recognizances (Ireland) Act 1809 (c.83)
Recognizances (Ireland) Act 1817 (c.56)
Record of Title (Ireland) Act 1865 (c.88)
Recorded Delivery Service Act 1962 (c.27)
Recorders' Courts of Quarter Sessions Act 1837 (c.19)
Recorders, Magistrates and Clerks of the Peace Act 1888 (c.23)
Recorders, Stipendiary Magistrates and Clerks of the Peace Act 1906 (c.46)
Recoveries in Copyhold, etc. Courts Act 1807 (c.8)
Recovery of Advowsons in Ireland Act 1844 (c.27)
Recovery of Alimony (Ireland) Act 1867 (c.11)
Recovery of Possession by Landlords Act 1820 (c.87)
Recovery of Small Tithes Act 1826 (c.15)
Recovery of Tenements, etc. (Ireland) Act 1816 (c.88)
Recovery of Tenements, etc. (Ireland) Act 1818 (c.39)
Recovery of Tenements (Ireland) Act 1820 (c.41)
Recovery of Tithes (Ireland) Act 1832 (c.41)
Recovery of Wages (Ireland) Act 1814 (c.116)
Recovery of Wages (Ireland) Act 1849 (c.15)
Recreation Grounds Act 1859 (c.27)
Recreational Charities Act 1958 (c.17)
Rectifying of Spirits (Ireland) Act 1807 (c.19)
Rectory of Ewelme Act 1871 (c.23)
Rectory of Ledbury Act 1855 (c.92)
Red Sea and India Telegraph Company Act 1861 (c.4)
Red Sea and India Telegraph Company Act 1862 (c.39)
Redemption of Rent (Ireland) Act 1891 (c.57)
Redemption of Standard Securities (Scotland) Act 1971 (c.45)
Redistribution of Seats Act 1885 (c.23)
Redistribution of Seats (Ireland) Act 1918 (c.65)
Redstone Bridge, Severn Act 1795 (c.108)
Reduction of Annuity Tax Act 1867 (c.107)
Reduction of Duty on Rum Act 1863 (c.102)
Reduction of National Debt 1809 (c.64)
Reduction of National Debt Act 1822 (c.9)

Reduction of National Debt Act 1858 (c.38)

Reduction of National Debt Act 1860 (c.71)

Reductions Ex Capite Lecti Abolished Act 1871 (c.81)

Redundancy Fund Act 1981 (c.5)

Redundancy Payments Act 1965 (c.62)

Redundancy Rebates Act 1969 (c.8)

Redundancy Rebates Act 1977 (c.22)

Redundant Churches and Other Religious Buildings Act 1969 (c.22)

Re-election of Ministers Act 1915 (c.50)

Re-election of Ministers Act 1916 (c.22)

Re-election of Ministers Act 1919 (c.2)

Re-election of Ministers Act (1919) Amendment 1926 (c.19)

Re-election of Ministers (No.2) Act 1916 (c.56)

Referendum Act 1975 (c.33)

Refined Sugar Bounties Act 1824 (c.35)

Reformatory and Industrial Schools Act 1891 (c.23)

Reformatory and Industrial Schools Acts Amendment Act 1872 (c.21)

Reformatory and Industrial Schools (Channel Islands Children) Act 1895 (c.17)

Reformatory and Industrial Schools (Manx Children) Act 1884 (c.40)

Reformatory, etc. Schools Act 1856 (c.109)

Reformatory Institutions (Ireland) Act 1881 (c.29)

Reformatory Schools Act 1856 (c.28)

Reformatory Schools Act 1866 (c.117)

Reformatory Schools Act 1893 (c.15)

Reformatory Schools Act 1893 (c.48)

Reformatory Schools Act 1899 (c.12)

Reformatory Schools (England) Act 1854 (c.74)

Reformatory Schools (England) Act 1857 (c.55)

Reformatory Schools (Ireland) Act 1858 (c.103)

Refreshment Houses Act 1860 (c.27)

Refreshment Houses Act 1964 (c.88)

Refreshment Houses Act 1967 (c.38)

Refreshment Houses (Ireland) Act 1860 (c.107)

Refuse Disposal (Amenity) Act 1978 (c.3)

Regency Act 1830 (c.2)

Regency Act 1840 (c.52)

Regency Act 1910 (c.26)

Regency Act 1937 (c.16)

Regency Act 1943 (c.42)

Regency Act 1953 (c.1)

Regency Act Amendment Act 1838 (c.24)

Regent's Park, Regent Street Act 1851 (c.95)

Regent's Park, Regent Street, etc. Act 1817 (c.24)

Regent's Park, Regent Street, etc. Act 1824 (c.100)

Regent's Park, Regent Street, etc. Act 1831 (c.29)

Regent's Park, Regent Street, etc. Act 1832 (c.56)

Regent's Quadrant Colonnade Act 1848 (c.50)

Regent Street, etc. Act 1825 (c.38)

Regent Street Act 1828 (c.64)

Regent Street Act 1829 (c.61)

Regent Street, Caslton Place Act 1826 (c.77)

Regent Street, etc. Act 1828 (c.70)

Regiment of Cornwall and Devon Miners Act 1798 (c.74)

Regimental Accounts Act 1808 (c.128)

Regimental Benefit Societies Act 1849 (c.71)

Regimental Charitable Funds Act 1935 (c.11)

Regimental Debts Act 1863 (c.57)

Regimental Debts Act 1893 (c.5)

Regimental Debts (Deposit of Wills) (Scotland) Act 1919 (c.89)

Regimental Exchange Act 1875 (c.16)

Regional Commissioners Act 1939 (c.76)

Regional Development Grants (Termination) Act 1988 (c.11)

Register of Sasines Act 1828 (c.19)

Register of Sasines (Scotland) Act 1987 (c.23)

Registered Designs Act 1949 (c.88)

Registered Establishments (Scotland) Act 1987 (c.40)

Registered Homes Act 1984 (c.23)

Registered Homes (Amendment) Act 1991 (c.20)

Registering of British Vessels Act 1845 (c.89)

Registering of Vessels Act 1823 (c.41)

Registers of Sasines (Scotland) Act 1848 (c.74)

Registrar General (Scotland) Act 1920 (c.69)

Registration Acceleration Act 1894 (c.32)

Registration Act 1885 (c.15)

Registration Act 1908 (c.21)

Registration Amendment (Ireland) Act 1868 (c.112)

Registration Amendment (Scotland) Act 1885 (c.)

Registration Appeals (Ireland) Act 1885 (c.66)

Registration (Ireland) Act 1898 (c.2)

Registration of Aliens Act 1836 (c.11)

Registration of Assurances (Ireland) Act 1850 (c.72)

Registration of Births and Deaths (Ireland) Act 1863 (c.11)

Registration of Births, Deaths and Marriages (Army) Act 1879 (c.8)

Registration of Births, Deaths and Marriages (Scotland) Act 1854 (c.80)

Registration of Births, Deaths and Marriages (Scotland) Act 1855 (c.29)

Registration of Births, Deaths and Marriages (Scotland) Act 1860 (c.85)

Registration of Births, Deaths and Marriages (Scotland) Act 1965 (c.49)

Registration of Births, Deaths and Marriages (Scotland) Amendment Act 1910 (c.32)

Registration of Births, Deaths and Marriages (Scotland) (Amendment) Act 1934 (c.19)

Registration of Births, Deaths and Marriages (Special Provisions) Act 1957 (c.58)

Registration of Births, etc. Act 1836 (c.1)

Registration of Burials Act 1864 (c.97)

Registration of Business Names Act 1916 (c.58)

Registration of Certain Writs (Scotland) Act 1891 (c.9)

Registration of Clubs (Ireland) Act 1904 (c.9)

Registration of County Electors (Extension of Time) Act 1889 (c.19)

Registration of County Voters (Ireland) Act 1864 (c.22)

Registration of Deeds (Ireland) Act 1864 (c.76)

Registration of Electors 1891 (c.18)

Registration of Leases (Scotland) Act 1857 (c.26)

Registration of Leases (Scotland) Amendment Act 1877 (c.36)

Registration of Marriages (Ireland) Act 1863 (c.90)

Registration of Still-Births (Scotland) Act 1938 (c.55)

Registration of Voters (Ireland) Act 1973 (c.30)

Registration Service Act 1953 (c.37)

Registry Courts (Ireland) Amendment Act 1879 (c.71)

Registry, etc. of Colonial Slaves Act 1819 (c.120)

Registry of Admiralty Court Act 1813 (c.151)

Registry of Boats, etc. Act 1795 (c.58)

Registry of Deeds Act 1822 (c.116)

Registry of Deeds Act 1832 (c.87)

Registry of Deeds Act 1875 (c.5)

Registry of Deeds, etc. (Ireland) Act 1828 (c.57)

Registry of Deeds Office (Ireland) Holidays Act 1883 (c.20)

Registry of Ships Act 1796 (c.112)

Registry of Ships Built in India Act 1815 (c.116)

Registry of Wool Act 1821 (c.81)

Regrating and Ingrossing of Oaken Bark Act 1807 (c.53)

Regular and Elders' Widows' Funds Act 1897 (c.11)

Regulation of Factories Act 1834 (c.1)

Regulation of Railways Act 1868 (c.119)

Regulation of Railways Act 1871 (c.78)

Regulation of Railways Act 1873 (c.48)

Regulation of Railways Acts, 1873 and 1874, Continuance Act 1879 (c.56)

Regulation of Railways Act 1889 (c.57)

Regulation of the Forces Act 1871 (c.86)

Regulation of the Forces Act 1881 (c.57)

Rehabilitation of Offenders Act 1974 (c.53)

Reinstatement in Civil Employment Act 1944 (c.15)

Reinstatement in Civil Employment Act 1950 (c.10)

Reinsurance (Acts of Terrorism) Act 1993 (c.18)

Released Persons (Poor Law Relief) Act 1907 (c.14)

Relief as to Transferable Stocks, etc. Act 1812 (c.158)

Relief of Bankers Act 1824 (c.73)

Relief of Certain Bishops Act 1843 (c.57)

Relief of Certain Curates (England) Act 1803 (c.2)

Relief of Certain Incumbents Act 1824 (c.89)

Relief of Debtors Act 1799 (c.50)

Relief of Debtors in Prison Act 1812 (c.160)

Relief of Discharged Soldiers and Sailors Act 1803 (c.61)

Relief of Distress Act 1849 (c.63)

Relief of Distress (Ireland) Act 1880 (c.4)

Relief of Distress (Ireland) Amendment Act 1880 (c.14)

Relief of Distressed Unions (Ireland) Act 1883 (c.24)

Relief of Families of Militiamen Act 1803 (c.47)

Relief of Families of Militiamen (Scotland) Act 1809 (c.90)

Relief of Families of Militiamen (Ireland) Act 1811 (c.78)

Relief of Families of Militiamen Act 1812 (c.28)

Relief of Insolvent Debtors Act 1797 (c.112)

Relief of Prisoners Act 1797 (c.85)

Relief of Prisoners for Debt Act 1809 (c.6)

Relief of the Poor Act 1795 (c.23)

Relief of the Poor Act 1810 (c.50)

Relief of the Poor Act 1812 (c.73)

Relief of Revenue Prisoners Act 1795 (c.96)

Relief of Rutson & Company Act 1820 (c.30)

Relief of Sailors Abroad Act 1818 (c.38)

Relief of Shipwrecked Mariners, etc. Act 1814 (c.126)

Relief of Stress (Ireland) Act 1849 (c.5)

Relief of Traders for Grenada, etc. Act (c.127)

Relief to Chelsea, etc. Pensioners Act 1825 (c. 27)

Relief to Holders of Certain Securities Act 1818 (c.93)

Religious Congregations, etc. (Scotland) Act 1850 (c.13)

Religious Disabilities Act 1846 (c.59)

Remedies Against the Hundred (England) Act 1827 (c.31)

Remission of Penalties Act 1859 (c.32)

Remission of Penalties Act 1875 (c.80)

Remission of Rates (London) Act 1940 (c.32)

Removal of Goods Act 1812 (c.142)

Removal of Goods for Exportation, etc. Act 1808 (c.126)

Removal of Indictments into King's Bench Act 1835 (c.33)

Removal of Offensive Matter Act 1906 (c.45)

Removal of Prisoners in Custody Act 1854 (c.115)

Removal of Slaves Act 1820 (c.50)

Removal of Wool Act 1814 (c.78)

Removal of Wrecks Act 1877 (c.16)

Removal of Wrecks Act, 1877, Amendment Act 1889 (c.5)

Removal Terms Act 1886 (c.50)

Removal Terms (Burghs) (Scotland) Act 1881 (c.39)

Removal Terms (Scotland) Act, 1886, Amendment Act 1890 (c.36)

Remuneration, Charges and Grants Act 1975 (c.57)

Remuneration of Teachers Act 1963 (c.20)

Remuneration of Teachers Act 1965 (c.3)

Remuneration of Teachers (Scotland) Act 1967 (c.36)

Renewable Leasehold Conversion Act 1849 (c.105)

Renewable Leasehold Conversion (Ireland) Act 1868 (c.62)

Renewal of Leases (Ireland) Act 1838 (c.62)

Rent Act 1957 (c.25)

Rent Act 1965 (c.75)

Rent Act 1968 (c.23)

Rent Act 1974 (c.51)

Rent Act 1977 (c.42)

Rent (Agricultural) Amendment Act 1977 (c.17)

Rent (Agriculture) Act 1976 (c.80)

Rent (Amendment) Act 1985 (c.24)

Rent and Mortgage Interest Restrictions Act 1923 (c.32)

Rent and Mortgage Interest Restriction Act 1939 (c.71)

Rent and Mortgage Interest Restrictions (Amendment) Act 1933 (c.32)

Rent and Mortgage Interest (Restrictions Continuance) Act 1925 (c.32)

Rent (Control of Increases) Act 1969 (c.62)

Rent of Furnished Houses Control (Scotland) Act 1943 (c.44)

Rent Rebate Act 1973 (c.28)

Rent Restrictions (Notices of Increase) Act 1923 (c.13)

Rent (Scotland) Act 1971 (c.28)

Rent (Scotland) Act 1984 (c.58)

Rentcharges Act 1977 (c.30)

Rents of the Rolls Estate, etc. Act 1820 (c.107)

Reorganisation of Offices (Scotland) Act 1928 (c.34)

Reorganisation of Offices (Scotland) Act 1939 (c.20)

Repair of Blenheim Palace Act 1840 (c.43)

Repair of Roads and Bridges (Ireland) Act 1825 (c.101)

Repair of War Damage Act 1941 (c.34)

Repatriation of Prisoners Act 1984 (c.47)

Repayment of Advances (Ireland) Act 1852 (c.16)

Repayment of Certain Loans Act 1802 (c.39)

Repayment of Duty in Certain Cases Act 1810 (c.39)

Repeal of Acts Concerning Importation Act 1822 (cc.41, 42)

Repeal of 39 Eliz. c.17 Act 1812 (c.31)

Repeal of 41 Geo. 3 (Great Britain) 1801 (c.4)

Repeal of Certain Duties Act 1800 (c.69)

Repeal of Certain Duties Act 1824 (c.22)

Repeal, etc. of Certain Duties Act 1802 (c.103)

Repeal of a Certain Tax Act 1801 (c.100)

Repeal of Obsolete Statutes Act 1856 (c.64)

Repeal of Part of 15 Geo.3.c.31 Act 1850 (c.80)

Repeal of Salt Duties Act 1824 (c.65)

Repeal of Sir J. Barnard's Act 1860 (c.28)

Repeal of Nore Tolls Act 1859 (c.29)

Representation of the People Act 1832 (c.45)

Representation of the People Act 1832 (c.88)

Representation of the People Act 1867 (c.102)

Representation of the People Act 1884 (c.3)

Representation of the People Act 1918 (c.64)

Representation of the People Act 1920 (c.15)

Representation of the People Act 1921 (c.34)

Representation of the People Act 1922 (c.12)

Representation of the People Act 1945 (c.5)

Representation of the People Act 1948 (c.65)

Representation of the People Act 1949 (c.68)

Representation of the People Act 1968 (c.15)

Representation of the People Act 1969 (c.15)

Representation of the People Act 1974 (c.10)

Representation of the People Act 1977 (c.9)

Representation of the People Act 1978 (c.32)

Representation of the People Act 1979 (c.40)

Representation of the People Act 1980 (c.3)

Representation of the People Act 1981 (c.34)

Representation of the People Act 1983 (c.2)

Representation of the People Act 1985 (c.50)

Representation of the People Act 1989 (c.28)

Representation of the People Act 1990 (c.32)

Representation of the People Act 1991 (c.11)

Representation of the People Act 1993 (c.29)

Representation of the People (Amendment) Act 1918 (c.50)

Representation of the People Amendment Act 1957 (c.43)

Representation of the People Amendment Act 1958 (c.9)

Representation of the People (Armed Forces) Act 1976 (c.29)

Representation of the People (Equal Franchise) Act 1928 (c.12)

Representation of the People (Ireland) Act 1850 (c.69)

Representation of the People (Ireland) Act 1861 (c.60)

Representation of the People (Ireland) Act 1868 (c.49)

Representation of the People (No. 2) Act 1920 (c.35)

Representation of the People (No. 2) Act 1922 (c.41)

Representation of the People (No. 2) Act 1974 (c.13)

Representation of the People (Reading University) Act 1928 (c.25)

Representation of the People (Returning Officers' Expenses) Act 1919 (c.8)

Representation of the People (Scotland) Act 1832 (c.65)

Representation of the People (Scotland) Act 1868 (c.48)

Representative Peers (Ireland) Act 1857 (c.33)

Representative Peers (Scotland) Act 1847 (c.52)

Representative Peers (Scotland) Act 1851 (c.87)

Representative Peers (Scotland) Act 1852 (c.35)

Reprisals Against Foreign Ships, etc. Act 1808 (c.132)

Reproductive Loan Fund Act 1874 (c.86)

Republic of Gambia Act 1970 (c.37)

Republic of South Africa (Temporary Provisions) Act 1961 (c.23)

Requisitioned Houses Act 1960 (c.20)

Requisitioned Houses and Housing (Amendment) Act 1955 (c.24)

Requisitioned Land and War Works Act 1945 (e.43)

Requisitioned Land and War Works Act 1947 (c.17)

Requisitioned Land and War Works Act 1948 (c.17)

Resale Prices Act 1964 (c.58)

Resale Prices Act 1976 (c.53)

Rescue Act 1821 (c.88)

Reserve and Auxiliary Forces Act 1939 (c.24)

Reserve and Auxiliary Forces (Protection of Civil Interests) Act 1951 (c.65)

Reserve and Auxiliary Forces (Training) Act 1951 (c.23)

Reserve Force Act 1859 (c.42)

Reserve Force Act 1867 (c.110)

Reserve Forces Act 1870 (c.67)

Reserve Forces Act 1882 (c.48)

Reserve Forces Act 1890 (c.42)

Reserve Forces Act 1899 (c.40)

Reserve Forces Act 1900 (c.62)

Reserve Forces Act 1906 (c.11)

Reserve Forces Act 1937 (c.17)

Reserve Forces Act 1966 (c.30)

Reserve Forces Act 1980 (c.9)

Reserve Forces Act 1982 (c.14)

Reserve Forces and Militia Act 1898 (c.9)

Reserve Forces (Safeguard of Employment) Act 1985 (c.17)

Reservoirs Act 1975 (c.23)

Reservoirs (Safety Provisions) Act 1930 (c.51)

Residence in France During the War Act 1798 (c.79)

Residence of Incumbents Act 1869 (c.109)

Residence on Benefices, etc. (England) Act 1814 (c.175)

Residence on Benefices, etc. (England) Act 1816 (c.6)

Residence on Benefices, etc. (England) Act 1816 (c.123)

Residence on Benefices, etc. (England) Act 1817 (c.99)

Resident Magistrates and Police Commissioners Salaries Act 1874 (c.23)

Resident Magistrates (Belfast) Act 1911 (c.58)

Resident Magistrates (Ireland) Act 1920 (c.38)

Resident Magistrates (Ireland) Act 1853 (c.60)

Residential Homes Act 1980 (c.7)

Resignation Bonds Act 1827 (c.25)

Responsibility of Shipowners Act 1813 (c.159)

Restoration of Order in Ireland Act 1920 (c.31)

Restoration of Order In Ireland (Indemnity) Act 1923 (c.12)

Restoration of Pre-War Practices Act 1919 (c.42)

Restoration of Pre-War Trade Practices Act 1942 (c.9)

Restoration of Pre-War Trade Practices Act 1950 (c.9)

Restriction of Advertisement (War Risks Insurance) Act 1939 (c.120)

Restriction of Offensive Weapons Act 1959 (c.37)

Restriction of Ribbon Development (Temporary Development) Act 1943 (c.34)

Restrictions of Ribbon Development Act 1935 (c.47)

Restriction on Cash Payments Act 1797 (c.1)

Restriction on Cash Payments Act 1797 (c.45)

Restriction on Cash Payments Act 1797 (c.91)

Restriction on Cash Payments Act 1802 (c.40)

Restriction on Cash Payments Act 1802 (c.45)

Restriction on Cash Payments Act 1803 (c.1)

Restriction on Cash Payments Act 1803 (c.18)

Restriction on Cash Payments Act 1803 (c.44)

Restriction on Cash Payments Act 1814 (c.99)

Restriction on Cash Payments Act 1814 (c.130)

Restriction on Cash Payments Act 1815 (c.28)

Restriction on Cash Payments Act 1815 (c.41)

Restriction on Cash Payments Act 1816 (c.40)

Restriction on Cash Payments Act 1816 (c.48)

Restriction on Cash Payments Act 1818 (c.37)

Restriction on Cash Payments Act 1818 (c.60)

Restriction on Cash Payments (Ireland) Act 1804 (c.21)

Restrictive Practices Court Act 1976 (c.33)

Restrictive Trade Practices Act 1956 (c.68)
Restrictive Trade Practices Act 1968 (c.66)
Restrictive Trade Practices Act 1976 (c.34)
Restrictive Trade Practices Act 1977 (c.19)
Restrictive Trade Practices (Stock Exchange) Act 1984 (c.2)
Resumption of Cash Payments Act 1819 (c.49)
Resumption of Cash Payments Act 1819 (c.99)
Retail Brewers Act 1828 (c.68)
Retail Meat Dealers' Shops (Sunday Closing) Act 1936 (c.30)
Retailing of Spirits (Scotland) Act 1818 (c.13)
Retail of Sweets, etc. Act 1834 (c.77)
Retired Officers (Civil Employment) Act 1919 (c.40)
Retirement of Officers on Half Pay Act 1811 (c.103)
Retirement of Officers on Half Pay Act 1812 (c.151)
Retirement of Teachers (Scotland) Act 1976 (c.65)
Return of Persons Committed, etc. Act 1815 (c.49)
Returning Officers Act 1854 (c.57)
Returning Officers (Scotland) Act 1886 (c.58)
Returning Officers (Scotland) Act 1891 (c.49)
Returning Officers (Scotland) Act 1977 (c.14)
Returns to Secretary of State Act 1858 (c.67)
Revenue Act 1845 (c.76)
Revenue Act 1862 (c.22)
Revenue Act 1863 (c.33)
Revenue Act 1865 (c.30)
Revenue Act 1866 (c.36)
Revenue Act 1867 (c.114)
Revenue Act 1867 (c.90)
Revenue Act 1868 (c.28)
Revenue Act 1869 (c.14)
Revenue Act 1883 (c.55)
Revenue Act 1884 (c.62)
Revenue Act 1889 (c.42)
Revenue Act 1898 (c.46)
Revenue Act 1903 (c.46)
Revenue Act 1906 (c.20)
Revenue Act 1909 (c.43)
Revenue Act 1911 (c.2)
Revenue Act 1968 (c.11)
Revenue Buildings, Liverpool Act 1832 (c.14)
Revenue Departments Accounts Act 1861 (c.93)
Revenue, Friendly Societies and National Debt Act 1882 (c.72)
Revenue (Ireland) Act 1806 (c.106)
Revenue (Ireland) Act 1821 (c.90)
Revenue Inquiry Act 1824 (c.7)
Revenue (No. 1) Act 1861 (c.21)
Revenue (No. 1) Act 1864 (c.18)
Revenue (No. 2) Act 1861 (c.91)
Revenue (No. 2) Act 1864 (c.56)
Revenue (No. 2) Act 1865 (c.96)
Revenue of Scotland Act 1718 (c.20)
Revenue Officers' Disabilities Act 1868 (c.73)

Revenue Officers' Disabilities Removal Act 1874 (c.22)
Revenue Offices (Scotland) Holidays Act 1880 (c.17)
Revenue Solicitors Act 1828 (c.25)
Revenue (Transfer of Charges) Act 1856 (c.59)
Revenues of Archbishopric of Armagh Act 1864 (c.81)
Reverend J. G. MacManaway's Indemnity Act 1951 (c.29)
Reverter of Sites Act 1987 (c.15)
Review of Justices' Decisions Act 1872 (c.26)
Revising Barristers Act 1866 (c.54)
Revising Barristers Act 1873 (c.70)
Revising Barristers Act 1874 (c.53)
Revising Barristers Act 1885 (c.57)
Revising Barristers Act 1886 (c.42)
Revising Barristers (Ireland) Act 1886 (c.43)
Revision of the Army and Air Force Acts (Transitional Provisions) Act 1955 (c.20)
Revival of Expired Laws, etc. Jamaica Act 1839 (c.26)
Rhodesia and Nyasaland Federation Act 1953 (c.30)
Rhodesia and Nyasaland Act 1963 (c.34)
Richmond Lunatic Asylum Act 1815 (c.107)
Richmond Lunatic Asylum Act 1830 (c.22)
Richmond Lunatic Asylum Act 1831 (c.13)
Richmond Penitentiary, etc. Act 1836 (c.51)
Richmond to Lancaster Road Act 1795 (c.157)
Riding Establishments Act 1939 (c.56)
Riding Establishments Act 1964 (c.70)
Riding Establishments Act 1970 (c.32)
Rifle Volunteer Grounds Act 1860 (c.140)
Rifle Volunteer Grounds Act 1862 (c.41)
Right of Light Act 1959 (c.56)
Rights of Entry (Gas and Electricity Boards) Act 1954 (c.21)
Rights of Way Act 1932 (c.45)
Rights of Way Act 1990 (c.24)
Rights of Way Near Aldershot Camp Act 1856 (c.66)
Riot Act 1714 (c.5)
Riot (Damages) Act 1886 (c.38)
Riotous Assemblies (Scotland) Act 1822 (c.33)
River Boards Act 1948 (c.32)
River Itchin: Navigation Act 1795 (c.86)
River Ivel: Navigation Act 1795 (c.105)
River Liffey, Dublin Act 1833 (c.26)
River Ness Act 1855 (c.113)
River Navigation Improvement (Ireland) Act 1914 (c.55)
River Ouze: Navigation Act 1795 (c.77)
River Poddle Act 1840 (c.58)
River Thames and Isis: Navigation Act 1795 (c.106)
Rivers Pollution Prevention Act 1876 (c.75)
Rivers Pollution Prevention Act 1893 (c.31)
Rivers Pollution Prevention (Border Councils) Act 1898 (c.34)

Rivers (Prevention of Pollution) Act 1951 (c.64)

Rivers (Prevention of Pollution) Act 1961 (c.50)

Rivers (Prevention of Pollution) (Scotland) Act 1951 (c.66)

Rivers (Prevention of Pollution) (Scotland) Act 1965 (c.13)

Road and Rail Traffic Act 1933 (c.53)

Road Haulage Wages Act 1938 (c.44)

Road Safety Act 1967 (c.30)

Road Traffic Act 1930 (c.43)

Road Traffic Act 1934 (c.50)

Road Traffic Act 1937 (c.44)

Road Traffic Act 1956 (c.67)

Road Traffic Act 1959 (c.16)

Road Traffic Act 1960 (c.16)

Road Traffic Act 1962 (c.59)

Road Traffic Act 1964 (c.45)

Road Traffic Act 1967 (c.21)

Road Traffic Act 1972 (c.20)

Road Traffic Act 1974 (c.50)

Road Traffic Act 1988 (c.52)

Road Traffic Act 1991 (c.40)

Road Traffic (Amendment) Act 1931 (c.32)

Road Traffic (Amendment) Act 1960 (c.51)

Road Traffic (Amendment) Act 1967 (c.70)

Road Traffic and Roads Improvement Act 1960 (c.63)

Road Traffic (Consequential Provisions) Act 1988 (c.54)

Road Traffic (Disqualification) Act 1970 (c.23)

Road Traffic (Driving Instruction by Disabled Persons) Act 1993 (c.31)

Road Traffic (Driver Licensing and Information Systems) Act 1989 (c.22)

Road Traffic (Drivers' Ages and Hours of Work) Act 1976 (c.3)

Road Traffic (Driving Instruction) Act 1967 (c.79)

Road Traffic (Driving Instruction) Act 1984 (c.13)

Road Traffic (Driving Licences) Act 1936 (c.23)

Road Traffic (Driving Licences) Act 1946 (c.8)

Road Traffic (Driving Licences) Act 1983 (c.43)

Road Traffic (Driving of Motor Cycles) Act 1960 (c.69)

Road Traffic (Foreign Vehicles) Act 1972 (c.27)

Road Traffic Offenders Act 1988 (c.53)

Road Traffic (Production of Documents) Act 1985 (c.34)

Road Traffic Regulation Act 1967 (c.76)

Road Traffic Regulation Act 1984 (c.27)

Road Traffic Regulation (Parking) Act 1986 (c.27)

Road Traffic Regulation (Special Events) Act 1994 (c.11)

Road Traffic (Temporary Restrictions) Act 1991 (c.26)

Road Transport Lighting Act 1927 (c.37)

Road Transport Lighting Act 1953 (c.21)

Road Transport Lighting Act 1957 (c.51)

Road Transport Lighting Act 1967 (c.55)

Road Transport Lighting (No. 2) Act (c.22)

Road Transport Lighting (Amendment) Act 1958 (c.22)

Roads Act 1920 (c.72)

Roads Amendment Act 1880 (c.7)

Roads and Bridges (Scotland) Act 1848 (c.40)

Roads and Bridges (Scotland) Act 1878 (c.51)

Roads and Bridges (Scotland) Amendment Act 1892 (c.12)

Roads and Bridges (Scotland) Act 1878 Amendment Act 1888 (c.9)

Roads and Streets in Police Burghs (Scotland) Act 1891 (c.32)

Roads and Streets in Police Burghs (Scotland) Act 1925 (c.82)

Roads between London and Holyhead Act 1819 (c.48)

Roads, etc. (Ireland) Act 1827 (c.23)

Roads, etc. (Ireland) Act 1829 (c.40)

Roads, etc. (Scotland) Act 1833 (c.33)

Roads (Ireland) Act 1835 (c.31)

Roads Improvement Act 1925 (c.68)

Roads in Lanarkshire, etc. Act 1823 (c.10)

Roads (London to Chirk) Act 1820 (c.70)

Roads (Scotland) Act 1970 (c.20)

Roads (Scotland) Act 1984 (c.54)

Roasted Malt for Colouring Beer Act 1842 (c.30)

Robbery from the Person Act 1837 (c.87)

Rochdale Canal Company Act 1798 (c.49)

Rochdale Road Act 1795 (c.160)

Rochdale and Bury Road Act 1797 (c.145)

Rochdale and Bury and Sudden Roads Act 1797 (c.146)

Rochdale to Bury Road Act 1794 (c.124)

Rochdale Vicarage Act 1866 (c.86)

Rochdale Vicarage Appointment Act 1865 (c.117)

Rock Salt Act 1811 (c.82)

Roe Deer (Close Seasons) Act 1977 (c.4)

Rogue Money Act (Scotland) 1839 (c.65)

Roll of Valuation (1748) (c.29)

Rolls Estate Act 1837 (c.46)

Rolls-Royce (Purchase) Act 1971 (c.9)

Roman Catholic Act 1844 (c.102)

Roman Catholic Charities Act 1831 (c.115)

Roman Catholic Charities Act 1856 (c.76)

Roman Catholic Charities Act 1857 (c.76)

Roman Catholic Charities Act 1858 (c.51)

Roman Catholic Charities Act 1859 (c.50)

Roman Catholic Charities Act 1860 (c.134)

Roman Catholic Relief Act 1791 (c.32)

Roman Catholic Relief Act 1803 (c.30)

Roman Catholic Relief Act 1813 (c.128)

Roman Catholic Relief Act 1829 (c.7)

Roman Catholic Relief Act 1926 (c.55)

Roosevelt Memorial Act 1946 (c.83)

Ropeworks Act 1846 (c.40)
Rothwell Gaol Act 1845 (c.72)
Royal and Parliamentary Titles Act 1927 (c.4)
Royal Arsenals, etc. Act 1862 (c.78)
Royal Assent Act 1967 (c.23)
Royal Burghs (Scotland) Act 1822 (c.91)
Royal Burghs (Scotland) Act 1833 (c.76)
Royal Burghs, etc. (Scotland) Act 1834 (c.87)
Royal Canal Act 1818 (c.35)
Royal Canal Company Act 1813 (c.101)
Royal Exchange Assurance Act 1796 (c.26)
Royal Household, etc., Act 1812 (c.8)
Royal Irish Constabulary Act 1873 (c.74)
Royal Irish Constabulary (Widows' Pensions) Act 1954 (c.17)
Royal (Late Indian) Ordinance Corps Act 1874 (c.61)
Royal Marines Act 1820 (c.91)
Royal Marines Act 1847 (c.63)
Royal Marines Act 1857 (c.1)
Royal Marines Act 1914 (c.16)
Royal Marines Act 1916 (c.23)
Royal Marines Act 1939 (c.88)
Royal Marines Act 1946 (c.4)
Royal Marines Act 1948 (c.25)
Royal Military Asylum, Chelsea Act 1854 (c.61)
Royal Military Asylum Chelsea (Transfer) Act 1884 (c.32)
Royal Military Canal Act 1837 (c.20)
Royal Military Canal Act 1867 (c.140)
Royal Military Canal Act 1872 (c.66)
Royal Naval Asylum Act 181 (c.105)
Royal Naval Asylum, etc. Act 1825 (c.26)
Royal Naval Reserve Act 1902 (c.5)
Royal Naval Reserve Act 1927 (c.18)
Royal Naval Reserve (Volunteer) Act 1859 (c.40)
Royal Naval Reserve Volunteer Act 1896 (c.33)
Royal Naval Volunteer Reserve Act 1917 (c.22)
Royal Naval Volunteer Reserve Act 1942 (c.18)
Royal Niger Company Act 1899 (c.43)
Royal Patriotic Fund Corporation Act 1949 (c.10)
Royal Pavilion, Brighton, etc. Act 1849 (c.102)
Royal Scottish Museum (Extension) Act 1912 (c.16)
Royal Signature by Commission Act 1830 (c.23)
Royal Tithes Act 1876 (c.10)
Royal Titles Act 1901 (c.15)
Royal Titles Act 1952 (c.9)
Royal University of Ireland Act 1881 (c.52)
Rules Publication Act 1893 (c.66)
Rural Water Supplies Act 1934 (c.7)
Rural Water Supplies and Sewerage Act 1944 (c.26)
Rural Water Supplies and Sewerage Act 1951 (c.45)

Rural Water Supplies and Sewerage Act 1955 (c.13)
Rural Water Supplies and Sewerage Act 1961 (c.29)
Rural Water Supplies and Sewerage Act 1965 (c.80)
Rural Water Supplies and Sewerage Act 1971 (c.49)
Rural Water Supplies and Sewerage (No. 2) Act 1955 (c.15)
Rural Water Supplies and Sewerage (Scotland) Act 1969 (c.6)
Russian Dutch Loan Act 1815 (c.115)
Russian Dutch Loan Act 1832 (c.81)
Russian Dutch Loan Act 1891 (c.26)
Russian Goods (Import Prohibition) Act 1933 (c.10)
Russian Government Securities Act 1854 (c.123)
Ruthin Charities Act 1863 (c.59)
Rye Harbour Act 1797 (c.130)

Sacramental Test Act 1828 (c.17)
Sacramental Test (Ireland) Act 1832 (c.7)
Sailcloth Manufacture, etc. Act 1805 (c.68)
Safety at Sea Act 1986 (c.23)
Safety of Sports Grounds Act 1975 (c.52)
Safeguarding of Industries Act 1921 (c.47)
Safeguarding of Industries (Customs Duties) Act 1925 (c.79)
Sailors and Soldiers (Gifts for Land Settlement) Act 1916 (c.60)
Salaries of Bishops, etc. in West Indies Act 1826 (c.4)
Salaries of Chief Baron, etc. Act 1809 (c.127)
Salaries of County Officers (Ireland) Act 1823 (c.43)
Salaries of County Officers (Ireland) Act 1824 (c.93)
Salaries of Judges (Scotland) Act 1806 (c.49)
Salaries of Scotch Judges Act 1800 (c.55)
Salary of Lord Lieutenant Act 1811 (c.89)
Salary of Sir J. Lawrence Act 1864 (c.2)
Salcey Forest Act 1825 (c.132)
Sale and Supply of Goods Act 1994 (c.35)
Sale of Advowsons Act 1856 (c.50)
Sale of Beer Act 1795 (c.113)
Sale of Beer, etc. on Sunday Act 1848 (c.49)
Sale of Beer, etc. Act 1854 (c.79)
Sale of Bread, etc. Act 1800 (c.16)
Sale of Bread Act 1800 (c.71)
Sale of Bread Act 1800 (c.18)
Sale of Bread Act 1801 (c.12)
Sale of Butter Act 1796 (c.86)
Sale of Certain Lands in Worcester Act 1819 (c.137)
Sale of Certain Stock Act 1812 (c.148)
Sale, etc. of Certain Stocks Act 1829 (c.48)
Sale of Church Patronages Belonging to Municipal Corporations Act 1838 (c.31)
Sale of Crown Lands Act 1826 (c.51)
Sale of Crown Rents (Ireland) Act 1806 (c.123)

Sale of Crown Rents, etc. (Ireland) Act 1807 (c.16)

Sale of Exhausted Parish Lands Act 1876 (c.62)

Sale of Farming Stock Act 1816 (c.50)

Sale of Fish Act 1834 (c.20)

Sale of Food and Drugs Act 1875 (c.63)

Sale of Food and Drugs Act 1899 (c.51)

Sale of Food and Drugs Act 1927 (c.5)

Sale of Food and Drugs Amendment Act 1879 (c.30)

Sale of Food (Weights and Measures) Act 1926 c.63)

Sale of Gas Act 1859 (c.66)

Sale of Gas Act 1860 (c.146)

Sale of Gas (Scotland) Act 1864 (c.96)

Sale of Goods Act 1893 (c.71)

Sale of Goods Act 1979 (c.54)

Sale of Goods (Amendment) Act 1994 (c.32)

Sale of Hares (Ireland) Act 1863 (c.19)

Sale of H. M.'s Bakehouse in Windsor Act 1862 (c.57)

Sale of Horseflesh, etc. Regulation Act 1889 (c.11)

Sale of Land by Auction Act 1867 (c.48)

Sale of Liquors by Retail (Ireland) Act 1807 (c.12)

Sale of Liquors on Sunday Act 1878 (c.72)

Sale of Mill Sites, etc. (Ireland) Act 1863 (c.42)

Sale of Muriate of Potash, etc. Act 1813 (c.97)

Sale of Offices Act 1809 (c.126)

Sale of Post Office Buildings Act 1831 (c.27)

Sale of Prize Ship Constantia Maria Act 1808 (c.147)

Sale of Spirits Act 1862 (c.38)

Sale of Spirits (England) Act 1820 (c.76)

Sale of Spirits, etc. (Ireland) Act 1839 (c.79)

Sale of Spirituous Liquors Act 1805 (c.50)

Sale of Spirituous Liquors, etc. Act 1813 (c.137)

Sale of Tea Act 1922 (c.29)

Sale of Venison (Scotland) Act 1968 (c.38)

Sale of Wine, etc. Act 1801 (c.48)

Sale of Workhouses Act 1821 (c.56)

Sales of Reversions Act 1867 (c.4)

Salmon Act 1696 (c.35)

Salmon Act 1986 (c.62)

Salmon Acts Amendment Act 1863 (c.10)

Salmon Acts Amendment Act 1870 (c.33)

Salmon and Fisheries Act 1965 (c.68)

Salmon and Freshwater Fisheries Act 1886 (c.39)

Salmon and Freshwater Fisheries Act 1892 (c.50)

Salmon and Freshwater Fisheries Act 1907 (c.15)

Salmon and Freshwater Fisheries Act 1921 (c.38)

Salmon and Freshwater Fisheries Act 1923 (c.16)

Salmon and Freshwater Fisheries Act 1923 (Amendment) Act 1964 (c.27)

Salmon and Freshwater Fisheries Act 1935 (c.43)

Salmon and Freshwater Fisheries Act 1972 (c.37)

Salmon and Freshwater Fisheries Act 1975 (c.51)

Salmon and Freshwater Fisheries (Amendment) Act 1929 (c.39)

Salmon and Freshwater Fisheries (Protection) (Scotland) Act 1951 (c.26)

Salmon Fisheries Act 1843 (c.33)

Salmon Fisheries Act 1848 (c.52)

Salmon Fisheries (England) Act 1818 (c.43)

Salmon Fisheries (Scotland) Act 1828 (c.39)

Salmon Fisheries (Scotland) Act 1844 (c.95)

Salmon Fisheries (Scotland) Act 1862 (c.97)

Salmon Fisheries (Scotland) Act 1863 (c.50)

Salmon Fisheries (Scotland) Act 1864 (c.118)

Salmon Fisheries (Scotland) Act 1868 (c.123)

Salmon Fishery Act 1861 (c.109)

Salmon Fishery Act 1865 (c.121)

Salmon Fishery Act 1873 (c.71)

Salmon Fishery Act 1876 (c.19)

Salmon Fishery Commissioners Act 1873 (c.13)

Salmon Fishery (Ireland) Act 1863 (c.114)

Salmon Fishery (Ireland) Act 1869 (c.9)

Salmon Fishery Law Amendment Act 1879 (c.26)

Salop Roads Act 1794 (c.123)

Salop Roads Act 1797 (c.172)

Salop and Hereford Roads Act 1794 (c.122)

Salt Duties Act 1798 (c.89)

Salt Duties Act 1799 (c.77)

Salt Duties Act 1805 (c.14)

Salt Duties Act 1813 (c.22)

Salt Duty Act 1813 (c.124)

Salt Duty Act 1815 (c.179)

Salt Duty Act 1816 (c.94)

Saltcoates Harbour 1797 (c.132)

Saltpetre Act 1800 (c.38)

Sand-Grouse Protection Act 1888 (c.55)

Sandhurst Act 1862 (c.33)

Sanitary Act 1866 (c.90)

Sanitary Act 1868 (c.115)

Sanitary Act 1870 (c.53)

Sanitary Act 1873 (c.78)

Sanitary Act, 1866, Amendment (Ireland) Act 1869 (c.108)

Sanitary Act (Dublin) Amendment Act 1870 (c.106)

Sanitary Inspectors (Change of Designation) Act 1956 (c.66)

Sanitary Law Amendment Act 1874 (c.89)

Sanitary Law (Dublin) Amendment Act 1875 (c.95)

Sanitary Loans Act 1869 (c.100)

Sardinia Loan Act 1855 (c.17)

Sardinian Loan Act 1856 (c.39)

Satisfied Terms Act 1845 (c.112)

Saving Banks Act 1824 (c.62)

Saving Bank Act 1828 (c.92)
Saving Bank Act 1833 (c.14)
Saving Bank Act 1835 (c.57)
Saving Bank Act 1844 (c.83)
Saving Banks Act 1852 (c.60)
Saving Banks Act 1880 (c.36)
Saving Banks Act 1887 (c.40)
Savings Banks Act 1891 (c.21)
Savings Bank Act 1893 (c.69)
Savings Bank Act 1904 (c.8)
Savings Banks Act 1920 (c.12)
Savings Banks Act 1929 (c.27)
Savings Banks Act 1949 (c.13)
Savings Banks and Friendly Societies Act 1854 (c.50)
Savings Banks (Barrister) Act 1876 (c.52)
Savings Bank (Charitable Societies) Act 1859 (c.53)
Savings Bank (England) Act 1817 (c.130)
Savings Bank (England) Act 1818 (c.48)
Savings Bank (England) Act 1820 (c.83)
Savings Bank Investment Act 1863 (c.25)
Savings Bank Investment Act 1866 (c.5)
Savings Bank Investment Act 1869 (c.59)
Savings Bank (Ireland) Act 1817 (c.105)
Savings Bank (Ireland) Act 1848 (c.133)
Savings Bank (Ireland) Act 1850 (c.110)
Savings Banks (Ireland) Act 1859 (c.17)
Savings Banks (Ireland) Cont. Act 1862 (c.75)
Savings Bank (Scotland) Act 1819 (c.62)
School Board Conference Act 1897 (c.32)
School Boards Act 1885 (c.38)
School Boards (Scotland) Act 1988 (c.47)
School Crossing Patrols Act 1953 (c.45)
School Districts Act 1850 (c.11)
School Grants Act 1855 (c.131)
School of Physic (Ireland) Amendment Act 1867 (c.9)
School Sites Act 1841 (c.38)
School Sites Act 1844 (c.37)
School Sites Act 1849 (c.49)
School Sites Act 1851 (c.24)
School Sites Act 1852 (c.49)
School Sites (Ireland) Act 1810 (c.32)
School Teachers Pay and Conditions Act 1991 (c.49)
School Teachers (Superannuation) Act 1918 (c.55)
School Teachers (Superannuation) Act 1922 (c.42)
School Teachers (Superannuation) Act 1924 (c.12)
Schools for Science and Art Act 1891 (c.61)
Science and Technology Act 1965 (c.4)
Scientific Societies Act 1843 (c.36)
Scotch and Irish Paupers Act 1840 (c.27)
Scotch and Irish Paupers Removal Act 1844 (c.42)
Scotch Distilleries Act 1797 (c.102)
Scotch Distilleries Act 1798 (c.92)
Scotch Whisky Act 1988 (c.22)
Scotland Act 1978 (c.51)

Scottish Board of Health Act 1919 (c.20)
Scottish Development Agency Act 1975 (c.69)
Scottish Development Agency Act 1987 (c.56)
Scottish Episcopal and other Clergy Act 1840 (c.33)
Scottish Episcopalians Act 1711 (c.10)
Scottish Episcopalians Relief Act 1792 (c.63)
Scottish Fisheries Advisory Council Act 1941 (c.1)
Scottish Land Court Act 1938 (c.31)
Scottish Land Court Act 1993 (c.45)
Scottish Universities (Emergency Powers) Act 1915 (c.78)
Scrabster Harbour Act 1841 (c.1)
Scrap Metal Dealers Act 1964 (c.69)
Sculpture Copyright Act 1814 (c.56)
Sea and Coast Fisheries Fund (Ireland) Act 1884 (c.21)
Sea Birds Preservation Act 1869 (c.17)
Sea Fish (Conservation) Act 1967 (c.84)
Sea Fish (Conservation) Act 1992 (c.60)
Sea Fish Industry Act 1938 (c.30)
Sea Fish Industry Act 1951 (c.30)
Sea Fish Industry Act 1959 (c.7)
Sea Fish Industry Act 1962 (c.31)
Sea Fish Industry Act 1970 (c.11)
Sea Fish Industry Act 1973 (c.3)
Sea Fish Industry Act 1980 (c.35)
Sea Fisheries Act 1817 (c.69)
Sea Fisheries Act 1843 (c.79)
Sea Fisheries Act 1868 (c.45)
Sea Fisheries Act 1875 (c.15)
Sea Fisheries Act 1883 (c.22)
Sea Fisheries Act 1884 (c.27)
Sea Fisheries Act 1967 (c.83)
Sea Fisheries Act 1968 (c.77)
Sea Fisheries (Clam and Bait Beds) Act 1881 (c.11)
Sea Fisheries (Compensation) (Scotland) Act 1959 (c.27)
Sea Fisheries (Ireland) Act 1818 (c.94)
Sea Fisheries (Ireland) Act 1883 (c.26)
Sea Fisheries Regulation Act 1888 (c.54)
Sea Fisheries Regulation Act 1966 (c.38)
Sea Fisheries (Regulation) Expenses Act 1930 (c.41)
Sea Fisheries Regulation (Scotland) Act 1895 (c.42)
Sea Fisheries (Scotland) Act 1810 (c.108)
Sea Fisheries (Scotland) Application of Penalties Act 1907 (c.42)
Sea Fisheries (Scotland) Act 1810 (c.108)
Sea Fisheries (Scotland) Amendment Act 1885 (c.70)
Sea Fisheries (Shellfish) Act 1967 (c.83)
Sea Fisheries (Shellfish) Act 1973 (c.30)
Sea Fisheries (Shellfish) Regulation Act 1894 (c.26)
Sea Fisheries (Wildlife Conservation) Act 1992 (c.36)
Sea Fishing Boats (Scotland) Act 1886 (c.53)

Sea Fishing Industry Act 1933 (c.45)

Sea Insurances (Stamping of Policies) Amendment Act 1876 (c.6)

Seal Fisheries (North Pacific) Act 1895 (c.21)

Seal Fisheries (North Pacific) Act 1912 (c.10)

Seal Fishery Act 1875 (c.18)

Seal Fishery (Behring's Sea) Act 1891 (c.19)

Seal Fishery (North Pacific) Act 1893 (c.23)

Seal Office in Courts of Queen's Bench and Common Pleas Act 1845 (c.34)

Seamen Act 1836 (c.15)

Seamen's and Soldiers' False Characters Act 1906 (c.5)

Seamen's Clothing Act 1869 (c.57)

Seamen's Fund Winding-up Act 1851 (c.102)

Seamen's Hospital Society Act 1832 (c.9)

Seamen's Savings Bank Act 1856 (c.41)

Seats for Shop Assistants Act 1899 (c.21)

Second Session (Explanation) Act 1899 (c.3)

Secret Service Money (Repeal) Act 1886 (c.2)

Secretary at War Abolition Act 1863 (c.12)

Secretary for Scotland Act 1885 (c.61)

Secretary for Scotland Act 1887 (c.52)

Secretary for Scotland Act 1889 (c.16)

Secretary for State 1904 (c.27)

Secretaries of State Act 1926 (c.18)

Securities (Validation) Act 1940 (c.55)

Securities (Validation) Act 1942 (c.10)

Security of Public Officers Act 1812 (c.66)

Security of Rents, Durham Act 1830 (c.11)

Security Service Act 1989 (c.5)

Seditious Meetings Act 1795 (c.8)

Seditious Meetings Act 1817 (c.19)

Seditious Meetings Act 1846 (c.33)

Seditious Meetings, etc. Act 1819 (c.6)

Seditious Meetings Prevention Act 1801 (c.30)

Seed Potatoes and Seed Oats Supply (Ireland) Act 1908 (c.19)

Seed Potatoes Supply (Ireland) Act 1891 (c.1)

Seed Potatoes Supply (Ireland) Act 1891 (c.7)

Seed Potatoes Supply (Ireland) Act 1895 (c.2)

Seed Potatoes Supply (Ireland) Act 1906 (c.3)

Seed Supply and Potato Spraying (Ireland) Act 1898 (c.50)

Seed Supply (Ireland) Act 1880 (c.1)

Seeds Act 1920 (c.54)

Seeds Amendment Act 1925 (c.66)

Sees of St. Asaph and Bangor Act 1842 (c.112)

Seizure of Arms Act 1819 (c.2)

Seizure of Crops (Ireland) Act 1863 (c.62)

Selective Employment Payments Act 1966 (c.32)

Self-Governing Schools etc. (Scotland) Act 1989 (c.39)

Senior Member of Council, India Act 1860 (c.87)

Senior Public Elementary Schools (Liverpool) Act (c.60)

Sentence of Death (Expectant Mothers) Act 1931 (c.24)

Separatists' Affirmations Act 1833 (c.82)

Sequestration Act 1849 (c.67)

Sequestration Act 1871 (c.45)

Sergeants at Law Act 1825 (c.95)

Servants' Characters Act 1792 (c.56)

Servants' Wages (Ireland) Act 1807 (c.43)

Service of Heirs (Scotland) Act 1847 (c.47)

Service of Process (Justices) Act 1933 (c.42)

Service of Process out of the Jurisdiction (England and Ireland) Act 1832 (c.33)

Service of Process out of the Jurisdiction (England and Ireland) Act 1834 (c.82)

Session Court (Scotland) Act 1810 (c.31)

Session of the Peace, Dublin Act 1843 (c.81)

Sessions Houses, Westminster, etc. Act 1804 (c.61)

Sessions of the Peace, Westminster Act 1828 (c.9)

Settled Estates Act 1840 (c.55)

Settled Estates Act 1856 (c.120)

Settled Estates Act 1858 (c.77)

Settled Estates Act 1876 (c.30)

Settled Estates Act 1877 (c.18)

Settled Estates Act Amendment Act 1864 (c.45)

Settled Land Act 1882 (c.38)

Settled Land Act 1884 (c.18)

Settled Land Act 1889 (c.36)

Settled Land Act 1890 (c.69)

Settled Land Act 1925 (c.18)

Settled Land Acts (Amendment) Act 1887 (c.30)

Settled Land and Trustee Acts (Courts General Powers) Act 1943 (c.25)

Settled Land (Ireland) Act 1847 (c.46)

Settlement of Estate on Lord Nelson Act 1813 (c.134)

Settlement of the Poor (England) Act 1819 (c.50)

Settlements on Coast of Africa and Falkland Islands Act 1843 (c.13)

Severn Bridge Tolls Act 1965 (c.24)

Severn Bridge Act 1992 (c.3)

Sewage Utilisation Act 1865 (c.75)

Sewage Utilisation Act 1867 (c.113)

Sewerage (Scotland) Act 1968 (c.47)

Sewers Act 1833 (c.22)

Sewers Act 1841 (c.45)

Sewers Act 1849 (c.50)

Sex Discrimination Act 1975 (c.65)

Sex Discrimination Act 1986 (c.59)

Sex Disqualification (Removal) Act 1919 (c.71)

Sexual Offences Act 1956 (c.69)

Sexual Offences Act 1967 (c.60)

Sexual Offences Act 1985 (c.44)

Sexual Offences Act 1993 (c.30)

Sexual Offences (Amendment) Act 1976 (c.82)

Sexual Offences (Amendment) Act 1992 (c.34)

Sexual Offences (Scotland) Act 1976 (c.67)

Seychelles Act 1976 (c.19)

Shannon Act 1874 (c.60)

Shannon Act 1885 (c.41)

Shannon Navigation Act 1839 (c.61)

Shannon Navigation Act 1847 (c.74)

Sharing of Church Buildings Act 1969 (c.38)

Sheep and Cattle Disease Prevention Act 1850 (c.71)

Sheep, etc. Diseases Act 1851 (c.69)

Sheep, etc. Disorders Prevention Act 1852 (c.11)

Sheep Stealers (Ireland) Act 1849 (c.30)

Sheep Stocks Valuation (Scotland) Act 1937 (c.34)

Sheffield University Act 1914 (c.4)

Sheriff and Sheriff Clerk of Chancery (Scotland) Act 1854 (c.72)

Sheriff Court Houses Act 1860 (c.79)

Sheriff Court Houses (Scotland) Act 1866 (c.53)

Sheriff Court Houses (Scotland) Amendment Act 1884 (c.42)

Sheriff Courts and Legal Officers (Scotland) Act 1927 (c.35)

Sheriff Courts (Civil Jurisdiction and Procedure) (Scotland) Act 1963 (c.22)

Sheriff Courts Consignations (Scotland) Act 1893 (c.44)

Sheriff Courts (Scotland) Act 1825 (c.23)

Sheriff Courts (Scotland) Act 1838 (c.119)

Sheriff Courts (Scotland) Act 1853 (c.80)

Sheriff Courts (Scotland) Act 1870 (c.86)

Sheriff Courts (Scotland) Act 1876 (c.70)

Sheriff Courts (Scotland) Act 1877 (c.50)

Sheriff Courts (Scotland) Act 1907 (c.51)

Sheriff Courts (Scotland) Act 1913 (c.28)

Sheriff Courts (Scotland) Act 1939 (c.98)

Sheriff Courts (Scotland) Act 1971 (c.58)

Sheriff Courts (Scotland) Amendment 1914 (c.5)

Sheriff Courts (Scotland) Extracts Act 1892 (c.17)

Sheriff Deputies, etc. Act 1799 (c.66)

Sheriff of Lanarkshire Act 1887 (c.41)

Sheriff of Selkirkshire Act 1832 (c.101)

Sheriff of Westmoreland Act 1849 (c.42)

Sheriff of Westmoreland Act 1850 (c.30)

Sheriff Substitute (Scotland) Act 1875 (c.81)

Sheriffs Act 1817 (c.68)

Sheriffs Act 1887 (c.55)

Sheriffs Fees Act 1837 (c.55)

Sheriffs (Ireland) Act 1835 (c.55)

Sheriffs (Ireland) Act 1920 (c.26)

Sheriffs of Edinburgh and Lanark Act 1822 (c.49)

Sheriffs' Pension (Scotland) Act 1961 (c.42)

Sheriffs (Scotland) Act 1853 (c.92)

Sheriff's Substitute Act 1864 (c.106)

Sheriff's Tenure of Office (Scotland) Act 1898 (c.8)

Sheriffs, Wales Act 1845 (c.11)

Sherwood Forest Act 1818 (c.100)

Shipbuilding Act 1979 (c.59)

Shipbuilding Act 1982 (c.4)

Shipbuilding Act 1985 (c.14)

Shipbuilding Credit Act 1964 (c.7)

Shipbuilding Industry Act 1967 (c.40)

Shipbuilding Industry Act 1968 (c.6)

Shipbuilding Industry Act 1971 (c.46)

Shipbuilding (Redundancy Payments) Act 1978 (c.11)

Shipowners' Liability for Losses by Fire Act 1836 (c.61)

Shipowners' Negligence (Remedies) Act 1904 (c.10)

Shipping Act 1795 (c.80)

Shipping Act 1799 (c.32)

Shipping Act 1816 (c.114)

Shipping Casualties Investigations Act 1879 (c.72)

Shipping Dues Exemption Act 1867 (c.15)

Shipping Dues Exemption Act Amendment Act 1869 (c.52)

Shipping Duties Exemption Act 1870 (c.50)

Shipping, etc. Act 1845 (c.88)

Shipping Offences Act 1793 (c.67)

Shipping under Treaties of Commerce Act 1826 (c.5)

Ships and Aircraft (Transfer Restriction) Act 1939 (c.70)

Shoeburyness Artillery Rangers Act 1862 (c.36)

Shooting Hares (Scotland) Act 1808 (c.94)

Shop Clubs Act 1902 (c.21)

Shop Hours Act 1892 (c.62)

Shop Hours Act 1893 (c.67)

Shop Hours Act 1895 (c.5)

Shop Hours Act 1904 (c.31)

Shop Hours Regulation Act 1886 (c.55)

Shops Act 1911 (c.54)

Shops Act 1912 (c.3)

Shops Act 1913 (c.24)

Shops Act 1934 (c.42)

Shops Act 1936 (c.28)

Shops Act 1950 (c.28)

Shops (Airports) Act 1962 (c.35)

Shops (Early Closing) Act 1920 (c.58)

Shops (Early Closing) Act (1920) Amendment Act 1921 (c.60)

Shops (Early Closing Days) Act 1965 (c.35)

Shops (Hours of Closing) Act 1928 (c.33)

Shops (Sunday Trading Restrictions) Act 1936 (c.53)

Shorncliffe Military Canal, etc. Act 1807 (c.70)

Short Titles Act 1892 (c.10)

Short Titles Act 1896 (c.14)

Shrewsbury and Holyhead Road Act 1845 (c.73)

Shrewsbury Improvement Act 1756 (c.78)

Shrewsbury to Bangor Road Act 1835 (c.21)

Shrewsbury to Holyhead Act 1819 (c.30)

Shubenaccasie Canal, Nova Scotia Act 1830 (c.34)

Siam and Straits Settlement Jurisdiction Act 1870 (c.55)
Sierra Leone Act 1853 (c.86)
Sierra Leone Company Act 1807 (c.44)
Sierra Leone Independence Act 1961 (c.16)
Sierra Leone Offences Act 1861 (c.31)
Sierra Leone Republic Act 1972 (c.1)
Sikes' Hydrometer Act 1816 (c.140)
Silk, etc. Bounties Act 1821 (c.91)
Silk Duties Act 1828 (c.23)
Silk Manufacture Act 1811 (c.7)
Silk Manufacture, etc. Act 1821 (c.11)
Silk Manufacture (Ireland) Act 1810 (c.27)
Silk Manufactures Act 1809 (c.20)
Silk Manufactures Act 1824 (c.21)
Silk Manufactures Act 1824 (c.66)
Silk Weavers Act 1845 (c.128)
Silver Coin Act 1798 (c.59)
Silver Plate Act 1790 (c.31)
Simony Act 1588 (c.6)
Singapore Act 1966 (c.29)
Sinking Fund Act 1875 (c.45)
Sir H. Pottinger's Annuity Act 1845 (c.49)
Sir J. Soane's Museum Act 1862 (c.9)
Sir John Port's Charity, Repton Act 1867 (c.99)
Sir R. Hitcham's Charity Act 1863 (c.58)
Site for Docks, etc. Dublin Act 1819 (c.82)
Site for Record Office (Ireland) Act 1826 (c.13)
Sites for Schoolrooms Act 1836 (c.70)
Sites of Parish Churches (Ireland) Act 1813 (c.66)
Six Clerks in Chancery (Ireland) Act 1813 (c.129)
Slander of Women Act 1891 (c.51)
Slate Mines (Gunpowder) Act 1882 (c.3)
Slaughter of Animals Act 1914 (c.75)
Slaughter of Animals Act 1933 (c.39)
Slaughter of Animals Act 1958 (c.8)
Slaughter of Animals (Amendment) Act 1951 (c.49)
Slaughter of Animals (Amendment) Act 1954 (c.59)
Slaughter of Animals (Pigs) Act 1953 (c.27)
Slaughter of Animals (Scotland) Act 1928 (c.29)
Slaughter of Animals (Scotland) Act 1949 (c.52)
Slaughter of Animals (Scotland) Act 1980 (c.13)
Slaughter of Poultry Act 1967 (c.24)
Slaughterhouses Act 1954 (c.42)
Slaughterhouses Act 1958 (c.70)
Slaughterhouses Act 1974 (c.3)
Slaughterhouses etc. (Metropolis) Act 1874 (c.67)
Slave Trade Act 1795 (c.90)
Slave Trade Act 1797 (c.104)
Slave Trade Act 1797 (c.118)
Slave Trade Act 1798 (c.88)
Slave Trade Act 1799 (c.80)
Slave Trade Act 1806 (c.52)

Slave Trade Act 1806 (c.119)
Slave Trade Act 1811 (c.23)
Slave Trade Act 1813 (c.112)
Slave Trade Act 1814 (c.59)
Slave Trade Act 1818 (c.36)
Slave Trade Act 1818 (c.49)
Slave Trade Act 1818 (c.85)
Slave Trade Act 1818 (c.98)
Slave Trade Act 1819 (c.97)
Slave Trade Act 1824 (c.17)
Slave Trade Act 1824 (c.113)
Slave Trade Act 1828 (c.84)
Slave Trade Act 1833 (c.72)
Slave Trade Act 1835 (cc.60, 61)
Slave Trade Act 1836 (c.81)
Slave Trade Act 1837 (c.62)
Slave Trade Act 1843 (c.46)
Slave Trade Act 1843 (c.98)
Slave Trade Act 1844 (c.26)
Slave Trade Act 1848 (c.116)
Slave Trade Act 1849 (c.84)
Slave Trade Act 1873 (c.88)
Slave Trade Act 1876 (c.46)
Slave Trade, Brazil Act 1845 (c.122)
Slave Trade Convention with Brazil Act 1827 (c.74)
Slave Trade (East African Courts) Act 1873 (c.59)
Slave Trade (East African Courts) Act 1879 (c.38)
Slave Trade Jurisdiction (Zanzibar) Act 1869 (c.75)
Slave Trade (Muscat) Act 1848 (c.128)
Slave Trade Suppression Act 1838 (c.47)
Slave Trade Suppression Act 1838 (c.102)
Slave Trade Suppression Act 1839 (c.57)
Slave Trade Suppression Act 1839 (c.73)
Slave Trade Suppression Act 1840 (c.64)
Slave Trade Suppression Act 1842 (c.42)
Slave Trade Suppression Act 1842 (c.59)
Slave Trade Suppression Act 1842 (c.91)
Slave Trade Suppression Act 1842 (c.101)
Slave Trade Suppression Act 1842 (c.114)
Slave Trade Suppression, African Treaty Act 1855 (c.85)
Slave Trade Suppression, Netherlands Act 1819 (c.16)
Slave Trade Suppression, Portugal Act 1819 (c.17)
Slave Trade Suppression Treaties with Sohar and New Grenada Act 1853 (cc.16, 17)
Slave Trade Suppression Treaty with Spain Act 1836 (c.6)
Slave Trade Suppression Treaty with Venezuela Act 1840 (c.67)
Slave Trade Treaties Act 1838 (cc.39–41)
Slave Trade Treaties Act 1838 (cc.83, 84)
Slave Trade Treaties Act 1843 (cc.50–53)
Slave Trade Treaties with Bolivia, Texas, Uruguay Act 1843 (cc.14-16)
Slave Trade, Treaty with Sweden Act 1827 (c.54)
Slavery Abolition Act 1833 (c.73)

Sligo and Cashel Disfranchisement Act 1870 (c.38)

Slough Roads Act 1796 (c.140)

Slum Clearance (Compensation) Act 1956 (c.57)

Small Debt Amendment (Scotland) Act 1889 (c.26)

Small Debt (Scotland) Act 1837 (c.41)

Small Debt (Scotland) Act 1924 (c.16)

Small Debt (Scotland) Act 1932 (c.38)

Small Debts Act 1795 (c.123)

Small Debts Act 1845 (c.127)

Small Debts Recovery (Ireland) Act 1837 (c.43)

Small Debts (Scotland) Act 1800 (c.46)

Small Debts (Scotland) Act 1825 (c.24)

Small Debts (Scotland) Act 1829 (c.55)

Small Dwellings Acquisition Act 1899 (c.44)

Small Estates (Representation) Act 1961 (c.37)

Small Holdings Act 1892 (c.31)

Small Holdings Act 1910 (c.34)

Small Holdings and Allotments Act 1907 (c.54)

Small Holdings and Allotments Act 1908 (c.36)

Small Holdings and Allotments Act 1926 (c.52)

Small Holding Colonies Act 1916 (c.38)

Small Holding Colonies (Amendment) Act 1918 (c.26)

Small Landholders and Agricultural Holdings (Scotland) Act 1931 (c.44)

Small Landholders (Scotland) Act 1911 (c.49)

Small Livings Act 1806 (c.60)

Small Lotteries and Gaming Act 1956 (c.45)

Small Lotteries and Gaming Act 1959 (c.35)

Small Penalties Act 1865 (c.127)

Small Penalties (Ireland) Act 1873 (c.82)

Small Tenements Recovery Act 1838 (c.74)

Small Testate Estates (Scotland) Act 1876 (c.24)

Smithfield Market Act 1851 (c.61)

Smoke Abatement, London Act 1853 (c.128)

Smoke Abatement, London Act 1856 (c.107)

Smoke Detectors Act 1991 (c.37)

Smoke Nuisance (Scotland) Act 1857 (c.73)

Smoke Nuisance (Scotland) Act 1865 (c.102)

Smoke of Furnaces (Scotland) Act 1861 (c.17)

Smugglers' Families Act 1830 (c.10)

Smuggling Act 1795 (c.31)

Smuggling Act 1802 (c.82)

Smuggling Act 1803 (c.157)

Smuggling Act 1805 (c.121)

Smuggling Act 1807 (c.66)

Smuggling Act 1819 (c.121)

Smuggling Act 1822 (c.110)

Smuggling Act 1834 (c.13)

Smuggling Customs Regulations etc. Act 1809 (c.62)

Smuggling, etc. Act 1805 (c.99)

Smuggling, etc. Act 1808 (c.84)

Smuggling, etc. Act 1818 (c.76)

Smuggling, etc. Act 1820 (c.43)

Soap Duty Allowances Act 1835 (c.15)

Soap Duties Act 1839 (c.32)

Soap Duties Allowances Act 1842 (c.16)

Soap Duties Allowances Act 1844 (c.51)

Soap Duties Allowances Act 1847 (c.41)

Soap Duties Allowances Act 1849 (c.40)

Soap Duties Allowances Act 1851 (c.59)

Soap Duties Repeal Act 1853 (c.39)

Social Fund (Maternity and Funeral Expenses) Act 1987 (c.7)

Social Security Act 1971 (c.73)

Social Security Act 1973 (c.38)

Social Security Act 1975 (c.14)

Social Security Act 1979 (c.18)

Social Security Act 1980 (c.30)

Social Security Act 1981 (c.33)

Social Security Act 1985 (c.53)

Social Security Act 1986 (c.50)

Social Security Act 1988 (c.7)

Social Security Act 1989 (c.24)

Social Security Act 1990 (c.27)

Social Security Act 1993 (c.3)

Social Security Administration Act 1992 (c.5)

Social Security Administration (Northern Ireland) Act 1992 (c.8)

Social Security Amendment Act 1974 (c.58)

Social Security and Housing Benefits Act 1982 (c.24)

Social Security and Housing Benefits Act 1983 (c.36)

Social Security Benefits Act 1975 (c.11)

Social Security (Consequential Provisions) Act 1975 (c.18)

Social Security (Consequential Provisions) Act 1992 (c.6)

Social Security (Consequential Provisions) (Northern Ireland) Act 1992 (c.9)

Social Security (Contributions) Act 1981 (c.1)

Social Security (Contributions) Act 1982 (c.2)

Social Security (Contributions) Act 1991 (c.42)

Social Security (Contributions) Act 1994 (c.1)

Social Security Contributions and Benefits Act 1992 (c.4)

Social Security Contributions and Benefits (Northern Ireland) Act 1992 (c.7)

Social Security (Incapacity for Work) Act 1994 (c.18)

Social Security (Miscellaneous Provisions) Act 1977 (c.5)

Social Security (Mortgage Interest Payments) Act 1992 (c.33)

Social Security (Northern Ireland) Act 1975 (c.15)

Social Security (No. 2) Act 1980 (c.39)

Social Security Pensions Act 1975 (c.60)

Social Services (Northern Ireland Agreement) Act 1949 (c.23)

Social Work (Scotland) Act 1968 (c.49)

Social Work (Scotland) Act 1972 (c.24)

Societies' Borrowing Powers Act 1898 (c.15)
Societies (Miscellaneous Provisions) Act 1940 (c.19)
Societies (Suspension of Meetings) Act 1917 (c.16)
Sodor and Man Act 1838 (c.30)
Solicitor (Ireland) Act 1822 (c.16)
Solicitors Act 1837 (c.56)
Solicitors Act 1843 (c.73)
Solicitors Act 1860 (c.127)
Solicitors Act 1877 (c.25)
Solicitors Act 1888 (c.65)
Solicitors Act 1894 (c.9)
Solicitors Act 1899 (c.4)
Solicitors Act 1906 (c.24)
Solicitors Act 1919 (c.56)
Solicitors Act 1922 (c.57)
Solicitors Act 1928 (c.22)
Solicitors Act 1932 (c.37)
Solicitors Act 1933 (c.24)
Solicitors Act 1934 (c.45)
Solicitors Act 1936 (c.35)
Solicitors Act 1941 (c.46)
Solicitors Act 1950 (c.6)
Solicitors Act 1957 (c.27)
Solicitors Act 1965 (c.31)
Solicitors Act 1974 (c.47)
Solicitors (Amendment) Act 1956 (c.41)
Solicitors (Amendment) Act 1959 (c.42)
Solicitors (Amendment) Act 1974 (c.26)
Solicitors (Articled Clerks) Act 1918 (c.16)
Solicitors (Articled Clerks) Act 1919 (c.27)
Solicitors (Clerks) Act 1839 (c.33)
Solicitors (Clerks) Act 1844 (c.86)
Solicitors (Disciplinary Committee) Act 1939 (c.110)
Solicitors (Emergency Provisions) Act 1940 (c.15)
Solicitors (Examination) Act 1917 (c.43)
Solicitors (Ireland) Act 1821 (c.48)
Solicitors (Ireland) Act 1849 (c.53)
Solicitors (Ireland) Act 1861 (c.68)
Solicitors (Ireland) Act 1898 (c.17)
Solicitors, Public Notaries, etc. Act 1949 (c.21)
Solicitors Remuneration Act 1881 (c.44)
Solicitors (Scotland) Act 1933 (c.21)
Solicitors (Scotland) Act 1958 (c.28)
Solicitors (Scotland) Act 1965 (c.29)
Solicitors (Scotland) Act 1976 (c.6)
Solicitors (Scotland) Act 1980 (c.46)
Solicitors (Scotland) Act 1988 (c.42)
Solitary Confinement Act 1837 (c.90)
Solomon Islands Act 1978 (c.15)
Solvent Abuse (Scotland) Act 1983 (c.33)
Somerset: Canal Act 1796 (c.48)
Somerset House Act 1853 (c.8)
Somerset House Act 1984 (c.21)
Somerset House (King's College Lease) Act 1873 (c.4)
Somersham Rectory Act 1882 (c.81)
Sound Broadcasting Act 1972 (c.31)
Sound Dues Redemption Act 1857 (c.12)

South Africa Act 1877 (c.47)
South Africa Act 1909 (c.9)
South Africa Act 1962 (c.23)
South African Loans and War Contribution Act 1903 (c.27)
South African Offences Act 1863 (c.35)
South American Loans Guarantee Act 1852 (c.4)
South Australia Act 1834 (c.95)
South Australia Act 1842 (c.61)
South Australia Government Act 1838 (c.60)
South Indian Railway Purchase Act 1890 (c.6)
South Sea Company Act 1807 (c.23)
South Sea Company Act 1815 (c.57)
South Sea Company Act 1820 (c.2)
South Sea Company's Privileges Act 1815 (c.141)
South Sea Trade Act 1821 (c.60)
South Wales Bridges Act 1881 (c.14)
South Wales Highways Act 1860 (c.68)
South Wales Highway Act Amendment Act 1878 (c.34)
South Wales Turnpike Roads Act 1847 (c.72)
South Wales Turnpike Roads Amendment Act 1882 (c.67)
South Wales Turnpike Trusts Amendment Act 1875 (c.35)
Southampton to New Sarum Canal Act 1795 (c.51)
Southampton, Portsmouth and Sheet Bridge Roads Act 1796 (c.135)
Southern Rhodesia Act 1965 (c.76)
Southern Rhodesia Act 1979 (c.52)
Southern Rhodesia (Constitution) Act 1961 (c.2)
Southern Whale Fisheries Act 1795 (c.92)
Southern Whale Fisheries Act 1797 (c.121)
Southern Whale Fisheries Act 1798 (c.57)
Southern Whale Fisheries Act 1808 (c.124)
Southern Whale Fishery Act 1802 (c.18)
Southern Whale Fishery Act 1802 (c.114)
Southern Whale Fishery Act 1803 (c.90)
Southern Whale Fishery Act 1805 (c.96)
Southern Whale Fishery Act 1811 (c.34)
Southern Whale Fishery Act 1812 (c.103)
Southern Whale Fishery Act 1813 (c.111)
Southern Whale Fishery Act 1815 (c.45)
Southern Whale Fishery Act 1819 (c.113)
Spalding Road Act 1795 (c.166)
Special Acts (Extension of Time) Act 1915 (c.72)
Special Areas (Amendment) Act 1937 (c.31)
Special Areas (Development and Improvement) Act 1935 (c.1)
Special Areas Reconstruction (Agreement) Act 1936 (c.19)
Special Commission Act 1888 (c.35)
Special Commission (Belfast Prison) Act 1918 (c.44)
Special Commission (Dardanelles and Mesopotamia) Act 1916 (c.34)
Special Constables Act 1831 (c.41)

Special Constables Act 1835 (c.43)
Special Constables Act 1838 (c.80)
Special Constables Act 1914 (c.61)
Special Constables Act 1923 (c.11)
Special Constables (Ireland) Act 1832 (c.108)
Special Constables (Ireland) Act 1845 (c.46)
Special Constables (Scotland) Act 1914 (c.53)
Special Constables (Scotland) Act 1915 (c.47)
Special Enactments (Extension of Time) Act 1940 (c.16)
Special Juries Act 1898 (c.6)
Special Roads Act 1949 (c.32)
Spencer Perceval's Pensions Act 1813 (c.122)
Spirit, etc. Licences (Ireland) Act 1806 (c.70)
Spirit Licences Act 1799 (c.86)
Spirit of Wine Act 1855 (c.38)
Spirit Trade Act 1814 (c.149)
Spirits Act 1805 (c.39)
Spirits Act 1832 (c.74)
Spirits Act 1860 (c.114)
Spirits Act 1880 (c.24)
Spirits (Ireland) Act 1809 (c.99)
Spirits (Ireland) Act 1815 (c.104)
Spirits (Ireland) Act 1844 (c.82)
Spirits (Ireland) Act 1845 (c.64)
Spirits (Ireland) Act 1849 (c.17)
Spirits (Ireland) Act 1854 (c.89)
Spirits (Ireland) Act 1855 (c.103)
Spirits (Scotland): Spirits (Ireland) Act 1832 (c.29)
Spirits (Strength Ascertainment) Act 1818 (c.28)
Spiritual Duties Act 1839 (c.30)
Spitalfields and Shoreditch New Street Act 1853 (c.52)
Spitalfields Improvements Act 1850 (c.109)
Sporting Events (Control of Alcohol etc.) Act 1985 (c.57)
Sporting Events (Control of Alcohol etc.) (Amendment) Act 1992 (c.57)
Sporting Lands Rating (Scotland) Act 1886 (c.15)
Spray Irrigation (Scotland) Act 1964 (c.90)
Spring Assizes Act 1879 (c.1)
Spring Guns Act 1827 (c.18)
Sri Lanka Republic Act 1972 (c.55)
St. Albans Bribery Commission Act 1851 (c.106)
St. Albans Roads Act 1794 (c.113)
St. Briavels Small Debts Court Act 1842 (c.83)
St. Bride's Church, City Act 1796 (c.35)
St. David's College Act 1824 (c.101)
St. Helena Act 1833 (c.85)
St. John's Church, Hackney Act 1795 (c.70)
St. John's, Newfoundland Act 1820 (c.51)
St. John's, Newfoundland, etc. Act 1811 (c.45)
St. Martin Outwich Church, City Act 1796 (c.103)

St. Mary Magdalen Hospital, Bath Act 1856 (c.45)
St. Mary Somerset's Church, London Act 1868 (c.127)
St. Marylebone: Improvement Act 1795 (c.73)
St. Marylebone Rectory, Purchase of Act 1817 (c.98)
St. Michael, Cornhill: Building Act 1716 (c.5)
St. Pancras: Improvements, etc. Act 1797 (c.80)
St. Paul, Covent Garden: Church Rebuilding Act 1796 (c.65)
St. Vincent and Grenada Constitution Act 1876 (c.47)
Stables at Windsor Castle Act 1839 (c.20)
Stafford Election Act 1833 (c.20)
Stafford Election Act 1836 (c.10)
Stafford Roads Act 1770 (c.113)
Staffordshire Potteries Stipendiary Justice Act 1839 (c.15)
Stage Carriages Act 1832 (c.120)
Stage Coach duties Act 1796 (c.16)
Stage Coaches, etc. Act 1806 (c.136)
Stage Coaches, etc. (Great Britain) Act 1810 (c.48)
Stage Coaches, etc. (Ireland) Act 1810 (c.32)
Stage Coaches (Scotland) Act 1820 (c.4)
Stamford to Greetham Road Act 1795 (c.152)
Stamp Act 1795 (c.30)
Stamp Act 1795 (c.55)
Stamp Act 1795 (c.63)
Stamp Act 1796 (c.19)
Stamp Act 1796 (c.80)
Stamp Act 1797 (c.60)
Stamp Act 1797 (c.90)
Stamp Act 1797 (c.111)
Stamp Act 1797 (c.136)
Stamp Act 1798 (c.56)
Stamp Act 1798 (c.85)
Stamp Act 1799 (c.39)
Stamp Act 1799 (c.92)
Stamp Act 1799 (c.107)
Stamp Act 1804 (c.98)
Stamp Act 1815 (c.184)
Stamp Act 1853 (c.59)
Stamp Act 1854 (c.83)
Stamp Act 1864 (c.90)
Stamp Act 1870 (c.97)
Stamp Act 1891 (c.39)
Stamp Duties Act 1828 (c.49)
Stamp Duties Act 1848 (c.9)
Stamp Duties Act 1850 (c.97)
Stamp Duties Act 1860 (c.111)
Stamp Duties, etc. (Ireland) Act 1812 (c.87)
Stamp Duties (Court of Chancery) (Ireland) Act 1823 (c.78)
Stamp Duties (Ireland) Act 1815 (c.100)
Stamp Duties (Ireland) Act 1826 (c.20)
Stamp Duties in Law Proceedings (Ireland) Act 1821 (c.112)
Stamp Duties (Ireland) Act 1842 (c.82)
Stamp Duties (Ireland) Act 1850 (c.114)

Stamp Duties Management Act 1870 (c.98)
Stamp Duties Management Act 1891 (c.38)
Stamp Duties on Cards and Dice Act 1828 (c.18)
Stamp Duties on Newspapers Act 1836 (c.76)
Stamp Duty Composition (Ireland) Act 1867 (c.89)
Stamp Duty on Certain Leases Act 1870 (c.44)
Stamp Duty (Temporary Provisions) Act 1992 (c.2)
Stamps Act 1800 (c.84)
Stamps Act 1801 (c.58)
Stamps Act 1802 (c.99)
Stamps Act 1803 (c.21)
Stamps Act 1803 (cc.126, 127)
Stamps Act 1810 (c.35)
Stamps Act 1813 (c.108)
Stamps Act 1814 (c.144)
Stamps Act 1815 (c.101)
Stamps Act 1821 (c.55)
Stamps Act 1822 (c.117)
Stamps Act 1824 (c.41)
Stamps Act 1825 (c.41)
Stamps Act 1826 (c.44)
Stamps Act 1832 (c.91)
Stamps Act 1833 (c.23)
Stamps Act 1834 (c.57)
Stamps Act 1838 (c.85)
Stamps Act 1840 (c.79)
Stamps Act 1841 (c.34)
Stamps Act 1843 (c.72)
Stamps Act 1844 (c.21)
Stamps Act 1845 (c.2)
Stamps Act 1849 (c.80)
Stamps Act 1851 (c.18)
Stamps Act 1852 (c.21)
Stamps Act 1856 (c.22)
Stamps Act 1856 (c.81)
Stamps Act 1858 (c.20)
Stamps Act 1858 (c.24)
Stamps Act 1871 (c.4)
Stamps and Excise Act 1836 (c.45)
Stamps and Taxes Act 1835 (c.20)
Stamps, etc. Act 1833 (c.97)
Stamps (Great Britain) Act 1814 (c.133)
Stamps (Ireland) Act 1804 (c.68)
Stamps (Ireland) Act 1805 (c.20)
Stamps (Ireland) Act 1805 (c.51)
Stamps (Ireland) Act 1806 (c.35)
Stamps (Ireland) Act 1806 (c.64)
Stamps (Ireland) Act 1807 (c.50)
Stamps (Ireland) Act 1810 (c.76)
Stamps (Ireland) Act 1812 (c.126)
Stamps (Ireland) Act 1814 (c.118)
Stamps (Ireland) Act 1815 (cc.78, 79)
Stamps (Ireland) Act 1815 (c.80)
Stamps (Ireland) Act 1815 (c.81)
Stamps on Fire Insurances Act 1828 (c.13)
Standards of Weights, Measures and Coinage Act 1866 (c.82)
Stanhope and Wolsingham Rectories Act 1858 (c.58)

Stannaries Act 1836 (c.106)
Stannaries Act 1839 (c.58)
Stannaries Act 1855 (c.32)
Stannaries Act 1869 (c.19)
Stannaries Act 1887 (c.43)
Stannaries Court (Abolition) Act 1896 (c.45)
Stannaries Court of Cornwall Act 1834 (c.42)
Starch and Soap Duties Allowances Act 1822 (c.25)
State Hospitals (Scotland) Act 1994 (c.16)
State Immunity Act 1978 (c.33)
State of Singapore Act 1958 (c.59)
Statement of Rates Act 1919 (c.31)
Statistics of Trade Act 1947 (c.39)
Status of Aliens Act 1914 (c.17)
Statute Duty Act 1804 (c.52)
Statute of Frauds Amendment Act 1828 (c.14)
Statute of Westminster Act 1932 (c.4)
Statute Law (Repeals) Act 1969 (c.52)
Statute Law (Repeals) Act 1971 (c.52)
Statute Law (Repeals) Act 1973 (c.39)
Statute Law (Repeals) Act 1974 (c.22)
Statute Law (Repeals) Act 1975 (c.10)
Statute Law (Repeals) Act 1976 (c.16)
Statute Law (Repeals) Act 1977 (c.18)
Statute Law (Repeals) Act 1978 (c.45)
Statute Law (Repeals) Act 1981 (c.19)
Statute Law (Repeals) Act 1986 (c.12)
Statute Law (Repeals) Act 1989 (c.43)
Statute Law (Repeals) Act 1993 (c.50)
Statute Law Revision Act 1861 (c.101)
Statute Law Revision Act 1863 (c.125)
Statute Law Revision Act 1867 (c.59)
Statute Law Revision Act 1870 (c.69)
Statute Law Revision Act 1871 (c.116)
Statute Law Revision Act 1872 (c.63)
Statute Law Revision Act 1873 (c.91)
Statute Law Revision Act 1874 (c.35)
Statute Law Revision Act 1875 (c.66)
Statute Law Revision Act 1878 (c.79)
Statute Law Revision Act 1883 (c.39)
Statute Law Revision Act 1887 (c.59)
Statute Law Revision Act 1888 (c.3)
Statute Law Revision Act 1890 (c.33)
Statute Law Revision Act 1891 (c.67)
Statute Law Revision Act 1892 (c.19)
Statute Law Revision Act 1893 (c.14)
Statute Law Revision Act 1894 (c.56)
Statute Law Revision Act 1898 (c.22)
Statute Law Revision Act 1908 (c.49)
Statute Law Revision Act 1927 (c.42)
Statute Law Revision Act 1948 (c.62)
Statute Law Revision Act 1950 (c.6)
Statute Law Revision Act 1953 (c.5)
Statute Law Revision Act 1958 (c.46)
Statute Law Revision Act 1959 (c.68)
Statute Law Revision Act 1960 (c.56)
Statute Law Revision Act 1963 (c.30)
Statute Law Revision Act 1964 (c.79)
Statute Law Revision Act 1966 (c.5)
Statute Law Revision Act 1969 (c.52)
Statute Law Revision Act 1971 (c.52)

Statute Law Revision and Civil Procedure Act 1881 (c.59)

Statute Law Revision and Civil Procedure Act 1883 (c.49)

Statute Law Revision (Consequential Repeals) Act 1965 (c.55)

Statute Law Revision (Ireland) Act 1872 (c.98)

Statute Law Revision (Ireland) Act 1878 (c.57)

Statute Law Revision (Ireland) Act 1879 (c.24)

Statute Law Revision (Isle of Man) Act 1991 (c.61)

Statute Law Revision (Northern Ireland) Act 1973 (c.55)

Statute Law Revision (Northern Ireland) Act 1976 (c.12)

Statute Law Revision (Northern Ireland) Act 1980 (c.59)

Statute Law Revision (No. 2) Act 1872 (c.97)

Statute Law Revision (No. 2) Act 1874 (c.96)

Statute Law Revision (No. 2) Act 1888 (c.57)

Statute Law Revision (No. 2) Act 1890 (c.51)

Statute Law Revision (No. 2) Act 1893 (c.54)

Statute Law Revision (Scotland) Act 1906 (c.38)

Statute Law Revision (Scotland) Act 1964 (c.80)

Statute Law Revision (Substituted Enactments) Act 1876 (c.20)

Statute of Frauds 1677 (c.3)

Statute of Frauds Amendment Act 1828 (c.14)

Statute of Westminster 1931 (c.4)

Statutes (Definition of Time) Act 1880 (c.9)

Statutory Commissioners Act 1823 (c.35)

Statutory Companies (Redeemable Stock) Act 1915 (c.44)

Statutory Corporations (Financial Provisions) Act 1974 (c.8)

Statutory Corporations (Financial Provisions) Act 1975 (c.55)

Statutory Declarations Act 1835 (c.62)

Statutory Gas Companies (Electricity Supply Powers) Act 1925 (c.44)

Statutory Instruments Act 1946 (c.36)

Statutory Orders (Special Procedure) Act 1945 (c.18)

Statutory Orders (Special Procedure) Act 1965 (c.43)

Statutory Salaries Act 1937 (c.35)

Statutory Salaries (Restoration) Act 1934 (c.24)

Statutory Sick Pay Act 1991 (c.3)

Statutory Sick Pay Act 1994 (c.2)

Statutory Undertakings (Temporary Increase of Charges) Act 1918 (c.34)

Statutory Water Companies Act 1991 (c.58)

Stealing from Bleaching Grounds (Ireland) Act 1811 (c.39)

Stealing from Gardens Act 1826 (c.69)

Stealing in Shops, etc. Act 1820 (c.117)

Stealing of Linen, etc. Act 1811 (c.41)

Stealing of Records, etc. Act 1824 (c.30)

Stealing Property from Mines Act 1816 (c.73)

Steam Engines Furnaces Act 1821 (c.41)

Steam Navigation Act 1846 (c.100)

Steam Navigation Act 1848 (c.81)

Steam Navigation Act 1851 (c.79)

Steam Trawling (Ireland) Act 1889 (c.74)

Steam Whistles Act 1872 (c.61)

Steeping of Barley Act 1801 (c.31)

Stepney: Improvements, Poor Relief Act 1797 (c.79)

Still-Birth (Definition) Act 1992 (c.29)

Still Licences Act 1846 (c.90)

Stipendiary Curates Act 1813 (c.149)

Stipendiary Magistrate, Manchester Act 1813 (c.72)

Stipendiary Magistrate, Manchester and Salford Act 1854 (c.20)

Stipendiary Magistrate, Staffs Act 1846 (c.65)

Stipendiary Magistrates Act 1858 (c.73)

Stipendiary Magistrates Act 1863 (c.97)

Stipendiary Magistrates Act 1869 (c.34)

Stipendiary Magistrates Jurisdiction (Scotland) Act 1897 (c.48)

Stipendiary Magistrate for Manchester Act 1844 (c.30)

Stirling Roads Act 1794 (c.138)

Stirling, Dumbarton and Perth Roads Act 1794 (c.129)

Stockbridge Roads Act 1797 (c.149)

Stockbrokers (Ireland) Act 1868 (c.31)

Stockbrokers (Ireland) Act 1918 (c.46)

Stock Exchange (Completion of Bargains) Act 1976 (c.47)

Stock Transfer Act 1963 (c.18)

Stock Transfer Act 1982 (c.41)

Stocks, etc. of Lunatics Act 1821 (c.15)

Stoke Poges Hospital Act 1856 (c.111)

Stoke to Newcastle Canal Act 1795 (c.87)

Straits Settlements Act 1866 (c.115)

Straits Settlements and Johore Territorial Waters (Agreement) Act 1928 (c.23)

Straits Settlements (Ecclesiastic) Act 1869 (c.88)

Straits Settlements Offences Act 1874 (c.38)

Straits Settlements (Repeal) Act 1946 (c.37)

Stratified Ironstone Mines (Gunpowder) Act 1881 (c.26)

Stratford and Long Compton Hill Roads Act 1797 (c.152)

Street Betting Act 1906 (c.43)

Street Collections Regulations (Scotland) Act 1915 (c.88)

Street from Coventry Street to Long Acre Act 1841 (c.12)

Street Offences Act 1959 (c.57)

Street Playgrounds Act 1938 (c.37)

Submarine Telegraph Act 1885 (c.49)

Submarine Telegraph Act 1886 (c.3)

Subscriptions to Loan Act 1797 (c.82)

Subscriptions to Loan Act 1847 (c.36)

Substitution of Punishments for Death Act 1841 (c.56)

Succession Duty Act 1853 (c.51)
Succession (Scotland) Act 1964 (c.41)
Succession (Scotland) Act 1973 (c.25)
Succession to the Crown Act 1707 (c.41)
Sudan (Special Payments) Act 1955 (c.11)
Sudbury Bribery Commission Act 1843 (c.97)
Sudbury Disfranchisement Act 1842 (c.52)
Sudbury Disfranchisement Act 1843 (c.11)
Suez Canal (Shares) Act 1876 (c.67)
Suffragan Bishops Act 1898 (c.11)
Suffragans Nomination Act 1888 (c.56)
Sugar Act 1956 (c.48)
Sugar Bounties, etc. Act 1811 (c.13)
Sugar Convention Act 1903 (c.21)
Sugar Duties Act 1828 (c.36)
Sugar Duties Act 1829 (c.39)
Sugar Duties Act 1830 (c.50)
Sugar Duties Act 1831 (c.23)
Sugar Duties Act 1832 (c.22)
Sugar Duties Act 1832 (c.95)
Sugar Duties Act 1834 (c.5)
Sugar Duties Act 1836 (c.26)
Sugar Duties Act 1837 (c.27)
Sugar Duties Act 1838 (c.33)
Sugar Duties Act 1839 (c.21)
Sugar Duties Act 1840 (c.23)
Sugar Duties Act 1840 (c.57)
Sugar Duties Act 1841 (c.29)
Sugar Duties Act 1842 (c.34)
Sugar Duties Act 1843 (c.27)
Sugar Duties Act 1844 (c.28)
Sugar Duties Act 1845 (c.5)
Sugar Duties Act 1846 (c.29)
Sugar Duties Act 1846 (c.41)
Sugar Duties Act 1846 (c.63)
Sugar Duties Act 1848 (c.97)
Sugar Duties Act 1854 (c.30)
Sugar Duties (Ireland) Act 1820 (c.80)
Sugar Duties and Exchequer Bills Act 1835 (c.12)
Sugar, etc. Act 1820 (c.64)
Sugar in Brewing Act 1847 (c.5)
Sugar Industry Act 1942 (c.16)
Sugar Industry (Reorganisation) Act 1936 (c.18)
Suicide Act 1961 (c.60)
Suits Against Spiritual Persons Act 1814 (c.54)
Summary Convictions, etc. Act 1824 (c.18)
Summary Convictions (Ireland) Act 1834 (c.93)
Summary Convictions (Ireland) Act 1849 (c.70)
Summary Jurisdiction Act 1848 (c.43)
Summary Jurisdiction Act 1857 (c.43)
Summary Jurisdiction Act 1863 (c.77)
Summary Jurisdiction Act 1879 (c.49)
Summary Jurisdiction Act 1884 (c.43)
Summary Jurisdiction Act 1899 (c.22)
Summary Jurisdiction (Appeals) Act 1933 (c.38)
Summary Jurisdiction Cinque Ports, etc. Act 1864 (c.80)

Summary Jurisdiction (Ireland) Act 1850 (c.102)
Summary Jurisdiction (Ireland) Act 1851 (c.92)
Summary Jurisdiction (Ireland) Act 1862 (c.50)
Summary Jurisdiction (Ireland) Act 1908 (c.24)
Summary Jurisdiction (Ireland) Act 1918 (c.18)
Summary Jurisdiction (Ireland) Amendment Act 1871 (c.76)
Summary Jurisdiction (Married Women) Act 1895 (c.39)
Summary Jurisdiction over Children (Ireland) Act 1884 (c.19)
Summary Jurisdiction (Process) Act 1881 (c.24)
Summary Jurisdiction (Scotland) Act 1881 (c.33)
Summary Jurisdiction (Scotland) Act 1908 (c.65)
Summary Jurisdiction (Scotland) Act 1909 (c.28)
Summary Jurisdiction (Scotland) Act 1954 (c.48)
Summary Jurisdiction (Separation and Main-tenance) Act 1925 (c.51)
Summary Proceedings Act 1822 (c.23)
Summary Procedure (Domestic Proceed-ings) Act 1937 (c.58)
Summary Procedure on Bills of Exchange Act 1855 (c.67)
Summary Procedure on Bills of Exchange (Ireland) Act 1861 (c.43)
Summary Procedure (Scotland) Act 1864 (c.53)
Summary Prosecutions Appeals (Scotland) Act 1875 (c.62)
Summer Time Act 1916 (c.14)
Summer Time Act 1922 (c.22)
Summer Time Act 1925 (c.64)
Summer Time Act 1947 (c.16)
Summer Time Act 1972 (c.6)
Summons and Process Servers' Fees (Ire-land) Act 1919 (c.4)
Sunday and Ragged Schools (Exemption from Rating) Act 1869 (c.40)
Sunday Cinema Act 1972 (c.19)
Sunday Closing (Wales) Act 1881 (c.61)
Sunday Entertainments Act 1932 (c.51)
Sunday Observance Act 1833 (c.31)
Sunday Observation Prosecution Act 1871 (c.87)
Sunday Performances (Temporary Regu-lation) Act 1931 (c.52)
Sunday Theatre Act 1972 (c.26)
Sunday Trading Act 1994 (c.20)
Sunderland Pilotage Order Confirmation Act 1865 (c.59)
Superannuation Act 1834 (c.24)
Superannuation Act 1859 (c.26)
Superannuation Act 1860 (c.89)

Superannuation Act 1866 (c.68)
Superannuation Act 1872 (c.12)
Superannuation Act 1875 (c.4)
Superannuation Act 1876 (c.53)
Superannuation Act 1881 (c.43)
Superannuation Act 1884 (c.57)
Superannuation Act 1887 (c.67)
Superannuation Act 1892 (c.40)
Superannuation Act 1909 (c.10)
Superannuation Act 1914 (c.86)
Superannuation Act 1935 (c.23)
Superannuation Act 1946 (c.60)
Superannuation Act 1949 (c.44)
Superannuation Act 1950 (c.2)
Superannuation Act 1957 (c.37)
Superannuation Act 1965 (c.74)
Superannuation Act 1972 (c.11)
Superannuation Allowances Act 1824 (c.104)
Superannuation Act Amendment Act 1834 (c.45)
Superannuation Acts Amendment Act 1873 (c.23)
Superannuation Amendment Act 1965 (c.10)
Superannuation and Other Trust Funds (Validation) Act 1927 (c.41)
Superannuation, etc. Act 1828 (c.79)
Superannuation (Diplomatic Service) Act 1929 (c.11)
Superannuation (Ecclesiastical Commissioners and Queen Anne's Bounty) Act 1914 (c.5)
Superannuation (Ecclesiastical Commissioners and Queen Anne's Bounty) Act 1933 (c.47)
Superannuation (Mercantile Marine Fund Officers) Act 1877 (c.44)
Superannuation (Metropolis) Act 1866 (c.31)
Superannuation (Miscellaneous Provisions) Act 1948 (c.33)
Superannuation (Miscellaneous Provisions) Act 1967 (c.28)
Superannuation Post Office and War Office Act 1876 (c.68)
Superannuation (President of Industrial Court) Act 1954 (c.37)
Superannuation (Prison Officers) Act 1919 (c.67)
Superannuation Schemes (War Service) Act 1940 (c.26)
Superannuation (Various Services) Act 1938 (c.13)
Superannuation (War Department) Act 1890 (c.18)
Superintending Magistrates, etc. (Ireland) Act 1814 (c.13)
Superintending Magistrates, etc. (Ireland) Act 1817 (c.22)
Superior Courts (Officers) Act 1837 (c.30)
Supplemental Customs Consolidation Act 1855 (c.96)
Supplemental War Loan Act 1900 (c.61)
Supplemental War Loan (No. 2) Act 1900 (c.1)

Supplementary Benefits Act 1976 (c.71)
Supplementary Benefit (Amendment) Act 1976 (c.56)
Supplementary Militia Act 1797 (c.18)
Supplementary Militia Act 1797 (c.19)
Supplementary Militia Act 1799 (c.14)
Supplies and Services (Defence Purposes) Act 1951 (c.25)
Supplies and Services (Extended Purpose) Act 1947 (c.55)
Supplies and Services (Translation Powers) Act 1945 (c.10)
Supply Act 1820 (c.10)
Supply Act 1821 (c.4)
Supply Act 1821 (c.7)
Supply Act 1823 (c.6)
Supply Act 1823 (c.21)
Supply Act 1824 (c.3)
Supply Act 1824 (c.42)
Supply Act 1825 (c.1)
Supply Act 1825 (c.14)
Supply Act 1826 (c.1)
Supply Act 1827 (c.16)
Supply Act 1827 (c.42)
Supply Act 1828 (c.1)
Supply Act 1828 (c.10)
Supply Act 1828 (c.19)
Supply Act 1828 (c.28)
Supply Act 1828 (c.30)
Supply Act 1829 (c.3)
Supply Act 1830 (c.1)
Supply Act 1830 (c.2)
Supply Act 1830 (c.4)
Supply Act 1830 (c.28)
Supply Act 1831 (cc.9–10)
Supply Act 1831 (c.28)
Supply Act 1832 (c.1)
Supply Act 1832 (c.6)
Supply Act 1832 (c.30)
Supply Act 1832 (c.55)
Supply Act 1833 (c.18)
Supply Act 1834 (c.2)
Supply Act 1834 (c.12)
Supply Act 1835 (c.3)
Supply Act 1835 (c.9)
Supply Act 1836 (c.1)
Supply Act 1836 (c.18)
Supply Act 1837 (c.6)
Supply Act 1837 (c.11)
Supply Act 1838 (c.11)
Supply Act 1838 (c.21)
Supply Act 1839 (c.2)
Supply Act 1839 (c.6)
Supply Act 1840 (c.4)
Supply Act 1840 (c.7)
Supply Act 1841 (c.4)
Supply Act 1842 (c.8)
Supply Act 1843 (c.5)
Supply Act 1843 (c.87)
Supply Act 1844 (c.6)
Supply Act 1845 (c.1)
Supply Act 1846 (c.7)
Supply Act 1846 (c.47)

Supply Act 1847 (c.8)
Supply Act 1848 (c.4)
Supply Act 1848 (c.33)
Supply Act 1849 (c.3)
Supply Act 1849 (c.44)
Supply Act 1850 (c.3)
Supply Act 1851 (c.3)
Supply Act 1852 (c.1)
Supply Act 1853 (c.12)
Supply Act 1853 (c.31)
Supply Act 1854 (c.2)
Supply Act 1854 (c.21)
Supply Act 1855 (cc.5, 6)
Supply Act 1855 (c.37)
Supply Act 1856 (c.4)
Supply Act 1856 (c.7)
Supply Act 1857 (c.4)
Supply Act 1858 (cc.5, 6)
Supply Act 1858 (c.17)
Supply Act 1859 (cc.6, 7)
Supply Act 1859 (c.2)
Supply Act 1860 (cc.2, 3)
Supply Act 1860 (c.12)
Supply Act 1860 (c.25)
Supply Act 1860 (c.103)
Supply Act 1861 (c.2)
Supply Act 1861 (c.6)
Supply Act 1861 (c.19)
Supply Act 1862 (cc.1, 2)
Supply Act 1862 (c.31)
Supply Act 1863 (c.6)
Supply Act 1863 (c.15)
Supply Act 1864 (cc.5, 6)
Supply Act 1864 (c.11)
Supply Act 1864 (c.73)
Supply Act 1865 (c.4)
Supply Act 1865 (c.10)
Supply Act 1866 (c.6)
Supply Act 1866 (c.13)
Supply Act 1867 (c.4)
Supply Act 1867 (c.7)
Supply Act 1867 (c.30)
Supply Act 1867 (c.1)
Supply Act 1868 (c.10)
Supply Act 1868 (c.13)
Supply Act 1868 (c.16)
Supply Act 1869 (c.1)
Supply Act 1869 (c.8)
Supply Act 1870 (c.5)
Supply Act 1870 (c.31)
Supply Act 1871 (cc.6, 7)
Supply Act 1871 (c.20)
Supply Act 1871 (c.51)
Supply Act 1872 (c.1)
Supply Act 1872 (c.11)
Supply Act 1872 (c.37)
Supply Act 1873 (c.26)
Supply Act 1873 (c.3)
Supply Act 1874 (cc.1, 2)
Supply Act 1874 (c.10)
Supply Act 1875 (cc.1, 2)
Supply Act 1875 (c.10)
Supply Act 1876 (c.2)

Supply Act 1876 (c.4)
Supply Act 1876 (c.15)
Supply Act 1877 (c.1)
Supply Act 1877 (c.6)
Supply Act 1877 (c.12)
Supply Act 1877 (c.24)
Supply Act 1878 (c.1)
Supply Act 1878 (c.9)
Supply Act 1878 (c.21)
Supply Act 1878 (c.45)
Supply, etc., Act 1742 (c.25)
Supply of Goods and Services Act 1982 (c.29)
Supply of Goods (Implied Terms) Act 1973 (c.13)
Supply of Seamen Act 1803 (c.64)
Supply of Water in Bulk Act 1934 (c.15)
Supply Powers Act 1975 (c.9)
Support of Captured Slaves Act 1815 (c.172)
Support of Commercial Credit (Ireland) Act 1820 (c.39)
Support of Commercial Credit (Ireland) Act 1822 (c.22)
Support of Commercial Credit (Ireland) Act 1822 (c.118)
Support of Commercial Credit (Ireland) Act 1823 (c.42)
Suppression of Insurrections (Ireland) Act 1822 (c.1)
Suppression of Insurrections (Ireland) Act 1822 (c.80)
Suppression of Insurrection, etc. (Ireland) Act 1810 (c.78)
Suppression of Rebellion Act 1801 (c.14)
Suppression of Rebellion Act 1801 (c.61)
Suppression of Rebellion Act 1801 (c.104)
Suppression of Rebellion, etc. Act 1803 (c.117)
Suppression of Rebellion, etc. (Ireland) Act 1803 (c.9)
Suppression of Rebellion, etc. (Ireland) Act 1803 (c.117)
Suppression of Terrorism Act 1978 (c.26)
Supreme Court Act 1981 (c.54)
Supreme Court Act (Northern Ireland) 1942 (c.2)
Supreme Court (England) Act 1850 (c.16)
Supreme Court (England) Act 1864 (c.15)
Supreme Court (Ireland) Act 1850 (c.18)
Supreme Court (Ireland) Act 1850 (c.19)
Supreme Court (Ireland) (Master of the Rolls) Act 1815 (c.114)
Supreme Court, Madras Act 1830 (c.75)
Supreme Court (Northern Ireland) Act 1942 (c.2)
Supreme Court of Judicature Act 1873 (c.66)
Supreme Court of Judicature Act 1875 (c.77)
Supreme Court of Judicature Act 1877 (c.9)
Supreme Court of Judicature Act 1881 (c.68)
Supreme Court of Judicature Act 1884 (c.61)
Supreme Court of Judicature Act 1890 (c.44)
Supreme Court of Judicature Act 1891 (c.53)
Supreme Court of Judicature Act 1899 (c.6)

Supreme Court of Judicature Act 1902 (c.31)

Supreme Court of Judicature Act 1910 (c.12)

Supreme Court of Judicature (Amendment) Act 1935 (c.2)

Supreme Court of Judicature (Amendment) Act 1938 (c.67)

Supreme Court of Judicature (Amendment) Act 1944 (c.9)

Supreme Court of Judicature (Amendment) Act 1948 (c.20)

Supreme Court of Judicature (Amendment) Act 1959 (c.39)

Supreme Court of Judicature (Circuit Officers) Act 1946 (c.78)

Supreme Court of Judicature (Commencement) Act 1874 (c.83)

Supreme Court of Judicature (Consolidation) Act 1925 (c.49)

Supreme Court of Judicature (Funds, etc.) Act 1883 (c.29)

Supreme Court of Judicature Act (Ireland) Act 1877 (c.57)

Supreme Court of Judicature (Ireland) Act 1882 (c.70)

Supreme Court of Judicature (Ireland) Act 1887 (c.6)

Supreme Court of Judicature (Ireland) Act 1897 (c.17)

Supreme Court of Judicature (Ireland) Act 1907 (c.44)

Supreme Court of Judicature (Ireland) Act 1877, Amendment Act 1878 (c.27)

Supreme Court of Judicature (Ireland) Amendment Act 1888 (c.27)

Supreme Court of Judicature (Ireland) (No. 2) Act 1897 (c.66)

Supreme Court of Judicature of Northern Ireland 1926 (c.44)

Supreme Court of Judicature (London Causes) Act 1891 (c.14)

Supreme Court of Judicature (Officers) Act 1878 (c.35)

Supreme Court of Judicature (Officers) Act 1879 (c.78)

Supreme Court of Judicature (Procedure) Act 1894 (c.16)

Supreme Court Officers (Pensions) Act 1954 (c.38)

Supreme Court Officers (Retirement, Pensions, etc.) Act 1921 (c.56)

Surrey Act 1856 (c.61)

Surrogacy Arrangements Act 1985 (c.49)

Survey Act 1870 (c.13)

Survey, Great Britain Act 1851 (c.22)

Survey (Great Britain) Continuance Act 1875 (c.32)

Suspension of Certain Appointments Act 1837 (c.71)

Suspensory Act 1914 (c.88)

Swansea Harbour Act 1796 (c.93)

Swaziland Independence Act 1968 (c.56)

Sydney Branch Mint Act 1863 (c.74)

Tancred's Charities 1871 (c.117)

Tanganyika Agricultural Corporation Act 1957 (c.54)

Tanganyika and British Honduras Loans Act 1932 (c.17)

Tanganyika Independence Act 1961 (c.1)

Tanganyika Republic Act 1962 (c.1)

Tanners, Curriers, Shoemakers, etc. Act 1808 (c.60)

Tanners' Indemnity, etc. Act 1799 (c.54)

Taking of Hostages Act 1982 (c.28)

Tanzania Act 1969 (c.29)

Tattooing of Minors Act 1969 (c.24)

Tavistock Canal Act 1796 (c.67)

Taxation Act 1797 (c.16)

Taxation Act 1798 (c.81)

Taxation Act 1801 (c.8)

Taxation Act 1801 (c.10)

Taxation Act 1801 (c.33)

Taxation Act 1801 (c.40)

Taxation Act 1801 (c.42)

Taxation Act 1801 (c.44)

Taxation Act 1801 (c.51)

Taxation Act 1801 (c.62)

Taxation Act 1801 (c.69)

Taxation Act 1801 (c.71)

Taxation Act 1801 (c.74)

Taxation Act 1801 (c.75)

Taxation Act 1805 (c.5)

Taxation Act 1806 (c.84)

Taxation of Chargeable Gains Act 1992 (c.12)

Taxation of Colonies Act 1778 (c.12)

Taxes Act 1797 (c.69)

Taxes Act 1803 (c.99)

Taxes Act 1805 (c.71)

Taxes Act 1810 (c.105)

Taxes Act 1821 (c.113)

Taxes Act 1856 (c.80)

Taxes Management Act 1880 (c.19)

Taxes Management Act 1970 (c.9)

Taxes on Carriages, etc., (Ireland) Act 1809 (c.75)

Taxes (Regulation of Remuneration) Act 1891 (c.13)

Taxes (Regulation of Remuneration) Amendment Act 1892 (c.25)

Taxes (Scotland) Act 1803 (c.150)

Taxes (Scotland) Act 1805 (c.95)

Taxes (Scotland) 1812 (c.95)

Taxes (Scotland) Act 1815 (c.161)

Taxing Masters (Ireland) Act 1848 (c.132)

Taxing Officer (Ireland) Act 1853 (c.55)

Tea Duties Act 1833 (c.101)

Tea Duties Act 1835 (c.32)

Tea Duties Act 1855 (c.9)

Teachers of Nursing Act 1967 (c.16)

Teachers of Schools (Ireland) Act 1844 (c.8)

Teachers' Pay and Conditions Act 1987 (c.1)

Teachers' (Superannuation) Act 1925 (c.59)

Teachers' (Superannuation) Act 1928 (c.10)

Teachers' (Superannuation) Act 1933 (c.22)

Teachers' (Superannuation) Act 1935 (c.35)

Teachers' (Superannuation) Act 1937 (c.47)

Teachers' (Superannuation) Act 1945 (c.14)
Teachers' Superannuation Act 1965 (c.83)
Teachers' Superannuation Act 1967 (c.12)
Teachers' Superannuation (Scotland) Act 1968 (c.12)
Teachers' Superannuation (War Service) Act 1939 (c.95)
Teaching Council (Scotland) Act 1965 (c.19)
Teaching Council (Scotland) Act 1970 (c.2)
Technical and Industrial Institutions Act 1892 (c.29)
Technical Instruction Act 1889 (c.76)
Technical Instruction Act 1891 (c.4)
Technical Instruction Amendment (Scotland) Act 1892 (c.63)
Technical Schools (Scotland) Act 1887 (c.64)
Teinds Act 1808 (c.138)
Teinds Act 1810 (c.84)
Teinds Act 1824 (c.72)
Telecommunications Act 1984 (c.12)
Telegraph Act 1869 (c.73)
Telegraph Act 1870 (c.88)
Telegraph Act 1873 (c.83)
Telegraph Act 1885 (c.58)
Telegraph Act 1954 (c.28)
Telegraph Act 1863 (c.112)
Telegraph Act 1868 (c.110)
Telegraph Act 1878 (c.76)
Telegraph Act 1892 (c.59)
Telegraph Act 1899 (c.38)
Telegraph Act 1943 (c.26)
Telegraph Act 1949 (c.80)
Telegraph Act 1951 (c.37)
Telegraph Act 1962 (c.14)
Telegraph Act Amendment Act 1866 (c.3)
Telegraph (Arbitration) Act 1909 (c.20)
Telegraph (Construction) Act 1908 (c.33)
Telegraph (Construction) Act 1911 (c.39)
Telegraph (Construction) Act 1916 (c.40)
Telegraph (Isle of Man) Act 1889 (c.34)
Telegraph (Money) Act 1871 (c.75)
Telegraph (Money) Act 1876 (c.5)
Telegraph (Money) Act 1896 (c.40)
Telegraph (Money) Act 1898 (c.33)
Telegraph (Money) Act 1904 (c.3)
Telegraph (Money) Act 1907 (c.6)
Telegraph (Money) Act 1913 (c.24)
Telegraph (Money) Act 1920 (c.37)
Telegraph (Money) Act 1921 (c.57)
Telegraph (Money) Act 1922 (c.45)
Telegraph (Money) Act 1924 (c.25)
Telegraph (Money) Act 1925 (c.65)
Telegraphs (Money) Act 1877 (c.30)
Telephone Act 1951 (c.52)
Telephone Transfer Act 1911 (c.26)
Telephone Transfer Amendment Act 1911 (c.56)
Television Act 1954 (c.55)
Television Act 1963 (c.50)
Television Act 1964 (c.21)
Temperance (Scotland) Act 1913 (c.33)
Temple Balsall Hospital Act 1861 (c.24)
Temple Bar, etc. Act 1795 (c.126)

Temporary Migration of Children (Guardianship) Act 1941 (c.23)
Temporary Removal of Convicts Act 1823 (c.82)
Tenancy of Shops (Scotland) Act 1949 (c.25)
Tenancy of Shops (Scotland) Act 1964 (c.50)
Tenants Compensation 1890 (c.57)
Tenants' Rights, etc. (Scotland) Act 1980 (c.52)
Tenants' Rights, etc. (Scotland) Amendment Act 1980 (c.61)
Tenants' Rights, etc. (Scotland) Amendment Act 1984 (c.18)
Tension's Charity Act 1860 (c.43)
Tenures Abolition Act 1660 (c.24)
Term and Quarter Days (Scotland) Act 1990 (c.22)
Termination of the Present War (Definition) Act 1918 (c.59)
Terms and Conditions of Employment Act 1959 (c.26)
Territorial and Reserve Forces Act 1907 (c.9)
Territorial Army and Militia Act 1921 (c.37)
Territorial Sea Act 1987 (c.49)
Territorial Waters Jurisdiction Act 1878 (c.73)
Test Abolition Act 1867 (c.62)
Textile Manufacturers (Ireland) Act 1840 (c.91)
Textile Manufacturers (Ireland) Act 1842 (c.68)
Textile Manufacturers (Ireland) Act 1867 (c.60)
Thames: Ballastage Act 1795 (c.84)
Thames and Isis, Navigation Act 1771 (c.45)
Thames and Severn Canal Act 1796 (c.34)
Thames Conservancy Act 1864 (c.113)
Thames Embankment Act 1852 (c.71)
Thames Embankment Act 1853 (c.87)
Thames Embankment Act 1862 (c.93)
Thames Embankment Act 1863 (c.75)
Thames Embankment Act 1873 (c.40)
Thames Embankment, etc. (Loans) Act 1864 (c.61)
Thames Embankment, etc. (Loans) Act 1868 (c.43)
Thames Navigation Act 1866 (c.89)
Thames Preservation Act 1885 (c.76)
Thatched House Court and Little St. James's Street, Westminster Act 1843 (c.19)
The Chest at Chatham Act 1803 (c.119)
Theatres Act 1843 (c.68)
Theatres Act 1968 (c.54)
Theatres Trust Act 1976 (c.27)
Theatres Trust (Scotland) Act 1978 (c.24)
Theatrical Employers Act 1928 (c.46)
Theatrical Employers Registration Act 1925 (c.50)
Theatrical Employers Registration (Amendment) Act 1928 (c.46)
Theft Act 1968 (c.60)
Theft Act 1978 (c.31)
Theft of Turnips, etc. Act 1802 (c.67)
Therapeutic Substances Act 1925 (c.60)

Therapeutic Substances Act 1953 (c.32)
Therapeutic Substances Act 1956 (c.25)
Thermal Insulation (Industrial Buildings) Act 1957 (c.40)
Third Parties (Rights against Insurers) Act 1930 (c.25)
Thirlage Act 1799 (c.55)
Thirsk Roads Act 1794 (c.118)
Thomas Macklin's Paintings Act 1797 (c.133)
Thread Lace Manufacture (England) Act 1806 (c.81)
Threatening Letters Act 1825 (c.19)
Threatening Letters, etc. Act 1847 (c.66)
Threshing Machines Act 1878 (c.12)
Threshing Machines, Remedies for Damage Act 1832 (c.72)
Timber (Ireland) Act 1888 (c.37)
Timber Ships Act 1845 (c.45)
Timber Ships, America Act 1842 (c.17)
Timber Ships, British North America Act 1839 (c.44)
Timber Ships, British North America Act 1840 (c.36)
Time (Ireland) Act 1916 (c.45)
Time of Service in the Army Act 1847 (c.37)
Timeshare Act 1992 (c.35)
Tithe Act 1832 (c.100)
Tithe Act 1836 (c.71)
Tithe Act 1837 (c.69)
Tithe Act 1838 (c.64)
Tithe Act 1839 (c.62)
Tithe Act 1840 (c.15)
Tithe Act 1842 (c.54)
Tithe Act 1846 (c.73)
Tithe Act 1847 (c.104)
Tithe Act 1860 (c.93)
Tithe Act 1878 (c.42)
Tithe Act 1891 (c.8)
Tithe Act 1918 (c.54)
Tithe Act 1925 (c.87)
Tithe Act 1936 (c.43)
Tithe Act 1951 (c.62)
Tithe Annuities Apportionment Act 1921 (c.20)
Tithe Arrears Act 1839 (c.3)
Tithe Commutation Acts Amendment Act 1873 (c.42)
Tithe Composition Act 1837 (c.58)
Tithe Compositions (Ireland) Act 1836 (c.95)
Tithe Compositions (Ireland) Act 1841 (c.37)
Tithe Compositions (Ireland) Act 1841 (c.6)
Tithe (Ireland) Act 1840 (c.13)
Tithe Rentcharge (Ireland) Act 1838 (c.109)
Tithe Rentcharge (Ireland) Act 1848 (c.80)
Tithe Rentcharge (Ireland) Act 1900 (c.58)
Tithe Rentcharge (Rates) Act 1899 (c.17)
Tithe Rentcharge Redemption Act 1885 (c.32)
Tithes Act 1841 (c.36)
Tithes Prescription Act 1834 (c.83)
Tithes Rating Act 1851 (c.50)
Title Act 1846 (c.73)
Title Act 1925 (c.87)

Title Act 1936 (c.43)
Title Act 1951 (c.62)
Tin Duties Act 1838 (c.120)
Titles Deprivation Act 1917 (c.47)
Titles to Land Consolidation (Scotland) Act 1868 (c.101)
Titles to Land Consolidation (Scotland) Amendment Act 1869 (c.116)
Titles to Land (Scotland) Act 1858 (c.76)
Titles to Land (Scotland) Act 1860 (c.143)
Tobacco Act 1840 (c.18)
Tobacco Act 1842 (c.93)
Tobacco Cultivation Act 1831 (c.13)
Tobacco Growing (Scotland) Act 1908 (c.10)
Tobacco Products Duty Act 1979 (c.7)
Tokens Act 1812 (c.157)
Tokens Act 1813 (c.4)
Tokens Act 1817 (c.46)
Tokens Act 1817 (c.113)
Tokens Act 1825 (c.98)
Tokyo Convention Act 1967 (c.52)
Tolls for Certain Carriages Act 1813 (c.82)
Tolls (Ireland) Act 1817 (c.108)
Tonga Act 1970 (c.22)
Tonnage Duties Act 1822 (c.48)
Tonnage, etc. of Ships Act 1835 (c.56)
Tonnage Rates (Port of London) Act 1834 (c.32)
Tonnage of Steam Vessels Act 1819 (c.5)
Tortola Trade Act 1802 (c.102)
Tortola Trade, etc. Act 1803 (c.133)
Tortola Trade Act 1806 (c.72)
Torts (Interference with Goods) Act 1977 (c.32)
Tourism (Overseas Promotion) (Scotland) Act 1984 (c.4)
Tourism (Overseas Promotion) (Wales) Act 1992 (c.26)
Towcaser to Hardington Road Act 1795 (c.153)
Tower Burial Ground Act 1811 (c.116)
Tower Hamlets Militia Act 1797 (c.75)
Town and Country Amenities Act 1974 (c.32)
Town and Country Planning Act 1932 (c.48)
Town and Country Planning Act 1943 (c.5)
Town and Country Planning Act 1944 (c.47)
Town and Country Planning Act 1947 (c.51)
Town and Country Planning Act 1953 (c.16)
Town and Country Planning Act 1954 (c.72)
Town and Country Planning Act 1959 (c.53)
Town and Country Planning Act 1962 (c.38)
Town and Country Planning Act 1963 (c.17)
Town and Country Planning Act 1968 (c.72)
Town and Country Planning Act 1969 (c.30)
Town and Country Planning Act 1971 (c.78)
Town and Country Planning Act 1984 (c.10)
Town and Country Planning Act 1990 (c.8)
Town and Country Planning (Amendment) Act 1951 (c.19)
Town and Country Planning (Amendment) Act 1972 (c.42)
Town and Country Planning (Amendment) Act 1977 (c.29)

Town and Country Planning (Amendment) Act 1985 (c.52)

Town and Country Planning (Compensation) Act 1985 (c.19)

Town and Country Planning (Interim Development) Act 1943 (c.29)

Town and Country Planning (Interim Development) (Scotland) Act 1943 (c.43)

Town and Country Planning (Minerals) Act 1981 (c.36)

Town and Country Planning Regulations (London) (Indemnity) Act 1970 (c.57)

Town and Coury Planning (Scotland) Act 1932 (c.49)

Town and Country Planning (Scotland) Act 1945 (c.33)

Town and Country Planning (Scotland) Act 1947 (c.53)

Town and Country Planning (Scotland) Act 1954 (c.73)

Town and Country Planning (Scotland) Act 1959 (c.70)

Town and Country Planning (Scotland) Act 1972 (c.52)

Town and Country Planning (Scotland) Act 1977 (c.10)

Town and Country (Scotland) Act 1969 (c.30)

Town Council and Local Bds. Act 1880 (c.17)

Town Councils (Scotland) Act 1900 (c.49)

Town Councils (Scotland) Act 1903 (c.34)

Town Councils (Scotland) Act 1923 (c.41)

Town Development Act 1952 (c.54)

Town Gardens Protection Act 1863 (c.13)

Town Planning Act 1925 (c.16)

Town Planning (Scotland) Act 1925 (c.17)

Town Police Clauses Act 1847 (c.89)

Town Police Clauses Act 1889 (c.14)

Town Tenants (Ireland) Act 1906 (c.54)

Towns Improvements Clauses Act 1847 (c.34)

Towns Improvement (Ireland) Act 1854 (c.103)

Towyn Trewan Common Act 1963 (c.4)

Trade Act 1807 (c.38)

Trade Act 1814 (c.72)

Trade Act 1822 (cc.44,45)

Trade, America, etc. Act 1817 (c.29)

Trade, American Colonies and West Indies Act 1823 (c.2)

Trade Between Bermuda and America Act 1817 (c.28)

Trade Between Great Britain and Ireland Act 1802 (c.14)

Trade Between Great Britain and Ireland Act 1803 (c.78)

Trade Between Europe and British America Act 1809 (c.47)

Trade Between Ireland and East Indies Act 1808 (c.30)

Trade Boards Act 1909 (c.22)

Trade Boards Act 1918 (c.32)

Trade Boards and Road Haulage Wages (Emergency Provisions) Act 1940 (c.7)

Trade Descriptions Act 1968 (c.29)

Trade Descriptions Act 1972 (c.34)

Trade Disputes Act 1906 (c.47)

Trade Disputes Act 1965 (c.48)

Trade Disputes and Trade Unions Act 1927 (c.22)

Trade Disputes and Trade Unions Act 1946 (c.52)

Trade During Hostilities Act 1803 (c.57)

Trade, East Indies and Mediterranean Act 1817 (c.36)

Trade, Europe and American Colonies Act 1811 (c.97)

Trade Facilities Act 1921 (c.65)

Trade Facilities Act 1924 (c.8)

Trade Facilities Act 1925 (c.13)

Trade Facilities Act 1926 (c.3)

Trade Facilities and Loans Guarantee Act 1922 (c.4)

Trade in Grain, etc. Act 1802 (c.35)

Trade in Spirits Act 1815 (c.132)

Trade in Spirits Act 1816 (c.105)

Trade in Spirits Act 1817 (c.72)

Trade in Spirits Act 1818 (c.26)

Trade in Spirits Act 1819 (c.75)

Trade in Spirits Act 1820 (c.77)

Trade Marks Act 1904 (c.15)

Trade Marks Act 1905 (c.15)

Trade Marks Act 1914 (c.16)

Trade Marks Act 1919 (c.79)

Trade Marks Act 1938 (c.22)

Trade Marks Act 1994 (c.26)

Trade Marks (Amendment) Act 1937 (c.49)

Trade Marks (Amendment) Act 1984 (c.19)

Trade Marks Registration Act 1875 (c.91)

Trade Marks Registration Amendment Act 1876 (c.33)

Trade Marks, Registration etc. Act 1877 (c.37)

Trade of British Possessions Act 1845 (c.93)

Trade of Canada Act 1812 (c.55)

Trade of Demerara, etc. Act 1816 (c.91)

Trade of Malta, etc. Act 1814 (c.182)

Trade of Malta, Act 1815 (c.29)

Trade of Nova Scotia, etc. Act 1809 (c.49)

Trade of West Indies Act 1812 (c.100)

Trade of West Indies Act 1814 (c.48)

Trade of West Indies, etc. Act 1814 (c.49)

Trade to the Levant Sea Act 1799 (c.99)

Trade Union Act 1871 (c.31)

Trade Union Act Amendment Act 1876 (c.22)

Trade Union Act 1913 (c.30)

Trade Union Act 1984 (c.49)

Trade Union (Amalgamation) Act 1917 (c.24)

Trade Union (Amalgamations, etc.) Act 1964 (c.24)

Trade Union and Labour Relations Act 1974 (c.52)

Trade Union and Labour Relations (Amendment) Act 1976 (c.7)

Trade Union and Labour Relations (Consolidation) Act 1992 (c.52)

Trade Union Commissions Act 1967 (c.8)

Trade Union Commissions Act Extension 1867 (c.74)

Trade Union (Provident Funds) Act 1893 (c.2)

Trade Union Funds Protection Act 1869 (c.61)

Trade Union Reform and Employment Rights Act 1993 (c.19)

Trade with America Act 1795 (c.26)

Trade with America Act 1796 (c.58)

Trade with America Act 1801 (c.95)

Trade with America Act 1808 (c.85)

Trade with British Possession Act 1831 (c.24)

Trade with French Colonies Act 1815 (c.146)

Trade with India Act 1797 (c.117)

Trade with New South Wales Act 1819 (c.122)

Trade with South America Act 1808 (c.109)

Trade with United States Act 1797 (c.37)

Trade with United States Act 1809 (c.59)

Trade with United States Act 1815 (c.193)

Trade of Tanners and Curriers Act 1816 (c.110)

Trading Partnerships Act 1841 (c.14)

Trading Representations (Disabled Persons) Act 1958 (c.49)

Trading Representations (Disabled Persons) Amendment Act 1972 (c.45)

Trading Stamps Act 1964 (c.71)

Trading with the Enemy Act 1914 (c.87)

Trading with the Enemy Act 1939 (c.89)

Trading with the Enemy Amendment Act 1914 (c.12)

Trading with the Enemy Amendment Act 1915 (c.79)

Trading with the Enemy Amendment Act 1916 (c.105)

Trading with the Enemy (Amendment) Act 1918 (c.31)

Trading with the Enemy and Export of Prohibited Goods Act 1916 (c.52)

Trading with the Enemy (Copyright) Act 1916 (c.32)

Trading with the Enemy (Extension of Powers) Act 1915 (c.98)

Trafalgar Estates Act 1947 (c.34)

Trafalgar Square Act 1844 (c.60)

Traffic Calming Act 1992 (c.30)

Tralee Navigation and Harbour Act 1844 (c.99)

Tralee Navigation Loan Act 1841 (c.46)

Tramway Act (1865) (c.74)

Tramways Act 1870 (c.78)

Tramways and Public Companies Act 1884 (c.5)

Tramways and Public Companies (Ireland) Act 1883 (c.43)

Tramways and Public Companies (Ireland) Amendment Act 1884 (c.28)

Tramways (Ireland) Act 1860 (c.152)

Tramways (Ireland) Act 1895 (c.20)

Tramways (Ireland) Act 1900 (c.60)

Tramways (Ireland) Amendment Act 1861 (c.102)

Tramways (Ireland) Amendment Act 1871 (c.114)

Tramways (Ireland) Amendment Act 1881 (c.17)

Tramways (Ireland) Amendment Act 1891 (c.42)

Tramways (Scotland) Act 1861 (c.69)

Tramways (Temporary Increase of Charges) Act 1920 (c.14)

Transfer of Aids Act 1853 (c.6)

Transfer of Property Act 1844 (c.76)

Transfer of Railways (Ireland) Act 1891 (c.2)

Transfer of Uster Canal Act 1865 (c.109)

Transfer of Balance of Fees Act 1830 (c.1)

Transfer of Contracts, etc. Act 1816 (c.31)

Transfer of Public Funds Act 1821 (c.73)

Transfer of Scotch Excise Charity, etc. Act (c.82)

Transfer of Singapore to East India Company, etc., Act 1824 (c.108)

Transfer of Stock Act 1800 (c.36)

Transfer of Stock (Ireland) Act 1820 (c.5)

Transfer of Stock of Hertford College Act 1816 (c.95)

Transfer of Stocks Act 1817 (c.79)

Transfer of Stocks Act 1818 (c.80)

Transfer of Trust Estates Act 1830 (c.60)

Transfer of Trust Estates, etc. (Ireland) Act 1826 (c.43)

Transfer of Works (Ireland) Act 1856 (c.37)

Transfer to Admiralty of Postal Contracts Act 1837 (c.3)

Transferrence of Lands (Scotland) Act 1847 (cc.48, 49)

Transitional Payments Act (Determination of Need) Act 1932 (c.54)

Transitional Payments Prolongation (Unemployed Persons) Act 1932 (c.19)

Transmission of Moveable Property (Scotland) Act 1862 (c.85)

Transport Act 1947 (c.49)

Transport Act 1953 (c.13)

Transport Act 1962 (c.46)

Transport Act 1968 (c.73)

Transport Act 1978 (c.55)

Transport Act 1980 (c.34)

Transport Act 1981 (c.56)

Transport Act 1982 (c.49)

Transport Act 1983 (c.10)

Transport Act 1985 (c.67)

Transport Act 1962 (Amendment) Act 1981 (c.32)

Transport and Works Act 1992 (c.42)

Transport (Borrowing Papers) Act 1954 (c.10)

Transport (Borrowing Papers) Act 1959 (c.16)

Transport Charges, etc. (Miscellaneous Provisions) Act 1954 (c.64)

Transport (Disposal of Road Haulage Property) Act 1956 (c.56)

Transport (Finance) Act 1982 (c.6)

Transport Finances Act 1966 (c.17)

Transport (Financial Provisions) Act 1977 (c.20)
Transport (Grants) Act 1972 (c.15)
Transport Holding Company Act 1968 (c.10)
Transport Holding Company Act 1972 (c.14)
Transport (London) Act 1969 (c.35)
Transport (London) Amendment Act 1969 (c.60)
Transport Police (Jurisdiction) Act 1994 (c.8)
Transport (Railway Finances) Act 1957 (c.9)
Transport (Scotland) Act 1989 (c.23)
Transportation Act 1799 (c.51)
Transportation Act 1802 (c.15)
Transportation Act 1802 (c.28)
Transportation, etc. Act 1806 (c.28)
Transportation Act 1813 (c.39)
Transportation Act 1813 (c.30)
Transportation Act 1815 (c.156)
Transportation Act 1816 (c.27)
Transportation Act 1819 (c.101)
Transportation Act 1821 (c.6)
Transportation Act 1824 (c.84)
Transportation Act 1825 (c.69)
Transportation Act 1830 (c.39)
Transportation Act 1834 (c.67)
Transportation Act 1843 (c.7)
Transportation Act 1846 (c.26)
Transportation Act 1847 (c.67)
Transportation (Ireland) Act 1849 (c.27)
Transvaal Loan (Guarantee) Act 1907 (c.37)
Travel Concessions Act 1964 (c.95)
Travel Concessions (London) Act 1982 (c.12)
Trawling in Prohibited Areas Prevention Act 1909 (c.8)
Treachery Act 1940 (c.21)
Treason Act 1708 (c.21)
Treason Act 1746 (c.30)
Treason Act 1795 (c.7)
Treason Act 1800 (c.93)
Treason Act 1814 (c.146)
Treason Act 1817 (c.6)
Treason Act 1842 (c.51)
Treason Act 1945 (c.44)
Treason Felony Act 1848 (c.12)
Treason (Ireland) Act 1821 (c.24)
Treason (Ireland) Act 1854 (c.26)
Treason in Scotland Act 1714 (c.20)
Treason Outlawries (Scotland) Act 1748 (c.48)
Treasurer of the Navy Act 1807 (c.56)
Treasurer of the Navy Act 1808 (c.8)
Treasurer of the Navy, etc. Act 1817 (c.121)
Treasurer of the Navy Act 1821 (c.74)
Treasurer of the Navy Act 1830 (c.42)
Treasurers of Counties (Ireland) Act 1855 (c.74)
Treasury Bills Act 1806 (c.32)
Treasury Bills Act 1807 (c.10)
Treasury Bills Act 1877 (c.2)
Treasury Bills Act 1899 (c.2)
Treasury Bills (Ireland) Act 1803 (c.114)
Treasury Bills (Ireland) Act 1804 (c.97)
Treasury Bills (Ireland) Act 1807 (c.72)

Treasury Bills (Ireland) Act 1808 (c.112)
Treasury Bills (Ireland) Act 1809 (c.79)
Treasury Bills (Ireland) Act 1810 (c.98)
Treasury Bills (Ireland) Act 1811 (c.5)
Treasury Bills (Ireland) Act 1811 (c.88)
Treasury Bills (Ireland) Act 1812 (c.90)
Treasury Bills (Ireland) Act 1812 (c.113)
Treasury Bills (Ireland) Act 1813 (c.80)
Treasury Bills (Ireland) Act 1814 (c.75)
Treasury Bills (Ireland) Act 1815 (c.40)
Treasury Bills (Ireland) Act 1816 (cc.41, 42)
Treasury Bills (Ireland) Act 1816 (c.47)
Treasury Bills (Ireland) Act 1817 (c.81)
Treasury Bills (Ireland) Act 1818 (c.87)
Treasury Bills (Ireland) Act 1819 (c.132)
Treasury Bills (Ireland) Act 1820 (c.46)
Treasury Bills (Ireland) Act 1821 (c.80)
Treasury Chest Fund Act 1861 (c.127)
Treasury Chest Fund Act 1873 (c.56)
Treasury Chest Fund Act 1877 (c.45)
Treasury Chest Fund Act 1893 (c.18)
Treasury Instruments (Signature) Act 1849 (c.89)
Treasury of the Ordnance Act 1806 (c.45)
Treasury Solicitor Act 1876 (c.18)
Treasury (Temporary Borrowing) Act 1910 (c.1)
Treaties of Peace (Austria and Bulgaria) Act 1920 (c.6)
Treaties of Peace (Italy, Roumania, Bulgaria, Hungary and Finland) Act 1947 (c.23)
Treaties of Washington Act 1922 (c.21)
Treaty of Commerce, etc. with America Act 1805 (c.35)
Treaty of Commerce, etc. with America Act 1806 (c.16)
Treaty of Commerce, etc. with America Act 1807 (c.2)
Treaty of Commerce, etc. with America Act 1808 (c.6)
Treaty of Peace Act 1919 (c.33)
Treaty of Peace (Hungary) Act 1921 (c.11)
Treaty of Peace (Turkey) Act 1924 (c.7)
Treaty of Washington Act 1872 (c.45)
Treaty with Hayti Act 1842 (c.41)
Treaty with United States 1797 (c.97)
Treaty with United States Act 1819 (c.54)
Trees Act 1970 (c.43)
Trent and Markham Bridges Act 1837 (c.15)
Trespass (Scotland) Act 1865 (c.56)
Trial of Felonies in Certain Boroughs Act 1834 (c.27)
Trial of Lunatics Act 1883 (c.38)
Trial of Offences (Ireland) Act 1833 (c.79)
Trial of Peers (Scotland) Act 1825 (c.66)
Trials for Felony Act 1836 (c.114)
Trials of Murders, etc., in Honduras Act 1819 (c.44)
Tribunals and Inquiries Act 1958 (c.66)
Tribunals and Inquiries Act 1966 (c.43)
Tribunals and Inquiries Act 1971 (c.62)
Tribunals and Inquiries Act 1992 (c.53)
Tribunals of Inquiry (Evidence) Act 1921 (c.7)

Trinidad and Tobago Act 1887 (c.44)
Trinidad and Tobago Independence Act 1962 (c.54)
Trinidad and Tobago Republic Act 1976 (c.54)
Trinity College, Dublin Act 1855 (c.82)
Trout (Scotland) Act 1845 (c.26)
Trout (Scotland) Act 1860 (c.45)
Trout (Scotland) Act 1933 (c.35)
Truck Act 1831 (c.37)
Truck Act 1837 (c.37)
Truck Act 1896 (c.44)
Truck Act 1940 (c.38)
Truck Amendment Act 1887 (c.46)
Truck Commission Act 1870 (c.105)
Trunk Roads Act 1936 (c.5)
Trunk Roads Act 1946 (c.30)
Truro Bishopric and Chapter Acts Amendment Act 1887 (c.12)
Truro Chapter Act 1878 (c.44)
Trust Investment Act 1889 (c.32)
Trust Property, Escheat Act 1834 (c.23)
Trust (Scotland) Amendment Act 1884 (c.63)
Trustee Act 1850 (c.60)
Trustee Act 1852 (c.55)
Trustee Act 1888 (c.59)
Trustee Act 1893 (c.53)
Trustee Act 1925 (c.19)
Trustee Act 1893 Amendment Act 1894 (c.10)
Trustee Appointment Act 1850 (c.28)
Trustee Appointment Act 1869 (c.26)
Trustee Churches (Ireland) Act 1884 (c.10)
Trustee Investments Act 1961 (c.62)
Trustee Savings Banks Act 1863 (c.87)
Trustee Savings Banks Act 1887 (c.47)
Trustee Savings Banks Act 1918 (c.4)
Trustee Savings Banks Act 1946 (c.6)
Trustee Savings Banks Act 1954 (c.63)
Trustee Savings Banks Act 1957 (c.8)
Trustee Savings Banks Act 1969 (c.50)
Trustee Savings Banks Act 1976 (c.4)
Trustee Savings Banks Act 1978 (c.16)
Trustee Savings Banks Act 1981 (c.65)
Trustee Savings Banks Act 1985 (c.58)
Trustee Savings Banks (Pensions) Act 1954 (c.12)
Trustee Savings Banks (Special Investments) Act 1934 (c.37)
Trustee (War Damage Insurance) Act 1941 (c.28)
Trustees Appointment Act 1890 (c.19)
Trustees Relief Act 1847 (c.96)
Trustees Relief Act 1849 (c.74)
Trustees Relief (Ireland) Act 1848 (c.68)
Trustees Savings Banks Act 1968 (c.6)
Trusts (Scotland) Act 1861 (c.84)
Trusts (Scotland) Act 1867 (c.97)
Trusts (Scotland) Act 1897 (c.8)
Trusts (Scotland) Act 1898 (c.42)
Trusts (Scotland) Act, 1867, Amendment Act 1887 (c.18)
Trusts (Scotland) Amendment Act 1891 (c.44)

Trustee (Scotland) Act 1910 (c.22)
Trusts (Scotland) Act 1921 (c.58)
Trusts (Scotland) Act 1961 (c.57)
Tuberculosis Prevention (Ireland) Act 1908 (c.56)
Tuberculosis Prevention (Ireland) Act 1913 (c.25)
Tumultuous Petitioning Act 1661 (c.5)
Tumultuous Risings (Ireland) Act 1831 (c.44)
Tunnel Between Devonport and Keyham Act 1854 (c.15)
Turbary (Ireland) Act 1891 (c.45)
Turkish Loan Act 1855 (c.99)
Turks and Caicos Islands Act 1873 (c.6)
Turnpike Acts Act 1843 (c.69)
Turnpike Acts Continuance 1800 (c.26)
Turnpike Acts Continuance Act 1831 (c.6)
Turnpike Acts Continuance Act 1834 (c.10)
Turnpike Acts Continuance Act 1835 (c.49)
Turnpike Acts Continuance Act 1836 (c.62)
Turnpike Acts Continuance Act 1837 (c.18)
Turnpike Acts Continuance Act 1838 (c.68)
Turnpike Acts Continuance Act 1839 (c.31)
Turnpike Acts Continuance Act 1840 (c.45)
Turnpike Acts Continuance Act 1841 (c.9)
Turnpike Acts Continuance Act 1842 (c.60)
Turnpike Acts Continuance Act 1845 (c.53)
Turnpike Acts Continuance Act 1848 (c.96)
Turnpike Acts Continuance Act 1849 (c.87)
Turnpike Acts Continuance Act 1857 (c.24)
Turnpike Acts Continuance Act 1858 (c.63)
Turnpike Acts Continuance Act 1866 (c.105)
Turnpike Acts Continuance (Ireland) Act 1851 (c.44)
Turnpike Acts, Great Britain Act 1844 (c.41)
Turnpike Acts, Great Britain Act 1846 (c.51)
Turnpike Acts, Great Britain Act 1847 (c.105)
Turnpike Acts, Great Britain Act 1852 (c.58)
Turnpike Acts, Great Britain Act 1855 (c.98)
Turnpike Acts, Great Britain Act 1856 (c.49)
Turnpike Acts (Ireland) Act 1838 (c.72)
Turnpike Acts (Ireland) Act 1842 (c.23)
Turnpike Acts (Ireland) Act 1843 (c.21)
Turnpike Acts (Ireland) Act 1844 (c.36)
Turnpike Acts (Ireland) Act 1845 (c.125)
Turnpike Acts (Ireland) Act 1848 (c.73)
Turnpike Acts (Ireland) Act 1849 (c.47)
Turnpike Acts (Ireland) Act 1852 (c.22)
Turnpike Acts (Ireland) Act 1853 (c.76)
Turnpike Acts (Ireland) Act 1854 (c.42)
Turnpike Acts (Ireland) Act 1855 (c.83)
Turnpike Acts, Ireland, Continuance Act 1836 (c.40)
Turnpike Acts, Ireland, Continuance Act 1840 (c.46)
Turnpike Acts, Ireland, Continuance Act 1850 (c.34)
Turnpike Acts, Ireland, Continuance Act 1856 (c.71)
Turnpike Debts Act 1852 (c.33)
Turnpike Roads Act 1815 (c.119)
Turnpike Roads Act 1817 (c.37)
Turnpike Roads Act 1822 (c.126)

Turnpike Roads Act 1823 (c.95)
Turnpike Roads Act 1824 (c.69)
Turnpike Roads Act 1827 (c.24)
Turnpike Roads Act 1828 (c.77)
Turnpike Roads (England) Act 1853 (c.135)
Turnpike Roads (England) Act 1854 (c.58)
Turnpike Roads in Yorkshire Act 1852 (c.45)
Turnpike Roads (Ireland) Act 1834 (c.91)
Turnpike Roads (Ireland) Act 1841 (c.6)
Turnpike Roads (Ireland) Act 1846 (c.89)
Turnpike Roads (Ireland) Act 1847 (c.35)
Turnpike Roads (Scotland) Act 1823 (c.49)
Turnpike Roads (Scotland) Act 1831 (c.43)
Turnpike Roads (Scotland) Act 1849 (c.31)
Turnpike Roads (Tolls on Lime) Act 1823 (c.16)
Turnpike Roads Trusts Act 1820 (c.95)
Turnpike Tolls Act 1835 (c.18)
Turnpike Tolls Act 1839 (c.46)
Turnpike Tolls Act 1840 (c.51)
Turnpike Tolls Act 1841 (c.33)
Turnpike Tolls (Allowance of Wagon Weights) Act 1834 (c.81)
Turnpike Trusts Act 1856 (c.12)
Turnpike Trusts Arrangements Act 1867 (c.66)
Turnpike Trusts Arrangements Act 1868 (c.66)
Turnpike Trusts Arrangements Act 1872 (c.72)
Turnpike Trusts: Making of Provisional Orders Act 1851 (c.38)
Turnpike Trusts Relief Act 1861 (c.46)
Turnpike Trusts Returns Act 1833 (c.80)
Turnpike Trusts, South Wales Act 1845 (c.61)
Turnpikes Abolition (Ireland) Act 1857 (c.16)
Turnpikes Act 1831 (c.25)
Turnpikes Act 1832 (c.124)
Turnpikes Act 1840 (c.39)
Turnpikes Acts Continuation Act 1849 (c.87)
Turnpikes (Provisional Orders Confirmation) Act 1865 (c.91)
Turnpikes (Provisional Orders Confirmation) Act 1866 (c.92)
Turnpikes (Provisional Orders Confirmation) Act 1870 (c.22)
Turnpikes, South Wales Act 1844 (c.91)
Tuvalu Act 1978 (c.20)
Tweed Fisheries Act 1797 (c.48)
Tyne Pilotage Order Confirmation Act 1865 (c.44)
Tyne Pilotage Order Confirmation Act 1867 (c.78)

Uganda Act 1964 (c.20)
Uganda Railway Act 1896 (c.38)
Uganda Railway Act 1900 (c.11)
Uganda Railway Act 1902 (c.40)
Ugandan Independence Act 1962 (c.57)
Ulster Defence Regiment Act 1969 (c.65)

Ulster Defence Regiment Act 1973 (c.34)
Ulster Society 1704 (c.19)
Ulverstone Canal Act 1793 (c.105)
Unclaimed Prize Money, etc. Act 1812 (c.132)
Under Secretaries of State Act 1929 (c.9)
Under Secretary of State Indemnity Act 1864 (c.21)
Underground Works (London) Act 1956 (c.59)
Unemployed Workers' Dependants (Temporary Provisions) Act 1921 (c.62)
Unemployed Workmen Act 1904 (c.18)
Unemployment Act 1934 (c.29)
Unemployment and Family Allowances (Northern Ireland Agreement) Act 1946 (c.3)
Unemployment Assistance (Emergency Powers) Act 1939 (c.93)
Unemployment Assistance (Temporary Provisions) Act 1935 (c.6)
Unemployment Assistance (Temporary Provisions) (Amendment) Act 1937 (c.10)
Unemployment Assistance (Temporary Provisions) (Extension) Act 1936 (c.7)
Unemployment Assistance (Temporary Provisions) (No. 2) Act 1935 (c.22)
Unemployment Insurance Act 1920 (c.30)
Unemployment Insurance Act 1921 (c.1)
Unemployment Insurance Act 1922 (c.7)
Unemployment Insurance Act 1923 (c.2)
Unemployment Insurance Act 1924 (c.1)
Unemployment Insurance Act 1925 (c.69)
Unemployment Insurance Act 1926 (c.12)
Unemployment Insurance Act 1927 (c.30)
Unemployment Insurance Act 1928 (c.1)
Unemployment Insurance Act 1929 (c.3)
Unemployment Insurance Act 1930 (c.16)
Unemployment Insurance Act 1931 (c.8)
Unemployment Insurance Act 1935 (c.8)
Unemployment Insurance Act 1938 (c.8)
Unemployment Insurance Act 1939 (c.29)
Unemployment Insurance Act 1940 (c.44)
Unemployment Insurance (Agriculture) Act 1936 (c.13)
Unemployment Insurance (Crediting of Contributions) Act 1935 (c.33)
Unemployment Insurance (Emergency Powers) Act 1939 (c.92)
Unemployment Insurance (Expiring Enactments) Act 1933 (c.26)
Unemployment Insurance (Eire Volunteers) Act 1946 (c.76)
Unemployment Insurance (Increase of Benefit) Act 1944 (c.42)
Unemployment Insurance (Northern Ireland Agreement) Act 1926 (c.4)
Unemployment Insurance (Northern Ireland Agreement) Act 1929 (c.18)
Unemployment Insurance (No. 2) Act 1921 (c.15)
Unemployment Insurance (No. 2) Act 1922 (c.30)

Unemployment Insurance (No. 2) Act 1924 (c.30)

Unemployment Insurance (No. 2) Act 1930 (c.19)

Unemployment Insurance (No. 2) Act 1931 (c.25)

Unemployment Insurance (No. 3) Act 1924 (c.6)

Unemployment Insurance (No. 3) Act 1930 (c.47)

Unemployment Insurance (No. 3) Act 1931 (c.36)

Unemployment Insurance (No. 4) Act 1931 (c.3)

Unemployment Insurance (Temporary Provisions Amendment) 1920 (c.82)

Unemployment Insurance (Transitional Provisions Amendment) Act 1929 (c.19)

Unemployment (Northern Ireland Agreement) Act 1936 (c.10)

Unemployment Relief Works 1920 (c.57)

Unfair Contract Terms Act 1977 (c.50)

Unfunded Debt Act 1761 (c.7)

Unfunded Debt Act 1765 (c.19)

Unfunded Debt Act 1766 (c.15)

Unfunded Debt Act 1766 (c.16)

Unfunded Debt Act 1768 (c.18)

Unfunded Debt Act 1769 (c.15)

Unfunded Debt Act 1770 (c.11)

Unfunded Debt Act 1772 (c.39)

Unfunded Debt Act 1772 (c.66)

Unfunded Debt Act 1801 (c.4)

Uniform Laws on International Sales Act 1967 (c.45)

Uniformity of Worship Act 1749 (c.28)

Uniforms Act 1894 (c.45)

Union and Parish Property Act 1837 (c.50)

Union Assessment Act 1880 (c.7)

Union Assessment Committee Act 1862 (c.103)

Union Assessment Committee Amendment Act 1864 (c.39)

Union Between England and Scotland Act 1702 (c.8)

Union Chargeability Act 1865 (c.79)

Union Loans Act 1869 (c.45)

Union of Benefices Act 1860 (c.142)

Union of Benefices Act 1898 (c.23)

Union of Benefices Act 1919 (c.98)

Union of Benefices Acts Amendment Act 1871 (c.90)

Union of Benefices, etc. Act 1855 (c.127)

Union of England and Scotland 1704 (c.6)

Union of England and Scotland 1705 (c.15)

Union of Parishes Act 1827 (c.43)

Union of Parishes, etc. (Ireland) Act 1832 (c.67)

Union of Turnpike Trusts Act 1849 (c.46)

Union Officers (Ireland) Act 1872 (c.89)

Union Officers (Ireland) Act 1885 (c.80)

Union Officers Superannuation (Ireland) Act 1865 (c.26)

Union Relief Aid Act 1862 (c.110)

Union Relief Aid Act 1863 (c.91)

Union Relief Aid Continuance Act 1863 (c.4)

Union Relief Aid Continuance Act 1864 (c.10)

Union with Ireland Act 1800 (c.67)

Union with Scotland Act 1706 (c.11)

Union with Scotland (Amendment) Act 1707 (c.40)

United Nations Act 1946 (c.45)

United Parishes (Scotland) Act 1868 (c.30)

United Parishes (Scotland) Act 1876 (c.11)

United States of America Veterans' Pensions (Administration) Act 1949 (c.45)

United States of America (Visiting Forces) Act 1942 (c.31)

Universities Act 1825 (c.97)

Universities and College (Emergency Powers) Act 1914 (c.22)

Universities and College (Emergency Provisions) Act 1939 (c.106)

Universities and College Estates Act 1858 (c.44)

Universities and College Estates Act 1898 (c.55)

Universities and College Estates Act 1925 (c.24)

Universities and College Estates Act 1964 (c.51)

Universities and College Estates Act Extension Act 1860 (c.59)

Universities and College Estates Amendment Act 1880 (c.46)

Universities and Colleges (Trust) Act 1943 (c.9)

Universities Election Act 1868 (c.65)

Universities Elections Amendment (Scotland) Act 1881 (c.40)

Universities of Oxford and Cambridge Act 1859 (c.19)

Universities of Oxford and Cambridge Act 1877 (c.48)

Universities of Oxford and Cambridge Act 1880 (c.11)

Universities of Oxford and Cambridge Act 1923 (c.33)

Universities (Scotland) Act 1853 (c.89)

Universities (Scotland) Act 1858 (c.83)

Universities (Scotland) Act 1859 (c.24)

Universities (Scotland) Act 1862 (c.28)

Universities (Scotland) Act 1889 (c.55)

Universities (Scotland) Act 1922 (c.31)

Universities (Scotland) Act 1932 (c.26)

Universities (Scotland) Act 1966 (c.13)

Universities Tests Act 1871 (c.26)

University Education (Ireland) Act 1879 (c.65)

University Elections Act 1861 (c.53)

University of Dublin Registration Act 1842 (c.74)

University of Dublin Tests 1873 (c.21)

University of Durham Act 1908 (c.20)

University of Durham Act 1935 (c.29)

University of Liverpool Act 1904 (c.11)

University of London Act 1898 (c.62)

University of London Act 1899 (c.24)
University of London Act 1926 (c.46)
University of London Medical Graduates Act 1854 (c.114)
University of Oxford Act 1869 (c.20)
University of St. Andrews Act 1746 (c.32)
University of St. Andrews Act 1953 (c.40)
University of Wales Act 1902 (c.14)
University of Wales (Medical Graduates) Act 1911 (c.43)
Universities (Wine Licences) Act 1743 (c.40)
Unlawful Combinations (Ireland) Act 1803 (c.86)
Unlawful Combinations (Ireland) Act 1814 (c.180)
Unlawful Combinations (Ireland) Act 1848 (c.89)
Unlawful Combinations of Workmen Act 1799 (c.81)
Unlawful Combinations of Workmen Act 1800 (c.106)
Unlawful Distillation, etc. (Ireland) Act 1814 (c.12)
Unlawful Drilling Act 1819 (c.1)
Unlawful Games Act 1728 (c.28)
Unlawful Oaths Act 1797 (c.123)
Unlawful Oaths Act 1810 (c.102)
Unlawful Oaths Act 1812 (c.104)
Unlawful Oaths Act 1823 (c.87)
Unlawful Oaths (Ireland) Act 1810 (c.102)
Unlawful Oaths (Ireland) Act 1844 (c.78)
Unlawful Oaths (Ireland) Act 1845 (c.55)
Unlawful Oaths (Ireland) Act 1851 (c.48)
Unlawful Oaths (Ireland) Act 1856 (c.78)
Unlawful Oaths (Ireland) Act 1862 (c.32)
Unlawful Pawning Act 1786 (c.92)
Unlawful Societies Act 1799 (c.79)
Unlawful Societies (Ireland) Act 1839 (c.74)
Unlawful Weights (Ireland) Act 1824 (c.110)
Unreasonable Withholding of Food Supplies Act 1914 (c.51)
Unsolicited Goods and Services Act 1971 (c.30)
Unsolicited Goods and Services (Amendment) Act 1975 (c.13)
Urban Development Corporations (Financial Limits) Act 1987 (c.57)
Use of Clarke's Hydrometer Act 1802 (c.97)
Use of Corn in Distillation of Spirits, etc. Act 1800 (c.3)
Use of Fine Flow Act 1801 (cc.1, 2)
Use of Fire on Steamboats Act 1828 (c.11)
Use of Highland Dress Act 1782 (c.63)
Use of Horsehides etc. Act 1800 (c.66)
Use of Plate Act 1769 (c.11)
Use of Rice in Distillation Act 1856 (c.51)
Use of Salt Duty Free, etc. Act 1800 (c.21)
Use of Sugar in Brewing Act 1800 (c.62)
Use of Sugar in Brewing Act 1812 (c.1)
Use of Sugar in Brewing Act 1812 (c.65)
Use of Wheat in Making Starch Act 1800 (c.25)
Usury Act 1713 (c.15)

Usury Act 1837 (c.80)
Usury Act 1839 (c.37)
Usury Act 1840 (c.83)
Usury Act 1841 (c.54)
Usury Act 1843 (c.45)
Usury Act 1845 (c.102)
Usury Act 1850 (c.56)
Usury Laws Repeal Act 1854 (c.90)
Uttoxeter to Stoke Road Act 1793 (c.131)
Uxbridge: Streets Act 1785 (c.16)

Vacant Ecclesiastical Dignities, etc. Act 1835 (c.30)
Vaccination Act 1840 (c.29)
Vaccination Act 1841 (c.32)
Vaccination Act 1853 (c.100)
Vaccination Act 1867 (c.84)
Vaccination Act 1871 (c.98)
Vaccination Act 1874 (c.75)
Vaccination Act 1898 (c.49)
Vaccination Act 1907 (c.31)
Vaccination Acts Amendment Act 1861 (c.59)
Vaccination Amendment (Ireland) Act 1868 (c.87)
Vaccination Amendment (Ireland) Act 1879 (c.70)
Vaccination (Ireland) Act 1858 (c.64)
Vaccination (Ireland) Act 1863 (c.52)
Vaccination (Scotland) Act 1863 (c.108)
Vaccination (Scotland) Act 1907 (c.49)
Vaccine Damage Payments Act 1979 (c.17)
Vagrance (Ireland) Amendment Act 1865 (c.33)
Vagrancy Act 1824 (c.83)
Vagrancy Act 1838 (c.38)
Vagrancy Act 1898 (c.39)
Vagrancy Act 1935 (c.20)
Vagrancy (England) Act 1822 (c.40)
Vagrancy (Ireland) Act 1847 (c.84)
Vagrant Act Amendment Act 1868 (c.52)
Vagrant Act Amendment Act 1873 (c.38)
Vagrants Act 1706 (c.32)
Vagrants Act 1713 (c.26)
Vagrants Act 1739 (c.24)
Vagrants Act 1821 (c.64)
Vagrants and Criminals Act 1787 (c.11)
Validation of Acts of Hate, Chief Justice of Bombay Act 1858 (c.32)
Validation of Elections Act 1955 (c.10)
Validation of Elections (No. 2) Act 1955 (c.12)
Validation of Elections (No. 3) Act 1955 (c.13)
Validation of Elections (Northern Ireland) Act 1956 (c.35)
Validation of War-time Leases Act 1944 (c.34)
Validity of Certain Contracts Act 1838 (c.10)
Validity of Certain Oaths Act 1812 (c.21)
Validity of Certain Orders in Council, etc. Act 1808 (c.37)
Validity of Certain Proceedings, etc. Act 1854 (c.37)
Validity of Proceedings in the House of Commons Act 1855 (c.33)

Valuation and Rating (Exempted Classes) (Scotland) Act 1976 (c.64)

Valuation and Rating (Scotland) Act 1956 (c.60)

Valuation (Ireland) Act 1834 (c.55)

Valuation (Ireland) Act 1852 (c.63)

Valuation (Ireland) Act 1853 (c.7)

Valuation (Ireland) Act 1854 (c.8)

Valuation (Ireland) Act 1864 (c.52)

Valuation (Ireland) Act 1901 (c.37)

Valuation (Ireland) Amendment Act 1874 (c.70)

Valuation (Metropolis) Act 1869 (c.67)

Valuation Metropolis Amendment Act 1884 (c.5)

Valuation Metropolis Amendment Act 1925 (c.40)

Valuation of Lands (Ireland) Act 1826 (c.62)

Valuation of Lands (Ireland) Act 1831 (c.51)

Valuation of Lands (Ireland) Act 1832 (c.73)

Valuation of Lands (Ireland) Act 1836 (c.84)

Valuation for Rating Act 1953 (c.42)

Valuation for Rating (Scotland) Act 1970 (c.4)

Valuation of Lands (Scotland) Acts Amendment Act 1894 (c.36)

Valuation of Lands (Scotland) Amendment Act 1867 (c.80)

Valuation of Lands (Scotland) Amendment Act 1879 (c.42)

Valuation of Lands (Scotland) Amendment Act 1887 (c.51)

Value Added Tax Act 1983 (c.55)

Value Added Tax Act 1994 (c.23)

Van Diemen's Land Act 1842 (c.3)

Van Diemen's Land Co. Act 1825 (c.39)

Van Diemen's Land Co. Act 1847 (c.57)

Vancouver's Island Act 1849 (c.48)

Variation of Trusts Act 1958 (c.53)

Vehicle and Driving Licences Act 1969 (c.27)

Vehicle Excise and Registration Act 1994 (c.22)

Vehicles (Excise) Act 1949 (c.89)

Vehicles (Excise) Act 1962 (c.13)

Vehicles (Excise) Act 1971 (c.10)

Vendor and Purchaser Act 1874 (c.78)

Venereal Disease Act 1917 (c.21)

Vessels Built at Malta, etc. Act 1820 (c.9)

Vessels Protection Act 1967 (c.85)

Vesting in Crown of Lands at Sandhurst Act 1812 (c.124)

Vestries Act 1818 (c.69)

Vestries Act 1819 (c.85)

Vestries Act 1831 (c.60)

Vestries Act 1850 (c.57)

Vestries Act 1853 (c.65)

Vesty Cess Abolition Act 1864 (c.17)

Veterinary Surgeons Act 1881 (c.62)

Veterinary Surgeons Act 1948 (c.52)

Veterinary Surgeons Act 1966 (c.36)

Veterinary Surgeons Act (1881) Amendment 1920 (c.20)

Veterinary Surgeons Amendment 1900 (c.24)

Veterinary Surgeons (Irish Free State Agreement) Act 1932 (c.10)

Vexatious Actions Act 1896 (c.51)

Vexatious Actions (Scotland) Act 1898 (c.35)

Vexatious Arrests Act 1747 (c.3)

Vexatious Arrests Act 1817 (c.101)

Vexatious Indictments Act 1859 (c.17)

Vice-Admiralty Courts Act 1816 (c.82)

Vice-Admiralty Courts Act 1832 (c.51)

Vice-Admiralty Courts Act 1863 (c.24)

Vice-Admiralty Courts Act Amendment Act 1867 (c.45)

Victoria Constitution Act 1855 (c.55)

Victoria Park Act 1842 (c.20)

Victoria Park Act 1872 (c.53)

Victoria University Act 1888 (c.45)

Victualling Establishment, Plymouth Act 1824 (c.49)

Video Recordings Act 1984 (c.39)

Video Recordings Act 1993 (c.24)

Vinegar Act 1844 (c.25)

Viscount Hardinge's Annuity Act 1846 (c.21)

Visiting Forces Act 1952 (c.67)

Visiting Forces (British Commonwealth) Act 1933 (c.6)

Voluntary Conveyances Act 1893 (c.21)

Voluntary Hospitals (Paying Patients) Act 1936 (c.17)

Voluntary Schools Act 1897 (c.5)

Volunteer Act 1863 (c.65)

Volunteer Act 1869 (c.81)

Volunteer Act 1895 (c.23)

Volunteer Act 1897 (c.47)

Volunteer Act 1900 (c.39)

Volunteer Act 1916 (c.62)

Volunteers Act 1780 (c.37)

Volunteers Act 1782 (c.79)

Volunteers Act 1861 (c.126)

Volunteers and Local Militia Act 1809 (c.113)

Volunteers and Yeomanry (Great Britain) Act 1803 (c.18)

Volunteer Corps Act 1794 (c.31)

Wadeshill and Royston Road Act 1796 (c.129)

Wages Act 1708 (c.16)

Wages Act 1986 (c.48)

Wages and Prize Money, etc. in the Navy Act 1809 (c.108)

Wages Arrestment Act 1845 (c.39)

Wages Arrestment Limitation (Amendment) (Scotland) Act 1960 (c.21)

Wages Arrestment Limitation (Scotland) Act 1870 (c.63)

Wages Attachment Abolition Act 1870 (c.30)

Wages Councils Act 1945 (c.17)

Wages Councils Act 1948 (c.7)

Wages Councils Act 1959 (c.69)

Wages Councils Act 1979 (c.12)

Wages Councils (Northern Ireland) Act 1945 (c.21)

Wages, etc. of Artificers, etc. Act 1813 (c.40)

Wages of Artificers, etc. Act 1820 (c.93)

Wages of Certain Deceased Seamen Act 1819 (c.59)

Wages of Merchant Seamen Act 1819 (c.58)

Wages (Temporary Regulations) Act 1918 (c.61)

Wages (Temporary Regulations) Extension Act 1919 (c.18)

Wakefield Church Act 1791 (c.74)

Wakefield, etc. Roads Act 1740 (c.19)

Wakefield and Halifax Roads Act 1793 (c.129)

Wakefield and Sheffield Road Act 1797 (c.159)

Wakefield (Improvement) Act 1771 (c.44)

Wakefield: Improvement Act 1796 (c.50)

Wakefield Roads Act 1778 (c.85)

Wakefield to Abberford Road Act 1789 (c.86)

Wakefield to Abberford Road Act 1793 (c.179)

Wakefield to Austerlands Road Act 1758 (c.48)

Wakefield to Sheffield Road Act 1778 (c.105)

Walcot, Somerset: Improvement Act 1793 (c.89)

Wales Act 1978 (c.52)

Wales and Berwick Act 1746 (c.42)

Wales, Chester, etc. (Courts) Act 1793 (c.68)

Wallingford: Improvement Act 1795 (c.75)

Walmer Vesting Act 1863 (c.54)

Walmore and Bearce Commons, Forest of Dean Act 1866 (c.70)

Walton - Shepperton Bridge (Building and Tolls) Act 1746 (c.22)

Walton - Shepperton Bridge (Rebuilding and Tolls) Act 1780 (c.32)

Wangford, Suffolk: Poor Relief Act 1764 (c.91)

Wapping, Stepney Act 1728 (c.30)

Wapping, Stepney: Poor Relief Act 1782 (c.35)

Wapping, Stepney: Poor Relief, etc. Act 1783 (c.32)

Wapping, Stepney: Improvement Act 1782 (c.86)

War Charges (Validity) Act 1925 (c.6)

War Charities Act 1916 (c.43)

War Charities Act 1940 (c.31)

War Charities Act (Scotland) 1919 (c.12)

War Crimes Act 1991 (c.13)

War Damage Act 1941 (c.12)

War Damage Act 1943 (c.21)

War Damage Act 1949 (c.36)

War Damage Act 1964 (c.25)

War Damage Act 1965 (c.18)

War Damage (Amendment) Act 1942 (c.28)

War Damages (Amendment) Act 1943 (c.12)

War Damage (Clearance Payments) Act 1960 (c.25)

War Damage (Extension of Risk Period) Act 1941 (c.37)

War Damage (Public Utility Undertakings, etc.) Act 1949 (c.36)

War Damage to Land (Scotland) Act 1939 (c.80)

War Damage to Land (Scotland) Act 1941 (c.40)

War Damage (Valuation Appeals) Act 1945 (c.8)

War Damaged Sites Act 1949 (c.84)

War Department Property Act 1938 (c.49)

War Department Stores Act 1867 (c.128)

War Department Tramway (Devon) Act 1865 (c.74)

War Emergency Laws (Continuance) Act 1920 (c.5)

War Loan Act 1900 (c.2)

War Loan Act 1914 (c.60)

War Loan Act 1915 (c.55)

War Loan Act 1916 (c.67)

War Loan Act 1917 (c.41)

War Loan Act 1918 (c.25)

War Loan Act 1919 (c.37)

War Loan (Redemption) Act 1910 (c.2)

War Loan (Supplemental Provisions) Act 1915 (c.93)

War Memorials (Local Authorities' Powers) Act 1923 (c.18)

War Office Act 1879 (c.17)

War Orphans Act 1942 (c.8)

War Pensions Act 1920 (c.23)

War Pensions Act 1921 (c.49)

War Pensions (Administrative Provisions) Act 1918 (c.57)

War Pensions (Administrative Provisions) Act 1919 (c.53)

War Risks Insurance Act 1939 (c.57)

War Risks (Insurance by Truskes) Act 1916 (c.6)

War Service Canteens (Disposal of Surplus) Act 1922 (c.53)

War Stores (Commission) Act 1904 (c.7)

Warden of Fleet Prison Act 1728 (c.32)

Warden of the Fleet Prison Act 1819 (c.64)

Wareham and Purbeck Roads Act 1786 (c.122)

Wareham: Improvement Act 1763 (c.54)

Warehoused British Spirits Act 1867 (c.27)

Warehoused Goods Act 1809 (c.106)

Warehoused Tobacco, etc. Act 1793 (c.57)

Warehousing of British Compounded Spirits Act 1865 (c.98)

Warehousing of British Spirits Act 1864 (c.12)

Warehousing of Foreign Goods, Manchester Act 1844 (c.31)

Warehousing of Goods Act 1799 (c.59)

Warehousing of Goods Act 1803 (c.132)

Warehousing of Goods Act 1823 (c.24)

Warehousing of Goods Act 1845 (c.91)

Warehousing of Spirits (Ireland) Act 1812 (c.30)

Warehousing of Wines, etc. Act 1795 (c.118)

Warminster Roads Act 1726 (c.16)

Warminster Roads Act 1742 (c.5)

Warminster Roads Act 1765 (c.62)

Warminster Roads Act 1792 (c.141)

Warrants of Attorney Act 1822 (c.39)
Warrants of Attorney Act 1843 (c.66)
Warrick Election Act 1834 (c.17)
Warrington and Wigan Road Act 1726 (c.10)
Warrington and Wigan Road Act 1770 (c.70)
Warrington to Wigan Road Act 1746 (c.8)
Warrington to Wigan Road Act 1793 (c.164)
Warwick and Birmingham Canal Act 1793 (c.38)
Warrington and Birmingham Canal Act 1796 (c.42)
Warwick and Gloucester Roads Act 1773 (c.97)
Warwick and Gloucester Roads Act 1791 (c.116)
Warwick and Napton Canal Act 1794 (c.38)
Warwick and Napton Canal Act 1796 (c.95)
Warwick and Northampton Road Act 1765 (c.107)
Warwick Assizes Act 1854 (c.35)
Warwick, etc. Roads Act 1739 (c.5)
Warwick to Northampton Road Act 1776 (c.80)
Warwick and Northampton Roads Act 1781 (c.106)
Warwick and Northamptonshire Roads Act 1759 (c.44)
Warwick and Oxford Roads Act 1755 (c.46)
Warwick and Oxford Roads Act 1780 (c.69)
Warwick and Worcester Roads Act 1754 (c.36)
Warwick and Worcester Roads Act 1767 (c.81)
Warwick and Worcester Roads Act 1780 (c.71)
Warwick and Worcester Roads Act 1781 (c.88)
Warwick Bridge Act 1788 (c.9)
Warwick Gaol Act 1777 (c.58)
Warwick, Stafford and Worcester Roads Act 1794 (c.117)
Warwick Roads Act 1723 (c.15)
Warwick Roads Act 1730 (c.9)
Warwick Roads Act 1738 (c.18)
Warwick Roads Act 1739 (c.22)
Warwick Roads Act 1742 (c.20)
Warwick Roads Act 1743 (c.12)
Warwick Roads Act 1744 (c.32)
Warwick Roads Act 1753 (c.73)
Warwick Roads Act 1760 (c.36)
Warwick Roads Act 1767 (c.77)
Warwick Roads Act 1770 (c.63)
Warwick Roads Act 1770 (c.69)
Warwick Roads Act 1770 (c.94)
Warwick Roads Act 1772 (c.91)
Warwick Roads Act 1780 (c.80)
Warwick Roads Act 1785 (c.115)
Warwick Roads Act 1788 (c.107)
Warwick Roads Act 1791 (c.98)
Warwick Roads Act 1792 (c.116)
Warwick Roads Act 1794 (c.115)
Warwick Roads Act 1794 (c.116)
Warwick Shire Hall Act 1757 (c.56)

Warwick, Stafford and Worcester Roads Act 1772 (c.110)
Warwick, Worcester and Stafford Roads Act 1787 (c.73)
Warwickshire and Northamptonshire Roads 1736 (c.11)
Warwickshire Roads Act 1744 (c.19)
Washington Treaty (Claims) Act 1875 (c.52)
Waste Lands, Australia Act 1846 (c.104)
Waste Lands, Van Diemen's Land Act 1845 (c.95)
Watch Rates in Boroughs Act 1840 (c.28)
Watching: City of London Act 1736 (c.22)
Watching: Holborn Act 1736 (c.25)
Watching, St. Margaret and St. John, Westminster 1735 (c.17)
Watching, St. Martin's in the Fields Act 1735 (c.8)
Watching, St. Paul (Covent Garden) 1735 (c.13)
Watching, Westminster 1735 (c.19)
Watchett (Somerset) Harbour Act 1707 (c.69)
Watchett (Somerset) Harbour Act 1720 (c.14)
Watchett Harbour Act 1770 (c.24)
Water Act 1945 (c.42)
Water Act 1948 (c.22)
Water Act 1958 (c.67)
Water Act 1973 (c.37)
Water Act 1981 (c.12)
Water Act 1983 (c.23)
Water Act 1989 (c.15)
Water Charges Act 1976 (c.9)
Water Charges Equalisation Act 1977 (c.41)
Water Companies (Regulation of Powers) Act 1887 (c.21)
Water Consolidation (Consequential Provisions) Act 1991 (c.60)
Water (Fluoridation) Act 1985 (c.63)
Water Industry Act 1991 (c.60)
Water Measure of Fruit 1702 (c.9)
Water Officers Compensation Act 1960 (c.15)
Water Rate Definition Act 1885 (c.34)
Water Resources Act 1963 (c.38)
Water Resources Act 1968 (c.35)
Water Resources Act 1971 (c.34)
Water Resources Act 1991 (c.57)
Water (Scotland) Act 1946 (c.42)
Water (Scotland) Act 1949 (c.31)
Water (Scotland) Act 1967 (c.78)
Water (Scotland) Act 1980 (c.45)
Water Supplies (Exceptional Shortage Orders) Act 1934 (c.20)
Water Supply, London Act 1747 (c.8)
Water Undertakings (Modification of Charges) Act 1921 (c.44)
Waterbeach Level (Cambridge, Isle of Ely): Drainage Act 1797 (c.88)
Waterbeach Level: Drainage Act 1790 (c.74)
Waterbeach Level, Northampton: Drainage Act 1740 (c.24)
Waterford Hospital Act 1839 (c.19)
Waterfront House of Industry Act 1838 (c.13)

Waterloo Subscription Fund Act 1819 (c.34)

Waterworks Clauses Act 1847 (c.17)

Waterworks Clauses Act 1863 (c.93)

Watford Churchyard and Workhouse Act 1772 (c.28)

Wear Coal Trade Act 1792 (c.29)

Wear Navigation Act 1758 (c.64)

Wear Navigation Act 1758 (c.65)

Wearmouth and Tyne Bridge Road Act 1796 (c.136)

Wedding Rings Act 1855 (c.60)

Wednesfield Chapel Act 1746 (c.27)

Weedon Barracks Act 1804 (c.78)

Weeds Act 1959 (c.54)

Weeds and Agricultural Seeds (Ireland) Act 1909 (c.31)

Weights and Measures Act 1795 (c.102)

Weights and Measures Act 1797 (c.143)

Weights and Measures Act 1815 (c.43)

Weights and Measures Act 1824 (c.74)

Weights and Measures Act 1825 (c.12)

Weights and Measures Act 1834 (c.49)

Weights and Measures Act 1855 (c.72)

Weights and Measures Act 1859 (c.56)

Weights and Measures Act 1862 (c.76)

Weights and Measures Act 1878 (c.49)

Weights and Measures Act 1889 (c.21)

Weights and Measures Act 1893 (c.19)

Weights and Measures Act 1904 (c.28)

Weights and Measures Act 1936 (c.38)

Weights and Measures Act 1963 (c.31)

Weights and Measures Act 1979 (c.45)

Weights and Measures Act 1985 (c.72)

Weights and Measures (Amendment) Act 1926 (c.8)

Weights and Measures, Dublin Act 1867 (c.94)

Weights and Measures etc. Act 1976 (c.77)

Weights and Measures (Ireland) Act 1860 (c.119)

Weights and Measures (Leather Measurement) Act 1919 (c.29)

Weights and Measures (Metric System) Act 1897 (c.46)

Weights and Measures (Northern Ireland) Act 1967 (c.6)

Weights and Measures (Purchase) Act 1892 (c.18)

Weights and Measures, Sale of Coal (Scotland) Act 1936 (c.54)

Weights in Sales of Bullion Act 1853 (c.29)

Weights for Coin in the Mint Act 1774 (c.92)

Weights for Coin in the Mint Act 1775 (c.30)

Welfare of Animals at Slaughter Act 1991 (c.30)

Welford and Leicester Road Act 1765 (c.78)

Welford Bridge to Milston Lane Road Act 1786 (c.148)

Wellingborough and Northampton Road Act 1797 (c.167)

Wellington Museum Act 1947 (c.46)

Wells Harbour Act 1769 (c.8)

Wells Roads Act 1753 (c.76)

Wells, Somerset: Improvement Act 1779 (c.31)

Welsh Cathedrals Act 1843 (c.77)

Welsh Church Act 1914 (c.91)

Welsh Church (Amendment) Act 1938 (c.39)

Welsh Church (Burial Grounds) Act 1945 (c.27)

Welsh Church (Temporalities) Act 1919 (c.65)

Welsh Courts Act 1942 (c.40)

Welsh Development Agency Act 1975 (c.70)

Welsh Development Agency Act 1988 (c.5)

Welsh Development Agency Act 1991 (c.69)

Welsh Intermediate Education Act 1889 (c.40)

Welsh Language Act 1967 (c.66)

Welsh Language Act 1993 (c.38)

Welsh National Opera Company 1971 (c.37)

Wendover and Buckingham Road Act 1766 (c.71)

Wern and Bron-y-Garth Road Act 1797 (c.151)

Wesleyan Methodists (Appointments During the War) Act 1917 (c.29)

West Africa Offences Act 1871 (c.8)

West Coast of Africa and Falkland Islands Act 1860 (c.121)

West Coast of Africa Possessions Act 1821 (c.28)

West Cowgate and Alemouth Road Act 1797 (c.163)

West Highland Railway Guarantee Act 1896 (c.58)

West India Island Relief Act 1845 (c.50)

West India Islands Relief Act 1840 (c.40)

West India Loans Act 1848 (c.38)

West India Loans Act 1855 (c.71)

West India Loans Act 1879 (c.16)

West India Relief Commissioners Act 1856 (c.35)

West Indian Bishops, etc. Act 1825 (c.88)

West Indian Court of Appeal Act 1919 (c.47)

West Indian Courts of Appeal Act 1850 (c.15)

West Indian Incumbered Estates Act 1854 (c.117)

West Indian Incumbered Estates Act 1858 (c.96)

West Indian Incumbered Estates Act 1862 (c.45)

West Indian Incumbered Estates Act 1864 (c.108)

West Indian Islands Relief Act 1844 (c.17)

West Indian Islands (Telegraph) Act 1924 (c.14)

West Indian Loans Act 1848 (c.130)

West Indian Mortgages Act 1772 (c.14)

West Indian Prisons Act 1838 (c.67)

West Indies Act 1806 (c.80)

West Indies Act 1962 (c.19)

West Indies Act 1967 (c.4)

West Indies (Encumbered Estates) Act 1872 (c.9)

West Indies (Encumbered Estates) Act 1886 (c.36)

West Indies Relief Act 1843 (c.63)
West Indies (Salaries) Act 1868 (c.120)
West Riding Inclosures Act 1712 (c.4)
West Riding: Small Debts Act 1780 (c.65)
West Riding: Small Debts Act 1793 (c.84)
Westbury, Wilts (Additional Oversees) Act 1786 (c.23)
Western Australia Constitution Act 1890 (c.26)
Western Australia Government Act 1835 (c.14)
Western Australia Government Act 1836 (c.68)
Western Australia Government Act 1838 (c.46)
Western Australia Government Act 1841 (c.43)
Western Australia Government Act 1842 (c.88)
Western Australia Government Act 1844 (c.57)
Western Australia Government Act 1846 (c.35)
Western Highlands and Islands (Transport Services) Act 1928 (c.6)
Western Highlands and Islands (Scotland) Works Act 1891 (c.58)
Westminster Act 1756 (c.25)
Westminster Act 1757 (c.17)
Westminster 1861 (c.78)
Westminster Abbey Act 1888 (c.11)
Westminster Bridge Act 1735 (c.29)
Westminster Bridge Act 1736 (c.16)
Westminster Bridge Act 1737 (c.25)
Westminster Bridge Act 1738 (c.33)
Westminster Bridge Act 1739 (c.16)
Westminster Bridge Act 1740 (c.40)
Westminster Bridge Act 1741 (c.26)
Westminster Bridge Act 1743 (c.32)
Westminster Bridge Act 1744 (c.29)
Westminster Bridge Act 1756 (c.38)
Westminster Bridge Act 1757 (c.34)
Westminster Bridge Act 1853 (c.46)
Westminster Bridge Act 1859 (c.58)
Westminster Bridge Act 1864 (c.88)
Westminster Corn and Grain Market Act 1757 (c.25)
Westminster Election Act 1813 (c.152)
Westminster Fish Market Act 1790 (c.54)
Westminster Fish Market Act 1802 (c.19)
Westminster: Improvement Act 1778 (c.72)
Westminster: Improvement Act 1787 (c.54)
Westminster: Improvements Act 1790 (c.53)
Westminster, Improvements Act 1821 (c.45)
Westminster, King's Street Act 1753 (c.101)
Westminster Market Act 1749 (c.14)
Westminster Offices Act 1855 (c.95)
Westminster Offices Act 1859 (c.19)
Westminster Offices Act 1861 (c.33)
Westminster Offices Act 1862 (c.74)
Westminster Offices Act 1864 (c.51)
Westminster Offices Act 1865 (c.31)
Westminster Offices Act 1865 (c.32)

Westminster Parliamentary Elections Act 1811 (c.126)
Westminster Parliamentary Elections Act 1819 (c.2)
Westminster Streets Act 1728 (c.11)
Westminster Streets Act 1763 (c.39)
Westminster Streets Act 1765 (c.50)
Westminster Streets Act 1777 (c.61)
Westminster: Streets Act 1782 (c.44)
Westminster: Streets Act 1783 (c.42)
Westminster: Streets Act 1783 (c.43)
Westminster: Streets Act 1783 (c.89)
Westminster: Streets Act 1783 (c.90)
Westminster: Streets Act 1786 (c.102)
Westminster: Watching Act 1774 (c.90)
Westminster: Watching Act 1786 (c.112)
Westminster (Water Supply) Act 1721 (c.26)
Westmoreland Canals Act 1792 (c.101)
Westmoreland Gaol, etc. Act 1776 (c.54)
Westmoreland Roads Act 1742 (c.3)
Westmoreland Roads Act 1760 (c.43)
Westmoreland Roads Act 1753 (c.67)
Westmoreland Roads Act 1758 (c.69)
Westmoreland Roads Act 1779 (c.106)
Westmoreland Roads Act 1779 (c.108)
Westmoreland Roads Act 1780 (c.88)
Westmoreland Roads Act 1782 (c.111)
Westmoreland and Yorkshire Roads Act 1784 (c.70)
Wetherby to Grassington Road Act 1758 (c.71)
Wetherby to Grassington Road Act 1774 (c.98)
Wetherby to Knaresborough Road Act 1783 (c.103)
Wexford Grand Jury Act 1867 (c.77)
Weyhill and Lyde Way Road Act 1762 (c.60)
Weymouth Harbour Act 1748 (c.22)
Weymouth: Improvement Act 1776 (c.57)
Weymouth: Water Supply Act 1797 (c.129)
Whale Fishery Act 1732 (c.33)
Whale Fishery Act 1748 (c.45)
Whale Fishery Act 1755 (c.20)
Whale Fishery Act 1763 (c.22)
Whale Fishery Act 1768 (c.27)
Whale Fishery, etc. Act 1776 (c.47)
Whale Fisheries Act 1789 (c.53)
Whale Fisheries (Scotland) Act 1907 (c.41)
Whale Fisheries (Scotland) Act Amendment 1922 (c.34)
Whales Fisheries (Ireland) Act 1908 (c.31)
Whaling Industry (Regulation) Act 1934 (c.49)
Wharves Between London Bridge and Temple Act 1821 (c.89)
Wheat Act 1932 (c.24)
Wheat (Amendment) Act 1939 (c.37)
Whichwood Disafforesting Act 1853 (c.36)
Whichwood Disafforesting Act 1856 (c.32)
Whipping Act 1820 (c.57)
Whipping Act 1862 (c.18)
Whipping of Female Offenders, Abolition Act 1817 (c.75)

Whitby Harbour Act 1734 (c.10)
Whitby Harbour Act 1749 (c.39)
Whitby Harbour Act 1766 (c.81)
Whitby Harbour Act 1780 (c.12)
Whitby Harbour Act 1796 (c.121)
Whitby: Improvement Act 1764 (c.73)
Whitby: Improvement Act 1789 (c.12)
Whitby Piers 1702 (c.13)
Whitby Piers Act 1708 (c.7)
Whitby Roads Act 1785 (c.111)
Whitchurch, Salop: Poor Relief Act 1792 (c.85)
White Cross and Beverley Roads Act 1760 (c.42)
White Fish and Herring Industries Act 1948 (c.51)
White Fish and Herring Industries Act 1953 (c.17)
White Fish and Herring Industries Act 1957 (c.22)
White Fish and Herring Industries Act 1961 (c.18)
White Herring Fisheries Act 1771 (c.31)
White Herring Fishery Act 1779 (c.26)
White Herring Fishery (Scotland) Act 1821 (c.79)
White Herring Fishery (Scotland) Act 1861 (c.72)
White Phosphorus Matches Prohibition Act 1908 (c.42)
Whitechapel Highways Act 1721 (c.30)
Whitechapel: Improvement Act 1778 (c.37)
Whitechapel: Improvement Act 1778 (c.80)
Whitechapel (Poor Relief) Act 1763 (c.53)
Whitechapel: Poor Relief Act 1766 (c.74)
Whitechapel Roads Act 1736 (c.36)
Whitechapel, Stepney: Improvement Act 1793 (c.82)
Whitechapel: Streets Act 1783 (c.91)
Whitechapel to Aldermaston Road Act 1770 (c.88)
Whitehaven Harbour Act 1708 (c.9)
Whitehaven Harbour Act 1710 (c.17)
Whitehaven Harbour Improvement Act 1739 (c.14)
Whitehaven Harbour Impovement Act 1760 (c.44)
Whitehaven Harbour Improvement Act 1762 (c.87)
Whitehaven: Improvement Act 1788 (c.61)
Whitgift, Yorks (Drainage) Act 1793 (c.108)
Whitney Bridge, Hereford Act 1797 (c.56)
Whitney Bridge, Wye Act 1780 (c.27)
Whittlesey Drainage Act 1797 (c.68)
Whittlewood Disafforesting Act 1853 (c.42)
Whittlewood Forest Act 1824 (c.99)
Wicklow Harbour Act 1897 (c.55)
Wide Streets and Coal Trade, Dublin Act 1809 (c.72)
Wide Streets, Dublin Act 1811 (c.10)
Widows', Orphans' and Old Age Contributory Pensions Act 1925 (c.70)
Widows', Orphans' and Old Age Contributory Pensions Act 1929 (c.10)

Widows', Orphans' and Old Age Contributory Pensions Act 1931 (c.19)
Widows', Orphans' and Old Age Contributory Pensions Act 1936 (c.33)
Widows', Orphans' and Old Age Contributory Pensions (Voluntary Contributors) Act 1937 (c.39)
Wigan to Preston Road Act 1726 (c.9)
Wigan to Preston Road Act 1779 (c.92)
Wigan to Preston Road Act 1795 (c.145)
Wigan: Water Supply Act 1764 (c.75)
Wiggenhall Drainage Act 1757 (c.32)
Wigtown Roads Act 1778 (c.7)
Wild Animals in Captivity Protection Act 1900 (c.33)
Wild Animals in Captivity Protection (Scotland) Act 1909 (c.33)
Wild Birds (Duck and Geese) Protection Act 1939 (c.19)
Wild Birds Protection Act 1880 (c.35)
Wild Birds Protection Act 1881 (c.51)
Wild Birds Protection Act 1894 (c.24)
Wild Birds (Protection) Act 1896 (c.56)
Wild Birds Protection Act 1902 (c.6)
Wild Birds Protection Act 1904 (c.4)
Wild Birds Protection Act 1908 (c.11)
Wild Birds Protection (St. Kilda) Act 1904 (c.10)
Wild Creatures and Forest Laws Act 1971 (c.47)
Wilden Ferry Bridge Act 1757 (c.59)
Wildlife and Countryside Act 1981 (c.69)
Wildlife and Countryside (Amendment) Act 1985 (c.31)
Wildlife and Countryside (Amendment) Act 1991 (c.39)
Wildlife and Countryside (Service of Notices) Act 1985 (c.59)
Will of Sir Joseph Jekyll Act 1746 (c.34)
Willian Preston Indemnity Act 1925 (c.7)
Wills Act 1703 (c.5)
Wills Act 1751 (c.6)
Wills Act 1837 (c.26)
Wills Act 1861 (c.114)
Wills Act 1963 (c.44)
Wills Act 1968 (c.28)
Wills Act Amendment Act 1852 (c.24)
Wills, etc. of Seamen, etc. Act 1815 (c.60)
Wills (Soldiers and Sailors) Act 1918 (c.58)
Wiltshire Highways 1706 (c.26)
Wiltshire Highways Act 1707 (c.76)
Wiltshire Highways Act 1713 (c.17)
Wiltshire Highways Act 1728 (c.12)
Wiltshire Roads Act 1724 (c.27)
Wiltshire Roads Act 1725 (c.7)
Wiltshire Roads Act 1725 (c.11)
Wiltshire Roads Act 1736 (c.6)
Wiltshire Roads Act 1740 (c.29)
Wiltshire Roads Act 1742 (c.10)
Wiltshire Roads Act 1743 (c.23)
Wiltshire Roads Act 1743 (c.27)
Wiltshire Roads Act 1744 (c.14)
Wiltshire Roads Act 1750 (c.9)

Wiltshire Roads Act 1751 (c.5)
Wiltshire Roads Act 1751 (c.12)
Wiltshire Roads Act 1753 (c.42)
Wiltshire Roads Act 1755 (c.44)
Wiltshire Roads Act 1756 (c.67)
Wiltshire Roads Act 1757 (c.41)
Wiltshire Roads Act 1757 (c.68)
Wiltshire Roads Act 1758 (c.63)
Wiltshire Roads Act 1760 (c.37)
Wiltshire Roads Act 1762 (c.49)
Wiltshire Roads Act 1762 (c.51)
Wiltshire Roads Act 1762 (c.59)
Wiltshire Roads Act 1762 (c.66)
Wiltshire Roads Act 1766 (c.57)
Wiltshire Roads Act 1768 (c.49)
Wiltshire Roads Act 1769 (c.48)
Wiltshire Roads Act 1769 (c.73)
Wiltshire Roads Act 1771 (c.81)
Wiltshire Roads Act 1772 (c.74)
Wiltshire Roads Act 1772 (c.85)
Wiltshire Roads Act 1773 (c.101)
Wiltshire Roads Act 1777 (c.72)
Wiltshire Roads Act 1777 (c.98)
Wiltshire Roads Act 1779 (c.111)
Wiltshire Roads Act 1780 (c.82)
Wiltshire Roads Act 1780 (c.98)
Wiltshire Roads Act 1783 (c.30)
Wiltshire Roads Act 1783 (c.111)
Wiltshire Roads Act 1788 (c.86)
Wiltshire Roads Act 1790 (c.96)
Wiltshire Roads Act 1790 (c.98)
Wiltshire Roads Act 1791 (c.121)
Wiltshire Roads Act 1792 (c.114)
Wiltshire Roads Act 1795 (c.136)
Wiltshire and Berkshire Roads Act 1757 (c.66)
Wiltshire, Dorset and Somerset Roads Act 1753 (c.60)
Wiltshire, Dorset and Somerset Roads Act 1756 (c.92)
Wiltshire, Dorset and Somerset Roads Act 1756 (c.54)
Wiltshire and Dorset Roads Act 1777 (c.83)
Wiltshire, Dorset and Somerset Roads Act 1779 (c.94)
Wiltshire and Gloucester Roads Act 1751 (c.59)
Wiltshire and Gloucester Roads 1778 (c.103)
Wiltshire and Hampshire Roads 1764 (c.47)
Wiltshire and Somerset Roads Act 1751 (c.17)
Wiltshire and Somerset Roads Act 1751 (c.52)
Wiltshire and Somerset Roads Act 1751 (c.24)
Wiltshire and Somerset Roads Act 1757 (c.46)
Wiltshire and Somerset Roads Act 1768 (c.49)
Wiltshire and Somerset Roads Act 1777 (c.93)
Wiltshire and Somerset Roads Act 1777 (c.99)

Wiltshire and Somerset Roads Act 1792 (c.137)
Wiltshire and Somerset Roads Act 1793 (c.155)
Wiltshire and Southampton Roads Act 1753 (c.66)
Wiltshire and Southampton Roads Act 1756 (c.45)
Wiltshire and Southampton Roads Act 1782 (c.110)
Wincanton Roads 1756 (c.49)
Winchester: Improvement Act 1771 (c.9)
Window Duties Act 1747 (c.10)
Window Duties Act 1753 (c.17)
Window Duties Act 1761 (c.8)
Window Duties (Scotland) Act 1817 (c.128)
Window Duty (Ireland) Act 1810 (c.75)
Windows Duties Act 1796 (c.117)
Windsor Bridge Act 1735 (c.15)
Windsor Castle Act 1848 (c.53)
Windsor Forest Act 1806 (c.143)
Windsor Forest Act 1813 (c.158)
Windsor Forest Act 1815 (c.122)
Windsor Forest Act 1816 (c.132)
Windsor Forest Boundary Commission Act 1807 (c.46)
Windsor Forest Road Act 1758 (c.46)
Windsor Lands Act 1702 (c.27)
Windward Islands Appeal Court Act 1889 (c.33)
Wine and Beerhouse Act 1869 (c.27)
Wine and Beerhouse Amendment Act 1870 (c.29)
Wine, etc. Duties Act 1825 (c.13)
Wine Licences Act 1758 (c.19)
Winfrith Heath Act 1957 (c.61)
Winter Assizes Act 1876 (c.57)
Winter Assizes Act 1877 (c.46)
Winterbourne Parish Act 1841 (c.42)
Wireless Telegraph (Blind Person' Facilities) Act 1926 (c.54)
Wireless Telegraphy Act 1904 (c.24)
Wireless Telegraphy Act 1906 (c.13)
Wireless Telegraphy Act 1949 (c.54)
Wireless Telegraphy Act 1955 (c.10)
Wireless Telegraphy Act 1967 (c.72)
Wireless Telegraphy (Explanation) Act 1925 (c.67)
Wireless Telegraphy (Validation of Charges) Act 1954 (c.2)
Wisbech Canal Act 1794 (c.92)
Wisbech Roads Act 1786 (c.133)
Witchcraft Act 1735 (c.5)
Witchcraft, etc. (Ireland) Act 1821 (c.18)
Witford, etc. Suffolk: Poor Relief Act 1765 (c.97)
Witham Drainage Act 1762 (c.32)
Witnesses Act 1806 (c.37)
Witnesses' Indemnity, Penryn Act 1828 (c.13)
Witnesses on Petitions Act 1801 (c.105)
Witnesses on Trial for Treason 1702 (c.9)
Witnesses (Public Inquiries) Protection Act 1892 (c.64)

Witney to Chanfield Road Act 1793 (c.137)
Wiveliscombe Roads Act 1786 (c.135)
Wolverhampton Church Act 1755 (c.34)
Wolverhampton: Improvements Act 1776 (c.25)
Wolverhampton Parish Act 1848 (c.95)
Wolverhampton Roads Act 1772 (c.101)
Wolverhampton Roads 1747 (c.25)
Wolverhampton Roads Act 1793 (c.147)
Wolverhampton Roads Act 1794 (c.133)
Wolverhampton Roads Act 1796 (c.146)
Women and Young Persons (Employment in Lead Processes) Act 1920 (c.62)
Woods and Forest Act 1803 (c.31)
Woods and Forests Act 1806 (c.142)
Woodstock, Oxford, Roads Act 1784 (c.61)
Wool Act 1738 (c.21)
Wool Act 1780 (c.55)
Wool Duties, etc. Act 1824 (c.47)
Woolcombers Act 1795 (c.124)
Woollen Cloths Act 1707 (c.43)
Woollen Cloths Act 1708 (c.13)
Woollen, etc. Manufacturers Act 1710 (c.32)
Woollen, etc. Manufacturers 1735 (c.4)
Woollen, etc. Manufactures Act 1720 (c.7)
Woollen, etc. Manufactures, Bedfordshire Act 1785 (c.40)
Woollen, etc. Manufactures, Norfolk Act 1791 (c.56)
Woollen Manufacturers Act 1702 (c.22)
Woollen Manufacture Act 1711 (c.26)
Woollen Manufacture Act 1714 (c.15)
Woollen Manufacture Act 1715 (c.41)
Woollen Manufactures Act 1725 (c.34)
Woollen Manufactures Act 1726 (c.23)
Woollen Manufactures Act 1731 (c.21)
Woollen Manufacture Act 1756 (c.33)
Woollen Manufactures Act 1757 (c.12)
Woollen Manufactures Act 1803 (c.136)
Woollen Manufacture Act 1804 (c.64)
Woollen Manufacture Act 1805 (c.83)
Woollen Manufacture Act 1806 (c.18)
Woollen Manufacture Act 1807 (c.43)
Woollen Manufacture Act 1808 (c.131)
Woollen Manufacture Act 1809 (c.109)
Woollen Manufacture Act 1810 (c.83)
Woollen Manufactures, Suffolk Act 1784 (c.3)
Woollen Trade Act 1833 (c.28)
Woolmer Forest Act 1812 (c.71)
Woolmer Forest Act 1855 (c.46)
Woolwich Church Act 1738 (c.9)
Woolwich Dockyard Act 1833 (c.65)
Woolwich Fortifications Act 1780 (c.46)
Worcester Roads Act 1725 (c.14)
Worcester Roads Act 1736 (c.5)
Worcester Roads act 1743 (c.13)
Worcester Roads Act 1753 (c.50)
Worcester Roads Act 1759 (c.50)
Worcester Roads Act 1767 (c.65)
Worcester Roads Act 1782 (c.95)
Worcester Roads Act 1783 (c.98)
Worcester Roads Act 1788 (c.88)
Worcester Roads Act 1789 (c.102)

Worcester Roads Act 1793 (c.175)
Worcester Roads Act 1795 (c.133)
Worcester and Birmingham Canal Act 1791 (c.59)
Worcester Bridge Act 1769 (c.84)
Worcester Bridge Act 1779 (c.42)
Worcester to Droitwich Road Act 1725 (c.20)
Worcester: Improvement Act 1770 (c.22)
Worcester: Poor Relief, Burial Ground and Hopmarket 1703 (c.8)
Worcester: Poor Relief, Burial Ground and Hopmarket Act 1730 (c.23)
Worcester: Poor Relief, Burial Ground and Hopmarket Act 1730 (c.25)
Worcester: Poor Relief, Burial Ground and Hopmarket Act 1792 (c.99)
Worcester and Salop Roads Act 1762 (c.78)
Worcester and Salop Roads Act 1763 (c.51)
Worcester, Salop and Stafford Roads Act 1790 (c.102)
Worcester: Streets Act 1780 (c.21)
Worcester and Warwick Roads Act 1767 (c.68)
Worcester and Warwick Roads Act 1771 (c.92)
Worcester and Warwick Roads Act 1773 (c.106)
Worcester and Warwick Roads Act 1773 (c.107)
Worcester and Warwick Roads Act 1788 (c.115)
Worcester and Warwick Roads Act 1789 (c.106)
Worcester and Warwick Roads Act 1792 (c.140)
Worcester and Warwick Roads Act 1794 (c.136)
Worcester, Warwick and Gloucester Roads Act 1757 (c.64)
Worcester: Water Supply, etc., Act 1771 (c.13)
Worcestershire Highways Act 1713 (c.27)
Worcestershire Roads Act 1748 (c.43)
Worcestershire Roads Act 1751 (c.60)
Worcestershire Roads Act 1755 (c.48)
Worcestershire Roads Act 17776 (c.78)
Worcestershire Roads Act 1779 (c.89)
Worcestershire, Staffordshire, Shropshire Roads Act 1781 (c.93)
Workhouses Act 1790 (c.49)
Workhouse Act 1816 (c.129)
Workhouses (Ireland) Act 1849 (c.86)
Workhouse Sites Act 1857 (c.13)
Workhouse, Westminster Act 1772 (c.34)
Working Classes Dwellings Act 1890 (c.16)
Working Men's Dwellings Act 1874 (c.59)
Working of Jews on Sunday Act 1871 (c.19)
Workmen's Compensation Act 1897 (c.37)
Workmen's Compensation Act 1900 (c.22)
Workmen's Compensation Act 1906 (c.58)
Workmen's Compensation Act 1909 (c.16)
Workmen's Compensation Act 1923 (c.42)
Workmen's Compensation Act 1925 (c.84)

Workmen's Compensation Act 1926 (c.42)
Workmen's Compensation Act 1931 (c.18)
Workmen's Compensation Act 1943 (c.6)
Workmen's Compensation (Amendment) Act 1938 (c.27)
Workmen's Compensation and Benefit (Amendment) Act 1965 (c.79)
Workmen's Compensation and Benefit (Byssinosis) Act 1940 (c.56)
Workmen's Compensation and Benefit (Supplementation) Act 1956 (c.51)
Workmen's Compensation (Coal Mines) Act 1934 (c.23)
Workmen's Compensation (Illegal Employment) Act 1918 (c.8)
Workmen's Compensation (Pneumoconiosis) Act 1945 (c.16)
Workmen's Compensation (Silicosis) Act 1918 (c.14)
Workmen's Compensation (Silicosis) Act 1924 (c.40)
Workmen's Compensation (Silicosis and Asbestosis) Act 1930 (c.29)
Workmen's Compensation (Supplementary Allowances) Act 1940 (c.47)
Workmen's Compensation (Supplementation) Act 1951 (c.22)
Workmen's Compensation (Temporary Increase) Act 1943 (c.49)
Workmen's Compensation (Transfer of Funds) Act 1927 (c.15)
Workmen's Compensation (War Addition) Act 1917 (c.42)
Workmen's Compensation (War Addition) Amendment Act 1919 (c.83)
Works and Public Buildings Act 1874 (c.84)
Works of Utility, etc. Indemnity Act 1858 (c.102)
Workshop Regulation Act 1867 (c.146)
Worksop and Attercliffe Road Act 1764 (c.52)
Worksop and Attercliffe Road Act 1786 (c.125)
Worsley Brook: Navigation Act 1736 (c.9)
Worstead Act 1776 (c.11)
Wreak and Eye: Navigation Act 1791 (c.77)
Wreck and Salvage Act 1846 (c.99)
Wrecking (Ireland) Act 1803 (c.79)
Wrexham to Barnhill Road Act 1782 (c.105)
Writ of Subpoena Act 1805 (c.92)
Writs Execution (Scotland) Act 1877 (c.40)
Writs of Assistance Act 1814 (c.46)
Writs of Error Act 1718 (c.13)
Writs of Error Act 1825 (c.96)
Writs of Execution Act 1833 (c.67)
Writs of Mandamus Act 1843 (c.67)
Writs Registration (Scotland) Act 1868 (c.34)

Yarmouth Coal Import Duties 1706 (c.10)
Yarmouth Coal Import Duties (Privileges of Freemen, etc.) 1782 (c.22)
Yarmouth Haven Act 1746 (c.40)
Yarmouth Haven and Pier Repairs 1702 (c.7)

Yarmouth Naval Hospital Act 1931 (c.15)
Yarmouth Naval Hospital Transfer Act 1957 (c.3)
Yarmouth: Small Debts Act 1757 (c.24)
Yarmouth to Gorleston Road Act 1775 (c.67)
Yarmouth to Gorleston Road Act 1795 (c.132)
Yaxley: Drainage Act 1772 (c.46)
Yeomanry Act 1804 (c.54)
Yeomanry Act 1817 (c.44)
Yeomanry Act 1826 (c.58)
Yeomanry (Accounts) Act 1804 (c.94)
Yeomanry Cavalry Act 1798 (c.51)
Yeomanry (Ireland) Act 1802 (c.68)
Yeomanry (Training) Act 1816 (c.39)
Yeomanry and Volunteers Act 1802 (c.66)
Yeomanry and Volunteers Act 1803 (c.121)
Yeomanry Corps, etc. (Ireland) Act 1814 (c.178)
Yeomanry Corps (Ireland) Act 1816 (c.72)
Yeomanry Corps (Ireland) Act 1818 (c.40)
Yeomanry Corps (Ireland) Act 1820 (c.48)
Yeomanry Corps (Ireland) Act 1823 (c.15)
Yeomanry Corps (Ireland) Act 1828 (c.30)
Yeomanry, etc. Act 1806 (c.125)
York and Boroughbridge Road Act 1749 (c.38)
York and Boroughbridge Road Act 1771 (c.66)
York and Boroughbridge Road Act 1797 (c.149)
York and Durham Roads Act 1753 (c.95)
York Buildings Company, Sale of Scottish Estates Act 1776 (c.24)
York Buildings: Rates Act 1756 (c.90)
York Butter Trade Supervision Act 1721 (c.27)
York House and Victoria Park Act 1841 (c.27)
York: Lighting and Watching Act 1763 (c.48)
York Roads Act 1765 (c.99)
York Roads Act 1792 (c.155)
Yorkshire Registries Act 1884 (c.54)
Yorkshire Registries Amendment Act 1884 (c.4)
Yorkshire Registries Amendment Act 1885 (c.26)
Yorkshire Roads Act 1740 (c.23)
Yorkshire Roads Act 1742 (c.7)
Yorkshire Roads Act 1743 (c.22)
Yorkshire Roads Act 1743 (c.25)
Yorkshire Roads Act 1744 (c.6)
Yorkshire Roads Act 1744 (c.16)
Yorkshire Roads Act 1748 (c.39)
Yorkshire Roads Act 1751 (c.47)
Yorkshire Roads Act 1751 (c.53)
Yorkshire Roads Act 1751 (c.58)
Yorkshire Roads Act 1755 (c.50)
Yorkshire Roads Act 1756 (c.71)
Yorkshire Roads Act 1756 (c.83)
Yorkshire Roads Act 1757 (c.54)
Yorkshire Roads Act 1758 (c.70)
Yorkshire Roads Act 1759 (c.55)
Yorkshire Roads Act 1760 (c.35)

Yorkshire Roads Act 1762 (c.71)
Yorkshire Roads Act 1764 (c.66)
Yorkshire Roads Act 1764 (c.69)
Yorkshire Roads Act 1765 (c.72)
Yorkshire Roads Act 1766 (c.59)
Yorkshire Roads Act 1766 (c.62)
Yorkshire Roads Act 1767 (c.71)
Yorkshire Roads Act 1768 (c.54)
Yorkshire Roads Act 1769 (c.54)
Yorkshire Roads Act 1769 (c.75)
Yorkshire Roads Act 1769 (c.79)
Yorkshire Roads Act 1771 (c.63)
Yorkshire Roads Act 1771 (c.68)
Yorkshire Roads Act 1771 (c.71)
Yorkshire Roads Act 1774 (c.117)
Yorkshire Roads Act 1777 (c.73)
Yorkshire Roads Act 1777 (c.77)
Yorkshire Roads Act 1777 (c.78)
Yorkshire Roads Act 1777 (c.80)
Yorkshire Roads Act 1777 (c.102)
Yorkshire Roads Act 1778 (c.96)
Yorkshire Roads Act 1780 (c.86)
Yorkshire Roads Act 1780 (c.89)
Yorkshire Roads Act 1781 (c.96)
Yorkshire Roads Act 1782 (c.97)
Yorkshire Roads Act 1783 (c.29)
Yorkshire Roads Act 1783 (c.95)
Yorkshire Roads Act 1786 (c.142)
Yorkshire Roads Act 1786 (c.144)
Yorkshire Roads Act 1787 (c.86)
Yorkshire Roads Act 1788 (c.106)
Yorkshire Roads Act 1788 (c.108)
Yorkshire Roads Act 1788 (c.110)
Yorkshire Roads Act 1789 (c.109)
Yorkshire Roads Act 1790 (c.99)
Yorkshire Roads Act 1792 (c.132)
Yorkshire Roads Act 1792 (c.133)
Yorkshire Roads Act 1792 (c.136)
Yorkshire Roads Act 1793 (c.157)
Yorkshire Roads Act 1794 (c.134)
Yorkshire and Chester Roads Act 1767 (c.94)
Yorkshire and Derby Roads Act 1757 (c.62)
Yorkshire and Derby Roads Act 1768 (c.47)
Yorkshire and Derby Roads Act 1771 (c.76)
Yorkshire and Derby Roads Act 1779 (c.96)
Yorkshire and Derby Roads Act 1795 (c.164)
Yorkshire, Derby and Chester Roads Act 1793 (c.140)
Yorkshire and Derbyshire Roads Act 1793 (c.184)
Yorkshire and Durham Roads Act 1746 (c.28)
Yorkshire and Durham Roads Act 1748 (c.32)
Yorkshire and Durham Roads Act 1755 (c.51)

Yorkshire and Durham Roads Act 1756 (c.80)
Yorkshire and Durham Roads Act 1760 (c.41)
Yorkshire and Durham Roads Act 1779 (c.80)
Yorkshire and Durham Roads Act 1782 (c.93)
Yorkshire and Durham Roads Act 1792 (c.118)
Yorkshire and Durham Roads Act 1792 (c.135)
Yorkshire and Lancaster Roads Act 1755 (c.59)
Yorkshire and Lancaster Roads Act 1755 (c.60)
Yorkshire and Lancaster Roads Act 1756 (c.91)
Yorkshire and Lancaster Roads Act 1759 (c.48)
Yorkshire and Lancaster Roads Act 1777 (c.90)
Yorkshire and Nottinghamshire Roads Act 1766 (c.67)
Yorkshire and Westmorland Roads Act 1753 (c.86)
Yorkshire and Westmorland Roads Act 1791 (c.122)
Yorkshire Coroners Act 1897 (c.39)
Yorkshire: Drainage Act 1789 (c.78)
Yorkshire (East Riding) Land Registry Act 1707 (c.62)
Yorkshire (North Riding) Land Registry Act 1734 (c.6)
Yorkshire: Small Debts Act 1776 (c.15)
Yorkshire (West Riding) Land Registry Act 1703 (c.4)
Yorkshire (West Riding) Land Registry 1706 (c.20)
Youghal Rectory Act 1827 (c.26)
Young Persons (Employment) Act 1938 (c.69)
Young Persons (Employment) Act 1964 (c.66)
Youthful Offenders Act 1855 (c.87)
Youthful Offenders Act 1901 (c.20)
Youthful Offenders, Great Britain Act 1854 (c.86)
Yule Vacance Act 1711 (c.22)
Yule Vacance Act 1714 (c.28)

Zambia Independence Act 1964 (c.65)
Zanzibar Act 1963 (c.55)
Zanzibar Indemnity Act 1894 (c.31)
Zimbabwe Act 1979 (c.60)
Zoo Licensing Act 1981 (c.37)

CURRENT LAW
STATUTE CITATOR 1994

This is the fifth part of the Current Law Statute Citator 1994 and is up to date to December 8, 1994. It comprises in a single table:

  (i) Statutes passed between January 1 and December 8, 1994;
  (ii) Statutes affected during this period by Statutory Instrument;
  (iii) Statutes judicially considered during this period;
  (iv) Statutes repealed and amended during this period.

  (S.) Amendments relating to Scotland only.

[Please Note: where legislation has been consolidated by a subsequent Act this is denoted by **C**. followed by the section/Schedule of the Act where the relevant provision can now be found.]

ACTS OF THE PARLIAMENT OF SCOTLAND

CAP.

10. Citation Act 1540.
  repealed: Act of Sederunt 94/1443.
5. Subscription of Deeds Act 1681.
  see *MacDougall* v. *Clydesdale Bank Trs.* (O.H.), 1993 S.C.L.R. 832.

CAP.

21. Citation Act 1693.
  repealed: Act of Sederunt 94/1443.
22. Real Rights Act 1693.
  see *Sharp* v. *Thomson* (O.H.), 1994 S.L.T. 1068.

ACTS OF THE PARLIAMENTS OF ENGLAND, GREAT BRITAIN AND THE UNITED KINGDOM

CAP.

34 & 35 Hen. 8 (1542)

26. Laws in Wales Act 1542.
  s. 47, repealed: 1994, c. 32, s. 2.

31 Car. 2 (1679)

2. Habeas Corpus Act 1679.
  s. 2, amended: 1994, c. 33, sch. 10.

2 Geo. 2 (1728)

22. Insolvent Debtors Relief Act 1728.
  s. 13, see *Aectra Refining and Marketing Inc.* v. *Exmar NV, The Times*, August 15, 1994, C.A.

14 Geo. 3 (1774)

48. Life Assurance Act 1774.
  s. 1, see *Fuji Finance Inc.* v. *Aetna Life Insurance, The Times*, July 21, 1994, Sir Donald Nicholls, V.-C.
  s. 2, see *Siu* v. *Eastern Insurance Co., The Times*, December 16, 1993, P.C.

CAP.

3 Geo. 4 (1822)

33. Riotous Assemblies (Scotland) Act 1822.
  s. 10, amended: 1994, c. 39, sch. 13.

6 Geo. 4 (1825)

120. Court of Session Act 1825.
  s. 53, repealed: Act of Sederunt 94/1443.

1 & 2 Will. 4 (1831)

32. Game Act 1831.
  ss. 30, 32, amended: 1994, c. 33, sch. 9.

2 & 3 Will. 4 (1832)

68. Game (Scotland) Act 1832.
  ss. 1, 6, amended: 1994, c. 33, sch. 9.

3 & 4 Will. 4 (1833)

41. Judicial Committee Act 1833.
  ss. 3, 4, see *Walker* v. *The Queen; Douglas* v. *The Queen; Glanville* v. *The Queen* [1993] 3 W.L.R. 1017, P.C.

(1)

CAP.

5 & 6 Will. (1835)

76. Municipal Corporations Act 1835.
s. 2, see *Peggs* v. *Lamb* [1994] 2 W.L.R.
1, Morritt J.

6 & 7 Will. 4 (1836)

13. Constabulary (Ireland) Act 1836.
s. 50, see *Toye* v. *Chief Constable of Royal Ulster Constabulary* [1991] NI 164, Carswell J.

7 Will. 4 & 1 Vict. (1837)

26. Wills Act 1837.
s. 9, see *Weatherhill* v. *Pearce, The Times*, November 7, 1994, H.H.J. Kolbert sitting as a deputy judge.

1 & 2 Vict. (1837–38)

114. Debtors (Scotland) Act 1838.
ss. 16, 18, 20, repealed: Act of Sederunt 94/1443.

2 & 3 Vict. (1839)

45. Highway (Railway Crossings) Act 1839.
s. 1, see *Tayside Regional Council* v. *British Railways Board, The Times*, December 30, 1993.

4 & 5 Vict. (1841)

38. School Sites Act 1841.
s. 2, see *Marchant* v. *Onslow* [1994] 2 All E.R. 707, Mr. David Neuberger, Q.C.

5 & 6 Vict. (1842)

94. Defence Act 1842.
s. 19, amended: 1994, c. 19, sch. 2.

7 & 8 Vict. (1844)

69. Judicial Committee Act 1844.
s. 1, see *Walker* v. *The Queen; Douglas* v. *The Queen; Glanville* v. *The Queen* [1993] 3 W.L.R. 1017, P.C.

8 & 9 Vict. (1845)

19. Lands Clauses Consolidation (Scotland) Act 1845.
s. 17, see *Emslie & Simpson* v. *City of Aberdeen District Council*, 1994 S.C.L.R. 69; *Rush* v. *Fife Regional Council*, 1994 S.C.L.R. 231.
20. Railways Clauses Consolidation Act 1845.
ss. 115–120, amended: order 94/857.
33. Railways Clauses Consolidation (Scotland) Act 1845.
ss. 108–113, amended: order 94/857.

CAP.

10 & 11 Vict. (1847)

27. Harbours, Docks and Piers Clauses Act 1847.
ss. 7, 8, amended(S.): 1994, c. 39, sch. 13.

11 & 12 Vict. (1848)

42. Indictable Offences Act 1848.
ss. 12, 14, 15, repealed: 1994, c. 33, sch. 11.

12 & 13 Vict. (1849)

51. Judicial Factors Act 1849.
ss. 34A, 40, Act of Sederunt 94/1443.

16 & 17 Vict. (1852–53)

30. Criminal Procedure (Scotland) Act 1853.
s. 9, amended: 1994, c. 33, sch. 4.

17 & 18 Vict. (1854)

91. Lands Valuation (Scotland) Act 1854.
s. 42, amended: 1994, c. 39, s. 152.
s. 43, added: *ibid.*, s. 152.

18 & 19 Vict. (1855)

68. Burial Grounds (Scotland) Act 1855.
ss. 4, 9, amended: 1994, c. 39, sch. 13.
s. 10, amended: *ibid.*; repealed in pt.: *ibid.*, schs. 13, 14.
s. 11, repealed in pt.: *ibid.*
111. Bills of Lading Act 1855.
s. 1, see *Future Express, The* [1993] 2 Lloyd's Rep. 542, C.A.

19 & 20 Vict. (1856)

2. Metropolitan Police Act 1856.
s. 2, amended: 1949, c. 29, s. 41; repealed in pt.: *ibid.*, s. 41, sch. 9.

22 Vict. (1859)

1. Burial Act 1859.
s. 1, amended: 1994, c. 19, sch. 16.

23 & 24 Vict. (1860)

90. Game Licences Act 1860.
s. 14, repealed in pt.: 1994, c. 19, schs. 16, 18.
100. Offences against the Person Act 1861.
ss. 18, 20, see *R.* v. *Maxwell (Nolan Andrew), The Times,* May 11, 1994, C.A.; *R.* v. *Field (Andrew John)* (1993) 97 Cr.App.R. 357, C.A.; *R.* v. *Mandair* [1994] 2 W.L.R. 700, H.L.
s. 20, see *R.* v. *Aitken (Thomas Adam); R.* v. *Bennet (Simon Christopher); R.* v. *Barson (Alan Robert)* (1992) 95 Cr.App.R. 304, Court Martial Appeal Ct.; *R.* v. *Orr* [1990] NI 287, C.A.(N.I.).

CAP.

23 & 24 Vict. (1860)—cont.

100. Offences against the Person Act 1861—*cont.*
s. 29, see *R.* v. *Howard* [1993] Crim.L.R. 213, C.A.
s. 47, see *R.* v. *Maxwell (Nolan Andrew), The Times,* May 11, 1994, C.A.; *R.* v. *Chan-Fook* [1994] 1 W.L.R. 689, C.A.

30 & 31 Vict. (1867)

17. Lyon King of Arms Act 1867.
sch. B, order 94/201; amended: *ibid.*

31 & 32 Vict. (1868)

100. Court of Session Act 1868.
s. 39, repealed: Act of Sederunt 94/1443.
101. Titles to Land Consolidation (Scotland) Act 1868.
s. 158, sch. QQ, repealed: Act of Sederunt 94/1443.
119. Regulation of Railways Act 1868.
s. 2, amended: order 94/857.

32 & 33 Vict. (1869)

62. Debtors Act 1869.
ss. 4, 5, see *Graham* v. *Graham* [1993] 1 F.C.R. 339, C.A.
s. 5, see *Woodley* v. *Woodley (No. 2)* [1993] 4 All E.R. 1010, C.A.; *M.* v. *M. (Enforcement: Judgment Summons)* [1993] Fam. Law 469, H.H.J. Kennedy, Q.C.
115. Metropolitan Public Carriage Act 1869.
s. 9, order 94/1087.

33 & 34 Vict. (1870)

52. Extradition Act 1870.
ss. 2, 21, order 94/2794.

34 & 35 Vict. (1871)

78. Regulation of Railways Act 1871.
ss. 2–4, 6, order 94/857.
ss. 2, 6, amended: order 94/2229.
96. Pedlars Act 1871.
s. 3, see *Prentice* v. *Normand,* 1994 S.C.C.R. 55.

37 & 38 Vict. (1874)

81. Great Seal (Offices) Act 1874.
s. 9, order 94/600.

38 & 39 Vict. (1875)

17. Explosives Act 1875.
s. 67, amended: 1994, c. 19, sch. 16.
ss. 110, 111, amended(S.): 1994, c. 39, sch. 13.

41 & 42 Vict. (1878)

73. Territorial Waters Jurisdiction Act 1878.
s. 4, amended: 1994, c. 33, sch. 4.

CAP.

42 & 43 Vict. (1879)

58. Public Offices Fees Act 1879.
ss. 2, 3, orders 93/3229; 94/1974.

43 & 44 Vict. (1880)

4. Judicial Factors (Scotland) Act 1880.
s. 5, Act of Sederunt 94/2354.

45 & 46 Vict. (1882)

61. Bills of Exchange Act 1882.
ss. 21, 29, see *Insurance Corporation of Ireland* v. *Dunluce Meats* [1991] NI 286, Carswell J.
s. 24, see *Strathmore Group* v. *Credit Lyonnais* (O.H.), 1994 S.L.T. 1023.
77. Citation Amendment (Scotland) Act 1882.
ss. 3, 4 (in pt.), 5, 6, schs. 1, 2, repealed: Act of Sederunt 94/1443.

46 & 47 Vict. (1883)

3. Explosive Substances Act 1883.
s. 4, see *R.* v. *Berry (No. 3)* [1994] 2 All E.R. 913, C.A.
s. 6, amended: 1994, c. 33, sch. 4.

49 & 50 Vict. (1886)

15. Sporting Lands Rating (Scotland) Act 1886.
repealed: 1994, c. 39, sch. 14.
38. Riot (Damages) Act 1886.
s. 9, repealed in pt.: 1994, c. 29, sch. 9.

50 & 51 Vict. (1887)

42. Public Libraries Consolidation (Scotland) Act 1887.
s. 2, substituted: 1994, c. 39, sch. 13.
55. Sheriffs Act 1887.
ss. 3, 6, amended: 1994, c. 19, s. 62.

52 & 53 Vict. (1889)

39. Judicial Factors Act 1889.
ss. 11B, 21, Act of Sederunt 94/1443.
45. Factors Act 1889.
s. 1, see *Forsythe International (U.K.)* v. *Silver Shipping Co. and Petroglobe International; Saetta, The* [1993] 2 Lloyd's Rep. 268, Clarke J.
57. Regulation of Railways Act 1889.
s. 5, amended: order 94/857.

CAP.

54 & 55 Vict. (1891)

38. Stamp Duties Management Act 1891.
s. 27, amended: 1994, c. 9, s. 239.

39. Stamp Act 1891.
s. 73, amended: 1994, c. 9, s. 241; repealed in pt.: *ibid.,* s. 241, sch. 26.
s. 122, amended: *ibid.,* s. 239.
sch. 1, amended: *ibid.,* s. 241; repealed in pt.: *ibid.,* sch. 26.

43. Forged Transfers Act 1891.
s. 2, repealed in pt.: 1994, c. 29, sch. 9.

50. Commissioners for Oaths Act 1891.
s. 1, repealed in pt.: 1994, c. 26, sch. 5.

55 & 56 Vict. (1892)

54. Allotments (Scotland) Act 1892.
s. 16, amended: 1994, c. 39, sch. 13.

57 & 58 Vict. (1894)

40. Nautical Assessors (Scotland) Act 1894.
ss. 2–5, repealed: Act of Sederunt 94/1443.

60. Merchant Shipping Act 1894.
ss. 110–112, repealed: 1994, c. 40, schs. 10, 17.
s. 427, rules 93/3161.
s. 503, see *Capitan San Luis, The* [1993] 2 Lloyd's Rep. 573, Clarke J.
ss. 544–546, repealed: 1994, c. 28, schs. 2, 4.
ss. 552, 555, 556, amended: *ibid.,* sch. 2.
s. 668, amended(S.): 1994, c. 39, sch. 13.

58 & 59 Vict. (1895)

14. Courts of Law Fees (Scotland) Act 1895.
s. 2, see *Muir* v. *Muir* (Sh.Ct.), 1944 S.C.C.R. 182.
s. 2, orders 93/2957; 94/498.

19. Court of Session Consignations (Scotland) Act 1895.
s. 3, repealed in pt.: Act of Sederunt 94/1443.
s. 4, Act of Sederunt 94/1443.

59 & 60 Vict. (1896)

48. Light Railways Act 1896.
s. 3, orders 94/691, 1761.
s. 7, orders 94/84, 691, 1331, 1761.
s. 8, order 94/1761.
s. 9, orders 94/84, 691, 1331, 1761.
ss. 10, 11, orders 94/84, 691, 1331, 1761.
s. 12, orders 94/84, 691, 1331, 1761.
s. 18, orders 94/84, 1331.
s. 24, orders 94/260, 1331.
s. 26, amended(S.): 1994, c. 39, sch. 13.

60 & 61 Vict. (1897)

26. Metropolitan Police Courts Act 1897.
ss. 3, 4, 7, 11, repealed: 1994, c. 29, sch. 9.

38. Public Health (Scotland) Act 1897.
s. 12, amended: 1994, c. 39, sch. 13.

CAP.

61 & 62 Vict. (1898)

36. Criminal Evidence Act 1898.
s. 1, see *R.* v. *Knutton (Beverley)* (1993) 67 Cr.App.R. 115, C.A.; *R.* v. *McLeod* [1994] 3 All E.R. 254, C.A.
s. 1, amended: 1994, c. 33, s. 31, sch. 10; repealed in pt.: *ibid.,* schs. 10, 11.

2 Edw. 7 (1902)

28. Licensing Act 1902.
s. 6, repealed in pt.: 1994, c. 29, sch. 9.

6 Edw. 7 (1906)

41. Marine Insurance Act 1906.
s. 18, see *Pan Atlantic Insurance Co.* v. *Pine Top Insurance Co., The Times,* July 27, 1994, H.L.
ss. 33, 78, see *Noble Resources and Unirise Development* v. *Greenwood (George Albert); Vasso, The* [1993] 2 Lloyd's Rep. 309, Hobhouse J.
ss. 55, 78, 86, see *National Oilwell (U.K.)* v. *Davy Offshore* [1993] 2 Lloyd's Rep. 582, Colman J.

55. Public Trustee Act 1906.
s. 9, order 94/714.
s. 14, rules 94/2519.

7 Edw. 7 (1907)

29. Patents and Designs Act 1907.
s. 62, amended: 1994, c. 26, sch. 4.
s. 63, amended: *ibid.,* repealed in pt.: *ibid.,* schs. 4, 5.

51. Sheriff Courts (Scotland) Act 1907.
s. 27, see *Cambridge Street Properties* v. *City of Glasgow District Licensing Board,* 1994 S.L.T.(Sh.Ct.) 4; *Anderson* v. *Woodend Communications* (Sh.Ct.), 1994 S.C.L.R. 658.
ss. 27, 28, see *Friel (H.L.) & Son* v. *Inverclyde District Council,* 1994 S.C.L.R. 561.
s. 28, see *Gupta* v. *Laurie,* 1994 S.C.L.R. 176.
s. 40, Acts of Sederunt 93/3080; 94/392, 1141, 1142.
sch., see *Hunter* v. *Hunter* (Sh.Ct.), 1993 S.C.L.R. 785; *McHardy* v. *Bawden International* (Sh.Ct.), 1993 S.C.L.R. 893; *Cairney* v. *Bulloch* (Sh.Ct.), 1993 S.C.L.R. 901; *Whiteway Laidlaw Bank* v. *Green* (Sh.Ct.), 1993 S.C.L.R. 968; *Halifax Building Society* v. *Gupta,* 1994 S.L.T. 339; *Patterson* v. *Patterson* (Sh.Ct.), 1994 S.C.C.R. 166; *Calder* v. *Simpson* (Sh.Ct.), 1994 S.C.L.R. 27; *Grier* v. *Wimpey Plant & Transport,* 1994 S.C.L.R. 186; *Singh* v. *Bank of Scotland,* 1994 S.C.L.R. 89;

7 Edw. 7 (1907)—cont.

51. Sheriff Courts (Scotland) Act 1907—cont.

Calder v. *Simpson,* 1994 S.L.T. (Sh.Ct.) 32; *Grier* v. *Wimpey Plant & Transport,* 1994 S.L.T. 714; *Cairney* v. *Bulloch,* 1994 S.L.T. (Sh.Ct.) 38; *McIlwraith* v. *Lochmaddy Hotel* (Sh.Ct.), 1994 S.C.L.R. 386; *Boyle* v. *Anderson* (Sh.Ct.), 1994 S.C.L.R. 543; *Mullen* v. *Harmac,* 1994 S.L.T. 926; *Rodgers* v. *Rodgers* (Sh.Ct.), 1994 S.C.L.R. 750; *Thorn Securities* v. *Calder Mechanical Services* (Sh.Ct.), 1994 S.C.L.R. 690.

55. London Cab and Stage Carriage Act 1907.

s. 1, order 94/1087.

8 Edw. 7 (1908)

16. Finance Act 1908.

s. 6, amended: 1994, c. 19, sch. 16; repealed in pt.: *ibid.,* schs. 16, 18.

44. Commons Act 1908.

s. 1, amended: 1994, c. 19, sch. 16.

1 & 2 Geo. 5 (1911)

6. Perjury Act 1911.

s. 13, see *R.* v. *Carroll, Perkins and Dickerson* [1993] Crim.L.R. 613, C.A.

27. Protection of Animals Act 1911.

s. 1, see *Stilgoe* v. *Eager, The Times,* January 27, 1994, D.C.; *Peterssen* v. *R.S.P.C.A.* [1993] Crim.L.R. 852, D.C.; *Hunt* v. *Duckering* [1993] Crim.L.R. 678, D.C.

28. Official Secrets Act 1911.

s. 3, order 94/968.

57. Maritime Conventions Act 1911.

ss. 6, 7, repealed: 1994, c. 28, schs. 2, 4.

s. 8, see *Al Tabith and Alanfushi, The* [1993] 2 Lloyd's Rep. 214, Sheen J.

s. 8, repealed in pt.: 1994, c. 28, schs. 2, 4.

4 & 5 Geo. 5 (1914)

59. Bankruptcy Act 1914.

ss. 38, 42, see *Dent (A Bankrupt), Re* [1994] 2 All E.R. 904, D.C.

91. Welsh Church Act 1914.

s. 19, amended: 1994, c. 19, sch. 16.

5 & 6 Geo. 5 (1914–15)

18. Injuries in War Compensation Act 1914 (Session 2).

s. 1, scheme 94/1012.

9 & 10 Geo. 5 (1919)

76. Church of England Assembly (Powers) Act 1919.

ss. 3, 4, see *Williamson, ex p., The Times,* March 9, 1994, C.A.

10 & 11 Geo. 5 (1920)

41. Census Act 1920.

s. 9, amended(S.): 1994, c. 39, sch. 13.

81. Administration of Justice Act 1920.

s. 11, Act of Sederunt 94/1443.

s. 14, order 94/1901.

12 & 13 Geo. 5 (1922)

35. Celluloid and Cinema Film Act 1922.

s. 9, amended: 1994, c. 19, sch. 9.

s. 10, amended(S.): 1994, c. 39, sch. 13.

52. Allotments (Scotland) Act 1922.

s. 19, amended: 1994, c. 39, sch. 13.

13 & 14 Geo. 5 (1923)

8. Industrial Assurance Act 1923.

s. 43, regs. 39/2826.

14 & 15 Geo. 5 (1924)

27. Conveyancing (Scotland) Act 1924.

s. 46, see *Short's Tr.* v. *Keeper of the Registers of Scotland,* 1994 S.L.T. 65.

15 & 16 Geo. 5 (1924–25)

18. Settled Land Act 1925.

s. 64, see *Hambro* v. *The Duke of Marlborough* [1994] 3 W.L.R. 341, Morritt J.

20. Law of Property Act 1925.

s. 30, see *Payne* v. *Zafiropoyloy,* October 20, 1993, H.H.J. Coltart, Eastbourne County Ct.; *Abbey National Building Society* v. *Moss* [1993] NPC 153, C.A.

s. 40, see *Pitt* v. *PHH Asset Management* [1993] 40 EG 149, C.A.

s. 62, see *Pretoria Warehousing Co.* v. *Shelton* [1993] NPC 98, C.A.; *Handel* v. *St. Stephens Close* [1994] 05 EG 159, D.C.

s. 76, repealed (with savings): 1994, c. 36, ss. 10, 21, sch. 2.

s. 77, amended: *ibid.,* sch. 1.

s. 84, see *Solarfilms (Sales) Application, Re (Ref: LP/73/1991)* (1993) 67 P. & C.R. 110, Lands Tribunal; *Hydeshire's Application, Re (Ref: LP/54/1992)* (1993) 67 P. & C.R. 93, Lands Tribunal; *Love's and Love's Application, Re (Ref: LP/42/1991)* (1993) 67 P. & C.R. 101, Lands Tribunal; *Hopcraft's Application, Re* (1993) 66 P. & C.R. 475, Lands Tribunal; *O'Reilly's Application, Re* (1993) 66 P. & C.R. 485, Lands Tribunal.

CAP.

15 & 16 Geo. 5 (1924–25)—cont.

20. Law of Property Act 1925—*cont.*

s. 91, see *Arab Bank* v. *Mercantile Holdings* [1994] 2 W.L.R. 307, Millett J.

s. 105, see *Mathew* v. *T.M. Sutton, The Times,* June 22, 1994, Chadwick J.

s. 109, see *Sargent* v. *Customs and Excise Commissioners* [1994] 1 W.L.R. 235, H.H.J. Paul Baker, Q.C., sitting as a deputy judge.

s. 146, see *John Lewis Properties* v. *Viscount Chelsea* [1993] 34 EG 116, Mummery J.

ss. 193, 194, amended: 1994, c. 19, sch. 16.

s. 205, see *Connell Estate Agents* v. *Begej* [1993] 39 EG 125, C.A.

sch. 2, repealed in pt.: 1994, c. 36, sch. 2.

21. Land Registration Act 1925.

s. 24, see *Stanhope Pension Trust* v. *Registrar of Companies* [1993] NPC 169, C.A.

s. 24, repealed in pt. (with savings): 1994, c. 36, ss. 10, 21, sch. 2.

s. 38, amended: *ibid.*, sch. 1.

s. 49, amended: 1994, c. 37, sch. 1; repealed in pt.: *ibid.*, schs. 1, 3.

s. 52, see *Mortgage Corp.* v. *Nationwide Credit Corp.* [1993] 3 W.L.R. 769, C.A.

s. 70, see *Barclay's Bank* v. *Khaira* [1993] 1 FLR 343, C.A.

s. 70, amended: 1994, c. 21, sch. 9.

s. 112, rules 93/3275, 3276.

s. 144, rules 93/3045, 3275, 3276; 94/1130, 1974.

s. 145, orders 93/3229; 94/1974.

23. Administration of Estates Act 1925.

s. 2, amended: 1994, c. 36, s. 16; repealed in pt.: *ibid.*, s. 16, sch. 2.

s. 9, substituted: *ibid.*, s. 14.

ss. 35, 36, repealed in pt.: *ibid.*, sch. 2.

38. Performing Animals (Regulation) Act 1925.

s. 6, amended: 1994, c. 39, sch. 13.

49. Supreme Court of Judicature (Consolidation) Act 1925.

s. 225, see *C.T. Bowring & Co. (Insurance)* v. *Corsi & Partners, The Times,* June 28, 1994, C.A.

86. Criminal Justice Act 1925.

ss. 13, 49, repealed in pt.: 1994, c. 33, sch. 11.

16 & 17 Geo. 5 (1926)

16. Execution of Diligence (Scotland) Act 1926.

s. 6, Acts of Sederunt 94/391, 392.

36. Parks Regulation (Amendment) Act 1926.

s. 2, regs. 94/432.

CAP.

18 & 19 Geo. 5 (1928)

19. Agricultural Produce (Grading and Marking) Act 1928.

s. 8, amended(S.): 1994, c. 39, sch. 13.

32. Petroleum (Consolidation) Act 1928.

s. 2, amended: 1994, c. 19, sch. 9.

s. 24, amended(S.): 1994, c. 39, sch. 13.

44. Rating and Valuation (Apportionment) Act 1928.

s. 3, see *Slivenson (J.B.)* v. *Assessor for Strathclyde Region (L.V.A.C.),* 1991 S.C. 272.

19 & 20 Geo. 5 (1929)

25. Local Government (Scotland) Act 1929.

s. 29, amended: 1994, c. 39, sch. 13.

20 & 21 Geo. 5 (1929–30)

25. Third Parties (Rights against Insurers) Act 1930.

s. 2, see *Woolwich Building Society* v. *Taylor, The Times,* May 17, 1994, Lindsay J.

43. Road Traffic Act 1930.

ss. 108, 109, 119, amended(S.): 1994, c. 39, sch. 13.

23 & 24 Geo. 5 (1932–33)

12. Children and Young Persons Act 1933.

s. 1, see *R.* v. *Young (Tara Moira Lisa)* (1993) 97 Cr.App.R. 280, C.A.

s. 3, see *R.* v. *Aziz* [1993] Crim.L.R. 708, C.A.

s. 7, see *Hereford and Worcester County Council* v. *T & S Stores, The Times,* November 4, 1994, D.C.

s. 11, amended: S.L.R. 1993.

s. 20, repealed in pt.: 1994, c. 20, schs. 4, 5.

s. 39, see *R. (A Minor) (Wardship: Restraint of Publication), Re, The Times,* April 25, 1994, C.A.; *R.* v. *Central Criminal Court, ex p. Godwin and Crook, The Times,* August 16, 1994, C.A.

s. 42, amended: 1994, c. 33, sch. 4.

s. 49, substituted: *ibid.*, s. 49.

s. 53, see *R.* v. *Secretary of State for the Home Office, ex p. T.; R.* v. *Same, ex p. H; R.* v. *Same, ex p. Hickey* [1994] 2 W.L.R. 190, D.C.; *R.* v. *Martins and Ellison* (1993) 14 Cr.App.R.(S.) 526, C.A.

s. 53, amended: 1994, c. 33, s. 16.

s. 55, see *North Yorkshire County Council* v. *Selby Youth Court Justices* (1994) 1 All E.R. 991, D.C.

s. 55, amended: 1994, c. 33, sch. 10.

s. 56, amended: *ibid.*, schs. 4, 10.

s. 96, amended: 1994, c. 19, sch. 10.

sch. 2, order 94/1695.

7 & 8 Geo. 6 (1943–44)—cont.

31. Education Act 1944—*cont.*
ss. 39, 55, see *R.* v. *Dyfed County Council, ex p. S. (Minors), The Independent,* December 21, 1993, May J.
s. 54, repealed in pt.: 1994, c. 19, sch. 16.
s. 55, regs. 94/1421, 2330.
s. 70, regs. 94/537.
s. 80, regs. 94/2128.
s. 100, regs. 94/156, 2036, 2102.
s. 111A, regs. 94/2330.
s. 114, amended: 1994, c. 19, s. 21; repealed in pt.: *ibid.,* s. 21, sch. 18.

8 & 9 Geo. 6 (1944–45)

28. Law Reform (Contributory Negligence) Act 1945.
see *Barclays Bank* v. *Fairclough Building, The Times,* May 11, 1994, C.A.
s. 1, see *Jones (Kenneth)* v. *Morgan (Jonathan),* May 10, 1994: Dyson J.: High Ct. Cardiff.
43. Requisitioned Land and War Works Act 1945.
s. 34, amended: 1994, c. 21, sch. 9.
s. 59, amended: 1994, c. 19, sch. 16.

9 & 10 Geo. 6 (1945–46)

15. Public Health (Scotland) Act 1945.
s. 1, amended: 1994, c. 33, sch. 13.
17. Police (Overseas Service) Act 1945.
ss. 2, 3, repealed in pt.: 1994, c. 29, sch. 9.
18. Statutory Orders (Special Procedure) Act 1945.
s. 11, repealed in pt.: 1994, c. 29, sch. 9.
45. United Nations Act 1946.
s. 1, orders 94/1323–1326, 1636, 1637, 2673–2675.
59. Coal Industry Nationalisation Act 1946.
s. 1, repealed (prosp.): 1994, c. 21, sch. 11, Pts. II, IV.
s. 2, repealed (prosp.): *ibid.,* sch. 11, Pts. III, IV.
s. 3, repealed in pt. (prosp.): *ibid.,* sch. 11, Pts. II, IV.
s. 4, repealed (prosp.): *ibid.,* sch. 11, Pt. III.
ss. 5–9, repealed (prosp.): *ibid.,* sch. 11, Pt. II.
ss. 27–28, repealed (prosp.): *ibid.,* sch. 11, Pt. III.
s. 29, repealed (prosp.): *ibid.,* sch. 11, Pt. IV.
s. 30, repealed (prosp.): *ibid.,* sch. 11, Pt. II.
ss. 31–33, repealed (prosp.): *ibid.,* sch. 11, Pt. IV.
ss. 34 (in pt.), 35, repealed (prosp.): *ibid.,* sch. 11, Pt. III.
s. 36, repealed in pt.: *ibid.,* sch. 11, Pt. I; repealed (prosp.): *ibid.,* sch. 11, Pt. II.
s. 37, repealed (prosp.): *ibid.,* sch. 11, Pt. III.

9 & 10 Geo. 6 (1945–46)—cont.

59. Coal Industry Nationalisation Act 1946—*cont.*
ss. 38, 39, repealed (prosp.): *ibid.,* sch. 11, Pt. II.
s. 41, repealed (prosp.): *ibid.,* sch. 11, Pt. III.
ss. 42, 44, repealed (prosp.): *ibid.,* sch. 11, Pt. II.
s. 45, repealed (prosp.): *ibid.,* sch. 11, Pt. III.
ss. 46, 47, repealed (prosp.): *ibid.,* sch. 11, Pt. IV.
s. 48, repealed (prosp.): *ibid.,* sch. 11, Pt. II.
s. 49, repealed in pt. (prosp.): *ibid.,* sch. 11, Pt. IV.
s. 52, repealed (prosp.): *ibid.,* sch. 11, Pt. III.
s. 53, repealed (prosp.): *ibid.,* sch. 11, Pt. II.
s. 54, repealed (prosp.): *ibid.,* sch. 11, Pt. IV.
ss. 55–65, repealed (prosp.): *ibid.,* sch. 11, Pt. III.
schs. 1, 2, repealed (prosp.): *ibid.,* sch. 11, Pt. II.
sch. 2A, repealed (prosp.): *ibid.,* sch. 11, Pt. III.
sch. 3, repealed (prosp.): *ibid.,* sch. 11, Pt. II.

10 & 11 Geo. 6 (1946–47)

39. Statistics of Trade Act 1947.
ss. 2, 11, order 93/3037.
s. 9, amended: 1994, c. 21, sch. 9.
41. Fire Services Act 1947.
s. 4, amended: 1994, c. 19, s. 23.
s. 15, amended(S.): 1994, c. 39, sch. 14; repealed in pt.(S.): *ibid.,* schs. 14, 15.
s. 18, regs. 93/2946, 3709.
s. 36, amended(S.): 1994, c. 39, sch. 14; repealed in pt.(S.): *ibid.,* schs. 14, 15.
s. 38, amended(S.): *ibid.,* sch. 13.
42. Acquisition of Land (Authorisation Procedure) (Scotland) Act 1947.
s. 6A, added: 1994, c. 21, sch. 9.
s. 7, amended: 1994, c. 39, sch. 13.
43. Local Government (Scotland) Act 1947.
ss. 237 (in pt.), 243, 243A, 243B, 244, repealed: 1994, c. 39, sch. 14.
44. Crown Proceedings Act 1947.
s. 3, repealed in pt.: 1994, c. 26, sch. 5.
s. 8, amended: 1994, c. 28, sch. 2.
s. 21, see *McDonald* v. *Secretary of State for Scotland, The Times,* February 2, 1994.
s. 40, see *Savage's Application, Re* [1991] NI 103, Carswell J.

CAP.

14 Geo. 6 (1950)—cont.

27. Arbitration Act 1950—*cont.*
s. 13A, see *L'Office Cherifien des Phosphates* v. *Yamashita Shinnihon Steam ship Co., Boucraa, The* [1994] 2 W.L.R. 39, H.L.
s. 22, see *Prudential Assurance Co.* v. *Grand Metropolitan Estate* [1993] 32 EG 74, H.H. Judge Michael Rich, Q.C.; *International Petroleum Refining & Supply Sdad* v. *Elpis Finance SA; Faith, The* [1993] 2 Lloyd's Rep. 408, Hobhouse J.; *Land Securities* v. *Westminster City Council* [1993] NPC 117, Jonathan Parker J.; *Arnold* v. *National Westminster Bank* [1994] NPC 37, C.A.
s. 23, see *Ashbank Property Co.* v. *Department of Transport, The Times,* July 25, 1994, H.H.J. Levy, Q.C. sitting as a deputy judge.
s. 27, see *Saris* v. *Westminster Transports SA and Kestrel Marine* [1994] 1 Lloyd's Rep. 115, Colman J.
28. Shops Act 1950.
repealed: 1994, c. 40, sch. 17.
Pt. I (ss. 1–16), repealed: *ibid.*, s. 23.
Pt. II (ss. 17–39), s. 67, repealed: *ibid.*, s. 24.
s. 73, amended(S.): 1994, c. 39, sch. 13.
38. Allotments (Scotland) Act 1950.
ss. 9, 13, amended: 1994, c. 39, sch. 13.

14 & 15 Geo. 6 (1950–51)

35. Pet Animals Act 1951.
s. 7, amended(S.): 1994, c. 39, sch. 13.
63. Rag Flock and Other Filling Materials Act 1951.
s. 35, amended: 1994, c. 19, sch. 9.
s. 36, amended(S.): 1994, c. 39, sch. 13.
65. Reserve and Auxiliary Forces (Protection of Civil Interests) Act 1951.
s. 48, repealed in pt.: 1994, c. 29, sch. 9.
66. Rivers (Prevention of Pollution) (Scotland) Act 1951.
ss. 6, 12, 13, 16, 17, 19, 35, amended: 1994, c. 39, sch. 13.

15 & 16 Geo. 6 & 1 Eliz. 2 (1951–52)

23. Miners' Welfare Act 1952.
repealed (prosp.): 1994, c. 21, sch. 11, Pt. III.
46. Hypnotism Act 1952.
s. 2, amended(S.): 1994, c. 39, sch. 13.
52. Prison Act 1952.
s. 3, amended: 1994, c. 33, sch. 10.
s. 8A, added: *ibid.*, s. 152.
s. 16A, added: *ibid.*, s.151.
s. 33, amended: *ibid.*, s. 100.
s. 37, amended: *ibid.*, sch. 10.

CAP.

15 & 16 Geo. 6 & 1 Eliz. 2 (1951–52)—cont.

52. Prison Act 1952—*cont.*
s. 43, amended: *ibid.*, ss. 5, 18, sch. 4; repealed in pt.: *ibid.*, schs. 4, 11.
s. 47, see *R.* v. *Secretary of State for the Home Department, ex p. Leech (No. 2)* [1993] 3 W.L.R. 1125, C.A.
s. 47, rules 93/3075, 3076.
s. 47, amended: 1994, c. 33, s. 6, sch. 4.
s. 49, amended: *ibid.*, sch. 10.
66. Defamation Act 1952.
s. 7, see *Tsikata* v. *Newspaper Publishing, The Times,* November 9, 1994, Mr Jonathan Sumption, Q.C. sitting as a deputy judge.
67. Visiting Forces Act 1952.
s. 8, order 94/1643.

1 & 2 Eliz. 2 (1952–53)

14. Prevention of Crime Act 1953.
s. 1, see *Houston* v. *Snape,* 1993 S.C.C.R. 995; *Owens* v. *Crowe,* 1994 S.C.C.R. 310.
20. Births and Deaths Registration Act 1953.
ss. 1, 5, 9, 10, 10A, 11, 12, 14, 29, 39, 41, regs. 94/1948.
36. Post Office Act 1953.
s. 51, amended(S.): 1994, c. 39, sch. 13.
37. Registration Service Act 1953.
ss. 20, 21, regs. 94/1948.
s. 21, amended: 1994, c. 19, sch. 16.
47. Emergency Laws (Miscellaneous Provisions) Act 1953.
s. 5, amended(S.): 1994, c. 39, sch. 13.

2 & 3 Eliz. 2 (1953–54)

40. Protection of Animals (Amendment) Act 1954.
s. 2, see *Royal Society for the Prevention of Cruelty to Animals* v. *Miller, The Times,* March 8, 1994, D.C.
49. Long Leases (Scotland) Act 1954.
s. 4, amended: 1994, c. 39, sch. 13.
56. Landlord and Tenant Act 1954.
s. 18, see *Hamid and Hamid* v. *Jeje,* May 19, 1994.
s. 23, see *Graysim Holdings* v. *P. & O. Property Holdings* [1994] 1 W.L.R. 992, C.A.
Pt. II (ss. 23–46), see *Ricci* v. *Masons* (A Firm) [1993] 38 EG 154, Mr. L. Swift, Q.C.
s. 24, see *City of London Corp.* v. *Fell* [1993] 3 W.L.R. 1164, H.L.
ss. 24–28, 38, see *Nicholls* v. *Kinsey* [1994] 16 EG 145, C.A.
ss. 25, 26, see *M. & P. Enterprises (London)* v. *Norfolk Square Hotels* [1994] 14 EG 128, H.H.J. Rich, Q.C.

2 & 3 Eliz. 2 (1953–54)—cont.

56. Landlord and Tenant Act 1954—*cont.*
s. 34, see *Baptist* v. *Masters of the Bench and Trustees of the Honourable Society of Gray's Inn* [1993] 42 EG 287, H.H.J. Aron Owen.
s. 37, see *Busby* v. *Co-operative Insurance Society* [1994] 06 EG 141, H.H.J. O'Brien.
s. 43, see *Taylor* v. *Courage* [1993] 44 EG 116, C.A.
s. 66, regs. 93/2409.
s. 69, repealed in pt. (prosp.): 1994, c. 21, schs. 9, 11.

64. Transport Charges etc. (Miscellaneous Provisions) Act 1954.
s. 6, amended(S.): 1994, c. 39, sch. 13.

3 & 4 Eliz. 2 (1954–55)

13. Rural Water Supplies and Sewerage Act 1955.
repealed(S.): 1994, c. 39, sch. 14.
18. Army Act 1955.
continued in force: order 94/1903.
s. 187, amended: 1994, c. 33, sch. 4.
s. 214, sch. 5A, amended(S.): 1994, c. 39, sch. 13.
19. Air Force Act 1955.
continued in force: order 94/1903.
s. 187, amended: 1994, c. 33, sch. 4.
s. 212, sch. 5A, amended(S.): 1994, c. 39, sch. 13.
21. Crofters (Scotland) Act 1955.
s. 12, see *Lochalsh Estates* v. *Crofters Sharing in Avernish Common Grazings,* 1993 S.L.C.R. 85.

4 & 5 Eliz. 2 (1955–56)

46. Administration of Justice Act 1956.
s. 47, amended: 1994, c. 28, sch. 2.
s. 48, repealed in pt.: *ibid.,* schs. 2, 4.
60. Valuation and Rating (Scotland) Act 1956.
s. 1, repealed: 1994, c. 39, sch. 14.
s. 3, repealed: *ibid.,* s. 162, sch. 14.
s. 6, amended: orders 94/911–913, 2068–2081.
s. 6A, added: 1994, c. 39, sch. 13.
s. 7, see *Twygen* v. *Assessor for Tayside Region (L.V.A.C.),* 1991 S.C. 98.
s. 22A, repealed: 1994, c. 39, sch. 14.
s. 43, amended: *ibid.,* sch. 13; repealed in pt.: *ibid.,* s. 162, sch. 14.
69. Sexual Offences Act 1956.
s. 1, substituted: 1994, c. 33, s. 142.
ss. 2, 3, repealed in pt.: *ibid.,* s. 33, schs. 9, 11.
s. 4, repealed in pt.: *ibid.,* schs. 9, 11.
s. 12, amended: *ibid.,* s. 143.

4 & 5 Eliz. 2 (1955–56)—cont.

69. Sexual Offences Act 1956—*cont.*
s. 13, see *D.P.P.* v. *Gawecki and Bazar* [1993] Crim.L.R. 202, D.C.
ss. 22, 23, repealed in pt.: 1994, c. 33, schs. 9, 11.
s. 30, see *R.* v. *McFarlane* [1994] 2 W.L.R. 494, C.A.
s. 32, see *D.P.P.* v. *Bull, The Times,* June 1, 1994, D.C.
s. 54, repealed in pt.: S.L.R. 1993.
sch. 2, amended: 1994, c. 33, s. 144.
sch. 3, repealed in pt.: S.L.R. 1993.
74. Copyright Act 1956.
s. 4, see *John Richardson Computers* v. *Flanders* [1993] F.S.R. 497, Ferris J.
ss. 5, 49, see *Monsoon* v. *India Imports of Rhode Island* [1993] F.S.R. 486, Sir Mervyn Davies sitting as a deputy judge.

5 & 6 Eliz. 2 (1957)

11. Homicide Act 1957.
s. 3, see *R.* v. *Morhall* [1993] 4 All E.R. 888, C.A.; *R.* v. *Cambridge* [1994] 2 All E.R. 760, C.A.
12. Public Trustee (Fees) Act 1957.
s. 1, order 94/714.
16. Nurses Agencies Act 1957.
s. 2, amended: 1994, c. 19, sch. 9.
31. Occupiers' Liability Act 1957.
see *Gesner* v. *Wallingford and District Labour Party Supporters Association Club, The Times,* June 2, 1994, C.A.
s. 2, see *Cotton* v. *Derbyshire Dales District Council, The Times,* June 20, 1994, C.A.; *McGeown* v. *Northern Ireland Housing Executive, The Times,* June 24, 1994, H.L.(N.I.).
52. Geneva Conventions Act 1957.
s. 5, amended: 1994, c. 33, sch. 4.
53. Naval Discipline Act 1957.
continued in force: order 94/1903.
s. 109, amended: 1994, c. 33, sch. 4.
sch. 4A, amended(S.): 1994, c. 39, sch. 13.

6 & 7 Eliz. 2 (1957–58)

24. Land Drainage (Scotland) Act 1958.
sch. 1, amended: 1994, c. 39, sch. 13.
33. Disabled Persons (Employment) Act 1958.
s. 3, amended: 1994, c. 19, sch. 10; repealed in pt.: *ibid.,* schs. 10, 18.
s. 3, amended(S.): 1994, c. 39, sch. 13.
40. Matrimonial Proceedings (Children) Act 1958.
ss. 10, 12, amended(S.): 1994, c. 39, sch. 13.

CAP.

6 & 7 Eliz. 2 (1957–58)—cont.

49. Trading Representations (Disabled Persons) Act 1958.
s. 1, amended: 1994, c. 19, sch. 16; c. 39, sch. 13(S.).

51. Public Records Act 1958.
s. 2, regs. 94/2353.
sch. 1, amended: 1994, c. 21, sch. 9; c. 30, sch. 2.

64. Local Government and Miscellaneous Provisions (Scotland) Act 1958.
s. 7, repealed: 1994, c. 39, sch. 14.

69. Opencast Coal Act 1958.
s. 3, repealed (prosp.): 1994, c. 21, s. 53, sch. 11.
s. 4, amended: *ibid.*, sch. 8; repealed in pt. (prosp.): *ibid.*, schs. 8, 11.
ss. 5, 7, 8, 10–12, amended: *ibid.*, sch. 8.
s. 13, repealed (prosp.): *ibid.*, schs. 8, 11.
ss. 14, 14A, 15, amended: *ibid.*, sch. 8.
s. 15A, amended: 1994, c. 19, sch. 16; c. 21, sch. 8; repealed in pt.: 1994, c. 19, schs. 16, 18; (prosp.) c. 21, schs. 8, 11.
s. 16, amended: *ibid.*, sch. 8; repealed in pt. (prosp.): *ibid.*, schs. 8, 11.
s. 17, amended: *ibid.*, sch. 8; repealed in pt. (prosp.): *ibid.*, schs. 8, 11, Pts. II, III.
s. 18, substituted (prosp.): *ibid.*, sch. 8.
ss. 19, 20, repealed (prosp.): *ibid.*, schs. 8, 11.
ss. 21, 23A, amended: *ibid.*, sch. 8.
s. 26, amended: *ibid.*, sch. 8; repealed in pt. (prosp.): *ibid.*, schs. 8, 11.
ss. 27, 29, amended: *ibid.*, sch. 8.
s. 31, amended: *ibid.*; repealed in pt. (prosp.): *ibid.*, schs. 8, 11.
s. 31A, added: *ibid.*, sch. 8.
ss. 32, 35, amended: *ibid.*; repealed in pt. (prosp.): *ibid.*, schs. 8, 11.
ss. 36, 38–40, 42, amended: *ibid.*, sch. 8.
s. 43, repealed in pt. (prosp.): *ibid.*, schs. 8, 11.
s. 44, amended: *ibid.*, sch. 8; repealed in pt. (prosp.): *ibid.*, schs. 8, 11.
s. 45, amended: *ibid.*, sch. 8.
s. 46, repealed in pt. (prosp.): *ibid.*, sch. 11.
s. 49, amended: *ibid.*, sch. 8.
s. 51, amended: *ibid.*; repealed in pt. (prosp.): *ibid.*, sch. 11.
s. 52, amended: *ibid.*, sch. 8.
sch. 2, amended: *ibid.*; repealed in pt. (prosp.): *ibid.*, schs. 8, 11.
schs. 3, 5, amended: *ibid.*, sch. 8.
sch. 6, amended: *ibid.*; repealed in pt. (prosp.): *ibid.*, sch. 11.
sch. 8, amended: *ibid.*, sch. 8; repealed in pt. (prosp.): *ibid.*, schs. 8, 11.

CAP.

7 & 8 Eliz. 2 (1958–59)

24. Building (Scotland) Act 1959.
ss. 3, 24, 29, sch. 4, regs. 94/1266.
s. 29, amended: 1994, c. 39, sch. 13.

40. Deer (Scotland) Act 1959.
s. 25A, amended: 1994, c. 39, sch. 13; repealed in pt.: *ibid.*, schs. 13, 14.
s. 25D, repealed in pt.: *ibid.*
s. 25F, amended: *ibid.*, sch. 13.

45. Metropolitan Magistrates' Courts Act 1959.
ss. 3, 4, repealed in pt.: 1994, c. 29, sch. 9.

54. Weeds Act 1959.
s. 5, amended: 1994, c. 19, sch. 16.

57. Street Offences Act 1959.
s. 1, see *D.P.P.* v. *Bull,* June 1, 1994, D.C.

66. Obscene Publications Act 1959.
see *R.* v. *Jack (Colin Mason),* July 4, 1994, Mr Recorder Lamb, Norwich Crown Ct.
s. 1, see *R.* v. *Taylor (Alan), The Times,* February 4, 1994, C.A.; *R.* v. *O'Sullivan, The Times,* May 3, 1994, C.A.
s. 1, amended: 1994, c. 33, sch. 9.

8 & 9 Eliz. 2 (1959–60)

16. Road Traffic Act 1960.
s. 233, amended: 1994, c. 40, sch. 13.

30. Occupiers' Liability (Scotland) Act 1960.
s. 2, see *Mallon* v. *Spook Erections* (Sh.Ct.), 1993 S.C.L.R. 845.

36. Game Laws (Amendment) Act 1960.
s. 4A, added: 1994, c. 33, sch. 9.

58. Charities Act 1960.
s. 13, see *Peggs* v. *Lamb* [1994] 2 W.L.R. 1, Morritt J.

62. Caravan Sites and Control of Development Act 1960.
s. 23, amended: 1994, c. 19, sch. 16.
s. 24, amended: *ibid.*; c. 33, s. 80; repealed in pt.: 1994, c. 19, schs. 16, 18.
s. 24, amended(S.): 1994, c. 39, sch. 13; repealed in pt.(S.): *ibid.*, schs. 13, 14.
s. 29, see *Carter* v. *Secretary of State for the Environment, The Times,* April 6, 1994, C.A.
s. 29, amended: 1994, c. 19, sch. 16.

65. Administration of Justice Act 1960.
s. 4, amended: 1994, c. 33, sch. 10.
s. 12, see *R. (A Minor) (Wardship: Restraint of Publication), Re, The Times,* April 25, 1994, C.A.

9 & 10 Eliz. 2 (1960–61)

27. Carriage by Air Act 1961.
s. 10, see *Gurtner* v. *Beaton* [1993] 2 Lloyd's Rep. 369, C.A.
sch. 1, see *Antwerp United Diamondbuba* v. *Air Europe* [1993] 4 All E.R. 469, Phillips J.

9 & 10 Eliz. 2 (1960–61)—cont.

33. Land Compensation Act 1961.
s. 32, regs. 94/468.
s. 39, amended: 1994, c. 19, sch. 16.

34. Factories Act 1961.
s. 29, see *Walsh* v. *Crown Decorative Products* [1993] P.I.Q.R. P194, C.A.; *Gunion* v. *Roche Products, The Scotsman,* October 19, 1994, Outer House; *Neil* v. *Greater Glasgow Health Board* (O.H.), 1994 S.C.L.R. 673.
s. 176, amended: 1994, c. 19, sch. 16; c. 39, sch. 13(S.).

39. Criminal Justice Act 1961.
s. 23, amended: 1994, c. 33, sch. 10.
ss. 28, 29, see *Advocate (H.M.)* v. *R., The Times,* October 21, 1994.
ss. 29, 30, 32, 38, amended: 1994, c. 33, sch. 10.

41. Flood Prevention (Scotland) Act 1961.
s. 1, amended: 1994, c. 39, sch. 13.
ss. 4, 12, repealed in pt.: *ibid.,* schs. 13, 14.
s. 15, amended: *ibid.,* sch. 13.

62. Trustee Investments Act 1961.
s. 11, amended: 1994, c. 19, sch. 16; c. 29, sch. 4.
s. 12, orders 94/265, 1908.
sch. 1, amended: 1994, c. 19, sch. 16; c. 29, sch. 4; orders 94/265, 1908.

64. Public Health Act 1961.
sch. 4, repealed in pt. (prosp.): 1994, c. 21, schs. 9, 11, Pt. IV.

10 & 11 Eliz. 2 (1961–62)

9. Local Government (Financial Provisions etc.) (Scotland) Act 1962.
s. 4, amended: 1994, c. 39, sch. 13.

12. Education Act 1962.
ss. 1, 4, regs. 93/3183; 94/1606.
s. 4, amended: 1994, c. 30, sch. 2.
sch. 1, regs. 93/3183.

19. West Indies Act 1962.
ss. 5, 7, orders 93/3143; 94/1638.

21. Commonwealth Immigrants Act 1962.
s. 2, see *R.* v. *Secretary of State for the Home Department, ex p. Miah (Nazmul)* [1994] Imm AR 279, Jowitt J.

22. Coal Consumers' Councils (Northern Irish Interests) Act 1962.
repealed (prosp.): 1994, c. 21, sch. 11, Pt. III.

35. Shops (Airports) Act 1962.
repealed: 1994, c. 40, sch. 17.

38. Town and Country Planning Act 1962.
s. 221, see *Lliw Valley Borough Council* v. *Secretary of State for Wales and Evans* [1993] J.P.L. 673, Mr. R. Vandermeer, Q.C.

47. Education (Scotland) Act 1962.
s. 145, amended: 1994, c. 39, sch. 13.

10 & 11 Eliz. 2 (1961–62)—cont.

56. Local Government (Records) Act 1962.
ss. 2, 8, amended: 1994, c. 19, sch. 16; c. 29, sch. 4.

58. Pipe-lines Act 1962.
s. 7, order 94/1994.
s. 35, amended: 1994, c. 19, sch. 16; repealed in pt.: *ibid.,* schs. 16, 18.

11 Eliz. 2 (1962)

6. Coal Industry Act 1962.
ss. 1, 2, 4, repealed (prosp.): 1994, c. 21, sch. 11, Pt. III.

1963

2. Betting, Gaming and Lotteries Act 1963.
s. 5, amended: 1994, c. 40, s. 20.
s. 31A, added: *ibid.,* s. 20.
schs. 1–3, amended(S.): 1994, c. 39, sch. 13.
sch. 4, amended: 1994, c. 40, s. 20.
sch. 5A, added: *ibid.,* s. 20, sch. 8.

12. Local Government (Financial Provisions) (Scotland) Act 1963.
ss. 7, 15, amended: 1994, c. 39, sch. 13.
s. 18, substituted: *ibid.*
s. 26, amended: *ibid.*

18. Stock Transfer Act 1963.
s. 4, repealed in pt.: 1994, c. 29, sch. 9.

33. London Government Act 1963.
s. 51, repealed in pt.: 1994, c. 20, sch. 5.

37. Children and Young Persons Act 1963.
s. 18, amended: 1994, c. 33, sch. 9.
s. 35, repealed in pt.: 1994, c. 20, sch. 5.
s. 56, amended: 1994, c. 19, sch. 10.
s. 57, repealed in pt.: 1994, c. 33, sch. 11.
s. 63, amended: 1994, c. 19, sch. 10.

41. Offices, Shops and Railway Premises Act 1963.
s. 90, amended: 1994, c. 29, sch. 5.

43. Animal Boarding Establishments Act 1963.
s. 5, amended(S.): 1994, c. 39, sch. 13.

51. Land Compensation (Scotland) Act 1963.
s. 11, see *Bisset* v. *Secretary of State for Scotland (No. 2),* 1994 S.L.T.(Lands Tr.) 21.
s. 12, see *Bisset* v. *Secretary of State for Scotland,* 1994 S.L.T.(Lands Tr.) 12.
ss. 32–34, 36, regs. 94/1187.
s. 40, regs. 94/469.

1964

5. International Headquarters and Defence Organisations Act 1964.
s. 1, order 94/1642.

9. Public Works Loans Act 1964.
s. 6, amended(S.): 1994, c. 39, sch. 13.

1964—cont.

14. Plant Varieties and Seeds Act 1964.
ss. 1, 3, 5, schemes 94/2776–2781.
ss. 4, 15, see *Germinal Holdings* v. *H.R. Fell & Sons* [1993] F.S.R. 343, H.H.J. Baker, Q.C., sitting as a deputy judge.
s. 5A, repealed in pt.: 1994, c. 26, sch. 5.
s. 7, schemes 93/2776–2778, 2780, 2781.
s. 9, scheme 93/2775; regs. 94/675.
s. 16, regs. 94/676, 1423.
s. 36, scheme 93/2775; regs. 94/675, 676, 1423.
s. 38, schemes 93/2775–2781.

26. Licensing Act 1964.
s. 10, see *R.* v. *Hastings Justices, ex p. McSpirit, The Times,* June 23, 1994, Sedley J.
s. 20, see *R.* v. *West London Licensing Justices, ex p. Davis, The Times,* March 16, 1994, Pill J.
s. 20A, see *R.* v. *Maidstone Crown Court, ex p. Harris, The Times,* July 21, 1994, Schiemann J.
s. 56, amended: 1994, c. 21, sch. 9.
s. 58, amended: 1994, c. 19, sch. 16.
s. 66, amended: *ibid.*; repealed in pt.: *ibid.*, schs. 16, 18.
s. 67, see *Unicorn Inns* v. *Secretary of State for the Environment and Chelmsford Borough Council* [1993] J.P.L. 932, Mr R. Vandermeer, Q.C. sitting as a deputy judge.
s. 67, amended: 1994, c. 19, sch. 16.
s. 85, amended: *ibid.*, sch. 2.
s. 86A, added: 1994, c. 40, s. 18.
s. 98, amended: 1994, c. 19, sch. 16.
s. 168, amended: 1994, c. 40, s. 19.
s. 168A, added: *ibid.*
s. 179, amended: *ibid.*, sch. 11.
s. 180, amended: 1994, c. 19, sch. 16.
ss. 188, 193, amended: *ibid.*, sch. 2.
s. 196A, amended: 1994, c. 40, sch. 11; repealed in pt.: *ibid.*, sch. 17.
ss. 201, 202, amended: *ibid.*, sch. 11.
sch. 2, see *R.* v. *Mid-Warwickshire Licensing Justices, ex p. Patel, The Times,* December 15, 1993, May J.
sch. 2, amended: 1994, c. 19, sch. 16.
sch. 8, amended: *ibid.*; repealed in pt.: *ibid.*, schs. 16, 18.
sch. 12A, added: 1994, c. 40, s. 19, sch. 7.

29. Continental Shelf Act 1964.
s. 1, repealed in pt. (prosp.): 1994, c. 21, sch. 11, Pt. II.

40. Harbours Act 1964.
s. 14, orders 93/2974; 94/1440, 1647, 1778, 2064, 2253, 2298, 2733, 2846.
s. 16, order 94/1693.
sch. 3, order 93/2908.
sch. 3, amended: 1994, c. 19, sch. 16; repealed in pt.: *ibid.*, schs. 16, 18.
sch. 3, amended(S.): 1994, c. 39, sch. 13.

42. Administration of Justice Act 1964.
sch. 3, repealed in pt.: 1994, c. 29, sch. 9.

1964—cont.

48. Police Act 1964.
s. 1, amended: 1994, c. 19, s. 24; repealed in pt.: *ibid.*, s. 24, sch. 18; substituted: 1994, c. 29, s. 1.
s. 2, amended: 1994, c. 19, s. 24.
ss. 2, 2A, 3, substituted as ss. 2, 3: 1994, c. 29, s. 2.
ss. 3A, 3B, added: *ibid.*, s. 3.
s. 4, substituted as ss. 4, 4A–4C: *ibid.*, s. 4.
s. 5, substituted as ss. 5, 5A: *ibid.*, s. 5.
s. 6, substituted: *ibid.*, s. 6.
s. 6A, repealed: *ibid.*, sch. 9.
s. 7, amended: *ibid.*, s. 7; repealed in pt.: *ibid.*, s. 7, sch. 9.
s. 8, substituted: *ibid.*, s. 8.
s. 8A, added: *ibid.*, s. 9.
s. 9, repealed: *ibid.*, sch. 9.
s. 10, substituted: *ibid.*, s. 10.
ss. 10A, 10B, added: *ibid.*, s. 11.
s. 11, substituted: *ibid.*, s. 12.
s. 12, amended: *ibid.*, sch. 5; repealed in pt.: *ibid.*, schs. 5, 9.
s. 13, amended: *ibid.*, sch. 5.
s. 15A, added: *ibid.*, s. 13.
s. 17, repealed in pt.: *ibid.*, schs. 5, 9.
s. 19, amended: *ibid.*, sch. 5; c. 33, s. 160.
s. 21, substituted as ss. 21, 21A–21C: 1994, c. 29, s. 14.
ss. 22–24, repealed: *ibid.*, sch. 9.
s. 25, repealed in pt.: *ibid.*, schs. 5, 9.
ss. 26, 27, repealed in pt.: *ibid.*, sch. 9.
s. 28, amended: *ibid.*, sch. 5.
s. 28A, order 94/2678.
ss. 28A–28D, added: 1994, c. 29, s. 15.
s. 29, amended: *ibid.*, sch. 5; repealed in pt.: *ibid.*, sch. 9.
s. 29A, added: *ibid.*, s. 16.
s. 30, amended: *ibid.*, sch. 5.
s. 31, substituted as ss. 31, 31A, 31B: *ibid.*, s. 17.
s. 33, regs. 94/1308, 2195, 2331.
s. 33, amended: 1994, c. 29, s. 17; repealed in pt.: *ibid.*, s. 18, sch. 9.
s. 37, see *R.* v. *Secretary of State for the Home Department, ex p. Barr, The Times,* March 18, 1994, C.A.
s. 37, substituted: 1994, c. 29, s. 19.
s. 37, sch. 5, see *R.* v. *Secretary of State for the Home Department, ex p. Harrison, The Times,* May 17, 1994, Potts J.
s. 38, amended: 1994, c. 29, s. 20.
s. 38A, added: *ibid.*, s. 21.
s. 39, amended: *ibid.*, s. 22.
s. 41, substituted: *ibid.*, s. 23.
s. 42, amended: *ibid.*, sch. 5.
s. 43, amended: *ibid.*; repealed in pt.: *ibid.*, sch. 9.
s. 44, amended: *ibid.*, sch. 5.
s. 48, amended: 1994, c. 33, sch. 10.

1964—cont.

48. Police Act 1964—cont.
s. 51, see *Kerr* v. *D.P.P., The Times*, August 5, 1994, D.C.; *Lunt* v. *D.P.P.* [1993] Crim.L.R. 534, D.C.
s. 51, amended: 1994, c. 33, sch. 10.
s. 53, repealed in pt.: 1994, c. 29, schs. 5, 9.
s. 53A, added: *ibid.,* s. 24.
s. 53B, added: *ibid.,* s. 25.
s. 53C, added: *ibid.,* s. 26.
s. 56, amended: *ibid.,* sch. 5.
s. 58, amended: *ibid.*; repealed in pt.: *ibid.,* sch. 9.
s. 60, repealed in pt.: *ibid.*
s. 62, substituted: *ibid.,* sch. 5.
sch. 1, substituted as sch. 1A: *ibid.,* s. 1, sch. 1.
schs. 1B, 1C, added: *ibid.,* s. 3, sch. 2.
sch. 1C, regs. 94/2023.
schs. 3, 4, repealed: 1994, c. 29, sch. 9.
sch. 5, substituted: *ibid.,* s. 19, sch. 3.
sch. 9, repealed in pt.: *ibid.,* sch. 9.

63. Law of Property (Joint Tenants) Act 1964.
s. 1, repealed in pt.: 1994, c. 36, schs. 1, 2.

65. Zambia Independence Act 1964.
s. 3, see *Patel (Rameshbhai), Patel (Girishbhai), Patel (Kantilal), Patel (Kanubhai) and Patel (Anilkumar)* v. *Secretary of State for the Home Department* [1993] Imm AR 508, C.A.

67. Local Government (Development and Finance) Act 1964.
s. 16, amended: 1994, c. 39, sch. 13.

69. Scrap Metal Dealers Act 1964.
s. 9, amended: 1994, c. 19, sch. 9; c. 22, sch. 3.

70. Riding Establishments Act 1964.
s. 6, amended: 1994, c. 19, sch. 9; c. 39, sch. 13(S.).

71. Trading Stamps Act 1964.
s. 4, amended: 1994, c. 35, sch. 2.

74. Obscene Publications Act 1964.
s. 1, see *R.* v. *O'Sullivan, The Times,* May 3, 1994, C.A.

75. Public Libraries and Museums Act 1964.
s. 4, amended: 1994, c. 19, sch. 16; repealed in pt.: *ibid.,* schs. 16, 18.
ss. 5 (in pt.), 6, 10 (in pt.), 11 (in pt.), 21, repealed: *ibid.*
s. 25, sch. 2, amended: *ibid.,* sch. 16.

81. Diplomatic Privileges Act 1964.
s. 2, amended: 1994, c. 23, sch. 14.

82. Education Act 1964.
s. 1, regs. 94/581.

1965

4. Science and Technology Act 1965.
s. 1, order 94/423–425.
s. 3, order 94/611.

1965—cont.

12. Industrial and Provident Societies Act 1965.
see *Gesner* v. *Wallingford and District Labour Party Supporters Association Club, The Times,* June 2, 1994, C.A.
s. 31, repealed in pt.: 1994, c. 29, sch. 9.
ss. 70, 71, regs. 94/658, 660.

14. Cereals Marketing Act 1965.
ss. 13, 23, 24, order 94/1424.

19. Teaching Council (Scotland) Act 1965.
sch. 1, order 94/1702.

25. Finance Act 1965.
s. 24, see *Marshall (Inspector of Taxes)* v. *Kerr* [1994] 3 W.L.R. 299, H.L.
s. 87, sch. 21, repealed: 1994, c. 9, sch. 26.

35. Shops (Early Closing Days) Act 1965.
repealed: 1994, c. 40, sch. 17.

36. Gas Act 1965.
s. 13, amended: 1994, c. 21, sch. 9.
s. 28, amended: 1994, c. 19, sch. 16; repealed in pt.: *ibid.,* schs. 16, 18.
s. 28, sch. 6, amended(S.): 1994, c. 39, sch. 13.

37. Carriage of Goods by Road Act 1965.
sch. 1, see *Noble* v. *The R.H. Group* [1993] P.I.Q.R. P235, C.A.

45. Backing of Warrants (Republic of Ireland) Act 1965.
s. 1, amended: 1994, c. 33, s. 159.
s. 2, order 94/1952.
s. 2, repealed in pt.: 1994, c. 33, s. 159, sch. 11.
s. 4, amended: *ibid.,* s. 159.
ss. 6A–6C, order 94/1952.
sch., amended: 1994, c. 33, s. 159.

49. Registration of Births, Deaths and Marriages (Scotland) Act 1965.
ss. 5, 8, amended: 1994, c. 39, s. 51.
s. 15, amended: *ibid.,* s. 51; repealed in pt.: *ibid.,* s. 51, sch. 14.
ss. 28A, 37, 38, 40, 43, 47, 54, 56, regs. 93/3153.
s. 56, amended: 1994, c. 39, s. 51.

51. National Insurance Act 1965.
s. 36, order 94/542.

56. Compulsory Purchase Act 1965.
ss. 4, 5, see *Cooperative Insurance Society* v. *Hastings Borough Council* 91 L.G.R. 608, Vinelott J.

57. Nuclear Installations Act 1965.
s. 16, order 94/909; amended: *ibid.*

63. Public Works Loans Act 1965.
s. 31, repealed in pt.: 1994, c. 29, sch. 9.

64. Commons Registration Act 1965.
ss. 1, 4–6, see *Dynevor* v. *Richardson, The Times,* May 26, 1994, Knox J.

69. Criminal Procedure (Attendance of Witnesses) Act 1965.
s. 1, repealed: 1994, c. 33, sch. 11.
s. 3, see *R.* v. *Lennock* (1993) 97 Cr.App.R. 228, C.A.

CAP.

1965—cont.

82. Coal Industry Act 1965.
s. 1, repealed (prosp.): 1994, c. 21, sch. 11, Pt. III.
s. 2, repealed in pt. (prosp.): *ibid.,* sch. 11, Pt. II.
s. 4, repealed in pt. (prosp.): *ibid.,* sch. 11, Pts. III, IV.
s. 5, sch. 1, repealed (prosp.): *ibid.,* sch. 11, Pt. III.

1966

4. Mines (Working Facilities and Support) Act 1966.
s. 1, amended: 1994, c. 21, sch. 9; repealed in pt. (prosp.): *ibid.,* schs. 9, 11, Pt. II.
s. 4, amended: *ibid.,* sch. 9.
s. 7A, added: *ibid.*
s. 9, sch. 2, repealed in pt. (prosp.): *ibid.,* sch. 11, Pt. II.

10. Commonwealth Secretariat Act 1966.
sch., amended: 1994, c. 23, sch. 14.

18. Finance Act 1966.
s. 2, amended: 1994, c. 22, sch. 3; repealed in pt.: *ibid.,* sch. 5.
schs. 5, 6, repealed in pt.: 1994, c. 9, sch. 26.

19. Law Reform (Miscellaneous Provisions) (Scotland) Act 1966.
s. 8, Act of Sederunt 94/1443.

35. Family Provision Act 1966.
s. 1, order 93/2906.

36. Veterinary Surgeons Act 1966.
s. 25, order 94/305.

38. Sea Fisheries Regulation Act 1966.
ss. 1–3, 19, amended: 1994, c. 19, sch. 16.

41. Arbitration (International Investments Disputes) Act 1966.
s. 7, Act of Sederunt 94/1443.

42. Local Government Act 1966.
s. 11, amended: 1994, c. 29, sch. 4.
s. 41, amended: 1994, c. 19, sch. 16.

47. National Coal Board (Additional Powers) Act 1966.
repealed (prosp.): 1994, c. 21, sch. 11, Pt. II.

51. Local Government (Scotland) Act 1966.
s. 11, substituted: 1994, c. 39, s. 166.
ss. 17, 20, repealed: *ibid.,* sch. 14.
s. 24, substituted: *ibid.,* s. 154.
ss. 24A, 24B, added: *ibid.,* s. 155.
s. 25, repealed in pt.: *ibid.,* schs. 13, 14.
s. 25A, added: *ibid.,* s. 156.
s. 44, amended: *ibid.,* sch. 13.
s. 46, sch. 3, amended: *ibid.;* repealed in pt.: *ibid.,* sch. 14.
sch. 5, repealed in pt.: *ibid.*

CAP.

1967

1. Land Commission Act 1967.
ss. 14, 15, amended: 1994, c. 21, sch. 9; repealed in pt. (prosp.): *ibid.,* schs. 9, 11, Pt. III.
ss. 58, 89, sch. 5, repealed in pt. (prosp.): *ibid.,* schs. 9, 11, Pt. II.
sch. 12, amended: 1994, c. 36, sch. 1; repealed in pt.: *ibid.,* schs. 1, 2.

7. Misrepresentation Act 1967.
s. 2, see *William Sindall* v. *Cambridgeshire County Council* [1994] 1 W.L.R. 1016, C.A.

8. Plant Health Act 1967.
ss. 1, 2, order 94/1441(S.).
s. 3, orders 93/3213; 94/1441(S.).
s. 4, order 93/3213.
s. 4A, order 94/1441(S.).
s. 5, amended: 1994, c. 19, sch. 16; c. 39, sch. 13(S.).

9. General Rate Act 1967.
s. 103, see *Trull* v. *Restormel Borough Council, The Times,* June 20, 1994, Latham J.

10. Forestry Act 1967.
s. 40, amended(S.): 1994, s. 39, sch. 13.

13. Parliamentary Commissioner Act 1967.
s. 5, amended: 1994, c. 14, s. 1.
ss. 5, 7, 10, see *R.* v. *Parliamentary Commissioner for Administration, ex p. Dyer* [1994] 1 All E.R. 375, D.C.
sch. 2, amended: 1994, c. 19, sch. 14; c. 21, sch. 1.
sch. 3, amended: *ibid.,* s. 1.
sch. 4, added: *ibid.*

19. Private Places of Entertainment (Licensing) Act 1967.
sch., amended: 1994, c. 19, sch. 16.

22. Agriculture Act 1967.
s. 75, amended: 1994, c. 19, sch. 16; repealed in pt.: *ibid.,* schs. 16, 18.

24. Slaughter of Poultry Act 1967.
s. 8, amended: 1994, c. 19, sch. 16; repealed in pt.: *ibid.,* schs. 16, 18.
s. 8, amended(S.): 1994, c. 39, sch. 13.

27. Merchant Shipping (Load Lines) Act 1967.
s. 26, regs. 94/502.

28. Superannuation (Miscellaneous Provisions) Act 1967.
s. 15, amended: 1994, c. 29, sch. 8.

41. Marine, etc., Broadcasting (Offences) Act 1967.
s. 10, order 94/1064.

45. Uniform Laws on International Sales Act 1967.
s. 1, amended: 1994, c. 35, sch. 2.

48. Industrial and Provident Societies Act 1967.
s. 7, regs. 94/658, 660.

54. Finance Act 1967.
s. 45, repealed in pt.: 1994, c. 22, sch. 5.

1967—cont.

60. Sexual Offences Act 1967.
s. 1, amended: 1994, c. 33, s. 145; repealed in pt.: *ibid.*, s. 146, sch. 11.
s. 2, repealed: *ibid.*, s. 146, sch. 11.
s. 3, repealed: *ibid.*, sch. 11.

64. Anchors and Chain Cables Act 1967.
s. 1, regs. 94/502.

65. Antarctic Treaty Act 1967.
repealed: 1994, c. 15, sch.

66. Welsh Language Act 1967.
s. 2, regs. 93/1511 (corrected by regs. 94/725).

72. Wireless Telegraphy Act 1967.
s. 8, amended: 1994, c. 22, sch. 3; repealed in pt.: *ibid.*, sch. 5.
s. 14, repealed in pt.: *ibid.*

77. Police (Scotland) Act 1967.
ss. 1, 2, amended: 1994, c. 39, sch. 13.
s. 3, substituted: 1994, c. 29, s. 47.
ss. 5, 5A, substituted as s. 5: *ibid.*, s. 48.
s. 6, repealed in pt.: *ibid.*, s. 63, sch. 9.
s. 7, amended: *ibid.*, s. 63; repealed in pt.: *ibid.*, s. 47, sch. 9.
s. 8, repealed in pt.: *ibid.*, s. 47, sch. 9.
s. 9, substituted: *ibid.*, s. 49.
s. 12A, added: *ibid.*, s. 50.
s. 14, repealed in pt.: *ibid.*, s. 47, sch. 9.
s. 15, amended: *ibid.*, s. 51.
s. 17, amended: 1994, c. 39, s. 160.
s. 18, amended: *ibid.*, sch. 13; repealed: 1994, c. 33, sch. 11.
s. 19, amended: 1994, c. 39, sch. 13; repealed in pt.: *ibid.*, schs. 13, 14.
s. 19A, added: *ibid.*, sch. 13.
s. 20, substituted: *ibid.*, s. 35.
s. 21, amended: *ibid.*, sch. 13.
s. 21A, repealed: *ibid.*, sch. 14.
s. 21B, added: *ibid.*, s. 34.
s. 22, amended: *ibid.*, sch. 13.
s. 23, amended: 1994, c. 29, s. 53; c. 39, sch. 13.
s. 24, amended: 1994, c. 29, s. 63; repealed in pt.: *ibid.*, s. 63, sch. 9.
s. 26, regs. 93/3031; 94/1953, 2095, 2231.
s. 26, amended: 1994, c. 29, ss. 52, 53; repealed in pt.: *ibid.*, ss. 47, 52, sch. 9.
ss. 26A–26C, added: *ibid.*, s. 54; amended: 1994, c. 39, sch. 13.
s. 27, regs. 94/2096.
s. 30, substituted: 1994, c. 29, s. 55.
s. 31, amended: *ibid.*, s. 63; repealed in pt.: *ibid.*, s. 63, sch. 9.
s. 32, amended: *ibid.*, s. 63; c. 39, sch. 13.
s. 32A, added: 1994, c. 29, s. 56; amended: 1994, c. 39, sch. 13.
s. 33, amended: 1994, c. 29, s. 57.
s. 34, amended: *ibid.*, s. 58.
s. 36, substituted: *ibid.*, s. 59; amended: 1994, c. 39, sch. 13.
s. 38, amended: 1994, c. 29, s. 63, sch. 9.
s. 38A, added: *ibid.*, s. 60.

1967—cont.

77. Police (Scotland) Act 1967—*cont.*
s. 39, amended: 1994, c. 33, sch. 10.
s. 40A, added: 1994, c. 29, s. 61.
s. 41, see *Gillespie* v. *Hamilton,* 1994 S.L.T. 761.
s. 41, amended: 1994, c. 33, sch. 10.
s. 42, repealed in pt.: 1994, c. 29, s. 63, sch. 9.
s. 47, amended: *ibid.*, s. 62.
s. 51, amended: *ibid.*, s. 63; c. 39, sch. 13; repealed in pt.: 1994, c. 29, s. 63, sch. 9.
sch. 2, amended: 1994, c. 39, sch. 13; repealed in pt.: 1994, c. 29, s. 63, sch. 9.
sch. 3, substituted: *ibid.*, s. 55, sch. 6.
sch. 4, repealed in pt.: *ibid.*, sch. 9.

78. Water (Scotland) Act 1967.
repealed: 1994, c. 39, sch. 14.

80. Criminal Justice Act 1967.
s. 7, repealed: 1994, c. 33, sch. 11.
s. 9, amended: *ibid.*, schs. 4, 9.
s. 10, see *R.* v. *Tredwen, The Times,* January 3, 1994, C.A.
s. 11, see *R.* v. *Johnson (Aldin), The Times,* March 22, 1994, C.A.
s. 11, amended: 1994, c. 33, schs. 4, 9, paras. 6, 7.
s. 17, see *R.* v. *Central Criminal Court, ex p. Spens* [1993] C.O.D. 194, D.C.
s. 22, amended: 1994, c. 33, sch. 10.
s. 36, repealed in pt.: *ibid.*, sch. 11.
s. 56, see *R.* v. *Keogh* [1993] Crim.L.R. 895, C.A.
s. 61, see *R.* v. *Secretary of State for the Home Department, ex p. Stroud* [1993] C.O.D. 75, Henry J.
s. 67, amended: 1994, c. 33, sch. 10; repealed in pt.: *ibid.*, sch. 11.
sch. 3, repealed in pt.: 1994, c. 26, sch. 4.

83. Sea Fisheries (Shellfish) Act 1967.
s. 1, orders 94/1946(S.), 2230, 2329.
ss. 3, 5, amended: 1994, c. 33, sch. 8.
s. 7, amended: *ibid.*; repealed in pt.: 1994, c. 32, s. 2.
s. 10, amended: 1994, c. 19, sch. 2.
ss. 14, 16, 17, amended: 1994, c. 33, sch. 8.

84. Sea Fish (Conservation) Act 1967.
ss. 4, 11, see *Wither* v. *Cowie,* 1994 S.L.T. 363, ECJ.
s. 4B, regs. 94/2813.
ss. 5, 15, orders 93/2465, 3063, 3192, 3195; 94/2169.
s. 20, order 93/2465.
s. 22, orders 93/3063, 3192, 3193; 94/2169; regs. 94/2813.

86. Countryside (Scotland) Act 1967.
ss. 46, 48A, amended: 1994, c. 39, sch. 13.
s. 49, repealed in pt.: *ibid.*, schs. 13, 14.
ss. 50, 54, amended: *ibid.*, sch. 13.
s. 61, repealed in pt.: *ibid.*, sch. 14.
s. 63, amended: *ibid.*, sch. 13; repealed in pt.: *ibid.*, schs. 13, 14.

1967—cont.

86. Countryside (Scotland) Act 1967—*cont.*
s. 65, repealed in pt.: *ibid.*
s. 78, amended: *ibid.*, sch. 13.

88. Leasehold Reform Act 1967.
s. 10, amended: 1994, c. 36, sch. 1; repealed in pt.: *ibid.*, schs. 1, 2.
s. 15, amended: *ibid.*, sch. 1.
s. 19, see *Estates Governors of Alleyn's College* v. *Williams, The Times*, January 21, 1994, Sir Donald Nicholls V.-C.
s. 28, amended: 1994, c. 19, sch. 8; c. 29, sch. 4.
sch. 1, amended: 1994, c. 36, sch. 1.
sch. 4A, amended: 1994, c. 19, sch. 8.

91. Coal Industry Act 1967.
ss. 4, 7, 8, repealed: 1994, c. 21, sch. 11, Pt. III.

1968

2. Provisional Collection of Taxes Act 1968.
s. 1, amended: 1994, c. 9, sch. 7; repealed in pt.: 1993, c. 34, sch. 23.
s. 5, repealed in pt.: *ibid.*

3. Capital Allowances Act 1968.
sch. 7, amended: 1994, c. 9, s. 119.

7. London Cab Act 1968.
s. 1, order 94/1087.

13. National Loans Act 1968.
sch. 1, repealed in pt. (prosp.): 1994, c. 21, sch. 11, Pt. III.
sch. 4, repealed in pt.: 1994, c. 29, sch. 9.
sch. 5, repealed in pt. (prosp.): 1994, c. 21, sch. 11, Pt. IV.

14. Public Expenditure and Receipts Act 1968.
s. 5. sch. 3, orders 93/3116, 3151; 94/201(S.).

16. New Towns (Scotland) Act 1968.
s. 1A, amended: 1994, c. 39, sch. 13.
s. 34, repealed in pt.: *ibid.*, sch. 14.
s. 35, amended: *ibid.*, sch. 13.
s. 36, orders 93/3060–3062; 94/200.
ss. 36, 47, sch. 1, amended: 1994, c. 39, sch. 13.

18. Consular Relations Act 1968.
s. 1, amended: 1994, c. 23, sch. 14.

19. Criminal Appeal Act 1968.
see *R.* v. *L. (Corroboration Direction), The Times,* March 16, 1994, C.A.; *R.* v. *Oransaye* [1993] Crim.L.R. 772, C.A.
s. 1, amended: 1994, c. 33, sch. 4.
ss. 1, 9, 35, see *R.* v. *Kearley (No. 2)* [1994] 3 W.L.R. 413, H.L.
s. 2, see *R.* v. *Guthrie, The Times,* February 23, 1994, C.A.; *R.* v. *Daghir; R.* v. *Speckman, The Times,* May 27, 1994, C.A.
ss. 8, 11, amended: 1994, c. 33, sch. 10.
ss. 11, 23, see *R.* v. *Guppy, The Times,* March 8, 1994, C.A.

1968—cont.

19. Criminal Appeal Act 1968—*cont.*
ss. 16, 19, amended: 1994, c. 33, sch. 10.
ss. 19, 51, see *R.* v. *Ofori; R.* v. *Tackie, The Times,* November 17, 1993, C.A.
s. 35, see *R.* v. *Mandair* [1994] 2 W.L.R. 700, H.L.
s. 36, amended: 1994, c. 33, sch. 10.
s. 50, see *Att.-Gen.'s Reference (No. 22 of 1992)* (1993) 97 Cr.App.R. 275, C.A.
s. 50, amended: 1994, c. 37, sch. 1.
sch. 2, repealed in pt.: 1994, c. 33, sch. 11.

27. Firearms Act 1968.
s. 16A, added: 1994, c. 31, s. 1.
s. 19, see *R.* v. *Jones (Terence Michael), The Times,* August 19, 1994, C.A.
s. 20, amended: 1994, c. 31, s. 2.
s. 21, see *Davis* v. *Buchanan*, 1994 S.C.C.R. 369.
s. 21, amended: 1994, c. 33, sch. 10.
s. 26, order 94/2614.
ss. 32, 35, amended: orders 94/2615, 2652(S.).
s. 43, orders 94/2615, 2652(S.).
s. 46, amended: 1994, c. 31, s. 2.
s. 52, amended: 1994, c. 33, sch. 10.
s. 54, amended: 1994, c. 29, s. 42.
s. 57, see *Boyd* v. *McGlennan*, 1994 S.L.T. 1148.
sch. 1, amended: 1994, c. 27, sch. 9.
sch. 6, amended: *ibid.*, schs. 4, 8; c. 31, ss. 1, 2.

29. Trade Descriptions Act 1968.
see *Airtours* v. *Shipley* (1994) 158 J.P.N. 319, D.C.; *Gale* v. *Dixon Stores Group* (1994) 158 J.P.N. 256, D.C.
ss. 1, 2, see *Bury Metropolitan Borough Council* v. *Real* [1993] C.O.D. 375, D.C.
ss. 2, 34, see *R.* v. *Veys* [1993] F.S.R. 366, C.A.
s. 34, amended and repealed in pt.: 1994, c. 26, sch. 4.

34. Agriculture (Miscellaneous Provisions) Act 1968.
s. 2, regs. 94/2126.

46. Health Services and Public Health Act 1968.
s. 45, amended: 1994, c. 19, sch. 10.
s. 63, amended(S.): 1994, c. 39, sch. 13.
s. 64, amended: 1994, c. 19, sch. 10.
s. 65, amended: *ibid.*; c. 39, sch. 13(S.).
s. 71, repealed in pt.(S): 1994, c. 39, sch. 14.

47. Sewerage (Scotland) Act 1968.
s. 1, amended: 1994, c. 39, sch. 13; modified (temp.): order 94/2850.
ss. 2, 3, amended: 1994, c. 39, sch. 13.
s. 3A, added: *ibid.*, s. 101; modified (temp.): order 94/2850.
ss. 4, 6, 7, amended: 1994, c. 39, sch. 13.
s. 10, substituted: *ibid.*, s. 102.

1968—cont.

47. Sewerage (Scotland) Act 1968—*cont.*
ss. 11–16, amended: *ibid.*, sch. 13.
s. 16A, added: *ibid.*; modified (temp.): order 94/2850.
s. 17, amended: 1994, c. 39, sch. 13.
s. 18, repealed: *ibid.*, schs. 13, 14.
s. 20, amended: *ibid.*, sch. 13; modified (temp.): order 94/2850.
s. 21, amended: 1994, c. 39, sch. 13.
ss. 22, 23, amended: *ibid.*; modified (temp.): order 94/2850.
ss. 24–37, amended: 1994, c. 39, sch. 13.
ss. 37A, 37B, added: *ibid.*, s. 103.
ss. 38, 39, amended: *ibid.*, sch. 13.
s. 40, repealed: *ibid.*, schs. 13, 14.
ss. 41, 42, 44, 45, amended: *ibid.*, sch. 13.
s. 47, repealed (with savings): *ibid.*, s. 179, sch. 14.
s. 48, amended: *ibid.*, sch. 13; modified (temp.): order 94/2850.
s. 50, amended: 1994, c. 39, s. 104.
s. 51, amended: *ibid.*, sch. 13.
s. 52, repealed: *ibid.*, schs. 13, 14.
s. 53, amended: *ibid.*, sch. 13.
s. 59, amended: *ibid.*; repealed in pt.: *ibid.*, schs. 13, 14.

48. International Organisations Act 1968.
s. 2, repealed in pt.: 1994, c. 22, sch. 5.
s. 10, order 94/1890.
sch. 1, amended: 1994, c. 23, sch. 14.

49. Social Work (Scotland) Act 1968.
s. 1, amended: 1994, c. 39, sch. 13.
s. 2, repealed: *ibid.*, sch. 14.
s. 3, substituted: *ibid.*, s. 45.
s. 5, amended: *ibid.*, sch. 13.
s. 5A, amended: *ibid.*, sch. 13; repealed in pt.: *ibid.*, schs. 13, 14.
ss. 5B, 6A, 10, 20A, 27, 33, amended: *ibid.*, sch. 13.
s. 34, repealed in pt.: *ibid.*, schs. 13, 14.
s. 36, amended: *ibid.*, sch. 13; repealed in pt.: *ibid.*, s. 127, schs. 13, 14.
s. 36A, amended: *ibid.*, sch. 13.
s. 38, amended: *ibid.*, s. 139, sch. 13.
s. 39, amended: *ibid.*, s. 139.
ss. 44, 47, 50, 54, amended: *ibid.*, sch. 13.
s. 58, see *McArdle* v. *Orr,* High Court of Justiciary, January 19, 1993.
ss. 58A, 58B, 58E, 73, 75, amended: 1994, c. 39, sch. 13.
s. 76, sch. 3, amended: *ibid.*; repealed in pt.: *ibid.*, schs. 13, 14.

50. Hearing Aid Council Act 1968.
s. 7, order 93/3052; amended: *ibid.*

52. Caravan Sites Act 1968.
Pt. II (ss. 6–12), repealed: 1994, c. 33, s. 80, sch. 11.
s. 12, orders 93/2644, 2980, 3032; 94/1189.

1968—cont.

52. Caravan Sites Act 1968—*cont.*
s. 16, see *R.* v. *South Hams District Council, ex p. Gibb; R.* v. *Gloucestershire County Council, ex p. Davies; R.* v. *Dorset County Council, ex p. Rolls, The Times,* June 8, 1994, C.A.
s. 16, repealed in pt.: 1994, c. 33, s. 80, sch. 11.

54. Theatres Act 1968.
s. 18, amended: 1994, c. 19, sch. 16; repealed in pt.: *ibid.*, schs. 16, 18.
s. 18, amended(S.): 1994, c. 39, sch. 13.

60. Theft Act 1968.
s. 1, see *Deutsche Genossenschaftsbank* v. *Burnhope* [1993] 2 Lloyd's Rep. 518, Hobhouse J.
s. 5, see *R.* v. *McHugh (Christopher John Patrick)* (1993) 97 Cr.App.R. 335, C.A.; *R.* v. *Clowes (No. 2)* [1994] 2 All E.R. 316, C.A.
s. 6, see *R.* v. *Cahill* [1993] Crim.L.R. 141, C.A.
s. 9, amended: 1994, c. 33, sch. 10.
s. 10, see *R.* v. *Kelly (Ronnie Peter)* (1993) 97 Cr.App.R. 245, C.A.
s. 12, see *D.P.P.* v. *Spriggs* [1994] RTR 1, D.C.
s. 12A, see *Dawes* v. *D.P.P.* [1994] RTR 209, D.C.; *R.* v. *Button, The Times,* October 21, 1994, C.A.
s. 15, see *R.* v. *Parker, The Times,* March 11, 1994, C.A.
s. 27, see *R.* v. *Duffus* (1994) 158 J.P. 224, C.A.
s. 28, amended: 1994, c. 33, sch. 4.

65. Gaming Act 1968.
s. 13, regs. 94/2899.
s. 14, regs. 94/958, 1042(S.).
s. 15, regs. 94/2899.
s. 20, orders 94/956, 1043(S.).
s. 20, amended: orders 94/956, 1043(S.).
s. 21, orders 94/957, 1043(S.).
s. 21, amended: orders 94/957, 1043(S.).
s. 44, amended(S.): 1994, c. 39, sch. 13.
s. 51, regs. 94/1042(S.), 2899; orders 94/956, 957, 958, 1043(S.).
s. 52, amended: 1994, c. 21, sch. 9.
sch. 2, repealed in pt.: 1994, c. 29, sch. 9.
schs. 2, 9, amended(S.): 1994, c. 39, sch. 13.

67. Medicines Act 1968.
s. 4, order 94/102.
ss. 7, 8, amended and repealed in pt.: regs. 94/101, 276.
s. 18, regs. 94/2157.
ss. 24, 28, amended: regs. 94/101, 276.
s. 40, regs. 94/1531.
s. 47, regs. 94/103.
s. 49, order 94/787.
s. 51, order 94/2410.
s. 53, regs. 94/2411.
s. 57, orders 94/599, 2409.
s. 58, orders 93/1890, 3256; 94/558.

1968—cont.

67. Medicines Act 1968—*cont.*
ss. 61, 66, regs. 94/1932.
ss. 75, 76, regs. 93/2902.
ss. 85, 86, regs. 94/104, 1932.
s. 86, amended: regs. 94/101, 276.
s. 87, regs. 94/1402.
s. 91, regs. 94/104, 1402, 1932.
s. 91, amended: regs. 94/101, 276.
s. 95, regs. 94/1932.
s. 108, amended: 1994, c. 19, sch. 16.
s. 109, amended(S.): 1994, c. 39, sch. 13.
s. 129, regs. 93/2398, 2399, 2538, 2539, 2902; 94/103, 1402, 1531, 1932, 2157, 2411; orders 93/1890, 3256; 94/558, 559, 787, 2409, 2410.
s. 132, regs. 93/2538.
s. 132, amended: regs. 94/101, 276.

71. Race Relations Act 1968.
s. 68, see *Ironside Ray & Vials, Re; Ironside Ray & Vials* v. *Lindsay, The Times*, January 28, 1994, E.A.T.

73. Transport Act 1968.
s. 9, amended(S.): 1994, c. 39, sch. 13.
s. 9A, repealed in pt.(S.): *ibid.*, schs. 13, 14.
ss. 9B, 10, amended(S.): *ibid.*, s. 13.
s. 13, substituted(S.): *ibid.*, s. 41.
s. 13A, added(S.): *ibid.*, s. 163.
s. 34, amended(S.): *ibid.*, sch. 13.
s. 56, amended(S.): *ibid.*; repealed in pt.(S.): *ibid.*, schs. 13, 14.
s. 61, amended: 1994, c. 40, s. 42.
s. 61A, added: *ibid.*
s. 62, amended: *ibid.*, sch. 13; repealed in pt.: *ibid.*, schs. 13, 17.
s. 63, amended: *ibid.*, s. 43, sch. 13; repealed in pt.: *ibid.*, schs. 13, 17.
s. 63, amended(S.): 1994, c. 39, sch. 13.
s. 64, substituted as ss. 64, 64A: 1994, c. 40, s. 44.
s. 64B, added: *ibid.*, s. 45.
s. 66, amended: *ibid.*, sch. 13.
s. 67, substituted as ss. 67, 67A: *ibid.*, s. 46.
s. 68, substituted as ss. 68, 68A; *ibid.*, s. 47.
s. 69, amended: *ibid.*, s. 48, sch. 13; repealed in pt.: *ibid.*, schs. 13, 17.
s. 69A, amended: *ibid.*, sch. 13.
s. 69B, amended: *ibid.*, s. 44, sch. 13; repealed in pt.: *ibid.*, schs. 13, 17.
s. 69C, amended: *ibid.*, sch. 13.
s. 69D, substituted: *ibid.*, s. 47.
s. 69E, substituted: *ibid.*, s. 49.
ss. 69EA–69ED, added: *ibid.*, s. 50.
s. 69F, repealed: *ibid.*, schs. 13, 17.
s. 69G, substituted as ss. 69G, 69H: *ibid.*, sch. 13.
s. 69I, added: *ibid.*, s. 51.
s. 69J, added: *ibid.*, s. 52.
s. 70, substituted: *ibid.*, s. 53.
ss. 82, 84, 85, amended: *ibid.*, sch. 13.

1968—cont.

73. Transport Act 1968—*cont.*
s. 85A, added: *ibid.*, s. 54.
s. 86, substituted: *ibid.*, s. 55.
s. 87, repealed in pt.: *ibid.*, schs. 13, 17.
s. 89, substituted: *ibid.*, s. 56.
ss. 89, 91, regs. 94/1209.
ss. 91, 92, amended: 1994, c. 40, sch. 13; repealed in pt.: *ibid.*, schs. 13, 17.
ss. 93, 94 (in pt.): repealed: *ibid.*, sch. 17.
ss. 96, 97A, see *R.* v. *Abergavenny Justices, ex p. Barratt* [1994] RTR 98, D.C.
s. 97, see *Bailey* v. *Department of Transport* [1993] C.O.D. 371, D.C.
s. 97, amended: regs. 94/1838.
s. 115, amended(S.): 1994, c. 39, sch. 13.
s. 121, order 94/1803.
ss. 123, 124, amended(S.): 1994, c. 39, sch. 13.
s. 125, amended: order 94/857.
s. 159, amended: 1994, c. 19, sch. 7.
sch. 5, amended(S.): 1994, c. 39, sch. 13.
sch. 8A, added: 1994, c. 40, s. 50, sch. 12.

1969

2. Local Government Grants (Social Need) Act 1969.
s. 1, amended: 1994, c. 29, sch. 4.

10. Mines and Quarries (Tips) Act 1969.
s. 11, amended: 1994, c. 19, sch. 16; repealed in pt.: *ibid.*, schs. 16, 18.
s. 11, amended(S.): 1994, c. 39, sch. 13.

22. Redundant Churches and other Religious Buildings Act 1969.
s. 1, order 94/962.

46. Family Law Reform Act 1969.
s. 8, see *E. (A Minor) (Wardship: Medical Treatment), Re* [1993] 1 FLR 386, Ward J.
s. 23, see *W.* v. *G. (Paternity), Re; A. (A Minor), Re, The Times*, May 18, 1994, C.A.

48. Post Office Act 1969.
s. 7, amended: 1994, c. 29, sch. 4.
s. 86, amended: 1994, c. 19, sch. 16; repealed in pt.: *ibid.*, schs. 16, 18.
s. 86, amended(S.): 1994, c. 39, sch. 13.
sch. 4, repealed in pt.: 1994, c. 20, sch. 5; c. 40, sch. 17.

51. Development of Tourism Act 1969.
s. 14, repealed in pt.: 1994, c. 29, sch. 9.

53. Late Night Refreshment Houses Act 1969.
s. 2, amended: 1994, c. 19, sch. 16.

54. Children and Young Persons Act 1969.
see *X. (Minors)* v. *Bedfordshire County Council, The Times*, November 24, 1993, Turner J.
s. 10, repealed in pt.: 1994, c. 33, sch. 11.
s. 23, see *North Yorkshire County Council* v. *Selby Youth Court Justices* [1994] 1 All E.R. 991, D.C.

1969—cont.

54. Children and Young Persons Act 1969—cont.

s. 23, amended: 1994, c. 33, ss. 19, 20, sch. 4.

s. 23A, added: *ibid.*, s. 23.

s. 34, amended: *ibid.*, sch. 9.

s. 57, repealed in pt.: *ibid.*, sch. 11.

s. 70, amended: 1994, c. 19, sch. 10.

57. Employers' Liability (Compulsory Insurance) Act 1969.

see *Richardson* v. *Pitt-Stanley, The Times,* August 11, 1994, C.A.

s. 3, amended: 1994, c. 19, sch. 16; c. 39, sch. 13(S.).

ss. 3, 6, regs. 94/520.

63. Police Act 1969.

s. 1, repealed: 1994, c. 33, sch. 11.

s. 2, repealed: 1994, c. 29, sch. 9.

ss. 3, 6, 7, repealed: 1994, c. 33, sch. 11.

1970

6. Rural Water Supplies and Sewerage (Scotland) Act 1970.

repealed: 1994, c. 39, sch. 14.

9. Taxes Management Act 1970.

ss. 1, 33, see *Franklin* v. *British Railways Board* [1993] IRLR 441, C.A.

s. 7, substituted (prosp.): 1994, c. 9, sch. 19.

s. 8, see *Alexander* v. *Wallington General Commissioners and I.R.C.* [1993] STC 588, C.A.

ss. 8, 8A, amended (prosp.): 1994, c. 9, s. 178.

s. 9, substituted (prosp.): *ibid.*, s. 179.

s. 9A, added (prosp.): *ibid.*, s. 180.

s. 10, see *Joint (Inspector of Taxes)* v. *Bracken Developments* [1994] STC 300, Vinelott J.

s. 11, amended (prosp.): 1994, c. 9, s. 181; repealed in pt. (prosp.): *ibid.*, sch. 26.

s. 11A, repealed (prosp.): *ibid.*

s. 11AA, added (prosp.): *ibid.*, s. 182.

s. 11AB, added (prosp.): *ibid.*, s. 183.

s. 12, repealed in pt. (prosp.): *ibid.*, sch. 26.

s. 12AA, added (prosp.): *ibid.*, s. 184.

s. 12AB, added (prosp.): *ibid.*, s. 185.

s. 12AC, added (prosp.): *ibid.*, s. 186.

s. 12A, amended (prosp.): *ibid.*, sch. 19.

s. 12B, added (prosp.): *ibid.*

s. 19A, added (prosp.): *ibid.*, s. 187.

s. 20, amended: *ibid.*, s. 255.

s. 28A, added (prosp.): *ibid.*, s. 188.

s. 28B, added (prosp.): *ibid.*, s. 189.

s. 28C, added (prosp.): *ibid.*, s. 190.

s. 29, substituted (prosp.): *ibid.*, s. 191.

s. 30, amended (prosp.): *ibid.*, sch. 19.

ss. 30A, 30B, added (prosp.): *ibid.*

s. 31, amended (prosp.): *ibid.*

1970—cont.

9. Taxes Management Act 1970—cont.

s. 33, amended: 1994, c. 9, sch. 19 (prosp.); regs. 94/1813; repealed in pt.: (prosp.): 1994, c. 9, sch. 26.

s. 33A, added (prosp.): *ibid.*, sch. 19.

s. 34, amended: 1994, c. 9, sch. 19 (prosp.); regs. 94/1813.

ss. 36, 40, amended (prosp.): 1994, c. 9, sch. 19.

s. 42, substituted (prosp.): *ibid.*

ss. 43, 43A, amended (prosp.): *ibid.*

s. 44, amended: regs. 94/1813.

s. 45, amended and repealed in pt.: *ibid.*

s. 46, amended: 1994, c. 9, sch. 19 (prosp.); regs. 94/1813.

s. 46A, regs. 94/1811–1813.

s. 50, amended (prosp.): 1994, c. 9, sch. 19; repealed in pt.: regs. 94/1813.

ss. 51, 52, repealed: *ibid.*

s. 53, see *Wilson* v. *Leek General Commissioners and I.R.C.* [1994] STC 147, Knox J.

s. 53, substituted: regs. 94/1813.

ss. 54, 55, see *R.* v. *I.R.C., ex p. Barker* [1994] STC 731, Latham J.

s. 55, amended: 1994, c. 9, sch. 19 (prosp.); regs. 94/1813; repealed in pt.: regs. 94/1813.

s. 56, see *Zielinski* v. *Pickering (Inspector of Taxes)* [1993] STC 418, Vinelott J.; *Franklin* v. *Holmes (Inspector of Taxes)* [1993] STC 720, C.A.; *Sutherland* v. *Gustar (Inspector of Taxes)*; *sub nom. Sutherland & Partners' Appeal, re* [1994] STC 387, C.A.; *Whittles (Inspector of Taxes)* v. *Uniholdings* [1993] STC 671, Jonathan Parker J.; *Whittles (Inspector of Taxes)* v. *Uniholdings (No. 2)* [1993] STC 767, Vinelott J.; *Petch* v. *Gurney (Inspector of Taxes); Gurney (Inspector of Taxes)* v. *Petch* [1994] STC 689, C.A.; *Kudehinbu* v. *Cutts (Inspector of Taxes)* [1994] STC 560, Vinelott J.

s. 56, amended and repealed in pt.: regs. 94/1813.

s. 56A, substituted: *ibid.*

s. 56B, regs. 94/1811–1813.

s. 56B, amended: 1994, c. 9, s. 254.

ss. 56C, 56D, regs. 94/1811.

s. 58, amended and repealed in pt.: regs. 94/1813.

s. 59A, added (prosp.): 1994, c. 9, s. 192.

s. 59B, added (prosp.): *ibid.*, s. 193.

s. 59C, added (prosp.): *ibid.*, s. 194.

s. 59D, added (prosp.): *ibid.*, s. 195.

s. 61, regs. 94/236.

ss. 65, 69, amended (prosp.): 1994, c. 9, sch. 19.

s. 70, amended (prosp.): *ibid.*, repealed in pt. (prosp.): *ibid.*

s. 70A, added (prosp.): *ibid.*

1970—cont.

9. Taxes Management Act 1970—*cont.*

s. 86, see *R. v. I.R.C., ex p. Barker* [1994]STC 731, Latham J.

s. 86, substituted (prosp.): 1994, c. 9, sch. 19.

s. 87A, amended (prosp.): *ibid.*

s. 88, see *Joint (Inspector of Taxes) v. Bracken Developments* [1994] STC 300, Vinelott J.

s. 93, see *Alexander v. Wallington General Commissioners and I.R.C.* [1993] STC 588, C.A.

s. 93, substituted (prosp.): 1994, c. 9, sch. 19.

s. 93A, added (prosp.): *ibid.*

s. 95, amended (prosp.): *ibid., repealed* in pt. (prosp.): *ibid.,* schs. 19, 26.

s. 95A, added (prosp.): *ibid.,* sch. 19.

s. 97AA, added (prosp.): *ibid.*

s. 98, see *Wilson v. Leek General Commissioners and I.R.C.* [1994] STC 147, Knox J.

s. 98, reg. 94/1813.

s. 98, amended: *ibid.,* ss. 97, 105, sch. 16; repealed in pt.: *ibid.,* sch. 26; regs. 94/1813.

s. 98B, amended: 1994, c. 9, sch. 19.

s. 100, repealed in pt.: regs. 94/1813.

s. 100B, amended: 1994, c. 9, sch. 19; regs. 94/1813.

s. 103, amended: 1994, c. 9, sch. 19.

s. 103A, added (prosp.): *ibid.*

s. 115, amended: regs. 94/1813.

s. 118, amended: 1994, c. 9, sch. 19 (prosp.); regs. 94/1813; repealed in pt.: 1994, c. 9, schs. 19, 26.

sch. 1A, added (prosp.): *ibid.,* sch. 19.

sch. 2, amended (prosp.): *ibid.*

sch. 4, repealed in pt.: *ibid.,* sch. 26.

10. Income and Corporation Taxes Act 1970.

s. 181, see *Hall (Inspector of Taxes) v. Lorimer, The Times,* November 18, 1993, C.A.

s. 189, see *Fitzpatrick v. I.R.C.* (H.L.), 1994 S.L.T. 836; *Fitzpatrick v. I.R.C. (No. 2); Smith (Inspector of Taxes) v. Abbott* [1994] 1 W.L.R. 306, H.L.

s. 273, see *NAP Holdings U.K. v. Whittles (Inspector of Taxes)* [1993] STC 592, C.A.

sch. 15, repealed in pt.: 1994, c. 9, sch. 26.

24. Finance Act 1970.

s. 21, see *Kelsall (Inspector of Taxes) v. Investment Chartwork* [1994] STC 33, Arden J.

s. 27, see *NAP Holdings U.K. v. Whittles (Inspector of Taxes)* [1993] STC 592, C.A.

27. Fishing Vessels (Safety Provisions) Act 1970.

s. 6, regs. 94/502.

1970—cont.

31. Administration of Justice Act 1970.

s. 11, sch. 8, see *M. v. M. (Enforcement: Judgment Summons* [1993] Fam. Law 469, H.H.J. Kennedy, Q.C.

s. 36, see *Cheltenham and Gloucester Building Society v. Grant, The Times,* May 9, 1994, C.A.; *Cheltenham and Gloucester Building Society v. Ofi,* June 23, 1994.

sch. 8, see *Symmons v. Symmons* [1993] 1 FLR 317, H.H.J. Hunter sitting as a deputy High Court Judge.

sch. 2, repealed in pt.: 1994, c. 36, sch. 2.

34. Marriage (Registrar General's Licence) Act 1970.

s. 1, amended: 1994, c. 34, sch.

35. Conveyancing and Feudal Reform (Scotland) Act 1970.

s. 1, see *Mackay v. Lord Burton,* 1994 S.L.T. (Lands Tr.) 35.

ss. 14, 16, 53, sch. 4, see *Sanderson's Trs. v. Ambion Scotland* (O.H.), 1994 S.L.T. 645.

s. 20, sch. 3, see *Clydesdale Bank v. Davidson* (Sh.Ct.), 1993 S.C.L.R. 984.

s. 24, see *Halifax Building Society v. Gupta,* 1994 S.L.T. 339.

s. 25, see *Gordaviran v. Clydesdale Bank* (Sh.Ct.), 1994 S.C.L.R. 248.

36. Merchant Shipping Act 1970.

s. 9, regs. 94/791.

s. 84, regs. 94/502.

s. 85, rules 94/1104.

39. Local Authorities (Goods and Services) Act 1970.

s. 1, orders 94/37, 1389.

s. 1, amended: 1994, c. 19, s. 25; c. 29, sch. 4; c. 39, sch. 13(S.).

40. Agriculture Act 1970.

ss. 28, 29, schemes 93/2901; 94/1302.

s. 38, amended: 1994, c. 19, sch. 16; repealed in pt.: *ibid.,* schs. 16, 18.

ss. 48, 60, 62, amended: *ibid.,* sch. 16.

s. 66, regs. 94/129, 1610; S.Rs. 1994 Nos. 123, 166, 309.

s. 67, amended: 1994, c. 19, sch. 16; repealed in pt.: *ibid.,* schs. 16, 18.

s. 67, amended(S.): 1994, c. 39, sch. 13.

ss. 68–70, 73, 74, S.R. 1994 No. 123.

s. 74A, regs. 94/129; S.Rs. 1994 Nos. 123, 166.

ss. 75, 76, S.R. 1994 No. 166.

ss. 77, 78, S.Rs. 1994 Nos. 166, 309.

s. 79, regs. 94/129, 1610; S.R. 1994 No. 166, 309.

s. 84, regs. 94/129, 499, 1610; S.Rs. 1994 Nos. 123, 166, 309.

s. 86, S.Rs. 1994 Nos. 123, 166, 309.

ss. 92, 94, amended(S.): 1994, c. 39, sch. 13.

CAP.
1970—cont.

41. Equal Pay Act 1970.
see *British Coal Corp.* v. *Smith; North Yorkshire County Council* v. *Ratcliffe, The Times,* May 11, 1994, C.A.
s. 1, see *Yorkshire Blood Transfusion Service* v. *Plaskitt* [1994] I.C.R. 74, E.A.T.

42. Local Authority Social Services Act 1970.
see *X. (Minors)* v. *Bedfordshire County Council, The Times,* November 24, 1993, Turner J.
s. 1, amended: 1994, c. 19, sch. 10.

44. Chronically Sick and Disabled Persons Act 1970.
s. 14, repealed in pt. (in prosp.): 1994, c. 21, sch. 11, Pt. III.
s. 21, amended: 1994, c. 19, sch. 10; repealed in pt.: *ibid.,* schs. 10, 18.
s. 21, amended(S.): 1994, c. 39, sch. 13.

1971

3. Guardianship of Minors Act 1971.
see *B. (Procedure: Family Proceedings Court), Re* [1993] Fam. Law 209, C.A.

10. Vehicles (Excise) Act 1971.
repealed: 1994, c. 22, sch. 5.
s. 16, regs. 94/1911.
ss. 19, 34, see *Naylor* v. *Hutson* [1994] F.S.R. 63, Maddocks J.
s. 23, regs. 94/1364.
s. 26, see *R.* v. *Johnson (Tony), The Times,* February 24, 1994, C.A.
s. 37, regs. 94/1911.

16. Coal Industry Act 1971.
s. 4, repealed (prosp.): 1994, c. 21, sch. 11, Pt. III.
s. 6, repealed (prosp.): *ibid.,* sch. 11, Pt. II.
s. 7, repealed (prosp.): *ibid.,* sch. 11, Pts. II, IV.
s. 8, repealed (prosp.): *ibid.,* sch. 11, Pt. IV.
ss. 9, 10, repealed (prosp.): *ibid.,* sch. 11, Pt. III.

23. Courts Act 1971.
s. 27, substituted: 1994, c. 40, sch. 16.
s. 53, repealed in pt.: 1994, c. 29, sch. 9.

29. National Savings Bank Act 1971.
s. 2, regs. 93/3130.

38. Misuse of Drugs Act 1971.
s. 4, see *R.* v. *Gill (Simon Imran)* (1993) 97 Cr.App.R. 215, C.A.
s. 5, see *McCrindle* v. *Walkingshaw,* 1994 S.C.C.R. 299.
s. 20, see *R.* v. *Lillie, The Times,* November 3, 1994, C.A.
s. 21, amended: 1994, c. 37, sch. 1.
s. 23, see *Annan* v. *McIntosh,* 1993 S.C.C.R. 938.
ss. 23, 27, amended: 1994, c. 37, sch. 1.

CAP.
1971—cont.

38. Misuse of Drugs Act 1971—cont.
s. 28, see *R.* v. *Rautamaki* [1993] Crim.L.R. 691, C.A.
ss. 30, 31, 37, regs. 94/535.
sch. 4, amended: 1994, c. 33, sch. 8.

40. Fire Precautions Act 1971.
ss. 12, 37, 40, regs. 94/2184.
s. 43, amended: 1994, c. 19, sch. 9; repealed in pt.: *ibid.,* schs. 9, 18.
s. 43, amended(S.): 1994, c. 39, sch. 13.

48. Criminal Damage Act 1971.
s. 1, see *Att.-Gen.'s Reference (No. 3 of 1992)* [1994] RTR 122, C.A.; *R.* v. *Parker* [1993] Crim.L.R. 856, C.A.
s. 2, see *R.* v. *Orgles (Kevin); R.* v. *Orgles (Julie)* [1993] 4 All E.R. 533, C.A.

49. Rural Water Supplies and Sewerage Act 1971.
repealed(S.): 1994, c. 39, sch. 14.

56. Pensions (Increase) Act 1971.
s. 13, regs. 93/3235(S.).
sch. 2, amended: 1994, c. 19, sch. 13; c. 29, schs. 5, 8.
sch. 3, repealed in pt.: 1994, c. 29, sch. 9.
sch. 6, regs. 93/3235(S.).
sch. 6, amended: 1994, c. 29, sch. 8.

58. Sheriff Courts (Scotland) Act 1971.
s. 32, Acts of Sederunt 93/3128, 3240; 94/2354.
s. 35, see *Rutherford* v. *Virtue* (Sh.Ct.), 1993 S.C.L.R. 886.
s. 36B, see *Hamilton* v. *Sullivan* (Sh.Ct.), 1993 S.C.L.R. 969; *Fenton* v. *Uniroyal Englebert Tyres* (Sh.Ct.), 1994 S.C.L.R. 127; *Milne* v. *Uniroyal Englebert Tyres* (Sh.Ct.), 1994 S.C.L.R. 532.
s. 38, see *Edinburgh District Council (City of)* v. *Robbin* (Sh.Ct.), 1994 S.C.L.R. 43.

59. Merchant Shipping (Oil Pollution) Act 1971.
amendments made by 1988, c. 12, sch. 4, restored: 1994, c. 28, s. 5.
s. 1, amended: *ibid.,* sch. 3, Pt. II.
s. 1A, added: *ibid.,* sch. 3, Pts. I, II.
ss. 1B, 1C, added: *ibid.,* sch. 3, Pt. I.
ss. 2, 3, amended: *ibid.,* sch. 3, Pt. II.
s. 9, amended: *ibid.,* sch. 3, Pts. I, II.
s. 12, amended: *ibid.,* s. 8.
s. 13, amended: *ibid.,* sch. 3, Pt. II.
s. 15, amended: *ibid.,* sch. 3, Pts. I, II; repealed in pt.: *ibid.,* schs. 3, Pt. II, 4.
s. 19, amended: *ibid.,* s. 5.
s. 20, amended: *ibid.,* sch. 3, Pts. I, II.

60. Prevention of Oil Pollution Act 1971.
s. 12, amended: 1994, c. 28, s. 8; repealed in pt.: *ibid.,* sch. 4.

64. Diplomatic and other Privileges Act 1971.
s. 1, amended: 1994, c. 23, sch. 14.

1971—cont.

68. Finance Act 1971.
ss. 44, 59, sch. 17, see *Melluish (Inspector of Taxes)* v. *BMI (No. 3), The Times,* August 17, 1994, C.A.

69. Medicines Act 1971.
s. 1, regs. 94/696, 1554.

77. Immigration Act 1971.
s. 1, see *R.* v. *Secretary of State for the Home Department, ex p. Miah (Nazmul)* [1994] Imm AR 279, Jowitt J.; *R.* v. *Secretary of State for the Home Department, ex p. Kwapong (Kwaku Boateng)* [1994] Imm AR 207, C.A.
s. 3, see *Marchon (Olavo)* v. *Immigration Appeal Tribunal, sub nom. R.* v. *Secretary of State for the Home Department, ex p. Marchon* [1993] Imm AR 384, C.A.; *Patel (Pushpaben Kiritbhai)* v. *Secretary of State for the Home Department, sub nom. R.* v. *Secretary of State for the Home Department, ex p. Patel (Pushpaben Kiritbhai)* [1993] Imm AR 392, C.A.; *R.* v. *Immigration Appeal Tribunal, ex p. Davis (Martin Sammy)* [1993] Imm AR 558, Jowitt J.; *R.* v. *Secretary of State for the Home Department, ex p. Figueiredo (Fernando de Milo)* [1993] Imm AR 606, Hutchison J.; *R.* v. *Secretary of State for the Home Department, ex p. Asumda (Patrick)* [1993] Imm AR 601, Sedley J.; *Hlomodor (Richard)* v. *Secretary of State for the Home Department* [1993] Imm AR 534, C.A.; *R.* v. *Secretary of State for the Home Department, ex p. Baskaran (John)* [1993] Imm AR 471, McCullough J.; *Akinde (Bolanle)* v. *Secretary of State for the Home Department* [1993] Imm AR 512, C.A.; *Samir (Rawda el Balah)* v. *Secretary of State for the Home Department* [1993] Imm AR 551, C.A.; *R.* v. *Secretary of State for the Home Department, ex p. Jahangeer (Shala), Rounag (Noorullamin Saeed Naderi) and Jahangeer (Mamora)* [1993] Imm AR 564, Jowitt J.; *Matondo (Fleur), Re; Finlay (Cecelia)* v. *Matondo (Kininga) and the Secretary of State for the Home Department* [1993] Imm AR 541, Bracewell J.; *R.* v. *Secretary of State for the Home Department, ex p. Okello (Paul)* [1993] Imm AR 531, Pill J.; *R.* v. *Secretary of State for the Home Department, ex p. Chahal (Karamjit Singh)* [1994] Imm AR 107, C.A.; *R.* v. *Secretary of State for the Home Department, ex p. Nijjar (Surrinder Singh)* [1994] Imm AR 50, Auld J.; *Nwafor (Michael), Re* [1994] Imm AR 91,

1971—cont.

77. Immigration Act 1971—*cont.*
Laws J.; *R.* v. *Secretary of State for the Home Department and Governor of H.M. Prison Hindley, ex p. Ali (Ifzal)* [1994] Imm AR 69, C.A.; *R.* v *Secretary of State for the Home Department, ex p. Iye (Jordan Abiodun)* [1994] Imm AR 63, C.A.; *R.* v. *Secretary of State for the Home Department, ex p. Chung (Tin Sang); Ku (Kurai Chi); Kuet (Shi Ping)* [1994] Imm AR 183, Laws J.; *R.* v. *Secretary of State for the Home Department, ex p. Butta (Mohammed)* [1994] Imm AR 197, Brooke J.; *R.* v. *Secretary of State for the Home Department, ex p. Kwapong (Kwaku Boateng)* [1994] Imm AR 207, C.A.; *R.* v. *Secretary of State for the Home Department, ex p. Oyeleye (Florence Jumoke)* [1994] Imm AR 268, Dyson J.
s. 3, amended: order 93/1813.
ss. 3, 4, see *R.* v. *Secretary of State for the Home Department, ex p. Butt (Awais Karni)* [1994] Imm AR 11, Pill J.; *R.* v. *Secretary of State for the Home Department, ex p. Okello (Paul) (No. 2)* [1994] Imm AR 261, Laws J.
ss. 3, 11, see *Akhtar (Raja Waheed)* v. *Governor of Pentonville Prison* [1993] Imm AR 424, C.A.
s. 4, see *R.* v. *Secretary of State for the Home Department, ex p. Coban (Mahmut)* [1994] Imm AR 53, Hutchison J.; *R.* v. *Secretary of State for the Home Department, ex p. Alzagha (Rashed Masoud)* [1994] Imm AR 20, C.A.
s. 4, amended and repealed in pt.: order 93/1813.
s. 6, see *Nwafor (Michael), Re* [1994] Imm AR 91, Laws J.
s. 7, see *R.* v. *Secretary of State for the Home Department, ex p. Butta (Mohammed)* [1994] Imm AR 197, Brooke J.
s. 8, amended: order 93/1813.
ss. 8, 16, 21, see *Matondo (Fleur), Re; Findlay (Cecelia)* v. *Matondo (Kininga) and the Secretary of State for the Home Department* [1993] Imm AR 541, Bracewell J.
s. 10, repealed in pt.: order 93/1813.
s. 11, amended and repealed in pt.: *ibid.*
s. 13, see *R.* v. *Secretary of State for the Home Department, ex p. Mostafa (Mohammed)* [1994] Imm AR 18, Pill J.; *R.* v. *Secretary of State for the Home Department, ex p. Alzagha (Rashed Masoud)* [1994] Imm AR 20, C.A.
s. 13, repealed in pt.: order 93/1813.

1971—cont.

77. Immigration Act 1971—cont.

ss. 13, 19, see *R.* v. *Secretary of State for the Home Department, ex p. Al-Zagha (Rashed Masoud)* [1993] Imm AR 555, Jowitt J.

s. 15, see *R.* v. *Secretary of State for the Home Department, ex p. Chahal (Karamjit Singh)* [1994] Imm AR 107, C.A.

ss. 16, 19, see *R.* v. *Secretary of State for the Home Department, ex p. Alzagha (Rashed Masoud)* [1994] Imm AR 20, C.A.

s. 24, see *R.* v. *Secretary of State for the Home Department and Governor of H.M. Prison Hindley, ex p. Ali (Ifzal)* [1994] Imm AR 69, C.A.

s. 24, amended: order 93/1813.

ss. 24, 25, 33, see *Rahman and Qadir* v. *D.P.P.* [1993] Crim.L.R. 874, D.C.

s. 25, amended and repealed in pt.: order 93/1813.

ss. 26, 33, see *Akinde (Bolanle)* v. *Secretary of State for the Home Department* [1993] Imm AR 512, C.A.; *Akhtar (Raja Waheed)* v. *Governor of Pentonville Prison* [1993] Imm AR 424, C.A.

s. 27, amended: orders 93/1813; 94/1405; repealed in pt.: order 93/1813.

s. 33, see *R.* v. *Secretary of State for the Home Department and Governor of H.M. Prison Hindley, ex p. Ali (Ifzal)* [1994] Imm AR 69, C.A.; *R.* v. *Secretary of State for the Home Department, ex p. Chung (Tin Sang); Ku (Kurai Chi); Kuet (Shi Ping)* [1994] Imm AR 183, Laws J.

s. 33, amended and repealed in pt.: orders 93/1813; 94/1405.

s. 34, repealed in pt.: S.L.R. 1993.

sch. 2, see *Singh, Petr.* (O.H.), 1988 S.C. 349; *R.* v. *Secretary of State for the Home Department, ex p. Yilmaz (Inan)* [1993] Imm AR 359, Auld J.; *Akhtar (Raja Waheed)* v. *Governor of Pentonville Prison* [1993] Imm AR 424, C.A.; *R.* v. *Secretary of State for the Home Department, ex p. Asumda (Patrick)* [1993] Imm AR 601, Sedley J.; *R.* v. *Secretary of State for the Home Department, ex p. Al-Zagha (Rashed Masoud)* [1993] Imm AR 555, Jowitt J.; *R.* v. *Secretary of State for the Home Department, ex p. Coban (Mahmut)* [1994] Imm AR 53, Hutchison J.; *R.* v. *Secretary of State for the Home Department, ex p. Iye (Jordan Abiodun)* [1994] Imm AR 63, C.A.; *R.* v. *Secretary of State for the Home Department, ex p. Butt (Awais Karni)* [1994] Imm AR 11, Pill J.; *R.* v. *Sec-*

1971—cont.

77. Immigration Act 1971—cont.

retary of State for the Home Department, ex p. Chung (Tin Sang); Ku (Kurai Chai); Kuet (Shi Ping) [1994] Imm AR 183, Laws J.; *R.* v. *Secretary of State for the Home Department, ex p. Zagha (Rashed Masoud)* [1994] Imm AR 20, C.A.; *R.* v. *Secretary of State for the Home Department, ex p. Akram (Mohammed)* [1994] Imm AR 8, Popplewell J.; *R.* v. *Secretary of State for the Home Department, ex p. Lawson (Vera)* [1994] Imm AR 58, Sedley J.; *R.* v. *Secretary of State for the Home Department, ex p. Nessa (Sayarun) and Akhtar (Shamina)* [1994] Imm AR 193, Schiemann J.

sch. 2, amended and repealed in pt.: orders 93/1813; 94/1405.

sch. 3, see *R.* v. *Ofori; R.* v. *Tackie, The Times*, November 17, 1993, C.A.; *Patel (Pushpaben Kiritbhai)* v. *Secretary of State for the Home Department, sub nom. R.* v. *Secretary of State for the Home Department, ex p. Patel (Pushpaben Kiritbhai)* [1993] Imm AR 392, C.A.: *R.* v. *Secretary of State for the Home Department, ex p. Ali (Akin)* [1993] Imm AR 610, Hutchison J.; *Nwafor (Michael), Re* [1994] Imm AR 91, Laws J.

sch. 3, amended: order 93/1813.

sch. 5, repealed in pt.: *ibid.*

78. Town and Country Planning Act 1971.

s. 52, see *Good* v. *Epping Forest District Council* [1994] 1 W.L.R. 376, C.A.

1972

6. Summer Time Act 1972.

s. 1, amended: order 94/2798.

s. 2, order 94/2798.

11. Superannuation Act 1972.

s. 7, regs. 93/2783, 3030, 3043, 3044(S.); 94/531(S.), 948, 963, 1909.

s. 9, regs. 94/1058, 2699(S.).

s. 12, regs. 93/2783, 3030, 3043, 3044(S.); 94/531(S.), 948, 1058, 2699(S.).

s. 24, regs. 93/2890; 94/1059, 1730.

sch. 1, amended: 1994, c. 21, sch. 1; c. 30, sch. 2.

sch. 3, regs. 94/1058, 2699(S.).

18. Maintenance Orders (Reciprocal Enforcement) Act 1972.

ss. 6, 8–10, see *R.* v. *West London Magistrates' Court, ex p. Emmett* [1993] 2 FLR 663, Ward J.

ss. 40, 45, order 94/1902.

27. Road Traffic (Foreign Vehicles) Act 1972.

s. 7, amended: 1994, c. 22, sch. 3.

1972—cont.

41. Finance Act 1972.
ss. 55, 128, repealed in pt.: 1994, c. 22, sch. 5.
s. 129, repealed: regs. 94/1813.

42. Town and Country Planning (Amendment) Act 1972.
s. 10C, amended(S.): 1994, c. 39, sch. 13.

48. Parliamentary and other Pensions Act 1972.
Pt. I (ss. 1–25), repealed, exc. ss. 1 (in pt.), 5, 23, 24 (in pt.): regs. 93/3253.
ss. 30, 33, 35, schs. 1, 2, repealed: *ibid.*

52. Town and Country Planning (Scotland) Act 1972.
s. 4, amended: 1994, c. 39, sch. 4; repealed in pt.: *ibid.*, sch. 14.
s. 4A, added: *ibid.*, s. 33.
s. 5, amended: *ibid.*, sch. 4; repealed in pt.: *ibid.*, sch. 14.
s. 6, amended: *ibid.*, sch. 4.
s. 6A, added: *ibid.*
s. 7, amended: *ibid.*
s. 8, repealed in pt.: *ibid.*, sch. 14.
s. 9, amended: *ibid.*, sch. 4.
s. 15, amended: *ibid.*, repealed in pt.: *ibid.*, schs. 4, 14.
s. 17, amended: *ibid.*, sch. 4.
s. 21, orders 94/1442, 2586.
ss. 22, 25, repealed in pt.: 1994, c. 39, sch. 14.
s. 26B, regs. 94/2012.
s. 28, order 94/2585.
s. 28, repealed in pt.: 1994, c. 39, sch. 14.
s. 31, see *Stirrat Park Hogg* v. *Dumbarton District Council* (O.H.), 1994 S.C.L.R. 631.
ss. 32 (in pt.), 49G, 50 (in pt.), 52 (in pt.), 56F (in pt.), 56K (in pt.), 84A, 87A (in pt.), repealed: 1994, c. 39, sch. 14.
s. 102, amended: *ibid.*, sch. 4, repealed in pt.: *ibid.*, sch. 14.
s. 169, repealed in pt.: *ibid.*
s. 181, repealed in pt. (prosp.): 1994, c. 21, schs. 9, 11, Pt. II.
ss. 201, 202, amended: 1994, c. 39, sch. 4.
s. 205, repealed in pt. (prosp.): 1994, c. 21, schs. 9, 11, Pt. II.
ss. 229A, 231 (in pt.): repealed: 1994, c. 39, sch. 14.
s. 232, see *Mackenzie's Trs.* v. *Highland Regional Council, The Times,* November 4, 1994.
ss. 242, 243, amended: 1994, c. 39, sch. 4.
s. 251, repealed in pt. (prosp.): 1994, c. 21, schs. 9, 11, Pt. III.
s. 254, repealed in pt.: 1994, c. 39, sch. 14.
s. 259, repealed (prosp.): 1994, c. 21, schs. 9, 11, Pt. III.
s. 265, repealed in pt.: 1994, c. 39, sch. 14.
s. 273, orders 94/1442, 2585, 2586.
s. 275, amended: 1994, c. 39, sch. 4; repealed in pt.: *ibid.*, sch. 14.
sch. 21, repealed in pt.: *ibid.*

1972—cont.

52. Town and Country Planning (Scotland) Act 1972—*cont.*
sch. 24, see *Emslie & Simpson* v. *City of Aberdeen District Council,* 1994 S.C.L.R. 69.

59. Administration of Justice (Scotland) Act 1972.
s. 1, see *Dailey Petroleum Services* v. *Pioneer Oil Tools, The Times,* December 3, 1993.
s. 1, Act of Sederunt 94/1443.

61. Land Charges Act 1972.
ss. 3, 5, 6, amended: 1994, c. 36, s. 15.
s. 9, rules 94/286.
ss. 10, 16, 17, rules 94/286, 287.

65. National Debt Act 1972.
s. 3, regs. 93/3131.
s. 11, regs. 93/3132, 3133; 94/343.

66. Poisons Act 1972.
s. 11, amended: 1994, c. 19, sch. 16; repealed in pt.: *ibid.*, schs. 16, 18.
s. 11, amended(S.): 1994, c. 39, sch. 13.

68. European Communities Act 1972.
see *R.* v. *Secretary of State for Foreign and Commonwealth Affairs, ex p. Rees-Mogg* [1994] 2 W.L.R. 115, D.C.
s. 1, orders 93/3157; 94/758–761.
s. 1, amended: 1994, c. 38, s. 1.
s. 2, regs. 93/2900, 2924, 3014, 3015, 3031, 3039–3042, 3050, 3053, 3071, 3074, 3083, 3127, 3173, 3194, 3225, 3227, 3228, 3234, 3245, 3247; 94/94, 101, 105, 106, 118, 141, 188, 232, 237, 249, 275, 276, 342, 440, 450, 452, 501, 608, 617, 672, 674, 677, 806, 899, 947, 979, 1002, 1056, 1134, 1230, 1386, 1447, 1448, 1515, 1516, 1528, 1529, 1570, 1696, 1701(S.), 1712, 1729, 1731–1736, 1806, 1838, 1932, 1933, 1981, 1984, 1985, 2012(S.), 2063, 2126, 2155, 2249, 2251, 2280, 2286, 2295, 2326, 2328, 2479, 2556, 2710(S.), 2716, 2841, 2842, 2783; orders 94/757, 1029, 1327, 1887, 1895, 1908, 2791; S.Rs. 1993 Nos. 424, 449, 467, 469, 474, 475, 478, 480, 483, 488, 757; 1994 Nos. 6, 44, 123, 133, 145, 147, 161, 174, 176, 181, 193, 211, 222–224, 240, 270, 316, 339, 346, 360, 370, 379, 384, 395.

70. Local Government Act 1972.
s. 20, substituted: 1994, c. 19, s. 1.
s. 21, substituted: *ibid.*, s. 2.
s. 22, amended: *ibid.*, sch. 15.
s. 25, amended: *ibid.*, s. 4.
s. 25A, added: *ibid.*, sch. 15.
s. 26, substituted: *ibid.*, s. 4.
s. 27, substituted: *ibid.*, s. 8.
s. 28, substituted: *ibid.*, s. 9.
s. 29, substituted: *ibid.*, s. 10.
s. 29A, added: *ibid.*, s. 11.
s. 29B, added: *ibid.*, s. 12.

1972—cont.

70. Local Government Act 1972—*cont.*

s. 30, amended: *ibid.*, sch. 15; repealed in pt.: *ibid.*, schs. 15, 18.

s. 31, amended: *ibid.*, sch. 15.

s. 33, substituted: *ibid.*, s. 13.

s. 33A, added: *ibid.*, s. 14.

s. 35, amended: *ibid.*, s. 15.

s. 37, substituted: *ibid.*, sch. 15.

s. 51, orders 93/2881, 2971, 3129; 94/330, 331.

ss. 51, 68, see *R*. v. *Secretary of State for the Environment, ex p. Almondsbury District Council, The Times,* March 11, 1994, Harrison J.

s. 54, amended: 1994, c. 19, schs. 2, 15; c. 29, s. 40.

s. 55, amended: 1994, c. 19, sch. 15; repealed in pt.: *ibid.*, schs. 15, 18.

s. 56, amended: *ibid.*, schs. 2, 15.

s. 58, orders 94/130, 142.

s. 58, amended: 1994, c. 19, sch. 15; c. 29, s. 40.

s. 59, amended: 1994, c. 19, sch. 15; repealed in pt.: *ibid.*, schs. 15, 18.

s. 60, amended: *ibid.*, sch. 15; c. 29, s. 40; repealed in pt.: 1994, c. 19, schs. 15, 18.

s. 61, amended: *ibid.*, sch. 15.

s. 64, substituted: *ibid.*, s. 6.

s. 67, orders 93/2881, 2971; 94/130, 142, 330, 331.

s. 67, amended: 1994, c. 29, s. 40; repealed in pt.: 1994, c. 19, schs. 15, 18.

s. 69, order 93/3129.

s. 69, amended: 1994, c. 19, sch. 15; repealed in pt.: *ibid.*, sch. 18.

s. 71, amended: *ibid.*, sch. 15.

s. 72, amended: *ibid.*; repealed in pt.: *ibid.*, schs. 15, 18.

s. 73, amended: *ibid.*, sch. 15.

ss. 74, 76, amended: *ibid.*; repealed in pt.: *ibid.*, schs. 15, 18.

s. 78, amended: *ibid.*, sch. 15.

s. 80, see *R*. v. *Tower Hamlets London Borough Council, The Times,* May 17, 1994, D.C.

ss. 83, 91, amended: 1994, c. 19, sch. 15.

s. 94, amended: 1994, c. 29, sch. 4.

s. 97, amended: 1994, c. 19, sch. 15; repealed in pt.: *ibid.*, schs. 15, 18.

ss. 98, 99, amended: 1994, c. 29, sch. 4.

s. 100B, see *R*. v. *Swansea City Council, ex p. Elitestone, sub nom. Elitestone's Application for Judicial Review* [1993] 46 EG 181, C.A.

s. 100J, amended: 1994, c. 29, sch. 4.

s. 101, amended: 1994, c. 19, sch. 15; repealed in pt.: 1994, c. 29, sch. 9.

s. 103, amended: 1994, c. 19, sch. 15.

s. 107, amended: 1994, c. 29, sch. 4; repealed in pt.: *ibid.*, sch. 9.

1972—cont.

70. Local Government Act 1972—*cont.*

s. 111, see *Credit Suisse* v. *Allerdale Borough Council, The Independent,* June 17, 1994, Colman J.; *Credit Suisse* v. *Waltham London Borough Council, The Times,* November 8, 1994, Gatehouse J.

s. 120, see *R*. v. *Somerset County Council, ex p. Fewings, The Times,* February 10, 1994, Laws J.

ss. 125, 134, 137, 140B, 141, 146, amended: 1994, c. 19, sch. 15.

s. 146A, amended: 1994, c. 29, sch. 4.

s. 148, amended: 1994, c. 19, sch. 12; regs. 94/2825.

s. 150, amended: 1994, c. 19, sch. 15.

s. 168, repealed in pt.: 1994, c. 29, sch. 9.

ss. 173, 175, regs. 94/615.

ss. 180, 181, amended: 1994, c. 19, sch. 15.

s. 184, amended: *ibid.*, sch. 6.

ss. 187, 189, 191, amended: *ibid.*, sch. 15.

s. 192, amended: *ibid.*, s. 21.

s. 195, amended: *ibid.*, sch. 15; repealed in pt.: *ibid.*, schs. 15, 18.

s. 196, repealed in pt.: 1994, c. 29, sch. 9.

s. 200, repealed: 1994, c. 19, sch. 18.

s. 204, amended: *ibid.*, sch. 15.

s. 207, repealed: *ibid.*, schs. 15, 18.

s. 213, amended: *ibid.*, sch. 15; repealed in pt.: *ibid.*, schs. 15, 18.

ss. 214, 215, amended: *ibid.*, sch. 15.

s. 219, amended: *ibid.*, sch. 2.

s. 223, amended: 1994, c. 29, sch. 4.

s. 224, amended: 1994, c. 19, sch. 2.

s. 225, amended: *ibid.*, sch. 15.

ss. 226, 227, amended: *ibid.*; repealed in pt.: *ibid.*, schs. 15, 18.

ss. 228, 229, 231–234, amended: 1994, c. 29, sch. 4.

ss. 235, 236, amended: 1994, c. 19, sch. 15.

s. 245, amended: *ibid.*; repealed in pt.: *ibid.*, schs. 15, 18.

s. 245A, substituted: *ibid.*, s. 5.

s. 245B, added: *ibid.*, s. 16.

ss. 246–249, amended: *ibid.*, sch. 15.

s. 247, order 94/1888.

s. 255, amended: 1994, c. 19, sch. 15.

s. 266, order 93/3129.

s. 269, substituted: 1994, c. 19, sch. 2.

s. 270, regs. 94/615.

s. 270, amended: 1994, c. 19, s. 1, sch. 15.

sch. 4, amended: *ibid.*, s. 1, sch. 1; repealed in pt.: *ibid.*, schs. 15, 18.

sch. 5, substituted: *ibid.*, s. 3, sch. 3.

sch. 8, amended: *ibid.*, sch. 15; repealed in pt.: *ibid.*, schs. 15, 18.

sch. 10, repealed: *ibid.*

sch. 11, amended: *ibid.*, s. 7; repealed in pt.: *ibid.*, s. 7, schs. 15, 18.

1972—cont.

70. Local Government Act 1972—*cont.*
sch. 12, amended: *ibid.,* s. 12, sch. 15;
c. 29, sch. 4.
schs. 14, 16, amended: 1994, c. 19, sch.
15.
sch. 17, amended: *ibid.,* s. 19, sch. 6.
sch. 26, amended: *ibid.,* sch. 15; repealed
in pt.: *ibid.,* schs. 15, 18.
sch. 29, amended: *ibid.,* sch. 15; repealed
in pt.: 1994, c. 40, sch. 17.

71. Criminal Justice Act 1972.
s. 46, repealed in pt.: 1994, c. 33, sch. 11.

1973

8. Coal Industry Act 1973.
s. 1, repealed (prosp.): 1994, c. 21, sch.
11, Pt. IV.
ss. 2, 10, repealed (prosp.): *ibid.,* sch. 11,
Pt. III.
ss. 11–14, repealed (prosp.): *ibid.,* sch.
11, Pt. IV.
sch. 1, repealed in pt. (prosp.): *ibid.,* sch.
11, Pts. III, IV.
sch. 2, repealed (prosp.): *ibid.,* sch. 11,
Pt. IV.

13. Supply of Goods (Implied Terms) Act 1973.
ss. 8–11, amended: 1994, c. 35, sch. 2.
s. 11A, added: *ibid.*
s. 12, substituted: *ibid.*
s. 12A, added: *ibid.*
s. 15, amended: *ibid.*; repealed in pt.:
ibid., schs. 2, 3.

15. Administration of Justice Act 1973.
s. 8, see *Cheltenham and Gloucester
Building Society* v. *Grant, The Times,*
May 9, 1994, C.A.

18. Matrimonial Causes Act 1973.
ss. 10, 24, see *Griffiths* v. *Dawson & Co.*
[1993] 2 FLR 315, Ewbank J.
Pt. II (ss. 21–40), see *Symmons* v.
Symmons [1993] 1 FLR 317, H.H.J.
Hunter sitting as a deputy High Court
judge.
ss. 23, 37, sch. 8, see *Graham* v. *Graham*
[1993] 1 F.C.R. 339, C.A.
ss. 24, 25, see *Brooks* v. *Brooks, The
Times,* May 27, 1994, C.A.
s. 25, see *R.* v. *R. (Financial Provision)*
[1993] Fam. Law 282, District Judge
Silverman.
s. 31, see *H.* v. *H. (Financial Provision)
(Application to Terminate Wife's
Right to Periodical Payments)* [1993] 2
FLR 35, Thorpe J.

21. Overseas Pensions Act 1973.
s. 2, amended: 1994, c. 29, sch. 5.

1973—cont.

26. Land Compensation Act 1973.
see *Harford* v. *Birmingham City Council
(Ref: 32/1991)* (1993) 66 P. & C.R. 468,
Lands Tribunal.
s. 2, see *Fallows* v. *Gateshead Metropolitan Borough Council (Ref: 206/1991)*
(1993) 66 P. & C.R. 460, Lands
Tribunal.
ss. 8, 15, 19, amended: 1994, c. 19, sch.
16.
s. 53, see *Ward Construction (Medway)*
v. *Barclays Bank, The Times,* July 20,
1994, C.A.

33. Protection of Wrecks Act 1973.
s. 1, orders 93/2895; 94/1842.
ss. 2, 3, order 94/2372(S.).

35. Employment Agencies Act 1973.
ss. 1–3, repealed: 1994, c. 40, schs. 10, 17.
ss. 3A–3C, added: *ibid.,* sch. 10.
s. 7, repealed: *ibid.,* sch. 17.
s. 9, amended: *ibid.,* sch. 10; repealed in
pt.: *ibid.,* sch. 17.
s. 10, repealed in pt.: *ibid.*
s. 13, amended: 1994, c. 19, sch. 16; c. 29,
sch. 4; c. 40, sch. 10, Pt. I; repealed in
pt.: 1994, c. 19, schs. 16, 18; c. 40,
schs. 10, Pt. II, 17.
s. 13, amended(S.): 1994, c. 39, sch. 13.

36. Northern Ireland Constitution Act 1973.
s. 38, order 94/763.

41. Fair Trading Act 1973.
ss. 48, 49, 54, see *R.* v. *Monopolies and
Mergers Commission, ex p. National
House Building Council, The Times,*
January 25, 1994, C.A.
s. 50, order 94/1922.
ss. 56A–56G, added: 1994, c. 40, s. 7.
s. 57, amended: *ibid.,* s. 8.
s. 64, order 94/72; amended: *ibid.*
s. 75B, amended: regs. 94/1934.
s. 75F, regs. 94/1934.
s. 75G, repealed in pt.: 1994, c. 40, s. 9,
sch. 17.
s. 75K, amended: *ibid.,* s. 9.
s. 77, 93A, amended: *ibid.,* sch. 11.
s. 133, amended: 1994, c. 21, sch. 9; c. 40,
sch. 11.
sch. 7, amended: order 94/1922.

45. Domicile and Matrimonial Proceedings Act 1973.
s. 16, see *Social Security Decision No.
R(G)* 1/94.
sch. 3, Act of Sederunt 94/1443.

51. Finance Act 1973.
s. 47, sch. 19, see *Guinness* v. *I.R.C.*
[1994] STC 86, Rattee J.
s. 56, regs. 93/2903, 3066–3068; 94/1265;
order 94/1441(S.); S.R. 1993 No. 470.

CAP.

1973—cont.

52. Prescription and Limitation (Scotland) Act 1973.

s. 1, see *Hamilton* v. *McIntosh Donald*, 1994 S.L.T. 793.

ss. 6, 9, see *Hogg* v. *Prentice* (Sh.Ct.), 1994 S.C.L.R. 426.

ss. 6, 11, see *Sinclair* v. *McDougall Estates* (O.H.), March 25, 1992.

s. 17, see *McArthur* v. *Strathclyde Regional Council, The Times,* May 20, 1994.

ss. 17, 19A, see *McHardy* v. *Bawden International* (Sh.Ct.), 1993 S.C.L.R. 893; *McCabe* v. *McLellan,* 1994 S.L.T. 346; 1994 S.C.L.R. 188.

s. 18, see *Paton* v. *Loffland Brothers North Sea* (O.H.), 1994 S.L.T. 784.

s. 19A, see *Kidd* v. *Grampian Health Board* (O.H.), 1994 S.L.T. 267; *McFarlane* v. *Breen* (O.H.), 1994 S.C.L.R. 382; *Clark* v. *McLean,* 1994 S.C.L.R. 564; *McCluskey* v. *Sir Robert McAlpine & Sons,* 1994 S.C.L.R. 650.

56. Land Compensation (Scotland) Act 1973.

ss. 34, 35, see *Bisset* v. *Secretary of State for Scotland,* 1994 S.L.T.(Lands Tr.) 12.

60. Breeding of Dogs Act 1973.

s. 5, amended: 1994, c. 19, sch. 16; repealed in pt.: *ibid.,* schs. 16, 18.

s. 5, amended(S.): 1994, c. 39, sch. 13.

62. Powers of Criminal Courts Act 1973.

ss. 5, 6, sch. 1, see *R.* v. *Brent Justices, ex p. Ward* [1993] C.O.D. 17, D.C.

s. 17, see *R.* v. *Fielding (Craig)* (1993) 14 Cr.App.R.(S.) 494; [1993] Crim.L.R. 229, C.A.

s. 21, amended: 1994, c. 33, sch. 4.

s. 22, see *R.* v. *McQuillan* [1993] Crim.L.R. 893, C.A.; *R.* v. *French* [1993] Crim.L.R. 893, C.A.; *R.* v. *Lowery (James)* (1993) 14 Cr.App.R.(S.) 485; [1993] Crim.L.R. 225, C.A.

s. 24, *see R.* v. *Keogh* [1993] Crim.L.R. 895, C.A.

s. 32, amended: 1994, c. 33, sch. 4; repealed in pt.: *ibid.,* schs. 4, 11.

s. 35, see *R.* v. *Crutchley; R.* v. *Tonks, The Times,* January 3, 1994, C.A.; *D.P.P.* v. *Scott, The Times,* August 15, 1994, D.C.; *Botrose* v. *Hammersmith and Fulham London Borough Council, The Times,* November 7, 1994, D.C.

s. 54, sch. 3, orders 93/2852, 2853, 3139, 3142.

sch. 1A, amended: 1994, c. 33, sch. 9.

63. Government Trading Funds Act 1973.

ss. 1, 6, order 94/1192.

s. 2B, repealed in pt.: 1993, c. 34, sch. 23.

CAP.

1973—cont.

65. Local Government (Scotland) Act 1973.

ss. 1–3, 3A, 4, 5, 11, repealed: 1994, c. 39, sch. 14.

ss. 14, 16, amended: *ibid.,* sch. 13.

s. 17, order 94/259.

ss. 20, 23, substituted: 1994, c. 39, sch. 13.

s. 24, amended: *ibid.,* sch. 13; repealed in pt.: *ibid.,* schs. 13, 14.

s. 28, amended: *ibid.,* sch. 13.

s. 31, amended: *ibid.;* repealed in pt.: *ibid.,* schs. 13, 14.

s. 38, amended: *ibid.,* sch. 13.

s. 47, amended: *ibid.;* repealed in pt.: *ibid.,* schs. 13, 14.

ss. 45, 47, 49A, regs. 94/630.

s. 50B, amended: 1994, c. 39, sch. 13.

ss. 50D, 50H, see *Stirral Park Hogg* v. *Dumbarton District Council* (O.H.), 1994 S.C.L.R. 631.

s. 50K, amended: 1994, c. 39, sch. 13.

s. 51, repealed in pt.: *ibid.,* sch. 14.

s. 55, amended: *ibid.,* sch. 13.

s. 56, amended: *ibid.;* repealed in pt.: *ibid.,* schs. 13, 14.

ss. 62A–62C, added: *ibid.,* s. 20.

s. 63, amended: 1994, c. 29, s. 64; c. 39, sch. 13; repealed in pt.: *ibid.,* schs. 13, 14.

s. 63A, added: *ibid.,* sch. 13.

s. 64, amended: *ibid.;* repealed in pt.: *ibid.,* schs. 13, 14.

s. 67, amended: *ibid.,* sch. 13.

s. 69, see *Morgan Guaranty Trust Company of New York* v. *Lothian Regional Council* (O.H.), 1994 S.C.L.R. 213.

s. 69, repealed in pt.: 1994, c. 39, sch. 14.

ss. 70, 71, amended (temp.): *ibid.,* s. 182.

s. 74, repealed in pt.: *ibid.,* sch. 14.

s. 83, see *Commission for Local Authority Accounts in Scotland* v. *Grampian Regional Council,* 1994 S.L.T. 1120.

s. 83, amended: 1994, c. 39, s. 164, sch. 13; repealed in pt.: *ibid.,* s. 164, schs. 13, 14.

s. 84, repealed in pt.: *ibid.*

s. 87, amended: *ibid.,* sch. 13; repealed in pt.: *ibid.,* schs. 13, 14.

s. 88, amended: *ibid.,* s. 140.

s. 90, substituted: *ibid.,* s. 176.

s. 90A, repealed: *ibid.,* sch. 14.

ss. 92–94, amended: *ibid.,* sch. 13.

s. 96, repealed in pt.: *ibid.,* sch. 14.

s. 100, amended: *ibid.,* sch. 13; repealed in pt.: *ibid.,* schs. 13, 14.

s. 102, amended: *ibid.,* sch. 13.

s. 103, see *Lawrie* v. *Commission for Local Authority Accounts in Scotland* (O.H.), 1994 S.L.T. 1185.

s. 103, amended: 1994, c. 39, sch. 13.

1973—cont.

65. Local Government (Scotland) Act 1973—cont.

s. 106, repealed in pt. (with savings): *ibid.*, s. 90, sch. 14.

ss. 109, 111 (in pt.), 116, 118 (in pt.), repealed: *ibid.*, sch. 14.

s. 122A, added: *ibid.*, s. 170.

s. 123, substituted: *ibid.*, sch. 13.

s. 124, substituted: *ibid.*, s. 31.

s. 126, substituted: *ibid.*, sch. 13.

s. 127, repealed: *ibid.*, sch. 14.

ss. 128, 130, amended: *ibid.*, sch. 13.

ss. 131, 132, repealed: *ibid.*, sch. 14.

ss. 133, 134, repealed in pt.: *ibid.*, schs. 13, 14.

s. 135, amended: *ibid.*, sch. 13; repealed in pt.: *ibid.*, schs. 13, 14.

s. 135A, amended: *ibid.*, sch. 13.

ss. 137 (in pt.), 138 (in pt.), 140, 142, 143, repealed: *ibid.*, schs. 13, 14.

s. 145, amended: *ibid.*, sch. 13.

s. 146, amended: *ibid.*; repealed in pt.: *ibid.*, sch. 14.

s. 147, substituted: *ibid.*, s. 36.

s. 148, repealed in pt.: *ibid.*

s. 150, substituted: *ibid.*, sch. 13.

ss. 153, 154, amended: *ibid.*; repealed in pt.: *ibid.*, schs. 13, 14.

ss. 154A, 154B, repealed: *ibid.*, sch. 14.

ss. 155, 156, repealed in pt.: *ibid.*, schs. 13, 14.

s. 157, repealed in pt.: *ibid.*; repealed: 1994, c. 40, sch. 17.

s. 159, repealed: 1994, c. 39, schs. 13, 14.

s. 161, repealed: *ibid.*, sch. 14.

s. 163, repealed in pt.: *ibid.*, schs. 13, 14.

s. 166, repealed in pt.: *ibid.*, sch. 14.

s. 168, repealed: *ibid.*, schs. 13, 14.

ss. 169, 170, amended: *ibid.*, sch. 13.

ss. 170A, 170B, amended: *ibid.*, repealed in pt.: *ibid.*, schs. 13, 14.

s. 171, repealed in pt.: *ibid.*

s. 172, substituted: *ibid.*, sch. 13.

ss. 173, 174, 176, 177, 179, 181–183, repealed: *ibid.*, sch. 14.

s. 188, substituted: *ibid.*, sch. 13.

s. 190, amended: *ibid.*

s. 193, repealed in pt.: *ibid.*, sch. 14.

s. 194, amended: *ibid.*, sch. 13.

s. 200, repealed in pt.: *ibid.*, sch. 14.

s. 201, amended: *ibid.*, sch. 13.

s. 202, repealed in pt.: *ibid.*, schs. 13, 14.

s. 206, amended: *ibid.*, sch. 13.

s. 211, amended: *ibid.*, s. 21.

ss. 215 (in pt.); 222–225, repealed: *ibid.*, sch. 14.

ss. 226, 230, repealed: *ibid.*, schs. 13, 14.

s. 235, amended: *ibid.*, sch. 13; repealed in pt.: *ibid.*, schs. 13, 14.

s. 235, regs. 94/630.

1973—cont.

65. Local Government (Scotland) Act 1973—cont.

s. 236, repealed in pt.: 1994, c. 39, sch. 14.

schs. 1, 2, repealed: *ibid.*

sch. 5, substituted: *ibid.*, sch. 13.

sch. 6, amended: *ibid.*; repealed in pt.: *ibid.*, sch. 14.

schs. 7, 8, amended: *ibid.*, sch. 13.

schs. 9 (in pt.), 10, repealed: *ibid.*, sch. 14.

schs. 13, 14, 17 (in pt.), repealed: *ibid.*, schs. 13, 14.

sch. 20, repealed: *ibid.*, sch. 14.

sch. 22, repealed: *ibid.*, schs. 13, 14.

sch. 27, repealed in pt.: *ibid.*, sch. 14.

1974

3. Slaughterhouses Act 1974.

s. 27, amended: 1994, c. 19, sch. 16; repealed in pt.: *ibid.*, schs. 16, 18.

ss. 34, 45, amended: *ibid.*, sch. 16.

7. Local Government Act 1974.

s. 25, amended: 1994, c. 29, sch. 4; regs. 94/1083.

s. 34, amended: 1994, c. 19, sch. 16.

23. Juries Act 1974.

s. 9B, added: 1994, c. 33, s. 41.

s. 10, repealed in pt.: *ibid.*, s. 11.

s. 13, substituted: *ibid.*, s. 43.

s. 20, amended: *ibid.*, sch. 10.

sch. 1, amended: 1994, c. 29, sch. 8; c. 33, s. 42, sch. 10; repealed in pt.: 1994, c. 29, sch. 9.

24. Prices Act 1974.

ss. 2, 4, order 94/1853.

s. 7, see *Allen* v. *Redbridge London Borough Council* [1994] 1 W.L.R. 139, D.C.

28. Northern Ireland Act 1974.

s. 1, order 94/1772.

sch. 1, S.R. 1994 No. 47.

37. Health and Safety at Work etc. Act 1974.

ss. 2, 3, see *R.* v. *Associated Octel, The Times*, August 3, 1994, C.A.

s. 3, see *RMC Roadstone Products* v. *Jester* [1994] I.C.R. 456, D.C.

s. 4, see *Moualem* v. *Carlisle City Council, The Times*, July 8, 1994, D.C.

ss. 7, 33, see *Skinner* v. *H.M. Advocate*, 1994 S.C.C.R. 316.

ss. 7, 52, see *Thomson* v. *Barbour*, 1994 S.C.C.R. 485.

s. 15, regs. 93/3050; 94/118, 237, 299, 669, 670, 1886.

s. 18, regs. 94/669.

s. 28, amended(S.): 1994, c. 39, sch. 13.

s. 43, regs. 93/3050; 94/397.

s. 53, amended: 1994, c. 19, sch. 9; repealed in pt.: *ibid.*, schs. 9, 16.

s. 53, amended(S.): 1994, c. 39, sch. 13.

s. 82, regs. 93/3050; 94/118, 237, 299, 397, 669, 670, 1886.

sch. 3, regs. 93/3050; 94/299, 669, 670, 1886.

1974—cont.

39. Consumer Credit Act 1974.
see *Legal and General Assurance Society* v. *Cooper*, August 5, 1994; H.H.J. Poulton; Medway County Ct.
s. 16, orders 93/2922; 94/2420.
s. 46, see *Clydesdale Group* v. *Normand*, 1993 S.C.C.R. 958; *Carrington Carr* v. *Leicestershire County Council* [1993] Crim.L.R. 938, D.C.
s. 56, see *Woodchester Leasing Equipment* v. *Clayton (R.M.) and Clayton (D.M.) t/a Sudbury Sports)*, October 22, 1993; H.H.J. Brandt: Colchester and Clacton County Ct.
ss. 87, 176, see *Lombard North Central* v. *Power-Hines*, June 7, 1994; H.H.J. Viljoen; Barnet County Ct.
s. 121, see *Mathew* v. *T.M. Sutton, The Times,* June 22, 1994, Chadwick J.
s. 139, see *Pye* v. *Ambrose* [1994] NPC 53, Arden J.
s. 174, amended: 1994, c. 21, sch. 9.
s. 176, amended: 1994, c. 36, s. 36.
s. 182, orders 93/2922; 94/2420.
s. 189, amended: 1994, c. 19, sch. 16; repealed in pt.: *ibid.,* schs. 16, 18.
s. 189, amended(S.): 1994, c. 39, sch. 13.
sch. 4, repealed in pt.: 1994, c. 22, sch. 5.

40. Control of Pollution Act 1974.
s. 3, see *Durham County Council* v. *Thomas Swan & Co., The Times,* July 27, 1994, D.C.
ss. 16, 30, 85, see *Friel (H.L.) & Son* v. *Inverclyde District Council*, 1994 S.C.L.R. 561.
s. 22, amended: 1994, c. 19, sch. 9.
s. 25, repealed (prosp.): 1994, c. 21, sch. 11, Pt. II.
s. 30, regs. 94/1056.
s. 30, amended: 1994, c. 19, sch. 9.
s. 32, amended(S.): 1994, c. 39, sch. 13; modified (temp.): order 94/2850; repealed in pt.(S.): 1994, c. 39, schs. 13, 14.
ss. 36, 55, 56, amended(S.): *ibid.,* sch. 13.
s. 58, see *Aitken* v. *South Hams District Council* [1994] 3 W.L.R. 333, H.L.; *R.* v. *Folkestone Magistrates' Court, ex p. Kibble* [1993] Crim.L.R. 704, D.C.
ss. 60, 61, see *Walter Lilley & Co.* v. *Westminster City Council, The Times,* March 1, 1994, D.C.
s. 62, amended(S.): 1994, c. 39, sch. 13.
s. 73, amended: 1994, c. 19, sch. 9; c. 22, sch. 3; repealed in pt.: 1994, c. 19, schs. 9, 18.
s. 73, amended(S.): 1994, c. 39, sch. 13.
ss. 91, 92, see *Polymeric Treatments* v. *Walsall Metropolitan Borough Council* [1993] C.O.D. 213, D.C.
s. 98, amended: 1994, c. 19, sch. 9; repealed in pt.: *ibid.,* schs. 9, 18.

1974—cont.

40. Control of Pollution Act 1974—*cont.*
s. 98, amended(S.): 1994, c. 39, sch. 13.
s. 104, regs. 94/1056.
s. 105, amended: 1994, c. 19, sch. 9.
s. 106, amended(S.): 1994, c. 39, sch. 13; repealed in pt.: *ibid.,* schs. 13, 14.
sch. 1A, amended(S.): *ibid.,* sch. 13.

43. Merchant Shipping Act 1974.
amendments made by 1988, c. 12, sch. 4, restored: 1994, c. 28, s. 5.
s. 1, order 94/2788.
s. 1, amended: 1994, c. 28, s. 5.
s. 4A, repealed in pt.: *ibid.*
s. 8, amended: 1994, c. 28, s. 7; repealed in pt.: *ibid.,* s. 7, sch. 4.
s. 17, regs. 94/502.
sch. 1, repealed in pt.: 1994, c. 28, s. 5.
sch. 5, regs. 94/502.

46. Friendly Societies Act 1974.
s. 104, regs. 94/657.

47. Solicitors Act 1974.
s. 22, amended: 1994, c. 26, sch. 4.
s. 23, amended: regs. 94/1696.
s. 25, see *Piper Double Glazing* v. *D.C. Contracts (1992) Co.* [1994] 1 All E.R. 177, Potter J.
s. 46, rules 94/288.
s. 49, see *Solicitor, A (No. 6119/92), Re, The Times,* May 4, 1994, C.A.
ss. 50, 51, see *Peasegood* v. *Meisel* [1994] 1 All E.R. 298, D.C.
s. 56, order 94/2616.
sch. 1A, see *R.* v. *The Law Society, ex p. Singh & Choudry (A Firm), The Times,* April 1, 1994, D.C.

48. Railways Act 1974.
s. 8, repealed in pt.: order 94/1649.
sch. 4, repealed in pt.: 1994, c. 40, sch. 17.

53. Rehabilitation of Offenders Act 1974.
ss. 4, 7, see *R.* v. *Hastings Justices, ex p. McSpirit, The Times,* June 23, 1994, Sedley J.
s. 5, amended: 1994, c. 33, schs. 9, 10; repealed in pt.: *ibid.,* schs. 9, 11.

1975

7. Finance Act 1975.
s. 38, see *Gray* v. *I.R.C.* [1994] STC 360, C.A.

14. Social Security Act 1975.
Pt. II (ss. 12–92), see *Social Security Decision No. R(P) 2/93.*
s. 15, see *Secretary of State for Social Security and Chief Adjudication Officer* v. *Graham (Rose),* January 18, 1994, C.A.
s. 35, see *Social Security Decision No. R(A) 1/94; Mallinson* v. *Secretary of State for Social Security* [1994] 1 W.L.R. 630, H.L.

1975—cont.

14. Social Security Act 1975—*cont.*

ss. 36, 165A, see *Social Security DecisionNo. R(S)* 2/91.

ss. 50, 107, see *Faulkner* v. *Chief Adjudication Officer, The Times,* April 8, 1994, C.A.

s. 82, see *Social Security Decision No. R(S)* 2/93; *Social Security Decision No. R(S)* 2/94.

s. 104, see *Social Security Decision No. R(SB)* 1/93.

s. 119, see *Plewa (Executrix of the Estate of Joseph Plewa, dec'd)* v. *Chief Adjudication Officer* [1994] 3 W.L.R. 317.

s. 134, amended: 1994, c. 1, s. 2.

sch. 2, amended and repealed in pt.: *ibid.,* s. 3.

15. Social Security (Northern Ireland) Act 1975.

sch. 2, amended and repealed in pt.: 1994, c. 1, s. 3.

20. District Courts (Scotland) Act 1975.

s. 1A, amended: 1994, c. 39, sch. 13.

s. 2, amended: *ibid.,* s. 48.

s. 7, repealed in pt.: *ibid.,* schs. 13, 14.

s. 12, amended: *ibid.,* sch. 13.

s. 18, repealed in pt.: *ibid.,* sch. 14.

s. 26, amended: *ibid.,* sch. 13.

21. Criminal Procedure (Scotland) Act 1975.

amended: 1994, c. 39, sch. 13.

s. 46, see *Mitchell* v. *H.M. Advocate,* 1994 S.C.C.R. 440.

s. 76, see *Baptie* v. *H.M. Advocate,* 1994 S.C.C.R. 104.

s. 77, see *Carruthers* v. *H.M. Advocate,* 1994 S.L.T. 900.

s. 77A, see *Advocate, H.M.* v. *Smith,* 1993 S.C.C.R. 987.

s. 101, see *Stewart* v. *H.M. Advocate,* 1993 S.C.C.R. 1010; *Millar* v. *H.M. Advocate,* High Court of Justiciary, October 8, 1993; *Advocate (H.M.)* v. *R., The Times,* October 21, 1994.

s. 147, see *Advocate, H.M.* v. *Hislop,* 1994 S.L.T. 333; *C.* v. *H.M. Advocate,* 1994 S.C.C.R. 560.

ss. 168, 173, 186, amended: 1994, c. 39, sch. 13.

s. 205A, see *Casey* v. *H.M. Advocate,* 1994 S.L.T. 44.

s. 212A, amended: 1994, c. 33, s. 132.

s. 218, see *Brooks* v. *H.M. Advocate,* 1994 S.L.T. 932.

s. 218, amended: 1994, c. 33, sch. 9.

s. 228, see *Ralton* v. *H.M. Advocate,* 1994 S.L.T. 321; *Hynes* v. *H.M. Advocate,* 1994 S.C.C.R. 602; *Carrington* v. *H.M. Advocate,* 1994 S.C.C.R. 567; *Cameron* v. *H.M. Advocate,* 1994 S.C.C.R. 502.

1975—cont.

21. Criminal Procedure (Scotland) Act 1975—*cont.*

ss. 228, 252, see *McLay* v. *H.M. Advocate,* 1994 S.C.C.R. 397; 1994 S.L.T. 873.

s. 252, see *Carrington* v. *H.M. Advocate,* 1994 S.C.C.R. 567.

s. 255, see *Friel* v. *Mailley* (Sh.Ct.), 1993 S.C.C.R. 928.

ss. 262, 263, 281, see *Windsor, Petr.,* 1994 S.C.C.R. 59.

s. 282, Act of Adjournal 94/1769.

s. 289, see *Robb* v. *Hamilton,* 1994, S.L.T. 423.

s. 289D, amended: 1994, c. 33, s. 157.

s. 290, see *Sim* v. *Lockhart,* 1994 S.C.C.R. 243.

s. 296, amended: 1994, c. 39, sch. 13.

s. 311, see *Milne* v. *Normand,* 1993 S.C.C.R. 1058; *Hutchison* v. *Normand,* 1993 S.C.C.R. 1000.

ss. 311, 335, see *Doonin Plant* v. *Carmichael,* 1994 S.L.T. 313.

s. 312, see *Clydesdale Group* v. *Normand,* 1993 S.C.C.R. 958; *Hamilton* v. *Normand,* 1994 S.L.T. 184; *Horsburgh* v. *Russell,* 1994 S.C.C.R. 237.

s. 314, see *Heywood* v. *McLennan* (Sh.Ct.), 1994 S.C.C.R. 1.

ss. 328, 334, see *Pearson* v. *Crowe,* 1994 S.L.T. 378.

s. 332A, see *Brawls* v. *Walkingshaw,* 1994 S.C.C.R. 7.

s. 334, see *Taylor* v. *Lees,* 1993 S.C.C.R. 947; *McLeay* v. *Hingston,* 1994 S.L.T. 720; *Kirkcubright Scallop Gear* v. *Walkingshaw,* 1994 S.C.C.R. 772.

s. 348, see *Hay* v. *McClory,* 1993 S.C.C.R. 1040.

s. 350A, see *MacGillivray* v. *Johnston (No. 2),* 1994 S.L.T. 1012.

s. 364, amended: 1994, c. 39, sch. 13.

s. 366, see *Heywood* v. *B.,* 1994 S.C.C.R. 554.

ss. 372, 373, amended: 1994, c. 39, sch. 13.

s. 380, see *Storie* v. *Friel,* 1993 S.C.C.R. 955; *Johnstone* v. *Lees,* 1993 S.C.C.R. 1050.

s. 387, amended: 1994, c. 39, sch. 13.

ss. 395, 442B, see *St. Clare* v. *Wilson,* 1994 S.C.C.R. 26; 1994 S.L.T. 564.

s. 403, see *McIntosh* (Sh.Ct.), 1994 S.C.C.R. 4.

s. 403, amended: 1994, c. 33, s. 47.

s. 413, amended: 1994, c. 39, sch. 13.

s. 431, amended: 1994, c. 33, sch. 9.

s. 447, see *Roberton* v. *McGlennan,* 1994 S.C.C.R. 394.

s. 457, Act of Adjournal 94/1769.

1975—cont.

21. Criminal Procedure (Scotland) Act 1975—cont.
s. 462, repealed in pt.: 1994, c. 39, sch. 13.
Sch. 5, amended: *ibid.*
Sch. 7D, repealed in pt.: *ibid.*, sch. 14.

22. Oil Taxation Act 1975.
s. 2, amended: 1994, c. 9, s. 235, schs. 23, 26.
s. 5, amended: *ibid., s.* 237.
sch. 2, amended: *ibid.,* sch. 23; regs. 94/1813; repealed in pt.: regs. 94/1813.
sch. 3, amended: 1994, c. 9, sch. 23; repealed in pt.: *ibid.,* schs. 23, 26.
sch. 5, amended: regs. 94/1813.

23. Reservoirs Act 1975.
s. 2, amended: 1994, c. 19, sch. 11; repealed in pt.: *ibid.,* schs. 11, 18.
s. 2, amended(S.): 1994, c. 39, sch. 13.
ss. 4, 5, regs. 94/1533.

24. House of Commons Disqualification Act 1975.
sch.-1, amended: 1994, c. 13, sch. 2; c. 19, schs. 13, 14; c. 21, sch. 1; c. 26, sch. 4; c. 30, sch. 2; repealed in pt.: 1994, c. 21, sch. 11, Pt. IV; (prosp.); c. 40, sch. 17.
sch. 1, amended(S.): 1994, c. 39, s. 177, sch. 13; repealed in pt.(S.): *ibid.*, sch. 14.

25. Northern Ireland Assembly Disqualification Act 1975.
sch. 1, amended: 1994, c. 13, sch. 2; c. 19, schs. 13, 14; c. 21, sch. 1; repealed in pt. (prosp.): 1994, c. 21, sch. 11, Pt. IV.

27. Ministerial and other Salaries Act 1975.
s. 1, order 93/3166.

30. Local Government (Scotland) Act 1975.
s. 1, repealed in pt.: 1994, c. 39, sch. 14.
s. 2, amended: orders 94/911–913, 2068–2081; 1994, c. 39, sch. 13.
s. 3, amended: orders 94/911, 2068–2071, 2073–2081.
s. 4, repealed: 1994, c. 39, sch. 14.
s. 6, orders 94/911–913, 2068–2081.
s. 6, amended: 1994, c. 39, ss. 157, 160; repealed in pt.: *ibid.*, sch. 14.
s. 7, repealed in pt.: *ibid.*
s. 7A, amended: *ibid.*, sch. 13; repealed in pt.: *ibid.*, schs. 13, 14.
s. 8, amended: *ibid.*, sch. 13.
s. 13, repealed: *ibid.*, sch. 14.
s. 15A, added: *ibid.*, s. 168.
s. 16, repealed in pt.: *ibid.*, sch. 14.
s. 23, amended: *ibid.*, sch. 13; repealed in pt.: *ibid.*, schs. 13, 14.
s. 28, amended: *ibid.*, sch. 13.
s. 29A, repealed in pt.: *ibid.*, sch. 14.
ss. 35, 37, orders 94/911–913, 2068–2081.
s. 37, amended: order 94/2072; 1994, c. 39, sch. 13.
sch. 3, see *Morgan Guaranty Trust Company of New York* v. *Lothian Regional Council* (O.H.), 1994 S.C.L.R. 213.

1975—cont.

30. Local Government (Scotland) Act 1975—cont.
sch. 3, amended: 1994, c. 39, sch. 13; repealed in pt.: *ibid.*, s. 168, sch. 14.
sch. 6, repealed in pt.: *ibid.*, sch. 14.

34. Evidence (Proceedings in Other Jurisdictions) Act 1975.
see *Dailey Petroleum Services* v. *Pioneer Oil Tools, The Times,* December 3, 1993.

41. Industrial and Provident Societies Act 1975.
s. 2, order 94/341.

45. Finance (No. 2) Act 1975.
s. 5, repealed in pt.: 1994, c. 22, sch. 5.
s. 67, repealed in pt. (prosp.): 1994, c. 9, sch. 26.

46. International Road Haulage Permits Act 1975.
s. 1, amended: 1994, c. 22, sch. 3.

47. Litigants in Person (Costs and Expenses) Act 1975.
s. 1, see *Nader (t/a Try Us)* v. *Customs and Excise Commissioners* [1993] STC 806, C.A.

50. Guard Dogs Act 1975.
s. 7, amended: 1994, c. 19, sch. 16; repealed in pt.: *ibid.,* schs. 16, 18.
s. 7, amended(S.): 1994, c. 39, sch. 13.

51. Salmon and Freshwater Fisheries Act 1975.
s. 4, see *R.* v. *CPC (U.K.), The Times,* August 4, 1994, C.A.; *National Rivers Authority* v. *Welsh Development Agency* (1994) 158 J.P. 506, D.C.

52. Safety of Sports Grounds Act 1975.
s. 1, order 94/2239.
ss. 3–5, 10, 10A, 11, amended: 1994, c. 19, sch. 16.
s. 17, amended: *ibid.*; repealed in pt.: *ibid.,* schs. 16, 18.
s. 17, amended(S.): 1994, c. 39, sch. 13.
s. 18, order 94/2239.

55. Statutory Corporations (Financial Provisions) Act 1975.
schs. 2, 4, repealed in pt. (prosp.): 1994, c. 21, sch. 11, Pt. III.

56. Coal Industry Act 1975.
s. 1, repealed (prosp.): 1994, c. 21, sch. 11, Pt. IV.
s. 2, see *Hepworth Building Products* v. *British Coal Corp., The Times,* March 18, 1994, C.A.
ss. 2 (in pt.), 3, schs. 1 (in pt.), 2, repealed (prosp.): 1994, c. 21, sch. 11, Pt. II.

57. Local Government (Miscellaneous Provisions) Act 1976.
ss. 46, 55, 80, see *Windsor and Maidenhead Royal Borough Council* v. *Khan (t/a Top Cabs)* [1994] RTR 87, D.C.

1975—cont.

60. Social Security Pensions Act 1975.
s. 52A, order 93/2904.
s. 59, order 94/776.

63. Inheritance (Provision for Family and Dependants) Act 1975.
see *Harlow* v. *National Westminster Bank, The Times,* January 3, 1994, C.A.
s. 9, see *Powell* v. *Osbourne* [1993] 1 FLR 1001, C.A.

65. Sex Discrimination Act 1975.
s. 1, see *Bhudi* v. *EMI Refiners* [1994] I.C.R. 307, E.A.T.
ss. 1, 5, 6, see *Dixon* v. *Rees; Hopkins* v. *Shepherd & Partners* [1993] IRLR 468, E.A.T.
ss. 1, 62, see *Wadman* v. *Carpenter Farrer Partnership* [1993] IRLR 374, E.A.T.
ss. 6, 76, see *Swithland Motors* v. *Clarke* [1994] I.C.R. 231, E.A.T.
s. 23A, amended: 1994, c. 30, sch. 2.
s. 23D, added: *ibid.*
s. 25, amended: *ibid.*
s. 53, see *R.* v. *Secretary of State for Employment, ex p. Equal Opportunities Commission* [1994] 2 W.L.R. 409, H.L.
s. 76, see *Gillick* v. *BP Chemicals* [1993] IRLR 437, E.A.T.

70. Welsh Development Agency Act 1975.
s. 16, amended: 1994, c. 19, sch. 16.
s. 27, repealed in pt. (prosp.): 1994, c. 21, schs. 9, 11, Pt. II.

71. Employment Protection Act 1975.
sch. 13, repealed in pt.: 1994, c. 40, sch. 17.

72. Children Act 1975.
s. 47, see *D.* v. *Grampian Regional Council,* 1994 S.L.T. 1038.
ss. 47, 48, Act of Sederunt 94/1443.
s. 99, amended(S.): 1994, c. 39, sch. 13; repealed in pt.(S): *ibid.,* sch. 14.
s. 102, Act of Sederunt: 94/1443.

75. Policyholders Protection Act 1975.
s. 3, amended: regs. 94/1696.
s. 4, see *Ackman* v. *Policyholders' Protection Board, Royal Insurance (U.K.) and New Hampshire Insurance Co.* [1993] 2 Lloyd's Rep. 533, H.L.
ss. 6, 8, see *Scher* v. *Policyholders Protection Board (Nos. 1 and 2) (Note)* [1994] 2 W.L.R. 593, H.L.

76. Local Land Charges Act 1975.
s. 3, amended: 1994, c. 19, sch. 16.

1976

1. National Coal Board (Finance) Act 1976.
ss. 2, 4, repealed (prosp.): 1994, c. 21, sch. 11, Pt. III.

1976—cont.

3. Road Traffic (Drivers' Ages and Hours of Work) Act 1976.
s. 2, amended: 1994, c. 40, sch. 13.

22. Freshwater and Salmon Fisheries (Scotland) Act 1976.
s. 1, orders 93/3126; 94/1949, 2621–2623.

25. Fair Employment (Northern Ireland) Act 1976.
s. 16, see *McCausland* v. *Dungannon District Council* [1993] IRLR 583, C.A. (N.I.).
s. 26, S.R. 1994 No. 50.

30. Fatal Accidents Act 1976.
see *Crabtree (Administratrix of the Estate of Crabtree)* v. *Wilson* [1993] P.I.Q.R. Q24, C.A.
s. 2, see *Byrne* v. *Graham,* March 4, 1994; Pill J.; Liverpool D.C.
ss. 3, 4, see *Greenhalgh* v. *Smith and R.W. Shaw Transport,* October 29, 1993, Mr. Recorder V.E. Hall, Peterborough County Ct.

32. Lotteries and Amusements Act 1976.
s. 12, regs. 93/3223.
ss. 18, 24, order 93/3224.
s. 23, schs. 1, 3, amended: 1994, c. 19, sch. 16; c. 39, sch. 13(S.).

34. Restrictive Trade Practices Act 1976.
s. 1, amended: 1994, c. 40, sch. 3.
s. 23, amended: *ibid.,* s. 11.
s. 24, amended: *ibid.,* sch. 3.
s. 25A, added: *ibid.*
s. 26, amended: *ibid.*
s. 27, regs. 94/1095.
s. 27A, added: 1994, c. 40, s. 10.
s. 35, see *Supply of Ready Mixed Concrete (No. 2)* [1994] I.C.R. 57, C.A.
s. 36, amended: 1994, c. 40, sch. 3.
s. 41, amended: 1994, c. 21, sch. 9.
s. 42, regs. 94/1095.
ss. 42, 43, amended: 1994, c. 40, s. 10.
sch. 2, amended: *ibid.,* sch. 3.
sch. 3, amended: 1994, c. 26, sch. 4.

35. Police Pensions Act 1976.
s. 1, regs. 94/641.
ss. 7, 11, amended: 1994, c. 29, sch. 5.
sch. 2, repealed in pt.: *ibid.,* sch. 9.

36. Adoption Act 1976.
ss. 6, 11, 57, see *W. (Adoption Application), Re* [1993] 1 F.C.R. 988, Douglas Brown J.
ss. 6, 12, modified: regs. 94/2767.
ss. 6, 16, see *E.H. and M.H. (Step-Parent Adoption), Re* [1993] Fam. Law 187, H.H.J. Heald.
ss. 6, 30, 31, see *C. (A Minor) (Adoption Notice: Local Authority), Re, The Times,* June 28, 1994, C.A.
ss. 12, 16, 18, 19, see *A. (A Minor) (Adoption: Contact Order), Re* [1993] 2 FLR 645, C.A.

1976—cont.

36. Adoption Act 1976—cont.

s. 13, see *K.T. (A Minor) (Adoption), Re* [1993] Fam. Law 567, Ward J.

ss. 16, 18, see *U. (A Minor), Re* [1993] 2 FLR 992, C.A.

ss. 24, 27, 29, modified: regs. 94/2767.

s. 39, see *S. (Adopted Child: Contact), Re* [1993] 2 F.C.R. 234, Thorpe J.

ss. 39, 42, 44–47, modified: regs. 94/2767.

s. 50, see *X. (A Minor) (Adoption Order), Re, The Times,* April 11, 1994, C.A.; *X. (A Minor) (Adoption Details: Disclosure), Re* [1994] 3 W.L.R. 327, C.A.

ss. 50, 51, 61, 63, 64, 67, modified: regs. 94/2767.

s. 72, amended: 1994, c. 19, sch. 10; modified: regs. 94/2767.

sch. 1, modified: regs. 94/2767.

38. Dangerous Wild Animals Act 1976.

s. 7, amended: 1994, c. 19, sch. 16; repealed in pt.: *ibid.,* schs. 16, 18.

s. 7, amended(S): 1994, c. 39, sch. 13.

39. Divorce (Scotland) Act 1976.

s. 1, see *Smith* v. *Smith* (Sh.Ct.), 1994 S.C.L.R. 244.

s. 11, Act of Sederunt 94/1443.

40. Finance Act 1976.

s. 11, amended: 1994, c. 9, sch. 2; repealed in pt.: *ibid.,* schs. 2, 26; c. 22, sch. 5.

s. 12, see *Naylor* v. *Hutson* [1994] F.S.R. 63, Maddocks J.

s. 12, repealed in pt.: 1994, c. 9, schs. 2, 26; repealed: 1994, c. 22, sch. 5.

50. Domestic Violence and Matrimonial Proceedings Act 1976.

s. 1, see *G.* v. *J. (Ouster Order); sub nom. Grant* v. *James* [1993] 1 FLR 1008, C.A.

55. Agriculture (Miscellaneous Provisions) Act 1976.

ss. 18, 20, see *Francis Perceval Saunders dec'd Trustees* v. *Ralph* [1993] 28 EG 127, Jowitt J.

57. Local Government (Miscellaneous Provisions) Act 1976.

s. 15, amended: 1994, c. 21, sch. 9.

s. 19, see *Credit Suisse* v. *Allerdale Borough Council, The Independent,* June 17, 1994, Colman J.

s. 26, amended: 1994, c. 21, sch. 9.

ss. 30, 44, amended: 1994, c. 29, sch. 4.

ss. 46, 55, 80, see *Dittah* v. *Birmingham City Council; Choudhry* v. *D.P.P.* [1993] RTR 356, D.C.

58. International Carriage of Perishable Foodstuffs Act 1976.

s. 19, amended: 1994, c. 22, sch. 3.

1976—cont.

63. Bail Act 1976.

s. 1, repealed in pt.: 1994, c. 33, sch. 11.

s. 3, amended: *ibid.,* s. 27, schs. 4, 9; repealed in pt.: *ibid.,* s. 27, sch. 11.

s. 3A, added: *ibid.,* s. 27.

s. 4, amended: *ibid.,* sch. 10.

s. 5, amended: *ibid.,* schs. 3, 4.

s. 5A, added: *ibid.,* sch. 3.

s. 5B, added: *ibid.,* s. 30.

ss. 6, 9, amended: *ibid.,* s. 4.

sch. 1, amended: *ibid.,* s. 26, sch. 10.

66. Licensing (Scotland) Act 1976.

s. 1, amended: 1994, c. 39, sch. 13; repealed in pt.: *ibid.,* schs. 13, 14.

ss. 3, 5, repealed in pt.: *ibid.,* schs. 13, 14.

s. 7, amended: *ibid.,* sch. 13; repealed in pt.: *ibid.,* schs. 13, 14.

s. 16, see *Khan* v. *City of Glasgow District Licensing Board* (O.H.), 1994 S.C.L.R. 529.

ss. 16, 31, see *Graham* v. *Cunninghame District Licensing Board* (Sh.Ct.), 1994 S.C.L.R. 179.

s. 17, see *Monklands District Licensing Board* v. *Forrestfield Hotel,* 1994 S.L.T. 823.

ss. 17, 18, see *Di Ciacca* v. *Lorn, Mid Argyll, Kintyre and Islay Divisional Licensing Board,* 1994 S.C.L.R. 152.

ss. 18, 64, see *J.A.E. (Glasgow)* v. *Glasgow District Licensing Board* (O.H.), 1994 S.C.L.R. 333.

s. 23, amended: 1994, c. 39, sch. 13.

s. 39, see *Cambridge Street Properties* v. *City of Glasgow District Licensing Board,* 1994 S.L.T.(Sh.Ct.) 4; *Latif* v. *Motherwell District Licensing Board,* 1994 S.L.T. 414.

ss. 58, 64, see *Cindarella's Rockafella's* v. *Glasgow District Licensing Board* (O.H.), 1994 S.C.L.R. 591.

s. 63A, added: 1994, c. 40, s. 18.

ss. 67, 101, see *Ahmed* v. *MacDonald,* 1994 S.C.L.R. 320.

ss. 90, 101, 121, 138, sch. 1, see *Standard Taverns* v. *McAneny* (O.H.), 1994 S.C.L.R. 1.

s. 105, amended: 1994, c. 39, sch. 13.

s. 117, see *Stephen* v. *Woodend Bowling Club,* 1994 S.L.T.(Sh.Ct.) 9.

s. 119, amended: 1994, c. 40, s. 22.

s. 120, amended: 1994, c. 39, sch. 13.

s. 129, see *Graham* v. *Cunninghame District Licensing Board* (Sh.Ct.), 1994 S.C.L.R. 179.

s. 139, amended: 1994, c. 39, sch. 13.

71. Supplementary Benefits Act 1976.

see *Social Security Decision No. R(SB)* 1/94.

s. 20, see *Plewa* v. *Chief Adjudication Officer* [1994] 3 W.L.R. 317, H.L.

1976—cont.

71. Supplementary Benefits Act 1976— *cont.*

sch. 5, amended: 1994, c. 19, sch. 10.
sch. 5, amended(S.): 1994, c. 39, sch. 13; repealed in pt.(S.): *ibid.*, schs. 13, 14.

74. Race Relations Act 1976.

see *Mukoro* v. *European Bank for Reconstruction and Development, The Times,* June 2, 1994, E.A.T.
s. 18A, amended: 1994, c. 30, sch. 2.
s. 18D, added: *ibid.*
s. 19, amended: *ibid.*
s. 19A, amended: 1994, c. 19, sch. 16.
s. 56, regs. 94/1748.
s. 56, amended: 1994, c. 10, s. 2; repealed in pt.: *ibid.,* s. 1, sch.
s. 68, see *Lindsay* v. *Ironsides Ray & Vials* [1994] I.C.R. 384, E.A.T.
s. 71, amended: 1994, c. 29, sch. 4; c. 39, sch. 13(S).
s. 74, amended: 1994, c. 10, s. 2.
s. 75, regs. 94/109, 1986.

75. Development of Rural Wales Act 1976.

s. 1, amended: 1994, c. 19, sch. 16.
s. 4, amended: 1994, c. 21, sch. 9.
s. 34, amended: 1994, c. 19, sch. 16; repealed in pt.: *ibid.,* schs. 9, 11, Pt. II.
sch. 1, amended: *ibid.,* sch. 16.
sch. 3, amended: *ibid.*; repealed in pt.: *ibid.,* schs. 16, 18; (prosp.) c. 21, schs. 9, 11, Pt. II.
s. 5, amended: 1994, c. 40, sch. 11.

80. Rent (Agriculture) Act 1976.

see *McPhail* v. *Greensmith* [1993] 2 EGLR 228, C.A.
s. 5, amended: 1994, c. 19, sch. 8; c. 29, sch. 4.

82. Sexual Offences (Amendment) Act 1976.

s. 1, amended: 1994, c. 33, sch. 10; repealed in pt.: *ibid.*, sch. 11.
s. 2, amended: *ibid.*, sch. 10.
s. 3, amended: *ibid.*, sch. 4.
s. 4, amended: *ibid.*, schs. 4, 9, 10.
s. 7, amended: *ibid.*, sch. 10; repealed in pt.: *ibid.*, sch. 11.

1977

5. Social Security (Miscellaneous Provisions) Act 1977.

s. 12, orders 94/771–773, 1906.
s. 24, order 94/772.

15. Marriage (Scotland) Act 1977.

ss. 3, 19, 25, 26, regs. 93/3152.

27. Presumption of Death (Scotland) Act 1977.

s. 4, amended: Act of Sederunt 94/1443.
s. 15, Act of Sederunt 94/1443.

30. Rentcharges Act 1977.

s. 11, amended: 1994, c. 36, sch. 1.

1977—cont.

36. Finance Act 1977.

s. 5, repealed in pt.: 1994, c. 22, sch. 5.

37. Patents Act 1977.

s. 3, see *Boehringer Mannheim GmbH* v. *Genzyme* [1993] F.S.R. 716, Aldous J.
s. 44, see *Chiron Corp.* v. *Organon Teknika (No. 2)*; *Chiron Corp.* v. *Murex Diagnostics* [1993] F.S.R. 567, C.A.
ss. 63, 75, see *PLG Research* v. *Ardon International (No. 2)* [1993] P.C.R. 698, Aldous J.
s. 65, see *Wellcome Foundation, The* v. *Discpharm (No. 2)* [1993] F.S.R. 444, Patents County Ct.
s. 67, see *Optical Coating Laboratory Inc.* v. *Pilkington PE* [1993] F.S.R. 310, H.H.J. Ford.
s. 70, see *Hong Kong Toy Centre* v. *Tomy U.K., The Times,* January 14, 1994, Aldous J.
s. 72, see *Mentor Corp.* v. *Hollister Inc.* [1993] R.P.C. 7, C.A.
s. 73, see *Citizen Watch's Patent* [1993] R.P.C. 1, Patent Office.
s. 92, Act of Sederunt 94/1443.

39. Coal Industry Act 1977.

ss. 1, 7, repealed (prosp.): 1994, c. 21, sch. 11, Pt. III.
s. 9, repealed in pt. (prosp.): *ibid.,* sch. 11, Pts. II, IV.
s. 10, repealed (prosp.): *ibid.,* sch. 11, Pt. IV.
s. 11, repealed (prosp.): *ibid.,* sch. 11, Pts. II–IV.
ss. 12 (in pt.), 13–16, schs. 1, 3, repealed (prosp.): *ibid.,* sch. 11, Pt. III.
sch. 4, repealed in pt.: *ibid.,* sch. 11, Pt. I, (prosp.) III, IV.
sch. 5, repealed (prosp.): *ibid.,* sch. 11, Pt. III.

42. Rent Act 1977.

s. 2, see *Vedmay, Re* (1994) 26 H.L.R. 70, Mr G. Lightman, Q.C.
s. 5, sch. 15, see *Dawncar Investments* v. *Plews* (1993) 25 H.L.R. 639, C.A.
s. 12, see *O'Sullivan* v. *Barnett, The Times,* May 25, 1994, C.A.
s. 14, amended: 1994, c. 19, schs. 8, 13; c. 29, sch. 4.
s. 62, amended: 1994, c. 19, sch. 8.
ss. 66, 67, 67A, 73, 74, 79, regs. 93/1511 (corrected by regs. 94/725).
ss. 83, 124, 149, amended: 1994, c. 19, sch. 8.
sch. 2, amended: 1994, c. 36, sch. 1.

43. Protection of Eviction Act 1977.

s. 1, see *Bolton Metropolitan Borough Council* v. *McKay (Gerrard),* April 18, 1994; H.H.J. Livesey, Q.C.; Preston Crown Ct.
ss. 3A, 6, amended: 1994, c. 19, sch. 8.

CAP.

1977—cont.

45. Criminal Law Act 1977.

s. 1, see *R.* v. *Daghir; R.* v. *Speckman, The Times*, May 27, 1994, C.A.

s. 2, see *R.* v. *Lovick (Sylvia)* [1993] Crim.L.R. 890, C.A.

s. 6, amended: 1994, c. 33, s. 72; repealed in pt.: *ibid.*, s. 72, sch. 11.

s. 7, substituted: *ibid.*, s. 73.

s. 12A, added: *ibid.*, s. 74.

s. 38, repealed: *ibid.*, sch. 11.

ss. 38A, 38B, amended: *ibid.*, sch. 9.

46. Insurance Brokers (Registration) Act 1977.

ss. 27, 28, order 94/2569.

49. National Health Service Act 1977.

ss. 3, 13, 14, see *Porter and Nanayakkara* v. *Queen's Medical Centre (Nottingham University Hospital)* [1993] IRLR 486, Sir Godfray le Quesne sitting as a deputy judge.

s. 7, order 94/545; amended: *ibid.*

s. 8, orders 94/680, 681, 683, 684, 1260, 1261, 2288, 2289.

s. 11, orders 94/589, 603, 1831.

s. 13, regs. 94/590, 682.

s. 14, regs. 94/590.

s. 15, regs. 93/3172; 94/284, 633.

s. 16, regs. 93/3172; 94/284, 682.

s. 17, regs. 94/281, 590, 682.

s. 18, regs. 94/590, 682.

s. 22, amended: 1994, c. 19, sch. 10.

ss. 23, 27, amended: 1994, c. 22, sch. 3.

s. 28A, amended: 1994, c. 19, sch. 10.

s. 29, regs. 93/2972; 94/633, 634.

ss. 30, 33, regs. 94/633.

s. 35, regs. 93/3172.

s. 36, regs. 93/2972, 3172; 94/634.

s. 39, regs. 93/2972; 94/634.

s. 41, regs. 94/2402.

s. 42, regs. 93/2972; 94/634, 682, 2402.

s. 43, regs. 94/2402.

s. 77, regs. 94/690, 2402.

s. 79A, regs. 94/530.

s. 92, orders 93/2857; 94/22–27, 29–36, 51–55, 59–62, 223–226, 278, 281, 318, 358–360, 481, 483–494, 619–625, 661–666, 679, 896, 945, 1913–1921, 2255–2258, 2332–2342, 2357–2370, 2412.

s. 121, regs. 94/1535.

s. 126, regs. 93/2972, 3172; 94/131, 284, 495, 590, 602, 633, 634, 640, 682, 690; orders 93/2815, 2834–2841, 2848, 2849, 3140, 3141; 94/195, 316, 317, 482, 589, 603, 680, 681, 683, 684, 745, 797, 827–833, 856, 858–863, 986–995, 1053, 1054, 1086, 1205, 1206, 1211, 1260, 1261, 1268, 1269, 1294–1301, 1309–1320, 1332–1341, 1343, 1388, 1534, 1555, 1559–1564, 2288, 2289, 2402, 2522, 2690.

s. 128, regs. 94/1262.

CAP.

1977—cont.

49. National Health Service Act 1977—cont.

s. 128, amended: 1994, c. 19, sch. 10.

sch. 2, amended: 1994, c. 22, sch. 3.

sch. 5, regs. 94/602; order 94/603.

sch. 7, amended: 1994, c. 19, sch. 10.

sch. 12, regs. 94/131, 495, 530.

50. Unfair Contract Terms Act 1977.

ss. 6, 11, sch. 11, see *W. Photoprint* v. *Forward Trust Group* (1993) 12 Tr.L.R. 146, D.B. Johnson, Q.C., sitting as a deputy judge of the High Court.

sch. 1, see *Cheltenham and Gloucester Building Society* v. *Ebbage*, May 27, 1994.

1978

2. Commonwealth Development Corporation Act 1978.

s. 3, order 94/2880.

3. Refuse Disposal (Amenity) Act 1978.

s. 11, amended: 1994, c. 19, sch. 9; c. 22, sch. 3.

s. 11, amended(S.): 1994, c. 39, sch. 13.

10. European Parliamentary Elections Act 1978.

s. 178, amended: regs. 94/342.

sch. 1, order 94/83; regs. 94/748, 782, 894.

schs. 1, 2, amended: 1994, c. 19, sch. 16; repealed in pt.: *ibid.*, schs. 16, 18.

schs. 1, 2, amended(S.): 1994, c. 39, sch. 13.

sch. 4, amended: regs. 94/342.

22. Domestic Proceedings and Magistrates' Courts Act 1978.

s. 20ZA, amended: order 94/731.

s. 30, amended: 1994, c. 29, sch. 8.

23. Judicature (Northern Ireland) Act 1978.

s. 31, see *Harper* v. *Associated British Foods* [1991] NI 244, C.A. (N.I.).

s. 55, S.R. 1994, No. 286.

s. 116, S.Rs. 1993 No. 418; 1994 Nos. 278–283.

sch. 5, repealed in pt.: 1994, c. 26, sch. 5.

26. Suppression of Terrorism Act 1978.

sch. 1, order 94/570.

28. Adoption (Scotland) Act 1978.

s. 2, amended: 1994, c. 39, sch. 13.

ss. 6, 16, see *D.* v. *F.*, 1994 S.C.L.R. 417.

ss. 12, 18, see *D.* v. *Grampian Regional Council* (O.H.), 1994 S.C.L.R. 515.

ss. 16, 59, see *X.* v. *Y.* (Sh.Ct.), 1994 S.C.L.R. 775.

s. 59, Act of Sederunt 94/1443.

s. 65, amended: 1994, c. 39, sch. 13.

29. National Health Service (Scotland) Act 1978.

s. 12A, orders 93/2926–2929, 2931–2934, 2936–2938, 3018–3026; 94/107, 1408, 1607; regs. 93/3057.

CAP.
1978—cont.

29. National Health Service (Scotland) Act 1978—cont.

s. 12E, order 94/496.

s. 12G, orders 94/510, 2485.

ss. 15, 16, amended: 1994, c. 22, sch. 3.

s. 16A, amended: 1994, c. 39, sch. 13; repealed in pt.: *ibid.*, schs. 13, 14.

s. 19, regs. 94/697, 884, 2624.

s. 26, regs. 94/635.

s. 27, regs. 94/697, 884, 2624.

s. 69, regs. 94/697.

s. 70, regs. 94/145, 635, 636, 2587.

ss. 71, 71A, regs. 94/636.

ss. 73, 74, regs. 94/635.

s. 75, regs. 94/697.

s. 98, regs. 94/1770.

s. 102, substituted: 1994, c. 16, s. 1.

s. 105, regs. 93/3057; 94/145, 635, 636, 697, 884, 1770, 2484; orders 94/1408, 2587.

s. 105, repealed in pt.: 1994, c. 16, s. 1.

s. 108, regs. 93/3057; 94/145, 635, 636, 884, 1770, 2587, 2624; order 94/1408.

s. 108, amended: 1994, c. 16, s. 1; c. 39, sch. 13.

sch. 7A, orders 94/1607, 2484.

sch. 11, regs. 94/635, 2587.

sch. 12, regs. 94/145.

30. Interpretation Act 1978.

s. 5, sch. 1, see *Pruden* v. *Cunard Ellerman* [1993] IRLR 317, E.A.T.

s. 16, see *Aitken* v. *South Hams District Council* [1994] 3 W.L.R. 333, H.L.

sch. 1, amended: 1994, c. 19, sch. 2; c. 33, sch. 4; repealed in pt.: *ibid.*, sch. 11.

33. State Immunity Act 1978.

s. 13, see *Soleh Boneh International* v. *Government of the Republic of Uganda and National Housing Corp.* [1993] 2 Lloyd's Rep. 208, C.A.

ss. 13, 14, see *Coreck Maritime* v. *Sevrybokholodflot* (O.H.), 1994 S.L.T. 893.

s. 14, order 13/2809.

37. Protection of Children Act 1978.

s. 1, amended: 1994, c. 33, s. 84; repealed in pt.: *ibid.*, s. 84, sch. 11.

s. 2, amended: *ibid.*, sch. 10.

s. 4, amended: *ibid.*; repealed in pt.: *ibid.*, schs. 9, 11.

s. 5, amended: *ibid.*, sch. 10.

s. 7, amended: *ibid.*, s. 84.

42. Finance Act 1978.

s. 8, amended: 1994, c. 9, sch. 2; repealed in pt.: 1994, c. 22, sch. 5.

44. Employment Protection (Consolidation) Act 1978.

see *R.* v. *Secretary of State for Employment, ex p. Equal Opportunities Commission, The Times,* March 4, 1994, H.L.

s. 1, see *Morley* v. *Heritage* [1993] IRLR 40, C.A.

CAP.
1978—cont.

44. Employment Protection (Consolidation) Act 1978—cont.

s. 18, order 94/1409.

s. 23, see *Wilson* v. *Associated Newspapers; Palmer* v. *Associated British Ports* [1993] IRLR 366, C.A.; *Department of Transport* v. *Gallacher, The Times,* March 25, 1994, C.A.

ss. 23, 55, see *Johnstone* v. *B.B.C. Enterprises* [1994] I.C.R. 180, E.A.T.

s. 33, see *Hilton International Hotels (U.K.)* v. *Kaissi, The Times,* March 7, 1994, E.A.T.

s. 55, see *Brown* v. *JBD Engineering* [1993] IRLR 568, E.A.T.

ss. 55, 57, see *Ely* v. *YKK Fasteners (U.K.)* [1993] IRLR 500, C.A.

s. 57, see *Heron* v. *Citylink-Nottingham* [1993] IRLR 372, E.A.T.; *Duffy* v. *Yeomans & Partners, The Independent,* July 15, 1994, C.A.

ss. 57–59, 74, see *Britool* v. *Roberts* [1993] IRLR 481, E.A.T.

ss. 57, 74, see *Steel Stockholders (Birmingham)* v. *Kirkwood* [1993] IRLR 515, E.A.T.; *Robertson* v. *Magnet (Retail Division)* [1993] IRLR 512, E.A.T.

s. 58, see *CGB Publishing* v. *Killey* [1993] IRLR 520, E.A.T.

ss. 58, 59, see *Driver* v. *Cleveland Structural Engineering Co.* [1994] I.C.R. 372, E.A.T.

s. 59, repealed in pt.: 1994, c. 40, s. 36, sch. 17.

s. 60A, amended: 1994, c. 20, sch. 4; c. 40, sch. 8.

ss. 62, 69, 73, 74, see *TNT Express (U.K.)* v. *Downes* [1993] IRLR 432, E.A.T.

s. 64, see *Northern General Hospital National Health Service Trust* v. *Gale* [1994] I.C.R. 426, C.A.

s. 65, amended: 1994, c. 20, sch. 4; c. 40, sch. 8.

s. 67, see *Gillick* v. *BP Chemicals* [1993] IRLR 437, E.A.T.; *Pruden* v. *Cunard Ellerman* [1993] IRLR 317, E.A.T.; *London International College* v. *Sen* [1993] IRLR 333, C.A.; *Capital Foods Retail* v. *Corrigan* [1993] IRLR 430, E.A.T.; *Marley (U.K.)* v. *Anderson* [1994] I.C.R. 295, E.A.T.

s. 68, see *Berry* v. *Ravensbourne National Health Service Trust* [1993] I.C.R. 871, E.A.T.

ss. 68, 69, see *Cowley* v. *Manson Timber* [1994] I.C.R. 252, E.A.T.

s. 74, see *Dunlop* v. *Farrell* [1993] I.C.R. 885, E.A.T.; *Devine* v. *Designer Flowers Wholesale Florist Sundries* [1993] IRLR 57, E.A.T.; *Hilton International Hotels (U.K.)* v. *Faraji* [1994] I.C.R. 259, E.A.T.

1978—cont.

44. Employment Protection (Consolidation) Act 1978—*cont.*

s. 76, repealed in pt.: 1994, c. 10, s. 1, sch.

s. 127, see *Morley* v. *Heritage* [1993] IRLR 400, C.A.

s. 128, regs. 94/536.

s. 129, amended: 1994, c. 20, sch. 4; c. 40, sch. 8.

s. 131, orders 94/1623, 1624.

ss. 133, 141, amended: 1994, c. 20, sch. 4; c. 40, sch. 8.

s. 149, orders 93/3167; 94/417.

s. 150, amended: 1994, c. 20, sch. 4; c. 40, sch. 8.

s. 154, regs. 94/536; rules 93/2854; orders 93/3167; 94/417, 1623, 1624.

sch. 3, amended: 1994, c. 18, sch. 1.

sch. 9, regs. 94/536.

sch. 11, rules 93/2854.

sch. 12, amended: 1994, c. 20, sch. 4; c. 40, sch. 8.

sch. 13, see *Justfern* v. *Skaife D'Ingerthorpe* [1994] I.C.R. 286, E.A.T.; *A. & G. Tuck* v. *Bartlett* [1994] I.C.R. 379, E.A.T.

sch. 16, repealed in pt.: 1994, c. 10, sch.

47. Civil Liability (Contribution) Act 1978.

see *Arab Monetary Fund* v. *Hashim (No. 9), The Times*, October 11, 1994, Chadwick J.

ss. 1, 2, see *Saipem SpA and Conoco (U.K.)* v. *Dredging VO2 BV and Geosite Surveys; Volvox Hollandia (No. 2), The* [1993] 2 Lloyd's Rep. 315, Tuckey J.

49. Community Service by Offenders (Scotland) Act 1978.

ss. 2, 12, amended: 1994, c. 39, sch. 13.

50. Inner Urban Areas Act 1978.

ss. 1, 2, 7, repealed in pt.(S).: 1994, c. 39, schs. 13, 14.

ss. 1, 2, 7, 17, sch., amended: 1994, c. 19, sch. 16.

56. Parliamentary Pensions Act 1978.

ss. 2–5, 6 (in pt.), 7, 11, 12 (in pt.), 18 (in pt.), repealed: regs. 93/3253.

60. Theft Act 1978.

s. 3, see *R.* v. *Aziz* [1993] Crim.L.R. 708, C.A.

1979

2. Customs and Excise Management Act 1979.

see *R.* v. *Cousins*, August 1, 1994; H.H.J. Prendergast; Inner London Crown Ct.

s. 1, amended: 1994, c. 23, sch. 14.

ss. 20, 20A, 22, 22A, 25, 25A, 27, 42, 75C, 77C, amended: regs. 93/3014.

ss. 92, 93, amended: 1994, c. 9, sch. 4.

1979—cont.

2. Customs and Excise Management Act 1979—*cont.*

s. 100A, orders 94/143, 144, 1410, 2216.

ss. 100B, 100C, repealed: 1994, c. 23, sch. 15.

ss. 100J, 101, amended: 1994, c. 9, sch. 4.

s. 102, amended: 1994, c. 22, sch. 3.

ss. 107, 108, amended: 1994, c. 9, sch. 4.

s. 111, amended: *ibid.*; repealed in pt.: *ibid.*, schs. 4, 26.

s. 113, repealed in pt.: *ibid.*, sch. 26.

ss. 114–116, amended: *ibid.*, sch. 4.

s. 116A, repealed: *ibid.*, sch. 26.

s. 117, amended: *ibid.*, s. 18.

s. 118A, regs. 94/1737.

s. 118A, amended: 1994, c. 9, s. 256; repealed in pt.: *ibid.*, s. 256, sch. 26.

s. 118G, amended: *ibid.*, sch. 4.

s. 127, repealed: *ibid.*, s. 18, sch. 26.

ss. 147, 155, amended: 1994, c. 33, sch. 4.

s. 170, see *R.* v. *Latif; R.* v. *Shahzad, The Times,* March 17, 1994, C.A.

s. 170A, amended: 1994, c. 9, sch. 4.

s. 172, regs. 94/1737.

sch. 4, repealed in pt.: 1994, c. 22, sch. 5.

3. Customs and Excise Duties (General Reliefs) Act 1979.

ss. 1, 4, orders 93/3254; 94/1739.

s. 13, order 94/955.

4. Alcoholic Liquor Duties Act 1979.

ss. 8, 10, amended: 1994, c. 9, sch. 4.

ss. 13, 15, amended: *ibid.*, repealed in pt.: *ibid.*, schs. 4, 26, Pt. III.

ss. 16, 18, amended: *ibid.*, sch. 4.

s. 19, amended: *ibid.*, repealed in pt.: *ibid.*, schs. 4, 26, Pt. III.

ss. 20–22, 24, 33–35, 41A, 44, 46, 47, 49, 54, 55, 55A, 56, 59, 61, amended: *ibid.*, sch. 4.

s. 62, amended: *ibid.*, s. 1, sch. 4.

ss. 64, 67, 69, 71, 75, 77, 78, 82, amended: *ibid.*, sch. 4.

sch. 1, substituted: *ibid.*, s. 1, sch. 1.

5. Hydrocarbon Oil Duties Act 1979.

s. 6, amended: 1994, c. 9, s. 3.

s. 10, amended: *ibid.*, sch. 4.

s. 11, amended: *ibid.*, s. 3.

s. 13, amended: *ibid.*, sch. 4.

s. 14, amended: *ibid.*, s. 3, sch. 4.

ss. 20AA, 21–24, amended: *ibid.*, sch. 4.

s. 24, regs. 94/694.

sch. 1, amended: 1994, c. 22, sch. 3.

sch. 4, regs. 94/694.

7. Tobacco Products Duty Act 1979.

s. 7, amended: 1994, c. 9, sch. 4.

s. 8, amended: *ibid.*, sch. 26, Pt. III.

sch. 1, substituted: *ibid.*, s. 2.

10. Public Lending Right Act 1979.

s. 3, order 93/3049.

CAP.

1979—cont.

14. Capital Gains Tax Act 1979.
ss. 78, 85, see *NAP Holdings U.K.* v. *Whittles (Inspector of Taxes)* [1993] STC 592, C.A.
ss. 101, 102, see *Griffin (Inspector of Taxes)* v. *Craig-Harvey* [1994] STC 54, Vinelott J.
s. 115, see *Campbell Connelly & Co.* v. *Barnett (Inspector of Taxes)* [1994] STC 50, C.A.

33. Land Registration (Scotland) Act 1979.
Commencement order: 94/2588.
ss. 2, 9, 12, see *Short's Tr.* v. *Keeper of the Registers of Scotland,* 1994 S.L.T. 65.
s. 21, see *MacLean's Exr.* v. *Kershaw,* 1993 S.L.C.R. 145.
s. 28, amended: 1994, c. 21, sch. 9.
s. 30, order 94/2588.

34. Credit Unions Act 1979.
s. 13, order 93/3100.
s. 31, regs. 94/658.

36. Nurses, Midwives and Health Visitors Act 1979.
s. 6, order 94/586.

38. Estate Agents Act 1979.
s. 10, amended: 1994, c. 21, sch. 9.
s. 18, see *Connell Estate Agents* v. *Begej* [1993] 39 EG 125, C.A.

39. Merchant Shipping Act 1979.
Commencement order: 94/2789.
s. 17, sch. 4, see *Capitan San Luis, The* [1993] 2 Lloyd's Rep. 573, Clarke J.
s. 20, amended: 1994, c. 28, ss. 2, 3.
s. 20A, added: *ibid.*, s. 4.
s. 21, regs. 93/3162–3164, 3231, 3232; 94/422, 502, 1383, 2013, 2014, 2082, 2464.
s. 22, regs. 93/3162–3164, 3231, 3232; 94/422, 1383, 2013, 2014, 2082, 2464.
s. 52, order 94/2789.
sch. 3, see *Higham* v. *Stena Sealink,* June 17, 1994; H.H.J. Bernstein; Liverpool County Ct.
sch. 6, repealed in pt.: 1994, c. 40, sch. 17.

42. Arbitration Act 1979.
see *International Petroleum Refining & Supply Sdad* v. *Elpis Finance SA; Faith, The* [1993] 2 Lloyd's Rep. 408, Hobhouse J.; *Thomas* v. *Countryside Council for Wales* [1994] 04 EG 138, Rougier J.
s. 1, see *Cohen* v. *Baram, The Times,* December 16, 1993, C.A.; *Prudential Assurance Co.* v. *Grand Metropolitan Estate* [1993] 32 EG 74, H.H. Judge Michael Rich, Q.C.; *Secretary of State for the Environment* v. *Euston Centre Investments, The Times,* July 6, 1994, C.A.; *Secretary of State for the Environment* v. *Reed International* [1994] 06 EG 137, Evans-Lombe J.;

CAP.

1979—cont.

42. Arbitration Act 1979—*cont.*
Secretary of State for the Environment v. *Euston Centre Investments* [1994] 1 W.L.R. 563, Mr. John Cherryman, Q.C. sitting as a deputy judge; *Cefetra B.V.* v. *Alfred C. Toepfer International GmbH* [1994] 1 Lloyd's Rep. 93, Colman J.
s. 5, see *Waverley S.F.* v. *Carnaud Metalbox Engineering* [1994] 1 Lloyd's Rep. 38, H.H.J. Kershaw, Q.C.; *Sumitomo Heavy Industries* v. *Oil and Natural Gas Commission* [1994] 1 Lloyd's Rep. 45, Potter J.

46. Ancient Monuments and Archaeological Areas Act 1979.
ss. 2, 3, order 94/1381.
s. 8, amended: 1994, c. 19, sch. 16.
s. 35, amended: *ibid.*; repealed in pt.: *ibid.*, schs. 16, 18.
s. 60, order 94/1381.
s. 61, amended: 1994, c. 19, sch. 16; repealed in pt.: *ibid.*, schs. 16, 18; (prosp.) c. 21, schs. 9, 11, Pt. II.

50. European Parliament (Pay and Pensions) Act 1979.
s. 3, substituted: order 94/1663.
s. 3A, order 94/1663.
s. 4, order 94/1662.

53. Charging Orders Act 1979.
s. 3, see *Ezekiel* v. *Orakpo, The Times,* November 8, 1994, Carnwath J.

54. Sale of Goods Act 1979.
s. 2, see *Connell Estate Agents* v. *Begej* [1993] 39 EG 125, C.A.
s. 11, amended: 1994, c. 35, sch. 2; repealed in pt.: *ibid.*, schs. 2, 3.
ss. 12, 13, amended: *ibid.*, sch. 2.
s. 14, see *Boyter* v. *Thomson,* 1994 S.C.L.R. 293.
s. 14, amended: 1994, c. 35, s. 1, sch. 2.
s. 15, amended: *ibid.*, sch. 2; repeated in pt.: *ibid.*, schs. 2, 3.
s. 15A, added (exc. S.): *ibid.*, s. 4.
s. 15B, added(S.): *ibid.*, s. 5.
s. 22, repealed in pt.: 1994, c. 32, s. 1.
s. 25, see *Forsythe International (U.K.)* v. *Silver Shipping Co. and Petroglobe International; Saetta, The* [1993] 2 Lloyd's Rep. 268, Clarke J.
s. 30, amended (exc. S.): 1994, c. 35, s. 4.
s. 30, amended(S.): *ibid.*, s. 5.
s. 34, amended: *ibid.*, s. 2; repealed in pt.: *ibid.*, s. 2, sch. 3.
s. 35, amended: *ibid.*, s. 2.
s. 35A, added: *ibid.*, s. 3.
s. 53, amended: *ibid.*, sch. 2.
s. 53A, added(S.): *ibid.*, s. 5.
s. 55, amended: *ibid.*, sch. 2.
s. 61, amended: *ibid.*, repealed in pt.: *ibid.*, schs. 2, 3.

1979—cont.

55. Justices of the Peace Act 1979.
ss. 1, 4, amended: 1994, c. 19, sch. 2.
s. 12, amended: 1994, c. 29, sch. 8; repealed in pt.: *ibid.*, sch. 9.
s. 17, see *R. v. Brent Justices, ex p. Richards* [1993] C.O.D. 196, D.C.
s. 17, amended: 1994, c. 29, sch. 8.
s. 18, amended: *ibid.*; repealed in pt.: *ibid.*, sch. 9.
s. 19, amended: 1994, c. 19, sch. 2; c. 29, s. 79, sch. 8; repealed in pt.: *ibid.*, schs. 8, 9.
s. 20, substituted: *ibid.*, s. 70.
s. 21, amended: *ibid.*, s. 71; repealed in pt.: *ibid.*, sch. 9.
s. 22, amended: *ibid.*, s. 72, sch. 8; repealed in pt.: *ibid.*, s. 72, sch. 9.
s. 22A, added: *ibid.*, s. 73.
s. 23, amended: *ibid.*, sch. 8; repealed in pt.: *ibid.*, sch. 9.
ss. 24, 24A, amended: *ibid.*, sch. 8; repealed in pt.: *ibid.*, schs. 8, 9.
s. 24B, amended: *ibid.*, sch. 8.
s. 24C, added: *ibid.*, s. 74.
ss. 24D, 24E, added: *ibid.*, s. 75.
s. 25, substituted: *ibid.*, s. 76.
s. 26, amended: *ibid.*, sch. 8; repealed in pt.: *ibid.*, schs. 8, 9.
s. 26A, added: *ibid.*, s. 77.
s. 27, amended: *ibid.*, sch. 8; repealed in pt.: *ibid.*, s. 91, schs. 8, 9.
ss. 28, 30, repealed in pt.: *ibid.*, schs. 8, 9.
s. 30A, added: *ibid.*, s. 78.
s. 32, amended: *ibid.*, sch. 8.
s. 34A, added: *ibid.*, s. 81.
s. 34B, added: *ibid.*, sch. 8.
s. 35, repealed: *ibid.*, s. 79, sch. 9.
s. 36, repealed in pt.: *ibid.*, s. 91, schs. 8, 9.
s. 36A, repealed in pt.: *ibid.*, s. 91, sch. 9.
s. 37, repealed: *ibid.*, s. 80.
s. 38, repealed in pt.: *ibid.*, s. 79, sch. 9.
s. 42, amended: *ibid.*, sch. 8.
s. 53, amended: *ibid.*; repealed in pt.: *ibid.*, sch. 9.
ss. 55, 56, substituted: *ibid.*, s. 83.
ss. 57, 58, repealed: *ibid.*, s. 83, sch. 9.
s. 59, amended: *ibid.*, sch. 8; repealed in pt.: *ibid.*, sch. 9.
s. 59A, added: *ibid.*, s. 84.
s. 62, amended: *ibid.*, sch. 8.
s. 62A, added: *ibid.*, s. 85.
s. 63, repealed in pt.: *ibid.*, sch. 9.
s. 64, amended: *ibid.*, sch. 4.
s. 69A, added: *ibid.*, s. 90.
s. 70, amended: 1994, c. 19, sch. 2; c. 29, sch. 8; repealed in pt.: *ibid.*, sch. 9.
sch. 1, amended: *ibid.*, sch. 8.

58. Isle of Man Act 1979.
ss. 1, 6, 14, amended: 1994, c. 23, sch. 14.

1980

4. Bail etc. (Scotland) Act 1980.
s. 10, amended: 1994, c. 39, sch. 13.

5. Child Care Act 1980.
s. 10, see *R. v. Kirklees Metropolitan Borough Council, ex p. C.* [1993] 2 FLR 187, C.A.

9. Reserve Forces Act 1980.
ss. 94, 130, amended: 1994, c. 19, s. 61.
s. 131, amended(S.): 1994, c. 39, sch. 13; repealed in pt.(S.): *ibid.*, schs. 13, 14.
s. 133, amended(S.): *ibid.*, sch. 13; repealed in pt.: 1994, c. 19, s. 61.
s. 156, amended(S.): 1994, c. 39, sch. 13.
sch. 5, amended: 1994, c. 33, sch. 4.
sch. 7, amended: 1994, c. 19, s. 61; c. 39, sch. 13(S.).
sch. 8, amended(S.): *ibid.*, sch. 13.

10. Police Negotiating Board Act 1980.
s. 1, amended: 1994, c. 29, sch. 5; repealed in pt.: *ibid.*, sch. 9.
s. 2, see *Police Association for Northern Ireland's Application, Re* [1990] NI 258, Carswell J.

11. Protection of Trading Interests Act 1980.
s. 7, order 94/1901.

12. Bees Act 1980.
s. 1, order 93/3249.

13. Slaughter of Animals (Scotland) Act 1980.
s. 22, amended: 1994, c. 39, sch. 13.

19. Highlands and Islands Air Services (Scotland) Act 1980.
s. 3, amended: regs. 93/3040.

20. Education Act 1980.
s. 8, regs. 93/2824; 94/1048, 1421, 2103, 2330.
ss. 12, 13, regs. 93/3113.
s. 17, regs. 94/2034.
s. 18, regs. 94/2035.
s. 35, regs. 93/2824; 94/1421, 2034, 2035, 2103, 2330.
ss. 49, 73, 74, regs. 93/3184.

21. Competition Act 1980.
s. 2, order 94/1557.
s. 2, repealed in pt.: 1994, c. 40, schs. 11, 17.
s. 3, repealed in pt.: *ibid.*, s. 12, sch. 17.
s. 4, amended: *ibid.*, s. 12.
s. 5, amended: *ibid.*, s. 12, sch. 11; repealed in pt.: *ibid.*, schs. 11, 17.
s. 6, amended: *ibid.*, s. 12; repealed in pt.: *ibid.*, sch. 17.
s. 11, amended(S.): 1994, c. 39, s. 72.
ss. 13, 15, repealed in pt.: 1994, c. 40, sch. 17.
s. 16, amended: *ibid.*, sch. 11.
s. 19, amended: 1994, c. 21, sch. 9; c. 40, sch. 11.
s. 29, amended: *ibid.*, sch. 11.

1980—cont.

34. Transport Act 1980.
ss. 52B, 52D, order 94/2388.

43. Magistrates' Courts Act 1980.
s. 1, see *R.* v. *Tower Bridge Metropolitan Stipendiary Magistrate, ex p. Chaudhry* [1993] 3 W.L.R. 1154, D.C.; *R.* v. *Bingley Magistrates' Court, ex p. Morrow, The Times,* April 28, 1994, D.C.

ss. 1, 2, see *R.* v. *Abergavenny Justices, ex p. Barratt* [1994] RTR 98, D.C.

s. 1, amended: 1994, c. 19, sch. 2.

s. 2, amended: *ibid.;* c. 33, sch. 4.

s. 3, amended: 1994, c. 19, sch. 2.

ss. 4–8, substituted as ss. 4–8C: 1994, c. 33; sch. 4.

s. 6, see *R.* v. *Ormskirk Justices, ex p. Davies, The Times,* June 23, 1994, D.C.; *R.* v. *Worcester Magistrates' Court, ex p. Bell* (1993) 157 J.P. 921, D.C.

s. 8, see *R.* v. *Beaconsfield Justices, ex p. Westminster Press, The Times,* June 28, 1994, Bell J.

s. 11, amended: 1994, c. 33, sch. 10.

s. 12, substituted: *ibid.,* sch. 5.

s. 12A, added: *ibid.*

s. 13, amended: *ibid.*

ss. 19–21, amended: *ibid.,* sch. 4.

ss. 19, 20, 25, see *R.* v. *West Norfolk Justices, ex p.* McMullen [1993] C.O.D. 25, D.C.

ss. 19, 38, see *R.* v. *Northamptonshire Magistrates' Court, ex p. Customs and Excise Commissioners, The Independent,* February 23, 1964, D.C.

s. 22, amended: 1994, c. 33, s. 46; repealed in pt.: *ibid.,* sch. 11.

s. 23, amended: *ibid.,* sch. 4.

s. 24, amended: *ibid.;* repealed in pt.: *ibid.,* sch. 11.

s. 25, see *R.* v. *Chorley Magistrates' Court, ex p. Darbyshire,* March 21, 1994; D.C.

s. 25, amended: 1994, c. 33, sch. 4.

s. 26, substituted: *ibid.*

s. 28, amended: *ibid.*

s. 29, amended: *ibid.,* schs. 4, 10.

s. 37, amended: *ibid.,* sch. 10.

s. 38, see *R.* v. *Dover Justices, ex p. Pamment, The Times,* March 3, 1994, D.C.; *R.* v. *Manchester City Magistrates' Court, ex p. Kaymanesh, The Times,* March 3, 1994, D.C.

s. 38, amended: 1994, c. 33, sch. 9; repealed in pt.: *ibid.,* schs. 9, 11.

s. 42, see *R.* v. *Brent Justices, ex p. Ward* [1993] C.O.D. 17, D.C.

s. 42, amended: 1994, c. 33, sch. 4.

s. 43, amended: *ibid.,* sch. 10.

s. 43B, added: *ibid.,* sch. 3.

1980—cont.

43. Magistrates' Courts Act 1980—*cont.*
s. 53, see *R.* v. *Basildon Justices, ex p. Holding & Barnes, The Times,* April 26, 1994, Schiemann J.

s. 59, amended: order 94/731.

s. 64, see *R.* v. *Southend Stipendiary Magistrates, ex p. Rochford District Council, The Times,* May 10, 1994, Judge J.

s. 68, repealed in pt.: 1994, c. 29, sch. 9.

s. 70, amended: *ibid.,* sch. 8.

ss. 82, 88, see *R.* v. *Exeter City Justices, ex p. Sugar* (1993) 157 J.P. 766, D.C.

ss. 89, 90, amended: 1994, c. 33, s. 47.

s. 97, amended: *ibid.,* sch. 4; repealed in pt.: *ibid.,* schs. 4, 11.

s. 102, see *Kelly* v. *C.P.S.; Williams* v. *C.P.S.,* June 16, 1994; H.H.J. Allardine; Stafford County Ct.

ss. 102, 103, 105, 106, repealed: 1994, c. 33, sch. 11.

s. 108, amended: *ibid.,* sch. 9.

s. 113, amended: *ibid.,* sch. 10.

ss. 128–130, amended: *ibid.,* sch. 4.

s. 128A, see *R.* v. *Noakes (Stephen James),* February 25, 1994; Buxton J.; Manchester Crown Ct.

s. 133, see *R.* v. *Davies (Paul Neil)* (1993) 157 J.P. 820, C.A.

s. 141, repealed in pt.: 1994, c. 29, sch. 9.

s. 142, see *R.* v. *Highbury Corner Magistrates' Court, ex p. Tann* [1994] RTR 5, D.C.

s. 143, amended: 1994, c. 33, s. 157.

s. 144, rules 94/809, 1481, 2166.

s. 145, amended: 1994, c. 33, sch. 4; repealed in pt.: 1994, c. 29, schs. 8, 9; c. 33, sch. 11.

s. 150, amended: 1994, c. 19, sch. 2; repealed in pt.: 1994, c. 33, sch. 11.

s. 155, amended: *ibid.,* sch. 5.

sch. 3, amended: *ibid.,* sch. 4.

sch. 5, amended: *ibid.,* repealed in pt.: *ibid.,* sch. 11.

sch. 7, repealed in pt.: 1994, c. 22, sch. 5.

44. Education (Scotland) Act 1980.
s. 2, regs. 94/351.

ss. 4, 6, repealed in pt.: 1994, c. 39, schs. 13, 14.

s. 19, regs. 94/351.

s. 22A, see *Hughes* v. *Strathclyde Regional Council,* 1994 S.C.L.R. 49.

s. 22D, amended: 1994, c. 39, s. 144.

s. 23, amended: *ibid.,* s. 32.

ss. 28B, 28I, regs. 94/351.

ss. 50, 51, amended: 1994, c. 39, s. 145.

s. 73, regs. 94/351, 1826.

s. 74, regs. 94/1826.

ss. 75A, 75B, regs. 94/1827.

ss. 78, 86 (in pt.), repealed: 1994, c. 39, schs. 13, 14.

1980—cont.

44. Education (Scotland) Act 1980—*cont.*
ss. 112, 122, 129, amended: *ibid.*, sch. 13.
s. 135, regs. 94/351.
s. 135, sch. A1, amended: 1994, c. 39, sch. 13.

45. Water (Scotland) Act 1980.
s. 1, substituted: 1994, c. 39, s. 65.
ss. 3–5, repealed: *ibid.*, schs. 13, 14.
s. 6, amended: *ibid.*, sch. 13.
s. 9, amended: *ibid.*, s. 105.
s. 9A, amended: *ibid.*, sch. 13.
s. 10, amended: *ibid.*, repealed in pt.: *ibid.*, schs. 13, 14.
s. 11, repealed in pt.: *ibid.*
s. 12, substituted: *ibid.*, s. 106.
s. 13, amended: *ibid.*, sch. 13; repealed in pt.: *ibid.*, schs. 13, 14.
s. 13A, added: *ibid.*, s. 107.
s. 15, amended (temp.): *ibid.*, s. 182; repealed: *ibid.*, schs. 13, 14.
s. 16, repealed in pt.: *ibid.*
s. 17, orders 94/810, 1556.
s. 17, repealed in pt.: 1994, c. 39, schs. 13, 14.
s. 18, amended: *ibid.*, sch. 13; repealed in pt.: *ibid.*, schs. 13, 14.
s. 20, repealed: *ibid.*, schs. 13, 14.
s. 21, substituted: *ibid.*, s. 108.
s. 22, repealed in pt.: *ibid.*, schs. 13, 14.
s. 23, amended: *ibid.*, s. 109, sch. 13; repealed in pt.: *ibid.*, schs. 13, 14.
s. 24, amended: *ibid.*, s. 110.
s. 24A, added: *ibid.*, s. 111.
s. 25, amended: *ibid.*, sch. 13; repealed in pt.: *ibid.*, schs. 13, 14.
s. 26, amended: *ibid.*, sch. 13.
s. 27, amended: *ibid.*, repealed in pt.: *ibid.*, sch. 14.
s. 28, repealed in pt.: *ibid.*, schs. 13, 14.
s. 29, order 94/1556.
s. 29, repealed in pt.: 1994, c. 39, schs. 13, 14.
s. 30, repealed: *ibid.*
ss. 32, 33, 35, 38, repealed in pt.: *ibid.*
ss. 40, 41, repealed: *ibid.*
s. 41A, substituted: *ibid.*, s. 112.
ss. 42, 43, repealed: *ibid.*, schs. 13, 14.
ss. 44, 45, repealed: *ibid.*, sch. 14.
s. 46, repealed: *ibid.*, schs. 13, 14.
s. 47, amended: *ibid.*, sch. 13; repealed in pt.: *ibid.*, schs. 13, 14.
ss. 48, 49, 54 (in pt.), repealed: *ibid.*
s. 55, amended: *ibid.*, sch. 13.
s. 58, amended: *ibid.*; repealed in pt.: *ibid.*, schs. 13, 14.
ss. 60, 61, repealed: *ibid.*
s. 63, amended: *ibid.*, sch. 13; repealed in pt.: *ibid.*, schs. 13, 14.

1980—cont.

45. Water (Scotland) Act 1980—*cont.*
ss. 64–67, repealed (with savings): *ibid.*, s. 179, schs. 13, 14.
s. 68, amended: *ibid.*, sch. 13; repealed in pt.: *ibid.*, schs. 13, 14.
s. 69, amended: *ibid.*, sch. 13.
s. 70, repealed in pt.: *ibid.*, schs. 13, 14.
s. 71, amended: *ibid.*, sch. 13; repealed in pt.: *ibid.*, schs. 13, 14.
ss. 72, 73, repealed in pt.: *ibid.*
s. 76, amended: *ibid.*, sch. 13; repealed in pt.: *ibid.*, schs. 13, 14.
s. 76E, amended: *ibid.*, s. 113.
s' 76F, amended: *ibid.*, s. 114, sch. 13.
s. 76H, amended: *ibid.*, sch. 13; repealed in pt.: *ibid.*, schs. 13, 14.
ss. 76I, 76J, amended: *ibid.*, sch. 13.
s. 76L (in pt.), 80–92, repealed: *ibid.*, schs. 13, 14.
s. 100, amended: *ibid.*, sch. 13.
s. 101, amended: *ibid.*, s. 115.
ss. 104, 106, amended: *ibid.*, sch. 13.
s. 107, orders 94/810, 2758.
s. 107, repealed in pt.: 1994, c. 39, schs. 13, 14.
s. 109, amended: *ibid.*, sch. 13; repealed in pt. (with savings): *ibid.*, s. 179, schs. 13, 14.
sch. 1, amended: *ibid.*, sch. 13; repealed in pt.: *ibid.*, schs. 13, 14.
sch. 2, repealed in pt.: *ibid.*
sch. 3, amended: *ibid.*, sch. 13; repealed in pt.: *ibid.*, schs. 13, 14.
sch. 4, amended: *ibid.*, sch. 13.
schs. 7, 8, repealed: *ibid.*, schs. 13, 14.
sch. 10, repealed in pt.: *ibid.*, sch. 14.

46. Solicitors (Scotland) Act 1980.
s. 57, Act of Sederunt 94/1443.

47. Criminal Appeal (Northern Ireland) Act 1980.
s. 28, amended: 1994, c. 33, s. 53.

48. Finance Act 1980.
s. 4, repealed in pt.: 1994, c. 22, sch. 5.
s. 80, see *Re Rothschild* v. *Lawrenson (Inspector of Taxes)* [1994] STC 8, Vinelott J.

50. Coal Industry Act 1980.
ss. 1, 2, 7, repealed (prosp.): 1994, c. 21, sch. 11, Pt. III.
s. 8, repealed (prosp.): *ibid.*, sch. 11, Pt. IV.
ss. 9–11, repealed (prosp.): *ibid.*, sch. 11, Pt. III.

55. Law Reform (Miscellaneous Provisions) (Scotland) Act 1980.
s. 17, order 93/3125.
sch. 1, amended: 1994, c. 33, sch. 10.

57. Imprisonment (Temporary Provisions) Act 1980.
s. 6, amended: 1994, c. 33, s. 94, sch. 10.

1980—cont.

58. Limitation Act 1980.

s. 14, see *Khan* v. *Ainslie* [1993] 4 Med LR 319, Waterhouse J.; *Broadley* v. *Guy Clapham & Co.* [1993] 4 Med LR 328, C.A.; *Felton* v. *Gaskill Osborne & Co.* [1993] 43 EG 118, H.H.J. O'Donoghue; *Dobbie* v. *Medway Health Authority, The Times,* May 18, 1994, C.A.

s. 20, see *Ezekiel* v. *Orakpo, The Times,* November 8, 1994, Carnwath J.

s. 32, see *Sheldon* v. *Outhwaite (R.H.M.) (Underwriting Agencies), The Times,* July 1, 1994, C.A.

s. 33, see *Yates* v. *Thakeham Tiles, The Times,* May 19, 1994, C.A.; *Higham* v. *Stena Sealink,* June 17, 1994; H.H.J. Bernstein; Liverpool County Ct.

s. 34, see *Triad Shipping Co.* v. *Stellar Chartering & Brokerage Inc.; Island Archon, The* [1993] 2 Lloyd's Rep. 388, Cresswell J.; *Petredec* v. *Tokumaru Kaiun Co.; Sargasso, The* [1994] 1 Lloyd's Rep. 162, Hobhouse J.

s. 35, see *Welsh Development Agency* v. *Redpath Dorman Long, The Times,* April 4, 1994, C.A.; *Clarke (E.) & Sons (Coaches)* v. *Axtell Yates Hallett* 30 Con LR 123, H.H.J. Esyr Lewis, Q.C.

62. Criminal Justice (Scotland) Act 1980.

s. 2, amended: 1994, c. 33, s. 129, sch. 10.

s. 3, amended: *ibid.,* sch. 10.

s. 26, see *Straker* v. *Orr,* 1994 S.C.C.R. 251; *Carr* v. *H.M. Advocate,* 1994 S.C.C.R. 521.

s. 78, see *Murray* v. *O'Brien,* 1994 S.L.T. 1051.

s. 80, amended: 1994, c. 33, ss. 145, 148; repealed in pt.: *ibid.,* s. 146, sch. 11.

63. Overseas Development and Co-operation Act 1980.

s. 2, repealed in pt. (prosp.): 1994, c. 21, schs. 9, 11, Pt. IV.

s. 11, repealed: 1994, c. 29, sch. 9.

sch. 1, repealed in pt. (prosp.): 1994, c. 21, schs. 9, 11, Pt. IV.

65. Local Government, Planning and Land Act 1980.

s. 2, amended: 1994, c. 29, sch. 4; repealed in pt.: *ibid.,* schs. 4, 9.

s. 2, amended(S.): 1994, c. 39, sch. 13.

s. 3, regs. 94/2422.

s. 4, amended: 1994, c. 19, sch. 16; repealed in pt.: *ibid.,* schs. 16, 18.

s. 7, regs. 94/338, 567, 1439.

s. 8, amended(S.): 1994, c. 39, sch. 13; repealed in pt.(S.): *ibid.,* schs. 13, 14.

s. 9, see *Colas Roads* v. *Lothian Regional Council* (O.H.), 1994 S.L.T. 397.

s. 9, regs. 93/848; 94/338, 1439.

1980—cont.

65. Local Government, Planning and Land Act 1980—*cont.*

s. 20, amended: 1994, c. 19, sch. 16; c. 29, sch. 4; repealed in pt.: 1994, c. 19, schs. 16, 18.

s. 20, amended(S.): 1994, c. 39, sch. 13; repealed in pt.(S.): *ibid.,* schs. 13, 14.

s. 23, regs. 94/338, 567, 1439.

s. 69, amended(S.): 1994, c. 39, s. 158.

s. 70, repealed: 1994, c. 33, s. 80.

s. 87, regs. 93/3211(S).

s. 87, repealed in pt.(S.): 1994, c. 39, sch. 14.

s. 98, amended: 1994, c. 19, sch. 16.

s. 99, amended: *ibid.,* c. 29, sch. 4.

ss. 100, 103, amended: 1994, c. 19, sch. 16.

s. 108, repealed in pt. (prosp.): 1994, c. 21, schs. 9, 11, Pt. II.

s. 116, amended: 1994, c. 19, sch. 16; repealed in pt.: *ibid.,* schs. 16, 18.

s. 120, repealed in pt. (prosp.): 1994, c. 21, schs. 9, 11, Pt. II.

s. 120, amended(S.): 1994, c. 39, sch. 13.

s. 134, order 94/2578.

s. 148, amended: 1994, c. 19, sch. 6.

s. 148, amended(S.): 1994, c. 39, sch. 13; repealed in pt.(S.): *ibid.,* schs. 13, 14.

s. 162, amended: 1994, c. 19, sch. 16.

s. 165, amended: *ibid.;* repealed in pt.: *ibid.,* schs. 16, 18.

s. 165, amended(S.): 1994, c. 39, sch. 13.

s. 170, repealed in pt. (prosp.): 1994, c. 21, schs. 9, 11, Pt. II.

s. 185, amended: 1994, c. 19, sch. 16.

sch. 4, repealed in pt.: 1994, c. 40, sch. 17.

sch. 16, amended: 1994, c. 19, sch. 16; c. 21, sch. 9; c. 29, sch. 4.

schs. 19–21, amended: 1994, c. 19, sch. 16.

sch. 28, amended: *ibid.,* sch. 6.

sch. 32, amended: *ibid.,* sch. 16; repealed in pt.: *ibid.,* schs. 16, 18.

sch. 32, amended(S.): 1994, c. 39, s. 159; repealed in pt.(S.): *ibid.,* s. 159, sch. 14.

66. Highways Act 1980.

s. 1, amended: 1994, c. 19, sch. 7.

ss. 6, 8, amended: 1994, c. 19, sch. 7.

s. 31, see *Jacques* v. *Secretary of State for the Environment, The Independent,* June 8, 1994, Laws J.; *R.* v. *Secretary of State for the Environment, ex p. Cowell* [1993] J.P.L. 851, C.A.

s. 36, amended: 1994, c. 19, sch. 7.

s. 41, see *Stovin* v. *Wise (Norfolk County Council, Third Party)* [1994] RTR 225, C.A.

ss. 47, 67, 69, 79, 100, amended: 1994, c. 19, sch. 7.

s. 105A, amended: regs. 94/1002.

1980—cont.

66. Highways Act 1980—*cont.*

s. 106, instruments 94/2086, 2087, 2170.

ss. 114, 116, 120, 151, 154, 166, 185, 204, 205, 210, 219, 220, 223, 232, 264, 272, amended: 1994, c. 19, sch. 7.

s. 278, see *Ward Construction (Medway) v. Barclays Bank, The Times,* July 20, 1994, C.A.

s. 287, amended: 1994, c. 19, sch. 7.

s. 290, amended: 1994, c. 21, sch. 9; repealed in pt. (prosp.): *ibid.,* schs. 9, 11, Pt. II.

s. 329, amended: 1994, c. 19, sch. 7.

sch. 6, repealed in pt.: 1994, c. 29, sch. 9.

schs. 9, 12, amended: 1994, c. 19, sch. 7.

1981

7. House of Commons Members' Fund and Parliamentary Pensions Act 1981.

s. 2, resolution 94/631; amended: *ibid.*

14. Public Passenger Vehicles Act 1981.

s. 5, amended(S.): 1994, c. 39, sch. 13.

s. 10, regs. 93/3012.

s. 14, amended: 1994, c. 40, s. 59, sch. 14.

s. 14A, amended: *ibid.,* s. 60; repealed in pt.: *ibid.,* schs. 14, 17.

s. 14A, amended(S.): 1994, c. 39, sch. 13.

s. 15, amended: *ibid.,* s. 61.

s. 16, amended: *ibid.,* s. 59; repealed in pt.: *ibid.,* schs. 14, 17.

s. 17, amended: *ibid.,* s. 59, sch. 14; repealed in pt.: *ibid.,* schs. 14, 17.

s. 18, amended: *ibid.,* s. 63, sch. 14.

s. 27, repealed: *ibid.,* s. 64, sch. 17.

s. 49A, added: *ibid.,* s. 65.

s. 50, amended: *ibid.,* s. 65, sch. 14; repealed in pt.: *ibid.,* schs. 14, 17.

s. 52, regs. 93/2753, 2754, 3012.

s. 52, amended: 1994, c. 40, s. 66.

s. 56A, added: *ibid.,* s. 65.

s. 60, regs. 93/2753, 2754, 3012.

s. 82, amended: 1994, c. 19, sch. 7.

s. 82, sch. 1, amended(S.): 1994, c. 39, sch. 13.

18. Disused Burial Grounds (Amendment) Act 1981.

sch., amended: 1994, c. 19, sch. 16.

20. Judicial Pensions Act 1981.

s. 21, order 94/350; amended: *ibid.*

s. 33A, sch. 1A, amended: regs. 94/1696.

22. Animal Health Act 1981.

s. 1, orders 93/3086, 3119, 3250; 94/472, 944, 1716.

s. 7, orders 93/3086, 3119, 3250.

s. 8, orders 93/3119, 3250; 94/944.

s. 10, orders 93/3250; 94/1716.

s. 10, amended: order 93/1813.

ss. 15, 17, order 93/3119.

s. 23, orders 93/3086, 3119.

s. 25, order 93/3119.

1981—cont.

22. Animal Health Act 1981—*cont.*

ss. 32, 34, order 94/673.

s. 35, order 93/3250.

s. 38, order 93/3119.

s. 50, amended: 1994, c. 19, sch. 16; 39, sch. 13(S.).

s. 72, order 94/472.

s. 83, order 93/3119.

s. 87, orders 93/3119, 3250.

s. 88, orders 93/3250; 94/472, 944.

s. 95, order 94/1716.

23. Local Government (Miscellaneous Provisions) (Scotland) Act 1981.

ss. 6, 11, 27, repealed: 1994, c. 39, sch. 14.

schs. 2, 3, repealed in pt.: *ibid.*

29. Fisheries Act 1981.

s. 4, amended: order 94/1390.

ss. 15, 18, scheme 94/1568.

s. 30, orders 94/451, 1679–1681.

35. Finance Act 1981.

s. 7, repealed in pt.: 1994, c. 22, sch. 5.

s. 80, see *Marshall (Inspector of Taxes) v. Kerr* [1994] 3 W.L.R. 299, H.L.

s. 107, amended: 1994, c. 29, sch. 5; c. 39, sch. 13(S.).

sch. 8, repealed in pt.: 1994, c. 9, sch. 26.

37. Zoo Licensing Act 1981.

s. 1, amended: 1994, c. 19, sch. 16; repealed in pt.: *ibid.,* schs. 16, 18.

s. 1, amended(S.): 1994, c. 39, sch. 13.

s. 3, amended: 1994, c. 19, sch. 16.

45. Forgery and Counterfeiting Act 1981.

s. 7, see *R. v. Leeds Magistrates' Court, ex p. Dumbleton* [1993] Crim.L.R. 866, D.C.

s. 9, see *R. v. Warneford; R. v. Gibbs, The Times,* May 18, 1994, C.A.

s. 17, see *R. v. Maltman, The Times,* June 28, 1994, C.A.

47. Criminal Attempts Act 1981.

s. 1, see *Att.-Gen.'s Reference (No. 3 of 1992)* [1994] RTR 122, C.A.

s. 2, repealed in pt.: 1994, c. 33, schs. 4, 11.

49. Contempt of Court Act 1981.

s. 4, see *R. v. Clerkenwell Justices, ex p. Trachtenberg* [1993] Crim.L.R. 222, D.C.; *R. v. Beaconsfield Justices, ex p. Westminster Press, The Times,* June 28, 1994, Bell J.

s. 4, amended: 1994, c. 33, sch. 4.

s. 8, see *Att.-Gen.* v. *Associated Newspapers,* [1994] 2 W.L.R. 277, H.L.

s. 10, see *Broadmoor Hospital* v. *Hyde, The Independent,* March 4, 1994, Sir Peter Pain.

s. 11, see *Birmingham Post and Mail* v. *Birmingham City Council, The Times,* November 25, 1993, D.C.

s. 12, see *Hooker (Patricia), Re* [1993] C.O.D. 190, D.C.

s. 14, see *Villiers* v. *Villiers* [1994] 2 All E.R. 149, C.A.

CAP.

1981—cont.

54. Supreme Court Act 1981.
s. 9, amended: 1994, c. 33, s. 52.
s. 20, amended: 1994, c. 28, sch. 2.
ss. 28, 29, 31, see *R.* v. *Chelmsford Crown Court, ex p. Chief Constable of Essex Police* [1994] 1 All E.R. 325, D.C.
s. 28A, see *R.* v. *Newcastle under Lyme Justices, ex p. Massey; R.* v. *Stoke on Trent Magistrates' Court, ex p. Knight, The Independent,* October 7, 1994, D.C.
s. 29, see *R.* v. *Manchester Crown Court, ex p. D.P.P.* [1993] 1 W.L.R. 1524, H.L.; *R.* v. *Central Criminal Court, ex p. Spens* [1993] C.O.D. 194, D.C.; *R.* v. *Southwark Crown Court, ex p. Ward, The Times,* August 19, 1994, D.C.
s. 31, see *R.* v. *Secretary of State for Health, ex p. Furneaux* [1994] 2 All E.R. 652, C.A.; *Patterson* v. *Greenwich London Borough Council* (1993) 26 H.L.R. 159, C.A.
s. 33, see *M.* v. *Plymouth Health Authority* [1993] P.I.Q.R. P223, Brooke J.
s. 35A, see *Suncorp Insurance and Finance* v. *Milano Assicurazioni SpA* [1993] 2 Lloyd's Rep. 225, Waller J.; *Mathew* v. *T.M. Sutton, The Times,* June 22, 1994, Chadwick J.
s. 37, see *O. (Minors) (Adoption: Injunction), Re; sub nom. O. (Adoption Order: Effect on Injunction), Re* [1993] 2 FLR 737, Ewbank J.; *Mercantile Group (Europe) AG* v. *Aiyela* [1993] F.S.R. 745, Hobhouse J.; *Naylor* v. *Hutson* [1994] F.S.R. 63, Maddocks J.
s. 42, see *Mephistopheles Debt Collection Service (A Firm)* v. *Lotay, The Times,* May 17, 1994, C.A.; *Ewing (No. 2), Re, The Times,* August 11, 1994, C.A.
ss. 42, 51, see *R.* v. *Darlington Borough Council, ex p. Association of Darlington Taxi Owners (No. 2), The Times,* April 14, 1994, Auld J.
s. 51, see *R.* v. *Secretary of State for the Home Department, ex p. Singh (Atrvinder)* [1993] Imm A R 450, Macpherson J.; *Shah* v. *Karanjia* [1993] 4 All E.R. 792, Vinelott J.; *Company, A (No. 0022 of 1993), Re* [1993] BCC 726, Knox J.; *Kleinwort Benson* v. *De Montenegro* [1994] NPC 46, Aldous J.; *Ridehalgh* v. *Horsefield; Allen* v. *Unigate Dairies; Roberts* v. *Coverite (Asphalters); Philex* v. *Golban; Watson* v. *Watson; Antonelli* v. *Wade Gery Farr (A Firm)* [1994] 3 W.L.R. 462, C.A.; *Wellcome Foundation, The* v.

CAP.

1981—cont.

54. Supreme Court Act 1981—*cont.*
Discpharm (No. 2) [1993] F.S.R. 444, Patents County Ct.; *R.* v. *Newcastle under Lyme Jutices, ex p. Massey; R.* v. *Stoke on Trent Magistrates' Court, ex p. Knight, The Independent,* October 7, 1994, D.C.
s. 51, rules 94/1975.
s. 55, amended: 1994, c. 33, s. 52.
ss. 56A, 56B, added: *ibid.*
s. 69, see *Racz* v. *Home Office* [1994] 2 W.L.R. 23, H.L.
ss. 76, 77, amended: 1994, c. 33, schs. 4, 9 (temp.).
s. 80, amended: *ibid.,* sch. 4.
s. 81, amended: *ibid.,* schs. 9, 10.
s. 84, rules 94/1480, 1975.
s. 85, rules 93/2760; 94/1975.
s. 86, rules 94/1480.
s. 90, see *P. (Minors) (Official Solicitor's Costs), Re* [1993] 2 F.C.R. 550, Booth J.
s. 104, order 94/1103.
s. 130, order 93/3191.
s. 133, regs. 94/601, 604.

56. Transport Act 1981.
s. 4, sch. 1, order 93/2805.
s. 35, amended: 1994, c. 19, sch. 7.

59. Matrimonial Homes (Family Protection) (Scotland) Act 1981.
ss. 3, 19, see *Milne* v. *Milne* (Sh.Ct.), 1994 S.C.L.R. 437; 1994 S.L.T. 57.
ss. 15, 18, see *Crossley* v. *Galletta* (Sh.Ct.), 1993 S.C.L.R. 780.
s. 18, see *Armour* v. *Anderson,* 1994 S.L.T.(Sh.Ct.) 14.

60. Education Act 1981.
ss. 1, 2, 4, 5, 7, 11, 13, 17, see *P.* v. *Harrow London Borough Council* [1993] 2 F.C.R. 341, Potter J.
ss. 4, 5, 7–9, sch. 2, see *R.* v. *Isle of Wight County Council, ex p. RS; R.* v. *Isle of Wight County Council, ex p. AS* [1993] 1 FLR 634, C.A.
ss. 5, 9, see *R.* v. *Surrey County Council, ex p. G.; R.* v. *Same, ex p. H., The Times,* May 24, 1994, Judge J.
ss. 7, 8, see *R.* v. *Clwyd County Council, ex p. A.* [1993] C.O.D. 35, Simon Brown J.
s. 8, see *R.* v. *Secretary of State for Education, ex p. J.* [1993] C.O.D. 146, Brooke J.; *R.* v. *Secretary of State for Education, ex p. S., The Times,* January 26, 1994, Sedley J.
s. 9, see *R.* v. *Hampshire County Council, ex p. W., The Times,* June 9, 1994, Sedley J.
s. 19, sch. 1, regs. 94/1047.
s. 72, see *P.* v. *Harrow London Borough Council* [1993] 2 F.C.R. 341, Potter J.

1981—cont.

61. British Nationality Act 1981.

s. 1, see *K. (A Minor) (Adoption Order: Nationality), Re* [1994] 3 W.L.R. 572, C.A.

s. 2, order 94/556.

ss. 6, 40, 42, see *R.* v. *Secretary of State for the Home Department, ex p. Ejaz (Naheed)* [1994] 2 W.L.R. 534, C.A.

s. 37, order 94/1634.

sch. 3, amended: *ibid.*

sch. 7, repealed in pt.: 1994, c. 15, sch.

63. Betting and Gaming Duties Act 1981.

s. 21, amended: 1994, c. 9, sch. 3.

ss. 21A, 22 (in pt.), repealed: *ibid.,* schs. 3, 26, Pt. II.

s. 23, substituted: *ibid.,* sch. 3.

s. 24, amended: *ibid.,* sch. 4; repealed in pt.: *ibid.,* schs. 3, 4, 26, Pts. II, III, V.

s. 26, amended: *ibid.,* sch. 3; repealed in pt.: *ibid.,* schs. 3, 26, Pt. II.

sch. 1, amended: *ibid.,* sch. 4; repealed in pt.: *ibid.,* schs. 4, Pt. V, 26, Pt. III.

sch. 2, amended: *ibid.,* sch. 4; repealed in pt.: *ibid.,* sch. 26, Pt. III.

sch. 3, amended: *ibid.,* sch. 4; repealed in pt.: *ibid.,* schs. 4, Pt. V, 26, Pt. III.

sch. 4, amended: *ibid.,* schs. 3, 4, Pt. V; repealed in pt.: *ibid.,* schs. 3, 4, Pt. V, 26, Pts. II, III.

64. New Towns Act 1981.

ss. 2, 7, 23, 33, 38, 39, 41, 77, amended: 1994, c. 19, sch. 16.

s. 80, repealed in pt.: 1994, c. 29, sch. 9.

sch. 1, amended: 1994, c. 19, sch. 16.

sch. 9, amended: 1994, c. 5, s. 1.

66. Compulsory Purchase (Vesting Declarations) Act 1981.

ss. 3, 4, see *Cooperative Insurance Society* v. *Hastings Borough Council* 91 L.G.R. 608, Vinelott J.

67. Acquisition of Land Act 1981.

s. 7, order 94/2145.

s. 7, repealed in pt.: 1994, c. 29, sch. 9.

ss. 10–12, 15, regs. 94/2145.

s. 17, amended: 1994, c. 19, sch. 6; c. 29, sch. 4; repealed in pt. (prosp.): 1994, c. 21, schs. 9, 11, Pt. II.

s. 22, regs. 94/2145.

s. 23, see *Burke* v. *Secretary of State for the Environment and Camden London Borough Council* (1994) 26 H.L.R. 10, C.A.

s. 26, see *Cooperative Insurance Society* v. *Hastings Borough Council* 91 L.G.R. 608, Vinelott J.

s. 29, amended: 1994, c. 21, sch. 9; repealed in pt. (prosp.): *ibid.,* schs. 9, 11, Pt. II.

sch. 1, regs. 94/2145.

sch. 2, amended: 1994, c. 21, sch. 9.

sch. 3, regs. 94/2145.

sch. 3, amended: 1994, c. 21, sch. 9.

sch. 4, repealed in pt.: 1994, c. 29, sch. 9.

1981—cont.

68. Broadcasting Act 1981.

s. 54, see *R.* v. *Broadcasting Complaints Commission, ex p. Lloyd* [1993] C.O.D. 137, Macpherson J.

69. Wildlife and Countryside Act 1981.

see *Thomas* v. *Countryside Commission for Wales* [1993] NPC 119, Rougier J.; *sub nom. Thomas* v. *Countryside Council for Wales* [1994] 04 EG 138, Rougier J.

s. 1, see *Seiga* v. *Walkingshaw,* 1994 S.C.C.R. 146.

s. 3, amended: 1994, c. 19, sch. 16.

s. 7, order 94/1152.

s. 22, order 94/1151.

s. 27, amended: 1994, c. 19, sch. 16; repealed in pt.: *ibid.,* schs. 16, 18.

s. 27, amended(S.): 1994, c. 39, sch. 13.

ss. 34, 36, amended: 1994, c. 19, sch. 16.

s. 36, amended(S.): 1994, c. 39, sch. 13.

s. 52, repealed in pt.: 1994, c. 19, schs. 16, 18.

s. 53, see *R.* v. *Secretary of State for the Environment, ex p. Kent County Council, The Times,* November 11, 1994, Turner J.

s. 53, sch. 14, see *R.* v. *Secretary of State for the Environment, ex p. Bagshaw; R.* v. *Same, ex p. Norton, The Times,* May 6, 1994, Owen J.

ss. 57, 66, 72, amended: 1994, c. 19, sch. 16.

sch. 4, amended: order 94/1151.

sch. 12, amended: 1994, c. 19, sch. 16.

sch. 14, amended: *ibid.;* repealed in pt.: *ibid.,* schs. 16, 18.

sch. 15, see *R.* v. *Cornwall County Council, ex p. Huntingdon; R.* v. *Devon County Council, ex p. Isaac* [1994] 1 All E.R. 694, C.A.

sch. 15, amended: 1994, c. 19, sch. 16; repealed in pt.: *ibid.,* schs. 16, 18.

1982

9. Agricultural Training Board Act 1982.

ss. 1, 3, order 94/555.

15. Coal Industry Act 1982.

ss. 3, 5, 6, repealed (prosp.): 1994, c. 21, sch. 11, Pt. III.

16. Civil Aviation Act 1982.

s. 17, regs. 93/3039.

s. 30, repealed in pt.(S.): 1994, c. 39, schs. 13, 14.

s. 36, amended(S.): *ibid.,* sch. 13.

s. 64, regs. 93/3039.

ss. 69A, regs. 93/3039; 94/1732.

s. 73, regs. 93/2970, 2975, 3098; 94/503, 1468, 1601, 2325.

s. 74, regs. 94/2325.

1982—cont.

16. Civil Aviation Act 1982—*cont.*

s. 78, see *R.* v. *Secretary of State for Transport, ex p. Richmond upon Thames London Borough Council* [1994] 1 W.L.R. 74, Laws J.

s. 79, repealed in pt.: 1994, c. 19, schs. 16, 18.

s. 84, regs. 93/3039.

s. 88, repealed in pt.(S): 1994, c. 39, schs. 13, 14.

s. 105, regs. 93/3039.

s. 105, amended: 1994, c. 19, sch. 16; regs. 94/1732; repealed in pt.: 1994, c. 19, schs. 16, 18.

s. 105, amended(S.): 1994, c. 39, sch. 13.

27. Civil Jurisdiction and Judgments Act 1982.

see *Charman (John Robert) and Brockbank (Mark E.)* v. *WOC Offshore B.V.* [1993] 2 Lloyd's Rep. 551, C.A.; *Barclays Bank* v. *Glasgow City Council* [1994] 2 W.L.R. 466, C.A.; *R.* v. *West London Magistrates' Court, ex p. Emmett* [1993] 2 FLR 663, Ward J.

s. 4, Act of Sederunt 94/1443.

s. 9, order 94/1901.

s. 12, Act of Sederunt 94/1443.

s. 18, amended: 1994, c.37, sch. 1.

s. 20, sch. 8, see *Timberwise Consultants* v. *Ross & Liddell* (Sh.Ct.), 1993 S.C.L.R. 972; *O'Neill* v. *Tebbett* (O.H.), 1994 S.L.T. 752.

s. 22, see *Kelly* v. *Renfrew District Council* (Sh.Ct.), 1994 S.C.L.R. 353; 1994 S.L.T.(Sh.Ct.) 46.

s. 27, sch. 7, see *Caledonian Newspapers, Re, The Times*, February 16, 1994.

s. 34, see *Republic of India* v. *India Steamship Co.; Indian Endurance and Indian Grace, The (No. 2), The Times*, June 9, 1994, Clarke J.

s. 38, order 94/1901.

s. 48, Act of Sederunt 94/1443.

sch. 1, see *Continental Bank NA* v. *Aeakos Compania Naviera SA* [1994] 1 W.L.R. 588, C.A.; *Neste Chemicals SA* v. *DK Line SA; Sargasso, The* [1994] 3 All E.R. 180, C.A.; *Kinnear* v. *Falconfilms N.V.* [1994] 3 All E.R. 42, Phillips J.

sch. 4, see *Clydesdale Bank* v. *Ions* (Sh.Ct.), 1993 S.C.L.R. 964.

sch. 8, see *Mann (B.J.) (Advertising)* v. *Ace Welding & Fabrications* (Sh.Ct.), 1994 S.C.L.R. 763.

29. Supply of Goods and Services Act 1982.

s. 1, amended: 1994, c. 35, sch. 2.

ss. 4, 5, amended: *ibid.*, repealed in pt.: *ibid.*, schs. 2, 3.

s. 5A, added: *ibid.*, sch. 2.

s. 6, amended: *ibid.*

1982—cont.

29. Supply of Goods and Services Act 1982—*cont.*

ss. 9, 10, amended: *ibid.*; repealed in pt.: *ibid.*, schs. 2, 3.

s. 10A, added: *ibid.*, sch. 2.

Pt. 1A (ss. 11A–11L), added(S.): *ibid.*, sch. 1.

s. 13, see *Society of Lloyd's* v. *Clementson; Same* v. *Mason, The Times*, January 11, 1994, Saville J.

Pt. 1A (ss. 11A–11L), added(S.): 1994, c. 35, sch. 1.

s. 17, repealed in pt.: *ibid.*, sch. 3.

s. 18, amended: *ibid.*, sch. 2; repealed in pt.: *ibid.*, sch. 3.

s. 18, amended(S.): *ibid.*, sch. 1; repealed in pt.(S.): *ibid.*

s. 20, amended(S.): *ibid.*

30. Local Government (Miscellaneous Provisions) Act 1982.

s. 33, amended: 1994, c. 19, sch. 13; c. 29, sch. 4.

s. 41, amended: 1994, c. 29, sch. 4.

sch. 1, see *Chichester District Council* v. *Ware* (1993) 157 J.P. 574, D.C.

32. Local Government Finance Act 1982.

ss. 12, 19, 20, amended: 1994, c. 29, sch. 4.

s. 28B, added: *ibid.*, sch. 4.

sch. 5, repealed in pt.: *ibid.*, sch. 9.

36. Aviation Security Act 1982.

s. 30, amended: 1994, c. 19, sch. 16; repealed in pt.: 1994, c. 29, sch. 9.

s. 31, amended: *ibid.*, sch. 5.

37. Merchant Shipping (Liner Conferences) Act 1982.

s. 9, Act of Sederunt 94/1443.

39. Finance Act 1982.

ss. 3, 5, 7, repealed in pt.: 1994, c. 22, sch. 5.

s. 134, amended: 1994, c. 9, s. 236.

schs. 3, 5 (in pt.) repealed: 1994, c. 22, sch. 5.

sch. 6, repealed in pt.: 1994, c. 9, sch. 26.

41. Stock Transfer Act 1982.

s. 5, repealed in pt.(S.): 1994, c. 39, sch. 14.

sch. 1, amended: 1994, c. 29, sch. 4; c. 39, sch. 13(S.).

43. Local Government and Planning (Scotland) Act 1982.

ss. 4, 6, 7, repealed: 1994, c. 39, sch. 14.

s. 9, substituted: *ibid.*, sch. 13.

s. 14, amended: *ibid.*; repealed in pt.: *ibid.*, schs. 13, 14.

ss. 15, 16, amended: *ibid.*, sch. 13.

s. 17, substituted: *ibid.*

ss. 18, 24–26, amended: *ibid.*

s. 27, amended: *ibid.*; repealed in pt.: *ibid.*, schs. 13, 14.

ss. 28, 30, amended: *ibid.*, sch. 13.

ss. 33, 34, 50 (in pt.), 56, repealed: 1994, c. 39, sch. 14.

1982—cont.

43. Local Government and Planning (Scotland) Act 1982—*cont.*
s. 67, amended: *ibid.*, sch. 13.
sch. 1, repealed in pt.: *ibid.*, schs. 13, 14.
sch. 3, repealed in pt.: *ibid.*, sch. 14.

45. Civic Government (Scotland) Act 1982.
s. 2, amended: 1994, c. 39, sch. 13.
ss. 7, 39, see *Prentice* v. *Normand*, 1994 S.C.C.R. 55.
s. 10, sch. 1, see *Cashley* v. *City of Dundee District Council*, 1994 S.C.L.R. 6.
s. 45, amended: 1994, c. 39, sch. 13.
s. 51, amended: 1994, c. 33, s. 87, sch. 9.
ss. 52, 52A, amended: *ibid.*, s. 84.
s. 58, see *Mathieson* v. *Crowe*, 1993 S.C.C.R. 1100.
ss. 62–64, amended: 1994, c. 33, sch. 13.
s. 87, see *Acorn Properties* v. *City of Edinburgh District Council* (Sh.Ct.), 1994 S.C.L.R. 370.
ss. 87, 89, repealed in pt.: 1994, c. 39, schs. 13, 14.
ss. 90–92, 94–97, 119, 10, amended: *ibid.*, sch. 13.
s. 121, amended: *ibid.*, s. 141, sch. 13; repealed in pt.: *ibid.*, s. 141, sch. 14.
s. 122, amended: *ibid.*, sch. 13; repealed in pt.: *ibid.*, schs. 13, 14.
s. 123, amended: *ibid.*, sch. 13; repealed in pt. (prosp.): 1994, c. 21, schs. 9, 11, Pt. II.
s. 133, sch. 2, amended: 1994, c. 39, sch. 13.

48. Criminal Justice Act 1982.
s. 1, amended: 1994, c. 33, sch. 4; repealed in pt.: *ibid.*, schs. 4, 11.
Pt. I (ss. 1–28), see *R.* v. *Newcastle Justices, ex p. Ashley* [1993] RA 264, Laws J.
s. 1B, see *R.* v. *Ward (Stephen), The Times*, July 9, 1994, C.A.
s. 1B, amended: 1994, c. 33, s. 17.
s. 1C, amended: *ibid.*, s. 18.
s. 3, amended: *ibid.*, schs. 4, 10.
s. 12, repealed in pt.: *ibid.*, s. 18, sch. 11.
s. 19, amended: *ibid.*, sch. 9.
s. 32, amended: *ibid.*, sch. 10.
s. 37, see *Botross* v. *Hammersmith and Fulham London Borough Council, The Times*, November 7, 1994, D.C.
s. 67, repealed in pt.: 1994, c. 33, sch. 11.
sch. 1, amended: order 94/1570; 1994, c. 37, sch. 1.
sch. 14, repealed in pt.: 1994, c. 33, sch. 11.

49. Transport Act 1982.
s. 21, sch. 4, repealed in pt.: 1994, c. 40, sch. 17.

1982—cont.

50. Insurance Companies Act 1982.
amended: regs. 93/3127.
ss. 1, 3, 9, see *NRG Victory Reinsurance, Re, The Times*, November 8, 1994, Lindsay J.
ss. 2, 5, regs. 94/1516.
ss. 2, 5, amended: regs. 94/1696.
s. 6, substituted: *ibid.*
ss. 7–9, amended and repealed in pt.: *ibid.*
ss. 7, 9, regs. 94/1516.
ss. 11, 12, amended: regs. 94/1696.
s. 12A, added: *ibid.*
ss. 13, 15, amended: *ibid.*
s. 15, regs. 94/1516.
s. 16, see *Fuji Finance Inc.* v. *Aetna Life Insurance, The Times*, July 21, 1994, Sir Donald Nicholls, V.-C.
ss. 17, 18, 20, 21, regs. 94/1515.
s. 21A, regs. 94/449.
ss. 32, 33, 35, regs. 94/1516.
ss. 32, 34, 35, amended: regs. 94/1696.
ss. 32, 37, 49, see *NRG Victory Reinsurance, Re, The Times*, November 8, 1994, Lindsay J.
ss. 35A, 35B, added: regs. 94/1696.
s. 37, amended and repealed in pt.: *ibid.*
ss. 38, 39, amended: *ibid.*
ss. 40A, 43A, added: *ibid.*
ss. 44, 45, amended: *ibid.*
s. 47A, substituted: *ibid.*
s. 47B, amended: *ibid.*
ss. 49–52, substituted as s. 49: *ibid.*
s. 52A, amended: *ibid.*
s. 52B, added: *ibid.*
ss. 54, 60, 61, amended: *ibid.*
ss. 60–62, regs. 94/1516.
ss. 61A, 61B, added: regs. 94/1696.
s. 62, amended: *ibid.*
s. 63, see *NRG Victory Reinsurance, Re, The Times*, November 8, 1994, Lindsay J.
s. 63, amended: regs. 94/1696.
s. 63A, repealed: *ibid.*
s. 66, amended: *ibid.*
s. 71, amended and repealed in pt.: *ibid.*
s. 72, regs. 94/1516.
ss. 72A, 72B, added: regs. 94/1696.
ss. 74, 78, regs. 94/1516.
ss. 74, 75, 78, amended: *ibid.*
s. 81A, substituted: *ibid.*
s. 81B, substituted for ss. 81B–81J: *ibid.*
ss. 82, 83A, 85, amended: *ibid.*
ss. 84, 86, 90, regs. 94/1516.
s. 94A, regs. 94/643.
s. 95, see *NRG Victory Reinsurance, Re, The Times*, November 8, 1994, Lindsay J.
s. 96, see *Scher* v. *Policyholders Protection Board (Nos. 1 and 2) (Note)* [1994] 2 W.L.R. 593, H.L.

1982—cont.

50. Insurance Companies Act 1982—*cont.*
s. 96, regs. 94/643, 1515, 1516.
ss. 96, 96A, amended: regs. 94/1696.
ss. 96C–96F, added: *ibid.*
s. 97, regs. 94/643, 1515, 1516.
sch. 1, amended: regs. 94/1696.
schs. 1, 2, see *NRG Victory Reinsurance, Re, The Times,* November 8, 1994, Lindsay J.
sch. 2A, added: *ibid.*
sch. 2B, added and applied: *ibid.*
schs. 2C–2G, added: *ibid.*
sch. 3, repealed: *ibid.*
sch. 3A, amended: *ibid.*

1983

2. Representation of the People Act 1983.
s. 8, amended(S.): 1994, c. 39, sch. 13.
ss. 8, 18, amended: 1994, c. 19, sch. 16; repealed in pt.: *ibid.*, schs. 16, 18.
s. 18, amended(S.): 1994, c. 39, s. 142; repealed in pt.(S.): *ibid.*, s. 142, sch. 14.
ss. 24, 28, amended: 1994, c. 19, sch. 16.
s. 25, amended(S.): 1994, c. 39, sch. 13; repealed in pt.(S.): *ibid.*, schs. 13, 14.
s. 29, orders 94/1044, 1379, 1412, 1413.
s. 31, amended: 1994, c. 19, sch. 16.
s. 31, amended(S.): 1994, c. 39, sch. 13; repealed in pt.(S.): *ibid.*, schs. 13, 14.
ss. 35, 36, 39, amended: 1994, c. 19, sch. 16; repealed in pt.: *ibid.*, schs. 16, 18.
s. 43, amended(S.): 1994, c. 39, s. 6.
s. 52, amended: 1994, c. 19, sch. 16; repealed in pt.: *ibid.*, schs. 16, 18.
s. 52, amended(S.): 1994, c. 39, sch. 13.
s. 57, Act of Sederunt 94/2483.
s. 69, amended: 1994, c. 19, sch. 16.
s. 76, amended: order 94/747.
s. 76A, order 94/747.
s. 82, amended: 1994, c. 19, sch. 16; c. 39, sch. 13(S.).
s. 96, amended(S.): *ibid.*, sch. 13.
ss. 121, 136, 138, 139, 146, 147, 152, 153, Act of Sederunt 94/1443.
s. 159, amended: 1994, c. 19, sch. 16.
s. 166, see *Thompson* v. *Dann; Local Government Election for Eel Brook Division of Hammersmith and Fulham London Borough Council, Re, The Times,* November 3, 1994, D.C.
s. 177, amended: 1994, c. 19, sch. 2.
s. 185, Act of Sederunt 94/1443.
s. 197, order 94/747; amended: *ibid.*
s. 203, amended: 1994, c. 19, sch. 16.
s. 204, amended(S.): 1994, c. 39, sch. 13; repealed in pt.(S.): *ibid.*, schs. 13, 14.
sch. 1, see *Sanders* v. *Chichester, The Guardian,* November 14, 1994, Election Ct.

1983—cont.

2. Representation of the People Act 1983—*cont.*
sch. 1, amended: 1994, c. 19, schs. 2, 16.
schs. 2, 3, 5, amended: *ibid.*, sch. 16.
sch. 5, amended(S.): 1994, c. 19, sch. 13.

7. Conwy Tunnel (Supplementary Powers) Act 1983.
s. 8, amended: 1994, c. 19, sch. 7.

14. International Transport Conventions Act 1983.
s. 1, amended: order 94/1907.
s. 8, order 94/1907.

16. Level Crossings Act 1983.
s. 1, amended: 1994, c. 19, sch. 7; repealed in pt.: *ibid.*, schs. 7, 18.
s. 1, amended(S.): 1994, c. 39, sch. 13.

19. Matrimonial Homes Act 1983.
s. 1, see *B.* v. *B.,* November 15, 1993; H.H.J. Hague, Reading County Ct.; *Pike* v. *Pike, The Times,* March 4, 1994, C.A.; *Friendship Housing Association* v. *Buchanon,* September 9, 1994; District Judge Owen; Birmingham County Ct.

20. Mental Health Act 1983.
ss. 2, 23, see *Hereford and Worcester County Council* v. *S.* [1993] 2 FLR 360, Connell J.
s. 3, see *R.* v. *South Western Hospital Managers, ex p. M.* [1994] 1 All E.R. 161, Laws J.
ss. 3, 16, 72, see *R.* v. *Canons Park Mental Health Review Tribunal, ex p. A* [1994] 2 All E.R. 659, C.A.
ss. 42, 47, 49, 50, 74, see *R.* v. *Secretary of State for the Home Department, ex p. Stroud* [1993] C.O.D. 75, Henry J.
s. 50, see *R.* v. *Secretary of State for the Home Office, ex p. T.; R.* v. *Same, ex p. H.; R.* v. *Same, ex p. Hickey* [1994] 2 W.L.R. 190, D.C.
s. 51, amended: 1994, c. 33, sch. 10.
s. 52, amended: *ibid.*, sch. 4.
s. 131, see *R.* v. *Kirklees Metropolitan Borough Council, ex p. C.* [1993] 2 FLR 187, C.A.
s. 145, repealed in pt.: 1994, c. 6, s. 1.

24. Licensing (Occasional Permissions) Act 1983.
s. 1, amended: 1994, c. 19, sch. 16.

28. Finance Act 1983.
s. 4, repealed in pt.: 1994, c. 22, sch. 5.
sch. 3, repealed in pt.: 1994, c. 9, sch. 26; c. 22, sch. 5.

29. Miscellaneous Financial Provisions Act 1983.
sch. 2, repealed in pt. (prosp.): 1994, c. 21, sch. 11, Pt. III.

35. Litter Act 1983.
ss. 4, 8, amended(S.): 1994, c. 39, sch. 13.
s. 10, amended: 1994, c. 19, schs. 6, 9.

1983—cont.

37. Agriculture Act 1983.
s. 2, order 93/3230.

40. Education (Fees and Awards) Act 1983.
s. 1, amended: 1994, c. 30, sch. 2.
ss. 1, 2, regs. 93/3183, 3184.

41. Health and Social Services and Social Security Adjudications Act 1983.
sch. 9, amended: 1994, c. 19, sch. 10.

44. National Audit Act 1983.
sch. 4, repealed in pt. (prosp.): 1994, c. 21, schs. 9, 11, Pt. IV.

54. Medical Act 1983.
sch. 1, order 94/2022.

55. Value Added Tax Act 1983.
repealed: 1994, c. 23, sch. 15.
s. 2, see *Robert Gordon's College* v. *Customs and Excise Commissioners* [1993] VATTR 159, Edinburgh Tribunal; *Gould and Cullen* v. *Customs and Excise Commissioners* [1993] VATTR 209, London Tribunal.
s. 3, order 93/2951.
ss. 3, 5, see *Nationwide Building Society* v. *Customs and Excise Commissioners* [1993] VATTR 205, London Tribunal.
s. 5, see *Broadwell Land* v. *Customs and Excise Commissioners* [1993] VATTR 346, London Tribunal; *Richmond Theatre Management* v. *Customs and Excise Commissioners* [1993] VATTR 339, London Tribunal.
s. 6, regs. 93/1224.
s. 7, order 93/2328.
s. 13, see *Feehan* v. *Customs and Excise Commissioners* [1993] VATTR 266, London Tribunal.
s. 14, see *Customs and Excise Commissioners* v. *Rosner* [1994] STC 228, Latham J.
s. 14, regs. 93/3028; order 93/2954.
s. 16, see *Bophuthatswana National Commercial Corp.* v. *Customs and Excise Commissioners* [1993] STC 702, C.A.
s. 16, order 94/686.
s. 17, orders 94/687, 1188.
s. 18, order 93/2951.
s. 20, amended: 1994, c. 19, sch. 16.
s. 23, regs. 23/1223.
s. 24, regs. 93/3027.
s. 29, see *Customs and Excise Commissioners* v. *Kingfisher* [1994] STC 63, Popplewell J.
s. 29A, amended: 1994, c. 9, s. 18.
s. 31, see *Sargent* v. *Customs and Excise Commissioners, The Times*, November 18, 1993, Judge Paul Baker, Q.C. sitting as a deputy judge of the High Court.

1983—cont.

55. Value Added Tax Act 1983—*cont.*
s. 37A, see *Independent Coach Travel (Wholesaling)* v. *Customs and Excise Commissioners* [1993] VATTR 357, London Tribunal.
s. 38, see *Advocate (Lord)* v. *Raj Restaurant* (Sh.Ct.), 1994 S.C.L.R. 467.
s. 38A, see *National Council of YMCAs Inc.* v. *Customs and Excise Commissioners* [1993] VATTR 299, London Tribunal.
s. 39, see *R.* v. *Northamptonshire Magistrates' Court, ex p. Customs and Excise Commissioners, The Independent*, February 23, 1994, D.C.
s. 40, see *Sitar Tandoori Restaurant* v. *Customs and Excise Commissioners* [1993] STC 582, Henry J.; *Customs and Excise Commissioners* v. *Lewis, The Times*, June 22, 1994, Brooke J.; *Fresh Pasta Products* v. *Customs and Excise Commissioners* [1993] VATTR 238, London Tribunal; *Camden London Borough Council* v. *Customs and Excise Commissioners* [1993] VATTR 73, London Tribunal; *Dollar Land (Feltham); Dollar Land (Cumbernauld); Dollar Land (Calthorpe House)* v. *Customs and Excise Commissioners* [1993] VATTR 30, London Tribunal.
s. 40, amended: 1994, c. 9, s. 18.
s. 46A, regs. 93/1224.
s. 46B, regs. 93/3027.
s. 48, orders 94/686, 687, 1188.
sch. 1, see *Customs and Excise Commissioners* v. *Trinity Factoring Services, The Times*, June 30, 1994.
schs. 1, 1B, order 93/2953.
sch. 3, amended: order 93/2328.
schs. 3, 5, see *Bophuthatswana National Commercial Corp.* v. *Customs and Excise Commissioners* [1993] STC 702, C.A.
sch. 4, see *Fine Art Developments* v. *Customs and Excise Commissioners, The Times*, June 1, 1994, C.A.; *Customs and Excise Commissioners* v. *Showmarch Marketing* [1994] STC 19, McCullough J.; *Beckbell* v. *Customs and Excise Commissioners* [1993] VATTR 212, Manchester Tribunal.
sch. 5, see *Customs and Excise Commissioners* v. *Lewis* [1994] STC 739, Brooke J.; *Virgin Atlantic Airways* v. *Customs and Excise Commissioners* [1993] VATTR 136, London Tribunal; *Whiteley (Simon)* v. *Customs and Excise Commissioners* [1993] VATTR 248, London Tribunal; *Smith Kline Beecham* v. *Customs and Excise*

1983—cont.

55. Valued Added Tax Act 1983—*cont.*
Commissioners [1993] VATTR 219, London Tribunal; *All Saints Tilsworth Parochial Church Council* v. *Customs and Excise Commissioners* [1993] VATTR 315, London Tribunal.
sch. 5, amended: orders 93/2498; 94/686.
sch. 6, see *Sargent* v. *Customs and Excise Commissioners, The Times,* November 18, 1993, Judge Paul Baker, Q.C. sitting as a deputy judge of the High Court; *Card Protection Plan* v. *Customs and Excise Commissioners* [1994] STC 199, C.A.; *Feehan* v. *Customs and Excise Commissioners* [1993] VATTR 266, London Tribunal; *Countrywide Insurance Marketing* v. *Customs and Excise Commissioners* [1993] VATTR 277, London Tribunal; *J.F. Greves* v. *Customs and Excise Commissioners* [1993] VATTR 127, London Tribunal; *Leightons* v. *Customs and Excise Commissioners* [1993] VATTR 1, London Tribunal.
sch. 6, amended: orders 94/687, 1188.
sch. 6A, see *Fencing Supplies* v. *Customs and Excise Commissioners* [1993] VATTR 302, Manchester Tribunal; *Robert Gordon's College* v. *Customs and Excise Commissioners; sub nom. Commissioners of Customs and Excise* v. *Robert Gordon's College, The Times,* September 6, 1994.
sch. 7, see *Sitar Tandoori Restaurant* v. *Customs and Excise Commissioners* [1993] STC 582, Henry J.; *Bjellica (t/a Eddy's Domestic Appliances)* v. *Customs and Excise Commissioners* [1993] STC 730, D.C.; *House* v. *Customs and Excise Commissioners* [1994] STC 211, May J.; *Far East Restaurants* v. *Customs and Excise Commissioners; Yuen Tung Restaurants* v. *Same* [1993] VATTR 226, Manchester Tribunal; *Broadwell Land* v. *Customs and Excise Commissioners* [1993] VATTR 346, London Tribunal; *John Dee* v. *Customs and Excise Commissioners* [1993] VATTR 196, Manchester Tribunal; *Advocate (Lord)* v. *Raj Restaurant* (Sh.Ct.), 1994 S.C.L.R. 467.
sch. 7, regs. 93/3027, 3028; 94/803.
sch. 7, amended: 1994, c. 9, s. 256; repealed in pt.: *ibid.,* s. 256, sch. 26.
sch. 8, see *Wine Warehouses Europe* v. *Customs and Excise Commissioners* [1993] VATTR 307, London Tribunal.
sch. 9, repealed in pt.: 1994, c. 22, sch. 5.

1983—cont.

56. Oil Taxation Act 1983.
sch. 2, amended: 1994, c. 9, s. 238.
60. Coal Industry Act 1983.
ss. 1, 2, 4–6, sch., repealed (prosp.): 1994, c. 21, sch. 11, Pt. III.

1984

8. Prevention of Terrorism (Temporary Provisions) Act 1984.
see *Brannigan and McBride* v. *U.K. (Nos. 14553/89 and 14554/89)* (1994) 17 E.H.R.R. 539, European Ct. H.R.
11. Education (Grants and Awards) Act 1984.
ss. 1, 3, regs. 94/612.
12. Telecommunications Act 1984.
s. 4, see *R.* v. *Effik (Godwin Eno); R.* v. *Mitchell (Graham Martin)* [1994] 3 W.L.R. 583, H.L.
s. 7, see *Mercury Communications* v. *Director General of Telecommunications, The Times,* August 3, 1994, C.A.
s. 9, orders 93/2897–2899; 94/1, 234, 874–876, 952–954, 1006–1008, 1071, 1072, 1190, 1202–1204, 2654, 2655.
s. 43, amended: 1994, c. 33, s. 92.
s. 50, amended: 1994, c. 40, schs. 2, 4; repealed in pt.: *ibid.,* sch. 17.
s. 65, order 94/744.
s. 69, order 94/2162.
s. 84, regs. 94/2250.
s. 97, amended: 1994, c. 19, sch. 16; repealed in pt.: *ibid.,* schs. 16, 18.
ss. 97, 98, amended(S.): 1994, c. 39, sch. 13.
s. 108, order 94/1064.
19. Trade Marks (Amendment) Act 1984.
repealed: 1994, c. 26, sch. 5.
s. 68, see *Fingals Trade Mark* [1993] R.P.C. 21, Trade Marks Registry.
22. Public Health (Control of Diseases) Act 1984.
s. 1, amended: 1994, c. 19, sch. 9.
ss. 11, 37, see *Birmingham Post and Mail* v. *Birmingham City Council, The Times,* November 25, 1993, D.C.
s. 13, regs. 94/311.
s. 13, amended: orders 93/1813; 94/1405; 1994, c. 19, sch. 9; repealed in pt.: order 93/1813.
ss. 53, 64, 74, amended: 1994, c. 19, sch. 9.
23. Registered Homes Act 1984.
s. 5, see *Swindells* v. *Cheshire County Council* 91 L.G.R. 582, D.C.
24. Dentists Act 1984.
sch. 5, repealed in pt.: 1994, c. 23, sch. 15.

1984—cont.

26. Inshore Fishing (Scotland) Act 1984.

s. 1, orders 94/326, 1828, 2613.

s. 1, amended and repealed in pt.: 1994, c. 27, s. 1.

s. 2, see *MacGillivray* v. *Johnston (No. 2),* 1994 S.L.T. 1012.

s. 2, repealed in pt.: 1994, c. 27, s. 4.

s. 4, amended: *ibid.*, s. 2.

s. 5, amended: *ibid.*, s. 3.

s. 9, amended: *ibid.*, s. 4.

27. Road Traffic Regulation Act 1984.

s. 8, see *Post Office* v. *Richmond upon Thames London Borough Council, The Times,* May 17, 1994, D.C.

ss. 16A–16C, added: 1994, c. 11, s. 1.

s. 17, regs. 94/2129.

s. 19, amended(S.): 1994, c. 39, sch. 13.

s. 26, amended(S.): *ibid.*; repealed in pt.(S.): *ibid.*, schs. 13, 14.

s. 28, regs. 94/1519.

ss. 32, 37, amended(S.): 1994, c. 39, sch. 13.

ss. 39, 44, 45, amended: 1994, c. 19, sch. 7; repealed in pt.: *ibid.*, schs. 7, 18.

ss. 44, 45, amended(S.): 1994, c. 39, sch. 13.

ss. 49 (in pt.), 54, repealed: 1994, c. 19, schs. 7, 18.

ss. 55, 59, amended: *ibid.*, sch. 7; repealed in pt.: *ibid.*, schs. 7, 18.

s. 62, regs. 94/432.

ss. 64, 65, regs. 94/1519.

s. 68, amended: 1994, c. 11, sch.

s. 85, regs. 94/1519.

s. 97, repealed in pt.: 1994, c. 29, sch. 9.

s. 99, regs. 94/1503.

s. 100, amended: 1994, c. 19, sch. 7; c. 39, sch. 13(S.).

s. 101, see *Bulbruin Limited* v. *Romanyszyn* [1994] RTR 273, C.A.

ss. 101, 111, amended: 1994, c. 22, sch. 3.

s. 121A, amended(S.): 1994, c. 39, sch. 13.

s. 124, amended: 1994, c. 11, sch.

s. 125, repealed in pt.: 1994, c. 19, schs. 7, 18.

ss. 130, 141A, amended: 1994, c. 11, sch.

s. 142, amended: 1994, c. 19, sch. 7.

sch. 5, repealed in pt. (prosp.): 1994, c. 21, schs. 9, 11, Pt. IV.

sch. 9, see *Strathclyde Buses* v. *Strathclyde Regional Council* (O.H.), 1994 S.L.T. 724.

sch. 9, amended: 1994, c. 11, sch.; c. 19, sch. 7; c. 40, sch. 11; repealed in pt.: 1994, c. 19, schs. 7, 18; c. 40, sch. 17.

sch. 12, amended: 1994, c. 22, sch. 3.

28. County Courts Act 1984.

s. 2, orders 93/3120; 94/706.

1984—cont.

28. County Courts Act 1984—*cont.*

s. 14, see *Blackburn* v. *Bowering* [1994] 3 All E.R. 380, C.A.; *Cottrell* v. *Hunt,* May 17, 1994; H.H.J. Edwards, Q.C.: Westminster County Ct.

s. 27, amended: 1994, c. 28, sch. 2.

s. 40, see *Groom* v. *Norman Motors (Wallisdown)* [1993] P.I.Q.R. P215, Turner J.; *Restrick* v. *Crickmore; Nisbet* v. *Granada Entertainment; Reed* v. *Department of Employment; Warren* v. *Hinchcliffe; Kazmi* v. *Wali* [1994] 1 W.L.R. 420, C.A.; *Composite Gutters* v. *Pre-formed Components* [1993] F.S.R. 305, Hoffmann J.

s. 42, see *Pharma Plast A/S* v. *Bard* [1993] F.S.R. 686, Patents County Ct.

s. 57, amended: 1994, c. 33, sch. 4.

s. 60, amended: 1994, c. 29, sch. 4.

s. 75, rules 93/3273; 94/306, 1288, 1403, 2403.

s. 77, order 93/2789.

s. 112, see *Wood (Jennifer Agnes), Re,* August 27, 1993; District Judge Brown in a reserved judgment; Tamworth County Court.

s. 128, order 94/1936.

30. Food Act 1984.

s. 61, amended: 1994, c. 19, sch. 9.

s. 68, order 94/407.

31. Rating and Valuation (Amendment) (Scotland) Act 1984.

ss. 6, 7, sch. 2 (in pt.), repealed: 1994, c. 39, sch. 14.

32. London Regional Transport Act 1984.

sch. 6, repealed in pt.: 1994, c. 40, sch. 17.

35. Data Protection Act 1984.

s. 5, see *R.* v. *Brown (Gregory Michael)* [1994] 2 W.L.R. 673, C.A.

ss. 5, 28, amended: 1994, c. 33, s. 161.

s. 30, amended: regs. 94/1696.

36. Mental Health (Scotland) Act 1984.

s. 25, order 94/1675.

s. 90, repealed: 1994, c. 16, s. 2.

s. 91, amended and repealed in pt.: *ibid.*

s. 125, amended: *ibid.*

37. Child Abduction Act 1984.

s. 1, see *R.* v. *Sherry; R.* v. *El Yamani* [1993] Crim.L.R. 536, C.A.

39. Video Recordings Act 1984.

s. 1, amended: 1994, c. 33, sch. 9; repealed in pt.: *ibid.*, sch. 11.

s. 2, amended: *ibid.*, s. 89.

s. 3, amended: 1994, c. 17, s. 39.

ss. 4A, 4B, added: 1994, c. 33, s. 90.

s. 7, amended: *ibid.*, s. 90.

ss. 9–12, amended: *ibid.*, s. 88.

s. 13, amended: *ibid.*, sch. 10.

s. 14, amended: *ibid.*, s. 88.

s. 15, substituted: *ibid.*, sch. 10.

s. 16A, amended: *ibid.*, s. 91.

ss. 16B–16D, added: *ibid.*

1984—cont.

39. Video Recordings Act 1984—*cont.*
s. 17, repealed in pt.: *ibid.*, schs. 9, 11.

40. Animal Health and Welfare Act 1984.
s. 10, regs. 93/2920, 2921, 3248.

42. Matrimonial and Family Proceedings Act 1984.
see *Hewitson* v. *Hewitson, The Independent,* October 7, 1994, C.A.
s. 40, rules 94/808, 2165.

43. Finance Act 1984.
ss. 10–13, repealed: 1994, c. 23, sch. 15.
sch. 3, repealed in pt.: 1994, c. 9, sch. 26.
sch. 6, repealed: 1994, c. 23, sch. 15.
sch. 22, repealed in pt.: regs. 94/1813.

51. Inheritance Tax Act 1984.
s. 8, order 93/2949.
s. 113B, amended: 1994, c. 9, s. 247.
ss. 115, 116, see *Starke* v. *I.R.C., The Times,* February 24, 1994, Blackburne J.
s. 124B, amended: 1994, c. 9, s. 247.
s. 224, repealed in pt.: regs. 94/1813.
s. 225, substituted: *ibid.*
ss. 245 (in pt.), 246, repealed: regs. 94/1813.
s. 251, substituted: *ibid.*
sch. 8, repealed in pt.: 1994, c. 23, sch. 15.

52. Parliamentary Pensions etc. Act 1984.
ss. 3 (in pt.)–5 (in pt.), 6, repealed: regs. 93/3253.

54. Roads (Scotland) Act 1984.
s. 4, repealed in pt.: 1994, c. 39, sch. 14.
s. 9, amended: *ibid.*, sch. 13.
ss. 12A–12F, added: *ibid.*, s. 38.
s. 20A, amended: regs. 94/2012.
s. 39B, regs. 94/2488.
s. 55, amended: 1994, c. 39, sch. 13.
s. 55A, amended: regs. 94/2012.
s. 60, see *McArthur* v. *Strathclyde Regional Council, The Times,* May 20, 1994.
s. 62, amended: 1994, c. 11, sch.
s. 81A, added: 1994, c. 39, s. 39.
s. 93, amended: *ibid.*, sch. 13.
s. 95, repealed in pt.: *ibid.*, schs. 13, 14.
s. 97, amended: *ibid.*, sch. 13.
s. 112, amended: *ibid.*, s. 38.
s. 113, amended: *ibid.*, sch. 13.
s. 113A, added: *ibid.*, s. 147.
s. 135, amended: *ibid.*, sch. 13.
s. 140, amended: 1994, c. 21, sch. 9; repealed in pt. (prosp.): *ibid.*. schs. 9, 11, Pt. II.
s. 143, regs. 94/2488.
s. 143, amended: 1994, c. 39, s. 38, sch. 13.
s. 151, amended: *ibid.*, s. 146, sch. 13.
sch. 1, amended: regs. 94/2012; 1994, c. 39, s. 148, sch. 13.
sch. 9, repealed in pt.: 1994, c. 21, sch. 11, Pt. II (prosp.); c. 22, sch. 5; c. 39, sch. 14.

1984—cont.

55. Building Act 1984.
s. 1, regs. 94/1850, 2020.
s. 3, regs. 94/1850.
s. 14, amended: 1994, c. 40, s. 32.
s. 16, regs. 94/2020.
s. 18, amended: 1994, c. 19, sch. 9.
ss. 34, 35, 50, regs. 94/2020.
s. 59, see *Swansea City Council* v. *Jenkins, The Times,* April 1, 1994, MacPherson of Cluny, J.
ss. 87, 126, amended: 1994, c. 19, sch. 9.
s. 126, regs. 94/1850.
sch. 1, regs. 94/1850, 2020.
sch. 1, amended: 1994, c. 40, s. 32.

56. Foster Children (Scotland) Act 1984.
s. 21, amended: 1994, c. 39, sch. 13.

58. Rent (Scotland) Act 1984.
s. 5, amended: 1994, c. 39, sch. 13.
s. 43, amended: *ibid.*; c. 40, sch. 13.
ss. 43A–43C, added: *ibid.*; sch. 16.
ss. 62, 63, 115, amended: 1994, c. 39, sch. 13.

60. Police and Criminal Evidence Act 1984.
see *Dudley Metropolitan Borough Council* v. *Debenhams, The Times,* August 16, 1994, D.C.; *Joy* v. *Federation against Copyright Theft* [1993] Crim.L.R. 588, D.C.; *R.* v. *Campbell and Williams* [1993] Crim.L.R. 448, C.A.; *R.* v. *Park* (1994) 158 J.P. 144, C.A.
s. 4, amended: 1994, c. 22, sch. 3.
s. 9, see *R.* v. *Acton Crown Court, ex p. Layton* [1993] Crim.L.R. 458, D.C.
ss. 9, 11, see *R.* v. *Singleton, The Times,* June 22, 1994, C.A.
s. 10, see *R.* v. *R.* [1994] 1 W.L.R. 758, C.A.; *R.* v. *Leeds Magistrates' Court, ex p. Dumbleton* [1993] Crim.L.R. 866, D.C.
s. 17, amended: 1994, c. 33, sch. 10.
s. 24, amended: *ibid.*, ss. 85, 155, 166, 167.
s. 25, see *Edwards* v. *D.P.P.* (1993) 97 Cr.App.R. 301, D.C.
s. 32, amended: 1994, c. 33, s. 59.
s. 34, amended: *ibid.*, s. 29.
s. 37, repealed in pt.: *ibid.*, s. 29, sch. 11.
s. 38, amended: *ibid.*, ss. 24, 28, sch. 10.
ss. 41–43, amended: *ibid.*, s. 29.
s. 43, see *R.* v. *Anderson* [1993] Crim.L.R. 447, C.A.
s. 46A, added: 1994, c. 33, s. 29.
s. 47, amended: *ibid.*, ss. 27, 29; repealed in pt.: *ibid.*, s. 29, sch. 11.
s. 54, amended: *ibid.*, sch. 10.
s. 58, see *R.* v. *Chief Constable of South Wales, ex p. Merrick* [1994] 1 W.L.R. 663, D.C.
s. 60, see *Darby* v. *D.P.P., The Times,* November 4, 1994, D.C.
s. 61, amended: 1994, c. 33, sch. 10.

1984—cont.

60. Police and Criminal Evidence Act 1984—*cont.*

s. 62, amended: *ibid.*, s. 54, schs. 4, 9, 10, paras. 57, 62; repealed in pt.: *ibid.*, sch. 11.

ss. 62, 64, see *R.* v. *Kelt (Stephen)* [1994] 1 W.L.R. 765, C.A.

s. 63, amended: 1994, c. 33, s. 55, sch. 10, paras. 58, 62.

ss. 63, 65, see *R.* v. *Cooke, (Stephen), The Times,* August 10, 1994, C.A.

s. 63A, amended: 1994, c. 33, s. 56.

s. 64, amended: *ibid.*, s. 57.

s. 65, amended: *ibid.*, ss. 58, 59; c. 37, sch. 1.

ss. 66, 67, see *R.* v. *Weekes (Trevor Dave)* (1993) 97 Cr.App.R. 222, C.A.

s. 67, repealed in pt.: 1994, c. 29, s. 37, sch. 9.

ss. 67, 78, see *Stilgoe* v. *Eager, The Times,* January 27, 1994, D.C.

s. 69, see *R.* v. *Hinds* [1993] Crim.L.R. 528, C.A.

s. 74, see *R.* v. *Hall* [1993] Crim.L.R. 527, C.A.

ss. 74, 78, see *R.* v. *Hillier (Brian); R.* v. *Farrar (Vivian Frederick)* (1993) 97 Cr.App.R. 349, C.A.

s. 76, see *R.* v. *Paris; R.* v. *Abdullah; R.* v. *Miller* (1993) 97 Cr.App.R. 99, C.A.

ss. 76, 78, see *R.* v. *Joseph* [1993] Crim.L.R. 206, C.A.; *R.* v. *Heaton* [1993] Crim.L.R. 593, C.A.

s. 77, see *R.* v. *Campbell, The Times,* July 13, 1994, C.A.

s. 78, see *R.* v. *Preston (Stephen); R.* v. *Clarke (Nicholas Henry); R.* v. *Austen (Anthony); R.* v. *Salter (Jeremy); R.* v. *Preston (Zena)* [1993] 3 W.L.R. 891, H.L.; *C.P.S.* v. *W.,* March 24, 1994; D.C.; *R.* v. *Smurthwaite; R.* v. *Gill* [1994] 1 All E.R. 898, C.A.; *R.* v. *Rogers* [1993] Crim.L.R. 386, C.A.; *R.* v. *Jones (M.A.); R.* v. *Dowling; R.* v. *Jones (D.H.); R.* v. *Brown* (1994) 158 J.P. 293, C.A.; *R.* v. *Konscol* [1993] Crim.L.R. 950, C.A.

s. 80, see *R.* v. *Director of the Serious Fraud Office, ex p. Johnson (Malcolm Keith)* [1993] C.O.D. 58, Auld J.

Pt. IX (ss. 83–105), see *R.* v. *Chief Constable of the West Midlands Police, ex p. Wiley; R.* v. *Chief Constable of Nottinghamshire Police, ex p. Sunderland* [1994] 3 W.L.R. 433, H.L.

s. 84, amended: 1994, c. 29, sch. 5.

s. 85, amended: *ibid.*, sch. 5; repealed in pt.: *ibid.*, schs. 5, 9.

s. 86, amended: *ibid.*, sch. 5.

s. 88, amended: *ibid.*, s. 34.

s. 89, amended: *ibid.*, sch. 5.

1984—cont.

60. Police and Criminal Evidence Act 1984—*cont.*

s. 90, amended: *ibid.*, sch. 35; repealed in pt.: *ibid.*, s. 35, sch. 9.

s. 91, repealed: *ibid.*, schs. 5, 9.

s. 92, repealed: *ibid.*, s. 37, sch. 9.

s. 93, amended: *ibid.*, s. 36.

s. 94, repealed: *ibid.*, s. 37, sch. 9.

ss. 95, 96, amended: *ibid.*, sch. 5.

s. 97, repealed in pt.: *ibid.*, s. 37, sch. 9.

s. 99, amended: *ibid.*, sch. 5; repealed in pt.: *ibid.*, sch. 9.

s. 100, amended: *ibid.*, sch. 5.

s. 101, repealed: *ibid.*, s. 37, sch. 9.

s. 102, substituted: *ibid.*, sch. 5.

s. 103, see *R.* v. *Secretary of State for the Home Department, ex p. Harrison, The Times,* May 17, 1994, Potts J.

s. 103, repealed: 1994, c. 29, sch. 9.

s. 104, repealed in pt.: *ibid.*, s. 37, sch. 9.

s. 105, amended: *ibid.*, sch. 5; repealed in pt.: *ibid.*, schs. 5, 9.

s. 107, amended: *ibid.*, sch. 5.

s. 108, repealed in pt.: *ibid.*, sch. 9.

s. 116, amended: 1994, c. 37, sch. 1; repealed in pt.: *ibid.*, schs. 1, 3.

s. 118, repealed in pt.: *ibid.*, sch. 11.

sch. 1, see *R.* v. *Singleton, The Times,* June 22, 1994, C.A.; *R.* v. *Acton Crown Court, ex p. Layton* [1993] Crim.L.R. 458, D.C.

sch. 4, amended: 1994, c. 29, sch. 5; repealed in pt.: *ibid.*, sch. 9.

sch. 5, order 94/570.

sch. 5, amended: 1994, c. 33, s. 85, sch. 10.

sch. 6, repealed in pt.: 1994, c. 23, sch. 15; c. 29, sch. 9.

Code C, see *R.* v. *Menard, The Times,* March 23, 1994, C.A.

1985

6. Companies Act 1985.

s. 90, see *Thundercrest, Re, The Times,* August 2, 1994, H.H.J. Paul Baker, Q.C. sitting as a deputy judge.

ss. 151, 153, see *Arab Bank* v. *Mercantile Holdings* [1994] 2 W.L.R. 307, Millett J.

s. 209, repealed in pt.: 1994, c. 36, sch. 2.

s. 228, amended: regs. 93/3246.

s. 240, amended: regs. 94/1935.

s. 245, regs. 94/1935; amended: *ibid.*

ss. 246, 248, amended: regs. 94/1696.

ss. 249A–249E, added: regs. 94/1935.

s. 254, amended: regs. 93/3246.

ss. 255, 255A, amended and repealed in pt.: *ibid.*

s. 255B, amended: *ibid.*

s. 255C, repealed: *ibid.*

s. 257, regs. 93/3246; 94/233, 1935.

1985—cont.

6. Companies Act 1985—*cont.*
s. 260, amended: regs. 93/3246.
s. 262A, amended: regs. 93/3246; 94/1935; repealed in pt.: regs. 94/233.
s. 268, amended: regs. 93/3246.
ss. 287, 288, regs. 94/117.
s. 330, see *A. & C. Group Services, Re* [1993] BCLC 1297, Sir Mervyn Davies sitting as a judge of the High Court.
s. 343, amended: regs. 94/233.
s. 349, see *Jenice* v. *Dan* [1993] BCLC 1349, R. Titheridge, Q.C. sitting as a deputy judge of the High Court.
s. 363, regs. 94/117.
s. 371, see *BML Group* v. *Harman* [1994] 1 W.L.R. 893, C.A.
ss. 371, 459, see *Whitchurch Insurance Consultants, Re* [1993] BCLC 1359, Harman J.
s. 384, amended: regs. 94/1935.
s. 388A, substituted: *ibid.*
s. 396, repealed in pt.: 1994, c. 26, sch. 5.
ss. 410, 415, 417, 464, see *A.I.B. Finance* v. *Bank of Scotland*, 1993 S.C.L.R. 851.
ss. 410, 419, see *Scottish & Newcastle* v. *Ascot Inns (In Receivership)* (O.H.), 1994 S.L.T. 1140.
s. 425, see *Bank of Credit and Commerce International SA (No. 3), Re* [1993] BCLC 1490, C.A.
s. 449, order 94/340.
ss. 449, 450, 451A, 452, amended: regs. 94/1696.
s. 459, see *Ghyll Beck Driving Range, Re* [1993] BCLC 1126, Vinelott J.; *Mountforest, Re* [1993] BCC 565, Harman J.
ss. 459, 726, see *Unisoft Group No. 1, Re; Saunderson Holdings* v. *Unisoft Group* [1993] BCLC 1292, C.A.
s. 460, amended: regs. 94/1696.
s. 462, see *Sharp* v. *Thomson* (O.H.), 1994 S.L.T. 1068.
ss. 464, 486, see *Grampian Regional Council* v. *Drill Stem (Inspection Services)* (Sh.Ct.), 1994 S.C.C.R. 36.
s. 466, see *Scottish & Newcastle* v. *Ascot Inns (In Receivership)* (O.H.), 1994 S.L.T. 1140.
ss. 475, 614, see *Turner* v. *I.R.C.* (O.H.), 1994 S.L.T. 811.
s. 651, see *Mixhurst, Re* [1993] BCC 748, Evans-Lombe J.; *Stanhope Pension Trust* v. *Registrar of Companies* [1993] NPC 169, C.A.
ss. 652A–652F, added: 1994, c. 40, sch. 5.
s. 653, amended: *ibid.*
s. 655, see *Allied Dunbar Insurance* v. *Fowler, The Times,* February 22, 1994, Garland J.

1985—cont.

6. Companies Act 1985—*cont.*
s. 704, amended: 1994, c. 40, sch. 16.
s. 708, regs. 94/2217.
s. 710B, regs. 94/117, 727.
s. 716, regs. 94/117, 644.
s. 725, see *Milestate* v. *Clarke*, April 19, 1994; H.H.J. Coltart; Brighton County Ct.
s. 726, see *C.T. Bowring & Co. (Insurance)* v. *Corsi & Partners, The Times*, June 28, 1994, C.A.
ss. 735A, 735B, amended: 1994, c. 40, sch. 16.
s. 744, regs. 94/117, 644, 727.
sch. 8, amended: regs. 94/1935.
sch. 9, amended and repealed in pt.: regs. 94/233.
sch. 9A, substituted: regs. 93/3246.
sch. 10, repealed: *ibid.*
sch. 11, amended: regs. 93/3246; 94/233.
sch. 19, see *Turner* v. *I.R.C.* (O.H.), 1994 S.L.T. 811.
sch. 22, repealed in pt.: regs. 93/3246.
sch. 24, amended: 1994, c. 40, sch. 5.

9. Companies Consolidation (Consequential Provisions) Act 1985.
sch. 2, repealed in pt. (prosp.): 1994, c. 21, sch. 11, Pts. III, IV.

13. Cinemas Act 1985.
s. 21, amended: 1994, c. 19, sch. 16; repealed in pt.: *ibid.*, schs. 16, 18.
s. 21, amended(S.): 1994, c. 39, sch. 13.
sch. 2, repealed in pt.: 1994, c. 40, sch. 17.

15. Hong Kong Act 1985.
sch., order 93/3145.

21. Films Act 1985.
sch. 1, orders 94/1065, 1904.

23. Prosecution of Offences Act 1985.
see *R.* v. *Croydon Crown Court, ex p. Lewis, The Times,* March 29, 1994, D.C.
s. 1, see *R.* v. *Crown Prosecution Service, ex p. Hogg, The Times,* April 14, 1994, C.A.
ss. 3, 6, see *R.* v. *Tower Bridge Metropolitan Stipendiary Magistrate, ex p. Chaudry* [1993] 3 W.L.R. 1154, D.C.
s. 10, see *R.* v. *D.P.P., ex p. C., The Times*, March 7, 1994, D.C.
s. 16, amended: 1994, c. 33, schs. 4, 9.
s. 18, amended: *ibid.*, sch. 9.
s. 19A, see *Barrister (Wasted Costs Order) (No. 4 of 1992), Re, The Times,* March 15, 1994, C.A.
s. 21, amended: 1994, c. 33, sch. 4.
s. 22, see *R.* v. *Norwich Crown Court, ex p. Cox* (1993) 97 Cr.App.R. 145, D.C.; *Kelly* v. *C.P.S.; Williams* v. *C.P.S.,* June 16, 1994; H.H.J. Allardice; Stafford County Ct.
s. 22, amended: 1994, c. 33, schs. 4, 9.

1985—cont.

23. Prosecution of Offences Act 1985—*cont.*
s. 23, amended: *ibid.*, sch. 4.
sch. 1, repealed in pt.: *ibid.*, sch. 11.

27. Coal Industry Act 1985.
s. 1, repealed (prosp.): 1994, c. 21, sch. 11, Pt. II.
ss. 3–5, repealed (prosp.): *ibid.*, sch. 11, Pt. III.

37. Family Law (Scotland) Act 1985.
ss. 8–10, 14, see *Muir* v. *Muir* (Sh.Ct.), 1994 S.C.L.R. 178.
ss. 8–11, 14, see *Welsh* v. *Welsh* (O.H.), 1994 S.L.T. 828.
ss. 9, 11, see *Louden* v. *Louden* (O.H.), 1994 S.L.T. 381.
s. 10, see *Davidson* v. *Davidson* (O.H.), July 9, 1993; *Ranaldi* v. *Ranaldi*, 1994 S.L.T.(Sh.Ct.) 25; *MacRitchie* v. *MacRitchie* (Sh.Ct.), 1994 S.C.L.R. 348; *Welsh* v. *Welsh* (O.H.), 1994 S.C.L.R. 360; 1994 S.L.T. 828; *Gribb* v. *Gribb*, 1994 S.L.T. (Sh.Ct.) 43; *Mitchell* v. *Mitchell*, 1994 S.C.L.R. 784.
ss. 11, 14, see *Welsh* v. *Welsh*, 1994 S.L.T. 828.
s. 16, see *Worth* v. *Worth* (Sh.Ct.) (1994) S.L.C.R. 362; *Gillon* v. *Gillon*, 1994 S.C.L.R. 278.

41. Copyright (Computer Software) Amendment Act 1985.
s. 1, see *John Richardson Computers* v. *Flanders* [1993] F.S.R. 497, Ferris J.

43. Local Government (Access to Information) Act 1985.
sch. 2, repealed in pt.: 1994, c. 29, sch. 9.

48. Food and Environment Protection Act 1985.
s. 1, orders 93/3058(S.); 94/50, 63, 65, 1950, 1977, 2029, 2144, 2193; S.Rs. 1993 No. 485; 1994 Nos. 204, 229.
s. 16, see *Thomson* v. *Barbour*, 1994 S.C.C.R. 485.
s. 16, regs. 94/1985.
s. 24, orders 93/3058(S.); 94/50, 63, 65, 1950, 1977, 2029, 2144, 2193; regs. 94/1985; S.Rs. 1993 No. 485; 1994 Nos. 204, 229.

50. Representation of the People Act 1985.
ss. 6, 9, amended: 1994, c. 19, sch. 16.
s. 8, see *Thompson* v. *Dann; Local Government Election for Eel Brook Division of Hammersmith and Fulham London Borough Council, Re, The Times,* November 3, 1994, D.C.
s. 21, amended: 1994, c. 19, repealed in pt.: *ibid.*, schs. 16, 18.

51. Local Government Act 1985.
s. 12, repealed in pt.: 1994, c. 29, sch. 9, Pt. II.
ss. 24, 25, repealed: *ibid.*, sch. 9, Pt. I.
ss. 29, 30, 32, 36, 37, 42, schs. 10, 11, repealed in pt.: *ibid.*

1985—cont.

54. Finance Act 1985.
s. 4, repealed in pt.: 1994, c. 9, sch. 26; c. 22, sch. 5.
s. 9, repealed: 1994, c. 22, sch. 5.
ss. 11–13, repealed: 1994, c. 23, sch. 15.
s. 14, see *Customs and Excise Commissioners* v. *P. & O. Steam Navigation Co.* [1994] STC 259, C.A.; *Customs and Excise Commissioners* v. *Nomura Property Management Services* [1994] STC 461, Sedley J.
s. 14, amended: 1994, c. 9, s. 45; repealed: 1994, c. 23, sch. 15.
ss. 14, 14A, regs. 94/803.
s. 15, see *Bjellica (t/a Eddy's Domestic Appliances)* v. *Customs and Excise Commissioners* [1993] STC 730, D.C.
ss. 15–17, repealed: 1994, c. 23, sch. 15.
s. 18, order 93/3168.
ss. 18, 19, repealed: 1994, c. 23, sch. 15.
s. 20, amended: 1994, c. 9, s. 46; repealed in pt.: *ibid.*, s. 46, sch. 26; repealed: 1994, c. 23, sch. 15.
s. 21, repealed: *ibid.*
s. 22, see *Customs and Excise Commissioners* v. *Le Rififi* [1993] STC 725, Leonard J.
ss. 22–33, repealed: 1994, c. 23, sch. 15.
s. 26, order 94/1978.
s. 69, see *Pepper (Inspector of Taxes)* v. *Daffurn* [1993] 41 EG 184, Jonathon Parker J.
s. 70, see *Clarke (Inspector of Taxes)* v. *Mayo, The Times,* June 8, 1994, Evans-Lombe J.
sch. 2, repealed in pt.: 1994, c. 22, sch. 5.
sch. 5, repealed in pt.: 1994, c. 9, sch. 26, Pts. II, III.
schs. 6–8, 26 (in pt.), repealed: 1994, c. 23, sch. 15.

56. Interception of Communications Act 1985.
ss. 1, 9, see *R.* v. *Effik (Godwin Eno); R.* v. *Mitchell (Graham Martin)* [1994] 3 W.L.R. 583, H.L.
ss. 2, 6, 9, see *R.* v. *Preston (Stephen); R.* v. *Clarke (Nicholas Henry); R.* v. *Austen (Anthony); R.* v. *Salter (Jeremy); R.* v. *Preston (Zena)* [1993] 3 W.L.R. 891, H.L.

57. Sporting Events (Control of Alcohol etc.) Act 1985.
s. 1A, amended: 1994, c. 22, sch. 3.

60. Child Abduction and Custody Act 1985.
see *B. (A Minor) (Child Abduction: Consent), Re, The Times,* May 12, 1994, C.A.; *N. (Child Abduction: Habitual Residence), Re* [1993] 2 FLR 124, C.A.
s. 1, sch. 1, see *Perrin* v. *Perrin*, 1993 S.C.L.R. 949; *Urness* v. *Minto* (O.H.), 1994 S.C.C.R. 109; *Findlay* v. *Findlay* (O.H.), 1994 S.C.L.R. 523.

1985—cont.

60. Child Abduction and Custody Act 1985—*cont.*
s. 2, orders 93/3144; 94/262, 1063, 1322, 1889.
s. 10, Act of Sederunt 94/1443.
s. 13, order 94/2792.
s. 24, Act of Sederunt 94/1443.
s. 27, amended: 1994, c. 39, sch. 13.
s. 28, order 94/2799.
sch. 1, see *AZ. (A Minor) (Abduction: Acquiescence), Re* [1993] 1 FLR 682, C.A.; *S. (Minors) (Convention on the International Aspects of International Child Abduction: Wrongful Retention), Re* [1994] 2 W.L.R. 228, Wall J.; *W. v. W. (Child Abduction: Acquiescence)* [1993] 2 FLR 211, Waite J.; *Urness v. Minto*, 1994 S.C.L.R. 392; *Findlay v. Findlay*, 1994 S.L.T. 709; *McCarthy v. McCarthy* (O.H.), 1994 S.L.T. 743; *B. v. K. (Child Abduction)* [1993] Fam. Law 17, Johnson J.; *F. v. F. (Abduction; Habitual Residence)* [1993] Fam. Law 199, Thorpe J.
sch. 2, see *H. (A Minor) (Foreign Custody Order: Enforcement), Re*, [1994] 2 W.L.R. 269, C.A.

63. Water (Fluoridation) Act 1985.
s. 1, amended(S.): 1994, c. 39, sch. 13.
s. 3, repealed(S.): *ibid.*, schs. 13, 14.
s. 4, amended(S.): *ibid.*, sch. 13; repealed in pt.: *ibid.*, schs. 13, 14.
s. 5, amended(S.): *ibid.*, sch. 13.

65. Insolvency Act 1985.
sch. 8, repealed in pt.: 1993, c. 48, sch. 5; S.L.R. 1993; 1994, c. 40, sch. 17.

66. Bankruptcy (Scotland) Act 1985.
s. 1A, Act of Sederunt 94/1443.
s. 5, see *Scottish & Newcastle Breweries v. Harvey-Rutherford* (Sh.Ct.), 1994 S.C.L.R. 131.
s. 5, amended: 1994, c. 37, sch. 1.·
ss. 5, 7, 11, see *Advocate (Lord) v. Thomson*, 1994 S.C.C.R. 96.
s. 7, amended: 1994, c. 37, sch. 1; repealed in pt.: *ibid.*, schs. 1, 3.
ss. 12, 14, 31–33, see *Alliance & Leicester Building Society v. MacGregor* (Sh.Ct.), 1994 S.C.C.R. 19.
s. 14, Act of Sederunt 94/1443.
s. 16, see *Brown v. Middlemas of Kelso*, 1994 S.C.L.R. 463.
s. 17, see *Martin v. Martin's Tr.* (O.H.), 1994 S.L.T. 261.
s. 32, see *Brown's Tr. v. Brown* (Sh.Ct.), 1994 S.C.L.R. 470.
s. 34, see *Short's Tr. v. Keeper of the Registers of Scotland*, 1994 S.L.T. 65; *MacFadyen's Tr. v. MacFadyen*, 1994 S.L.T. 1245.
s. 36, see *Balcraig House's Tr. v. Roosevelt Property Services* (O.H.), 1994 S.L.T. 1133.

1985—cont.

66. Bankruptcy (Scotland) Act 1985—*cont.*
s. 40, see *Simpson's Tr. v. Simpson* (Sh.Ct.), 1993 S.C.L.R. 867.
s. 54, see *Clydesdale Bank v. Davidson*, 1994 S.L.T. 225.
s. 62, Act of Sederunt 94/1443.
s. 73, repealed in pt.: S.L.R. 1993.
sch. 3, amended: 1994, c. 9, sch. 7; repealed in pt.: 1994, c. 23, sch. 14.
sch. 5, Act of Sederunt 94/1443.

67. Transport Act 1985.
s. 6, amended: order 94/1649.
s. 12, repealed in pt.: 1994, c. 40, schs. 14, 17.
s. 24, repealed in pt.: *ibid.*, sch. 17.
s. 28, amended: *ibid.*, s. 67.
s. 35, amended: order 94/1649.
ss. 63, 64, repealed in pt.: 1994, c. 19, schs. 7, 18.
ss. 66, 81, 87, amended: *ibid.*, sch. 7.
s. 91, regs. 94/1227.
s. 93, amended(S.): 1994, c. 39, sch. 13.
s. 105, amended: 1994, c. 19, sch. 7.
s. 129, orders 93/2797, 2909.
s. 137, amended: 1994, c. 19, sch. 7.
sch. 2, repealed in pt.: 1994, c. 40, sch. 17.

68. Housing Act 1985.
ss. 1, 2, amended: 1994, c. 19, sch. 8.
s. 4, amended: *ibid.*; c. 29, sch. 4; repealed in pt.: *ibid.*, schs. 4, 9.
ss. 14, 16, amended: 1994, c. 19, sch. 8.
s. 17, see *Burke v. Secretary of State for the Environment and Camden London Borough Council* (1994) 26 H.L.R. 10, C.A.
s. 22, see *R. v. Northavon District Council, ex p. Smith* [1994] 3 W.L.R. 403, H.L.
ss. 27, 27AB, regs. 94/627.
s. 28, amended: 1994, c. 19, sch. 8.
Pt. III (ss. 58–78), see *R. v. Northavon District Council, ex p. Palmer* (1993) 25 H.L.R. 674, Sedley J.; *R. v. Barnet London Borough Council, ex p. Rughooputh* (1993) 25 H.L.R. 607, C.A.; *R. v. Rushcliffe Borough Council, ex p. Summerson and Buckley* (1992) (1993) 25 H.L.R. 577, Sir Louis Blom-Cooper, Q.C.; *R. v. Shrewsbury and Atcham Borough Council, ex p. Griffiths* (1993) 25 H.L.R. 613, Anthony Lester, Q.C.; *R. v. Brent London Borough Council, ex p. McManus* (1993) 25 H.L.R. 643, Tucker J.; *R. v. Rugby Borough Council, ex p. Hunt* (1994) 26 H.L.R. 1, Hutchinson J.; *R. v. City of Westminster, ex p. Moozary-Oraky* (1993) 26 H.L.R. 213, Sir Louis Blom-Cooper, Q.C., sitting as a deputy judge; *Hobbs v. Sutton London Borough Council*

1985—cont.

68. Housing Act 1985—*cont.*

(1993) 26 H.L.R. 132, C.A.; *R.* v. *Exeter City Council, ex p. Tranckle* (1993) 26 H.L.R. 244, C.A.; *Patterson* v. *Greenwich London Borough Council* (1993) 26 H.L.R. 159, C.A.; *R.* v. *Lambeth London Borough Council, ex p. Walters* (1993) 26 H.L.R. 170, Sir Louis Blom-Cooper, Q.C., sitting as a deputy judge.

Pt. III (ss. 58–78), ss. 82, 85, see *R.* v. *Newham London Borough Council, ex p. Campbell* (1993) 26 H.L.R. 183, Sir Louis Blom-Cooper, Q.C., sitting as a deputy judge.

ss. 59, 65, see *R.* v. *Sheffield City Council, ex p. Leek (Martin)* [1993] NPC 161, C.A.

s. 60, see *R.* v. *Wandsworth London Borough Council, ex p. Hawthorne, The Times,* July 14, 1994, C.A.

ss. 62, 63, 65, see *R.* v. *Northavon District Council, ex p. Palmer, The Independent,* February 22, 1994, *The Times,* March 16, 1994, Roger Toulson, Q.C., sitting as a deputy judge.

s. 65, see *R.* v. *Northavon District Council, ex p. Smith* [1994] 3 W.L.R. 403, H.L.; *R.* v. *Brent London Borough Council, ex p. Awna, The Times,* April 26, 1994, C.A.; *Credit Suisse* v. *Waltham Forest London Borough Council, The Times,* November 8, 1994, Gatehouse J.

s. 75, see *R.* v. *Newham London Borough Council, ex p. Dada, The Times,* July 29, 1994, Sir Louis Blom-Cooper, Q.C. sitting as a deputy judge.

s. 76, amended(S.): 1994, c. 39, sch. 13.

s. 79, see *Hughes* v. *Greenwich London Borough Council* [1993] 3 W.L.R. 821, H.L.

ss. 81, 84, see *Bruce* v. *Worthing Borough Council* (1993) 26 H.L.R. 223, C.A.

s. 84, see *Woking Borough Council* v. *Bystram* [1993] EGCS 208, C.A.

s. 85, see *Hammersmith and Fulham London Borough Council* v. *Hill, The Times,* April 25, 1994, C.A.

s. 96, regs. 94/133, 844.

s. 99A, regs. 94/613.

ss. 105, 106, amended: 1994, c. 19, sch. 8.

s. 118, see *Hughes* v. *Greenwich London Borough Council* [1993] 3 W.L.R. 821, H.L.

Pt. V (ss. 118–188), see *Savill* v. *Goodall* (1992) (1993) 25 H.L.R. 588, C.A.

s. 156, orders 93/2757; 94/1762.

Pts. VI (ss. 189–208), IX (ss. 264–323), see *R.* v. *Southwark London Borough Council, ex p. Cordwell* (1993) 26 H.L.R. 107, Auld J.

1985—cont.

68. Housing Act 1985—*cont.*

s. 386, sch. 13, see *Burke* v. *Secretary of State for the Environment and Camden London Borough Council* (1994) 26 H.L.R. 10, C.A.

s. 444, orders 93/2758; 94/1763.

s. 464, see *R.* v. *Parker, The Times,* March 11, 1994, C.A.

ss. 536, 537, see *R.* v. *Sandwell Metropolitan Borough Council, ex p. Cashmore* (1993) 25 H.L.R. 544, Owen J.

s. 573, amended: 1994, c. 19, sch. 6; c. 21, sch. 9.

s. 622, amended: regs. 94/1696.

sch. 1, see *Hughes* v. *Greenwich London Borough Council* [1993] 3 W.L.R. 821, H.L.

sch. 4, amended(S.): 1994, c. 39, sch. 13.

sch. 6, see *Coventry City Council* v. *Cole* (1993) 25 H.L.R. 555, C.A.

sch. 6, amended: 1994, c. 36, sch. 1; repealed in pt.: *ibid.,* schs. 1, 2.

sch. 24, see *Samrai* v. *Sandwell Metropolitan Borough Council (Ref.: 170/1990)* (1993) 66 P. & C.R. 494, Lands Tribunal.

69. Housing Associations Act 1985.

s. 24, order 94/668.

s. 34, amended: 1994, c. 19, sch. 8.

ss. 58, 60, see *Credit Suisse* v. *Waltham Forest London Borough Council, The Times,* November 8, 1994, Gatehouse J.

s. 59, repealed in pt.(S.): 1994, c. 39, schs. 13, 14.

ss. 104, 106, amended(S.): *ibid.,* sch. 13.

s. 106, amended: 1994, c. 19; c. 29, sch. 4; regs. 94/1696.

70. Landlord and Tenant Act 1985.

s. 11, see *Ager* v. *Liverpool City Council,* April 5, 1994; District Judge Knopf; Liverpool County Ct.; *Leather* v. *Liverpool City Council; Morgan* v. *Same,* July 13, 1994; H.H.J. Marshall Evans, Q.C.; Liverpool County Ct.; *Windever (Christine)* v. *Liverpool City Council,* June 13, 1994; Mr. Recorder Stockdale; Liverpool County Ct.

s. 38, amended: 1994, c. 19, sch. 8; c. 29, sch. 4.

72. Weights and Measures Act 1985.

s. 4, regs. 94/1851.

s. 5, regs. 94/1259, 1851.

s. 8, order 94/1883; amended: *ibid.*

s. 11, regs. 94/1259, 1851.

s. 15, regs. 94/1851, 1852.

s. 22, orders 94/1883, 1884.

s. 23, regs. 94/1852.

s. 24, order 94/1884.

s. 43, repealed: 1994, c. 40, s. 14, sch. 17.

ss. 48, 49, regs. 94/1258, 1852.

s. 65, regs. 94/1852.

s. 66, regs. 94/1258, 1852.

1985—cont.

72. Weights and Measures Act 1985—cont.
s. 68, regs. 94/1852.
s. 69, amended: 1994, c. 19, sch. 16; c. 39, sch. 13.
s. 86, orders 94/1258, 1259, 1883, 1884.
s. 86, repealed in pt.: 1994, c. 40, sch. 17.
s. 94, regs. 94/1258, 1851, 1852.
s. 99, repealed in pt.: 1994, c. 40, sch. 17.
sch. 3, amended: order 94/1883.
sch. 5, repealed in pt. (prosp.): 1994, c. 21, schs. 9, 11, Pt. II.
sch. 6, amended: order 94/1884.

73. Law Reform (Miscellaneous Provisions) (Scotland) Act 1985.
s. 8, see *Bank of Scotland* v. *Brunswick Developments* (1987) (O.H.), 1994 S.C.C.R. 102.

1986

5. Agricultural Holdings Act 1986.
see *Hannaford* v. *Smallacombe* [1994] 15 EG 155, C.A.
s. 2, see *Evans* v. *Tompkins* [1993] 33 EG 86, C.A.
s. 36, see *Welby* v. *Casswell, The Times,* April 1, 1994, Popplewell J.
ss. 37, 39, see *Francis Perceval Saunders dec'd Trustees* v. *Ralph* [1993] 28 EG 127, Jowitt J.; *sub nom. Trustees of Saunders* v. *Ralph* (1993) 66 P. & C.R. 335, Jowitt J.
sch. 3, see *Dallhold Estates (U.K.) Pty (in administration)* v. *Lindsey Trading Properties* [1994] 17 EG 148, C.A.
sch. 3, repealed in pt. (prosp.): 1994, c. 21, schs. 9, 11, Pt. II.
sch. 6, order 94/2183.
sch. 11, amended: 1994, c. 33, sch. 4.

9. Law Reform (Parent and Child) (Scotland) Act 1986.
s. 3, see *Patterson* v. *Patterson* (Sh.Ct.), 1994 S.C.C.R. 166.
ss. 3, 9, see *D.* v. *Grampian Regional Council* (O.H.), 1994 S.C.L.R. 515; 1994 S.L.T. 1038.

10. Local Government Act 1986.
s. 2, see *Commission for Local Authority Accounts in Scotland* v. *Grampian Regional Council,* 1994 S.L.T. 1120.
s. 6, amended(S.): 1994, c. 39, sch. 13.
ss. 6, 9, amended: 1994, c. 29, sch. 4.

12. Statute Law (Repeals) Act 1986.
sch. 2, repealed in pt.: 1994, c. 26, sch. 5.

14. Animals (Scientific Procedures) Act 1986.
ss. 1, 7, S.R. 1993 No. 407.
s. 8, order 93/2956.

22. Civil Protection in Peacetime Act 1986.
s. 1, amended(S.): 1994, c. 39, sch. 13.

24. Health Service Joint Consultative Committee (Access to Information) Act 1986.
s. 1, amended: 1994, c. 19, sch. 16.

1986—cont.

31. Airports Act 1986.
s. 12, amended: 1994, c. 19, sch. 16; repealed in pt.: *ibid.,* schs. 16, 18.
s. 12, amended(S.): 1994, c. 39, sch. 13.
s. 70, sch. 5 (in pt.), repealed: 1994, c. 20, sch. 5.

32. Drug Trafficking Offences Act 1986.
repealed, except ss. 24 (in pt.), 32, 34, 40 (in pt.): 1994, c. 37, sch. 3.
s. 1A, amended: 1994, c. 33, sch. 9.
ss. 3, 14, see *R.* v. *Tredwen, The Times,* January 3, 1994, C.A.
s. 26, orders 93/3158; 94/1641.
s. 36B, regs. 94/1757.
s. 40, amended: 1994, c. 37, sch. 1.

33. Disabled Persons (Services, Consultation and Representations) Act 1986.
s. 2, amended(S.): 1994, c. 39, sch. 13.
s. 16, amended(S.): *ibid.,* sch. 13; repealed in pt.: *ibid.,* schs. 13, 14.

39. Patents, Designs and Marks Act 1986.
ss. 2, 4 (in pt.), schs. 1 (in pt.), 2, repealed: 1994, c. 26, sch. 5.

41. Finance Act 1986.
s. 3, repealed in pt.: 1994, c. 22, sch. 5.
ss. 9–15, repealed: 1994, c. 23, sch. 15.
s. 98, regs. 93/3110.
s. 109, amended: 1994, c. 9, s. 236.
sch. 1, repealed: 1994, c. 22, sch. 5.
sch. 2, repealed in pt.: 1994, c. 9, sch. 26; c. 22, sch. 5.
sch. 6, order 93/2952.
sch. 6, amended: order 93/2952; 1994, c. 22, sch. 3; repealed: 1994, c. 23, sch. 15.

44. Gas Act 1986.
ss. 13, 16, amended: 1994, c. 40, sch. 16.
s. 17, amended: *ibid.;* repealed in pt.: *ibid.,* schs. 6, 7.
sch. 7, amended: 1994, c. 19, sch. 16; repealed in pt.: *ibid.,* schs. 16, 18; (prosp.) c. 21, sch. 11, Pt. II.
sch. 7, amended(S.): 1994, c. 39, sch. 13.

45. Insolvency Act 1986.
see *Chohan* v. *Saggar* [1993] EGCS 194, C.A.
ss. 3, 6, see *Cranley Mansions, Re, The Times,* June 23, 1994, Ferris J.
ss. 8–10, see *Secretary of State for Trade and Industry* v. *Palmer, The Times,* November 4, 1994.
s. 11, see *Carr* v. *British International Helicopters* [1994] I.C.R. 18, E.A.T.
s. 19, amended: 1994, c. 7, s. 1; repealed in pt.: *ibid.,* s. 1, sch. 2.
ss. 19, 27, see *Powdrill* v. *Watson, The Times,* March 1, 1994, C.A.
s. 35, see *Sargent* v. *Customs and Excise Commissioners, The Times,* November 18, 1993, Judge Paul Baker, Q.C. sitting as a deputy judge of the High Court.

1986—cont.

45. Insolvency Act 1986—*cont.*

s. 40, see *New Bullas Trading, Re, The Times*, January 12, 1994, C.A.

s. 44, see *Ferranti International, Re; Leyland Daf, Re, The Times*, August 11, 1994, Lightman J.

s. 44, amended: 1994, c. 7, s. 2.

s. 53, see *Secretary of State for Trade and Industry* v. *Houston* (O.H.), 1994 S.L.T. 775; *Sharp* v. *Thomson* (O.H.), 1994 S.L.T. 1068.

ss. 55, 70, see *Grampian Regional Council* v. *Drill Stem (Inspection Services)* (Sh.Ct.), 1994 S.C.C.R. 36.

s. 57, amended:1994, c. 7, s. 3.

ss. 57, 60, see *McKillop and Walters, Petrs., The Times*, April 14, 1994.

s. 124, see *Dollar Land Holdings, Re* [1993] BCC 823, Sir Donald Nicholls, V.-C.

ss. 124A, 220, see *Company, A (No. 007946 of 1993), Re* [1994] 2 W.L.R. 438, Morritt J.

ss. 124A, 220, 221, see *Normandy Marketing, Re* [1993] BCC 879, Morritt J.

s. 125, see *Bank of Credit and Commerce International SA (No. 3), Re* [1993] BCLC 1490, C.A.

s. 127, see *Mountforest, Re* [1993] BCC 565, Harman J.

s. 130, see *Fordham* v. *National Employers Mutual General Insurance Association*, September 22, 1994; Rattee J.

ss. 167, 242, see *Dyer* v. *Hyslop* (Sh.Ct.), 1994 S.C.C.R. 171.

s. 178, see *W.H. Smith* v. *Wynham Investments, The Times*, May 26, 1994; H.H.J. Paul Baker, Q.C., sitting as a deputy judge; *Hindcastle* v. *Barbara Attenborough Associates, The Times*, July 6, 1994, C.A.

ss. 178, 182, see *Vedmay, Re* (1994) 26 H.L.R. 70, Mr G. Lightman, Q.C.

s. 220, see *Western Counties Construction* v. *Witney Town Football and Social Club*, sub nom. *Witney Town Football and Social Club, Re* [1993] BCC 874, Morritt J.

s. 234, see *Leyland Daf (No. 2), Re, The Times*, January 19, 1994, C.A.

s. 236, see *Company, A (No. 005374 of 1993), Re* [1993] BCC 734, Harman J.

s. 241, amended: 1994, c. 12, s. 1.

s. 242, see *Rae (John E.) (Electrical Services) Linlithgow* v. *Lord Advocate* (O.H.), 1994 S.L.T. 788.

s. 245, see *Shoe Lace, Re; Power* v. *Sharp Investment* [1993] BCC 609, C.A.

s. 252, see *McMullen & Sons* v. *Cerrone* (1993) 66 P. & C.R. 351, Mr. Roger Kaye, Q.C.

1986—cont.

45. Insolvency Act 1986—*cont.*

ss. 257, 260, 267, see *Debtor, A (No. 64 of 1992), Re* [1994] 1 W.L.R. 264, Colin Rimer, Q.C. sitting as a deputy judge.

s. 267, see *Wood (Jennifer Agnes), Re*, August 27, 1993; District Judge Brown in a reserved judgment; Tamworth County Ct.

ss. 267, 270, see *Debtor, A (No. 22 of 1993), Re* [1994] 1 W.L.R. 46, Mummery J.

s. 268, see *Debtor, A (No. 340 of 1992), Re; The Debtor* v. *First National Commercial Bank* [1994] 3 All E.R. 269, Aldous J.; *Section 263(4) of the Insolvency Act 1986, Re*, September 26, 1994; District Judge Vincent; Truro County Ct.

s. 271, see *Debtor, A (No. 32 of 1993), Re* [1994] 1 W.L.R. 899, Mr. Timothy Lloyd, Q.C., sitting as a deputy judge.

ss. 278, 283, 306, 421, see *Palmer (Gavin), (dec'd) (a Debtor), Re* [1994] 3 W.L.R. 420, C.A.

ss. 306, 354, see *Woodley* v. *Woodley (No. 2)* [1993] 4 All E.R. 1010, C.A.

s. 315, see *MEPC* v. *Scottish Amicable Life Assurance Society; Neville Richard Eckley (Third Party)* [1993] 36 EG 133, C.A.

s. 342, amended: 1994, c. 12, s. 2.

s. 386, amended: 1994, c. 9, sch. 7.

s. 388, amended and repealed in pt.: order 94/2421.

ss. 414, 415, orders 93/3191; 94/2541.

s. 420, order 94/2421.

s. 423, see *TSB Bank* v. *Katz and Katz, The Times*, May 2, 1994, Arden J.; *Agricultural Mortgage Corp.* v. *Woodward, The Times*, May 30, 1994, C.A.; *Alsop Wilkinson (A firm)* v. *Neary, The Times*, November 4, 1994, Lightman J.

s. 426, see *Bank of Credit and Commerce International, Re; Bank of Credit and Commerce International (Overseas), Re* [1993] BCC 787, Rattee J.

s. 441, see *Normany Marketing, Re* [1993] BCC 879, Morritt J.

sch. 4, see *Dyer* v. *Hyslop* (Sh.Ct.), 1994 S.C.C.R. 171.

sch. 6, amended: 1994, c. 9, sch. 6; c. 23, sch. 14.

46. Company Directors Disqualification Act 1986.

see *Rex Williams Leisure (In Administration), Re, The Times*, May 4, 1994, C.A.; *Manlon Trading, Re, The Times*, August 15, 1994, Evans-Lombe J.

ss. 1, 7, see *Moonbeam Cards, Re* [1993] BCLC 1099, Vinelott J.

s. 2, amended: 1994, c. 40, sch. 11.

1986—cont.

46. Company Directors Disqualification Act 1986—*cont.*

s. 6, see *A. & C. Group Services, Re* [1993] BCLC 1297, Sir Mervyn Davies sitting as a judge of the High Court; *Burnham Marketing Services, Re; Secretary of State for Trade and Industry* v. *Harper* [1993] BCC 518, District Judge Sonnex; *Synthetic Technology, Re; Secretary of State for Trade and Industry* v. *Joiner* [1993] BCC 549, Edward Evans-Lombe, Q.C. sitting as a deputy judge of the High Court.

ss. 6, 7, see *Copecrest, Re* [1993] BCLC 1118, Mervyn Davies, J.; *Polly Peck International, Re; Secretary of State for Trade and Industry* v. *Ellis (No. 2)* [1993] BCC 890, Lindsay J.; *Secretary of State for Trade and Industry* v. *Houston* (O.H.), 1994 S.L.T. 775; *Secretary of State for Trade and Industry* v. *Palmer, The Times,* November 4, 1994.

ss. 6, 22, see *Seagull Manufacturing Co. (No. 2), Re* [1993] BCC 833, Mary Arden Q.C., sitting as a deputy judge.

s. 7, see *Walter L. Jacob, Re; Official Receiver* v. *Jacob* [1993] BCC 512, Hoffmann J.; *Polly Peck International, Re; Secretary of State for Trade and Industry* v. *Ellis* [1993] BCC 886, Jonathan Parker J.; *Secretary of State for Trade and Industry* v. *Houston* (O.H.), 1994 S.C.L.R. 209; *Secretary of State for Trade and Industry* v. *Normand* (O.H.), 1994 S.L.T. 1249.

ss. 11, 13, see *R.* v. *Brockley, The Times,* November 25, 1993, C.A.

s. 21, order 94/2421.

47. Legal Aid (Scotland) Act 1986.

ss. 4, 33, see *Advocate, H.M.* v. *Birrell,* 1994 S.L.T. 480.

s. 8, amended: regs. 94/997.

s. 9, regs. 93/3186, 3187; 94/1000.

s. 11, regs. 94/997; amended: *ibid.*

s. 12, regs. 94/1061.

ss. 15, 17, amended: regs. 94/998, 1001.

s. 17, regs. 94/1049.

s. 18, see *Ferguson* v. *Povah* (Sh.Ct.), 1993 S.C.L.R. 634; *Handy* v. *Chief Constable, Tayside Police* (Sh.Ct.), 1993 S.C.L.R. 790.

s. 19, 20, see *Moss* v. *Penman,* 1994 S.C.L.R. 15.

s. 21, regs. 94/1001.

s. 33, regs. 94/1018, 1019, 1233.

s. 36, regs. 93/3017, 3187; 94/997, 998, 1000, 1001, 1016–1019, 1049, 1050, 1061, 1233.

s. 37, regs. 93/3017, 3186, 3187; 94/997, 998, 1000, 1001, 1049, 1061.

s. 42, regs. 94/1061.

1986—cont.

48. Wages Act 1986.

s. 1, see *S.I.P. Industrial Products* v. *Swinn* [1994] I.C.R. 473, E.A.T.

49. Agriculture Act 1986.

s. 1, amended: 1994, c. 40, sch. 16.

s. 16, see *Broadland Properties Estates* v. *Mann,* 1994 S.L.T.(Land Ct.) 7.

s. 18, orders 93/3136(S.), 3149(S.), 3150(S.); 94/238–241, 707–712, 918–933, 1989, 1990.

s. 18, amended: regs. 94/249.

50. Social Security Act 1986.

ss. 20–22, see *Bolstridge* v. *Chief Adjudication Officer* [1993] 2 FLR 657, C.A.

ss. 32–35, see *R.* v. *Social Fund Inspector, ex p. Ali Waris* [1993] C.O.D. 263, Brooke J.

s. 51, see *Social Security Decision No. R(S) 3/94.*

s. 53, see *Jones* v. *Chief Adjudication Officer; Sharples* v. *Same* [1994] 1 W.L.R. 62, C.A.; *Plewa (Executrix of the Estate of Josef Plewa, dec'd)* v. *Chief Adjudication Officer* [1994] 3 W.L.R. 317, H.L.; *Riches* v. *Secretary of State for Social Security,* 1994 S.L.T. 730.

53. Building Societies Act 1986.

s. 2, regs. 94/656.

s. 7, amended: 1994, c. 40, s. 15.

ss. 7, 8, rules 93/2833.

ss. 10, 11, amended: 1994, c. 40, s. 16, sch. 11.

s. 12, amended: *ibid.*, s. 16.

s. 13, amended: *ibid.*, sch. 11; repealed in pt.: *ibid.*, schs. 11, 17.

s. 14, order 94/655.

s. 14A, added: 1994, c. 40, s. 17.

s. 16, amended: *ibid.*, s. 16.

s. 18, order 93/2706.

s. 20, rules 93/2833.

s. 45, orders 94/749, 750.

s. 82, order 94/525.

ss. 97, 100, see *Cheltenham and Gloucester Building Society* v. *Building Societies Commission, The Times,* June 10, 1994, Sir Donald Nicholls, V.-C.

s. 116, regs. 94/656.

s. 119, amended: 1994, c. 40, sch. 11.

sch. 2, modified: *ibid.*, s. 17.

sch. 8, amended: 1994, c. 19, sch. 16; repealed in pt.: *ibid.*, schs. 16, 18.

55. Family Law Act 1986.

ss. 1–3, see *F.* v. *S. (Wardship: Jurisdiction)* [1993] 2 FLR 686, C.A.

s. 2, see *S. (A Minor) (Residence Order: Jurisdiction), Re, The Times,* October 21, 1994, Thorpe J.

ss. 2, 3, see *R.* v. *Secretary of State for the Home Department, ex p. Mehari* [1994] 2 W.L.R. 349, Laws J.

1986—cont.

55. Family Law Act 1986—*cont.*
s. 5, see *H.* v. *H. (Minors) (Forum Conveniens) (Nos. 1 and 2)* [1993] 1 FLR 958, Waite J.
ss. 27, 28, Act of Sederunt 94/1443.
s. 43, order 94/2800.

56. Parliamentary Constituencies Act 1986.
s. 6, amended: 1994, c. 19, sch. 16.
s. 6, amended(S.): 1994, c. 39, sch. 13.
sch. 2, amended: 1994, c. 19, sch. 2.

60. Financial Services 1986.
s. 22, amended: regs. 94/1696.
s. 45, amended: 1994, c. 36, sch. 1.
s. 46, order 94/1517.
ss. 47A, 48, 52, amended: regs. 94/1696.
s. 64, repealed in pt.: *ibid.*
ss. 65, 104, 107, amended: *ibid.*
s. 109, rules 94/526.
ss. 119, 121, amended: regs. 94/1696.
s. 125, repealed in pt.: 1994, c. 40, schs. 11, 17.
ss. 129, 132, 139, amended: regs. 94/1696.
s. 134, repealed: *ibid.*
s. 179, see *Melton Medes* v. *Securities and Investments Board, The Times,* July 27, 1994, Lightman J.
s. 180, order 94/340.
s. 180, schs. 2, 7, 10, amended: regs. 94/1696.

61. Education (No. 2) Act 1986.
s. 8, regs. 93/3107.
s. 30, orders 94/692 (corrected by order 94/2732), 2732.
s. 30, amended and repealed in pt.: order 94/692.
s. 50, regs. 94/2016.
s. 50, amended: 1994, c. 30, s. 13; repealed in pt.: *ibid.*
s. 54, regs. 93/3113.
s. 63, regs. 93/3107; 94/2016; order 94/2092.
sch. 3, orders 93/2827; 94/2092.
sch. 3, amended: order 94/2092.

62. Salmon Act 1986.
ss. 3, 10, regs. 94/2524(S.).

63. Housing and Planning Act 1986.
s. 42, regs. 94/642.
sch. 5, repealed in pt.: 1994, c. 29, sch. 9.
sch. 8, repealed in pt. (prosp.): 1994, c. 21, sch. 11, Pts. II, III.

64. Public Order Act 1986.
s. 2, see *R.* v. *Rothwell and Barton* [1993] Crim.L.R. 626, C.A.
s. 3, see *D.P.P.* v. *Cotcher and Cotcher* [1993] C.O.D. 181, D.C.; *R.* v. *Robinson* [1993] Crim.L.R. 581, C.A.; *R.* v. *Dixon* [1993] Crim.L.R. 579, C.A.
ss. 3, 4, see *R.* v. *Stanley and Knight* [1993] Crim.L.R. 618, C.A.
ss. 4, 8, see *Rukwira, Rukwira, Musoke and Johnson* v. *D.P.P.* [1993] Crim. L.R. 882, D.C.

1986—cont.

64. Public Order Act 1986—*cont.*
s. 4A, added: 1994, c. 33, s. 154.
s. 5, see *Poku (Kwasi)* v. *D.P.P.* [1993] Crim.L.R. 705, D.C.
ss. 14A, 14B, added: 1994, c. 33, s. 70.
s. 14C, added: *ibid.,* s. 71.
s. 15, amended: 1994, c. 29, sch. 5; c. 33, sch. 10.
ss. 39, 42 (in pt.), repealed: *ibid.,* sch. 11.

1987

3. Coal Industry Act 1987.
s. 1, repealed in pt. (prosp.): 1994, c. 21, sch. 11, Pt. IV.
s. 2, repealed (prosp.): *ibid.,* sch. 11, Pt. II.
s. 3, order 94/1422.
s. 3, amended: *ibid.;* repealed (prosp.): 1994, c. 21, sch. 11, Pt. III.
s. 4, repealed (prosp.): *ibid.*
s. 5, amended: *ibid.,* sch. 9.
ss. 6, 9, 10 (in pt.), schs. 2, 3, repealed (prosp.): *ibid.,* sch. 11, Pt. III.

4. Ministry of Defence Police Act 1987.
s. 1, regs. 94/1102.

12. Petroleum Act 1987.
s. 22, orders 94/372, 1836.

15. Reverter of Sites Act 1987.
s. 1, see *Marchant* v. *Onslow* [1994] 2 All E.R. 707, Mr. David Neuberger, Q.C.

16. Finance Act 1987.
s. 2, repealed in pt.: 1994, c. 22, sch. 5.
ss. 4, 5 (in pt.), repealed: 1994, c. 9, sch. 26.
ss. 11–19, repealed in pt.: 1994, c. 22, sch. 5.
s. 61, regs. 93/2939; 94/939.
sch. 1, repealed: 1994, c. 9, sch. 26; c. 22, sch. 5.
sch. 2, repealed: 1994, c. 23, sch. 15.
sch. 10, regs. 93/2939; 94/939.
sch. 10, amended: 1994, c. 9, s. 235.

18. Debtors (Scotland) Act 1987.
ss. 1, 5, amended: 1994, c. 39, sch. 13.
ss. 47, 49, 73, see *Feeney* v. *United Biscuits* (Sh.Ct.), 1993 S.C.C.R. 965.
ss. 90, 102, Act of Sederunt 94/1443.
s. 106, amended: 1994, c. 39, sch. 13.
sch. 4, repealed in pt.: 1994, c. 23, sch. 15.
sch. 5, see *Irvine* v. *Strathclyde Regional Council* (Sh.Ct.), 1994 S.C.L.R. 388.
sch. 5, amended: 1994, c. 39, sch. 13.

21. Pilotage Act 1987.
ss. 2, 16, see *Oceangas (Gibraltar)* v. *Port of London Authority; Cavendish, The* [1993] 2 Lloyd's Rep. 292, Clarke J.

22. Banking Act 1987.
s. 47, regs. 94/524.
s. 58, see *Deposit Protection Board* v. *Dalia, The Times,* May 20, 1994, H.L.

1987—cont.

22. Banking Act 1987—*cont.*
s. 59, see *Deposit Protection Board* v. *Barclays Bank* [1994] 2 W.L.R. 732, H.L.
s. 84, sch. 2, amended: regs. 94/1696.

26. Housing (Scotland) Act 1987.
s. 26, see *Robson* v. *Kyle and Carrick District Council* (O.H.), 1994 S.L.T. 259.
ss. 26, 28, see *Speck* v. *Kyle and Carrick District Council* (O.H.), 1994 S.L.T. 1007.
ss. 31, 32, 35, see *Bradley* v. *Motherwell District Council* (O.H.), 1994 S.C.L.R. 160.
ss. 44, 61, see *McLoughlin's Curator Bonis* v. *Motherwell District Council*, 1994 S.L.T. (Lands Tr.) 31.
s. 58A, regs. 94/632.
s. 60, regs. 94/1046.
s. 61, see *Dundee District Council, City of* v. *Kelly*, 1994 S.C.L.R. 494.
s. 61, order 94/2097.
s. 61, amended: 1994, c. 39, sch. 13; repealed in pt.: *ibid.*, schs. 13, 14.
ss. 61, 62, see *Ross and Cromarty District Council* v. *Patience* (O.H.), 1994 S.C.L.R. 779.
ss. 61, 68, see *Fernie* v. *Strathclyde Regional Council*, 1994 S.L.T.(Lands Tr.) 11.
s. 64, amended: 1994, c. 39, sch. 13.
s. 68, see *Henderson* v. *City of Glasgow District Council*, 1994 S.L.T. 263.
s. 70, amended: 1994, c. 39, sch. 13.
ss. 72, 73, see *Clydebank District Council* v. *Keeper of the Registers of Scotland*, 1994 S.L.T.(Lands Tr.) 2.
ss. 162, 163, see *Pearson* v. *City of Glasgow District Council* (Sh.Ct.), 1994 S.C.L.R. 444.
ss. 191, 192, order 94/430.
s. 204, order 94/106.
s. 212, amended: 1994, c. 39, sch. 13; repealed in pt.: *ibid.*, schs. 13, 14.
s. 229, order 94/2030.
s. 235, repealed: 1994, c. 39, sch. 14.
s. 300, amended: *ibid.*, sch. 13.
s. 338, regs. 94/632, 1046.
s. 338, amended: regs. 94/1696; 1994, c. 39, sch. 13.
sch. 3, amended: *ibid.*, sch. 13.
schs. 15, 23, repealed in pt.: *ibid.*, sch. 14.

27. Fire Safety and Safety of Places of Sport Act 1987.
ss. 28–30, 35, amended: 1994, c. 19, sch. 16.
s. 41, amended: *ibid.*; repealed in pt.: *ibid.*, schs. 16, 18.
s. 41, amended(S.): 1994, c. 39, sch. 13.

1987—cont.

31. Landlord and Tenant Act 1987.
ss. 43, 46, 48, 60, see *Dallhold Estates (U.K.) Pty (in administration)* v. *Lindsey Trading Properties* [1994] 17 EG 148, C.A.
s. 48, see *Milestate* v. *Clarke*, April 19, 1994; H.H.J. Coltart; Brighton County Ct.; *Rogan* v. *Woodfield Building Services, The Times*, August 10, 1994, C.A.
s. 58, amended: 1994, c. 19, sch. 8; c. 29, sch. 4.

37. Access to Personal Files Act 1987.
sch. 1, amended: 1994, c. 19, sch. 13.
sch. 2, amended(S.): 1994, c. 39, sch. 13.

38. Criminal Justice Act 1987.
s. 2, see *R.* v. *Clerkenwell Justices, ex p. Trachtenberg* [1993] Crim.L.R. 222, D.C.; *R.* v. *Director of the Serious Fraud Office, ex p. Johnson (Malcolm Keith)* [1993] C.O.D. 58, Auld J.; *R.* v. *Metropolitan Stipendiary Magistrate, ex p. Serious Fraud Office, The Independent*, June 24, 1994, D.C.; *Harris, Complainer*, 1994 S.L.T. 906.
s. 2, amended: 1994, c. 33, s. 164.
s. 3, amended: regs. 94/1696.
s. 4, amended: 1994, c. 33, schs. 4, 9.
ss. 5, 6, amended: *ibid.*, sch. 4.
s. 7, amended: *ibid.*, sch. 9.
s. 9, see *R.* v. *Smithson, The Times,* May 10, 1994, C.A.; *Case Statements Made Under s.9 of the Criminal Justice Act 1987* (1993) 97 Cr.App.R. 417, C.A.
sch. 2, repealed in pt.: 1994, c. 33, sch. 11.

41. Criminal Justice (Scotland) Act 1987.
ss. 1–6, see *Advocate, H.M.* v. *McLean*, 1993 S.C.C.R. 917.
s. 2, see *Advocate, H.M., Petr.*, 1994 S.C.C.R. 136.
ss. 3, 7, amended: 1994, c. 37, sch. 1.
s. 8, Act of Sederunt: 94/1443.
ss. 10, 11, amended: 1994, c. 37, sch. 1.
s. 22, Act of Sederunt: 94/1443.
ss. 23, 27, amended: 1994, c. 37, sch. 1.
s. 28, Act of Sederunt: 94/1443.
s. 28, amended: 1994, c. 37, sch. 1.
s. 30, orders 93/3156; 94/1644.
s. 31, repealed: 1994, c. 37, sch. 3.
s. 35, amended: *ibid.*, sch. 1.
s. 45, repealed in pt.: *ibid.*, sch. 3.
s. 46, Act of Sederunt 94/1443.
s. 46A, regs. 94/1808.
ss. 48, 49, amended: 1994, c. 33, s. 129.
ss. 51, 52, amended: *ibid.*, s. 164.
s. 54, amended: regs. 94/1696.

43. Consumer Protection Act 1987.
s. 11, regs. 93/2877, 2923; 94/1768.
s. 20, see *Toys 'R' Us* v. *Gloucestershire County Council* (1994) 158 J.P. 338, D.C.; *Clydesdale Group* v. *Normand*, 1993 S.C.C.R. 958.

1987—cont.

43. Consumer Protection Act 1987—*cont.*
s. 39, see *Turtington* v. *United Co-operatives* [1993] Crim.L.R. 376, D.C.
s. 45, repealed in pt.: 1994, c. 26, sch. 5.

45. Parliamentary and other Pensions Act 1987.
s. 2, regs. 93/3252, 3253.

47. Abolition of Domestic Rates Etc. (Scotland) Act 1987.
s. 2, see *Lothian Region (Assessor for)* v. *Rowe* (L.V.A.C.), 1991 S.C. 257.
sch. 4, order 94/529.

49. Territorial Sea Act 1987.
s. 2, repealed in pt. (prosp.): 1994, c. 21, sch. 11, Pt. II.

51. Finance (No. 2) Act 1987.
s. 102, order 94/1859(S.).

53. Channel Tunnel Act 1987.
s. 11, orders 94/570, 1390, 1405, 1813, 2478.
s. 13, order 94/1390.
s. 14, amended: 1994, c. 29, sch. 5.
s. 23, orders 94/970, 1667.

1988

1. Income and Corporation Taxes Act 1988.
s. 1, order 93/2948.
s. 1, amended (temp.): 1994, c. 9, s. 75.
s. 5, repealed (prosp.): *ibid.*, sch. 26.
s. 8, repealed in pt.: 1993, c. 34, sch. 23.
s. 10, repealed (prosp.): 1994, c. 9, sch. 26.
s. 13, amended: *ibid.*, s. 86, sch. 16.
s. 13A, see *Lord (Inspector of Taxes)* v. *Tustain; Same* v. *Chapple* [1993] STC 755, Vinelott J.
s. 14, amended: 1994, c. 9, sch. 16.
s. 19, see *Hall (Inspector of Taxes)* v. *Lorimer* [1994] 1 All E.R. 250, C.A.
s. 20, amended: 1994, c. 9, s. 219.
s. 43, repealed in pt.: *ibid.*, schs. 17, 26.
s. 60, substituted (prosp.): *ibid.*, s. 200.
s. 61, substituted (prosp.): *ibid.*, s. 201.
s. 62, substituted (prosp.): *ibid.*, s. 202.
s. 62A, added (prosp.): *ibid.*, s. 203.
s. 63, substituted (prosp.): *ibid.*, s. 204.
s. 63A, added (prosp.): *ibid.*, s. 205.
s. 64, substituted (prosp.): *ibid.*, s. 206.
s. 65, amended (prosp.): *ibid.*, s. 207; repealed in pt. (prosp.): *ibid.*, s. 207, sch. 26.
ss. 66, 67, repealed (prosp.): *ibid.*, s. 207, sch. 26.
s. 68, amended (prosp.): *ibid.*, s. 207.
s. 69, substituted: *ibid.*, s. 208.
s. 74, see *Earlspring Properties* v. *Guest (Inspector of Taxes)* [1993] STC 473, Vinelott J.; *Prior (Inspector of Taxes)* v. *Saunders* [1993] STC 562, Sir Mervyn Davies.

1988—cont.

1. Income and Corporation Taxes Act 1988—*cont.*
s. 74, amended: 1994, c. 9, s. 144, sch. 9.
s. 75, amended: *ibid.*, sch. 16.
ss. 79, 79A, amended: *ibid.*, s. 145.
s. 83, repealed in pt.: 1994, c. 26, sch. 5.
s. 94, amended: 1994, c. 9, s. 144.
s. 96, amended (prosp.): *ibid.*, sch. 19; repealed in pt. (prosp.): *ibid.*, ss. 214, 216, sch. 26.
s. 103, amended: *ibid.*, s. 144.
s. 111, substituted (prosp.): *ibid.*, s. 215.
s. 113, see *Maidment (Inspector of Taxes)* v. *Kibby* [1993] STC 494, Sir Donald Nicholls, V.-C.
s. 113, amended (prosp.): 1994, c. 9, s. 216; repealed in pt. (prosp.): *ibid.*, s. 216, sch. 26.
s. 114, amended (prosp.): *ibid.*, s. 215; repealed in pt. (prosp.): *ibid.*, s. 215, sch. 26.
s. 115, repealed in pt. (prosp.): *ibid.*, s. 215, sch. 26.
s. 141, amended: *ibid.*, s. 89; repealed in pt.: *ibid.*, s. 89, sch. 26.
ss. 142–144, amended: *ibid.*, s. 89.
s. 144A, added: *ibid.*, s. 132.
s. 158, amended: *ibid.*, s. 87; c. 22, sch. 3.
s. 160, regs. 94/1307, 1567.
s. 160, amended: 1994, c. 9, sch. 9; repealed in pt.: *ibid.*, sch. 26.
s. 161, amended: *ibid.*, sch. 9.
s. 167, repealed in pt.: *ibid.*, sch. 26.
s. 168, amended: 1994, c. 22, sch. 3.
s. 168E, regs. 94/777.
s. 185, see *I.R.C.* v. *Reed International; Reed International* v. *I.R.C.*, *The Times,* March 10, 1994, Blackburne J.
ss. 188, 189, repealed in pt. (with savings): 1994, c. 9, s. 108, sch. 26.
s. 191B, repealed in pt.: *ibid.*, sch. 26.
s. 201A, repealed in pt.: 1994, c. 40, sch. 17.
s. 203, regs. 94/775, 1212.
s. 203, repealed in pt. (prosp.): 1994, c. 9, sch. 19, 26.
s. 203B, added: *ibid.*, s. 125.
ss. 203C–203E, added: *ibid.*, s. 126.
s. 203F, added: *ibid.*, s. 127.
s. 203G, added: *ibid.*, s. 128.
s. 203H, added: *ibid.*, s. 129.
s. 203I, added: *ibid.*, s. 130.
s. 203J–203L, added: *ibid.*, s. 131.
ss. 206, 331, see *Walters (Inspector of Taxes)* v. *Tickner* [1993] STC 624, C.A.
s. 237, amended: *ibid.*, sch. 9.
Pt. VI, Chap. VA (ss. 246A–246Y), added: *ibid.*, sch. 16.
s. 247, amended: *ibid.*, sch. 16.
s. 257A, amended: *ibid.*, s. 77, sch. 8.

1988—cont.

1. Income and Corporation Taxes Act 1988—*cont.*

s. 257BA, amended: *ibid.*, sch. 8.

s. 257BB, amended: *ibid.*, sch. 8; repealed in pt.: *ibid.*, schs. 8, 26.

s. 257C, order 93/2948.

s. 257D, repealed in pt.: 1994, c. 9, schs. 8, 10, 26, Pt. V(1)(2)(3)(17).

s. 257F, amended: *ibid.*, sch. 8.

s. 259, amended: *ibid.*, s. 77, sch. 8.

s. 260, amended: *ibid.*, sch. 8.

ss. 261A, 262, amended: *ibid.*, s. 77, sch. 8.

s. 265, amended: *ibid.*, s. 82; repealed in pt.: *ibid.*, schs. 8, 10, 26, Pt. V(1)(2)(3)(17).

s. 271, repealed in pt.: *ibid.*, schs. 17, 26.

s. 276, amended: *ibid.*, sch. 8.

s. 277, repealed in pt. (prosp.): *ibid.*, s. 215, sch. 26.

ss. 289, 289A, 289B, substituted for s.289: *ibid.*, sch. 15.

ss. 289, 299A, see *National Westminster Bank* v. *I.R.C.; Barclays Bank* v. *Same* [1994] 3 W.L.R. 159, H.L.

s. 290, amended: 1994, c. 9, sch. 15.

s. 290A, amended: *ibid.*, repealed in pt.: *ibid.*, schs. 15, 26.

ss. 291, 291A, 291B, substituted for s. 291: *ibid.*, sch. 15.

s. 292, amended: *ibid.*

s. 293, amended: *ibid.*, repealed in pt.: *ibid.*, schs. 15, 26.

s. 294, amended: *ibid.*, sch. 15.

s. 296, repealed in pt.: *ibid.*, schs. 15, 26.

ss. 297, 298, amended: *ibid.*, sch. 15; repealed in pt.: *ibid.*, schs. 15, 26.

s. 299, substituted: *ibid.*, sch. 15.

ss. 299A, 300, amended: *ibid.*

s. 301, amended: *ibid.*, repealed in pt.: *ibid.*, schs. 15, 26.

s. 302, amended: *ibid.*, sch. 15.

s. 303, amended: *ibid.*, repealed in pt.: *ibid.*, schs. 15, 26.

ss. 304, 305, substituted: *ibid.*, sch. 15.

s. 305A, added: *ibid.*

ss. 306–308, amended: *ibid.*, repealed in pt.: *ibid.*, schs. 15, 26.

s. 309, repealed: *ibid.*

s. 310, amended: *ibid.*, sch. 15; repealed in pt.: *ibid.*, schs. 15, 26.

s. 311, amended: *ibid.*, sch. 15.

s. 312, amended: *ibid.*, repealed in pt.: *ibid.*, schs. 15, 26.

ss. 339, 660, see *Racal Group Services* v. *Ashmore* [1994] STC 416, Vinelott J.

s. 347A, amended: 1994, c. 9, s. 79.

s. 347B, amended: *ibid.*, s. 79; repealed in pt.: *ibid.*, s. 79, sch., 26.

s. 353, amended: *ibid.*, s. 81; repealed in pt.: *ibid.*, schs., 9, 26.

1988—cont.

1. Income and Corporation Taxes Act 1988—*cont.*

ss. 353, 360, see *Lord (Inspector of Taxes)* v. *Tustain; Same* v. *Chapple* [1993] STC 755, Vinelott J.

ss. 355, 356, 356A, amended: 1994, c. 9, sch. 9.

s. 356D, amended: *ibid.*, schs. 9, 17.

ss. 357, 357A–357C, 358, amended: *ibid.*, sch. 9.

s. 369, amended: *ibid.*, s. 81.

ss. 370, 375, amended: *ibid.*, sch. 9.

s. 376, order 93/3055.

s. 376, amended: 1994, c. 9, s. 142; repealed in pt.: *ibid.*, s. 142, sch. 26.

s. 376A, added: *ibid.*, s. 142.

s. 379, repealed in pt.: *ibid.*, sch. 26.

ss. 380, 381, amended (prosp.): *ibid.*, s. 209; repealed in pt. (prosp.): *ibid.*, s. 216, sch. 26.

s. 381, see *Gallagher* v. *Jones (Inspector of Taxes); Threlfall* v. *Jones (Inspector of Taxes)* [1993] STC 537, C.A.

s. 382, amended (prosp.): 1994, c. 9, s. 209.

s. 383, repealed (prosp.): *ibid.*, s. 214, sch. 26.

s. 384, amended (prosp.): *ibid.*, s. 214; repealed in pt. (prosp.): *ibid.*, ss. 214, 216, sch. 26.

s. 385, amended (prosp.): *ibid.*, s. 209; repealed in pt. (prosp.): *ibid.*, ss. 209, 216, sch. 26.

s. 386, repealed in pt. (prosp.): *ibid.*, s. 216, sch. 26.

s. 388, amended (prosp.): *ibid.*, s. 209; repealed in pt. (prosp.): *ibid.*, s. 214, sch. 26.

s. 389, amended (prosp.): *ibid.*, s. 217; repealed in pt. (prosp.): *ibid.*, ss. 214, 217, sch. 26.

s. 397, amended (prosp.): *ibid.*, s. 214; repealed in pt. (prosp.): *ibid.*, s. 214, sch. 26.

s. 419, see *Earlspring Properties* v. *Guest (Inspector of Taxes)* [1993] STC 473, Vinelott J.; *Joint (Inspector of Taxes)* v. *Bracken Developments* [1994] STC 300, Vinelott J.

s. 431, amended (prosp.): 1994, c. 9, s. 143, schs. 16, 17; repealed in pt.: *ibid.*, s. 143, sch. 26.

s. 431AA, added: *ibid.*, s. 143.

s. 434, amended: *ibid.*, s. 176, sch. 16; repealed in pt.: *ibid.*, sch. 26.

s. 438, amended: *ibid.*, sch. 16; repealed in pt.: *ibid.*, schs. 16, 26.

s. 451, regs. 94/728.

s. 458, amended: 1994, c. 9, sch. 16.

s. 463, regs. 93/3111.

s. 468, amended: 1994, c. 9, s. 113, sch. 14; repealed in pt.: *ibid.*, schs. 14, 26.

1988—cont.

1. Income and Corporation Taxes Act 1988—*cont.*

s. 468E, amended: *ibid.*, s. 111.
s. 468EE, added: *ibid.*
s. 468F, repealed: *ibid.*, sch. 26, Pt. V; repealed in pt.: *ibid.*, s. 251, sch. 26, Pt. VIII.
s. 468G, repealed: *ibid.*, schs. 14, 26.
ss. 468H–468R, added: *ibid.*, sch. 14.
ss. 468O, 468P, regs. 94/2318.
s. 469, regs. 94/1479.
s. 469, amended: 1994, c. 9, s. 113, sch. 14.
s. 477A, regs. 94/296.
s. 478, repealed (prosp.): 1994, c. 9, sch. 26.
s. 480B, regs. 94/295.
s. 490, amended: 1994, c. 9, sch. 16.
s. 520, amended (prosp.): *ibid.*, s. 214.
ss. 521, 528, repealed in pt. (prosp.): *ibid.*, s. 214, sch. 26.
s. 530, amended (prosp.): *ibid.*, s. 214; repealed in pt. (prosp.): *ibid.*, s. 214, sch. 26.
ss. 534, 537A, amended (prosp.): *ibid.*, sch. 19.
s. 561, amended: *ibid.*, sch. 17.
s. 574, amended (prosp.): *ibid.*, s. 210.
s. 576, amended: *ibid.*, sch. 17.
s. 577A, amended: *ibid.*, s. 141.
s. 590C, order 93/2950.
s. 591, regs. 93/2813.
s. 591, amended: 1994, c. 9, s. 107; repealed in pt.: *ibid.*, s. 107, sch. 26.
s. 592, see *Kelsall (Inspector of Taxes)* v. *Investment Chartwork* [1994] STC 33, Arden J.
s. 596A, amended: 1994, c. 9, s. 107.
s. 597, amended: *ibid.*, s. 110.
s. 605, amended: *ibid.*, s. 105; repealed in pt.: *ibid.*, s. 105, sch. 26.
s. 605A, added: *ibid.*, s. 106.
s. 606, substituted: *ibid.*, s. 104.
s. 607, amended: *ibid.*
s. 611AA, added: *ibid.*, s. 103.
s. 612, repealed in pt.: *ibid.*, s. 103, sch. 26.
s. 614, repealed in pt.: *ibid.*, sch. 26.
ss. 619, 623, see *Koenigsberger* v. *Mellor (Inspector of Taxes)* [1993] STC 408, Lindsay J.
ss. 627, 641 (in pt.), repealed (prosp.): 1994, c. 9, s. 228, sch. 26.
s. 648A, added (prosp.): *ibid.*, s. 109.
ss. 687, 701, amended: *ibid.*, sch. 16.
s. 705, repealed in pt.: regs. 94/1813.
ss. 705A, 705B, added: *ibid.*
s. 715, amended: 1994, c. 9, s. 123.
s. 731, amended: *ibid.*, sch. 16; repealed in pt.: *ibid.*, schs. 16, 26.
s. 737, amended: *ibid.*, sch. 16.
ss. 737A–737C, added: *ibid.*, s. 122.
ss. 742, 745, 749, 751, repealed in pt.: *ibid.*, s. 251, sch. 26.

1988—cont.

1. Income and Corporation Taxes Act 1988—*cont.*

ss. 767A, 767B, added: *ibid.*, s. 135.
s. 768, amended: *ibid.*, sch. 17.
s. 769, amended: *ibid.*, s. 135.
s. 788, orders 94/767–770.
s. 791, regs. 94/1418.
s. 796, amended: 1994, c. 9, sch. 8.
s. 802, amended: *ibid.*, sch. 16.
s. 804, amended (prosp.): *ibid.*, s. 217; repealed in pt. (prosp.): *ibid.*, s. 217, sch. 26.
s. 808, amended: *ibid.*, s. 140; repealed in pt.: *ibid.*, s. 140, sch. 26.
s. 824, amended (prosp.): *ibid.*, sch. 19; repealed in pt. (prosp.): *ibid.*, schs. 19, 26.
s. 826, amended: *ibid.*, schs. 16, 19 (prosp.).
s. 827, amended: *ibid.*, s. 18, sch. 7; c. 23, sch. 14.
s. 828, repealed in pt.: 1994, c. 9, sch. 26.
s. 834, amended: *ibid.*, sch. 14.
s. 842, amended: *ibid.*, sch. 17.
s. 842A, amended(S.): 1994, c. 39, sch. 13; repealed in pt.: 1994, c. 29, sch. 9.
s. 843, amended: 1994, c. 9, sch. 17.
sch. 5, amended (prosp.): *ibid.*, sch. 19.
sch. 6, regs. 94/778.
sch. 7, amended: 1994, c. 9, s. 88; repealed in pt.: *ibid.*, s. 88, sch. 26.
sch. 8, amended: *ibid.*, ss. 98, 99.
sch. 9, see *I.R.C.* v. *Reed International; Reed International* v. *I.R.C.* [1994] STC 396, Blackburne J.
sch. 9, amended: 1994, c. 9, s. 101.
sch. 10, amended: *ibid.*, s. 100; repealed in pt.: *ibid.*, s. 100, sch. 26.
sch. 11, repealed in pt.: *ibid.*, schs. 17, 26.
sch. 13, amended: *ibid.*, sch. 16.
sch. 19, see *Massmould Holdings* v. *Payne (Inspector of Taxes)* [1994] STC 717, C.A.
sch. 19A, regs. 94/728.
sch. 19AB, regs. 93/3109.
sch. 23, regs. 93/3219.
sch. 23A, amended: 1994, c. 9, ss. 123, 124, sch. 16; repealed in pt.: *ibid.*, sch. 26.
sch. 25, amended: *ibid.*, s. 134; repealed in pt.: *ibid.*, s. 134, sch. 26.
sch. 27, amended: *ibid.*, s. 176.

7. Social Security Act 1988.
s. 13, regs. 94/2004.

8. Multilateral Investment Guarantee Agency Act 1988.
s. 7, Act of Sederunt 94/1443.

9. Local Government Act 1988.
s. 1, amended: 1994, c. 29, sch. 4.
s. 1, amended(S.): 1994, c. 39, sch. 13; repealed in pt.(S.): *ibid.*, schs. 13, 14.

1988—cont.

9. Local Government Act 1988—*cont.*

s. 2, orders 93/2813, 3035; 94/15, 339, 569, 902, 1167, 1671, 2154, 2196, 2296, 2744, 2884, 2888.

s. 2, amended: orders 94/1671, 2884, 2888; repealed in pt.: order 94/1671.

s. 2, amended(S.): 1994, c. 39, sch. 13.

ss. 4, 5, amended: order 94/1671.

s. 6, regs. 94/2297.

s. 7, see *R.* v. *Secretary of State for the Environment, ex p. Haringey London Borough Council, The Times,* March 2, 1994, C.A.

s. 8, regs. 93/848.

s. 15, orders 93/2813, 3035; 94/15, 339, 569, 902, 1167, 1671, 2154, 2196, 2296, 2297, 2744, 2884, 2888.

ss. 15, 24, amended(S.): 1994, c. 39, sch. 13.

sch. 1, amended: orders 94/1671, 2884, 2888.

sch. 2, amended(S.): 1994, c. 39, sch. 13; repealed in pt.(S.): *ibid.,* sch. 14.

sch. 6, repealed in pt.(S.): *ibid.*

sch. 12, amended: 1994, c. 19, sch. 6; c. 29, sch. 4.

12. Merchant Shipping Act 1988.

Commencement order: 94/1201.

s. 31, see *Seaboard Offshore* v. *Secretary of State for Transport* [1994] 1 W.L.R. 541, H.L.

ss. 33, 53, regs. 94/2013.

s. 58, order 94/1201.

sch. 4 (as repealed by 1993, c. 22, sch. 5, Pt. II) restored: 1994, c. 28, s. 5; repealed in pt.: *ibid.,* sch. 4.

sch. 5, repealed in pt.: *ibid.*

13. Coroners Act 1988.

ss. 1, 2, 4, amended: 1994, c. 19, sch. 16.

s. 4A, added: *ibid.*

s. 8, see *R.* v. *Coroner for Western District of East Sussex, ex p. Homberg, The Independent,* January 27, 1994, C.A.

s. 11, see *R.* v. *H.M. Coroner for North Humberside and Scunthorpe, ex p. Jamieson* [1994] 3 W.L.R. 82, C.A.

ss. 16, 17, amended: 1994, c. 33, sch. 4.

ss. 22, 27, 31, 35, amended: 1994, c. 19, sch. 16.

14. Immigration Act 1988.

Commencement order: 94/1923.

s. 3, see *R.* v. *Secretary of State for the Home Department, ex p. Mostafa (Mohammed)* [1994] Imm AR 18, Pill J.

s. 8, repealed in pt.: order 93/1813.

s. 12, order 94/1923.

20. Dartford–Thurrock Crossing Act 1988.

s. 17, order 94/2033.

s. 19, amended: 1994, c. 22, sch. 3.

ss. 25, 26, 44, 46, regs. 94/2031.

1988—cont.

26. Landlord and Tenant Act 1988.

s. 1, see *CIN Properties* v. *Gill* [1993] 38 EG 152, Sir Godfray Le Quesne, Q.C.

s. 4, see *S. Ayers* v. *Long Acre Securities,* October 3, 1994; District Judge Freedman; Uxbridge County Ct.

30. Finance Act 1988.

sch. 10, see *De Rothschild* v. *Lawrenson (Inspector of Taxes)* [1994] STC 8, Vinelott J.

32. Civil Evidence (Scotland) Act 1988.

s. 2, see *Lenaghan* v. *Ayrshire and Arran Health Board,* 1994 S.L.T. 765; *Sanderson* v. *McManus* (Sh.Ct.), 1994 S.C.L.R. 537.

33. Criminal Justice Act 1988.

s. 23, see *R.* v. *McGillivray* (1993) 97 Cr.App.R. 232, C.A.; *R.* v. *Jiminez-Paez (Carmenza)* [1993] Crim.L.R. 596, C.A.; *R.* v. *Wilson,* February 24, 1994; H.H.J. Cockcroft; Leeds Crown Ct.

ss. 23, 26, see *R.* v. *Patel; R.* v. *Javed; R.* v. *Hurree; R.* v. *McCormick* (1993) 97 Cr.App.R. 294, C.A.; *R.* v. *French and Gowhar* (1993) 97 Cr.App.R. 421, C.A.

ss. 24–26, see *R.* v. *Hinds* [1993] Crim. L.R. 528, C.A.

s. 25, amended: 1994, c. 33, sch. 9; repealed in pt.: *ibid.,* sch. 11.

s. 32, amended: *ibid.,* sch. 9.

s. 32A, amended: *ibid.,* s. 50; repealed in pt.: *ibid.,* sch. 11.

s. 33A, amended: *ibid.,* sch. 9.

s. 34, repealed in pt.: *ibid.,* s. 32, sch. 11.

s. 35, order 94/119.

s. 35, amended: 1994, c. 33, sch. 9.

ss. 35, 36, see *Att.-Gen.'s Reference (No. 22 of 1992)* (1993) 97 Cr.App.R. 274, C.A.; *Att.-Gen's Reference (No. 3 of 1992)* [1994] RTR 122, C.A.

s. 36, see *R.* v. *Chadwick (Barry John), The Times,* August 10, 1994, C.A.

s. 40, amended: 1994, c. 33, schs. 4, 9.

s. 41, see *R.* v. *Davies (Paul Neil)* (1993) 157 J.P. 820, C.A.

s. 41, amended: 1994, c. 33, sch. 4.

s. 71, amended: 1994, c. 37, sch. 1.

s. 72A, amended: 1994, c. 33, sch. 9.

s. 83, see *S. (Confiscation Order), Re, The Times,* November 1, 1994, Dyson J.

s. 91, Act of Sederunt 94/1443.

s. 93G, regs. 94/1759.

s. 96, orders 93/3147; 94/1639.

s. 103, repealed in pt.: 1994, c. 37, sch. 3.

s. 126, repealed: 1994, c. 33, sch. 11.

s. 133, see *R.* v. *Secretary of State for the Home Department, ex p. Howse; R.* v. *Same, ex p. Bateman, The Times,* July 1, 1994, C.A.

CAP.

1988—cont.

33. Criminal Justice Act 1988—*cont.*
s. 151, amended: 1994, c. 37, sch. 1.
s. 160, amended: 1994, c. 33, ss. 84, 86; repealed in pt.: *ibid.*, s. 84, sch. 11.
ss. 164 (in pt.), 165, repealed 1994, c. 29, sch. 9.
sch. 5, repealed in pt.:1994, c. 37, sch. 3.

34. Legal Aid Act 1988.
s. 2, see *R. v. Legal Aid Board, ex p. Higgins, The Times*, November 19, 1993, D.C.; *R. v. Legal Aid Board, ex p. Gilchrist, The Times*, March 8, 1994, C.A.
s. 8, regs. 94/2768.
s. 9, regs. 94/805.
s. 14, regs. 94/2768.
s. 15, see *R. v. Legal Aid Board, ex p. Woolcock* [1993] C.O.D. 246, Owen J.
s. 15, regs. 94/806.
s. 16, see *Parkes* v. *Legal Aid Board, The Times*, May 24, 1994, Thorpe J.
s. 16, regs. 94/806, 1822.
s. 17, see *Jones* v. *Goldsack*, October 8, 1993; H.H. Judge Moseley, Q.C., Chancery Division, Cardiff; *Parr* v. *Smith* [1994] NPC 5, C.A.; *Williams (Ronald) and Williams (Lynne)* v. *Walklett (Barry)*, March 18, 1994; Mr. Recorder Digney, Medway County Ct.
s. 18, see *Jones* v. *Zahedi* [1993] 1 W.L.R. 1445, C.A.; *Middleton* v. *Middleton* [1994] 3 All E.R. 236, C.A.
ss. 19, 21, see *R. v. Recorder of Liverpool, ex p. McCann, The Times*, May 4, 1994, D.C.
ss. 19, 21, 26, see *R. v. Crawley Justices, ex p. Ohakwe, The Times*, May 26, 1994, D.C.
s. 20, amended: 1994, c. 33, sch. 4; repealed in pt.: *ibid.*, sch. 11.
s. 21, see *British Waterways Board* v. *Norman* (1993) 26 H.L.R. 232, D.C.
s. 21, regs. 94/807.
s. 21, amended: 1994, c. 33, sch. 4.
s. 22, see *R. v. Liverpool City Magistrates, ex p. McGhee* [1993] Crim.L.R. 609, D.C.
s. 23, regs. 94/807.
s. 25, regs. 94/1477, 1825, 2218.
s. 31, regs. 94/228–230.
s. 34, regs. 94/228–230, 805–807, 1477, 1822–1825, 2218.
s. 43, regs. 94/228–230, 805–807, 1477, 1822–1825, 2218, 2218, 2768.
sch. 2, amended: regs. 94/2768.
sch. 3, amended: 1994, c. 33, sch. 4.

36. Court of Session Act 1988.
s. 1, order 93/3154; amended: *ibid.*
s. 5, Acts of Sederunt 94/391, 1139, 1140, 1443, 2310.
s. 6, Act of Sederunt 94/1443.

CAP.

1988—cont.

36. Court of Session Act 1988—*cont.*
s. 10, see *Tonner* v. *F.T. Everard & Sons*, 1994 S.L.T. 1033.
ss. 26, 28, 29, 34, Act of Sederunt 94/1443.
s. 45, see *Tayside Regional Council* v. *British Railways Board, The Times*, December 30, 1993.
s. 46, see *Five Oaks Properties* v. *Granite House* (O.H.), 1994 S.C.L.R. 740.
ss. 46, 47, see *Church Commissioners for England* v. *Abbey National*, 1994 S.L.T. 959.
ss. 48, 51, Act of Sederunt 94/1443.

39. Finance Act 1988.
s. 4, repealed in pt.: 1994, c. 22, sch. 5.
ss. 13–20, repealed: 1994, c. 23, sch. 15.
s. 21, amended: 1994, c. 9, s. 47; repealed: 1994, c. 23, sch. 15.
s. 22, repealed: *ibid.*
s. 38, amended: 1994, c. 9, s. 79.
s. 50, repealed: *ibid.*, sch. 26.
s. 135, repealed in pt.: regs. 94/1813.
s. 141, see *Guinness* v. *I.R.C., The Times*, December 17, 1993, Rattee J.
sch. 2, repealed in pt.: 1994, c. 22, sch. 5.
schs. 3 (in pt.), 4, repealed: 1994, c. 9, sch. 26.

40. Education Reform Act 1988.
s. 3, orders 94/1814, 1818.
s. 3, amended and repealed in pt.: order 94/1814.
s. 4, orders 94/646, 647, 1520, 1743, 1744, 1815–1817, 2099–2101, 2226–2228.
s. 9, amended: 1994, c. 30, sch. 2.
s. 17, regs. 94/2112, 2206.
s. 22, regs. 93/2824; 94/959, 1420, 1421, 2254, 2330.
s. 28, regs. 93/3113.
s. 38, regs. 94/277.
s. 42, regs. 93/3070; 94/323.
s. 43, regs. 93/3104.
ss. 63, 89, 92, regs. 93/3113.
s. 106, amended: 1994, c. 30, sch. 2; regs. 94/1083.
ss. 109, 110, amended: regs. 94/1083.
s. 122A, orders 94/2017–2019.
s. 187, order 94/580.
s. 214, order 93/2828.
s. 218, regs. 94/222.
s. 218, amended: 1994, c. 30, s. 14, sch. 2.
s. 220, amended and repealed in pt.: *ibid.*, sch. 2.
s. 231, orders 94/580, 1255, 2163.
s. 232, regs. 93/2824, 3104; 94/222, 323, 959; orders 94/580, 646, 647, 1420, 1421, 1743, 1744, 1815, 1818, 2099–2101, 2206, 2226–2228, 2254, 2330.
s. 232, repealed in pt.: 1994, c. 30, s. 14.
s. 235, amended: 1994, c. 19, sch. 16.
sch. 4, regs. 93/3104.
sch. 11, order 93/3056.

(69)

1988—cont.

41. Local Government Finance Act 1988.
see *Wood (Jennifer Agnes), Re,* August 27, 1993; District Judge Brown in a reserved judgment; Tamworth County Ct.
s. 41A, added: 1994, c. 19, sch. 37.
s. 53, regs. 94/834.
s. 55, regs. 94/1809.
s. 55, amended: 1994, c. 19, sch. 16.
s. 58, amended: 1994, c. 3, s. 2.
ss. 64, 65, regs. 94/834.
s. 74, amended: 1994, c. 19, sch. 6; regs. 94/2825.
s. 88, amended: 1994, c. 19, sch. 16.
s. 89, amended: regs. 94/2825.
s. 89A, added: 1994, c. 19, sch. 12.
ss. 91, 92, amended: regs. 94/2825.
s. 99, regs. 94/246.
s. 111, amended: 1994, c. 19, sch. 12; c. 29, s. 31; repealed in pt.: *ibid.*, sch. 9.
ss. 112, 114, amended: *ibid.*, sch. 4.
s. 128, repealed(S.): 1994, c. 39, sch. 14.
s. 140, regs. 93/3077, 3082; 94/246, 415, 421, 547, 834, 1431, 1742; order 94/999.
s. 143, regs. 93/3077, 3082; 94/246, 415, 421, 547, 834, 1431, 1742; orders 94/903, 999.
s. 146, regs. 94/246, 415, 421, 504, 547.
sch. 4, regs. 94/504.
sch. 6, orders 94/903, 999.
sch. 7A, amended (temp.): 1994, c. 3, s. 1.
sch. 8, regs. 93/3077, 3082; 94/421, 547, 1431, 1742.
sch. 8 (amended: 1992, c. 46, ss. 4, 5), continued and amended: 1994, c. 3, s. 3.
sch. 9, regs. 94/415.
sch. 9, amended: 1994, c. 19, sch. 16.
sch. 12, repealed in pt.(S.): 1994, c. 39, sch. 14.

43. Housing (Scotland) Act 1988.
ss. 43, 45, amended: 1994, c. 39, sch. 13.
s. 55, amended: *ibid.*; repealed in pt.: *ibid.*, schs. 13, 14.
s. 56, amended: *ibid.*, sch. 13.
s. 57, amended: *ibid.*; repealed in pt.: *ibid.*, sch. 14.
s. 70, order 94/582.
sch. 4, amended: 1994, c. 39, sch. 13.

45. Firearms (Amendment) Act 1988.
s. 15, orders 94/2615, 2652(S.).
s. 15, amended: orders 94/2615, 2652(S.).
s. 22, order 93/2919.

47. School Boards (Scotland) Act 1988.
s. 5, amended: 1994, c. 39, sch. 13.
s. 22, sch. 2, amended: *ibid.*; repealed in pt.: *ibid.*, sch. 14.

1988—cont.

48. Copyright, Designs and Patents Act 1988.
ss. 1, 3, 9, 11, 21, sch. 1, see *John Richardson Computers* v. *Flanders* [1993] F.S.R. 497, Ferris J.
ss. 107, 110, see *Thames and Hudson* v. *Design and Artists Copyright Society, The Times,* August 10, 1994, Evans-Lombe J.
s. 107A, added: 1994, c. 33, s. 165.
s. 114, Act of Sederunt 94/1443.
s. 114, amended: 1994, c. 26, sch. 4.
s. 143, orders 93/2755; 94/247.
s. 159, order 94/263.
s. 198A, added: 1994, c. 33, s. 165.
s. 204, Act of Sederunt 94/1443.
s. 204, amended: 1994, c. 26, sch. 4.
s. 208, order 94/264.
s. 231, Act of Sederunt 94/1443.
s. 231, amended: 1994, c. 26, sch. 4.
s. 279, rules 94/362.
s. 280, amended: 1994, c. 26, sch. 4.
s. 282, repealed: *ibid.*, sch. 5.
s. 283, rules 94/363.
ss. 283, 284, 286 (in pt.), repealed: 1994, c. 26, sch. 5.
s. 287, see *McDonald* v. *Graham, The Times,* January 12, 1994, C.A.
s. 287, order 94/1609.
ss. 288, 289, see *Chaplin Patents Holdings Co.* v. *Group Lotus, The Times,* January 12, 1994, C.A.
s. 289, see *Pharma Plast A/S* v. *Bard* [1993] F.S.R. 686, Patents County Ct.; *Composite Gutters* v. *Pre-formed Components* [1993] F.S.R. 305, Hoffmann J.
s. 300, repealed: 1994, c. 26, sch. 5.

50. Housing Act 1988.
s. 27, see *Nwokorie* v. *Mason* (1994) 26 H.L.R. 60, C.A.
ss. 27, 28, see *Rowlands (Sandra)* v. *Liverpool City Council,* January 13, 1994; H.H.J. Mackay; Liverpool County Ct.; *Bain* v. *Stimpson,* February 10, 1994; H.H.J. Viner, Q.C.; *Sampson* v. *Wilson* [1994] EGCS 5, H.H.J. Roger Cook; *Farthing and Hughes* v. *Colisanti,* June 14, 1994; District Judge Cooper; Southampton County Ct.; *Shafer* v. *Yagambrun,* October 4, 1994; Mr Recorder Whiteman; Cardiff County Ct.
s. 34, see *Goringe* v. *Twinsectra,* April 20, 1994; Mr. Recorder Mackie; Staines County Ct.
s. 55, order 94/668.
ss. 60, 62, order 94/1987.
s. 66, amended: 1994, c. 19, sch. 8.
ss. 74, 75, orders 94/566, 695.
ss. 104, 111, 114, regs. 94/266.
s. 121, order 94/568.

1988—cont.

50. Housing Act 1988—*cont.*
 sch. 1, amended: 1994, c. 19, schs. 8, 13; c. 29, sch. 4; c. 36, sch. 1.
 sch. 9, repealed in pt. (prosp.): 1994, c. 21, schs. 9, 11, Pt. II.
 sch. 17, repealed in pt.: 1994, c. 37, sch. 3.

52. Road Traffic Act 1988.
 see *Rush* v. *D.P.P.* [1994] RTR 268, D.C.
 s. 2, see *Learmont* v. *D.P.P.* [1994] RTR 286, D.C.
 ss. 2, 2A, see *Abbas* v. *Houston*, 1993 S.C.C.R. 1019.
 ss. 2, 3, see *Rodger* v. *Normand, The Scotsman*, November 10, 1994.
 s. 3A, see *R.* v. *Shepherd (Att.-Gen.'s Reference (No. 14 of 1993)); R.* v. *Wernet (Att.-Gen.'s Reference (No. 24 of 1993)), The Times*, December 27, 1993, C.A.
 s. 4, see *R.* v. *Ealing Magistrates' Court, ex p. Woodman* [1994] RTR 189, D.C.; *Lunt* v. *D.P.P.* [1993] Crim.L.R. 534, D.C.
 ss. 4, 5, 7, see *D.P.P.* v. *Butterworth* [1994] 3 W.L.R. 538, H.L.
 s. 5, see *D.P.P.* v. *Johnson, The Times*, March 15, 1994, D.C.; *Drake* v. *D.P.P., The Times*, April 4, 1994, D.C.; *D.P.P.* v. *Snook* [1993] Crim. L.R. 883, D.C.; *Gunnell* v. *D.P.P.* [1994] RTR 151, D.C.
 ss. 5, 7, 8, see *Hayes* v. *D.P.P.* [1994] RTR 163, D.C.
 s. 7, see *Ogburn* v. *D.P.P.* [1994] RTR 241, C.A.; *D.P.P.* v. *Thomas (Elwyn Kenneth)* (1993) 157 J.P. 480, D.C.; *McLaren* v. *MacLeod*, 1994 S.C.C.R. 493; *Duncan* v. *Normand*, 1994 S.C.C.R. 508.
 s. 13, regs. 94/2653(S.).
 s. 27, amended(S.): 1994, c. 39, sch. 13.
 s. 31, regs. 94/1226.
 s. 33, amended(S.): 1994, c. 39, sch. 13.
 s. 34, see *McClelland* v. *Whitelaw*, 1993 S.C.C.R. 1113.
 s. 36, regs. 94/1519.
 s. 39, amended(S.): 1994, c. 39, sch. 13.
 s. 41, regs. 93/3048; 94/14, 329, 2192, 2280.
 s. 43, amended: 1994, c. 22, sch. 3.
 ss. 45, 46, regs. 93/3011; 94/2136.
 s. 47, amended: 1994, c. 9, sch. 2; c. 22, sch. 3.
 ss. 49, 51, regs. 93/3013; 94/326.
 s. 54, regs. 94/2190, 2191.
 s. 61, regs. 94/1265, 2190, 2191.
 s. 63, regs. 94/2190.
 ss. 64A, 65A, 66, amended: 1994, c. 22, sch. 3.
 s. 67B, amended(S.): 1994, c. 39, sch. 13.
 s. 69A, amended: 1994, c. 22, sch. 3.

1988—cont.

52. Road Traffic Act 1988—*cont.*
 s. 73, amended: 1994, c. 40, sch. 13.
 s. 88, order 94/116.
 s. 89, order 94/116; regs. 94/638, 639.
 s. 92, regs. 94/1862.
 ss. 105, 108, regs. 94/638, 639, 1862.
 s. 124, amended(S.): 1994, c. 39, sch. 13.
 ss. 125, 132, 141, regs. 94/554.
 s. 143, see *Heywood* v. *O'Connor*, 1994 S.L.T. 254.
 s. 144, amended(S.): 1994, c. 39, sch. 13.
 ss. 148, 156, amended: 1994, c. 22, sch. 3.
 s. 170, see *Cunningham* v. *Crowe*, 1994 S.C.C.R. 330.
 ss. 172, 183, amended: 1994, c. 22, sch. 3.
 s. 192, regs. 94/638, 639.
 s. 192, amended: 1994, c. 19, sch. 7.
 sch. 2, amended: *ibid.*; repealed in pt.: *ibid.*, schs. 7, 18.
 sch. 2, amended(S.): 1994, c. 39, sch. 13.

53. Road Traffic Offenders Act 1988.
 s. 1, amended: 1994, c. 33, sch. 9.
 s. 2, see *Bremner* v. *Westwater*, 1993 S.C.C.R. 1023.
 s. 4, amended: 1994, c. 19, sch. 7; repealed in pt.: *ibid.*, schs. 7, 18.
 s. 6, see *Hampson* v. *Carmichael*, 1993 S.C.C.R. 1030.
 s. 15, see *D.P.P.* v. *Snook* [1993] Crim. L.R. 883, D.C.
 s. 16, see *Thorn* v. *D.P.P.* [1994] RTR 11, D.C.
 s. 20, see *Roberts* v. *D.P.P.* [1994] RTR 31, D.C.
 s. 21, repealed in pt.: 1994, c. 22, sch. 5.
 s. 28, see *Reith* v. *Thomson* (Sh.Ct.), 1994 S.C.C.R. 577.
 s. 33, see *Robb* v. *Hamilton*, 1994 S.L.T. 423.
 s. 34, see *Learmont* v. *D.P.P.* [1994] RTR 286, D.C.
 s. 35, see *Edmonds* v. *Buchanan*, 1993 S.C.C.R. 1048; *Ewen* v. *Orr*, 1993 S.C.C.R. 1015.
 ss. 35, 44, see *Scott* v. *Ross*, 1994 S.L.T. 945.
 s. 44, see *Heywood* v. *O'Connor*, 1994 S.L.T. 254.
 s. 71, amended: 1994, c. 22, sch. 3.
 s. 75, see *Reith* v. *Thomson* (Sh.Ct.), 1994 S.C.C.R. 577.
 ss. 85, 89, amended: 1994, c. 22, sch. 3.
 sch. 2, see *Robb* v. *Hamilton*, 1994 S.L.T. 423.
 sch. 2, amended: 1994, c. 11, s. 1.
 sch. 3, amended: 1994, c. 22, sch. 3; repealed in pt.: *ibid.*, sch. 5.
 sch. 5, repealed in pt.: 1994, c. 9, sch. 26.

54. Road Traffic (Consequential Provisions) Act 1988.
 sch. 2, repealed in pt.: 1994, c. 9, sch. 26.
 sch. 3, repealed in pt.: *ibid.*; c. 22, sch. 5; c. 23, sch. 15; c. 40, sch. 17.

CAP.

1989

4. Prevention of Terrorism (Temporary Provisions) Act 1989.
continued in force (pt.): order 94/835.
see *R.* v. *Secretary of State for the Home Department, ex p. Gallagher, The Times*, February 16, 1994, C.A.; *R.* v. *Secretary of State for the Home Department, ex p. McQuillan, The Independent,* September 23, 1994, Sedley J.
s. 13A, added: 1994, c. 33, s. 81.
Pt. IV (ss. 14–16), title, substituted: *ibid.*
s. 15, amended: *ibid.,* sch. 10.
Pt. IV (ss. 16A, 16B), added: *ibid.,* s. 82.
ss. 17, 19, amended: *ibid.,* sch. 10.
s. 19A, regs. 94/1758.
s. 20, repealed in pt.: order 93/1813.
s. 27, orders 94/835, 1569.
s. 28, amended: 1994, c. 33, sch. 10, paras. 62, 63.
sch. 4, Act of Sederunt 94/1443.
sch. 5, amended: orders 93/1813; 94/1405; repealed in pt.: order 93/1813.
sch. 7, amended: 1994, c. 33, s. 83.

5. Security Services Act 1989.
ss. 2, 4, sch. 1, amended: 1994, c. 13, sch. 4.
s. 3, repealed: 1994, c. 13, s. 6.

6. Official Secrets Act 1989.
s. 4, amended: 1994, c. 13, sch. 4.

14. Control of Pollution (Amendment) Act 1989.
s. 1, regs. 94/1056.
s. 2, regs. 94/1056, 1137.
s. 3, regs. 94/1137.
s. 8, regs. 94/1056.
s. 9, regs. 94/1056, 1137.

15. Water Act 1989.
s. 107, see *R.* v. *Yorkshire Water Services, The Times,* July 19, 1994, C.A.; *National Rivers Authority* v. *Welsh Development Agency* (1994) 158 J.P. 506, D.C.
ss. 107, 108, see *National Rivers Authority* v. *Yorkshire Water Services, The Times,* November 24, 1993, D.C.
ss. 107, 148, see *National Rivers Authority* v. *Harcross Timber and Building Supplies* [1993] Crim.L.R. 221, D.C.
s. 148, see *Att.-Gen.'s Reference (No. 2 of 1994), The Times,* August 4, 1994, C.A.
sch. 25, repealed in pt. (prosp.): 1994, c. 21, sch. 11, Pt. II.
sch. 25, repealed in pt.(S.): 1994, c. 39, sch. 14.

21. Antarctic Minerals Act 1989.
ss. 1–13, 15–19, sch., repealed: 1994, c. 15, sch.

CAP.

1989—cont.

24. Social Security Act 1989.
Commencement order: 94/1661.
s. 22, see *Morrison* v. *Laidlaw* (O.H.), 1994 S.L.T. 359.
s. 33, order 94/1661.

26. Finance Act 1989.
Commencement orders: 94/87, 2508.
ss. 6 (in pt.), 7–10, repealed: 1994, c. 22, sch. 3.
ss. 11, 12, amended: 1994, c. 5, sch. 2; repealed: 1994, c. 22, sch. 3.
ss. 13, 14 (in pt.), repealed: *ibid.*
s. 15, repealed: 1994, c. 9, sch. 26.
s. 16, repealed in pt.: 1994, c. 22, sch. 3.
ss. 18–26, repealed: 1994, c. 23, sch. 15.
s. 54, regs. 94/1518, 1527.
s. 54, amended: 1994, c. 9, sch. 10.
s. 55, regs. 94/1518.
s. 55, amended: 1994, c. 9, sch. 10; repealed in pt.: *ibid.,* schs. 10, 26.
s. 56, regs. 94/1518.
s. 57, regs. 94/1527.
s. 69, amended: 1994, c. 9, sch. 13.
s. 89, amended: *ibid.,* sch. 16.
s. 92, regs. 94/728.
s. 152, order 94/87.
s. 165, order 94/2508.
s. 168, repealed in pt.: regs. 94/1813.
s. 178, regs. 93/3171; 94/1307, 1567, 2657.
s. 178, amended (prosp.): 1994, c. 9, sch. 19, 2657.
schs. 1, 2, repealed in pt.: 1994, c. 22, sch. 3.
sch. 3, repealed: 1994, c. 23, sch. 15.
sch. 5, amended: 1994, c. 9, sch. 13.
sch. 6, regs. 93/3220, 3221.

29. Electricity Act 1989.
s. 5, orders 94/1070, 1683.
s. 29, regs. 94/533.
s. 43, amended: 1994, c. 40, schs. 2, 4; repealed in pt.: *ibid.,* sch. 17.
s. 57, amended: 1994, c. 21, sch. 9; repealed in pt. (prosp.): *ibid.,* sch. 11, Pt. III.
s. 60, regs. 94/533.
s. 84, order 93/2825.
s. 111, orders 94/1070, 1683.
sch. 5, amended(S.): 1994, c. 39, sch. 13; repealed in pt.: *ibid.,* sch. 14.
sch. 7, see *Singh* v. *Normand,* 1994 S.C.C.R. 247.
sch. 8, amended: 1994, c. 19, schs. 6, 18.
sch. 16, repealed in pt. (prosp.): 1994, c. 21, sch. 11, Pt. II.

32. Fair Employment (Northern Ireland) Act 1989.
s. 25, S.R. 1993 No. 459.

33. Extradition Act 1989.
see *Bartley, Re, The Times,* July 22, 1994, D.C.
s. 2, amended: 1994, c. 33, sch. 9.

1989—cont.

33. Extradition Act 1989—*cont.*

ss. 2, 7, 9, see *Evans, Re; sub nom. R. v. Governor of Brixton Prison, ex p. Evans* [1994] 1 W.L.R. 1006, H.L.

s. 4, order 94/2794.

s. 4, amended: 1994, c. 33, s. 158.

s. 7, see *R. v. Secretary of State for the Home Department, ex p. Schmidt* [1994] 2 All E.R. 784, D.C.

s. 7, amended: 1994, c. 33, s. 158, sch. 9.

ss. 8, 9, amended: *ibid.*, s. 158.

s. 11, see *Schmidt v. Federal Government of Germany; sub nom. R. v. Secretary of State for the Home Department, ex p. Schmidt; sub nom. Schmidt, Re* [1994] 3 All E.R. 65, H.L.

s. 12, see *Schmidt, Re, The Times,* July 1, 1994, H.L.

s. 22, order 94/2794.

s. 22, amended: 1994, c. 33, s. 158; c. 37, sch. 1.

s. 30, order 94/2794.

s. 35, amended: 1994, c. 33, s. 158.

s. 37, order 94/2794.

sch. 1, amended: 1994, c. 33, s. 158; c. 37, sch. 1.

sch. 1, see *Mullin, Re* [1993] Crim.L.R. 390, D.C.

34. Law of Property (Miscellaneous Provisions) Act 1989.

s. 2, see *Pitt v. PHH Asset Management* [1993] 40 EG 149, C.A.; *Payne v. Zafiropoyloy,* October 20, 1993, H.H.J. Coltart, Eastbourne County Ct.; *Commission for New Towns v. Cooper (Great Britain)* [1993] NPC 115, H.H.J. Micklem, Q.C.; *United Bank of Kuwait, The Times,* July 7, 1994, Chadwick J.; *Wright v. Robert Leonard (Developments)* [1994] NPC 49, C.A.

37. Football Spectators Act 1989.

s. 11, order 94/1666.

s. 13, amended: 1994, c. 19, sch. 16.

38. Employment Act 1989.

sch. 3, repealed in pt.: 1994, c. 20, sch. 5.

sch. 6, repealed in pt.: 1994, c. 40, sch. 17.

39. Self-Governing Schools etc. (Scotland) Act 1989.

s. 7, regs. 94/351.

ss. 13, 21, see *Hughes v. Strathclyde Regional Council,* 1994 S.C.L.R. 49.

s. 14, amended: 1994, c. 39, s. 143.

s. 23, regs. 94/351.

ss. 26–28, regs. 94/431.

s. 30, regs. 94/478.

s. 78, regs. 94/431.

s. 80, regs. 94/351.

sch. 7, regs. 94/478.

40. Companies Act 1989.

s. 87, amended: regs. 94/1696.

s. 130, regs. 94/950.

1989—cont.

40. Companies Act 1989—*cont.*

sch. 10, repealed in pt. regs. 94/233; repealed in pt. (prosp.): 1994, c. 21, sch. 11, Pt. IV.

sch. 14, repealed in pt.: 1994, c. 40, schs. 11, 17.

sch. 18, repealed in pt.: 1994, c. 21, sch. 11, Pts. III, IV (prosp.); c. 23, sch. 15.

41. Children Act 1989.

see *Oxfordshire County Council v. M., The Times,* November 2, 1993, C.A.

s. 1, see *H. (A Minor) (Care Proceedings: Child's Wishes), Re* [1993] 1 FLR 440, Thorpe J.; *F. v. Leeds City Council, The Times,* March 10, 1994, C.A.; *B. (A Minor: Contact Order), Re, The Times,* April 8, 1994, Ewbank J.; *M. (A Minor) (Care Order: Threshold Conditions), Re* [1994] 3 W.L.R. 558, H.L.; *K. v. H. (Child Maintenance)* [1993] 2 FLR 61, Sir Stephen Brown P.; *A. v. A. (Children: Shared Residence Order), The Times,* February 23, 1994, C.A.; *P. (Minors) (Interim Order), Re; sub nom. Cheshire County Council v. P.* [1993] 2 FLR 742, C.A.; *North Yorkshire County Council v. G.* [1993] 2 FLR 732, Douglas Brown J.; *M. (A Minor) (Justices' Discretion), Re; sub nom. M. (Child) (Ascertaining Wishes and Feelings), Re* [1993] 2 FLR 706, Booth J.; *M. v. A. (Wardship: Removal from Jurisdiction)* [1993] 2 FLR 715, Bracewell J.; *G. (Minors) (Interim Care Order), Re* [1993] 2 FLR 839, C.A.; *M. (Minors), Re, The Independent,* November 2, 1994, C.A.

s. 2, see *R. v. Northavon District Council, ex p. Smith* [1993] 3 W.L.R. 776, C.A.

s. 3, see *North Yorkshire County Council v. Selby Youth Court Justices* [1994] 1 All E.R. 991, D.C.

s. 4, see *W. v. Ealing London Borough Council; sub nom. W. (Children in Care) (Contact and Parental Responsibility Orders), Re* [1993] 2 FLR 788, C.A.; *A. (Minors) (Parental Responsibility), Re* [1993] Fam. Law 464, H.H.J. Davies.

s. 5, see *A., J. and J. (Minors) (Residence and Guardianship Orders), Re* [1993] Fam. Law 568, Birmingham Family Proceedings Ct.

s. 8, see *Camden London Borough Council v. R. (A Minor) (Blood Transfusion)* 91 L.G.R. 623, Booth J.; *A. (A Minor) (Adoption: Contact Order), Re* [1993] 2 FLR 645, C.A.; *C. (A Minor) (Child Support Agency: Disclosure), Re, The Times,* October 7, 1994, Ewbank J.; *A. (Minors) (Par-*

CAP.

1989—cont.

41. Children Act 1989—cont.

ental Responsibility), Re [1993] Fam. Law 464, H.H.J. Davies; *S. (A Minor) (Stay of Proceedings), Re* [1993] 2 FLR 912, C.A.

ss. 8, 9, 13, see *Matondo (Fleur), Re; Findlay (Cecelia)* v. *Matondo (Kininga) and the Secretary of State for the Home Department* [1993] Imm AR 541, Bracewell J.

ss. 8, 15, see *Pearson* v. *Franklin* [1994] 1 W.L.R. 370, C.A.; *K.* v. *H. (Child Maintenance* [1993] 2 FLR 61, Sir Stephen Brown P.

ss. 9, 10, see *G. (Minors) (Interim Care Order), Re* [1993] 2 FLR 839, C.A.

s. 10, see *A. (A Minor) (Residence Order: Leave to Apply), Re, sub nom. A.* v. *A. and Newham London Borough Council* [1993] 1 FLR 425, Hollings J.; *G.* v. *Kirklees Metropolitan Borough Council* [1993] 1 FLR 805, Booth J.; *S. (Adopted Child: Contact), Re* [1993] 2 F.C.R. 234, Thorpe J.; *North Yorkshire County Council* v. *G.* [1993] 2 FLR 732, Douglas Brown J.

s. 11, see *A.* v. *A. (Children: Shared Residence Order), The Times,* February 23, 1994, C.A.; *G.* v. *G. (Joint Residence Order)* [1993] Fam. Law 615, H.H.J. Lauriston, Q.C. sitting as a deputy judge.

s. 15, see *J.* v. *J. (A Minor: Property Transfer)* [1993] 2 FLR 56, Eastham J.

s. 17, see *X. (Minors)* v. *Bedfordshire County Council, The Times,* November 24, 1993, Turner J.; *R.* v. *Northavon District Council, ex p. Smith* [1994] 3 W.L.R. 403, H.L.; *Oldham Metropolitan Borough Council* v. *E., The Times,* March 16, 1994, C.A.; *D.B. and C.B. (Minors), Re* [1993] 2 F.C.R. 607, C.A.

s. 21, amended: 1994, c. 33, sch. 9.

s. 22, see *S. (J.) (A Minor) (Care or Supervision Order), Re* [1993] Fam. Law 621, H.H.J. Coningsby, Q.C. sitting as a deputy judge.

ss. 23, 26, see *R.* v. *Brent London Borough Council, ex p. Sawyers* (1994) 26 H.L.R. 44, Owen J.

ss. 24, 26, regs. 93/3069.

s. 25, see *C. (A Minor)* v. *Humberside County Council, The Times,* May 24, 1994, Bracewell J.; *B. (A Minor) (Secure Accommodation Order), Re, The Times,* May 27, 1994, C.A.; *W.* v. *North Yorkshire County Council* [1993] 1 F.C.R. 693, Booth J.; *C. (A Minor) (Secure Accommodation Order: Bail), Re, The Times,* July 5,

CAP.

1989—cont.

41. Children Act 1989—cont.

1994, Hollis J.; *Hereford and Worcester County Council* v. *S.* [1993] 2 FLR 360, Connell J.

s. 26, see *X. (Minors)* v. *Bedfordshire County Council, The Times,* November 24, 1993, Turner J.

s. 27, see *R.* v. *Northavon District Council, ex p. Smith* [1994] 3 W.L.R. 403, H.L.

ss. 27, 29, see *R.* v. *Tower Hamlets London Borough, ex p. B.* [1993] 2 FLR 605, C.A.

s. 31, see *T. (A Minor) (Care Order: Conditions), Re, The Times,* May 5, 1994, C.A.; *Essex County Council* v. *R.* (Note) [1994] 2 W.L.R. 407, Thorpe, J.; *Oxfordshire County Council* v. *M.* [1994] 2 W.L.R. 393, C.A.; *B.* v. *Humberside County Council* [1993] 1 F.C.R. 613, Booth J.; *M. (A Minor) (Care Order: Threshold Conditions), Re* [1994] 3 W.L.R. 558, H.L.

ss. 31, 33–35, see *S. (J.) (A Minor) (Care or Supervision Order), Re* [1993] Fam. Law 621, H.H.J. Coningsby, Q.C. sitting as a deputy judge.

ss. 31, 34, see *S. (Children: Interim Care Order), Re* [1993] 2 F.C.R. 475, Johnson J.

ss. 31, 38, see *O. (Minors) (Medical Examination), Re* [1993] 1 FLR 860, Rattee J.; *P. (Minors) (Interim Order), Re; sub nom. Cheshire County Council* v. *P.* [1993] 2 FLR 742, C.A.

s. 32, see *Oldham Metropolitan Borough Council* v. *E., The Times,* March 16, 1994, C.A.

s. 33, see *North Yorkshire County Council* v. *Selby Youth Court Justices* [1994] 1 All E.R. 991, D.C.

s. 34, see *West Glamorgan County Council* v. *P. (No. 2)* [1993] 1 FLR 407, Rattee J.; *Birmingham City Council* v. *H. (A Minor)* [1994] 2 W.L.R. 31, H.L.; *U. (T.) (A Minor) (Care Order Contact), Re* [1993] 2 F.C.R. 565, Douglas Brown J.; *W.* v. *Ealing London Borough Council; sub nom. W. (Children in Care) (Contact and Parental Responsibility Orders), Re* [1993] 2 FLR 788, C.A.; *P. (Minors) (Contact with Children in Care), Re* [1993] Fam. Law 394, Ewbank J.

s. 37, see *H. (A Minor) (Section 37 Direction), Re; sub nom. H. (Child's Circumstances: Direction to Investigate), Re* [1993] 2 FLR 541, Scott Baker J.; *X. (Minors)* v. *Bedfordshire County Council, The Times,* November 24, 1993, Turner J.

1989—cont.

41. Children Act 1989—*cont.*

s. 38, see *Gateshead Metropolitan Borough Council* v. *N.* [1993] 1 FLR 811, Connell J.; *South Glamorgan County Council* v. *B.* [1993] 1 F.C.R. 626, Douglas Brown J.; *C. (Minors) (Care: Procedure), Re* [1993] Fam. Law 288, Johnson J.

s. 41, see *P. (Minors) (Official Solicitor's Costs), Re* [1993] 2 F.C.R. 550, Booth J.

s. 42, see *Manchester City Council* v. *T.* [1994] 2 W.L.R. 594, C.A.

s. 44, see *North Yorkshire County Council* v. *Selby Youth Court Justices* [1994] 1 All E.R. 991, D.C.

s. 45, see *Essex County Council* v. *F.* [1993] 1 FLR 847, Douglas Brown J.

s. 47, see *X. (Minors)* v. *Bedfordshire County Council, The Times,* November 24, 1993, Turner J.

s. 53, amended: 1994, c. 33, s. 22.

ss. 59, 60, 62–64, regs. 93/3069.

s. 71, see *Sutton London Borough Council* v. *Davis* [1994] 2 W.L.R. 721, Wilson J.

s. 84, see *X. (Minors)* v. *Bedfordshire County Council, The Times,* November 24, 1993, Turner J.; *R.* v. *Brent London Borough Council, ex p. Sawyers* (1994) 26 H.L.R. 44, Owen J.

ss. 87A, 87B, added: 1994, c. 40, s. 38.

s. 91, see *F.* v. *Kent County Council* [1993] 1 FLR 432, Sir Stephen Brown P.; *W.* v. *Ealing London Borough Council; sub nom. W. (Children in Care) (Contact and Parental Responsibility Orders), Re* [1993] 2 FLR 788, C.A.

s. 94, see *S.* v. *S. (Children: Financial Provision)* [1993] 1 F.C.R. 805, Thorpe J.

s. 98, see *Kent County Council* v. *K.; sub nom. K. (Minors) (Disclosure of Privileged Material), Re* [1994] 1 W.L.R. 912, Booth J.

s. 100, see *S. (A Minor) (Medical Treatment), Re* [1993] 1 FLR 377, Thorpe J.; *O. (Minors) (Adoption: Injunction), Re; sub nom. O. (Adoption Order: Effect on Injunction, Re* [1993] 2 FLR 737, Ewbank J.; *D.B. and C.B. (Minors), Re* [1993] 2 F.C.R. 607, C.A.

s. 104, regs. 93/3069.

s. 105, amended: 1994, c. 19, sch. 10; repealed in pt.: *ibid.,* schs. 10, 18.

sch. 1, see *Pearson* v. *Franklin* [1994] 1 W.L.R. 370, C.A.; *H.* v. *P. (Illegitimate Child: Capital Provision)* [1993] Fam. Law 515, H.H.J. Collins; *K.* v. *H. (Child Maintenance)* [1993] 2 FLR 61,

1989—cont.

41. Children Act 1989—*cont.*

Sir Stephen Brown P.; *J.* v. *J. (A Minor: Property Transfer)* [1993] 2 FLR 56, Eastham J.

sch. 1, amended: order 94/731.

sch. 2, see *P. (Minors) (Interim Order), Re; sub nom. Cheshire County Council* v. *P.* [1993] 2 FLR 742, C.A.; *X. (Minors)* v. *Bedfordshire County Council, The Times,* November 24, 1993, Turner J.

sch. 3, see *S. (J.) (A Minor) (Case or Supervision Order), Re* [1993] Fam. Law 621, H.H.J. Coningsby, Q.C. sitting as a deputy judge.

sch. 4, regs. 93/3069; 94/1511.

sch. 4, amended: 1994, c. 33, s. 22.

schs. 5, 6, regs. 93/3069; 94/1511.

schs. 5, 6, amended: 1994, c. 33, s. 19; repealed in pt.: *ibid.,* s. 19, sch. 11.

sch. 11, order 94/2164.

42. Local Government and Housing Act 1989.

ss. 2, 4, amended(S.): 1994, c. 39, sch. 13; repealed in pt.(S.): *ibid.,* schs. 13, 14.

s. 5, amended: 1994, c. 29, sch. 4; repealed in pt.: *ibid.,* sch. 9.

s. 5, repealed in pt.(S.): 1994, c. 39, schs. 13, 14.

s. 8, amended(S.): *ibid.,* sch. 13.

s. 9, amended(S.): *ibid.;* repealed in pt.(S.): *ibid.,* schs. 13, 14.

s. 13, regs. 94/901, 961.

s. 13, amended: 1994, c. 29, sch. 4; repealed in pt.: *ibid.,* sch. 9.

s. 14, amended(S.): 1994, c. 39, sch. 13; repealed in pt.(S.): *ibid.,* schs. 13, 14.

s. 18, regs. 94/615, 630(S.).

s. 18, amended: 1994, c. 29, sch. 4.

s. 21, amended: 1994, c. 19, sch. 6; c. 29, sch. 4; repealed in pt.: *ibid.,* sch. 9.

ss. 21, 31, amended(S.): 1994, c. 39, sch. 13.

s. 39, order 93/2875.

s. 39, amended: 1994, c. 19, schs. 6, 16; c. 29, s. 30; regs. 94/2825; repealed in pt.: 1994, c. 29, sch. 9.

s. 48, regs. 93/3054.

s. 49, regs. 94/560.

ss. 59, 61, regs. 93/3054.

s. 67, amended: 1994, c. 19, sch. 6; c. 29, sch. 4; repealed in pt.: *ibid.,* sch. 9.

ss. 74, 79, 80, see *R.* v. *Secretary of State for the Environment, ex p. Enfield London Borough Council, The Times,* May 20, 1994, H.L.

s. 86, amended: regs. 94/2825.

s. 101, amended: 1994, c. 29, sch. 4.

ss. 101, 103, 113, 115, see *R.* v. *Bristol City Council, ex p., Naqvi, The Times,* May 9, 1994, Harrison J.

s. 102, regs. 94/435, 565, 693.

1989—cont.

42. Local Government and Housing Act 1989—*cont.*

s. 109, regs. 94/648.

ss. 114, 127, amended: 1994, c. 19, sch. 8.

s. 137, regs. 94/565, 648, 693.

s. 138, regs. 94/435, 565, 693.

s. 150, regs. 94/1885.

s. 151, amended(S.): 1994, c. 39, sch. 13.

s. 152, regs. 94/1885.

s. 152, amended: 1994, c. 19, sch. 6; repealed in pt.: 1994, c. 29, schs. 4, 9.

s. 152, amended(S.): 1994, c. 39, sch. 13.

s. 155, amended: 1994, c. 29, sch. 4.

s. 155, amended(S.): 1994, c. 39, sch. 13; repealed in pt.(S.): *ibid.*, schs. 13, 14.

s. 157, amended: 1994, c. 29, sch. 4.

ss. 157, 170, amended(S.): 1994, c. 39, sch. 13.

s. 171, order 94/548.

s. 172, regs. 94/1005.

s. 172, amended: 1994, c. 19, sch. 8.

s. 190, regs. 93/3054; 94/435, 553, 565, 615, 630(S.), 648, 693, 961, 1005.

s. 191, regs. 94/435, 693.

sch. 1, amended: 1994, c. 29, sch. 4; repealed in pt.: *ibid.*, sch. 9.

sch. 1, repealed in pt.(S.): 1994, c. 39, sch. 14.

sch. 3, regs. 94/553.

sch. 6, repealed in pt.(S.): 1994, s. 39, sch. 14.

sch. 7, see *Busby* v. *Co-operative Insurance Society* [1994] 06 EG 141, H.H.J. O'Brien.

sch. 11, repealed in pt.(S.): 1994, c. 39, sch. 14.

44. Opticians Act 1989.

s. 10, order 94/729.

s. 24, order 94/70.

s. 34, orders 94/70, 729.

s. 37, repealed in pt.: 1994, c. 23, sch. 15.

45. Prisons (Scotland) Act 1989.

s. 3, modified: 1994, c. 33, s. 110.

s. 7, amended: *ibid.*, s. 103.

s. 8, amended: 1994, c. 39, sch. 13.

s. 9, modified: 1994, c. 33, s. 110.

ss. 11, 13, modified: *ibid.*, ss. 110, 111.

s. 14, amended: 1994, c. 39, sch. 13; repealed in pt.: *ibid.*, schs. 13, 14.

s. 15, modified: 1994, c. 33, s. 110.

s. 16, amended: 1994, c. 39, sch. 13; repealed in pt.: *ibid.*, schs. 13, 14.

s. 19, amended: 1994, c. 33, s. 116, sch. 10.

s. 33, repealed: *ibid.*, s. 116, sch. 11.

s. 33A, added: *ibid.*, s. 116; modified: *ibid.*, ss. 110, 111.

ss. 34, 36, 37, modified: *ibid.*, s. 110.

s. 39, rules 94/1931.

s. 39, amended: 1994, c. 33, ss. 116, 130; modified: *ibid.*, s. 110.

s. 40, modified: *ibid.*, ss. 110, 111.

1989—cont.

45. Prisons (Scotland) Act 1989—*cont.*

s. 41, amended: *ibid.*, s. 153; modified: *ibid.*, ss. 110, 111.

s. 41A, added: *ibid.*, s. 152; modified: *ibid.*, s. 110.

s. 41B, added: *ibid.*, s. 151; modified: *ibid.*, s. 110.

1990

1. Capital Allowances Act 1990.

repealed in pt.: 1994, c. 9, s. 213.

s. 3, amended (prosp.): *ibid.*, repealed in pt. (prosp.): *ibid.*, sch. 26.

s. 4, amended (prosp.): *ibid.*, s. 120, repealed in pt. (prosp.): *ibid.*, sch. 26.

s. 4A, added: *ibid.*, s. 120.

ss. 5, 6, amended: *ibid.*

s. 7, repealed in pt. (prosp.): *ibid.*, sch. 26.

s. 8, amended: *ibid.*, ss. 120, 213 (prosp.); repealed in pt. (prosp.): *ibid.*, s. 213, sch. 26.

ss. 9, 19, 21, 23, repealed in pt. (prosp.): *ibid.*, sch. 26.

s. 24, amended (prosp.); *ibid.*, s. 213; repealed in pt. (prosp.): *ibid.*, sch. 26.

ss. 25, 33, repealed in pt. (prosp.): *ibid.*

ss. 34, 35, amended (prosp.): *ibid.*, s. 213.

ss. 37, 42, 46–49, 61, 62A, 67, 73, 79, repealed in pt. (prosp.): *ibid.*, sch. 26.

s. 83, amended: *ibid.*, s. 117.

s. 85, amended (prosp.): *ibid.*, s. 213; repealed in pt. (prosp.): *ibid.*, sch. 26.

ss. 87, 93, repealed in pt. (prosp.): *ibid.*

s. 98, amended (prosp.): *ibid.*, s. 213.

ss. 99, 101, 121, 124, 126, 128, 129, repealed in pt. (prosp.): *ibid.*, sch. 26.

s. 134, repealed in pt. (prosp.): *ibid.*, s. 213, sch. 26.

s. 137, amended (prosp.): *ibid.*, s. 213.

s. 138, repealed in pt. (prosp.): *ibid.*, sch. 26.

s. 140, substituted (prosp.): *ibid.*, s. 211.

s. 148, repealed in pt. (prosp.): *ibid.*, sch. 26.

s. 158, amended: *ibid.*, s. 119.

s. 159, repealed in pt. (prosp.): *ibid.*, sch. 26.

s. 159A, amended: 1994, c. 23, sch. 4; repealed in pt. (prosp.): 1994, c. 9, sch. 26.

s. 160, substituted (prosp.): *ibid.*, s. 212.

s. 161, amended (prosp.): *ibid.*, ss. 212, 213.

sch. AAI, added: *ibid.*, s. 117.

3. Coal Industry Act 1990.

ss. 1–3, repealed (prosp.): 1994, c. 21, sch. 11, Pt. III.

s. 4, repealed in pt.: *ibid.*, sch. 11, Pt. I; repealed (prosp.): *ibid.*, sch. 11, Pt. II.

1990—cont.

3. Coal Industry Act 1990—*cont.*
s. 5, repealed (prosp.): *ibid.*
s. 6, repealed (prosp.): *ibid.*, sch. 11, Pts. II, III.
5. Criminal Justice (International Co-operation) Act 1990.
s. 4, amended: 1994, c. 33, s. 164.
s. 7, see *R.* v. *Secretary of State for the Home Department, ex p. Propend Finance Pty; R.* v. *Central Criminal Court, ex p. Same; R.* v. *Secretary of State for the Home Department, ex p. Stein Richards & Co. (A Firm); R.* v. *Central Criminal Court, ex p. Same, The Independent,* March 29, 1994, D.C.
s. 9, orders 93/3148, 3155(S.); 94/1640, 1645(S.).
ss. 9, 13, amended: 1994, c. 37, sch. 1.
s. 14, repealed: *ibid.*, sch. 3.
s. 15, amended: *ibid.*, sch. 1; repealed in pt.: *ibid.*, schs. 1, 3.
s. 16, see *Barretto, Re* [1994] 2 W.L.R. 149, C.A.
s. 16, repealed: 1994, c. 37, sch. 3.
s. 23A, regs. 94/1756.
s. 23A, repealed 1994, c. 37, sch. 3.
s. 24, amended: *ibid.*, sch. 1.
s. 25, see *R.* v. *Uxbridge Magistrates' Court, ex p. Henry, The Times,* February 24, 1994, D.C.; *R.* v. *Crawley Justices, ex p. Ohakwe, The Times,* May 26, 1994, D.C.
ss. 25–29, repealed: 1994, c. 37, sch. 3.
ss. 30, 31, repealed in pt.: *ibid.*
s. 32, order 94/1635.
s. 32, amended: 1994, c. 37, sch. 1.
sch. 4, repealed in pt.: *ibid.*, sch. 3.
6. Education (Student Loans) Act 1990.
s. 1, regs. 93/1214, 2915, 3183.
s. 1, amended: 1994, c. 30, sch. 2.
sch. 2, regs. 93/1214, 2915.
8. Town and Country Planning Act 1990.
s. 1, amended: 1994, c. 19, s. 18; repealed in pt.: *ibid.*, s. 18, sch. 18.
s. 2, amended: *ibid.*, s. 19; repealed in pt.: *ibid.*, s. 19, sch. 18.
s. 4, amended: *ibid.*, sch. 6.
s. 10A, added: *ibid.*, s. 20.
ss. 12, 15, 18, amended: *ibid.*, sch. 5.
ss. 23A–23C, added: *ibid.*
s. 26, amended: *ibid.*
s. 27, amended: order 94/1210.
s. 27A, added: 1994, c. 19, sch. 5.
s. 28A, added: *ibid.*, s. 20.
s. 29, substituted: *ibid.*, sch. 5.
s. 54A, see *Devon County Council* v. *Secretary of State for the Environment and Striding* [1993] J.P.L. 40, Hutchison J.; *British Railways Board* v. *Slough Borough Council* [1993] J.P.L.

1990—cont.

8. Town and Country Planning Act 1990—*cont.*
678, Mr. David Widdicombe, Q.C.; *Sainsbury* v. *Secretary of State for the Environment and Bexley London Borough Council* [1993] J.P.L. 651, Mr. Malcolm Spence, Q.C.; *South Lakeland District Council* v. *Secretary of State for the Environment* [1993] J.P.L. 644, Mr. M.G.V. Harrison, Q.C.; *Loup* v. *Secretary of State for the Environment and Salisbury District Council* [1994] NPC 51, Mr. Moriarty Q.C. sitting as a deputy judge; *Spelthorne Borough Council* v. *Secretary of State for the Environment* [1994] EGCS 38, Mr. David Keene, Q.C.
s. 55, see *Bennett* v. *Secretary of State for the Environment and East Devon District Council* [1993] J.P.L. 134, Mr. Lionel Read, Q.C.
s. 55, order 94/724.
ss. 59–61, order 94/678.
s. 62, see *Hallinan* v. *Secretary of State for the Environment and Barnet London Borough Council* [1993] J.P.L. 584, Mr. Malcolm Spence, Q.C.
s. 65, order 94/678.
ss. 70, 106, see *R.* v. *Plymouth City Council; J. Sainsbury, Tesco Stores, ex p. Plymouth and South Devon Cooperative Society* [1993] 36 EG 135, C.A.
s. 74, order 94/678.
s. 78, see *Barnet Meeting Room Trust* v. *Secretary of State for the Environment and Barnet London Borough Council* [1993] J.P.L. 739, Auld J.
s. 106, see *Ealing London Borough Council* v. *Secretary of State for the Environment and Brixton Estates* [1993] J.P.L. 638, Popplewell J.; *Wimpey Homes Holdings* v. *Secretary of State for the Environment and Winchester City Council* [1993] J.P.L. 919, Mr Moriarty, Q.C. sitting as a deputy judge.
ss. 110, 137, 140, amended: 1994, c. 19, sch. 6.
s. 172, see *Newbury District Council* v. *Secretary of State for the Environment* [1993] NPC 112; (1993) 67 P. & C.R. 68, C.A.
s. 179, see *Holmes* v. *Bradford Metropolitan City Council, The Times,* May 19, 1994, D.C.
s. 187, see *Runnymede Borough Council* v. *Harwood, The Times,* February 22, 1994, C.A.; *Croydon London Borough Council* v. *Gladden, The Times,* February 22, 1994, C.A.

1990—cont.

8. Town and Country Planning Act 1990—*cont.*

s. 187A, see *Quinton* v. *North Cornwall District Council*, May 11, 1994; H.H.J. Anthony Thompson, Q.C.; Truro Crown Ct.

s. 188, amended: 1994, c. 19, sch. 6.

s. 191, see *Bailey* v. *Secretary of State for the Environment and Sedgemoor District Council* [1993] J.P.L. 774, Mr Moriarty, Q.C. sitting as a deputy judge.

ss. 220, 221, regs. 94/2351.

s. 224, see *Wycombe District Council* v. *Michael Shanly Group* [1994] 02 EG 112, D.C.; *Merton London Borough Council* v. *Edmonds; sub nom. Edmonds* v. *Merton London Borough Council; Tyndall* v. *Same* (1993) 157 J.P. 1129, D.C.

ss. 226, 227, 231, amended: 1994, c. 19, sch. 4.

ss. 233, 336, see *R.* v. *Thurrock Borough Council, ex p. Blue Circle Industries, The Times,* October 11, 1994, C.A.

s. 247, amended: 1994, c. 19, sch. 6.

s. 252, amended: *ibid.*, schs. 6, 12; c. 29, sch. 4.

s. 253, amended: 1994, c. 19, schs. 6, 12; repealed in pt. (prosp.): 1994, c. 21, schs. 9, 11, Pt. II.

s. 287, see *British Railways Board* v. *Slough Borough Council* [1993] J.P.L. 678, Mr. David Widdicombe, Q.C.

s. 288, see *Mendip District Council* v. *Secretary of State for the Environment and Castle Housing Society* [1993] J.P.L. 434, Schiemann J.; *Camden London Borough Council* v. *Secretary of State for the Environment, NFC Properties and Hyperion Properties* [1993] J.P.L. 466, Mr. Lionel Read, Q.C.; *Sainsbury* v. *Secretary of State for the Environment and Bexley London Borough Council* [1993] J.P.L. 651, Mr. Malcolm Spence, Q.C.; *South Lakeland District Council* v. *Secretary of State for the Environment* [1993] J.P.L. 644, Mr. M.G.V. Harrison, Q.C.; *Bailey* v. *Secretary of State for the Environment and Sedgemoor District Council* [1993] J.P.L. 774, Mr. Moriarty, Q.C. sitting as a deputy judge; *Barnet Meeting Room Trust* v. *Secretary of State for the Environment and Barnet London Borough Council* [1993] J.P.L. 739, Auld J.; *Northavon District Council* v. *Secretary of State for the Environment and the Trustees of the Congregation of Jehovah's Witnesses* [1993] J.P.L. 761, Auld J.;

1990—cont.

8. Town and Country Planning Act 1990—*cont.*

Barnet London Borough Council v. *Secretary of State for the Environment and C.F. Cox, A. Archdeacon and Pointon York Trustees* [1993] J.P.L. 767, Auld J.; *Robson* v. *Secretary of State for the Environment, Tynedale District Council and Troldahl* [1993] J.P.L. 938, Sir Frank Layfield, Q.C. sitting as a deputy judge.

s. 289, see *R.* v. *Secretary of State for Wales, ex p. Rozhon* 91 L.G.R. 667, C.A.; *Leyshon* v. *Secretary of State for Wales and Monmouth Borough Council* [1993] J.P.L. 581, Mr. Malcolm Spence, Q.C.; *Deitsch and Deitsch* v. *Secretary of State for the Environment and Richmond-upon-Thames London Borough Council* [1993] J.P.L. 579, Rose J.; *K.G. Diecasting (Weston)* v. *Secretary of State for the Environment and Woodspring District Council* [1993] J.P.L. 925, Potts J.; *Small and D.W.S. Car Breakers* v. *Secretary of State for the Environment and Chelmsford Borough Council* [1993] J.P.L. 923, Henry J.

s. 303, regs. 93/3170.

s. 307, amended: 1994, c. 19, sch. 6.

ss. 315 (in pt.), 317, repealed (prosp.): 1994, c. 21, schs. 9, 11, Pt. III.

s. 333, regs. 94/267, 678, 724, 2351.

s. 336, see *Powell* v. *Secretary of State for the Environment* [1993] J.P.L. 455, Mr. D. Widdicombe, Q.C.

s. 336, regs. 94/267.

s. 336, amended: 1994, c. 19, sch. 6; repealed in pt.: 1994, c. 29, sch. 9.

sch. 1, repealed in pt.: 1994, c. 19, schs. 6, 18.

sch. 1A, added: *ibid.*, s. 18, sch. 4.

sch. 2, amended: *ibid.*, sch. 5.

sch. 7, regs. 94/267.

sch. 13, amended: 1994, c. 19, sch. 6; repealed in pt. (prosp.): 1994, c. 21, schs. 9, 11, Pt. II.

schs. 14, 16, 17, amended: *ibid.*, sch. 6.

9. Planning (Listed Buildings and Conservation Areas) Act 1990.

s. 2, amended: 1994, c. 19, sch. 6; repealed in pt.: *ibid.*, schs. 6, 18.

ss. 3, 32, 34, 46, 47, 52, 57, 59, amended: *ibid.*, sch. 6.

s. 60, order 94/1771.

s. 72, see *Chorley and James* v. *Secretary of State for the Environment and Basingstoke and Deane Borough Council* [1993] J.P.L. 927, Mr. R. Vandermeer, Q.C. sitting as a deputy judge.

1990—cont.

9. Planning (Listed Buildings and Conservation Areas) Act 1990—cont.
s. 75, order 94/1771.
s. 85, repealed (prosp.): 1994, c. 21, schs. 9, 11, Pt. II.
s. 93, order 94/1771.
sch. 4, amended: 1994, c. 19, sch. 6.

10. Planning (Hazardous Substances) Act 1990.
ss. 1, 3, amended: 1994, c. 19, sch. 6.

11. Planning (Consequential Provisions) Act 1990.
sch. 2, repealed in pt.: 1994, c. 21, sch. 11, Pt. II (prosp.); c. 23, sch. 15.
sch. 3, amended: 1994, c. 19, sch. 6.

16. Food Safety Act 1990.
s. 5, amended: 1994, c. 19, sch. 9; repealed in pt.: *ibid.*, schs. 9, 18.
s. 5, amended(S.): 1994, c. 39, sch. 13.
s. 6, regs. 94/298, 743, 804, 1446, 2465, 2783.
s. 6, amended: 1994, c. 40, schs. 9, 16.
ss. 8, 21, see *Carrick District Council* v. *Taunton Vale Meat Traders* (1994) 158 J.P. 347, D.C.
s. 10, see *Bexley London Borough* v. *Gardiner Merchant* [1993] C.O.D. 383, D.C.
s. 16, regs. 93/2759; 94/298, 804, 960(S.), 1029, 2465, 2544(S.), 2783.
s. 17, regs. 94/298, 734, 1029, 2127, 2465, 2783.
s. 18, regs. 94/2783.
s. 19, regs. 94/1029.
s. 26, regs. 94/298, 734, 743, 804, 960(S.), 1029, 2127, 2783.
s. 27, amended: regs. 94/867; 1994, c. 19, sch. 9.
ss. 27, 28, amended(S.): 1994, c. 39, sch. 13.
s. 37, regs. 94/1029.
s. 42, amended: 1994, c. 40, sch. 16.
s. 48, regs. 93/2759; 94/298, 743, 804, 960(S.), 1029, 2127, 2465, 2783.
s. 49, regs. 94/1029, 2783.
ss. 50, 53, amended: 1994, c. 40, sch. 16.
sch. 1, regs. 94/1029, 2783.

18. Computer Misuse Act 1990.
ss. 10, 17, amended: 1994, c. 33, s. 162.

19. National Health Service and Community Care Act 1990.
Commencement order: 94/2658.
s. 4, see *Porter and Nanayakkara* v. *Queen's Medical Centre (Nottingham University Hospital)* [1993] IRLR 486, Sir Godray le Quesne sitting as a deputy judge.
s. 5, orders 93/2816, 2834–2841, 2848, 2849, 2856, 2896, 3140, 3141; 94/161–185, 194–198, 307–309, 400–404, 482, 745, 797, 827–833, 848–856, 858–863, 1268, 1269, 1534, 1555, 1831, 2522, 2690.

1990—cont.

19. National Health Service and Community Care Act 1990—cont.
s. 6, see *Northern General Hospital National Health Service Trust* v. *Gale* [1994] I.C.R. 426, C.A.
s. 9, order 94/405.
ss. 14–16, regs. 94/640.
s. 46, amended: 1994, c. 19, sch. 10.
s. 61, repealed in pt.: 1994, c. 23, sch. 15.
s. 67, orders 94/2658, 2773.
sch. 1, regs. 94/682, 1262.
sch. 2, orders 93/2633 (corrected by order 94/856), 2816, 2834–2841, 2848, 2849, 2856, 2896, 3140, 3141; 94/161–185, 194, 196–198, 307–309, 400–404, 745, 827–833, 848–856, 858–863.
sch. 8, repealed in pt.: 1994, c. 22, sch. 5; c. 23, sch. 15.

23. Access to Health Records Act 1990.
s. 2, amended: 1994, c. 17, s. 38.
s. 8, Act of Sederunt 94/1443.

27. Social Security Act 1990.
s. 15, regs. 93/2799; 94/637.

29. Finance Act 1990.
ss. 5 (in pt.), 6, repealed: 1994, c. 22, sch. 5.
ss. 10–16, repealed: 1994, c. 23, sch. 15.
ss. 66, 67 (in pt.), 73, 75, repealed: 1994, c. 9, sch. 26.
s. 128, orders 93/3191, 3229; 94/1974; regs. 94/1265.
sch. 2, repealed in pt.: 1994, c. 22, sch. 5.

35. Enterprise and New Towns (Scotland) Act 1990.
ss. 21, 36, amended: 1994, c. 39, sch. 13.
s. 23, order 94/1976.

36. Contracts (Applicable) Law Act 1990.
s. 1, amended: order 94/1900.
s. 2, amended and repealed in pt.: *ibid.*
s. 4, order 94/1900.
sch. 1, amended and repealed in pt.: *ibid.*
sch. 3A, added: *ibid.*

37. Human Fertilisation and Embryology Act 1990.
Commencement order: 94/1776.
s. 3, order 94/2618.
s. 3A, added: 1994, c. 33, s. 156.
s. 30, regs. 94/2804.
s. 41, amended: 1994, c. 33, s. 156.
s. 45, regs. 94/2767, 2804.
s. 49, order 94/1776.

40. Law Reform (Miscellaneous Provisions) (Scotland) Act 1990.
s. 6, amended: 1994, c. 39, sch. 13.
s. 9, see *Smart, Petr.*, 1993 S.C.L.R. 958; *Mining Institute of Scotland Benevolent Fund Trs., Petrs.* (O.H.), 1994 S.L.T. 785.
s. 19, amended: regs. 94/1696.

CAP.

1990—cont.

40. Law Reform (Miscellaneous Provisions) (Scotland) Act 1990—*cont.*

s. 47, see *Cindarella's Rockafella's* v. *Glasgow District Licensing Board*, 1994 S.C.L.R. 591; *Bass Taverns* v. *Clydebank District Licensing Board* (O.H.), 1994 S.C.L.R. 601.

sch. 6, amended: 1994, c. 39, sch. 13.

sch. 8, repealed in pt.: 1994, c. 15, sch.

41. Courts and Legal Services Act 1990.

s. 2, see *Pharma Plast A/S* v. *Bard* [1993] F.S.R. 686, Patents County Ct.

s. 10, repealed in pt.: 1994, c. 29, sch. 9, Pt. II.

ss. 37, 38, amended: regs. 94/1696.

s. 41, see *British Waterways Board* v. *Norman* (1993) 26 H.L.R. 232, D.C.

ss. 113, 119, regs. 94/1380.

sch. 10, repealed in pt.: 1994, c. 23, sch. 15; c. 29, sch. 9, Pt. I.

sch. 18, repealed in pt.: 1994, c. 29, sch. 9, Pt. II.

42. Broadcasting Act 1990.

see *R.* v. *The Radio Authority, ex p. Guardian Media Group; R.* v. *Same, ex p. Trans World Communications, The Times*, November 11, 1994, Schiemann J.

s. 43, order 93/3046; 94/454.

s. 79, order 93/3047; 94/453.

ss. 143, 150, see *R.* v. *Broadcasting Complaints Commission, ex p. B.B.C., The Times*, May 26, 1994, Laws J.

s. 194, order 94/2540.

s. 204, order 94/1064.

sch. 2, order 93/3199.

sch. 2, amended: 1994, c. 19, sch. 16; repealed in pt.: *ibid.*, schs. 16, 18.

sch. 2, amended(S.): 1994, c. 39, sch. 13.

sch. 20, repealed in pt.: 1994, c. 23, sch. 15; c. 33, sch. 11.

43. Environmental Protection Act 1990.

Commencement orders: 94/780, 1096, 2487, 2854.

see *R.* v. *Folkestone Magistrates' Court, ex p. Kibble* [1993] Crim.L.R. 704, D.C.

s. 4, amended: 1994, c. 19, sch. 9; c. 39, sch. 13(S.).

s. 29, regs. 94/1056.

s. 30, amended: 1994, c. 19, sch. 9; repealed in pt.: *ibid.*, schs. 9, 18.

s. 30, amended(S.): 1994, c. 39, sch. 13.

s. 33, regs. 94/1056.

s. 34, amended: 1994, c. 40, s. 33.

ss. 35, 36, 39, regs. 94/1056.

ss. 36, 39, amended(S.): 1994, c. 39, sch. 13; repealed in pt.(S.): *ibid.*, schs. 13, 14.

ss. 40, 43, 45, regs. 94/1056.

s. 45, amended(S.): 1994, c. 39, sch. 13; repealed in pt.: *ibid.*, schs. 13, 14.

CAP.

1990—cont.

43. Environmental Protection Act 1990—*cont.*

s. 50, regs. 94/1056.

s. 50, repealed in pt.: 1994, c. 19, schs. 9, 18.

s. 50, repealed in pt.(S.): 1994, c. 39, sch. 14.

s. 52, regs. 94/522.

s. 53, amended(S.): 1994, c. 39, sch. 13; repealed in pt.: *ibid.*, schs. 13, 14.

s. 54, regs. 94/1056.

s. 54, amended(S.): 1994, c. 39, sch. 13; repealed in pt.: *ibid.*, schs. 13, 14.

s. 58, see *Aitken* v. *South Hams District Council* [1994] 3 W.L.R. 333, H.L.

s. 64, regs. 94/1056.

s. 74, regs. 94/1056, 1137.

s. 75, regs. 94/1056.

s. 79, see *Network Housing Association* v. *Westminster City Council, The Times*, November 8, 1994, D.C.

s. 79, amended: 1994, c. 19, sch. 9; c. 22, sch. 3.

ss. 79, 82, see *Botross* v. *Hammersmith and Fulham London Borough Council, The Times*, November 7, 1994, D.C.

s. 82, see *British Waterways Board* v. *Norman* (1993) 26 H.L.R. 232, D.C.

s. 86, amended: 1994, c. 19, sch. 9.

s. 86, amended(S.): 1994, c. 39, sch. 13.

s. 88, amended: 1994, c. 19, schs. 6, 9; repealed in pt.: *ibid.*, schs. 6, 18.

s. 88, amended(S.): 1994, c. 39, sch. 13.

ss. 90, 92, 93, 95, 99, amended: 1994, c. 19, sch. 9.

ss. 90, 92, 93, 95, 99, amended(S.): 1994, c. 39, sch. 13.

s. 140, regs. 93/199.

ss. 143, 149, amended: 1994, c. 19, sch. 9; repealed in pt.: *ibid.*, schs. 9, 18.

s. 149, amended(S.): 1994, c. 39, sch. 13.

s. 156, regs. 94/1056.

s. 164, orders 94/780, 1096, 2487, 2854.

sch. 1, regs. 94/1329.

sch. 15, repealed in pt.: 1994, c. 40, sch. 17.

44. Caldey Island Act 1990.

s. 1, amended: 1994, c. 19, sch. 16; repealed in pt.: *ibid.*, schs. 16, 18.

ss. 2, 4 (in pt.), repealed: *ibid.*

1991

13. War Crimes Act 1991.

s. 1, sch. 1, repealed in pt.: 1994, c. 33, schs. 4, 11.

21. Disability Living Allowance and Disability Working Allowance Act 1991.

sch. 2, repealed in pt.: 1994, c. 22, sch. 5; c. 23, sch. 15.

1991—cont.

22. New Roads and Street Works Act 1991.
s. 13, amended: 1994, c. 22, sch. 3.
s. 27, amended(S.): 1994, c. 39, s. 148.
s. 36, amended: 1994, c. 22, sch. 3.
s. 94, amended: 1994, c. 19, sch. 7.
ss. 108, 109, amended(S.): 1994, c. 39, sch. 13.
s. 112, amended(S.): *ibid.*, s. 149.
ss. 117, 148, 149, amended(S.): *ibid.*, sch. 13.
s. 153, repealed in pt.(S.): *ibid.*, schs. 13, 14.
s. 164, amended(S.): *ibid.*, sch. 3.
sch. 2, amended: 1994, c. 19, sch. 7.
sch. 6, amended(S.): 1994, c. 39, sch. 3.

23. Children and Young Persons (Protection from Tobacco) Act 1991.
s. 6, amended(S.): 1994, c. 39, sch. 13.

24. Northern Ireland (Emergency Provisions) Act 1991.
s. 48, amended: 1994, c. 33, sch. 9.
s. 55A, regs. 94/1760.
s. 61, order 93/2788.
s. 69, order 94/1569.
s. 71, order 94/764.
sch. 1, amended: order 94/570.
sch. 5, amended: regs. 94/1696; 1994, c. 33, s. 83.
sch. 7, repealed in pt.: *ibid.*, sch. 11.

28. National Heritage (Scotland) Act 1991.
s. 20, amended: 1994, c. 39, sch. 13.
ss. 22, 24, amended: *ibid.*, sch. 13; repealed in pt.: *ibid.*, schs. 13, 14.
sch. 7, repealed in pt.: *ibid.*, schs. 13, 14.
sch. 8, amended: *ibid.*, sch. 13; repealed in pt.: *ibid.*, schs. 13, 14.

31. Finance Act 1991.
ss. 4 (in pt.), 8–10, repealed: 1994, c. 22, sch. 5.
ss. 13–18, repealed: 1994, c. 23, sch. 15.
ss. 27 (in pt.) 31, repealed: 1994, c. 9, sch. 26.
s. 32, regs. 93/3118.
s. 32, amended: 1994, c. 9, s. 84; repealed in pt.: *ibid.*, sch. 26.
s. 72, repealed in pt. (prosp.): *ibid.*
s. 110, repealed in pt.: *ibid.*
sch. 3, repealed in pt.: *ibid.*, Pt. I (1)(3); c. 22, sch. 5.
sch. 6, repealed in pt.: 1994, c. 9, sch. 26.

34. Planning and Compensation Act 1991.
Commencement order: 94/398.
s. 67, see *Cooperative Insurance Society* v. *Hastings Borough Council* 91 L.G.R. 608, Vinelott J.
s. 84, order 94/398.
sch. 13, repealed in pt.(S.): 1994, c. 39, sch. 14.

40. Road Traffic Act 1991.
Commencement orders: 93/2803, 3238; 94/81, 1482, 1484, 1487–1502, 1504–1510.

1991—cont.

40. Road Traffic Act 1991—*cont.*
ss. 1, 24, see *Fraser* v. *H.M. Advocate*, 1994 S.C.C.R. 334.
s. 47, amended: 1994, c. 19, sch. 7.
s. 76, orders 93/2804, 3239; 94/82, 689, 1376–1378, 1487–1502, 1504–1510, 1613.
s. 77, orders 93/2804, 3239; 94/689, 1376–1378, 1487–1502, 1504–1510, 1613.
ss. 79, 82, amended: 1994, c. 22, sch. 3.
s. 84, orders 93/2803, 3238; 94/81, 1482, 1484.
sch. 3, amended: 1994, c. 19, sch. 7; repealed in pt.: *ibid.*, schs. 7, 18.
sch. 3, amended(S.): 1994, c. 39, sch. 13.
sch. 4, repealed in pt.: 1994, c. 22, sch. 5.

45. Coal Mining Subsidence Act 1991.
s. 1, amended (prosp.): 1994, c. 21, s. 42.
s. 8, amended (prosp.): *ibid.*, sch. 6.
s. 10, repealed in pt. (prosp.): *ibid.*, schs. 6, 11, Pt. II.
s. 16, amended (prosp.): *ibid.*, sch. 6; repealed in pt. (prosp.): *ibid.*, schs. 6, 11, Pt. II.
s. 17, repealed in pt. (prosp.): *ibid.*, schs. 6, 11, Pt. II.
s. 25, regs. 94/2564.
s. 27, amended: 1994, c. 21, sch. 9.
s. 29, regs. 94/2564.
s. 30, amended: 1994, c. 21, sch. 9; repealed in pt. (prosp.): *ibid.*, sch. 11, Pt. II.
s. 31, repealed in pt. (prosp.): *ibid.*
s. 33, repealed in pt. (prosp.): *ibid.*, sch. 6.
ss. 34, 35, repealed (prosp.): *ibid.*, s. 42, sch. 11, Pt. II.
ss. 37, 38, amended (prosp.): *ibid.*
s. 39, repealed (prosp.): *ibid.*, sch. 11, Pt. II.
ss. 40–42, amended (prosp.): *ibid.*, sch. 6.
s. 43, repealed (prosp.): *ibid.*, sch. 11, Pt. II.
s. 44, amended (prosp.): *ibid.*, sch. 6.
s. 45, repealed (prosp.): *ibid.*, sch. 11, Pt. II.
s. 46, regs. 94/2565.
s. 46, amended: 1994, c. 21, s. 45, sch. 6 (prosp.); repealed in pt. (prosp.): *ibid.*, sch. 11, Pt. II.
s. 47, amended: 1994, c. 19, sch. 16; c. 21, s. 45, sch. 6 (prosp.); repealed in pt.: 1994, c. 19, schs. 16, 18; (prosp.) c. 21, sch. 11, Pt. II.
s. 47, amended(S.): 1994, c. 39, sch. 13.
s. 48, repealed (prosp.): *ibid.*
s. 49, amended (prosp.): *ibid.*, sch. 6; repealed in pt. (prosp.): *ibid.*, sch. 11, Pt. III.
s. 50, regs. 94/2563–2566.

1991—cont.

45. Coal Mining Subsidence Act 1991—*cont.*

s. 51, substituted: 1994, c. 21, sch. 9.

sch. 2, repealed in pt. (prosp.): *ibid.*, schs. 6, 11, Pt. II.

schs. 6, 7, amended: *ibid.*, sch. 9.

48. Child Support Act 1991.

see *Crozier* v. *Crozier* [1994] 2 W.L.R. 444, Booth J.

ss. 16, 17, 32, 35, 47, 51, regs. 94/227.

s. 50, see *C. (A Minor) (Child Support Agency: Disclosure), Re, The Times,* October 7, 1994, Ewbank J.

s. 52, regs. 94/227; order 94/731.

s. 58, order 94/731.

sch. 1, regs. 94/227.

49. School Teachers' Pay and Conditions Act 1991.

s. 1, see *Wandsworth London Borough Council* v. *National Association of Schoolmasters/Union of Women Teachers* [1993] IRLR 344, C.A.

ss. 2, 5, orders 94/910, 1673.

52. Ports Act 1991.

s. 7, orders 93/2916(S.); 94/818.

53. Criminal Justice Act 1991.

s. 1, see *R.* v. *Dorries and Dorries* (1993) 14 Cr.App.R.(S.) 608, C.A.; *R.* v. *Moriarty (Terence Patrick)* (1993) 14 Cr.App.R.(S.) 575, C.A.; *R.* v. *Ailie (Mark Clayton)* (1993) 14 Cr.App.R.(S.) 598, C.A.; *R.* v. *Hill (Andrew Paul)* (1993) 14 Cr.App.R.(S.) 556, C.A.; *R.* v. *Corkhill (Neil Robert)* (1993) 14 Cr.App.R.(S.) 543, C.A.; *R.* v. *McQuillan* [1993] Crim.L.R. 893, C.A.

s. 2, see *R.* v. *Mansell, The Times,* February 22, 1994, C.A.; *R.* v. *Oudkerk, The Times,* June 9, 1994, C.A.; *R.* v. *O'Brien, The Times,* July 21, 1994, C.A.; *R.* v. *Joszko, The Times,* August 11, 1994, C.A.; *R.* v. *Thomas (Ian), The Times,* November 8, 1994, C.A.

s. 3, amended: 1994, c. 33, sch. 9; repealed in pt.: *ibid.*, schs. 9, 11.

s. 5, see *R.* v. *French* [1993] Crim. L.R. 893, C.A.

ss. 7, 12, 18, amended: 1994, c. 33, sch. 9.

s. 20, amended: *ibid.*, schs. 9, 10.

s. 20A, added: *ibid.*, sch. 9.

s. 24, amended: 1994, c. 18, sch. 1; c. 22, sch. 3; c. 33, s. 47.

s. 25, see *R.* v. *Manchester Magistrates' Court, ex p. Kaymanesh* (1994) 158 J.P. 401, D.C.

s. 29, see *R.* v. *Kyle (Joseph)* (1993) 14 Cr.App.R.(S.) 613 C.A.

s. 29, amended: 1994, c. 33, sch. 9.

s. 31, see *R.* v. *Joszko, The Times,* August 11, 1994, C.A.

1991—cont.

53. Criminal Justice Act 1991—*cont.*

s. 31, amended: 1994, c. 33, schs. 9, 10.

s. 32, amended: *ibid.*, s. 149.

s. 34, see *R.* v. *Secretary of State for the Home Department, ex p. McCartney, The Times,* May 25, 1994, C.A.; *R.* v. *Parole Board, ex p. Lodomez, The Times,* August 3, 1994, D.C.; *R.* v. *Sanderson (Nicholas)* [1993] Crim.L.R. 983, C.A.

s. 34, amended: 1994, c. 33, sch. 9.

ss. 34, 35, see *R.* v. *Secretary of State for the Home Office, ex p. T.; R.* v. *Same, ex p. H.; R.* v. *Same, ex p. Hickey* [1994] 2 W.L.R. 190, D.C.

s. 39, see *R.* v. *Secretary of State for the Home Department, ex p. MacNeill, The Times,* May 26, 1994, D.C.

s. 40, amended: 1994, c. 33, schs. 9, 10.

s. 47, amended: *ibid.*, sch. 9.

s. 50, amended: *ibid.*, s. 150; repealed in pt.: *ibid.*, s. 150, sch. 11.

s. 52, repealed in pt.: *ibid.*, sch. 11.

s. 53, amended: *ibid.*, schs. 4, 9.

s. 57, repealed in pt.: *ibid.*, schs. 9, 11.

s. 58, amended: *ibid.*, sch. 9.

s. 61, amended: *ibid.*, s. 19.

s. 61A, added: *ibid.*, s. 21.

s. 64, repealed: *ibid.*, sch. 11.

s. 76, amended: 1994, c. 29, sch. 8; repealed in pt.: *ibid.*, schs. 8, 9.

s. 77, amended: *ibid.*, sch. 8.

s. 79, repealed: *ibid.*, sch. 9.

s. 80, amended: 1994, c. 33, s. 93.

s. 82, amended: *ibid.*, s. 94.

s. 83, substituted: *ibid.*, s. 95.

s. 84, substituted: *ibid.*, s. 96.

s. 85, amended: *ibid.*, ss. 97, 101.

s. 87, amended: *ibid.*, s. 97, sch. 10.

s. 88, amended: *ibid.*, s. 101.

s. 88A, added: *ibid.*, s. 99.

ss. 89–91, amended: *ibid.*, s. 101.

s. 92, amended: *ibid.*, ss. 93, 98, 101.

s. 93, repealed in pt.: 1994, c. 29, sch. 9.

s. 102, amended: 1994, c. 33, s. 101.

sch. 3, amended(S.): 1994, c. 39, sch. 13.

sch. 5, substituted: 1993, c. 33, sch. 10.

sch. 6, amended: *ibid.*, schs. 4, 10.

sch. 10, amended: *ibid.*, s. 101.

sch. 11, repealed in pt.: 1994, c. 22, sch. 5; c. 29, sch. 9.

sch. 12, see *R.* v. *Secretary of State for the Home Department, ex p. Chapman, The Times,* October 25, 1994, D.C.; *R.* v. *Secretary of State for the Home Office, ex p. T.; R.* v. *Same, ex p. H; R.* v. *Same, ex p. Hickey* [1994] 2 W.L.R. 190, D.C.

sch. 12, amended: 1994, c. 33, sch. 9.

54. Deer Act 1991.

s. 11, amended: 1994, c. 19, sch. 16.

1991—cont.

55. Agricultural Holdings (Scotland) Act 1991.
s. 13, see *Broadland Properties Estates* v. *Mann*, 1994 S.L.T.(Land Ct.) 7.
ss. 21, 22, see *Kildrummy (Jersey)* v. *Calder* (O.H.), 1994 S.L.T. 888.

56. Water Industry Act 1991.
s. 31, amended: 1994, c. 40, sch. 2.
s. 33, regs. 93/73; amended: *ibid.*
ss. 191, 219, amended: 1994, c. 19, sch. 11.
sch. 2, order 94/1650.
sch. 13, amended: 1994, c. 21, sch. 9.

57. Water Resources Act 1991.
ss. 10, 13, amended: 1994, c. 19, sch. 11.
s. 82, regs. 94/1057.
s. 85, see *Taylor Woodrow Property Management* v. *National Rivers Authority, The Times*, July 4, 1994, D.C.; *R.* v. *CPC (U.K.), The Times*, August 4, 1994, C.A.
s. 94, order 93/3198.
ss. 140, 167, 184, amended: 1994, c. 19, sch. 11.
s. 209, see *Att.-Gen.'s Reference (No. 2 of 1994), The Times*, August 4, 1994, C.A.
s. 219, regs. 94/1057.
s. 221, amended: 1994, c. 19, sch. 11.
sch. 3, order 94/245.
schs. 8, 14–16, 19, amended: 1994, c. 19, sch. 11.
schs. 22, 24, amended: 1994, c. 21, sch. 9.

58. Statutory Water Companies Act 1991.
ss. 12, 14, order 94/2205.

59. Land Drainage Act 1991.
s. 3, orders 94/310, 723, 1411.
s. 10, amended: 1994, c. 19, sch. 11.
ss. 12, 13, repealed: 1994, c. 25, s. 2.
ss. 14–16, 18, 20, 55, 57, 58, amended: 1994, c. 19, sch. 11.
Pt. IVA (ss. 61A–61E), added: 1994, c. 25, s. 1.
ss. 62, 66, 72, schs. 2–4, amended: 1994, c. 19, sch. 11.
sch. 6, amended: 1994, c. 21, sch. 9.

62. Armed Forces Act 1991.
s. 1, order 94/1903.

65. Dangerous Dogs Act 1991.
see *D.P.P.* v. *Kellett, The Times*, July 14, 1994, D.C.; *R.* v. *Metropolitan Police and the Index of Exempted Dogs, ex p. Wheeler* [1993] Crim.L.R. 942, D.C.
s. 1, see *R.* v. *Knightsbridge Crown Court, ex p. Dunne; Brock* v. *D.P.P.* [1993] 4 All E.R. 491, D.C.
ss. 1, 10, see *Bates* v. *D.P.P.* (1993) 157 J.P. 1004, D.C.
s. 3, see *W.* v. *C.I.C.B.*, August 10, 1993; C.I.C.B.; Plymouth.
ss. 3, 4, see *Stewart* v. *Donnelly*, 1994 S.C.C.R. 545.

1991—cont.

65. Dangerous Dogs Act 1991—*cont.*
ss. 3, 10, see *McGeachy* v. *Normand*, 1993 S.C.C.R. 951; *D.P.P.* v. *Fellowes* [1993] Crim.L.R. 523, D.C.

68. Consolidated Fund (No. 3) Act 1991.
repealed: 1994, c. 24, sch. (C.).

1992

1. Consolidated Fund Act 1992.
repealed: 1994, c. 24, sch. (C.).

3. Severn Bridges Act 1992.
s. 8, amended: 1994, c. 22, sch. 3.
s. 9, order 93/3135.
s. 21, regs. 94/1777.
s. 39, sch. 2, amended: 1994, c. 19, sch. 7.
sch. 3, amended: *ibid.*; repealed in pt.: *ibid.*, schs. 7, 18.

4. Social Security Contributions and Benefits Act 1992.
see *Social Security Decision No. R(I) 3/93.*
s. 1, regs. 94/667, 2299.
s. 2, regs. 94/726.
s. 3, regs. 93/2925; 94/2194.
s. 4, repealed in pt.: 1994, c. 18, schs. 1, 2.
s. 5, regs. 94/563.
s. 7, regs. 94/726.
s. 8, amended: 1994, c. 1, s. 1.
s. 9, amended: order 94/544.
ss. 10, regs. 94/667; amended: *ibid.*
ss. 11, 13, 15, amended: order 94/544.
s. 16, amended (prosp.): 1994, c. 9, sch. 19.
s. 20, see *Fullwood* v. *Chesterfield Borough Council* (1993) 26 H.L.R. 126, C.A.
s. 20, amended: 1994, c. 18, sch. 1.
s. 21, regs. 94/704.
s. 21, amended: 1994, c. 18, sch. 1.
s. 22, regs. 94/1837.
s. 25, amended: 1994, c. 18, sch. 1.
ss. 25A, 25B, added: *ibid.*
s. 28, amended(S.): 1994, c. 39, sch. 13.
s. 30, amended: 1994, c. 18, sch. 1.
s. 30A, added: *ibid.*, s. 1.
s. 30B, added: *ibid.*, s. 2.
ss. 30B–30E, regs. 94/2946.
ss. 30C–30E, added: 1994, c. 18, s. 3.
ss. 31–34, repealed: *ibid.*, schs. 1, 2.
s. 35, regs. 94/1367, 1882.
s. 35, amended: regs. 94/1230.
ss. 40–42, substituted: 1994, c. 18, sch. 1.
s. 44, amended: regs. 94/542; 1994, c. 18, sch. 1.
s. 46, repealed in pt.: *ibid.*, schs. 1, 2.
s. 47, amended: *ibid.*, sch. 1.
s. 57, regs. 94/559, 1101.
s. 57, repealed: 1994, c. 18, schs. 1, 2.
s. 58, amended: 1994, c. 19, sch. 16; repealed: 1994, c. 18, schs. 1, 2.
s. 58, amended(S.): 1994, c. 39, sch. 13.

1992—cont.

4. Social Security Contributions and Benefits Act 1992—*cont.*

s. 59, repealed: 1994, c. 18, schs. 1, 2.

s. 61, amended: 1994, c. 18, sch. 1; repealed in pt.: *ibid.*, schs. 1, 2.

s. 64, see *Mattinson* v. *Secretary of State for Social Security, The Times,* April 28, 1994, H.L.

s. 67, regs. 94/1779.

s. 68, regs. 94/1101.

s. 68, amended: 1994, c. 18, s. 9, sch. 1; regs. 94/2556; repealed in pt.: 1994, c. 18, schs. 1, 2; regs. 94/2556.

s. 70, amended and repealed in pt.: regs. 94/2556.

ss. 72, 73, regs. 94/1779.

s. 80, amended: order 94/542; 1994, c. 18, s. 2.

s. 82, amended: *ibid.*, sch. 1; repealed in pt.: *ibid.*, schs. 1, 2.

s. 83, repealed in pt.: *ibid.*

s. 84, amended: *ibid.*, sch. 1.

ss. 85 (in pt.), 86, repealed: *ibid.*, schs. 1, 2.

s. 86A, added: *ibid.*, s. 2.

s. 87, amended: *ibid.*, sch. 1; repealed in pt.: *ibid.*, schs. 1, 2.

s. 88, substituted: *ibid.*, sch. 1.

ss. 89, 91, 93, amended: *ibid.*

s. 102, repealed: *ibid.*, schs. 1, 2.

ss. 108, 109, regs. 94/2343.

s. 113, regs. 94/268, 559, 1832.

s. 119, regs. 94/563, 1367.

s. 122, regs. 93/2925; 94/559, 667, 726, 1779, 1837, 2194, 2299, 2343, 2946.

s. 122, amended: 1994, c. 18, sch. 1.

s. 123, regs. 94/527, 578, 1003, 1608, 1924, 2137, 2139.

s. 123, amended(S.): 1994, c. 39, sch. 13.

ss. 123, 130, see *R.* v. *Haringey London Borough Council, ex p. Ayub (Azad)* (1992) (1993) 25 H.L.R. 566, Schiemann J.

s. 124, regs. 94/527.

s. 126, amended: order 94/542; repealed in pt.: 1994, c. 18, schs. 1, 2.

ss. 128, 129, regs. 94/2139.

s. 129, amended: 1994, c. 18, s. 10, sch. 1.

s. 130, regs. 94/578, 1003, 1608.

s. 130, amended(S.): 1994, c. 39, sch. 13.

s. 131, regs. 94/470, 1807, 2137.

s. 135, regs. 94/527, 1003, 1004, 1807, 2137, 2139.

s. 136, regs. 94/527, 578, 1608, 1924, 2137, 2139.

s. 137, regs. 94/470, 527, 578, 1003, 1004, 1608, 1807, 1924, 2137.

s. 137, repealed in pt.(S.): 1994, c. 39, sch. 13.

s. 138, regs. 94/506.

ss. 150, 151, amended: 1994, c. 18, sch. 1.

1992—cont.

4. Social Security Contributions and Benefits Act 1992—*cont.*

s. 153, regs. 94/1367.

s. 155, amended: 1994, c. 18, s. 8.

s. 157, order 94/562.

s. 157, amended: orders 94/542, 562; 1994, c. 18, s. 8.

s. 158, regs. 94/561, 730.

s. 158, amended: 1994, c. 18, s. 8; repealed in pt.: 1994, c. 2, s. 1.

s. 159A, added: *ibid.*, s. 3.

s. 163, regs. 94/561, 730.

s. 163, amended: 1994, c. 18, sch. 1; repealed in pt.: *ibid.*, schs. 1, 2.

s. 164, repealed in pt.: regs. 94/1230.

ss. 164, 165, regs. 94/1367.

s. 165, amended: regs. 94/1230.

s. 166, regs. 94/1367.

s. 166, amended and repealed in pt.: regs. 94/1230.

s. 167, regs. 94/592, 1882.

s. 167, amended: regs. 94/1230.

s. 171, regs. 94/592, 1367, 1882.

ss. 171A–171C, added: 1994, c. 18, s. 5.

ss. 171D–171G, added: *ibid.*, s. 6.

s. 175, regs. 93/2925; 94/268, 470, 506, 527, 559, 561, 563, 578, 592, 667, 704, 726; order 94/562, 1003, 1004, 1101, 1367, 1608, 1779, 1807, 1832, 1837, 1882, 1924, 2004, 2137, 2139, 2194, 2299, 2343, 2946.

s. 175, amended: 1994, c. 18, sch. 1.

s. 176, amended: 1994, c. 2, s. 3; c. 18, sch. 1; repealed in pt.: *ibid.*, schs. 1, 2.

sch. 1, regs. 94/667.

sch. 2, amended and repealed in pt.: 1994, c. 1, s. 3.

sch. 3, regs. 94/704.

sch. 3, amended: regs. 94/1230; 1994, c. 18, ss. 1, 3, sch. 1.

sch. 4, amended: order 94/542; regs. 94/1230; 1994, c. 18, s. 2, sch. 1; repealed in pt.: *ibid.*, schs. 1, 2.

sch. 5, amended: *ibid.*, sch. 1.

sch. 6, repealed in pt.: regs. 94/2556.

sch. 7, amended: 1994, c. 18, sch. 1; repealed in pt.: *ibid.*, schs. 1, 2.

sch. 8, scheme 94/671.

sch. 8, amended: order 94/542; 1994, c. 18, sch. 1.

sch. 11, regs. 94/1367.

sch. 11, amended: 1994, c. 2, s. 1; c. 18, sch. 1; repealed in pt.: *ibid.*, schs. 1, 2.

schs. 12, 13, amended: *ibid.*, sch. 1.

5. Social Security Administration Act 1992.

s. 5, regs. 94/2137, 2139.

s. 15A, amended: 1994, c. 19, sch. 8.

s. 15A, amended(S.): 1994, c. 39, sch. 13; repealed in pt.(S.): *ibid.*, schs. 13, 14.

ss. 20, 25, 27, amended: 1994, c. 18, sch. 1.

1992—cont.

5. Social Security Administration Act 1992—*cont.*

ss. 27, 33, regs. 94/2139.

s. 36, see *Social Security Decision No. R(IS)* 11/93.

s. 46, regs. 94/1082.

s. 54, amended: 1994, c. 40, sch. 16.

s. 59, regs. 94/1082.

s. 61A, added: 1994, c. 18, s. 6.

s. 63, regs. 94/578, 2137.

s. 73, regs. 94/1779.

s. 75, see *R.* v. *Haringey London Borough Council, ex p. Ayub (Azad)* (1992) (1993) 25 H.L.R. 566, Schiemann J.

ss. 76, 77, amended(S.): 1994, c. 39, sch. 13.

s. 81, regs. 94/730.

s. 81, repealed in pt.: 1994, c. 2, s. 1.

Pt. IV (ss. 81–104), see *R. (Social Security Claimant), Re* [1993] P.I.Q.R. P252, M.H. Johnson, Commissioner.

s. 91, regs. 94/730.

s. 123, amended: 1994, c. 40, sch. 16.

ss. 127, 128, regs. 94/578, 1925, 2137.

ss. 127, 128, amended: 1994, c. 40, sch. 16.

s. 128, amended(S.): 1994, c. 39, sch. 13.

ss. 130, 132, amended: 1994, c. 18, sch. 1.

s. 134, order 94/579.

ss. 135, 136, order 94/523.

s. 137, regs. 94/781.

ss. 138–140, amended(S.): 1994, c. 39, sch. 13.

s. 139, regs. 94/2137; order 94/2138.

s. 140, regs. 94/781; order 94/523.

ss. 141–143, 145, order 94/544.

s. 148, order 94/1105.

s. 150, order 94/542.

s. 150, amended: 1994, c. 18, ss. 2, 9.

s. 162, amended: 1994, c. 1, s. 2.

s. 170, amended: 1994, c. 18, sch. 1.

s. 179, orders 94/1646, 2802.

s. 184, regs. 94/2343.

s. 189, regs. 94/532, 542, 781, 1082, 1779, 1925, 2137, 2139; orders 94/523, 544, 578, 579, 2138.

s. 191, regs. 94/730, 781, 1082, 1779.

s. 191, amended: 1994, c. 19, sch. 16; repealed in pt.: 1994, c. 18, schs. 1, 2; c. 19, schs. 16, 18.

s. 191, amended(S.): 1994, c. 39, sch. 13; repealed in pt.: *ibid.*, schs. 13, 14.

sch. 2, amended: 1994, c. 18, sch. 1.

sch. 3, regs. 94/1082.

sch. 9, scheme 94/671.

6. Social Security (Consequential Provisions) Act 1992.

sch. 2, repealed in pt.: 1994, c. 29, sch. 9.

7. Social Security Contributions and Benefits (Northern Ireland) Act 1992.

amended: S.R. 1994 No. 176.

s. 2, S.R. 1994 No. 92.

1992—cont.

7. Social Security Contributions and Benefits (Northern Ireland) Act 1992—*cont.*

s. 3, S.Rs. 1994 Nos. 219, 328.

s. 5, S.R. 1994 No. 78.

s. 7, S.R. 1994 No. 92.

s. 10, S.R. 1994 No. 94.

s. 21, S.R. 1994 No. 89.

s. 22, S.R. 1994 No. 265.

s. 35, S.Rs. 1994 Nos. 191, 271.

s. 57, S.Rs. 1994 Nos. 75, 152.

s. 67, S.R. 1994 No. 263.

s. 68, S.R. 1994 No. 152.

ss. 72, 73, S.R. 1994 No. 263.

ss. 108, 109, S.R. 1994 No. 347.

s. 113, S.Rs. 1994 Nos. 45, 75, 269.

s. 119, S.Rs. 1994 Nos. 78, 191.

s. 122, S.Rs. 1993 Nos. 414, 479; 1994 Nos. 77, 80, 81, 88, 137, 138, 233, 266, 274, 327, 335.

s. 123, S.R. 1994 No. 77.

ss. 127, 128, S.R. 1994 No. 327.

s. 129, S.Rs. 1994 Nos. 81, 137, 233.

s. 131, S.Rs. 1993 Nos. 414, 479; 1994 Nos. 77, 81, 137, 138, 266, 327, 335.

s. 132, S.Rs. 1993 Nos. 414; 1994 Nos. 77, 88, 233, 274, 327, 335.

s. 133, S.Rs. 1994 No. 77, 80, 266, 327.

s. 134, S.Rs. 1993 Nos. 413; 1994 Nos. 68, 383.

s. 149, S.R. 1994 No. 191.

s. 153, S.R. 1994 No. 82.

s. 154, S.Rs. 1994 Nos. 76, 103.

ss. 160, 162, S.R. 1994 No. 191.

s. 163, S.Rs. 1994 No. 84, 271.

s. 171, S.Rs. 1994 Nos. 77, 83, 89, 274, 327, 347.

sch. 1, S.Rs. 1994 Nos. 94, 219, 343.

sch. 2, amended and repealed in pt.: 1994, c. 1, s. 3.

sch. 3, S.R. 1994 No. 89.

sch. 7, S.R. 1994 No. 75.

sch. 8, S.R. 1994 No. 83.

sch. 11, S.R. 1994 No. 191.

8. Social Security Administration (Northern Ireland) Act 1992.

s. 5, S.Rs. 1994 Nos. 335, 345, 432.

ss. 25, 30, 33, S.R. 1994 No. 21.

s. 44, S.R. 1994 No. 150.

s. 52, amended: 1994, c. 40, sch. 16.

s. 57, S.R. 1994 No. 150.

s. 59, S.Rs. 1994 Nos. 21, 396.

s. 61, S.Rs. 1994 Nos. 88, 335.

s. 71, S.R. 1994 No. 263.

s. 77, S.R. 1994 No. 103.

s. 117, amended: 1994, c. 40, sch. 16.

s. 120, S.R. 1994 No. 335.

s. 129, S.R. 1994 No. 79.

s. 130, S.R. 1994 No. 155.

s. 131, S.R. 1994 No. 76.

s. 132, S.R. 1994 No. 74.

CAP.

1992—cont.

8. **Social Security Administration (Northern Ireland) Act 1992**—*cont.*
s. 135, S.R. 1994 No. 75.
s. 155, S.R. 1994 No. 262.
sch. 3, S.R. 1994 No. 150.
9. **Social Security (Consequential Provisions) (Northern Ireland) Act 1992.**
sch. 3, S.R. 1994 No. 432.
12. **Taxation of Chargeable Gains Act 1992.**
s. 3, order 93/2947.
s. 3, amended (temp.): 1994, c. 9, s. 90.
s. 6, repealed in pt.: *ibid.*, sch. 26.
s. 35, amended: *ibid.*, schs. 24, 25; repealed in pt.: *ibid.*, schs. 24, 26.
ss. 53, 55, amended: *ibid.*, s. 93.
s. 56, amended: *ibid.*; repealed in pt.: *ibid.*, sch. 26.
s. 98A, added: *ibid.*, s. 97.
s. 103, repealed: *ibid.*, sch. 26.
s. 110, amended: *ibid.*, s. 93.
s. 111, repealed: *ibid.*, sch. 26.
ss. 127, 135, 171, see *NAP Holdings U.K. v. Whittles (Inspector of Taxes)* [1993] STC 592, C.A.
s. 139, repealed in pt.: 1994, c. 9, s. 251, sch. 26.
s. 143, amended: *ibid.*, s. 95; repealed in pt.: *ibid.*, s. 95, sch. 26.
s. 144A, added: *ibid.*, 96.
s. 150, amended: *ibid.*, sch. 15.
s. 150A, added: *ibid.*
s. 160, repealed: *ibid.*, s. 251, sch. 26.
ss. 163, 164, see *Clarke (Inspector of Taxes)* v. *Mayo* [1994] STC 570, Evans-Lombe J.
s. 164A, amended: 1994, c. 9, sch. 11; repealed in pt.: *ibid.*, schs. 11, 26.
s. 164B, substituted: *ibid.*, sch. 11.
s. 164BA, added: *ibid.*, sch. 11.
ss. 164C–164E, repealed: *ibid.*, schs. 11, 26.
s. 164F, amended: *ibid.*, sch. 11; repealed in pt.: *ibid.*, schs. 11, 26.
s. 164H, amended: *ibid.*, s. 91; repealed in pt.: *ibid.*, sch. 11, 26.
s. 164L, amended: *ibid.*, sch. 11.
s. 164M, amended: *ibid.*, sch. 15.
s. 164MA, added: *ibid.*
s. 164N, amended: *ibid.*, schs. 11, 15.
ss. 166, 171, 172, 175, repealed in pt.: *ibid.*, s. 251, sch. 26.
ss. 182–184, repealed: *ibid.*, s. 93, sch. 26.
ss. 186, 187 (in pt.), 188, repealed: *ibid.*, s. 251, sch. 26.
s. 200, repealed: *ibid.*, s. 93, sch. 26.
s. 209, regs. 94/728.
s. 211, repealed in pt.: 1994, c. 9, s. 251, sch. 26.
s. 231, repealed in pt.: *ibid.*, schs. 15, 26.
s. 275, repealed in pt.: 1994, c. 26, sch. 5.
s. 283, amended (prosp.): 1994, c. 9, sch. 19; repealed in pt. (prosp.): *ibid.*, schs. 19, 26.

CAP.

1992—cont.

12. **Taxation of Chargeable Gains Act 1992**—*cont.*
sch. 5, repealed in pt.: *ibid.*, s. 97, sch. 26.
sch. 5A, added: *ibid.*, s.97.
sch. 6, amended: *ibid.*, s. 91.
sch. 7A, amended: *ibid.*, ss. 93, 94; repealed in pt.: *ibid.*, s. 93, sch. 26.
sch. 9, order 94/2656.
sch. 10, repealed in pt.: 1994, c. 23, sch. 15.
13. **Further and Higher Education Act 1992.**
ss. 16, 17, orders 94/1434, 1449.
ss. 20, 21, regs. 94/1435, 1450.
s. 27, orders 94/1478, 1741, 1754, 1755, 1830.
s. 50, regs. 94/1321.
s. 61, regs. 94/1435, 1450.
s. 70, repealed in pt.: 1994, c. 30, sch. 2.
s. 89, regs. 94/1321, 1435, 1450.
s. 90, amended: 1994, c. 19, sch. 16; c. 30, sch. 2.
sch. 4, regs. 94/1435.
14. **Local Government Finance Act 1992.**
s. 1, regs. 94/1747.
s. 1, amended: 1994, c. 12, s. 35.
s. 4, order 94/539.
s. 13, regs. 94/135.
s. 19, amended: 1994, c. 19, sch. 13; c. 29, sch. 4; repealed in pt.: *ibid.*, sch. 9.
s. 21, regs. 94/1747.
s. 22A, added: 1994, c. 19, s. 36.
s. 24, regs. 94/1746.
ss. 24, 28, amended: 1994, c. 19, sch. 16.
ss. 32, 33, regs. 94/246.
ss. 32, 33, amended: *ibid.*; 1994, c. 19, sch. 12.
ss. 35, 37, amended: *ibid.*
s. 39, amended: *ibid.*, s. 35; c. 29, s. 27.
s. 43, see *R.* v. *Secretary of State for Wales, ex p. Gwent County Council, The Times*, March 16, 1994, C.A.
ss. 43, 44, regs. 94/246; amended: *ibid.*
s. 46, amended: 1994, c. 29, sch. 8; repealed in pt.: *ibid.*, sch. 9.
s. 54, order 94/1419.
s. 54, amended: 1994, c. 19, sch. 16; c. 29, s. 27; regs. 94/2825.
s. 55, amended: regs. 94/2825.
s. 57, order 94/1419.
ss. 60, 62, amended: 1994, c. 19, sch. 12.
s. 70, amended(S.): 1994, c. 39, sch. 13.
s. 72, order 94/628(S.).
s. 74, repealed in pt.(S.): 1994, c. 39, sch. 14.
s. 78, amended(S.): *ibid.*, sch. 13.
s. 80, regs. 93/3236(S.).
ss. 80, 81, amended(S.): 1994, c. 39, sch. 13.
s. 84, amended(S.): *ibid.*; repealed in pt.(S.): *ibid.*, sch. 14.
ss. 85–87, repealed in pt.(S.): *ibid.*

1992—cont.

14. Local Government Finance Act 1992—*cont.*
s. 90, amended(S.): *ibid.*, sch. 13; repealed in pt.: *ibid.*, sch. 14.
s. 91, amended(S.): *ibid.*, sch. 13.
s. 93, repealed in pt.(S.): *ibid.*, sch. 14.
s. 94, amended(S.): *ibid.*, sch. 13; repealed in pt.: *ibid.*, sch. 14.
s. 94A, added(S.): *ibid.*, s. 24.
s. 95, repealed(S.): *ibid.*, sch. 14.
s. 97, amended(S.): *ibid.*, sch. 13; repealed in pt.(S.): *ibid.*, schs. 13, 14.
s. 98, amended(S.): *ibid.*, sch. 13.
ss. 99, 107, amended(S.): repealed in pt.: *ibid.*, schs. 13, 14.
s. 108A, added(S.): *ibid.*, s. 167.
ss. 109, 111, amended(S.): *ibid.*, sch. 13.
s. 112, repealed in pt.(S.): *ibid.*, sch. 14.
s. 113, regs. 93/3059, 3236(S.); 94/135, 246, 505, 582(S.), 629(S.), 1746, 1747; orders 94/543, 626(S.).
s. 114, order 94/582(S.).
s. 116, regs. 93/3059, 3236(S.); 94/540, 629(S.).
sch. 1, regs. 92/540, 629(S.); orders 94/543, 626(S.).
sch. 2, regs. 93/3059; 94/505.
sch. 2, amended(S.): 1994, c. 39, sch. 13; repealed in pt.(S.): *ibid.*, sch. 14.
sch. 3, amended(S.): *ibid.*, sch. 13.
sch. 7, repealed in pt.(S.): *ibid.*, sch. 14.
sch. 8, amended(S.): *ibid.*, sch. 13; repealed in pt.(S.): *ibid.*, sch. 14.
schs. 9, 11, repealed in pt.(S.): *ibid.*
sch. 11, order 94/628(S.).
sch. 12, order 94/528(S.).
sch. 12, amended(S.): 1994, c. 39, sch. 13.
sch. 13, repealed in pt.(S.): *ibid.*, sch. 14.

17. Coal Industry Act 1992.
repealed (prosp.): 1994, c. 21, sch. 11, Pt. III.

19. Local Government Act 1992.
Commencement order: 93/3169; 94/1445.
s. 9, regs. 93/848.
s. 13, see *R.* v. *Secretary of State for the Environment, ex p. Lancashire County Council; R.* v. *Same, ex p. Derbyshire County Council, The Times,* February 3, 1994, Jowitt J.
s. 14, amended: 1994, c. 29, s. 39; repealed in pt.: *ibid.*, sch. 19.
s. 15, amended: *ibid.*, s. 39.
s. 17, see *R.* v. *Local Government Commission for England, ex p. Cleveland County Council, The Times,* July 4, 1994, D.C.
s. 17, order 94/1210.
s. 17, amended: 1994, c. 29, s. 39.
s. 18, repealed in pt.: *ibid.*, s. 39, sch. 9.
s. 19, regs. 94/867, 2825.
s. 19, amended: 1994, c. 29, s. 39.

1992—cont.

19. Local Government Act 1992—*cont.*
s. 26, regs. 94/867, 2825; order 94/1210.
s. 30, orders 93/3169; 94/1445.
s. 30, amended(S.): 1994, c. 39, sch. 13.
sch. 3, repealed in pt.: 1994, c. 29, sch. 9.

20. Finance Act 1992.
s. 4, repealed in pt.: 1994, c. 22, sch. 5.
ss. 6, 7, repealed: 1994, c. 23, sch. 15.

21. Consolidated Fund (No. 2) Act 1992.
repealed: 1994, c. 24, sch. (C.).

22. Appropriation Act 1992.
repealed: 1994, c. 24, sch. (C.).

28. Medicinal Products: Prescription by Nurses etc. Act 1992.
Commencement order: 94/2408.
s. 6, order 94/2408.

34. Sexual Offences (Amendment) Act 1992.
s. 2, amended: 1994, c. 33, sch. 9.
s. 6, amended: *ibid.*, schs. 4, 9.

37. Further and Higher Education (Scotland) Act 1992.
s. 45, orders 93/2969; 94/1980, 2371.
s. 47, order 94/1715.
s. 48, order 94/1125.
s. 60, orders 93/2969; 94/1125, 1715, 1980, 2371.

38. Education (Schools) Act 1992.
s. 1, order 94/1633.
s. 12, regs. 94/717.
s. 16, regs. 93/2824; 94/1186, 1420, 1421, 2254.
s. 19, regs. 93/2824, 2968, 2973; 94/1186, 1420, 1421, 2254.
sch. 2, regs. 93/2968, 2973.
sch. 2, amended: regs. 94/1083.
sch. 3, regs. 94/717.

40. Friendly Societies Act 1992.
Commencement orders: 93/3226; 94/2543.
s. 1, amended: regs. 94/1984.
s. 2, regs. 94/657.
ss. 32, 34, amended: regs. 94/1984.
s. 40, amended and repealed in pt.: *ibid.*
s. 41, amended: *ibid.*
ss. 45, 46, 48, regs. 94/1981.
s. 48, repealed in pt.: regs. 94/1984.
s. 49, regs. 94/1981.
ss. 49A, 49B, added: regs. 94/1984.
ss. 50, 52, amended: *ibid.*
ss. 52A, 55A, added: *ibid.*
s. 56, regs. 94/1981.
ss. 57, 57A, substituted: regs. 94/1984.
ss. 62, 64, 65, 67, amended: *ibid.*
ss. 67A–67D, added: *ibid.*
ss. 70, 71, regs. 94/1983.
s. 79, order 94/132.
ss. 87, 88, amended: regs. 94/1984.
s. 90A, added: *ibid.*
s. 114, regs. 94/657.
ss. 117, 119, amended: regs. 94/1984.
ss. 119A, 119B, added: *ibid.*

1992—cont.

40. Friendly Societies Act 1992—*cont.*
s. 121, regs. 94/1981, 1982.
s. 123, regs. 93/3084.
s. 126, orders 93/3226; 94/2543.
sch. 13, regs. 94/1982.
sch. 13, amended: regs. 94/1984.
schs. 13A–13C, added: *ibid.*
sch. 14, regs. 94/1983.
sch. 15, amended: *ibid.*

41. Charities Act 1992.
s. 58, amended: 1994, c. 40, s. 25.
s. 63, amended: *ibid.*, s. 26.
s. 65, amended: 1994, c. 19, sch. 16.
s. 67, repealed in pt.: 1994, c. 40, s. 27, sch. 17.

42. Transport and Works Act 1992.
Commencement order: 94/718.
s. 1, orders 94/371, 701, 1039, 1532, 1803.
s. 3, order 94/1753.
s. 5, orders 94/1039, 1532, 1753, 1803.
ss. 11, 14, amended: 1994, c. 19, sch. 7.
s. 41, regs. 94/157.
s. 48, amended: 1994, c. 19, sch. 7.
s. 70, order 94/718.

47. Appropriation (No. 2) Act 1992.
repealed: 1994, c. 24, sch. (C.).

46. Non-Domestic Rating Act 1992.
s. 2, amended: 1994, c. 3, s. 1.

48. Finance (No. 2) Act 1992.
ss. 11 (in pt.), 12, 13, repealed: 1994, c. 22, sch. 5.
ss. 14 (in pt.), 15–17, repealed: 1994, c. 23, sch. 15.
ss. 19 (in pt.), 38–40, sch. 2 (in pt.), repealed: 1994, c. 9, sch. 26.
sch. 3, repealed in pt.: 1994, c. 22, sch. 5; c. 23, sch. 15.
sch. 5, repealed in pt.: 1994, c. 9, sch. 26.

52. Trade Union and Labour Relations (Consolidation) Act 1992.
s. 108, regs. 94/546.
s. 146, see *Wilson* v. *Associated Newspapers; Palmer* v. *Associated British Ports* [1993] IRLR 366, C.A.
ss. 178, 179, see *Lee* v. *GEC Plessey Telecommunications* [1993] IRLR 383, Connell J.
ss. 219, 244, see *Wandsworth London Borough Council* v. *National Association of Schoolmasters/Union of Women Teachers* [1993] IRLR 344, C.A.
s. 293, regs. 94/546.
sch. 2, repealed in pt.: 1994, c. 23, sch. 15.

53. Tribunals and Inquiries Act 1992.
s. 7, amended: 1994, c. 29, sch. 5.
s. 8, regs. 94/1811–1813, 1910.
s. 11, see *Henderson* v. *City of Glasgow District Council*, 1994 S.L.T. 263.
s. 13, order 93/3258.

1992—cont.

53. Tribunals and Inquiries Act 1992—*cont.*
sch. 1, amended: 1994, c. 9, s. 7; c. 23, sch. 14; c. 26, sch. 4; c. 29, sch. 5; regs. 94/1083; c. 39, sch. 13(S.).
sch. 3, repealed in pt.: 1994, c. 23, sch. 15.

1993

1. Gas (Exempt Supplies) Act 1993.
Commencement order: 94/2568.
s. 4, order 94/2568.

2. British Coal and British Rail (Transfer Proposals) Act 1993.
repealed: 1994, c. 21, sch. 11, Pt. III.

3. Social Security Act 1993.
s. 2, order 94/544.

8. Judicial Pensions and Retirement Act 1993.
s. 10, amended: regs. 94/1696.
s. 21, amended: 1994, c. 19, sch. 16.
sch. 2, amended: regs. 94/1696.
schs. 6, 8, repealed in pt.: 1994, c. 23, sch. 15.

9. Prisoners and Criminal Proceedings (Scotland) Act 1993.
s. 1, see *McKinlay* v. *H.M. Advocate, The Scotsman*, February 16, 1994.
s. 7, amended: 1994, c. 33, s. 130.
s. 10, amended: *ibid.*, s. 133.
s. 12, amended: *ibid.*, s. 131.
s. 18, amended: *ibid.*, s. 134; c. 39, sch. 13(S.).
s. 22, amended: 1994, c. 33, s. 134.
s. 27, amended(S.): 1994, c. 39, sch. 13.
s. 28, amended: 1994, c. 33, s. 134.
s. 41, see *Brooks* v. *H.M. Advocate*, 1994 S.L.T. 932.
s. 42, amended: 1994, c. 33, s. 134.
s. 45, amended: *ibid.*, s. 130.
sch. 6, see *McKinlay* v. *H.M. Advocate, The Scotsman*, February 19, 1994.

10. Charities Act 1993.
s. 17, orders 94/1235, 2181.
s. 33, see *Gunning* v. *Buckfast Abbey Trustees Registered, The Times*, June 9, 1994, Arden J.
s. 43, amended: 1994, c. 40, s. 28.
s. 45, amended: *ibid.*, s. 29; regs. 94/1935.
s. 46, amended: 1994, c. 40, s. 29.
s. 47, amended: *ibid.*, sch. 11; regs. 94/1935; repealed in pt.: 1994, c. 40, schs. 11, 17.
s. 48, amended: *ibid.*, s. 30.
s. 49, amended: *ibid.*, s. 28.
ss. 76–79, amended: 1994, c. 19, sch. 16.
sch. 2, order 94/1905.
sch. 3, amended: 1994, c. 19, sch. 16.

11. Clean Air Act 1993.
ss. 30, 63, regs. 94/2295.

1993—cont.

11. Clean Air Act 1993—*cont.*
s. 64, amended: 1994, c. 19, sch. 9; repealed in pt.: *ibid.*, schs. 9, 18.
s. 64, amended(S.): 1994, c. 39, sch. 13.

12. Radioactive Substances Act 1993.
s. 47, amended: 1994, c. 19, sch. 16; repealed in pt.: *ibid.*, schs. 16, 18.
s. 47, amended(S.): 1994, c. 39, sch. 13.

13. Carrying of Knives etc. (Scotland) Act 1993.
s. 1, see *Lister* v. *Lees*, 1994 S.C.C.R. 548.

17. Non-Domestic Rating Act 1993.
s. 4, regs. 93/3077, 3082.

19. Trade Union Reform and Employment Rights Act 1993.
Commencement order: 94/1365.
s. 52, sch. 9, order 94/1365.
sch. 8, repealed in pt.: 1994, c. 40, sch. 17.

21. Osteopaths Act 1993.
ss. 9, 13, amended and repealed in pt.: 1994, c. 17, sch. 2.
ss. 18, 20, amended: *ibid.*
ss. 22, 27, 28, amended and repealed in pt.: *ibid.*
ss. 30, 31, 41, sch., amended: *ibid.*

22. Merchant Shipping (Registration, etc.) Act 1993.
Commencement order: 93/3137.
ss. 2, 3, regs. 93/3138; 94/502, 541.
s. 5, regs. 93/3138.
s. 7, regs. 93/3138; 94/541; order 94/774.
s. 9, regs. 93/3138.
s. 10, order 93/3137.
sch. 1, regs. 93/3138; 94/541.
sch. 4, repealed in pt.: 1994, c. 28, s. 5, sch. 4.

23. Asylum and Immigration Appeals Act 1993.
ss. 1, 2, 8, sch. 2, see *R.* v. *Secretary of State for the Home Department, ex p. Thavatherathasan (Manickavasar)* [1994] Imm AR 249, C.A.
s. 2, sch. 2, see *R.* v. *Secretary of State for the Home Department, ex p. Cokezici (Ali)* [1994] Imm AR 224, Laws J.
s. 8, see *R.* v. *Special Adjudicator, ex p. Kandasamy, The Times*, March 11, 1994, Hidden J.; *R.* v. *Secretary of State for the Home Department, ex p. Kazmi, The Independent*, September 30, 1994, Dyson J.
s. 8, sch. 2, see *R.* v. *Secretary of State for the Home Department, ex p. Abdi; R.* v. *Same, ex p. Gawe, The Times*, April 25, 1994, C.A.; *R.* v. *Secretary of State for the Home Department, ex p. Sop (Biljana)* [1994] Imm AR 204, Macpherson J.
s. 9, see *R.* v. *Special Adjudicator, ex p. Arthur (Frank)* [1994] Imm AR 246, Harrison J.

1993—cont.

23. Asylum and Immigration Appeals Act 1993—*cont.*
s. 10, see *R.* v. *Secretary of State for the Home Department, ex p. Kaur (Nauranga Singh Balwant); Same* v. *Same, ex p. Lizzie (Nauranga Singh)* [1994] Imm AR 180, Schiemann J.
sch. 2, see *R.* v. *Secretary of State for the Home Department, ex p. Mehari* [1994] 2 W.L.R. 349, Laws J.

24. Video Recordings Act 1993.
s. 3, repealed: 1994, c. 33, sch. 11.

25. Local Government (Overseas Assistance) Act 1993.
s. 1, amended: 1994, c. 19, schs. 6, 16; repealed in pt.: 1994, c. 29, sch. 9.
s. 1, amended(S.): 1994, c. 39, sch. 13.

26. Bail (Amendment) Act 1993.
Commencement order: 94/1437.
s. 1, see *R.* v. *Governor of Pentonville Prison, ex p. Bone, The Times*, November 15, 1994, D.C.
s. 1, order 94/1438.
s. 2, order 94/1437.

28. Leasehold Reform, Housing and Urban Development Act 1993.
Commencement orders: 93/2762; 94/935.
s. 13, regs. 94/1263.
ss. 34, 57, rules 93/3045.
ss. 34, 57, amended: 1994, c. 36, sch. 1.
s. 78, regs. 94/1263.
s. 128, order 94/42.
s. 161, amended: 1994, c. 19, sch. 16; repealed in pt. (prosp.): 1994, c. 21, schs. 9, 11, Pt. IV.
s. 188, orders 93/2762; 94/935.
schs. 7, 9, amended: 1994, c. 36, sch. 1.

32. European Communities (Amendment) Act 1993.
see *R.* v. *Secretary of State for Foreign and Commonwealth Affairs, ex p. Rees-Mogg* [1994] 2 W.L.R. 115, D.C.

34. Finance Act 1993.
Commencement orders: 93/2446, 2782, 2831.
ss. 15, 16 (in pt.), repealed: 1994, c. 9, sch. 26. Pt. II.
s. 17, amended: order 93/2452; repealed in pt.: 1994, c. 9, sch. 26, Pt. I; c. 22, sch. 5.
s. 18, order 93/2446.
s. 18, repealed: 1994, c. 22, sch. 5.
s. 19, repealed in pt.: 1994, c. 9, sch. 26, Pt. I; repealed: 1994, c. 22, sch. 5.
s. 20, repealed in pt.: 1994, c. 9, sch. 26, Pt. I; c. 22, sch. 5.
s. 21, order 93/2215.
ss. 21, 23, repealed: 1994, c. 22, sch. 5.
ss. 24, 26–29, regs. 93/3212.
ss. 27–29, amended: 1994, c. 9, sch. 4.
s. 35, amended: *ibid.*, s. 18.

1993—cont.

34. Finance Act 1993—*cont.*
s. 38, regs. 93/3212.
ss. 42–50, repealed: 1994, c. 23, sch. 15.
s. 57, repealed in pt.: 1994, c. 9, schs. 9, 26.
s. 61, repealed in pt.: *ibid.*, sch. 26.
s. 94A, added: *ibid.*, s. 136.
s. 95, amended: *ibid.*
s. 121, regs. 93/3112.
ss. 126, 146, amended: 1994, c. 9, s. 115.
ss. 154, 155, amended: *ibid.*, s. 114.
s. 164, amended: *ibid.*, s. 115.
s. 171, amended (prosp.): *ibid.*; repealed in pt. (prosp.): *ibid.*, schs. 21, 26.
s. 172, amended: *ibid.*, sch. 21.
s. 174, amended (prosp.): *ibid.*
s. 177, amended: *ibid.*
s. 178, amended (prosp.): *ibid.*
s. 179, repealed in pt. (prosp.): *ibid.*, sch. 26.
s. 179A, added: *ibid.*, sch. 21.
s. 182, repealed in pt. (prosp.): *ibid.*, schs. 21, 26.
s. 183, repealed in pt. (prosp.): *ibid.*, s. 228, sch. 26.
s. 184, amended (prosp.): *ibid.*, sch. 21; repealed in pt. (prosp.): *ibid.*, sch. 26.
s. 190, repealed in pt.: *ibid.*
s. 211, order 93/2831.
s. 211, repealed in pt.: 1994, c. 9, s. 251.
sch. 2, order 93/2782.
sch. 2, repealed: 1994, c. 23, sch. 15.
sch. 6, repealed in pt.: 1994, c. 9, sch. 26, Pt. V (2), (13).
sch. 15, amended: *ibid.*, s. 116.
sch. 17, repealed in pt.: *ibid.*, sch. 26.
schs. 19, 20, amended: *ibid.*, sch. 21; repealed in pt.: *ibid.*, schs. 21, 26 (prosp.).

35. Education Act 1993.
Commencement orders: 93/3106; 94/436, 507, 1414, 1558, 2038 (corrected by order 94/2248).
s. 8, repealed: regs. 94/1083.
s. 12, amended: *ibid.*
s. 21, regs. 94/1256.
s. 24, order 94/1861.
s. 28, regs. 94/1232.
ss. 32, 48, 49, regs. 93/3113.
s. 56, regs. 94/2094.
ss. 60, 61, regs. 94/654.
ss. 72, 73, regs. 93/3113; 94/2167.
s. 77, regs. 93/3188.
s. 78, regs. 94/654.
ss. 81–83, regs. 94/610, 938, 2111.
s. 84, regs. 94/938, 2111.
ss. 88–90, regs. 94/610.
s. 94, regs. 94/610, 938, 2111.
ss. 96, 97, 104, 105, regs. 93/3113.
s. 117, regs. 94/1041.
ss. 118, 119–124, regs. 94/2896.

1993—cont.

35. Education Act 1993—*cont.*
ss. 119, 120, 122, 123, modified: regs. 94/2281.
s. 126, regs. 94/1195.
s. 127, regs. 94/1041, 2281.
s. 153, regs. 94/1048, 1421, 2330.
s. 158, order 94/1414.
s. 161, regs. 94/1048.
s. 161, amended: regs. 94/1083.
s. 162, regs. 94/650, 2156.
s. 166, regs. 94/1047.
s. 166, amended: 1994, c. 19, sch. 16.
s. 168, regs. 94/1047.
s. 172, regs. 94/651, 652, 1047.
ss. 177, 178, 180, regs. 94/1910.
s. 183, regs. 94/652, 653 (corrected by regs. 94/1231), 1231, 2003.
s. 186, regs. 94/653 (corrected by regs. 94/1231), 1231.
s. 187, regs. 94/779, 1041, 2281.
s. 187, amended: regs. 94/1083.
s. 188, regs. 94/652.
s. 189, regs. 94/651.
ss. 210, 211, regs. 93/2968, 2973.
s. 223, regs. 93/3101; 94/1085.
s. 228, regs. 93/3103; 94/1083, 1084 (corrected by regs. 94/2848).
s. 234, regs. 93/3113.
s. 242, regs. 94/1270, 2206; orders 94/1814–1817.
ss. 247, 248, order 93/3105.
s. 252, order 94/645.
s. 258, regs. 94/1304.
s. 261, repealed in pt.: regs. 94/1083.
s. 262, regs. 94/1697.
s. 265, regs. 94/1321.
s. 267, regs. 94/1303.
s. 268, amended: regs. 94/1083.
s. 272, regs. 93/3113.
s. 273, amended: regs. 94/1083.
s. 298, regs. 94/2103, 2330.
s. 301, regs. 93/2968, 2973, 3072, 3101, 3103, 3188; 94/610, 650–652, 653 (corrected by regs. 94/1231), 654, 938, 1041, 1047, 1083, 1084 (corrected by regs. 94/2848), 1085, 1231, 1232, 1256, 1304, 1321, 1421, 1910, 2003, 2094, 2103, 2104, 2111, 2156, 2167, 2330; orders 93/3106; 94/436, 507, 1861, 2038 (corrected by order 94/2248).
s. 305, regs. 94/1048, 1321, 1910.
s. 305, amended: 1994, c. 19, sch. 16.
s. 308, orders 93/3106; 94/436, 507, 1558, 2038 (corrected by order 94/2248).
s. 310, regs. 94/1231, 2093.
sch. 3, regs. 93/3113.
sch. 4, regs. 93/3072.
sch. 5, regs. 94/654.
sch. 8, modified: regs. 94/2281.
sch. 9, regs. 94/1047, 1251.
sch. 10, regs. 94/1047.

CAP.

1993—cont.

35. Education Act 1993—*cont.*
sch. 11, regs. 94/653 (corrected by regs. 94/1231), 1048, 1231, 2003, 2104, 2247.
sch. 18, regs. 94/2103, 2330.
sch. 19, regs. 94/2093.
sch. 20, order 94/507.

36. Criminal Justice Act 1993.
Commencement orders: 94/71, 242, 700, 1951.
ss. 7–16, 18, repealed: 1994, c. 37, sch. 3.
ss. 20, 21, 22, 24, repealed in pt.: *ibid.*
ss. 25, 26 (in pt.), repealed: *ibid.*
ss. 54, 60, 62, 64, order 94/187.
s. 67, repealed in pt.: 1994, c. 33, sch. 11.
s. 78, orders 94/71, 242, 700, 1951.
s. 78, amended: 1994, c. 33, sch. 9; repealed in pt.: 1994, c. 37, sch. 3.
s. 79, amended: *ibid.*, sch. 1; repealed in pt.: *ibid.*, schs. 1, 3.
schs. 4, 5, repealed in pt.: *ibid.*, sch. 3.

37. Agriculture Act 1993.
s. 1, orders 94/282, 685(S.), 2900.
s. 1, amended: orders 94/282, 685(S.).
s. 2, order 94/951.
s. 14, regs. 94/2589(S.)–2591(S.).
s. 50, scheme 94/1403; order 94/1404.
s. 62, sch. 2, regs. 94/2460.

38. Welsh Language Act 1993.
Commencement order: 94/115.
ss. 6, 25, amended: 1994, c. 19, sch. 16.
ss. 25, 27, order 94/2736.
s. 26, regs. 94/117, 415, 693, 725, 1989, 1990.
s. 36, order 94/115.

39. National Lottery etc. Act 1993.
Commencement orders: 94/1055, 2659.
s. 7, order 94/1200.
s. 12, regs. 94/189.
s. 23, amended: order 94/1342.
s. 29, order 94/1342.
s. 60, regs. 94/1170; orders 94/406, 1055, 1200.
s. 65, orders 94/406, 1055, 2659.
sch. 3, regs. 94/1170.

40. Noise and Statutory Nuisance Act 1993.
ss. 8, 9, amended(S.): 1994, c. 39, sch. 13.

41. European Parliamentary Elections Act 1993.
Commencement order: 94/1089.
s. 3, order 94/1089.

43. Railways Act 1993.
Commencement orders: 93/3237; 94/202, 447, 571, 1648, 2142.
s. 7, orders 94/573, 574, 606.
s. 8, regs 94/572.
ss. 20, 24, orders 94/573, 374, 606.
s. 49, orders 94/573, 574, 606, 607.
s. 67, amended: 1994, c. 40, schs. 2, 4, paras. 2, 4; repealed in pt.: *ibid.*, sch. 17.
ss. 72, 73, order 94/575.
s. 125, order 94/2032.

CAP.

1993—cont.

43. Railways Act 1993—*cont.*
s. 130, regs. 94/576.
s. 132, repealed in pt.: 1994, c. 8, s. 2, sch.
s. 136, amended(S.): 1994, c. 39, sch. 13.
s. 143, regs. 94/572, 576; orders 94/571, 573, 574, 606, 607, 609, 1432, 1433, 1648, 2005.
s. 151, orders 94/573, 574, 606.
s. 151, amended: 1994, c. 19, sch. 16.
s. 151, amended(S.): 1994, c. 39, sch. 13; repealed in pt.(S.): *ibid.*, schs. 13, 14.
s. 153, orders 94/857, 1649, 2229, 2520.
s. 154, orders 93/3237; 94/202, 447, 571, 1648, 2142.
sch. 10, order 94/609.
sch. 10, repealed in pt.: 1994, c. 8, sch.
sch. 11, orders 94/1432, 1433, 2005, 2150.

44. Crofters (Scotland) Act 1993.
ss. 42, 46, schemes 94/1013, 1014.

46. Health Service Commissioners Act 1993.
s. 19, amended: 1994, c. 19, sch. 16; repealed in pt.: *ibid.*, schs. 16, 18.

47. Probation Service Act 1993.
s. 2, orders 94/471, 473, 969, 1542, 1543.
s. 4, amended: 1994, c. 33, sch. 10.
s. 9, rules 94/1228.
s. 17, amended: 1994, c. 33, sch. 10.
s. 25, rules 94/1228.
s. 29, amended: 1994, c. 19, sch. 16.

48. Pension Schemes Act 1993.
Commencement order: 94/86.
ss. 6–12, 19–24, regs. 94/1062.
ss. 26, 27, regs. 94/1062.
s. 28, regs. 94/1062, 1751.
ss. 29, 30, 32, 34–36, 39, 43–45, regs. 94/1062.
s. 46, amended: 1994, c. 18, sch. 1; repealed in pt.: *ibid.*, schs. 1, 2.
s. 47, repealed in pt.: *ibid.*
s. 48, regs. 94/1062.
s. 48, amended: 1994, c. 18, sch. 1.
ss. 50, 51, 55–57, 59–63, 71, 73, 75, 77, 82, 88, 95, 97, 98, regs. 94/1062.
s. 109, order 94/500.
ss. 111–114, 116–119, 135, 136, 138, regs. 94/1062.
s. 144, regs. 94/895, 1062.
s. 146, regs. 94/1062.
s. 153, regs. 94/895, 1062.
ss. 154, 156, 160, 163, 165, 172, 175, 178, regs. 94/1062.
s. 181, regs. 94/895.
s. 182, regs. 94/895, 1751.
s. 183, regs. 94/1062.
s. 193, order 94/86.
schs. 1, 2, regs. 94/1062.
sch. 3, regs. 94/1062, 2891.
sch. 6, regs. 94/1062.
sch. 8, repealed in pt.: 1994, c. 29, sch. 9.

1993—cont.

49. Pension Schemes (Northern Ireland) Act 1993.
Commencement order: S.R. 1994 No. 17.
S.R. 1994 No. 300.
s. 24, S.R. 1994 No. 261.
s. 105, S.R. 1994 No. 69.
s. 186, S.R. 1994 No. 17.

51. European Economic Area Act 1993.
s. 2, regs. 93/2915, 3183, 3225.

1994

1. Social Security (Contributions) Act 1994.
Royal Assent, February 10, 1994.

2. Statutory Sick Pay Act 1994.
Royal Assent, February 10, 1994.
s. 2, regs. 94/730.

3. Non-Domestic Rating Act 1994.
Royal Assent, February 24, 1994.

4. Consolidated Fund Act 1994.
Royal Assent, March 24, 1994.

5. New Towns (Amendment) Act 1994.
Royal Assent, March 24, 1994.

6. Mental Health (Amendment) Act 1994.
Royal Assent, March 24, 1994.

7. Insolvency Act 1994.
Royal Assent, March 24, 1994.

8. Transport Police (Jurisdiction) Act 1994.
Royal Assent, March 24, 1994.

9. Finance Act 1994.
Royal Assent, May 3, 1994.
Commencement orders: 94/1253, 1257, 1773, 2143, 2679.
s. 4, repealed: 1994, c. 22, sch. 5.
s. 7, amended: 1994, c. 23, sch. 14; repealed in pt.: *ibid.*, sch. 15.
s. 17, amended: 1994, c. 22, sch. 3.
s. 18, repealed: 1994, c. 23, sch. 15.
s. 19, orders 94/2143, 2679.
s. 30, order 94/1821.
ss. 31–35, 38, regs. 94/1738.
s. 42, regs. 94/1738, 1821.
s. 43, regs. 94/1738.
s. 45, order 94/1257.
s. 45, repealed: 1994, c. 23, sch. 15.
s. 47, order 94/1253.
s. 47, repealed: 1994, c. 23, sch. 15.
ss. 53–55, 57, 58, regs. 94/1774.
s. 61, order 94/1773.
ss. 62, 65, 68, regs. 94/1774.
s. 69, amended: order 94/1698.
s. 70, amended and repealed in pt.: *ibid.*
s. 71, order 94/1698.
s. 73, repealed in pt.: order 94/1698.
s. 74, orders 94/1698, 1773, 1819; regs. 94/1774.
s. 118, repealed in pt. (prosp.): 1994, c. 9, sch. 26.
sch. 2, repealed in pt.: 1994, c. 22, sch. 5.
sch. 6, order 94/1820; regs. 94/1737.

1994—cont.

9. Finance Act 1994—*cont.*
sch. 7, order 94/1819; regs. 94/1774.
sch. 7A, added: order 94/1698.
sch. 19, amended and repealed in pt.: regs. 94/1813.

10. Race Relations (Remedies) Act 1994.
Royal Assent, May 3, 1994.

11. Road Traffic Regulation (Special Events) Act 1994.
Royal Assent, May 3, 1994.

12. Insolvency (No. 2) Act 1994.
Royal Assent, May 26, 1994.

13. Intelligence Services Act 1994.
Royal Assent, May 26, 1994.
Commencement order: 94/2734.
s. 12, order 94/2734.

14. Parliamentary Commissioner Act 1994.
Royal Assent, July 5, 1994.

15. Antarctic Act 1994.
Royal Assent, July 5, 1994.

16. State Hospitals (Scotland) Act 1994.
Royal Assent, July 5, 1994.

17. Chiropractors Act 1994.
Royal Assent, July 5, 1994.

18. Social Security (Incapacity for Work) Act 1994.
Royal Assent, July 5, 1994.
Commencement order: 94/2926.
ss. 2, 3, regs. 94/2946.
s. 16, order 94/2926.
schs. 1, 2, amended: regs. 94/2556.

19. Local Government (Wales) Act 1994.
Royal Assent, July 5, 1994.
Commencement order: 94/2109, 2790.
s. 24, repealed: 1994, c. 29, sch. 9.
s. 63, order 94/2790.
s. 66, orders 94/2109, 2790.

20. Sunday Trading Act 1994.
Royal Assent, July 5, 1994.
Commencement order: 94/1841.
s. 1, order 94/1841.
s. 5, sch. 4, repealed in pt.: 1994, c. 40, sch. 17.

21. Coal Industry Act 1994.
Royal Assent, July 5, 1994.
Commencement orders: 94/2189, 2552.
s. 7, order 94/2553.
s. 22, regs. 94/2576.
s. 45, regs. 94/2565.
s. 46, regs. 94/2563.
s. 47, regs. 94/2566.
s. 68, orders 94/2189, 2552.
sch. 5, regs. 94/2576.
sch. 7, regs. 94/2562.
sch. 10, regs. 94/2564, 2565.

22. Vehicle Excise and Registration Act 1994.
Royal Assent, July 5, 1994.
sch. 2, amended: 1994, c. 23, sch. 14.
sch. 3, repealed in pt.: *ibid.*, sch. 15.

1994—cont.

23. Value Added Tax Act 1994.
Royal Assent, July 5, 1994.
s. 4, see *Durham Aged Mineworkers' Homes Association* v. *Customs and Excise Commissioners* [1994] STC 553, Auld J.
s. 6, see *B.J. Rice & Associates* v. *Customs and Excise Commissioners* [1994] STC 565, Macpherson J.
s. 24, see *Customs and Excise Commissioners* v. *Plant Repair and Services (South Wales)* [1994] STC 232, Laws J.
ss. 63, 76, see *Customs and Excise Commissioners* v. *Nomura Property Management Services* [1994] STC 461, Sedley J.
s. 73, see *Ridgeons Bulk* v. *Customs and Excise Commissioners* [1994] STC 427, Popplewell J.
s. 74, order 94/2542.
sch. 6, see *Fine Art Developments* v. *Customs and Excise Commissioners* [1994] STC 668, C.A.
sch. 9, see *R.* v. *Ryan (Edmund Joseph); R.* v. *Ryan (James Joseph); R.* v. *Ryan (Patrick Edmund)* [1994] STC 446, C.A.
sch. 11, see *Customs and Excise Commissioners* v. *Peachtree Enterprises* [1994] STC 747, Dyson J.

24. Appropriation Act 1994.
Royal Assent, July 21, 1994.

25. Land Drainage Act 1994.
Royal Assent, July 21, 1994.

26. Trade Marks Act 1994.
Royal Assent, July 21, 1994.
Commencement order: 94/2550.
ss. 4, 13, 25, 34, 35, 38–41, 43–45, 63–69, 76, 78, 80–82, 88, rules 94/2583.
s. 109, order 94/2550.
schs. 1–3, rules 94/2583.

27. Inshore Fishing (Scotland) Act 1994.
Royal Assent, July 21, 1994.
Commencement order: 94/2124.
s. 5, order 94/2124.

1994—cont.

28. Merchant Shipping (Salvage and Pollution) Act 1994.
Royal Assent, July 21, 1994.
Commencement order: 94/1988.
s. 10, order 94/1988.

29. Police and Magistrates' Courts Act 1994.
Royal Assent, July 21, 1994.
Commencement orders: 94/2095, 2151, 2594.
s. 94, orders 94/2095, 2151, 2594.

30. Education Act 1994.
Royal Assent, July 21, 1994.
Commencement order: 94/2204.
ss. 17, 23, order 94/2463.
s. 26, order 94/2204.

31. Firearms (Amendment) Act 1994.
Royal Assent, July 21, 1994.

32. Sale of Goods (Amendment) Act 1994.
Royal Assent, November 3, 1994.

33. Criminal Justice and Public Order Act 1994.
Royal Assent, November 3, 1994.
sch. 9, repealed in pt.: 1994, c. 37, sch. 3.

34. Marriage Act 1994.
Royal Assent, November 3, 1994.

35. Sale and Supply of Goods Act 1994.
Royal Assent, November 3, 1994.

36. Law of Property (Miscellaneous Provisions) Act 1994.
Royal Assent, November 3, 1994.

37. Drug Trafficking Act 1994.
Royal Assent, November 3, 1994.

38. European Union (Accessions) Act 1994.
Royal Assent, November 3, 1994.

39. Local Government etc. (Scotland) Act 1994.
Royal Assent, November 3, 1994.
Commencement order: 94/2850.
ss. 182, 184, order 94/2850.

40. Deregulation and Contracting Out Act 1994.
Royal Assent, November 3, 1994.

CURRENT LAW
STATUTORY INSTRUMENT CITATOR 1994

This is the fifth part of the Statutory Instrument Citator 1994. It details how Statutory Instruments have been affected by other Statutory Instruments and by Acts and also notes where the provisions of Statutory Instruments have been judicially considered.

The material is arranged in chronological order, by year. Part 5 is up to date to December 19, 1994 (materials received in house).

C. indicates that the provision has been consolidated by the Act or Instrument noted.

NO.

1912

348. Public Trustee Rules 1912.
rule 30, amended: rules 94/2519, rule 2.

1922

210. Enrolment of Deeds (Fees) Regulations 1922.
revoked: regs. 94/601, reg. 7.

1925

1093. Land Registration Rules 1925.
rule 1, amended: rules 94/1130, rule 2.
Sch., Form 19, substituted: *ibid.*, rule 3.

1934

703. North of Scotland Milk Marketing Scheme 1934.
revoked: ord. 94/2900, art. 2.
1346. London Cab Order 1934:
para. 40, substituted: ord. 94/1087, art. 3.

1939

404. London–Fishguard Trunk Road (Whitland By-Pass) Order 1939.
revoked in pt.: ord. 94/1614, art. 5.

1946

1331. Double Taxation Relief (Taxes on Income) (USA) Regulations 1946.
reg. 2, amended: regs. 94/1418, reg. 3.
reg. 3, revoked: *ibid.*, reg. 4.
reg. 4, amended: *ibid.*, reg. 5.
2198. Coal Industry Nationalisation (Superannuation) Regulations 1946.
continuation: regs. 94/2576, reg. 3.

NO.

1948

1888. Conway Mussel Fishery (Amendment) Order 1948.
art. 10, revoked: regs. 94/275, reg. 2.

1949

140. British Protectorates, Protected States and Protected Persons Order 1949.
art. 9(1)(a), see *Patel* v. *Secretary of State for the Home Department* [1993] Imm. A.R. 508, C.A.
1896. Act of Sederunt (Court of Session Jury Trials) 1949.
revoked: Act 94/1443, para. 3.

1950

376. Coal Industry Nationalisation (Superannuation) Regulations 1950.
continuation: regs. 94/2577, reg. 3.

1951

1937. Enrolment of Deeds (Fees) (Amendment) Regulations 1951.
revoked: regs. 94/601, reg. 7.

1952

565. Prison (Scotland) Rules 1952.
revoked: rules 94/1931, rule 143.

1954

240. Prison (Scotland) Rules 1954.
revoked: rules 94/1931, rule 143.

1955

690. Potato Marketing Scheme Order 1955.
para. 1, amended: ord. 94/2404, art. 2.
para. 4, amended: *ibid.*
para. 8, amended: *ibid.*
para. 9, amended: *ibid.*
para. 10, amended: *ibid.*
para. 11, amended: *ibid.*
para. 12, revoked: *ibid.*

(1)

1955—cont.

690. Potato Marketing Scheme Order 1955—cont.
para. 13, amended: *ibid.*
para. 14, amended: *ibid.*
para. 16, amended: *ibid.*
sch. A, substituted: *ibid.*

1956

357. Pupils' Registration Regulations 1956.
applied: regs. 94/2254, reg. 3.
552. Rules of the Supreme Court (Non-Contentious Probate Costs) 1956.
revoked: rules 94/1975, rule 24.
671. Prison (Scotland) Rules 1956.
revoked: rules 94/1931, rule 143.
894. Schools (Scotland) Code 1956.
reg. 24A, inserted: regs. 94/351, reg. 2.

1958

301. London Traffic (40 mph Speed Limit) (No. 1) Regulations 1958.
sch., para. 1, amended: ord. 94/2787, art. 7.
886. Saundersfoot Harbour Order 1958.
art. 38, amended: ord. 94/2253, art. 2.

1959

413. Food Hygiene (Scotland) Regulations 1959.
reg. 13, amended: regs. 94/2783, reg. 5.
reg. 31A, inserted: *ibid.*
452. Tribunals and Inquiries (Revenue Tribunals) Order 1959.
art. 2, amended: regs. 94/1813, reg. 2.
art. 3, amended: *ibid.*
955. General Optical Council (Companies Committee Rules) Order of Council 1959.
revoked: ord. 94/2579, art. 10.
1335. Diseases of Animals (Ascertainment of Compensation) Order 1959.
art. 3, referred to: ord. 94/673, art. 3.
art. 4, referred to: *ibid.*

1960

250. Cycle Racing on Highways Regulations 1960.
reg. 5, modified: regs. 94/1226, reg. 3.
1602. Food Hygiene (Docks, Carriers, etc.) Regulations 1960.
reg. 4, amended: regs. 94/2783, reg. 6.
reg. 4A, substituted: regs. 94/1029, reg. 27.
reg. 4B, inserted: regs. 94/2783, reg. 6.

1961

1580. Construction (General Provisions) Regulations 1961.
regs. 3, 32, 37, see *Morris* v. *Breaverglen (t/a Anzac Construction Co.)* [1993] I.C.R. 766, C.A.

1961—cont.

1580. Construction (General Provisions) Regulations 1961—cont.
reg. 14(2), see *Blackman* v. *C. J. Pryor (Earth Moving Contractors)*, The *Times*, July 5, 1994.
2291. East Anglian Water Order 1961.
art. 16, revoked: ord. 94/978, art. 3.

1962

1550. Jamaica (Constitution) Order in Council 1962.
s. 94(3)(a), (6), see *Brooks (Lloyd)* v. *D.P.P.* [1994] 2 W.L.R. 381, P.C.
sch. 2, see *Pratt* v. *Att.-Gen. for Jamaica* [1993] 3 W.L.R. 995, P.C.; see *Brooks (Lloyd)* v. *D.P.P.* [1994] 2 W.L.R. 381, P.C.

1963

1710. Weights and Measures Regulations 1963.
reg. 1, amended: regs. 94/1259, reg. 2.
sch. 1, pt. II, amended: *ibid.*

1964

388. Prison Rules 1964.
rule 33(3), see *R.* v. *Secretary of State for the Home Department*, ex p. *Leech (No. 2)* [1993] 3 W.L.R. 1125, C.A.
1456. British Transport Police Force Scheme 1963 (Approval) Order 1964.
art. 1, amended: ord. 94/609, art. 3.
art. 2A, inserted: *ibid.*, art. 4.
art. 3B, amended: *ibid.*, art. 5.
art. 4, amended: *ibid.*, art. 6.
art. 5, substituted: *ibid.*, art. 7.
art. 6, substituted: *ibid.*, art. 8.
1901. Act of Sederunt (Rules of Court Amendment No. 5) 1964.
revoked: Act 94/1443, para. 3.

1965

195. Young Offenders (Scotland) Rules 1965.
revoked: rules 94/1931, rule 143.
321. Rules of the Court of Session 1965.
revoked: Act 94/1443, para. 3.
rule 35.11(1), see *Tonner* v. *F. T. Everard & Sons*, 1994 S.L.T. 1033.
rule 101, see *Tonner* v. *F. T. Everard & Sons*, 1994 S.L.T. 1033.
rule 108A, see *Lenaghan* v. *Ayrshire and Arran Health Board*, 1994 S.L.T. 765.
rule 260B, see *Strathclyde Buses* v. *Strathclyde Regional Council* (O.H.), 1994 S.L.T. 724.
rule 262(c), see *Marsh* v. *Baxendale*, 1994 S.C.L.R. 239

NO.

1965—cont.

321. Rules of the Court of Session 1965—*cont.*
rule 264(c), see *Marsh* v. *Baxendale*, 1994 S.C.L.R. 239.
rule 347, amended: Act of Sederunt 94/1139, rule 2, Act of Sederunt 94/1140, rule 2 see *Clark* v. *Laddows*, 1994 S.L.T. 792.
rule 347(a), see *Mitchell (J. M.) & Sons* v. *Lord Advocate*, 1994 S.C.L.R. 522.
rule 347(d), see *Boal* v. *Newalls Insulation Co.*, 1994 S.C.L.R. 534.

460. Zetland County Council (Laxa Burn, Mid Yell, Yell) Water Order 1965.
art. 4, amended: ord. 94/2758, art. 2.
art. 5, amended: *ibid.*

1090. Act of Sederunt (Rules of Court Amendment No. 1) 1965.
revoked: Act 94/1443, para. 3.

1266. Act of Sederunt (Rules of Court Amendment No. 2) 1965.
revoked: Act 94/1443, para. 3.

1405. Act of Sederunt (Rules of Court Amendment No. 3) 1965.
revoked: Act 94/1443, para. 3.

1410. London–Fishguard Trunk Road (Whitland By-Pass) (Variation) Order 1965.
revoked: ord. 94/1614, art. 6.

1535. International Headquarters and Defence Organisations (Designation and Privileges) Order 1965.
sch., amended: ord. 94/1642, art. 2.

1536. Visiting Forces and International Headquarters (Application of Law) Order 1965.
art. 3, amended: ord. 94/61643, art. 2.

1776. Rules of the Supreme Court 1965.
see *Thomson* v. *Omal* (O.H.), 1993 S.C.L.R. 974.
Ord. 1,
rule 2(1), see *R.* v. *Darlington Borough Council*, ex p. *Association of Darlington Taxi Owners (No. 2)*, *The Times*, April 14, 1994.
rule 10, see *Yates* v. *Marr*, December 16, 1993, Oldham County Ct.
Ord. 3,
rule 5, see *Mendip District Council* v. *Secretary of State for the Environment and Castle Housing Society* [1993] J.P.L. 434.
Ord. 5,
rule 6, see *Peasegood* v. *Meiser* [1994] 1 All E.R. 298, D.C.
rule 6(2), see *Radford* v. *Samuel* [1993] BCC 870, C.A.
Ord. 6,
rule 8, amended: rules 94/1975, rule 3.
rule 8(1)(4), see *Saris* v. *Westminster Transports SA and Kestrel Marine* [1994] 1 Lloyd's Rep. 115.

NO.

1965—cont.

1776. Rules of the Supreme Court 1965—*cont.*
Ord. 6—*cont.*
rule 8(2), (2A), see *Singh (Joginder)* v. *Duport Harport Foundries* [1994] 1 W.L.R. 769, C.A.
Ord. 9,
rule 6, see *Yates* v. *Marr*, December 1993, Oldham County Ct.
Ord. 11,
rule 1(1)(d), (e), see *Seaconsar Far East* v. *Bank Markazi Jomhouri Islam Iran* [1993] 4 All E.R. 456, H.L.; *MB Pyramid Sound N.V.* v. *Briese Schiffahrts GmbH & Co., K.G.M.S. "Sina" and Latvian Shipping Association; Ines, The* [1993] 2 Lloyd's Rep. 492.
rule 4(2), see *MB Pyramid Sound N.V.* v. *Briese Schiffahrts GmbH & Co., K.G.M.S. "Sina" and Latvian Shipping Association; Ines, The* [1993] 2 Lloyd's Rep. 492.
Ord. 12,
rule 6(2), see *Sumitomo Heavy Industries* v. *Oil and Natural Gas Commission* [1994] 1 Lloyd's Rep. 45.
rule 8, see *Saris* v. *Westminster Transports SA and Kestrel Marine* [1994] 1 Lloyd's Rep. 115.
Ord. 13,
see *Cambro Contractors* v. *John Kennelly Sales, The Times*, April 14, 1994, C.A.
Ord. 14,
see *Cohen* v. *Baram* [1994] 13 EG 111, C.A.
rule 1, see *Macmillan Publishers* v. *Thomas Reed Publications* [1993] F.S.R. 455, Patents County Ct,
rule 3, see *Macmillan Publishers* v. *Thomas Reed Publications* [1993] F.S.R. 455, Patents County Ct.
Ord. 14A,
see *Polly Peck International, Re*; *Secretary of State for Trade and Industry* v. *Ellis* [1993] BCC 886.
Ord. 15,
rule 7, see *Toprak Enerji Sanay; AS* v. *Sale Tilney Technology* [1994] 1 W.L.R. 840.
rule 12A, inserted: rules 94/1975, rule 4.
rule 16, see *C. (Mental Patient: Contact), Re* [1993] 1 FLR 940.
Ord. 16,
rule 1(1), see *Kinnear* v. *Falcon Films N.V.* [1994] 3 All E.R. 42.
Ord. 18,
see *W.* v. *Ealing London Borough Council sub nom. W. (Children in Care) (Contact and Parental Responsibility Orders), Re* [1993] 2 FLR 788, C.A.

NO.

1965—cont.

1776. Rules of the Supreme Court
1965—*cont.*
Ord. 18—*cont.*
rule 19, see *X. (Minors)* v. *Bedford-shire County Council, The Times,* November 24, 1993; see *Petch* v. *Gurney (Inspector of Taxes); Gurney* v. *Petch (Inspector of Taxes)* [1994] STC 689, C.A.
Ord. 19,
see *W.* v. *Ealing London Borough Council; sub nom. W. (Children in Care) (Contact and Parental Responsibility Orders) Re* [1993] 2 FLR 788, C.A.
rules 3(1), 4, see *Mannon* v. *Khan,* April 13, 1994, Mold County Court.
Ord. 20,
rule 5(2), see *Clarke (E.) & Sons (Coaches)* v. *Axtell Yates Hallet* 30 Con LR 123.
rule 5(5), see *Welsh Development Agency* v. *Redpath Dorman Long, The Times,* April 4, 1994, C.A.; see *Sion* v. *Hampstead Health Authority, The Times,* June 10, 1994, C.A.
rule 10, see *Milano Assicurazioni SpA* v. *Walbrook Insurance Co.* [1994] 1 W.L.R. 977.
Ord. 21,
rule 2, see *Fakih Brothers* v. *A. P. Moller (Copenhagen)* [1994] 1 Lloyd's Rep. 103.
Ord. 22,
rule 1(1), (5), see *Walker v. Turpin* [1993] 4 All E.R. 865, C.A.
rule 8, amended: rules 94/1975, rule 6.
rule 13, applied: regs. 94/1516, reg. 7.
rule 14, see *Singh* v. *Parkfield Group, The Times,* May 27, 1994.
Ord. 23,
rule 1, see *C. T. Bowring & Co. (Insurance)* v. *Corsi & Partners, The Times,* June 28, 1994, C.A.
rule 1(1)(a), see *Little Olympian Eachways, Re, The Times,* July 29, 1994.
Ord. 24,
rule 1, see *Glaverbel SA* v. *British Coal Corp. (No. 2)* [1993] R.P.C. 90.
rule 2(1), see *G.E. Capital Corporate Finance Group* v. *Bankers Trust Co., The Times,* August 3, 1994, C.A.
rules 10, 13, see *Polly Peck International, Re: Secretary of State for Trade and Industry* v. *Ellis* [1993] BCC 886.

NO.

1965—cont.

1776. Rules of the Supreme Court
1965—*cont.*
Ord. 24—*cont.*
rule 17, see *Partenreederei M/S "Heidberg" (A Body Corporate)* v. *Grosvenor Grain and Feed Co.; Heidberg, The* [1993] 2 Lloyd's Rep. 324.
Ord. 28,
rule 4(1), see *Sumitomo Heavy Industries* v. *Oil and Natural Gas Commission* [1994] 1 Lloyd's Rep. 45.
Ord. 29,
rule 11, see *Stringman* v. *McArdle, The Times,* November 19, 1993, C.A.
Ord. 31,
rule 1, see *Green* v. *Green* [1993] 1 FLR 326.
Ord. 32,
rule 3, substituted: rules 94/1975, rule 7.
rule 7, amended: *ibid.,* rule 17.
rule 11, amended: *ibid.,* rule 11.
rule 14, amended: *ibid.*
Ord. 35,
rule 2, see *R.* v. *Newcastle under Lyme Justices, ex p. Massey; R.* v. *Stoke on Trent Magistrates' Court, ex p. Knight, The Independent,* October 7, 1994, D.C.
Ord. 38,
rules 2, 3, see *R.* v. *Horseferry Magistrates' Court,* ex p. *Bennett (No. 3), The Times,* January 14, 1994, D.C.
rule 5, see *Kearns* v. *Furlong and Parkes,* July 13, 1993, Liverpool District Registry; *Khan* v. *Armguard, The Times,* March 4, 1994, C.A.
Ord. 38,
rule 5, see *Jones* v. *Heald,* January 7, 1994, Chester District Ct.
Ord. 39,
rule 2, see *Panayioutou* v. *Sony Music Entertainment (U.K.)* [1994] 2 W.L.R. 241.
Ord. 41,
rule 5, amended: rules 94/1975, rule 18.
Ord. 42,
rule 3(2), see *Kuwait Airways Corp.* v. *Iraqi Airways Co. (No. 2)* [1994] 1 W.L.R. 985, C.A.
Ord. 49, see *A. Co.* v. *Republic of X and E.C. Commission* [1994] 1 Lloyd's Rep. 111.
Ord. 53,
rule 1(2), see *R.* v. *Secretary of State for Employment,* ex p. *Equal Opportunities Commission* [1994] 2 W.L.R. 409, H.L.

NO.

1965—cont.

1776. Rules of the Supreme Court 1965—*cont.*
Ord. 53—*cont.*
rule 3, see *R.* v. *Northavon District Council*, ex p. *Palmer* (1993) 25 H.L.R. 674.
rule 4, see *Patterson* v. *Greenwich London Borough Council* (1993) 26 H.L.R. 159, C.A.
rule 4(1), see *R.* v. *Secretary of State for Health*, *ex p. Furneaux* [1994] 2 All E.R. 652, C.A.
Ord. 58,
rule 4(b), see *Virgin Group* v. *De Morgan Group*, *The Times*, March 9, 1994, C.A.
Ord. 59,
rule 1, see *S. (A Minor) (Contact Order)*, Re, *The Times*, January 12, 1994, C.A.
rule 1A, amended: rules 94/1975, rule 14.
rule 10(2), see *Royal Bank of Scotland* v. *Binnell and Binnell*, October 28, 1993; D.C. Manchester.
rule 18, see *Hamid and Hamid* v. *Jeje*, May 19, 1994, C.A.
Ord. 62,
see *McDonald* v. *Horn*, *The Times*, August 10, 1994, C.A.
rule 2(2)(g), see *Piper Double Glazing* v. *D.C. Contracts (1992) Co.* [1994] 1 All E.R. 177.
rule 2(4), see *R.* v. *Darlington Borough Council*, ex p. *Association of Darlington Taxi Owners (No. 2)*, *The Times*, April 14, 1994.
rule 3(3), see *Van der Lely NV* v. *Ruston's Engineering Co.* [1993] R.P.C. 45, C.A.
rule 11, see *R.* v. *Secretary of State for the Home Department*, ex p. *Singh* [1993] Imm. A.R. 450; *Ridehalgh* v. *Horsefield; Allen* v. *Unigate Dairies*; *Roberts* v. *Coverite (Asphalters); Philex* v. *Golban*; *Watson* v. *Watson*; *Antonelli* v. *Wade Gerry Farr (A Firm)*, *The Times*, January 28, 1994.
rule 12, see *L.* v. *L. (Legal Aid Taxation)* [1993] 2 FLR 84.
rule 17, amended: rules 94/1975, rule 8.
Ord. 65,
rule 5(ZB)(c), see *Mayes* v. *Gayton International*, November 3, 1993; District Court, Manchester.
Ord. 67,
rule 1, amended: rules 94/1975, rule 9.
rule 7, see *Al-Tobaishi* v. *Aung*, *The Times*, March 10, 1994, C.A.
Ord. 73,
rule 2, see *Cohen* v. *Baram*, *The Times*, December 16, 1993, C.A.

NO.

1965—cont.

1776. Rules of the Supreme Court 1965—*cont.*
Ord. 73—*cont.*
rule 7, amended: rules 94/1975, rule 10.
rule 7(1), see *Sumitomo Heavy Industries* v. *Oil and Natural Gas Commission* [1994] 1 Lloyd's Rep. 45.
Ord. 75,
rule 5, see *International Petroleum Refining and Supply SDAD* v. *Elpis Finance SA, Faith, The* [1993] 2 Lloyd's Rep. 408; *Varna, The* [1993] 2 Lloyd's Rep. 253, C.A.
Ord. 77,
rule 16, amended: rules 94/1975, rule 12.
Ord. 82,
rule 3, amended: rules 94/1975, rule 13.
Ord. 82,
rule 3A, inserted: *ibid.*
Ord. 92,
rule 3, revoked: rules 94/1975, rule 20.
rule 5, amended: *ibid.*, rule 15.
Ord. 93,
rule 3, revoked: rules 94/1975, rule 21.
rules 7, 8, revoked: *ibid.*
rule 10, amended: *ibid.*
rule 11, amended: *ibid.*
rule 12, *ibid.*
rule 14, revoked: *ibid.*
rule 18, amended: *ibid.*
Ord. 94,
rule 12, see *R.* v. *Secretary of State for Wales*, ex p. *Rozhon* 91 L.G.R. 667, C.A.
Ord. 104,
rules 3, 6, see *Rediffusion Simulation* v. *Lint-Miles* [1993] F.S.R. 369.
rules 6, 16, see *Glaverbel SA* v. *British Coal Corp.* (No. 3) [1993] F.S.R. 478.
Ord. 106,
rule 2, amended: rules 94/1975, rule 16.
rule 3, amended: *ibid.*
rule 4, revoked: *ibid.*
rule 5, substituted: *ibid.*
Ord 108,
rule 1, amended: rules 94/1975, rule 22.
rule 3, amended: *ibid.*
rule 4, amended: *ibid.*
Ord. 114,
rule 2, see *BLP Group* v. *Customs and Excise Commissioners; Swallowfield* v. *Customs and Excise Commissioners* [1994] STC 41, C.A.

NO.

1965—cont.

1776. Rules of the Supreme Court 1965—cont.
Ord. 114—cont.
app. A, amended: rules 94/1975, rule 23.

1995. Industrial and Provident Societies Regulations 1965.
sch. 2, substituted: regs. 94/660, reg. 2.

1966

335. Act of Sederunt (Rules of Court Amendment No. 1) 1966.
revoked: Act 94/1443, para. 3.

791. Food Hygiene (Markets, Stalls and Delivery Vehicles) Regulations 1966.
reg. 2, amended: regs. 94/1029, reg. 27.
reg. 2A, substituted: regs. 94/2783, reg. 7.

868. Act of Sederunt (Rules of Court Amendment No. 2) 1966.
revoked: Act 94/1443, para. 3.

969. Industrial Training (Agricultural, Horticultural and Forestry Boards) Order 1966.
revoked: ord. 94/554, art. 3.

1283. Act of Sederunt (Rules of Court Amendment No. 3) 1966.
revoked: Act 94/1443, para. 3.

1298. Crofters etc. Livestock Purchase Loans (Scotland) Scheme 1966.
revoked: scheme 94/1014, para. 2.

1471. Commons Registration (General) Regulations 1966.
reg. 9, amended: ord. 94/2567, art. 2.

1531. Act of Sederunt (Rules of Court Amendment No. 4) 1966.
revoked: Act 94/1443, para. 3.

1551. Young Offenders (Scotland) (Amendment) Rules 1966.
revoked: rules 94/1931, rule 143.

1552. Prison (Scotland) (Amendment) Rules 1966.
revoked: rules 94/1931, rule 143.

1620. Act of Sederunt (Rules of Court Amendment No. 5) 1966.
revoked: Act 94/1443, para. 3.

1967

149. Capital Gains Tax Regulations 1967.
regs. 6, 7, revoked: regs. 94/1813, reg. 2.
reg. 8, revoked in pt.: ibid.
reg. 10, revoked in pt.: ibid.
reg. 11, applied: regs. 94/1811, reg. 22, regs. 94/1812, reg. 18; revoked in pt.: regs. 94/1813, reg. 2.

387. Act of Sederunt (Rules of Court Amendment No. 1) 1967.
revoked: Act 94/1443, para. 3.

395. Veterinary Surgeons and Veterinary Practitioners (Registration Regulations) Order of Council 1967.
reg. 16, amended: regs. 94/305, reg. 2.
reg. 20, amended: ibid., reg. 3.
reg. 23, amended: ibid., reg. 4.

NO.

1967—cont.

480. Carriage by Air Act (Application of Provisions) Order 1967.
see Gurtner v. Beaton [1993] 2 Lloyd's Rep. 369, C.A.

487. Act of Sederunt (Appointment of Judicial Factors and Rules of Court Amendment No. 2) 1967.
paras. 5–8, revoked: Act 94/1443, para. 3.

532. Lancaster Port Commission Revision Order 1967.
arts. 18–23, applied: ord. 94/1647, art. 9.
art. 38, amended: ibid., art. 4.
art. 27, amended: ibid., art. 5.
art. 35, revoked: ibid., art. 6.

1090. Act of Sederunt (Rules of Court Amendment No. 3) 1967.
revoked: Act 94/1443, para. 3.

1199. School Premises (General Requirements and Standards) (Scotland) Regulations 1967.
reg. 27, inserted: regs. 94/351, reg. 3.

1310. Industrial and Provident Societies Regulations 1967.
reg. 5, amended: regs. 94/660, reg. 3.

1789. Act of Sederunt (Rules of Court Amendment No. 4) 1967.
revoked: Act 94/1443, para. 3.

1968

17. Police (Promotion) (Scotland) Regulations 1968.
reg. 3, amended: regs. 94/1953, reg. 2.
reg. 6A, inserted: ibid., reg. 3.

208. Police Cadets (Scotland) Regulations 1968.
sch. 1, amended: regs. 94/2096, reg. 2.
sch. 2, amended: ibid., reg. 3.

1016. Act of Sederunt (Rules of Court Amendment No. 1) 1968.
revoked: Act 94/1443, para. 3.

1122. Act of Sederunt (Form of Extract Decree of Divorce) 1968.
revoked: Act 94/1443, para. 3.

1150. Act of Sederunt (Rules of Court Amendment No. 2) 1968.
revoked: Act 94/1443, para. 3.

1222. Partnerships (Unrestricted Size) No. 1 Regulations 1968.
reg. 1, amended: regs. 94/644, reg. 3.

1558. Customs Duty (Personal Reliefs) (No. 1) Order 1968.
revoked: ord. 94/955, art. 5.

1602. Act of Sederunt (Rules of Court Amendment No. 3) 1968.
revoked: Act 94/1443, para. 3.

1759. Act of Sederunt (Rules of Court Amendment No. 4) 1968.
revoked: Act 94/1443, para. 3.

1760. Act of Sederunt (Rules of Court Amendment No. 5) 1968.
revoked: Act 94/1443, para. 3.

NO.

1969

310. Electrical Appliances (Colour Code) Regulations 1969.
revoked: regs. 94/1768, reg. 2.

474. Act of Sederunt (Rules of Court Amendment No. 1) 1969.
revoked: Act 94/1443, para. 3.

475. Act of Sederunt (Rules of Court Amendment No. 2) 1969.
revoked: Act 94/1443, para. 3.

699. Asbestos Regulations 1969.
regs. 3(2), 15(1)(a), see *Edgson* v. *Vickers, The Times*, April 8, 1994.

945. South-East of Scotland Water Board (Galashiels Mill Lade) Water Order 1969.
art. 6, substituted: ord. 94/810, art. 2.

1487. Traffic Signs (Speed Limits) Regulations and General Directions 1969.
revoked: regs. 94/1519, reg. 2.

1702. Act of Sederunt (Rules of Court Amendment No. 3) 1969.
revoked: Act 94/1443, para. 3.

1703. Act of Sederunt (Rules of Court Amendment No. 4) 1969.
revoked: Act 94/1443, para. 3.

1819. Act of Sederunt (Rules of Court Amendment No. 5) 1969.
revoked: Act 94/1443, para. 3.

1843. Commons Registration (New Land) Regulations 1969.
reg. 5, amended: ord. 94/2567, art. 2.

1970

31. Electrical Appliances (Colour Code) Regulations (Northern Ireland) 1970.
revoked: regs. 94/1768, reg. 2.

96. Act of Sederunt (Rules of Court Amendment No. 1) 1970.
revoked: Act 94/1443, para. 3.

134. Act of Sederunt (Rules of Court Amendment No. 2) 1970.
revoked: Act 94/1443, para. 3.

180. Electrical Appliances (Colour Code) (Amendment) Regulations (Northern Ireland) 1970.
revoked: regs. 94/1768, reg. 2.

212. Trade Marks (Customs) Regulations 1970.
revoked: regs. 94/2625, reg. 7.

231. Justices' Clerks Rules 1970.
sch., para. 18, inserted: rules 94/1481, rule 2.

682. Act of Sederunt (Rules of Court Amendment No. 3) 1970.
revoked: Act 94/1443, para. 3.

803. Gaming Clubs (Bankers' Games) Regulations 1970.
revoked: regs. 94/2899, reg. 3.

804. Gaming Clubs (Bankers' Games) Regulations (Scotland) 1970.
revoked: regs. 94/2899, reg. 3.

NO.

1970—cont.

811. Electrical Appliances (Colour Code) (Amendment) Regulations 1970.
revoked: regs. 94/1768, reg. 2.

1058. Act of Sederunt (Rules of Court Amendment No. 4) 1970.
revoked: Act 94/1443, para. 3.

1152. Drainage Rates (Appeals) Regulations 1970.
reg. 5, amended: ord. 94/2567, art. 2.

1172. Food Hygiene (General) Regulations 1970.
reg. 3, amended: regs. 94/1029, reg. 27.
reg. 3A, substituted: regs. 94/2783, reg. 8.
reg. 27, amended: *ibid.*

1746. Act of Sederunt (Rules of Court Amendment No. 5) 1970.
revoked: Act 94/1443, para. 3.

1790. Three Valleys Water Order 1970.
arts. 16–24, revoked: ord. 94/977, art. 3.
art. 26, revoked: *ibid.*
sch. 2, revoked: *ibid.*

1947. Double Taxation Relief (Taxes on Income) (Austria) Order 1970.
sch., art. 17, substituted: ord. 94/768, sch., art. 1.

2013. Prison (Scotland) (Amendment) Rules 1970.
revoked: rules 94/1931, rule 143.

1971

66. Act of Sederunt (Rules of Court Amendment No. 1) 1971.
revoked: Act 94/1443, para. 3.

198. Act of Sederunt (Rules of Court Amendment No. 5 1970) (Alteration of Fees to Shorthand Writers) 1971.
revoked: Act 94/1443, para. 3.

201. Act of Sederunt (Rules of Court Amendment No. 1) (Alteration by Operative Date) 1971.
revoked: Act 94/1443, para. 3.

202. Act of Sederunt (Rules of Court Amendment No. 2) 1971.
revoked: Act 94/1443, para. 3.

203. Act of Sederunt (Rules of Court Amendment No. 3) 1971.
revoked: Act 94/1443, para. 3.

218. Lands Tribunal for Scotland Rules 1971.
sch. 2, substituted: rules 94/497, rule 2.

265. Act of Sederunt (Rules of Court Amendment No. 4) 1971.
revoked: Act 94/1443, para. 3.

450. Road Vehicles (Registration and Licensing) Regulations 1971.
reg. 3, amended: regs. 94/1911, reg. 4.
reg. 15, amended: regs. 94/1364, reg. 2.
reg. 28A, substituted: regs. 94/1911, reg. 4.

NO.

1971—cont.

450. Road Vehicles (Registration and Licensing) Regulations 1971—*cont.*
reg. 38, amended: *ibid.*, reg. 5.
reg. 41, revoked: *ibid.*, reg. 3.
sch. 4, revoked: *ibid.*

972. Medicines (Standard Provisions for Licences and Certificates) Regulations 1971.
reg. 2, amended: regs. 94/103, reg. 2.
reg. 3, revoked in pt.: reg. 94/2852, reg. 9.
sch. 2, para. 16, amended: regs. 94/103, reg. 3; revoked in pt.: regs. 94/2852, reg. 9.
sch. 3, para. 6, amended: *ibid.*, reg. 4.
sch. 3, para. 8, amended: *ibid.*, reg. 4.

1161. Act of Sederunt (Rules of Court Amendment No. 5) 1971.
revoked: Act 94/1443, para. 3.

1162. Act of Sederunt (Rules of Court Amendment No. 6) 1971.
revoked: Act 94/1443, para. 3.

1165. Act of Sederunt (Edictal Citations, Commissary Petitions and Petitions of Service) 1971.
para. 1, revoked: Act 94/1443, para. 3.

1198. Medicines (Exportation of Specified Products for Human Use) Order 1971.
revoked: ord. 94/787, art. 4.

1200. Medicines (Control of Substances for Manufacture) Order 1971.
sch. 1, amended: ord. 94/787, art. 2.
sch. 2, amended: *ibid.*

1215. Act of Sederunt (Rules of Court Amendment No. 7) 1971.
revoked: Act 94/1443, para. 3.

1253. Indictment Rules 1971.
s. 9, see *R.* v. *Baird (Paul)* (1993) 97 - Cr.App.R. 308, C.A.

1525. General Optical Council (Companies Committee Rules) (Amendment) Order of Council 1971.
revoked: ord. 94/2579, art. 10.

1714. Act of Sederunt (Rules of Court Amendment No. 8) 1971.
revoked: Act 94/1443, para. 3.

1797. Act of Sederunt (Rules of Court Amendment No. 9) 1971.
revoked: Act 94/1443, para. 3.

1809. Act of Sederunt (Rules of Court Amendment No. 10) 1971.
revoked: Act 94/1443, para. 3.

1933. Employers' Liability (Compulsory Insurance) Exemption Regulations 1971.
reg. 2, amended: regs. 94/520, reg. 2.
reg. 3, amended: *ibid.*
reg. 4, inserted: *ibid.*

NO.

1972

164. Act of Sederunt (Rules of Court Amendment No. 1) 1972.
revoked: Act 94/1443, para. 3.

674. Hovercraft (General) Order 1972.
art. 35, applied: regs. 94/1382.

917. Highly Flammable Liquids and Liquefied Petroleum Gases Regulations 1972.
reg. 6, applied: regs. 94/669, reg. 15.
reg. 7, applied: *ibid.*

1139. Solicitors' Remuneration Order 1972.
revoked: ord. 94/2616, art. 1.

1148. Value Added Tax (Supplies by Retailers) Regulations 1972.
reg. 2, see *Gus Merchandise Corp.* v. *Customs and Excise Commissioners (No. 2)*; *Customs and Excise Commissioners* v. *Gus Merchandise (No. 2)* [1993] STC 738; *Customs and Excise Commissioners* v. *Kingfisher* [1994] STC 63.
reg. 6, see *Gus Merchandise Corp.* v. *Customs and Excise Commissioners (No. 2)*; *Customs and Excise Commissioners* v. *Gus Merchandise Corp. (No. 2)* [1993] STC 738.

1265. Health and Personal Social Services (Northern Ireland) Order 1972.
art. 30, applied: 1994, c. 22, sch. 2, para. 19.
art. 30, amended: *ibid.*, sch. 3.

1530. Act of Sederunt (Rules of Court Amendment No. 2) 1972.
revoked: Act 94/1443, para. 3.

1672. Act of Sederunt (Rules of Court Amendment No. 3) 1972 (Alteration of Fees to Shorthand Writers) 1972.
revoked: Act 94/1443, para. 3.

1700. Merchant Shipping (Seamen's Wages and Accounts) Regulations 1972.
reg. 6, substituted: regs. 94/791, reg. 2.

1770. Customs Duty (Personal Reliefs) (No. 1) Order 1968 (Amendment) Order 1972.
revoked: ord. 94/955, art. 5.

1835. Act of Sederunt (Rules of Court Amendment No. 4) 1972.
revoked: Act 94/1443, para. 3.

1981. Act of Sederunt (Rules of Court Amendment No. 5) 1972.
revoked: Act 94/1443, para. 3.

1982. Act of Sederunt (Rules of Court Amendment No. 6) 1972.
revoked: Act 94/1443, para. 3.

2021. Act of Sederunt (Rules of Court Amendment No. 7) 1972.
revoked: Act 94/1443, para. 3.

2022. Act of Sederunt (Rules of Court Amendment No. 8) 1972.
revoked: Act 94/1443, para. 3.

NO.

1972—cont.

2050. East Anglian Water (Capital Powers) Order 1972.
revoked: ord. 94/978, art. 3.

1973

145. Act of Sederunt (Rules of Court Amendment No. 1) 1973.
revoked: Act 94/1443, para. 3.

334. Income Tax (Employments) Regulations 1973.
reg. 3, referred to: 1994, c. 9, s. 133.

360. Act of Sederunt (Rules of Court Amendment No. 2) 1973.
revoked: Act 94/1443, para. 3.

540. Act of Sederunt (Rules of Court Amendment No. 3) 1973.
revoked: Act 94/1443, para. 3.

541. Act of Sederunt (Rules of Court Amendment No. 4) 1973.
revoked: Act 94/1443, para. 3.

950. Registration of Restrictive Trading Agreements (EEC Documents) Regulations 1973.
revoked: regs. 94/1095, reg. 2.

984. Act of Sederunt (Rules of Court Amendment No. 5 1973) (Alteration of Fees to Shorthand Writers) 1973.
revoked: Act 94/1443, para. 3.

1085. Family Allowances (Jersey) Order 1973.
revoked: ord. 94/2802, art. 3.

1311. Hydrocarbon Oil Regulations 1973.
reg. 18, substituted: regs. 94/694, reg. 4.
reg. 20, amended: *ibid.*, reg. 5.
reg. 21, amended: *ibid.*
reg. 28, amended: *ibid.*, reg. 6.
reg. 29, amended: *ibid.*

1522. Magistrates' Courts Committees (Constitution) Regulations 1973.
revoked: regs. 94/2811, reg. 2.

1776. Occupational Pensions Board (Determinations and Review Procedure) Regulations 1973.
reg. 1, amended: regs. 94/1062, reg. 2.
reg. 2, amended: *ibid.*
reg. 5, amended: *ibid.*
reg. 7, amended: *ibid.*

1991. Act of Sederunt (Rules of Court Amendment No. 6) 1973.
revoked: Act 94/1443, para. 3.

1974

160. National Health Service (General Medical and Pharmaceutical Services) Regulations 1974.
art. 3, C.: 1994, c. 22, sch. 2.

168. National Health Service (Vehicles) Order 1974.
revoked: 1994, c. 22, sch. 5.

NO.

1974—cont.

419. Town and Country Planning (Inquiries Procedure) Rules 1974.
see *Portsmouth Water* v. *Secretary of State for the Environment* (1993) 66 P. & C.R. 410.

467. National Health Service (Functions of Common Services Agency) (Scotland) Order 1974.
referred to: 1994, c. 39, s. 43.

506. National Health Service (General Medical and Pharmaceutical Services) (Scotland) Regulations 1974.
reg. 16, amended: regs. 94/884, reg. 2.
reg. 23, amended: *ibid.*, reg. 3.
reg. 27, amended: *ibid.*, reg. 4.
reg. 27A, inserted: *ibid.*, reg. 5.
reg. 32, amended: *ibid.*, reg. 6.
sch. 1, para. 4, amended: *ibid.*, reg. 7.
sch. 1, para. 7A, amended: *ibid.*
sch. 1, para. 12, amended: *ibid.*
sch. 2A, amended: regs. 94/2624, reg. 2.
sch. 2B, amended: *ibid.*, reg. 3.

845. Act of Sederunt (Rules of Court Amendment) 1974.
revoked: Act 94/1443, para. 3.

945. Act of Sederunt (Rules of Court Amendment No. 2) 1974.
revoked: Act 94/1443, para. 3.

946. Act of Sederunt (Rules of Court Amendment No. 3) 1974.
revoked: Act 94/1443, para. 3.

1286. Land Charge Rules 1974.
rule 16, amended: rules 94/287, rule 3.
rule 19, amended: *ibid.*, rule 4.

1329. General Optical Council (Rules on the Testing of Sight by Persons Training as Ophthalmic Opticians) Order of Council 1974.
revoked: ord. 94/70, art. 5.

1491. National Health Service (Vehicles) (Scotland) Order 1974.
art. 3, C.: 1994, c. 22, sch. 2.
revoked: 1994, c. 22, sch. 5.

1603. Act of Sederunt (Rules of Court Amendment No. 4) 1974.
revoked: Act 94/1443, para. 3.

1628. Act of Sederunt (Rules of Court Amendment No. 5) (Alteration of Fees to Shorthand Writers) 1974.
revoked: Act 94/1443, para. 3.

1686. Act of Sederunt (Rules of Court Amendment No. 6) 1974.
revoked: Act 94/1443, para. 3.

1919. Merchant Shipping (Radio) (Fishing Vessels) Rules 1974.
rule 1, amended: rules 94/1104, rule 3.
rule 3, amended: *ibid.*, rule 4.
rule 4, amended: *ibid.*, rule 5.
rule 6, amended: *ibid.*, rules 6, 7.
rule 8, amended: *ibid.*, rule 8.
rule 11A, inserted: *ibid.*, rule 9.
rule 12, amended: *ibid.*, rule 10.
rule 13, amended: *ibid.*, rule 11.

NO.

1974—cont.

2034. Agriculture (Tractor Cabs) Regulations 1974.
applied: regs. 94/397, reg. 4.

2090. Act of Sederunt (Rules of Court Amendment No. 7) 1974.
revoked: Act 94/1443, para. 3.

2211. Rabies (Importation of Dogs, Cats and Other Mammals) Order 1974.
art. 2, amended: ord. 94/1405, art. 8.
art. 4, amended: ord. 94/1716, art. 2.
art. 4A, inserted: *ibid.*

1975

89. Act of Sederunt (Rules of Court Amendment) 1975.
revoked: Act 94/1443, para. 3.

182. Official Secrets (Prohibited Places) Order 1975.
revoked: ord. 94/968, art. 2.

353. Coroners (Compensation) Regulations 1975.
applied: regs. 94/867, reg. 23.
reg. 2, amended: regs. 94/867, reg. 23.

529. Social Security (Mariners' Benefits) Regulations 1975.
applied: regs. 94/648, reg. 24.

536. Trade Union and Employers' Associations (Amalgamations, etc.) Regulations 1975.
reg. 11, amended: regs. 94/546, regs. 2, 3.
reg. 12, amended: *ibid.*, reg. 4.

555. Social Security (Hospital In-Patients) Regulations 1975.
referred to: regs. 94/648, sch. 1, para. 14.

556. Social Security (Credits) Regulations 1975.
reg. 9, amended: regs. 94/1837, reg. 2.
reg. 9A, substituted: *ibid.*, reg. 3.
reg. 9B, amended: *ibid.*, reg. 4.

563. Social Security Benefit (Persons Abroad) Regulations 1975.
reg. 2, amended: regs. 94/268, reg. 2.
reg. 2(1), see *Chief Adjudication Officer* v. *Ahmed, The Times,* April 6, 1994, C.A.
reg. 2(1)(a), see *Social Security Decision No. R(S) 2/93.*
reg. 2(1)(b)(c)(d), see *Social Security Decision No. R(S) 2/94.*
reg. 5, applied: regs. 94/559, reg. 3; amended: regs. 94/1832, reg. 2.
sch., inserted: regs. 94/1832, reg. 3.

590. Social Security (Attendance Allowance) (No. 2) Regulations 1975.
reg. 2(1), see *Social Security Decision No. R(A) 1/94.*

1023. Rehabilitation of Offenders Act 1974 (Exceptions) Order 1975.
sch. 1, pt. I, amended: 1994, c. 17, s. 40.
sch. 1, pt. IV, amended: *ibid.*

NO.

1975—cont.

1092. Further Education Regulations 1975.
reg. 3, applied: 1994, c. 30, s. 18.

1100. National Health Service (Constitution of Regional Health Authorities) Order 1975.
revoked: ord. 94/684, art. 5.

1106. Act of Sederunt (Rules of Court Amendment No. 2) 1975.
revoked: Act 94/1443, para. 3.

1135. Schools General (Scotland) Regulations 1975.
reg. 10, amended: regs. 94/351, reg. 8.
reg. 13A, inserted: *ibid.*, reg. 4.

1326. Medicines (Advertising of Medicinal Products) (No. 2) Regulations 1975.
reg. 2, amended: regs. 94/1932, reg. 24.

1385. Juvenile Courts (London) Order 1975.
revoked: ord. 94/1695, art. 2.

1585. Act of Sederunt (Rules of Court Amendment No. 3) (Alteration of Fees to Shorthand Writers) 1975.
revoked: Act 94/1443, para. 3.

2000. Medicines (Child Safety) Regulations 1975.
reg. 2, amended: regs. 94/1402, reg. 2.

2212. Veterinary Surgeons and Veterinary Practitioners (Registration) (Amendment) Regulations (No. 2) Order of Council 1975.
revoked: ord. 94/305.

1976

137. Act of Sederunt (Rules of Court Amendment) 1976.
revoked: Act 94/1443, para. 3.

142. Occupational Pension Schemes (Equal Access to Membership) Regulations 1976.
reg. 1, amended: regs. 94/1062, reg. 2.
reg. 2 amended: *ibid.*
reg. 3, amended: *ibid.*
reg. 13, amended: *ibid.*
reg. 14, amended: *ibid.*

185. Occupational Pensions Board (Determinations and Review Procedure) Regulations 1976.
reg. 1, amended: regs. 94/1062, reg. 2.
reg. 2, amended: *ibid.*
reg. 3, amended: *ibid.*
reg. 4, amended: *ibid.*

282. Act of Sederunt (Rules of Court Amendment No. 2) 1976.
revoked: Act 94/1443, para. 3.

372. Act of Sederunt (Rules of Court Amendment No. 3) (Alteration of Fees to Shorthand Writers) 1976.
revoked: Act 94/1443, para. 3.

409. Social Security (Invalid Care Allowance) Regulations 1976.
reg. 2, amended: regs. 94/2556, reg. 5.

NO.

1976—cont.

409. Social Security (Invalid Care Allowance) Regulations 1976—*cont.*
reg. 10, amended: *ibid.*
reg. 10A, inserted: *ibid.*
reg. 11, amended: *ibid.*
reg. 11A, inserted: *ibid.*

476. Act of Sederunt (Summary Cause Rules, Sheriff Court) 1976.
rule 27, see *Scottish Homes* v. *Hamilton* (Sh.Ct.), 1993 S.C.L.R. 771.

582. Solicitors (Northern Ireland) Order 1976.
art. 22, referred to: 1994, c. 26, s. 86.

615. Social Security (Medical Evidence) Regulations 1976.
reg. 2, applied: regs. 94/648, sch. 1, para. 12.

745. Act of Sederunt (Rules of Court Amendment No. 4) 1976.
revoked: Act 94/1443, para. 3.

779. Act of Sederunt (Rules of Court Amendment No. 5) 1976.
revoked: Act 94/1443, para. 3.

847. Act of Sederunt (Rules of Court Amendment No. 6) (Appeals under Consumer Credit Act 1974) 1976.
revoked: Act 94/1443, para. 3.

867. Act of Sederunt (Rules of Court Amendment No. 7) (Solicitor's Admission Fees) 1976.
revoked: Act 94/1443, para. 3.

963. Child Benefit (Residence and Persons Abroad) Regulations 1976.
sch., amended: ord. 94/2802, art. 3.

1043. Industrial Relations (Northern Ireland) Order 1976.
applied: 1994, c. 33, s. 126.
art. 22C, amended: 1994, c. 40, s. 36.

1073. Police (Scotland) Regulations 1976.
reg. 21, amended: regs. 94/2231, reg. 2.
reg. 21A, amended: *ibid.*, reg. 3.
reg. 21B, amended: *ibid.*, reg. 4.
reg. 22, amended: *ibid.*, reg. 5.
reg. 23, amended: *ibid.*, reg. 6.
reg. 23A, inserted: *ibid.*, reg. 7.
reg. 27A, inserted: *ibid.*, reg. 8.
reg. 28A, inserted: regs. 94/2095, reg. 4.
regs. 42–42D, revoked: regs. 94/2231, reg. 12.
regs. 43–45, revoked: *ibid.*
reg. 47, amended: regs. 94/2095, reg. 5.
regs. 48–49, revoked: regs. 94/2231, reg. 12.
reg. 51, amended: *ibid.*, reg. 9.
regs. 55–56, revoked: *ibid.*, reg. 12.
reg. 58, amended: *ibid.*, reg. 10.
reg. 62, revoked: *ibid.*, reg. 12.
reg. 66, revoked: *ibid.*
sch. 1A, para. 4, amended: *ibid.*, reg. 11.
sch. 3, Table A, substituted: regs. 94/2095, reg. 6.
sch. 3, Table B, substituted: *ibid.*
sch. 10, para. 1, amended: *ibid.*, reg. 2.

NO.

1976—cont.

1073. Police (Scotland) Regulations 1976—*cont.*
sch. 9, para. 4, revoked in pt.: regs. 94/2231, reg. 12.
schs. 6–7, revoked: *ibid.*

1221. Poultry Meat (Hygiene) Regulations 1976.
revoked: regs. 94/1029, reg. 26.

1276. Child Benefit and Social Security (Fixing and Adjustment of Rates) Regulations 1976.
reg. 2, amended: regs. 94/542, reg. 13.

1572. Immigration (Variation of Leave) Order 1976.
art. 3(1), see *R.* v. *Secretary of State for the Home Department, ex P. Oyeleye (Florence Jumoke)* [1994] Imm AR 268.

1605. Act of Sederunt (Rules of Court Amendment No. 9) (Alteration of Fees to Shorthand Writers No. 2) 1976.
revoked: Act 94/1443, para. 3.

1726. Medicines (Labelling) Regulations 1976.
reg. 3, amended: regs. 94/104, reg. 2.
reg. 4F, inserted: *ibid.*, reg. 3.
sch. 9, inserted: *ibid.*, reg. 4.

1849. Act of Sederunt (Rules of Court Amendment No. 10) (Revenue Appeals) 1976.
revoked: Act 94/1443, para. 3.

1989. Motor Fuel (Sulphur Content of Gas Oil) Regulations 1976.
revoked: regs. 94/2295, reg. 12.

1994. Act of Sederunt (Rules of Court Amendment No. 11) (Consistorial Appeals) 1976.
revoked: Act 94/1443, para. 3.

2019. Motor Vehicles (Competitions and Trials) (Scotland) Regulations 1976.
sch. 2, amended: regs. 94/2653, reg. 2.
sch. 3, amended: *ibid.*

2145. Virgin Islands (Constitution) Order 1976.
art. 26, amended: ord. 94/1638, art. 2.
art. 27, amended: *ibid.*, art. 3.
art. 40, amended: *ibid.*, art. 4.
art. 48, amended: *ibid.*, art. 5.

2147. Industrial Relations (No. 2) (Northern Ireland) Order 1976.
applied: 1994, c. 33, s. 126.

2196. Act of Sederunt (Rules of Court Amendment No. 13) (Medical Witnesses' Fees) 1976.
revoked: Act 94/1443, para. 3.

2197. Act of Sederunt (Rules of Court Amendment No. 14) (Third Party Procedure) 1976.
revoked: Act 94/1443, para. 3.

NO.

1977

158. Guarantee Payments (Exemption) (No. 3) Order 1977.
revoked: ord. 94/1409, art. 3.

176. General Optical Council (Registration and Enrolment Rules) Order of Council 1977.
amended: ord. 94/729, art. 2.

238. Lotteries (Scotland) Regulations 1977.
revoked: regs. 93/3223, reg. 1.
revoked: regs. 93/3223, reg. 1.

295. East Anglian Water (Capital Powers) Order 1977.
revoked: ord. 94/978, art. 3.

301. Electrical Appliances (Colour Code) (Amendment) Regulations (Northern Ireland) 1977.
revoked: regs. 94/1768, reg. 2.

343. Social Security (Dependency) Regulations 1977.
reg. 1, amended: regs. 94/2943, reg. 15.
reg. 3, amended: *ibid.*
reg. 8, amended: *ibid.*
reg. 10, amended: *ibid.*
reg. 11, amended: *ibid.*
reg. 12, substituted: *ibid.*
reg. 13, amended: *ibid.*

472. Act of Sederunt (Rules of Court Amendment No. 2) (Adoption Proceedings) 1977.
revoked: 94/1443, para. 3.

486. Offshore Installations (Life-saving Appliances) Regulations 1977.
reg. 11, amended: regs. 94/397, reg. 16.
sch., revoked: *ibid.*

500. Safety Representatives and Safety Committee Regulations 1977.
reg. 2, applied: regs. 94/237, reg. 2.

592. Child Benefit (Guernsey) Order 1977.
revoked: ord. 94/2802, art. 3.

815. Town and Country Planning (New Towns in Rural Wales) Special Development Order 1977.
referred to: ord. 94/2567, art. 4.
art. 8, amended: *ibid.*, art. 2.

931. Electrical Appliances (Colour Code) (Amendment) Regulations 1977.
revoked: regs. 94/1768, reg. 2.

952. Traffic Signs (Speed Limits) (Amendment) Regulations and General Directions 1977.
revoked: regs. 94/1519, reg. 2.

974. Act of Sederunt (Rules of Court Amendment No. 3) (Applications under Companies and Insolvencies Act 1976) 1977.
revoked: Act 94/1443, para. 3.

978. Act of Sederunt (Rules of Court Amendment No. 4) (Shorthand Writers' Fees) 1977.
revoked: Act 94/1443, para. 3.

NO.

1977—cont.

1055. Medicines (Leaflets) Regulations 1977.
reg. 2, amended: regs. 94/104, reg. 5.
reg. 3, amended: *ibid.*, reg. 6.
reg. 3B, inserted: *ibid.*, reg. 7.
reg. 4, amended: *ibid.*, reg. 8.
reg. 5, amended: *ibid.*, reg. 9.
sch. 3, inserted: *ibid.*, reg. 10.

1247. Criminal Damage (Compensation) (Northern Ireland) Order 1977.
art. 9, amended: 1994, c. 22, sch. 3.

1621. Act of Sederunt (Rules of Court Amendment No. 5) (Miscellaneous Amendments) 1977.
revoked: Act 94/1443, para. 3.

1978

41. Medicines (Labelling and Advertising to the Public) Regulations 1978.
reg. 1A, inserted: regs. 94/1932, reg. 24.

106. Act of Sederunt (Rules of Court Amendment No. 1) (Consistorial Causes) 1978.
revoked: Act 94/1443, para. 3.

161. Act of Sederunt (Rules of Court Amendment No. 3) (Presumption of Death) 1978.
revoked: Act 94/1443, para. 3.

277. South Africa (United Nations Arms Embargo) (Prohibited Transactions) Order 1978.
revoked: ord. 94/1636, art. 2.

393. Social Security (Graduated Retirement Benefit) (No. 2) Regulations 1978.
reg. 3, see *Social Security Decision No. R(P) 2/93.*
sch. 2, amended: regs. 94/542, reg. 11.

508. Social Security Pensions (Home Responsibilities and Miscellaneous Amendments) Regulations 1978.
reg. 1, amended: regs. 94/704, reg. 3.
reg. 2, revoked: *ibid.*

611. Offshore Installations (Fire-fighting Equipment) Regulations 1978.
reg. 20, amended: regs. 94/397, reg. 16.
sch., revoked: *ibid.*

690. Act of Sederunt (Rules of Court Amendment No. 4) (Commercial Causes) 1978.
revoked: 94/1443, para. 3.

799. Act of Sederunt (Rules of Court Amendment No. 5) (Depute Clerks of Session) 1978.
revoked: Act 94/1443, para. 3.

891. Parliamentary and Other Pensions (Contracted-Out Provisions) Order 1978.
revoked: regs. 93/3253, reg. R5.

925. Act of Sederunt (Rules of Court Amendment No. 6) (Shorthand Writers' Fees) 1978.
revoked: Act 94/1443, para. 3.

NO.
1978—cont.

955. Act of Sederunt (Rules of Court Amendment No. 8) (Patent Rules) 1978.
revoked: Act 94/1443, para. 3.

1020. Medicines (Advertising to Medical and Dental Practitioners) Regulations 1978.
revoked: regs. 94/1932, reg. 24.

1034. South Africa (United Nations Arms Embargo) (Prohibited Transactions) (Amendment) Order 1978.
revoked: ord. 94/1636, art. 2.

1039. Health and Safety at Work (Northern Ireland) Order 1978.
referred to: 1994, c. 40, s. 37.

1047. Protection of Children (Northern Ireland) Order 1978.
art. 2, amended: 1994, c. 33, s. 84.
art. 3, amended: *ibid*.
art. 4, amended: *ibid*., sch. 10, para. 38.
art. 5, amended: *ibid*.

1049. Pollution Control and Local Government (Northern Ireland) Order 1978.
art. 36, amended: 1994, c. 22, sch. 3.

1052. South Africa (United Nations Arms Embargo) (Prohibited Transactions) (Guernsey) Order 1978.
revoked: ord. 94/1636, art. 2.

1053. South Africa (United Nations Arms Embargo) (Prohibited Transactions) (Isle of Man) Order 1978.
revoked: ord. 94/1636, art. 2.

1054. South Africa (United Nations Arms Embargo) (Prohibited Transactions) (Jersey) Order 1978.
revoked: ord. 94/1636, art. 2.

1087. London–Holyhead Trunk Road (Gwalchmai By-Pass) Order 1978.
revoked: ord. 94/108, art. 1.

1373. Act of Sederunt (Rules of Court Amendment No. 9) (Convention Adoption Rules) 1978.
revoked: Act 94/1443, para. 3.

1394. Insurance Brokers Registration Council (Code of Conduct) Approval Order 1978.
revoked: ord. 94/2569, art. 3.

1524. State Immunity (Merchant Shipping) (Union of Soviet Socialist Republics) Order 1978.
arts. 3, 4, see *Coreck Maritime* v. *Sevrybokholod-oflot*, 1994 S.L.T. 893.

1527. Social Security (Jersey and Guernsey) Order 1978.
revoked: ord. 94/2802, art. 3.

1624. South Africa (Prohibited Exports and Transactions) (Overseas Territories) Order 1978.
revoked: ord. 94/1636, art. 2.

NO.
1978—cont.

1689. Social Security (Categorisation of Earners) Regulations 1978.
reg. 1, amended: regs. 94/726, reg. 2.
sch. 1, pt. III, amended: *ibid*., reg. 3.
sch. 3, para. 9, inserted: *ibid*., reg. 4.

1804. Act of Sederunt (Rules of Court Amendment No. 10) (Induciae) 1978.
revoked: Act 94/1443, para. 3.

1837. Parliamentary Pensions (Purchase of Added Years) Order 1978.
revoked: regs. 93/3253, reg. R5.

1883. Customs Duty (Personal Reliefs) (No. 1) Order 1968 (Amendment) Order 1978.
revoked: ord. 94/955, art. 5.

1895. South Africa (United Nations Arms Embargo) (Prohibited Transactions) (Amendment No. 2) Order 1978.
revoked: ord. 94/1636, art. 2.

1896. South Africa (United Nations Arms Embargo) (Prohibited Transactions) (Guernsey) (Amendment) Order 1978.
revoked: ord. 94/1636, art. 2.

1897. South Africa (United Nations Arms Embargo) (Prohibited Transactions) (Isle of Man) (Amendment) Order 1978.
revoked: ord. 94/1636, art. 2.

1898. South Africa (United Nations Arms Embargo) (Prohibited Transactions) (Jersey) (Amendment) Order 1978.
revoked: ord. 94/1636, art. 2.

1979

195. Rehabilitation of Offenders (Exceptions) Order (Northern Ireland) 1979.
sch. 1, pt. I, amended: 1994, c. 17, s. 40.
sch. 1, pt. IV, amended: *ibid*.

516. Act of Sederunt (Rules of Court Amendment No. 2) (European Assembly Election Petitions) 1979.
revoked: Act 94/1443, para. 3.

591. Social Security (Contributions) Regulations 1979.
reg. 7, amended: regs. 94/563, reg. 2.
reg. 18, amended: regs. 94/2194, reg. 2.
reg. 22C, amended: regs. 94/667, reg. 2.
reg. 22D, amended: *ibid*.
reg. 22F, amended: *ibid*.
reg. 25, amended: regs. 94/1553, reg. 2.
reg. 38, amended: *ibid*., reg. 3.
reg. 123D, amended: regs. 94/563, reg. 2.
sch. 1, reg. 30, amended: regs. 94/667, reg. 2.
sch. 1, para. 3, amended: regs. 94/2299, reg. 2.

NO.

1979—cont.

591. Social Security (Contributions) Regulations 1979—*cont.*
sch. 1A, para. 5, amended: regs. 94/2194, reg. 3.
sch. 1A, para. 9A, amended: *ibid.*
sch. 1A, para. 9ZA, inserted: *ibid.*
sch. 1A, para. 9ZB, inserted: *ibid.*
sch. 1A, para. 17, inserted: *ibid.*
sch. 1A, para. 18, inserted: *ibid.*
sch. 3, para. 9, substituted: regs. 94/1553, reg. 4.

597. Social Security (Overlapping Benefits) Regulations 1979.
referred to: regs. 94/648, sch. 1, para. 15; applied: regs. 94/826, reg. 1.

642. Social Security (Widow's Benefit and Retirement Pensions) Regulations 1979.
reg. 4(1)(b), see *Social Security Decision No. R(P) 2/93.*

670. Act of Sederunt (Rules of Court Amendment No. 3) (International Oil Pollution Compensation Fund) 1979.
revoked: Act 94/1443, para. 3.

693. Poultry Meat (Hygiene) (Amendment) Regulations 1979.
revoked: regs. 94/1029, reg. 26.

937. Industrial and Provident Societies (Credit Unions) Regulations 1979.
sch. 2, substituted: regs. 94/658, reg. 2.

1033. Act of Sederunt (Rules of Court Amendment No. 4) (Shorthand Writers' Fees) 1979.
revoked: Act 94/1443, para. 3.

1087. Conwy Mussel Fishery (Variation) Order 1979.
sch., para. 4, revoked: regs. 94/275, reg. 2.

1410. Act of Sederunt (Rules of Court Amendment No. 5) 1979.
revoked: Act 94/1443, para. 3.

1551. Customs Duty (Personal Reliefs) (No. 1) Order 1968 (Amendment) Order 1979.
revoked: ord. 94/955, art. 5.

1573. Statutory Rules (Northern Ireland) Order 1979.
referred to: 1994, c. 40, s. 37, s. 82.

1596. Brucellosis (Scotland) Order 1979.
art. 8A, inserted: ord. 94/2770, art. 2.

1630. Prison (Scotland) Amendment Rules 1979.
revoked: rules 94/1931, rule 143.

1980

136. Dangerous Substances and Preparations (Safety) Regulations 1980.
revoked: regs. 94/2844, reg. 7.

NO.

1980—cont.

290. Act of Sederunt (Rules of Court Amendment No. 1) (Adoption Proceedings) 1980.
revoked: Act 94/1443, para. 3.

440. Value Added Tax (Fuel and Power) Order 1980.
revoked: 1994, c. 23, sch. 15.

456. HMSO Trading Fund Order 1980.
sch., para. (a), substituted: ord. 94/1192, art. 2.
sch., para. (b), substituted: *ibid.*, art. 3.

535. Merchant Shipping (Passenger Ship Construction) Regulations 1980.
reg. 11, amended: regs. 94/1383, reg. 3; amended: regs. 94/422, reg. 3.

891. Act of Sederunt (Rules of Court Amendment No. 3) (Protection of Trading Interests Act 1980) 1980.
revoked: Act 94/1443, para. 3.

892. Act of Sederunt (Rules of Court Amendment No. 4) (Applications under section 85 of Fair Trading Act 1973) 1980.
revoked: Act 94/1443, para. 3.

909. Act of Sederunt (Rules of Court Amendment No. 5) (Witnesses' Fees) 1980.
revoked: Act 94/1443, para. 3.

918. Education (Middle Schools) Regulations 1980.
reg. 2, amended: ord. 94/580, art. 2.

958. Novelties (Safety) Order 1980.
revoked: regs. 94/2844, reg. 7.

979. Anti-Competitive Practices (Exclusions) Order 1980.
art. 2, amended: ord. 94/1557, art. 2.
art. 3, amended: *ibid.*, art. 3.
sch. 2, amended: *ibid.*, art. 4.

1016. Act of Sederunt (Rules of Court Amendment No. 6) (Shorthand Writers' Fees) 1980.
revoked: Act 94/1443, para. 3.

1089. Summer Time Order 1980.
revoked: ord. 94/2798, art. 5.

1144. Act of Sederunt (Rules of Court Amendment No. 7) (Miscellaneous Amendments) 1980.
revoked: Act 94/1443, para. 3.

1183. Vehicle Licences (Duration and Rate of Duty) Order 1980.
art. 5, C. in pt.: 1994, c. 22, ss. 3, 4.

1248. Control of Lead at Work Regulations 1980.
applied: regs. 94/397, regs. 3, 8.

1258. Magistrates' Courts Committees (Constitution) (Amendment) Regulations 1980.
revoked: regs. 94/2811, reg. 2.

1450. European Parliament (United Kingdom Representatives) Pensions Order 1980.
revoked: ord. 94/1662, art. 32.
art. 4, amended: ord. 94/1664, *ibid.*
art. 8B, inserted: ord. 94/1662, *ibid.*

NO.

1980—cont.

1450. European Parliament (United Kingdom Representatives) Pensions Order 1980—cont.
art. 9, amended: *ibid.*
art. 10, amended: *ibid.*
art. 12, amended: *ibid.*
art. 15, amended: *ibid.*
art. 17, applied: *ibid.*
art. 18, applied: *ibid.*
sch. 6, amended: *ibid.*
sch. 7, substituted: *ibid.*

1709. Control of Pollution (Special Waste) Regulations 1980.
reg. 2, applied: regs. 94/1056, reg. 1.
reg. 7, substituted: regs. 94/1137, reg. 18.
reg. 13, applied: regs. 94/1056, reg. 10.
reg. 14, applied: *ibid.*

1754. Act of Sederunt (Rules of Court Amendment No. 8) (Leave to appeal and appeals from Social Security Commissioners) 1980.
revoked: Act 94/1443, para. 3.

1801. Act of Sederunt (Rules of Court Amendment No. 9) (Remits from Sheriff Court) 1980.
revoked: Act 94/1443, para. 3.

1923. Medicines (Sale or Supply) (Miscellaneous Provisions) Regulations 1980.
reg. 8, amended: regs. 94/2411, reg. 2.

1924. Medicines (Pharmacy and General Sale—Exemption) Order 1980.
art. 2, amended: ord. 94/2409, art. 2.

1981

15. Public Bodies' Land (Appropriate Ministers) Order 1981.
referred to: ord. 94/2567, art. 8.
art. 2, amended: *ibid.*, art. 2.

109. Lotteries (Amendment) Regulations 1981.
revoked: regs. 93/3223, reg. 1.

154. Road Traffic (Northern Ireland) Order 1981.
art. 28, applied: 1994, c. 22, s. 61, sch. 1, para. 6.
art. 29, amended: *ibid.*, sch. 3.
art. 31D, amended: *ibid.*
art. 33, applied: *ibid.*, sch. 2, para. 22.
art. 34, amended: 1994, c. 9, sch. 2, para. 24; 1994, c. 22, sch. 3.
art. 89, amended: *ibid.*
art. 188, amended: 1994, c. 22, sch. 3.
art. 189, amended: *ibid.*

155. Firearms (Northern Ireland) Order 1981.
art. 18, applied: 1994, c. 33, s. 123.

156. Housing (Northern Ireland) Order 1981.
pt. VII, applied: 1994, c. 23, sch. 10, para. 3.

NO.

1981—cont.

226. Judgments Enforcement (Northern Ireland) Order 1981.
art. 2, applied: 1994, c. 23, s. 87.

252. Pollution Control (Special Waste) Regulations (Northern Ireland) 1981.
reg. 8, substituted: regs. 94/1137, reg. 18.

303. Lotteries (Scotland) (Amendment) Regulations 1981.
revoked: regs. 93/3223, reg. 1.

330. Social Security Pensions (Home Responsibilities and Graduated Retirement Benefit) Amendment Regulations 1981.
revoked: regs. 94/704, reg. 3.

552. Magistrates' Courts Rules 1981.
rule 11, amended: rules 94/1481, rule 3.
rule 12(1), see *D.P.P.* v. *Butterworth* [1994] 3 W.L.R. 538, H.L.
rule 17, amended: rules 94/1481, rule 3.
rule 93A, inserted: *ibid.*
rule 100, see *D.P.P.* v. *Butterworth* [1994] 3 W.L.R. 538, H.L.

553. Magistrates' Courts (Forms) Rules 1981.
sch. 2, amended: rules 94/1481, rule 4.

800. Parliamentary Pensions (Purchase of Added Years) (Amendment) Order 1981.
revoked: regs. 93/3253, reg. R5.

839. Employment (Miscellaneous Provisions) (Northern Ireland) Order 1991.
arts. 3, 4, 5, revoked: 1994, c. 40, sch. 10, para. 2.
art. 5A, inserted: *ibid.*
art. 5B, inserted: *ibid.*
art. 5C, inserted: *ibid.*
art. 11, amended: *ibid.*, para. 5.

859. Traffic Signs Regulations and General Directions 1981.
revoked: regs. 94/1519, reg. 2.

1086. Education (Schools and Further Education) Regulations 1981.
applied: regs. 94/651, sch., para. 7.
reg. 15, applied: 1994, c. 30, s. 18.
reg. 16, applied: *ibid.*

1115. Diseases of Animals (Northern Ireland) Order 1981.
art. 12, applied: regs. 94/672, reg. 13.

1137. Act of Sederunt (Rules of Court Amendment No. 3) (Shorthand Writers' Fees) 1981.
revoked: Act 94/1443, para. 3.

1168. Poultry Meat (Hygiene) (Scotland) Amendment Regulations 1981.
revoked: regs. 94/1029, reg. 26.

1222. Prisons (Scotland) (Amendment) Rules 1981.
revoked: rules 94/1931, rule 143.

1223. Young Offenders (Scotland) (Amendment) Rules 1981.
revoked: rules 94/1931, rule 143.

NO.

1981—cont.

1302. Ancient Monuments (Class Consents) Order 1981.
revoked: ord. 94/1381, art. 3.

1468. Ancient Monuments (Class Consents) (Scotland) Order 1981.
sch., class II, amended: ord. 94/2567, art. 2.

1523. Motor Fuel (Lead Content of Petrol) Regulations 1981.
revoked: regs. 94/2295, reg. 12.

1529. Supplementary Benefit (Urgent Cases) Regulations 1981.
see *Social Security Decision No. R(SB) 1/94.*

1654. Insurance Companies Regulations 1981.
revoked: regs. 94/1516, reg. 86.

1671. South Africa (United Nations Arms Embargo) (Prohibited Transactions) (Amendment) Order 1981.
revoked: ord. 94/1636, art. 2.

1675. Magistrates' Courts (Northern Ireland) Order 1981.
art. 2, applied: 1994, c. 9, s. 27, sch. 7, para. 6; 1994, c. 22, ss. 51, 55.
art. 10, applied: 1994, c. 33, s. 120.
art. 16, applied: *ibid.*, s. 91.
art. 114, applied: ord. 94/451, art. 5; applied: ord. 94/1679, art. 5, ord. 94/1681, art. 4.
art. 146, applied: 1994, c. 26, s. 97.
art. 154, applied: ord. 94/451, art. 5; applied: ord. 94/1679, art. 5, ord. 94/1681, art. 4.
sch. 4, applied: 1994, c. 26, s. 101.

1687. County Court Rules.
Ord. 1,
rule 3, amended: rules 94/2403, rule 16.
rule 10, see *Trace* v. *Kedward*, May 9, 1994, Cardiff County Court.
rule 13, substituted: rules 94/2403, rule 2.
Ord. 7,
rule 10(1), see *Willowgreen* v. *Smithers* [1994] 1 W.L.R. 832, C.A.
rule 20, amended: rules 94/2403, rule 3.
Ord. 9,
rules 2, 6 see *Cooper* v. *Price*, July 21, 1994, Birmingham County Court.
rule 6(2), see *Bevis* v. *Tarmey*, July 19, 1993, Walsall County Court.
rule 9, see *Cooper* v. *Price*, July 21, 1994, Birmingham County Court.
rule 14, see *Rooney* v. *Smith*, September 20, 1993; Liverpool County Court; see *Kinetsu World Express (U.K.)* v. *Advance Mouldings Component*, May 10, 1994, Uxbridge County Court.

NO.

1981—cont.

1687. County Court Rules—*cont.*
Ord. 11,
rule 3, see *Trace* v. *Kedward*, May 9, 1994, Cardiff County Court.
rule 10, see *Ager* v. *Liverpool City Council*, April 5, 1994, Liverpool County Court.
Ord. 13,
rule 2, amended: rules 94/2403, rule 4.
rule 4, see *Kelliher* v. *E.H. Savill Engineering*, The Times, May 10, 1994, C.A.
rule 10, see *Sandle* v. *Lewis*, July 11, 1994, Brentwood County Court.
Ord. 17,
rule 11, see *Gough* v. *Birdseye Walls*, May 11, 1994, Sheffield County Court; amended: rules 94/1288, rule 2.
rule 11(2)(b), (9), see *Nelson and Guy* v. *Infil Housing Co-op*; *Rastin* v. *British Steel*; *Todd* v. *Evans*; *Adams* v. *Geest*; *Byrne* v. *Webber*; *Donaldson* v. *Canavan*; *Ayres* v. *British Steel*, March 7, 1994, Central London County Court.
rule 11(9), see *Rastin* v. *British Steel*; *Todd* v. *Evans*; *Adams* v. *Geest*; *Byrne* v. *Webber*; *Donaldson* v. *Canavan*; *Ayres* v. *British Steel*, The Times, February 14, 1994, C.A.; *Carter* v. *Hirst*, April 25, 1994, Exeter County Court: see *Rastin* v. *British Steel*; *Todd* v. *Evans*; *Adams* v. *Geest*; *Byrne* v. *Webber*; *Donaldson* v. *Canavan*; *Ayres* v. *British Steel* [1994] 1 W.L.R. 732, C.A.; see *Sandle* v. *Lewis*, July 11, 1994, Brentwood County Court.
Ord. 19,
see *Starmer* v. *Bradbury*, The Times, April 11, 1994, C.A.; *Smith* v. *Sanson*, April 26, 1994, Lambeth County Court.
rule 2, see *James* v. *Royal Ordnance*, March 24, 1994, Nottingham County Court.
rule 3, see *Hoptroff* v. *TNT Express (U.K.)*, April 14, 1994, Oldham County Court.
rule 3(1), (2)(d), (3)(b), see *King (Colin)* v. *Hickman (Gabrielle)*, September 6, 1994, Hastings County Court.
Ord. 22,
rule 8, amended: rules 94/2403, rule 6.

NO.

1981—cont.

1687. County Court Rules—*cont.*
Ord. 24,
  see *Friendship Housing Association*
    v. *Buchanan*, September 9, 1994,
    Birmingham County Court.
Ord. 25,
  rule 2, amended: rules 94/2403, rule
    5.
  rule 3, amended: *ibid.*, rule 13.
  rule 11, amended: *ibid.*, rule 8.
  rule 12, substituted: *ibid.*, rule 9.
  rule 13, amended: *ibid.*, rule 7.
Ord. 27,
  rule 7B, inserted: rules 94/2403, rule
    12.
  rule 8, amended: *ibid.*
Ord. 28,
  rule 4, amended: rules 94/2403, rule
    14.
Ord. 31,
  rule 1, amended: rules 94/2403, rule
    15.
Ord. 37,
  rule 4, see *Cooper* v. *Price*, July 21,
    1994, Birmingham County Court.
  rule 6, see *Leather* v. *Liverpool City
    Council*, July 13, 1994, Liverpool
    County Court.
  rule 8(1), see *Hammersmith and Ful-
    ham London Borough Council* v.
    Hill, The Times, April 25, 1994,
    C.A.
Ord. 38,
  rule 1(2), see *The Wellcome Foun-
    dation* v. *Discpharm (No. 2)*
    [1993] F.S.R. 444, Patents County
    Court.
  rule 2, amended: rules 94/306, rule 2.
  rule 4(6), see *Sutherland* v. *Wall and
    Wall*, May 3, 1993, Dartford
    County Court.
  rule 14(1), see *Leather* v. *Liverpool
    City Council*, July 13, 1994, Liver-
    pool County Court.
Ord. 44,
  rule 4, amended: rules 94/2403, rule
    10.
Ord. 48A,
  see *The Wellcome Foundation* v.
    Discpharm [1993] F.S.R. 433, Pat-
    ents County Court.
Ord. 48C,
  inserted: rules 94/1288, rule 3.
  app. B, Pt. I, amended: rules 94/2403,
    rule 11.
**1741. Value Added Tax (Special Provisions)
  Order 1981.**
  art. 9(1), see *Customs and Excise Com-
    missioners* v. *P & O Steam Navi-
    gation Co.* [1994] STC 259, C.A.;
    Thorn EMI v. *Customs and Excise
    Commissioners* [1994] STC 469.

NO.

1981—cont.

**1794. Transfer of Undertakings (Protection
  of Employment) Regulations 1981.**
  see *Longden* v. *Ferrari and Kennedy
    International, The Times*, February
    14, 1994, E.A.T.; *Dines* v. *Initial
    Health Care Services*, May 27, 1994,
    C.A.; *Ibex Trading Co.* v. *Walton,
    The Times*, July 29, 1994, E.A.T.;
    applied: 1994, c. 21, sch. 2, para. 7.
  regs. 2(1), 3(1), see *Dines* v. *Initial
    Healthcare Services* [1993] I.C.R.
    978, E.A.T.; *Wren* v. *Eastbourne
    Borough Council* [1993] I.C.R. 955,
    E.A.T.
  reg. 3(4), see *Longden* v. *Ferrari and
    Kennedy International* [1994] I.C.R.
    443, E.A.T.
  reg. 5(1)(3), see *Harrison Bowden* v.
    Bowden [1994] I.C.R. 186, E.A.T.
  reg. 5(2), see *Allen* v. *Stirling District
    Council* [1994] I.C.R. 434, E.A.T.
  regs. 5(3), 8(1), see *Longden* v. *Ferrari
    and Kennedy International* [1994]
    I.C.R. 443, E.A.T.
  reg. 7, see *Walden Engineering Co.* v.
    Warrener [1993] I.C.R. 967, E.A.T.
  reg. 8, see *Wren* v. *Eastbourne Bor-
    ough Council* [1993] I.C.R. 955,
    E.A.T.
  reg. 8(1), see *Harrison Bowden* v. *Bow-
    den* [1994] I.C.R. 186, E.A.T.; *Allen*
    v. *Stirling District Council* [1994]
    I.C.R. 434, E.A.T.
**1836. National Health Service (Determi-
  nation of Regions) Order 1981.**
  revoked: ord. 94/683, art. 14.
**1837. National Health Service (Determi-
  nation of Districts) Order 1981.**
  art. 2, applied: ord. 94/681, art. 1.
  art. 3, amended: *ibid.*, art. 2.
  sch. 1, substituted: *ibid.*
  sch. 1, pt. I, amended: ord. 94/1261, art.
    2.
  sch. 1, pt. II, amended: *ibid.*; ord.
    94/2289, art. 2.

1982

**133. European Parliament (United King-
  dom Representatives) Pensions
  (Amendment) Order 1982.**
  revoked: ord. 94/1662, art. 32.
**153. South Africa (United Nations Arms
  Embargo) (Prohibited Transactions) (Isle of Man) (Amendment) Order 1982.**
  revoked: ord. 94/1636, art. 2.
**154. South Africa (United Nations Arms
  Embargo) (Prohibited Transactions) (Jersey) (Amendment)
  Order 1982.**
  revoked: ord. 94/1636, art. 2.

NO.

1982—cont.

343. National Health Service (Determination of Regions) Amendment Order 1982.
revoked: ord. 94/683, art. 14.

379. District Probate Registries Order 1982.
sch., amended: ord. 94/1103, art. 3.

521. Wells and Walsingham Railway Light Railway Order 1982.
amended: ord. 94/260, art. 2.

555. Town and Country Planning (Structure and Local Plans) Regulations 1982.
regs. 29(1), 31(1), see *British Railways Board* v. *Slough Borough Council* [1993] J.P.L. 678.

586. County Court (Forms) Rules 1982.
sch., amended: rules 94/1289, rule 2; rules 94/2110, rules 2–7.

654. Act of Sederunt (Rules of Court Amendment No. 3) 1982.
revoked: Act 94/1443, para. 3.

675. Insurance Companies (Amendment) Regulations 1982.
revoked: regs. 94/1516, reg. 86.

804. Act of Sederunt (Rules of Court Amendment No. 4) (Shorthand Writers' Fees) 1982.
revoked: Act 94/1443, para. 3.

844. Seeds (National Lists of Varieties) Regulations 1982.
applied: regs. 94/676, reg. 3.

876. Merchant Shipping (Safety Officials and Reporting of Accidents and Dangerous Occurrences) Regulations 1982.
reg. 1, amended: regs. 94/2014, reg. 2.
reg. 5, amended: *ibid.*
regs. 9–11, revoked: *ibid.*
reg. 12, revoked in pt.: *ibid.*
sch., revoked: *ibid.*

894. Statutory Sick Pay (General) Regulations 1982.
reg. 2(1)(a), see *Social Security -Decision No. R(S) 4/93.*
reg. 3, amended: regs. 94/1367, reg. 9.

950. Education (School and Placing Information) (Scotland) Regulations 1982.
sch. 1, pt. II, amended: regs. 94/351, reg. 9.

1004. British Citizenship (Designated Service) Order 1982.
sch., para. 10, revoked: ord. 94/556, art. 2.
sch., para. 12, revoked: *ibid.*
sch., para. 13, amended: *ibid.*
sch., paras. 15–18, revoked: *ibid.*

1080. Agricultural Marketing (Northern Ireland) Order 1982.
art. 29, applied: regs. 94/672, reg. 24.

1109. Crown Court Rules 1982.
rule 6, amended: rules 94/1480, rule 3.
rule 11A, inserted: *ibid.*, rule 4.

NO.

1982—cont.

1109. Crown Court Rules 1982—*cont.*
rule 27, amended: *ibid.*, rule 5.
schs. 9, 10, inserted: *ibid.*, rule 6.

1144. Feedingstuffs (Sampling and Analysis) Regulations 1982.
sch. 2, amended: regs. 94/1610, reg. 3.

1221. Wildlife and Countryside (Registration and Ringing of Certain Captive Birds) Regulations 1982.
reg. 5, amended: regs. 94/1152, reg. 2.

1271. Motor Vehicles (Type Approval for Goods Vehicles) (Great Britain) Regulations 1982.
sch. 1B, para. 1, substituted: regs. 94/2191, reg. 3.
sch. 1B, Pt. IV, inserted: *ibid.*

1381. Act of Sederunt (Rules of Court Amendment No. 5) (Application under Matrimonial Homes (Family Protection) (Scotland) Act 1981) 1982.
revoked: Act 94/1443, para. 3.

1408. Social Security (General Benefit) Regulations 1982.
reg. 16, amended: regs. 94/559, reg. 5.
reg. 19, referred to: regs. 92/1409, reg. 2.

1489. Workmen's Compensation (Supplementation) Scheme 1982.
art. 5, amended: scheme 94/671, art. 2.
sch. 1, substituted: *ibid.*, art. 3.

1527. Social Security (Jersey and Guernsey) Order 1982.
revoked: ord. 94/2802, art. 3.

1531. South Africa (United Nations Arms Embargo) (Prohibited Transactions) (Guernsey) (Amendment) Order 1982.
revoked: ord. 94/1636, art. 2.

1536. Homosexual Offences (Northern Ireland) Order 1982.
art. 3, amended: 1994, c. 33, ss. 145, 147.
art. 5, amended: *ibid.*, s. 147.

1591. Customs Duty (Personal Reliefs) (No. 1) Order 1968 (Amendment) Order 1982.
revoked: ord. 94/955, art. 5.

1673. Summer Time Order 1982.
revoked: ord. 94/2798, art. 5.

1679. Act of Sederunt (Rules of Court Amendment No. 6) (Simplified Divorce Procedure) 1982.
revoked: Act 94/1443, para. 3.

1706. County Court Fees Order 1982.
art. 4, substituted: ord. 94/1936, art. 2.
sch. 1, para. 4, revoked: *ibid.*, art. 3.
sch. 1, para. 4, renumbered: *ibid.*, art. 4.
sch. 1, para. 5, inserted: *ibid.*
fee 1, amended: *ibid.*, arts. 5, 6.
fee 2A, inserted: *ibid.*, art. 7.
fee 2A, renumbered: *ibid.*, art. 8.
fee 3, amended: *ibid.*, art. 3.
fee 4, amended: *ibid.*, art. 9.
fee 8, amended: *ibid.*, art. 9.

NO.

1982—cont.

1723. **Act of Sederunt (Rules of Court Amendment No. 7) (Witnesses' Fees) 1982.**
revoked: Act 94/1443, para. 3.

1727. **Food (Revision of Penalties) Regulations 1982.**
sch. 2, amended: regs. 94/1029, reg. 26.

1730. **Education (Particulars of Independent Schools) Regulations 1982.**
reg. 2, amended: regs. 94/537, reg. 2.
sch., para. 10, substituted: *ibid.*

1824. **Act of Sederunt (Rules of Court Amendment No. 8) (Court Fees in Simplified Divorce Procedure) 1982.**
revoked: Act 94/1443, para. 3.

1825. **Act of Sederunt (Rules of Court Amendment No. 9) (Miscellaneous Amendments) 1982.**
revoked: Act 94/1443, para. 3.

1879. **Traffic Signs (Amendment) Regulations 1982.**
revoked: regs. 94/1519, reg. 2.

1880. **Traffic Signs General (Amendment) Directions 1982.**
revoked: regs. 94/1519, reg. 2.

1983

8. **Local Government (Publication of Manpower Information) (England) Regulations 1983.**
revoked: regs. 94/2422, reg. 2.

29. **Education (Special Educational Needs) Regulations 1983.**
see *P. v. Harrow London Borough Council* [1993] 2 F.C.R. 341.
revoked: regs. 94/1047, reg. 20.
reg. 10, see *R. v. Clwyd County Council*, ex p. *A* [1993] C.O.D. 35.

224. **Insurance (Lloyd's) Regulations 1983.**
reg. 2, amended: regs. 94/1516, reg. 85.
reg. 3, amended: *ibid.*
sch. 1, amended: *ibid.*
sch. 3, para. 4, amended: *ibid.*
sch. 3, para. 5, amended: *ibid.*

376. **Statutory Sick Pay (Compensation of Employers) and Miscellaneous Provisions Regulations 1983.**
reg. 2, amended: regs. 94/730, reg. 2.

396. **Insurance Companies (Advertisements) (Amendment) (No. 2) Regulations 1983.**
revoked: regs. 94/1516, reg. 86.

397. **Act of Sederunt (Rules of Court Amendment No. 1) (Appeals Under Social Security Acts) 1983.**
revoked: Act 94/1443, para. 3.

398. **Act of Sederunt (Rules of Court Amendment No. 2) (Interest in Decrees or Extracts) 1983.**
revoked: Act 94/1443, para. 3.

NO.

1983—cont.

506. **Redundant Mineworkers and Concessionary Coal (Payments Schemes) Order 1983.**
sch., amended: ord. 94/2567, art. 2.
art. 10, amended: *ibid.*

604. **Social Security (Jersey and Guernsey) Order 1983.**
revoked: ord. 94/2802, art. 3.

615. **Local Government (Publication of Manpower Information) (Wales) (Revocation) Regulations 1983.**
revoked: regs. 94/2677, reg. 2.

656. **Act of Sederunt (Rules of Court Amendment No. 3) (Letters of Request) 1983.**
revoked: Act 94/1443, para. 3.

680. **Enrolment of Deeds (Change of Name) Regulations 1983.**
revoked: regs. 94/604, reg. 9.

686. **Personal Injuries (Civilians) Scheme 1983.**
art. 14, applied: regs. 94/648, reg. 2.
art. 15, applied: *ibid.*
art. 16, applied: *ibid.*
art. 18, amended: scheme 94/715, art. 2.
art. 25A, referred to: regs. 94/648, sch. 3, para. 7; applied: 1994, c. 9, s. 70; applied: 1994, c. 23, sch. 8, group 11.
art. 27, amended: scheme 94/2021, art. 2.
art. 43, applied: regs. 94/648, reg. 2.
art. 44, applied: *ibid.*
art. 76, amended: scheme 94/715, art. 3.
art. 76A, inserted: *ibid.*, art. 4.
art. 76B, inserted: *ibid.*
art. 76C, inserted: *ibid.*
sch. 3, substituted: *ibid.*, art. 5.
sch. 4, substituted: *ibid*: para. 1, amended: scheme 94/2021, art. 2.

704. **Meat and Poultry Meat (Staining and Sterilisation) (Scotland) Regulations 1983.**
reg. 28, amended: regs. 94/1029, reg. 27.

713. **Civil Courts Order 1983.**
sch. 1, amended: ord. 94/1536, arts. 3, 4, 5; ord. 94/2626, art. 3; ord. 94/2893, art. 4.
sch. 3, amended: ord. 94/706, art. 3; ord. 94/1536, arts. 4, 6; ord. 94/2626, art. 3; ord. 94/2893, art. 5.
sch. 4, amended: ord. 94/706, art. 4; ord. 94/2893, art. 6.

826. **Act of Sederunt (Rules of Court Amendment No. 4) (Taxation of Accounts) 1983.**
revoked: Act 94/1443, para. 3.

883. **Naval, Military and Air Forces etc. (Disablement and Death) Service Pensions Order 1983.**
art. 5(4), see *R. v. Secretary of State for Social Security*, ex p. *Edwards* [1993] C.O.D. 68, D.C.

NO.

1983—cont.

883. Naval, Military and Air Forces etc. (Disablement and Death) Service Pensions Order 1983—cont.
art. 18, amended: ord. 94/772, art. 2.
art. 26A, applied: 1994, c. 9, s. 70; referred to: regs. 94/648, sch. 3, para. 7; 1994, c. 23, sch. 8, group 11.
art. 67, amended: ord. 94/772, art. 3.
art. 67A, inserted: *ibid.*, art. 4.
art. 67B, inserted: *ibid.*
art. 67C, inserted: *ibid.*
sch. 1, amended: *ibid.*, art. 5.
sch. 2, amended: *ibid.*
sch. 4, amended: *ibid.*

914. Weighing Equipment (Beltweighers) Regulations 1983.
reg. 2, amended: regs. 94/1851, reg. 2.
reg. 12, amended: *ibid.*
reg. 12A, inserted: *ibid.*

1086. Traffic Signs General (Amendment) Directions 1983.
revoked: 94/1519, reg. 2.

1088. Traffic Signs (Amendment) Regulations 1983.
revoked: regs. 94/1519, reg. 2.

1140. Clarification and Labelling of Explosives Regulations 1983.
applied: regs. 94/670, reg. 8.

1160. Redundancy Payments (Local Government) (Modification) Order 1983.
art. 1, amended: ord. 94/417, art. 2.
art. 4, amended: *ibid.*
sch. 1, amended: *ibid.*

1210. Act of Sederunt (Rules of Court Amendment No. 6) (Simplified Divorce Procedure) 1983.
revoked: Act 94/1443, para. 3.

1390. Measuring Equipment (Liquid Fuel Delivered from Road Tankers) Regulations 1983.
reg. 3, amended: regs. 94/1851, reg. 2.
reg. 11, amended: *ibid.*
reg. 11A, inserted: *ibid.*
reg. 16A, inserted: *ibid.*
reg. 24, amended: *ibid.*

1398. Merchant Shipping (Prevention of Oil Pollution) Regulations 1983.
reg. 1, amended: regs. 94/2085, reg. 3.
reg. 4, amended: *ibid.*, reg. 4.
reg. 4A, inserted: *ibid.*, reg. 5.
reg. 7, amended: *ibid.*, reg. 6.
reg. 16, amended: *ibid.*, reg. 7.
sch. 1, revoked: *ibid.*, reg. 8.

1399. Supplementary Benefit (Requirements) Regulations 1983.
reg. 19, referred to: regs. 94/648, sch. 3, para. 36, sch. 4, para. 28.

1499. Education (Approval of Special Schools) Regulations 1983.
see *P. v. Harrow London Borough Council* [1993] 2 F.C.R. 341.
revoked: regs. 94/652, reg. 3.

NO.

1983—cont.

1598. Social Security (Unemployment, Sickness and Invalidity Benefit) Regulations 1983.
reg. 3, amended: regs. 94/559, reg. 4; regs. 94/1101, reg. 2.
reg. 7(1)(o), see *Social Security Decision No. R(U) 2/93.*

1642. Act of Sederunt (Rules of Court Amendment No. 7) (Shorthand Writers' Fees) 1983.
revoked: Act 94/1443, para. 3.

1649. Asbestos (Licensing) Regulations 1983.
applied: regs. 94/397, reg. 6.

1656. Measuring Equipment (Intoxicating Liquor) Regulations 1983.
reg. 2, amended: regs. 94/1851, reg. 2.
reg. 7, amended: *ibid.*
reg. 7A, inserted: *ibid.*
reg. 14, amended: *ibid.*

1716. County Court (Amendment No. 2) Rules 1983.
see *Willowgreen* v. *Smithers* [1994] 1 W.L.R. 832, C.A.

1717. Value Added Tax (Charities Etc.) Order 1983.
C.: 1994, c. 23, sch. 8.
revoked: 1994, c. 23, sch. 15.

1794. Equal Pay (Amendment) Regulations 1983.
reg. 2(2), see *Yorkshire Blood Transfusion Service* v. *Plaskitt* [1994] I.C.R. 74, E.A.T.

1811. Insurance Companies (Accounts and Statements) Regulations 1983.
applied: regs. 94/1516, reg. 79.
reg. 2, amended: regs. 94/1515, reg. 2.
reg. 3, amended: *ibid.*, reg. 3, applied: regs. 94/1774, reg. 20.
reg. 6, amended: regs. 94/1515, reg. 4.
reg. 11, amended: *ibid.*, regs. 5, 6.
reg. 14, substituted: *ibid.*, reg. 7.
reg. 22A, amended: *ibid.*, reg. 2.
reg. 22B, inserted: *ibid.*, reg. 9.
reg. 22C, inserted: *ibid.*, reg. 10.
reg. 24, amended: *ibid.*, reg. 11.
reg. 25, amended: *ibid.*, reg. 12.
reg. 27, amended: *ibid.*, reg. 13.
reg. 30, substituted: *ibid.*, reg. 14.
sch. 1, para. 3, amended: *ibid.*, reg. 15.
sch. 1, para. 8, amended: *ibid.*
sch. 1, Forms, amended: *ibid.*
sch. 3, amended: *ibid.*, reg. 16.
sch. 4, para. 1, amended: *ibid.*, reg. 17.
sch. 4, para. 4, amended: *ibid.*
sch. 4, para. 5, amended: *ibid.*
sch. 4, para. 7, amended: *ibid.*
sch. 4, para. 8, amended: *ibid.*
sch. 6, para. 1, amended: *ibid.*, reg. 18.
sch. 6, para. 4, amended: *ibid.*, reg. 2.
sch. 6, para. 6A, inserted: *ibid.*, reg. 18.
sch. 6, para. 11, amended: *ibid.*
sch. 6, para. 12, inserted: *ibid.*

NO.

1983—cont.

1964. Adoption Agencies Regulations 1983.
referred to: regs. 94/648, reg. 7.
1969. Adoption Agencies Regulations 1983.
reg. 14, see *Manchester City Council* v.
T., *The Times*, January 12, 1994,
C.A.

1984

176. Goods Vehicles (Operators' Licences, Qualifications and Fees) Regulations 1984.
reg. 35, amended: regs. 94/1209, reg. 2.
218. Race Relations (Prescribed Public Bodies) Regulations 1984.
revoked: regs. 94/109, reg. 3.
222. Ancient Monuments (Class Consents) (Amendment) Order 1984.
revoked: ord. 94/1381, art. 3.
235. Act of Sederunt (Rules of Court Amendment No. 1).
revoked: Act 94/1443, para. 3.
248. Gaming Clubs (Hours and Charges) Regulations 1984.
reg. 5, amended: regs. 94/958, reg. 2.
265. Adoption Rules 1984.
rule 18, see *S. (A Minor) (Adoption Order: Conditions)*, *Re*, *The Times*, April 26, 1994, C.A.
380. Occupational Pension Schemes (Contracting-out) Regulations 1984.
reg. 1, amended: regs. 94/1062, reg. 2.
reg. 14, amended: *ibid.*
reg. 15, amended: *ibid.*
reg. 16, amended: *ibid.*
reg. 18, amended: *ibid.*
reg. 18A, amended: *ibid.*
reg. 19, amended: *ibid.*
reg. 20, amended: *ibid.*
reg. 21, amended: *ibid.*
reg. 22, amended: *ibid.*
reg. 22A, amended: *ibid.*
reg. 23, amended: *ibid.*
reg. 23A, amended: *ibid.*
reg. 24, amended: *ibid.*
reg. 26A, amended: *ibid.*
reg. 27, amended: *ibid.*
reg. 28, amended: *ibid.*
reg. 29, amended: *ibid.*
reg. 30, amended: *ibid.*
reg. 31, amended: *ibid.*
reg. 33A, amended: *ibid.*
reg. 33B, amended: *ibid.*
reg. 33C, amended: *ibid.*
reg. 33D, amended: *ibid.*
reg. 34, amended: *ibid.*
reg. 35, amended: *ibid.*
reg. 36, amended: *ibid.*
reg. 37, amended: *ibid.*
reg. 38, amended: *ibid.*
reg. 40, amended: *ibid.*
reg. 41, amended: *ibid.*
reg. 42, amended: *ibid.*
reg. 43, amended: *ibid.*

NO.

1984—cont.

380. Occupational Pension Schemes (Contracting-out) Regulations 1984—cont.
reg. 44, amended: *ibid.*
reg. 45, amended: *ibid.*
reg. 47, amended: *ibid.*
reg. 48, amended: *ibid.*
reg. 49, amended: *ibid.*
reg. 50, amended: *ibid.*
464. Aberdeen and District Milk Marketing Scheme 1984.
revoked: ord. 94/2900, art. 2.
457. Redundant Mineworkers and Concessionary Coal (Payments Scheme) Order 1984.
sch., amended: ord. 94/2567, art. 2.
art. 10, amended: *ibid.*
470. Gaming Clubs (Hours and Charges) (Scotland) Regulations 1984.
reg. 5, amended: regs. 94/1042, reg. 2.
472. Act of Sederunt (Rules of Court Amendment No. 2) (Miscellaneous) 1984.
revoked: Act 94/1443, para. 3.
489. Value Added Tax (Handicapped Persons) Order 1984.
C.: 1994, c. 23, sch. 8.
revoked: 1994, c. 23, sch. 15.
499. Act of Sederunt (Rules of Court Amendment No. 3) (Summary Decree and Other Amendments) 1984.
revoked: Act 94/1443, para. 3.
544. European Parliamentary Constituencies (England) Order 1984.
constituencies substituted: ord. 94/427, art. 2.
545. European Parliamentary Constituencies (Wales) Order 1984.
constituencies substituted: ord. 94/428, art. 2.
552. Coroners Rules 1984.
rule 36, see *R.* v. *Coroner for North Humberside and Scunthorpe*, ex p. *Jamieson*, *The Times*, April 28, 1994, C.A.
rules 36, 42, see *R.* v. *H.M. Coroner for North Humberside and Scunthorpe, ex p. Jamieson* [1994] 3 W.L.R. 82, C.A.
rules 36, 41, 42, 43, see *R.* v. *Coroner for Western District of East Sussex*, ex p. *Homberg*, *The Independent*, January 27, 1994, D.C.
rules 40, 42, 43, 60, sch. 4, see *R.* v. *Coroner for North Humberside and Scunthorpe*, ex p. *Jamieson*, *The Times*, April 28, 1994, C.A.
571. European Parliamentary Elections (Returning Officers) (England and Wales) Order 1984.
revoked: ord. 94/894, art. 3.

NO.

1984—cont.

631. Value Added Tax (Lifeboats) Order 1984.
revoked: 1994, c. 23, sch. 15.

647. Probation Rules 1984.
rule 41A, inserted: rules 94/1228, rule 2.

703. Fines and Penalties (Northern Ireland) Order 1984.
art. 17, amended: 1994, c. 33, s. 157.

713. Juvenile Courts (London) (Amendment) Order 1984.
revoked: ord. 94/1695, art. 2.

718. Customs Duty (Personal Reliefs) (No. 1) Order 1968 (Amendment) Order 1984.
revoked: ord. 94/955, art. 5.

766. Value Added Tax (Charities Etc.) Order 1984.
C.: 1994, c. 23, sch. 8.
revoked: 1994, c. 23, sch. 15.

767. Value Added Tax (Marine Etc. Insurance) Order 1984.
revoked: 1994, c. 23, sch. 15.

769. Medicines (Products Other Than Veterinary Drugs) (General Sale List) Order 1984.
art. 1, amended: ord. 94/2410, art. 2.
sch. 1, amended: *ibid.* art. 3.

785. Three Valleys Water Order 1984.
art. 3, amended: ord. 94/977, art. 3.

919. Act of Sederunt (Amendment of Rules of Court No. 4) (Provisional Damages) 1984.
revoked: Act 94/1443, para. 3.

920. Act of Sederunt (Amendment of Rules of Court No. 5) (Intimation in fatal accident cases) 1984.
revoked: Act 94/1443, para. 3.

959. Value Added Tax (Handicapped Persons) (No. 2) Order 1984.
C.: 1994, c. 23, sch. 8.
revoked: 1994, c. 23, sch. 15.

966. Traffic Signs (Amendment) Regulations and General Directions 1984.
revoked: regs. 94/1519, reg. 2.

981. Motor Vehicles (Type Approval) (Great Britain) Regulations 1984.
sch. 1B, para. 1, substituted: regs. 94/2190, reg. 3.
sch. 1B, Pt. IV, inserted: *ibid.*

988. Adoption Agencies (Scotland) Regulations 1984.
referred to: regs. 94/648, reg. 7.

997. Act of Sederunt (Rules of Court Amendment No. 6) (Adoption Proceedings) 1984.
revoked: Act 94/1443, para. 3.

1095. Mental Health (Prescription of Class of Nurse) (Scotland) Order 1984.
revoked: ord. 94/1675, art. 3.

1133. Act of Sederunt (Rules of Court Amendment No. 8) (Shorthand Writers' Fees) 1984.
revoked: Act 94/1443, para. 3.

NO.

1984—cont.

1216. Merchant Shipping (Passenger Ship Construction and Survey) Regulations 1984.
reg. 11A, amended: regs. 94/1383, reg. 3; amended: regs. 94/422, reg. 3.

1303. Social Security (Severe Disablement Allowance) Regulations 1984.
reg. 2, amended: regs. 94/1101, reg. 3.
reg. 2, amended: regs. 94/2556, reg. 4; regs. 94/2947, reg. 2.
reg. 3, amended: *ibid.*
reg. 4, amended: regs. 94/2556, reg. 4.
reg. 4A, inserted: *ibid.*
reg. 5, amended: *ibid.*
reg. 5A, inserted: *ibid.*
reg. 6, amended: regs. 94/2947, reg. 2.
reg. 7, amended: regs. 94/2556, reg. 4; regs. 94/2947, reg. 2.
reg. 7A, revoked: regs. 94/2947, reg. 3.
reg. 8A, amended: *ibid.* reg. 2.
reg. 9, amended: regs. 94/1101, reg. 3.
revoked: regs. 94/2947, reg. 3.
reg. 20, amended: regs. 94/2556, reg. 4; regs. 94/2947, reg. 2.

1305. Food Labelling Regulations 1984.
see *Cheshire County Council* v. *Mornflake Oats* (1993) 12 Tr.L.R. 111, D.C.
reg. 2, amended: regs. 94/804, reg. 3; regs. 94/1486, reg. 3.
reg. 15, amended: *ibid.*
pt. IV, title, substituted: regs. 94/804, reg. 4.
reg. 37, amended: *ibid.*, reg. 5.
sch. 1, para. 1, amended: regs. 94/2127, reg. 6.
sch. 1, para. 4, amended: regs. 94/804, reg. 6.
sch. 4, amended: regs. 94/1486, reg. 3.
sch. 6, pt. II, amended: *ibid.*, reg. 7.
sch. 6A, inserted: *ibid.*, reg. 8.
sch. 7, amended: *ibid.*, reg. 9.

1506. Valuation Appeal Committee Procedure (Scotland) Regulations 1984.
reg. 4(3)(d), see *Ashbourne Homes* v. *Assessor for Central Region*, 1994 S.L.T. (Lands Tr.) 24.

1509. Food Labelling (Scotland) Regulations 1984.
sch. 1, para. 1, amended: regs. 94/2127, reg. 6.

1519. Food Labelling (Scotland) Regulations 1984.
reg. 2, amended: regs. 94/960, reg. 3; regs. 94/1486, reg. 3.
pt. IV, title, substituted: regs. 94/960, reg. 4.
reg. 15, amended: regs. 94/1486, reg. 3.
reg. 37, amended: regs. 94/960, reg. 5.
sch. 1, para. 4, amended: *ibid.*, reg. 6.
sch. 4, amended: regs. 94/1486, reg. 3.
sch. 6, pt. II, amended: regs. 94/960, reg. 7.
sch. 6A, inserted: *ibid.*, reg. 8.

NO.

1984—cont.

1519. Food Labelling (Scotland) Regulations 1984—cont.
sch. 7, amended: *ibid.*, reg. 9.

1784. Value Added Tax (Optical Appliances) Order 1984.
revoked: 1994, c. 23, sch. 15.

1821. Fire Services (Northern Ireland) Order 1984.
applied: 1994, c. 22, sch. 2, para. 4.

1890. Freight Containers (Safety Convention) Regulations 1984.
applied: regs. 94/397, reg. 5.

1902. Control of Industrial Major Accident Hazards Regulations 1984.
reg. 3, amended: regs. 94/118, reg. 3.

1907. Parliamentary Pensions (Purchase of Added Years) (Amendment) Order 1984.
revoked: regs. 93/3253, reg. R5.

1908. Parliamentary Pensions (Added Years and Rates of Accrual) (Further Provisions) Order 1984.
revoked: regs. 93/3253, reg. R5.

1909. Parliamentary Pensions (Maximum and Abated Pensions and Pension Commutation) Order 1984.
revoked: regs. 93/3253, reg. R5.

2024. Hill Livestock (Compensatory Allowances) Regulations 1984.
referred to: regs. 94/2740, reg. 2.

2040. Immigration Appeals (Notices) Regulations 1984.
regs. 2(1), 3(1), 4(1), 5(1), *R. v. Secretary of State for the Home Department, ex p. Zagha (Rashed Masoud)* [1994] Imm AR 20, C.A.
regs. 3(1), 4, see *R. v. Secretary of State for the Home Department*, ex p. *Al-Zagha (Rashed Masoud)* [1993] Imm. A.R. 555.

2041. Immigration Appeals (Procedure) Rules 1984.
rule 2, amended: ord. 94/1405, art. 8.
rule 4, amended: *ibid.*
rule 6, amended: *ibid.*
rules 8, 25, see *R. v. Secretary of State for the Home Department*, ex p. *Abdi, Same* v. *Same*, ex p. *Game, The Times*, April 25, 1994, C.A.
rule 34(2), see *R. v. Immigration Appeal Tribunal*, ex p. *Davis (Martin Sammy)* [1993] Imm. A.R. 558.

2058. Prison (Scotland) Amendment Rules 1984.
revoked: rules 94/1931, rule 143.

1985

16. Industrial Tribunal (Rules of Procedure) Regulations 1985.
rules 8(1), 14(1), see *Reddington* v. *Straker & Sons* [1994] I.C.R. 172, E.A.T.

NO.

1985—cont.

16. Industrial Tribunal (Rules of Procedure) Regulations 1985—cont.
rule 10(1)(e), see *Ironside Ray & Vials*, Re; *Ironside Ray & Vials* v. *Lindsay, The Times*, January 28, 1994, E.A.T.
sch. 1, rule 10(1)(e), see *Lindsay* v. *Ironsides Ray & Vials* [1994] I.C.R. 384, E.A.T.

17. Industrial Tribunal (Rules of Procedure) (Scotland) Regulations 1985.
rules 1, 2, 10, 13(1), 14, see *Gillick* v. *BP Chemicals* [1993] I.R.L.R. 437, E.A.T.

18. Value Added Tax (Protected Buildings) Order 1985.
revoked: 1994, c. 23, sch. 15.

67. Food (Revision of Penalties) Regulations 1985.
sch., pt. II, amended: regs. 94/1029, reg. 26.

127. Dangerous Substances and Preparations (Safety) (Amendment) Regulations 1985.
revoked: regs. 94/2844, reg. 7.

128. Novelties (Safety) (Amendment) Regulations 1985.
revoked: regs. 94/2844, reg. 7.

226. Solicitors (Disciplinary Proceedings) Rules 1985.
revoked: rules 94/288, rule 1.

227. Act of Sederunt (Rules of Court Amendment No. 1) (Operational Procedure in Certain Actions of Reparation) 1985.
revoked: Act 94/1443, para. 3.

240. East Anglian Water (Capital Powers) Order 1985.
revoked: ord. 94/978, art. 3.

304. Community Health Council Regulations 1985.
reg. 19(1), see *R. v. North West Thames Regional Health Authority; Riverside Health Authority; Secretary of State for Health*, ex p. *Daniels* [1993] 4 Med L.R. 364.

373. Public Trustee (Fees) Order 1985.
art. 17, amended: ord. 94/714, arts. 2, 3.

431. Value Added Tax (Charities Etc.) Order 1985.
C.: 1994, c. 23, sch. 8.
revoked: 1994, c. 23, sch. 15.

432. Value Added Tax (Finance) Order 1985.
C.: 1994, c. 23, sch. 9.
revoked: 1994, c. 23, sch. 15.

500. Act of Sederunt (Rules of Court Amendment No. 2) (Judicial Review) 1985.
revoked: Act 94/1443, para. 3.

698. Town and Country Planning (Compensation for Restrictions on Mineral Working) Regulations 1985.
reg. 1, amended: ord. 94/2567, art. 2.

NO.

1985—cont.

722. Motor Vehicles (Exemption from Vehicles Excise Duty) Order 1985.
art. 3, applied: 1994, c. 9, s. 70; 1994, c. 23, sch. 8, group 11.

723. Motor Vehicles (Exemption from Vehicles Excise Duty) (Northern Ireland) Order 1985.
art. 3, applied: 1994, c. 9, s. 70; 1994, c. 23, sch. 8, group 11.

760. Act of Sederunt (Rules of Court Amendment No. 4) (Shorthand Writers' Fees) 1985.
revoked: Act 94/1443, para. 3.

782. Unfair Dismissal (Variation of Qualifying Period) Order 1985.
see *Northern General Hospital National Health Service Trust* v. *Gale* [1994] I.C.R. 426, C.A.

799. Value Added Tax (Hiring of Goods) Order 1985.
revoked: 1994, c. 23, sch. 15.

855. Fishing Vessels (Reporting of Accidents) Regulations 1985.
revoked: regs. 94/2013, reg. 1.

886. Value Added Tax (General) Regulations 1985.
reg. 11(1)(3), see *Sargent* v. *Customs and Excise Commissioners* [1994] 1 W.L.R. 235.
reg. 23, see *B. J. Rice & Associates* v. *Customs and Excise Commissioners* [1994] STC 565.

919. Value Added Tax (Handicapped Persons) Order 1985.
C.: 1994, c. 23, sch. 8.
art. 3, revoked: 1994, c. 23, sch. 15.

967. Social Security (Industrial Injuries) (Prescribed Diseases) Regulations 1985.
reg. 1, amended: regs. 94/2343, reg. 2.
reg. 14A, inserted: *ibid.*, reg. 3.
regs. 37, 38, revoked: *ibid.*, reg. 5.
regs. 41, 42, revoked: *ibid.*
sch. 1, pt. I, amended: *ibid.*, reg. 4.

975. Fodder Plant Seeds Regulations 1985.
reg. 4(3), see *Germinal Holdings* v. *H. R. Fell & Sons* [1993] F.S.R. 343.

1068. Food (Revision of Penalties and Mode of Trial) (Scotland) Regulations 1985.
sch. 1, pt. I, amended: regs. 94/1029, reg. 26.

1116. European Parliament (United Kingdom Representatives) Pensions (Amendment) Order 1985.
revoked: ord. 94/1662, art. 32.

1178. Act of Sederunt (Rules of Court Amendment No. 5) (Interest in Decrees or Extracts) 1985.
revoked: Act 94/1443, para. 3.

NO.

1985—cont.

1309. Race Relations (Prescribed Public Bodies) (Amendment) Regulations 1985.
revoked: regs. 94/109, reg. 3.

1319. Fish Farming and Shellfish Farming Businesses Order 1985.
art. 5, amended: regs. 94/1447, reg. 16.
sch. 3, pt. I, substituted: *ibid.*

1323. Contracting-out (Transfer) Regulations 1985.
reg. 1, amended: regs. 94/1062, reg. 2.
reg. 2, amended: *ibid.*
reg. 2A, amended: *ibid.*
reg. 2B, amended: *ibid.*
reg. 3, amended: *ibid.*
reg. 3A, amended: *ibid.*
sch. 2, para. 1, amended: *ibid.*
sch. 2, para. 3, amended: *ibid.*
sch. 2, para. 4, amended: *ibid.*
sch. 2A, para. 1, amended: *ibid.*
sch. 3, para. 1, substituted: *ibid.*
sch. 3, para. 2, amended: *ibid.*
sch. 3, para. 4, substituted: *ibid.*
sch. 3, para. 5, substituted: *ibid.*
sch. 3, para. 6, amended: *ibid.*
sch. 3, para. 7, revoked: *ibid.*
sch. 3, para. 8, substituted: *ibid.*
sch. 3A, para. 1, substituted: *ibid.*
sch. 3A, para. 2, amended: *ibid.*
sch. 3A, para. 3, substituted: *ibid.*
sch. 3A, para. 4, substituted: *ibid.*
sch. 3A, para. 5, substituted: *ibid.*

1333. Ionising Radiations Regulations 1985.
applied: regs. 94/397, regs. 3, 9.

1375. Customs Duty (Personal Reliefs) (No. 1) Order 1968 (Amendment) Order 1985.
revoked: ord. 94/955, art. 5.

1383. Local Government (Magistrates' Courts etc.) Order 1985.
sch., para. 5, revoked: ord. 94/2812, art. 2.

1403. Medicines (Control of Substances for Manufacture) Order 1985.
sch. 1, amended: ord. 94/787, art. 3.

1426. Act of Sederunt (Rules of Court Amendment No. 6) (Election Petitions) 1985.
revoked: Act 94/1443, para. 3.

1419. Insurance Companies (Amendment) Regulations 1985.
revoked: regs. 94/1516, reg. 86.

1576. Building (Prescribed Fees etc.) Regulations 1985.
revoked: regs. 94/2020, reg. 16.

1600. Act of Sederunt (Rules of Court Amendment No. 7) (Miscellaneous Amendments) 1985.
revoked: Act 94/1443, para. 3.

1699. Deposits in the Sea (Exemptions) Order 1985.
art. 3, applied: regs. 94/1056, reg. 20.
art. 3, amended: *ibid.*, reg. 21.

NO.

1985—cont.

1699. Deposits in the Sea (Exemptions) Order 1985—*cont.*
reg. 4, inserted: *ibid.*
reg. 5, inserted: *ibid.*

1728. Motor Fuel (Lead Content of Petrol) (Amendment) Regulations 1985.
revoked: regs. 94/2295, reg. 12.

1757. Race Relations (Prescribed Public Bodies) (Amendment) (No. 2) Regulations 1985.
revoked: regs. 94/109, reg. 3.

1765. Diseases of Animals (Ascertainment of Disease) Order 1985.
art. 2, amended: ord. 94/2627, art. 2.
art. 3, amended: *ibid.*

1799. Boarding-out and Fostering of Children (Scotland) Regulations 1985.
reg. 9, referred to: regs. 94/648, sch. 3, para. 24.

1900. Value Added Tax (Welfare) Order 1985.
C.: 1994, c. 23, sch. 9.
revoked: 1994, c. 23, sch. 15.

1921. Service Subsidy Agreements (Tendering) Regulations 1985.
reg. 3, amended: regs. 94/1227, reg. 2.

1929. Occupational Pension Schemes (Discharge of Liability) Regulations 1985.
reg. 1, amended: regs. 94/1062, reg. 2.
reg. 1A, amended: *ibid.*
reg. 2, amended: *ibid.*
reg. 3, amended: *ibid.*
reg. 4, amended: *ibid.*
reg. 5, amended: *ibid.*
reg. 6, amended: *ibid.*
sch., amended: *ibid.*

1931. Occupational Pension Schemes (Transfer Values) Regulations 1985.
reg. 1, amended: regs. 94/1062, reg. 2.
reg. 2, amended: *ibid.*
reg. 2A, amended: *ibid.*
reg. 2B, amended: *ibid.*
reg. 2C, amended: *ibid.*
reg. 2D, amended: *ibid.*
reg. 3, amended: *ibid.*
reg. 4, amended: *ibid.*
reg. 5, amended: *ibid.*
reg. 6, amended: *ibid.*
reg. 7, amended: *ibid.*
reg. 8, amended: *ibid.*

2023. Reporting of Injuries, Diseases and Dangerous Occurrences Regulations 1985.
sch. 1, Pt. I, amended: regs. 94/669, reg. 15.

2068. London–Fishguard Trunk Road (Pontyfenni–Whitland Diversion) Order 1985.
revoked: ord. 94/1614, art. 7.

NO.

1986

24. Local Government Superannuation Regulations 1986.
reg. P14, applied: regs. 94/948, reg. 2.

26. Textile Products (Indications of Fibre Content) Regulations 1986.
reg. 5, amended: regs. 94/450, reg. 2.

60. Inshore Fishing (Prohibition of Carriage of Monofilament Gill Nets) (Scotland) Order 1986.
art. 3, see *MacGillivray* v. *Johnston (No. 2)*, 1994 S.L.T. 1012.

183. Removal and Disposal of Vehicles Regulations 1986.
reg. 15, see *Bulbruin Ltd.* v. *Romanyszyn* [1994] RTR 273, C.A.
sch. 1, amended: regs. 94/1503, reg. 2.

223. Summer Time Order 1986.
revoked: ord. 94/2798, art. 5.

416. Misuse of Drugs (Licence Fees) Regulations 1986.
reg. 3, amended: regs. 94/535, reg. 2.

514. Act of Sederunt (Rules of Court Amendment No. 1) (Bankruptcy Forms) 1986.
revoked: Act 94/1443, para. 3.

515. Act of Sederunt (Rules of Court Amendment No. 2) (Custody of Children) 1986.
revoked: 94/1443, para. 3.

524. National Health Service (Transfer of Officers) (No. 2) Regulations 1986.
referred to: ord. 94/683, art. 3.

530. Value Added Tax (Handicapped Persons and Charities) Order 1986.
C.: 1994, c. 23, sch. 8.
revoked: 1994, c. 23, sch. 15.

590. Value Added Tax Tribunals Rules 1986.
rule 2, amended: rules 94/2617, rule 4.
rule 3, amended: *ibid.*, rule 5.
rule 7, amended: *ibid.*, rule 6.
rule 8, amended: *ibid.*, rule 7.
rule 12, amended: *ibid.*, rule 8.
rule 13, substituted: *ibid.*, rule 9.
rule 16, amended: *ibid.*, rule 10.
rule 19, amended: *ibid.*, rules 11, 12.
rule 20, amended: *ibid.*, rules 13, 14.
rule 21, amended: *ibid.*, rule 15.
rule 22, amended: *ibid.*, rule 16.
rule 26, amended: *ibid.*, rule 17.
rule 27, amended: *ibid.*, rules 18, 19, 20.
rule 29, see *Nader (t/a Try Us)* v. *Customs and Excise Commissioners* [1993] STC 806, C.A.
rule 29, amended: rules 94/2617, rules. 21, 22.
rule 30, amended: *ibid.*, rule 23.
rule 30A, amended: *ibid.*, rule 24.

594. Education and Libraries (Northern Ireland) Order 1986.
applied: 1994, c. 23, sch. 9, group 6.

595. Mental Health (Northern Ireland) Order 1986.
applied: 1994, c. 33, s. 118.

1986—cont.

625. Redundant Mineworkers and Concessionary Coal (Payments Schemes) Order 1986.
sch., amended: ord. 94/2567, art. 2.
art. 10, amended: *ibid.*

694. Act of Sederunt (Rules of Court Amendment No. 3) (Companies and Insolvency) 1986. ⟨
revoked: Act 94/1443, para. 3.

799. Act of Sederunt (Rules of Court Amendment No. 4) (Liner Conferences) 1986.
revoked: Act 94/1443, para. 3.

967. Act of Sederunt (Rules of Court Amendment No. 5) (Solicitors' Fees) 1986.
revoked: Act 94/1443, para. 3.

1015. Insolvency (Scotland) Rules 1986.
rules 4, 5, see *International Factors* v. *Ves Voltech Electronic Services,* 1994 S.L.T. (Sh.Ct.) 40.

1032. Companies (Northern Ireland) Order 1986.
art. 4, applied: regs. 94/1516, reg. 38.
art. 266, applied: *ibid.*, reg. 44.
art. 403, applied: 1994, c. 26, s. 106.
art. 403, amended: *ibid.*
art. 418, applied: 1994, c. 9, s. 144.
art. 603A, inserted: 1994, c. 40, sch. 6, para. 2.
art. 603B, inserted: *ibid.*
art. 603C, inserted: *ibid.*
art. 603D, inserted: *ibid.*
art. 603E, inserted: *ibid.*
art. 603F, inserted: *ibid.*
art. 604, amended: *ibid.*
sch. 4, Pt. I, applied: 1994, c. 26, s. 106.
sch. 9, Pt. I, applied: *ibid.*
sch. 23, amended: 1994, c. 40, sch. 6, para. 4.

1046. Occupational Pension Schemes (Disclosure of Information) Regulations 1986.
reg. 1, amended: regs. 94/1062, reg. 2.
reg. 2, amended: *ibid.*
reg. 6, amended: *ibid.*
reg. 8, amended: *ibid.*
sch. 1, para. 7, amended: *ibid.*
sch. 1, para. 16A, amended: *ibid.*
sch. 1, para. 19, amended: *ibid.*
sch. 2, para. 4C, amended: *ibid.*
sch. 2, para. 8, amended: *ibid.*
sch. 2, para. 9, amended: *ibid.*
sch. 2, para. 10, amended: *ibid.*
sch. 2, para. 11, amended: *ibid.*
sch. 2, para. 14, amended: *ibid.*
sch. 2, para. 15, amended: *ibid.*
sch. 2, para. 16, amended: *ibid.*
sch. 3, para. 6, amended: *ibid.*
sch. 5, para. 8, amended: *ibid.*
sch. 5, para. 16, amended: *ibid.*

1986—cont.

1073. Merchant Shipping (Gas Carriers) Regulations 1986.
revoked: regs. 94/2464, reg. 1.

1078. Road Vehicles (Construction and Use) Regulations 1986.
reg. 3, amended: regs. 94/329, reg. 3.
reg. 4, amended: regs. 94/14, reg. 3.
reg. 9, amended: regs. 94/329, reg. 4.
reg. 36B, amended: *ibid.*, reg. 5.
reg. 37, amended: ord. 94/2567, art. 2.
reg. 54, amended: regs. 94/329, reg. 5.
reg. 55, amended: *ibid.*
reg. 57, substituted: *ibid.*
reg. 58, amended: *ibid.*
reg. 59, amended: *ibid.*
reg. 61, amended: regs. 94/2192, reg. 3.
reg. 71, amended: regs. 94/329, reg. 6.
reg. 76, amended: *ibid.*, reg. 7.
reg. 77, amended: *ibid.*, reg. 8.
reg. 80, amended: *ibid.*, reg. 9.
sch. 2, amended: regs. 94/14, reg. 4.
sch. 7A, inserted: *ibid.*
sch. 10B, inserted: regs. 94/329, reg. 10.
sch. 10C, inserted: *ibid.*
sch. 11, amended: *ibid.*
sch. 11A, inserted: *ibid.*, reg. 12.

1081. Representation of the People Regulations 1986.
reg. 4, amended: regs. 94/342, reg. 17.
reg. 14A, inserted: *ibid.*
reg. 16, amended: *ibid.*
reg. 20, amended: *ibid.*
reg. 29, amended: *ibid.*
reg. 29A, inserted: *ibid.*; modified: *ibid.*, reg. 18.
reg. 30, amended: *ibid.*, reg. 17.
reg. 32, amended: *ibid.*; modified: *ibid.*, reg. 18.
reg. 33, amended: *ibid.*, reg. 17.
reg. 35, modified: *ibid.*, reg. 18.
reg. 38, modified: *ibid.*
reg. 40, modified: *ibid.*
reg. 41, amended: *ibid.*, reg. 17; modified: *ibid.*, reg. 18.
reg. 50, amended: *ibid.*, reg. 17.
reg. 51, modified: *ibid.*, reg. 18.
reg. 52, amended: *ibid.*, reg. 17.
reg. 58, amended: *ibid.*

1091. Representation of the People (Northern Ireland) Regulations 1986.
reg. 4, amended: regs. 94/342, reg. 17.
reg. 14A, inserted: *ibid.*
reg. 16, amended: *ibid.*
reg. 20, amended: *ibid.*
reg. 29, amended: *ibid.*
reg. 29A, inserted: *ibid.*; modified: *ibid.*, reg. 18.
reg. 30, amended: *ibid.*, reg. 17.
reg. 32, amended: *ibid.*
reg. 33, amended: *ibid.*; modified: *ibid.*, reg. 18.

1986—cont.

1091. Representation of the People (Northern Ireland) Regulations 1986—cont.

reg. 35, modified: *ibid.*
reg. 38, modified: *ibid.*
reg. 39, amended: *ibid.*, reg. 17.
reg. 40, modified: *ibid.*, reg. 18.
reg. 41, amended: *ibid.*, reg. 17; modified: *ibid.*, reg. 18.
reg. 50, amended: *ibid.*, reg. 17.
reg. 51, modified: *ibid.*, reg. 18.
reg. 52, amended: *ibid.*, reg. 17.
reg. 58, amended: *ibid.*

1111. Representation of the People (Scotland) Regulations 1986.

reg. 4, amended: regs. 94/342, reg. 17.
reg. 13A, inserted: regs. 94/382, reg. 17.
reg. 15, amended: regs. 94/342, reg. 17.
reg. 19, amended: *ibid.*
reg. 28, amended: *ibid.*
reg. 28A, inserted: *ibid.*; modified: *ibid.*, reg. 18.
reg. 29, amended: *ibid.*, reg. 17.
reg. 31, amended: *ibid.*
reg. 35, modified: *ibid.*, reg. 18.
reg. 36, modified: *ibid.*
reg. 37, amended: *ibid.*, reg. 17.
reg. 38, modified: *ibid.*, reg. 18.
reg. 39, amended: *ibid.*, reg. 17; modified: *ibid.*, reg. 18.
reg. 48, amended: *ibid.*, reg. 17.
reg. 49, modified: *ibid.*, reg. 18.
reg. 50, amended: *ibid.*, reg. 17.
reg. 56, amended: *ibid.*

1128. Act of Sederunt (Rules of Court Amendment No. 6) (Shorthand Writers' Fees) 1986.

revoked: Act 94/1443, para. 3.

1159. Child Abduction and Custody (Parties to Conventions) Order 1986.

sch. 2, substituted: ord. 94/2792, art. 2.

1202. Civil Aviation (Canadian Navigation Services) Regulations 1986.

revoked: regs. 94/2325, reg. 3.
reg. 4, amended: regs. 94/1601, reg. 2.

1231. Act of Sederunt (Rules of Court Amendment No. 7) (Consistorial Causes) 1986.

revoked: Act 94/1443, para. 3.

1272. Sea Fish (Marketing Standards) Regulations 1986.

reg. 2, amended: regs. 94/452, reg. 3.
reg. 3, amended: *ibid.*, reg. 4.
reg. 4, amended: *ibid.*, reg. 5.
reg. 5, amended: *ibid.*, reg. 6.
sch., amended: *ibid.*, reg. 7.

1319. Trade Marks and Services Marks Rules 1986.

revoked: rules 94/2583, reg. 69.
rule 36, see *Cos Trade Mark* [1993] R.P.C. 67.
rule 59, amended: rules 94/2549, rule 2.
rule 60, amended: *ibid.*, rule 3.
rule 89, see *Seaforth Maritime's Trade Mark* [1993] R.P.C. 72.

1986—cont.

1320. Weighing Equipment (Filling and Discontinuous Totalising Automatic Weighing Machines) Regulations 1986.

reg. 2, amended: regs. 94/1320, reg. 2.
reg. 12, amended: regs. 94/1851, reg. 2.
reg. 12A, inserted: *ibid.*

1338. Petroleum Revenue Tax (Nomination Scheme for Disposals and Appropriations) Regulations 1987.

reg. 2A, amended: regs. 94/939, reg. 3.

1367. Trade Marks and Service Marks (Forms) Rules 1986.

revoked: rules 94/2582, rule 2.
sch., amended: rules 94/2551, rule 2.

1390. General Medical Council (Constitution of Fitness to Practise Committees) Rules 1986.

rule 2, amended: rules 94/2022, rule 2.
rule 4, amended: *ibid.*
rule 6, substituted: *ibid.*

1510. Control of Pesticides Regulations 1986.

reg. 6(b), see *Thomson* v. *Barbour*, 1994, S.C.C.R. 485.

1682. Measuring Equipment (Measures of Length) Regulations 1986.

reg. 17A, inserted: regs. 94/1851, reg. 2.
reg. 2, amended: *ibid.*
reg. 17, amended: *ibid.*
reg. 24, substitute: *ibid.*

1684. Weights and Measures (Local and Working Standard Linear Measures) Regulations 1986.

reg. 3, amended: regs. 94/1851, reg. 2.
sch. 1, amended: *ibid.*

1685. Weights and Measures (Local and Working Standard Weights and Testing Equipment) Regulations 1986.

sch. 1, substituted: regs. 94/1851, reg. 2.
sch. 2, amended: *ibid.*

1711. Stamp Duty Reserve Tax Regulations 1986.

reg. 8, amended: regs. 94/1813, reg. 2.
reg. 10, substituted: *ibid.*
sch., amended: *ibid.*

1713. Combined Probation Areas Order 1986.

sch. 2, amended: ord. 94/471, art. 2, ord. 94/473, art. 2; ord. 94/969, art. 2; ord. 94/1543, art. 2.

1718. Occupational Pension Schemes (Managers) Regulations 1986.

reg. 1, amended: regs. 94/1062, reg. 2.
reg. 2, inserted: *ibid.*
reg. 3, amended: *ibid.*

1859. Traffic Signs (Amendment) Regulations 1986.

revoked: regs. 94/1519, reg. 2.

1925. Insolvency Rules 1986.

rule 1.17, see *Cranley Mansions*, Re, *The Times*, June 23, 1994.

NO.

1986—cont.

1925. Insolvency Rules 1986—*cont.*

rule 2.2, see *Practice Note (D.C.) (Administration Order Applications: Independent Reports)*, *The Times*, January 25, 1994.

rule 4.90, see *Bank of Credit and Commerce International SA, Re*; *The Times*, March 22, 1994.

rule 6.1, see *Debtor, A (No. 64 of 1992)*, Re [1994] 1 W.L.R. 264.

rules 6.4, 6.5, 6.8(2)(b)(ii), 7.55, see *Debtor, A (No. 22 of 1993)*, Re [1994] 1 W.L.R. 46.

rule 6.5(4)(d), see *Debtor, A (No. 415/SD/1993)*, *Re* [1994] 1 W.L.R. 917.

rule 7.47, see *Secretary of State for Trade and Industry* v. *Langley* [1993] BCLC 1340; *Midrome* v. *Shaw* [1993] BCC 659, C.A.; *SN Group, Re* [1993] BCC 808.

rule 12.3, see *Woodley* v. *Woodley (No. 2)* [1993] 4 All E.R. 1010, C.A.

1937. Act of Sederunt (Rules of Court Amendment No. 8) (Miscellaneous) 1986.

revoked: Act 94/1443, para. 3.

1941. Act of Sederunt (Rules of Court Amendment No. 9) (Jurisdiction and Enforcement) 1986.

revoked: Act 94/1443, para. 3.

1955. Act of Sederunt (Rules of Court Amendment No. 10) (Miscellaneous Amendments) 1986.

revoked: Act 94/1443, para. 3.

1960. Statutory Maternity Pay (General) Regulations 1986.

reg. 2, amended: regs. 94/1367, reg. 2.

reg. 4, amended: *ibid.*, reg. 3.

reg. 6, amended: regs. 94/542, reg. 10; *ibid.*, reg. 4.

reg. 21, amended: regs. 94/1367, reg. 5.

reg. 23, amended: *ibid.*, reg. 6.

1994. Insolvency Regulations 1986.

revoked: regs. 94/2507, reg. 2.

1999. Administration of Insolvent Estates of Deceased Persons Order 1986.

art. 3. see *Palmer (Dec'd) (A Debtor)*, *Re* [1994] 3 W.L.R. 420, C.A.

sch. 1, pt. II, paras. 10, 12, see *Palmer (Dec'd) (A Debtor)*, Re [1993] 3 W.L.R. 877.

2030. Insolvency Fees Order 1986.

art. 2, amended: ord. 94/2541, art. 3.

art. 4, amended: *ibid.*

art. 4A, inserted: *ibid.*

art. 9, amended: *ibid.*

art. 12, amended: *ibid.*

sch., amended: *ibid.*

2049. Weights and Measures (Packaged Goods) Regulations 1986.

sch. 1, pt. I, amended: regs. 94/1258, reg. 2.

NO.

1986—cont.

2049. Weights and Measures (Packaged Goods) Regulations 1986—*cont.*

sch. 1, pt. II, amended: *ibid.*, reg. 3.

2090. Sea Fishing (Enforcement of Community Conservation Measures) Order 1986.

art. 2, amended: ord. 94/1680, art. 3.

2105. Customs Duty (Personal Reliefs) (No. 1) Order 1968 (Amendment) Order 1986.

revoked: ord. 94/955, art. 5.

2142. Insolvent Partnerships Order 1986.

revoked: ord. 94/2421, art. 20.

2194. Housing (Right to Buy) (Prescribed Forms) Regulations 1986.

sch. 1, amended: ord. 94/2567, art. 2.

2209. European Parliamentary Elections Regulations 1986.

reg. 4, amended: regs. 94/342, regs. 5, 15.

reg. 5, amended: *ibid.*, reg. 15; regs. 94/748, reg. 2.

reg. 8, inserted: regs. 94/34, reg. 5.

sch. 1, amended: regs. 94/748, reg. 3.

sch. 4, pt. II, amended: regs. 94/34, reg. 15.

2218. Social Security (Adjudication) Regulations 1986.

reg. 1, amended: regs. 94/1082, reg. 2.

reg. 5, amended: *ibid.*, reg. 3.

reg. 7, amended: *ibid.*, reg. 4.

reg. 11(1)(c), see *Social Security Decision No. R(SB) 1/92.*

reg. 25(2)(b), see *Social Security Decision No. R(IS) 3/94.*

reg. 64, amended: regs. 94/2686, reg. 2.

regs. 69, 71, see *Social Security Decision No. R(IS) 11/93.*

regs. 69, 72, see *Social Security Decision No. R(SB) 1/93.*

sch. 2, para. 3, substituted: regs. 94/1082, reg. 5.

2250. European Parliamentary Elections (Northern Ireland) Regulations 1986.

reg. 4, amended: regs. 94/342, regs. 6, 16.

reg. 5, amended: *ibid.*, reg. 16.

reg. 7, inserted: *ibid.*, reg. 6.

2251. Environmentally Sensitive Areas (West Penwith) Designation Order 1986.

art. 2, amended: ord. 94/933, art. 4.

art. 4A, inserted: *ibid.*, art. 5.

art. 6, amended: *ibid.*, art. 6.

sch. 1A, inserted: *ibid.*, art. 7.

sch. 2, para. 2, amended: *ibid.*, art. 7.

sch. 2, para. 9, inserted: *ibid.*, art. 7.

2287. Building (Amendment of Prescribed Fees) Regulations 1986.

revoked: regs. 94/2020, reg. 16.

NO.

1986—cont.

2289. Rules of the Supreme Court (Amendment) (No. 3) Order 1986.
see *Varna, The* [1993] 2 Lloyd's Rep. 253, C.A.

2297. Act of Sederunt (Sheriff Court Company Insolvency Rules) 1986.
rules 22, 23(5), see *International Factors* v. *V.E.S. Voltech Electronic Services* (Sh.Ct.), 1993 S.C.L.R. 906.

2298. Act of Sederunt (Rules of Court Amendment No. 11) (Companies) 1986.
revoked: Art 94/1443, para. 3.

1987

12. Act of Sederunt (Rules of Court Amendment No. 1) (Drug Trafficking) 1987.
revoked: Art 94/1443, para. 3.

37. Dangerous Substances in Harbour Areas Regulations 1987.
applied: regs. 94/397, reg. 12.
reg. 2, applied: regs. 94/237, reg. 2; amended: regs. 94/669, reg. 15.
reg. 3, amended: regs. 94/669, reg. 15.
reg. 24, amended: *ibid.*
reg. 25, amended: *ibid.*
sch. 1, amended: *ibid.*
sch. 3, amended: *ibid.*
sch. 3, inserted: ord. 94/241, art. 3.
sch. 4, inserted: *ibid.*

91. Statutory Maternity Pay (Compensation of Employers) Regulations 1987.
revoked: regs. 94/1882, art. 8.
reg. 3, amended: regs. 94/592, reg. 2.

133. Authorised Officers (Meat Inspection) Regulations 1987.
sch., para. 3, applied: regs. 94/1029, sch. 16.

257. Police Pensions Regulations 1987.
reg. B8, amended: regs. 94/641, reg. 2.
reg. E4, amended: *ibid.*, reg. 3.
reg. E8, amended: *ibid.*, reg. 4.
reg. G6, inserted: *ibid.*, reg. 5.
reg. J1, amended: *ibid.*, reg. 6.
sch. C, pt. I, amended: *ibid.*, reg. 7.
sch. C, pt. III, amended: *ibid.*, reg. 8.
sch. C, pt. IV, amended: *ibid.*, reg. 9.
sch. C, pt. V, amended: *ibid.*, reg. 10.

299. Prosecution of Offences (Custody Time Limits) Regulations 1987.
reg. 4, see *R.* v. *Waltham Forest Justices,* ex p. *Lee* (1993) 97 Cr.App.R. 287.
reg. 5(3), see *R.* v. *Norwich Crown Court,* ex p. *Cox* (1993) 97 Cr.App.R. 145, D.C.
reg. 6(6), see *R.* v. *Croydon Crown Court,* ex p. *Lewis, The Times,* March 29, 1994, D.C.

NO.

1987—cont.

307. Criminal Legal Aid (Scotland) Regulations 1987.
reg. 2, amended: regs. 94/1050, reg. 3.
reg. 4, amended: *ibid.*, reg. 4.

381. Civil Legal Aid (Scotland) Regulations 1987.
reg. 3, amended: regs. 94/1049, reg. 3.
reg. 5, amended: *ibid.*, reg. 4.
reg. 10, amended: *ibid.*, reg. 5.
reg. 18, substituted: *ibid.*, reg. 6.
reg. 28A, amended: *ibid.*, reg. 7.
reg. 32, amended: *ibid.*, reg. 8.
reg. 35, see *Ferguson* v. *Povah* (Sh.Ct.), 1993 S.C.L.R. 634.
reg. 40A, revoked: regs. 94/1049, reg. 9.

382. Advice and Assistance (Scotland) Regulations 1987.
reg. 15, amended: regs. 94/1061, reg. 3.
sch. 2, amended: *ibid.*, reg. 4.

384. Legal Aid (Scotland) (Children) Regulations 1987.
reg. 2, amended: regs. 94/1017, reg. 4.

416. Social Security (Maternity Allowance) Regulations 1987.
reg. 3, amended: regs. 94/1367, reg. 7; amended: regs. 94/1882, art. 9.

417. Social Security (Maternity Allowance) (Work Abroad) Regulations 1987.
reg. 2, amended: regs. 94/1367, reg. 8.

433. Town and Country Planning (Compensation for Restrictions on Mineral Workings) (Scotland) Regulations 1987.
reg. 1, amended: ord. 94/2567, art. 2.

437. Value Added Tax (Charities) Order 1987.
C.: 1994, c. 23, sch. 8.
revoked: 1994, c. 23, sch. 15.

470. Merchant Shipping (IBC Code) Regulations 1987.
reg. 1, amended: regs. 94/2082, regs. 3, 4, 5.
reg. 3, amended: *ibid.*, reg. 6.
reg. 7, amended: *ibid.*, reg. 7.
reg. 10, amended: *ibid.*, reg. 8.
sch., revoked: *ibid.*, reg. 9.

481. Social Fund Maternity and Funeral Expenses (General) Regulations 1987.
reg. 3, amended: regs. 94/506, reg. 2.
reg. 7, amended: *ibid.*, reg. 3.
reg. 7(1)(b), see *Social Security Decision No. R(IS) 9/93.*
reg. 8, amended: regs. 94/506, reg. 4.

517. Value Added Tax (Betting, Gaming and Lotteries) Order 1987.
C.: 1994, c. 23, sch. 9.
revoked: 1994, c. 23, sch. 15.

518. Value Added Tax (International Services) Order 1987.
revoked: 1994, c. 23, sch. 15.

NO.

1987—cont.

550. Merchant Shipping (BCH Code) Regulations 1987.
reg. 1, amended: regs. 94/2084, regs. 3–5.
reg. 3, substituted: *ibid.*, reg. 6.
reg. 7, amended: *ibid.*, reg. 7.
reg. 10, amended: *ibid.*, reg. 8.
sch. revoked: *ibid.*, reg. 9.

551. Merchant Shipping (Control of Pollution by Noxious Liquid Substances in Bulk) Regulations 1987.
reg. 1, amended: regs. 94/2083, reg. 3.
reg. 2A, inserted: *ibid.*, reg. 5.
reg. 4, amended: *ibid.*, reg. 6.
reg. 26, amended: *ibid.*, reg. 7.
reg. 29, amended: *ibid.*, reg. 8.
schs. 1, 2, 3, revoked: *ibid.*, reg. 3.

603. Plugs and Sockets etc. (Safety) Regulations 1987.
revoked: regs. 94/1768, reg. 2.

701. Town and Country Planning (Appeals) (Written Representations Procedure) Regulations 1987.
reg. 5, see *Mancetter Developments* v. *Secretary of State for the Environment, Peterborough City Council and Kesteven Fruit Co.* [1993] J.P.L. 439.

710. Agricultural Holdings (Arbitration on Notices) Order 1987.
art. 10(a), see *Robinson* v. *Moody, The Times,* February 23, 1994, C.A.

764. Town and Country Planning (Use Classes) Order 1987.
art. 3, amended: ord. 94/724, art. 2.

827. Public Telecommunication System Designation (British Cable Services Limited) Order 1987.
revoked: ord. 94/1006, art. 3.

851. Police Regulations 1987.
reg. 8A, amended: regs. 94/2195, reg.' 2.
reg. 26, amended: *ibid.*, reg. 3.
reg. 26A, amended: *ibid.*, reg. 4.
reg. 27, amended: *ibid.*, reg. 5.
reg. 28, amended: *ibid.*, reg. 6.
reg. 29, amended: *ibid.*, reg. 7.
reg. 29A, inserted: *ibid.*, reg. 8.
reg. 35A, inserted: regs. 94/1308, reg. 2.
reg. 37, amended: regs. 94/2331, reg. 2.
reg. 39, amended: regs. 94/1308, reg. 3.
reg. 43A, inserted: regs. 94/2195, reg. 9.
regs. 49–49D, revoked: *ibid.*, reg. 14.
regs. 50–52, revoked: *ibid.*
reg. 52B, substituted: regs. 94/1308, reg. 4; revoked: regs. 94/2195, reg. 14.
reg. 53, amended: regs. 94/1308, reg. 5; amended: regs. 94/2195, reg. 10.
regs. 54–55, revoked: *ibid.*, reg. 14.
reg. 57, revoked in pt.: *ibid.*
regs. 61–62, revoked: *ibid.*
reg. 64, amended: *ibid.*, reg. 11.

NO.

1987—cont.

851. Police Regulations 1987—*cont.*
reg. 66, revoked: *ibid.*, reg. 14.
reg. 72, revoked: *ibid.*, reg. 14.
sch. 1A, para. 1, amended: *ibid.*, reg. 12.
sch. 1A, para. 6, amended: *ibid.*
sch. 1A, para. 12A, *ibid.*, reg. 6.
sch. 1A, para. 7, amended: *ibid.*
sch. 1A, paras. 16–18, revoked: *ibid.*, reg. 14.
sch. 1A, para. 22, amended: *ibid.*, reg. 12.
sch. 2A, para. 4, amended: *ibid.*, reg. 13.
sch. 4, para. 4, revoked in pt.: *ibid.*, reg. 14.
sch. 5, para. 1, amended: regs. 94/2331, reg. 3.
sch. 5, para. 2, revoked: *ibid.*
sch. 5, para. 3, amended: *ibid.*
schs. 9, 10, revoked: regs. 94/2195, reg. 14.
sch. 11, amended: regs. 94/2331, reg. 4.
sch. 12, para. 4, revoked: regs. 94/2195, reg. 14.

860. Value Added Tax (Finance) Order 1987.
amended: 1994, c. 23, sch. 9.
revoked: 1994, c. 23, sch. 15.

871. Act of Sederunt (Rules of Court Amendment No. 2) (Solicitor's Fees) 1987.
revoked: Act 94/1443, para. 3.

905. Marek's Disease (Restriction on Vaccination) Order 1987.
revoked: ord. 94/472, art. 2.

1072. Value Added Tax (Construction of Buildings) (No. 2) Order 1987.
art. 2, revoked: 1994, c. 23, sch. 15.

1079. Act of Sederunt (Rules of Court Amendment No. 3) (Shorthand Writers' Fees) 1987.
revoked: Act 94/1443, para. 3.

1086. Value Added Tax (Tour Operators) Order 1987.
applied: 1994, c. 23, sch. 8, group 8.

1101. Money Purchase Contracted-out Schemes Regulations 1987.
reg. 1, amended: regs. 94/1062, reg. 2.
reg. 2, amended: *ibid.*
reg. 3, amended: *ibid.*
reg. 4, amended: *ibid.*
reg. 5, amended: *ibid.*
reg. 6, amended: *ibid.*

1102. Occupational Pension Schemes (Auditors) Regulations 1987.
reg. 1, amended: regs. 94/1062, reg. 2.

1103. Occupational Pension Schemes (Contracted-out Protected Rights Premiums) Regulations 1987.
reg. 2, amended: regs. 94/1062, reg. 2.

NO.

1987—cont.

1106. Occupational Pension Schemes (Qualifying Service—Consequential and Other Provisions) Regulations 1987.
reg. 6, amended: regs. 94/1062, reg. 2.

1108. Pension Schemes (Voluntary Contributions Requirements and Voluntary and Compulsory Membership) Regulations 1987.
reg. 1, amended: regs. 94/1062, reg. 2.
reg. 2, amended: *ibid.*
reg. 2A, amended: *ibid.*
reg. 3, amended: *ibid.*

1110. Personal Pension Schemes (Disclosure of Information) Regulations 1987.
reg. 1, amended: regs. 94/1062, reg. 2.
reg. 5, amended: *ibid.*
sch. 1, para. 14, amended: *ibid.*
sch. 2, para. 1, amended: *ibid.*

1111. Personal Pension Schemes (Personal Pension Protected Rights Premiums) Regulations 1987.
reg. 1, amended: regs. 94/1062, reg. 2.
reg. 2, amended: *ibid.*
reg. 3, amended: *ibid.*
reg. 4, amended: *ibid.*
reg. 5, amended: *ibid.*
reg. 6, amended: *ibid.*
reg. 7, amended: *ibid.*
reg. 8, amended: *ibid.*

1112. Personal Pension Schemes (Transfer Values) Regulations 1987.
reg. 1, amended: regs. 94/1062, reg. 2.
reg. 2, amended: *ibid.*
reg. 2A, amended: *ibid.*
reg. 3, amended: *ibid.*
reg. 4, amended: *ibid.*

1113. Personal and Occupational Pension Schemes (Abatement of Benefit) Regulations 1987.
reg. 1, amended: regs. 94/1062, reg. 2.
reg. 2, amended: *ibid.*
reg. 3, amended: *ibid.*
reg. 4, amended: *ibid.*
reg. 5, amended: *ibid.*

1117. Personal and Occupational Pension Schemes (Protected Rights) Regulations 1987.
reg. 1, amended: regs. 94/1062, reg. 2.
reg. 2, amended: *ibid.*
reg. 3, amended: *ibid.*
reg. 4, amended: *ibid.*
reg. 5, amended: *ibid.*
reg. 6, amended: *ibid.*
reg. 7, amended: *ibid.*
reg. 8, amended: *ibid.*
reg. 9, amended: *ibid.*
reg. 10, amended: *ibid.*
reg. 15, amended: *ibid.*

1118. Protected Rights (Transfer Payment) Regulations 1987.
reg. 1, amended: regs. 94/1062, reg. 2.

NO.

1987—cont.

1118. Protected Rights (Transfer Payment) Regulations 1987—*cont.*
reg. 2, amended: *ibid.*
reg. 3, amended: *ibid.*
reg. 4, amended: *ibid.*
sch. 1, amended: regs. 94/1751, reg. 2.
sch. 3, para. 2, amended: regs. 94/1062, reg. 2.

1120. General Medical Council (Constitution of Fitness to Practise Committees) (Amendment) Rules 1987.
rule 2, revoked in pt.: rules 94/2022, rule 3.

1206. Act of Sederunt (Rules of Court Amendment No. 4) (Miscellaneous) 1987.
revoked: Act 94/1843, para. 3.

1253. Commonwealth Development Corporation (Additional Enterprises) Order 1987.
revoked: ord. 94/2880, art. 3.

1259. Value Added Tax (Education) Order 1987.
revoked: 1994, c. 23, sch. 15.

1343. Town and Country Planning (Black Country Urban Development Area) Special Development Order 1987.
referred to: ord. 94/2567, art. 3.
art. 6, amended: *ibid.*, art. 2.

1345. Town and Country Planning (Tyne and Wear Urban Development Area) Special Development Order 1987.
applied: ord. 94/2567, art. 3.
art. 6, amended: *ibid.*, art. 2.

1378. Motor Vehicles (Driving Licences) Regulations 1987.
reg. 19, amended: regs. 94/638, reg. 3.
reg. 21, amended: *ibid.*
reg. 24, amended: regs. 94/1862, reg. 3.

1427. Value Added Tax (Cash Accounting) Regulations 1987.
reg. 11, C.: 1994, c. 23, s. 83.

1532. Town and Country Planning (Simplified Planning Zones) (Scotland) Regulations 1987.
referred to: ord. 94/2567, art. 5.
art. 4, amended: *ibid.*, art. 2.

1683. Social Security (Hospital In-Patients) Amendment (No. 2) Regulations 1987.
reg. 3, referred to: regs. 94/648, sch. 3, para. 37.

1706. Traffic Signs General (Amendment) Directions 1987.
revoked: regs. 94/1519, reg. 2.

1806. Value Added Tax (Tour Operators) Order 1987.
C.: 1994, c. 23, sch. 8.
revoked: 1994, c. 23, sch. 15.

1850. Local Government Superannuation (Scotland) Regulations 1987.
reg. B6, amended: regs. 94/531, reg. 3.

NO.

1987—cont.

1850. Local Government Superannuation (Scotland) Regulations 1987—*cont.*

reg. C3, amended: *ibid.*, reg. 4.
reg. C3A, amended: *ibid.*, reg. 5.
sch. 3, pt. I, para. 6, inserted: *ibid.*, reg. 6.

1903. Data Protection (Subject Access Modification) (Health) Order 1987.

sch., amended: 1994, c. 17, s. 38.

1911. Approval of Safety Standards Regulations 1987.

revoked: refs. 94/2328, reg. 6.

1959. Insolvency (Amendment) Regulations 1987.

revoked: regs. 94/2507, reg. 2.

1967. Income Support (General) Regulations 1987.

reg. 2, see *Social Security Decision No. R(IS) 11/94.*
reg. 5A, inserted: regs. 94/1004, reg. 2.
reg. 17, amended: regs. 94/542, reg. 16.
reg. 18, amended: *ibid.*, regs. 94/1807, reg. 4.
reg. 19, amended: regs. 94/527, reg. 2.
reg. 21, amended: regs. 94/527, reg. 3, regs. 94/542, reg. 16.
reg. 38(3), see *Social Security Decision No. R(IS) 13/91.*
reg. 42, amended: regs. 94/527, reg. 4.
reg. 51(1), see *Social Security Decision No. R(IS) 9/92.*
reg. 54(d), see *Bolstridge* v. *Chief Adjudication Officer* [1993] 2 FLR 657, C.A.
reg. 62, amended: regs. 94/1608, reg. 2.
reg. 66, amended: regs. 94/527, reg. 5.
reg. 71, amended: *ibid.*, reg. 6, regs. 94/542, reg. 16.
sch. 1, para. 5, substituted: regs. 94/527, reg. 7.
sch. 2, see *Social Security Decision No. R(IS) 10/94.*
sch. 2, pt. I, amended: regs. 94/542, reg. 16.
sch. 2, pt. II, amended: *ibid.*
sch. 2, pt. III, amended: *ibid.*
sch. 2, pt. IV, amended: *ibid.*
sch. 3, para. 7, see *Social Security Decision No. R(IS) 2/94*; amended: regs. 94/527, reg. 8.
sch. 3, para. 11, amended: regs. 94/542, reg. 16; see *Social Security Decisions No. R(IS) 19/93; No. R(IS) 11/94; No. R(IS) 6/94; No. R(IS) 3/94; No. R(IS) 13/92; No. R(IS) 10/93.*
sch. 4, pt. I, amended: *ibid.*
sch. 7, amended: *ibid.*
sch. 8, amended: *ibid.*
sch. 9, para. 15, amended: regs. 94/527, reg. 9.
sch. 9, para. 19, substituted: *ibid.*
sch. 9, para. 20, substituted: *ibid.*
sch. 9, para. 53, inserted: *ibid.*

NO.

1987—cont.

1968. Social Security (Claims and Payments) Regulations 1987.

see *Social Security Decision No. R(SB) 1/94.*
reg. 3, amended: regs. 94/2943, reg. 2.
reg. 6, amended: regs. 94/2319, reg. 2.
reg. 7(1), see *Social Security Decision No. R(IS) 4/93.*
reg. 10, amended: regs. 94/2943, reg. 3.
reg. 11, amended: *ibid.*, reg. 4.
reg. 13, amended: regs. 94/2319, reg. 3.
reg. 15, amended: regs. 94/2943, reg. 5.
reg. 16, amended: *ibid.*, reg. 6.
reg. 17(4), see *Social Security Decision No. R(S) 3/94.*
reg. 18, amended: regs. 94/2943, reg. 7.
reg. 21, amended: regs. 94/2319, reg. 4; regs. 94/2943, reg. 8.
reg. 24, substituted: regs. 94/2943, reg. 9.
reg. 30, amended: regs. 94/2319, reg. 5.
reg. 37AA, inserted: *ibid.*, reg. 6.
reg. 37AB, inserted: *ibid.*, reg. 6.
reg. 38(2A), see *Social Security Decision No. R(P) 3/93.*
sch. 1, pt. I, amended: regs. 94/2943, reg. 10.
sch. 3, amended: *ibid.*, reg. 11.
sch. 4, para. 2, substituted: *ibid.*, reg. 12.
sch. 5, para. 2, substituted: *ibid.*, reg. 13.
sch. 7, para. 2, amended: *ibid.*
sch. 7, para. 3, amended: *ibid.*
sch. 7, para. 4, amended: *ibid.*
sch. 9, para. 1, amended: *ibid.*, reg. 15.
sch. 9, para. 6, amended: regs. 94/2319, reg. 7.
sch. 9, para. 7, amended: *ibid.*, reg. 7.
sch. 9, para. 8, amended: *ibid.*
sch. 9A, para. 5, amended: regs. 94/2943, reg. 16.

1969. Income Support (Transitional) Regulations 1987.

reg. 14(1)(a), see *Social Security Decision No. R(IS) 6/93.*
reg. 15, amended: regs. 94/542, reg. 17.

1971. Housing Benefit (General) Regulations 1987.

see *R.* v. *Haringey London Borough Council, ex p. Ayub* (1992) (1993) 25 H.L.R. 566; referred to ord. 94/523, art. 2.
reg. 2, amended: regs. 94/578, reg. 2; regs. 94/1924, reg. 5.
reg. 3, see *Fullwood* v. *Chesterfield Borough Council* (1993) 26 H.L.R. 126, C.A.
reg. 7A, inserted: regs. 94/470, reg. 3; regs. 94/1807, reg. 3.
reg. 10, applied: regs. 94/648, reg. 28, sch. 3, para. 13.

NO.

1987—cont.

1971. Housing Benefit (General) Regulations 1987—cont.

reg. 10(3), sch. 1, para. 1(f), see *R. v. North Cornwall District Council*, ex p. *Singer*; *Same* v. *Same*, ex p. *Barrett*; *Same* v. *Same*, ex p. *Bateman*, *The Times*, January 12, 1994, D.C.

reg. 11(3), see *R. v. Housing Benefit Review Board for East Devon District Council*, ex p. *Gibson and Gibson* (1993) 25 H.L.R. 487, C.A.

reg. 16, amended: regs. 94/542, reg. 19.

reg. 17, amended: *ibid.*

reg. 18, amended: *ibid.*, reg. 18.

reg. 21, amended: regs. 94/1924, reg. 5.

reg. 21A, inserted: *ibid.*

reg. 25, amended: regs. 94/578, reg. 3.

reg. 29, amended: *ibid.*, reg. 4.

reg. 30, amended: *ibid.*, reg. 5.

reg. 31, amended: *ibid.*, reg. 6.

reg. 35, amended: *ibid.*, reg. 7.

reg. 49, revoked: regs. 94/470, reg. 3.

reg. 51, amended: regs. 94/1608, reg. 3.

reg. 53, amended: *ibid.*, reg. 2.

reg. 55, amended: regs. 94/578, reg. 8.

reg. 61, applied: regs. 94/579, reg. 1.

reg. 61, amended: regs. 94/578, reg. 10.

reg. 63, amended: regs. 94/542, reg. 19.

reg. 68, amended: regs. 94/578, reg. 11.

reg. 69, amended: *ibid.*, reg. 12.

reg. 83, see *R. v. Solihull Metropolitan Borough Council Housing Benefit Review Board*, ex p. *Simpson*, *The Times*, July 19, 1994, C.A.

regs. 79, 81, 93, 94, see *R. v. Stoke City Council*, ex p. *Highgate Projects*; *R. v. Birmingham City Council*, ex p. *Connolly*, *The Independent*, April 14, 1994, D.C.

sch. 1, pt. I, amended: regs. 94/542, reg. 19.

sch. 1, pt. II, amended: *ibid.*

sch. 1, para. 1, amended: regs. 94/1003, reg. 2.

sch. 2, pt. I, amended: regs. 94/542, reg. 19.

sch. 2, pt. II, amended: *ibid.*

sch. 2, pt. III, amended: *ibid.*

sch. 2, pt. IV, amended: *ibid.*

sch. 4, para. 20, substituted: regs. 94/578, reg. 13.

sch. 4, para. 42, substituted: *ibid.*

sch. 4, para. 52, inserted: *ibid.*

1973. Family Credit (General) Regulations 1987.

reg. 2, amended: regs. 94/527, reg. 10; regs. 94/1924, reg. 4.

reg. 13, amended: regs. 94/1924, reg. 4.

reg. 13A, inserted: *ibid.*

reg. 14, amended: regs. 94/527, reg. 11.

reg. 14A, inserted: *ibid.*, reg. 12.

reg. 15, amended: *ibid.*, reg. 13.

reg. 17, substituted: *ibid.*, reg. 14.

reg. 18, amended: *ibid.*, reg. 15.

NO.

1987—cont.

1973. Family Credit (General) Regulations 1987—cont.

reg. 20, amended: *ibid.*, reg. 16.

reg. 20ZA, inserted: *ibid.*, reg. 17.

reg. 20A, amended: *ibid.*, reg. 18.

reg. 22, amended: *ibid.*, reg. 19.

reg. 26, amended: *ibid.*, reg. 20.

reg. 38, amended: regs. 94/1608, reg. 2.

reg. 42, amended: regs. 94/527, reg. 21.

reg. 46, amended: regs. 94/542, reg. 14.

reg. 47, amended: *ibid.*

sch. 2, para. 19, substituted: regs. 94/527, reg. 22.

sch. 2, para. 40, substituted: *ibid.*

sch. 2, para. 51, inserted: *ibid.*

sch. 4, amended: regs. 94/542, reg. 14.

2023. Insolvent Companies (Disqualification of Unfit Directors) Proceedings Rules 1987.

see *Moonbeam Cards*, Re [1993] BCLC 1099.

2026. Environmentally Sensitive Areas (Cambrian Mountains—Extension) Designation Order 1987.

rule 3(2), see *Homes Assured Corp.*, Re [1993] BCC 573.

art. 2, amended: ord. 94/240, art. 3.

art. 3, amended: *ibid.*

art. 4, substituted: *ibid.*

art. 5, amended: *ibid.*

art. 6, substituted: *ibid.*

sch. 1, inserted: *ibid.*

sch. 2, inserted: *ibid.*

sch. 3, inserted: *ibid.*

sch. 4, inserted: *ibid.*

2027. Environmentally Sensitive Areas (Lleyn Peninsula) Designation Order 1987.

art. 2, amended: ord. 94/241, art. 3.

art. 3, amended: *ibid.*

art. 5, amended: *ibid.*

art. 6, substituted: *ibid.*

sch. 1, inserted: *ibid.*

sch. 2, inserted: *ibid.*

2049. Consumer Protection (Northern Ireland) Order 1987.

art. 5, applied: 1994, c. 26, s. 106.

2088. Registration of Births and Deaths Regulations 1987.

reg. 2, amended: regs. 94/1948, reg. 2.

reg. 9, amended: *ibid.*, reg. 3.

reg. 19, amended: *ibid.*, reg. 4.

reg. 34, amended: *ibid.*, reg. 5.

reg. 36, amended: *ibid.*, reg. 6.

reg. 56, amended: *ibid.*, reg. 7.

sch. 2, amended: *ibid.*, reg. 8.

2115. Control of Asbestos at Work Regulations 1987.

applied: regs. 94/397, reg. 3.

reg. 18, amended: regs. 94/669, reg. 15.

sch. 2, para. 1, amended: *ibid.*

2116. Benzene in Toys (Safety) Regulations 1987.

revoked: regs. 94/2844, reg. 7.

NO.

1987—cont.

2132. Friendly Societies (Long Term Insurance Business) Regulations 1987.
reg. 11, applied: regs. 94/1981, reg. 9.
2160. Act of Sederunt (Rules of Court Amendment No. 5) (Miscellaneous) 1987.
revoked: Act 94/1443, para. 3.
2203. Adoption (Northern Ireland) Order 1987.
applied: regs. 94/2767, reg. 3.
2231. Prison (Scotland) Amendment Rules 1987.
revoked: rules 94/1931, rule 143.

1988

110. Act of Adjournal (Consolidation) 1988.
rule 73A, amended: Act 94/1769, rule 2.
rule 122A, amended: *ibid.*
sch. 1, form 93, substituted: *ibid.*
120. Capacity Serving Measures (Intoxicating Liquor) Regulations 1988.
reg. 10, amended: regs. 94/1851, reg. 2.
reg. 2, amended: *ibid.*
reg. 3, amended: *ibid.*
sch., amended: *ibid.*
128. Measuring Equipment (Liquid Fuel and Lubricants) Regulations 1988.
reg. 7A, inserted: regs. 94/1851, reg. 2.
reg. 2, amended: *ibid.*
reg. 17, amended: *ibid.*
reg. 24, amended: *ibid.*
137. Personal Pension Schemes (Appropriate Schemes) Regulations 1988.
reg. 1, amended: regs. 94/1062, reg. 2.
reg. 2, amended: *ibid.*
reg. 7, amended: *ibid.*
reg. 8, amended: *ibid.*
reg. 9, amended: *ibid.*
reg. 10, amended: *ibid.*
reg. 12, amended: *ibid.*
reg. 13, amended: *ibid.*
reg. 14, amended: *ibid.*
reg. 16, amended: *ibid.*
reg. 17, amended: *ibid.*
reg. 17A, amended: *ibid.*
reg. 19, amended: *ibid.*
reg. 20, amended: *ibid.*
sch. 2, para. 2, amended: *ibid.*
267. Income Tax (Definition of Unit Trust Scheme) Regulations 1988.
reg. 7, amended: regs. 94/1479, reg. 2.
350. Financial Services Act 1986 (Miscellaneous Exemptions) Order 1988.
sch. 2, para. 7, revoked: ord. 94/1517, art. 3.
395. Registered Housing Associations (Accounting Requirements) Order 1988.
revoked in pt.: ord. 94/668, art. 1.

NO.

1988—cont.

412. Aycliff and Peterlee Development Corporation (Transfer of Property and Dissolution) Order 1988.
see *Optilon* v. *Commission for New Towns* [1993] EG 125.
507. Value Added Tax (Confectionary) Order 1988.
C.: 1994, c. 23, sch. 8.
revoked: 1994, c. 23, sch. 15.
536. Welfare Food Regulations 1988.
reg. 2, amended: regs. 94/2004, reg. 2.
reg. 4, amended: *ibid.*, reg. 3.
reg. 5, amended: *ibid.*, reg. 4.
reg. 9, referred to: regs. 94/648, sch. 3, para. 44, sch. 4, para. 39.
reg. 10, referred to: *ibid.*, sch. 3, para. 44, sch. 4, para. 39.
reg. 11, referred to: *ibid.*, sch. 3, para. 44, sch. 4, para. 39.
reg. 13, referred to: *ibid.*, sch. 3, para. 44, sch. 4, para. 39.
sch. 1, amended: regs. 94/2004, reg. 5.
sch. 3, amended: *ibid.*, reg. 6.
537. Prison (Scotland) Amendment Rules 1988.
revoked: rules 94/1931, rule 143.
538. European Communities (Iron and Steel Employees Re-adaptation Benefits Scheme) (No. 2) Regulations 1988.
scheme, terminated: regs. 94/141, reg. 3.
546. National Health Service (Travelling Expenses and Remission of Charges) (Scotland) Regulations 1988.
reg. 3, referred to: regs. 94/648, sch. 3, para. 43.
reg. 5, referred to: *ibid.*, sch. 3, para. 43, sch. 4, para. 38.
reg. 8, referred to: *ibid.*, sch. 3, para. 43, sch. 4, para. 38.
551. National Health Service (Travelling Expenses and Remission of Charges) Regulations 1988.
reg. 3, referred to: regs. 94/648, sch. 3, para. 43, sch. 4, para. 38.
reg. 5, referred to: *ibid.*, sch. 3, para. 43, sch. 4, para. 38.
reg. 8, referred to: *ibid.*
559. Crofting Counties Agricultural Grants (Scotland) Scheme 1988.
para. 5, amended: Scheme 94/1013, para. 3.
para. 6, amended: *ibid.*, para. 4.
para. 12A, inserted: *ibid.*, para. 5.
para. 12B, inserted: *ibid.*
sch., amended: *ibid.*, para. 6.
sch. 5, amended: *ibid.*, reg. 7.
591. Social Security (Reciprocal Agreements) Order 1988.
sch., amended: ord. 94/2802, art. 3.

NO.

1988—cont.

615. Act of Sederunt (Rules of the Court of Session Amendment No. 1) (Family Law) 1988.
revoked: Act 94/1443, para. 3.

623. Social Security Pensions (Home Responsibilities and Miscellaneous Amendments) Amendment Regulations 1988.
revoked: regs. 94/704, reg. 3.

646. Banking Act 1987 (Exempt Transactions) Regulations 1988.
sch. 2, amended: ord. 94/2567, art. 2.

662. Housing Benefit (Supply of Information) Regulations 1988.
reg. 1, amended: regs. 94/1925, reg. 2.
reg. 2, amended: *ibid.*
reg. 3, amended: *ibid.*
reg. 4, inserted: regs. 94/578, reg. 14.

673. Insurance Companies (Amendment) Regulations 1988.
revoked: regs. 94/1516, reg. 86.

684. Act of Sederunt (Rules of the Court of Session Amendment No. 2) (Solicitors' Fees) 1988.
revoked: Act 94/1443, para. 3.

722. Civil Aviation (Canadian Navigation Services) (Amendment) Regulations 1988.
revoked: regs. 94/2325, reg. 3.

819. Control and Disposal of Waste Regulations 1988.
reg. 3, amended: regs. 94/1056, reg. 22.
reg. 6, amended: *ibid.*
reg. 7, amended: *ibid.*
reg. 7A, inserted: *ibid.*

871. Building (Amendment of Prescribed Fees) Regulations 1986.
revoked: regs. 94/2020, reg. 16.

876. Weighing Equipment (Non-automatic Weighing Machines) Regulations 1988.
reg. 2, amended; regs. 94/1851, reg. 2.
reg. 14, amended; *ibid.*
reg. 16, amended: *ibid.*
reg. 16A, inserted: *ibid.*
reg. 18, substituted: *ibid.*
reg. 29, revoked: *ibid.*
sch. 2, para. 11, amended: *ibid.*
sch. 2, para. 13, amended: *ibid.*
sch. 2, para. 15, amended: *ibid.*
sch. 2, para. 17, amended: *ibid.*

900. Urban Development Corporations (Appropriate Ministers) Order 1988.
art. 2, amended: ord. 94/2567, art. 2.

931. Summer Time Order 1988.
revoked: 94/2798, art. 5.

944. Town and Country Planning (Inquiries Procedure) Rules 1988.
rule 16(4), see *Portsmouth Water* v. *Secretary of State for the Environment* (1993) 66 P. & C.R. 410.

NO.

1988—cont.

945. Town and Country Planning Appeals (Determination by Inspectors) (Inquiries Procedure) Rules 1988.
rule 16(2), see *Hallinan* v. *Secretary of State for the Environment and Barnet London Borough Council* [1993] J.P.L. 584.

950. Insurance Brokers Registration Council (Conduct of Investment Brokers) Rules 1988.
applied: ord. 94, 2569, art. 2.

1032. Act of Sederunt (Rules of the Court of Session Amendment No. 3) (Shorthand Writers' Fees) 1988.
revoked: Act 94/1443, para. 3.

1057. Electricity Supply Regulations 1988.
reg. 34, substituted: regs. 94/533, reg. 3.
sch. 4, pt. I, amended: *ibid.*, reg. 4.

1067. Education (Special Educational Needs) (Amendment) Regulations 1988.
revoked: regs. 94/1047, reg. 20.

1098. Ministry of Defence Police (Police Committee) Regulations 1988.
reg. 3, amended: regs. 94/1102, reg. 3.

1112. Trade Marks and Service Marks (Forms) (Amendment) Rules 1988.
revoked: rules 94/2582, rule 2; rules 94/2583, rule 69.

1126. Criminal Legal Aid (Scotland) Amendment Regulations 1988.
reg. 4, amended: regs. 94/1050, reg. 5.

1171. Civil Legal Aid (Scotland) Amendment (No. 2) Regulations 1988.
reg. 6, revoked: regs. 94/1049, reg. 9.

1180. Pig Carcase (Grading) Regulations 1988.
revoked: regs. 94/2155, reg. 13.

1199. Town and Country Planning (Assessment of Environmental Effects) Regulations 1988.
reg. 2, amended: regs. 94/677, reg. 2.
reg. 3, amended: *ibid.*
reg. 4, amended: *ibid.*
reg. 5, amended: *ibid.*
reg. 6, amended: *ibid.*
reg. 8, amended: *ibid.*
reg. 9, amended: *ibid.*
reg. 14, amended: *ibid.*
reg. 15, amended: *ibid.*
reg. 19, amended: *ibid.*
reg. 21, amended: *ibid.*
sch. 2, para. 3, amended: *ibid.*
sch. 2, para. 10, amended: *ibid.*

1221. Environmental Assessment (Scotland) Regulations 1988.
reg. 4, amended: regs. 94/2012, reg. 2.
reg. 5, amended: *ibid.*
reg. 6, amended: *ibid.*
reg. 16, amended: *ibid.*
reg. 18, amended: *ibid.*
reg. 21, amended: *ibid.*

NO.

1988—cont.

1221. Environmental Assessment (Scotland) Regulations 1988—cont.
reg. 22, amended: *ibid.*
reg. 28, amended: *ibid.*
reg. 29, substituted: *ibid.*
reg. 35, amended: *ibid.*
reg. 36, amended: *ibid.*
reg. 40, amended: *ibid.*
reg. 43, amended: *ibid.*
reg. 48, amended: *ibid.*
reg. 49, amended: *ibid.*
reg. 53, amended: *ibid.*
reg. 54, amended: *ibid.*
reg. 59, amended: *ibid.*
reg. 60, amended: *ibid.*
reg. 64, amended: *ibid.*
reg. 65, amended: *ibid.*
reg. 67, amended: *ibid.*
reg. 68, amended: *ibid.*
sch. 2, para. 3, amended: *ibid.*
sch. 2, para. 10, amended: *ibid.*
sch. 6, inserted: *ibid.*

1282. Value Added Tax (Training) Order 1988.
revoked: 1994, c. 23, sch. 15.

1291. Farm Woodland Scheme 1988.
referred to: regs. 94/1292, reg. 2.

1328. Matrimonial Causes (Costs) Rules 1988.
see *L. v. L. (Legal Aid Taxation)* [1993] 2 FLR 84.

1352. Set-Aside Regulations 1988.
applied: regs. 94/1292, reg. 2.

1372. Local Government Act 1988 (Defined Activities) (Exemptions) (England) Order 1988.
art. 3, amended: ord. 94/2296, art. 2.

1378. Pesticides (Maximum Residue Levels in Food) Regulations 1988.
revoked: regs. 94/1985, reg. 9.

1397. Education (Bursaries for Teacher Training) Regulations 1988.
applied: 1994, c. 30, s. 13; revoked: regs. 94/2016, reg. 2.

1469. Local Government Act 1988 (Defined Activities) (Exemptions) (Wales) Order 1988.
art. 3, amended: ord. 94/2296, art. 2.

1478. Goods Vehicles (Plating and Testing) Regulations 1988.
reg. 3, amended: regs. 94/328, reg. 3.
reg. 19, amended: *ibid.*, reg. 4.
reg. 20, amended: *ibid.*, reg. 5.

1521. Act of Sederunt (Rules of the Court of Session Amendment No. 4) (Commercial Actions) 1988.
revoked: Act 94/1443, para. 3.

1562. Transfrontier Shipment of Hazardous Waste Regulations 1988.
applied: regs. 94/1056, reg. 3; revoked: regs. 94/1137, reg. 21.

NO.

1988—cont.

1652. Teachers' Superannuation (Consolidation) Regulations 1988.
reg. B2, amended: regs. 94/1058, reg. 3.
reg. B5, amended: *ibid.*, reg. 4.
reg. B7, amended: *ibid.*, reg. 5.
reg. C3, amended: *ibid.*, reg. 6.
reg. C4, amended: *ibid.*, reg. 7; regs. 94/2774, reg. 2.
reg. C8, amended: regs. 94/1058, reg. 8.
reg. C12, amended: *ibid.*, reg. 9.
reg. C14, amended: *ibid.*, reg. 10.
reg. D1, amended: *ibid.*, reg. 11.
reg. E9, amended: *ibid.*, reg. 12.
reg. E14, amended: *ibid.*, reg. 13.
reg. E19, amended: *ibid.*, reg. 14.
reg. E20, amended: *ibid.*, reg. 15.
reg. E21, amended: *ibid.*, reg. 16.
reg. E22, amended: *ibid.*, reg. 17.
reg. E29, amended: regs. 94/2876, reg. 2.
reg. G6, amended: regs. 94/1058, reg. 18.
reg. H1, amended: *ibid.*, reg. 19.
sch. 1, amended: *ibid.*, reg. 20.
sch. 2, para. 2, amended: *ibid.*, reg. 21.
sch. 2, para. 3, amended: *ibid.*
sch. 2, para. 3A, inserted: *ibid.*
sch. 2, para. 24, amended: *ibid.*
sch. 2, para. 26, substituted: *ibid.*
sch. 4, pt. IV, revoked: *ibid.*, reg. 22.
sch. 5, para. 3, amended: *ibid.*, reg. 23.
sch. 5, para. 3A, inserted: *ibid.*
sch. 7, para. 6, inserted: *ibid.*, reg. 24.
sch. 11, pt. I, amended: *ibid.*, reg. 25.
sch. 12, pt. III, amended: *ibid.*, reg. 26.

1657. Control of Substances Hazardous to Health Regulations 1988.
applied: regs. 94/397, reg. 3.

1715. Central Institutions (Scotland) Regulations 1988.
revoked in pt.: ord. 94/1715, art. 8; ord. 94/1980, art. 42; ord. 94/2371, art. 20.

1724. Social Fund Cold Weather Payments (General) Regulations 1988.
reg. 3, amended: regs. 94/2593, reg. 2.
sch. 1, amended: *ibid.*, reg. 3.
sch. 2, amended: *ibid.*, reg. 4.

1739. Insolvency (Amendment) Regulations 1988.
revoked: regs. 94/2507, reg. 2.

1790. Control of Pollution (Special Waste) (Amendment) Regulations 1988.
revoked: regs. 94/1137, reg. 21.

1813. Town and Country Planning General Development Order 1988.
applied: ord. 94/238, art. 4; ord. 94/239, art. 4.
referred to: regs. 94/1291, sch. 2, regs. 94/1292, sch.
art. 12, amended: ord. 94/678, art. 2.
art. 13, amended: ord. 94/2595, art. 2.
art. 14, amended: ord. 94/678, art. 3.
art. 18, amended: ord. 94/2595, art. 3.

NO.

1988—cont.

1813. Town and Country Planning General Development Order 1988—*cont.*
art. 25, amended: ord. 94/678.
sch. 2, see *Wycombe District Council* v. *Secretary of State for the Environment and Trevor* [1994] NPC 45.
sch. 2, para. 19, amended: ord. 94/2595, art. 4.
sch. 2, pt. 20, substituted: *ibid.*, art. 5.
sch. 2, pt. 21, amended: *ibid.*, art. 6.
sch. 2, pt. 24, amended: ord. 94/678, art. 4.

1847. Criminal Justice (Evidence etc.) (Northern Ireland) Order 1988.
pt. II, applied: 1994, c. 9, s. 22, sch. 7, para. 1; 1994, c. 23, sch. 11, para. 6.
art. 15, amended: 1994, c. 33, ss. 84, 86.

1891. Civil Legal Aid (Scotland) Amendment (No. 3) Regulations 1988.
reg. 3, revoked: regs. 94/1049, reg. 9.

1987. Criminal Evidence (Northern Ireland) Order 1988.
art. 3, amended: 1994, c. 33, sch. 10, para. 61.
art. 4, amended: *ibid.*, sch. 11.
art. 5, amended: *ibid.*
art. 6, amended: *ibid.*

2059. Act of Sederunt (Form of charge for payment) 1988.
revoked in pt.: Act 94/1443, para. 3.

2060. Act of Sederunt (Rules of the Court of Session Amendment No. 5) (Time to pay directions) 1988.
revoked: Act 94/1443, para. 3.

2161. Lotteries (Amendment) Regulations 1988.
revoked: regs. 93/3223, reg. 1.

2193. Lotteries (Scotland) Amendment Regulations 1988.
revoked: regs. 93/3223, reg. 1.

2238. Personal Pension Schemes (Compensation) Regulations 1988.
reg. 1, amended: regs. 94/1062, reg. 2.
reg. 3, amended: *ibid.*

2290. Advice and Assistance (Assistance by Way of Representation) (Scotland) Regulations 1988.
reg. 3, amended: regs. 94/1000, reg. 3.
reg. 5, amended: *ibid.*, reg. 4.
reg. 5A, inserted: *ibid.*, reg. 5.

2292. Merchant Shipping (Prevention of Pollution by Garbage) Regulations 1988.
applied: regs. 94/1056, reg. 3.

1989

28. Financial Services Act 1986 (Single Property Schemes) (Exemption) Regulations 1989.
reg. 2, applied: 1994, c. 23, sch. 9, group 5.

NO.

1989—cont.

115. Transfrontier Shipment of Hazardous Waste Regulations (Northern Ireland) 1989.
revoked: regs. 94/1137, reg. 21.

128. Farm and Conservation Grant Scheme 1989.
para. 3, amended: scheme 94/1302, para. 3.
para. 5, amended: *ibid.*, para. 4.
sch. 1, para. 9A, inserted: *ibid.*, para. 5.
sch. 1, para. 9B, inserted: *ibid.*

206. Access to Personal Files (Social Services) Regulations 1989.
sch., amended: 1994, c. 17, s. 38.

251. Access to Personal Files (Social Work) (Scotland) Regulations 1989.
sch., amended: 1994, c. 17, s. 38.

265. Adoption Rules 1989.
see *X. (A Minor) (Adoption Order), Re, The Times,* April 11, 1994, C.A.

267. Value Added Tax (Education) Order 1989.
revoked: 1994, c. 23, sch. 15.

298. Teachers (Compensation for Redundancy and Premature Retirement) Regulations 1989.
reg. 2, amended: regs. 94/1059, reg. 3.
reg. 3, amended: *ibid.*, reg. 4.
reg. 4, amended: *ibid.*, reg. 5.
reg. 9, amended: *ibid.*, reg. 6.
reg. 10, amended: *ibid.*, reg. 7.
reg. 11, amended: *ibid.*, reg. 8.
reg. 17, amended: *ibid.*, reg. 9.
sch., amended: *ibid.*, reg. 10.

306. National Health Service (Charges to Overseas Visitors) Regulations 1989.
reg. 1, amended: regs. 94/1535, reg. 2.
reg. 3, amended: *ibid.*, reg. 3.
reg. 4, amended: *ibid.*, reg. 4.
sch. 1, Pt. I, amended: *ibid.*, reg. 5.
sch. 1, Pt. II, amended: *ibid.*
sch. 2, amended: *ibid.*

326. National Health Service (Charges for Drugs and Appliances) (Scotland) Regulations 1989.
reg. 3, amended: regs. 94/697, reg. 2.
reg. 8, amended: *ibid.*
sch. 1, substituted: *ibid.*
sch. 2, substituted: *ibid.*
sch. 3, substituted: *ibid.*

327. Registered Housing Associations (Accounting Requirements) (Amendment) Order 1989.
revoked in pt.: ord. 94/668, art. 1.

338. Civil Legal Aid (Assessment of Resources) Regulations 1989.
reg. 4, amended: regs. 94/806, reg. 4.

339. Civil Legal Aid (General) Regulations 1989.
reg. 2, substituted: regs. 94/1822, reg. 5.

1989—cont.

339. Civil Legal Aid (General) Regulations 1989—cont.

reg. 3, amended: regs. 94/229, reg. 4; regs. 94/1822, reg. 6.

reg. 3(1), see *Jones* v. *Zahedi* [1993] 1 W.L.R. 1445, C.A.

reg. 4, amended: regs. 94/1822, reg. 7.

reg. 7(2), see *Middleton* v. *Middleton* [1994] 3 All E.R. 236, C.A.

reg. 21, see *R.* v. *Legal Aid Board*, ex p. *Higgins, The Times*, November 19, 1993, D.C.

reg. 35, amended: regs. 94/1822, reg. 8.

reg. 41, amended: *ibid.*, reg. 9.

reg. 50, amended: *ibid.*, reg. 10.

reg. 51(a)(f), see *R.* v. *Legal Aid Board*, ex p. *Nicolson, The Times*, June 24, 1994.

reg. 54, amended: regs. 94/1822, reg. 11.

reg. 61, amended: *ibid.*, reg. 12.

reg. 82, amended: *ibid.*, reg. 13.

reg. 90, amended: regs. 94/229, reg. 5; regs. 94/1822, reg. 14.

reg. 91, amended: regs. 94/229, reg. 6; regs. 94/1822, reg. 15.

reg. 92, substituted: *ibid.*, reg. 7.

reg. 92A, inserted: regs. 94/1822, reg. 16.

reg. 95, amended: *ibid.*, reg. 17.

reg. 96, amended: regs. 94/229, reg. 8; regs. 94/1822, reg. 18.

reg. 97, amended: regs. 94/1822, reg. 19.

reg. 98, amended: *ibid.*, reg. 20.

reg. 99, amended: *ibid.*, reg. 21.

reg. 100, amended: reg. 9; regs. 94/1822, reg. 22.

reg. 103, amended: regs. 94/229, reg. 14.

reg. 104, amended: *ibid.*, reg. 10.

reg. 105, amended: *ibid.*, reg. 11.

reg. 106, revoked: *ibid.*, reg. 12.

reg. 106A, inserted: *ibid.*, reg. 13.

reg. 107, amended: *ibid.*, reg. 14.

reg. 107A, inserted: *ibid.*, reg. 15.

reg. 107B, inserted: *ibid.*

reg. 111, amended: *ibid.*, reg. 14.

reg. 113, amended: *ibid.*, reg. 16.

reg. 115, amended: regs. 94/1822, reg. 23.

reg. 121, amended: *ibid.*

regs. 124, 130, see *National Westminster Bank* v. *Daniel* [1993] 1 W.L.R. 1453, C.A.

reg. 142(a), see *Middleton* v. *Middleton* [1994] 3 All E.R. 236, C.A.

reg. 152, substituted: regs. 94/1822, reg. 24.

340. Legal Advice and Assistance Regulations 1989.

reg. 3, amended: regs. 94/1823, reg. 4.

reg. 3A, inserted: *ibid.*, reg. 5.

reg. 5A, inserted: regs. 94/805, reg. 5.

reg. 9, amended: regs. 94/1823, reg. 6.

reg. 11, amended: regs. 94/805, reg. 6.

reg. 12, amended: *ibid.*, reg. 7.

1989—cont.

340. Legal Advice and Assistance Regulations 1989—cont.

reg. 30, amended: regs. 94/1823, reg. 7.

reg. 30A, amended: *ibid.*, reg. 8.

342. Legal Advice and Assistance at Police Stations (Remuneration) Regulations 1989.

reg. 2, amended: regs. 94/1824, reg. 3.

reg. 5, amended: *ibid.*, reg. 4.

sch., para. 2, amended: *ibid.*, para. 5.

343. Legal Aid in Criminal and Care Proceedings (Costs) Regulations 1989.

reg. 2, amended: regs. 94/1825, reg. 4.

reg. 4E, inserted: *ibid.*, reg. 5.

reg. 5, amended: regs. 94/2218, reg. 3.

reg. 6, amended: regs. 94/1477, reg. 2.

reg. 7A, amended: regs. 94/2218, reg. 4.

reg. 9, amended: regs. 94/1477, reg. 2.

sch. 1, Pt. I, amended: regs. 94/2218, reg. 7.

sch. 1, pt. 1, para. 3(b), see *R.* v. *Legal Aid Board*, ex p. *R.M. Broudie & Co (A Firm), The Times*, April 11, 1994, D.C.

sch. 1, Pt. III, amended: *ibid.*, regs. 5, 6.

344. Legal Aid in Criminal and Care Proceedings (General) Regulations 1989.

reg. 10, see *R.* v. *Liverpool City Magistrates' Court, ex p. Pender (No. 2)* [1994] 2 All E.R. 897, D.C.

reg. 23, amended: regs. 94/807, reg. 4.

reg. 24, amended: *ibid.*, reg. 5.

sch. 4, amended: *ibid.*, reg. 6.

363. National Health Service (Dental Charges) (Scotland) Regulations 1989.

reg. 4, amended: regs. 94/636, reg. 2.

364. National Health Service (Charges to Overseas Visitors) (Scotland) Regulations 1989.

reg. 1, amended: regs. 94/1770, reg. 2.

reg. 3, amended: *ibid.*, reg. 3.

reg. 4, amended: *ibid.*, reg. 4.

sch. 1, amended: *ibid.*, reg. 5.

sch. 2, amended: *ibid.*, reg. 6.

392. National Health Service (Optical Charges and Payments) (Scotland) Regulations 1989.

reg. 1, amended: regs. 94/145, reg. 2; regs. 94/2587, reg. 2.

reg. 20, amended: regs. 94/635, reg. 2.

sch. 1, amended: *ibid.*, reg. 3.

sch. 2, substituted: *ibid.*

sch. 3, amended: *ibid.*

394. National Health Service (Dental Charges) Regulations 1989.

reg. 4, amended: regs. 94/530, reg. 2.

396. National Health Service (Optical Charges and Payments) Regulations 1989.

reg. 1, amended: regs. 94/131, reg. 2; regs. 94/2619, reg. 2.

reg. 20, amended: regs. 94/495, reg. 2.

NO.

1989—cont.

396. National Health Service (Optical Charges and Payments) Regulations 1989—*cont.*
sch. 1, amended: *ibid.*, reg. 3.
sch. 2, para. 1, amended: *ibid.*
sch. 2, para. 2, amended: *ibid.*
sch. 3, substituted: *ibid.*

398. Education (School Hours and Policies) (Information) Regulations 1989.
applied: regs. 94/653, reg. 42; applied with modifications: 94/1084, reg. 9.
reg. 2, modified: *ibid.*

419. National Health Service (Charges for Drugs and Appliances) Regulations 1989.
reg. 2, amended: regs. 94/2402, reg. 3.
reg. 3, amended: regs. 94/690, reg. 2.
reg. 4, amended: *ibid.*
reg. 5, amended: *ibid.*
reg. 8, amended: *ibid.*
sch. 1, amended: *ibid.*

421. Lloyd's Underwriters (Tax) Regulations 1989.
reg. 9, amended: regs. 94/1813, reg. 2.

434. Act of Sederunt (Fees of Solicitors in the Sheriff Court) 1989.
regs. 6, 8, 11, see *Clydesdale Bank* v. *Andrew* (Sh.Ct.), 1993 S.C.L.R. 754.

435. Act of Sederunt (Rules of the Court of Session Amendment No. 1) (Written Statements) 1989.
revoked: Act 94/1443, para. 3.

438. Community Charge (Administration and Enforcement) Regulations 1989.
reg. 41, amended: regs. 94/504, reg. 3.
regs. 41, 42(7), see *R.* v. *Newcastle Justices*, ex p. *Ashley* [1993] R.A. 264.
regs. 43, 61, see *Wood*, Re, August 24, 1993; Tamworth County Court.
sch. 6, inserted: *ibid.*, reg. 4.

441. Valuation for Rating (Plant and Machinery) Regulations 1989.
revoked: regs. 94/2680, reg. 4.

445. Act of Sederunt (Rules of the Court of Session Amendment No. 2) (Solicitors' Fees) 1989.
revoked: Act 94/1443, para. 3.

470. Value Added Tax (Fund Raising Events and Charity) Order 1989.
C.: 1994, c. 23, sch. 8, sch. 9.
revoked: 1994, c. 23, sch. 15.

486. European Parliamentary Constituencies (England) (Miscellaneous Changes) Order 1989.
constituencies substituted: ord. 94/427, art. 2.

487. European Parliamentary Constituencies (Wales) (Miscellaneous Changes) Order 1989.
constituencies substituted: ord. 94/428, art. 2.

NO.

1989—cont.

502. European Parliamentary Elections (Northern Ireland) (Amendment) Regulations 1989.
reg. 2, amended: regs. 94/782, reg. 3.

503. Access to Personal Files (Housing) Regulations 1989.
sch., amended: 1994, c. 17, s. 38.

547. Motor Fuel (Lead Content of Petrol) (Amendment) Regulations 1989.
revoked: regs. 94/2295, reg. 12.

550. Legal Advice and Assistance (Scope) Regulations 1989.
reg. 2, amended: regs. 94/2768, reg. 3.

615. Road Traffic (Carriage of Explosives) Regulations 1989.
reg. 7, amended: regs. 94/669, reg. 15.

633. European Paliamentary Elections (Amendment) Regulations 1989.
reg. 2, amended: regs. 94/748, reg. 4.

644. Pig Carcase (Grading) (Amendment) Regulations 1989.
revoked: regs. 94/2155, reg. 13.

778. Act of Sederunt (Rules of the Court of Session Amendment No. 3) (Shorthand Writers' Fees) 1989.
revoked: Act 94/1443, para. 3.

869. Consumer Credit (Exempt Agreements) Order 1989.
sch. 1, pt. I, amended: ord. 94/2420, art. 2.
sch. 1, pt. III, substituted: ord. 94/2420, art. 2.

950. European Economic Interest Grouping Regulations 1989.
reg. 2, applied: regs. 94/2327, reg. 3.
sch., amended: *ibid.*, reg. 2.

954. Education (School Curriculum and Related Information) Regulations 1989.
applied: regs. 94/653, reg. 42; applied with modifications: regs. 94/1084, reg. 9.
reg. 4, modified: *ibid.*

985. Summer Timer Order 1988.
revoked: 94/2798, art. 5.

992. Transfer of Functions (Economic Statistics), Order 1989.
C.: 1994, c. 23, s. 90.

1058. Non-Domestic Rating (Collection and Enforcement) (Local Lists) Regulations 1989.
see *ELS (formerly English Lifestyle), Re* [1994] 2 All E.R. 833.
reg. 15, see *R.* v. *Basildon Justices*, ex p. *Holding & Barnes, The Times*, April 26, 1994.
reg. 16, see *R.* v. *Highbury Corner Justices*, ex p. *Uchendu, The Times*, January 28, 1994.

1117. Trade Marks and Service Marks (Amendment) Rules 1989.
revoked: rules 94/2583, rule 69.

1118. Building (Amendment of Prescribed Fees) Regulations 1989.
revoked: regs. 94/2020, reg. 16.

NO.

1989—cont.

1125. Consumer Credit (Advertisements) Regulations 1989.
reg. 8(1)(b)(i), see Clydesdale Group v. Normand, 1993 S.C.C.R. 958.

1133. Education (Assisted Places) (Scotland) Regulations 1989.
reg. 13, amended: regs. 94/1827, reg. 2.
reg. 15, amended: ibid., reg. 3.
reg. 16, amended: ibid., reg. 4.
reg. 17, amended: ibid., reg. 5.
sch. 2, substituted: ibid., reg. 6.

1134. St Mary's Music School (Aided Places) Regulations 1989.
sch. 1, para. 13, amended: regs. 94/1826, reg. 2.
sch. 1, para. 14, amended: ibid., reg. 3.
sch. 1, para. 18, amended: ibid., reg. 4.
sch. 1, para. 24, amended: ibid., reg. 5.

1172. Merchant Shipping (Accident Investigation) Regulations 1989.
revoked: regs. 94/2013, reg. 1.

1181. Education (National Curriculum) (Temporary Exceptions for Individual Pupils) Regulations 1989.
applied: regs. 94/653, reg. 42; regs. 94/1084, reg. 9.

1235. Education (Assisted Places) Regulations 1989.
reg. 11, amended: regs. 94/2034, reg. 2.
sch. 2, para. 1, amended: ibid., reg. 3.
sch. 2, para. 2, amended: ibid.

1236. Education (Grants) (Music and Ballet Schools) Regulations 1989.
reg. 8D, substituted: regs. 94/2036, reg. 2.
reg. 8F, amended: ibid.
reg. 8G, amended: ibid.

1237. Education (Assisted Places) (Incidental Expenses) Regulations 1989.
reg. 3, amended: regs. 94/2035, reg. 2.
reg. 4, amended: ibid., reg. 3.
reg. 7, amended: ibid., reg. 7.

1261. Education (School Records) Regulations 1989.
reg. 9, applied: regs. 94/653, reg. 42; regs. 94/1084, reg. 9.

1263. Sludge (Use in Agriculture) Regulations 1989.
applied: regs. 94/1056, sch. 3, para. 8.

1297. Taxes (Interest Rate) Regulations 1989.
reg. 5, substituted: regs. 94/1307, reg. 2; amended: regs. 94/1567, reg. 2; regs. 94/2657, reg. 2.

1321. Community Charge Benefits (General) Regulations 1989.
referred to: ord. 94/523, art. 14.

1341. Police and Criminal Evidence (Northern Ireland) Order 1989.
art. 6, amended: 1994, c. 22, sch. 3.
art. 12, applied: regs. 94/674, reg. 8; 1994, c. 33, s. 139.

NO.

1989—cont.

1341. Police and Criminal Evidence (Northern Ireland) Order 1989—cont.
art. 13, applied: regs. 94/674, reg. 8.
art. 16, applied: ibid.
art. 26, amended: 1994, c. 33, s. 85; applied: 1994, c. 33, s. 140.
art. 27, applied: 1994, c. 33, s. 140.
art. 63, amended: ibid., sch. 9, para. 39.
art. 68, applied: 1994, c. 9, s. 22, sch. 7, para. 1; 1994, c. 23, sch. 11, para. 6.
sch. 5, pt. II, amended: 1994, c. 33, s. 85.

1352. Education (Financial Delegation to Schools) (Mandatory Exceptions) Regulations 1989.
revoked: regs. 94/277, reg. 2.

1401. Fire Precautions (Sub-surface Railway Stations) Regulations 1989.
reg. 12, amended: regs. 94/2184, reg. 2.

1451. Education (Bursaries for Teacher Training) (Amendment) Regulations 1989.
revoked: regs. 94/2016, reg. 2.

1490. Civil Legal Aid (Scotland) (Fees) Regulations 1989.
reg. 2, amended: regs. 94/1015, reg. 3.
reg. 5, amended: ibid., reg. 4.
reg. 10, amended: ibid., reg. 5.
reg. 11, amended: regs. 94/1233, reg. 3.
sch. 2, amended: regs. 94/1015, reg. 6.
sch. 4, para. 1, substituted: ibid., reg. 7.

1491. Criminal Legal Aid (Scotland) (Fees) Regulations 1989.
reg. 2, amended: regs. 94/1019, reg. 4.
reg. 10, sch. 2, see Advocate H.M. v. Birrell, 1994 S.L.T. 480.

1507. European Convention on Extradition Order 1990.
see Bartley, Re, The Times, July 22, 1994, D.C.

1588. Local Government (Direct Labour Organisations) (Competition) Regulations 1989.
revoked in pt.: regs. 94/338, reg. 10.
reg. 2, amended: regs. 94/1439, reg. 5.
reg. 6, amended: ibid., reg. 3.
reg. 7, amended: ibid., reg. 4.
reg. 9, amended: ibid.

1796. Road Vehicles Lighting Regulations 1989.
reg. 3, amended: regs. 94/2280, reg. 3; ord. 94/2567, art. 2.
reg. 3A, inserted: ibid., reg. 4.
reg. 11, amended: ibid., reg. 5.
reg. 14, amended: ibid., reg. 8.
reg. 17A, inserted: ibid., reg. 6.
reg. 21, amended: ibid., reg. 17.
reg. 23, amended: ibid., reg. 17.
reg. 27, amended: ibid., reg. 9.
sch. 1, amended: ibid., reg. 10.
sch. 2, Pt. I, amended: ibid., regs. 11, 17.
sch. 3, Pt. I, amended: ibid., reg. 12.
sch. 7, Pt. I, amended: ibid., regs. 13, 16, 17.
sch. 10, Pt. I, amended: ibid., reg. 14.
sch. 19, substituted: ibid., reg. 15.

NO.

1989—cont.

1806. Scottish Milk Marketing Scheme 1989.
revoked: ord. 94/2900, art. 2.
1882. Merchant Shipping (Sterling Equivalents) (Merchant Shipping Act 1974) Order 1989.
revoked: ord. 94/2788, art. 2.
1903. Health and Safety (Enforcing Authority) Regulations 1989.
applied: regs. 94/2479, reg. 3.
reg. 2, amended: regs. 94/669, reg. 15.
sch. 1, para. 1, amended: *ibid.*
2004. Air Navigation Order 1989.
art. 69, applied: regs. 94/1444.
2057. Motor Cars (Driving Instruction) Regulations 1989.
reg. 4, amended: regs. 94/554, reg. 2.
reg. 13, amended: *ibid.*
2061. Bovine Offal (Prohibition) Regulations 1989.
reg. 2, amended: regs. 94/2628, reg. 3.
reg. 3, amended: *ibid.*, reg. 4.
reg. 7, amended: *ibid.*, reg. 5.
2139. Traffic Signs (Amendment) Regulations and General Directions 1989.
revoked: regs. 94/1519, reg. 2.
2203. Town and Country Planning (Central Manchester Urban Development Area) Special Development Order 1987.
referred to: ord. 94/2567, art. 3.
sch., amended: *ibid.*, art. 2.
2204. Town and Country Planning (Sheffield Urban Development Area) Special Development Order 1989.
referred to: ord. 94/2567, art. 3.
sch., amended: ord. 94/2567, art. 2.
2205. Town and Country Planning (Bristol Urban Development Area) Special Development Order 1989.
referred to: ord. 94/2567, art. 3.
sch., amended: *ibid.*, art. 2.
2206. Town and Country Planning (Leeds Urban Development Area) Special Development Order 1989.
referred to: ord. 94/2567, art. 3.
sch., amended: *ibid.*, art. 2.
2220. Civil Aviation (Canadian Navigation Services) (Second Amendment) Regulations 1989.
revoked: regs. 94/2325, reg. 3.
2233. Cosmetic Products (Safety) Regulations 1989.
reg. 2, amended: regs. 94/1529, reg. 2.
sch. 1, amended: *ibid.*
sch. 2, Pt. II, amended: *ibid.*
sch. 4, Pt. II, amended: *ibid.*
sch. 5, Pt. I, amended: *ibid.*
sch. 5, Pt. II, amended: *ibid.*
sch. 6, para. 1, amended: *ibid.*
sch. 6, para. 6, amended: *ibid.*
2248. Value Added Tax (Accounting and Records) Regulations 1989.
reg. 5, amended: regs. 94/803, reg. 2.

NO.

1989—cont.

2252. Customs Duty (Personal Reliefs) (Amendment) Order 1989.
revoked: ord. 94/955, art. 5.
2263. Central Rating Lists Regulations 1989.
sch., pt. 4, amended: regs. 94/834, reg. 3.
2271. Finance Act 1989 (Recovery of Overpaid Tax and Administration (Appointed Days) Order 1989.
C.: 1994, c. 23, s. 80.
2272. Value Added Tax (Finance, Health and Welfare) Order 1989.
C.: 1994, c. 23, sch. 9.
revoked: 1994, c. 23, sch. 15.
2307. Inshore Fishing (Prohibition of Fishing and Fishing Methods) (Scotland) Order 1989.
art. 8, amended: ord. 94/326, art. 2.
art. 8A, inserted: *ibid.*, art. 3.
sch. 1, amended: *ibid.*, art. 4.
sch. 3, amended: *ibid.*, art. 5.
2364. Commonwealth Development Corporation (Additional Enterprise) (Variation) Order 1989.
revoked: ord. 94/2880, art. 3.
2372. Dartford–Thurrock Crossing Regulations 1989.
revoked: regs. 94/2031, reg. 12.
2376. Export of Goods (Control) Order 1989.
see *R.* v. *Daghir; R.* v. *Speckman, The Times*, May 27, 1994, C.A.
2387. Private Medical Insurance (Tax Relief) Regulations 1989.
reg. 2, amended: regs. 94/1527, reg. 3.
reg. 3, amended: *ibid.*, reg. 4.
reg. 4, amended: *ibid.*, reg. 5.
reg. 7, amended: *ibid.*, reg. 6.
reg. 8, amended: *ibid.*, reg. 7.
reg. 9, amended: *ibid.*, reg. 8.
reg. 9A, inserted: *ibid.*, reg. 9.
reg. 10, amended: *ibid.*, reg. 10.
reg. 12, amended: *ibid.*, reg. 11.
regs. 15–17, revoked: *ibid.*, reg. 12.
reg. 18, inserted: *ibid.*, reg. 13.
2389. Private Medical Insurance (Disentitlement to Tax Relief and Approved Benefits) Regulations 1989.
revoked: regs. 94/1518, reg. 9.
2405. Insolvency (Northern Ireland) Order 1989.
applied: 1994, c. 9, s. 144.
pt. VIII, applied: 1994, c. 23, s. 81.
art. 31, amended: 1994, c. 7, schs. 1, 2.
art. 54, amended: *ibid.*, sch. 1.
art. 205, amended: 1994, c. 12, s. 3.
art. 315, amended: *ibid.*, s. 4.
art. 346, amended: 1994, c. 7, sch. 7, para. 7.
art. 378, applied: 1994, c. 12, s. 5.
2406. Education Reform (Northern Ireland) Order 1989.
applied: 1994, c. 23, sch. 9, group 6.

1989—cont.

2471. British Gas plc (Rateable Values) Order 1989.
art. 9, amended: 1994, c. 3, s. 1.

2475. Electricity Supply Industry (Rateable Values) Order 1989.
art. 9, amended: 1994, c. 3, s. 1.

2477. Railways (Rateable Values) Order 1989.
art. 12, amended: 1994, c. 3, s. 1.
art. 17, revoked: ord. 94/999, art. 2.
art. 19, inserted: *ibid.*

2478. Telecommunications Industry (Rateable Values) Order 1989.
art. 5, amended: ord. 94/903, art. 2.

2479. Water Undertakers (Rateable Values) Order 1989.
art. 9, amended: 1994, c. 3, s. 1.

1990

112. Bovine Offal (Prohibition) (Scotland) Regulations 1990.
reg. 2, amended: reg. 94/2544, reg. 2.
reg. 3, amended: *ibid.*

124. Education (Inner London Education Authority) (Property Transfer) Order 1990.
art. 4, amended: ord. 94/1255, art. 3.
sch. 9, *ibid.*

161. Household Appliances (Noise Emission) Regulations 1990.
reg. 1, amended: regs. 94/1386, reg. 2.
reg. 2, amended: *ibid.*, reg. 3.
reg. 3, amended: *ibid.*
reg. 4, amended: *ibid.*
reg. 6, inserted: *ibid.*
reg. 8, inserted: *ibid.*
reg. 6, amended and renumbered as reg. 7: *ibid.*

193. Electricity (Class Exemptions from the Requirement for a Licence) Order 1990.
art. 2, amended: ord. 94/1683, art. 3.
art. 4, amended: ord. 94/1070, art. 2.
art. 5, amended: *ibid.*, art. 3.
sch. 2, class A save for para. A.1, substituted: *ibid.*, art. 4.
sch. 3, class B, substituted: *ibid.*, art. 5.
sch. 3, para. B.1, substituted: *ibid.*
sch. 3, class C, amended: *ibid.*, art. 6.
sch. 3, para. C.2, revoked: *ibid.*
sch. 3, para. C.3, amended: *ibid.*

200. Official Secrets Act 1989 (Prescription) Order 1990.
sch. 3, amended: 1994, c. 13, sch. 4.

222. Bovine Spongiform Encephalopathy Compensation Order 1990.
revoked: ord. 94/673, art. 4.

266. Fossil Fuel Levy Regulations 1990.
sch. 1, applied: regs. 94/947, reg. 13.

1990—cont.

290. Firearms (Variation of Fees) Order 1990.
revoked: ord. 94/2615, art. 3.

295. Schools (Safety and Supervision of Pupils) (Scotland) Regulations 1990.
reg. 5, inserted: regs. 94/351, reg. 5.

304. Dangerous Substances (Notification and Marking of Sites) Regulations 1990.
reg. 2, amended: regs. 94/669, reg. 15.
sch. 1, para. 1, amended: *ibid.*

322. Social Security (Recoupment) Regulations 1990.
reg. 2, amended: regs. 94/730, reg. 3.

325. Firearms (Variation of Fees) (Scotland) Order 1990.
revoked: ord. 94/2652, art. 9.

327. Land Charges Fees Rules 1990.
rule 1, amended: rules 94/286, rule 3.
rule 4, amended: *ibid.*, rule 4.
sch. 1, para. 5, amended: *ibid.*, rule 5.
sch. 1, para. 6, amended: *ibid.*, rule 6.

355. Companies Act 1989 (Commencement No. 4 and Transitional and Saving Provisions) Order 1990.
sch. 2, pt. I, amended: ord. 93/3246, art. 5.

379. Act of Sederunt (Fees of Messengers-at-Arms) 1990.
revoked: Act 94/391, para. 3.

381. Act of Sederunt (Fees of Sheriff Officers) 1990.
revoked: Act 94/392, para. 3.

390. Electricity Supply (Amendment) Regulations 1990.
sch., para. 11, revoked: regs. 94/533, reg. 5.

396. Rent Officers (Additional Functions) (Scotland) Order 1990.
referred to: ord. 94/523, art. 2.
art. 5, amended: ord. 94/582, art. 2.
sch. 1, para. 2A, inserted: *ibid.*
sch. 2, para. 1, amended: *ibid.*

424. Education (National Curriculum) (Attainment Targets and Programmes of Study in Technology) Order 1990.
art. 5, amended: ord. 94/1815, art. 3.

426. Local Authorities (Capital Finance) (Approved Investments) Regulations 1990.
sch., pt. II, amended: ord. 94/2567, art. 2.

428. Rent Officers (Additional Functions) Order 1990.
referred to: ord. 94/523, art. 2.
art. 5, amended: ord. 94/568, art. 2.
sch. 1, para. 2A, inserted: *ibid.*
sch. 1, para. 3, amended: *ibid.*
sch. 1, para. 5, amended: *ibid.*
sch. 2, para. 1, amended: *ibid.*

NO.

1990—cont.

432. Local Authorities (Capital Finance) Regulations 1990.
reg. 26, amended: regs. 94/553, reg. 2.

534. Housing Benefit (Permitted Totals) Order 1990.
revoked: ord. 94/579, art. 4.

549. Education (Grant-maintained Schools) (Finance) Regulations 1990.
revoked: regs. 94/610, reg. 3.

593. Companies (Northern Ireland) Order 1990.
art. 28, applied: 1994, c. 17, s. 41.

613. Compulsory Purchase of Land Regulations 1990.
revoked: regs. 94/2145, reg. 5.

617. Seeds (National Lists of Varieties) (Fees) Regulations 1990.
revoked: regs. 94/676, reg. 5.

618. Plant Breeders' Rights (Fees) Regulations 1990.
sch., substituted: regs. 94/675, reg. 2.

627. Lloyd's Underwriters (Tax) (1987-88) Regulations 1990.
reg. 9, amended: regs. 94/1813, reg. 2.

631. Civil Legal Aid (Scotland) Amendment Regulations 1990.
reg. 5, revoked: regs. 94/1049, reg. 9.

682. Value Added Tax (Increase of Registration Limits) Order 1990.
revoked: 1994, c. 23, sch. 15.

704. Traffic Signs (Amendment) Regulations and General Directions 1990.
revoked: regs. 94/1519, reg. 2.

705. Act of Sederunt (Roles of the Court of Session Amendment No. 1) (Miscellaneous) 1990.
revoked: Act 94/1443, para. 3.

717. Act of Sederunt (Rules of the Court of Session Amendment No. 2) (Solicitors' Fees) 1990.
revoked: Act 94/1443, para. 3.

750. Value Added Tax (Charities) Order 1990.
C.: 1994, c. 23, sch. 8.
revoked: 1994, c. 23, sch. 15.

752. Value Added Tax (Transport) Order 1990.
C.: 1994, c. 23, sch. 8.
revoked: 1994, c. 23, sch. 15.

766. Juvenile Courts (London) (Amendment) Order 1990.
revoked: ord. 94/1695, art. 2.

798. Act of Sederunt (Rules of the Court of Session Amendment No. 3) (Shorthand Writers' Fees) 1990.
revoked: Act 94/1443, para. 3.

879. Copyright (Certification of Licensing Scheme for Educational Recording of Broadcasts and Cable Programmes) (Educational Recording Agency Limited) Order 1990.
sch., amended: ord. 94/247, art. 2.

NO.

1990—cont.

1019. Housing (Change of Landlord) (Payment of Disposal Cost by Instalments) Regulations 1990.
reg. 3, amended: ord. 94/266, art. 2; regs. 94/2916, reg. 2.

1036. Civil Legal Aid (Scotland) (Fees) Amendment (No. 2) Regulations 1990.
revoked: regs. 94/1015, reg. 8.

1096. Oil Fuel (Sulphur Content of Gas Oil) Regulations 1990.
revoked: regs. 94/2249, reg. 4.

1097. Motor Fuel (Sulphur Content of Gas Oil) (Amendment) Regulations 1990.
revoked: regs. 94/2295, reg. 12.

1140. Personal Pension Schemes (Advertisements) Regulations 1990.
reg. 1, amended: regs. 94/1062, reg. 2.
reg. 3, amended: *ibid.*

1143. Personal and Occupational Pension Schemes (Perpetuities) Regulations 1990.
reg. 2, amended: regs. 94/1062, reg. 2.
reg. 3, amended: *ibid.*
reg. 4, amended: *ibid.*
reg. 5, amended: *ibid.*

1160. Insurance Companies (Legal Expenses Insurance) (Application for Authorisation) Regulations 1990.
revoked: regs. 94/1516, reg. 86.

1181. Insurance Companies (Credit Insurance) Regulations 1990.
revoked: regs. 94/1516, reg. 86.

1189. Housing Renovation etc. Grants (Reduction of Grant) Regulations 1990.
revoked: regs. 94/648, reg. 45.

1199. Drug Trafficking Offences Act 1986 (Designated Countries and Territories) Order 1990.
sch. 1, amended: ord. 94/1641, art. 2.
sch. 3, amended: *ibid.*, art. 3.

1236. Housing Renovation etc. Grants (Prescribed Forms and Particulars) Regulations 1990.
revoked: regs. 94/565, reg. 5.

1262. Act of Sederunt (Rules of the Court of Session Amendment No. 4) (Solicitors' Fees) 1990.
revoked: Act 94/1443, para. 3.

1331. Regional and District Health Authorities (Membership and Procedure) Regulations 1990.
applied: regs. 94/602, regs. 3, 5, 6.
sch. 1, pt. I, substituted: regs. 94/682, reg. 3; amended: regs. 94/1262, reg. 2.

1459. Trade Marks and Service Marks (Amendment) Rules 1990.
revoked: rules 94/2583, rule 69.

NO.

1990—cont.

1496. Patents County Court (Designation and Jurisdiction) Order 1990.
see *McDonald* v. *Graham, The Times,* January 12, 1994, C.A.
revoked: ord. 94/1609, art. 5.

1507. European Convention on Extradition Order 1990.
sch. 2, pt. I, amended: ord. 94/2796, art. 2.
sch. 3, pt. 1A, inserted: *ibid.*

1524. Education (Special Educational Needs) (Amendment) Regulations 1990.
revoked: regs. 94/1047, reg. 20.

1551. School Pupil Records (Scotland) Regulations 1990.
reg. 11A, inserted: regs. 94/351, reg. 6.

1584. Milk and Dairies and Milk (Special Designation) (Charges) Regulations 1990.
reg. 2, amended: regs. 94/1446, reg. 3.
reg. 3, amended: *ibid.,* reg. 4.
reg. 4, substituted: *ibid.,* reg. 5.
sch., substituted: *ibid.,* reg. 6.

1598. Dartford–Thurrock Crossing (Amendment) Regulations 1990.
revoked: regs. 94/2031, reg. 12.

1599. Education (Bursaries for Teacher Training) (Amendment) Regulations 1990.
revoked: regs. 94/2016, reg. 2.

1755. National Health Service (Determination of Regions and Districts) Amendment Order 1990.
art. 3, amended: ord. 94/683, art. 14.

1756. National Health Service (District Health Authorities) Order 1990.
art. 3, amended: ord. 94/680, art. 4.
sch. 1, substituted: *ibid.*
sch. 1, pt. I, amended: ord. 94/1260, art. 4.
sch. 1, pt. 8, amended: ord. 94/2288, art. 4.

1764. County Court (Amendment No. 3) Rules 1990.
rule 14, see *Rastin* v. *British Steel; Todd* v. *Evans; Adams* v. *Geest; Byrne* v. *Webber; Donaldson* v. *Canavan; Ayres* v. *British Steel* [1994] 1 W.L.R. 732, C.A.

1799. Trade Marks and Service Marks (Amendment) (No. 2) Rules 1990.
revoked: rules 94/2583, rule 69.

1811. Trade Marks and Service Marks (Forms) (Amendment) Rules 1990.
revoked: rules 94/2582, rule 2.

1972. Act of Sederunt (Registration Appeal Court) 1990.
revoked: Act 94/2483, rule 2.

1989. Education (Grant) Regulations 1990.
reg. 16A, inserted: regs. 94/2102.

NO.

1990—cont.

2021. Occupational Pension Schemes (Modification) Regulations 1990.
reg. 2, amended: regs. 94/1062, reg. 2.
reg. 3, amended: *ibid.*
reg. 4, amended: *ibid.*

2037. Value Added Tax (Insurance) Order 1990.
C.: 1994, c. 23, sch. 9.
revoked: 1994, c. 23, sch. 15.

2075. Occupational Pension Schemes (Independent Trustee) Regulations 1990.
reg. 2, amended: regs. 94/1062, reg. 2.
reg. 3, amended: *ibid.*
reg. 4, amended: *ibid.*
reg. 5, amended: *ibid.*
reg. 7, amended: *ibid.*

2129. Value Added Tax (Charities) (No. 2) Order 1990.
C.: 1994, c. 23, sch. 8.
revoked: 1994, c. 23, sch. 15.

2167. Channel Tunnel (Customs and Excise) Order 1990.
art. 2, amended: ord. 94/1405, art. 8.
art. 5, amended: *ibid.*
sch., amended: *ibid.*

2179. Building Standards (Scotland) Regulations 1990.
reg. 2, amended: regs. 94/1266, reg. 2.
reg. 11, amended: *ibid.*
reg. 25, amended: *ibid.*
reg. 27, amended: *ibid.*
reg. 33, amended: *ibid.*

2231. Income Tax (Building Societies) (Dividends and Interest) Regulations 1990.
reg. 4, amended: regs. 94/296, reg. 4.
reg. 5, amended: *ibid.,* reg. 5.
reg. 11, amended: *ibid.*

2232. Income Tax (Deposit-takers) (Interest Payments) Regulations 1990.
reg. 5, amended: regs. 94/295, reg. 2.

2277. Occupational and Personal Pension Schemes (Levy) Regulations 1990.
reg. 1, amended: regs. 94/1062, reg. 2.
reg. 2, amended: *ibid.*

2278. Register of Occupational and Personal Pension Schemes Regulations 1990.
reg. 1, amended: regs. 94/1062, reg. 2.
reg. 2, amended: *ibid.*
reg. 6, amended: *ibid.*

2319. Crown Office Fees Order 1990.
revoked: ord. 94/600, art. 3.

2329. Non-Domestic Rating (Transitional Period) (Amendment and Further Provision) Regulations 1990.
referred to: 1994, c. 3, s. 1.

2384. Patent Rules 1990.
rule 97, see *R.* v. *Comptroller-General of Patents,* ex p. *Archibald Kenrick & Sons, The Times,* August 2, 1994.

2427. Mount Vernon Hospital National Health Service Trust (Establishment) Order 1990.
revoked: ord. 94/860, art. 2.

NO.

1990—cont.

2428. Newcastle Mental Health National Health Service Trust (Establishment) Order 1990.
revoked: ord. 94/861, art. 2.

2438. Royal London Hospital and Associated Community Services National Health Service Trust (Establishment) Order 1990.
revoked: ord. 94/830, art. 2.

2452. West Dorset Community Health National Health Service Trust (Establishment) Order 1990.
revoked: ord. 94/833, art. 2.

2454. West Dorset Mental Health National Health Service Trust (Establishment) Order 1990.
revoked: ord. 94/831, art. 2.

2471. Enrolment of Deeds (Change of Name) (Amendment) Regulations 1990.
revoked: regs. 94/604, reg. 9.

2486. Food Safety Act 1990 (Consequential Modifications) (England and Wales) Order 1990.
reg. 18, amended: regs. 94/1029, reg. 26.
sch. 4, pt. I, amended: regs. 94/2486, reg. 26.
sch. 5, revoked: regs. 94/1029, reg. 26.
sch. 10, revoked: *ibid.*

2494. Fresh Meat and Poultry Meat (Hygiene, Inspection and Examinations for Residues) (Charges) Regulations 1990.
reg. 2, amended: regs. 94/1029, reg. 27.
reg. 9, amended: *ibid.*
reg. 13, revoked: *ibid.*

2551. Special Schools (Scotland) Grant Regulations 1990.
reg. 3, amended: regs. 94/351, reg. 10.

2553. Value Added Tax (Construction of Dwellings and Land) Order 1990.
C.: 1994, c. 23, sch. 9.
revoked: 1994, c. 23, sch. 15.

2588. Criminal Justice (Confiscation) (Northern Ireland) Order 1990.
sch. 2, para. 9, C.: 1994, c. 37, s. 48.

2600. Building (Amendment of Prescribed Fees) Regulations 1989.
revoked: regs. 94/2020, reg. 16.

2612. Motor Vehicles (Driving Licences) (Large Goods and Passenger Carrying Vehicles) Regulations 1990.
reg. 15, amended: regs. 94/639, reg. 3.
reg. 18, amended: *ibid.*, reg. 4.

2615. Quick-frozen Foodstuffs Regulations 1990.
reg. 2, amended: regs. 94/298, reg. 2.
reg. 3, amended: *ibid.*
reg. 6A, inserted: *ibid.*
reg. 7A, inserted: *ibid.*
sch. 2, inserted: *ibid.*

NO.

1990—cont.

2625. Food Safety Act 1990 (Consequential Modifications) (Scotland) Order 1990.
sch. 3, pt. I, amended: regs. 94/1029, reg. 26.
sch. 7, amended: *ibid.*

2626. Weights and Measures (Local and Working Standard Capacity Measures and Testing Equipment) Regulations 1990.
reg. 2, amended: regs. 94/1851, reg. 2.
reg. 3, amended: *ibid.*
reg. 4, amended: *ibid.*
sch. 3, amended: regs. 94/1259, reg. 3; regs. 94/1851, reg. 2.
sch. 4, amended: regs. 94/1851, reg. 2.

1991

3. Apple Orchard Grubbing Up Regulations 1991.
reg. 2, amended: regs. 94/2731, reg. 2.
reg. 5, amended: *ibid.*
reg. 7, amended: *ibid.*
reg. 8, substituted: *ibid.*
reg. 8A, inserted: *ibid.*
reg. 8B, inserted: *ibid.*
reg. 9, amended: *ibid.*
reg. 10, substituted: *ibid.*
regs. 10A, 10B, 10C, inserted: *ibid.*
reg. 13, substituted: *ibid.*

5. Food Protection (Emergency Prohibitions) (Radioactivity in Sheep) (Wales) Order 1991.
revoked in pt.: ord. 94/63, art. 2.

6. Food Protection (Emergency Prohibitions) (Radioactivity in Sheep) (England) Order 1991.
revoked in pt.: ord. 94/65, art. 2.

20. Food Protection (Emergency Prohibitions) (Radioactivity in Sheep) Order 1991.
revoked in pt.: ord. 94/50, art. 2.

80. Housing Renovation etc. Grants (Prescribed Forms and Particulars) (Welsh Forms and Particulars) Regulations 1991.
revoked: regs. 94/693, reg. 3.
sch. 1, amended: regs. 94/435, reg. 2.

166. Contracting-out (Protection of Pensions) Regulations 1991.
reg. 1, amended: regs. 94/1062, reg. 2.
reg. 2, amended: *ibid.*
reg. 3, amended: *ibid.*
reg. 4, amended: *ibid.*
reg. 5, amended: *ibid.*
reg. 6, amended: *ibid.*
reg. 7, amended: *ibid.*
reg. 8, amended: *ibid.*
reg. 9, amended: *ibid.*

NO.

1991—cont.

167. Occupational Pension Schemes (Preservation of Benefit) Regulations 1991.
reg. 1, amended: regs. 94/1062, reg. 2.
reg. 2, amended: *ibid.*
reg. 3, amended: *ibid.*
reg. 4, amended: *ibid.*
reg. 5, amended: *ibid.*
reg. 6, amended: *ibid.*
reg. 7, amended: *ibid.*
reg. 9, amended: *ibid.*
reg. 11, amended: *ibid.*
reg. 12, amended: *ibid.*
reg. 13, amended: *ibid.*
reg. 14, amended: *ibid.*
reg. 16, amended: *ibid.*
reg. 17, amended: *ibid.*
reg. 18, amended: *ibid.*
reg. 20, amended: *ibid.*
reg. 21, amended: *ibid.*
reg. 22, amended: *ibid.*
reg. 25, amended: *ibid.*
reg. 26, amended: *ibid.*
reg. 27, amended: *ibid.*

168. Occupational Pension Schemes (Revaluation) Regulations 1991.
reg. 2, amended: regs. 94/1062, reg. 2.
reg. 3, amended: *ibid.*
reg. 4, amended: *ibid.*
reg. 5, amended: *ibid.*
reg. 6, amended: *ibid.*
reg. 7, amended: *ibid.*
reg. 8, amended: *ibid.*
reg. 9, amended: *ibid.*
reg. 10, amended: *ibid.*
reg. 11, amended: *ibid.*
reg. 12, amended: *ibid.*
reg. 13, amended: *ibid.*

172. Public Telecommunication System Designation (British Cable Services Limited) (Cardiff) Order 1991.
revoked: ord. 94/1007, art. 3.

194. Health and Personal Social Services (Northern Ireland) Order 1991.
art. 7, applied: 1994, c. 22, sch. 2, para. 7; 1994, c. 23, s. 41.

195. Health and Personal Social Services (Northern Ireland Consequential Amendments) Order 1991.
art. 5, C.: 1994, c. 23, s. 41.

198. Civil Aviation (Canadian Navigation Services) (Third Amendment) Regulations 1991.
revoked: regs. 94/2325, reg. 3.

235. Oil Fuel (Sulphur Content of Gas Oil) Regulations (Northern Ireland) 1991.
revoked: regs. 94/2249, reg. 4.

272. Act of Sederunt (Rules of the Court of Session Amendment No. 1) (Fees of Solicitors) 1991.
revoked: Act 94/1443, para. 3.

NO.

1991—cont.

290. Act of Sederunt (Fees of Sheriff Officers) 1991.
revoked: Act 94/392, para. 3.

291. Act of Sederunt (Fees of Messengers-at-Arms) 1991.
revoked: Act 94/391, para. 3.

351. Local Authorities (Members' Allowances) Regulations 1991.
reg. 12, amended: regs. 94/615, reg. 2.
reg. 17, amended: *ibid.*
reg. 18, amended: *ibid.*

380. Insolvency (Amendment) Regulations 1991.
revoked: regs. 94/2507, reg. 2.

397. Local Authorities Etc. (Allowances) (Scotland) Regulations 1991.
reg. 13, amended: regs. 94/630, reg. 2.
reg. 19, amended: *ibid.*
reg. 22, amended: *ibid.*
reg. 23, amended: *ibid.*
reg. 24, amended: *ibid.*
sch. 2, substituted: *ibid.*

428. Statutory Sick Pay (Small Employers' Relief) Regulations 1991.
reg. 2, amended: regs. 94/561, reg. 2.
reg. 3, amended: *ibid.*

436. Wireless Telegraphy (Television Licence Fees) Regulations 1991.
sch. 2, amended: regs. 94/595, reg. 2.
sch. 3, amended: *ibid.*

439. London Government Reorganisation (Capital Money) (Greater London) Order 1991.
art. 4, amended: ord. 94/580, art. 3.

441. Housing Benefit and Community Charge Benefit (Subsidy) Regulations 1991.
revoked: regs. 94/781, reg. 5.

449. Education (Special Educational Needs) (Approval of Independent Schools) Regulations 1991.
revoked: regs. 94/651, reg. 6.

450. Education (Approval of Special Schools) (Amendment) Regulations 1991.
revoked: regs. 94/652, reg. 3.

470. Civil Aviation (Navigation Services Charges) Regulations 1991.
reg. 2, amended: regs. 94/503, reg. 2.
reg. 6, amended: *ibid.*
reg. 7, amended: *ibid.*

506. Statutory Sick Pay (Rate of Payment) Order 1991.
revoked: ord. 94/562, art. 4.

535. National Health Service Trusts (Membership and Procedure) (Scotland) Regulations 1991.
reg. 8, amended: regs. 94/1408, reg. 2.

542. Wireless Telegraphy (Licence Charge) Regulations 1991.
reg. 3, amended: regs. 94/659, reg. 3.
reg. 4, amended: *ibid.*, reg. 4.
reg. 9, inserted: *ibid.*, reg. 5.
sch., substituted: *ibid.*, reg. 6.

NO.

1991—cont.

554. National Health Service Functions (Directions to Authorities and Administration Arrangements) Regulations 1991.
reg. 2, amended: regs. 94/590, reg. 2.
reg. 5, amended: *ibid.*
sch., amended: *ibid.*

565. Civil Legal Aid (Scotland) (Fees) Amendment Regulations 1991.
reg. 4, amended: regs. 94/1015, reg. 8.

588. Personal and Occupational Pension Schemes (Pensions Ombudsman) Regulations 1991.
reg. 1, amended: regs. 94/1062, reg. 2.
reg. 2, amended: *ibid.*

609. Parliamentary Pensions (Amendment) Regulations 1991.
revoked: regs. 93/3253, reg. R5.

657. Seeds (National Lists of Varieties) (Fees) (Amendment) Regulations 1991.
revoked: regs. 94/676, reg. 5.

681. Education (National Curriculum) (Attainment Targets and Programmes of Study in History) (England) Order 1991.
applied: regs. 94/653; reg. 42; regs. 94/1084, reg. 9.
art. 1, amended: ord. 94/1816, art. 2.
art. 5, revoked: *ibid.*
art. 6, amended: *ibid.*
art. 7, amended: *ibid.*
art. 8, amended: *ibid.*
art. 8A, inserted: *ibid.*

702. Building Societies (Designated Capital Resources) (Permanent Interest Bearing Shares) Order 1991.
art. 2, amended: ord. 94/749, art. 6.

724. (L.5). High Court and County Courts Jurisdiction Order 1991.
art. 7(5), see *Chaplin Patents Holdings Co.* v. *Group Lotus, The Times,* January 12, 1994, C.A.; *Pharma Plast A/S* v. *Bard* [1993] F.S.R. 686.

737. Value Added Tax (Charities) Order 1991.
C.: 1994, c. 23, sch. 8.
revoked: 1994, c. 23, sch. 15.

738. Value Added Tax (Increase of Registration Limits) Order 1991.
revoked: 1994, c. 23, sch. 15.

751. Education (National Curriculum) (Attainment Targets and Programmes of Study in Geography) (Wales) Order 1991.
applied: regs. 94/653, reg. 42; regs. 94/1084, reg. 9.
art. 1, amended: ord. 94/1744, art. 3.
art. 5, revoked: *ibid.,* art. 4.
art. 6, amended: *ibid.,* art. 5.
art. 7, amended: *ibid.,* art. 6.
art. 8, amended: *ibid.,* art. 7.
art. 9, amended: *ibid.,* art. 8.

NO.

1991—cont.

751. Education (National Curriculum) (Attainment Targets and Programmes of Study in Geography) (Wales) Order 1991—cont.
art. 10, inserted: *ibid.,* art. 9.
sch. 1, amended: *ibid.,* art. 10.
sch. 2, amended: *ibid.,* art. 11.

752. Education (National Curriculum) (Attainment Targets and Programmes of Study in History) (Wales) Regulations 1991.
applied: regs. 94/653, reg. 42; regs. 94/1084, reg. 9.
art. 1, amended: ord. 94/1743, art. 2.
art. 5, revoked: *ibid.*
art. 6, amended: *ibid.*
art. 7, amended: *ibid.*
art. 8, amended: *ibid.*
sch. 1, amended: *ibid.*
sch. 2, amended: *ibid.*
sch. 4, inserted: *ibid.,* art. 3.

762. Food Safety (Northern Ireland) Order 1991.
art. 2, applied: regs. 94/674, reg. 2.

784. Merchant Shipping (Fees) Regulations 1991.
reg. 4, amended: regs. 94/502, reg. 3.
sch., pt. I, amended: *ibid.,* regs. 4–6.
sch., pt. IV, amended: *ibid.,* reg. 7.
sch., pt. V, substituted: *ibid.,* reg. 8.

789. Costs in Criminal Cases (General) (Amendment) Regulations 1991.
reg. 3, see *Barrister (Wasted Costs Order) (No. 4 of 1992), Re, The Times,* March 15, 1994, C.A.

846. Act of Sederunt (Rules of the Court of Session Amendment No. 3) (Solicitors' Fees) 1991.

851. Lloyd's Underwriters (Tax) (1988-89) Regulations 1991.
reg. 7, amended: regs. 94/1813, reg. 2.

895. Review of Children's Cases Regulations 1991.
see *B. (A Minor) (Care Order: Review),* Re [1993] 1 FLR 421.

897. Housing Renovation etc. Grants (Reduction of Grant) (Amendment) Regulations 1991.
revoked: regs. 94/648, reg. 45.

898. Housing Renovation etc. Grants (Prescribed Forms and Particulars) (Amendment) Regulations 1991.
revoked: regs. 94/565, reg. 5.

973. Fertilisers (Sampling and Analysis) Regulations 1991.
reg. 6, amended: regs. 94/129, reg. 3.
sch. 2, pt. I, *ibid.,* reg. 4.

1031. Savings Certificates Regulations 1991.
reg. 2, amended: regs. 94/343, reg. 3.
reg. 5, amended: *ibid.,* reg. 4.
reg. 6, amended: *ibid.,* reg. 5.
reg. 21, amended: *ibid.,* reg. 6.

NO.

1991—cont.

1115. Children (Admissibility of Hearsay Evidence) Order 1991.

see *C. (Minors) (Contempt Proceedings), Re* [1993] 1 F.C.R. 820, C.A.

1155. Specified Diseases (Notification) Order 1991.

art. 4A, inserted: ord. 94/2627, art. 3.

art. 6, amended: *ibid.*

art. 8, amended: *ibid.*

1157. Act of Sederunt (Rules of the Court of Session Amendment No. 2) (Miscellaneous) 1991.

revoked: Act 94/1443, para. 3.

1206. Companies (Fees) Regulations 1991.

sch., amended: regs. 94/2217, reg. 3.

1220. Planning (Northern Ireland) Order 1991.

C.: 1994, c. 23, sch. 8.

applied: 1994, c. 23, sch. 8, group 6.

1222. (L.8). County Courts Remedies Regulations 1991.

see *McDonald* v. *Graham, The Times,* January 12, 1994, C.A.

1247. (L.20). Family Proceedings Rules 1991.

see *A. (A Minor) (Residence Order: Leave to Apply), Re; sub nom. A.* v. *A. and Newham London Borough Council* [1993] 1 FLR 425; *Kent County Council* v. *K.; sub nom K. (Minors) (Disclosure of Privileged Material), Re* [1994] 1 W.L.R. 912; *U. (T.) (A Minor) (Care Order Contact), Re* [1993] 2 F.C.R. 566.

Pt. IVA, inserted: rules 94/2165, rule 4.

rule 2.62(7), (8), see *Frary* v. *Frary* [1993] 2 F.L.R. 696, C.A.

rule 4.5. see *D.B. and C.B. (Minors), Re* [1993] 2 F.C.R. 607, C.A.

rule 4.11, see *P (Minors) (Official Solicitors' Costs), Re* [1993] 2 F.C.R. 550.

rule 6, amended: rules 94/2890, rules 3-6.

rule 7, amended: *ibid.*, rules 7-11.

rule 9.2A, see *T. (Child Case: Application by Child), Re* [1993] 1 F.C.R. 646.

appendix 1, amended: rules 94/808, rule 3; amended: rules 94/2165, rule 5.

appendix 3, amended: rules 94/2165, rule 6.

1286. Customs Duty (Personal Reliefs) (Amendment) Order 1991.

revoked: ord. 94/955, art. 5.

1382. Price Marking Order 1991.

arts. 3, 8, see *Allen* v. *Redbridge London Borough Council* [1994] 1 W.L.R. 139, D.C.

NO.

1991—cont.

1395. (L.17). Family Proceedings Courts (Children Act 1989) Rules 1991.

Pt. IIA, inserted: rules 94/2166, rule 4.

rule 5, see *F. (A Minor) (Care Order: Withdrawal of Proceedings), Re* [1993] 2 FLR 9.

rule 10(7)(c), see *Devon County Council* v. *S* [1993] 1 FLR 842.

rule 11, see *F. (A Minor) (Care Order: Withdrawal of Proceedings) Re,* [1993] 2 FLR 9.

rules 11(3), 12(1), 21(6), see *H. (A Minor) (Care Proceedings: Child's Wishes), Re* [1993] 1 FLR 440.

rule 17, see *R.* v. *Nottinghamshire County Council* [1993] 1 F.C.R. 576.

rule 21, see *R.* v. *Nottinghamshire County Council* [1993] 1 F.C.R. 576; *S.* v. *S. (Children: Financial Provision)* [1993] 1 F.C.R. 805; *W.* v. *L. (Family Proceedings: Reasons)* [1993] 1 F.C.R. 591.

rule 21(5), see *W.* v. *North Yorkshire County Council* [1993] 1 F.C.R. 693.

rule 21(6), see *S.* v. *Oxfordshire County Council* [1993] 1 FLR 452.

rule 22, see *Sutton London Borough Council* v. *Davis (No. 2), The Times,* June 15, 1994.

sch. 1, amended: rules 94/809, rule 2.

1403. Housing Renovation etc. Grants (Prescribed Forms and Particulars) (Welsh Forms and Particulars) (Amendment) Regulations 1991.

revoked: regs. 94/693, reg. 3.

1431. Trade Marks and Service Marks (Amendment) Rules 1991.

revoked: rules 94/2583, rule 69.

1463. Criminal Justice (International Co-operation) Act 1990 (Enforcement of Overseas Forfeiture Orders) Order 1991.

art. 3, amended: ord. 94/1640, art. 2.

art. 12, amended: *ibid.*

sch. 1, amended: *ibid.*, art. 3.

sch. 2, amended: *ibid.*, art. 4.

sch. 3, amended: *ibid.*, art. 5.

1464. Criminal Justice (International Co-operation) Act 1990 (Enforcement of Overseas Forfeiture Orders) (Northern Ireland) Order 1991.

art. 3, amended: ord. 94/1640, art. 2.

art. 12, amended: *ibid.*

sch. 1, amended: *ibid.*, art. 3.

sch. 2, amended: *ibid.*, art. 4.

sch. 3, amended: *ibid.*, art. 5.

1467. Confiscation of the Proceeds of Drug Trafficking (Designated Countries and Territories) (Scotland) Order 1991.

sch. 1, amended: ord. 94/1644, art. 2.

sch. 3, amended: *ibid.*, art. 3.

NO.

1991—cont.

1468. Criminal Justice (International Co-operation) Act 1990 (Enforcement of Overseas Orders) (Scotland) Order 1991.
art. 3, amended: ord. 94/1645, art. 2.
art. 21, amended: *ibid.*
sch. 1, amended: *ibid.*
sch. 2, amended: *ibid.*, art. 4.

1474. Medicines (Products for Human Use—Fees) Regulations 1991.
reg. 2, amended: regs. 94/696, reg. 3.
reg. 5, amended: *ibid.*, reg. 4.
reg. 6, amended: *ibid.*, reg. 2.
reg. 8, amended: *ibid.*, reg. 5.
reg. 9A, revoked: *ibid.*, reg. 11.
reg. 10, amended: *ibid.*, reg. 2.
reg. 11, amended: *ibid.*
reg. 14, amended: *ibid.*, reg. 6.
sch. 1, pt. I, amended: *ibid.*, reg. 7.
sch. 1, pt. II, amended: *ibid.*, regs. 2, 7.
sch. 1, pt. III, amended: *ibid.*
sch. 2, para. 1, amended: *ibid.*, reg. 8.
sch. 2, para. 2, amended: *ibid.*, reg. 2.
sch. 2, para. 2A, amended: *ibid.*, reg. 8.
sch. 2, para. 4, amended: *ibid.*, reg. 2.
sch. 3, pt. I, amended: *ibid.*, reg. 9.
sch. 3, pt. III, amended: *ibid.*, regs. 2, 9.
sch. 4, para. 2A, revoked: *ibid.*, reg. 11.
sch. 5, para. 2, amended: *ibid.*, reg. 10.

1505. Children (Secure Accommodation) Regulations 1991.
see *W.* v. *North Yorkshire County Council* [1993] 1 F.C.R. 693.
reg. 11, see *C. (A Minor)* v. *Humberside County Council, The Times,* May 24, 1994, C.A.

1506. Children's Homes Regulations 1991.
reg. 14, amended: regs. 94/1511, reg. 2.

1511. Education (School Teacher Appraisal) Regulations 1991.
applied: regs. 94/653, reg. 42; applied with modifications: regs. 94/1084, reg. 8.

1624. Controlled Waste (Registration of Carriers and Seizure of Vehicles) Regulations 1991.
applied: regs. 94/1056, sch. 5, para. 1.
reg. 2, amended: regs. 94/1056, reg. 23.
reg. 4, amended: *ibid.*
sch. 1, amended: regs. 94/1137, reg. 19.

1658. Education (School Curriculum and Related Information) (Wales) Regulations 1991.
applied: regs. 94/653, reg. 42; applied with modifications: regs. 94/1084, reg. 9.
revoked: regs. 94/2330, reg. 2.
reg. 8, modified: *ibid.*

1677. (L.21). Children (Allocation of Proceedings) Order 1991.
art. 3, amended: ord. 94/2164, art. 3.
art. 6, amended: *ibid.*, art. 4.

NO.

1991—cont.

1677. (L.21). Children (Allocation of Proceedings) Order 1991—cont.
art. 8, see *R.* v. *South East Hampshire Family Proceedings Court,* ex p. *D.* [1994] 1 W.L.R. 611.
art. 10, amended: ord. 94/2164, art. 4.
art. 12, amended: *ibid.*
art. 13, amended: *ibid.*
rule 7, see *S.* v. *Oxfordshire County Council* [1993] 1 FLR 452.
rule 8, see *R.* v. *South East Hampshire Family Proceedings Court,* ex p. *D., The Times,* January 26, 1994.
sch. 2, amended: ord. 94/2164, art. 5.

1701. Extradition (Drug Trafficking) Order 1991.
art. 4, substituted: ord. 94/2794, art. 2.
sch. 4, inserted: *ibid.*
sch. 5, inserted: *ibid.*

1709. Broadcasting Act 1990 (Guernsey) (No. 2) Order 1991.
art. 3, amended: ord. 94/1064, art. 4.
sch., para. 41, revoked: *ibid.*
sch., para. 57, revoked: *ibid.*

1712. Disability Living Allowance and Disability Working Allowance (Northern Ireland) Order 1991.
sch. 2, para. 1, revoked: 1994, c. 22, sch. 5.

1723. Family Law Act 1986 (Dependent Territories) Order 1991.
sch. 2, para. 19, amended: ord. 94/2800, art. 2.

1737. Free Zone (Birmingham Airport) Designation Order 1991.
art. 3, amended: ord. 94/2509, art. 2.

1739. Free Zone (Prestwick Airport) Designation Order 1991.
art. 2, amended: ord. 94/143, art. 3.

1740. Free Zone (Southampton) Designation Order 1991.
amended: ord. 94/1410, art. 2.

1776. Banking Act 1987 (Meaning of Deposit) Order 1991.
see *Depositors' Protection Fund* v. *Dalia* [1994] 1 All E.R. 539, C.A.; *Deposit Protection Board* v. *Barclays Bank* [1994] 2 W.L.R. 732, H.L.

1804. Education (Bursaries for Teacher Training) (Amendment) Regulations 1991.
revoked: regs. 94/2016, reg. 2.

1805. Dartford–Thurrock Crossing (Amendment) Regulations 1991.
revoked: regs. 94/2031, reg. 12.

1813. Education (School Curriculum and Related Information) (Wales) (Amendment) Regulations 1991.
revoked: regs. 94/2330, reg. 2.

1820. Broadcasting (Prescribed Countries) Order 1991.
revoked: ord. 94/454, art. 3.

NO.

1991—cont.

1991. Family Proceedings Courts (Matrimonial Proceedings etc.) Rules 1991.
sch. 1, amended: rules 94/809, rule 3.

1999. Insurance Company Regulations 1981 (Amendment) Regulations 1991.
revoked: regs. 94/1516, reg. 86.

2038. Legal Aid in Family Proceedings (Remuneration) Regulations 1991.
reg. 2, amended: regs. 94/230, reg. 4.
reg. 3, amended: *ibid.*, regs. 5, 6.

2097. Packaging of Explosives for Carriage Regulations 1991.
applied: regs. 94/670, reg. 8.
reg. 2, amended: regs. 94/669, reg. 15.

2124. Broadcasting (Foreign Satellite Programmes) (Specified Countries) Order 1991.
revoked: ord. 94/453, art. 3.

2206. Seed Potatoes Regulations 1991.
reg. 2, amended: regs. 94/2592, reg. 2.
reg. 6, amended: *ibid.*
reg. 7A, inserted: *ibid.*

2234. Rivers Tweed and Eye Protection (Renewal) Order 1991.
art. 4, amended: ord. 94/2621, art. 2.

2235. River Tummel Catchment Area Protection (Renewal) Order 1991.
art. 4, amended: ord. 94/2623, art. 2.

2236. River Lunan Catchment Area Protection (Renewal) Order 1991.
art. 4, amended: ord. 94/2622, art. 2.

2242. Beef Carcase (Classification) Regulations 1991.
reg. 2, amended: regs. 94/2853, reg. 2.
reg. 5, amended: *ibid.*
reg. 6, amended: *ibid.*
reg. 14, amended: *ibid.*
sch. 3, revoked: *ibid.*

2246. Bovine Spongiform Encephalopathy Order 1991.
art. 4, amended: ord. 94/2627, art. 4.
art. 5, amended: *ibid.*
art. 12, amended: *ibid.*
art. 14, substituted: *ibid.*
art. 15, amended: *ibid.*
art. 17, amended: *ibid.*
sch., amended: *ibid.*

2336. Dacorum and St. Albans Community National Health Service Trust (Establishment) Order 1991.
revoked: ord. 94/862, art. 2.

2351. Gateshead Community Health National Health Service Trust (Establishment) Order 1991.
revoked: ord. 94/827, art. 2.

2355. Harrow Community Health Services National Health Service Trust (Establishment) Order 1991.
revoked: ord. 94/858, art. 2.

2359. Hillingdon Community Health National Health Service Trust (Establishment) Order 1991.
revoked: ord. 94/863, art. 2.

NO.

1991—cont.

2366. Liverpool Obstetric and Gynaecology Services National Health Service Trust (Establishment) Order 1991.
art. 1, amended: ord. 94/2784, art. 2.
art. 2, amended: *ibid.*

2379. Northgate National Health Service Trust (Establishment) Order 1991.
revoked: ord. 94/829, art. 2.

2388. Premier Health National Health Service Trust (Establishment) Order 1991.
revoked: ord. 94/832, art. 2.

2393. Royal Victoria Infirmary and Associated Hospitals National Health Service Trust (Establishment) Order 1991.
revoked: ord. 94/859, art. 2.

2437. Rules of the Air Regulations 1991.
sch., rule 5, amended: regs. 94/1444, reg. 2.
sch., rule 25, amended: *ibid.*
sch., rule 40, revoked: *ibid.*
sch., rule 44, amended: *ibid.*

2486. Imported Food and Feedingstuffs (Safeguards against Cholera) Regulations 1991.
reg. 1, amended: regs. 94/2783, reg. 9.
reg. 3, revoked: *ibid.*
reg. 3A, revoked: *ibid.*
reg. 5, amended: *ibid.*
reg. 6, amended: *ibid.*
sch. 2, revoked: *ibid.*
sch. 4, revoked: *ibid.*

2511. Insurance Companies (Linked Contracts) (Amendment) Regulations 1991.
revoked: regs. 94/1516, reg. 86.

2534. Value Added Tax (Piped Gas) (Metrication) Order 1991.
revoked: 1994, c. 23, sch. 15.

2562. Education (National Curriculum) (Attainment Targets and Programmes of Study in Geography) (England) Order 1991.
applied: regs. 94/653, reg. 42; regs. 94/1084, reg. 9.
art. 1, amended: ord. 94/1817, art. 2.
art. 5, revoked: *ibid.*
art. 6, amended: *ibid.*
art. 7, amended: *ibid.*
art. 8A, inserted: *ibid.*

2563. Education (National Curriculum) (Attainment Targets and Programmes of Study in Modern Foreign Languages) Order 1991.
applied: regs. 94/653, reg. 42; regs. 94/1084, reg. 9.
art. 3, amended: ord. 94/1815, art. 2.
art. 3, substituted: *ibid.*

2567. Education (National Curriculum) (Modern Foreign Languages) Order 1991.
art. 3, amended: ord. 94/1818, art. 2.

1991—cont.

2569. Value Added Tax (Buildings and Land) Order 1991.
C.: 1994, c. 23, sch. 9, sch. 10.
revoked: 1994, c. 23, sch. 15.

2589. Education (Bursaries for Teacher Training) (Amendment) (No. 2) Regulations 1991.
revoked: regs. 94/2016, reg. 2.

2679. Public Supply Contracts Regulations 1991.
reg. 2, amended: regs. 93/3228, reg. 33.
reg. 7, amended: *ibid.*

2680. Public Works Contracts Regulations 1991.
regs. 10, 12, 14, see *General Building and Maintenance* v. *Greenwich London Borough Council* 92 L.G.R. 21.

2724. Customs Controls on Importation of Goods Regulations 1991.
reg. 5, applied: 1994, c. 23, sch. 8, group 13; ord. 94/1739, art. 2.

2727. Free Zone Regulations 1991.
C.: 1994, c. 23, s. 4.

2740. Social Security (Attendance Allowance) Regulations 1991.
reg. 7, amended: regs. 94/1779, reg. 2.
reg. 7A, inserted: *ibid.*
reg. 8A, inserted: *ibid.*
reg. 8B, inserted: *ibid.*

2768. Building Regulations 1991.
reg. 6, amended: regs. 94/1850, reg. 2.
reg. 13A, inserted: *ibid.*
reg. 14A, inserted: *ibid.*

2825. Food Premises (Registration) Regulations 1991.
reg. 3, amended: regs. 94/1029, reg. 27.

2840. Feeding Stuffs Regulations 1991.
reg. 13, amended: regs. 94/2510, reg. 3.
sch. 1, pt. I, amended: *ibid.*, reg. 4.
sch. 4, para. 12, inserted: *ibid.*
sch. 4, pt. II, substituted: *ibid.*
sch. 4, pt. III, amended: regs. 94/499, reg. 3; regs. 94/2510, reg. 4.
sch. 4, pt. VII, amended: regs. 94/499, reg. 3.
sch. 4, pt. IX, amended: regs. 94/2510, reg. 4.
sch. 4, pt. X, inserted: *ibid.*
sch. 5, pt. I, amended: *ibid.*
sch. 7, amended: regs. 94/499, reg. 3.
sch. 8, pt. I, amended: regs. 94/2510, reg. 4.
sch. 8, pt. II, amended: *ibid.*

2843. Animals, Meat and Meat Products (Examination for Residues and Maximum Residue Limits) Regulations 1991.
reg. 2, amended: regs. 94/2465, reg. 2.
reg. 4A, inserted: *ibid.*
reg. 6, amended: *ibid.*
reg. 8, amended: *ibid.*
reg. 13, amended: *ibid.*
reg. 14, amended: *ibid.*
reg. 15, amended: *ibid.*

1991—cont.

2843. Animals, Meat and Meat Products (Examination for Residues and Maximum Residue Limits) Regulations 1991—cont.
reg. 20, inserted: *ibid.*
sch. 1, substituted: *ibid.*

2873. Criminal Justice Act 1988 (Designated Countries and Territories) Order 1991.
art. 2, amended: ord. 94/1639, art. 2.
art. 5A, inserted: *ibid.*, art. 3.
sch. 1, amended: *ibid.*, art. 4.
sch. 2, amended: *ibid.*, art. 5.
sch. 3, amended: *ibid.*, art. 6.

2887. Disability Working Allowance (General) Regulations 1991.
reg. 2, amended: regs. 94/1924, reg. 3.
reg. 15, amended: *ibid.*
reg. 15A, inserted: *ibid.*
reg. 22, amended: regs. 94/527, reg. 23.
reg. 23, amended: *ibid.*, reg. 24.
reg. 25, amended: *ibid.*, reg. 25.
reg. 29, amended: *ibid.*, reg. 26.
reg. 42, amended: regs. 94/1608, reg. 2.
reg. 46, amended: regs. 94/527, reg. 27.
reg. 51, amended: regs. 94/542, reg. 15.
reg. 52, amended: *ibid.*
sch. 3, para. 19, substituted: regs. 94/527, reg. 28.
sch. 3, para. 38, substituted: *ibid.*, reg. 23.
sch. 3, para. 49, substituted: *ibid.*
sch. 5, amended: regs. 94/542, reg. 15.

2890. Social Security (Disability Living Allowance) Regulations 1991.
reg. 4, amended: regs. 94/542, reg. 12.
reg. 9, amended: regs. 94/1779, reg. 3.
reg. 9A, inserted: *ibid.*
reg. 10A, amended: *ibid.*
reg. 10B, inserted: *ibid.*

2897. Education (National Curriculum) (Attainment Targets and Programmes of Study in Science) Order 1991.
art. 7, amended: ord. 94/1520, art. 2.
art. 7A, inserted: *ibid.*

1992

33. Medicines (Veterinary Drugs) (Pharmacy and Merchants' List) Order 1992.
art. 3, amended: ord. 94/599, art. 2.
art. 4, amended: *ibid.*
art. 13, amended: *ibid.*
art. 16, amended: *ibid.*
schs. 1–4, substituted: *ibid.*

52. Environmentally Sensitive Areas (South Downs) Designation Order 1992.
art. 2, amended: ord. 94/931, art. 4.
art. 4A, inserted: *ibid.*, art. 5.
art. 6, amended: *ibid.*, art. 6.
sch. 1A, inserted: *ibid.*, art. 7.
sch. 3, para. 10, inserted: *ibid.*

NO.

1992—cont.

54. Environmentally Sensitive Areas (The Broads) Designation Order 1992.
art. 2, amended: ord. 94/929, art. 4.
art. 4A, inserted: *ibid.*, art. 5.
art. 6, amended: *ibid.*, art. 6.
sch. 1A, inserted: *ibid.*, art. 7.
sch. 5, para. 11, inserted: *ibid.*

55. Environmentally Sensitive Areas (Pennine Dales) Designation Order 1992.
art. 2, amended: ord. 94/930, art. 4.
art. 4A, inserted: *ibid.*, art. 5.
art. 6, amended: *ibid.*, art. 6.
sch. 1A, inserted: *ibid.*, art. 7.
sch. 4, para. 8, inserted: *ibid.*

82. Act of Sederunt (Fees of Sheriff Officers) 1992.
revoked: Act 94/392, para. 3.

87. Act of Sederunt (Fees of Messengers-at-Arms) 1992.
revoked: Act 94/391, para. 3.

94. Lotteries (Gaming Board Fees) Order 1992.
revoked: ord. 93/3224, art. 8.

155. Education (National Curriculum) (Exceptions) Regulations 1992.
revoked: regs. 94/2112, reg. 2.

156. Education (National Curriculum) (Exceptions in History and Geography at Key Stage 4) Regulations 1992.
applied: regs. 94/653, reg. 42; regs. 94/1084, reg. 9; revoked: regs. 94/2112, reg. 2.

157. Education (National Curriculum) (Exceptions from Science at Key Stage 4) Regulations 1992.
revoked: regs. 94/212, reg. 2.

176. A564 Trunk Road (Stoke–Derby Route) (Derby Southern Bypass and Slip Roads) (No. 2) Order 1992.
art. 2, amended: ord. 94/801, art. 2.
art. 5, amended: *ibid.*
sch. 2, amended: *ibid.*

179. A564 Trunk Road (Stoke–Derby Route) (Derby Southern Bypass and Slip Roads) (No. 1) Order 1992.
art. 2, amended: ord. 94/801, art. 2.
art. 4, amended: *ibid.*
sch. 2, amended: *ibid.*

180. A564 Trunk Road (Stoke–Derby Route) (Derby Southern Bypass) (Burnaston Slip Roads) Order 1992.
art. 4, amended: ord. 94/801, art. 2.

223. Town and Country Planning (General Permitted Development) (Scotland) Order 1992.
art. 2, amended: ord. 94/2586, art. 2.
sch. 1, pt. 16, amended: *ibid.*, art. 3.
sch. 1, pt. 17, amended: *ibid.*, art. 4.
sch. 1, pt. 18, amended: *ibid.*, art. 5.
sch. 1, class 54, amended: ord. 94/1442, art. 2.
sch. 1, class 58, substituted: *ibid.*, art. 3.

NO.

1992—cont.

224. Town and Country Planning (General Development Procedure) (Scotland) Order 1992.
art. 15, amended: ord. 94/2585, art. 2.

231. Electricity (Northern Ireland) Order 1992.
art. 46, applied: 1994, c. 40, sch. 2, para. 5.
art. 46, amended: *ibid.*, sch. 4, para. 2.

233. European Parliamentary Constituencies (England) (Miscellaneous Changes) Order 1992.
constituencies substituted: ord. 94/427, art. 2.

246. Occupational Pension Schemes (Investment of Scheme's Resources) Regulations 1992.
reg. 1, amended: regs. 94/1062, reg. 2.
reg. 4, amended: *ibid.*
reg. 5, amended: *ibid.*

269. Hill Livestock (Compensatory Allowances) Regulations 1992.
referred to: regs. 94/2740, reg. 2.

272. Act of Sederunt (Judicial Factors Rules) 1992.
rule 6, amended: Act 94/2354, rule 2.

280. Teachers' Superannuation (Scotland) Regulations 1992.
reg. B7, amended: regs. 94/2699, reg. 3.
reg. C3, amended: *ibid.*, reg. 4.
reg. C4, amended: *ibid.*, reg. 5.
reg. C12, amended: *ibid.*, reg. 6.
reg. C13, amended: *ibid.*, reg. 7.
reg. D1, amended: *ibid.*, reg. 8.
reg. E15, amended: *ibid.*, reg. 9.
reg. E19, amended: *ibid.*, reg. 10.
reg. E20, amended: *ibid.*, reg. 11.
reg. E21, amended: *ibid.*, reg. 12.
reg. E22, amended: *ibid.*, reg. 13.
reg. E27, amended: *ibid.*, reg. 14.
reg. H1, amended: *ibid.*, reg. 15.
sch. 1, amended: *ibid.*, reg. 16.
sch. 4, para. 3, amended: *ibid.*, reg. 17.
sch. 4, pt. IV, revoked: *ibid.*.
sch. 5, para. 1, amended: *ibid.*, reg. 18.
sch. 10, para. 1, amended: *ibid.*, reg. 19.

355. New Town (East Kilbride) Winding Up Order 1992.
art. 2, amended: ord. 94/200, art. 2.
art. 6, inserted: *ibid.*
art. 7, inserted: *ibid.*

359. Building Societies (Accounts and Related Provisions) Regulations 1992.
reg. 9, amended: regs. 94/2459, reg. 2.
sch. 5, para. 5, amended: *ibid.*
sch. 5, para. 12, amended: *ibid.*
sch. 5, para. 13, amended: *ibid.*
sch. 5, para. 15, amended: *ibid.*
sch. 5, para. 15A, inserted: *ibid.*
sch. 8, para. 9, inserted: *ibid.*
sch. 9, para. 3, amended: *ibid.*
sch. 9, para. 3A, inserted: *ibid.*

NO.

1992—cont.

372. Civil Legal Aid (Scotland) (Fees) Amendment Regulations 1992.
reg. 3, revoked: regs. 94/1015, reg. 8.

429. Gaming Act (Variation of Monetary Limits) (No. 2) Order 1992.
revoked: ord. 94/957, art. 3.

445. Insurance Companies (Amendment) Regulations 1992.
revoked: regs. 94/1516, reg. 86.

456. Family Proceedings (Amendment) Rules 1992.
rule 9.2A(4)(6), see *K, W and H (Minors) (Medical Treatment), Re* [1993] 1 FLR 854.

462. Environmental Protection (Waste Recycling Payments) Regulations 1992.
reg. 2, amended: regs. 94/522, reg. 2.
sch., substituted, *ibid.*

478. Hovercraft (Fees) Regulations 1992.
sch., amended: regs. 94/1382, reg. 2.

483. Home Energy Efficiency Grants Regulations 1992.
reg. 3, amended: regs. 94/637, reg. 2.
reg. 10A, inserted: *ibid.*

511. Lloyd's Underwriters (Tax) (1989–90) Regulations 1992.
reg. 7, amended: regs. 94/1813, reg. 2.

529. Act of Sederunt (Fees of Messengers-at-Arms) (Amendment) 1992.
revoked: Act 94/391, para. 3.

530. Environmentally Sensitive Areas (Somerset Levels and Moors) Designation Order 1992.
art. 2, amended: ord. 94/932, art. 4.
art. 4A, inserted: *ibid.*, art. 5.
art. 6, amended: *ibid.*, art. 6.
art. 9, renumbered as art. 7: *ibid.*, art. 7.
sch. 1A, inserted: *ibid.*, art. 8.
sch. 5, para. 15, inserted: *ibid.*

548. Council Tax (Discount Disregards) Order 1992.
art. 3, amended: ord. 94/543, art. 2.
art. 4, amended: *ibid.*
sch. 1, para. 7, amended: *ibid.*

550. Council Tax (Situation and Valuation of Dwellings) Regulations 1992.
reg. 3, amended: regs. 94/1747, reg. 3.
reg. 6, amended: *ibid.*, reg. 4.

552. Council Tax (Additional Provisions for Discount Disregards) Regulations 1992.
sch., para. 3, amended: regs. 94/540, reg. 2.

558. Council Tax (Exempt Dwellings) Order 1992.
art. 2, amended: ord. 94/539, art. 3.
art. 3, amended: *ibid.*, art. 4.

562. Housing Renovation etc. Grants (Prescribed Forms and Particulars) (Amendment) Regulations 1992.
revoked: regs. 94/565, reg. 5.

NO.

1992—cont.

588. Control of Waste Regulations 1992.
reg. 1, applied: regs. 94/1056, reg. 4.

597. Education (National Curriculum) (Attainment Targets and Programmes of Study in Music) (England) Order 1992.
applied: regs. 94/653, reg. 42; regs. 94/1084, reg. 9.

598. Education (National Curriculum) (Attainment Targets and Programmes of Study in Art) (England) Order 1992.
applied: regs. 94/653, reg. 42; regs. 94/1084, reg. 9.

599. Parliamentary Pensions (Amendment) Regulations 1992.
regs. 3, 4, 5, revoked: regs. 93/3253, reg. R5.
reg. 7, revoked: *ibid.*

613. Council Tax (Administration and Enforcement) Regulations 1992.
reg. 23, amended: regs. 94/505, reg. 3.
reg. 28, amended: *ibid.*, reg. 4.
reg. 33, amended: *ibid.*, reg. 5.
reg. 47, amended: *ibid.*, reg. 6.
reg. 52, amended: *ibid.*, reg. 7.
reg. 54, amended: *ibid.*, reg. 8.
sch. 6, inserted: *ibid.*, reg. 9.

628. Value Added Tax (Charities and Aids for Handicapped Persons) Order 1992.
C.: 1994, c. 23, sch. 8.
revoked: 1994, c. 23, sch. 15.

629. Value Added Tax (Increase of Registration Limits) Order 1992.
revoked: 1994, c. 23, sch. 15.

631. Telecommunications Act 1984 (Government Shareholding) Order 1992.
revoked: ord. 94/744, art. 3.

635. National Health Service (General Medical Services) Regulations 1992.
reg. 5, amended: regs. 94/633, reg. 2.
reg. 12, amended: *ibid.*, reg. 3.
reg. 12A, inserted: *ibid.*, reg. 4.
reg. 13, amended: *ibid.*, reg. 5.
reg. 19, amended: *ibid.*, reg. 6.
reg. 21, amended: *ibid.*, reg. 7.
sch. 2, para. 4, amended: *ibid.*, reg. 8.
sch. 2, para. 9, amended: *ibid.*, reg. 8.
sch. 2, para. 9A, inserted: *ibid.*
sch. 10, amended: regs. 94/2620, reg. 2.
sch. 11, amended: *ibid.*

637. Welfare Food Amendment Regulations 1992.
reg. 2, amended: regs. 94/2004, reg. 8.
reg. 3, revoked: *ibid.*

649. Building Societies (Designation of Qualifying Bodies) Order 1992.
referred to: 1994, c. 40, s. 17.

656. Planning (Hazardous Substances) Regulations 1992.
referred to: ord. 94/2567, art. 6.
art. 10, amended: *ibid.*, art. 2.

NO.

1992—cont.

659. National Health Service Functions (Administration Arrangements and Amendment of Directions) Regulations 1992.
reg. 2, amended: regs. 94/590, reg. 3.

660. National Health Service (Appellate and Other Functions) Regulations 1992.
reg. 2, amended: regs. 94/682, reg. 2.
reg. 3, amended: *ibid.*
reg. 4, amended: *ibid.*

662. National Health Service (Pharmaceutical Services) Regulations 1992.
reg. 2, amended: regs. 94/2402, reg. 2.
sch. 2, pt. II, amended: *ibid.*
sch. 2, pt. III, amended: *ibid.*

664. National Health Service (Service Committees and Tribunal) Regulations 1992.
reg. 5, amended: regs. 94/634, reg. 2.
reg. 6, amended: *ibid.*, reg. 3.
reg. 10, amended: *ibid.*, reg. 4.
reg. 11, amended: *ibid.*, reg. 5.
sch. 4, para. 2, amended: *ibid.*, reg. 6.
sch. 4, para. 3, amended: *ibid.*
sch. 4, para. 4, amended: *ibid.*
sch. 4, para. 7, amended: *ibid.*
sch. 4, para. 10, amended: *ibid.*

666. Town and Country Planning (Control of Advertisements) Regulations 1992.
reg. 2, amended: regs. 94/2351, reg. 3.
reg. 3A, see *R. v. Mann and Co. (Thames Valley)*, Guildford Crown Ct.
sch. 2, class F, amended: regs. 94/2351, reg. 4.
sch. 3, pt. I, see *R. v. Mann and Co. (Thames Valley)*, Guildford Crown Ct.; amended: regs. 94/2351, regs. 5–8.
sch. 3, pt. II, amended: *ibid.*, reg. 9.

694. Medicines (Fees Relating to Medicinal Products for Animal Use) Regulations 1992.
revoked: regs. 94/1554, reg. 17.

701. Housing Benefit and Community Charge Benefit (Subsidy) Amendment Regulations 1992.
revoked: regs. 94/781, reg. 5.

705. Housing Renovation etc. Grants (Reduction of Grant) (Amendment) Regulations 1992.
revoked: regs. 94/648, reg. 45.

706. Representation of the People (Variation of Limits of Candidates' Election Expenses) Order 1992.
revoked: ord. 94/747, art. 9.

717. Returning Officers' Charges Order 1992.
revoked: ord. 94/1044, art. 1.
reg. 4, amended: regs. 94/542, reg. 12.

NO.

1992—cont.

730. Returning Officer's Charges (Northern Ireland) Order 1992.
revoked: ord. 94/1413, art. 1.

733. Value Added Tax (Increase for Consideration for Fuel) Order 1992.
revoked: 1994, c. 23, sch. 15.

741. Building (Prescribed Fees etc.) (Amendment) Regulations 1989.
revoked: regs. 94/2020, reg. 16.

742. Road Traffic (Carriage of Dangerous Substances in Packages etc.) Regulations 1992.
reg. 2, amended: regs. 94/669, reg. 15.
reg. 3, amended: *ibid.*
reg. 16, amended: *ibid.*
sch., revoked: *ibid.*

743. Road Traffic (Carriage of Dangerous Substances in Road Tankers and Tank Containers) Regulations 1992.
reg. 2, amended: regs. 94/669, reg. 15.
sch. 1, amended: *ibid.*
sch. 2, amended: *ibid.*

744. Road Traffic (Training of Drivers of Vehicles Carrying Dangerous Goods) Regulations 1992.
applied: regs. 94/397, reg. 14.
reg. 1, amended: regs. 94/669, reg. 15.
reg. 5, amended: regs. 94/397, reg. 16.
reg. 8, amended: *ibid.*
sch. 2, pt. I, amended: regs. 94/669, reg. 15.
sch. 2, pt. II, amended: *ibid.*

751. Gaming Act (Variation of Monetary Limits) (Scotland) Order 1992.
revoked: ord. 94/1043, art. 5.

753. Civil Legal Aid (Scotland) Amendment Regulations 1992.
regs. 2, 3, revoked: regs. 94/1049, reg. 9.

756. Medicines (Products for Human Use—Fees) Regulations 1992.
reg. 4, revoked: regs. 94/696, reg. 11.
reg. 11, revoked: *ibid.*

757. Education (National Curriculum) (Attainment Targets and Programmes of Study in Art) (Wales) Order 1992.
applied: regs. 94/653, reg. 42; regs. 94/1084, reg. 9.

758. Education (National Curriculum) (Attainment Targets and Programmes of Study in Music) (Wales) Order 1992.
applied: regs. 94/653, reg. 42; regs. 94/1084, reg. 9.

759. Housing Renovation etc. Grants (Prescribed Forms and Particulars) (Welsh Forms and Particulars) (Amendment) Regulations 1992.
revoked: regs. 94/693, reg. 3.

773. Act of Sederunt (Fees of Sheriff Officers) (Amendment) 1992.
revoked: Act 94/392, para. 3.

NO.

1992—cont.

807. Industrial Relations (Northern Ireland) Order 1992.
applied: 1994, c. 33, s. 126.

835. Education (National Curriculum) (Assessment Arrangements for English, Mathematics, Science, Technology, History and Geography) (Key Stage 1) Order 1992.
applied: regs. 94/1084, reg. 9.

905. Farm Woodland Premium Scheme 1992.
referred to: regs. 94/1292, reg. 2.

1069. Trade Marks and Service Marks (Fees) Rules 1992.
revoked: rules 94/2584, rule 5.
sch., amended: rules 94/2581, rule 2.

1197. European Parliament (United Kingdom Representatives) Pensions (Amendment) Order 1992.
revoked: ord. 94/1662, art. 32.

1227. Legal Aid in Contempt of Court Proceedings (Scotland) Regulations 1992.
reg. 2, amended: regs. 94/1016, reg. 4.

1228. Legal Aid in Contempt of Court Proceedings (Scotland) (Fees) Regulations 1992.
reg. 2, amended: regs. 94/1018, reg. 4.

1295. Education (Chief Inspector of Schools in England) Order 1992.
revoked: ord. 94/1633, art. 3.

1302. Serbia and Montenegro (United Nations Sanctions) Order 1992.
applied: ord. 94/2673, art. 7.

1303. Serbia and Montenegro (United Nations Sanctions) (Dependent Territories) Order 1993.
applied: ord. 94/2674, art. 7.

1308. Serbia and Montenegro (United Nations Sanctions) (Channel Islands) Order 1992.
applied: ord. 94/2675, art. 7.

1333. Council Tax (Exempt Dwellings) (Scotland) Order 1992.
sch., para. 17, substituted: ord. 94/628, art. 2.

1408. Council Tax (Discounts) (Scotland) Order 1992.
art. 4, amended: ord. 94/626, art. 2.
art. 7, amended: ibid., art. 3.

1409. Council Tax (Discounts) (Scotland) Regulations 1992.
reg. 2, amended: regs. 94/629, reg. 2.

1507. Food Safety (Fishery Products) (Derogations) Regulations 1992.
reg. 2, amended: regs. 94/2783, reg. 10.
sch., amended: ibid.

1520. Medicines (Medicated Animal Feeding Stuffs) (No. 2) Regulations 1992.
reg. 3, substituted: regs. 94/1531, reg. 3.
reg. 6, amended: ibid., reg. 4.
reg. 8, amended: ibid., reg. 5.
reg. 9, substituted: ibid., reg. 6.

NO.

1992—cont.

1520. Medicines (Medicated Animal Feeding Stuffs) (No. 2) Regulations 1992—cont.
sch. 2, amended: ibid., reg. 7.
sch. 3, inserted: ibid., reg. 8.

1527. Reservoirs (Panel of Civil Engineers) (Applications and Fees) Regulations 1992.
reg. 2, amended: regs. 94/1533, reg. 2.

1555. Occupational Pension Schemes (Deficiency on Winding Up etc.) Regulations 1992.
revoked: regs. 94/895, reg. 5.

1586. Civil Legal Aid (Financial Conditions) (Scotland) Regulations 1992.
reg. 2, revoked: regs. 94/998, reg. 5.

1601. Imported Food (Bivalve Molluscs and Marine Gastropods from Japan) Regulations 1992.
reg. 1, amended: regs. 94/2783, reg. 11.

1611. Building Societies (Designated Capital Resources) Order 1992.
art. 2, amended: ord. 94/750, art. 2.
art. 7, amended: ibid.

1619. Private Medical Insurance (Disentitlement to Tax Relief and Approved Benefits) (Amendment) Regulations 1992.
revoked: regs. 94/1518, reg. 9.

1629. Revenue Support Grant (Scotland) (No. 2) Order 1992.
revoked: ord. 94/529, art. 5.

1703. Housing (Right to Buy) (Prescribed Persons) Order 1992.
sch., amended: ord. 94/2567, art. 2.

1735. Social Security (Jersey and Guernsey) Order 1992.
revoked: ord. 94/2802, art. 3.

1752. Health and Safety (Fees) Regulations 1992.
revoked: regs. 94/397, reg. 16.

1812. Child Support (Information, Evidence and Disclosure) Regulations 1992.
see C. (A Minor) (Child Support Agency: Disclosure), Re, The Times, October 7, 1994.

1813. Child Support (Maintenance Assessment Procedure) Regulations 1992.
reg. 10, amended: regs. 94/227, reg. 2.
reg. 20, amended: ibid.
reg. 21, amended: ibid.
reg. 31, amended: ibid.

1814. Council Tax Benefit (General) Regulations 1992.
referred to: ord. 94/523, art. 14.
reg. 2, amended: regs. 94/578, reg. 15; regs. 94/1924, reg. 2.
reg. 4A, inserted: regs. 94/470, reg. 2; amended: regs. 94/1807, reg. 2.
reg. 8, amended: regs. 94/542, reg. 20.
reg. 9, amended: ibid.
reg. 10, amended: ibid.
reg. 13, amended: regs. 94/1924, reg. 2.

NO.

1992—cont.

1814. Council Tax Benefit (General) Regulations 1992—*cont.*
  reg. 13A, inserted: *ibid.*
  reg. 17, amended: regs. 94/542, reg. 20.
  reg. 20, amended: *ibid.*, reg. 17.
  reg. 21, amended: *ibid.*, reg. 18.
  reg. 22, amended: *ibid.*, reg. 19.
  reg. 26, amended: *ibid.*, reg. 20.
  reg. 41, revoked: regs. 94/470, reg. 2.
  reg. 42, amended: regs. 94/1608, reg. 2.
  reg. 44, amended: regs. 94/578, reg. 21.
  reg. 46, amended: *ibid.*, reg. 22.
  reg. 52, amended: regs. 94/542, reg. 20.
  reg. 59, amended: regs. 94/578, reg. 23.
  reg. 71, applied: regs. 94/135, reg. 9.
  reg. 72, applied: *ibid.*
  reg. 92, amended: regs. 94/1925, reg. 3.
  reg. 93, amended: *ibid.*
  reg. 94, inserted: regs. 94/578, reg. 24.
  sch. 1, pt. I, amended: regs. 94/542, reg. 20.
  sch. 1, pt. II, amended: *ibid.*
  sch. 1, pt. III, amended: *ibid.*
  sch. 1, pt. IV, amended: *ibid.*
  sch. 2, para. 1, amended: *ibid.*
  sch. 4, para. 20, substituted: regs. 94/578, reg. 25.
  sch. 4, para. 21, substituted: *ibid.*, reg. 25.
  sch. 4, para. 51, inserted: *ibid.*

1815. Child Support (Maintenance Assessments and Special Cases) Regulations 1992.
  reg. 3, amended: regs. 94/227, reg. 4.
  reg. 6, amended: *ibid.*
  reg. 11, amended: *ibid.*
  reg. 23, amended: *ibid.*

1829. Parole Board (Transfer of Functions) Order 1992.
  art. 3, amended: 1994: c. 33, sch. 11.

1852. Access to Personal Files (Housing) (Scotland) Regulations 1992.
  sch., amended: 1994, c. 17, s. 38.

1857. Education (National Curriculum) (Assessment Arrangements for English, Mathematics, Science, Technology, History and Geography) (Key Stage 1) Order 1992.
  applied: regs. 94/653, reg. 42.

1878. Act of Sederunt (Fees of Witnesses and Shorthand Writers in the Sheriff Court) 1992.
  sch. 2, amended: Act of Sederunt 94/1141, rule 2.

1934. Dartford–Thurrock Crossing (Amendment) Regulations 1992.
  revoked: regs. 94/2031, reg. 12.

1971. Flavourings in Food Regulations 1992.
  reg. 5, amended: regs. 94/1486, reg. 2.

1974. Salmon (Definition of Methods of Net Fishing and Construction of Nets) (Scotland) Regulations 1992.
  reg. 8A, inserted: regs. 94/111, reg. 2.

NO.

1992—cont.

1989. Child Support (Collection and Enforcement) Regulations 1992.
  reg. 9, amended: regs. 94/227, reg. 3.
  sch. 2, amended: *ibid.*

2036. Poultry Meat (Hygiene) (Amendment) Regulations 1992.
  revoked: regs. 94/1029, reg. 26.

2037. Fresh Meat (Hygiene and Inspection) Regulations 1992.
  applied: regs. 94/1029, sch. 6.

2047. Magistrates' Courts Committees (Constitution) (Amendment) Regulations 1992.
  revoked: regs. 94/2811, reg. 2.

2051. Management of Health and Safety at Work Regulations 1992.
  reg. 1, amended: regs. 94/2865, reg. 2.
  reg. 13A, inserted: *ibid.*
  reg. 13A, applied: ord. 94/2930, art. 2.
  reg. 13B, inserted: regs. 94/2865, reg. 2; applied: ord. 94/2930, art. 2.
  reg. 13C, inserted: regs. 94/2865, reg. 2.
  reg. 14, amended: *ibid.*
  reg. 15, amended: *ibid.*

2061. Poultry Meat (Hygiene) (Scotland) Amendment Regulations 1992.
  revoked: regs. 94/1029, reg. 26.

2078. Housing Renovation etc. Grants (Prescribed Forms and Particulars (Welsh Forms and Particulars) (Amendment) (No. 2) Regulations 1993.
  revoked: regs. 94/693, reg. 3.

2079. Building (Amendment of Prescribed Fees) Regulations 1992.
  revoked: regs. 94/2020, reg. 16.

2111. Organic Products Regulations 1992.
  reg. 2, amended: regs. 94/2286, reg. 3.
  reg. 3, amended: *ibid.*, reg. 4.
  reg. 4, revoked: *ibid.*, reg. 5.
  reg. 5, amended: *ibid.*, reg. 6.
  reg. 10, amended: *ibid.*, reg. 7.

2257. Education (London Residuary Body) (Transfer of Functions and Property) (No. 2) Order 1992.
  art. 1, amended: ord. 94/580, art. 4.
  art. 13, amended: *ibid.*

2274. Education (School Performance Information) (Wales) Order 1992.
  applied: regs. 94/653, reg. 42.
  reg. 7, modified: *ibid.*

2323. British Railways (Penalty Fares) Act 1989 (Activating No. 4) Order 1992.
  revoked: ord. 94/577, art. 2.

2324. British Railways (Penalty Fares) Act 1989 (Activating No. 5) Order 1992.
  revoked: ord. 94/577, art. 2.

2338. Royal Scottish National Hospital and Community National Health Service Trust (Establishment) Order 1992.
  revoked: ord. 94/2484, art. 2.

NO.

1992—cont.

2364. Imported Food and Feedingstuffs (Safeguards against Cholera) (Amendment) Regulations 1992.
reg. 2, revoked in pt.: regs. 94/2783, reg. 16.

2414. Town and Country Planning (Simplified Planning Zones) Regulations 1992.
reg. 2, amended: regs. 94/267, reg. 3.
reg. 3, amended: *ibid.*, reg. 4.

2428. Local Authorities (Funds) (England) Regulations 1992.
sch. 2, pt. I, amended: regs. 94/246, reg. 7.

2429. Billing Authorities (Alteration of Requisite Calculations) (England) Regulations 1992.
revoked: regs. 94/246, reg. 6.

2471. West Lindsey National Health Service Trust (Establishment) Order 1992.
art. 4, amended: ord. 94/1534, art. 2.

2514. Mid Essex Community Health National Health Service Trust (Establishment) Order 1992.
revoked: ord. 94/745, art. 2.

2537. Northwick Park Hospital National Health Service Trust (Establishment) Order 1992.
art. 1, amended: ord. 94/195, art. 2.
art. 2, amended: *ibid.*

2586. Mancunian Community Health National Health Service Trust (Establishment) Order 1992.
revoked: ord. 94/828, art. 2.

2589. British Railways (Penalty Fares) Act 1989 (Activating No. 6) Order 1992.
revoked: ord. 94/577, art. 2.

2598. Education (Parental Ballots for Acquisition of Grant-maintained Status) (Prescribed Body) Regulations 1992.
referred to: regs. 94/1041, reg. 6.

2882. Faculty Jurisdiction Rules 1992.
rules 24, 25(1), see *St. James's, New Malden, Re* [1993] 3 W.L.R. 861.

2890. Insurance Companies (Amendment) Regulations 1992.
regs. 13–15, revoked: regs. 94/1516, reg. 85.

2902. Transport and Works (Applications and Objections Procedure) Rules 1992.
referred to: ord. 94/2567, art. 7.
sch. 2, amended: *ibid.*, art. 2.
sch. 5, amended: *ibid.*

2921. Meat Hygiene Appeals Tribunal (Procedure) Regulations 1992.
reg. 1, amended: regs. 94/1029, reg. 27.
reg. 2, substituted: *ibid.*

2932. Provision and Use of Work Equipment Regulations 1992.
sch. 1, para. 31, amended: regs. 94/2326, reg. 2.

NO.

1992—cont.

2936. Sea Fishing (Enforcement of Community Conservation Measures) (Amendment) (No. 5) Order 1992.
revoked: ord. 94/1680, art. 4.

2945. British Railways (Penalty Fares) Act 1989 (Activating No. 7) Order 1992.
revoked: ord. 94/577, art. 2.

2966. Personal Protective Equipment at Work Regulations 1992.
sch. 1, amended: regs. 94/2326, reg. 3.

2977. National Assistance (Assessment of Resources) Regulations 1992.
sch. 1, pt. III, amended: regs. 94/825, reg. 2.
sch. 3, pt. I, amended: regs. 94/2386, reg. 2.
sch. 3, para. 28A, inserted: regs. 94/825, reg. 3.
sch. 4, para. 1, substituted: *ibid.*, reg. 4.

3047. Police Cadets (Scotland) Amendment (No. 2) Regulations 1992.
revoked: regs. 94/2096, reg. 4.

3060. Railway Regulations 1992.
reg. 2, amended: regs. 94/608, reg. 3.
reg. 4, amended: *ibid.*, reg. 4.
reg. 6, amended: *ibid.*, reg. 5.
reg. 8, amended: regs. 94/237, reg. 13; regs. 94/608, reg. 6.
reg. 9, amended: regs. 94/237, reg. 13; regs. 94/608, reg. 7.
reg. 14, amended: regs. 94/237, reg. 13.
reg. 15, revoked: *ibid.*
sch. 1, rules 1–5, substituted: regs. 94/608, reg. 8.

3065. Value Added Tax (Motor Vehicles for the Handicapped) Order 1992.
C.: 1994, c. 23, sch. 8.
revoked: 1994, c. 23, sch. 15.

3072. Public Record Office (Fees) Regulations 1992.
revoked: regs. 94/2353, reg. 3.

3082. Non-Domestic Rating Contributions (England) Regulations 1992.
reg. 7A, amended: regs. 94/421, reg. 2.
regs. 8, 8A, 9, 9A, substituted: regs. 94/1431, reg. 2.

3092. Export of Goods (Control) Order 1992.
revoked in pt.: ord. 94/1191, art. 9.
sch. 3, pt. III, amended: ord. 94/534, art. 2.

3094. Child Support Fees Regulations 1992.
reg. 1, amended: regs. 94/227, reg. 5.
reg. 3, amended: *ibid.*
reg. 4, amended: *ibid.*

3095. Customs and Excise (Single Market Etc.) Regulations 1992.
C.: 1994, c. 23, sch. 8.

3107. Motor Vehicles (EC Type Approval) Regulations 1992.
reg. 2, amended: regs. 94/617, reg. 3.
reg. 14, amended: *ibid.*, reg. 4.
sch. 1, amended: *ibid.*, reg. 5; regs. 94/1570, reg. 2.

NO.

1992—cont.

3121. Value Added Tax (Place of Supply of Services) Order 1992.
applied: 1994, c. 23, sch. 8, group 8.

3126. Value Added Tax (Transport) Order 1992.
C.: 1994, c. 23, sch. 8.
revoked: 1994, c. 23, sch. 15.

3127. Value Added Tax (Means of Transport) Order 1992.
C.: 1994, c. 23, s. 95.
revoked: 1994, c. 23, sch. 15.

3128. Value Added Tax (Reverse Charge) Order 1992.
C.: 1994, c. 23, sch. 5.

3131. Value Added Tax (Tax Free Shops) Order 1992.
C.: 1994, c. 23, sch. 8.
revoked: 1994, c. 23, sch. 15.

3139. Personal Protective Equipment (EC Directive) Regulations 1992.
sch. 1, para. 31, amended: regs. 94/2326, reg. 3.

3147. Social Security Benefits (Amendments Consequential Upon the Introduction of Community Care) Regulations 1992.
reg. 7, revoked in pt.: regs. 94/1779, reg. 4.
reg. 8, revoked in pt.: *ibid.*

3163. Food Safety (Fishery Products) Regulations 1992.
applied: regs. 94/2782, reg. 2.
reg. 2, amended: regs. 94/2783, reg. 12.
reg. 3, inserted: *ibid.*
reg. 5, substituted: *ibid.*
reg. 6, substituted: *ibid.*
reg. 9, amended: *ibid.*
reg. 11, amended: *ibid.*
reg. 11A, inserted: *ibid.*
reg. 13, amended: *ibid.*
reg. 14, amended: *ibid.*
reg. 15, amended: *ibid.*
reg. 16, amended: *ibid.*
reg. 18, amended: *ibid.*
reg. 20, amended: *ibid.*
regs. 21, 22, revoked: *ibid.*, reg. 16.
reg. 23, amended: *ibid.*
reg. 24, revoked: *ibid.*
sch. 1, pt. I, amended: *ibid.*, reg. 12.
sch. 1, pt. II, amended: *ibid.*
sch. 5, amended: *ibid.*

3164. Food Safety (Live Bivalve Molluscs and Other Shellfish) Regulations 1992.
reg. 2, amended: regs. 94/2782, reg. 5.
reg. 3, amended: *ibid.*
reg. 7, amended: *ibid.*, reg. 3.
reg. 9, amended: *ibid.*, reg. 5.
reg. 10, amended: *ibid.*
reg. 11, substituted: *ibid.*
reg. 11A, inserted: *ibid.*
reg. 12, amended: *ibid.*

NO.

1992—cont.

3164. Food Safety (Live Bivalve Molluscs and Other Shellfish) Regulations 1992—*cont.*
reg. 14, amended: *ibid.*
reg. 15, revoked: *ibid.*
reg. 18, amended: *ibid.*
reg. 19, amended: *ibid.*
reg. 22, amended: *ibid.*, reg. 8.
sch. 1, para. 1, amended: *ibid.*, reg. 5.
sch. 1, para. 4, inserted: *ibid.*
sch. 3, pt. 2, amended: *ibid.*
sch. 6, para. 3, amended: *ibid.*
sch. 9, para. 1, amended: *ibid.*
sch. 9, para. 2, amended: *ibid.*
sch. 9, para. 5, amended: *ibid.*

3165. Food Safety (Fishery Products on Fishing Vessels) Regulations 1992.
reg. 7, amended: regs. 94/2783, reg. 13.

3170. Police (Scotland) Amendment (No. 2) Regulations 1992.
regs. 8, 9, revoked: regs. 94/2095, reg. 9.

3183. Acquisition of Land (Rate of Interest after Entry) Regulations 1992.
revoked: regs. 94/468, reg. 3.

3192. Customs Duty (Personal Reliefs) (Amendment) Order 1992.
revoked: ord. 94/955, art. 5.

3218. Banking Coordination (Second Council Directive) Regulations 1992.
applied: 1994, c. 9, s. 177.

3223. Value Added Tax (International Services and Transport) Order 1992.
C.: 1994, c. 23, sch. 8.
revoked: 1994, c. 23, sch. 15.

3225. Acquisition of Land (Rate of Interest after Entry) (Scotland) (No. 2) Regulations 1992.
revoked: regs. 94/469, reg. 3.

3238. Non-Domestic Rating Contributions (Wales) (Amendment) Regulations 1994.
reg. 7A, amended: regs. 94/547, reg. 2.
reg. 8, substituted: regs. 94/1742, reg. 2.
reg. 8A, substituted: *ibid.*
reg. 9, substituted: *ibid.*

3275. Education Support Grants Regulations 1992.
revoked: regs. 94/612, reg. 12.

3298. Products of Animal Origin (Import and Export) Regulations 1992.
reg. 1, amended: regs. 94/2783, reg. 14.
reg. 5, substituted: *ibid.*
reg. 7, amended: *ibid.*
reg. 13, amended: *ibid.*
reg. 15, amended: *ibid.*
reg. 16, amended: *ibid.*
reg. 17, amended: *ibid.*
reg. 18, amended: *ibid.*
reg. 19, amended: *ibid.*

3300. Fish Health Regulations 1992.
applied: regs. 94/1447, reg. 2.
referred to: regs. 94/2782, reg. 3.
reg. 2, amended: regs. 94/1448, reg. 2.

NO.

1992—cont.

3300. Fish Health Regulations 1992—cont.
reg. 3, amended: *ibid.*, reg. 3.
reg. 7, amended: *ibid.*, reg. 4.
reg. 9A, inserted: *ibid.*, reg. 5.
reg. 16, amended: *ibid.*, reg. 6.
sch. 1, substituted: *ibid.*, reg. 7.
sch. 2, substituted: *ibid.*, reg. 2.
sch. 3, substituted: *ibid.*, reg. 9.
sch. 7, pt. I, amended: *ibid.*, reg. 10.

3301. Shellfish and Specified Fish (Third Country Imports) Order 1992.
referred to: regs. 94/2782, reg. 3.

3303. Controlled Waste Regulations 1992.
reg. 1, amended: regs. 94/1056, reg. 24.
reg. 2, amended: *ibid.*
reg. 5, amended: *ibid.*
reg. 6, amended: *ibid.*
reg. 7A, inserted: *ibid.*

3305. Export of Goods (Control) Order 1992 (Amendment) Order 1992.
revoked: ord. 94/1191, art. 9.

1993

82. Environmentally Sensitive Areas (North Kent Marshes) Designation Order 1993.
art. 2, amended: ord. 94/918, art. 4.
art. 4A, inserted: *ibid.*, art. 5.
art. 6, amended: *ibid.*, art. 6.
sch. 1A, inserted: *ibid.*, art. 7.
sch. 4, para. 7, inserted: *ibid.*

83. Environmentally Sensitive Areas (Exmoor) Designation Order 1993.
art. 2, amended: ord. 94/928, art. 4.
art. 4A, inserted: *ibid.*, art. 5.
art. 6, amended: *ibid.*, art. 6.
sch. 1A, inserted: *ibid.*, art. 7.
sch. 5, para. 7, inserted: *ibid.*

84. Environmentally Sensitive Areas (Avon Valley) Designation Order 1993.
art. 2, amended: ord. 94/927, art. 4.
art. 4A, inserted: *ibid.*, art. 5.
art. 6, amended: *ibid.*, art. 6.
sch. 1A, inserted: *ibid.*, art. 7.
sch. 4, para. 7, inserted: *ibid.*

85. Environmentally Sensitive Areas (Lake District) Designation Order 1993.
art. 2, amended: ord. 94/925, art. 4.
art. 4A, inserted: *ibid.*, art. 5.
art. 6, amended: *ibid.*, art. 6.
sch. 1A, inserted: *ibid.*, art. 7.
sch. 5, para. 7, inserted: *ibid.*

86. Environmentally Sensitive Areas (South Wessex Downs) Designation Order 1993.
art. 2, amended: ord. 94/924, art. 4.
art. 4A, inserted: *ibid.*, art. 5.
art. 6, amended: *ibid.*, art. 6.
sch. 1A, inserted: *ibid.*, art. 7.
sch. 3, para. 7, inserted: *ibid.*

NO.

1993—cont.

87. Environmentally Sensitive Areas (South West Peak) Designation Order 1993.
art. 2, amended: ord. 94/926, art. 4.
art. 4A, inserted: *ibid.*, art. 5.
art. 6, amended: *ibid.*, art. 6.
sch. 1A, inserted: *ibid.*, art. 7.
sch. 5, para. 8, inserted: *ibid.*

113. Education (School Financial Statements) (Prescribed Particulars etc.) Regulations 1993.
revoked: regs. 94/323, reg. 1.

115. British Railways (Penalty Fares) Act 1989 (Activating No. 8) Order 1993.
revoked: ord. 94/577, art. 2.

118. Act of Sederunt (Fees of Messengers-at-Arms) 1993.
revoked: Act 94/391, para. 3.

120. Act of Sederunt (Fees of Sheriff Officers) 1993.
revoked: Act 94/392, para. 3.

143. Food Protection (Emergency Prohibitions) (Oil and Chemical Pollution of Fish) (No. 2) Order 1993.
revoked in pt.: ord. 94/2555, art. 2.

176. Motor Vehicles (Wearing of Seat Belts) Regulations 1993.
see *Jones (Kenneth)* v. *Morgan (Jonathon)*, May 10, 1994; High Ct., Cardiff.

199. Protection of Wrecks (MV Braer) Order 1993.
revoked: ord. 94/2372, art. 2.

209. Poultry Meat (Hygiene) (Amendment) Regulations 1993.
revoked: regs. 94/1029, reg. 26.

220. Superannuation (Children's Pensions) (Earnings Limit) Order 1993.
revoked: ord. 94/350, art. 3.

235. Poultry Meat (Hygiene) (Scotland) Amendment Regulations 1993.
revoked: regs. 94/1029, reg. 26.

252. Non-Domestic Rating (Demand Notices) (Wales) Regulations 1993.
sch. 2, pt. I, amended: regs. 94/415, rég. 3.
sch. 2, pt. II, amended: *ibid.*

290. Council Tax (Alteration of Lists and Appeals) Regulations 1993.
reg. 4, amended: ord. 94/1746, art. 2.
reg. 14, amended: *ibid.*

291. Non-Domestic Rating (Alteration of Lists and Appeals) Regulations 1993.
reg. 13, amended: regs. 94/1809, reg. 2.
reg. 15, amended: *ibid.*, reg. 3.

296. Lands Tribunal for Scotland (Amendment) (Fees) Rules 1993.
revoked: rules 94/497, rule 3.

297. Scottish Land Court (Fees) Order 1993.
revoked: ord. 94/498, art. 4.

NO.

1993—cont.

298. Lyon Court and Office Fees (Variation) Order 1993.
revoked: ord. 94/201, art. 4.

322. Revenue Support Grant (Scotland) Order 1993.
revoked: ord. 94/529, reg. 5.

323. Town and Country Planning (Hazardous Substances) (Scotland) Regulations 1993.
referred to: ord. 94/2567, art. 6.
reg. 11, amended: *ibid.*, art. 2.

341. Local Government Finance (Scotland) Order 1993.
art. 2, revoked: ord. 94/528, art. 5.
sch. 1, revoked: *ibid.*

343. Council Tax (Discounts) (Scotland) Amendment Order 1993.
revoked: ord. 94/626, art. 4.

345. Council Tax (Exempt Dwellings) (Scotland) Amendment Order 1993.
revoked: ord. 94/628, art. 3.

349. Social Security Benefits Up-rating Order 1993.
revoked: regs. 94/542, reg. 22.

350. Statutory Sick Pay (Rate of Payment) Order 1993.
revoked: ord. 94/562, art. 4.

387. Sea Fishing (Enforcement of Community Quota Measures) Order 1993.
revoked: ord. 94/1679, art. 14.
art. 4, see *Holmneilson* v. *Wilson*, 1994 S.C.C.R. 427.

401. Billing Authorities (Alteration of Requisite Calculations and Transitional Reduction Scheme) (England) Regulations 1993.
regs. 2, 3, 4, revoked: regs. 94/246, reg. 6.

415. Lloyd's Underwriters (Tax) (1990–91) Regulations 1993.
reg. 7, amended: regs. 94/1813, reg. 2.

416. Seeds (National Lists of Varieties) (Fees) (Amendment) Regulations 1993.
revoked: regs. 94/676, reg. 5.

430. Plant Breeders' Rights (Fees) (Amendment) Regulations 1993.
revoked: regs. 94/675, reg. 3.

455. Environmentally Sensitive Areas (Breckland) Designation Order 1993.
art. 2, amended: ord. 94/923, art. 4.
art. 4A, inserted: *ibid.*, art. 5.
art. 6, amended: *ibid.*, art. 6.
sch. 6A, inserted: *ibid.*, art. 7.
sch. 6, heading, substituted: *ibid.*
sch. 7, para. 13, inserted: *ibid.*

456. Environmentally Sensitive Areas (Clun) Designation Order 1993.
art. 2, amended: ord. 94/921, art. 4.
art. 4A, inserted: *ibid.*, art. 5.

NO.

1993—cont.

456. Environmentally Sensitive Areas (Clun) Designation Order 1993—*cont.*
art. 6, amended: *ibid.*, art. 6.
sch. 1A, inserted: *ibid.*, art. 7.
sch. 8, para. 9, inserted: *ibid.*

457. Environmentally Sensitive Areas (North Peak) Designation Order 1993.
art. 2, amended: ord. 94/922, art. 4.
art. 4A, inserted: *ibid.*, art. 5.
art. 6, amended: *ibid.*, art. 6.
sch. 1A, inserted: *ibid.*, art. 7.
sch. 4, para. 10, inserted: *ibid.*

458. Environmentally Sensitive Areas (Suffolk River Valleys) Designation Order 1993.
art. 2, amended: ord. 94/920, art. 4.
art. 4A, inserted: *ibid.*, art. 5.
art. 6, amended: *ibid.*, art. 6.
sch. 1A, inserted: *ibid.*, art. 7.
sch. 6, para. 10, inserted: *ibid.*, art. 7.

459. Environmentally Sensitive Areas (Test Valley) Designation Order 1993.
art. 2, amended: ord. 94/919, art. 4.
art. 4A, inserted: *ibid.*, art. 5.
art. 6, amended: *ibid.*, art. 6.
sch. 1A, inserted: *ibid.*, art. 7.
sch. 3, para. 9, inserted: *ibid.*, art. 7.

462. National Assistance (Sums for Personal Requirements) Regulations 1993.
revoked: regs. 94/826, reg. 3.

483. General Optical Council (Registration and Enrolment (Amendment) Rules) Order of Council 1993.
revoked: ord. 94/729, art. 3.

517. Common Agricultural Policy (Wine) Regulations 1993.
revoked: regs. 94/674, reg. 2.

518. Social Security Benefits (Miscellaneous Amendments) Regulations 1993.
reg. 4, amended: regs. 94/1779, reg. 4.

528. Legal Aid in Contempt of Court Proceedings (Scotland) Amendment Regulations 1993.
revoked: regs. 94/1016, reg. 5.

529. Legal Aid in Contempt of Court Proceedings (Scotland) (Fees) Amendment Regulations 1993.
revoked: regs. 94/1018, reg. 5.

530. Criminal Legal Aid (Scotland) (Fees) Amendment Regulations 1993.
revoked: regs. 94/1019, reg. 5.

531. Civil Legal Aid (Scotland) (Fees) Amendment Regulations 1993.
revoked: regs. 94/1015, reg. 8.

532. Criminal Legal Aid (Scotland) Amendment Regulations 1993.
revoked: regs. 94/1050, reg. 5.

NO.

1993—cont.

534. Legal Aid (Scotland) (Children) Amendment Regulations 1993.
reg. 3, revoked: regs. 94/1017, reg. 5.

535. Civil Legal Aid (Scotland) Amendment Regulations 1993.
reg. 3, revoked: regs. 94/1049, reg. 9.

543. Education (Teachers) Regulations 1993.
reg. 3, amended: regs. 94/222, reg. 2.
reg. 7, substituted: *ibid.*, reg. 3.
sch. 3, para. 1, amended: *ibid.*, reg. 4;
regs. 94/651, regs. 3, 4.
sch. 3, para. 2, amended: 1994, c. 30, s. 14.

545. Local Authorities (Members' Allowances) (Amendment) Regulations 1993.
revoked: regs. 94/615, reg. 3.

546. Building Societies (General Charge and Fees) Regulations 1993.
revoked: regs. 94/656, reg. 11.

547. Friendly Societies (General Charge and Fees) Regulations 1993.
reg. 3A, inserted: regs. 94/657, reg. 3.
sch. 1, para. 1, amended: *ibid.*, reg. 4.
sch. 2, substituted: *ibid.*, reg. 5.
sch. 3, substituted: *ibid.*, reg. 6.

548. Industrial and Provident Societies (Credit Unions) (Amendment of Fees) Regulations 1993.
revoked: regs. 94/658, reg. 3.

549. Industrial and Provident Societies (Amendment of Fees) Regulations 1993.
revoked: regs. 94/660, reg. 4.

551. Housing Renovation etc. Grants (Reduction of Grant) (Amendment) Regulations 1991.
revoked: regs. 94/648, reg. 45.

552. Housing Renovation etc. Grants (Prescribed Forms and Particulars) (Amendment) Regulations 1993.
revoked: regs. 94/565, reg. 5.

567. National Health Service (Fund-holding Practices) Regulations 1993.
reg. 8, substituted: regs. 94/640, reg. 2.
reg. 10, amended: *ibid.*, reg. 3.
reg. 13, amended: *ibid.*, reg. 4.
reg. 21, amended: *ibid.*, reg. 5.
sch. 2, para. 5, substituted: *ibid.*, reg. 6.

568. Education (Grant-maintained Schools) (Finance) Regulations 1993.
revoked: regs. 94/938, reg. 3.

571. National Health Service (Determination of Regions) Amendment Order 1993.
revoked: order 94/683, art. 14.

581. Housing (Change of Landlord) (Payment of Disposal Cost by Instalments) (Amendment) Regulations 1993.
revoked: ord. 94/266, art. 3.

NO.

1993—cont.

585. National Blood Authority (Establishment and Constitution) Order 1993.
art. 1, amended: ord. 94/589, art. 2.
art. 3, amended: *ibid.*
art. 6, amended: *ibid.*

593. Reciprocal Enforcement of Maintenance Orders (Hague Convention Countries) Order 1993.
sch. 1, amended: ord. 94/1902, art. 2.

601. Insurance (Fees) Regulations 1993.
revoked: regs. 94/643, reg. 2.

610. Veterinary Surgeons and Veterinary Practitioners (Registration) (Amendment) Regulations Order of Council 1993.
regs. 2, 3, 4, revoked: regs. 94/305, reg. 5.

629. National Board for Nursing, Midwifery and Health Visiting for England (Constitution and Administration) Order 1993.
art. 12, amended: ord. 94/586, art. 2.

630. Motor Vehicles (Type Approval and Approval Marks) (Fees) Regulations 1993.
revoked: regs. 94/1265, reg. 2.

646. Rent Officers (Additional Functions) (Scotland) Amendment Order 1993.
art. 2, amended: ord. 94/582, art. 3.

652. Rent Officers (Additional Functions) (Amendment) Order 1993.
art. 2, amended: ord. 94/568, art. 3.

715. Housing Renovation etc. Grants (Prescribed Forms and Particulars) (Welsh Forms and Particulars) (Amendment) Regulations 1993.
revoked: regs. 94/693, reg. 3.

723. Social Security Benefits (General Benefit) Regulations 1993.
revoked: regs. 94/559, reg. 6.

744. Income Tax (Employments) Regulations 1993.
reg. 5, amended: regs. 94/775, reg. 3.
reg. 11, amended: regs. 94/1813, reg. 2.
reg. 14, amended: regs. 94/1212, reg. 9.
reg. 15, amended: *ibid.*
reg. 46, amended: *ibid.*, regs. 10, 11, 12.
reg. 46A, inserted: regs. 94/775, reg. 4.

765. Value Added Tax (Increase for Consideration for Fuel) Order 1993.
Table A, C.: 1994, c. 23, s. 57.
revoked: 1994, c. 23, sch. 15.

766. Value Added Tax (Increase of Registration Limits) Order 1993.
C.: 1994, c. 23, schs. 1, 3.
revoked: 1994, c. 23, sch. 15.

767. Value Added Tax (Protective Boots and Helmets) Order 1993.
C.: 1994, c. 23, sch. 8.
revoked: 1994, c. 23, sch. 15.

774. Income Tax (Employments) Regulations 1993.
reg. 4, revoked: 1994, c. 9, s. 133.

NO.

1993—cont.

780. British Railways (Penalty Fares) Act 1989 (Activating No. 9) Order 1993.
revoked: ord. 94/577, art. 2.

781. British Railways (Penalty Fares) Act 1989 (Activating No. 10) Order 1993.
revoked: ord. 94/577, art. 2.

835. Education (Individual Pupils' Achievements) (Information) (Wales) Regulations 1993.
applied: regs. 94/653, reg. 42; regs. 94/1084, reg. 9.
revoked save for reg. 8: regs. 94/959, reg. 1.

863. Official Secrets (Prohibited Places) (Amendment) Order 1993.
revoked: ord. 94/968, art. 2.

874. Electricity Generators (Rateable Values) (Scotland) Order 1993.
revoked: ord. 94/2072, art. 11.

875. Scottish Hydro-Electric plc (Rateable - Values) (Scotland) Order 1993.
revoked: ord. 94/2076, art. 10.

876. Industrial and Freight Transport (Rateable Values) (Scotland) Order 1993.
revoked: ord. 94/913, art. 8.

877. Scottish Nuclear Limited (Rateable Values) (Scotland) Order 1993.
revoked: ord. 94/2077, art. 10.

878. Scottish Power plc (Rateable Values) (Scotland) Order 1993.
revoked: ord. 94/2078, art. 10.

879. British Gas plc (Rateable Values) (Scotland) Order 1993.
revoked: ord. 94/2069, art. 10.

880. British Railways Board (Rateable Values) (Scotland) Order 1993.
revoked: ord. 94/2070, art. 10

881. British Telecommunications plc (Rateable Values) (Scotland) Order 1993.
revoked: ord. 94/2071, art. 10.

882. Glasgow Underground (Rateable Values) (Scotland) Order 1993.
revoked: ord. 94/2073, art. 9.

883. Lochaber Power Company (Rateable Values) (Scotland) Order 1993.
revoked: ord. 94/2074, art. 10.

884. Mercury Communications Ltd (Rateable Values) (Scotland) Order 1993.
revoked: ord. 94/2075, art. 10.

885. Mines and Quarries (Rateable Values) (Scotland) Order 1993.
revoked: ord. 94/912, art. 8.

886. Water Undertakings (Rateable Values) (Scotland) Order 1993.
revoked: ord. 94/2079, art. 9.

923. Dairy Produce Quotas Regulations 1993.
revoked: regs. 94/672, reg. 36.
reg. 2, amended: regs. 94/160, reg. 4.
reg. 8, amended: *ibid.*, reg. 5.

NO.

1993—cont.

923. Dairy Produce Quotas Regulations 1993—*cont.*
reg. 30B, inserted: *ibid.*, reg. 6.
reg. 32, amended: *ibid.*, reg. 7.

936. Certification Officer (Amendment of Fees) Regulations 1993.
revoked: regs. 94/546, reg. 8.

941. Local Elections (Variation of Limits of Candidates' Election Expenses) (Northern Ireland) Order 1993.
revoked: ord. 94/763, art. 3.

942. Copyright (Application to Other Countries) Order 1993.
art. 3, amended: ord. 94/263, art. 2.
art. 4, amended: *ibid.*
sch. 1, amended: *ibid.*
sch. 2, amended: *ibid.*
sch. 3, amended: *ibid.*
sch. 4, para. 1, substituted: *ibid.*

943. Performances (Reciprocal Protection) (Convention Countries) Order 1993.
revoked: ord. 94/264, art. 3.

945. Housing Benefit and Community Charge Benefit (Subsidy) Amendment (No. 2) Regulations 1993.
revoked: regs. 94/781, reg. 5.

967. Gaming Act (Variation of Monetary Limits) Order 1993.
art. 3, revoked: ord. 94/956, art. 3.

968. Gaming Clubs (Hours and Charges) (Amendment) Regulations 1993.
revoked: regs. 94/958, reg. 3.

970. Civil Legal Aid (Financial Conditions and Contributions) (Scotland) Regulations 1993.
reg. 3, amended: regs. 94/998, reg. 5.

971. Advice and Assistance (Financial Conditions) (Scotland) Regulations 1993.
revoked: regs. 94/997, reg. 6.

985. Building Societies (Designation of Qualifying Bodies) Order 1993.
art. 3, amended: ord. 94/2457, art. 2.
sch. 1, pt. I, amended: *ibid.*
sch. 1, pt. II, para. 2A, inserted: *ibid.*

998. Education (School Curriculum and Related Information) (Wales) (Amendment) Regulations 1993.
revoked: regs. 94/2330, reg. 2.

1020. Export of Goods (Control) (Amendment) Order 1993.
revoked: ord. 94/1191, art. 9.

1037. Gaming Act (Variation of Monetary Limits) (Scotland) Order 1993.
art. 3, revoked: ord. 94/1043, art. 4.

1040. Gaming Clubs (Hours and Charges) (Scotland) Amendment Regulations 1993.
revoked: regs. 94/1042, reg. 3.

1092. Insurance Companies (Cancellation No. 2) Regulations 1993.
revoked: regs. 94/1516, reg. 86.

NO.

1993—cont.

1105. Welfare Food Amendment Regulations 1993.
reg. 4, amended: regs. 94/2004, reg. 8.

1124. Value Added Tax (Education) (No. 2) Order 1993.
revoked: 1994, c. 23, sch. 15.

1188. Serbia and Montenegro (United Nations Sanctions) Order 1993.
applied: ord. 94/2673, art. 7.
art. 7, amended: *ibid.*, art. 15.
art. 9, amended: *ibid.*

1189. Export of Goods (Control) (Croatian and Bosnian Territories) Order 1993.
applied: ord. 94/2673, art. 3, ord. 94/2676, arts. 3, 9.

1191. Lothian Region (Electoral Arrangements) Order 1993.
sch., amended: ord. 94/259, art. 2.

1195. Serbia and Montenegro (United Nations Sanctions) (Dependent Territories) Order 1993.
applied: ord. 94/2674, art. 7.
art. 7, amended: *ibid.*, art. 15.
art. 9, amended: *ibid.*

1197. Third Country Fishing (Enforcement) Order 1993.
revoked: ord. 94/1681, art. 11.

1243. Child Abduction and Custody (Parties to Conventions) (Amendment) Order 1993.
revoked: ord. 94/2792, art. 1.

1250. Access to Health Records (Northern Ireland) Order 1993.
art. 4, amended: 1994, c. 17, s. 38.

1253. Serbia and Montenegro (United Nations Sanctions) (Channel Islands) Order 1993.
applied: ord. 94/2675, art. 7.

1254. Serbia and Montenegro (United Nations Sanctions) (Isle of Man) Order 1993.
applied: ord. 94/2675, art. 7.

1317. Integrated Administration and Control System Regulations 1993.
reg. 2, amended: regs. 94/1134, reg. 2.
reg. 4, substituted: *ibid.*
reg. 4A, inserted: *ibid.*

1320. Plant Health (Great Britain) Order 1993.
referred to: ord. 94/1441, art. 2.

1321. Health and Safety (Fees) Regulations 1993.
revoked: regs. 94/397, reg. 16.

1441. Suckler Cow Premium Regulations 1993.
reg. 2, amended: regs. 94/1528, reg. 2.
reg. 3, amended: *ibid.*, reg. 2.
reg. 3A, inserted: *ibid.*
reg. 5, amended: *ibid.*
reg. 6, amended: *ibid.*
reg. 9, amended: *ibid.*

NO.

1993—cont.

1452. Housing Renovation etc. Grants (Prescribed Forms and Particulars) (Amendment No. 2) Regulations 1993.
revoked: regs. 94/565, reg. 5.

1474. Road Traffic (Special Parking Areas) (London Borough of Wandsworth) Order 1993.
art. 2, amended: ord. 94/2786, art. 3.
art. 3, revoked: *ibid.*
art. 4, substituted: *ibid.*
art. 5, amended: *ibid.*
schs. 1, 2, 3, substituted: *ibid.*

1477. Plant Health Fees (Scotland) Order 1993.
revoked: ord. 94/1441, art. 5.

1502. Education (School Information) (England) Regulations 1993.
revoked: regs. 94/1421, reg. 2.
reg. 3, applied: regs. 94/653, reg. 42.

1511. Rent Act 1977 (Forms etc.) (Welsh Forms and Particulars) Regulations 1993.
reg. 2, amended: regs. 94/725, reg. 2.
sch., amended: *ibid.*

1591. Wireless Telegraphy (Short Range Devices) (Exemption) Regulations 1993.
reg. 3, amended: regs. 94/2250, reg. 3.
reg. 4, substituted: *ibid.*, reg. 4.
- sch., para. 4, substituted: *ibid.*, reg. 5.
sch., para. 8, revoked: *ibid.*
sch., para. 9, substituted: *ibid.*
sch., para. 14, substituted: *ibid.*

1595. Severn Bridge Regulations 1993.
reg. 12, amended: regs. 94/1777, reg. 2.

1605. Education (Provision of Information as to Schools) (Scotland) Regulations 1993.
reg. 4, inserted: regs. 94/351, reg. 7.

1625. Right to Purchase (Prescribed Persons) (Scotland) Order 1993.
art. 2, amended: ord. 94/2097, art. 2.

1644. Alcan Aluminium UK Ltd (Rateable Values) (Scotland) Order 1993.
revoked: ord. 94/2068, art. 9.

1645. Forth Ports plc (Rateable Values) (Scotland) Order 1993.
revoked: ord. 94/2081, art. 10.

1646. Caledonian MacBrayne Limited (Rateable Values) (Scotland) Order 1993.
revoked: ord. 94/2080, art. 10.

1661. Asylum Appeals (Procedure) Rules 1993.
see *R.* v. *Special Adjudicator, ex p. Arthur (Frank)* [1994] Imm AR 246.
rule 4(1)(4), see *R.* v. *Secretary of State for the Home Department, ex p. Thavathevathasan (Manickavasagar)* [1994] Imm AR 249, C.A.

NO.

1993—cont.

1661. Asylum Appeals (Procedure) Rules 1993—*cont.*
rule 5(6), see *R. v. Secretary of State for the Home Department*, ex p. *Abdi, Same* v. *Same*, ex p. *Gawe, The Times*, April 25, 1994, C.A.

1692. Export of Goods (Control) (Amendment No. 2) Order 1993.
revoked: ord. 94/1191, art. 9.

1709. Inshore Fishing (Prohibition of Fishing for Cockles) (Scotland) Order 1993.
revoked: ord. 94/1828, art. 5.

1746. Chemical (Hazard Information and Packaging) Regulations 1993.
reg. 2, amended: regs. 94/669, reg. 15.
reg. 3, amended: *ibid.*
reg. 7, revoked: *ibid.*
reg. 8, amended: *ibid.*
reg. 9, amended: *ibid.*
regs. 10–12, revoked: *ibid.*
reg. 14, amended: *ibid.*
reg. 17, amended: *ibid.*
reg. 19, amended: *ibid.*
reg. 21, amended: *ibid.*
reg. 22, revoked: *ibid.*
sch. 1, pt. III, amended: *ibid.*
sch. 3, revoked: *ibid.*
sch. 7, pt. II, amended: *ibid.*
schs. 8, 9, revoked: *ibid.*
sch. 11, revoked: *ibid.*

1755. Education (School Teachers' Pay and Conditions) (No. 2) Order 1993.
document, para. 4, substituted: ord. 94/910, art. 3.
document, para. 5, amended: *ibid.*
document, para. 6, amended: *ibid.*
document, para. 8, amended: *ibid.*
document, para. 9, amended: *ibid.*

1775. Education (Bursaries for Teacher Training) (Amendment) Regulations 1993.
revoked: regs. 94/2016, reg. 2.

1784. Haiti (United Nations Sanctions) Order 1993.
revoked: ord. 94/1323, art. 19.

1785. Haiti (United Nations Sanctions) (Dependent Territories) Order 1993.
revoked: ord. 94/1324, art. 20.

1787. United Nations Arms Embargoes (Liberia, Somalia and the Former Yugoslavia) Order 1993.
art. 2, amended: ord. 94/1637, art. 2.
art. 8, amended: *ibid.*
sch., para. 4, amended: *ibid.*

1793. Haiti (United Nations Sanctions) (Channel Islands) Order 1993.
revoked: ord. 94/1325, art. 20.

1794. Haiti (United Nations Sanctions) (Isle of Man) Order 1993.
revoked: ord. 94/1326, art. 20.

NO.

1993—cont.

1808. Development Board for Rural Wales (Transfer of Housing Stock) Regulations 1993.
reg. 2, amended: regs. 94/1005, reg. 2.
reg. 4, amended: *ibid.*, reg. 3.
reg. 5, amended: *ibid.*, reg. 4.
reg. 6, amended: *ibid.*, reg. 5.
reg. 10, amended: *ibid.*, reg. 6.
reg. 11, amended: *ibid.*, reg. 7.
reg. 12, amended: *ibid.*, reg. 8.
reg. 13, amended: *ibid.*, reg. 9.
reg. 15, amended: *ibid.*, reg. 10.
reg. 16, amended: *ibid.*, reg. 11.

1813. Channel Tunnel (International Arrangements) Order 1993.
applied: ord. 94/570, art. 3.
art. 5, amended: ord. 94/1405, art. 8.
sch. 3, pt. I, applied with modifications: *ibid.*, art. 6.
sch. 3, pt. I, amended: *ibid.*, art. 8.
sch. 4, amended: *ibid.*

1825. Export of Goods (Control) (Amendment No. 4) Order 1993.
revoked: ord. 94/1191, art. 9.

1842. Ecclesiastical Judges and Legal Officers (Fees) Order 1993.
revoked: ord. 94/2009, art. 2.

1843. Legal Officers (Annual Fees) Order 1993.
revoked: ord. 94/2010, art. 3.

1844. Parochial Fees Order 1993.
revoked: ord. 94/2011, art. 3.

1850. Education (Mandatory Awards) Regulations 1993.
reg. 23, amended: regs. 94/1606, reg. 4.
reg. 26, amended: *ibid.*, reg. 5.
sch. 5, para. 1, applied: regs. 94/648, reg. 38.

1933. Money Laundering Regulations 1993.
reg. 4, applied: regs. 94/1808, reg. 2.

1961. Dartford–Thurrock Crossing (Amendment) Regulations 1993.
revoked: regs. 94/2031, reg. 12.

1969. Education (Teachers) (Amendment) Regulations 1993.
revoked: regs. 94/222, reg. 1.

1987. Education (Further Education in Schools) Regulations 1993.
applied: regs. 94/653, reg. 42; applied: regs. 94/1084, reg. 8.

2007. Oil and Fibre Plant Seeds Regulations 1993.
sch. 4, pt. I, amended: regs. 94/1423, reg. 2.

2016. Sea Fishing (Enforcement of Community Control Measures) Order 1993.
revoked: ord. 94/451, art. 13.

2037. Agricultural Holdings (Units of Production) Order 1993.
revoked: ord. 94/2183, art. 3.

NO.

1993—cont.

2077. Education (School Performance Information) (England) (No. 2) Regulations 1993.
applied: regs. 94/653, reg. 42; regs. 94/1084, reg. 9; revoked: regs. 94/1420, reg. 4.

2169. Education (Further Education Institutions Information) (Wales) Regulations 1993.
reg. 2, amended: regs. 94/1321, reg. 7.

2172. Public Telecommunication System Designation (Bradford Cable Communications Limited) Order 1993.
revoked: ord. 94/1190, art. 3.

2190. Education (National Curriculum) (Assessment Arrangements for English, Welsh, Mathematics and Science) (Key Stage 1) (Wales) Order 1993.
applied: regs. 94/653, reg. 42; regs. 94/1084, reg. 9.
art. 3, amended: ord. 94/646, art. 2.

2191. Education (National Curriculum) (Assessment Arrangements for English, Welsh, Mathematics and Science) (Key Stage 3) (Wales) Order 1993.
applied: regs. 94/653, reg. 42; regs. 94/1084, reg. 9.
art. 3, amended: ord. 94/646, art. 2.

2194. Education (School Performance Information) (Wales) Regulations 1993.
applied with modifications: regs. 94/1084, reg. 9.
revoked: regs. 94/2254, reg. 2.

2214. Finance Act 1993 (Appointed Day) Order 1993.
revoked: 1994, c. 23, sch. 15.

2227. Prison (Scotland) (Amendment) Rules 1993.
revoked: rules 94/1931, rule 143.

2228. Young Offenders (Scotland) (Amendment) Rules 1993.
revoked: rules 94/1931, rule 143.

2237. Road Traffic (Special Parking Areas) (London Boroughs of Bromley, Hammersmith and Fulham and Lewisham) (London Borough of Wandsworth) (Amendment) Order 1993.
art. 4, amended: ord. 94/1376, art. 3.

2272. Finance (No. 2) Act 1992 (Commencement No. 6 and Transitional Provisions and Savings) Order 1993.
sch., C.: 1994, c. 22, sch. 4.

2320. Civil Aviation (Canadian Navigation Services) (Fourth Amendment) Regulations 1993.
revoked: regs. 94/2325, reg. 3.

2328. Value Added Tax (Reverse Charge) Order 1993.
C.: 1994, c. 23, sch. 5.
revoked: 1994, c. 23, sch. 15.

NO.

1993—cont.

2330. Telecommunications (Leased Lines) Regulations 1993.
reg. 2, amended: regs. 94/2251, reg. 3.
sch. 2, substituted: *ibid.*, reg. 4.

2344. Plant Health Fees (Scotland) Amendment Order 1993.
revoked: ord. 94/1441, art. 5.

2398. Medicines (Veterinary Medicinal Products) (Applications for Product Licences) Regulations 1993.
reg. 2, amended: regs. 94/2157, reg. 2.
reg. 4, amended: *ibid.*

2452. Vehicles Excise Duty (Simplification of Goods Vehicles Rates) Order 1993.
sch. 1, C. in pt.: 1994, c. 22, sch. 1.

2498. Value Added Tax (Beverages) Order 1993.
revoked: 1994, c. 23, sch. 15.

2515. Export of Goods (Control) (Amendment No. 5) Order 1993.
revoked: ord. 94/1191, art. 9.

2519. Friendly Societies (Amendment) Regulations 1993.
reg. 2, revoked in pt.: regs. 94/1984, reg. 11.
reg. 4, revoked: *ibid.*, reg. 15.
reg. 5, revoked: *ibid.*, reg. 25.
regs. 8–13, revoked: regs. 94/1981, reg. 63.

2520. Friendly Societies (Insurance Business No. 2) Regulations 1993.
revoked: regs. 94/1981, reg. 63.

2521. Friendly Societies (Authorisation No. 2) Regulations 1993.
revoked: regs. 94/1982, reg. 6.

2543. South Birmingham Community Health National Health Service Trust (Establishment) Order 1993.
art. 1, amended: ord. 94/798, art. 2.
art. 2, amended: *ibid.*

2544. Churchill John Radcliffe National Health Service Trust (Establishment) Order 1993.
art. 1, amended: ord. 94/482, art. 2.
art. 2, amended: *ibid.*

2613. Community Health Care: North Durham National Health Service Trust (Establishment) Order 1993.
art. 3, amended: ord. 94/194, art. 2.

2631. Hill Livestock (Compensatory Allowances) Regulations 1993.
revoked: regs. 94/2740, reg. 17.
reg. 3, amended: regs. 94/94, reg. 3.
reg. 9, amended: *ibid.*, reg. 4.
reg. 10, amended: *ibid.*, reg. 5.

2633. South East London Mental Health National Health Service Trust (Establishment) Order 1993.
art. 3, amended: ord. 94/856, art. 3.
art. 4, amended: *ibid.*

NO.

1993—cont.

2639. North Kent Healthcare National Health Service Trust (Establishment) Order 1993.
art. 3, amended: ord. 94/797, art. 2.

2687. Industrial Tribunals (Constitution and Rules of Procedure) Regulations 1993.
applied: regs. 94/1806, reg. 6.
sch. 1, rule 6, amended: regs. 94/536, reg. 2.
sch. 1, rule 7, amended: *ibid.*, reg. 3.
sch. 1, rule 10, amended: *ibid.*, reg. 4.
sch. 1, rule 17, amended: *ibid.*, reg. 5.
sch. 2, rule 9, amended: *ibid.*, reg. 6.

2688. Industrial Tribunals (Constitution and Rules of Procedure) (Scotland) Regulations 1993.
applied: regs. 94/1806, reg. 6.
sch. 1, rule 4, amended: regs. 94/538, reg. 3.
sch. 1, rule 6, amended: *ibid.*, reg. 2.
sch. 1, rule 7, amended: *ibid.*, reg. 4.
sch. 1, rule 10, amended: *ibid.*, reg. 5.
sch. 2, rule 9, amended: *ibid.*, reg. 6.

2706. Building Societies (Designation of Qualifying Bodies) (No. 3) Order 1993.
referred to: 1994, c. 40, s. 17.
art. 3, amended: ord. 94/2457, art. 2.
sch., pt. I, amended: *ibid.*
sch., pt. II, amended: *ibid.*

2797. Transport Act 1985 (Modifications in Schedule 4 to the Transport Act 1968) (Further Modification) Order 1993.
art. 1, amended: ord. 93/2909, art. 2.

2804. Road Traffic (Special Parking Areas) (London Boroughs of Camden, Hackney and Hounslow) Order 1993.
art. 3, amended: ord. 94/1378, art. 3.

2814. British Railways (Penalty Fares) Act 1989 (Activating No. 11) Order 1993.
revoked: order 94/577, art. 2.

2824. Education (School Information) (Amendment) (England) Regulations 1993.
revoked: regs. 94/1421, reg. 2.

2833. Building Societies (Aggregation) Rules 1993.
rule 2, amended: rules 94/2458, rule 2.
rule 7, amended: *ibid.*

2903. Motor Vehicles (Type Approval and Approval Marks) (Fees) (Amendment) Regulations 1993.
revoked: regs. 94/1265, reg. 2.

2914. Education (Mandatory Awards) (No. 2) Regulations 1993.
reg. 9, amended: regs. 94/1606, reg. 3.
reg. 23, amended: *ibid.*, reg. 4.
reg. 26, amended: *ibid.*, reg. 5.

NO.

1993—cont.

2924. Hill Livestock (Compensatory Allowances) (Amendment) Regulations 1993.
revoked: 94/2740, reg. 17.

2935. Glasgow Community and Mental Health Services National Health Service Trust (Establishment) Order 1993.
art. 2, amended: ord. 94/107, art. 3.

2952. Value Added Tax (Increase for Consideration for Fuel) (No. 2) Order 1993.
C.: 1994, c. 23, s. 57.
revoked: 1994, c. 23, sch. 15.

2953. Value Added Tax (Increase of Registration Limits) (No. 2) Order 1993.
C.: 1994, c. 23, schs. 1, 3.
revoked: 1994, c. 23, sch. 15.

3029. Trade Marks and Service Marks (Fees) (Amendment) Rules 1993.
revoked: 94/2584, rule 5.

3046. Broadcasting (Prescribed Countries) Order 1991.
revoked: ord. 94/454, art. 3.

3047. Broadcasting (Foreign Satellite Programmes) (Specified Countries) (Amendment) Order 1993.
revoked: ord. 94/453, art. 3.

3069. Children (Homes, Arrangements for Placement, Reviews and Representations) (Miscellaneous Amendments) Regulations 1993.
reg. 2, amended: regs. 94/1511, reg. 3.

3071. Common Agricultural Policy (Wine) (Amendment) Regulations 1993.
revoked: regs. 94/674, reg. 2.

3072. Education (Acquisition of Grant-Maintained Status) (Transitional Functions) Regulations 1993.
applied: regs. 94/653, reg. 42; regs. 94/1084, reg. 4.

3074. Personal Protective Equipment (EC Directive) (Amendment) Regulations 1993.
reg. 2, revoked: regs. 94/2326, reg. 1.

3080. Act of Sederunt (Fees of Solicitors in the Sheriff Court) 1993.
sch. 1, amended: Act of Sederunt 94/1142, rule 2.

3081. Police (Scotland) Amendment Regulations 1993.
reg. 9, revoked: regs. 94/2095, reg. 9.

3101. Education (Schools Conducted by Education Associations) (Initial Articles of Government) Regulations 1993.
revoked: regs. 94/2849, reg. 4.
sch., amended: regs. 94/1085, reg. 2.

3102. Education (Grant-maintained Schools) (Initial Governing Instruments) Regulations 1993.
sch. 1, para. 3, amended: regs. 94/2094, reg. 2.
sch. 1, para. 16, amended: *ibid.*

NO.

1993—cont.

3102. Education (Grant-maintained Schools) (Initial Governing Instruments) Regulations 1993—cont.
sch. 1, para. 25, amended: *ibid.*
sch. 1, para. 38, amended: *ibid.*
sch. 1, para. 40, amended: *ibid.*
sch. 1, appendix 1, amended: *ibid.*
sch. 1, appendix 2, amended: *ibid.*
sch. 2, art. 1, amended: *ibid.*, reg. 3.
sch. 2, art. 2, revoked: *ibid.*
sch. 2, art. 7, amended: *ibid.*, reg. 2.
sch. 2, art. 8, amended: *ibid.*, reg. 3.
sch. 2, art. 8A, inserted: *ibid.*
sch. 2, art. 8B, inserted: *ibid.*
sch. 2, art. 10, amended: *ibid.*
sch. 2, art. 11, amended: *ibid.*
sch. 2, art. 12, amended: *ibid.*
sch. 2, art. 12A, inserted: *ibid.*
sch. 2, art. 16, amended: *ibid.*
sch. 2, art. 17, amended: *ibid.*
sch. 2, art. 21, amended: *ibid.*
sch. 2, appendix 1, revoked: *ibid.*
sch. 2, appendix 2, amended: *ibid.*

3103. Education (Schools Conducted by Education Associations) Regulations 1993.
reg. 4A, inserted: regs. 94/1083, reg. 2.
sch. 1, substituted: *ibid.*, reg. 3.
sch. 3, amended: *ibid.*, reg. 4.

3106. Education Act 1993 (Commencement No. 2 and Transitional Provisions) Order 1993.
sch. 2, para. 2, amended: ord. 94/436, art. 436.

3138. Merchant Shipping (Registration of Ships) Regulations 1993.
reg. 7, amended: regs. 94/541, reg. 3.
reg. 8, amended: *ibid.*, reg. 4.
reg. 22, amended: *ibid.*, reg. 5.
reg. 24, amended: *ibid.*, reg. 6.
reg. 49, amended: *ibid.*, reg. 7.
reg. 57, amended: *ibid.*, reg. 8.
reg. 60, substituted: *ibid.*, reg. 9.
reg. 61, substituted: *ibid.*, reg. 10.
reg. 65, amended: *ibid.*, reg. 11.
reg. 81, amended: *ibid.*, reg. 12.
reg. 85, amended: *ibid.*
reg. 108, amended: *ibid.*, reg. 13.
reg. 115, amended: *ibid.*, reg. 14.
reg. 120, amended: *ibid.*, reg. 15.
sch. 1, para. 1, amended: *ibid.*, reg. 16.
sch. 5, para. 3, amended: *ibid.*, reg. 17.

3140. Mid Essex Community Health National Health Service Trust Dissolution Order 1993.
revoked: ord. 94/745, art. 3.

3144. Child Abduction and Custody (Parties to Conventions) Order 1993.
sch., substituted: ord. 94/262, art. 2; ord. 94/1322, art. 3.

3160. Roads (Northern Ireland) Order 1993.
referred to: 1994, c. 33, s. 68.

NO.

1993—cont.

3182. Education (Individual Pupils' Achievements) (Information) Regulations 1993.
applied: regs. 94/653, reg. 42; regs. 94/1084, reg. 9.

3229. Land Registration Fees Order 1993.
replaced: ord. 94/1974, art. 1.

3234. Dairy Produce Quotas (Amendment) Regulations 1993.
revoked: regs. 94/672, reg. 36.

3239. Road Traffic (Special Parking Areas) (London Boroughs of Richmond upon Thames and Southwark) Order 1993.
art. 1, amended: ord. 94/82, art. 2.
art. 3, amended: *ibid.*; ord. 94/1377, art. 3.
sch. 2, pt. II, revoked: ord. 94/82, art. 2.

3247. Animals and Animal Products (Import and Export) Regulations 1993.
reg. 12, amended: regs. 94/1029, reg. 27.

3253. Parliamentary Pensions (Consolidation and Amendment) Regulations 1993.
reg. N5, applied: ord. 94/1662, art. 30.
reg. R1, applied: *ibid.*, art. 28.
reg. R2, applied: *ibid.*, art. 29.

3256. Medicines (Products Other Than Veterinary Drugs) (Prescription Only) Order 1993.
art. 4, amended: ord. 94/558, art. 2.

3264. Export of Goods (Control) (Amendment No. 6) Order 1993.
revoked: ord. 94/1191, art. 9.

1994

94. Hill Livestock (Compensatory Allowances) (Amendment) Regulations 1993.
revoked: 94/2740, reg. 17.

101. Medicines Act 1968 (Amendment) Regulations 1994.
revoked: regs. 94/276, reg. 2.

105. Medicines (Homoeopathic Medicinal Products for Human Use) Regulations 1994.
reg. 5, amended: regs. 94/899, reg. 2.
reg. 9, amended: *ibid.*, reg. 3.
sch. 4, amended: *ibid.*, reg. 4.

109. Race Relations (Prescribed Public Bodies) Regulations 1994.
revoked: regs. 94/1986, reg. 3.

117. Companies (Welsh Language Forms and Documents) Regulations 1994.
reg. 4, amended: regs. 94/727, reg. 2.

133. Secure Tenants of Local Housing Authorities (Right to Repair) Regulations 1994.
reg. 2, amended: regs. 94/844, reg. 2.
reg. 11, substituted: *ibid.*

160. Dairy Produce Quotas (Amendment) Regulations 1994.
revoked: regs. 94/672, reg. 36.

NO.

164. Salford Hospitals National Health Service Trust (Establishment) Order 1994.
art. 1, amended: ord. 94/1269, art. 2.
art. 2, amended: *ibid.*

182. Surrey Ambulance National Health Service Trust (Establishment) Order 1994.
art. 1, amended: ord. 94/1268, art. 2.
art. 2, amended: *ibid.*

250. Environmentally Sensitive Areas (West Penwith) Designation (Amendment) Order 1994.
revoked: ord. 94/933, art. 2.

251. Environmentally Sensitive Areas (Somerset Levels and Moors) Designation (Amendment) Order 1994.
revoked: ord. 94/932, art. 2.

252. Environmentally Sensitive Areas (South Downs) Designation (Amendment) Order 1994.
revoked: ord. 94/931, art. 2.

253. Environmentally Sensitive Areas (Pennine Dales) Designation (Amendment) Order 1994.
revoked: ord. 94/930, art. 2.

254. Environmentally Sensitive Areas (The Broads) Designation (Amendment) Order 1994.
revoked: ord. 94/929, art. 2.

262. Child Abduction and Custody (Parties to Conventions) (Amendment) Order 1994.
sch., substituted: ord. 94/1063, art. 2; revoked: ord. 94/1322, art. 2.

266. Housing (Change of Landlord) (Payment of Disposal Costs by Instalments) (Amendment) Regulations 1994.
revoked: regs. 94/2916, reg. 3.

311. Public Health (International Trains) Regulations 1994.
reg. 2, amended: regs. 94/1405, reg. 8.
reg. 5, amended: *ibid.*
reg. 6, amended: *ibid.*

361. Hydrocarbon Oil (Amendment) Regulations 1994.
revoked: regs. 94/361, reg. 2.

422. Merchant Shipping (Ro-Ro Passenger Ship Survivability) Regulations 1994.
revoked: regs. 94/1383, reg. 1.

435. Housing Renovation etc. Grants (Prescribed Forms and Particulars) (Welsh Forms and Particulars) (Amendment) Regulations 1994.
revoked: regs. 94/693, reg. 3.

534. Export of Goods (Control) (Amendment No. 7) Order 1994.
revoked: ord. 94/1191, art. 9.

573. Railways (London Regional Transport) (Exemptions) Order 1994.
art. 6, referred to: ord. 94/607, art. 2.

NO.

603. Microbiological Research Authority (Establishment and Constitution) Order 1994.
applied: regs. 94/602, reg. 5.

606. Railways (Class and Miscellaneous Exemptions) Order 1994.
art. 7, referred to: ord. 94/607, art. 2.

612. Education (Grants for Education Support and Training) Regulations 1994.
reg. 5, amended: regs. 94/2446, reg. 2.
reg. 6, amended: *ibid.*
reg. 11, amended: *ibid.*
sch., para. 3, amended: *ibid.*
sch., para. 18, amended: *ibid.*
sch., para. 19, amended: *ibid.*

650. Education (Payment for Special Educational Needs Supplies) Regulations 1994.
reg. 2, amended: regs. 94/2156, reg. 2.

653. Education (Grant-maintained Special Schools) Regulations 1994.
reg. 2, amended: regs. 94/1231, reg. 2.
reg. 6, amended: *ibid.*, reg. 3.
reg. 8A, inserted: *ibid.*, reg. 4.
reg. 11, amended: *ibid.*, reg. 5.
reg. 13, amended: regs. 94/2003, reg. 6; regs. 94/1231, reg. 6.
reg. 13A, inserted: regs. 94/2003, reg. 6.
reg. 15A, inserted: regs. 94/1231, reg. 7.
reg. 18, amended: *ibid.*, reg. 8.
reg. 19, amended: *ibid.*, reg. 9.
reg. 21, amended: regs. 94/2003, reg. 6.
reg. 22A, inserted: regs. 94/1231, reg. 10.
reg. 23, substituted: *ibid.*, reg. 11.
sch., pt. II, amended: *ibid.*, reg. 12.

669. Carriage of Dangerous Goods by Road and Rail (Classification, Packaging and Labelling) Regulations 1994.
applied: regs. 94/670, reg. 8.

672. Dairy Produce Quotas Regulations 1994.
reg. 6, amended: regs. 94/2448, reg. 3.
reg. 25, amended: *ibid.*, reg. 4.
reg. 33, amended: *ibid.*, reg. 5.

680. National Health Service (District Health Authorities) Order 1994.
applied: ord. 94/681, art. 1.

681. National Health Service (Determination of Districts) Order 1994.
referred to: ord. 94/680, art. 3.

683. National Health Service (Determination of Regions) Order 1994.
applied: ord. 94/684, art. 1.

684. National Health Service (Regional Health Authorities) Order 1994.
sch. 2, applied: ord. 94/683, art. 1.

686. Value Added Tax (Tax Free Shops) Order 1994.
revoked: 1994, c. 23, sch. 15.

NO.

1994—cont.

1601. Civil Aviation (Canadian Navigation Services) (Fifth Amendment) Regulations 1994.
revoked: regs. 94/2325, reg. 3.

1692. Customs Duties (ECSC) (Quota and other Reliefs) Order 1994.
revoked: ord. 94/1739, art. 6.

1828. Inshore Fishing (Prohibition of Fishing for Cockles) (Scotland) Order 1994.
revoked: ord. 94/2613, art. 5.

1912. Education (School Performance Information) (Wales) (Amendment) Regulations 1994.
revoked: regs. 94/2254, reg. 2.

1950. Food Protection (Emergency Prohibitions) (Paralytic Shellfish Poisoning) Order 1994.
revoked: ord. 94/2193, art. 2.

1982. Friendly Societies (Authorisation) Regulations 1994.
applied: regs. 94/1983, sch. 6, para. 38.

1983. Friendly Societies (Accounts and Related Provisions) Regulations 1994.
sch. 6, Pt. VI, applied: regs. 94/1981, reg. 37.

2029. Food Protection (Emergency Prohibitions) (Paralytic Shellfish Poisoning) (No. 3) Order 1994.
revoked: ord. 94/2193, art. 2.

NO.

1994—cont.

2038. Education Act 1993 (Commencement No. 5 and Transitional Provisions) Order 1994.
sch. 4, para. 2, amended: ord. 94/2248, art. 2.
sch. 4, para. 6, amended: *ibid.*
sch. 4, para. 7, amended: *ibid.*

2195. Police (Amendment) (No. 2) Regulations 1994.
reg. 10, revoked: regs. 94/2331, reg. 5.
sch., pt. II, amended: *ibid.*

2549. Trade Marks and Service Marks (Amendment) Rules 1994.
revoked: rules 94/2583, rule 69.

2551. Trade Marks and Service Marks (Forms) (Amendment) Rules 1994.
revoked: rules 94/2582, rule 2.

2581. Trade Marks and Service Marks (Fees) (Amendment) Rules 1994.
revoked: rules 94/2584, rule 5.

2583. Trade Marks Rules 1994.
applied: rules 94/2584, rule 2.

2804. Parental Orders (Human Fertilisation and Embryology) (Scotland) Regulations 1994.
sch. 1, para. 15, applied: rules 94/2805, rules 94/2806.

INDEX

This is the third part of the Current Law Statutes Index 1994 and is up to date to December 21, 1994. References, e.g. 12/2, are to the Statutes of 1994, Chapter 12, section 2.

INDEX

INDEX

[3]

INDEX

INDEX

INDEX

[7]

INDEX

INDEX

INDEX